A DIRECTORY OF AMERICAN POETS AND FICTION WRITERS

2001–2002 Edition

A DIRECTORY OF AMERICAN POETS AND FICTION WRITERS

2001–2002 Edition

Names and addresses of over 7,400 contemporary poets,
fiction writers, and performance writers.

PUBLISHED BY POETS & WRITERS, INC.

Acknowledgments

A Directory of American Poets and Fiction Writers is compiled and edited by the Literary Horizons program at Poets & Writers, Inc., Heather Shayne Blakeslee, Co-Director, and Amy Holman, Director.

We would like to express our gratitude to the poets, fiction writers, and performance writers who responded on time to the *Directory* update mailing, assisted us in locating lost authors, and who, between editions, keep their address and publication listings up-to-date.

We thank the seven writers listed in the *Directory* who granted us permission to put their faces on the cover of the 2001–2002 edition, the photographers and the agent who granted us permission to use their photographs or to contact an author, including Janet Landay, Diana Solis, and Susan Bergholz.

We are also grateful to Anna Cerami, Guy LeCharles Gonzalez, Dika Lam, Connie Lovatt, and Yolanda Wilkinson for their help with the monstrous tasks of data entry from 3,500 update forms, proofing all 7,473 Directory listings and making corrections from the resulting proofs.

This year's edition of *A Directory of American Poets and Fiction Writers* includes additional indices reflecting new information in many of the individual writer's listings. We are grateful to Jason Chapman, our MIS administrator at Poets & Writers, and to both our data specialist, Melissa Colbert, and printer, Jerry Balan, at ATLIS.

Cover Photographs, clockwise from lower left: Sandra Cisneros (Diana Solis, photo), Edward Hirsch (Janet Landay, photo), Daniela Gioseffi, W.P. Kinsella, Dagoberto Gilb, Fay Chiang, and N. Scott Momaday.

Original book redesign by Leah Kalotay at HPlus, Inc, 2001–2002 edition by David Opie at HPlus, Inc.

Typeset and Manufactured in the United States of America by ATLIS, Silver Spring, MD.

ISSN 0734-0605
ISBN 0-913734-62
Price: $29.95; $27.95 for institutions.

Poets & Writers, Inc.
72 Spring Street
New York, New York 10012
Tel. (212) 226-3586
Fax (212) 226-3963
http://www.pw.org

CONTENTS

Preface

The 2001–2002 edition of *A Directory of American Poets and Fiction Writers* offers its writers a place to advertise themselves and gives the conference directors, reading series curators, publicists, editors, agents and other writers who use this reference guide a means by which to contact them. As Peter Davison, poetry editor at *The Atlantic Monthly,* puts it, "It's an indispensable tool for any publishing person who needs a fingertips guide to the whereabouts of every substantial writer of verse or prose in the United States."

Every two years, we send update forms to all the writers listed in the *Directory* so that each can make changes to his or her listing. Roughly half respond with changes or to acknowledge "ok as is." This was the first update to allow writers to indicate their language fluency, race, cultural or other self-identification, and audience preferences. Microphone and airplane icons appear after the writer's name if he/she answered yes to giving readings and traveling to them, even though we recognize that many readings are unmiked and travel could be by car, train, bus, or ferry. Not every one of the Directory's over 7,470 living poets, fiction writers, and performance writers chose to answer these questions. And we leave it up to the writers and the reading series hosts to negotiate how much payment, how far the travel, and how fluent their Czech.

This country often accuses itself of caring little for children or the elderly, but I'd like to point out the generosity of spirit in the 143 listed writers interested in working with children, and 146 who are interested in reading to seniors. While the subject of self-identification can be tricky, we mean only to help both unify and broaden the communities. If you are looking for Latino/a writers for your bilingual reading series in Brownsville, Texas, you can use both the Language and Self-Identification indices in the *Directory.* But, since we did not put more than a number limit on the writers' choices, we discovered that there was an almost limitless way for writers to interpret themselves. Perhaps it is a sign of the times that there is only one hedonist and one anarchist among them.

In the Literary Horizons program at Poets & Writers, we encourage writers to think like detectives and use the success of others to find publishers, agents, and publicity for their own work. You can use the Directory to look up the most recent publications of writers with similar style to yours. With our new Literary Agent index, you can determine the interests of agencies based on the writers they represent. To help promote her first novel, *Mama,* Terry McMillan used the *Directory* to find the addresses of writers she admired who reviewed books, and then sent letters that introduced them to the story and publication date of her book. *Mama* was reviewed in more than thirty periodicals. If you've lost touch with writers you've met through the years at conferences and workshops and want to invite them to your book party, chances are you will find them listed in the *Directory.*

But don't do what Bech did in John Updike's short story "Bech Noir." Insulted by old, bad reviews, Bech sets about eliminating his critics. When he can't find one of them, he looks her up in "P&W's Directory."

Amy Holman
Director, Literary Horizons

General Information about the *Directory:*

The 2001–2002 edition of the *Directory* contains information on 4,142 poets, 1,884 fiction writers and 1,273 poets and fiction writers. Some additional poets and fiction writers are also listed as performance poets. The three largest numbers of listed writers are in New York, California, and Massachusetts.

As of November 1, 2000, the *Directory* is as complete and accurate as possible. Additions and changes are received frequently. A portion of the *Directory* is also online at our web site, http://www.pw.org/directry. (No misprint—leave out the 'o'.) Only those who okayed their online listing will be found in this searchable Web version, which is updated monthly. Newly listed writers who okay an online listing will also be accessible here. No telephone numbers are included.

As a supplement to *A Directory of American Poets and Fiction Writers,* specialized up-to-date computer mailing labels are available on magnetic tape, pressure-sensitive, and Cheshire formats. These mailing labels are a resource for individuals and organizations that wish to do targeted mailings to specific groups of writers. Call Direct Communications in Vermont at 802-747-3322 for details on mailing lists.

How To Use A Directory of American Poets and Fiction Writers

A Directory of American Poets and Fiction Writers is organized geographically by state and country, and alphabetically within state and country. New York is divided into two sections: writers listed in the five boroughs of New York City and writers listed elsewhere in New York state. The District of Columbia and Puerto Rico are included in the state listings. Writers who live outside the United States can be found following the Wyoming section. If you are looking up a particular writer, check the complete alphabetical index of all writers.

Each entry in the *Directory* includes the name of the writer, his/her genre, contact information, and publications. Some entries also include optional information—icons of microphone and airplane if writer is willing to give readings and travel for them; and language fluency for readings, self-identification, and community group reading interests.

Below is a sample listing:

Maria Arrillaga 🎤 ✈   P&W
140 Charles St, #8E,
New York, NY 10014, 212-928-4046.
Mariagjo@banet.cnet
Pubs: *Manana Valentina* (Room of One's Own,
    1995), *These are Not Sweet Girl* (White Pine Pr,
    1994), *Cascada de Sol* (Inst of Puerto Rican
    Culture, 1977), *Yo Soy Fili Mele: Anth* (U PR Pr,
    1999), Festa Da Palabra, Cupey, Tercer Milenio,
    Confrontation, PEN Int'l
Lang: Spanish; ID: Puerto Rican; Groups: Women,
Latino/Latina.

Name: This is the name under which the writer writes, not necessarily the legal/full name.

Icons: 🎤 for willingness to read and ✈ for willingness to travel to read.

Genre: Letter symbols to the right of entry indicate the type(s) of writing for which the writer is listed.

P	=	poet
W	=	fiction writer
PP	=	performance poet/writer (Those who create works intended for performance or multimedia presentation.)
P&W	=	poet and fiction writer
PP&P	=	performance poet and poet
PP&W	=	performance poet and fiction writer
PP&P&W	=	performance poet, poet, and fiction writer

Contact information: Every entry has a mailing address for the writer—home, business address, post office box, agent, or publisher. Telephone numbers, e-mail, or Internet addresses are optional.

Publications (Pubs): Every poet or fiction writer listed has had work published. The order of listing is 1. Books; 2. Anthologies; and 3. Magazines. Books and anthologies are listed with book titles followed by the publisher and date. Only magazine titles are listed, not the titles of the works published in them.

Languages (Lang): One or two, other than English, in which writer can read their work.

Self-Identification (I.D.): One or two categories of identification, such as race, culture, gender, etc.

Community Groups (Groups): One or two categories of groups to whom writer is interested in reading.

This edition has new indices following the general index:

Performance Index: includes performance poets who are also listed in other categories, such as Daniela Gioseffi, PP&P&W.

Index of Languages: those other than English in which writers can read their work.

Index of Self-Identification: categories of identification, which may include race, culture, political interest, home, social group, gender, and employment.

Index of Community Groups: groups to whom writers will read their work, or teach.

Index of Literary Agents: alphabetical listing of agents, followed by alphabetical listing of writers who listed his or her address in care of that agent.

All information is provided by the listed writers, who are given an opportunity to change or amend their listing with an update mailing every two years, and who must send changes of address at any other time of the year. If a writer does not update the listing, the entry from the last edition of the *Directory* is retained—unless we know the address to be incorrect, in which case we cut the listing from that edition. Space is increased for new information in the 2001–2002 edition, but is still limited in some cases to the most recent publications. Performance poets may list performance pieces and venues where their work has been performed, as well as audiotape/CD recordings.

A list of Frequently Used Abbreviations precedes the listings in the *Directory*.

Please note that all writers listed in the *Directory* must meet the publication requirements. We screen applications on a quarterly basis, and once a writer is accepted, his or her listing continues for life. Check your eligibility for listing in the next section.

How to Apply for Listing with Poets & Writers, Inc.

Writers interested in being listed should request an application by calling the Literary Horizons program at Poets & Writers, 212-226-3586. All applications must be accompanied by a one-time screening fee, so don't be surprised by the $10 requirement.

Requirements for Eligibility
To be eligible for listing you must be a U.S. citizen or permanent resident. If you are applying in one genre (poetry, fiction, or performance) you must have 12 points, as established in the following point system. If you are applying for both poet and fiction print designation, you will need only 12 combined print points. If you are a performance poet/writer who qualifies with 12 performance points and you would also like to be considered for print designation, you must have an additional 12 print points.

Print Points
2 pts each poem published in a literary periodical*, anthology, or book

3 pts each work of fiction published in a literary periodical, anthology, or book

12 pts each standard length book of poetry, novel, novella, story collection, or chapbook

Up to 1/3 of the 12 points required may be forthcoming work; collaborations with two or more writers count for half the normal credits for each writer.

*A literary periodical is defined as a distributed magazine that regularly publishes poetry or fiction.

Performance Points Only
2 pts each for spoken word performance

This may not be a regular reading, play reading, or singing, and may not be an open mike performance, unless you were the featured performer

These Do Not Count As Points for Listing
- Nonfiction of ANY kind
- Self-published work
- Publications and awards from vanity presses
- Translations
- Plays or dramatic treatments
- Works that you have edited
- Teaching positions
- Credits with publications that do not regularly publish poetry or fiction
- Writing for children under the age of 12
- High school/college/university/membership publications if more than 50 percent of work is native faculty, students, or society members.

Who We Are

The mission of Poets & Writers is to foster the professional development of poets and writers, to promote communication throughout the U.S. literary community, and to help create an environment in which literature can be appreciated by the widest possible public. Poets & Writers believes in literature's fundamental contribution to contemporary culture. Since its founding in 1970, it has focused on the source of literature, providing information, support, and exposure to writers at all stages in their careers.

Poets & Writers is a national, nonprofit service organization sustained by contributions from individuals, foundations, corporations, and government funding agencies. We invite your participation in Poets & Writers' programs, and we welcome your support.

Programs

Poets & Writers Magazine delivers to its readers profiles of noted authors and publishing professionals, practical how-to articles, a comprehensive listing of grants and awards for writers, and special sections on subjects ranging from small presses to writers conferences. Now in its fourteenth year of publication and with a circulation exceeding 70,000, the bimonthly magazine is the leading journal of its kind for creative writers.

Literary Horizons offers how-to-publish seminars, in person, online, and on audiotape panel discussions, a lecture series, and conferences. The program also provides a publishing information packet free of charge and compiles this biennial *A Directory of American Poets and Fiction Writers.*

Poets & Writers Online was launched in 1996 to make Poets & Writers' resources available on the Internet. Included are a searchable database consisting of more than 3,500 listings from *A Directory of American Poets and Fiction Writers,* news from the writing world, information on contests, and excerpts from *Poets & Writers Magazine.* Another popular feature is The Speakeasy, which provides a forum for the exchange of information, news, and ideas and serves as a central meeting place and community center for writers.

The Readings/Workshops Program supports public literary events through matching grants to community organizations. The program helps to bring literary events to libraries, bookstores, senior citizens' centers, prisons, and other venues and helps to increase the public's awareness of literature as a living art. Poets & Writers also provides technical assistance to event organizers. The program distributes more than $160,000 annually to some 1,000 writers from 35 states, reaching 120,000 people at readings and workshops held throughout New York and California, as well as in Chicago and Detroit.

The Writers Exchange was established in 1984 to introduce emerging writers to literary communities outside their home states and provide them with a network for professional advancement. Each year writers from a different state are invited to apply. To date, more than 45 writers from 19 states have traveled to New York to give readings and meet with publishers, editors, and well-known authors. As a result of this experience, many have had books published, received fellowships, and secured teaching positions.

Writers on Site offers multi-disciplinary residencies for writers working in partnership with visual arts organizations in California. Drawing inspiration from the collections of participating museums and galleries, writers explore the intersection of literature and visual art through readings, workshops, and panel discussions. As a cofounder of The Literary Network, Poets & Writers continues to champion the cause of freedom of expression and advocates on behalf of writers for public funding of literature and the arts.

The Friends of Poets & Writers help make all of these programs possible with annual contributions of $25 or more. For information on the Friends, please contact the Development Office at the New York address below.

National office
Poets & Writers, Inc.
72 Spring Street, Suite 301
New York, NY 10012
phone (212) 226-3586 fax (212) 226-3963

California office
Poets & Writers, Inc.
580 Washington Street, Suite 308
San Francisco, CA 94111
phone (415) 986-9577 fax (415) 986-9575

On the World Wide Web
http://www.pw.org

Subscription orders and information
Poets & Writers Magazine
P.O. Box 543
Mount Morris, IL 61054
(815) 734-1123

Abbreviations Frequently Used

Space limitations have made it necessary to use abbreviations in listing author addresses and publication credits. Some are standard mailing abbreviations, some others are used by the publications they represent. Because some of these abbreviations may seem cryptic, the following list has been created to serve as a general guide.

Acad	Academy	Lang	Language
ACM	Another Chicago Magazine	LIQ	Long Island Quarterly
ALR	American Literary Review	Lit	Literary or Literature
Amer	American	Little, Brown	Little, Brown & Company
Anth	Anthology	LSU	Louisiana State University
APR	American Poetry Review	Ldt	Limited
Assn	Association	Mag	Magazine
Assoc	Associates	Morrow	William Morrow & Company
Ave	Avenue	MPR	Manhattan Poetry Review
Bk	Book	Mtn	Mountain
BkMk	BookMark	MWPA	Maine Writers & Publishers Alliance
Bldg	Building	NAL	New American Library
BPJ	Beloit Poetry Journal	NAR	North American Review
c/o	care of	NER	New England Review
CCC	Cross-Cultural Communications	Norton	W. W. Norton & Company
Cir	Circle	NW	Northwest
Ctr	Center	NYQ	New York Quarterly
Cnty	County	Pitt	Pittsburgh
Co	Company	Pl	Place
CQ	California State Poetry Quarterly	PO	Post Office
CSM	Christian Science Monitor	Pr	Press
Ct	Court	Pub	Publications
Dr	Drive	Pubs	Publishers
Edtn	Edition	QRL	Quarterly Review of Literature
Fdn	Foundation	Qtly	Quarterly
FSG	Farrar, Straus and Giroux	Rev	Review
H Holt	Henry Holt	Rm	Room
H&R	Harper & Row	Rte	Route
HB	Harcourt Brace & Co	S&S	Simon & Schuster
HBJ	Harcourt, Brace, Jovanovich	SPR	Southern Poetry Review
HC	HarperCollins Publishers	St	Street
HM	Houghton Mifflin	Sta	Station
HR&W	Holt, Rinehart & Winston	Ste	Suite
Hse	House	SW	Southwest
Hwy	Highway	TLS	Times Literary Supplement
Inc	Incorporated	TriQtly	TriQuarterly
Inst	Institute	U/Univ	University
Intl	International	Unldt	Unlimited
Jrnl	Journal	VLS	Voice Literary Supplement
Knopf	Alfred A. Knopf		

ALABAMA

Robin Behn 🎤 ✈   P
Univ of Alabama, English Department, Tuscaloosa, AL
35487-0244, 205-348-0766
Internet: rbehn@english.as.ua.edu
   Pubs: *The Red Hour* (HC, 1993), *Paper Bird* (Texas
   Tech U, 1988), *Iowa Rev, Field, Missouri Rev,
   Crazyhorse, Denver Qtly, Indiana Rev*

Richard G. Beyer   P
1131 Hermitage Dr
Florence, AL 35630, 205-764-6312
   Pubs: *Alabama Poets: Anth* (Livingston U Pr, 1990),
   Negative Capability, Panhandler, Potato Eyes

Margaret Key Biggs   P
Country Rd Box 852
Heflin, AL 36264, 205-748-3203
   Pubs: *Parnassus of India: Anth* (Parnassus of India,
   1995), *Pen Woman, Pelican Tracks, Earthwise,
   Negative Capability*

Robert Boliek 🎤 ✈   P
1301 Panorama Dr
Birmingham, AL 35216, 205-979-6500
Internet: rboliek@home.com
   Pubs: *The Formalist, MacGuffin, Hellas, RE:AL,
   Troubadour, Edge City Rev*

Kelly Cherry 🎤 ✈   P&W
Univ of Alabama, Humanities Center, Huntsville, AL 35899,
256-890-6583
Internet: kcherry@facstaff.wisc.edu
   Pubs: *The Society of Friends: Stories, Writing the
   World* (U Missouri Pr, 1999, 1995), *Augusta Played,
   Death & Transfiguration, God's Loud Hand* (LSU Pr,
   1998, 1997, 1993), *Lovers & Agnostics* (Carnegie
   Mellon U Pr, 1995), *Atlantic, Commentary, Ms., Poetry*

William Cobb   W
200 Shady Hill Dr
Montevallo, AL 35115, 205-665-7959
   Pubs: *A Walk Through Fire* (Crane Hill, 2000), *A
   Spring of Souls* (Crane Hill, 1999), *Somewhere in All
   This Green, Harry Reunited* (Black Belt Pr, 1998,
   1995), *Amaryllis, Orpheus, Story, Southern Living,
   Arete, Shenandoah*

Robert Collins   P
205 Humanities Building, English Dept UAB, Birmingham,
AL 35294, 205-934-4250
   Pubs: *Lives We Have Chosen* (Middle Tennessee State
   U Pr, 1998), *The Glass Blower* (Pudding Hse, 1997),
   The Inventor (Glass Blower Pr, 1981), *Prairie Schooner,
   SPR, Portland Rev, Connecticut Rev*

Michael Driver   W
PO Box 6406
Montgomery, AL 36106-0406, 205-271-6384
   Pubs: *Infinity Ltd, Pearl, Road King Mag, Rockford Rev,
   Nihilistic Rev, NOMOS*

Charles Ghigna   P
204 W Linwood Dr
Homewood, AL 35209-3926, 205-870-4261
   Pubs: *Mice Are Nice* (Random Hse, 1999), *Plastic
   Soup: Dream Poems* (Black Belt Pr, 1998), *Speaking in
   Tongues* (Livingston U Pr, 1994), *Tickle Day: Poems
   from Father Goose* (Disney/Hyperion, 1994), *Harper's,
   Playboy, McCall's, Highlights for Children*

Virginia Gilbert   P
Alabama A&M Univ, Box 453, English Dept, Normal, AL
35762, 205-464-9130
   Pubs: *That Other Brightness* (Black Star Pub, 1996),
   The Earth Above (Catamount Pr, 1993), *Prairie
   Schooner, Mss., PSA Poetry Rev, NAR*

Ralph Hammond   P
Box 486
Arab, AL 35016, 205-586-4151
   Pubs: *Vincent Van Gogh: A Narrative Journey*
   (Livingston Pr, 1997), *Crossing Many Rivers: Poems
   Along the Way, Upper Alabama: Poems of Light*
   (Clemmons Creek Pr, 1995, 1993), *Wolfe Rev,
   Amaryllis, Harp-String*

Peter Huggins 🎤 ✈   P
English Dept, Auburn Univ, 9030 Haley, Auburn Univ, AL
36849-5203, 334-844-4620
Internet: huggipm@mail.auburn.edu
   Pubs: *Hard Facts* (Livingston Pr, 1998), *Solo, Texas
   Rev, Colorado Rev, Cumberland Poetry Rev, Negative
   Capability, New Virginia Rev, SPR, Zone 3*

Sandy Huss 🎤 ✈   W
Univ Alabama, English Dept, Box 870244, Tuscaloosa, AL
35487, 205-348-5065
Internet: shuss@bama.ua.edu
   Pubs: *Labor for Love: Stories* (U Missouri Pr, 1992),
   *Georgia Rev, TriQtly, Crazyhorse, River Styx, 2 Girls
   Rev, Spelunker Flophouse, Chain, Pearl*

Honoree Fanonne Jeffers   PW
812 W Battle St #D
Talladega, AL 35160, 256-761-1590
   Pubs: *The Gospel of Barbeque* (Kent State U Pr,
   2000), *Dark Matter: Anth* (Warner/Aspect, 2000), *Catch
   the Fire: Anth* (Riverhead/Putnam, 1998), *Identity
   Lesson: Anth* (Viking/Penguin, 1998), *The
   Massachusetts Rev, Callaloo, Brilliant Corners, African
   Amer Rev*

Hank Lazer 🎤 ✈   P
2945 N Hampton Dr
Tuscaloosa, AL 35406-2701, 205-345-1543
Internet: hlazer@bama.ua.edu
  Pubs: *As It Is* (Diaeresis, 1999), *3 of 10* (Chax Pr,
  1996), *Doublespace* (Segue Bks, 1992),
  INTER(IR)RUPTIONS (Generator Pr, 1992), *Chicago
  Rev, Boxkite, Facture, Salt, Tinfish, Virginia Qtly Rev,
  Hambone, New Orleans Rev, Mythosphere*

Susan Militzer Luther 🎤 ✈   P
2115 Buckingham Dr SW
Huntsville, AL 35803-2017, 256-881-2245
Internet: smluther@hiwaay.net
  Pubs: *Breathing in the Dark* (Banyon Swamp Creek Pr,
  2000), *And What Rough Beast: Anth* (Ashland Poetry
  Pr, 1999), *Ordinary & Sacred as Blood Anth* (River's
  Edge, 1999), *Alabama Horizons: Anth* (Mulberry River
  Pr, 1998), *Amaryllis, Jrnl of Poetry Therapy*
Groups: Schools, Women

Fred A. Marchman 🎤 ✈   P
1803 Clearmont St
Mobile, AL 36606
  Pubs: *Dox Dixie Duograms* (Mail Pr, 1993), *Dr. Jo-Mo's
  Handy Holy Home Remedy Remedial Reader* (Nail Pr,
  1973), *Sparks of Fire: Anth* (North Atlantic Bks, 1982),
  Mobile Bay Monthly, For the Love of Life

Michael Martone 🎤 ✈   W
PO Box 21179
Tuscaloosa, AL 35402-1300, 205-344-5059
Internet: mmartone@english.as.ua.edu
  Pubs: *Seeing Eye* (Zoland Bks, 1996), *Pensees*
  (Broadripple Pr, 1995), *Flyway, Epoch, Iowa Rev, Story,
  Harper's*

Marianne Merrill Moates   W
640 Peckerwood Creek Trail
Sylacuaga, AL 35151, 205-249-4225
  Pubs: *Writer's Digest, Seventeen, Birmingham, Sewanee
  News*

Georgette Perry 🎤   P
2519 Roland Rd SW
Huntsville, AL 35805-4147, 256-536-9801
  Pubs: *Bramblecrown* (Cedar Hill Pubs, 1999), *Ordinary
  & Sacred as Blood: Anth* (River's Edge Pub, 1999),
  Edge City Rev, Hiram Poetry Rev, Lilliput Rev

Carol J. Pierman 🎤 ✈   P
1508 13 St
Tuscaloosa, AL 35401
Internet: cpierman@tenhoor.as.ua.edu
  Pubs: *The Age of Krypton* (Carnegie Mellon U Pr,
  1989), *Naturalized Citizen* (New Rivers, 1981), *Iowa
  Rev, Carolina Qtly, Black Warrior Rev*

Thomas Rabbitt   P
Star Rte, Box 58
Elrod, AL 35458, 205-339-3548
  Pubs: *The Abandoned Country* (Carnegie Mellon, 1988),
  The Booth Interstate (Knopf, 1981), *Poetry*

Charles Bernard Rodning 🎤 ✈   P
Univ South Alabama Med Center, 2451 Fillingim St,
Mobile, AL 36617-2293, 334-471-7034
  Pubs: *Tradition of Excellence, Love Knot* (American
  Literary Pr, 1994), *Swaying Grass, Papering Dreams*
  (Scots Plaid Pr, 1998, 1994), *Negative Capability, Ko,
  Mayfly, Modern Haiku, New Cicada, Brussels Sprout*

Sue Scalf 🎤 ✈   P
152 Lawrence St
Prattville, AL 36067, 334-365-9661
  Pubs: *South by Candlelight* (Elk River Pr, 1997),
  Ceremony of Names (Druid Pr, 1990), *Devil's Wine*
  (Troy State U Pr, 1978), *Southern Rev, America, Elk
  River Rev, Carolina Qtly, English Jrnl, Poem*

Carolynne Scott 🎤 ✈   W
5305 9th Ave S
Birmingham, AL 35212-4120, 205-595-3228
  Pubs: *The Green & the Burning Alike* (Portals Pr,
  1994), *Belles' Letters: Anth* (Livingston Pr, 1999),
  *Outerbridge, Short Story Intl, Flannery O'Connor
  Bulletin, Aura, The Distillery, Noccalula*

Anne Nall Stallworth   P&W
4316 Wilderness Rd
Birmingham, AL 35213, 205-871-0140
  Pubs: *Go, Go, Said the Bird, This Time Next Year*
  (Vanguard Pr, 1984, 1972), *McCall's, Birmingham Mag,
  This Week*

Lorraine Standish   P&W
10478 County Rd 99
Lillian, AL 36549-0657, 334-961-3259
  Pubs: *Life's Seasons: Anth* (Southern Poetry
  Association, 1994), *The Lillian News, Onlooker, The
  Legend, SPR, Best Poetry of 1997*

Joe Taylor 🎤 ✈   W
RR2, Box 90-D
Coatopa, AL 35470-9642, 205-652-3470
Internet: jwt@univ.westal.edu
  Pubs: *Oldcat & Ms. Puss* (Black Belt Pr, 1997), *TriQtly,
  Montana Rev, Cimarron Rev, Florida Rev, Virginia Qtly
  Rev*

Jeanie Thompson 🎤 ✈   P
c/o Alabama Writers' Forum, 846 Park Ave, Montgomery,
AL 36106, 3342424076x236
Internet: jeanie@arts.state.al.us
  Pubs: *White for Harvest, Witness* (Black Belt Pr, 2001,
  1995), *How to Enter the River* (Holy Cow! Pr, 1985),
  *NAR, Poem, Missouri Rev, Ploughshares, Black Warrior
  Rev, Southern Rev, NER, Southern Humanities Rev*
Groups: A.A.U.W., Teenagers

Sandra S. Thompson   P
316 Woodland Dr
Birmingham, AL 35209, 205-879-3800

Natasha Trethewey   P
Department of English, 9030 Haley Center, Auburn
University, AL 36849, 334-844-9013
    Pubs: *Domestic Work* (Graywolf Pr, 2000), *The Best
Amer Poetry: Anth* (Scribner, 2000), *The New Young
Amer Poets: Anth* (Southern Illinois U Pr, 2000),
Boomer Girls: Anth (U Iowa Pr, 1999), *Giant Steps:
Anth* (HC, 2000), *NER, Southern Rev*

Sue Walker   P
Univ South Alabama, Humanities/English Dept, Mobile, AL
36688, 205-460-6146
    Pubs: *Baker's Dozen* (Druid Pr, 1988), *Traveling My
Shadow* (Negative Capability Pr, 1982), *Kentucky Rev*

Wallace Whatley   P&W
826 Tullahoma
Auburn, AL 36830, 205-821-1399
    Pubs: *New Stories from the South: Best of 1986 Anth*
(Algonquin Pr, 1986), *Minnesota Rev, Outerbridge,
Virginia Qtly Rev, SPR, Kansas Qtly, Greensboro Rev*

James P. White ♪ ✈   P&W
PO Box 428
Montrose, AL 36559-0428, 334-928-3711
    Pubs: *Where Joy Resides* (FSG, 1993), *Clara's Call*
(Texas Ctr for Writers Pr, 1991), *Birdsong, The Persian
Oven & California Exit* (Methuen, 1990, 1989)

William J. Wilson   P&W
1239 Blevins Gap Rd SE
Huntsville, AL 35802, 205-881-8002
    Pubs: *Horror Story: Anth* (Underwood-Miller, 1990),
*Poem, Haunts, Old Hickory Rev, The Scribbler, Black
Lotus*

A. J. Wright   P
119 Pintail Dr
Pelham, AL 35124-2121, 205-663-3403
    Pubs: *Right Now I Feel Like Robert Johnson*
(Timberline Pr, 1981), *Alabama Poets: A Contemporary
Anth* (Livingston U, 1990), *Aura, Morpo Rev, Semiotext
(e)*

ALASKA

Jean Anderson ♪ ✈   W
509 Aquila St
Fairbanks, AK 99712-1320, 907-457-7692
    Pubs: *In Extremis* (Plover Pr, 1989), *Inroads: Anth*
(ASCA, 1988), *Prairie Schooner, Sugar Mule, Northern
Rev, Polyarnya Izvezda, Alaska Qtly Rev, Chariton Rev,
Stories, Connotations*
I.D.: Women. Groups: Literacy, Adults

Ann Fox Chandonnet   P
6552 Lakeway Dr
Anchorage, AK 99502-1949, 907-243-9172
    Pubs: *Alaska's Arts, Crafts & Collectibles, Whispered
Secrets* (Sedna Pr, 1998, 1991), *Last New Land*
(Alaska Northwest Bks, 1996), *Canoeing in the Rain:
Poems for my Aleut-Athabascan Son* (Mr. Cogito Pr,
1990), *Alaska, Lands' End Catalog*

Richard Dauenhauer   P
3740 N Douglas Hwy
Juneau, AK 99801, 907-586-4708
    Pubs: *Phenologies* (Thorp Springs Pr, 1988), *Frames of
Reference* (Black Current Pr, 1987), *Haa Tuwunaagu
Yis, For Healing Our Spirit: Anth* (U Washington Pr,
1990)

Tim Jones ♪ ✈   W
Box 1644
Valdez, AK 99686-1644, 907-835-4125
Internet: tjones@alaska.net
    Pubs: *Keep the Round Side Down* (McRoy &
Blackburn, 1996), *Soundings*

Carolyn S. Kremers   P
3754 Frenchman Rd
Fairbanks, AK 99709, 907-455-6557
    Pubs: *Place of the Pretend People: Gifts from a Yup'ik
Eskimo Village, Last New Land: Stories of Alaska Past
& Present: Anth* (Alaska Northwest Bks, 1996, 1996),
Life on the Line: Anth (Negative Capability Pr, 1992),
Alaska Qtly Rev

Nancy Lord   W
PO Box 558
Homer, AK 99603
    Pubs: *Survival* (Coffee Hse Pr, 1991), *The Compass
Inside Ourselves* (Fireweed Pr, 1984), *NAR,
Ploughshares, High Plains Literary Rev, Passages
North, Other Voices*

Donna Mack   W
5000 Vi St
Anchorage, AK 99507, 907-349-2680
    Pubs: *The Whole Apple, Essence, Raven*

Linda McCarriston   P
1746 Alder Dr
Anchorage, AK 99508, 907-786-4378
    Pubs: *Eva-Mary* (TriQtly Bks, 1991), *Talking Soft Dutch*
(Texas Tech U Pr, 1984), *Atlantic, Sojourner, TriQtly,
Poetry, Georgia Rev, Seneca Rev*

John Morgan ♪ ✈   P
3240 Rosie Creek Rd
Fairbanks, AK 99709-2818, 907-479-4936
Internet: ffjwm@aurora.alaska.edu
    Pubs: *Walking Past Midnight, The Arctic Herd* (U
Alabama Pr, 1989, 1984), *New Yorker, APR, Poetry,
Paris Rev, New Republic, Kenyon Rev*

Sheila Nickerson   P&W
540 W 10 St
Juneau, AK 99801, 907-586-6553
    Pubs: *In an August Garden* (Black Spruce Pr, 1997),
Feast of the Animals (Old Harbor Pr, 1991), *In the
Compass of Unrest* (Trout Creek Pr, 1988)

James Ruppert   P
3266 Bluebird Ave
Fairbanks, AK 99709, 907-479-3132
    Pubs: *Natural Formations* (Blue Cloud Qtly Pr, 1981),
Contact II, New Mexico Humanities Rev, Blue Mesa

Tom Sexton   P
1972 Wildwood Ln
Anchorage, AK 99517, 907-272-1060
    Pubs: *Leaving for a Year* (Adastra Pr, 1998), *The Bend
Toward Asia* (Salmon Run, 1993), *Late August on the
Kenai River* (Limner Pr, 1992), *Terra Incognita* (Solo Pr,
1974), *Hayden's Ferry Rev, Paris Rev, Zone 3,
Zyzzyva, Chariton Rev*

Peggy Shumaker 🎤 ✈   P
100 Cushman St #210
Fairbanks, AK 99701, 907-456-4098
Internet: peggyzoe@sprynet.com
    Pubs: *Wings Moist from the Other World, The Circle of
Totems* (U Pitt Pr, 1994, 1988), *Braided River* (Limner
Pr, 1993), *APR, NAR, Alaska Qtly Rev*

John E. Smelcer 🎤 ✈   P
4101 University Dr, #328
Anchorage, AK 99508-4625
    Pubs: *Songs from an Outcast* (UCLA, 2000),
Riversongs (CPR, 2000), *Changing Seasons* (South
Head Pr, 1995), *Kesugi Ridge* (Aureole Pr, 1995), *Here
First: Anth* (RH, 2000), *Poetry Comes Up: Anth* (Utah
U Pr, 2000), *Poetry Editor, Rosebud Mag, Atlantic,
CSM*

Ronald Spatz   W
Dept of Creative Writing & Literary Arts, Univ Alaska
Anchorage, Anchorage, AK 99508, 907-786-4361
    Pubs: *Fiction, Transatlantic Rev, New Letters, Panache,
Telescope, The Wayne Rev, Third Coast, In the
Dreamlight, Inroads*

Ken Waldman   P&W
3705 Arctic, #1511
Juneau, AK 99503, 907-258-1051
    Pubs: *MacGuffin, High Plains Literary Rev, Yankee,
Exquisite Corpse, Manoa, BPJ, West End Pr*

Mark Arvid White   P&W
PO Box 1771
Palmer, AK 99645, 907-746-2566
    Pubs: *Readers Break Vol III: Anth* (Pine Grove Pr,
1996), *Haiku Moment: Anth* (C. Tuttle Co, 1993),
Windows of the Soul: Anth (Nat'l Arts Society, 1990),
*Webster Rev, Modern Haiku, Candelabrum, Riverrun,
Woodnotes, Arnazella, Minas Tirith Evening-Star*

ARIZONA

Ai   P
6125 E Indian School Rd, #108
Scottsdale, AZ 85251
    Pubs: *Vice, Greed* (Norton, 1999, 1993), *Fate, Sin,
Killing Floor, Cruelty* (HM, 1991, 1986, 1979, 1973),
APR, Iowa Rev, Caprice, Poetry Int'l, Agni, Onthebus

Karl Arthur 🎤 ✈   W
Ravenhawk Books, 7739 E Broadway Blvd, #95, Tucson,
AZ 85710, 520-886-9885
Internet: ravenhawk6dof@yahoo.com
    Pubs: *Desert Dogs, Stalked to Death, Bank of Satan*
(Ravenhawk Bks, 2001, 2000, 2000)

Dick Bakken   P
3 Old Douglas Rd
Bisbee, AZ 85603, 520-432-2771
    Pubs: *Feet with the Jesus* (Lynx Hse, 1989), *The Other
Side* (Brushfire, 1986), *Ironwood, Ploughshares, Yellow
Silk, Poetry NW, Poetry Flash, Willow Springs*

Diane Beeson   P
685 S La Posada Cir, #1701
Green Valley, AZ 85614, 520-648-7949
    Pubs: *Tiny Tales, Vols. 6, 4-5, 1-3* (Co-author; Mangold
Santillana, 1991, 1990, 1989), *Parnassus of World
Poets: Anth* (Venus Printers, 1994), *Poets & Peace
International, Vol. 2: Anth* (Arc Pr, 1984)

Jay Boyer   P&W
MFA Program, English Dept, Arizona State Univ, Tempe,
AZ 85287-0302, 480-965-7644
Internet: j.boyer@asu.edu
    Pubs: *As Far Away As China* (Pratt, 1990), *Newsweek,
Paris Rev, Nation*

Sandra Braman   P
1865 Gun Fury Rd
Sedona, AZ 86336
    Pubs: *A True Story* (Tansy/Zelot, 1985), *Spokehearts*
(Longspoon, 1983), *Exquisite Corpse, Island*

Charles Brownson W
Arizona State Univ Library, Tempe, AZ 85287,
602-965-5250
　Pubs: *In Uz* (Noumenon Pr, 1985), *Ancestors* (Jump
River Pr, 1984)

Linda Cargill W
515 E Grant Rd, Ste 141-204
Tucson, AZ 85705-5774
　Pubs: *Pool Party* (Scholastic, 1996), *Hang Loose* (HC,
1996), *The Witch of Pungo* (Cora Verlag, 1991), *To
Follow the Goddess* (Cheops Bks, 1991)

Ron Carlson 🎤 ✈ W
Arizona State Univ, 8839 E Thoroughbred Trail,
Scottsdale, AZ 85258-1335, 602-596-8376
Internet: ron.carlson@asu.edu
　Pubs: *The Hotel Eden, Plan B for the Middle Class,
The News of the World, Betrayed by F. Scott
Fitzgerald, Truants, Contemporary Fiction: Anth,* (Norton,
1997, 1992, 1987, 1984, 1981, 1997), *GQ, Harper's,
Story, Esquire, New Yorker, Carolina Qtly*

Jefferson Carter P
Pima Community College, 1255 N Stone, Box 5027,
Tucson, AZ 85709-3000, 520-884-6135
　Pubs: *Tough Love* (Riverstone Pr, 1993), *None of This
Will Kill Me* (Moon Pony Pr, 1987), *Gentling the Horses*
(Maguey, 1979), *Metro, Carolina Qtly*

Emily Pritchard Cary 🎤 ✈ W
27653 N 72nd Way
Scottsdale, AZ 85255-1105, 480-502-0528
Internet: empcary@cs.com
　Pubs: *The Ghost of Whitaker Mountain, My High Love
Calling* (Bouregy, 1979, 1977), *British Heritage, Phi
Delta Kappan, Dog Fancy, Pittsburgh Pr Sunday Mag*

James V. Cervantes P
Univ of Arizona Press, 1230 N Park Ave, #102, Tucson,
AZ 85719-4140
　Pubs: *The Headlong Future* (New Rivers, 1990), *Pacific
Rev, Altadena Rev, Northern Arizona Rev*

Virgil Chabre P
7166 E Lindner Ave
Mesa, AZ 85208-4986
　Pubs: *San Fernando Poetry Jrnl, The Archer, Prophetic
Voices, Deros, Poetica, Pub 9, Manna*

David Chorlton 🎤 ✈ P
118 W Palm Ln
Phoenix, AZ 85003, 602-253-5055
　Pubs: *Assimilation* (Main St Rag, 2000), *Outposts*
(Taxus Pr, 1994), *Forget the Country You Came From*
(Singular Street, 1992), *Fever Dreams: Anth* (U Arizona
Pr, 1997), *Devil's Millhopper, Green Fuse, Heaven
Bone, Poet Lore, Webster Rev, Lucid Stone*

Joel Climenhaga P&W
115 San Jose Dr
Bisbee, AZ 85603-3009, 520-432-3410
　Pubs: *Exploration of the Great Northwest While
Traveling with the Fat Man* (Transient Pr, 1997), *Moan
of Raping Bees, Bottom of the Spittoon, The Treachery
of Innocence* (Shadow Pr, 1996, 1995, 1994),
Ascending Shadows, Mirage, Lucid Stone

Paul Cook P
1108 W Cornell
Tempe, AZ 85283, 602-831-7062
　Pubs: *Fortress on the Sun* (Penguin, 1997), *On the
Rim of the Mandala, Halo, Duende Meadow* (Bantam
Bks, 1987, 1986, 1985), *Amazing Stories, Mag of
Sci-Fi, New Letters*

David Coy P
The Writing School, Arizona Western College, PO Box
929, Yuma, AZ 85364-0929, 602-344-7577
　Pubs: *Lean Creatures* (Church of the Head Pr, 1994),
Rural Views (Mother of Ashes Pr, 1991), *Antioch Rev,
Widener Rev, Colorado North Rev, Slant*

Barbara Cully 🎤 ✈ P
Univ Arizona, Dept of English, ML 445, Tucson, AZ
85721, 520-621-1836
Internet: cullyb@u.arizona.edu
　Pubs: *The New Intimacy* (Penguin 1997), *Shoreline
Series* (Kore Pr, 1997)

Linda Lee Curtis P
1919 W Adams
Phoenix, AZ 85009-5240, 602-254-2876
　Pubs: *Head Shots* (Winter Wheat Pr, 1993), *Arizona
Journal: Anth* (High Desert Pub, 1995), *Voices, True
Liberty, Muse of Fire, It's Not Qtly, Quickenings,
Roadrunner, Life Scribes*

Alison Hawthorne Deming 🎤 ✈ P
Univ of Arizona, Department of English, Tucson, AZ
85719, 520-621-3866
Internet: aldeming@aol.com
　Pubs: *Writing the Sacred Into the Real* (Milkweed,
2000), *The Edges of the Civilized World, Temporary
Homelands* (Picador, 1998, 1996), *The Monarchs: A
Poem Sequence, Science & Other Poems* (Louisiana
State U Pr, 1997, 1994)

Laura Deming W
2929 N 70 St, #3025
Scottsdale, AZ 85251-6301, 330-423-1109
　Pubs: *Descant, Cimarron Rev, Crosscurrents, San Jose
Studies*

Wally Depew P&W
PO Box 215
Patagonia, AZ 85624-0215, 520-394-2779
    Pubs: *Girltalk, Pure Flip, Quatrains, Fortune, Book of the Dead, Dead Birds, Toxic* (Bright Moments, 1996, 1996, 1991, 1991, 1991, 1991, 1991)

Marvin Diogenes 🎤 ✈ W
Univ Arizona, English Dept, Modern Languages 445, Tucson, AZ 85721, 520-621-5976
Internet: diogenes@u.arizona.edu
    Pubs: *In Praise of Pedagogy: Anth* (Calendar Island Pub, 2000), *O. Henry Festival Stories: Anths* (Trans-Verse Pr, 2000, 1993), *American Fiction: Anth* (Birch Lane, 1991), *Other Voices*
I.D.: Jewish. Groups: Teenagers, Writing Groups

Norman Dubie P
700 W Brown #6
Tempe, AZ 85281, 603-965-3168
    Pubs: *Selected & New Poems* (Norton, 1983), *The City of Olesha Fruit* (Doubleday, 1979)

John Duncklee 🎤 ✈ P&W
PO Box 1357
Oracle, AZ 85623, 520-896-3116
    Pubs: *Genevieve of Tombstone* (Leisure Bks, 1999), *Quest for the Eagle Feather* (Northland, 1997), *Connection, High Country, Huerfano, Satire, Tombstone Epitaph*

Sally Ehrman P
PO Box 777
Bisbee, AZ 85603, 602-432-3995
    Pubs: *Fennel Stalk, Clarion, Z Misc, Piedmont Literary Rev, San Fernando Poetry Jrnl, Archer*

Elizabeth Evans W
English Dept, Univ Arizona, Modern Language Bldg, Tucson, AZ 85721, 520-621-1836
    Pubs: *Carter Clay* (HC, 1999), *The Blue Hour* (Algonquin, 1994), *Locomotion* (New Rivers, 1986), *The Qtly, Prairie Schooner, Crazyhorse, American Fiction, Sonora Rev*

Anne U. Forer W
4765 E Baker St
Tucson, AZ 85711-2116, 602-795-6245
    Pubs: *Hot Type: Anth* (Collier Bks, 1988), *Heresies, Green Mountains Rev, Exquisite Corpse, Minotaur*

Rita Garitano P
3109 E Circulo Del Tenis
Tucson, AZ 85716-1074, 520-319-0877
    Pubs: *Rainy Day Man* (Norton, 1985), *Feeding the Hungry Heart* (Bobbs-Merrill, 1982), *Walking the Twilight: Anth* (Northland Pr, 1994), *Tucson Guide Qtly*

Michael Gessner P&W
Central Arizona College, 8470 N Overfield Rd, Coolidge, AZ 85228, 520-836-1274
    Pubs: *American Literary Rev, Wallace Stevens Jrnl, Sycamore Rev, Pacific Rev, Poem, Wisconsin Rev*

Beckian Fritz Goldberg 🎤 ✈ P
Arizona State Dept of English, Box 870302, Tempe, AZ 85287, 480-965-3663
Internet: beckian@asu.edu
    Pubs: *Never Be the Horse* (U Akron Pr, 1999), *In the Badlands of Desire, Body Betrayer* (Cleveland St U Pr, 1993, 1991), *Pushcart Prize: Anth* (Pushcart Pr, 1998), *Best American Poetry: Anth* (Scribner, 1995), *New Amer Poets of the 90's: Anth* (Godine, 1991)
I.D.: Jewish

Drummond Hadley P
Guadalupe Ranch, Box 1093, Douglas, AZ 85607
    Pubs: *Tierra: Contemporary Short Fiction of New Mexico: Anth* (Cinco Puntos Pr, 1989)

Catherine Hammond P&W
1503 E Greentree Dr
Tempe, AZ 85284, 602-961-3337
    Pubs: *Contemporary Arizona Poets: Anth* (U Arizona, 1997), *Chicago Rev, Mississippi Rev, NAR, Puerto del Sol, Laurel Rev, Passages North*

Alan Harrington W
2831 N Orlando Ave
Tucson, AZ 85712, 602-326-4559
    Pubs: *The White Rainbow, Paradise I* (Little, Brown, 1981, 1977), *Harper's, Atlantic, Chicago Rev*

Mark Harris W
2014 E Balboa Dr
Tempe, AZ 85282
    Pubs: *The Tale Maker, The Diamond: Baseball Writings, Speed* (Donald I. Fine, 1994, 1994, 1990), *Arizona Qtly, Denver Qtly, Virginia Qtly Rev, Sequoia, Esquire*

Dorothy L. Hatch P
2314 E Montecito Ave
Phoenix, AZ 85016-6218
    Pubs: *The Curious Act of Poetry, Waking to the Day* (Stone Hse Pr, 1990, 1985)

Simon Hawke W
2080 W Speedway Blvd, Apt 2166
Tucson, AZ 85745-2171
    Pubs: *War, The Seeker* (TSR, Inc, 1996, 1994), *Whims of Creation* (Warner Bks, 1994)

Robert Haynes P
6117 E Nisbet Rd
Scottsdale, AZ 85254
　　Pubs: *Poetry NW, Poet Lore, New Letters, Zone 3,
　　Kentucky Poetry Rev, Cape Rock, Cimarron Rev, Atom
　　Mind*

Laraine Herring W
4407 W Caron Dr
Glendale, AZ 85302-3817, 623-934-2001
　　Pubs: *Monsoons* (Duality Pr, 1999), *Women Writers of
　　the Southwest: Walking the Twilight: Anth* (Northland Pr,
　　1994)

Robert Houston W
Univ Arizona, English Dept, Tucson, AZ 85721
　　Pubs: *The Fourth Codex* (HM, 1988), *The Line*
　　(Ballantine, 1986), *NER/BLQ, New York Times*

Will Inman ♪ P&W
2551 W Mossman Rd
Tucson, AZ 85746-5102, 520-883-3419
　　Pubs: *Other Eye, Other Ear, End of the Ceaseless
　　Road, What Friend in the Labyrinth* (Minotaur, 2000,
　　2000, 1999), *you whose eyes enter me naked* (Mille
　　Grazie, 1999), *Surfing the Dark Sound* (Pudding Hse
　　Pr, 1998), *Blackbird: Anth* (Phoenix Pr, 1998), *5 P.M.*

Nadine Kachur ♪ ✈ P
PO Box 2648
Prescott, AZ 86302, 520-541-9736
　　Pubs: *Sun Tennis, Art-Rag, Trails to Black Canyon,
　　exsanguinate, South Ash Pr, Ignis Fatuus Rev, Twisted
　　Nipples, Damaged Wine, Mirage*

Barbara Kingsolver P&W
PO Box 31870
Tucson, AZ 85751-1870
　　Pubs: *The Poisonwood Bible, High Tide in Tucson,
　　Pigs in Heaven, Animal Dreams* (HC, 1998, 1995,
　　1993, 1990), *Another America* (Seal Pr, 1992)

John Levy ♪ ✈ P
8987 E Tanque Verde Rd, Box 111
Tucson, AZ 85749-9399, 520-749-4188
　　Pubs: *Scribble & Expanse* (Tel-Let, 1995), *We Don't Kill
　　Snakes Where We Come From* (Querencia Pr, 1994),
　　Origin, Shearsman, Longhouse

Charlotte Ocean Lowe P&W
1530 N Blue Ridge Rd
Tucson, AZ 85745, 520-743-7596
　　Pubs: *Amer Poetry Rev, The Tucson Poet, Changes
　　Mag*

Jonathan F. Lowe P&W
PO Box 26073
Tucson, AZ 85726, 520-326-3007
　　Pubs: *Dark Fire, Postmarked for Death*
　　(www.e-pulp.com, 1998, 1998), *Snapshots* (Atlantic Disk
　　Pub, 1996), *Ghost Rider* (Spectravision Electronic Pub,
　　1994), *Arizona Highways, Rider, Porthole*

Delma Luben P
906 Forest Hylands Dr
Prescott, AZ 86303, 602-778-7860
　　Pubs: *Ghost Writers in the Sky* (Vision Pr, 1990),
　　*Parnassus, Heartland Jrnl, New Jersey Rev of
　　Literature*

Nancy Mairs ♪ ✈ P&W
1527 E Mabel St
Tucson, AZ 85719-4223, 602-623-2388
Internet: nmairs@earthlink.net
　　Pubs: *Waist-High in the World, Voice Lessons, Ordinary
　　Time* (Beacon, 1997, 1994, 1993), *Glamour, American
　　Voice, TriQtly, Mss.*

Robert Matte, Jr. P
5741 E Waverly St
Tucson, AZ 85712, 602-721-4445
　　Pubs: *Asylum Picnic* (Duck Down Pr, 1979), *Star
　　Kissing* (Vagabond Pr, 1975), *Bellingham Rev*

Patricia McConnel W
Bldg 300-417, 2700 Woodlands Village Blvd, Dead Cat,
AZ 86001
　　Pubs: *Eye of the Beholder* (Logoria, 1998), *Sing Soft,
　　Sing Loud* (Atheneum, 1989), *Neon, Catalyst,
　　Crosscurrents, Passages North, 13th Moon*

Judith McDaniel ♪ ✈ P
1412 S Moonflower Ln
Tucson, AZ 85748-7431, 520-721-8915
　　Pubs: *Yes I Said Yes I Will* (Naiad Pr, 1996), *Just Say
　　Yes, Metamorphosis, Sanctuary* (Firebrand, 1991, 1989,
　　1987)
Groups: G/L/B/T, Seniors

Christopher McIlroy ♪ ✈ W
2309 W Sumaya Pl
Tucson, AZ 85741-3708
Internet: mcilroyfamily@theriver.com
　　Pubs: *All My Relations* (U Georgia Pr, 1994), *Best
　　American Short Stories: Anth* (HM, 1986), *TriQtly,
　　Missouri Rev, Fiction, Story Qtly, Ploughshares, Puerto
　　del Sol*

Gregory McNamee P&W
1128 E 10 St
Tucson, AZ 85719, 520-882-4340
　　Pubs: *Christ on the Mount of Olives, Inconstant History*
　　(Broken Moon Pr, 1991, 1990)

Jane Miller   P
4990 N Acacia Ln
Tucson, AZ 85745-9262, 520-743-7474
    Pubs: *Wherever You Lay Your Head, Memory at These
    Speeds: Selected Poems, American Odalisque* (Copper
    Canyon Pr, 1999, 1996, 1987), *American Voice, Kenyon
    Rev, Ploughshares, APR*

Patricia Murphy   P
2333 E Geneva Dr
Tempe, AZ 85282-4146, 480-413-0371
    Pubs: *Seattle Rev, Qtly West, APR, Green Mountains
    Rev, Indiana Rev, Iowa Rev*

Sheila Ellen Murphy ☕ ✈   P
3701 E Monterosa St, #3
Phoenix, AZ 85018-4848
Internet: shemurph@aol.com
    Pubs: *Arbitrariums* (Broken Boulder Pr, 2000), The
    Immersion Tones (Luna Bisonte Prods Pr, 2000),
    *Indelible Occasion, Falling in Love Falling in Love with
    You Syntax* (Potes & Poets Pr, 2000, 1998), *A Clove
    of Gender* (U.K.; Stride, 1995), *Facture, NYQ*
I.D.: Irish-American

Tenney Nathanson   P
English Dept, Univ Arizona, 445 Modern Languages Bldg,
Tucson, AZ 85721, 520-621-1836
    Pubs: *Rif/t, Social Text, Ironwood, Tamarisk, Caterpillar,
    Massachusetts Rev*

John L. Natkie   P
Publisher-Editor, The Crazy Polack's Press, 5750 E Azalea
Ave, Mesa, AZ 85206
    Pubs: *Screams! From an Unpadded Cell* (Cosmep
    Prison Project, 1979), *Greenfield Rev*

Rodney Nelson   P&W
PO Box 22271
Flagstaff, AZ 86002-2271, 520-774-2829
    Pubs: *Villy Sadness* (New Rivers Pr, 1987), *Thor's
    Home* (Holmganger's Pr, 1984), *American Letters &
    Comments*

Steve Orlen   P
Univ Arizona, English Dept, Tucson, AZ 85721,
520-621-7405
    Pubs: *Happy As I Am* (Ausable Pr, 2000), *Kisses, The
    Bridge of Sighs* (Miami U Pr, 1997, 1992), *New Bread
    Loaf Anth* (U Pr New England, 1999), *Best American
    Poetry: Anth* (Scribner, 1989), *A Place at the Table*
    (HR&W, 1982)

Simon J. Ortiz   P&W
3535 N 1st Ave #R-10
Tucson, AZ 85719-1725
    Pubs: *A Good Journey* (Sun Tracks/U Arizona Pr,
    1984), *Fightin'* (Thunder's Mouth Pr, 1983)

Diane Payne ☕ ✈   W
PO Box 52
Tumacacori, AZ 85640-0052
Internet: dpayne2555@aol.com
    Pubs: *Burning Tulips* (Red Hen Pr, 2001), *To Honor a
    Teacher: Anth* (Andrews McMeel, 1999), *Limestone
    Circle, Potomac Rev, Medicinal Purposes, Maverick
    Mag, The Bridge, Poetry Heaven Qtly, Reverse, Moxie
    Mag, Abundance, Kimera, Pike Creek Rev*

Jonathan Penner ☕ ✈   W
2232 E Seneca St
Tucson, AZ 85719-3834, 520-327-6961
Internet: exlibris@u.arizona.edu
    Pubs: *Natural Order* (Poseidon, 1990), *Private Parties*
    (U Pitt Pr, 1983), *Harper's, Commentary, Paris Rev,
    Antaeus, Grand Street, Ploughshares*

Melissa Pritchard ☕ ✈   P&W
Arizona State Univ, English Dept, MFA Program, Tempe,
AZ 85282, 480-965-7295
Internet: melissap@asu.edu
    Pubs: *Selene of the Spirits* (Ontario Review Pr, 1998),
    The Instinct for Bliss (Zoland Bks, 1997), *Prize Stories
    2000: The O. Henry Awards* (Anchor, 2000),
    Prentice-Hall Anth of Women's Literature (Prentice-Hall,
    2000), *Paris Rev, Blvd*
Groups: Children, Prisoners

Michael Rattee ☕ ✈   P
2833 E Kaibab Vista
Tucson, AZ 85713-4011, 520-884-9392
Internet: mrattee@worldnet.att.net
    Pubs: *Calling Yourself Home* (Cleveland St U Pr,
    1986), *Men of Our Time: Anth* (U Georgia Pr, 1992),
    *Pivot, Laurel Rev, Poet Lore, Santa Clara Rev, The
    Signal*

David Ray ☕ ✈   P&W
2033 E 10 St
Tucson, AZ 85719-5925, 520-622-6332
Internet: djray@gci-net.com
    Pubs: *Demons in the Diner* (Ashland Poetry Pr, 1999),
    Kangaroo Paws (Thomas Jefferson U Pr, 1995), *Wool
    Highways* (Helicon Nine Edtns, 1993), *New Yorker,
    Paris Rev, Atlantic, Nation, Grand Street*
Groups: Medical Students, Teenagers

Judy Ray ☕ ✈   P&W
2033 E 10 St
Tucson, AZ 85719-5925, 520-622-6332
Internet: djray@gci-net.com
    Pubs: *Pigeons in the Chandeliers* (Timberline Pr, 1993),
    The Jaipur Sketchbook (Chariton Rev Pr, 1991),
    Fathers: Anth (St Martin's Pr, 1997), *Stiletto, American
    Voice, Westerly, Helicon Nine, New Millennium*

A. E. Reiff   P&W
2532 N Foote Dr
Phoenix, AZ 85008-1920
    Pubs: *Nineteen Women Without a Husband* (Papago
    Pr, 1997), *Living Jewels: A Treasury of Lyric Poetry*
    (Fine Arts Pr, 1993), *Planet 3: Help Send This Book
    Into Space* (Newfoundland Bks, 1986), *Broken Streets
    IV*

Del Reitz   P
c/o Newsletter Inago, PO Box 26244, Tucson, AZ
85726-6244, 520-294-7031
    Pubs: *Little Lieu & Other Waifs, Second Inago Anth of
    Poetry, First Inago Anth of Poetry* (Inago Pr, 1996,
    1995, 1985), *Various Artists, Mendocino Rev, South
    Ash Pr, Blue Unicorn*

Jewell Parker Rhodes 🎤 ✈   W
Arizona State Univ, English Dept, Box 870302, Tempe, AZ
85287-0302, 602-965-6856
Internet: jprhodes90@aol.com
    Pubs: *Magic City* (HC, 1997), *Voodoo Dreams* (St.
    Martin's Pr, 1993), *Seattle Rev, Callaloo, Feminist
    Studies, Calyx*

Alberto Alvaro Rios   P
English Dept, Arizona State Univ, Tempe, AZ 85287,
602-965-3168
    Pubs: *Teodoro Luna's Two Kisses* (Norton, 1990), *The
    Lime Orchard Woman, Five Indiscretions* (Sheep
    Meadow Pr, 1988, 1985), *New Yorker, Story, APR,
    Paris Rev*

Lois Roma-DeeLey   P
Paradise Valley Community College, 18401 N 32nd St,
Phoenix, AZ 85032, 602-493-2667
    Pubs: *Looking for Home: Women Writing about Exile:
    Anth* (Milkweed Edtns, 1990), *Classical Antiquity Street:
    Anth* (Pig Iron Pr, 1994), *la bella figura: A Choice: Anth*
    (malafemmina pr, 1993), *Faultline, Pinyon Rev,
    Confluence, Oregon Rev, Chants, CQ*

William Pitt Root   P
2022 E 5 St
Tucson, AZ 85719-5203, 602-791-2816
    Pubs: *Trace Elements from a Recurring Kingdom*
    (Confluence Pr, 1994), *Faultdancing* (U Pitt Pr, 1986),
    Manoa, Commonweal, Switched-On Guttenberg

Yvette A. Schnoeker-Shorb   P
PO Box 12226
Prescott, AZ 86304-2226
    Pubs: *Midwest Qtly, New Thought Jrnl, Green Hills
    Literary Lantern, Slant, Sulphur River Rev, Eureka
    Literary Mag, Blueline, Puerto del Sol, Concho River
    Rev, Pleiades, Pendragon, Sucarnochee Rev, Widener
    Rev*

Susanne Shaphren   W
823 E Brook Hollow Dr
Phoenix, AZ 85022
    Pubs: *Authorship, Crosscurrents, Hibiscus, The Writer*

Richard Shelton 🎤 ✈   P
Univ Arizona, English Dept, Tucson, AZ 85721,
602-743-7864
    Pubs: *Going Back to Bisbee* (U Arizona Pr, 1992), *The
    Other Side of the Story* (Confluence Pr, 1987),
    Hohokam (Sun/Gemini Pr, 1986)
Groups: Prisoners

Shirley Sikes 🎤 ✈   W
PO Box 65496
Tucson, AZ 85728-5496, 520-299-5733
Internet: sikes7@juno.com
    Pubs: *Suns Go Down* (Sunflower U Pr, 2000), *A Line
    of Cutting Women: Anth* (Calyx Pr, 1998), *O. Henry
    Prize Stories: Anth* (Doubleday, 1973), *Sonora Rev,
    Denver Qtly, Remark, Kansas Qtly, Calyx, Travelin
    Woman*

Leslie Marmon Silko   P&W
8000 W Camino del Cerro
Tucson, AZ 85745
    Pubs: *Almanac of the Dead* (S&S, 1991), *Storyteller*
    (Seaver Bks, 1981), *Ceremony* (Viking, 1977)

Beverly Silva   P&W
624 S Crows Nest Dr
Gilbert, AZ 85233-7129, 602-545-5842
    Pubs: *The Cat, The Second Street Poems* (Bilingual Pr,
    1986, 1983), *Infinite Divisions: An Anth of Chicana
    Literature* (U Arizona Pr, 1992)

Jim Simmerman 🎤 ✈   P
Northern Arizona Univ, Box 6032, English Dept, Flagstaff,
AZ 86011, 520-523-6269
Internet: jim.simmerman@nau.edu
    Pubs: *Kingdom Come, Moon Go Away, I Don't Love
    You No More* (Miami U Pr, 1999, 1994), *Dog Music:
    Anth* (St. Martin's Pr, 1996), *Antaeus, Antioch Rev,
    Iowa Rev, Laurel Rev, New Letters, Poetry, Prairie
    Schooner*

Linda Smukler   P&W
544 S 5th Ave, Apt E
Tucson, AZ 85701
    Pubs: *Normal Sex* (Firebrand Bks, 1994), *Love's
    Shadow: Anth* (Crossing Pr, 1993), *Ploughshares,
    American Voice, Prose Poem: Intl Jrnl, Kenyon Rev*

John Spaulding 🎤 ✈   P
4140 W Lane Ave
Phoenix, AZ 85051-5759
    Pubs: *Walking in Stone* (Wesleyan, 1989), *Poet Lore,
    Poetry East, Yankee, APR, Poetry, Iowa Rev, Prairie
    Schooner*

Laurel Speer P&W
PO Box 12220
Tucson, AZ 85732-2220, 520-747-2047
  Pubs: *Descant, Hollins Critic, Southern Humanities Rev,
  Massachusetts Rev, Prairie Schooner, Santa Barbara
  Rev*

Lawrence Sturhahn W
PO Box 50704
Tucson, AZ 85703, 520-887-8878
  Pubs: *NAR*

Virginia Chase Sutton 🎤 ✈ P
1714 E Del Rio Dr
Tempe, AZ 85282, 480-839-5411
  Pubs: *Fever Dreams: Contemporary Arizona Poetry
  Anth* (U Arizona Pr, 1997), *Paris Rev, Ploughshares,
  Witness, Antioch Rev, Boulevard, Poet Lore, Qtly West,
  Puerto del Sol, BPJ, Spoon River Poetry Rev*

Rhoda S. Tagliacozzo W
4748 E Quail Creek Dr
Tuscon, AZ 85718
  Pubs: *Saving Graces* (St. Martin's, 1979), *New York
  Woman, Cosmopolitan*

Tobi Taylor 🎤 ✈ P&W
6022 E Redbird Rd
Cave Creek, AZ 85331-6814, 480-585-9752
Internet: tobi.taylor@worldnet.att.net
  Pubs: *Layers of History* (Northland Research, 1995), *An
  Apple a Day: Anth* (Half Halt Pr, 2001), *In My Life:
  Anth* (Fromm Intl, 1998), *Rockford Rev, Oregon Rev,
  South Ash Pr, Gryphon, Colorado North Rev, Ripples*

Pamela Uschuk P
2022 E 5 St
Tucson, AZ 85719-5203, 520-791-2816
  Pubs: *Without Birds, Without Flowers, Without Trees*
  (Flume, 1991), *Light from Dead Stars* (Full Count,
  1981), *American Voice, Parnassus Rev, Agni, Poetry,
  Nimrod, Parabola*

Anna Lee Walters P&W
PO Box 276
Tsaile, AZ 86556, 602-724-3311
  Pubs: *Ghost Singer* (U New Mexico Pr, 1995), *Talking
  Indian* (Firebrand Bks, 1992), *The Spirit Seekers*
  (Chronicle Bks, 1989)

Frank Waters W
5630 N Blue Bonnet Rd
Tucson, AZ 85743
  Pubs: *The Man Who Killed the Deer* (U Ohio Pr,
  1992), *Book of the Hopi* (Viking, 1992)

Ramona Martinez Weeks P
326 W Dobbins Rd
Phoenix, AZ 85041
  Pubs: *Her Work* (Shearer Pub, 1982), *Lincoln County
  Poems* (Konocti Pr, 1973), *Virginia Qtly Rev, Forum*

Dana Weimer P
324 E 14 St
Tempe, AZ 85281, 602-966-2852
  Pubs: *Moving Bodies* (Sun/Gemini Pr, 1992), *Gargoyle
  Mag, Onthebus, Hayden's Ferry Rev, New Laurel Rev,
  Zone Mag*

Peter Wild P
Univ Arizona, English Dept, Modern Languages, Tucson,
AZ 85721, 602-621-1836
  Pubs: *The Desert Reader* (U Utah Pr, 1991), *The
  Brides of Christ* (Mosaic, 1991), *APR, Iowa Rev*

Allen Woodman 🎤 ✈ W
PO Box 23310
Flagstaff, AZ 86002-2310
Internet: allen.woodman@nau.edu
  Pubs: *Saved By F. Scott Fitzgerald* (Livingston Pr,
  1997), *All-You-Can-Eat, Alabama* (Apalachee Pr, 1994),
  The Bear Who Came to Stay (Bradbury Pr, 1994),
  Cows Are Going to Paris (Boyd Mills Pr, 1991),
  Sudden Fiction (Continued): Anth (Norton, 1996), *Story,
  Mirabella, Flash Fiction*

George T. Wright 🎤 ✈ P
2617 W Crown King Dr
Tucson, AZ 85741-2569, 520-575-1130
Internet: twright@u.arizona.edu
  Pubs: *Aimless Life* (North Stone Edtns, 1999), *New
  Yorker Book of Poetry: Anth* (Viking, 1969), *New
  Yorker, American Rev, Sewanee Rev, Esquire, Dacotah
  Territory*

Leilani Wright 🎤 ✈ P
247 W 9th St
Mesa, AZ 85201, 480-964-5211
Internet: laniw@aztec.asu.edu
  Pubs: *A Natural Good Shot* (White Eagle Coffee Store
  Pr, 1994), *Contemporary Arizona Poets: Anth* (U
  Arizona Pr, 1997), *Atlanta Rev, Tampa Rev, Hawaii
  Rev, Hayden's Ferry Rev, South Carolina Rev, Blue
  Mesa Rev, CSM*

Ofelia Zepeda 🎤 ✈ P
Univ of Arizona, Dept of Linguistics, PO Box 210028,
Tucson, AZ 85721-0028, 520-621-8294
  Pubs: *Jewed I-hoi/Earth Movement* (Kore Pr, 1997),
  Ocean Power, Home Places (U Arizona Pr, 1995,
  1995), *Poetry of the American Southwest: Anth*
  (Columbia U Pr, 1997), *Reinventing the Enemy's
  Language: Anth* (Norton Pr, 1997)
Lang: Tohono O'Odham. I.D.: Tohono O'Odham

ARKANSAS

Lee Barwood   P&W
PO Box 519
Salem, AR 72576, 501-895-3182
    Pubs: *Sisters in Fantasy II: Anth* (NAL, 1992),
Horsefantastic: Anth (DAW Bks, 1991), *Weirdbook,
Fantasy, Ellery Queen's Mag, Paradox, Haunts*

Mark Blaeuer 🎤 ✈   P
414 Veranda Trail
Pearcy, AR 71964-9318, 501-525-4798
    Pubs: *The Small Pond, Lilliput Rev, Mockingbird,
Tapjoe, Rag Shock, The Plastic Tower, Slant, Wind,
Hiram Poetry Rev, Poetry Motel*

Sue Abbott Boyd   P
2301 Quarry Dr
Van Buren, AR 72956-6440, 501-782-7642

Andrea Hollander Budy   P
PO Box 1107
Mountain View, AR 72560-1107, 870-269-4586
    Pubs: *House Without a Dreamer* (Story Line Pr, 1993),
What the Other Eye Sees (Wayland Pr, 1991), *NER,
Poetry, Georgia Rev, Kenyon Rev, SPR*

Ralph Burns 🎤 ✈   P
Univ Arkansas, English Dept, Little Rock, AR 72204,
501-569-3160
    Pubs: *Swamp Candles* (U Iowa Pr, 1996), *Mozart's
Starling* (Ohio Rev Bks, 1990), *Us* (Cleveland St U Pr,
1985), *Any Given Day* (U Alabama Pr, 1985), *Poetry,
Atlantic*

Crescent Dragonwagon   W
Rte 4, Box 7, 1 Frisco St
Eureka Springs, AR 72632-9401
    Pubs: *Dairy Hollow House Soup & Bread* (Workman,
1992), *Home Place, The Year It Rained* (Macmillan,
1991, 1984), *Lear's, New York Times Book Rev, Ms.,
Mode*

Ellen Gilchrist   P&W
834 Easwood Dr
Fayetteville, AR 72701
    Pubs: *Light Can Be Both Wave & Particle, The Anna
Papers* (Little, Brown, 1989, 1988)

Michael Heffernan   P
English Dept, Univ Arkansas, Fayetteville, AR 72701,
501-575-5990
    Pubs: *The Man at Home* (U Arkansas Pr, 1988), *To
the Wreakers of Havoc* (U Georgia Pr, 1984), *Iowa
Rev, The Qtly, Shenandoah*

David Jauss 🎤 ✈   P&W
English Dept, Univ Arkansas, 2801 S University, Little
Rock, AR 72204, 501-569-8316
    Pubs: *Black Maps* (U Massachusetts Pr, 1996),
Improvising Rivers (Cleveland State U Pr, 1995),
*Nation, Missouri Rev, Iowa Rev, Paris Rev, Poetry,
Georgia Rev, NER*

Paul Lake   P&W
400 S Commerce Ave
Russellville, AR 72801, 501-967-2174
    Pubs: *Among the Immortals* (Story Line Pr, 1994),
Another Kind of Travel (U Chicago Pr, 1988), *Paris
Rev, Yale Rev, New Republic*

Norman Lavers 🎤 ✈   W
3068 CR 901
Jonesboro, AR 72401-0754, 870-935-8543
    Pubs: *Growing Up in Berkeley with the Bomb* (Summer
Hse, 1998), *The Northwest Passage* (Fiction Collective,
1984), *APR, NAR, Short Story Intl, Missouri Rev*

Jo McDougall 🎤 ✈   P
6 Perdido Cir
Little Rock, AR 72211-2142, 501-223-3540
    Pubs: *From Darkening Porches, Towns Facing
Railroads, The Made Thing: An Anth of Contemporary
Southern Poetry, A New Geography of Poets: Anth* (U
Arkansas Pr, 1996, 1991, 1999, 1993), *Hudson Rev,
New Orleans Rev, New Letters, Kenyon Rev, Controlled
Burn*

Phillip H. McMath   W
711 W 3 St
Little Rock, AR 72201, 501-664-8990
    Pubs: *Arrival Point* (M&M Pr, 1991), *Native Ground*
(August Hse, 1984)

Rebecca Newth   P&W
611 Oliver Ave
Fayetteville, AR 72701
    Pubs: *Great North Woods* (Will Hall Bks, 1994), *19
Poems* (Picadilly Pr, 1993), *Cries of the Spirit: Anth*
(Beacon Pr, 1991), *Iris, Lamia Ink, Qtly West*

Carter Patteson   W
2700 Harrisburg Rd
Jonesboro, AR 72401, 501-932-8453
    Pubs: *Texas Qtly, Wind, Mississippi Valley Rev,
Roanoke Rev*

James Whitehead   P&W
517 E Lafayette
Fayetteville, AR 72707, 501-575-4301

Miller Williams 🎤 ✈ P
1111 Valley View Dr
Fayetteville, AR 72701-1603, 501-521-2934
Internet: mwms1000@aol.com
    Pubs: *Some Jazz a While* (U Illinois Pr, 1999), *Patterns of Poetry* (LSU Pr, 1986)

Terry Wright P
Univ Central Arkansas, English Dept, Conway, AR 72035, 501-450-5108
    Pubs: *No More Nature* (Kairos Edtns Pr, 1993), *Pig Iron, Rolling Stone, Urbanus, Puerto del Sol, Sequoia, Plastic Tower*

CALIFORNIA

William H. Abbott W
5000 Coldwater Canyon #4
Sherman Oaks, CA 91423, 818-761-3630
    Pubs: *Cat's Eye, Seems, Trace, Sunset Palms Hotel, Citadel*

Steve Abee P&W
1614 Lucretia Ave
Los Angeles, CA 90026, 213-481-2677
    Pubs: *King Planet* (Bork Press/Incommunicado, 1997), *Revival: Anth* (Manic D Press, 1994), *Quarry West, Poet's Fest, Spillway*

Elmaz Abinader P
4200 Park Blvd 138
Oakland, CA 94602, 510-444-4389
    Pubs: *Children of the Roojine* (U Wisconsin Pr, 1997), *Grape Leaves: A Century of Arab-American Poetry: Anth* (U Utah Pr, 1988)

SDiane Adamz-Bogus P&W
PO Box 2087
Cupertino, CA 95015-2087, 408-279-6626
    Pubs: *Buddhism in the Classroom, The Chant of the Woman of Magdalena, Dykehands* (Woman in the Moon Pubs, 1996, 1994, 1994), *The New Age Reader: Anth* (S&S, 1998), *MLA Newsletter, Connexions, Spirit, Sinister Wisdom, Common Lives, Black Scholar*

Kim Addonizio 🎤 ✈ P&W
1725 Quintara St
San Francisco, CA 94116-1234
Internet: http://addonizio.home.mindspring.com
    Pubs: *Tell Me, Jimmy & Rita, The Philosopher's Club* (BOA Edtns, 2000, 1997, 1994), *In the Box Called Pleasure* (Fiction Collective 2, 1999), *The Best American Poetry 2000: Anth* (Scribner, 2000), *The Beacon Best of 1999* (Beacon, 1999)
Groups: Seniors, Prisoners

Opal Palmer Adisa 🎤 ✈ P&W
PO Box 10625
Oakland, CA 94610-0625, 510-268-0704
Internet: opalpro@aol.com
    Pubs: *Leaf of Life, Traveling Woman* (Jukebox Pr, 2000, 1979), *It Begins with Tears* (Heinemann, 1997), *Tamarind & Mango Women* (Sister Vision Pr, 1992), *Bake-Face & Other Guava Stories* (Kelsey Str Pr, 1986), *Zyzzyva, Obsidian II, Frontiers, Sage*

Frances Payne Adler P
California State Univ, Monterey Bay, 100 Campus Ctr, Seaside, CA 93955-8001, 831-582-3982
    Pubs: *Raising the Tents* (Calyx, 1993), *When the Bough Breaks* (Newsage Pr, 1993), *Progressive, Women's Rev of Bks, Prism Intl, Ms., Exquisite Corpse*

Mandy Aftel W
1518 Walnut
Berkeley, CA 94709, 510-841-2111
    Pubs: *Out of Step & Out of Detroit* (Inkblot, 1986)

Pancho Aguila P
c/o Esperanza Farr, 3341 18 St, San Francisco, CA 94110

Ellery Akers 🎤 ✈ P&W
1592 Union, #211
San Francisco, CA 94123
    Pubs: *Knocking on the Earth* (Wesleyan, 1989), *Sierra, APR, Ploughshares, Intro 6*

Askia Akhnaton 🎤 ✈ P
656 Lytton Ave #G123
Palo Alto, CA 94301, 650-326-3381
    Pubs: *Concurencie: This Season for Love, Sing When the Spirit Says Sing* (Vision Victory People, 2001, 2000), *The Last Black Man* (Soul Visions, 1994), *Indianapolis U Mag*
I.D.: African-American

Mimi Albert 🎤 ✈ W
English Dept, Napa Valley College, 2100 Napa Vallejo Hwy, Napa, CA 94558, 510-918-5514
Internet: abriel@well.com
    Pubs: *Skirts* (Baskerville, 1994), *A Different Beat: Anth* (Serpent's Tail Pr, 1997), *The House on Via Gambito: Anth* (Two Rivers Pr, 1991), *Fiction Intl, Crazyquilt, SF Chronicle, Poetry Flash, Caprice, Southern Lights*
Groups: Mentally III, Women

Adele Aldridge P
6363 Christie Ave, #2106
Emeryville, CA 94608-1945
    Pubs: *Once I Was a Square, Notpoems* (Magic Circle Pr, 1974, 1972)

Jean Aldriedge P
1020 Bay St, Apt C
Santa Monica, CA 90405, 213-396-0825
   Pubs: *Circus Maximus, Interstate, Encore, Village Idiot, Dekalb Literary Arts Jrnl, Pig Iron*

Karl Alexander W
c/o Polly Fox, 1380 Manzanita Ave, Palm Springs, CA 92264, 760-327-2988
   Pubs: *Papa & Fidel* (Tor/St. Martin's Pr, 1989), *Curse of the Vampire* (Pinnacle, 1982), *Time After Time* (Delacorte/Dell, 1979)

T. Diener Allen W
PO Box 2775
Carmel-By-The-Sea, CA 93921

Dorothy Allison ♀ ✈ P&W
PO Box 460908
San Francisco, CA 94146-0908
Internet: karlsbergm@aol.com
   Pubs: *Cavedweller, Two or Three Things I Know for Sure, Bastard Out of Carolina* (Dutton, 1998, 1995, 1992), *Trash* (Firebrand, 1988)

Norma Almquist ♀ ✈ P
415 W Ave 42
Los Angeles, CA 90065, 323-223-8257
   Pubs: *Traveling Light* (Fithian Pr, 1997), *Where Icarus Falls: Anth* (Santa Barbara Rev, 1998), *Only Morning in Her Shoes: Anth* (Utah U Pr, 1990), *Crosscurrents, New Orleans Rev*

David Alpaugh P
Small Poetry Press, PO Box 5342, Concord, CA 94524, 510-798-1411
   Pubs: *Counterpoint* (Story Line Pr, 1994), *The Literature of Work: Anth* (U Phoenix Pr, 1991), *Asylum, BPR, Exquisite Corpse, Poets On, Poet & Critic, Wisconsin Rev*

Cathryn Alpert ♀ ✈ W
Box 624
Aptos, CA 95001
Internet: cathryn@alpert.com
   Pubs: *Rocket City* (Vintage, 1996), *Walking the Twilight I & II: Anth* (Northland Pub, 1996), *Sudden Fiction (Continued): Anth, Best of the West: Anth* (Norton, 1996, 1992), *Puerto del Sol, Zyzzyva*

Alta ♀ ✈ P&W
PO Box 5540
Berkeley, CA 94705, 510-547-7545
   Pubs: *Traveling Tales* (Acapella, 1990), *Deluged with Dudes* (Shameless Hussy Pr, 1989)
I.D.: Feminist

Alurista P
California Polytechnic State, Foreign Languages Dept, San Luis Obispo, CA 93407, 805-546-2992
   Pubs: *Z Eros, Et Tu, Raza?, Return* (Bilingual Pr, 1997, 1997, 1982), *Spik in glyph?* (Arte Publico Pr, 1981), *Calafia, Caracol*

Jorge Alvarez P
1004 S Ferris Ave
Los Angeles, CA 90022, 213-262-7120
   Pubs: *Homenaje a la Ciudad de Los Angeles: Anth* (Xismearte Pr, 1982), *El Espejo: Selected Chicano Literature: Anth* (Quinto Sol Pubs, 1972)

Ameen Alwan P
992 N Madison Ave
Pasadena, CA 91104-3625, 213-684-4002
   Pubs: *Nation, Kenyon Rev, New Republic, Michigan Qtly Rev, TriQtly, Chelsea, Epoch, Kayak*

Georgia Alwan P
992 N Madison Ave
Pasadena, CA 91104-3625
   Pubs: *Paris Rev, Boundary 2, Canto*

Jan Lee Ande ♀ ✈ P
8591C Via Mallorca
La Jolla, CA 92037-2599, 858-623-2748
Internet: ande@poetrywriter.com
   Pubs: *Place of Passage: Anth* (Story Line Pr, 2000), *Poetry Intl, Mississippi Rev, New Letters, Image, Sheila-Na-Gig, Nimrod*
Groups: Spiritual/Religious

Karla M. Andersdatter ♀ ✈ P
PO Box 790
Sausalito, CA 94966-0790, 415-383-8447
Internet: butterflytree@outrageous.net
   Pubs: *Tambourine, White Moon Woman or the Education of Imogene Love* (In Between Bks, 2000, 1999), *Wild Onions, The Broken String* (Plain View Pr, 1994, 1990)
I.D.: Californian. Groups: Seniors

Douglas Anderson P
Pitzer College, 1050 N Mills Ave, Claremont, CA 91711-6110, 909-621-8000
   Pubs: *The Moon Reflected Fire* (Alice James Bks, 1994), *The Four Way Reader: Anth* (Four Way Bks, 1996), *Virginia Qtly Rev, Ploughshares, Southern Rev, Massachusetts Rev*

Susan D. Noyes Anderson P
PO Box 2250
Saratoga, CA 95070-0250
   Pubs: *At the End of Your Rope, There's Hope* (Deseret Bks, 1997), *Age Happens: Anth, For Better & for Worse: Anth, The Funny Side of Parenthood: Anth* (Meadowbrook Pr, 1996, 1995, 1994), *Lyric, Poetpourri, Perceptions, Comstock Rev, Mobius, Ensign*

Caron Andregg P
1710 Panorama Rd
Vista, CA 92083, 760-643-0907
    Pubs: *Of Chemistry & Voodoo* (Inevitable Press, 1997),
*Spillway, Rattle, Sheila-Na-Gig, Talus & Scree, Poetry
Intl, The Maverick Press*

Michael Andrews P&W
1092 Loma Dr
Hermosa Beach, CA 90254, 310-374-7672
    Pubs: *In Country, The Poet from the City of the Angels*
(Bombshelter Pr, 1994, 1991), *Arizona Qtly, Onthebus,
Exquisite Corpse, Wormwood Rev*

Ralph Angel P
838 Bank St
South Pasadena, CA 91030, 213-259-9049
    Pubs: *Neither World* (Miami U Pr, 1995), *Anxious
Latitudes* (Wesleyan U Pr, 1986), *APR, Antioch Rev,
New Yorker, Partisan Rev, Poetry*

Roger R. Angle P&W
2225 Pacific Ave, Apt D
Costa Mesa, CA 92627, 949-642-9523
    Pubs: *Caprice, California State Poetry Qtly, Kryptogame,
StarWeb Paper, Italia America, Los Angeles Rev,
Center, Fiction West, Coldspring Jrnl, El Corno
Emplumado*

David Antin P&W
Visual Arts Dept, B-027, Univ California/San Diego, La
Jolla, CA 92093, 619-534-6552
    Pubs: *What It Means to Be Avant Garde* (New
Directions, 1993), *Selected Poems 1963-1973* (Sun &
Moon Pr, 1991), *Conjunctions, Critical Inquiry, Genre*

Eleanor Antin PP&P
Visual Arts Dept, B-027, Univ California/San Diego, La
Jolla, CA 92093, 619-755-4619
    Pubs: *Eleanora Antinova Plays* (Sun & Moon Pr, 1994),
Being Antinova (Astro Artz Pr, 1984)

Gloria E. Anzaldua 🎤 ✈ P&W
126 Centennial St
Santa Cruz, CA 95060-6502, 831-429-6041
Internet: anzaldua@pacbell.net
    Pubs: *Prietita & the Ghost Woman/Prietita y la Llorona,
Friends from the Other Side/Amigos del otro lado*
(Children's Bk Pr, 1995, 1993), *Borderlands/La Frontera*
(Spinsters/Aunt Lute, 1987), *Sinister Wisdom*

Roger Aplon P
16776 Bernardo Ctr Dr, Ste 110B
San Diego, CA 92128, 619-746-5250
    Pubs: *It's Mother's Day* (Barracuda Pr, 1996), *By
Dawn's Early Light at 120 MPH, Stiletto* (Dryad Pr,
1983, 1976)

Samuel Appelbaum 🎤 ✈ P
3929 Poppyseed Pl
Calabasas, CA 91302-2947, 818-880-0183
Internet: appelsam@pacbell.net
    Pubs: *Chtcheglov, Judea Capta* (Asylum Arts, 1998,
1995), *Saturn* (Quixote Pr, 1978)
I.D.: Jewish. Groups: Jewish

Jacki Apple PP
3532 Jasmine Ave #2
Los Angeles, CA 90034-4947, 310-836-2771
    Pubs: *Errant Bodies: Anth* (Brandon LaBelle, 1996),
*Ghost Dances/On the Event Horizon, Thank You for
Flying American* (CDs; Cactus, 1996, 1995), *Public Art
Rev, Performing Arts Jrnl, Revista de arte sonora*

Helen Arana P
405 King Dr
South San Francisco, CA 94080, 415-877-8046

Ivan Arguelles 🎤 ✈ P
1740 Walnut St, #4
Berkeley, CA 94709, 510-848-6846
    Pubs: *Madonna Septet* (Potes & Poets, 2000), *Enigma
& Variations* (Pantograph Pr, 1996), *Primary Trouble:
Anth* (Talisman Hse Pubs, 1996), *Lost & Found Times*
Lang: Spanish, Italian. I.D.: Latino/Latina

Rae Armantrout P
4774 E Mountain View Dr
San Diego, CA 92116, 619-563-3598
    Pubs: *Made to Seem, Necromance* (Sun & Moon,
1995, 1990), *Poems for the Millennium, Vol. 2: Anth* (U
California, 1998), *Postmodern American Poetry: Anth*
(Norton, 1994), *NAR, Iowa Rev, River City, Salt,
Boxkite, Conjunctions, Grand Street, Zyzzyva*

Linda "Gene" Armstrong P
5243 Lincoln Ave
Los Angeles, CA 90042, 213-257-4016
    Pubs: *Early Tigers* (Bellowing Ark Pr, 1995),
*Birmingham Poetry Rev, Rockford Rev, Bitterroot,
Earth's Daughters, Slant, Spirit That Moves Us*

Mary Armstrong P
PO Box 571
Woodland Hills, CA 91365, 818-348-9668
    Pubs: *Grand Passion: Anth* (Red Wind Bks, 1995),
Harbinger: Anth (L.A. Festival, 1990), *Spoon River
Poetry Rev, Kalliope, Zone 3, Birmingham Rev, Cream
City Rev*

Alfred Arteaga 🎤 ✈ P
Chicano Studies, Univ of California, 506 Barrows,
Berkeley, CA 94720-2570, 510-642-3563
Internet: bluebed@hotmail.com
    Pubs: *Red* (Bilingual Rev Pr, 2000), *Love in the Time
of Aftershocks, Cantos* (Chusma Hse, 1997, 1991),
House with the Blue Bed (Mercury Hse, 1997), *Chicano
Poetics: Anth* (Cambridge U Pr, 1997), *New Chicano
Writing: Anth* (U Arizona Pr, 1992), *Chispa*
Lang: Spanish. I.D.: Chicano/Chicana. Groups: Minorities,
Latino/Latina

Kenneth John Atchity P
435 S Curson, #8E
Los Angeles, CA 90036
Pubs: *A Writer's Time* (Norton, 1988), *Sleeping with an Elephant* (Valkyrie Pr, 1978), *Poetry/L.A., Southern Poetry, Huron Rev, Kansas Qtly, Ball State Forum*

Hope Athearn P
32 Bretano Way
Greenbrae, CA 94904, 415-461-0621
Pubs: *Asimov's, Amazing, Star*Line, Ploughshares, Blue Unicorn, Gaia*

Charles O. Atkinson P
142 Hagar Ct
Santa Cruz, CA 95064
Pubs: *The Best of Us on Fire* (Wayland, 1992), *The Only Cure I Know* (San Diego Poets Pr, 1991), *Nimrod, Pennsylvania Rev, SPR, River Styx, Poet Lore*

Mark Axelrod P&W
Dept of English & Comparative Literature, Chapman University, Orange, CA 92866, 714-997-6586
Pubs: *Cardboard Castles, Bombay California or Hollywood, Somewhere West of Vine* (Pacific Writers Pr, 1996, 1994), *Exquisite Corpse, Thanatos, Americas Rev, La Fusta, Iowa Rev, Splash, New Novel Rev, Pannus Index, Rev of Contemporary Fiction*

Hillary Ayer P
944 Fletcher Ln, #9
Hayward, CA 94544, 415-841-9032

Dale Alan Bailes P
5318 Breakers Way
Oxnard, CA 93035-1009, 805-984-1573
Pubs: *Recycling in L.A.* (Select Poets Series, 1996), *Ashes in the Grate* (South Carolina Arts Commission, 1983), *SPR, River Talk, Permafrost, Jrnl of Quantum Pataphysis*

Jane Bailey P
24 Kempton Ave
San Francisco, CA 94132
Pubs: *Tuning* (Slow Loris, 1978), *Pomegranate* (Black Stone, 1976), *Calyx, Columbia*

Eric Baizer P
PO Box 23042
Santa Barbara, CA 93121, 805-687-4067
Pubs: *Woodstock Poetry Rev, Coldspring Jrnl, Northern Pleasure, Cumberland Jrnl*

Laura Baker W
79 Roble Rd
Berkeley, CA 94705-2826
Pubs: *New Letters, San Francisco Focus, West Branch, Poetry East*

Charlene Baldridge 🎤 ✈ P
4435 Hamilton St, #5
San Diego, CA 92116-3079, 619-296-8044
Internet: charb81@home.com
Pubs: *Winter Roses* (Wordsperson Pr, 1990), *Poetry Conspiracy, Thirteen, Broomstick, Time of Singing, Sunrust, Song, Christianity Today*
Groups: Seniors, Feminist

Sheila Ballantyne W
Mills College, English Dept, 5000 MacArthur, Oakland, CA 94613, 510-430-2217
Pubs: *Life on Earth* (Linden Pr, 1988), *Imaginary Crimes, Norma Jean the Termite Queen* (Penguin, 1983, 1983)

Baloian P
PO Box 429
Half Moon Bay, CA 94019-0429
Pubs: *Eclipses* (Dark Sky Pr, 1995), *Ararat Papers* (Ararat Pr, 1979), *Anth of Mag Verse & Yearbook of American Poetry* (Monitor Bks, 1997), *Antioch Rev, Whole Notes, Poets On, Green Fuse, Ararat, Sensations, Midwest Qtly, Midwest Poetry Rev, Rain City Rev*

George Bamber W
2057 Willow Glen Rd
Fallbrook, CA 92028, 760-728-6786
Pubs: *The Sea Is Boiling Hot* (Ace Bks, 1971), *Rogue Mag*

Joan Baranow 🎤 ✈ P
73 Hillside Ave
Mill Valley, CA 94941-1180
Pubs: *Living Apart* (Plain View Pr, 1999), *Morning: Three Poems* (Radiolarian Pr, 1997), *Western Humanities Rev, Antioch Rev, Spoon-River Poetry Rev, Cream City Rev, U.S. 1 Worksheets*

Ramon Sender Barayon W
3922 23rd St
San Francisco, CA 94114, 415-821-2090
Pubs: *A Death in Zamora* (U New Mexico Pr, 1989), *Zero Weather* (Family Pub Co, 1981)

John Barbato P
20391 New Rome Rd
Nevada City, CA 95959, 916-265-8757
Pubs: *Wild Duck Rev, Northern Contours, Tule Rev, Glyphs, Community Endeavor, Deepest Valley Rev, Zyzzyva*

George Barlow P
English Dept, DeAnza College, 21250 Stevens Creek Blvd, Cupertino, CA 95014, 408-996-4547
Pubs: *Gumbo* (Doubleday, 1981), *Gabriel* (Broadside Pr, 1974), *Iowa Rev, River Styx, Antaeus, APR*

Dick Barnes P
English Dept, Pomona College, 140 W 6 St, Claremont,
CA 91711-6335, 909-621-8873
   Pubs: *Few & Far Between* (Ahsahta Pr, 1995), *A Lake
on the Earth* (Momentum Pr, 1982), *Poetry, Paris Rev,
Santa Monica Rev, Antioch, APR, Harvard*

Tony Barnstone P
Box 634
Whittier, CA 90608, 562-907-4200
   Pubs: *Impure* (U Pr Florida, 1999), *Seattle Rev, Literary
Rev, Agni 38, Nimrod*

Dorothy Barresi 🎤 ✈ P
English Dept, California State Univ, Northridge, CA
91330-8248, 818-677-3431
Internet: dorothy.barresi@csun.edu
   Pubs: *The Post-Rapture Diner* (U Pittsburgh Pr, 1996),
All of the Above (Beacon Pr, 1991), *Kenyon Rev,
Antioch, Gettysburg Rev, Parnassus, Michigan Qtly Rev,
Harvard Rev*

Anita Barrows P
546 The Alameda
Berkeley, CA 94707, 510-525-4899
   Pubs: *The Road Past the View* (QRL, 1992), *No More
Masks* (Doubleday, 1973), *Nation, Revision, Bridges,
Metis, Wild Duck Rev, Sonoma Mandala, Blind Donkey,
Montemora, Aphra*

Ellen Bass 🎤 ✈ P
PO Box 5296
Santa Cruz, CA 95063-5296, 831-426-8006
Internet: ebellenb@aol.com
   Pubs: *Our Stunning Harvest* (New Society, 1985), *No
More Masks!: Anth* (HC, 1993), *DoubleTake, Field,
Nimrod, Ms., Atlantic, Greensboro Rev, Calyx,
Ploughshares*
I.D.: Jewish, G/L/B/T

Peter S. Beagle 🎤 ✈ W
2135 Humboldt Ave
Davis, CA 95616-3084, 916-753-8538
Internet: psbeagle@juno.com
   Pubs: *A Dance for Emilia, Tamsin, Giant Bones*
(Dutton/Signet, 2000, 1999, 1997), *The Rhinoceros Who
Quoted Nietzsche* (Tachyon Pub, 1997), *The Unicorn
Sonata* (Turner Pub, 1996), *In the Presence of
Elephants* (Capra Pr, 1995), *Harper's, Saturday Evening
Post*

Beau Beausoleil 🎤 ✈ P
719 Lisbon St
San Francisco, CA 94112-3523
   Pubs: *Against the Brief Heavens* (Philos Pr, 2000), *Has
That Carrying* (Jungle Garden Pr, 1985), *Aleppo*
(Sombre Reptiles Pr, 1984)

Richard Beban P
Box 676
Santa Monica, CA 90406-0676, 310-535-2559
   Pubs: *Bedside Prayers: Anth* (HC, 1997), *Soul
Moments: Anth* (Conari Pr, 1997), *Caffeine, Rattle,
Spillway, Sabado Gigante, Neon Qtly, Blue Satellite,
51%*

Art Beck P
2528 25th Ave
San Francisco, CA 94116, 415-661-8502
   Pubs: *Simply to See* (Poltroon Pr, 1990), *Literature of
Work: Anth* (U Phoenix Pr, 1992), *Once More with
Feeling: Anth* (Vagabond, 1990), *Rilke* (Elysian Pr,
1983), *Alaska Qtly, Artful Dodge, Painted Bride Qtly,
Passages North, Invisible City, Sequoia*

Merle Ray Beckwith P
3732 Monterey Pine, #A109
Santa Barbara, CA 93105, 805-687-0310
   Pubs: *Abingdon Speeches & Recitations: Anth*
(Abingdon, 1994)

Robin Beeman 🎤 ✈ W
PO Box 963
Occidental, CA 95465-0963, 707-874-2091
Internet: robinbee@wclynx.com
   Pubs: *A Minus Tide, A Parallel Life & Other Stories*
(Chronicle Bks, 1995, 1992), *Gettysburg Rev, Puerto
del Sol, NAR, Crazyhorse, Ascent, Cutbank, Fiction
Network, Other Voices, PEN Syndicated Fiction*

James Scott Bell P
22136 Clarendon St
Woodland Hills, CA 91367, 818-703-7875
   Pubs: *The Night Carl Sagan Stepped on My Cat*
(Compendium Pr, 1988), *Broken Streets II*

Molly Bendall P
English Dept, Univ of Southern California, Los Angeles,
CA 90089-0354, 213-740-3748
   Pubs: *Dark Summer* (Miami U Pr, 1999), *After
Estrangement* (Peregrine Smith Bks, 1992), *Paris Rev,
Poetry, Colorado Rev, APR*

Karen Benke P&W
92 LaVerne Ave
Mill Valley, CA 94941, 415-380-9266
   Pubs: *Marin Poetry Center Press, Convolvulus, Conari
Press, Santa Clara Rev, Crown, Ploughshares,
California Qtly, Iris Edtns, Arctos Press*

Joyce Lorentzson Benson P
1220 Hampel St
Oakland, CA 94602-1112
   Pubs: *Lift, Io, Caterpillar, Redhandbook II, Boundary II,
Rolling Stock, Exquisite Corpse*

Rachelle Benveniste 🎤 ✈   P
5215 Sepulveda Blvd, #8-D
Culver City, CA 90230-5241, 310-398-9316
    Pubs: *Rapunzel, Rapunzel* (McBooks Pr, 1980),
    Gridlock: An Anth About Southern California (Applezaba
    Pr, 1990), *13th Moon, Sing Heavenly Muse,*
    Mindscapes, Playgirl
Groups: Jewish, Spiritual/Religious

Marsha Lee Berkman   W
1600 Hopkins Ave
Redwood City, CA 94062, 415-368-6516
    Pubs: *Mothers: Anth* (Northpoint Pr, 1996), *The*
    Schocken Book of Contemporary Jewish Fiction: Anth
    (Schocken Pr, 1992), *Other Voices, Sifrut Rev*

Bill Berkson 🎤 ✈   P
25 Grand View Ave
San Francisco, CA 94114, 415-826-2947
Internet: berkson@pacbell.net
    Pubs: *Serenade* (Zoland, 2000), *A Copy of the*
    Catalogue (Labyrinth, 1999), *Young Manhattan* (w/A.
    Waldman; Erudite Fangs, 1999), *Lush Life* (Z Pr, 1984),
    Red Devil (Smithereens, 1983), *Start Over*
    (Tombouctou, 1983), *Chicago Rev, Arshile, Blue Book,*
    Shiny

Christopher Bernard 🎤 ✈   P&W
400 Hyde St, #606
San Francisco, CA 94109-7445
    Pubs: *The Dilettante of Cruelty: Deserts* (Meridien
    Pressworks, 1996), *Gilded Abattoir: Wreckage from a*
    Journey (Small Poetry Pr, 1986), *ACM, Caesura,*
    Ampersand, Caveat Lector, The Drummer, Metier,
    Haight-Ashbury Jrnl

Mira-Lani Bernard   W
Art Options, PO Box 29476, Los Angeles, CA 90029-0476,
213-655-8433
    Pubs: *Athena Louise Replies* (Coffee Hse Pr, 1990),
    Word of Mouth: Anth (Crossing Pr, 1990), *Exquisite*
    Corpse, Fiction Intl, Los Angeles 1956, Fizz

Jeff Berner   P
PO Box 244
Dillon Beach, CA 94929-0244
    Pubs: *The Joy of Working from Home* (Berret-Koehler,
    1994), *The Photographic Experience* (Doubleday/Anchor,
    1975), *Kayak, Stolen Paper Rev, Antioch Rev,*
    Liberation

Alan Bernheimer   P
1613 Virginia St
Berkeley, CA 94703
    Pubs: *State Lounge* (Tuumba, 1981), *Up Late: Anth* (4
    Walls 8 Windows, 1987)

Elizabeth A. Bernstein   P
PO Box 94
Paradise, CA 95967-0094
    Pubs: *Pull of the Tides* (Chiron Review, 1998), *Silver*
    Quill: Anth (The Scriveners, 1995), *Black Buzzard Rev,*
    CQ, Watershed, New Press, Piedmont, Poetalk/Bay
    Area Poets Coalition, Taproot, Chiron Rev,
    Contemporary Rev

Lisa (Lisa B) Bernstein 🎤 ✈   P
PO Box 20663
Oakland, CA 94620-0663, 510-336-3276
Internet: www.lisabmusic.com
    Pubs: *Free Me for the Joy* (Piece of Pie Records,
    1999), *The Transparent Body* (Wesleyan, 1989),
    Anorexia (Five Fingers, 1985), *Lilith: Anth* (Orpheus &
    Co, 1999), *Brilliant Corners, Poetry Intl, Zyzzyva, Calyx,*
    Tikkun, Ploughshares, Kenyon Rev
Groups: Women, Performance

John Berry   P&W
579 Crane Blvd
Los Angeles, CA 90065
    Pubs: *Flight of White Crows, Krishna Fluting*
    (Macmillan, 1960, 1959), *Chelsea, Manhattan Poetry*
    Rev

Jane Besen   P&W
1540 Arriba Dr
Monterey Park, CA 91754, 626-284-1161
    Pubs: *Happy Org*

Maur Bettman   W
Sonoma Mountain Rd
Petaluma, CA 94952, 707-763-3341
    Pubs: *Chicago Rev, Confrontation, Ascent, Virginia Qtly*
    Rev, Kansas Qtly, Apalachee Qtly

Michael F. Biehl   P
615 Central Ave, #301
Alameda, CA 94501-3875, 510-521-4063
    Pubs: *Graham House Rev, Concho River Rev, Great*
    River Rev, Plains Poetry Jrnl, Creeping Bent, Bitterroot,
    Interim, Image: A Jrnl of Arts & Religion, Callaloo

Duane Big Eagle   P&W
210 Cleveland Ave
Petaluma, CA 94952-1775, 707-778-3107
    Pubs: *America Street: Anth* (Persea Bks, 1993),
    Zyzzyva, Mattoid, Headlands Jrnl, Inside Osage

Judith Bishop 🎤 ✈   P
240 Fulton St
Palo Alto, CA 94301, 650-324-1379
Internet: jbishop1@earthlink.net
    Pubs: *Wheel of Breath* (Green Way Pr, 1994), *The*
    Burning Place (Fithian Pr, 1994), *The Longest Light*
    (Five Fingers Rev Pr, 1991), *Muse Strikes Back: Anth*
    (Story Line Pr, 1997), *Coastlight: Anth* (Coastlight Pr,
    1981), *Americus Rev, Kalliope*
Lang: French, Welsh. I.D.: Native American,
Nature/Environment. Groups: Multicultural

Bette-Jean Black P&W
3747-105 Vista Campana S
Oceanside, CA 92057, 619-754-6832
 Pubs: *Hawaii Rev, Tide Pools, Green's Mag, Pig Iron, Mississippi Valley Rev, Northwoods Jrnl, Dekalb Literary Arts Jrnl, Family Living*

David Black W
c/o David Wirtschafter, ICM, 8942 Wilshire Blvd, Beverly Hills, CA 90211, 310-550-4000
 Pubs: *Peep Show* (Doubleday, 1986), *The Plague Years* (S&S, 1985), *Murder at the Met* (Dial, 1983), *Smart, Rolling Stone, Harper's*

Clark Blaise W
130 Rivoli St
San Francisco, CA 94117
 Pubs: *If I Were Me, Man & His World, Lunar Attractions* (Porcupine's Quill, 1997, 1992, 1990), *I Had a Father* (Addison-Wesley, 1993), *Resident Alien* (Penguin, 1986), *Mother Jones, Bomb, Descant*

Ella Blanche P
6817 Adolphia Dr
Carlsbad, CA 92009
 Pubs: *Whispering to God, Searching the Shadows* (Realities Library, 1986, 1984), *Maize, Poetry View, Impetus, Realities, Poetic Justice*

Douglas Blazek 🎤 ✈ P
2751 Castro Way
Sacramento, CA 95818-2709, 916-456-5734
 Pubs: *We Sleep As the Dream Weaves Outside Our Minds* (Alantansi Pr, 1994), *TriQtly, Seattle Rev, Prose Poem, Zyzzyva, APR, Poetry, Nation*

Lucy Jane Bledsoe W
1226 Cedar St
Berkeley, CA 94702, 510-526-7771
 Pubs: *Working Parts, Sweat: Stories & a Novella* (Seal Pr, 1997, 1995), *Newsday, Fiction Intl, Northwest Literary Forum, Wig, Lambda Book Report, The Writer*

Chana Bloch 🎤 ✈ P
12 Menlo Pl
Berkeley, CA 94707-1533, 510-524-8459
Internet: chana@mills.edu
 Pubs: *Mrs. Dumpty* (U Wisconsin Pr, 1998), *The Song of Songs* (U California, 1998), *The Past Keeps Changing* (Sheep Meadow, 1992), *Poetry, Field, Iowa Rev, Ploughshares, Poetry NW, Atlantic, Nation, New Yorker, Marlboro Rev, Salmagundi*

Robert Bloch W
4450 Placidia Ave, #2
Toluca Lake, CA 91602-2434

Layeh Bock Pallant P
642 Alcatraz Ave #106
Oakland, CA 94609, 510-547-5360
 Pubs: *Through the Hill Anthology, Poetry Flash, Yellow Silk, Haight-Ashbury Literary Jrnl, Beatitude*

Maclin Bocock W
635 Gerona Rd
Stanford, CA 94305, 415-327-6687
 Pubs: *New Directions 51 & 46: Anths* (New Directions, 1987, 1983), *Southern Rev, Sequoia, Fiction*

Deborah Boe P
PO Box 23851
Santa Barbara, CA 93121
 Pubs: *Mojave* (Hanging Loose Pr, 1987), *Poetry, Poetry NW, Hanging Loose, Ohio Rev*

Laurel Ann Bogen 🎤 ✈ P
836 N La Cienega Blvd, #217
West Hollywood, CA 90069
Internet: labogen@mindspring.com
 Pubs: *Fission* (Red Dancefloor Pr, 1998), *The Last Girl in the Land of the Butterflies, The Burning* (Red Wind Bks, 1996, 1991), *Outlaw Bible of American Poetry: Anth* (Thunder's Mouth Pr, 1999), *The Stand-Up Poetry Anth* (California State U Pr, 1994), *Solo*

Abby Lynn Bogomolny 🎤 ✈ P&W
PO Box 9636
Oakland, CA 94613-0636
 Pubs: *People Who Do Not Exist* (Woman in the Moon, 1997), *Black of Moonlit Sea, Nauseous in Paradise* (HerBooks, 1991, 1986), *Sexual Harrassment: Anth* (Crossing Pr, 1987) *Quarry West, Genre 10*
Groups: Women, Social Justice

Lucile Bogue W
2611 Brooks Ave
El Cerrito, CA 94530-1416, 510-232-0346
 Pubs: *One Woman, One Ranch, One Summer* (Strawberry Hill Pr, 1997), *I Dare You! How to Stay Young Forever* (Bristol Pub, 1990), *Pegasus Anth Series* (Kendall Hunt Pub, 1992), *Pen Woman, Blue Unicorn, Galley Sail Rev*

Margot Bollock P
2015 Belle Monte Ave
Belmont, CA 94002, 415-593-7753

Maryetta Kelsick Boose P
1537 W 20 St
San Bernardino, CA 92411, 714-887-6170
 Pubs: *Fragrant African Flowers* (Guild Pr, 1988), *Mosaic, Essence, Black American Lit Forum*

Millicent C. Borges 🎤 ✈   P
16 Thorton Ave #105
Venice, CA 90291
   Pubs: *Leading Me Towards Desperation* (Partisan Pr,
   2000), *Boomer Girls: Anth* (U Iowa Pr, 1999),
   Sycamore Rev, Tampa Rev, Seattle Rev, Laurel Rev,
   Madison Rev, Interim, Hubbub
I.D.: Portuguese. Groups: Seniors, Hispanic

David Borofka   W
Reedley College, 995 N Reed Ave, Reedley, CA
93654-2099, 209-638-3641
   Pubs: *The Island* (MacMurray & Beck, 1997), *Hints of*
   His Mortality (U Iowa Pr, 1996), *Black Warrior Rev,*
   Santa Monica Rev, West Branch, South Dakota Rev,
   Carolina Qtly, Greensboro Rev, Crosscurrents, Missouri
   Rev, Southern Rev, Gettysburg Rev, Witness

Terry Borst   P
23515 Lyons Ave, #280
Santa Clarita, CA 91355
   Pubs: *Gargoyle, Asylum, American Classic Anth, Nebo,*
   Blue Unicorn, Oyez Rev, Tequila Poetry Rev

Greg Boyd 🎤 ✈   P&W
c/o Asylum Arts Publishing, 5847 Sawmill Rd, Paradise,
CA 95969, 530-876-1454
   Pubs: *Modern Love & Other Tall Tales* (Red Hen Pr,
   2000), *Sacred Hearts* (Hi Jinx Pr, 1996), *Water &*
   Power (Asylum Arts, 1991), *Puppet Theatre, The*
   Masked Ball (Unicorn Pr, 1989, 1987), *Fiction Intl,*
   Caliban, Bakunin, Asylum, Poet Lore

Ray Bradbury   W
10265 Cheviot Dr
Los Angeles, CA 90064

Cecilia Manguerra Brainard   W
PO Box 5099
Santa Monica, CA 90409, 310-392-0541
   Pubs: *When the Rainbow Goddess Wept* (U Michigan
   Pr, 1999), *Acapulco at Sunset & Other Stories,*
   Contemporary Fiction by Filipinos in America: Anth
   (Anvil, 1995, 1998), *Filipinas Mag, Sunstar, Mirror*
   Weekly, West/Word Jrnl, Philippine Graphic

Donn Brannon   P
Box 105
Castella, CA 96017, 916-235-2303
   Pubs: *Bread Jrnl*

Charles Brashear   W
5025 Old Cliffs Rd
San Diego, CA 92120, 619-287-0850
   Pubs: *Contemporary Insanities* (MacDonald & Reinecke,
   1990), *Aniyunwiya: Contemporary Cherokee Prose: Anth*
   (Greenfield Rev Pr, 1995), *Vignette, Callaloo*

Luke Breit 🎤 ✈   P
2119 7th Ave
Sacramento, CA 95818-4312, 916-446-7638
Internet: lwb@quiknet.com
   Pubs: *Unintended Lessons, Messages: New & Selected*
   Poems (QED Pr, 1998, 1989), *Words the Air Speaks*
   (Wilderness Poetry Pr, 1978), *New Yorker, Pacific*
   Coast, Talkhard!, HaightAshbury Literary Rev, Poetry
   Now, One Dog Press, Oro Madre

Summer Brenner 🎤 ✈   W
1727 Addison St
Berkeley, CA 94703-1501, 510-644-3099
   Pubs: *Ivy: Tale of a Homeless Girl in San Francisco*
   (Creative Arts, 2000), *Presque nulle part* (France;
   Gallimard, 1999), *One Minute Movies* (Thumbscrew Pr,
   1996), *Dancers & the Dance* (Coffee Hse Pr, 1990)

David Breskin 🎤 ✈   P&W
1061 Francisco St
San Francisco, CA 94109-1126, 415-921-3354
Internet: db233@msn.com
   Pubs: *Fresh Kills* (Cleveland St U Pr, 1997), *The Real*
   Life Diary of a Boomtown Girl (Viking Penguin, 1989),
   Parnassus, New American Writing, Qtly West, American
   Letters & Commentary, New Yorker, TriQtly, Paris Rev,
   Boulevard, Nimrod, Salmagundi, NAW
I.D.: Multicultural, Activists. Groups: Prisoners, Basketball

Peter Brett   P
PO Box 1771
Ross, CA 94957-1771, 415-459-2566
   Pubs: *Borrowing the Sky* (Kastle, 1979), *Seneca Rev,*
   Kansas Qtly, Zyzzyva, Olympia Rev, Florida Rev,
   Wisconsin Rev, Rain City, Acorn, Red Owl, Silver Black
   Qtly, Lactuca

Armand Brint   P
215 Thompson St
Ukiah, CA 95482, 707-468-8906
   Pubs: *Plowman, Five Fingers Poetry, Lactuca, Pearl,*
   Poetry Flash, North Atlantic Rev

Mae Briskin   W
3604 Arbutus Dr
Palo Alto, CA 94303
   Pubs: *The Tree Still Stands, A Boy Like Astrid's Mother*
   (Norton, 1991, 1988), *Ascent, Chicago Tribune Mag,*
   San Francisco Chronicle Mag, St. Anthony Messenger,
   Western Humanities Rev, Mid-American Rev

Bill Broder   W
68 Central Ave
Sausalito, CA 94965, 415-332-4364
   Pubs: *Remember This Time* (w/G.K. Broder; Newmarket
   Bks, 1983)

Leslie Brody   P&W
238 San Jose Ave
San Francisco, CA 94110, 415-641-1795
  Pubs: *Monsieur Dada, Boxcar, Isthmus*

David Bromige   P&W
461 High St
Sebastopol, CA 95472
  Pubs: *A Cast of Tens* (Avec Bks, 1994), *From the
Other Side of the Century* (Sun & Moon Bks, 1994),
Avec, Object Permanence, River City, Sulfur, Fragmente

Lynne Bronstein 🎤 ✈   P
215 Bay St, #1
Santa Monica, CA 90405-1003, 310-392-2728
  Pubs: *Thirsty in the Ocean* (Graceful Dancer Pr, 1980),
Gridlock: Anth (Applezaba Pr, 1990), *Caffeine, California
Poetry Calendar*
I.D.: Jewish, Feminist

Beverly J. Brown   W
121 Sierra St
Escondido, CA 92025
  Pubs: *True Story, True Love, True Confessions, True
Life Secrets, Intimate Story*

Cecil Brown   W
38 Panoramic Way
Berkeley, CA 94704

Diana Brown   W
PO Box 2846
Carmel, CA 93921-2846
  Pubs: *The Blue Dragon, The Hand of a Woman, The
Sandalwood Fan* (St. Martin's, 1988, 1984, 1983)

James Brown   W
English Dept, California State Univ, 5500 University Pkwy,
San Bernardino, CA 92407, 909-880-5894
  Pubs: *Lucky Town* (HB, 1994), *Second Story Theatre &
Two Encores* (Story Line Pr, 1993), *Final Performance*
(Morrow, 1988), *Chicago Tribune, L.A. Times Mag*

Linda A. Brown   P
1006 Hermes Ave
Leucadia, CA 92024
  Pubs: *Contemporary Women Poets* (Merlin, 1977),
Canta Una Mujer (Athena, 1973), *Ms., Malahat Rev*

Stephanie Brown   P
2818 Via Blanco
San Clemente, CA 92673
  Pubs: *Allegory of the Supermarket* (U Georgia, 1998),
Best American Poetry: Anths (Scribner, 1997, 1995,
1993), *American Poetry Review*

Lennart Bruce   P
31 Los Cerros Pl
Walnut Creek, CA 94598-3106, 925-932-8234
Internet: lensonb@aol.com
  Pubs: *The Coffee Break, The Ways of a Carpetbagger*
(Symposion, 1995, 1993), *Speak to Me* (The Spirit That
Moves Us Pr, 1990)

Bruce-Novoa   P&W
Dept of Spanish & Portuguese, Univ California, Irvine, CA
92717, 714-856-7265
  Pubs: *RetroSpace* (Arte Publico, 1990), *Inocencia
Perversa* (Baleen, 1976), *Periodico de Poesia,
Confluencia, Plural, Quimera, Hispania*

John J. Brugaletta   P
California State Univ, 800 N State College Blvd, Fullerton,
CA 92634, 714-773-2723
  Pubs: *The Tongue Angles* (Negative Capability Pr,
1990), *Random House Treasury of Light Verse: Anth*
(Random Hse, 1995), *Formalist, Hellas Rev*

Christopher Buckley   P
Univ California Riverside, Creative Writing Department,
Riverside, CA 92521-0118, 909-787-2414
  Pubs: *Fall from Grace* (BkMk Pr, 1998), *Camino Cielo*
(Orchises Pr, 1997), *Dark Matter* (Copper Beech Pr,
1993), *APR, Poetry, Iowa Rev, Qtly West, Hudson Rev,
Crazyhorse, Kenyon Rev*

Y. Stephan Bulbulian 🎤 ✈   P
113 Carter Way
Fowler, CA 93625-2000
  Pubs: *Saroyan's World* (William Saroyan Society, 1998),
Poets of the Vineyard: Anths (Vintage, 1999, 1998,
1997, 1996, 1995), *Ararat, Armenian Weekly, Hye
Sharzoom, Asbarez, Poets of the Vineyard, Nor
Hayastan*

Richard Alan Bunch   P
248 Sandpiper Dr
Davis, CA 95616-7546
  Pubs: *Sacred Space* (Dry Bones Pr, 1998), *South By
Southwest* (Cedar Bay Pr, 1997), *Wading the Russian
River* (Norton Coker Pr, 1993), *Black Moon: Anth*
(Dream Tyger Prod, 1996), *Fugue, Windsor Rev, Hawaii
Rev, Coe Rev, Poetry Nottingham, Black Mountain Rev*

Claire Burch   P&W
Regent Press, 6020A Adeline, Oakland, CA 94608,
510-547-7602
  Pubs: *Homeless in the '90s, You Be the Mother Follies*
(Regent Pr, 1994, 1994), *Life, McCall's, Redbook, SW
Rev*

Jean Burden 🎤   P
1129 Beverly Way
Altadena, CA 91001
  Pubs: *Taking Light from Each Other* (U Pr Florida,
1992), *American Scholar, Georgia Rev, Poetry*

E.P. Burr   W
1241 Irving Ave
Glendale, CA 91201, 818-956-5395
    Pubs: *Utah Spring, Lightning in the Fog* (Herald House,
    1979, 1977), *Cimarron Rev, Forum, South, Writers' Jrnl*
I.D.: Nature/Environment, Music/Arts

Robert A. Burton   W
1 Daniel Burnham Ct, #335-C
San Francisco, CA 94109, 415-922-0605
    Pubs: *Cellmates* (Russian Hill Pr, 1997), *Final Therapy*
    (Berkley, 1994), *Doc-in-a-Box* (Soho Pr, 1991)

Mary Bucci Bush   W
1007 Palm Terr
Pasadena, CA 91104, 818-797-6642
    Pubs: *A Place of Light* (Morrow, 1990), *The Voices We
    Carry: Anth* (Guernica Edtns, 1994), *Ploughshares,
    Missouri Rev, Black Warrior Rev*

Emilya Cachapero   P
1101 Plymouth Ave
San Francisco, CA 94112

Michael Cadnum ✈   P
555 Pierce St #143
Albany, CA 94706
    Pubs: *Redhanded, The Book of the Lion, Rundown,
    Heat, Taking It* (Viking, 2000, 2000, 1999, 1998, 1995),
    In a Dark Wood (Orchard Bks, 1998), *The Judas Glass*
    (Carroll & Graf, 1996), *America, Commonweal, SPR,
    Poetry NW, Writers' Forum, The Literary Rev*

Stratton F. Caldwell   P
80 N Kanan Rd
Agoura, CA 91301-1105
    Pubs: *Somatics, Quest, Fat Tuesday, Parnassus
    Literary Jrnl, Yellow Butterfly, Pinchpenny, Arete,
    Mendocino Rev*

Pat Califia   W
2215R Market St, #261
San Francisco, CA 94114
    Pubs: *Doc & Fluff* (Alyson, 1990), *Macho Sluts* (Alyson,
    1988), *The Advocate, On Our Backs*

Camincha   P
723 Moana Way
Pacifica, CA 94044, 415-359-0890
    Pubs: *Hard Love: Anth* (Queen of Swords Pr, 1997),
    Apocalypse 4: Anth (Northeastern Illinois U Pr, 1997),
    Four By Four: Anth (Amaranth Edtns, 1993), *Cups,
    Passager*

Janine Canan 🎤 ✈   P
772 Ernest Dr
Sonoma, CA 95476-4614, 707-939-2771
Internet: jancanan@vom.com
    Pubs: *Changing Woman* (Scars Pubs, 2000), *Elegy in
    the Lotus* (Emily Dickinson, 2000), *Her Magnificent
    Body* (Manroot, 1986), *Exquisite Corpse*

Patricia E. Canterbury 🎤 ✈   P
PO Box 160127
Sacramento, CA 95816-0127, 916-483-1046
Internet: patmyst@aol.com
    Pubs: *The Secret of St. Gabriel's Tower* (Regeje Pr,
    1998), *Dreams of 21st Century – Rivers V* (Sacramento
    Poetry Ctr, 1993), *Shadowdrifters... Images of China*
    (Georgia State Poetry Society, 1990)
I.D.: African-American. Groups: Children, Women

Jo-Anne Cappeluti   P&W
Fullerton, CA
Internet: jcappeluti@fullerton.edu
    Pubs: *Short Story, Literary Rev, Negative Capability,
    The Jrnl, Lyric, NYQ, South Coast Poetry Jrnl, Mosaic,
    Plains Poetry Rev, Bluegrass Lit Rev*

Eve La Salle Caram 🎤 ✈   P&W
The Writers' Program, UCLA Extension, Dept of Arts,
10995 Le Conte Ave, Los Angeles, CA 90024,
323-663-1095
    Pubs: *Rena: A Late Journey, Wintershine, Dear Corpus
    Christi* (Plain View Pr, 2000, 1994, 1991), *Avocet,
    Snowy Egret, Greenfield Rev, Sou'wester, Wisconsin
    Rev, Cottonwood*

Henry Carlisle   W
1100 Union St, #301
San Francisco, CA 94109-2019
Internet: hccarlisle@aol.com
    Pubs: *The Jonah Man, The Idealists* (w/O. Carlisle),
    (St. Martin's Pr, 2000, 1999)

R. S. Carlson 🎤 ✈   P
English Dept, Azusa Pacific Univ, 901 E Alosta Ave,
Azusa, CA 91702-4052, 818-815-6000
Internet: rcarlson@apu.edu
    Pubs: *Pacific Rev, Viet Nam Generation, Poet Lore,
    Hawaii Rev, Cape Rock, Hollins Critic*

Josephine Carson   W
PO Box 210240
San Francisco, CA 94121-0240
    Pubs: *Dog Star & Other Stories, Where Icarus Falls:
    Anth* (Santa Barbara Rev Pub, 1998), *Listening to
    Ourselves: Anth* (Anchor Bks, 1994), *New Yorker,
    American Short Fiction, Poetry USA, auto/bio*

Marie Cartier 🎤 ✈   P
974 Haverford Ave, #4
Pacific Palisades, CA 90272, 310-459-7601
  Pubs: *Freeze Count, Come Out, Come Out, Wherever You Are Stumbling Into Light* (Dialogos Pr, 1995 1995), *I Am Your Daughter, Not Your Lover* (Clothespin Fever Pr, 1995), *Sinister Wisdom, Heresies, Colorado Rev*
Groups: G/L/B/T, College/Univ

Peter Cashorali   P
857 1/2 N Hayworth
Los Angeles, CA 90046
  Pubs: *Bachy, Rara Avis, Poetry/L.A., Barney, Magazine, Beyond Baroque, Mouth of the Dragon*

Marsh G. Cassady 🎤 ✈   P&W
MCD R-03, PO Box 439016, San Diego, CA 92143
Internet: gary@telnor.com
  Pubs: *The Times of the Double Star, Perverted Proverbs & Sudden Drama* (Spectrum Pr, 1994, 1994), *Brussels Sprout, Chiron Rev*

Cyrus Cassells   P
c/o Mary Cassells, 2190 Belden Pl, Escondido, CA 92029, 619-745-9156
  Pubs: *The Mud Actor* (H Holt, 1982), *Under 35: The New Generation of American Poets: Anth* (Doubleday, 1989), *Kenyon Rev, Ploughshares, Callaloo, Agni*

Irene Chadwick   P
4336 Copper Cliff Ln
Modesto, CA 95355-8967, 209-524-3066
  Pubs: *Dawn Pearl* (Ietje Kooi Pr, 1994), *Mindprint Rev, Napa Rev, INA Coolbrith Circle, Images of Oracle*

Pamela Herbert Chais   W
611 N Oakhurst Dr
Beverly Hills, CA 90210, 213-276-6215

Jeffrey Paul Chan   W
Asian American Studies Program, San Francisco State Univ, 1600 Holloway, San Francisco, CA 94132-1700, 415-338-1796
Internet: jefchan@sfsu.edu
  Pubs: *The Big Aiiieeeee!: Anth* (NAL, 1990)

Janet Carncross Chandler   P
c/o Dan Chandler, 436 Old Wagon Rd, Trinidad, CA 95570, 916-448-6248
  Pubs: *Why Flowers Bloom, Flight of the Wild Goose* (Papier-Mache Pr, 1994, 1989), *Significant Relationships* (Chandler, 1988)

Kosrof Chantikian 🎤 ✈   P
20 Millard Rd
Larkspur, CA 94939-1918
  Pubs: *Prophecies & Transformations, Imaginations & Self-Discoveries* (KOSMOS, 1978, 1974)

Elizabeth Biller Chapman 🎤 ✈   P
121 Fulton St
Palo Alto, CA 94301-1320, 650-323-9331
Internet: thisbmagic@aol.com
  Pubs: *First Orchard* (Bellowing Ark Pr, 1999), *Creekwalker* (Mother Tongue Pr, 1995), *Poetry, American Tanka, GMR, Texas Observer, Prairie Schooner, Yankee*

Maxine Chernoff 🎤 ✈   P&W
369 Molino Ave
Mill Valley, CA 94941-2767, 415-389-1877
Internet: maxpaul@sfsu.edu
  Pubs: *A Boy in Winter* (Crown, 1999), *American Heaven* (Coffee Hse Pr, 1996), *Signs of Devotion, Plain Grief* (S&S, 1993, 1991), *NAR, Sulfur, Chicago Rev, TriQtly*

Justin Chin 🎤 ✈   P&W
250-B Guerrero St
San Francisco, CA 94103-2313, 415-552-6542
Internet: sloth3@slip.net
  Pubs: *Bite Hard* (Manic D Pr, 1997), *American Poetry: Anth* (Carnegie Mellon, 2000), *The World in Us: Anth* (St Martin's, 2000), *Chick for a Day: Anth* (S&S, 2000), *Outlaw Bible: Anth* (Thunder's Mouth, 1999), *A Day for a Lay: Anth* (Barricade, 1999), *Zyzzyva*
I.D.: Asian-American, G/L/B/T. Groups: Asian-American, G/L/B/T

Marilyn Chin   P
English Dept, San Diego State Univ, San Diego, CA 92182-8140, 619-697-1941
  Pubs: *The Phoenix Gone, The Terrace Empty* (Milkweed, 1994), *Dwarf Bamboo* (Greenfield Rev Pr, 1987), *Best American Poetry: Anth* (S&S, 1996), *Pushcart Prize XX: Anth* (Pushcart Pr, 1996), *Kenyon Rev, Parnassus, Iowa Rev, Ploughshares, Zyzzyva*

John Christgau   W
2704 Comstock
Belmont, CA 94002, 415-591-4045
  Pubs: *The Origins of the Jump Shot* (U Nebraska Pr, 1999), *Mower County Poems, Sierra Sue II* (Great Plains Pr, 1998, 1994), *Spoon* (Viking, 1978), *Amelia, Window, Rainbow City Express, Camellia, Cream City Rev, Great River Rev*

Martha J. Cinader 🎤 ✈   PP&P&W
200 Brighton Dr
Vallejo, CA 94591-7035, 707-643-1893
Internet: mc@cinader.com
  Pubs: *When the Body Calls* (Harlem River Pr, 1999), *Dreamscape* (Tenth Avenue Edtns, 1995), *Dick for a Day: 1-800-YOR-DICK,* (Villard Bks, 1997), *A Gathering of the Tribes*
I.D.: New Media, Single Mother. Groups: Teenagers, Women

Leonard J. Cirino 🎤 ✈   P
2434 C St
Eureka, CA 95501-4111, 707-268-1274
Internet: ljc.pf@humboldt.com
    Pubs: *War Horses, The Sane Man Speaks* (Anabasis,
2000, 2000), *American Minotaur, 96 Sonnets Facing
Conviction, The Terrible Wilderness of Self* (Cedar Hill
Pub, 2000, 1999, 1998), *Henry's Will* (Mandrake Pr,
1995), *Wallace Stevens Jrnl, Lungfish*
I.D.: Italian-American. Groups: Prisoners, Seniors

Ralph Cissne 🎤 ✈   W
409 N Pacific Coast Hwy, #465
Redondo Beach, CA 90277-2870, 310-281-7341
Internet: cissne@earthlink.net
    Pubs: *American Way, Playboy, Writing on the Wall, Info*

Kevin Clark   P
Dept of English, California Polytech State U, San Luis
Obispo, CA 93407, 805-756-2596
    Pubs: *Window Under a New Moon* (Owl Creek Pr,
1990), *Granting the Wolf* (State St Pr, 1984), *The
Georgia Rev, Denver Qtly, College English, Black
Warrior Rev, Faultline, The Literary Rev, Qtly West*

Tom Clark   P&W
1740 Marin Ave
Berkeley, CA 94707
    Pubs: *Junkets on a Sad Planet: Scenes from the Life
of John Keats* (Black Sparrow Pr, 1994), *The Exile of
Celine* (Random Hse, 1987)

Killarney Clary 🎤 ✈   P
2517 Kenilworth Ave
Los Angeles, CA 90039
    Pubs: *By Common Salt* (Oberlin College Pr, 1996),
Who Whispered Near Me (FSG, 1989), *Ploughshares,
APR, Yale Rev, Colorado Rev, Paris Rev, Partisan*

Karen Claussen 🎤 ✈   P
PO Box 188
Crescent City, CA 95531-0188, 707-465-3228
    Pubs: *R. C. Lion, Primer, Poetry &, Altadena Rev,
Janus/Seth*

Paul Clayton   W
PO Box 280353
San Francisco, CA 94128, 408-735-3438
    Pubs: *Calling Crow Nation* (Berkley 1997), *Flight of the
Crow* (Berkley/Jove 1996), *Calling Crow*
(Putnam/Berkley 1995)

Richard Cloke   P&W
San Fernando Poetry Journal, 18301 Halsted St,
Northridge, CA 91325
    Pubs: *Earth Ovum* (Cerulean Pr, 1982), *Yvar* (Kent
Pub, 1981), *San Fernando Poetry Jrnl, Quindaro,
Abraxas, Ptolomy*

Peter Clothier   P
2341 Ronda Vista Dr
Los Angeles, CA 90027, 213-661-6349
    Pubs: *David Hockney* (Abbeville Pr, 1995), *Dirty-Down*
(Atheneum, 1987), *Chiaroscuro* (St. Martin's Pr, 1985),
Art News, Artspace

Jeanette Marie Clough 🎤 ✈   P
1330 Yale St #6
Santa Monica, CA 90404-2440
Internet: jclough@getty.edu
    Pubs: *Celestial Burn* (Sacred Beverage Pr, 1999),
Dividing Paradise (Inevitable Pr, 1998), *13th Moon,
Atlanta Rev, Fine Madness, Ohio Rev, Paterson Lit
Rev, Spillway, Wisconsin Rev*

Cathy Cockrell   W
3917 Elston Ave
Oakland, CA 94602-1620, 510-336-0484
    Pubs: *A Simple Fact, Undershirts & Other Stories*
(Hanging Loose Pr, 1987, 1982), *Croton Rev, Hanging
Loose Mag*

Judith Cody 🎤 ✈   P
Box 1107
Los Altos, CA 94023-1107
    Pubs: *Woman Magic* (Kikimora Pub, 1977), *Atlantic
Monthly Anth* (Atlantic Monthly Pr, 1973), *Cicada,
Brussels Sprouts, Amelia, Haiku Headlines, Palo Alto
Times, Lost & Found Times, Sequoia, Foreground,
Poetry Project Four, Stonecloud, Androgyne,
Amphichroia*

Tony Cohan 🎤   W
c/o Bonnie Nadell, Frederick Hill Associates, 1842 Union
St, San Francisco, CA 94173, 415-921-2910
Internet: tobo101@cs.com
    Pubs: *On Mexican Time* (Broadway Bks, 2000),
Mexicolor (Chronicle Bks, 1998), *Opium* (S&S, 1984),
Canary (Doubleday, 1981)

Wanda Coleman   P
Black Sparrow Press, 24 10th St, Santa Rosa, CA 95401,
707-597-4011
Internet: wcoleman44@hotmail.com
    Pubs: *Mambo Hips & Make Believe, Bathwater Wine,
Hand Dance, African Sleeping Sickness* (Black Sparrow,
1999, 1998, 1993, 1990), *Best American Poetry 1996:
Anth* (Scribner, 1996), *Postmodern American Poetry:
Anth* (Norton, 1994), *Critical Condition, ACM*
I.D.: African-American. Groups: Adults

Michael R. Collings   P&W
Humanities Division, Pepperdine Univ, Malibu, CA 90263,
805-469-3032
    Pubs: *Matrix* (White Crow, 1995), *Dark Transformation*
(Starmont, 1990), *In the Image of God* (Greenwood,
1990), *Georgetown Rev, Poet, Dialogue, Star*Line*

Julia Connor 🎤 ✈   P
2265 2nd Ave
Sacramento, CA 95818-3116, 916-737-2736
   Pubs: *Chrysanthemum* (Arcturus Edtns, 2000), *A Canto for the Birds* (Tule Pr, 1995), *New American Writing, First Intensity, Tyuonyi*

Andree Connors   W
PO Box 273
Mendocino, CA 95410
   Pubs: *Amateur People* (Fiction Collective, 1977)

Geoffrey Cook   P
PO Box 4233
Berkeley, CA 94704-0233, 510-654-9251
   Pubs: *The Heart of the Beast* (Hiram Poetry Rev, 1995), *Azrael* (Androgyne Pr, 1992), *Nation, Tropos, Poetpourri, Tight, Volume Number, Studia Mystica*

Carolyn Cooke   W
25524 Ten Mile Cutoff, PO Box 462, Point Arena, CA 95468-0462, 707-882-2106
   Pubs: *The Bostons, Best American Short Stories: Anth* (HM, 2001, 1997), *Prize Stories: The O. Henry Awards: Anth* (Anchor, 1998, 1997), *Breaking Up Is Hard to Do: Anth* (Crossing Pr, 1994), *Paris Rev, Ploughshares, NER*

Ellen Cooney   P
919 Sutter, #9
San Francisco, CA 94109
   Pubs: *Within the Labyrinth All, House Holding, The Quest for the Holy Grail, The Silver Rose* (Duir Pr, 1992, 1984, 1981, 1979)

M. Truman Cooper   P
6575 Camino Caseta
Goleta, CA 93117-1533, 805-683-2340
   Pubs: *Substantial Holdings* (Pudding Hse, 1987), *Poetry NW, New Letters, Prairie Schooner, South Dakota Rev, Tar River Poetry*

Lise King Couchot   P&W
808 Mission St
San Luis Obispo, CA 93405-2343
   Pubs: *Thin Scars/Purple Leaves* (Mudborn Pr, 1981), *Crosscurrents, Amelia, Connexions*

Michael Covino   P&W
2525 Ashby Ave #4
Berkeley, CA 94705-2218
   Pubs: *The Off-Season* (Persea Bks, 1985), *Unfree Associations* (Berkeley Poets Pr, 1982)

Lindsey Crittenden 🎤 ✈   W
268 Frederick St
San Francisco, CA 94117-4050
Internet: lindsc@pacbell.net
   Pubs: *The View from Below* (Mid-List Pr, 1999), *Berkeley Fiction Rev, Faultline, River City, Qtly West*

Irene Culver   P
2858 Westwood Ln #6
Carmichael, CA 95608, 916-486-9507
   Pubs: *Word Weavers Seven, Bellowing Ark, Sulphur River, The Plastic Tower, Poems for Nobody, Black Buzzard Rev*

Barney Currer   W
10280 Brooks Rd
Windsor, CA 95492-9464
   Pubs: *Free Fire Zone Anth* (McGraw-Hill, 1973), *Hawaii Rev, Aboriginal Sci Fi, Antioch Rev, Thema*

Daniel Curzon 🎤 ✈   W
City College San Francisco, L 196, San Francisco, CA 94112, 415-585-3410
   Pubs: *Superfag* (Igna Bks, 1996), *Queer View Mirror* (Arsenal Pump Pr, 1996), *Curzon in Love* (Knights Pr, 1988), *Kenyon Rev*

Bruce Cutler   P
260 High St #110
Santa Cruz, CA 95060, 408-420-1443
   Pubs: *Seeing the Darkness* (BkMk Pr, 1998), *Afterlife* (Juniper Pr, 1997), *The Massacre at Sand Creek* (U Oklahoma Pr, 1995), *Poetry, Shenandoah, New Letters*

Jane Cutler   W
352 27th St
San Francisco, CA 94131
   Pubs: *FM Five, Medical Heritage, Wind, Central Park West, Epoch, NAR, Ascent, Plainswoman*

Beverly Dahlen   P
15 Mirabel Ave
San Francisco, CA 94110-4614, 415-824-6649
   Pubs: *A Reading 8-10* (Chax Press, 1992), *Moving Borders: Anth* (Talisman House, 1998), *The Art of Practice: Anth* (Potes & Poets, 1994), *River City, Bombay Gin, Iowa Rev, Temblor, Camerawork, Poetics Jrnl, Fourteen Hills, Mirage*

Ruth Daigon 🎤 ✈   P
86 Sandpiper Cir
Corte Madera, CA 94925-1057, 415-924-0568
Internet: ruthart@aol.com
   Pubs: *Greatest Hits of Ruth Daigon* (Pudding Hse, 2000), *The Moon Inside* (Newton's Baby Pr, 2000), *Electronic Chapbook* (Alsop Rev, 1999), *ELF, Kansas Qtly, Atlanta Rev, Poet Lore, Tikkun, Mudlark, CrossConnect, Switched-On-Gutenberg, Recursive Angel*

Catherine Daly 🎤 ✈   P
533 S Alandele
Los Angeles, CA 90036-3250, 323-933-3880
Internet: http://members.aol.com/cadaly
    Pubs: *The Last Canto* (Duration Pr, 1999), *Piers
    Plowman Marginalia* (Potes & Poets, Pr, 1999),
    *American Letters & Commentary, Combo, East Village,
    Hollins Critic, Gulf Coast, Hubbub, Limestone, Ascent,
    Lullwater Rev, Paper Salad, Lucid Stone, Small Pond*
Groups: Women, Teenagers

Saralyn R. Daly   W
6211 Gyral Dr
Tujunga, CA 91042-2533
    Pubs: *Love's Joy, Love's Pain* (Fawcett, 1983), *Book of
    True Love* (Pennsylvania State U Pr, 1978), *A Shout in
    the Street, Western Humanities Rev, Beyond Baroque,
    Epos, Descant, Bywords*

John M. Daniel 🎤 ✈   W
PO Box 21922
Santa Barbara, CA 93121-1922, 805-962-1780
Internet: jmd@danielpublishing.com
    Pubs: *The Woman by the Bridge* (Dolphin-Moon Pr,
    1991), *Play Melancholy Baby* (Perseverance Pr, 1986),
    *Fish Stories, Qtly West, Zyzzyva, Amelia, Ambergris,
    Crosscurrents, Sequoia, Aberrations, Vignette*

Karen M. Daniels 🎤 ✈   P&W
46040 Paseo Gallante
Temecula, CA 92592
Internet: www.karendaniels.com
    Pubs: *Dancing Suns, Mentor's Lair, Mindspark*
    (Vivisphere Pub, 2000, 2000, 2000), *Tenacity*
Groups: Science Fiction Clubs, Spiritual/Religious

Keith Allen Daniels 🎤 ✈   P&W
PO Box 95
Ridgecrest, CA 93556, 760-375-8555
Internet: kdaniels@ix.netcom.com
    Pubs: *The Weird Sonneteers, I Think Therefore Iamb,
    Haiku by Unohu, Satan Is a Mathematician, What
    Rough Book* (Anamnesis Pr, 2000, 2000, 2000, 1998,
    1992), *Loopy Is the Inner Ear* (Quick Glimpse Pr,
    1993), *Analog, Asimov's SF, Recursive Angel, Weird
    Tales*

Jonathan Daunt   P
609 D St
Davis, CA 95616
    Pubs: *Stone Age Robin Hood* (Allegany Mtn Pr, 1979),
    Coyote's Jrnl: Anth (Wingbow Pr, 1982), *BPJ, Denver
    Qtly, Mississippi Rev, Prairie Schooner*

Michael Davidson   P
Dept of Literature, Univ California, San Diego, 9500
Gilman Dr, Dept 0410, La Jolla, CA 92093-0410,
619-534-2101
    Pubs: *The Arcades* (O Bks, 1999), *Post Hoc* (Avenue
    B Pr, 1990), *Analogy of the Ion* (The Figures, 1988)

Angela J. Davis   P
505 S Beverly, #488
Beverly Hills, CA 90212, 310-277-3976
    Pubs: *Eureka Anth* (U Iowa Pr, 1995), *Art/Life,
    Onthebus, Permafrost, Yellow Silk, Sequoia, Cream City
    Rev*

Lucille Lang Day 🎤 ✈   P
1057 Walker Ave
Oakland, CA 94610-1511, 510-763-3874
Internet: lucyday@autobahn.org
    Pubs: *Wild One* (Scarlet Tanager Bks, 2000), *Fire in
    the Garden* (Mother's Hen, 1997), *Self-Portrait with
    Hand Microscope* (Berkley Pr, 1982), *Blue Unicorn,
    Hudson Rev, Threepenny Rev, Portland Rev,
    Chattahoochee Rev, Hawaii Pacific Rev, Poet Lore*

Richard Cortez Day   W
PO Box 947
Arcata, CA 95518-0947, 707-822-8877
    Pubs: *When in Florence* (Doubleday, 1986), *Imagining
    Worlds: Anth* (McGraw-Hill, 1995), *Kenyon Rev, Qtly
    West, Redbook, Carolina Qtly, NER, Witness*

Jacqueline De Angelis   P&W
3244 Madera Ave
Los Angeles, CA 90039
    Pubs: *The Main Gate* (Paradise, 1984), *Hers: Anth*
    (Faber & Faber, 1996), *In a Different Light: Anth*
    (Clothespin Fever Pr, 1988), *Agni, Intl Qtly, Rara Avis,
    Momentum Mag*

Viviana Chamberlin De Aparicio   P&W
1769 Las Lunas St
Pasadena, CA 91106, 213-793-8379

Steve De France 🎤 ✈   P
5460 Las Lomas St
Lona Beach, CA 90815-4137, 562-494-4161
Internet: poet2000@gte.net
    Pubs: *Chiron Rev, Cimarron Rev, Higginsville Reader,
    IMAGO, Lynx Eye, ORBIS, Pegasus Spring, Poetry
    Motel, The Sun*

Marsha de la O 🎤 ✈   P
1296 Placid Ave
Ventura, CA 93004-2068, 805-647-3018
    Pubs: *Black Hope* (New Issues Pr, 1997), *Intimate
    Nature: Anth* (Ballantine, 1998), *Beyond the Valley:
    Anth* (Sacred Beverage Pr, 1998), *Solo, Third Coast,
    Art/Life*

Terri de la Peña 🎤 ✈   W
College of Letters & Science, Univ California, 405 Hilgard
Ave, Los Angeles, CA 90095-1438, 310-206-1853
    Pubs: *Faults* (Alyson Bks, 1999), *A Is for the Americas*
    (Orchard Bks, 1999), *Latin Satins, Margins* (Seal Pr,
    1994, 1992), *Chicana Lesbians: Anth* (Third Woman Pr,
    1992), *Lesbian Rev of Bks, Conmocion, Matrix*
I.D.: Latino/Latina, G/L/B/T. Groups: Latino/Latina, G/L/B/T

Ruth de Menezes   P
2821 Arizona Ave
Santa Monica, CA 90404, 510-828-2868
 Pubs: *The Heart's Far Cry* (Small Poetry Pr, 1996),
Love Ascending (Trinity Comm, 1987), *Woman Songs*
(Claremont Pr, 1982), *Poetic Voices of America: Anth*
(Sparrowgrass Poetic Forum, 1998), *America, Catholic
World, Magnificat, St. Anthony Messenger, Visions*

Richard De Mille   W
960 Lilac Dr
Santa Barbara, CA 93108, 805-969-4887
 Pubs: *Two Qualms & A Quirk* (Capra Pr, 1973),
Antioch Rev

John Deming   W
16634 McCormick
Encino, CA 91436, 818-501-5059
 Pubs: *Descant, Crosscurrents, Chariton Rev, Richmond
Qtly, Uncommon Reader, Missouri Rev, Other Voices*

W.S. Di Piero 🎤 ✈   P
225 Downey St #5
San Francisco, CA 94117, 415-731-6795
 Pubs: *Shooting the Works, Shadows Burning* (TriQtly
Bks, 1996, 1995), *The Restorers* (U Chicago, 1992),
Out of Eden (U Chicago, 1991), *The Dog Star* (U
Massachusetts Pr, 1989)

Diane di Prima 🎤 ✈   P&W
78 Niagara Ave
San Francisco, CA 94112-3335, 415-841-0717
 Pubs: *Loba* (Peguin, 1998), *Pieces of a Song* (City
Lights, 1990), *Unsettling America: Anth* (Viking, 1994),
*L.A. Times Book Rev, Disclosure, Paterson Lit Rev,
Yoga Jrnl, Heaven Bone, First Intensity, Mother Jones,
Long News in a Short Century*

N. A. Diaman   W
Persona Press, Box 14022, San Francisco, CA
94114-0022, 415-775-6143
 Pubs: *Private Nation, Castro Street Memories, Reunion,
Ed Dean Is Queer* (Persona Pr, 1997, 1988, 1983,
1978)
I.D.: Mediterranean. Groups: G/L/B/T

Ray Clark Dickson   P&W
Kerouac Connection/Beloit Poetry Jrnl, 1978 Oceanaire Dr,
San Luis Obispo, CA 93405-6829, 805-773-6530
 Pubs: *Saturday Evening Post, Wormwood Rev,
HaightAshbury Literary Jrnl, Coffeehouse Poets' Qtly,
BPJ*

Millicent G. Dillon   W
83 6th Ave
San Francisco, CA 94118-1323
Internet: www.millicentdillon.com
 Pubs: *Harry Gold* (The Overlook Pr, 2000), *Dance of
the Mothers* (Dutton, 1991), *The One in the Back Is
Medea, Baby Perpetua & Other Stories* (Viking, 1973,
1971), *SW Rev, Ascent, Threepenny Rev*

Chitra Banerjee Divakaruni   P&W
Foothill College, English Dept, Los Altos, CA 94022,
415-949-7250
 Pubs: *Black Candle* (Calyx Bks, 1991), *The Reason for
Nasturtiums* (Berkeley Poets Pr, 1990), *Ms., BPJ,
Chicago Rev, Zyzzyva, Chelsea*

Mario Divok   P
5 Misty Meadow
Irvine, CA 92715, 714-854-1322
 Pubs: *Forbidden Island: Complete Works Two, The
Birthday* (Triton, 1986, 1984), *Poetalk, California: A Qtly
Mag, American Poetry*

Carl Djerassi   P&W
Dept of Chemistry, Stanford Univ, Stanford, CA
94305-5080, 650-723-2783
 Pubs: *Menachem's Seed, The Bourbaki Gambit*
(Penguin, 1998, 1996), *No, Marx, Deceased* (U Georgia
Pr, 1998, 1996), *The Clock Runs Backwards* (Story
Line Pr, 1991), *Hudson Rev, Southern Rev, New
Letters, Grand Street, Kenyon Rev, Midwest Rev*

Harriet Doerr   W
494 Bradford St
Pasadena, CA 91105
 Pubs: *The Tiger in the Grass, Stones for Ibarra* (Viking,
1995, 1984), *Consider This, Senora* (HB, 1993), *Under
an Aztec Sun* (Yolla Bolly Pr, 1990)

Richard Dokey 🎤 ✈   W
4471 W Kingdon Rd
Lodi, CA 95242-9507, 209-463-8314
 Pubs: *The Hollow Man* (DeltaWest, 1999), *Late Harvest*
(Paragon Hse, 1992), *Intro to Literature: Anth, Intro to
Fiction: Anth* (Norton, 1995, 1995), *TriQtly, Missouri
Rev, SW Rev, New Letters*

Diane C. Donovan   P
12424 Mill St
Petaluma, CA 94952-9728
 Pubs: *General Store, Tightrope, Owlflight, Night
Voyages, The Bookwatch, Kliatt Book Guide*

Carol Dorf   P&W
1400 Delaware St
Berkeley, CA 94702, 510-848-4701
 Pubs: *A Breath Would Destroy That Symmetry* (E.G.
San Francisco, 1989), *Feminist Studies, Five Fingers
Rev, Liberty Hill, Heresies, Caprice, Metaphors*

Sharon Doubiago 🎤 ✈   P
1575 C Pershing Dr
San Francisco, CA 94129, 415-386-0139
    Pubs: *Body & Soul* (Cedar Hill Pubs, 2000), *Hard
Country* (West End Pr, 1999), *The Husband Arcane,
The Arcane of O* (Gorda Plate Pr, 1996), *South
America Mi Hija* (U Pitt Pr, 1992), *Psyche Drives the
Coast* (Empty Bowl Pr, 1990), *El Nino* (Lost Roads Pr,
1989)
I.D.: Feminist, Environmentalist. Groups: College/Univ

Philip Dow   P
2193 Ethel Porter Dr
Napa, CA 94558, 707-224-9463
    Pubs: *19 New American Poets of the Golden Gate:
Anth* (HBJ, 1985), *Boundary 2*

Frank Dwyer   P
768 Canyon Wash Dr
Pasadena, CA 91107

Kathryn Eberly   P&W
301 Precita Ave, #2
San Francisco, CA 94110, 415-824-5809
    Pubs: *Women & Death* (Ground Torpedo Pr, 1996), *It's
All the Rage: Anth* (Andrew Mountain Pr, 1997), *If I
Had a Hammer: Women's Work in Poetry & Fiction:
Anth* (Papier-Mache Pr, 1990), *Rhino, Evergreen
Chronicles, Ruah*

Bart Edelman   P
394 Elmwood Dr
Pasadena, CA 91105, 213-340-8121
    Pubs: *Under Damaris' Dress* (Lightning Pub, 1996),
Crossing the Hackensack (Prometheus Pr, 1993)

Nancy Edwards   P
English Dept, Bakersfield College, 1801 Panorama Dr,
Bakersfield, CA 93305, 805-831-1067
    Pubs: *The Woman Within* (Bakersfield College, 1994),
*Network Africa, Orpheus, Amelia, Roadrunner, The
Plastic Tower, CQ, Little Balkans Rev, The Forum*

Susan Efros   P
41 Pine Dr
Fairfax, CA 94930
    Pubs: *Two Way Streets* (Jungle Garden Pr, 1976), *This
Is Women's Work: Anth* (Panjandrum Pr, 1974), *Amelia,
Footwork, Lowell Pearl, Ascent, Paris Transcontinental,
Christopher Street*

Terry Ehret 🎤 ✈   P
924 Sunnyslope Rd
Petaluma, CA 94952-4747, 707-762-2698
Internet: tehret99@msn.com
    Pubs: *How We Go on Living* (Protean Pr, 1995), *Lost
Body* (Copper Canyon Pr, 1993), *Suspensions* (White
Mountain Pr, 1990), *Nimrod*

Samuel A. Eisenstein 🎤 ✈   P&W
1015 Prospect Blvd
Pasadena, CA 91103-2811
Internet: sameisenstein@hotmail.com
    Pubs: *Nudibranchia* (Red Hen Pr, 2000), *Rectification of
Eros, Price of Admission, The Inner Garden* (Sun &
Moon Pr, 2000, 1992, 1986)

Gary Elder   P&W
95 Carson Ct, Shelter Cove
Whitethorn, CA 95589, 707-986-7700
    Pubs: *Arnulfsaga* (Dustbooks, 1979), *The Far Side of
the Storm: Anth* (San Marcos, 1975)

Sergio D. Elizondo   P
627 Lilac Ln
Imperial, CA 92251, 619-353-8233
    Pubs: *Suruma* (Dos Pasos, 1990), *Muerte en una
Estrella* (Sainz-Luiselli, 1984)

Ellen 🎤   P
6353 Malibu Park Ln
Malibu, CA 90265, 310-457-3585
    Pubs: *Isis Rising: Anth* (Temple of Isis, 2000), *In the
Garden: Anth* (International Forum, 1996), *Women of
the 14th Moon: Anth* (Crossing Pr, 1991), *ACM, Slant,
COE Rev, Coastal Forest Rev, Prime Time, Blue
Unicorn, ArtLife, Spillway*

Ella Thorp Ellis   W
1438 Grizzly Peak
Berkeley, CA 94708, 510-549-9871
    Pubs: *Swimming with the Whales* (H Holt, 1995), *Hugo
& the Princess Nina, Sleepwalkers Moon* (Atheneum,
1983, 1980), *Mademoiselle*

Kenneth Ellsworth   P&W
6055 Calmfield Ave
Agoura Hills, CA 91301, 818-991-4757
    Pubs: *Christian Blues: Anth* (Amador Pub, 1995), *Black
Buzzard Rev, Rivertalk, Toast, Illya's Honey, California
Qtly, Farmer's Market, Atom Mind, Sell Outs, Gargoyle,
Iconoclast, Bohemian Chronicle, Verve, Buffalo Bones,
Etcetera, Knocked*

Alan C. Engebretsen   P
8220 Rayford Dr
Los Angeles, CA 90045, 310-649-1645
    Pubs: *A Rage of Blue* (Poetic Justice, 1985), *California
State Poetry Qtly, Wind, Pudding Mag, Prophetic
Voices, Orphic Lute, Proof Rock, Amelia*

Charles Entrekin   P&W
10736 Indian Shack Rd
Nevada City, CA 95959
    Pubs: *In This Hour, Casting for the Cutthroat* (Berkeley
Poets, 1988, 1980), *Madison Rev, Passager, Xanadu,
Literature of Work, Birmingham Poetry Rev*

Catherine Henley Erickson 🎤 ✈   P
764 Valparaiso
Claremont, CA 91711, 909-593-3511 x4352
   Pubs: *Contemporary Women Poets: Anth* (Merlin Pr,
   1977), *Rara Avis, Beyond Baroque, Poetry/L.A.*

María Amparo Escandón 🎤 ✈   W
2231 Overland Ave
Los Angeles, CA 90064
Internet: escandon@acento.com
   Pubs: *Las Mamis* (Knopf, 2000), Esperanza's Box of
   Saints (S&S, 1998), *Palm Readings: Anth* (Plain View
   Pr, 1998), *Onthebus, Manoa, Prairie Schooner, Herman
   Rev, WestWord*

John Espey   W
English Dept, Univ California, 405 Hilgard Ave, Los
Angeles, CA 90024, 213-825-4173
   Pubs: *Winter Return, Two Schools of Thought* (w/C.
   See), *Strong Drink, Strong Language* (Daniel, 1992,
   1991, 1990), *The Nine Lives of Algernon* (Capra Pr,
   1988)

Maria Espinosa   W
3396 Orchard Valley Ln
Lafayette, CA 94549, 510-283-4314
   Pubs: *Dark Plums, Longing, Three Day Flight: Anth*
   (Arte Publico Pr, 1995, 1995, 1994)

Rudy Espinosa   W
250 Drake St
San Francisco, CA 94112, 415-585-0395

David Evanier   W
2213 Glendon Ave
Los Angeles, CA 90064-2008, 310-470-9525
   Pubs: *Red Love* (Scribner, 1991), *Congregation* (HBJ,
   1988), *The One-Star Jew* (North Point, 1983), *New
   Republic, Paris Rev, Antioch Rev, NAW*

George Evans   P
1590 21st Ave
San Francisco, CA 94122
   Pubs: *Sudden Dreams: New & Selected Poems* (Coffee
   Hse Pr, 1991), *Conjunctions, New Directions, Sulfur*

Martha Evans 🎤 ✈   P
1022 57th St
Oakland, CA 94608-2706, 415-653-5566
   Pubs: *Landing Signals: Anth* (Sacramento Poetry Ctr,
   1985), *New Letters, Chelsea, NYQ, Chicago Rev,
   CutBank, Synapse, Ironwood*

Mary Fabilli   P
2445 Ashby Ave
Berkeley, CA 94705, 510-841-6300
   Pubs: *Winter Poems* (Inverno Pr, 1983), *Aurora Bligh &
   Early Poems* (Oyez, 1968), *Talisman, To, Sierra Jrnl*

B. H. Fairchild   P
706 W 11th St
Claremont, CA 91711
   Pubs: *The Art of the Lathe* (Alice James Bks 1998),
   Local Knowledge (QRL, 1991), *The Arrival of the
   Future* (Swallow's Tale Pr, 1986), *The System of Which
   the Body Is One Part* (State Street Pr, 1988), *Flight*
   (Persimmon Fork Road, 1985)

Marcia Falk 🎤 ✈   P
2905 Benvenue Ave
Berkeley, CA 94705, 510-548-8018
Internet: www.marciafalk.com
   Pubs: *Book of Blessings, Song of Songs* (Harper, 1996,
   1990), *This Year in Jerusalem* (State Street, 1986),
   Nice Jewish Girls: Anth (Plume, 1996), *APR, Women's
   Rev of Bks, Tikkun, PSA Bulletin, Anth of Mag Verse &
   Yearbook of American Poetry*
Lang: Hebrew. I.D.: Jewish. Groups: Jewish, Women

Jennifer Crystal Fang-Chien 🎤 ✈   P
617 Fallon St
Oakland, CA 94607, 510-405-2053
Internet: www.art.net/poets/jennifer
   Pubs: *Axe Factory Rev, Haight-Ashbury Lit Jrnl, Kimera,
   Perceptions, Shades of December, Writing for Our Lives*
Groups: Teenagers, Minorities

Thomas Farber 🎤 ✈   W
Box 2, 1678 Shattuck Ave
Berkeley, CA 94709, 510-644-4193
   Pubs: *A Lover's Question: Selected Stories* (Creative
   Arts, 2000), *The Face of the Deep* (Mercury Hse,
   1998), *Through a Liquid Mirror* (Editions Limited, 1997),
   On Water (Ecco Pr, 1994), *Learning to Love It* (Capra
   Pr, 1993)

Dion N. Farquhar 🎤 ✈   P&W
249 Dickens Way
Santa Cruz, CA 95064-1064, 408-425-8680
Internet: dnfarquhar@aol.com
   Pubs: *The Other Machine* (Routledge, 1996), *Sulfur,
   Crazyquilt, Poet Lore, Visions, Hawaii Rev, Red Bass,
   Painted Bride Qtly, Alea, Asylum, boundary 2, Burning
   Cloud Rev, Juxta, New Novel Rev*

Curtis Faville   P
34 Franciscan Way
Kensington, CA 94707, 415-526-3412

Jean Femling   W
2384 Cornell Dr
Costa Mesa, CA 92626
Internet: jfemling@earthlink.com
   Pubs: *Getting Mine, Hush, Money* (St. Martin's, 1991,
   1989), *Interfaces: Anth* (Ace, 1980), *Backyard* (H&R,
   1975), *Descant*

Paul Fericano   P&W
Yossarian Universal News, PO Box 236, Millbrae, CA
94030-0236
    Pubs: *The One-Minute President* (w/Ligi), *Sinatra
    Sinatra* (Poor Souls Pr, 1987, 1982), *Stoogism: Anth*
    (Scarecrow Bks, 1977), *Wormwood Rev, Realist,
    Krokodil, Second Coming, Free Lunch, Wine Rings*

Lawrence Ferlinghetti   P&W
City Lights Books, 261 Columbus Ave, San Francisco, CA
94133, 415-362-1901
    Pubs: *These Are My Rivers: New & Selected Poems
    1955-1993* (New Directions, 1993), *Love in the Days of
    Rage* (Dutton/Penguin, 1989)

Anne Finger ♀ ✈   W
5809 Fremont
Oakland, CA 94608, 510-594-6870
Internet: AnnieDigit@altavista.com
    Pubs: *Bone Truth* (Coffee Hse Pr, 1994), *Past Due*
    (Seal Pr, 1990), *Kenyon Rev, Southern Rev, Antioch
    Rev, 13th Moon, Feminist Studies, Kaleidoscope*
I.D.: Disabled. Groups: Disabled, Children

Molly Fisk ♀ ✈   P
10068 Newtown Rd
Nevada City, CA 95959
Internet: molly@oro.net
    Pubs: *Listening to Winter* (California Poetry Series,
    2000), *Terrain* (w/D. Bellm, et al; Hip Pocket Pr, 1998),
    Salt Water Poems (Jungle Garden Pr, 1994)

Lawrence Fixel ♀   P&W
1496 Willard St
San Francisco, CA 94117-3721, 415-661-3870
    Pubs: *Unlawful Assembly: Poems 1940-1992* (Cloud
    Forms, 1994), *Truth, War, & The Dream-Game:
    Selected Prose Poems & Parables* (Coffee Hse Pr,
    1992)

Ted Fleischman   P
293 Glorietta Blvd
Orinda, CA 94563, 510-376-3431
    Pubs: *Half a Bottle of Catsup, Berkeley Poets
    Cooperative Anth* (Berkeley Poets Pr, 1978, 1980),
    Berkeley Poets Co-op, Outerbridge, In a Nutshell

Gerald Fleming ♀ ✈   P
PO Box 529
Lagunitas, CA 94938-0529, 415-488-4226
    Pubs: *Seeds Flying in a Fresh Light* (Allyn & Bacon,
    1990), *New Letters, Volt, Five Fingers Rev, Puerto del
    Sol, Americas Rev, Pequod*

Stewart Florsheim ♀ ✈   P
170 Sandringham Rd
Piedmont, CA 94611
    Pubs: *And What Rough Beast: Anth* (Ashland Poetry
    Pr, 1999), *Unsettling America: Anth* (Viking Penguin,
    1994), *Ghosts of the Holocaust: Anth* (Wayne State U
    Pr, 1989), *DoubleTake, Karamu, Dimension, Round
    Table, Blue Unicorn, Slipstream*
Groups: Jewish

Jack Foley   P&W
2569 Maxwell Ave
Oakland, CA 94601-5521, 510-532-3737
    Pubs: *Advice to the Lovelorn* (Texture Pr, 1998), *New
    Poetry from California: Dead/Requiem* (w/Ivan
    Arquelles), *Exiles, Adrift* (Pantograph Pr, 1998, 1996,
    1993), *O Her Blackness Sparkles* (3300 Club Pr, 1995),
    Gershwin (Norton Coker Pr, 1991), *Juxta*

CB Follett   P
PO Box 401
Sausalito, CA 94966-0401, 415-331-2503
    Pubs: *Visible Bones* (Plain View Pr, 1998), *Gathering
    the Mountains, The Latitude of Their Going* (Hot Pepper
    Pr, 1995, 1993), *MacGuffin, Cumberland Rev, The
    Bridge, Confluence, Calyx, Heaven Bone, New Letters,
    Birmingham Poetry Rev*

Elizabeth Foote-Smith   P&W
2635 Regent St
Berkeley, CA 94704, 510-849-0800
    Pubs: *Never Say Die, Gentle Albatross* (Putnam, 1980,
    1978), *Michigan Qtly Rev*

Jeanne Foster   P
St. Mary's College, PO Box 4700, Moraga, CA
94575-4700, 925-631-4511
    Pubs: *A Blessing of Safe Travel* (QRL, 1980), *Great
    Horned Owl* (White Pine, 1980), *Ploughshares, Hudson
    Rev, TriQtly, NAR, APR, Paris Rev*

William L. Fox ♀ ✈   P
503 S Fuller Ave
Los Angeles, CA 90036, 323-692-0889
Internet: wlfox@earthlink.net
    Pubs: *One Wave Standing* (La Alameda Pr, 1998),
    Silence & License (Light & Dust, 1994), *Geograph*
    (Black Rock Pr, 1994), *TumbleWords: Anth* (U Nevada
    Pr, 1995), *Caliban, Chain*

Peter Frank   P
PO Box 24 A36
Los Angeles, CA 90024-1036, 310-271-9740
    Pubs: *New, Used & Improved* (Abbeville Pr, 1987),
    Travelogues (Sun & Moon Pr, 1982)

Thaisa Frank   W
459 66thSt
Oakland, CA 94609, 510-658-1225
   Pubs: *Enchanted Men, A Brief History of Camouflage* (Black Sparrow Pr, 1994, 1991), *Whole Earth Rev, City Lights Rev, Forehead*

Kathleen Fraser   P
1936 Leavenworth St
San Francisco, CA 94133, 415-474-8911
   Pubs: *il cuore: the heart, Selected Poems 1970-1997* (Wesleyan U Pr, 1997), *When New Time Folds Up* (Chax, 1993), *Chicago Rev, Conjunctions, Talisman*

Devery Freeman   W
320 N La Peer Dr, Apt 401
Beverly Hills, CA 90211
   Pubs: *Father Sky* (Morrow, 1979), *American Mag, Liberty*

Melvyn Freilicher   PP&P
3945 Normal St, #5
San Diego, CA 92103, 619-299-4859
   Pubs: *120 Days in the FBI: My Untold Story by Jane Eyre* (Standing Stones Pr, 1998), *River Styx, New Novel Rev, Fiction Intl, Frame-Work: Jrnl of Images & Culture, Central Park, Crawl Out Your Window*

Elliot Fried 🎤 ✈   P
Cal State Univ, Long Beach, English Dept, Long Beach, CA 90840
Internet: efried@csulb.edu
   Pubs: *Marvel Mystery Oil* (Red Wind Pr, 1991), *New Geography of Poets: Anth* (U Arkansas Pr, 1993), *Movie Poetry: Anth* (Faber & Faber, 1993), *Green Mtns Rev*

Paula Naomi Friedman 🎤 ✈   P&W
5522 Tehama Ave
Richmond, CA 94804-5041, 510-527-3857
Internet: pnfpnf@aol.com
   Pubs: *Touched By Adoption: Anth* (Green River Pr, 1999), *Word Hustler: Anth* (Word Hustler Pr, 1976) *The Open Cell, Buffalo Bones, Chain of Life, Work, Quantum Tao, NeoVictorian/Cochlea*
Lang: French. I.D.: Women, Health-Related. Groups: Homeless, Seniors

S. L. Friedman   P
732 N June St
Los Angeles, CA 90038, 213-464-5802
   Pubs: *Hanging by Our Teeth & Rising by Our Bootstraps, Some Light Through the Blindfold* (Friedman, 1991, 1988), *Wordsworth's Socks, Plains Poetry Jrnl, California Poetry Jrnl, Quartet, Epos*

Gloria Frym 🎤 ✈   P&W
2119 Eunice St
Berkeley, CA 94709-1416, 510-524-6069
Internet: gfrym@newcollege.edu
   Pubs: *Distance No Object* (City Lights Bks, 1999), *How I Learned* (Coffee Hse Pr, 1992), *By Ear* (Sun & Moon Pr, 1991), *The World, Before Columbus, Exquisite Corpse, Zyzzyva*

Blair Fuller   W
565 Connecticut St
San Francisco, CA 94107, 415-824-8132
   Pubs: *A Butterfly Net & a Kingdom* (Creative Arts Bk Co, 1989), *Birth of a Fan: Anth* (Macmillan, 1993)

Len Fulton   W
Box 100
Paradise, CA 95967-0100, 530-877-6110
   Pubs: *Dark Other Adam Dreaming* (Dustbooks, 1976), *The Grassman* (Penguin, 1975)

Robert Funge 🎤 ✈   P
PO Box 1225
San Carlos, CA 94070-1225, 650-592-7720
   Pubs: *The Passage* (Ireland; Elo Pr, 2000), *What Have You Lost?: Anth* (Greenwillow Bks, 1999), *Lit Rev, Tampa Rev, Seattle Rev, Chariton Rev, Libido*

Gary G. Gach 🎤 ✈   P
1243 Broadway, #4
San Francisco, CA 94109-2771, 415-771-7793
Internet: http://word.to
   Pubs: *Visions: Anth* (Nat'l Geographic, 2000), *The Book of Luminous Things: Anth* (Harcourt, 1998), *What Book!?: Anth* (Parallax, 1998), *Two Lines, APR, Zyzzyva*
I.D.: Zen Judaist. Groups: Children, Prisoners

Diane Gage   P
PO Box 881453
San Diego, CA 92168-1453
   Pubs: *Prayers to Protest: Anth, The Unitarian Universalist Poets: Anth* (Pudding Hse Pub, 1998, 1996), *Pikeville Rev, Phoebe, Puerto del Sol*

Susan M. Gaines   W
1046 Elsbree Lane
Windsor, CA 95492
   Pubs: *Carbon Dreams* (Creative Arts, 2000), *Sacred Ground: Writings About Home: Anth* (Milkweed Edtns, 1996), *Best of the West: Anth* (Norton, 1992), *Cream City Rev, NAR, Missouri Rev*

Kate Gale   P&W
Red Hen Press, PO Box 902582, Palmdale, CA 93590-2582, 818-831-0649
   Pubs: *Where Crows & Men Collide, Blue Air* (Red Hen Pr, 1995, 1995), *Water Moccasins* (Tidal Wave Pr, 1994)

Sally M. Gall   P
5820 Folsom Dr
La Jolla, CA 92037-7323
   Pubs: *Eleanor Roosevelt* (Oxford U Pr, 1996), *Kill Bear Comes Home* (VM Music, 1994), *Southern Rev, Ploughshares, Confrontation, Present Tense, Missouri Rev, The Humanist, Footwork*

Dick Gallup   P
1450 Castro St, #17
San Francisco, CA 94114, 415-550-0638
   Pubs: *Plumbing the Depths of Folly* (Smithereens Pr, 1983), *Where I Hang My Hat* (H&R, 1967)

Reymundo Gamboa   P&W
408 Chaparral
Santa Maria, CA 93454, 805-922-1339
   Pubs: *Cenzotle: Chicano Literary Prize* (U California Irvine, 1988), *The Baby Chook & Other Remnants* (Other Voices, 1976), *Chicanos: Antologia Historica de Literatura* (Fondo de Cultura Economica, 1980), *Denver Qtly, Morning of '56, El Oficio, Script*

evvy garrett   P
San Diego, CA
Internet: egarrett@peoplepc.com
   Pubs: *NYQ, AKA, Pearl, Capper's, Arizona Unconservative, Rant, Alura, December Rose, Copper Hill Qtly, Poetic Space, Radiant Woman*

Phyllis Gebauer 🎙 ✈   W
515 W Scenic Dr
Monrovia, CA 91016
   Pubs: *The Pagan Blessing* (Viking, 1979), *Iowa English Bulletin, Modern Maturity, Sight Lines*

Merrill Joan Gerber   W
542 Santa Anita Ct
Sierra Madre, CA 91024-2623, 626-355-0384
   Pubs: *Anna in Chains* (Syracuse U Pr, 1998), *Old Mother, Little Cat, The Kingdom of Brooklyn* (Longstreet Pr, 1995, 1992), *New Yorker, Atlantic, Redbook, Sewanee Rev, Shenandoah, Commentary*

Amy Gerstler 🎙 ✈   P&W
4430 Palo Verde Terr
San Diego, CA 92115
   Pubs: *Medicine* (Penguin Putnam, 2000), *Crown of Weeds, Nerve Storm* (Viking Penguin, 1997, 1993), *Bitter Angel* (North Point Pr, 1990)

Art Gibney   W
PO Box 711
Fairfax, CA 94978-0771
   Pubs: *Story Qtly, Zyzzyva, Estero, Clockwatch Rev, Tennessee Qtly, Intl Qtly, South Dakota Rev*

Barry Gifford 🎙 ✈   P&W
833 Bancroft Way
Berkeley, CA 94710, 510-848-4956
   Pubs: *Wyoming* (Arcade, 2000), *My Last Martini* (Crane Hill, 2000), *Night People* (Grove Pr, 1993), *First Intensity, Esquire, Rolling Stone, Speak, Shenandoah, Projections, Panta, Exquisite Corpse*

D.H.L. Gilbert   W
514 Lighthouse Ave
Santa Cruz, CA 95060
   Pubs: *Iowa Rev, NW Rev, NAR, Antioch Rev, Quarry West*

Jack Gilbert   P
136 Montana St
San Francisco, CA 94112, 415-585-6055
   Pubs: *Kochan* (Tamarack Pr, 1984), *Monolithos* (Knopf, 1983), *Views of Jeopardy* (Yale U Pr, 1962)

Jeremiah Gilbert 🎙 ✈   P&W
PO Box 11644
San Bernardino, CA 92423-1644, 909-825-7648
Internet: mersault@sprynet.com
   Pubs: *Atom Mind, Potpourri, Mind in Motion, Grasslands Rev, Parnassus*
Groups: G/L/B/T, Atheist/Agnostic

Sandra M. Gilbert 🎙 ✈   P&W
Univ California, English Dept, Davis, CA 95616,
916-752-2257
Internet: sgilbert@ucdavis.edu
   Pubs: *Kissing the Bread, Ghost Volcano* (Norton, 2000, 1995), *Poetry, Ontario Rev, Kenyon Rev, Poetry NW, Field, APR*

Elizabeth Gilchrist 🎙 ✈   W
1915 El Camino de la Luz
Santa Barbara, CA 93109-1926, 805-963-3108
   Pubs: *Second Chances* (Dell, 1986), *Your Cheatin' Heart* (Macmillan, 1979)

Molly Giles   W
PO Box 137
Woodacre, CA 94973
   Pubs: *Rough Translations* (U Georgia Pr, 1985), *Caprice, San Jose Studies, Real Fiction, Manoa, Greensboro Rev, McCall's, Sundog, Shenandoah*

S. E. Gilman   P&W
1725 Lehigh Dr
Davis, CA 95616, 916-757-1920
   Pubs: *Letters to our Children* (Franklin Watts, 1997), *Anyone Can Be a Target, Even Margaret* (Consummated Productions, 1978), *Americas Rev, Modern Words*

Dana Gioia 🎤 ✈   P
7190 Faught Rd
Santa Rosa, CA 95403-7835, 707-836-0354
    Pubs: *The Gods of Winter, Daily Horoscope* (Graywolf
    Pr, 1991, 1986), *Hudson Rev, Poetry, New Yorker*

Robert Franklin Gish   W
PO Box 947
San Luis Obispo, CA 93406, 805-756-2304
    Pubs: *Dreams of Quivira* (Clear Light Pub, 1998), *Bad
    Boys & Black Sheep, First Horses* (U Nevada Pr,
    1993), *North Dakota Qtly, New Mexico Mag, Mirage,
    Urbanus*

David Gitin 🎤 ✈   P
PO Box 505
Monterey, CA 93942-0505, 831-646-9181
Internet: dgitin@mbay.net
    Pubs: *Fire Dance, This Once* (Blue Wind, 1989, 1979),
    Vacuum Tapestries (BB Bks, 1981), *Intent, Paideuma,
    Poetry Flash*

Maria Gitin   P
287 La Vida Rd
Aptos, CA 95003, 408-722-8535
    Pubs: *Night Shift* (Blue Wind Pr, 1978), *The Melting
    Pot* (Crossing Pr, 1977), *Little Movies* (Ithaca Hse,
    1976), *In Celebration of the Muse: Anth* (Quarry
    West/UC Santa Cruz, 1997), *Poetry Flash, Alternative
    Press, Telephone, Sun & Moon, Hanging Loose*

Jan Glading   P
1536 9th St #D
Alameda, CA 94501, 510-521-7366
    Pubs: *Gridlock: Anth* (Applezaba Pr, 1990), *Peace or
    Perish: Anth* (Poets for Peace, 1983), *Napa Rev,
    Kaleidoscope, Disability*

David Glotzer   P
1648 Waller
San Francisco, CA 94117, 415-752-1278
    Pubs: *Occasions of Grace* (Heron Pr, 1979), *Mulch,
    River Styx, Lillabulero, Works, B'way Boogie*

Robert Gluck 🎤 ✈   P&W
4303 20th St
San Francisco, CA 94114-2816, 415-821-3004
Internet: chrisko@sirius.com
    Pubs: *Jack the Modernist, Margery Kempe* (Serpent's
    Tail/High Risk, 1995, 1994), *Reader* (Lapis Pr, 1989)

Dale Going 🎤 ✈   P
541 Ethel Ave
Mill Valley, CA 94941-3327, 415-381-1243
Internet: dalegoing@aol.com
    Pubs: *Leaves from a Gradual* (Potes & Poets, 2000),
    The View They Arrange (Kelsey Street Pr, 1994), *She
    Pushes with Her Hands, Or Less* (Em Pr, 1992, 1991)

Herbert Gold 🎤 ✈   W
1051-A Broadway
San Francisco, CA 94133
    Pubs: *She Took My Arm As If She Loved Me,
    Daughter Mine* (St. Martin's, 2000, 1997), *Bohemia:
    Digging the Roots of Cool, Best Nightmare on Earth: A
    Life in Haiti* (S&S, 1993, 1991)

Reuven Goldfarb   P
2020 Essex St
Berkeley, CA 94703, 510-848-0965
    Pubs: *To Be a Jew...* (Inter-oco Pr, 1977), *New
    Menorah, Exquisite Corpse, Oxygen, Voice of the
    Trees, Agada, Robert Frost Rev*

Juan Gomez-Quinones   P
507 Grande Vista Ave
Los Angeles, CA 90063
    Pubs: *5th & Grande Vista* (Editorial Mensaje, 1974),
    Revista Chicano-Riquena

Rafael Jesus Gonzalez   P&W
2514 Woolsey St
Berkeley, CA 94705, 510-841-5903
    Pubs: *El Hacedor De Juegos/The Maker of Games*
    (Casa Editorial, 1978), *West Coast Rev, Contact II*

Cesar A. Gonzalez-T. 🎤 ✈   P&W
San Diego Mesa College, 7250 Mesa College Dr, San
Diego, CA 92111, 619-627-2751
    Pubs: *Unwinding the Silence* (Lalo-Bilingual Pr, 1987),
    Paper Dance: Anth (Persea Bks, 1995), *Ventana
    Abierto, RiverSedge, Prairie Schooner, Bilingual Rev*
Lang: Spanish. I.D.: Chicano/Chicana, Latino/Latina

Mary Lee Gowland   P
49386 Cavin Ln
Coarsegold, CA 93614, 209-683-6876
    Pubs: *Remembering August* (Mountain Arts Council,
    1994), *Fresno Bee, Onthebus, Z Miscellaneous, Rag
    Mag, Poetry/L.A. Sculpture Gardens Rev, Fat Tuesday*

Taylor Graham 🎤 ✈   P
PO Box 39
Somerset, CA 95684-0039, 530-621-1833
Internet: piper@innercite.com
    Pubs: *Next Exit* (Cedar Hill Pub, 1999), *Casualties*
    (Coal City, 1995), *Ascent, MacGuffin, Maryland Poetry
    Rev, Santa Clara Rev, Willow Springs, America, Iowa
    Rev, Passages North, Southern Humanities Rev, 1997
    Anth of Mag Verse*

Toni Graham   W
345 Prospect Ave
San Francisco, CA 94110, 415-641-7858
    Pubs: *The Daiquiri Girls* (U Massachussetts Pr, 1998),
    *Mississippi Rev, American Fiction, Ascent, Clockwatch
    Rev, Worcester Rev, Green Mountains Rev, Writers'
    Forum, Mississippi Mud, The Bridge*

Judy Grahn   P&W
4221 Terrace St
Oakland, CA 94611-5127
    Pubs: *Mundane's World* (Crossing Pr, 1988), *The
    Queen of Swords, Another Mother Tongue* (Beacon Pr,
    1987, 1984)

Cynthia D. Grant 🎤 ✈   W
Box 95
Cloverdale, CA 95425-0095, 707-894-3420
    Pubs: *The White Horse, Mary Wolf, Uncle Vampire,
    Shadow Man, Keep Laughing* (Atheneum, 1998, 1995,
    1993, 1993, 1991)

Jack Grapes 🎤 ✈   P
6684 Colgate Ave
Los Angeles, CA 90048, 323-651-5488
    Pubs: *Lucky Finds, Breaking Down the Surface of the
    World, Trees, Coffee, & the Eyes of Deer* (Bombshelter
    Pr, 2000, 1998, 1987), *Men of Our Time: Anth* (U
    Georgia Pr, 1992), *The Maverick Poets: Anth* (Gorilla
    Pr, 1988), *Poetry East, Japanese American Mag*
Groups: Children, Jewish

Wallace Graves   W
English Dept, California State Univ, Northridge, CA 91330,
818-885-3431

Alice Wirth Gray 🎤 ✈   P&W
1001 Merced St
Berkeley, CA 94707-2521, 510-524-8958
Internet: awgray@aol.com
    Pubs: *What the Poor Eat* (Cleveland St U Poetry Ctr,
    1993), *American Scholar, Atlantic, Poetry*

Benjamin Green 🎤 ✈   P&W
3415 Patricks Point Dr #3
Trinidad, CA 95570-9769, 707-677-3084
    Pubs: *The Sound of Fish Dreaming* (Bellowing Ark,
    1996), *Green Grace* (Punla Pub, 1993), *Monologs from
    the Realm of Silence* (Ransom Note Pub, 1990)
Groups: Schools, Seniors

Geoffrey Green 🎤 ✈   W
English Dept, San Francisco State Univ, 1600 Holloway
Ave, San Francisco, CA 94132-1700, 415-338-7414
Internet: ggreen@sfsu.edu
    Pubs: *Fiction*

Suzanne Greenberg   W
257 1/2 Park Ave
Long Beach, CA 90803
    Pubs: *New Virginia Rev, Indiana Rev, Turnstile,
    Mississippi Rev, The Washington Rev, Florida Rev*

Linda Gregg   P
PO Box 475
Forest Knolls, CA 94933-0475, 415-488-9587
    Pubs: *Chosen by the Lion, The Sacraments of Desire*
    (Graywolf, 1994, 1991), *Paris Rev, Atlantic, The Qtly,
    TriQtly, Columbia Rev, Partisan Rev, Ploughshares*

Arpine Konyalian Grenier 🎤 ✈   P
990 S Marengo Ave
Pasadena, CA 91106-4255, 626-441-3249
    Pubs: *Whores from Samarkand* (Florida Literary Fdtn
    Pr, 1993), *St. Gregory's Daughter* (U La Verne Pr,
    1991), *Columbia Poetry Rev, Iowa Rev, Tinfish, Sulfur,
    CQ, Kiosk*
Lang: Armenian. I.D.: Armenian-American. Groups:
Prisoners, Scientist

Susan Griffin 🎤 ✈   P&W
904 Keeler Ave
Berkeley, CA 94708-1420, 510-528-9296
Internet: sgriffinca@earthlink.net
    Pubs: *What Her Body Thought* (HarperSF, 1999),
    *Bending Home Poems Selected & New, Unremembered
    Country* (Copper Canyon, 1998, 1988), *Women and
    Nature, The Poetry Inside Her: Anth* (Sierra Club Bks,
    2000), *APR, Mother Jones, City Lights Rev, Utne
    Reader*
Groups: G/L/B/T, Environmentalist

Morton Grinker   P
1367 Noe St
San Francisco, CA 94131
    Pubs: *The Gran Phenician Rover: Book 5, Books 1-4,
    To the Straying Aramaean* (Thorp Springs, 1994, 1992,
    1972)

Hugh Gross   W
880 N Hilldale Ave #16
West Hollywood, CA 90069, 310-652-5844
    Pubs: *16 Bananas, Same Bed, Different Dreams*
    (Mid-List Pr, 1995, 1991)

Richard Grossinger   W
258 Yale Ave
Kensington, CA 94708
    Pubs: *Out of Babylon, New Moon* (Frog Ltd, 1997,
    1996), *The Night Sky* (J.P. Tarcher, 1988),
    Embryogenesis (North Atlantic Bks, 1986)

Richard Grossman 🎤 ✈   P
2000 DeMille Dr
Los Angeles, CA 90027, 323-665-2116
Internet: http://www.richardgrossman.com
    Pubs: *The Book of Lazarus* (FC2, 1997), *The Alphabet
    Man* (Fiction Collective, 1993), *The Animals* (Graywolf,
    1990), *Tycoon Boy* (Kayak, 1977)
Groups: Children

Mark Grover P&W
3525 Del Mar Heights Rd Box 273
San Diego, CA 92130
    Pubs: *What Touched His Life* (Noble Crown, 1995),
    Words & Poets (Revorg, 1994)

Albert J. Guerard W
English Dept, Stanford Univ, Stanford, CA 94305,
415-327-6687
    Pubs: *The Hotel in the Jungle* (Baskerville Pub, 1996),
    Gabrielle (Donald I. Fine, 1992), *Christine/Annette*
    (Dutton, 1985), *Fiction*

Judith Guest W
Patricia Karlan Agency, 3575 Cahvenga Blvd Suite 210,
Los Angeles, CA 90068
    Pubs: *Errands* (Ballantine Bks, 1997), *The Mythic
    Family* (Milkweed Edtns, 1988), *Ordinary People*
    (Viking-Penguin Pr, 1976)

Thom Gunn 🎤 ✈ P
1216 Cole St
San Francisco, CA 94117
    Pubs: *Boss Cupid, Collected Poems, The Man with
    Night Sweats* (FSG, 2000, 1994, 1992), *Threepenny
    Rev, TLS*

Carol L. Gunther P
PO Box 876
Sutter Creek, CA 95685, 209-267-0332
    Pubs: *The Return of Mr. Trespass* (Black Tape Pr,
    1990), *Cincinnati Poetry Rev, Boston Literary Rev*

Katharine Haake 🎤 ✈ W
California State Univ, English Dept, Northridge, CA
91330-0001
    Pubs: *The Height & Depth of Everything* (U Nevada Pr,
    2001), *No Reason on Earth* (Dragon Gate, 1986), *Iowa
    Rev, Mississippi Rev, Minnesota Rev, Michigan Qtly
    Rev, Qtly West, Witness, NER/BLQ*

Philip Hackett 🎤 ✈ P
PO Box 330168
San Francisco, CA 94133-0168
    Pubs: *Two American Poets* (Little City Pr, 1997), *Iraq,
    Jordan, & Egypt Poems, Poems to My Son Dylan*
    (Pegasus, 1994, 1992), *SF Call, The Monthly,
    Beatitude, SF Bay Guardian, Boston Mag, Electrum,
    Stone Country, Deep Valley, A Publications,
    Haight-Ashbury*

Ray Hadley 🎤 ✈ P
PO 16696
South Lake Tahoe, CA 96151, 800-541-6967
    Pubs: *Smoking Mt. Shasta* (Blackberry, 1975), *Dacotah
    Territory, Kyoi, Kuksu, MidAtlantic, Sierra Nevada Rev,
    Scree 6, South & West, Yellow Brick Road*

D. R. Hakim P
Prometheus Press, PO Box 1569, Glendale, CA 91209
    Pubs: *Posed Perfectly in Dreams, Smoke of Signal
    Dreams* (Prometheus Pr, 1992, 1989), *Verve, L.A.
    Driver, The Moment, Counterfeit Monday, Red Dance
    Floor*

Jane Hall P&W
1516 Euclid Ave
Berkeley, CA 94708, 510-849-2540
    Pubs: *Anth of New England Writers* (New England
    Writers, 1997), *Fourteen Hills, Berkeley Poetry Rev,
    Ruah, Sonoma Literary Rev, Americas Rev*

Judith Hall P
28239 Via Acero
Malibu, CA 90265
    Pubs: *Anatomy, Errata* (Ohio State, 1998), *To Put the
    Mouth To* (Morrow, 1992)

Irving Halperin W
San Francisco State Univ, 1600 Holloway Ave, San
Francisco, CA 94132, 415-338-2578
    Pubs: *Here I Am: A Jew in Today's Germany*
    (Westminster Pr, 1971), *Prairie Schooner,
    Massachusetts Rev, NER*

James A. Hamby P
Drawer 1124
Arcata, CA 95521, 707-826-4189
    Pubs: *New Mexico Mag, Idaho Heritage, Pandora,
    Western Rev, South Dakota Rev*

Forrest Hamer 🎤 ✈ P
5275 Miles Ave
Oakland, CA 94618-1044, 510-601-6334
Internet: FHamer8580@aol.com
    Pubs: *Middle Ear* (Roundhouse, 2000), *Call &
    Response* (Alice James Bks, 1995), *Word of Mouth:
    Anth* (Talisman Hse, 2000), *Best American Poetry: Anth*
    (Scribner, 2000, 1994), *Geography of Home: Anth*
    (Heyday Bks, 1999)

Rose Hamilton-Gottlieb W
2997 Lakeview Way
Fullerton, CA 92835, 714-526-6395
    Pubs: *At Our Core: Women Writing About Power: Anth,
    Grow Old Along with Me: Anth, The Best Is Yet to Be:
    Anth* (Papier-Mache Pr, 1998, 1997, 1996), *Farm Wives
    & Other Iowa Stories: Anth* (Mid-Prairie Bks, 1995), *The
    Ear, Room of One's Own*

Sam Hamod 🎤 ✈ P
PO Box 1722
San Marcos, CA 92079, 760-746-0619
Internet: hshamod@yahoo.com
    Pubs: *Love Songs, The Arab Poems, The Muslim
    Poems* (Cedar Creek Pr, 2001, 2000, 2000), *Unsettling
    America: Anth* (Viking Penguin, 1994), *Konch*
Lang: Arabic. Groups: Ethnic, Seniors

Stephanie Han   P&W
55 Navy St #204
Venice, CA 90291, 310-396-3991
    Pubs: *L.A.(Lovers Anonymous)* (LaLa Pr, 1995), *In the
    Moment* (SheilaNaGig, 1994)

Joseph Hansen   P&W
2638 Cullen St
Los Angeles, CA 90034, 213-870-2604
    Pubs: *Living Upstairs* (Dutton, 1993), *Bohannon's
    Country* (Viking, 1993), *Ellery Queen's Mystery, Alfred
    Hitchcock's Mystery, South Dakota Rev*

C. G. Hanzlicek 🎤 ✈   P
738 E Lansing Way
Fresno, CA 93704-4223, 209-226-1528
Internet: charles_hanzlicek@csufresno.edu
    Pubs: *The Cave* (U Pitt Pr, 2001), *Against Dreaming* (U
    Missouri Pr, 1994), *When There Are No Secrets,
    Calling the Dead* (Carnegie Mellon U Pr, 1986, 1982)

Maria Harris 🎤 ✈   W
29377 Quail Run Dr
Agoura Hills, CA 91301, 818-889-8238
    Pubs: *Die, Die My Darling, Bullseye* (Books in Motion,
    1999, 1997), *Baroni, The Joseph File* (Putnam, 1975,
    1974)
Lang: German. I.D.: German-American. Groups: Children,
Seniors

Mark Jonathan Harris 🎤 ✈   W
School of Cinema-TV, Univ Southern California, Los
Angeles, CA 90089, 213-740-3317
    Pubs: *Into the Arms of Strangers* (Bloomsbury, 2000),
    Solay, Come the Morning (Bradbury Pr, 1993, 1989)

William Harrison   W
William Morris Agency, 151 El Camino Dr, Beverly Hills,
CA 90212, 310-274-7451
    Pubs: *Three Hunters* (Random Hse, 1989), *Burton &
    Speke* (St. Martin's Pr, 1982)

John Hart 🎤 ✈   P
PO Box 4262
San Rafael, CA 94913-4166, 415-507-9230
Internet: jh@johnhart.com
    Pubs: *The Climbers* (U Pitt Pr, 1978), *Ascent, Aethlon,
    Blue Unicorn, Interim, SPR*

William Hart 🎤 ✈   P&W
2721 Piedmont #3
Montrose, CA 91020
    Pubs: *Paris, Monsoon* (Timberline Pr, 1996, 1991),
    *Commonweal, Black Bear Rev, Florida Rev, Ko, Lilliput
    Rev, Brussels Sprout, Poetry Nippon*

Suzanne Hartman   W
17290 Redwood Springs Dr
Fort Bragg, CA 95437
    Pubs: *Kansas Qtly, Mississippi Valley Rev, Ladies
    Home Jrnl, Confrontation, Woman's Day, Gamut*

Gerald Haslam 🎤 ✈   W
PO Box 969
Penngrove, CA 94951-0969, 707-792-2944
Internet: www.geraldhaslam.com
    Pubs: *Manuel & the Madman, The Great Tejon Club
    Jubilee* (Devil Mountain Bks, 2000, 1996), *Straight
    White Male, Condor Dreams & Other Fictions* (U
    Nevada Pr, 2000, 1994), *L.A. Times Mag, Nation,
    Sierra, This World, Sky*

Robert Hass   P
Box 807
Inverness, CA 94937
    Pubs: *Human Wishes, Twentieth Century Pleasures,
    Praise* (Ecco Pr, 1988, 1984, 1979)

Barbara Hauk 🎤   P
10181 Beverly Dr
Huntington Beach, CA 92646-5426, 714-968-7530
    Pubs: *Confetti* (Event Horizon Pr, 1993), *Pearl, Chiron
    Rev, Onthebus, Cape Rock, Genre, BPJ*

Juanita Havill   P
PO Box 194
Sonoita, CA 85637
Internet: lemotjuste@theriver.com
    Pubs: *Jamaica's Blue Marker, Jamaica & Brianna* (HM,
    1995, 1993), *Saving Owen's Toad* (Hyperion, 1994),
    The Most Wonderful Books: Anth (Milkweed Edtns,
    1997), *Blossoms & Blizzards: Anth* (Pegasus Prose,
    1986), *The Inkling Selection: Anth* (Inkling Pub, 1984)

Marjorie Hawksworth   P
2516 Selrose Ln
Santa Barbara, CA 93109
    Pubs: *Silent Voices* (Ally Pr, 1978), *Connecticut Poetry
    Rev, Centennial Rev, Pulpsmith, Spectrum, NYQ*

Gwen Head 🎤 ✈   P
72 Eucalyptus Rd
Berkeley, CA 94705-2802, 510-654-4270
Internet: fireshadow@prodigy.net
    Pubs: *Frequencies: A Gamut of Poems* (U Utah Pr,
    1992), *The Ten Thousandth Night* (U Pitt Pr, 1979),
    Southern Rev, APR, NAR

Eloise Klein Healy 🎤 ✈   P
Antioch Univ Los Angeles, 13274 Fiji Way, Marina Del
Rey, CA 90292, 310-578-1080
Internet: eloise_klein_healy@antiochla.edu
    Pubs: *Artemis in Echo Park* (Firebrand, 1991), *The
    World in Us: Anth* (St Martin's Pr, 2000), *Geography of
    Home: Anth* (Heyday Bks, 1999), *Women's Studies
    Chronicles, Solo, High Plains Literary Rev, 51%,
    nerve.com*
I.D.: G/L/B/T. Groups: Women

Kevin Hearle ⚲ ⚼ P
102 Hobart Ave
San Mateo, CA 94402-2808, 650-571-6390
Internet: kevinhearle@earthlink.net
  Pubs: *Each Thing We Know Is Changed Because We Know It & Other Poems* (Ahsahta Pr, 1994), *Organization & Enviroment, Georgia Rev, Yale Rev, Qtly West, Windsor Rev, Poetry Flash*

Susan Hecht ⚲ ⚼ P&W
PO Box 4361
Mission Viejo, CA 92690, 949-363-2057
Internet: sahecht@home.com
  Pubs: *Beware of Islands* (Inevitable Pr, 1998), *Devil's Millhopper, Calyx, Onionhead, Sou'wester, Hawaii Pacific Rev*

Mary Hedin P&W
182 Oak Ave
San Anselmo, CA 94960, 415-454-4422
  Pubs: *Direction* (West Country, 1982), *Fly Away Home* (U Iowa, 1980)

Anne Hedley P
5870 Birch Ct
Oakland, CA 94618, 510-655-1430

Leslie Woolf Hedley ⚲ ⚼ P&W
Exile Press, 112 Chadwick Way, Cotati, CA 94931-5164
  Pubs: *The Holocaust Memorial Cantata* (CD; Polygram, 1996), *& Other Stories* (Exile Pr, 1992), *Blood to Remember: Poems* (U Texas Tech Pr, 1991), *Baseball: The Game of Life* (Birchbook Pr, 1990)
I.D.: American

Lyn Hejinian ⚲ ⚼ P
2639 Russell St
Berkeley, CA 94705-2131, 510-548-1817
  Pubs: *The Language of Inquiry* (U California Pr, 2000), *Happily* (Post-Apollo Pr, 2000), *Sight* (Edge Bks, 1999), *The Cold of Poetry, My Life* (Sun & Moon Pr, 1994, 1987), *Oxota* (The Figures, 1991)

Padma Hejmadi ⚲ ⚼ W
2135 Humboldt Ave
Davis, CA 95616-3084, 530-753-8538
Internet: padma@dcn.davis.ca.us
  Pubs: *Birthday Deathday* (Penguin Bks India, 1992), *Dr. Salaam & Other Stories* (Capra Pr, 1978), *Mirrorwork: Anth* (Owl Pr, 1997), *New Yorker, Parabola, American Book Rev, Southern Rev*
I.D.: South Asian, Women

Carol Henrie ⚲ ⚼ P
24929 Minnie Ct
Hayward, CA 94541-6910, 510-886-1018
Internet: reachus@pacbell.net
  Pubs: *Field, Nation, Ironwood, Poetry, Poetry NW, New Republic, Prairie Schooner*

Barbara Hernandez P
1432 Celis St
San Fernando, CA 91340

Juan Felipe Herrera ⚲ ⚼ P
5340 N Campus Dr
Fresno, CA 93740-0097, 559-278-7934
  Pubs: *Thunderweavers, Border-Crosser with Lamborghini Dream, Night Train to Tuxtla* (U Arizona Pr, 2000, 1999, 1994), *Erashbloomlove* (U New Mexico Pr, 1999), *Love After the Riots* (Curbstone Pr, 1997)
Lang: Spanish. I.D.: Chicano/Chicana. Groups: Latino/Latina, Children

Elizabeth Carothers Herron P&W
PO Box 41
Bodega, CA 94922
  Pubs: *The Stones the Dark Earth* (Harlequin Ink, 1995), *While the Distance Widens* (Floating Island, 1994), *Desire Being Full of Distances* (Calliopea, 1983)

John Herschel P
Univ California, Q-022, La Jolla, CA 92093, 619-534-3068
  Pubs: *The Floating World* (New Rivers Pr, 1979), *Minnesota Rev, Invisible City, Seattle Rev, APR*

Jerry Hicks ⚲ ⚼ P
2614 W 181 St
Torrance, CA 90504, 310-532-1200
Internet: beach.poet@worldnet.att.net
  Pubs: *California Poetry Calendar, Traffic Report Mag, Rattle Mag, Spillway Mag, One* (Dog) *Press Mag, ZamBomba, California Qtly*

Marvin R. Hiemstra ⚲ ⚼ PP
166 Bonview St
San Francisco, CA 94110-5147, 415-826-4485
  Pubs: *I Mouse Therefore I Am!* (Rhyme & Reason, 2000), *In Deepest USA* (Prairie Lights Bks, 1996), *A Turquoise Coyote Under Your Pillow* (Zippy Digital Prdns, 1997), *Marvin R. Hiemstra at Spoken Word Café* (Carmel Perf Arts Fstvl, 1998)
Groups: Seniors, G/L/B/T

Jamake Highwater P&W
c/o The Native Land Foundation, 8491 Sunset Blvd, Ste 424, Los Angeles, CA 90069
Internet: http://home.earthlink.net/~nativeland
  Pubs: *Journey to the Sky, The Sun, He Dies* (Replica Bks, 1999, 1999), *Anpao* (HC, 1999), *Dark Legend, Kill Hole* (Grove Pr, 1994, 1992), *Shadow Show* (Van Der Marck Edtns, 1987), *Native Land* (Little, Brown, 1986), *Moonsong Lullaby* (Morrow, 1985)

Donna Hilbert 🎤 ✈   P&W
5615 E Seaside Walk
Long Beach, CA 90803-4454, 562-434-4172
Internet: donnahilbert@earthlink.net
    Pubs: *Transforming Matter* (Pearl Edtns, 2000), *Deep
    Red, Mansions* (Event Horizon Pr, 1993, 1990), *Boomer
    Girls: Anth* (U Iowa Pr, 1999)

Nellie Hill 🎤 ✈   P&W
16 The Crescent
Berkeley, CA 94708, 510-540-0886
    Pubs: *Having Come This Far* (Keeler, 1978), *Coast &
    Ocean, Teacup, Sideshow, Aikido Today, Harvard Mag,
    Studia Mystica, Margin, American Writing*

Brenda Hillman   P
St. Mary's College, Moraga, CA 94575, 925-631-4472
    Pubs: *Loose Sugar, Bright Existence, Death Tractates,
    Fortress* (Wesleyan, 1997, 1993, 1992, 1989), *APR*

Mimi Walter Hinman   P
1085 Normington Way
San Jose, CA 95136, 408-723-0522
    Pubs: *Autumn Sun* (Zapizdat Pubs, 1995), *Wind
    Five-Folded* (AHA Bks, 1994), *Marilyn, My Marilyn: Anth*
    (Pennywhistle Pr, 1998), *Poetpourri, Japanophile, Poet,
    Pearl, Cicada, Thema*

Jack Hirschman   P
1314 Kearny St
San Francisco, CA 94133, 415-398-1953
    Pubs: *The David Arcane, The Donmeh* (Amerus Pr,
    1982, 1980)

Jane Hirshfield 🎤 ✈   P
Michael Katz, 367 Molino Ave, Mill Valley, CA
94941-2767, 415-381-2319
Internet: jh@well.com
    Pubs: *Given Sugar, Given Salt, The Lives of the Heart,
    The October Palace* (HC, 2000, 1997, 1994), *Of Gravity
    & Angels* (Wesleyan, 1988), *Atlantic, New Yorker*

Sandra Hoben   P
129 Sunnyside
Mill Valley, CA 94941, 415-388-7641
    Pubs: *Snow Flowers* (Westigan Rev Pr, 1979), *Partisan
    Rev, Ironwood, Qtly West, Mickle Street Rev*

Marilyn Hochheiser 🎤 ✈   P
5406 E Los Angeles Ave, #93
Simi Valley, CA 93063-4167, 805-527-5534
    Pubs: *Anthology Issue, A View Through the Thicket*
    (Outpost Pubs, 1990, 1977), *Last Words, California
    Confederation of the Arts, Art/Life, Crosscurrents*
I.D.: Jewish, Christian. Groups: Prisoners, Seniors

Cecelia Holland   W
520 Palmer Blvd
Fortuna, CA 95540

Scott C. Holstad   P
PO Box 10608
Glendale, CA 91209-3608
    Pubs: *Places* (Sterling Hse, 1995), *Distant Visions,
    Again & Again* (Poet Tree, 1994), *Poetry Ireland Rev,
    Textual Studies in Canada, Arkansas Rev, Minnesota
    Rev, Wisconsin Rev, Southern Rev*

Paul Hoover 🎤 ✈   P&W
369 Molino Ave
Mill Valley, CA 94941-2767, 415-389-1877
Internet: viridian@hotmail.com
    Pubs: *Totem & Shadow* (Talisman Hse, 1999), *Viridian*
    (U Georgia Pr, 1997), *Postmodern American Poetry:
    Anth* (Norton, 1994), *APR, Conjunctions, New Republic,
    Boston Rev, Stand*

Toke Hoppenbrouwers 🎤 ✈   W
Psychology Dept, California State Univ, 1811 Nordhoff St,
Northridge, CA 91330-8255, 818-667-2827
Internet: hcpsy009@csun.edu
    Pubs: *Autumn Sea* (Astarte Shell Pr, 1996)
Lang: Dutch. Groups: G/L/B/T

Bill Hotchkiss   P&W
Sierra College, 5000 Rocklin Rd, Rocklin, CA 95677,
916-624-3333
    Pubs: *Yosemite, Sierra Santa Cruz, To Fell the Giants*
    (Bantam, 1995, 1992, 1991)

Lindy Hough   P
258 Yale Ave
Kensington, CA 94708-1048
    Pubs: *Outlands & Inlands* (Truck Pr, 1984), *Nuclear
    Strategy & the Code of the Warrior: Anth* (North
    Atlantic Bks, 1984)

Sevrin Housen   P
3408 L St
Sacramento, CA 95816-5334, 916-451-7659
    Pubs: *Feathers & Bones* (Halcyon Pr, 1981),
    Bellingham Rev, Quercus, Suttertown News

James D. Houston 🎤 ✈   W
2-1130 E Cliff Dr
Santa Cruz, CA 95062-4836
Internet: jhouston@cruzio.com
    Pubs: *Snow Mountain Passage* (Knopf, 2001), *The Last
    Paradise* (U Oklahoma Pr, 1998), *In the Ring of Fire*
    (Mercury Hse, 1997), *Continental Drift* (U California Pr,
    1996), *Wild Duck Rev, Zyzzyva, Utne Reader, Manoa,
    Ploughshares, Common Boundary*

Noni Howard   P
New World Press, 744 Stoneyford Dr, Daly City, CA
94015-3642, 650-758-1437
    Pubs: *Tiger Balm, The Politics of Love* (New World Pr,
    1997, 1996), *Share My Fantasies* (Beatitude, 1996),
    Bloodjet Literary Mag, Haight-Ashbury Literary Jrnl

Fanny Howe   P
Literature Dept 0410, Univ California, La Jolla, CA 92093
  Pubs: *De Ultima Die* (O Bks, 1992), *Saving History,
  The Deep North* (Sun & Moon Pr, 1992, 1988), *Grand
  Street, Ploughshares*

George F. Howell   P&W
3342 Hamilton Way
Los Angeles, CA 90026
  Pubs: *The Sartre Situation* (Howell, 1984), *Working
  Book* (Periplus Pr, 1978), *Angle of Repose*

Mary Hower   P
1831 Castro St
San Francisco, CA 94131
  Pubs: *The World Between Women: Anth* (Her Bks,
  1987), *Virginia Qtly Rev, Threepenny Rev, Pacific Intl,
  California Qtly, Iowa Rev, Hubbub, Bellingham Rev*

Andrew Hoyem   P
460 Bryant St
San Francisco, CA 94107, 415-777-9651
  Pubs: *What If: Poems 1969-87, Picture/Poems* (Arion
  Pr, 1987, 1975)

Elias N. Hruska   P
PO Box 2157
Los Gatos, CA 95031-2157, 408-866-2229
  Pubs: *Perceptions Volume III: Anth* (The Wright
  Experience, 1992), *Many Voices/Many Lands: Anth*
  (Poetry Ctr, 1989), *Cafe Solo Anth* (Solo Pr, 1974),
  Poetry Mag

Richard G. Hubler   W
PO Box 793
Ojai, CA 93023, 805-646-3200
  Pubs: *Inside Ojai, Wheeler* (Creek Hse, 1976, 1970),
  Soldier & Sage (Crown Pub, 1966)

Barbara Hull   P
9449 Manzanita Ave
Ben Lomond, CA 95005-9422, 408-336-4240
  Pubs: *This House She Dreams In* (Kuhn Spit Pr, 1990),
  *California Qtly, Seattle Rev, Interim, Poet Lore, Poetry
  Seattle, Footwork*

Nan Hunt 🎤 ✈   P&W
23301 Clarendon St
Woodland Hills, CA 91367-4162, 818-887-0031
Internet: huntnanwritr@earthlink.net
  Pubs: *The Wrong Bride* (Plain View, 1999), *If I Had My
  Life to Live Over: Anth* (Papier-Mache Pr, 1992), *To Be
  a Woman: Anth* (J.P. Tarcher/St. Martin's Pr, 1991),
  *Slant, Daybreak, Rivertalk, SheilaNaGig, BPJ,
  Borderlands, Crosscurrents*
I.D.: Czech-American, Unitarian-Universalist. Groups:
Children, A.A.U.W.

Terryl Hunter   P
415 15th St, #12
Huntington Beach, CA 92648
  Pubs: *Poetry Loves Poetry: Anth* (Momentum Pr, 1985),
  Rara Avis, Magazine, Gramercy Rev, Onthebus

Maureen Hurley   P
7491 Mirabel Rd, #5
Forestville, CA 95436, 707-887-2046
  Pubs: *Atomic Ghost: Poets Respond to the Nuclear
  Age: Anth* (Coffee Hse Pr, 1995), *Poems on the
  Korean War Conflict: Anth* (Ctr for Korean Studies,
  1995), *House on Via Gambito: Women Writers Abroad:
  Anth* (New Rivers Pr, 1991)

Paula Huston 🎤 ✈   W
California Poly, San Luis Obispo, English Dept, San Luis
Obispo, CA 93407, 805-756-2596
Internet: www.tgrady.com
  Pubs: *Daughters of Song* (Random Hse, 1995), *Story,
  American Short Fiction, NAR, Missouri Rev, Mss.,
  Massachusetts Rev*

Kathleen Iddings 🎤 ✈   P
3366 Via Alicante
La Jolla, CA 92037-2743, 858-457-1399
  Pubs: *Here's to Humanity: Anth* (People's Pr, 2000),
  Streams: Anth (Pudding Hse Pr, 2000), *The Muse
  Strikes Back: Anth* (Story Line Pr, 1997), *Poet's Market,
  L.A. Times, Writer's Digest, English Jrnl, Crosscurrents*

Momoko Iko   W
c/o J. McCloden, PO Box 172, Hollywood, CA 90028

Ruth G. Iodice   P
22 Avon Rd
Kensington, CA 94707, 510-526-8439
  Pubs: *And What Rough Beast: Poems at the End of
  the Century* (Ashland Poetry Pr 1999), *Out of Season:
  Anth* (Amagansett Pr, 1993), *South Coast Poetry Jrnl,
  Blue Unicorn, Poet Lore, Long Pond Rev, Negative
  Capability*

Susan K. Ito 🎤 ✈   P&W
6034 Valley View Rd
Oakland, CA 94611-2026, 510-339-0622
Internet: skito@sprintmail.com
  Pubs: *A Ghost at Heart's Edge: Anth* (North Atlantic Pr,
  1999), *Making More Waves: Anth* (Beacon Pr, 1997),
  Growing Up Asian American: Anth (Morrow, 1993), *Two
  Worlds Walking: Anth* (New Rivers, 1992), *Side Show:
  Anth* (Somersault Pr, 1992), *Hip Mama*

Spoon Jackson   P
B-92377, #2184, CMC-East Box 8101, San Luis Obispo,
CA 93409-8101
    Pubs: *African American Wisdom* (New World Library,
1994), *Rivers* (Sacramento Poetry Review, 1992), *No
Distance Between Two Points* (Month of Mondays Pr,
1987), *Brother's Keeper: Anth* (M. Datcher, 1992),
Exquisite Corpse, Community Endeavor

Kelley Reynolds Jacquez 🎤 ✈   W
2828 W Compton
Fresno, CA 93711-1181, 559-439-0406
    Pubs: *Fantasmas: Anth* (Bilingual Pr, 2000), *Walking
the Twilight II: Anth* (Northland Pub, 1996), *Eratica,
Writing for Our Lives*

Harold Jaffe   P&W
3551 Granada Ave
San Diego, CA 92104, 619-294-4924
    Pubs: *Straight Razor* (Black Ice Bks, 1995), *Eros
Anti-Eros* (City Lights, 1990), *Fiction Intl, Chicago Rev,
New Directions Annual, City Lights Rev*

Maggie Jaffe   P
3551 Granada Ave
San Diego, CA 92104-4144, 619-294-4924
    Pubs: *7th Circle* (Cedar Hill Pub, 1998), *How the West
Was One, Continuous Performance* (Burning Cities Pr,
1996, 1992), *Getting By: Anth* (Bottom Dog Pr, 1996),
*Cedar Hill Rev, Rattle, Pemmican Pr, Viet Nam
Generation, Green Fuse, Intl Qtly*

Frances Jaffer   P
801 27th St
San Francisco, CA 94131
    Pubs: *Alternate Endings* (How/Ever, 1985), *She Talks to
Herself in the Language of an Educated Woman*
(Kelsey Street Pr, 1980)

T. R. Jahns   P
21141 Canada Rd, #1D
Lake Forest, CA 92630-7703
    Pubs: *Poetry NW, Denver Qtly, SW Rev, Ohio Rev*

Marnell Jameson   W
3957 Pacheco Dr
Sherman Oaks, CA 91403, 818-784-2204
    Pubs: *The Book of Blessings, The Song of Songs*
(Harper, 1995, 1990), *California Palms* (Sunstone Pr,
1990), *L.A. Times, Valley Mag, Cimarron Rev, APR,
Tikkun*

Jean Janzen 🎤 ✈   P
5508 East Ln
Fresno, CA 93727, 559-251-9006
Internet: jjanzen@qnis.net
    Pubs: *Tasting the Dust, Snake in the Parsonage* (Good
Bks, 2000, 1995), *The Upside Down Tree* (Windflower
Comm, 1992), *Piecework: Anth* (Silver Snakes Pr,
1987), *Poetry, Gettysburg Rev, Antioch Rev*

Estelle Jelinek   P&W
1301 Bonita Ave #3
Berkeley, CA 94709-1983
Internet: ejel@uclink.berkeley.edu
    Pubs: *Berkeley Poets Collective, Berkeley Works,
Dream Machinery, Razorslit*

Joyce Jenkins 🎤 ✈   P
1450 4th St #4
Berkeley, CA 94710-1328, 510-525-5476
Internet: www.poetryflash.org
    Pubs: *Portal* (Pennywhistle Pr, 1993), *Prayers at 3 AM:
Anth* (HC, 1995), *Berkeley Poetry Rev, Zyzzyva*

Francisco Jimenez 🎤 ✈   W
Santa Clara Univ, Modern Languages & Literatures, Santa
Clara, CA 95053-0001, 408-554-4533
Internet: fjimenez@scu.edu
    Pubs: *Cajas de Carton, The Christmas Gift, La
Mariposa* (HM, 2000, 2000, 1998), *The Circuit: Stories
from the Life of a Migrant Child* (U New Mexico Pr,
1997), *Mosaico de la Vida* (HBJ, 1984), *Riversedge,
L.A. Times Book Rev*
Lang: Spanish. I.D.: Latino/Latina, Mexican

Donas John 🎤 ✈   P&W
1629 Cimarron St
Los Angeles, CA 90019-6317, 323-732-3359
Internet: donaswest2@aol.com
    Pubs: *Peace Is Our Profession* (East River Pr, 1981),
*Now Times, Rainbow City Pr, Gypsy, Connecticut
Fireside, Poet Lore, Archer*

Diane Johnson   W
24 Edith
San Francisco, CA 94133
    Pubs: *Le Divorce* (Dutton, 1997), *Natural Opium, Health
& Happiness, Persian Nights* (Knopf, 1993, 1990, 1987)

Robin Johnson   P
Wide Awake Ranch, Rd 208
Madera, CA 93638, 209-822-2528
    Pubs: *Denver Qtly, Massachusetts Rev, Poetry NW,
Antioch Rev, SW Rev, Outerbridge*

Sheila Goldburgh Johnson 🎤 ✈   P&W
1498 Tunnel Rd
Santa Barbara, CA 93105-2139, 805-682-4618
Internet: chtodel@humanitas.ucsb.edu
    Pubs: *After I Said No, Santa Barbara Stories: Anth,
Shared Sightings: Anth* (John Daniel & Co, 2000, 1998,
1996), *Walking the Twilight II: Anth* (Northland Pub,
1996), *Atlanta Rev, Puerto Del Sol, Negative Capability,
Crosscurrents*
I.D.: Jewish. Groups: Teenagers, Seniors

Alice Jones P
6239 College Ave, #304
Oakland, CA 94618-1384, 510-420-8803
Internet: ajones@idiom.com
  Pubs: *Isthmus, The Knot* (Alice James Bks, 2000,
  1992), *Best American Poetry: Anth* (Scribner, 1994),
  *Volt, Colorado Rev, Poetry, Kenyon Rev, Zyzzyva,
  Denver Qtly, Ploughshares*

Silas Jones W
7818 S Hobart Blvd
Los Angeles, CA 90047, 213-971-8443
  Pubs: *Children of All* (Funkshunal Features, 1978), *The
  Price of Dirt* (Accent, 1974), *Black World*

June Jordan ♦ ✈ P
Univ of California, African American Studies, Berkeley, CA
94720-0001, 510-642-2743
  Pubs: *Soldier* (Basic Bks, 2000), *Affirmative Acts,
  Kissing God Good-bye* (Doubleday, 1999, 1998), *Living
  Room* (Thunder's Mouth Pr, 1985), *Civil Wars* (Beacon
  Pr, 1981)

Jorg P
125 Beach, #44
Santa Cruz, CA 95060
  Pubs: *Revolution Fruit Pie, Honking Geese* (Stone Pr,
  1978, 1978), *Sitting Frog*

Andrew Joron ♦ ✈ P
2009 Cedar St
Berkeley, CA 94709, 510-843-7853
Internet: ajoron@earthlink.net
  Pubs: *The Removes* (Hard Pr, 1998), *Primary Trouble*
  (Talisman Hse, 1996), *Science Fiction* (Pantograph Pr,
  1992), *Force Fields* (Starmont Hse, 1987), *Sulfur, New
  American Writing*

Natasha Josefowitz ♦ ✈ P
2235 Calle Guaymas
La Jolla, CA 92037-6915, 858-456-2366
Internet: natashaj@mail.sdsu.edu
  Pubs: *If I Eat I Feel Guilty, If I Don't I'm Deprived, Too
  Wise to Want to Be Young Again* (Blue Mountain Pr,
  1999, 1995)
Groups: Seniors, Women

David Joseph P&W
298 9th Ave
San Francisco, CA 94118, 415-387-3412
  Pubs: *Homeless But Not Helpless: Anth* (Harvest,
  1988), *Central Park, Rolling Stone*

Mifanwy Kaiser P
20592 Minerva Ln
Huntington Beach, CA 92646, 714-968-0905
  Pubs: *News from Inside, Raising the Roof: Anth*
  (Bombshelter Pr, 1996, 1999)

Gerald Kaminski ♦ P&W
883 Chamise Way
Redding, CA 96002, 530-221-8979
  Pubs: *People Wanting Children, Circumstantial Evidence*
  (Cove View Pr, 1998, 1993), *Iconoclast, Main Street
  Rag, University Rev*

Howard Kaplan W
2242 Guthrie Dr
Los Angeles, CA 90034-1030
  Pubs: *Passage to Baalbek* (Atheneum, 1979), *The
  Damascus Cover* (Dutton, 1977)

Pamala Karol ♦ ✈ P
Loyola Marymount Univ, Dept of Film & Television, #8230,
Los Angeles, CA 90045-2660, 310-338-3033
Internet: pamala.karol@mciworld.com
  Pubs: *Adventures on the Isle of Adolescence* (City
  Lights Bks, 1989), *Scars: Anth* (U Alabama Pr, 1996),
  AMC, Threepenny Rev, City Lights Rev, Jacaranda Rev

Pearl L. Karrer ♦ P
570 Kingsley Ave
Palo Alto, CA 94301-3224
  Pubs: *Weathering: Anth, River Poems: Anth* (Slapering
  Hol Pr, 1993, 1992), *Slant, Whetstone, Visions Intl,
  Poets On, CQ, Berkeley Poetry Rev, Devil's Millhopper*

Hiroshi Kashiwagi P&W
4314 Pacheco St
San Francisco, CA 94116-1056
  Pubs: *Only What We Could Carry: Anth* (Heyday Bks,
  2000), *The Big Aiiieeeee: Anth* (Meridian-Penguin Bks,
  1991), *On a Bed of Rice: Anth* (Anchor Bks, 1995)
I.D.: Asian-American, Japanese-American

Michael J. Katz W
1631 Barry Ave #6
Los Angeles, CA 90025, 213-826-9475
  Pubs: *The Big Freeze, Last Dance in Redondo Beach*
  (Putnam, 1990, 1989)

Sam Keen W
16321 Norrbom Rd
Sonoma, CA 95476, 707-996-9010
  Pubs: *Faces of the Enemy* (H&R, 1987)

George Keithley ♦ ✈ P&W
1302 Sunset Ave
Chico, CA 95926-2650, 530-345-0865
  Pubs: *Living Again* (Bear Star Pr, 1997), *Earth's Eye*
  (Story Line Pr, 1994), *The Donner Party* (Braziller,
  1989), *Harper's, Sewanee Rev, Alaska Qtly Rev, Agni,
  Kenyon Rev, TriQtly, NAR, Ekphrasis*

Robert Kelsey   W
650 N McPherson St
Fort Bragg, CA 95437, 707-964-7649
    Pubs: *Virginia Qtly Rev, Massachusetts Rev, The Sun,
    New Press, Snake Nation Rev*

Troxey Kemper   P&W
3108 W Bellevue Ave
Los Angeles, CA 90026-3717, 213-413-0789
    Pubs: *Last Bastion, All But Lost* (Derivations, 2000,
    1999), *Lean into the Wind* (Morris Pub, 1997), *Mood
    Swings* (Small Poetry Pr, 1996), *Part Comanche*
    (Bennet & Kitchel, 1991), *Tucumcari Lit Rev*

Robert Kendall 🎤 ✈   P
1800 White Oak Dr
Menlo Park, CA 94025-6129
Internet: www.wordcircuits.com/kendall
    Pubs: *A Life Set for Two* (Eastgate Systems, 1996), *A
    Wandering City* (Cleveland State U Poetry Ctr, 1992),
    WPWF Poetry: Anth (Bunny & Crocodile Pr, 1992),
    *Iowa Rev Web, Cortland Rev, Contact II, River Styx,
    NYQ, Indiana Rev*

Susan Kennedy   P
PO Box 108
Duncans Mills, CA 95430, 707-865-9536
    Pubs: *Cazadero Poems* (Floating Island Pr, 1994), *A
    New Geography of Poets: Anth* (U Arkansas Pr, 1992),
    *The Temple, White Heron Poetry Rev, Ruah, The
    Tomcat, Haight-Ashbury Literary Jrnl, Zyzzyva*

Joseph Kent   P
1372 Pine St
San Francisco, CA 94109
    Pubs: *Streams, White Wind* (Sunlight Pub, 1996, 1989),
    The Irreversible Man: Anth (Ars Poetica Pr, 1991), *In
    the Company of Poets, CQ*

Rolly Kent 🎤 ✈   P
5501 Tuxedo Terrace
Los Angeles, CA 90068, 323-462-3332
    Pubs: *Queen of Dreams* (S&S, 1991), *Spirit, Hurry*
    (Confluence Pr, 1985), *The Wreck in the Post Office
    Canyon* (Maguey Pr, 1977)
Lang: French. Groups: Teachers, Parents

Roger Lee Kenvin 🎤 ✈   W
575 Fairview Ave
Arcadia, CA 91007, 626-445-4420
Internet: jlybl@earthlink.net
    Pubs: *Trylons & Perispheres, The Cantabrigian Rowing
    Society's Saturday Night Bash, Harpo's Garden* (July
    Blue Pr, 1999, 1998, 1997), *South Carolina Rev, Garm
    Lu, Spindrift, Roanoke Rev, Oasis, The Distillery, ELF,
    Crescent Rev, Other Voices, New Letters*

Karen Kenyon 🎤 ✈   P
PO Box 12604
La Jolla, CA 92039-2604, 858-587-9027
    Pubs: *Writing By Heart* (Sunshower, 1989), *Sunshower*
    (Putnam/Marek, 1981), *Redbook, Ladies Home Jrnl,
    CSM, British Heritage, Westways, Writer's Digest*

T. S. Kerrigan 🎤 ✈   P
14651 Morrison St
Sherman Oaks, CA 91403-1650, 818-905-8084
Internet: tkerrigan@hq.dir.ca.gov
    Pubs: *Another Bloomsday at Molly Malone's Pub &
    Other Poems* (Inevitable Pr, 1999), *Branches Among
    the Stars* (Aran Pr, 1988), *Drastic Measures, Kansas
    Qtly, The Epigrammatist, Pacific Rev, Southern Rev,
    Tennessee Qtly, Intl Poetry Rev*
I.D.: Irish-American

Jascha Kessler 🎤 ✈   P&W
218 16th St
Santa Monica, CA 90402-2216
Internet: jkessler@ucla.edu
    Pubs: *Siren Songs: 50 Stories* (McPherson & Co,
    1992), *Catullan Games: Poems* (Marlboro Pr, 1989)

David Kherdian   P
284 Hutchins Ave
Sebastopol, CA 95472, 707-823-6671
    Pubs: *I Called It Home, My Racine* (Forkroads Pr,
    1997, 1994), *Friends: A Memoir* (Globe Press Bks,
    1993), *Asking the River* (Orchard Bks, 1993)

Kathy Kieth   P
4708 Tree Shadow Pl
Fair Oaks, CA 95628, 916-966-8620
    Pubs: *The Acorn, Limestone Circle, Nanny Fanny,
    Northern Stars*

Daphne Rose Kingma   P
PO Box 5244
Santa Barbara, CA 93150-5244, 805-969-4171
    Pubs: *Kansas Qtly, Spectrum, Circus Maximus*

Maxine Hong Kingston   W
Univ California, English Dept, Berkeley, CA 94720,
510-643-5127
    Pubs: *China Men, Tripmaster Monkey* (Knopf, 1990,
    1989), *Hawaii One Summer* (Meadow Pr, 1987)

Diane Kirsten-Martin 🎤 ✈   P
68 Ashton Ave
San Francisco, CA 94112-2206, 415-337-7408
Internet: martin3@best.com
    Pubs: *Left-Hand Maps: Anth* (Small Garlic Pr, 1998),
    *Five A.M., Crazyhorse, Santa Clara Rev, Zyzzyva,
    Yellow Silk, Hayden's Ferry, Blue Mesa, Onthebus,
    Bellingham Rev*

Ed Kissam P
Box 2041
Sebastopol, CA 95473, 707-829-5696
    Pubs: *Poems of the Aztec Peoples* (Bilingual Rev Pr,
    1983), *Jerusalem & the People* (Anvil, 1975)

Pat Kite W
5318 Stirling Ct
Newark, CA 94560-1352
    Pubs: *Highlights, Prime Monthly, Botanical Garden*

Carolyn Kizer ♀ ✈ P
19772 8th St E
Sonoma, CA 95476-3849
    Pubs: *Cool, Calm & Collected, Harping on Poems:
    1985-1995, The Nearness of You, Mermaids in the
    Basement* (Copper Canyon Pr, 2000, 1996, 1986,
    1984), *Pro Femina* (BkMk Pr, 2000), *100 Great Poems
    By Women: Anth* (Ecco Pr, 1995), *Paris Rev, Michigan
    Qtly Rev*

Sheila Solomon Klass ♀ ✈ W
Ruth Cohen, Inc, PO Box 7626, Menlo Park, CA 94025
    Pubs: *Little Women Next Door, The Uncivil War, A
    Shooting Star* (Holiday Hse, 2000, 1997, 1996), *In a
    Cold Open Field* (Black Heron Pr, 1997), *Next Stop
    Nowhere, Rhino, Kool Ada* (Scholastic, 1995, 1993,
    1991)

Edward Kleinschmidt Mayes ♀ ✈ P
1700 Monterey Blvd
San Francisco, CA 94127-1928
Internet: girasole@pacbell.net
    Pubs: *Works & Days* (U Pitt Pr, 1999), *Bodysong*
    (Heyeck Pr, 1999), *Speed of Life* (Apogee Pr, 1999),
    *New Yorker, APR, Poetry, NER, Massachusetts Rev,
    Volt*

August Kleinzahler P
325A Frederick St
San Francisco, CA 94117
    Pubs: *Live from the Hong Kong Nile Club, Red Sauce,
    Whiskey & Snow* (FSG, 2000, 1995), *New York Times,
    London Rev of Bks, New Yorker, Harper's*

Mary Julia Klimenko ♀ ✈ P
1392 West K St
Benicia, CA 94510-2445, 707-746-1645
Internet: vescamaria@aol.com
    Pubs: *Territory* (Brighton Pr, 1993), *New Letters,
    Transfer Mag, Suisun Valley Rev, Transfer 45, Berkeley
    Poetry Rev, Art Well, Psychopoetica*

Arthur Winfield Knight ♀ ✈ P&W
PO Box 544
Citrus Heights, CA 95621, 916-721-1827
Internet: www.geocities.com/Athens/Forum/2188
    Pubs: *Outlaw Voices* (CC Marimbo Comm, 2000),
    Johnnie D. (Forge Bks, 2000), *The Darkness Starts Up
    Where You Stand* (Depth Charge, 1996), *The Secret
    Life of Jesse James* (Burnhillwolf, 1996), *NYQ, Poet
    Lore, Windsor Rev*

Kit Knight ♀ ✈ P
PO Box 2580
Citrus Heights, CA 95611, 916-721-1827
Internet: www.geocities.com/Athens/Forum/2188
    Pubs: *Women of Wanted Men* (Potpourri Pr, 1994),
    *Redneck Rev, Caprice, Pittsburgh Qtly, Waterways,
    Green's Mag*

Chris Kobayashi P
298 Coleridge St
San Francisco, CA 94110, 415-821-3012
    Pubs: *Networks* (Vortex Edtns, 1979), *Azumi* (Japanese
    American Anth Committee, 1979)

Michael Koepf ♀ ✈ W
PO Box 1055
Elk, CA 95432, 707-877-3518
Internet: bigfish1@saber.net
    Pubs: *The Fisherman's Son* (Broadway Bks, 1998),
    Icarus (w/M. Crawford; Atheneum, 1987), *Save the
    Whale* (McGraw-Hill, 1978)
I.D.: American. Groups: Prisoners

Phyllis Koestenbaum ♀ ✈ P
982-E La Mesa Terr
Sunnyvale, CA 94086-2402, 408-732-2756
    Pubs: *Criminal Sonnets* (Writer's Ctr Edns, 1998), *A
    Formal Feeling Comes: Anth* (Story Line Pr, 1999),
    Best American Poetry: Anth (Macmillan, 1993, 1992),
    *Michigan Qtly Rev, Epoch, Amer Letters &
    Commentary, Brooklyn Rev, Poetry NY, Prairie
    Schooner, Verse*
Groups: Jewish, Women

Ken Kolb W
PO Box 30022
Cromberg, CA 96103, 530-836-2332
    Pubs: *Night Crossing* (Playboy, 1974), *Couch Trip*
    (Random Hse, 1970), *Redbook, Esquire, Playboy*

Susan Kolodny ♀ ✈ P
6239 College Ave Ste 304
Oakland, CA 94618, 510-339-2877
Internet: www.thecaptivemuse.com
    Pubs: *Outsiders: Anth, Verse & Universe: Anth*
    (Milkweed Edtns, 1999, 1998), *Anthology of Magazine
    Verse: Anth* (Yrbk of American Poetry, 1997), *NER,
    Bellingham Rev, River Styx*

Lynda Koolish 🎙 ✈   P
1020 Grizzly Peak Blvd
Berkeley, CA 94708-1526, 510-524-4994
    Pubs: *Journeys on the Living* (Ariel, 1973), *Mosaic,
    Networks, Yellow Silk, Berkeley Poets Co-op*
I.D.: Jewish, G/L/B/T

Stephen Kopel   P
187 Beaver St
San Francisco, CA 94114-1516, 415-626-1395
    Pubs: *Family Celebrations: Anth* (Andrews McMeel,
    1999), *Troubadour, Acorn, Mockingbird, Asspants,
    Comstock Rev, Skylark, Burning Cloud Rev, Ship of
    Fools, Mediphors, Buffalo Bones, Chaminade Literary
    Rev, Aurorean, Lyric, Wild Cat*

Steve Koppman   W
1960 Magellan Dr
Oakland, CA 94611, 510-339-6339
    Pubs: *The Literature of Work: Anth* (U Phoenix Pr,
    1991), *Zyzzyva, Berkeley Monthly, Jewish Currents,
    Agada, Sifrut, Wind*

Dennis Koran   P
6156 Wilkinson Ave
North Hollywood, CA 91606
    Pubs: *After All* (Norton Coker Pr, 1992), *Vacancies*
    (Mother Hen, 1975), *Poetry Now, Beatitudes, Abraxas,
    Panjandrum*

Steve Kowit   P
PO Box 184
Potrero, CA 91963-0184, 619-478-2129
    Pubs: *Pranks* (Bloody Twin Pr, 1990), *Lurid
    Confessions* (Carpenter Pr, 1983), *The Maverick Poets:
    Anth* (Gorilla Pr, 1988)

Michael H. Krekorian 🎙 ✈   W
San Diego State Univ, English Dept/Comparative
Literature, San Diego, CA 92182-8140, 619-594-5443
Internet: mkrekorian@juno.com
    Pubs: *Channel Zero* (Plover Pr, 1996), *Corridor* (Ashod
    Pr, 1989), *New Novel Rev, Fiction Intl, AM Lit, Bateria,
    Central Park, Mississippi Mud*
I.D.: Armenian-American. Groups: Armenian-American

Ian Krieger 🎙 ✈   P
216 Westminster Ave
Venice, CA 90291-3306, 310-392-1156
    Pubs: *An Unnamed Aesthetic* (Stolen Images, 1987),
    Pavans (Ommation Pr, 1985)

S. Allyx Kronenberg 🎙 ✈   PP&P&W
PO Box 5323
Santa Monica, CA 90409-5323, 310-399-4245
Internet: jardine3@juno.com
    Pubs: *Incantations of the Grinning Dream Woman*
    (Sagittarius Pr, 1990), *Always I Was Getting Ready to
    Go* (Black Heron Pr, 1989), *California Qtly, MPR*

Judy Kronenfeld 🎙 ✈   P
3314 Celeste Dr
Riverside, CA 92507-4051, 909-682-5096
Internet: jkronen@citrus.ucr.edu
    Pubs: *Disappeared Down Dark Wells & Still Falling*
    (Inevitable Pr, 2000), *Shadow of Wings* (Bellflower Pr,
    1991), *Essential Love: Anth* (Grayson Bks, 2000),
    Wilshire *Rev, Poets On, Light, Cape Rock, Verse,
    Kansas Qtly, Passages North, Chariton Rev, NAR, MPR*

Lewis Kruglick   P
118 Calera Canyon Rd
Salinas, CA 93908
    Pubs: *Spring Bandits* (Leviathan Pr, 1981), *The
    Unknown Angel* (Tree Bks, 1971)

James Krusoe   P
504 Pier Ave
Santa Monica, CA 90405
    Pubs: *Hotel de Dream,
    ABCDEFGHIJKLMNOPQRSTUVWXYZ* (Illuminati, 1991,
    1984), *Jungle Girl* (Little Caesar, 1982), *APR, Field,
    Denver Qtly*

Geraldine Kudaka   P
4470-107 Sunset Blvd, Ste 331
Los Angeles, CA 90027
    Pubs: *Persona* (Street Agency Pub, 1988), *Numerous
    Avalanches at the Point of Intersection* (Greenfield Rev
    Pr, 1979), *Y'Bird*

Joanne Kyger 🎙 ✈   P
PO Box 688
Bolinas, CA 94924-0688, 415-868-0272
    Pubs: *Some Life* (Post Apollo Pr, 2000), *Patzcuaro*
    (Blue Millennium Pr, 1999), *Just Space* (Black Sparrow
    Pr, 1991), *Phenomological* (Further Studies, 1989),
    Going On (Dutton, 1983)

Joan La Bombard 🎙   P
814 Teakwood Rd
Los Angeles, CA 90049-1330, 310-476-5437
    Pubs: *The Winter Watch of the Leaves, The Counting
    of Grains* (San Diego Poets Pr, 1993, 1990), *Wherever
    Home Begins: Anth* (Orchard Bks, 1995), *Poetry NW,
    Tar River Poetry, Colorado Rev, Nation, Virginia Qtly,
    Prairie Schooner*

Joyce La Mers 🎙 ✈   P
2514 Greencastle Ct
Oxnard, CA 93035-2901, 805-985-6336
    Pubs: *Grandma Rationalizes an Enthusiasm for
    Skydiving* (Mille Grazie Pr, 1996), *The Muse Strikes
    Back: Anth* (Story Line Pr, 1997), *Sometime the Cow
    Kick Your Head: Anth* (Bits Pr, 1988), *Plains Poetry
    Jrnl, Piedmont Literary Rev, Light Qtly, Formalist*

Salvatore La Puma W
PO Box 20147
Santa Barbara, CA 93210-0147, 805-569-1633
    Pubs: *A Time for Wedding Cake* (Norton, 1991), *The Boys of Bensonhurst* (U Georgia, 1987)

Jennifer Lagier 🎤 ✈ P&W
165 Dolphin Cir
Marina, CA 93933-2220, 408-883-9587
Internet: pcmc@igc.org
    Pubs: *Second-Class Citizen* (Bordighera, 2000), *Where We Grew Up* (Small Poetry Pr, 1999), *Coyote Dream Cantos* (Iota Pr, 1992), *New to North America: Anth* (Burning Bush Pub, 1998), *At Our Core: Anth* (Papier-Mache Pr, 1998)
I.D.: Italian-American

Philip Lamantia P
c/o City Lights Bookstore, 261 Columbus Ave, San Francisco, CA 94113, 415-362-1901
    Pubs: *Bed of Sphinxes, Meadowlark West, Becoming Visible* (City Lights Bks, 1997, 1986, 1981), *Sulfur, City Lights Rev, Arsenal, Exquisite Corpse, Caliban*

Jeanne Lance 🎤 ✈ P
218 Appleton Dr
Aptos, CA 95003-5002, 408-685-9518
    Pubs: *Water Burial* (e.g. Pr, 1985), *Mass Psychosis* (Jungle Garden Pr, 1983), *Red Wheelbarrow, 6ix, Switched-On Gutenberg, Santa Cruz County Sentinel, North Beach Now*

Maxine Landis P
553 N Pacific Coast Hwy #B130
Redondo Beach, CA 90277
    Pubs: *News from Inside: Anth* (Hand Maid Bks 1994), *San Fernando Poetry Jrnl, Voices, Volno, Struggle, Onthebus, Earth Bound, Blood Pudding, Quill, Spillway*

Mervin Lane P
258 E Mountain Dr
Santa Barbara, CA 93108, 805-969-2990
    Pubs: *Going to Town* (Sadhe Pr, 1987), *Black Mountain College: Sprouted Seeds: Anth* (U Tennessee, 1990)

A. J. Langguth W
Univ Southern California, ASC102, Los Angeles, CA 90089-0281, 213-740-3919
Internet: langguth@usc.edu
    Pubs: *Saki: Life of Hector Munro* (S&S, 1981)

Daniel J. Langton 🎤 ✈ P
1673 Oak St
San Francisco, CA 94117-2013, 415-552-2994
    Pubs: *Life Forms, The Inheritance* (Cheltenham, 1995, 1989)

Marina deBellagente LaPalma PP&P
329 Pope St
Menlo Park, CA 94025, 650-326-4981
    Pubs: *Half-Life* (The Present Pr, 1990), *Persistence: Anth* (Diderot Pr, 1994), *Rooms, Antigones, Afterimage, Resolutions*

John Laue 🎤 P
8 Morehouse Dr
La Selva Beach, CA 95076-1629, 408-684-0854
    Pubs: *Paradises Lost* (North Star Pr, 1997), *Snapshots of Planet Earth: Anth* (Oxford U Pr, 1998), *Grow Old Along with Me: Anth* (Papier-Mache Pr, 1996), *English Jrnl, Chiron Rev, Santa Barbara Rev, New Press Qtly, Modern Poetry, Chaminade Rev*

J. T. Ledbetter 🎤 ✈ P
California Lutheran Univ, Thousand Oaks, CA 91360, 805-492-2411
    Pubs: *Sewanee Rev, Sou'wester, Laurel Rev, Nimrod, Atlanta Rev, Puerto del Sol, The Formalist, Kansas Qtly, Poetry*

Stellasue Lee 🎤 ✈ P
4169 Greenbush Ave
Sherman Oaks, CA 91423-4305, 818-986-3274
Internet: stellasuel@aol.com
    Pubs: *Crossing the Double Yellow Line, Over to You, After I Fall: Anth* (Bombshelter Pr, 2000, 1991, 1991), *Sheila Na-Gig, Cedar Hill Rev, Raising the Roof, Onthebus, Herman Rev, On Target, Voices, Bloodpudding, Inky Blue, Rattle, Spillway*

Diane Lefer 🎤 ✈ W
7955 Blackburn Ave
Los Angeles, CA 90048-4461
Internet: desilef@cs.com
    Pubs: *Very Much Like Desire* (Carnegie Mellon U Pr, 2000), *The Circles I Move in* (Zoland Bks, 1994), *KGB Bar Reader: Anth* (Quill, 1998), *Breaking Up Is Hard to Do: Anth* (Crossing Pr, 1994), *Kenyon Rev, Manoa, Western Humanities Rev, Boulevard*

John Leggett P&W
1781 Partrick Rd
Napa, CA 94558
    Pubs: *Making Believe, Gulliver House* (HM, 1986, 1979), *Ross & Tom* (S&S, 1974)

Carolyn Lei-lanilau 🎤 ✈ P
6167 Harwood Ave
Oakland, CA 94618-1339
    Pubs: *Ono Ono Girl's Hula* (U Wisconsin, 1997), *Best American Poetry: Anth* (Scribner, 1996), *APR, Chicago Rev, Blue Mesa, Manoa, Raven Chronicles, American Voice, Occident, NAW*
I.D.: Polynesian/Hawaiian, Asian-American

Emily Wortis Leider   P
PO Box 210105
San Francisco, CA 94121
    Pubs: *WPFW 89.3 FM Anth, Rapid Eye Movement:
Anth* (Bunny & Crocodile Pr, 1992, 1976), *Chicago Rev,
Poets On, Mockingbird, Berkeley Poetry Rev, Hurricane
Alice*

Cornel Adam Lengyel 🎤 ✈   P&W
El Dorado National Forest, 7700 Wentworth Springs Rd,
Georgetown, CA 95634-9534, 916-333-4224
    Pubs: *Late News from Adam's Acres* (Dragon's Teeth,
1985), *Blood to Remember: Anth* (Texas Tech U Pr,
1991), *Old Crow, Confrontation, CQ, Dusty Dog,
Mandrake, Poetry Rev*

George H. Leong   P
1819 25th Ave
San Francisco, CA 94122, 415-441-2458
    Pubs: *A Lone Bamboo Doesn't Come from Jackson
Street* (Isthmus, 1977), *Califia, Time to Greez*

Russell C. Leong 🎤 ✈   P&W
3924 Tracy St
Los Angeles, CA 90027-3208, 310-825-2974
Internet: rleong@ucla.edu
    Pubs: *Phoenix Eyes & Other Stories* (U Washington,
2000), *Country of Dreams & Dust* (West End Pr, 1993),
Strange Attraction: Anth (U Nevada, 1995), *The Open
Boat: Anth* (Doubleday, 1993), *Charlie Chan Is Dead:
Anth* (Penguin, 1993), *Tricycle Buddhist Rev*
Lang: Chinese

Arthur Lerner   P
13511 Contour Dr
Sherman Oaks, CA 91423-4701, 213-936-4992
    Pubs: *Words for All Seasons* (Being Bks, 1983), *Spring,
Literary Rev, Poet & Critic, Poet, Orbis*

Eugene Lesser   P
Box 656
Woodacre, CA 94973, 415-488-4760

Ken Letko 🎤 ✈   P
College of the Redwoods, 883 W Washington Blvd,
Crescent City, CA 95531-8361, 707-465-2360
Internet: ken-letko@delnorte.redwoods.cc.ca.us
    Pubs: *All This Tangling* (Mardi Gras Pr, 1995), *Shelter
for Those Who Need It* (O2 Pr, 1985), *Greenfield Rev,
Cottonwood, Permafrost, World Order*

Bob Levin   W
2039 Shattuck, #201
Berkeley, CA 94704, 510-848-3868
    Pubs: *Fully Armed* (Baskerville, 1995), *The Best Ride
to New York* (H&R, 1978), *Karamu, Comics Jrnl,
Massachusetts Rev, Berkeley Insider, Cavalier, Carolina
Qtly*

Philip Levine   P
4549 N Van Ness Blvd
Fresno, CA 93704, 209-226-3361
    Pubs: *The Simple Truth, What Work Is* (Knopf, 1994,
1991), *New Yorker, Atlantic, Poetry, Paris Rev, Nation,
Hudson Rev*

Frieda L. Levinsky 🎤 ✈   P&W
1697 Calle Leticia
La Jolla, CA 92037
    Pubs: *Writers of the Desert Sage, La Jolla Village
News, Heritage, San Diego Jewish Pr, Chiron Rev,
Pegasus Rev, Poetic Liberty, Tucumcari Rev, San
Fernando Poetry Jrnl, Dog River, Parnassus, Atticus,
Hob-Nob, Omnific, Poetpourri*

Aurora Levins-Morales   W
1678 Shattuck Ave, Box 133
Berkeley, CA 94709, 510-524-0617
    Pubs: *Getting Home Alive* (Co-author; Firebrand, 1986),
In Other Words: Anth (Arte Publico, 1994), *Ms.,
American Voice, Bridges, Callaloo*

James Heller Levinson 🎤 ✈   P&W
21727 Tuba St
Chatsworth, CA 91311-2931, 818-882-9331
    Pubs: *Another Line* (Watermark Pr, 1990), *Bad Boy
Poems* (Bombshelter Pr, 1993), *Pulled Apart* (Third
Lung Pr, 1989), *Sulfur, Hawaii Rev, Dog River Rev,
Spoon River Poetry Rev, Center, Bakunin, Nexus*

Janet Lewis   P&W
143 W Portola Ave
Los Altos, CA 94022
    Pubs: *The Legend, Libretto* (John Daniel, 1987),
Numbers, Ohio Rev, Pennsylvania Rev, Southern Rev

John L'Heureux 🎤 ✈   P&W
Stanford Univ, Dept of English, Stanford, CA 94305-2087,
650-725-1209
Internet: jlx@leland.stanford.edu
    Pubs: *Having Everything* (Atlantic, 1999), *The Handmaid
of Desire* (Soho Pr, 1996), *The Shrine at Altamira*
(Penguin, 1995), *An Honorable Profession* (Viking,
1991), *Atlantic, New Yorker*

Genny Lim   P
New College of California, 766 Valencia St, San
Francisco, CA 94110
    Pubs: *The Politics of Experience* (Temple U, 1993),
Two Plays: Paper Angels & Bitter Cane (Kalamaku,
1991), *Winter Place* (Kearney Street Wkshp, 1991),
Wings for Lai Ho (East/West, 1982), *Oxford Book of
Women's Writing: Anth* (Oxford U, 1995)

Jim Lindsey   P
PO Box 1470
Ukiah, CA 95482, 704-849-1822
    Pubs: *The Difficult Days* (Princeton U Pr, 1984), *In Lieu
of Mecca* (U Pittsburgh Pr, 1976)

Shelley List W
2919 Grand Canal
Venice, CA 90291

Leo Litwak W
246 Chattanooga St
San Francisco, CA 94114

Myra Cohn Livingston P
9308 Readcrest Dr
Beverly Hills, CA 90210, 310-273-2909
Pubs: *Flights of Fancy & Other Poems, I Never Told & Other Poems* (Macmillan, 1994, 1992)

D. H. Lloyd W
Applezaba Press, PO Box 4134, Long Beach, CA 90804
Pubs: *Bible Bob Responds to a Jesus Honker* (Applezaba Pr, 1986), *Wormwood Rev, AKA Mag, Pearl*

Mona Locke 🎤 ✈ P
PO Box 1800
Paradise, CA 95969-2926, 530-872-4934
Internet: mmlocke@netzero.net
Pubs: *Coffeehouse Poetry: Anth* (Bottom Dog Pr, 1996), *Sculpture Gardens Rev III: Anth* (Pacific Voices Pr, 1991), *New Los Angeles Poets: Anth* (Bombshelter Pr, 1990), *South Dakota Rev, Onthebus, Negative Capability, CQ, Poets On, Blue Unicorn*

Gerald Locklin P&W
English Dept, California State Univ, Long Beach, CA 90840, 310-985-5285
Pubs: *Go West, Young Toad, Charles Bukowski: A Sure Bet* (Water Row Pr, 1998, 1992), *The Firebird Poems* (Event Horizon Pr, 1992), *Gold Rush & Other Stories* (Applezaba Pr, 1989), *Pearl, Chiron Rev*

Rachel Loden 🎤 ✈ P
3072 Stelling Dr
Palo Alto, CA 94303-3968, 650-493-4799
Internet: rloden@concentric.net
Pubs: *Hotel Imperium* (U Georgia Pr, 1999), *The Last Campaign* (Slapering Hol Pr, 1998), *An Exaltation of Forms: Anth* (U Michigan Pr, 2000), *Best American Poetry: Anth* (Scribner, 1995), *Paris Rev, NAW, Antioch Rev, Chelsea, Boulevard*

Ron Loewinsohn P
University of California, Department of English, Berkeley, CA 94702
Pubs: *Goat Dances* (Black Sparrow Pr, 1975), *Meat Air* (HBJ, 1970)

Jonathan London P
PO Box 537
Graton, CA 95444, 707-823-4003
Pubs: *The Candystore Man* (Morrow, 1998), *Hip Cat* (Chronicle Bks, 1993), *The Owl Who Became the Moon* (Dutton, 1993), *All My Roads* (Beehive Pr, 1981), *Gargoyle*

Cathleen Long 🎤 ✈ P
English Dept, Santa Monica College, 1900 Pico Blvd, Santa Monica, CA 90405, 310-434-4300
Pubs: *Truth & Lies That Press for Life: Anth* (Artifact Pr, 1991), *The New Los Angeles Poets: Anth* (Bombshelter Pr, 1989), *Sculpture Gardens Rev*

Perie J. Longo 🎤 ✈ P
9 East Mission
Santa Barbara, CA 93101, 805-687-9535
Pubs: *The Privacy of Wind, Milking the Earth* (John Daniel & Co, 1997, 1986), *Prairie Schooner, Lucid Stone, CQ, Pudding, Prattle, Embers*

David Wong Louie W
30155 S Barrington Ave #B
Los Angeles, CA 90066-1133
Pubs: *Pangs of Love* (Knopf, 1991), *Best American Short Stories: Anth* (HM, 1989), *Chicago Rev, Ploughshares, Fiction Intl*

Iven Lourie P
PO Box 2119
Nevada City, CA 95959, 530-272-0180
Pubs: *Miro's Dream* (Gateways Bks, 1988), *Alternatives, Poetry, Hanging Loose, Midstream*

B. D. Love 🎤 ✈ P&W
3740 Valleybrink Rd
Los Angeles, CA 90039-1427, 323-669-1332
Internet: bdlove@earthlink.net
Pubs: *Meat Wisdom* (Pudding Hse Pr, 2000), *Cut Salt Fire Grace* (Rhythm Dog Edtns, 1995), *Sweet Nothings: Anth* (Indiana U Pr, 1994), *New Orleans Rev, Tennessee Qtly, Many Mountains Moving, Lit Rev, Writers' Forum, Pacific Coast Jrnl*

Bia Lowe P&W
2252 Bronson Hill Dr
Los Angeles, CA 90068
Pubs: *Wild Ride* (HC, 1995), *Helter Skelter: Anth* (Los Angeles Museum of Contemporary Art, 1993), *Kenyon Rev, Witness, Harper's, Salmagundi*

Naomi Ruth Lowinsky 🎤 P
241 Courtney Ln
Orinda, CA 94563-3630
Internet: www.redclayistalking.com
Pubs: *red clay Is talking* (Scarlet Tanager Bks, 2000), *American Writing, Crab Creek Rev, Daybreak, Sheila-Na-Gig*
I.D.: Jewish, Spiritual/Religious

Suzanne Lummis 🎤 ✈   P
PO Box 27924
Los Angeles, CA 90027, 323-255-5223
Internet: www.lapoetryfestival.org
    Pubs: *In Danger* (Roundhouse Pr 1999), *Stand Up
Poetry: Anth* (California State U Pr, 1994),
Ploughshares, Solo, SPR, Poetry Daily, Poetry Intl

Kirk Lumpkin 🎤 ✈   P
1133-B Filbert St
San Francisco, CA 94109-1711, 415-474-6159
    Pubs: *Earth First! Campfire Poems* (Feral Pr, 1998),
Co-Hearing (Zyga Multimedia Research, 1983), *Peace
Or Perish: Anth* (Poets for Peace, 1983), *Earth First
Jrnl, Tenderloin Times, Am Here Forum, Terrain,
Temenos, Hazmat Rev*
Groups: Environmentalist, Progressive

Rick Lupert   P
5336 Kester Ave #103
Sherman Oaks, CA 91411, 818-995-4457
    Pubs: *Beyond the Valley of the Contemporary Poets,
You'll Wonder How You Ever Got Along Without It,
51%, Blue Satellite, Caffeine*

Toby Lurie   P
2022 High St, #B
Alameda, CA 94501-1726, 415-221-2446

Glenna Luschei   P
5146 Foothill Rd
Carpinteria, CA 93013, 805-543-1058
Internet: berrypress@aol.com
    Pubs: *Matriarch* (The Smith, 1992), *Bare Roots
Seasons* (Oblong, 1990), *Farewell to Winter* (Daedalus,
1988), *Blue Mesa Rev, Calapooya Collage*

Celia S. Lustgarten 🎤 ✈   P&W
317 3rd Ave
San Francisco, CA 94118-2402, 415-386-3592
Internet: cswilldfi@pacbell.net
    Pubs: *Shock Treatment* (Peak Output Unltd, 1988),
Apocalypse 3: Anth (Apocalypse Literary Arts Coalition,
1997), *For Poets Only, Perceptions, Chanticleer, New
Canadian Rev, Z Misc, Grasslands Rev*

William Luvaas   W
25593 1st St
Hemet, CA 92544, 619-739-1817
    Pubs: *Going Under* (Putnam, 1994), *The Seductions of
Natalie Bach* (Little, Brown, 1986), *Glimmer Train,
Village Voice, American Literary Rev, Confrontation*

Annette Peters Lynch   P
833 Garfield Ave
South Pasadena, CA 91030-2819, 626-799-7836
    Pubs: *Christmas Blues: Anth* (Amador Pub, 1995),
*Spectrum, CQ, Blue Unicorn, Pointed Circle, Poem,
Maryland Poetry Rev*

Kathleen Lynch 🎤 ✈   P&W
4807 Miners Cove Circle
Loomis, CA 95650-7112, 916-652-7315
Internet: kalynch@aol.com
    Pubs: *How to Build an Owl, Times Ten: Anth* (Small
Poetry Pr, 1995, 1997), *The Next River Over* (New
Rivers Pr, 1993), *Poetry, Nimrod, Qtly West, Poetry
East, Spoon River Poetry Rev, Sycamore Rev, Midwest
Qtly, Poetry NW*

Susan Macdonald   P
Printers Inc. Bookstore, 310 California Ave, Palo Alto, CA
94025, 415-323-7342
    Pubs: *A Smart Dithyramb* (Heyeck Pr, 1979),
Dangerous As Daughters (Five Trees Pr, 1976)

Samuel Maio   P
Univ San Jose
San Jose, CA 95129-0090, 408-924-4483
    Pubs: *The Burning of Los Angeles* (Thomas Jefferson
U Pr), *Antioch Rev, Bloomsbury Rev, Chariton Rev,
Formalist, Southern California Anth*

Clarence Major 🎤 ✈   P&W
Univ California, English Dept, Davis, CA 95616-7532,
916-752-5677
    Pubs: *Configurations* (Copper Canyon Pr, 1998), *Dirty
Bird Blues, Such Was the Season* (Mercury Hse, 1996,
1989), *Painted Turtle: Woman with Guitar* (Sun &
Moon, 1988)

devorah major   P
PO Box 423634
San Francisco, CA 94102, 415-621-1664
    Pubs: *Street Smarts* (Curbstone, 1996), *An Open
Weave* (Seal Pr, 1995), *Zyzzyva, Onthebus, Black
Scholar, Shooting Star, Caprice, Callaloo*

River Malcolm   W
625 Serpentine Dr
Del Mar, CA 92014, 619-755-7845
    Pubs: *Womanspirit, Sinister Wisdom, Thursday's Child*

Lee Mallory 🎤 ✈   P
Santa Ana College, 17th at Bristol, Santa Ana, CA 92706,
714-564-6526
    Pubs: *Two Sides Now* (w/M. Mallory; FarStarFire Pr,
1999), *Holiday Sheer* (Inevitable Pr, 1997), *Full Moon,
Empty Hands* (Lightning Pubs, 1994), *Invisible City,
Mojo Navigator, Hyperion, The Smith, Forum, Riverside
Qtly*

Eileen Malone 🎤 ✈   P&W
1544 Sweetwood Dr
Colma, CA 94015-2029, 650-756-5279
Internet: http://hometown.aol.com/eilymalone/index/html
    Pubs: *Mudfish, Salt Hill, Madison Rev, Americas Rev,
SPR, New Millennium, Half Tones to Jubilee, Louisville
Rev, Briar Cliff Rev, Abiko Qtly, Icarus, Ariel, Lucid
Stone, Fugue, Sun Dog, West Wind Rev, Disquieting
Muses, Poetry Mag*

Marvin Malone   P
722 Bedford Rd
Stockton, CA 95204-5214
  Pubs: *Bucolics & Cheromanics* (Callahan, 1963), *TriQtly*,
*Vagabond, Wormwood, December, Nihilistic Rev,
Stovepiper*

Oscar Mandel 🎤 ✈   P&W
California Inst Technology, Humanities & Social Sciences,
Pasadena, CA 91125, 626-395-4078
Internet: om@hss.caltech.edu
  Pubs: *Blossoms & Incantations, Prince Poupon Needs a
Wife,* (onlineoriginals.com, 1997, 1997), *Sigismund* (U
Pr America, 1988), *Antioch Rev, Kenyon Rev, Prairie
Schooner*
Lang: French

Angela Consolo Mankiewicz 🎤 ✈   P
752 N Mansfield Ave
Los Angeles, CA 90038-3406
Internet: acmank@earthlink.net
  Pubs: *Cancer Poems* (UBP-Los Angeles, 1995),
*Artword, Orange Willow, Yefief, Chiron Rev, Comstock
Rev, Slipstream, Hawaii Rev, Amelia, Phase & Cycle,
Karamu, The Lyric*
Groups: Prisoners, Teenagers

Victoria Lena Manyarrows 🎤 ✈   P
PO Box 411403
San Francisco, CA 94141-1403
Internet: earrows@itsa.ucsf.edu
  Pubs: *Songs from the Native Lands* (Nopal Pr, 1995),
Visit Teepee Town: Anth (Coffee Hse Pr, 1999), *The
Arc of Love: Anth* (Scribner, 1996), *Indigenous Woman,
Callaloo, XCP*

Adrianne Marcus 🎤 ✈   P&W
79 Twin Oaks
San Rafael, CA 94901-1915, 415-454-6062
Internet: medea999@aol.com
  Pubs: *Carrion House World of Gifts* (St. Martin's Pr,
1993), *Potomac Rev, Poetry Ireland, Crescent Rev,
Confrontation, Solo, Cosmopolitan*
I.D.: Jewish

Morton Marcus 🎤 ✈   P
1325 Laurel St
Santa Cruz, CA 95060, 831-429-9085
  Pubs: *Moments Without Names* (New Rivers Pr, 2001),
When People Could Fly (Hanging Loose Pr, 1997),
Geography of Home: Anth (Heyday Bks, 1999), *TriQtly,
Ploughshares, The Prose Poem, Denver Qtly, Hanging
Loose, Fiction*

William J. Margolis   P
1507 Cabrillo Ave
Venice, CA 90291-3709
  Pubs: *A Book of Touch & Other Poems* (Mendicant
Edtns, 1988), *Beat Voices: Anth* (H Holt, 1995), *Black
Ace 5, Grist On-Line, Venice West Rev, Galley Sail*

Stefanie Marlis   P
36 Madrone Ave
San Anselmo, CA 94960, 415-459-2920
  Pubs: *Rife* (Sarabande Bks, 1998), *Sheet of Glass*
(Floating Island Pr, 1994), *Slow Joy* (U Wisconsin Pr,
1989), *APR, Manoa, Plum Rev, Poetry, Poetry East,
Zyzzyva, Arshile, Five Fingers Rev, Gettysburg Rev,
Ploughshares, Volt*

Jack Marshall   P
4248 Moraga St
San Francisco, CA 94122
  Pubs: *Sesame, Arabian Nights* (Coffee Hse Pr, 1993,
1987), *APR, Talisman, Zyzzyva, Exquisite Corpse,
Caliban, Sifrut*

Jim Martin   P
303 Estrella Dr
Scotts Valley, CA 95066
  Pubs: *Shadows of My World* (Rush-Franklin Pub, 1993)

Joan M. Martin   P
670 Walton Dr
Red Bluff, CA 96080
  Pubs: *Z Miscellaneous, The Courier, Times-Argus,
Prophetic Voices, Yellow Butterfly, Deros*

Eliud Martinez 🎤 ✈   W
137 Nisbet Way
Riverside, CA 92507-4627, 909-682-5396
  Pubs: *Voice-Haunted Journey* (Bilingual Rev Pr, 1990),
Grow Old Along with Me: Anth (Papier-Mache Pr, 1996)

Jack Matcha   W
7716 Teesdale Ave
North Hollywood, CA 91605
  Pubs: *No Trumpets, No Drums* (Powell, 1970), *Prowler
in the Night* (Fawcett, 1959), *Gamma*

David Matlin   P&W
4635 56th St
San Diego, CA 92115, 619-583-7572
  Pubs: *How the Night Is Divided* (McPherson & Co,
1993), *Dressed in Protective Fashion* (Other Wind,
1990), *Avant-Pop: Fiction Anth* (Black Ice Bks, 1993),
Apex of the M

Clive Matson 🎤 ✈   P
472 44th St
Oakland, CA 94609-2136, 510-654-6495
Internet: clive@matson.ford.com
  Pubs: *Squish Boots* (Broken Shadow, 2000), *Hourglass*
(Seagull Pr, 1988), *Equal in Desire* (Manroot, 1983),
Exquisite Corpse, Nimrod, Visions Intl, Fine Madness

George Mattingly 🎤 ✈ P
820 Miramar Ave
Berkeley, CA 94707-1807, 510-525-2098
Internet: gmd@dnai.com
Pubs: *Driven, Breathing Space* (Blue Wind Pr, 2000, 1975), *Big Bridge, MSNBC Poetry Anthology*

Frances Mayes P&W
Creative Writing Program, San Francisco State Univ, San Francisco, CA 94132
Pubs: *Under the Tuscan Sun* (Broadway Bks, 1997), *Ex Voto, Hours* (Lost Roads, 1995, 1984), *Atlantic, Virginia Qtly, Southern Rev, Iowa Rev, Gettysburg Rev*

Sara McAulay W
California State Univ, English Dept, Hayward, CA 94542
Pubs: *Chance, Catch Rides* (Knopf, 1982, 1975), *Hot Flashes: Anth* (Faber & Faber, 1996), *Zyzzyva, Third Coast, Chili Verde Rev, Southern Ocean Rev, Black Warrior Rev, Real Fiction, California Qtly*

Kate McCarthy W
14854 Sutton St
Sherman Oaks, CA 91403, 818-784-0711
Pubs: *Calliope, Exquisite Corpse, Sewanee Rev*

Lee McCarthy P&W
8200 Kroll Way, #174
Bakersfield, CA 93311
Pubs: *Combing Hair with a Seashell* (Ion Bks, 1992), *Desire's Door* (Story Line Pr, 1991), *Intro 8: Anth* (Anchor Bks, 1977), *Raccoon 24/25, Solo, Daybreak*

Michael McClintock 🎤 ✈ P
807 Prospect Ave, Suite 107
South Pasadena, CA 91030-2448, 626-441-1853
Pubs: *Maya* (Seer Ox, 1976), *Man with No Face* (Shelters Pr, 1974), *The Haiku Anthology* (Norton, 2000), *Up Against the Window: Anth* (Redmoon Pr, 2000), *Tundra*

Frances Ruhlen McConnel P
Mary Routt Hall, Scripps College, Claremont, CA 91711, 714-621-8000
Pubs: *Gathering Light, One Step Closer* (Pygmalion Pr, 1979, 1975), *Iowa Rev, Seattle Rev, The Nation*

Brian McCormick P&W
c/o Martin Baum, Creative Artists Agency, 9830 Wilshire Blvd, Beverly Hills, CA 90212
Pubs: *The Immortality Project* (Word Made Flesh/Printed Matter Bks, 1991), *Atlantic, Permafrost, Blueline, Zyzzyva, Fine Madness, Harper's, Santa Monica Rev*

Jennifer McDowell P
PO Box 5602
San Jose, CA 95150
Pubs: *Ronnie Goose Rhymes for Grownups, Contemporary Women Poets: Anth* (Merlin Pr, 1984, 1977), *Chock, Snowy Egret, X, Tigris & Euphrates, Open Cell*

Whitman McGowan 🎤 ✈ P
PO Box 471493
San Francisco, CA 94147-1493, 415-441-0846
Pubs: *Contents May Have Shifted* (Viridiana, 1994), *No, I Am Not Walt Whitman's Great Grandson* (Mel Thompson Pub, 1993), *Left Hand Maps: Anth* (Small Garlic Pr, 1998), *Kinky Verse: Anth* (Daedalus, 1996), *poetry.about.com, Lord Buckley Online, Smoke & Mirrors*

Thomas R. McKague P&W
2306 Market St
San Francisco, CA 94114, 315-469-7741
Pubs: *Waterlight Dreams* (New Pr, 1995), *A Natural Beauty* (Florida Pr, 1991), *Poetpourri, New Press Literary Qtly, Blue Unicorn*

Michael McLaughlin 🎤 ✈ P&W
c/o Don't Trip Press, PO Box 14244, San Luis Obispo, CA 93401
Pubs: *Southern California Anthology* (MPW, 1988, 1984), *Crack, Coffeehouse Poet's Qtly, convolvus, Asylum Annual, Frank*
Groups: Prisoners, Mentally Ill

Elnora McNaughton 🎤 ✈ P
PO Box 7054
Oxnard, CA 93031, 805-485-5425
Pubs: *Hold the Moon Bursting* (Mille Grazie Pr, 1999), *Rivertalk: Anth* (Little Horse Pr, 1997-1994), *Verve, Embers, Art/Life, Wind, CQ, Daybreak*

Sandra McPherson P
2052 Calaveras Ave
Davis, CA 95616-3021, 530-753-9672
Pubs: *The Spaces Between Birds, Edge Effect: Trails & Portrayals* (Wesleyan/UPNE, 1996, 1996), *The God of Indeterminacy* (U Illinois Pr, 1993), *New Yorker*

Kat Meads 🎤 ✈ P&W
144 Walti St
Santa Cruz, CA 95060-4265
Internet: katmeads@aol.com
Pubs: *Night Bones, The Queendom* (Linear Arts Pr, 2000, 1998), *Born Southern & Restless* (Duquesne U Pr, 1996), *Wayward Women* (Illinois Writers Inc, 1995), *Women & Death: Anth* (Ground Torpedo Pr, 1994)

Maude Meehan P
2150 Portola Dr
Santa Cruz, CA 95062, 408-476-6164
    Pubs: *Washing the Stones: A Collection 1975-1995*
(Papier-Mache Pr, 1996), *Before the Snow* (Moving
Parts, 1991), *Chipping Bone* (Embers Pr, 1988)

Ib J. Melchior W
8228 Marmont Ln
Los Angeles, CA 90069, 213-654-6679
    Pubs: *Quest* (Presidio Pr, 1990), *Steps & Stairways*
(Co-author; Rizzoli, 1989)

David Meltzer 🎤 ✈ P&W
Poetics Dept, New College of California, 776 Valencia St,
San Francisco, CA 94110, 415-626-1694
Internet: dmelt@ccnet.com
    Pubs: *No Eyes, Arrows* (Black Sparrow Pr, 2000,
1993), *Under* (Rhinoceros Bks, 1998), *Writing Jazz:
Anth, Reading Jazz: Anth* (Mercury Hse, 1999, 1994),
Washington Post, Davka

Roger Ladd Memmott 🎤 P&W
512 S Crawford Ave
Willows, CA 95988-3313, 530-934-7062
Internet: rlmstory@aol.com
    Pubs: *Catharsis* (Millennium Pr, 1980), *Blue Unicorn,
Colorado Qtly, Confrontation, Sou'wester, Bachy,
Cumberland Poetry Rev, Cincinnati Poetry Rev*

Ann Menebroker P
10 Azorean Court
Sacramento, CA 95833
    Pubs: *Mailbox Boogie* (w/Robertson; Zerx Pr, 1991),
Time Capsule: Anth (Creative Time, 1995), *Caprice,
Atom Mind, Pearl, Painted Bride Qtly, Bogg, Smell
Feast, Thunders Mouth Press*

Sarah Menefee P
1655 Sacramento #1
San Francisco, CA 94109
    Pubs: *This Perishable Hand* (Multimedia Edizioni, 1995),
Please Keep My Word (Worm in the Rain Pub, 1991),
*The Blood About the Heart, I'm Not Thousandfurs,
Poetry Like Bread: Anth* (Curbstone Press, 1992, 1986,
1994)

Douglas Messerli P
Sun & Moon Press, 6026 Wilshire Blvd, Los Angeles, CA
90036, 213-857-1115
    Pubs: *The Walls Come True: An Opera for Spoken
Voices, Along Without: A Film for Fiction in Poetry*
(Littoral, 1994, 1993)

Deena Metzger P&W
PO Box 186
Topanga, CA 90290, 213-455-1089
    Pubs: *Tree: Essays & Pieces* (North Atlantic Bks,
1997), *A Sabbath Among the Ruins* (Parallax Pr, 1992),
What Dinah Thought (Viking, 1989), *Intimate Nature:
Anth* (Ballantine, 1998), *Anima, Turning Wheel, Poetry
Flash, Creation, Jacaranda Rev, Lilith*

Robert Mezey 🎤 ✈ P
English Dept, Pomona College, 140 W 6 St, Claremont,
CA 91711-6335, 909-607-2809
Internet: rmezey@pomona.edu
    Pubs: *Collected Poems* (U Arkansas Pr, 2000), *Evening
Wind* (Wesleyan, 1987), *New Criterion, Raritan, Paris
Rev, New Yorker, Hudson Rev, NYRB*

Leonard Michaels W
English Dept, Univ California, Berkeley, CA 94720,
415-642-2764
    Pubs: *I Would Have Saved Them If I Could* (FSG,
1975)

Jack Micheline P&W
41 Sutter St, Box 1269
San Francisco, CA 94104
    Pubs: *The Last Round Up, Poems of Fire & Light*
(Midnight Special Edtns, 1992, 1990), *Letter to Kerouac
in Heaven* (Zeitgeist Pr, 1991)

Rondo Mieczkowski 🎤 ✈ P&W
PO Box 29478
Los Angeles, CA 90029-0478, 323-661-0478
    Pubs: *Sundays at Seven: Anth* (Alamo Square Pr,
1996), *Sonora Rev, James White Rev, Wisconsin Rev,
Modern Words, Poetry/L.A.*
I.D.: G/L/B/T, HIV/AIDS. Groups: G/L/B/T, HIV/AIDS

Sara Miles P
824 Shotwell St
San Francisco, CA 94110-3213
    Pubs: *Native Dancer* (Curbstone Pr, 1986), *Ordinary
Women* (Ow Bks, 1984), *Opposite Sex: Anth* (NYU Pr,
1998), *Iowa Rev, Essence, Ms., XXXFruit, Nation, New
Yorker, Wired, Essence*

Adam David Miller 🎤 ✈ P
PO Box 162
Berkeley, CA 94701-0162, 510-845-8098
Internet: eliseadm@sirius.com
    Pubs: *Land Between, New & Selected Poems,
Apocalypse Is My Garden* (Eshu Hse Pub, 2000, 1997),
Forever Afternoon (Michigan State U Pr, 1994),
Neighborhood & Other Poems (Mina Pr, 1993), *Dices
or Black Bones* (HM, 1973)

Brown Miller P
English Dept, City College of San Francisco, 50 Phelan
Ave, San Francisco, CA 94112, 415-239-4793
   Pubs: *Hiroshima Flows Through Us* (Cherry Valley
   Edtns, 1977), *New Letters, Xanadu, Ohio Rev*

Lorraine Millings ♪ ✈ P
PO Box 2291
Lancaster, CA 93539-2291, 805-949-8687
Internet: PoetRaini@aol.com
   Pubs: *America at the Millennium, Verve, Plaza, Pirate
   Writings, Poetic Eloquence, Friendship Rose*

Paul L. Mills PP
3426 Keystone Ave #4
Los Angeles, CA 90034-4731
   Pubs: *The Co-op Songbook* (New York Musicians
   Co-op, 1983), *Think & Do* (Co-op Records, 1983),
   Boston Phoenix, Creem, Fusion, Outpost, Stroker

Stephen Minot ♪ W
2225 Mt Vernon Ave
Riverside, CA 92507-2500, 909-369-3938
Internet: s.minot@juno.com
   Pubs: *Surviving the Flood* (Second Chance Pr, 1986),
   Ghost Images (H&R, 1979), *Virginia Qtly Rev, Sewanee
   Rev, Harper's, Agni, Paris Rev, Atlantic*

Janice Mirikitani P
Glide Foundation, 330 Ellis St, San Francisco, CA 94102,
415-771-6300
   Pubs: *We the Dangerous, Shedding Silence: Anth*
   (Celestial Arts Pub, 1995, 1990), *Awake in the River*
   (Isthmus Pr, 1982)

Hayley R. Mitchell ♪ ✈ P
23106 Kent Ave
Torrance, CA 90505-3527
Internet: grimmgirl@aol.com
   Pubs: *Bite to Eat: Anth* (Redwood Coast Pr, 1995),
   *Black Buzzard Rev, Cimarron Rev, SPR, New Delta
   Rev, Poetry NW, Wordwrights*
Groups: Women

Mark J. Mitchell ♪ ✈ P
2547 California St
San Francisco, CA 94115, 415-567-0206
   Pubs: *Blue Unicorn, Spelunker Flophouse, Verve,
   Tucumari Literary Rev, Medicinal Purposes, Kayak,
   Black Bough, Chachalaca Poetry Rev, Blue Violin, Lynx,
   Ekphrasis, Santa Barbara Rev*

Bill Mohr ♪ ✈ PP&P
9246 Regents Rd, #E
La Jolla, CA 92037-1437, 858-587-4836
   Pubs: *Thoughtful Outlaw* (Inevitable Pr, 2000),
   Vehemence (Cassette/CD; New Alliance, 1992), *hidden
   proofs* (Bombshelter, 1982), *Zyzzyva, Wormwood Rev,
   Antioch Rev, Blue Mesa Rev, Santa Monica Rev,
   Sonora Rev, Onthebus*

Peter Money ♪ ✈ P
1412 Martin Luther King Jr Way
Berkeley, CA 94709-1915, 510-558-1476
Internet: www.neca.com/~bjones/poetry
   Pubs: *Finding It* (Mille Grazie, 2000), *Between
   Ourselves* (Backwoods, 1997), *These Are My Shoes*
   (Boz, 1991), *The Sun, Solo, Provincetown Arts, APR,
   North Dakota Qtly, Writer's Almanac*

Leslie Monsour ♪ ✈ P
2062 Stanley Hills Dr
Los Angeles, CA 90046, 323-654-9363
Internet: metermade@hotmail.com
   Pubs: *Earth's Beauty, Desire & Loss* (RLB Pr, 1998),
   Indelibility (Aralia Pr, 1999), *Visiting Emily: Anth* (U
   Iowa Pr, 2000), *A Formal Feeling Comes: Anth* (Story
   Line Press, 1994), *Edge City Rev, DarkHorse, Fourteen
   Hills, Hellas, Lyric, Plum Rev, Poetry*
Groups: College/Univ, Seniors

R. Bruce Moody W
PO Box 9555
Berkeley, CA 94709, 415-787-2706
   Pubs: *The Decline & Fall of Daphne Finn* (Coward,
   1966), *New Yorker, Bottege Oscure, Michigan Qtly*

Raylyn Moore W
302 Park St
Pacific Grove, CA 93950, 408-372-0113
   Pubs: *What Happened to Emily Goode After the Great
   Exhibition* (Donning, 1978)

Rod Val Moore ♪ ✈ W
5800 Fulton Ave
Van Nuys, CA 91401, 818-947-2800
   Pubs: *Igloo Among Palms* (Hinterlands, 1997)

Rosalie Moore P
1130 7th St, #B-26
Novato, CA 94945, 415-892-3073
   Pubs: *Learned & Leaved* (Marin Poetry Center, 1989),
   Of Singles & Doubles (Woolmer/Brotherson, 1979)

Cherrie Moraga P&W
1042 Mississippi St
San Francisco, CA 94107
   Pubs: *Loving in the War Years* (South End Pr, 1983)

Dorinda Moreno P
c/o Rose Gabaldon, 5505 Esplanada, Orcutt, CA 93455,
805-937-3067

Richard W. Morris P
2421 Buchanan St
San Francisco, CA 94115-1927
   Pubs: *Adventures of God* (Ghost Dance Pr, 1994),
   Assyrians (The Smith, 1991)

Henry J. Morro 🎤 ✈ P
2209 Dufour St, #A
Redondo Beach, CA 90278-1414, 310-370-9659
Internet: hjmorro@aol.com
Pubs: *Corpses of Angels* (Bombshelter Pr, 2000),
Outlaw Bible of Amer Poetry: Anth (Thunder's Mouth
Pr, 1999), *Invocation L.A.: Anth* (West End Pr, 1989),
*New Letters, Seneca Rev, Black Warrior Rev, Pacific
Rev*
I.D.: Latino/Latina

Carlos Morton P&W
San Francisco Mime Troupe, 855 Treat St, San Francisco,
CA 94110
Pubs: *White Heroin Winter* (One Eye Pr, 1971)

Lois Moyles P
4243 Norton Ave
Oakland, CA 94602, 510-531-1375
Pubs: *Alleluia Chorus* (Woolmer/Brotherson, 1979),
*Partisan Rev, Shenandoah, Delos, Hawaii Pacific Rev,
New Yorker, Manhattan Rev*

Frederick Mugler, Jr. W
580 St Francis Pl
Menlo Park, CA 94025, 650-322-9650
Pubs: *Pavilion* (Putnam, 1982), *Emergency Room*
(Delacorte 1975)

Harryette Mullen P
UCLA English Dept, 405 Hilgard Ave, Los Angeles, CA
90095, 310-825-7553
Pubs: *Muse & Drudge* (Singing Horse Pr, 1995),
Trimmings (Tender Buttons Bks, 1991), *Callaloo, Agni,
Chain, Antioch, World, Bombay Gin*

Alejandro Murguia W
1799 Revere Ave
San Francisco, CA 94124-2345, 415-822-2543
Pubs: *Southern Front* (Bilingual Rev Pr, 1988), *Farewell
to the Coast* (Heirs Pr, 1980)

Merilene M. Murphy 🎤 ✈ P
Telepoetics, Inc, 1939 1/4 W Washington Blvd, Los
Angeles, CA 90018-1635, 323-419-0001
Internet: http://this.is/telepoetics/la
Pubs: *darchitecture* (Love Is a House Lightshow, 1999),
under peace rising (Woman in the Moon Pubs, 1994),
Trouble: Anth (Kavayantra Pr, 1995), *Coffee House
Poets Qtly, L.A. Mag*

Pat Murphy W
c/o Exploratorium, 3601 Lyon St, San Francisco, CA
94123, 415-561-0336
Pubs: *Points of Departure, The Shadow Hunter, The
City, Not Long After* (Bantam, 1990, 1990, 1989)

William K. Murphy P
6635 Sepulveda Blvd
Van Nuys, CA 91411-1204, 818-787-2764
Pubs: *Nightland, Walk Along the Seashore* (Solo Pr,
1988, 1987), *Redstart, Cafe Solo, Kite*

Carol Muske-Dukes P&W
English Dept, Univ Southern California, University Park
Campus, Los Angeles, CA 90089-0354, 213-740-2808
Pubs: *An Octave Above Thunder: New & Selected*
(Penguin, 1997), *Women & Poetry* (U Michigan Pr,
1997), *Red Trousseau, Saving St. Germ* (Viking, 1993,
1993), *Dear Digby* (Washington Square Pr, 1991), *Paris
Rev, APR, New Yorker, Field, Poetry, Nation*

Edward Mycue P
PO Box 640543
San Francisco, CA 94164-0543, 415-922-0395
Pubs: *Rainbow Behind Irene* (Panjandrum Pr/Nuomenal
Edtns, 2000), *Night Boats, Split-Life Is Built from the
Inside Out* (w/Jim Grove) (Norton Coker Pr, 1999,
1994), *Because We Speak the Same Language*
(Spectacular Diseases Pr, 1994)

Majid Naficy P
1144 12th St #103
Santa Monica, CA 90403, 310-395-6993
Pubs: *In a Tiger's Skin* (Amir Kabir, 1969), *The Literary
Rev*

Peter Najarian W
1521 Stuart St
Berkeley, CA 94703
Pubs: *Daughters of Memory* (City Miner, 1986),
Voyages (Ararat, 1980), *Wash Me on Home, Mama*

Martin Nakell P&W
3787 Maplewood Ave
Los Angeles, CA 90066
Pubs: *The Library of Thomas Rivka* (Sun & Moon Pr,
1996), *The Myth of Creation* (Parenthesis Writing
Series, 1993), *Literal Latte, Hanging Loose, Hyper Age*

Rochelle Nameroff 🎤 ✈ P
1102 Neilson St
Albany, CA 94706-2400, 510-524-2477
Internet: rnameroff@earthlink.net
Pubs: *Body Prints* (Ithaca Hse, 1972), *Hard Choices:
Anth* (U Iowa Pr, 1996), *Diamonds Are a Girl's Best
Friend: Anth* (Faber & Faber, 1995), *Sweet Nothings:
Anth* (Indiana U Pr, 1994), *Iowa Rev, Qtly West,
Antioch Rev, Poetry NW, Michigan Qtly Rev*
I.D.: Jewish. Groups: Seniors

Brenda Nasio P
216 Fair Oaks St
San Francisco, CA 94110
Pubs: *Paris Rev, Open Places, Amelia, Negative
Capability, CutBank, Crab Creek Rev, Pudding*

Jim Natal 🎤 ✈ P
311 Bora Bora Way #205
Marina del Rey, CA 90292-8305, 310-821-3906
    Pubs: *In the Bee Trees* (Archer Bks, 2000), *Oil on Paper, Explaining Water with Water* (Inevitable Pr, 2000, 1997), *What Have You Lost: Anth* (Greenwillow Bks, 1999), *Paterson Lit Rev, Rattle, SOLO, Spillway, Yalobusha Rev*

Leonard Nathan P
40 Beverly Rd
Kensington, CA 94707
    Pubs: *The Potato Eaters* (Orchises Pr, 1997), *Diary of a Left-Handed Birdwatcher* (Graywolf Pr, 1996), *Carrying On: New & Selected Poems* (U Pitt Pr, 1985), *Manoa, Poet Lore, Salmagundi, Atlantic, Southwestern Rev, New Yorker, Wilderness*

Opal Louis Nations P
c/o KFPA, 1939 M L King Jr Way, Berkeley, CA 94704
    Pubs: *Neo-Absurdities* (Changed Species Pr, 1988), *Coach House Poets Collection: Anth* (Norton, 1988), *Rampike*

Louise Nayer 🎤 ✈ P
1165 Bosworth St
San Francisco, CA 94131-2801, 415-587-4475
Internet: lnayer50@aol.com
    Pubs: *The Houses Are Covered in Sound* (Blue Light Pr, 1990), *Keeping Watch* (Birthstone Pr, 1981)

Crawdad Nelson P&W
PO Box 219
Bayside, CA 95524-0219, 707-268-1274
    Pubs: *The Bull of the Woods, When the Eagle Shits* (Gorda Plate Pr, 1997, 1996), *Truth Rides to Work* (Poetic Space Bks, 1993), *Rosebud, The Sun, Poetry Flash, Mockingbird, Cedar Hills Rev, Rain City Rev, American Voice, Oxygen*

Mildred Nelson P&W
3448 Amber Ln
Oceanside, CA 92056-4841
    Pubs: *The Island* (Pocket Bks, 1973), *Light Year: Anth* (Bits Pr, 1986), *Mediphors, Georgia Rev, McCall's, San Fernando Poetry Jrnl, Writers Jrnl, Crosscurrents*

Peter E. Nelson P
1303 Allesandro St
Los Angeles, CA 90026
    Pubs: *Spring Into Light* (Green Tree Pr, 1978), *Between Lives* (Ironwood Pr, 1974), *Choice, Poetry*

Ray Faraday Nelson 🎤 ✈ W
333 Ramona Ave
El Cerrito, CA 94530, 510-526-7378
    Pubs: *Virtual Zen* (Avon, 1996), *Dog Headed Death* (Strawberry Hill, 1988), *Timequest* (Tor, 1985)
I.D.: Unitarian-Universalist

David Nemec 🎤 ✈ W
1517 Irving St
San Francisco, CA 94122-1908, 415-564-6506
    Pubs: *Stonesifer* (Robert D. Reed, 1999), *Early Dreams* (Baseball Pr, 1999), *The Beer & Whisky League* (Lyons & Burford, 1994), *The Systems of M.R. Shurnas* (John Calder, 1986), *Mad Blood* (Dial Pr, 1983), *Transatlantic Rev, Playgirl, Twilight Zone*
Groups: Prisoners

Peter Neumeyer P&W
45 Marguerita Rd
Kennsington, CA 94707-1019, 619-463-2229
    Pubs: *The Phantom of the Opera, Homage to John Clare* (Peregrine Smith, 1988, 1980), *Donald & The...* (Addison-Wesley, 1969), *New Mexico Qtly*

Rebecca Newman W
20 Bali Ln
Pacific Palisades, CA 90272, 310-573-2028
    Pubs: *Ely & the Komodo Dragon* (Ancient Mariners Pr, 1991), *Adam the Detective* (Midwest Express, 1991), *The Divorce of Mrs. Dracula* (Redstart, 1988)

Jeanne M. Nichols 🎤 ✈ P
4234 Camino Real
Los Angeles, CA 90065-3958, 323-222-0014
Internet: jeannenichols@mymailstation.com
    Pubs: *Leaning Over the Edge* (Fithian Pr, 1993), *Where Icarus Falls: Anth* (Santa Barbara Rev Pub, 1998), *Only Morning in Her Shoes: Anth* (Utah State U Pr, 1990), *College English, Nimrod, West Word*

Kristy Nielsen 🎤 ✈ P&W
1586 Winding Way
Belmont, CA 94002-1953, 650-654-1594
Internet: nielsen@concentric.net
    Pubs: *Two Girls* (Thorngate Road, 1997), *The Party Train: Anth* (New Rivers Pr, 1996), *Mid-American Rev, Spoon River Poetry Rev*

Ann Nietzke 🎤 ✈ W
466 N Hobart Blvd, #12
Los Angeles, CA 90004-1851, 323-660-5983
    Pubs: *Solo Spinout, Windowlight* (Soho Pr, 1996, 1996), *Shenandoah, Other Voices, Massachusetts Rev*

Nona Nimnicht P
303 Adams, #210
Oakland, CA 94610
    Pubs: *In the Museum Naked* (Second Coming Pr, 1978), *Ploughshares, Poetry NW, Qtly West, Crosscurrents, Prairie Schooner, Nimrod*

Larry Niven W
3961 Vanalden Ave
Tarzana, CA 91356

Rick Noguchi   P
5315 Etheldo Ave
Culver City, CA 90230
    Pubs: *The Ocean Inside Kenji Takezo* (U Pittsburgh Pr
1996), *The Wave He Caught* (Pearl Edtns 1995)

Harold Norse   P&W
c/o Bright Tyger, 537 Jones St, Box 263, San Francisco,
CA 94102, 415-863-7208
    Pubs: *Memoirs of a Bastard Angel* (Morrow, 1989), *The
Love Poems: 1940-85* (Crossing Pr, 1986)

John Norton ♦ ⊁   P&W
444A 14th St
San Francisco, CA 94103-2359, 415-558-9066
Internet: jnorton@us.oracle.com
    Pubs: *Re: Marriage, The Light at the End of the Bog*
(Black Star Series, 2000, 1992), *Posthum* (or)*ous* (e.g.
Pr, 1986), *Before Columbus Fdn: Anth* (Norton, 1991),
NAW, Oxygen, CrossConnect, Coracle

John Noto ♦ ⊁   P&W
PO Box 420803
San Francisco, CA 94142-0803
    Pubs: *Simulcast Yearning* (Wordcraft of Oregon, 1999),
Psycho-Motor Breathscapes (Vatic Hum Pr, 1997), *Volt,
Talisman, Caliban, Central Park, Fiction Intl, First
Intensity, NAW, Ctheory, American Letters &
Commentary*

Susan Nunes ♦ ⊁   W
Berkeley, CA 94708-1925
Internet: suminu@aol.com
    Pubs: *The Last Dragon* (Clarion, 1995), *A Small
Obligation & Other Stories of Hilo, Intersecting Circles:
Anth* (Bamboo Ridge, 1982, 2000), *Graywolf Annual:
Anth* (Graywolf, 1991), *Home to Stay: Anth* (Greenfield
Rev, 1990)
I.D.: Multicultural. Groups: Children

Heidi Nye   P
2273 Euclid Ave
Long Beach, CA 90815-2518
    Pubs: *Water from the Moon* (Forever a Foreigner Pr,
1992), *Australian Wellbeing, California Poetry Qtly, L.A.
View, Pearl, Natural Health, Bad Haircut*

Mark O'Brien   P
c/o Helen McGrath, 1406 Idaho Ct, Concord, CA 94521,
510-672-6211
    Pubs: *Staring Back* (Dutton, 1997), *Breathing* (LittleDog
Pr, 1990), *Our Mothers' Spirits: Anth* (HC, 1997), *Whole
Earth Rev, Tight, Expressions, The Sun, St. Andrews
Rev*

Raymond Obstfeld   W
2936 Ballesteros Ln
Tustin, CA 92680
    Pubs: *The Remington Contract* (Worldwide, 1988), *The
Reincarnation of Reece Erikson* (Tor, 1988)

Philip F. O'Connor   W
821 Gonzalez Dr
San Francisco, CA 94123-2235
    Pubs: *Martin's World* (Bottom Dog Pr, 1993), *Finding
Brendan* (S&S, 1991), *Defending Civilization* (Weidenfeld
& Nicolson, 1988)

Joyce Odam   P
2432 48th Ave
Sacramento, CA 95822
    Pubs: *Lemon Center for Hot Buttered Roll* (Hibiscus Pr,
1975), *Blue Unicorn, Impulse*

Ron Offen   P
28182 Via Chocano
Mission Viejo, CA 92692, 949-770-2239
    Pubs: *Answers/Questions* (Inevitable Pr, 1996), *Instead
of Gifts* (Pudding Hse, 1995), *Poet As Bad Guy*
(Cyfoeth Pubs, 1963), *Interim, Pearl, Mockingbird,
Pacific Coast Jrnl, Zyzzyva, Cedar Hill Rev, Interim,
Lightning & Ash, Parting Gifts, Whole Notes*

Jamie O'Halloran   P
8446 Fenwick St
Sunland, CA 91040, 818-353-7203
    Pubs: *The Landscape from Behind* (V.C. Pr, 1997),
Grand Passion: Poets of Los Angeles: Anth (Red Wind
Bks, 1995), *Cream City Rev, Southern California Anth,
Blue Satellite, Seattle Rev, Blue Moon Rev, 51%,
Snakeskin*

Diana O'Hehir   P
2855 Jackson St, #301
San Francisco, CA 94115, 415-928-1261
    Pubs: *Spells for Not Dying Again* (Eastern Washington
U Pr, 1997), *Home Free, The Bride Who Ran Away, I
Wish This War Were Over* (Atheneum, 1988, 1988,
1984), *Poetry, Kenyon Rev, American Voice, Poetry
NW, Shenandoah*

Jennifer Olds   P
1403 W Locust St
Ontario, CA 91762-5327
    Pubs: *Rodeo & the Mimosa Tree* (Event Horizon Pr,
1991), *Gypsy, Tsunami, Pearl, Slipstream, Staple,
Onthebus, Envoi, New Spokes*

Carole Simmons Oles ♦ ⊁   P
California State Univ, English Dept, Chico, CA
95929-0001, 530-898-5240
Internet: coles@csuchico.edu
    Pubs: *Sympathetic Systems* (Lynx Hse, 2000), *Stunts*
(GreenTower, 1992), *The Deed* (LSU Pr, 1991), *Field,
Kenyon Rev, Poetry, NER, Prairie Schooner, APR,
Georgia Rev*

Beverly Olevin   W
2252 Beverly Glen Pl
Los Angeles, CA 90077-2506, 310-474-0959
   Pubs: *The Breath of Juno* (Elk Horn Pr, 1996), *Sweet
   Peas* (Juno Pr, 1991), *Ms., America West, Sun Dog:
   SE Rev, Oxford Mag, Portland Rev, MacGuffin*

Robert Oliphant   W
English Dept, California State Univ, Northridge, CA 91330
   Pubs: *A Trumpet for Jackie, A Piano for Mrs. Cimino*
   (Prentice-Hall, 1983, 1980)

Daniel A. Olivas ♣ ✈   P&W
24638 Canyonwood Dr
West Hills, CA 91307, 213-897-2705
Internet: olivasdan@aol.com
   Pubs: *Fantasmas: Anth* (Bilingual Rev Pr, 2001), *Red
   River Rev, Exquisite Corpse, Foliage, Octavo,
   Paumanok Rev, PULSE, Sparks, THEMA*
I.D.: Latino/Latina, Jewish. Groups: Children

David Oliveira ♣ ✈   P
820A W Victoria St
Santa Barbara, CA 93101-4782, 805-963-8408
   Pubs: *In the Presence of Snakes* (Brandenburg Pr,
   2000), *A Near Country* (Solo Pr, 1999), *Geography of
   Home: Anth* (Heyday Bks, 1999), *Poetry Intl, Third
   Coast, Cafe Solo, Americas Rev*

Tillie Olsen ♣ ✈   W
2333 Ward St
Berkeley, CA 94705, 510-649-7472
   Pubs: *Mother to Daughter, Daughter to Mother*
   (Feminist Pr, 1986), *Silences* (Delacorte, 1978), *Tell Me
   a Riddle* (Bantam/Doubleday/Dell, 1962), *Yonnondio:
   From the Thirties* (Bantam/Doubleday/Dell, 1978), *First
   Words: Anth:* (Algonquin, 1998), *Iowa Rev*
I.D.: Feminist, Jewish. Groups: Prisoners, Schools

Sharon Olson   P
Palo Alto Main Library, 1213 Newell Rd, Palo Alto, CA
94303, 650-329-2438
Internet: slopoet@well.com
   Pubs: *Clouds Brushed in Later* (San Jose Poetry Ctr
   Pr, 1987), *Fire in the Hills: Anth* (Adler, 1992), *Kalliope,
   Santa Clara Rev, Palo Alto Rev, Kansas Qtly, Seattle
   Rev, American Literary Rev, Worcester Rev*

Regina O'Melveny   P
3071 Crest Rd
Rancho Palos Verde, CA 90275, 310-833-6580
   Pubs: *Blue Wolves* (Bright Hill Pr, 1997), *Cathedrals of
   the Spirit: Anth* (Harper Perennial, 1996), *Spreading the
   Word/L.A. Poetry Contest Winners: Anth* (Red Wind
   Bks, 1993), *Yellow Silk Anth* (Crown Pubs, 1990), *The
   Sun, Jacaranda Rev, Poetry/L.A.*

Philip D. Ortego   P&W
English Dept, San Jose State Univ, San Jose, CA 95912,
408-277-2242

Antonio G. Ortiz   P
2006 S Genesee Ave
Los Angeles, CA 90016
   Pubs: *Flor y Canto II & I* (U Southern California Pr,
   1978, 1976), *Urbis Mag, New Mexico Mag*

Mark Osaki ♣ ✈   P
6615 Fordham Way
Sacramento, CA 95831-2246, 916-421-4090
Internet: m.osaki@worldnet.att.net
   Pubs: *Carrying the Darkness: Anth* (Texas Tech U,
   1989), *Hawaii Rev, Berkeley Poetry Rev, South
   Carolina Rev, Georgia Rev*

John Jay Osborn   W
14 Fair Oaks St
San Francisco, CA 94110, 415-282-1629
   Pubs: *The Associates, The Man Who Owned New York*
   (HM, 1982, 1981)

Ernest John Oswald   P
Thumb Tree Poetry Service, 128 Laguna St, San
Francisco, CA 94102, 415-431-8791
   Pubs: *Apricot Two Step* (E. Oswald, 1976), *NYQ, Small
   Pond, Cincinnati Rev, Offerta Speciale*

Mary Overton   W
La Questa Press, 211 La Questa Way, Woodside, CA
94062
Internet: http://communities.msn.com/OvertonFiction
   Pubs: *The Wine of Astonishment* (La Questa Pr, 1997),
   *Glimmer Train, Potomac Rev, Wordwrights, Belletrist
   Rev, Spelunker Flophouse, Southern Anth*

Louis Owens ♣ ✈   W
Univ of California, English Dept, Davis, CA 95616
   Pubs: *Dark River, Bone Game* (U Oklahoma Pr, 1999,
   1994), *Nightland* (Dutton, 1996)

Rosella Pace   P
2750 Hilltop Ct
Arcata, CA 95521-5221
   Pubs: *Portugal: The Villages, Anth of Los Angeles
   Poets* (Red Hill Pr, 1977, 1972), *Cafe Solo, Bachy,
   Beyond Baroque, San Marcos Rev*

Javier Pacheco   PP&P
5162 Berryman Ave
Culver City, CA 90230, 213-390-2579
   Pubs: *Canciones De La Raza* (Fuego De Aztlan, 1978),
   Chismearte, Rayas, Electrum, Maize

Barbara Gordon Paine ♣   P
Chaspaine, 803 15th Ave, Menlo Park, CA 94025-1947,
650-326-2212
Internet: chaspaine@aol.com
   Pubs: *To Shout at the Fog* (Chaspaine, 1998), *Eidolon*
   (Ligda, 1962), *Reading & Interpreting: Anth* (Wadsworth,
   1968), *Prairie Schooner, NYQ*

Charlotte Painter 🎤 ✈   W
6450 Mystic St
Oakland, CA 94618, 510-595-3901
Internet: holywrit@pacbell.net
    Pubs: *Conjuring Tibet* (Mercury Hse, 1997), *Who Made the Lamb* (Creative Arts Bks, 1988), *Gifts of Age* (Chronicle Bks, 1986)

Michael Palmer 🎤 ✈   P
265 Jersey St
San Francisco, CA 94114-3822, 415-282-8522
    Pubs: *The Promises of Glass, The Lion Bridge, At Passages* (New Directions, 2000, 1998, 1995), *Grand Street, Sulfur, Chicago Rev, NAW, Chain, Avec, Common Knowledge*

Nicole Panter   W
PO Box 862
Venice, CA 90294, 310-396-5937
    Pubs: *Mr. Right On & Other Stories, Unnatural Disasters: Recent Writings from the Golden State: Anth* (Incommunicado Pr, 1994, 1996)

Richard Parque 🎤 ✈   P&W
PO Box 327
Verdugo City, CA 91046-0327
    Pubs: *A Distant Thunder, Flight of the Phantom, Firefight, Hellbound, Sweet Vietnam* (Zebra Bks, 1988, 1987, 1986, 1985, 1984)
I.D.: Veterans. Groups: Veterans

John B. Passerello   P
6825 Ashfield Way
Fair Oaks, CA 95628-4207
    Pubs: *Homeless Not Helpless: Anth* (Fox Sparrow, 1989), *We Speak for Peace: Anth* (KIT, 1993), *Tapjoe, Peace & Freedom, Pudding, Feelings, Aristos, CQ*

Louis Patler   P
36 Shell Rd
Mill Valley, CA 94941, 415-388-8344
    Pubs: *An American Ensemble* (Poltroon Pr, 1980), *Acts, Intent, Rootdrinker, Convivid, Mill Valley Mag, Pacific Poetry & Fiction Rev*

Jim Paul   P&W
1170 Guerrero St, Loft
San Francisco, CA 94110, 415-641-5308
    Pubs: *Medieval in L.A.* (Counterpoint, 1996), *Catapult: Harry & I Build a Siege Weapon* (Villard Bks, 1991), *Antioch Rev, Paris Rev, Mss.*

Walter Pavlich   P
2052 Calaveras Ave
Davis, CA 95616, 916-753-9672
    Pubs: *Running Near the End of the World* (U Iowa Pr, 1992), *Atlantic, APR, Yale Rev, Poetry, Manoa, Iowa Rev, Antioch Rev*

Paul J. J. Payack   P&W
5046 Blackhawk Dr
Danville, CA 94506, 650-812-6229
    Pubs: *New Letters, Paris Rev, Boulevard, Creative Computing, New Infinity Rev*

Gerrye Payne   P
10582 Barnett Valley Rd
Sebastopol, CA 95472
    Pubs: *The Year-God* (Ahsahta Pr, 1992), *An Amateur Plays Satie* (Loon Pr, 1984), *Dog River Rev, Kansas Qtly, Kalliope, Creeping Bent, Loon, Primavera, Fish Drum, Karamu, Hayden's Ferry Rev*

Sherman Pearl 🎤 ✈   P
941 26th St
Santa Monica, CA 90403, 310-453-0183
    Pubs: *Working Papers* (Pacific Writers Pr, 1999), *Anth of New England Writers* (New England Writers, 1998), *Grand Passion: Anth* (Red Wind Bks, 1995), *Atlanta Rev, Buffalo Bones, CQ, Ledge, Passager, Peregrine, Slant, Verve*

Victor Pearn   P
215 1/2 Hollister Ave
Santa Monica, CA 90405, 310-450-4156
    Pubs: *Pyromaniac* (The Plowman, 1995), *Swans Pausing* (Foothills Pub, 1994), *Negative Capability, Long Islander, Midwest Qtly, Mind Matters Rev, Sulphur River Literary Rev, Whole Notes*

Noel Peattie 🎤 ✈   P&W
23311 County Rd 88
Winters, CA 95694-9008, 530-662-3364
Internet: nrpeattie@earthlink.net
    Pubs: *In the Dome of Saint Laurence Meteor, Amy Rose, Western Skyline* (Regent Pr, 1999, 1995, 1994), *Cape Rock, Second Coming, Cayo, Tule Rev, Poetry Now, Poetry Motel Wallpaper, Hammers*

Oscar Penaranda   P&W
Logan High School, 1800 H St, Union City, CA 94587, 510-471-2520
    Pubs: *Fiction By Filipinos in America: Anth* (New Day Pubs, 1993), *Filipinas Mag, Bay-Loot*

James Pendergast   P
685 Fano Ln
Sonoma, CA 95476, 707-996-7743
    Pubs: *Anth of Mag Verse* (Monitor Book Co, 1981), *The New Mag, Ruhtra, Hyperion*

Sam Pereira 🎤 ✈   P
1548 Canal Farm Ln #1C
Los Banos, CA 93635-4425, 209-826-2072
Internet: litsam@telis.org
    Pubs: *Brittle Water* (Penumbra Pr, 1987), *The Marriage of the Portuguese* (L'Epervier Pr, 1978), *The Body Electric: Anth* (Norton, 2000), *Piecework: Anth* (Silver Skates Publishing, 1987), *APR, Poetry, Antioch Rev*

Anne S. Perlman   P
41 Fifth Ave
San Francisco, CA 94118, 415-752-2517
  Pubs: *Sorting It Out* (Carnegie Mellon, 1984), *Songs from Unsung Worlds: Anth* (Aviva, 1987)

Robert Peters   P
9431 Krepp Dr
Huntington Beach, CA 92646, 714-968-7546
  Pubs: *Feather: A Child's Death & Life* (U Wisconsin Pr, 1997), *Selected Poems 1967-1994* (Asylum Arts Pr, 1994), *American Bk Rev, James White Rev, Chiron Rev, Bakunin, Small Press Rev, Chicago Rev*

Geoff Peterson   P
25 San Juan Ave
San Francisco, CA 94112, 415-585-4808
  Pubs: *Medicine Dog* (St. Martin's Pr, 1989), *Letter from Wyoming: Anth* (Wyoming Council on the Arts, 1991), *Peregrine, Z Miscellaneous, Aileron, NYQ*

Robert Peterson 🎤 ✈   P
PO Box 417
Fairfax, CA 94978-0417, 415-455-8209
  Pubs: *All the Time in the World* (Hanging Loose Pr, 1996), *The Only Piano Player in La Paz* (Black Dog, 1985)

Dennis Phillips   P
Sun & Moon Press, 6026 Wilshire Blvd, Los Angeles, CA 90036, 213-857-1115
  Pubs: *20 Questions* (Jahbone, 1992), *Arena, A World* (Sun & Moon Pr, 1992, 1989), *The Hero Is Nothing* (Kajun Pr, 1985), *o.blek, Tyuonyi, Hambone*

Frances Phillips   P
194 Onondaga Ave
San Francisco, CA 94112, 415-626-2787
  Pubs: *Up at Two, For a Living* (Hanging Loose Pr, 1991, 1981), *Hanging Loose, Five Fingers Rev, Volt, NYQ, Zyzzyva, Feminist Studies, Hungry Mind Rev*

Felice Picano   P&W
386 S Burnside Ave 9L
Los Angeles, CA 90036
  Pubs: *A House on the Ocean, A House on the Bay* (Faber & Faber, 1997), *Like People in History* (Viking, 1995), *Window Elegies* (Close Grip Pr, 1985), *Ambidextrous* (Gay Press of New York, 1985), *No Apologies, San Francisco Examiner, Harvard Gay Rev*

Gg Poetrescr   P
PO Box 191261
San Francisco, CA 94119-1261, 415-626-6298
  Pubs: *Fanorama, 247*

Susan Lewis Policoff   P&W
2807 Milvia St
Berkeley, CA 94703
  Pubs: *Love's Shadow* (Crossing Pr, 1993), *Life on the Line* (Negative Capability, 1993), *Folio, Reed, Sequoia, Oxygen, Other Voices, First/For Women*

James Polster   W
3311 Mandeville Canyon Rd
Los Angeles, CA 90049, 310-471-1805
  Pubs: *Brown* (Longstreet Pr, 1995), *A Guest in the Jungle* (Mercury Hse, 1987), *Smoke, New Orleans Rev*

Melinda Popham   W
12179 Greenock Ln
Los Angeles, CA 90049, 310-471-4336
  Pubs: *Skywater* (Graywolf, 1990), *A Blank Book* (Bobbs-Merrill, 1974)

Michael Porges   P
850 Tucson Ct
San Dimas, CA 91773-1852
  Pubs: *Songs, Portraits, Poems, Songs Out of Season* (Landor Pr, 1981, 1979), *Verve*

Paul C. Portuges   P
3888 Fairfax Rd
Santa Barbara, CA 93110, 805-682-2060
  Pubs: *Paper Song* (Ross-Erikson, 1984), *The Turquoise Mockingbird of Light* (Mudborn, 1979), *Eye*

Evelyn Posamentier   P
210 Hoffman Ave
San Francisco, CA 94114-3128, 415-285-0477
Internet: ejp@justice.com
  Pubs: *Ghosts of the Holocaust: Anth* (Wayne State U Pr, 1989), *Processed World, APR, Chrysalis*

Jonathan V. Post   P&W
3225 N Marengo Ave
Altadena, CA 91001, 818-398-1673
  Pubs: *Project Solar Sail* (NAL, 1990), *Nebula Awards Anth 23* (HBJ, 1989), *Amazing Stories, Analog, Fantasy Book, Omni, Quantum, Science*

Holly Prado 🎤 ✈   P&W
1256 N Mariposa Ave
Los Angeles, CA 90029-1416, 213-664-3640
  Pubs: *Esperanza, Specific Mysteries* (Cahuenga Pr, 1998, 1990), *Gardens* (HBJ, 1985), *Grand Passion: Anth* (Red Wind Bks, 1995), *Exquisite Corpse, Denver Qtly, Kenyon Rev, Colorado Rev, Poetry Intl, Tule Rev*

Jean Pumphrey 🎤 ✈ P
650 Main St
Sausalito, CA 94965-2338, 415-332-5436
Internet: ajp397@cs.com
    Pubs: *Sheltered at the Edge* (Solo Pr, 1982), *Beside the Sleeping Maiden: Anth* (Arctos Pr, 1997), *Stones & Amulets: Anth* (Wordsworth, 1996)
Groups: Mentally Ill, Seniors

Barbara Quick P&W
17 Edgecroft Rd
Kensington, CA 94707-1412
    Pubs: *Northern Edge: A Novel of Survival in Alaska's Arctic* (HC West, 1994), Ms.

Leroy V. Quintana 🎤 ✈ P
9230-C Lake Murray
San Diego, CA 92119-1471, 619-589-1171
Internet: thequintanas@aol.com
    Pubs: *Great Whirl of Exile* (Curbstone Pr, 1999), *My Hair Turning Gray Among Strangers, History of Home* (Bilingual Pr, 1995, 1993), *Interrogations* (Viet Nam Generation, 1992), *Ploughshares, Progressive, Prairie Schooner, Puerto del Sol*
I.D.: Chicano/Chicana, Native American. Groups: Prisoners, Children

Frederick A. Raborg, Jr. P&W
329 E St
Bakersfield, CA 93304-2031, 661-323-4064
Internet: amelia@lightspeed.net
    Pubs: *Posing Nude, Hakata, Tule* (Amelia Pr, 1989, 1988, 1986), *Westways, Cimarron Rev, Tendril, Crazyquilt, Prairie Schooner*
Groups: Seniors, G/L/B/T

Charles Radke W
7722 N Angus #204
Fresno, CA 93720-0919
Internet: chuckradke@hotmail.com
    Pubs: *Gulf Stream Mag, Hayden's Ferry Rev, South Dakota Rev*

Rebecca Radner 🎤 ✈ P
3025 Steiner, #12
San Francisco, CA 94123-3911, 415-563-8746
Internet: rebeccar@sirius.com
    Pubs: *What Book!?: Anth* (Parallax Pr, 1998), *Harvard Mag, NER/BLQ, Berkeley Poets' Co-op, Iowa Rev, Minnesota Rev, California Qtly, Central Park, Caliban*

James Ragan 🎤 ✈ P
1516 Beverwil Dr
Los Angeles, CA 90035-2911, 310-277-1914
    Pubs: *Lusions, The Hunger Wall* (Grove Pr, 1996, 1995), *Womb Weary* (Carol Pub, 1990), *Ohio Rev, Antioch Rev, NAR, Poetry, Nation*

Carl Rakosi 🎤 ✈ P
1456 17th Ave
San Francisco, CA 94122-3403, 415-566-3425
    Pubs: *Old Poet's Tale, Earth Suite* (England; Etruscan Bks, 1999, 1997), *Poems 1923-1941* (Sun & Moon Pr, 1995), *Collected Poems, Collected Prose* (Nat Poetry Fdn, 1986, 1983), *American Poetry: Anth* (LOA, 2000), *Poems for the Millennium: Anth* (U Cal Pr, 1995)

Karen Randlev 🎤 ✈ P
20 Sunnyside Ave, #A153
Mill Valley, CA 94941, 415-389-1534
Internet: readk@earthlink.net
    Pubs: *Light Runner* (Fireweed Pr, 1987), *The Last New Land: Anth* (Alaska Northwest Bks, 1996), *A New Geography of Poets: Anth* (U Arkansas Pr, 1992), *Exquisite Corpse, CSM*

Jerry Ratch 🎤 ✈ P
1185 Glen Ave
Berkeley, CA 94708, 510-981-3033
    Pubs: *Wild Dreams of Reality* (Creative Arts Bks, 2001), *Light* (O Bks, 1990), *How the Net Is Gripped: Anth* (Stride, 1992), *Avec, Tight, Sonoma Mandala, Carolina Qtly, Contact II, Seems*

Stephen Ratcliffe P
Mills College, 5000 MacArthur Blvd, Oakland, CA 94613, 510-430-2245
    Pubs: *Sculpture* (Littoral Bks, 1996), *Present Tense* (The Figures, 1995), *Conjunctions, Talisman, Chain, New American Writing, o.blek, Avec*

Susan Rawlins P
1517 Ada St
Berkeley, CA 94703, 510-527-1244
    Pubs: *Grand Street, Shenandoah, Zyzzyva, Feminist Studies, The Qtly, Poet & Critic*

Dennis J. Reader P
2045 Green Valley Rd
Watsonville, CA 95076, 408-728-1988
    Pubs: *Coming Back Alive* (Avon, 1983), *Virginia Qtly Rev*

Ishmael Reed P&W
PO Box 3288
Berkeley, CA 94703
    Pubs: *The Terrible Threes, The Terrible Twos* (St. Martin's Pr, 1989, 1982), *God Made Alaska for the Indians* (Garland, 1982), *Yardbird Reader*

Diane Reichick P
2058 Ardenwood Ave
Simi Valley, CA 93063
    Pubs: *Color Wheel, Vol No, Verve, Orphic Lute, CQ, Red Dancefloor*

Gay Beste Reineck P
1425 Cole St
San Francisco, CA 94117

Lois Larrance Requist 🎤 ✈ P&W
485 Fernwood Dr
Moraga, CA 94556-2119, 925-376-0447
Internet: Loqu@aol.com
    Pubs: *A Family: From Fence to Fax through the
    Twentieth Century* (NTPWA, 1999), *Alaska Qtly Rev,
    Black Maria, Connecticut River Rev*

Ingrid Reti 🎤 P
1650 Descanso St
San Luis Obispo, CA 93405-6109, 805-544-3605
    Pubs: *Each in Her Own Way: Anth* (Queen of Swords
    Pr, 1994), *We Speak for Peace: Anth* (KIT, 1993), *Iowa
    Woman, Portlandia, San Luis Obispo Mag*

Doug Rice W
California State U English Dept., 6000 J St, Sacramento,
CA 95819-6075, 916-278-5989
Internet: drice@csus.edu
    Pubs: *Blood of Mugwump* (Black Ice Bks, 1996),
    Avant-Pop: Anth (Illinois State U, 1993), *collages &
    bricolages, 2 Girls Rev, Black Ice Mag, Spitting Image,
    Fiction Intl, New Novel Rev*

Marilee Richards P
1725 San Jose Ave
Alameda, CA 94501, 510-865-2533
    Pubs: *Poetry NW, National Forum, The Jrnl, Literary
    Rev, Sou'wester, Cimarron Rev, Poet Lore*

Cena Golder Richeson W
PO Box 268
Knightsen, CA 94548, 510-672-5229
    Pubs: *Tombstone Epitaph, Horse Tales: Anth*
    (Wordware, 1994), *The West That Was: Anth* (Random
    Hse, 1993), *Daughters of Our Land: Anth* (Maverick
    Pub, 1988)

Steve Richmond P
137 Hollister Ave
Santa Monica, CA 90405, 213-396-1996

John M. Ridland 🎤 ✈ P
1725 Hillcrest Rd
Santa Barbara, CA 93103-1844, 805-965-9613
    Pubs: *John the Valiant* (Budapest; Corrina Pr, 1999),
    Life with Unkie (Mille Grazie Pr, 1999), *Palms* (Buckner
    Pr, 1993), *The Formalist, Into the Teeth of the Wind,
    Hudson Rev, Sticks, Light, Overland, Quadrant*

Agnes Riedmann W
233 W Morris Ave
Modesto, CA 95354
    Pubs: *The Story of Adamsville* (Wadsworth Publishing
    Co, 1977), *Dismal River Rev, Intro*

Tom Riley P
1441 Brown St
Napa, CA 94559
    Pubs: *Writing Poems: Anth* (Little, Brown, 1987), *Byline,
    Art Times, Dialogue, The Lyric, The Formalist, Blue
    Unicorn*

Doren Robbins P
4161 Alla Rd
Los Angeles, CA 90066
Internet: pantagruli@aol.com
    Pubs: *The Donkey's Tale* (Red Wind Pr, 1998), *Driving
    Face Down* (Eastern Washington Univ, 2001), *Under
    the Black Moth's Wings* (Ameroot Pr, 1988),
    Sympathetic Manifesto (Perivale Pr, 1987), *APR,
    Sulphur, 5am, Indiana Rev*

Stuart Robbins P&W
660 Santa Ray Ave
Oakland, CA 94610
    Pubs: *Poetry Now, Berkeley Poet's Co-op, Paragraph,
    Amazing Stories, Berkeley Poetry Rev, Ararat*

Gillian Roberts W
PO Box 423
Tiburon, CA 94920
    Pubs: *Time & Trouble* (St. Martin's Pr, 1998), *The
    Bluest Blood, The Mummers' Curse, In the Dead of
    Summer* (Ballantine Bks, 1998, 1996, 1995)

Lillian S. Robinson P
1520 O'Farrell St
San Francisco, CA 94115, 415-567-4195
    Pubs: *The Old Life* (SUNY Buffalo, 1977)

Shelba Cole Robison W
PO Box 6359
Los Osos, CA 93412, 805-528-4182
    Pubs: *Appalachian Heritage, Pembroke Mag,
    Poughkeepsie*

Alfred A. Robles P
520 6th Ave
San Francisco, CA 94118, 415-387-5783
    Pubs: *Rappin' with Ten Thousand Carabaos in the
    Dark* (U California Pr, 1996), *Looking for Ifugao
    Mountain* (Children's Pr, 1976), *Amerasia Jrnl, Bridge*

Julia Park Rodrigues 🎤 P
1280 Oakes Blvd
San Leonardo, CA 94577, 510-635-2973
    Pubs: *Two Worlds Walking* (New Rivers Pr, 1994),
    *Caprice, Green Fuse Poetry, Poetry Nippon, Ruah,
    Spectrum*
Lang: Spanish. I.D.: Scottish. Groups: Children, Abuse
Victims

Aleida Rodriguez P
1811 Baxter St
Los Angeles, CA 90026-1935, 323-953-6372
   Pubs: *Garden of Exile* (Sarabande, 1999), *Not for the
   Academy: Anth* (Only Women Pr, 1999), *Sleeping with
   One Eye Open* (Georgia Pr, 1999), *In Short: Anth*
   (Norton, 1996), *Grand Passion: Anth* (Red Wind Bks,
   1995), *Ploughshares, Prairie Schooner, Kenyon Rev*

Zack Rogow P
358 27th St
San Francisco, CA 94131
   Pubs: *The Epistolary Form & the Letter as Artifact* (Pig
   Iron Pr, 1991), *Left-Hand Maps: San Francisco Bay
   Area Poets: Anth* (A Small Garlic Pr, 1998), *Time Is
   the Longest Distance: Anth* (HC, 1991), *Rhino, Calliope,
   APR, Switched-On Gutenberg*

Richard Ronan P
4845 17 St
San Francisco, CA 94117
   Pubs: *A Radiance Like Wind or Water, Narratives from
   America* (Dragon Gate Bks, 1984, 1982), *APR*

Wendy Rose P
41070 Lilley Mountain Dr
Coarsegold, CA 93614-9622, 209-658-8018
   Pubs: *Bone Dance: New & Selected Poems* (U Arizona
   Pr, 1994), *Now Poof She Is Gone* (Firebrand Pr, 1994),
   Going to War with All My Relations (Northland Pr,
   1993)

Gerald Rosen ⬤ W
320 Winfield St
San Francisco, CA 94110-5512, 415-648-2140
Internet: jerrydutch@aol.com
   Pubs: *Growing Up Bronx, Mahatma Gandhi in a
   Cadillac* (North Atlantic Bks, 2000, 1995), *Carmen
   Miranda Memorial Flagpole* (Avon, 1978)

Sylvia Rosen P
9 Hillary Ln
Chico, CA 95973, 530-894-0686
   Pubs: *Dreaming the Poems, A Dream Journal* (Red
   Wind Bks, 1994), *Stand-Up Poetry: Anth* (USCLB Pr,
   1994), *Onthebus, Pegasus*

Lee Rossi P
1341 Centinela Ave, #103
Santa Monica, CA 90404, 213-453-6303
   Pubs: *Grand Passion: Anth* (Red Wind Bks, 1995),
   Beyond Rescue (Bombshelter Pr, 1991), *Apalachee
   Qtly, Chelsea, Bakunin, Faultline, Poetry East, L.A.
   Times*

Alexis Rotella P
16651 Marchmont Dr
Los Gatos, CA 95032-5608
   Pubs: *Looking for a Prince* (Jade Mountain Pr, 1991),
   Haiku Moment: Anth (Tuttle, 1993), *Blue Mesa Rev,
   New Letters, Median Literary Rev*

Jerome Rothenberg ⬤ ✈ PP&P
1026 San Abella
Encinitas, CA 92024-3948, 619-436-9923
Internet: jrothenb@ucsd.edu
   Pubs: *A Paradise of Poets, Seedings & Other Poems*
   (New Directions, 1999, 1996), *A Book of the Book:
   Anth* (Granary Bks, 2000), *Poems for the Millennium:
   Anth* (U California Pr, 1998, 1995), *Jacket, Sulfur,
   Conjunctions, Apex of the M, Poesie*

Eugene Ruggles P
106 Washington St, #326
Petaluma, CA 94952-2308
   Pubs: *The Lifeguard in the Snow* (U Pittsburgh, 1977),
   Passages North: Anth (Milkweed Edtns, 1990), *Poetry
   Now, New Yorker, Poetry, Nation, Manoa, Poetry NW,
   Field*

Kay Ryan ⬤ ✈ P
60 Taylor Dr
Fairfax, CA 94930-1237, 415-453-2765
   Pubs: *Say Uncle, Elephant Rocks* (Grove Pr, 2000,
   1996), *Flamingo Watching* (Copper Beech Pr, 1994),
   *New Yorker, Atlantic, New Republic, Paris Rev, Georgia
   Rev, Yale Rev*

Michael Ryan ⬤ ✈ P
Univ California, English Dept, Irvine, CA 92697-0001,
949-824-8773
Internet: mryan@uci.edu
   Pubs: *Secret Life* (Vintage, 1995), *God Hunger* (Viking,
   1989), *In Winter* (HRW, 1981), *Threats Instead of Trees*
   (Yale, 1974)

Floyd Salas ⬤ ✈ P&W
1206 Delaware St
Berkeley, CA 94702-1407, 510-527-2594
Internet: www.floydsalas.com
   Pubs: *Color of My Living Heart, State of Emergency,
   What Now My Love* (Arte Publico Pr, 1996, 1996,
   1994), *Tattoo the Wicked Cross* (Second Chance Pr,
   1982), *Lay My Body on the Line* (Y Bird Pr, 1978)
I.D.: Hispanic, Boxer. Groups: Prisoners

Dixie Salazar ⬤ ✈ P&W
704 E Brown
Fresno, CA 93704-5509, 559-227-6914
   Pubs: *Reincarnation of the Commonplace* (Salmon Run
   Pr, 1999), *Limbo* (White Pine Pr, 1995), *Hotel Fresno*
   (Blue Moon, 1988), *Unsettling America: Anth* (Viking,
   1994)
I.D.: Hispanic, Multicultural. Groups: Prisoners

Rachel Salazar 🎤 ✈   W
PO Box 6173
Albany, CA 94706-6173
    Pubs: *Spectator: A Novel* (Fiction Collective, 1986),
    Chick-Lit 2: Anth (FC2, 1996), *Mondo Elvis: Anth* (St.
    Martin's Pr, 1994), *American Letters & Commentary*

Dennis Saleh   P
1996 Grandview
Seaside, CA 93955-3203, 831-394-4288
    Pubs: *Rhymses' Book* (Quicksilver, 2000), *This Is Not
    Surrealism* (Willamette River Bks, 1993), *First Z Poems*
    (Bieler Pr, 1980), *Artlife, Ozone, Bitter Oleander,
    Nedge, Poetry, Paris Rev, Santa Barbara Rev, Happy,
    Artword Qtly*

Mark Salerno   P
PO Box 3749
Los Angeles, CA 90078-3749
    Pubs: *Hate* (96 Tears Pr, 1995), *Exquisite Corpse,
    Ribot, Arshile, Oxygen, Galley Sail Rev, First Intensity,
    Apex of the M, Explosive, Membrane, Mike & Dale's
    Younger Poets*

Louis Omar Salinas   P
2009 9th St
Sanger, CA 93657, 209-875-4747
    Pubs: *Follower of Dusk* (Flume Pr, 1991), *Sadness of
    Days* (Arte Publico Pr, 1989)

Benjamin Saltman   P
English Dept, California State Univ, Northridge, CA 91330,
818-885-3431
    Pubs: *Deck* (Ithaca Hse, 1980), *The Leaves The
    People* (Red Hill Pr, 1974), *Event, Hudson Rev*

Steve Sanfield 🎤 ✈   P
22000 Lost River Rd
Nevada City, CA 95959-8559, 530-292-3353
Internet: sands@oro.net
    Pubs: *Bit By Bit* (Penguin Putnam, 1999), *In One Year
    & Out the Other, American Zen By a Guy Who Tried It*
    (Larkspur Pr, 1999, 1994), *No Other Business Here* (La
    Alameda Pr, 1999), *The Great Turtle Drive* (Knopf,
    1996), *The Girl Who Wanted a Song* (HB, 1996)
I.D.: Jewish

R. A. Sasaki 🎤 ✈   W
5916 Santa Cruz Ave
Richmond, CA 94804
Internet: rasasaki@aol.com
    Pubs: *The Loom & Other Stories* (Graywolf Pr, 1991),
    Selected Shorts: Anth (Radio; NPR, 1994), *Pushcart
    Prize: Anth* (Pushcart Pr, 1992), *Story*
I.D.: Asian-American, Japanese-American

Sally Love Saunders 🎤 ✈   P
2030 Vallejo St, #501
San Francisco, CA 94123-4854, 415-673-7213
    Pubs: *Manna, New York Times, Times Intl, London
    Times*

Minas Savvas   P
San Diego State Univ, English & Comparative Literature,
San Diego, CA 92182, 619-582-5873
    Pubs: *The House Vacated* (Parentheses Series, 1989),
    TriQtly, Seneca Rev, Antioch Rev, APR

Gilbert Schedler   P
Univ of the Pacific, Stockton, CA 95211, 209-946-2161
    Pubs: *Starting Over* (Pisces Pr, 1992), *Waking Before
    Dawn* (Wampeter Pr, 1978), *CQ, Blue Unicorn,
    Christian Century, California English, Minotaur, The
    Windless Orchard*

Linda Scheller   P
3125 Freitas Rd
Newman, CA 95360, 209-862-3819
    Pubs: *Poem, Aethlon, Notre Dame Rev, Ledge, Seattle
    Rev, Wisconsin Rev, Poetry East*

James Schevill 🎤 ✈   P&W
1309-1311 Oxford St
Berkeley, CA 94709-1424, 510-845-2802
    Pubs: *New & Selected Poems, The Complete American
    Fantasies* (Swallow/Ohio U Pr, 2000, 1996)

Tom Schmidt   P
8036 California Ave
Fair Oaks, CA 95628
    Pubs: *Watching from the Sky: Anth* (Pinyon Pine Pr,
    1989), *The Salmon, Pinchpenny, Poet News*

Dennis Schmitz 🎤 ✈   P
1348 57th St
Sacramento, CA 95819-4242, 916-456-6641
    Pubs: *About Night* (Field Edtns, 1993), *Eden* (U Illinois
    Pr, 1989), *Singing, String* (Ecco Pr, 1985, 1980)

Roy Schneider   W
PO Box 151388
San Diego, CA 92175
    Pubs: *I Know What You Look Like Naked* (Graffiti
    Comix, 1987), *Suburban Graffiti* (Second Coming Pr,
    1986), *City Lights Rev, Fiction Intl*

Darrell g. h. Schramm   P&W
473 28th Ave
San Francisco, CA 94121, 415-221-8779
    Pubs: *A Member of the Family: Anth* (Dutton, 1992),
    Silences, Bones & Angled Rain (Bogota, 1974), *Alaska
    Qtly Rev, Pittsburgh Qtly, Carolina Qtly, Illinois Rev,
    North Dakota Qtly*

Ruth Wildes Schuler P&W
94 Santa Maria Dr
Novato, CA 94947-3737
   Pubs: *Mistress of the Darkened Rooms & Other Short
   Stories, Shades of Salem* (Heritage Trails, 1988, 1988),
   *Greens Mag, Kavita India, Potpourri, Tears in the
   Fence, Yomimono, Timber Creek Rev*

Carol Schwalberg ⏚ ✈ P&W
629 Palisades Ave
Santa Monica, CA 90402-2723, 310-451-0098
   Pubs: *Sailing on Land: Anth* (New Voices, 1993), *If I
   Had My Life to Live Over I Would Pick More Daisies:
   Anth* (Papier-Mache Pr, 1992), *Potpourri, The Sunday
   Suitor, Palo Alto Rev, West, Wordplay, Black River
   Rev, Black Buzzard Rev, Yet Another Small Mag*

Ruth L. Schwartz P
6035 Majestic Ave
Oakland, CA 94605, 510-638-2956
   Pubs: *Accordion Breathing & Dancing* (U Pitt Pr, 1996),
   *Outlook, Nimrod, Yellow Silk, Zone Three, Sow's Ear,
   Confrontation, Evergreen Chronicles, Prairie Schooner,
   Chelsea, The Sun, Marlboro Rev, New Letters*

Leah Schweitzer ⏚ ✈ P&W
171 N Church Ln, Unit 606
Los Angeles, CA 90049-2068, 310-471-3817
Internet: leyeleh@aol.com
   Pubs: *Without a Single Answer* (Judah L. Magnes
   Museum, 1990), *Only Morning in Her Shoes* (Utah
   State U Pr, 1990), *Jrnl of the Skirball Cultural Ctr,
   Literary Monitor, Apalachee Qtly, Shirim, Confrontation,
   Slipstream, CQ*
Lang: Yiddish. I.D.: Jewish. Groups: Seniors, Jewish

Edward Scott ⏚ ✈ P
6020-A Adeline
Oakland, CA 94608, 510-594-2467
Internet: GHayes3327@aol.com
   Pubs: *The Metamorphi of the Phenomeni* (Regent Pr,
   1998), *The Afterbirth, No Reasonable Explanation
   Required* (Ebony Juan Pr, 1995, 1991)
Groups: Prisoners, Substance Abusers

James Scully P
2865 Bryant St
San Francisco, CA 94110
   Pubs: *Raging Beauty* (Azul Edtns, 1994), *Line Break:
   Poetry as Social Practice* (Bay Pr, 1988)

Anna Sears ⏚ ✈ W
1440 Guerrero St
San Francisco, CA 94110-4325, 415-285-3136
   Pubs: *Exile* (Goddesses We Ain't Pr, 1996), *Caveat
   Lector, Furious Fictions, Alchemy, Other Voices, Volition
   One*
I.D.: G/L/B/T. Groups: Disabled, Women

Carolyn See W
17339 Tramonto #303
Pacific Palisades, CA 90272
   Pubs: *Making History* (HM, 1991), *Golden Days, 110
   Shanghai Road* (McGraw-Hill, 1986, 1986)

Hubert Selby, Jr. ⏚ ✈ W
550 N Orlando, #102
West Hollywood, CA 90048-2547
   Pubs: *The Willow Tree, Song of the Silent Snow*
   (Marion Boyars, 1998, 1988), *Requiem for a Dream,
   The Demon* (Playboy, 1979, 1976), *Last Exit to
   Brooklyn* (Grove, 1964)

Bárbara Selfridge ⏚ ✈ W
476 43rd St
Oakland, CA 94609-2138, 510-658-8351
Internet: banterw8@aol.com
   Pubs: *Serious Kissing* (Glad Day Bks, 1999), *Pushcart
   Prize XVIII: Anth* (Pushcart Pr, 1994), *Witness,
   American Voice, Global City Rev, The Sun, Caribbean
   Writer, Other Voices*
I.D.: White, Leftist. Groups: Multicultural, Disabled

Peter Serchuk P
10366 Lorenzo Dr
Los Angeles, CA 90064, 213-477-3947
   Pubs: *Waiting for Poppa at the Smithtown Diner* (U
   Illinois Pr, 1990), *Manhattan Poetry Rev, Indiana Rev,
   Poetry*

Judith Serin ⏚ ✈ P
259 Staples Ave
San Francisco, CA 94112-1836
   Pubs: *Hiding in the World* (Eidolon Edtns, 1998),
   *Breaking Up Is Hard to Do: Anth, What's a Nice Girl
   Like You Doing in a Relationship Like This?: Anth*
   (Crossing Pr, 1994, 1992), *Barnabe Mountain Rev*

Nina Serrano P
551 Radnor Rd
Oakland, CA 94606, 415-832-6603
   Pubs: *Madison: The Adventure of Exile* (Temple U Pr,
   1989), *Heart Songs* (Poncho Che, 1980)

Bruce W. Severy P
827 Oxford Ave
Marina Del Rey, CA 90292-5431, 213-820-4111
   Pubs: *The Woman's Lib* (Plirto Pr, 1979)

Patty Seyburn ⏚ ✈ P
2042-F Santa Ana Ave
Costa Mesa, CA 92627-2178, 949-646-5439
Internet: PSeyburn@aol.com
   Pubs: *Diasporadic* (Helicon Nine Edtns, 1998), *American
   Poetry: Anth* (Carnegie Mellon U Pr, 2000), *American
   Diaspora: Anth* (U Iowa Pr, 2000), *Bellingham Rev,
   Crazyhorse, CutBank, Gulf Coast, NER, New Letters,
   Paris Rev, Qtly West, Third Coast*

Shaka Aku Shango   P&W
c/o Horace Coleman, 334 Gladys Ave, Apt 105, Long
Beach, CA 90814-2431, 714-841-1293
    Pubs: *Incoming* (Island Pubs, 1994), *Between a Rock &
    a Hard Place* (BkMk Pr, 1978), *Catalyst, Sacrifice the
    Common Sense, New Letters, Iowa Rev, Poets On*

Helen Shanley 🎤 ✈   P&W
6601 Eucalyptus Dr, #97
Bakersfield, CA 93306-6829, 661-366-8693
    Pubs: *Poetry, Cream City Rev, CQ, Ecphorizer,
    Bohemian Chronicle, Reach, Arts Connection*

Karl Shapiro   P&W
904 Radcliffe Dr
Davis, CA 95616, 916-753-0988
    Pubs: *The Younger Son* (Algonquin, 1988), *New &
    Selected Poems: 1940-1986* (U Chicago Pr, 1987)

Deirdre Sharett   P
106 Candlewood Dr
Petaluma, CA 94954, 707-763-3850
    Pubs: *Language of a Small Space* (Hartmus Pr, 1980),
    *Poetry Now, Footwork, Eleventh Muse, Telephone,
    Sheaf, Star Route Jrnl*

Saundra Sharp   P
Poets Pay Rent, Too, PO Box 75796, Sanford Sta, Los
Angeles, CA 90075, 213-993-6006
    Pubs: *On the Sharp Side* (Poets Pay Rent, Too, 1993),
    Black Women for Beginners (Writers & Readers, 1993),
    I Hear a Symphony: Anth (Anchor Bks, 1994),
    Healthquest, Black Film Rev, Essence, Crisis

Robin Shectman 🎤 ✈   P
1863 N Craig Ave
Altadena, CA 91001-3429
Internet: robin@ociw.edu
    Pubs: *NER, Berkeley Rev, Santa Barbara Rev, Poetry,
    American Scholar, Kenyon Rev, BPJ, Cumberland
    Poetry Rev, Literary Rev, Seneca Rev, Yankee*
Groups: Scientist

Martha A. Shelley   P
705 Shrader St
San Francisco, CA 94117
    Pubs: *Haggadah: A Celebration of Freedom* (Aunt Lute
    Bks, 1997), *Lovers & Mothers* (Sefir Pub, 1981),
    Crossing the DMZ (Women's Pr Collective, 1974), *On
    the Issues, Common Lives/Lesbian Lives, Amazon Qtly*

Jack Shields   PP
PO Box 36
Railroad Flat, CA 95248, 209-293-4437
Internet: shieldsmusic@depot.net
    Pubs: *Heritage Festival, Lord Buckley Festival of Poetry
    & Music, KDVS Radio, Whole Earth Fair*

Ruth Shigezawa   W
34 Cresthaven
Irvine, CA 92604, 714-786-6722
    Pubs: *Celeste* (Candlelight Pr, 1993), *The Women Who
    Walked Through Fire: Anth* (Crossing Pr, 1990), *Amelia,
    Cicada, Outerbridge, Pulpsmith*

P. Shneidre 🎤 ✈   P
2000 Ivar
Hollywood, CA 90068, 323-463-5683
Internet: tadbooks@earthlink.net
    Pubs: *Thus Spake the Corpse: An Exquisite Corpse
    Reader 1988-1998, Vol I-Poetry & Essays* (Black
    Sparrow Pr, 1999), *God Stole My Brain, The Idea of
    Light* (Tadbooks, 1995, 2000), *Zyzzyva, Rolling Stone,
    Paris Rev, Exquisite Corpse, Antioch Rev*
Groups: Spiritual/Religious, Children

Max Shulman   W
1100 Alta Loma Rd, #1505
Los Angeles, CA 90069

Al Shultz 🎤 ✈   P
1422 Selborn Pl
San Jose, CA 95126-2151, 408-289-9555
Internet: alshultz@earthlink.net
    Pubs: *Phantasm, New Laurel Rev, California Oranges,
    Sheaf, Dacotah Territory, Mango, Transfer*

Aaron Shurin   P
1661 Oak St
San Francisco, CA 94117, 415-552-0991
    Pubs: *Unbound: A Book of AIDS, Into Distances* (Sun
    & Moon Pr, 1997, 1993), *A's Dream* (O Bks, 1989),
    Grand Street, Sulfur, Talisman, Hambone

Noelle Sickels 🎤 ✈   P&W
3424 Larissa Dr
Los Angeles, CA 90026-6212
Internet: noelvic@earthlink.net
    Pubs: *The Shopkeeper's Wife, Walking West* (St.
    Martin's Pr, 1998, 1995), *American Fiction: Anth* (Birch
    Lane Pr, 1991), *Kalliope, Women's Words, Mediphors,
    Fathoms, Ignis Fatuus Rev*

Alan Siegler   W
c/o Dorothy Demke, 581 Baughman, Claremont, CA 91811
    Pubs: *Icarus, Midstream*

Richard Silberg 🎤 ✈   P&W
2140 Haste St
Berkeley, CA 94704-2019, 510-848-5156
    Pubs: *Doubleness* (Roundhouse Pr, 2000), *Totem Pole*
    (3300 Rev Pr, 1996), *The Fields* (Pennywhistle Pr,
    1989), *APR, Denver Qtly, Zyzzyva*

John Oliver Simon 🎤 ✈　　　　　　　P
2209 California
Berkeley, CA 94703-1607, 510-549-2456
Internet: josimon@lanminds.com
   Pubs: *Son Caminos* (Hotel Ambosmundos, 1997), *Lord of the House of Dawn* (Bombshelter, 1991), *Zyzzyva, Elysian Fields Qtly, The Temple, Two Lines, Poetry Flash, Onthebus, Artful Dodge, Caliban, APR*
Lang: Spanish

Maurya Simon 🎤 ✈　　　　　　　P
Creative Writing Dept, Univ California Riverside, Riverside, CA 92521-0318, 909-787-5312
Internet: maurya.simon@ucr.edu
   Pubs: *The Golden Labyrinth* (U Missouri Pr, 1995), *Days of Awe, The Enchanted Room* (Copper Canyon, 1989, 1986), *New Yorker, Gettysburg Rev, Poetry*

Willie Sims　　　　　　　　　　　PP
11369 Gladstone Ave
Lake View Terrace, CA 91342, 818-899-7209
   Pubs: *Beyond the Valley of Contemporary Poets: Anth* (Sacred Beverage Pr, 1996), *Grand Passion: Poets of Los Angeles: Anth* (Red Wind Bks, 1995), *Beyond Baroque, McGroarty Arts Ctr, UCLA Wight Art Gallery, Fullerton Art Museum, Los Angeles Cty Art Museum*

Bobbi Sinha-Morey　　　　　　　P
30 Canyon View Dr
Orinda, CA 94563, 510-254-7442
   Pubs: *Quantum Tao: Anth* (Blue Heron Pr, 1996), *Dreams of Decadence, Roswell Lit Rev, Penny Dreadful, Pirate Writings, Pablo Lenis, Calliope, Muse Portfolio, Contortions, Potpourri, Rouge et Noir, Rolling Paper Rev, Musing Magazine, Talebones*

Jean Sirius　　　　　　　　　　　P
PO Box 9665
Oakland, CA 94613
Internet: www.bayscenes.com/ac/sirius/
   Pubs: *And Every One of Us a Witch* (Sirius Bks, 1982), *Poetry of Sex: Anth* (Banned Bks, 1992), *Wanting Women: Anth* (Sidewalk Revolution Pr, 1992)

G. P. Skratz　　　　　　　　　P&W
5524 Vicente Way
Oakland, CA 94609, 510-428-2915
   Pubs: *Sundae Missile* (Generator Pr, 1992), *The Gates of Disappearance* (Konglomerati Pr, 1982), *Exquisite Corpse, High Performance, Score, Paragraph*

Richard Slota 🎤 ✈　　　　　　　P
1058 Century Dr
Napa, CA 94558-4227, 707-258-0108
   Pubs: *Famous Michael* (Samisdat Pr, 1989), *Abraxas, Blue Buildings, Plainswoman, Deros, Quercus, Yellow Silk*

Edward Smallfield 🎤 ✈　　　　　P&W
1009 Peralta Ave
Albany, CA 94706-2401, 510-524-1308
   Pubs: *Trio* (Specter Pr, 1995), *Seven Hundred Kisses: Anth* (HarperSF, 1997), *Fourteen Hills, Santa Clara Rev, Sarasota Poetry Rev, Barnabe Mountain Rev, Yellow Silk, Fiction, Ironwood, Zyzzyva, Margin, Five Fingers Rev, Caliban, Manoa*

D. James Smith 🎤 ✈　　　　　　　P
62 E Fedora
Fresno, CA 93704-4507
   Pubs: *Fast Company* (DK Ink, 1999), *Prayers for the Dead Ventriloquist* (Ahsahta Pr, 1995), *The Qtly, Qtly West, SPR, Carolina Qtly, Green Mountains Rev, Laurel Rev, New Virginia Rev, Stand*
Groups: Teenagers

Lawrence R. Smith 🎤 ✈　　　　　P&W
PO Box 561
Laguna Beach, CA 92652-0561
   Pubs: *The Map of Who We Are* (U Oklahoma Pr, 1997), *The Plain Talk of the Dead* (Montparnasse Edtns, 1988), *River Styx, Paris Rev, Iowa Rev, Pacific Rev*
Lang: Italian

Rick Smith　　　　　　　　　　　P
8591 Hamilton St
Alta Loma, CA 91701
   Pubs: *Hand to Mouth* (Deep Dish, 1981), *Exhibition Game* (G Sack Pr, 1973), *Poetry/L.A.*

Steven Phillip Smith　　　　　　　W
1847 S Sherbourne Dr
Los Angeles, CA 90035, 213-559-9370
   Pubs: *American Flyers* (Bantam, 1985), *First Born* (Pocket Bks, 1984), *American Boys* (Avon, 1984)

Clifton Snider 🎤 ✈　　　　　　　P
2719 Eucalyptus Ave
Long Beach, CA 90806-2515, 562-426-3669
Internet: www.csulb.edu/~csnider
   Pubs: *The Alchemy of Opposites* (Chiron Rev Pr, 2000), *The Age of the Mother* (Laughing Coyote, 1992), *Impervious to Piranhas* (Academic & Arts Pr, 1989), *Sundays at Seven: Anth* (Alamo Square Pr, 1996)
I.D.: Latino/Latina, Farmer. Groups: Scandinavian-American, G/L/B/T

Gary Snyder　　　　　　　　　　　P
English Dept, Univ California, Davis, CA 95616
   Pubs: *No Nature* (Pantheon, 1992), *The Practice of the Wild, Left Out in the Rain* (North Point Pr, 1990, 1986), *Yale Rev, Grand Street*

Margery Snyder 🎤 ✈   P
PO Box 471493
San Francisco, CA 94147-1493
Internet: http://www.poetry.about.com
   Pubs: *The Gods, Their Feathers* (Blue Beetle Pr, 1992),
Loving Argument (Viridiana, 1991), The *Astrophysicist's
Tango Partner Speaks, Bee Hive, Perihelion, Wise
Woman's Garden, Coracle, Lynx Eye*

Mary Ellen Solt   P
25520 Wilde Ave
Stevenson Ranch, CA 91381, 805-287-0089
   Pubs: *The People Mover 1968: A Demonstration Poem*
(West Coast Poetry Rev, 1978), *A Book of Women
Poets From Antiquity to Now: Anth* (Schocken Bks,
1980), *Poor Old Tired Horse, Poetry, 13th Moon,
Redstart, BPJ*

Scott A. Sonders 🎤 ✈   PP&P&W
PO Box 17897
Encino, CA 91416
Internet: news7@letterbox.com
   Pubs: *Orange Messiahs* (Yale Pr, 1999), *Prisoners
Rules* (Mangrove, 1998), *Litany* (Caravan Pr, 1987),
Meet the People (Perf; PBS Special, 1995), *Write On!
Best Short Stories: Anth* (Center Pr, 1995), *L.A. Times,
Concordia Rev, Atlantic, Parnassus, Chiron Rev*

R. Soos, Jr. 🎤 ✈   P
2745 Monterey Rd #76
San Jose, CA 95111-3130, 408-578-3546
Internet: soos@soos.com
   Pubs: *Guitars, Moaning & Groaning, California Breeze*
(Redwood Family, 2000, 1999, 1998), *Garden Songs,
The Son Is Breaking Through, His Power* (Carpenter's
Creative Rev, 1995, 1992, 1988)

Gary Soto 🎤 ✈   P&W
43 The Crescent
Berkeley, CA 94708-1701, 510-845-4718
   Pubs: *Poetry Lover, Nickel & Dime* (U New Mexico Pr,
2001, 2000), *A Natural Man, Junior College, New &
Selected Poems* (Chronicle Bks, 1999, 1997, 1995),
Buried Onions, Jesse (HB, 1997, 1994)
I.D.: Chicano/Chicana

Lily Iona Soucie   P
619 39th St
Richmond, CA 94805
   Pubs: *Ink Mag, Berkeley Poetry Rev, Lip Service Mag,
Green's Mag, Crazyquilt Qtly, Earth's Daughters, San
Francisco Qtly*

Barry Spacks   P&W
1111 Bath St
Santa Barbara, CA 93101
   Pubs: *Brief Sparrow* (Illuminati, 1988), *Spacks Street*
(Johns Hopkins, 1982)

Roswell Spafford   P
Kresge College, Univ California, Santa Cruz, CA 95064
   Pubs: *Networks, Mississippi Rev, Room, Berkeley Poets
Co-op Mag, Umbral, Sunbury*

Rona Spalten   W
6815 Paso Robles
Oakland, CA 94611, 415-339-2978
   Pubs: *New Worlds* (Avon, 1975), *City Miner, Fiction*

Roberta L. Spear   P
3712 E Balch St
Fresno, CA 93702
   Pubs: *The Pilgrim Among Us* (Wesleyan, 1991), *Talking
to Water* (HRW, 1985), *Ploughshares, Field*

Carol Speed   W
375 S 3 St, #511
San Jose, CA 95112-3649
   Pubs: *Inside Black Hollywood* (Holloway Hse, 1980),
Buffalo Soldier Mag

James Spencer 🎤 ✈   P&W
785 Berkeley Ave
Menlo Park, CA 94025, 650-323-0633
Internet: spencerjj@aol.com
   Pubs: *Best American Short Stories* (HM, 1999), *The
Girl in the Black Raincoat: Anth* (Duell, Sloan, Pearce,
1966), *Virginia Qtly Rev, Ontario Rev, Gettysburg Rev,
American Literary Rev, Hawaii Rev, Greensboro Rev,
BPJ*
I.D.: Buddhist, Abuse Victims. Groups: Psychotherapists

Lawrence P. Spingarn   P&W
Perivale Press & Agency, 13830 Erwin St, Van Nuys, CA
91401-2914
   Pubs: *Elegy for Amelia* (Typographeum Bks, 1994),
Journey to the Interior, Going Like Seventy (Perivale
Pr, 1992, 1988), *Sephardic American Voices: Anth*
(Brandeis U Pr, 1997), *Critical Qtly, Harper's, New
Yorker, The European, Transatlantic Rev*

Susan St. Aubin 🎤 ✈   P&W
5 Pastori Ave
San Anselmo, CA 94960-1815, 415-459-2100
Internet: st_aubin@sfsu.edu
   Pubs: *Best American Erotica: Anth* (S&S, 2000, 1995),
Herotica 6: Anth (Down There Pr, 1999), *Herotica 5:
Anth* (Penguin/Plume, 1998), *Going Down: Anth*
(Chronicle Bks, 1998), *Libido*
I.D.: G/L/B/T. Groups: Erotica

David St. John 🎤 ✈   P
Univ Southern California, University Park, English Dept,
Los Angeles, CA 90089-0354, 213-740-3748
Internet: dstjohn@usc.edu
   Pubs: *In the Pines, Where the Angels Come Toward
Us* (White Pine Pr, 1999, 1995), *The Red Leaves of
Night, Study for the World's Body* (HC, 1999, 1994),
Terrace of Rain (Recursos Bks, 1991)

Mia K. Stageberg 🎤 ✈ W
633 York St
San Francisco, CA 94110, 415-821-4708
  Pubs: *Chameleon 7 1/2, Dream Machinery, Furious
  Fiction, Kameleon, New Directions, Oxygen*

Jayne Lyn Stahl 🎤 ✈ P
1441 S Beverly Glen, #302
Los Angeles, CA 90024-6149
Internet: jstahl33@aol.com
  Pubs: *The Stiffest of the Corpse: Anth* (City Lights Bks,
  1989), *NYQ, Big Bridge, Sic: Vice & Verse, L.A.
  Woman, Beatitude, Exquisite Corpse, Jacaranda Rev,
  City Lights Rev, Pulpsmith*

Hans Jorg Stahlschmidt 🎤 P&W
1446 Scenic Ave
Berkeley, CA 94708-1834, 510-848-4040
Internet: stahlschmidt@home.com
  Pubs: *The Practice of Peace: Anth, XY Files: Anth*
  (Sherman Asher Publishing, 1998, 1997), *Anthology of
  Mag Verse, Yearbook of American Verse: Anth* (Monitor
  Bk Co, 1997, 1997), *Atlanta Rev, Cumberland Poetry
  Rev, Nightsun*

Albert Stainton P
478 Bartlett St
San Francisco, CA 94110
  Pubs: *The Crossing* (Puckerbrush Pr, 1974), *Paris Rev,
  Poetry, Chelsea, Poetry Now, Wormwood Rev*

Domenic Stansberry W
4104 24th St, #355
San Francisco, CA 94114, 415-821-7879
  Pubs: *Exit Paradise* (Lynx Hse Pr, 1991), *The Spoiler*
  (Atlantic Monthly Pr, 1987), *Ploughshares, Colorado
  State Rev, Mississippi Mud*

Elaine Starkman P&W
PO Box 4071
Walnut Creek, CA 94596, 925-932-1144
  Pubs: *Learning to Sit in the Silence* (Papier-Mache Pr,
  1993), *Vital Lines* (St. Martin's Pr, 1990), *Shaking Eve's
  Tree: Anth* (Jewish Pub Soc, 1991)

Marian Steele 🎤 P
1371 Marinette Rd
Pacific Palisades, CA 90272-2627, 310-454-1887
Internet: cmszego@ucla.edu
  Pubs: *The American Dream: Anth* (Pig Iron Pr, 1999),
  Life on the Line: Anth (Negative Capability Pr, 1992),
  *Ellipsis, South Dakota Rev, Black Buzzard Rev, Press
  Ltd, New Renaissance, Connecticut River Rev, Poets
  On*

Timothy Steele 🎤 ✈ P
1801 Preuss Rd
Los Angeles, CA 90035-4313
  Pubs: *All the Fun's in How You Say a Thing* (Ohio U
  Pr/Swallow, 1999), *Sapphics & Uncertainties, Missing
  Measures* (U Arkansas Pr, 1995, 1990), *The Color
  Wheel* (Johns Hopkins U Pr, 1994)

Dona Luongo Stein P
318 Cliff Dr
Aptos, CA 95003
  Pubs: *Heavenly Bodies* (Jacaranda Pr, 1995), *Women
  of the 14th Moon* (Crossing Pr, 1994), *Children of the
  Mafiosi* (West End Pr, 1977), *Prairie Schooner*

Hannah Stein P
1118 Bucknell Dr
Davis, CA 95616, 530-753-5382
  Pubs: *Earthlight* (La Questa Pr, 2000), *GRRR: Anth*
  (Arctos Pr, 1999), *Schools of Flying Fish* (State Street
  Pr, 1990), *American Literary Rev, American Voice, BPJ,
  Calyx, Kalliope, Kansas Qtly, Literary Rev, Poetry
  Flash, Prairie Schooner, Solo*

Julia Stein P
1233 1/2 N Genesse Ave
Los Angeles, CA 90046
  Pubs: *Desert Soldiers* (California Classics, 1992), *Under
  the Ladder to Heaven* (West End, 1984), *Calling Home:
  Anth* (Rutgers, 1990), *Ikon, Onthebus, Women's Studies
  Qtly, Pearl, American Book Rev*

Gary C. Sterling P&W
Marshall Secondary School, 990 N Allen Ave, Pasadena,
CA 91104, 818-798-0713
  Pubs: *Puerto del Sol, The Clearing House, Oyez Rev,
  Palo Alto Rev, Reading Improvement, Habersham Rev*

Janet Sternburg 🎤 ✈ P
16065 Royal Oak Rd
Encino, CA 91436-3913
Internet: janet.sternburg@calarts.edu
  Pubs: *Prairie Schooner, Cargo, Between Women,
  Tangled Vines*
Groups: Women, Cancer Survivors

Doreen Stock P&W
PO Box 442
Stinson Beach, CA 94970, 415-460-9296
  Pubs: *The Politics of Splendor* (Alcatraz Edtns, 1984),
  Poetry Greece, Kerem, Redwood Coast Rev, NASHIM

Ben Stoltzfus 🎤 ✈ W
Univ California, Comparative Literature Dept, Riverside, CA
92521, 909-787-5007
  Pubs: *La Belle Captive* (U California Pr, 1995), *Red
  White & Blue* (York Pr, 1989), *The Eye of the Needle*
  (Viking, 1967), *Fiction Intl, NAR, Nobodaddies, North
  Carolina Qtly, Collages & Bricolages, New Novel Rev,
  Alaluz, Chelsea, Mosaic*
Lang: French

Earle Joshua Stone P
72-685 Haystack Rd
Palm Desert, CA 92260
    Pubs: *Song of the Toad* (Paige Pub, 1989), *Pub Mirrors, Pine Needles, Arts of Asia Mag, Haiku Headlines, Poetry Nippon, Intl Art Collectors Mag*

Jennifer Stone P&W
KPFA Pacifica Public Radio, 2207 Shattuck Ave, Berkeley, CA 94704, 415-848-6767
    Pubs: *Stone's Throw* (North Atlantic, 1989), *Mind Over Media* (Cayuse, 1988), *Mother Jones, Realist*

Robert Joe Stout P&W
PO Box 5074
Chico, CA 95927, 916-894-7024
    Pubs: *They Still Play Baseball the Old Way* (White Eagle Coffee Store Pr, 1994), *City Lights* (Stout, 1992), *Notre Dame Mag, Penthouse, Christian Century*

Phyllis Stowell 🎤 ✈ P
1256 Queens Rd
Berkeley, CA 94708-2112
Internet: pstowell@stmarys-ca.edu
    Pubs: *Who Is Alice?* (Pennywhistle, 1989), *Pleiades, Slant, American Poetry Rev, Virginia Qtly Rev, Wallace Stevens Rev, Phoebe, Poet Lore, Volt, Columbia, International Qtly, Five Fingers Rev, 13th Moon*
I.D.: Feminist, Spiritual/Religious

Austin Straus P
PO Box 29154
Los Angeles, CA 90029
    Pubs: *Laureate Without a Country: Poems 1976-89* (Ambrosia Pr, 1992), *Hollywood Rev, Slipstream*

Jane Strong P&W
50 Sunset Ln
Berkeley, CA 94708, 510-527-0569
    Pubs: *Blue Unicorn, Primavera, Crosscurrents*

Joseph Stroud 🎤 ✈ P
144 Hunolt St
Santa Cruz, CA 95060, 831-429-6614
    Pubs: *Below Cold Mountain* (Copper Canyon Pr, 1998), Pushcart *Prize XXIV: Anth* (Pushcart Pr, 2000), *The Geography of Home: Anth* (Heyday Bks, 1999)

Dorothy Stroup 🎤 ✈ W
10 Claremont Crescent
Berkeley, CA 94705-2324, 415-841-9758
Internet: dstroup@uclink4.berkeley.edu
    Pubs: *In the Autumn Wind* (Scribner, 1987)

Denver Stull P&W
318 Cliff Dr
Aptos, CA 95003, 408-662-0197
    Pubs: *It Only Hurts When I Smile* (Modern Images, 1988), *Women of the 14th Moon: Anth* (Crossing Pr, 1991), *Looking for Home: Anth* (Milkweed Pr, 1990)

Evelin Sullivan 🎤 W
4050 Farm Hill Blvd, #8
Redwood City, CA 94061-1023, 415-367-7770
Internet: evelinsull@aol.com
    Pubs: *Four of Fools, Games of the Blind* (Fromm Intl Pub Corp, 1995, 1994), *The Dead Magician* (Dalkey Archive Pr, 1989)

Amber Coverdale Sumrall 🎤 ✈ P&W
434 Pennsylvania Ave
Santa Cruz, CA 95062-2434, 408-459-9377
Internet: ambers@sasquatch.com
    Pubs: *Litany of Wings* (Many Names Pr, 1998), *Atomic Ghost* (Coffee House Pr, 1995), *Storming Heaven's Gate: Anth* (Plume, 1997), *Quarry West*

David Swanger 🎤 ✈ P
Univ California–Santa Cruz, 301 Dickens Way, Santa Cruz, CA 95064, 408-426-1292
Internet: dswanger@cats.ucsc.edu
    Pubs: *Style* (Pudding Hse, 2000), *This Waking Unafraid* (U Missouri Pr, 1995), *Geography of Home: Anth* (Heyday Bks, 1999), *Georgia Rev, Poetry NW, Chariton Rev, Kansas Qtly, Poet & Critic*

Robert Sward 🎤 ✈ P&W
PO Box 7062
Santa Cruz, CA 95061-7062, 831-426-5247
    Pubs: *A Much Married Man* (Ekstasis Edtns, 1996), *Four Incarnations: New & Selected Poems* (Coffee House Pr, 1991), *New Yorker, Paris Rev, Poetry Chicago*

Robert Burdette Sweet W
1761 Edgewood Rd
Redwood City, CA 94062
    Pubs: *Writing Towards Wisdom: The Writer as Shaman* (Helios Hse, 1990)

Cole Swensen P
PO Box 927
Fairfax, CA 94978, 415-453-3331
    Pubs: *Noon* (Sun & Moon Pr, 1996), *Numen* (Burning Deck, 1995), *Conjunctions, Zyzzyva, Five Fingers Rev, Common Knowledge, Avec, o.blek*

Ruth Swensen 🎤 P&W
2587 Daisy Ln
Fallbrook, CA 92028-8479, 760-728-1203
Internet: rswensen@nctimes.net
    Pubs: *Magee Park Poets Anth* (Carlsbad Library, 2000), *Tide Pools Anth* (Mira Costa College, 1993)

Rob Swigart P&W
2995 Woodside Rd, Ste 400
Woodside, CA 94062, 415-851-5490
  Pubs: *Venom, Toxin, Portal* (St. Martin's Pr, 1991,
  1989, 1988), *NER, Poetry NW*

Michael Sykes P
PO Box 296
Cedarville, CA 96104-0296, 530-279-2337
  Pubs: *From an Island in Time* (Jungle Garden Pr,
  1984), *Neon, Northern Contours, Barnabe Mountain
  Rev, Floating Island, Fallow Deer, Estero*

Luis Salvador Syquia P
574 8th Ave
San Francisco, CA 94118

Barbara Szerlip P
532-B Lombard St
San Francisco, CA 94133, 415-398-3112
  Pubs: *The Ugliest Woman in the World & Other
  Histories* (Gallimaufry, 1978), *The Party Train: A
  Collection of North American Prose Poetry: Anth* (New
  Rivers Pr, 1996), *National Geographic, Elle*

Phil Taggart P
PO Box 559
Ventura, CA 93002, 805-672-1756
  Pubs: *Opium Wars* (Mille Grazie Pr, 1997)

William Talcott P
1331 26th Ave
San Francisco, CA 94122, 415-566-3367
  Pubs: *Benita's Book* (Thumbscrew Pr, 1997), *Kidstuff*
  (Norton Coker Pr, 1992), *Calling in Sick* (End of the
  Century Bks, 1989), *Exquisite Corpse, NAW, 33 Rev*

Elizabeth Tallent W
Univ California, English Dept, Davis, CA 95616,
916-752-6388
  Pubs: *Time with Children, Museum Pieces, In Constant
  Flight* (Knopf, 1987, 1985, 1983), *New Yorker*

Judith Tannenbaum P
3120 Yosemite Ave
El Cerrito, CA 94530-3430
  Pubs: *In the Crook of Grief's Arm, Songs in the Night*
  (Nehama Pr, 1993, 1988), *Poetry Flash, Tule Rev, Rain
  City Rev, Steelhead Special, Ink, Sequoia*

Carol Tarlen P&W
1001 Bridgeway #729
Sausalito, CA 94965, 415-332-0305
  Pubs: *Homeless Not Helpless: Anth* (Canterbury Pr,
  1991), *Calling Home: Anth* (Rutgers U Pr, 1990),
  Exquisite Corpse, Rain City Rev, Hurricane Alice

Roger Taus P
1418 Stanford St, #7
Santa Monica, CA 90404-3147
  Pubs: *If You Ask Me Where I've Been* (Igneus Pr,
  1998), *Poems from the Combat Zone* (Tao Anarchy
  Bks, 1984), *Going for Coffee: Anth* (Canada; Harbour
  Pub, 1981), *Neologisms, Left Curve, Third Rail*

Judith Taylor 🎤 ✈ P
3252 Mandeville Canyon Rd
Los Angeles, CA 90049-1016
Internet: judithtay@aol.com
  Pubs: *Curios* (Sarabande Bks, 2000), *Burning*
  (Portlandia Group, 1999), *Ravishing DisUnities: Real
  Ghazals in English: Anth* (Wesleyan, 2000), *APR,
  Crazyhorse, Witness, Qtly West, Antioch Rev, Poetry*
I.D.: Women

Kent Taylor 🎤 ✈ P
1450 10th Ave
San Francisco, CA 94122-3603, 415-665-8073
  Pubs: *Rabbits Have Fled, Late Show at the Starlight
  Laundry* (Black Rabbit, 1991, 1989), *Rattapallax, The
  Qtly, Abraxas, Onthebus*

Susan Terence P
65 Manchester St, #2
San Francisco, CA 94110-5214, 415-995-2659
  Pubs: *Nebraska Rev, San Francisco Bay Guardian,
  Halftones to Jubilee, SPR, Negative Capability, Lake
  Effect*

Susan Terris 🎤 ✈ P&W
11 Jordan Ave
San Francisco, CA 94118-2502, 415-386-7333
Internet: sdt11@aol.com
  Pubs: *Angels of Bataan, Killing in the Comfort Zone*
  (Pudding Hse Pubs, 1999, 1995), *Eye of the Holocaust*
  (Arctos Pr, 1999), *Curved Space* (La Jolla Poets Pr,
  1998), *Nell's Quilt, Author! Author!* (FSG, 1996, 1990),
  Missouri Rev, Nimrod, Antioch Rev

Roland Tharp P
307 Dickens Way
Santa Cruz, CA 95064
  Pubs: *Highland Station* (Poetry Texas Pr, 1977), *Prairie
  Schooner, Hawaii Rev, SW Rev*

Raul Thomas W
116 San Jose, #2
San Francisco, CA 94110, 415-641-8766
  Pubs: *Las Caras de la Luna, dicen que soy..., y
  aseguran que estoy* (Spain; Betania, 1996, 1993)

Joanna Thompson P
1515 Umeo Rd
Pacific Palisades, CA 90272
  Pubs: *American Scholar, California Qtly, SW Rev, New
  Orleans Rev, Phantasm, America*

Sabina Thorne   W
PO Box 1413
Bethel Island, CA 94511-2413
    Pubs: *Of Gravity & Grace* (Janus Pr, 1982), *Reruns*
(Viking Pr, 1981)

Sheila Thorne   W
1326 Spruce St
Berkeley, CA 94709-1435, 510-848-3826
Internet: MSapir@compuserve.com
    Pubs: *Literal Latte, Nimrod, Primavera, Stand Mag*
Groups: Prisoners, Seniors

Terry Tierney   P
1185 Glencourt Dr
Oakland, CA 94611, 510-339-0704
    Pubs: *Abraxas, Blue Buildings, California Qtly,
Centennial Rev, Chattahoochee Rev, Concerning Poetry,
Contact II, Cottonwood Rev, Great River Rev, Kalliope,
Kansas Qtly, Milkweed Chronicle, Poetry at 33, Poetry
NW, Puerto del Sol, South Dakota Rev*

JoAnn Byrne Todd   P
21627 Ocean Vista Dr
South Laguna, CA 92677, 714-499-2112
    Pubs: *Voices Intl, Wind Chimes, Modern Haiku, Pulp,
Blue Grass, Literary Rev*

Sotere Torregian   P
PO Box 163
San Carlos, CA 94070-3746, 415-592-6079
    Pubs: *The Young Englishwoman* (Printmasters, 1989),
The Age of Gold (Kulchur, 1976), *Paris Rev*

Paul Trachtenberg   P
9431 Krepp Dr
Huntington Beach, CA 92646, 714-968-7546
    Pubs: *Alphabet Soup: A Laconic Lexicon* (Wordworks,
1997), *Ben's Exit, Making Waves* (Cherry Valley Edtns,
1994, 1990)

Truong Tran   P
337 10th Ave, #5
San Francisco, CA 94118, 415-387-1121
    Pubs: *Zyzzyva, ACM, American Voice, Crazyhorse,
Poetry East, Onthebus, Prairie Schooner, Berkeley
Poetry Rev, Blue Mesa Rev, Fourteen Hills, North
Dakota Qtly, Reed*

Laurel Trivelpiece   P&W
23 Rocklyn Ct
Corte Madera, CA 94925, 415-924-9130
    Pubs: *Just a Little Bit Lost* (Scholastic, 1988), *Blue
Holes* (Alice James Bks, 1987), *Poetry*

Quincy Troupe 🎤 ✈   P
1655 Nautilus St
La Jolla, CA 92037-6412, 858-534-3210
    Pubs: *Choruses: New Poems, Avalanche: New Poems*
(Coffee Hse Pr, 1999, 1996), *Weather Reports: New &
Selected Poems* (Harlem River Pr, 1991) *Tin House,
Review: Latin Amer Lit & Arts, Long Shot, Kenyon Rev,
Ploughshares, Pequod*

Kitty Tsui   P
c/o Sheryl B. Fullerton, 1010 Church St, San Francisco,
CA 94114, 415-824-8460
    Pubs: *Breathless* (Firebrand, 1996)

Mike Tuggle   P
PO Box 421
Cazadero, CA 95421, 707-632-5818
    Pubs: *Cazadero Poems* (Floating Island Pub, 1994),
*White Heron Rev, Temple, Poetry Flash, Zyzzyva,
Manoa, Americas Rev, CPITS Anth, Psychological
Perspectives, Floating Island, Slant*

David L. Ulin   P&W
8126 Blackburn Ave
Los Angeles, CA 90048
    Pubs: *Cape Cod Blues* (Red Dust, 1992), *Unbearables:
Anth* (Autonomedia, 1995), *Exquisite Corpse, Rampike,
Vignette, Brooklyn Rev, B City, Sensitive Skin*

Charles Upton   P
245 Nova Albion Way
San Rafael, CA 94903-3529, 415-454-2343
    Pubs: *Snake of Mute River* (Artaud's Elbow, 1979),
Panic Grass (City Lights Bks, 1968), *Longhouse*

Amy Uyematsu 🎤 ✈   P
10535 Zelzah Ave
Granada Hills, CA 91344
Internet: uyematsua@aol.com
    Pubs: *Nights of Fire, Nights of Rain; 30 Miles from
J-Town* (Story Line Pr, 1998, 1992), *Geography of
Home: Anth* (Heyday, 1999), *What Book?: Anth*
(Parallax, 1998), *Bamboo Ridge Jrnl, Rattle, disOrient,
Art/Life*

Lequita Vance-Watkins   P
PO Box 221847
Carmel, CA 93922, 408-624-5068
    Pubs: *White Flash/Black Rain* (Milkweed Edtns, 1995),
Dark with Stars (High Coo Pr, 1984), *Out of the Dark:
Anth* (Queen of Swords Pr, 1995)

Paul Vangelisti   P
2060 Escarpa Dr
Los Angeles, CA 90041
    Pubs: *Nemo* (Sun & Moon Pr, 1995), *Villa* (Littoral Bks,
1991), *Another You* (Red Hill, 1981)

Cherry Jean Vasconcellos 🎤 ✈ P
436 Elmwood Dr
Pasadena, CA 91105-1329, 323-255-1770
    Pubs: *Before Our Very Eyes* (Pearl Edtns, 1997),
    Matchbook: Anth, Grand Passion: Anth (Red Wind Bks,
    1999, 1995), *Jitters: Anth* (Fossil Pr, 1996), *Poetry/L.A.
    Pearl, CQ, Wormwood Rev, NYQ*

Richard Vasquez W
3345 Marengo
Altadena, CA 91001, 213-794-9825

Katherine Vaz W
522 D St
Davis, CA 95616, 530-758-1219
    Pubs: *Mariana* (HC/Flamingo, 1997), *Fado & Other
    Stories* (U Pittsburgh Pr, 1997), *Saudade* (St. Martin's
    Pr 1994), *Nimrod, Gettysburg Rev, American Voice,
    Other Voices, TriQtly*

Bob Vickery W
769 Cole St #2
San Francisco, CA 94117, 415-386-3088
    Pubs: *Cock Tales* (Leyland Pub, 1997), *Up All Hours*
    (Alyson Bks, 1997), *Butch Boys, Skin Deep*
    (Masquerade Bks, 1997, 1994), *Advocate Men*

Alma Luz Villanueva 🎤 ✈ P
4135 Gladys Ave
Santa Cruz, CA 95062-4507
Internet: almaluzia@cs.com
    Pubs: *Vida* (Wings Pr, 2001), *Luna's California Poppies,
    Desire, Weeping Woman, Naked Ladies, Planet*
    (Bilingual Pr, 2001, 1998, 1994, 1993, 1993), *The
    Ultraviolet Sky* (Doubleday, 1993)
I.D.: Native American, Latino/Latina

Marianne Villanueva 🎤 ✈ W
2431 Hopkins Ave
Redwood City, CA 94032-2157
Internet: hf.mrv@forsythe.stanford.edu
    Pubs: *Tilting the Continent: Anth* (New Rivers Pr,
    2000), *Ginseng & Other Tales from Manila* (Calyx Bks,
    1991), *The Nuyorasian Anth, Flippin: Filipinos in
    America: Anth* (AAWW, 1998, 1996), *Charlie Chan Is
    Dead: Anth* (Viking, 1993)

Victor Edmundo Villasenor W
Rancho Villasenor, 1302 Stewart St, Oceanside, CA
92054, 619-454-1550
    Pubs: *Walking Star* (Arte Publico Pr, 1994), *Rain of
    Gold* (Dell, 1992), *Jury* (Little, Brown, 1978), *Macho*
    (Bantam, 1973)

Stephen Vincent P
3514 21st St
San Francisco, CA 94114, 415-641-0739
    Pubs: *Walking* (Junction Bks, 1993)

Gerald Robert Vizenor P
American Studies, Univ California, 301 Campbell Hall,
Berkeley, CA 94720, 510-642-6593
Internet: vizenor@uclink4.berkeley.edu
    Pubs: *Fugitive Poses* (U Nebraska Pr, 1998), *Hotline
    Healers* (Wesleyan U Pr, 1997)

Eric B. Vogel P
29190 Verdi Rd
Hayward, CA 94544, 510-538-1638
    Pubs: *Antigonish Rev, Stand, Envoi, Poetry Motel,
    Encodings, Sublime Odyssey, Raindog Rev, Mobius,
    Parting Gifts*

Arthur Vogelsang 🎤 ✈ P
1730 N Vista St
Los Angeles, CA 90046-2235, 323-874-2220
    Pubs: *Cities & Towns* (U Mass Pr, 1996), *Twentieth
    Century Women* (U Georgia Pr, 1988), *A Planet* (H
    Holt, 1983)

Christy Wagner 🎤 ✈ W
PO Box 1628
Mendocino, CA 95460-1628, 707-964-0350
Internet: cwagner@mcn.org
    Pubs: *Mustang Je T'aime* (Gorde Plata Pr, 1996)

Jeanne Wagner P
23 Edgecroft Rd
Kensington, CA 94707, 510-526-4190
    Pubs: *Denny Poems, Ekphrasis, Poet's Guild, Blue
    Unicorn, Lucid Stone, Silver Quill, Spoon River*

Marilyn Schoefer Wagner 🎤 ✈ W
PO Box 860
Fort Bragg, CA 95437-0860, 707-964-5063
Internet: lwagner@mcn.org
    Pubs: *Cats & Other Tales:* (Genesis Pr, 1999), *Coast
    Magazine, OutLook*

John Walke W
5671 E Waverly Ln
Fresno, CA 93727-5437, 209-456-9255
    Pubs: *Nethula Jrnl, Pulp, Apalachee Qtly, Bachy,
    Bridge, Backwash, Second Coming, Tandava*

Mary Alexander Walker W
PO Box 151615
San Rafael, CA 94915, 415-461-1025
    Pubs: *Scathach & Maeve's Daughters, Brad's Box,
    Maggot, To Catch a Zombie* (Atheneum, 1990, 1988,
    1980, 1979)

David Foster Wallace W
Frederick Hill Associates, 1842 Union St, San Francisco,
CA 94123
    Pubs: *Girl with Curious Hair* (Norton, 1989), *Broom of
    the System* (Viking, 1987), *Harper's*

William Wallis 🎤 ✈   P
English Dept, Los Angeles Valley College, 5800 Fulton
Ave, Van Nuys, CA 91401-4062, 818-781-1200
Internet: walliswg@laccd.cc.ca.us
   Pubs: *Selected Poems 1969-99, Dutton's Books, Eros*
   (Stone & Scott Pubs, 2000, 1995, 1994), *Biographer's
   Notes* (Yellow Barn Pr, 1984)

Diane Ward 🎤 ✈   P
1023 Centinela Ave
Santa Monica, CA 90403-2315, 310-828-1060
Internet: dianeward@yahoo.com
   Pubs: *Portraits & Maps* (NLF editori, 2000), *Human
   Ceiling* (Roof Bks, 1996), *Tripwire, Philly Talks*

Lynn Watson 🎤 ✈   P&W
PO Box 1253
Occidental, CA 95465-1253
   Pubs: *Catching the Devil* (Keegan Pr, 1994), *Amateur
   Blues* (Taurean Horn Pr, 1990), *Oxygen*

Charles Harper Webb   P&W
English Dept, California State Univ, 1250 Bellflower Blvd,
Long Beach, CA 90840, 562-985-4244
   Pubs: *Reading the Water* (Northeastern U Pr, 1998),
   Best American Poetry 1995: Anth (S&S, 1995), *Stand
   Up Poetry: Anth* (University Pr, 1994), *Iowa Rev, Paris
   Rev, Michigan Qtly Rev, Ploughshares, APR,
   Gettysburg Rev*

Brenda Webster   W
2671 Shasta Rd
Berkeley, CA 94708, 510-548-2618
   Pubs: *Tattoo Bird* (Fiction Net, 1996), *Sins of the
   Mothers* (Baskerville Pr, 1993), *Chariton Rev, Women's
   Studies, Crazyquilt*

Richard J. Weekley   P
24721 Newhall Ave
Newhall, CA 91321-1729, 805-254-0851
   Pubs: *Small Diligences* (L.A. Poets Pr, 1988), *Mayan
   Night* (Domina Bks, 1981), *These Things Happen: Anth*
   (Inevitable Pr, 1997), *Blue Buildings, Crosscurrents,
   Gryphon, Kansas Qtly, Poetry/L.A., Literary Rev*

Florence Weinberger 🎤 ✈   P
17143 Albers St
Encino, CA 91316-2602, 818-789-3786
Internet: flopetw@earthlink.net
   Pubs: *The Invisible Telling Its Shape* (Fithian Pr, 1997),
   Breathing Like a Jew (Chicory Blue Pr, 1997), *Grand
   Passion: Anth* (Red Wind Bks, 1995), Truth *& Lies That
   Press for Life: Anth* (Artifact Pr, 1991), *Solo, Lit Rev,
   Art/Life, Tikkun, ACM, Calyx*
Groups: Jewish, Seniors

Kenneth Weisner   P
528 Windham St
Santa Cruz, CA 95062, 408-426-5172
   Pubs: *Porter Gulch Rev, Oyez, Berkeley Poetry Rev,
   Brooklyn Rev, Antioch Rev, Lighthouse Point, Eye
   Prayers, New Honolulu Rev*

Jason Lee Weiss   P
1101 Spruce St
Berkeley, CA 94707, 415-655-9694

Mark Weiss 🎤 ✈   P
Box 40537
San Diego, CA 92164-0537, 619-282-0371
Internet: junction@earthlink.net
   Pubs: *Fieldnotes* (Junction Pr, 1995), *A Blockprint by
   Kuniyoshi* (Four Zoas/Night Hse, 1994)

ruth weiss 🎤 ✈   P
PO Box 509
Albion, CA 95410-0509, 707-937-5619
Internet: www.leftcoastart.com
   Pubs: *A New View of Matter* (Mata Pub, 1999), *For
   These Women of the Beat* (3300 Pr, 1997), *Ragged
   Lion: Anth* (Vagabond Pr, 1998), *Women of the Beat
   Generation: Anth* (Conari Pr, 1996), *Gargoyle*

David Weissmann   P
Creative Writing Program, Stanford Univ, Stanford, CA
94305, 415-497-1700
   Pubs: *Poetry, Southern Rev, Poetry NW, Antioch Rev,
   Shenandoah, Epoch, Stand*

Michael Dylan Welch 🎤 ✈   P
248 Beach Park Blvd
Foster City, CA 94404-2710, 650-571-9428
Internet: welchm@aol.com
   Pubs: *Global Haiku: Anth* (Iron/Mosaic Pr, 2000), *The
   Haiku Anth* (Norton, 1999), *Haiku World: Anth*
   (Kodansha, 1996), *Haiku Moment: Anth* (Charles E.
   Tuttle Co, 1993), *American Tanka, Frogpond, Spring,
   Woodnotes, Modern Haiku, Tundra*

Marion deBooy Wentzien   W
19801 Merribrook Ct
Saratoga, CA 95070, 408-867-0306
   Pubs: *Desert Shadows* (Avalon Bks, 1988), *Seventeen,
   New Letters, This World, Fact & Fiction*

Michael West   P
323 Martin
Rio del Mar, CA 95003, 408-688-6253
   Pubs: *Odes & Other Modes, Eye Quilt* (Wire Wind Ink,
   1984, 1971), *Street, Lost & Found Times, Paper Radio,
   Swift Kick, Bird Effort, Abbey*

David Westheimer   W
11722 Darlington Ave, #2
Los Angeles, CA 90049
    Pubs: *Death Is Lighter Than a Feather* (U North Texas
    Pr, 1995), *Sitting It Out* (Rice U Pr, 1992), *My Sweet
    Charlie* (Doubleday, 1965)

Philip Whalen   P&W
Hartford Street Zen Center, 57 Hartford St, San Francisco,
CA 94114
    Pubs: *You Didn't Even Try & Imaginary Speeches for a
    Brazen Head* (Zephyr, 1985)

Jackson Wheeler ♀ ⊀   P
PO Box 954
Ventura, CA 93002-0954, 805-483-1905
Internet: jw@tri-counties.org
    Pubs: *Swimming Past Iceland* (Mille Grazie Pr, 1993),
    A Near Country: Anth (Solo Pr, 1999), *And What
    Rough Beast: Anth* (Ashland U Pr, 1999), *Beyond the
    Valley of the Contemporary Poets: Anth* (Sacred
    Beverage Pr, 1997), *Cider Press Rev, Carolina Qtly*
Groups: G/L/B/T, Teenagers

Betty Coon Wheelwright   P
PO Box 1359
Pt Reyes Station, CA 94956-1359
    Pubs: *Seaward* (Berkeley Poets Co-op, 1978), *Calyx,
    SPR, Psych Perspectives, Women's Qtly Rev, Wooster
    Rev*

Robin White   W
English Dept, California State Polytechnic, 3801 W Temple
Ave, Pomona, CA 91768, 714-869-3940
    Pubs: *Moses the Man* (Monograph, 1981), *San
    Francisco, Focus, Spring Harvest, Pulpsmith, Hard
    Copies, Portfolio, Arizona Qtly*

Theresa Whitehill ♀ ⊀   P
1751 Cameron Rd
Elk, CA 95432-9204, 707-877-1816
Internet: writing@coloredhorse.com
    Pubs: *Napa Valley* (Stags Leap Winery, 1998), *A
    Natural History of Mill Towns* (Pygmy Forest Pr, 1993),
    Wood, Water, Air & Fire: Anth (Pot Shard Pr, 1998),
    *Montserrat Rev, Semi-Dwarf Rev, Art/Life, Yellow Silk,
    Oxygen*

William Wiegand   W
Writing Dept, San Francisco State Univ, 1600 Holloway
Ave, San Francisco, CA 94132
    Pubs: *The Chester A. Arthur Conspiracy* (Dial Pr,
    1983), *School of Soft Knocks* (Lippincott, 1968)

Rosemary C. Wilkinson ♀ ⊀   P
3146 Buckeye Ct
Placerville, CA 95667-8334, 530-626-4166
    Pubs: *Calendar Poetry, Spiritual, Nature, Collected
    Poems* (E.J. Co, 2000, 1997, 1996, 1994), *Cambrian
    Zephyr* (Amarin Printing Group, 1994), *Poetry Anth for
    World Peace: Anth* (England; Chinese World Pub, 2000)

Sylvia Wilkinson   W
514 Arena St
El Segundo, CA 90245-3016, 310-322-2814
    Pubs: *On the 7th Day God Created the Chevrolet, Cale*
    (Algonquin Bks, 1993, 1986)

Daniel Williams ♀ ⊀   P
General Delivery
Yosemite, CA 95389-9999, 209-375-6721
    Pubs: *Grrrr: Anth* (Arctos Pr, 2000), *XY Files: Anth*
    (Sherman Asher Pub, 1997), *North Dakota Qtly,
    Midwest Qtly, Seattle Rev, Manzanita, Kerf*
I.D.: Nature/Environment

Paul Osborne Williams ♀ ⊀   P
2718 Monserat Ave
Belmont, CA 94002-1448, 415-591-2733
Internet: powms@aol.com
    Pubs: *Outside Robins Sing* (Brooks Bks, 1999),
    Footsteps in the Fog, Fig Newtons: Anth (Press Here,
    1994, 1993), *Modern Haiku, Frogpond, Woodnotes*

Sherley Anne Williams   P
Literature Dept, Univ California, La Jolla, CA 92093,
619-534-3210
    Pubs: *Working Cotton* (HBJ, 1992), *Dessa Rose, Some
    One Sweet Angel Chile* (Morrow, 1986, 1982)

Paul Willis ♀ ⊀   P&W
Westmont College, English Dept, Santa Barbara, CA
93108-1099, 805-565-7174
Internet: willis@westmont.edu
    Pubs: *Poison Oak* (Mille Grazie, 1999), *No Clock in the
    Forest* (Avon Bks, 1993), *Best Spiritual Writing: Anth*
    (Harper SF, 1999), *Best American Poetry: Anth*
    (Scribner, 1996), *Weber Studies, Christian Century,
    Image, Poetry*
Groups: Environmentalist, Christian

Eric Wilson   W
1319 Pearl St
Santa Monica, CA 90405, 213-452-3452
    Pubs: *Prize Stories 1985: The O. Henry Awards: Anth*
    (Doubleday, 1985), *Witness, Massachusetts Rev, Epoch*

Dick Wimmer ♀ ⊀   W
c/o James Leonard, 4215 Glencoe Ave, 2nd Flr, Marina
Del Rey, CA 90292, 310-821-9000
    Pubs: *The Irish Wine Trilogy* (Penguin, 2001), *Boyne's
    Lassie* (Zoland, 1998), *Irish Wine* (Mercury Hse, 1989),
    Tales of the Heart, Nassau Rev, Flash-Bopp

A. D. Winans 🎤 ✈ P&W
PO Box 31249
San Francisco, CA 94131-0249, 415-826-1768
  Pubs: *North Beach Revisited* (Green Bean Pr, 2000),
  America (Black Bear Pr, 1998), *San Francisco Streets*
  (Ye Olde Font Shoppe, 1997), *Outlaw Bible of Amer
  Poetry: Anth* (Thunder's Mouth Pr, 1999), *APR, NYQ,
  Kansas Qtly, Confrontation, Karamu*

Mary Wings W
168 1/2 Precita Ave
San Francisco, CA 94110
  Pubs: *She Came by the Book* (Berkley Prime Crime,
  1996), *Divine Victim, She Came in a Flash* (NAL, 1993,
  1989), *She Came Too Late* (Crossing Pr, 1987)

Bayla Winters 🎤 P
2700 Scott Rd
Burbank, CA 91504-2314, 818-846-1879
  Pubs: *Seeing Eye Wife, Shooting from the Lip* (Gideon
  Pr, 1997, 1995), *Sacred & Propane* (Croton Rev, 1989),
  Life on the Line: Anth (Negative Capability Pr, 1992),
  *Graffiti Rag, Convolvulus, Maverick Pr, El Locofoco,
  Iconoclast, Phoenix, Fuel*
Groups: Women

Sandra Adelmund Witt P&W
120 Camellia Ter
Los Gatos, CA 95032-350
  Pubs: *Aerial Studies* (New Rivers Pr, 1994), *40 Days &
  40 Nights* (Iowa Arts Council, 1994), *Chaminade
  Literary Rev, Colorado Qtly, Cream City Rev,
  Confluence, CutBank*

Anne F. Wittels P
2116 Via Alamitos
Palos Verdes Estates, CA 90274, 213-378-5812
  Pubs: *Lost & Found* (Coco Palm Tree Pr, 1982),
  Bitterroot, Palos Verdes Rev, Women

Maia Wojciechowska W
Pebble Beach Press, PO Box 1171, Pebble Beach, CA
93953-1171
  Pubs: *Dreams of World Cup, Dreams of Wimbledon,
  Dreams of Golf* (Pebble Beach Pr, 1994, 1994, 1993)

Tad Wojnicki P&W
PO Box 3198
Carmel, CA 93921, 408-770-0107
  Pubs: *Lie Under the Fig Trees* (Angels by the Sea Pr,
  1998), *Scrawls on a Crate of Oranges* (Pomost Pubs,
  1987), *Mosaic, Leviathan, Coffeehouse, Poets' Paper,
  The Literary Jrnl*

Murray E. Wolfe 🎤 ✈ P
PO Box 280550
Northridge, CA 91328-0550, 818-885-0101
Internet: mw@america2000.com
  Pubs: *Blessed Be the Beast* (Ambrosia Pr, 1981)
Lang: Yiddish

Geoffrey Wolff W
202 S Orange Dr
Los Angeles, CA 90036, 949-824-3745
  Pubs: *Providence, The Duke of Deception* (Vintage,
  1991, 1990), *Granta, Esquire, Paris Rev, TriQtly,
  Atlantic*

Jean Walton Wolff P&W
PO Box 275
Aptos, CA 95001-0275, 831-475-4221
  Pubs: *Storming Heaven's Gate: Anth* (Plume, 1997),
  Sleeping with Dionysis: Anth (Crossing Pr, 1992), *Porter
  Gulch Rev, Milvia Street, Bakunin*

Tobias Wolff W
Creative Writing Program, Dept of English, Stanford
University, Stanford, CA 94305-2087, 650-723-2635
  Pubs: *In Pharaoh's Army* (Knopf, 1994), *This Boy's Life*
  (Atlantic Monthly Pr, 1989)

Blema Wolin 🎤 P
1400 Geary Blvd #1803
San Francisco, CA 94109-9311, 415-673-6846
  Pubs: *Elephant, Noodles & Feathers, Holy Bob-Jo*
  (Anths: Zapizdat Pub, 1994), *CQ, The Squaw Rev,
  Hawai'i Rev, Virginia, Antioch Rev, Bellowing Ark*

Joel M. Y. Wolk PP
1343 Oak St
San Francisco, CA 94117, 415-552-3883
  Pubs: *The Jazz Poetry Anthology* (Indiana U Pr, 1991),
  *Tree 3, Sou'wester, Monument, Poetry Bag, Off the
  Wall, Sala De Puerto Rico at MIT, Hayden Gallery at
  MIT, Writers' Forum, Old Red Kimono, Focus Midwest*

Cecilia Woloch P
5921 Whitworth Dr #201
Los Angeles, CA 90019, 213-933-8718
  Pubs: *Sacrifice* (Cahuenga Pr, 1997), *Grand Passion:
  Anth* (Red Wing Bks, 1995), *Breaking Up Is Hard to
  Do: Anth* (Crossing Pr, 1994), *Catholic Girls: Anth*
  (Penguin/Plume, 1992), *Prose Poem, Antioch Rev,
  Zyzzyva, Literal Latte, Chelsea Hotel*

Ko Won P
11754 Castillo Ln
Northridge, CA 91326, 818-363-5325
  Pubs: *Some Other Time* (Bombshelter Pr, 1990), *The
  Turn of Zero* (CCC, 1974), *Amerasia, Chicago Rev,
  The Literary Realm, Bitter Oleander*

Nanying Stella Wong P
1537 Comstock Ct
Berkeley, CA 94703-1030, 510-524-2229
  Pubs: *Bearing Dreams, Shaping Visions: Anth*
  (Washington State U Pr, 1993), *Peace & Pieces:
  Contemporary American Poetry: Anth* (Peace & Pieces
  Pr, 1973), *Sunset Mag, California Living*

Nellie Wong 🎤 ✈ P
549 Chenery St
San Francisco, CA 94131-3031, 415-584-7097
    Pubs: *Stolen Moments, Crimson Edge: Anth* (Chicory
    Blue Pr, 1997, 2000), *The Death of Long Steam Lady*
    (West End Pr, 1986), *Dreams in Harrison Railroad Park*
    (Kelsey Street Pr, 1977), *Forkroads, Open Boat,*
    Dissident Song, Long Shot

Alice F. Worsley P
California State College, English/Foreign Languages Dept,
Turlock, CA 95380, 209-633-2361

Elizabeth Wray P
834 Elizabeth St
San Francisco, CA 94114
    Pubs: *Partisan Rev, Kayak, Epoch, Denver Qtly, Pacific*
    Sun Literary Qtly, Berkeley Poets Co-op

Kirby Wright P&W
3259 Alma St
Palo Alto, CA 94306
    Pubs: *Artful Dodge, Blue Mesa Rev, Santa Clara Rev,*
    Hawaii Rev, Welter Mag, West Mag

Mark Wunderlich 🎤 ✈ P
3164 22nd St #19
San Francisco, CA 94110-3244, 415-824-0941
Internet: markwunderlich@aol.com
    Pubs: *The Anchorage* (U Mass Pr, 1999), *New*
    American Poets: Anth (U Pr of New England, 2000),
    American Poetry: Anth (Carnegie Mellon U Pr, 2000),
    The World in Us: Anth (St. Martin's Pr, 2000), *Paris*
    Rev, Boston Rev, Poetry, Fence, SW Rev
Groups: G/L/B/T

Robert Wynne P
10041 Benares Pl
Sun Valley, CA 91352-4207, 818-545-9846
    Pubs: *Northridge Rev, Caffeine, Verve, Sheila-Na-Gig,*
    Red Dancefloor, Convergence, Paper Radio

Mitsuye Yamada P&W
6151 Sierra Bravo Rd
Irvine, CA 92715, 714-854-8699
    Pubs: *Camp Notes & Other Poems, Desert Run:*
    Poems & Stories (Kitchen Table Pr, 1992, 1988),
    Sowing Ti Leaves: Anth (Multicultural Women Writers,
    1991)

Hisaye Yamamoto DeSoto W
4558 Mont Eagle Pl
Los Angeles, CA 90041
    Pubs: *Seventeen Syllables & Other Stories* (Rutgers U
    Pr, 1998), *Charlie Chan Is Dead: Anth* (Penguin, 1993),
    The Big Aiiieeeee!: Anth (Meridian, 1991), *Rafu*

Stephen Yenser 🎤 ✈ P
10322 Tennessee Ave
Los Angeles, CA 90064-2508, 310-203-9833
Internet: yenser@humnet.ucla.edu
    Pubs: *The Fire in All Things* (LSU Pr, 1993), *Best*
    American Poetry: Anth (Scribner, 1995, 1992), *Paris*
    Rev

Al Young P&W
514 Bryant St
Palo Alto, CA 94301, 415-329-1189
    Pubs: *Heaven: Collected Poems, 1956-1990* (Creative
    Arts Bk Co, 1992), *Seduction By Light* (Delacorte,
    1988)

C. Dale Young P
4210 Judah St, #303
San Francisco, CA 94122-1016
    Pubs: *The Day Underneath the Day* (TriQtly
    Bks/Northwestern U Pr, 2001), *The Best American*
    Poetry 1996: Anth (Scribner, 1996), *Paris Rev, Partisan*
    Rev, Ploughshares, Poetry, Southern Rev, Yale Rev

Gary Young 🎤 ✈ P
3965 Bonny Doon Rd
Santa Cruz, CA 95060-9706, 831-426-4355
Internet: gyounggrp@aol.com
    Pubs: *Braver Deeds* (Gibbs-Smith Pub, 1999), *Days*
    (Silverfish Rev Pr, 1997), *The Dream of a Moral Life*
    (Copper Beech Pr, 1990), *Antaeus, APR, Kenyon Rev*

John A. Youril P
8420 Olivine Ave
Citrus Heights, CA 95610, 916-729-7072
    Pubs: *Realm of the Vampire, Mixed Bag, Haunted Jrnl,*
    Bitterroot, Stone Country, Metrosphere, Poetry & Fiction,
    Lapis, Poetry Today, The Archer
I.D.: Seniors

Rich Yurman 🎤 ✈ P
2514 24th Ave
San Francisco, CA 94116-3036, 415-665-8649
Internet: clomax@pacbell.net
    Pubs: *A Perfect Pair: he whispered/she shouted* (Secon
    Avenyuh Pr, 1989), *Parting Gifts, The Ledge,*
    Slipstream, NYQ, Small Pond, Mudfish
I.D.: Jewish, Seniors. Groups: Seniors, Teenagers

Jeffrey A. Z. Zable P&W
50 Parnassus Ave
San Francisco, CA 94117, 415-731-5250
    Pubs: *Zable's Fables* (Androgyne Pr, 1990), *Wormwood*
    Rev, Writ, Long Shot, Central Park, Caliban, NYQ

Stella Zamvil P&W
821 Thornwood Dr
Palo Alto, CA 94303-4437, 650-494-7791
    Pubs: *In the Time of the Russias* (John Daniel, 1985),
    Harpoon, Greensboro Rev, Palo Alto Rev, Canadian
    Jewish Outlook, Louisville Rev

Franklin Zawacki   W
915 Sanchez St
San Franciso, CA 94114-3322, 916-457-1123
   Pubs: *Hell Coal Annual, Cowhunting*

Andrena Zawinski 🎤 ✈   P
1100 Pacific Marina, Apt 508
Alameda, CA 94501-1124
Internet: andrenaz@earthlink.net
   Pubs: *Elegies for My Mother* (TPQ/Autumn House,
   1999), *Traveling in Reflected Light* (Pig Iron Pr, 1996),
   *Nimrod Intl, Santa Clara Rev, Talking River Rev, Qtly
   West*
Groups: Teenagers, Seniors

Paul Zelevansky   PP&P
5625 Valley Oak Dr
Los Angeles, CA 90068-2556
   Pubs: *The Shadow Architecture at the Crossroads
   Annual 19__*(CNC, 1988)

Merla Zellerbach   W
Fred Hill Literary Agency, 1842 Union St, San Francisco,
CA 94123, 415-751-4535
   Pubs: *Rittenhouse Square* (Random Hse, 1991), *Sugar,
   Cavett Manor* (Ballantine, 1989, 1987), *Reader's Digest,
   Cosmopolitan*

Rafael Zepeda 🎤 ✈   P&W
English Dept, California State Univ, Long Beach, CA
90840, 562-985-4243
   Pubs: *The Witchita Poems* (Pearl Pr, 1997), *Horse
   Medicine* (Applezaba Pr, 1993), *The Yellow Ford of
   Texas* (Vergin Pr, 1993), *Higher Elevations: Anth*
   (Swallow Pr, 1993), *A New Geography of Poets: Anth*
   (U Arkansas Pr, 1993), *Wormwood Rev, Pearl Mag*

Paul Edwin Zimmer   P&W
Greyhaven, 90 El Camino Real, Berkeley, CA 94705,
510-658-6033
   Pubs: *La Chramata Degli Eroi* (Casa Editrice Nord,
   1993), *Return to Avalon: Anth* (Daw Bks, 1996), *Mythic
   Circle, Berserkrgangr*

Lloyd Zimpel   W
38 Liberty St
San Francisco, CA 94110-2319, 415-647-2868
   Pubs: *Literature, Class & Culture: Anth*
   (Addison-Wesley, 2000), *A Good Deal: Anth* (U Mass
   Pr, 1988), *Threepenny Rev, Missouri Rev, Alaska Qtly
   Rev, ACM, Arkansas Rev, North Dakota Qtly, South
   Dakota Rev*

Harriet Ziskin   W
187 Ney St
San Francisco, CA 94112
   Pubs: *The Adventures of Mona Pinsky* (Calyx Bks,
   1995), *Broomstick, Jacob's Letter, Ceilidh, Outerbridge*

Bonnie ZoBell   W
English Dept, Mesa College, 7250 Mesa College Dr, San
Diego, CA 92111, 619-627-2912
   Pubs: *American Fiction: Anth* (New Rivers, 1997),
   *Greensboro Rev, San Diego Writers Monthly, PEN
   Syndicated Project, Cimarron Rev, Bellingham Rev, Gulf
   Stream Mag*

Al Zolynas   P
2380 Viewridge Pl
Escondido, CA 92026, 760-740-9098
   Pubs: *Under Ideal Conditions* (Laterthanever Pr, 1994),
   A Book of Luminous Things: Anth (HB, 1996), *A New
   Geography of Poets: Anth* (U Arkansas Pr, 1992)

COLORADO

Keith Abbott 🎤 ✈   P&W
Naropa Writing Dept, 2130 Arapahoe, Boulder, CO
80302-6602, 303-682-9664
   Pubs: *Downstream from Trout Fishing in America*
   (Capra Pr, 1989), *The First Thing Coming* (Coffee Hse
   Pr, 1987)

Joe Amato 🎤 ✈   P
Univ of Colorado at Boulder, Hellems 101 Campus Box
226, Boulder, CO 80309-0226, 303-492-3401
   Pubs: *Bookend: Anatomies of a Virtual Self* (SUNY Pr,
   1997), *Symptoms of a Finer Age* (Viet Nam Generation
   & Burning Cities Pr, 1994), *Jacket, New American
   Writing, Crayon*

Mark Amerika   W
PO Box 241
Boulder, CO 80306, 303-499-9331
   Pubs: *Sexual Blood, The Kafka Chronicles* (Fiction
   Collective Two, 1995, 1993), *Lettre Intl, Fiction Intl,
   Witness, Central Park, American Book Rev*

Nancy Andrews   P
1942 Mt Zion Dr
Golden, CO 80401, 303-279-1277
   Pubs: *Kansas Qtly*

Dana W. Atchley   P
Box 183
Crested Butte, CO 81224, 303-349-6506

Leslee Becker   W
English Dept, Colorado State Univ, 359 Eddy, Fort Collins,
CO 80523, 970-491-7374
   Pubs: *The Sincere Cafe* (Mid-List Pr, 1996),
   Contemporary West Coast Fiction: Anth (Globe Pequot
   Pr, 1993), *American Fiction: Anth* (Wesley Pr, 1988),
   *Sonora Rev, Atlantic, Ploughshares, Iowa Rev,
   Gettysburg Rev*

Esther G. Belin   P
3549 W 2nd Ave
Durango, CO 81301, 970-247-2966
    Pubs: *From the Belly of My Beauty* (U Arizona Pr, 1999)

Don Bendell   P&W
PO Box 276
Canon City, CO 81215, 719-269-3929
    Pubs: *Blazing Colts, The Matched Colts Series* (Dutton-Signet, 1999, 1990-1999), *The B-52 Overture, Valley of Tears* (Dell, 1992, 1992), *Crossbow* (Berkley Pub Group, 1990), *Pembroke Mag, Bowhunter*

Bruce Berger   P
Box 482
Aspen, CO 81612-0482, 970-925-1647
    Pubs: *Almost an Island* (U Arizona Pr, 1998), *The Telling Distance* (Anchor/Doubleday, 1991), *Poetry, Negative Capability, Poetry NW, New Letters, Sierra, Orion*

Paul Bergner   P
PO Box 20512
Boulder, CO 80308
    Pubs: *Off the Beaten Track: Anth* (Quiet Lion Pr, 1992), *Portlander, Plazm, Stanza, Rain City Rev, Spoon, Sufi*

Rita Brady Kiefer 🎤 ✈   P
2120 Fairway Ln
Greeley, CO 80634-3635
Internet: rbkiefe@bentley.unco.edu
    Pubs: *Nesting Doll* (U Pr Colorado, 1999), *Trying on Faces* (Monkshood Pr, 1995), *Unveiling* (Chicory Blue Pr, 1993), *Beyond Lament: Anth* (Northwestern U Pr, 1998), *Ploughshares, Kansas Qtly, SW Rev, Bloomsbury Rev*

Edward Bryant   W
PO Box 18349
Denver, CO 80218-0349, 303-480-5363
    Pubs: *Flirting with Death* (Deadline Bks, 1996), *Strangeness & Charm* (Voyager Bks, 1996), *Evening's Empires* (Nemo Pr, 1989), *Omni, Penthouse*

Reed Bye   P
2227 W Nicholl St
Boulder, CO 80304, 303-440-4091
    Pubs: *Nice to See You: Homage to Ted Berrigan* (Coffee Hse, 1990), *Out of This World: Anth* (Crown, 1991), *Up Late: Anth* (4 Walls 8 Windows, 1989)

Lorna Dee Cervantes   P
820 33rd St
Boulder, CO 80303-2410, 303-938-9176
    Pubs: *From the Cables of Genocide: Poems on Love & Hunger* (Arte Publico Pr, 1990), *Red Dirt*

Jack Collom   P
1838 Pine St
Boulder, CO 80302, 303-444-1886
    Pubs: *Entering the City* (The Backwaters Pr, 1997), *Calluses of Poetry* (CD; Treehouse Pr, 1996), *Arguing with Something Plato Said* (Rocky Ledge, 1990), *The Fox* (United Artists, 1981)

Robert Cooperman 🎤 ✈   P
2061 S Humboldt St
Denver, CO 80210, 303-722-2107
    Pubs: *In the Colorado Gold Fever Mountains* (Western Reflections, 1999), *A Tale of the Grateful Dead* (Artword, 2000), *In the Household of Percy Bysshe Shelley* (U Pr Florida, 1993), *Centennial Rev, Literary Rev, Poetry East, Santa Clara Rev, Comstock Rev*
I.D.: Jewish. Groups: Seniors

Michele Corriel   P
807 Foxtail St
Fort Collins, CO 80524, 303-221-2925
    Pubs: *ABC No Rio: Anth* (1986), *Natl Poetry Mag of the Lower East Side, Che*

Mary Crow 🎤 ✈   P
English Dept, Colorado State Univ, Fort Collins, CO 80523, 970-491-6428
    Pubs: *I Have Tasted the Apple, Borders* (BOA Edtns, 1996, 1989), *APR, Ploughshares, NAR, New Letters, Graham House Rev, Prairie Schooner*

Robert Dassanowsky   P
Dept of Languages/Cultures, Univ Colorado, Colorado Springs, CO 80933
    Pubs: *Telegrams from the Metropole: Selected Poems 1980-1998* (U Salzburg Pr, 1999), *Verses of a Marriage* (Event Horizon, 1996), *Osiris, Poet's Voice, Rampike, Salz, Poesie Europe, High Performance*
Lang: German. I.D.: A.A.U.W.

Edward Dorn   P
English Dept/Campus Box 226, Univ Colorado, Boulder, CO 80309, 303-442-7631

James Doyle   P
PO Box 271156
Fort Collins, CO 80527-1156
    Pubs: *The Silk At Her Throat* (Cedar Hill, 1999), *Literature: An Intro to Critical Reading: Anth* (Prentice-Hall, 1996), *Ohio Rev, Poetry, Carolina Qtly, Midwest Qtly, Chelsea, Northwest Rev, Montserrat Rev*

Jean Dubois   P
PO Box 1430
Golden, CO 80402
    Pubs: *The Same Sweet Yellow, Silent Stones, Empty Passageways* (San Miguel Pr, 1994, 1992, 1992), *Wind Five-Folded: Anth* (AHA Bks, 1994), *Cicada, Mayfly, Modern Haiku, Passager, Poets On, Sijo West, Still, Frogpond, Lynx, Black Bough*

Mark DuCharme P
2965 13th St
Boulder, CO 80304, 303-938-9346
  Pubs: *Cosmopolitan Tremble* (Pavement Saw Pr, 2001), *Near to* (Poetry NY, 1999), *Desire Series* (Dead Metaphor Pr, 1999), *Contracting Scale* (Standing Stones Pr, 1996), *i, a series* (Burning Pr, 1995), *The Germ, Ixnay, Combo, Kerring, First Intensity, ACM*

Bruce Ducker ♪ ⊀ P&W
1560 Broadway
Denver, CO 80202
  Pubs: *Bloodlines, Lead Us Not Into Penn Station, Marital Assets* (Permanent Pr, 2000, 1994, 1993), *Yale Rev, The Qtly, Poetry, Commonweal, NYQ*

Rikki Ducornet W
Denver Univ, University Park, Denver, CO 80208-0001, 303-871-2890
  Pubs: *The Word "Desire"* (H Holt, 1997), *Phospor in Dreamland, The Stain, The Complete Butcher's Tales, The Jade Cabinet* (Dalkey Archive, 1995, 1995, 1994, 1993), *Conjunctions, Parnassus, Sulphur*

Lawrence Dunning W
1655 Leyden
Denver, CO 80220-1621, 303-321-2658
Internet: leehlarryd@aol.com
  Pubs: *Taking Liberty* (Avon, 1981), *Stories from Virginia Qtly Rev: Anth* (U Pr Virginia, 1990), *High Plains Lit Rev, Weber Studies, Margin, Virginia Qtly Rev, Colorado Qtly, Aspen Anth, Carolina Qtly, Descant, Rio Grande Rev*

Jacqui Earley P
Metamorphosis Arts, 1331 Marshall St, Boulder, CO 80302-5803
  Pubs: *Love for the Journey, Earthwoman, Healer of the Mind* (Earley, 1978, 1978, 1975)

Jacqueline Eis ♪ ⊀ W
1006 Hinsdale Dr
Fort Collins, CO 80526-3902, 970-229-9790
  Pubs: *Imaginary Lives: Anth* (Mica Pr, 1996), *CSM, MacGuffin, Crescent Rev, Crosscurrents, Prairie Schooner, Writers' Forum, Happy, Minimus, Greensboro Rev*

Larry Fagin P
Naropa Institute, 2130 Arapahoe Ave, Boulder, CO 80302, 303-444-0202
  Pubs: *Complete Fragments* (Z Pr, 1983), *I'll Be Seeing You* (Fullcourt Pr, 1978)

Ida Fasel P
165 Ivy St
Denver, CO 80220-5846, 303-377-4498
Internet: www.thaddeusbooks.com
  Pubs: *The Difficult Inch, All Real Living Is Meeting, Where Is the Center of the World?* (Small Poetry Pr, 2000, 1999, 1998), *On the Meanings of "Cleave"* (Eakin Pubs, 1979), *Blue Unicorn, Lucid Stone, Poet Lore, Half Tones to Jubilee*

Fred Ferraris ♪ ⊀ P
PO Box 65
Lyons, CO 80540-0065, 303-823-9362
Internet: ferr@imagenet.com
  Pubs: *Older Than Rain* (Selva Ed, 1997), *Marpa Point* (Blackberry Bks, 1976), *Heaven Bone, Measure, Kuksu, Glassworks, Rocky Mountain Rev, Phase & Cycle*

Rick Fields P
c/o Da Vajradehatu Sun, 1345 Spruce St, Boulder, CO 80302, 303-444-0190

Merrill Gilfillan ♪ ⊀ P&W
PO Box 18194
Boulder, CO 80308
  Pubs: *Grasshopper Falls* (Hanging Loose, 2000), *Chokecherry Places* (Johnson Bks, 1998), *Satin Street: Poems* (Moyer Bell, 1997), *Sworn Before Cranes* (Orion Bks, 1994), *Magpie Rising: Sketches from the Great Plains* (Vintage, 1991)

Sidney Goldfarb P
English Dept, Univ Colorado, Boulder, CO 80302, 303-443-2211

Art Goodtimes ♪ ⊀ P
Cloud Acre, Box 160, Norwood, CO 81423, 970-327-4767
  Pubs: *As If the World Really Mattered* (Conundrum Pr, 2000), *Mushroom Cloud Redeye* (Western Eye Pr, 1990), *Slow Rising Smoke* (Blackberry Bks, 1987), *Upriver Downriver, Word, The Sun, Petroglyph, Poiesis, Wild Earth*
Groups: Children, Seniors

Robert O. Greer, Jr. ♪ ⊀ W
180 Adams St, Ste 250
Denver, CO 80206-5215, 303-320-6827
  Pubs: *Limited Time, The Devil's Backbone, The Devil's Red Nickel, The Devil's Hatband* (Warner/Mysterious Pr, 2000, 1998, 1997, 1996)

Aimee Grunberger P
2100 Mesa Dr
Boulder, CO 80304
  Pubs: *Ten Degrees Cooler Inside* (Dead Metaphor Pr, 1992), *American Poets Say Goodbye to the 20th Century: Anth* (Four Walls Eight Windows, 1995)

Danielle D'Ottavio Harned W
27657 Timber Trail
Conifer, CO 80433
    Pubs: *The Perimeter of Light* (New Rivers Pr, 1992),
Sing Heavenly Muse, Kansas Qtly, Permafrost

Joan Harvey W
1100 Stage Rd
Aspen, CO 81611
    Pubs: *Between C&D: Anth* (Penguin, 1988), *Another
Chicago Mag, To: A Jrnl of Poetry, Prose & Visual
Arts, Global City Rev, Mississippi Mud, Bomb, Osiris,
Tampa Rev*

Bobbie Louise Hawkins P&W
2515 Bluff St
Boulder, CO 80304
    Pubs: *My Own Alphabet, One Small Saga* (Coffee Hse
Pr, 1988, 1984)

Jana Hayes P
c/o Janice Hays, 4835 St Anton Rd, Colorado Springs,
CO 80918-3909, 719-599-9633
    Pubs: *New House, A Book of Women* (San Marcos Pr,
1972), *Wingbone: Anth* (Sudden Jungle Pr, 1986), *BPJ,
Writers' Forum, Ithaca Women's Anth, South Dakota
Rev, Eleventh Muse, Hamline Jrnl, Frontiers, Ekphrasis*

Lois Beebe Hayna P
403 Locust Dr
Colorado Springs, CO 80907, 719-599-0502
    Pubs: *Northern Gothic* (Morgan Pr, 1992), *Never Trust
a Crow* (James Andrews Pub, 1990), *The Bridge,
Nimrod*

James B. Hemesath W
117 Poncha Ave
Alamosa, CO 81101-2166, 719-589-9374
    Pubs: *Where Past Meets Present: Anth* (U Colorado Pr,
1994), *Best of Wind: Anth* (Wind Pub, 1994), *Redneck
Rev of Literature, New Mexico Humanities Rev, Wind*

Jane Hilberry ♀ ✈ P
Colorado College, English Dept, 14 E Cache la Poudre,
Colorado Springs, CO 80903, 719-389-6501
    Pubs: *The Girl with the Pearl Earring* (Jones Alley Pr,
1995), *Denver Qtly Rev, Mid-American Rev, Virginia
Qtly Rev, Michigan Qtly Rev*

Linda Hogan ♀ ✈ W
PO Box 141
Idledale, CO 80453-0141, 303-697-9097
    Pubs: *Power* (Norton, 1998), *Solar Storms* (Scribner,
1996), *Book of Medicines* (Coffee Hse Pr, 1993), *Mean
Spirit* (Atheneum, 1990), *Ms., American Voice, Denver
Qtly*
I.D.: Native American, Environmentalist. Groups: Children,
Native American

Anselm Hollo ♀ ✈ P
c/o Poetics, Naropa Univ, 2130 Arapahoe Ave, Boulder,
CO 80302, 303-449-0691
Internet: jdhollo@aol.com
    Pubs: *Rue Wilson Monday* (La Alameda Pr, 2000),
Postmodern American Poetry: Anth (Norton, 1994),
*Exquisite Corpse, Lingo, NAW, Puerto del Sol,
Talisman, World, Conjuctions, Sulfur, Gare Du Nord,
Arshile, Gas*

Margaret Honton P
421 W 20th St
Pueblo, Co 81003-2509
    Pubs: *The Visionary Mirror, I Name Myself Daughter*
(Sophia Bks, 1983, 1982), *Hyperion, Pudding*

Joseph Hutchison ♀ ✈ P
PO Box 266
Indian Hills, CO 80454-0266, 303-697-3344
Internet: www.citylim.com/hutchbio.html
    Pubs: *The Rain at Midnight* (Sherman Asher, 2000),
The Heart Inside the Heart (Wayland Pr, 1999), *Bed of
Coals* (U Colorado Pr, 1996), *House of Mirrors* (J.
Andrews & Co, 1992), *Poetry, Tar River Poetry,
Northeast, Hubbub, Midwest Qtly*

Mark Irwin ♀ ✈ P
3875 S Cherokee St
Englewood, CO 80110-3511, 303-762-6336
Internet: irwin@bel-rea.com
    Pubs: *White City, Quick, Now, Always* (BOA Edtns,
2000, 1996), *Against the Meanwhile* (Wesleyan U Pr,
1988), *Antaeus, Kenyon Rev, Atlantic, Nation, APR*
Lang: French

Don Jones P
2221 S Prairie Ave, Lot 84
Pueblo, CO 81005-2800, 719-561-0676
    Pubs: *Medical Aid* (Samisdat, 1978), *Miss Liberty, Meet
Crazy Horse* (Swallow, 1972), *Massachusetts Rev, SPR,
Prairie Schooner, Poet & Critic*

Suzanne Juhasz P
English Dept, Univ Colorado, Boulder, CO 80309,
303-492-8948
    Pubs: *Benita to Reginald: A Romance* (Out of Sight Pr,
1978), *Conditions, San Jose Studies*

Steve Katz ♀ ✈ P
669 Washington St #602
Denver, CO 80203-3837, 303-832-2534
Internet: elbonoz@earthlink.net
    Pubs: *Swanny's Ways, 43 Fictions* (Sun & Moon Pr,
1995, 1992)

Jessica Kawasuna Saiki   W
1901 E 13 Ave, #9-C
Denver, CO 80206-2041
    Pubs: *From the Lanai & Other Hawaii Stories, Once, A
Lotus Garden, The Talking of Hands: Anth* (New Rivers
Pr, 1991, 1987, 1998)

Bruce F. Kawin   P
English Dept, Univ Colorado, Boulder, CO 80309-0226,
303-449-4845
    Pubs: *How Movies Work* (U California Pr, 1992), *The
Mind of the Novel* (Princeton U Pr, 1982), *Film Qtly,
Rolling Stock*

Eleanor Keats   PP&P
9261 E Berry Ave
Greenwood Village, CO 80111, 303-779-1297
    Pubs: *A Water Cycle, Touching This Earth: Anth* (Dawn
Valley Pr, 1986, 1977), *Antioch Rev, Sojourner, Denver
Qtly, Bloomsbury Rev, Sunrust, St. Andrews Rev*

Baine Kerr ⏺ ✈   W
411 Spruce
Boulder, CO 80302
    Pubs: *Harmful Intent* (Scribner, 1999), *Where Past
Meets Present: Anth* (U Colorado, 1994), *Jumping-Off
Place* (U Missouri Pr, 1981), *Best American Short
Stories: Anth* (HM, 1977), *Stanford Mag, Southwest
Rev, Shenandoah, Denver Qtly, Many Mountains
Moving*

Patricia Dubrava Keuning   P
2732 Williams St
Denver, CO 80205
    Pubs: *Holding the Light* (James Andrews & Co, 1994),
These Are Not Sweet Girls: Anth (White Pine Pr,
1994), *Intl Qtly, Sulphur River Literary Rev*

Karl Kopp   P
1517 S Dexter Way
Denver, CO 80222, 303-759-5985
    Pubs: *Crossing the River: Anth* (Permanent Pr, 1987),
City Kite on a Wire: Anth (Mesilla, 1986), *Chiron Rev,
Bloomsbury Rev, Chariton Rev*

Leota Korns   P&W
PO Box 1617
Durango, CO 81302, 970-247-4468
    Pubs: *Kansas Mag, Women: A Jrnl of Liberation, San
Juan Voices, Matrix, Raindrops of Spring*

Marilyn Krysl ⏺ ✈   P&W
2003 Mesa Dr #4
Boulder, CO 80304, 303-444-6643
    Pubs: *How to Accommodate Men* (Coffee Hse Pr,
1998), *Warscape with Lovers* (Cleveland State Poetry
Ctr, 1997), *Soulskin* (NLN Pr, 1996), *Mozart,
Westmoreland & Me* (Thunder's Mouth Pr, 1985),
Honey, You've Been Dealt a Winning Hand (Capra Pr,
1980)

R. D. Lakin   P
405 Scott
Ft Collins, CO 80521
    Pubs: *American Passport, The MacDowell Poems*
(Typographeum Pr, 1992, 1977), *Kansas Qtly, West
Coast Rev, Antioch Rev, Nation, Cottonwood Rev,
Michigan Qtly*

Marcela Lucero   P
8614 Princeton St
Westminster, CO 80030
    Pubs: *The Third Woman* (HM, 1979)

Russell Martin   W
15201 County Rd 25
Dolores, CO 81323, 970-882-4775
    Pubs: *Beautiful Islands* (S&S, 1988), *New Writers of the
Purple Sage: Anth* (Penguin, 1992)

David Mason ⏺ ✈   P&W
English Dept, Colorado College, 14 E Cache La Poudre,
Colorado Springs, CO 80903-3298, 719-389-6502
Internet: dmason@coloradocollege.edu
    Pubs: *The Country I Remember, The Buried Houses*
(Story Line Pr, 1996, 1991), *Irish Times, Hudson Rev,
Georgia Rev, Poetry, New Criterion, Harvard Rev,
American Scholar*

Katherine "Kaki" May   P
111 Emerson St, #1423
Denver, CO 80218-3791
    Pubs: *Some Inhuman Familiars* (Cabbage Head Pr,
1983), *Brandings* (Cummington, 1968), *New York Times*

Mary McArthur ⏺ ✈   P
622 W Pine St
Louisville, CO 80027-1083, 303-665-7605
Internet: mary.mcarthur@colorado.edu
    Pubs: *Midwest Qtly, Nation, Luminaria, Maryland Poetry
Rev, Light Year, Portland, Feminist Renaissance*

Peter Michelson   P
Univ Colorado, Box 226, English Dept, Boulder, CO
80309, 303-492-7381
    Pubs: *Speaking the Unspeakable* (SUNY Pr, 1993),
Pacific Plainsong (Another Chicago Pr, 1987), *Rolling
Stock, Boundary 2, ACM, Notre Dame Rev, Exquisite
Corpse, Cincinnati Poetry Rev, Spoon River Rev, Many
Mountains Moving*

Tony Moffeit   P
1501 E 7th
Pueblo, CO 81001, 719-549-2751
    Pubs: *Poetry Is Dangerous, The Poet Is an Outlaw*
(Floating Island Pubs, 1995), *Neon Peppers* (Cherry
Valley Edtns, 1992), *Amelia, Taos Rev, Chiron Rev*

Laura Mullen 🎤 ✈   P
English Dept, Colorado State Univ, 359 Eddy Hall, Ft
Collins, CO 80523, 303-419-6845
Internet: afteriwasdead@yahoo.com
    Pubs: *The Tales of Horror* (Kelsey Street Pr, 1999),
    After I was Dead (U Georgia, 1999), *The Surface* (U
    Illinois Pr, 1991), *American Letters & Commentary,
    Agni, Denver Qtly, Antaeus, Volt*

David J. Nelson   PP
PO Box 2993
Denver, CO 80201, 302-294-0653
    Pubs: *Cracking the Pavement* (Baculite Pub Co, 1990),
    Rocky Mountain Arsenal

Kent Nelson   W
PO Box 40
Ouray, CO 81427, 970-325-4791
    Pubs: *Discoveries* (Western Reflections, 1998), *Toward
    the Sun* (Breakaway Bks, 1998), *Language in the
    Blood, The Middle of Nowhere* (Gibbs Smith, 1992,
    1992), *Virginia Qtly Rev, Sewanee Rev, Gettysburg
    Rev, Glimmer Train, Southern Rev, Shenandoah*

Tom Parson   P
157 S Logan
Denver, CO 80209, 303-777-8951
    Pubs: *Some Trouble* (Now It's Up To You Pr, 1980),
    City Kite on a Wire: Anth (Mesilla Pr, 1986)

Veronica Patterson 🎤 ✈   P
11 Gregg Dr
Loveland, CO 80538-3850, 303-669-7010
Internet: rpatterson@duke.com
    Pubs: *Swan, What Shores?* (NYU Pr, 2000), *The
    Bones Remember* (Stone Graphics, 1992), *How to
    Make a Terrarium* (Cleveland State U Poetry Ctr,
    1987), *Many Mountains Moving, Willow Springs,
    Georgia Rev, Louisville Rev, Caliban, Malahat Rev*

Naomi Rachel 🎤 ✈   P&W
954 Arroyo Chico
Boulder, CO 80302-9730, 303-449-4031
    Pubs: *The Temptation of Extinction* (Senex Pr, 1993),
    *Yale Rev, Nimrod, NAR, Hampden-Sydney Poetry Anth,
    Canadian Literature, Hawaii Rev*

Bin Ramke 🎤 ✈   P
Univ Denver, English Dept, Denver, CO 80208,
303-871-2889
Internet: bramke@du.edu
    Pubs: *Wake, Massacre of the Innocents* (U Iowa Pr,
    1999, 1995), *The Erotic Light of Gardens* (Wesleyan,
    1989), *The Language Student* (LSU Pr, 1986)

Carson Reed   P&W
2271 W 54th Pl
Denver, CO 80221, 303-477-7058
    Pubs: *Tie Up the Strong Man* (Bread & Butter Pr,
    1989), *Eros: Anth* (Stewart, Tabori & Chang, 1996),
    The Book of Eros (Harmony Bks, 1995), *Neon Qtly,
    Artisan, Bizara, Western Pocket, Open Minds, Sun,
    Yellow Silk, New Censorship, Spilled Ink, Harp, Rant*

Deborah Robson 🎤 ✈   W
PO Box 484
Fort Collins, CO 80522-0484, 970-226-3590
Internet: debrobson@fortnet.org
    Pubs: *Nantucket Rev, Seattle Post-Intelligencer, Writers'
    Forum, Twigs, Dogsoldier, Port Townsend Jrnl*

Pattiann Rogers 🎤 ✈   P
7412 Berkeley Cir
Castle Rock, CO 80104-9278, 303-660-0851
Internet: www.mindspring.com/~pattiann_rogers
    Pubs: *A Covenant of Seasons* (Hudson Hills Pr, 1998),
    *Eating Bread & Honey, Firekeeper: New & Selected
    Poems* (Milkweed Edtns, 1997, 1994), *Hudson Rev,
    Paris Rev, Poetry, Georgia Rev, Gettysburg Rev, Prairie
    Schooner*

Reg Saner 🎤 ✈   P
Univ Colorado, English Dept, Box 226, Boulder, CO
80309, 303-494-8951
    Pubs: *Four-Cornered Falcon* (Johns Hopkins U Pr,
    1993), *Red Letters* (QRL, 1989), *Essay on Air* (Ohio
    Rev Bks, 1984), *Poetry Comes Up Where It Can: Anth*
    (U Utah Pr, 2000), *Orpheus & Company: Anth* (U Pr of
    New England, 1999), *Generations: Anth* (Penguin, 1998)

Bienvenido N. Santos   W
2524 W 13 St
Greeley, CO 80631, 303-356-1121
    Pubs: *What the Hell For You Left Your Heart in San
    Francisco* (New Day, 1987)

Andrew Schelling 🎤 ✈   P
Naropa Univ, 2130 Arapahoe Ave, Boulder, CO
80302-6697, 303-543-1166
    Pubs: *The Road to Ocosigno* (Smokeproof Pr, 1998),
    The Cane Groves of Narmada River (City Lights, 1998),
    Old Growth (Rodent Pr, 1995), *Moon Is a Piece of Tea*
    (Last Generation, 1993), *Sulfur, Terra Nova, NAW,
    Grand Street*

Joel Scherzer   P
PO Box 222
Pueblo, CO 81002
    Pubs: *More Bronx Zen* (Baculite Pub, 1992), *Bronx Zen*
    (Academic & Arts Pr, 1989), *Rocky Mountain Arsenal of
    the Arts, Blue Light Rev, Apalachee Qtly*

Jay Schneiders   P
3955 E Exposition Ave #316
Denver, CO 80209-5032, 303-649-6651
   Pubs: *Georgia Rev, Qtly West, Manoa, The Jrnl,
Tampa Rev, Prism Intl*

Gary Schroeder   P
1429 N Castlewood Dr
Franktown, CO 80116-9015, 303-470-9952
   Pubs: *Adjacent Solitudes* (Wayland Pr, 1991), *Only
Morning in Her Shoes: Anth* (Utah State U Pr, 1990),
Eleventh Muse, Environment Essence & Issue, JAMA

Steven Schwartz 🎤 ✈   W
2943 Skimmerhorn St
Fort Collins, CO 80526-6288, 970-282-8755
   Pubs: *A Good Doctor's Son* (Morrow, 1998), *Therapy:
A Novel* (Penguin/Plume, 1995), *Lives of the Fathers* (U
Illinois Pr, 1991), *Ploughshares, Tikkun, Redbook,
Virginia Qtly, Antioch Rev, Epoch, Missouri Rev*

Sandra Shwayder   P&W
1955 Holly
Denver, CO 80220, 303-399-5927
   Pubs: *The Nun* (Plainview Pr, 1992), *Connections, The
Long Story, The Dream, COE Rev*

Charles Squier   P
English Dept, Univ Colorado, Campus Box 226, Boulder,
CO 80309, 303-492-7381
   Pubs: *Mrs. Beaton's Tea Party* (Reading Dog Pr, 1996),
*Sniper Logic, Ohio Rev, Open Places, Midwest Qtly,
Midwest Rev, Rolling Stock, Light Year, Chinook*

Stephanie Stearns   P&W
3980 W Radcliff
Denver, CO 80236
   Pubs: *The Saga of the Sword That Sings & Other
Realities* (Dubless Pr, 1981), *Eldritch Tales*

Roger Steigmeier   P
2770 Moorhead Ave, #204
Boulder, CO 80303
   Pubs: *Light Traveling Dark Traveling Light* (First East
Coast Theater & Pub Co, 1984), *Poet*

Constance E. Studer 🎤 ✈   P&W
1617 Parkside Cir
Lafayette, CO 80026-1967, 303-665-3818
Internet: cstjal@prodigy.net
   Pubs: *The Age of Koestler: Anth* (Practices of the
Wind, 1994), *Birmingham Poetry Rev, Earth's
Daughters, Zone 3*

Ronald Sukenick   W
Univ Colorado, English Dept, Box 226, Boulder, CO
80309, 303-492-7381
   Pubs: *Up, 98.6* (FC 2, 1998, 1994), *Doggy Bag*
(FC2/Black Ice Bks, 1994), *Blown Away* (Sun & Moon
Pr, 1986)

Steve Rasnic Tem   P&W
2500 Irving St
Denver, CO 80211, 303-477-0235
   Pubs: *Excavation* (Avon, 1987), *The Umbral Anth of
Science Fiction Poetry* (Umbral Pr, 1982)

James Tipton   P&W
1742 DS Rd
Glade Park, CO 81523, 970-245-5760
   Pubs: *The Wizard of Is* (Bread & Butter Pr, 1995), *The
Third Coast Anth, Cimarron Rev, Greensboro Rev, High
Plains Literary Rev, American Literary Rev, Writers'
Forum, Pinyon Poetry, Woodnotes, South Dakota Rev,
Nation, Esquire, APR*

Rawdon Tomlinson   P
2020 S Grant
Denver, CO 80210
   Pubs: *Deep Red* (U Pr Florida, 1995), *Spreading the
Word: Anth* (Bench Pr, 1990), *Sewanee Rev,
Commonweal, Kansas Qtly, Poetry NW, SPR, Ohio
Rev, Midwest Qtly*

Bill Tremblay 🎤 ✈   P
3412 Lancaster Dr
Fort Collins, CO 80525-2817, 970-226-0311
Internet: watremblay@aol.com
   Pubs: *The June Rise* (Utah State U Pr, 1994), *A
Gathering of Poets: Anth* (Kent State U Pr, 1993), *Jazz
Poetry Anth* (Indiana U Pr, 1993), *Manoa, Spoon River
Poetry Rev, Connecticut Poetry Rev, High Plains
Literary Rev, Massachusetts Rev, Willow Springs*

Robert von Dassanowsky 🎤 ✈   PP&P
Univ Colorado, Dept of Languages/Cultures, Colorado
Springs, CO 80933-7150, 719-262-3562
Internet: rvondass@mail.uccs.edu
   Pubs: *Telegrams from the Metropole* (U Salzburg,
1999), *Phantom Empires* (Ariadne, 1996), *Verses of a
Marriage* (Event Horizon, 1996), *Osiris, Poesie Europe,
High Performance*
Lang: German

Anne Waldman   PP&P
375 S 45 St
Boulder, CO 80303, 303-444-0202
   Pubs: *Fast Speaking Woman* (City Lights, 1997), *Iovis:
All Is Full of Jove: Bks II & I, A Poem* (Coffee Hse Pr,
1997, 1993), *Kill Or Cure* (Penguin, 1996),
*Conjunctions, Sulfur, City Lights Jrnl, Apex of the M,
Poetry Project Newsletter, APR*

Gail Waldstein, M.D. ✈   P&W
108 Cook St, #308
Denver, CO 80206-5307, 303-321-1137
    Pubs: *Slipstream, Mutant Mule, Sheila-Na-Gig, Inklings,
    Explorations 1998, High Plains Lit Rev, Nimrod,
    Negative Capability, Women: A Jrnl of Liberation*
I.D.: Jewish. Groups: Children, Prisoners

David L. Wann   P&W
PO Box 714
Indian Hills, CO 80454, 303-679-8089
    Pubs: *Log Rhythms* (North Atlantic Bks, 1983), *NYQ,
    Lake Superior Rev, Samisdat*

Marc Weber   P
2 N 24 St
Colorado Springs, CO 80904, 719-634-8010
    Pubs: *Quest* (Lion's Roar, 1989), *Circle of Light* (San
    Marcos, 1976)

Robert Lewis Weeks   P
6767 E Dartmouth Ave
Denver, CO 80224, 303-756-4274
    Pubs: *As a Master of Clouds* (Juniper Pr, 1971), *APR,
    Sewanee Rev, Prairie Schooner, West Branch, Georgia
    Rev, The Qtly, Shenandoah, BPJ*

Thomas A. West, Jr.   P&W
6282 Chimney Rock Trail
Morrison, CO 80465-2151, 303-697-4772
    Pubs: *Writing Under Fire: Anth* (Dell, 1978), *Chiron
    Rev, Open Bone Rev, Wisconsin Rev, Cimarron Rev,
    Four Quarters, Connecticut River Rev, Panhandler, New
    Mexico Qtly Rev, Touchstone, Oxford Mag, Short Story
    Intl, Shorelines, Nebraska Mag, New Renaissance*

Richard Wilmarth ♒ ✈   P
PO Box 2076
Boulder, CO 80306-2076, 303-417-9398
    Pubs: *Alphabetical Order, Voices in the Room* (Dead
    Metaphor Pr, 1998, 1993), *More! Henry Miller Acrostics:
    Anth* (Standish Bks, 1996), *Shiny, Nedge, Napalm
    Health Spa, Lummox Jrnl, Tangents, Fan, Bombay Gin,
    Third Lung Rev, Fell Swoop*

Renate Wood ♒ ✈   P
1900 King Ave
Boulder, CO 80302-8038, 303-447-2796
Internet: rwood38@juno.com
    Pubs: *Patience of Ice* (TriQtly Bks/Northwestern U Pr,
    2000), *Raised Underground, Carnegie Mellon Poetry:
    Anth* (Carnegie Mellon U Pr, 1991, 1993), *APR, TriQtly,
    Ploughshares, NER*

James Yaffe   W
1215 N Cascade
Colorado Springs, CO 80903
    Pubs: *Mom Among the Liars, Mom Doth Murder Sleep,
    Mom Meets Her Maker* (St. Martin's Pr, 1992, 1991,
    1990)

William Zaranka   P&W
Univ Denver, Denver, CO 80110, 303-871-2966
    Pubs: *Blessing* (Wayland Pr, 1988), *Brand-X Anth of
    Fiction, Brand-X Anth of Poetry* (Apple-wood Pr, 1984,
    1983), *Poetry, TriQtly, Prairie Schooner*

CONNECTICUT

Dick Allen ♒ ✈   P
74 Fern Cir
Trumbull, CT 06611-4910, 203-375-1927
Internet: rallen10@snet.net
    Pubs: *Ode to the Cold War: New & Selected Poems*
    (Sarabande Bks, 1997), *The Best American Poetry:
    Anths* (Scribner, 1999, 1998), *Ontario Rev, Gettysburg
    Rev, Boulevard, Poetry, Hudson Rev, Image, American
    Arts Qtly*

Talvikki Ansel   P
PO Box 4
Old Mystic, CT 06372
    Pubs: *My Shining Archipelago* (Yale U Pr 1997)

Dennis Barone ♒ ✈   P&W
Saint Joseph College, 1678 Asylum Ave, West Hartford,
CT 06117, 860-231-5379
Internet: dbarone@sjc.edu
    Pubs: *Temple of the Rat, Separate Objects: Selected
    Poems* (Left Hand Bks, 2000, 1998), *Echoes* (Potes &
    Poets Pr, 1997), *The Returns* (Sun & Moon Pr, 1996),
    Waves of Ice, Waves of Rumor (Zasterle Pr, 1993)

Lou Barrett ♒ ✈   P
40 Meadow View Dr
Westport, CT 06880, 203-227-6384
Internet: louhalprin@aol.com
    Pubs: *Israel Horizons, Midstream, Connecticut River
    Rev*

Wendy Battin   P
15 Rogers Dr
Mystic, CT 06355, 860-572-9323
    Pubs: *Little Apocalypse* (Ashland Poetry Pr, 1997), *In
    the Solar Wind* (Doubleday, 1984), *The Sacred Place:
    Anth* (U Utah Pr, 1996), *Yale Rev, Nation, Gettysburg
    Rev, Threepenny Rev, Poetry, NER*

Paul Beckman   W
PO Box 609
Madison, CT 06443, 203-245-0835
    Pubs: *Come! Meet My Family & Other Stories*
    (Weighted Anchor Pr, 1995), *Cat's Meow! An Anth of
    Cat Tales* (Maine Rhode Pubs, 1996), *The Artful Mind,
    Verve, Maverick Pr, Other Voices, Parting Gifts,
    Northeast Mag*

Ted Bent   W
60 Hinkle Rd
Washington, CT 06793-1001
    Pubs: *The Girl in the Black Raincoat* (Duell, Sloan &
Pearce, 1966), *Massachusetts Rev*

April Bernard 🎙 ✈   P&W
96 Everit Str
New Haven, CT 06511-1321, 203-787-9012
    Pubs: *By Herself* (Graywolf, 2000), *Psalms, Pirate
Jenny* (Norton, 1993, 1990), *Blackbird Bye Bye*
(Random Hse, 1989), *Joyful Noise: Anth* (Little Brown,
1998)

Elaine Bissell   W
10-B Heritage Village
Southbury, CT 06488
    Pubs: *Empire* (Worldwide Library, 1990), *Family
Fortunes* (St. Martin's Pr, 1986), *Let's Keep in Touch*
(Pocket Bks, 1983), *Women Who Wait* (Popular Library,
1979)

Blanche McCrary Boyd   W
Connecticut College, Box 5421, 270 Mohegan Ave, New
London, CT 06320
    Pubs: *The Revolution of Little Girls, The Redneck Way
of Knowledge* (Knopf, 1991, 1981), *VLS, Esquire*

George Bradley   P
82 W Main St
Chester, CT 06412, 203-526-3900
    Pubs: *The Fire Fetched Down, Of the Knowledge of
Good & Evil* (Knopf, 1996, 1991), *Terms to Be Met*
(Yale U Pr, 1986), *New Yorker, Paris Rev*

Brian Butterick   P
31 Friendship St
Willimantic, CT 06226

Jamie Callan 🎙 ✈   W
438 Whitney Ave
New Haven, CT 06511-2349, 203-787-4558
Internet: jamiecatcallan@aol.com
    Pubs: *Story, Missouri Rev, Buzz, American Letters &
Commentary, American Way, Baffler*

Michael Casey 🎙 ✈   P
Yale Univ Press, 92A Yale Sta, New Haven, CT 06520
    Pubs: *The Million Dollar Hole* (Carnegie Mellon, 2001),
Millrat (Adastra, 1996), *Obscenities* (Yale U Pr, 1972),
*College English, TriQtly, Michigan Qtly Rev, Rolling
Stone, Panhandler, America, Salmagundi, Ohio Rev*

Ina B. Chadwick   P
2 Redcoat Rd
Westport, CT 06880, 203-221-0655
    Pubs: *Considerate Gestures of Love* (Greens Farms Pr,
1979), *Jewish Forward, Namat Woman, New York
Times, Antioch Rev*

David Chura   P
477 Newtown Turnpike
Redding, CT 06896-2017
Internet: dchura@ntplx.net
    Pubs: *Essential Love: Anth* (Grayson Bks/Poetworks,
2000), *Queer Dharma: Anth* (Gay Sunshine Pr, 1998),
*Adirondack, Turning Wheel, English Jrnl, Blueline,
Connecticut River Rev, Embers, Earth's Daughters*

Gene Coggshall   W
The Perkin-Elmer Corp M/S 887, 100 Wooster Heights Rd,
Danbury, CT 06810, 203-744-4000

Stanley I. Cohen   W
322 Pine Tree Dr
Orange, CT 06477, 203-795-4058
    Pubs: *Angel Face* (St. Martin's Pr, 1982), *330 Park*
(Putnam, 1977), *Year's Best Mystery & Suspense
Stories: Anth* (Walker, 1991), *Best Detective Stories of
the Year: Anth* (Dutton, 1975), *Alfred Hitchcock's
Mystery, Ellery Queen's Mystery*

James Coleman   W
Three Rivers C-T College, 7 Mahan Dr, English Dept,
Norwich, CT 06360, 860-823-2896
    Pubs: *South Dakota Rev, Elkhorn Rev, December,
Centennial Rev, St. Andrews Rev, Red Fox Rev,
Information*

Martha Collins 🎙 ✈   P&W
c/o Space, 59 Prospect St, Bloomfield, CT 06002
Internet: martha.collins@oberlin.edu
    Pubs: *Some Things Words Can Do* (Sheep Meadow,
1998), *A History of Small Life on A Windy Planet* (U
Georgia Pr, 1993), *The Arrangement of Space*
(Peregrine Smith, 1991)

Leo Connellan   P
PO Box 224
Hanover, CT 06350, 860-822-6884
    Pubs: *Short Poems-City Poems 1944-1998* (Hanover Pr,
1999), *Maine Poems* (Blackberry Pr, 1999),
Provincetown & Other Poems (Curbstone Pr, 1995),
The Clear Blue Lobster–Water Country (HBJ, 1985),
Harper's, Georgia Rev, NER, Chelsea, Nation

Tony Connor   W
44 Brainerd Ave
Middletown, CT 06457, 860-344-0815
    Pubs: *Metamorphic Adventures, Spirits of the Place*
(Anvil Poetry Pr, 1996, 1986), *Best American Short
Plays 1992-93* (Applause Theatre Bks, 1993)

Robert Cording 🎙 ✈   P
100 Shields Rd
Woodstock, CT 06281-2820, 860-974-0874
    Pubs: *Life-List* (Ohio State U Pr, 1988), *What Binds Us
to This World* (Copper Beech, 1991), *Heavy Grace*
(Alice James, 1996), *Poetry, New Yorker, Paris Rev,
NER, Southern Rev*

Charlotte Garrett Currier ♀ ✈   P
12 Long Hill Farm
Guilford, CT 06437, 203-453-5472
Internet: ccurrier@cshore.com
  Pubs: *Not to Look Back* (CD; w/D. Currier), *Poem Box*
(Trefoil Arts, 1998, 1993), *Presences* (The Pr of Night
Owl, 1977), *Southern Rev, Southern Humanities Rev*
Groups: Seniors, Teenagers

David Curtis   P
126 Ardmore Rd
Milford, CT 06460, 203-874-5102
  Pubs: *Update from Pahrump* (Wyndam Hall, 1992),
*Four Quarters, Dalhousie Rev, Descant, The Writer,
Poem, Pegasus Rev, Potato Eyes, Inlet*

Cortney Davis ♀ ✈   P
PO Box 678
West Redding, CT 06896-0678
  Pubs: *Details of Flesh* (Calyx Bks, 1997), *The Body
Flute* (Adastra Pr, 1994), *Between the Heartbeats: Anth*
(U Iowa Pr, 1995), *Hudson Rev, Crazyhorse, Poetry
East, Witness, Prairie Schooner, Hanging Loose, Poetry,
Ontario Rev*

Ellen Kitzes Delfiner ♀ ✈   P
1 Strawberry Hill Ct #6J
Stamford, CT 06902-2531
Internet: eskd@juno.com
  Pubs: *Response, Art Times, New Authors Jrnl, Jam
Today, Treasure House, Aura, Slant*

Concetta Ciccozzi Doucette ♀ ✈   P&W
2799 Ellington Rd
South Windsor, CT 06074-1703, 860-644-2352
  Pubs: *Footwork: Anth* (Passaic County Community
College, 1995), *AIM, Italian Americana, Beanfeast,
Mediphors, Apostrophe, Women's Words*

Franz Douskey ♀ ✈   P
50 Ives St
Mount Carmel, CT 06518-2202, 203-248-4615
Internet: inwalkedlike@yahoo.com
  Pubs: *Archaeological Nights* (Pharos Bks, 1982),
*Yankee, Nation, Rolling Stone, Die Hard, Colorado Qtly,
Carolina Qtly, Cavalier, Yellow Silk, Colorado Qtly,
NYQ, New Yorker, Georgia Rev, Minnesota Rev*

Johanna Drucker   W
324 Yale Ave
New Haven, CT 06515
  Pubs: *Simulant Portrait, History of the/my World*
(Druckwerk, 1990, 1990), *Italy* (The Figures Pr, 1980),
Big Allis, o.blek, Generator, Raddle Moon

Russell Edson ♀ ✈   P&W
29 Ridgeley St
Darien, CT 06820-4110, 203-655-1575
  Pubs: *The Tormented Mirror* (U Pittsburgh Pr, 2001),
The Tunnel (Oberlin College Pr, 1994), *The Song of
Percival Peacock* (Coffee Hse Pr, 1992)

Resurreccion Espinosa ♀ ✈   P&W
265 Gardner Ave
New London, CT 06320, 860-443-8703
  Pubs: *Bilingual Rev, INTI, Teatra*
Lang: Spanish. I.D.: Hispanic. Groups: Children, Hispanic

James Finnegan ♀ ✈   P
18 Woodrow St
West Hartford, CT 06107, 860-521-0358
  Pubs: *Poetry NW, Shenandoah, Tar River Poetry,
Southern Rev, Chelsea, Ploughshares, Poetry East,
Virginia Qtly Rev, Willow Springs*

Henry George Fischer ♀ ✈   P
29 Mauweehoo Hill
Sherman, CT 06784-2312, 860-354-2719
  Pubs: *Light & Night & the Half-Light* (Pocahontas Pr,
1999), *More Timely Rhymes, Timely Rhymes from the
Sherman Sentinel* (Singular Speech Pr, 1996, 1993),
Treasury of Light Verse: Anth (Random Hse, 1995),
Light, Pivot, Verbatim, Lyric, Sparrow, ELF

Eleni Fourtouni   P
1218 Forest Rd
New Haven, CT 06515, 203-397-3902
  Pubs: *Greek Women in Resistance, Watch the Flame*
(Thelphini Pr, 1985, 1983)

Vernon Frazer ♀ ✈   PP&P&W
132 Woodycrest Dr
East Hartford, CT 06118, 860-569-3101
Internet: http://members.home.net/vfrazer
  Pubs: *Demolition Fedora, Free Fall* (Potes & Poets,
1999, 1999), *Stay Tuned to This Channel, Sing Me
One Song of Evolution* (Beneath the Underground,
1999, 1998), *Demon Dance* (Nude Beach, 1995),
Massacre, Plain Brown Wrapper, Knitting Factory

William T. Freeman   P
205 Orange St
Waterbury, CT 06704, 203-753-7743
  Pubs: *Obsidian, Greenfield Rev, Pudding, Parnassus,
Laurels*

Jim Furlong   W
57 Fishtown Ln
Mystic, CT 06355-2007, 860-572-4186
  Pubs: *Local Action* (Cozy Detective Mystery Mag,
1999), *Literature of Work: Anth* (U Phoenix Pr, 1991),
Licking River Rev, Palo Alto Rev

Margaret Gibson 🎙 ✈   P
152 Watson Rd
Preston, CT 06365-8837, 860-886-1777
Internet: margibson@juno.com
   Pubs: *Earth Elegy, The Vigil, Out in the Open,
   Memories of the Future, Long Walks in the Afternoon*
   (LSU Pr, 1997, 1993, 1989, 1986, 1982), *Southern
   Rev, Georgia Rev, Shenandoah, Iowa Rev, Gettysburg
   Rev*

John Gilmore   P
c/o Walter Pitkin, 11 Oakwood Dr, Weston, CT 06883,
203-227-3684

Jody Gladding   P
Yale Univ Pr, PO Box 209040, New Haven, CT
06520-9040, 203-432-0960
   Pubs: *Stone Crop* (Yale U Pr, 1995), *Best American
   Poetry: Anth* (S&S, 1995), *Paris Rev, Wilderness, Agni,
   Poetry NW, Yale Rev*

Ruth Good   P
119 Old Rd
Westport, CT 06880
   Pubs: *SPR, Literary Rev, Carleton Miscellany, Prairie
   Schooner, Chariton Rev*

Antoni Gronowicz   P&W
128 Brookmoor Rd
Avon, CT 06001
   Pubs: *God's Broker* (Richardson & Snyder, 1984), *An
   Orange Full of Dreams* (Dodd, Mead, 1973)

Jayseth Guberman 🎙 ✈   P
PO Box 270357
West Hartford, CT 06127-0357
   Pubs: *Voices Israel, Martyrdom & Resistance, European
   Judaism, Rashi, Prophetic Voices, Poet, Black Buzzard
   Rev, Jewish Spectator*
I.D.: Jewish

Joan Joffe Hall   P&W
64 Birchwood Heights
Storrs, CT 06268
   Pubs: *Summer Heat: Three Stories* (Kutenai Pr, 1991),
   Romance & Capitalism at the Movies (Alice James Bks,
   1985), *Kansas Qtly, Alaska Qtly, North Dakota Qtly,
   Fiction Intl*

Jay Halpern   W
58 Jackson Cove Rd
Oxford, CT 06478, 203-888-4976
   Pubs: *The Jade Unicorn* (Macmillan, 1979), *Icarus,
   Hobo Jungle, Noiseless Spider, Tapestry, Enigma*

Richard F. Harteis   P&W
337 Kitemaug Rd
Uncasville, CT 06382, 860-848-8486
   Pubs: *Keeping Heart* (Orpheus Hse, 1996), *Marathon*
   (Norton, 1989), *Internal Geography, Window on the
   Black Sea: Anth* (Carnegie Mellon U Pr, 1987, 1992),
   Virginia Rev, Ploughshares, Seneca Rev, New Letters

Dolores Hayden 🎙 ✈   P
125 Prospect Ave
Guilford, CT 06437-3114
Internet: dolores.hayden@yale.edu
   Pubs: *Playing House* (Robert Barth, 1998), *Yale Rev,
   Michigan Qtly Rev, Witness, Poetry NW, Radcliffe Qtly,
   Formalist, Landscape Jrnl*
Groups: Schools, Visual Arts

Hank Heifetz 🎙 ✈   W
548 Orange St #406
New Haven, CT 06511-3866, 203-865-8801
   Pubs: *The Four Hundred Songs of War & Wisdom*
   (w/G.L. Hart; Columbia U Pr, 1999), *The Origin of the
   Young God, For the Lord of the Animals* (U California
   Pr, 1990, 1987), *Where Are the Stars in New York?*
   (Dutton, 1973), *Evergreen Rev, VLS*
Lang: Spanish

Peggy Heinrich 🎙 ✈   P
625 Gilman St
Bridgeport, CT 06605-3608, 203-333-3938
Internet: pheinrich@gateway.net
   Pubs: *Sharing the Woods* (Old Sandal Pr, 1992), *A
   Patch of Grass* (High/Coo Pr, 1984), *Negative
   Capability, Texas Rev, Blue Unicorn, Rio Grande Rev,
   Passager*

Madeleine Hennessy   P
70 Puritan Rd
Trumbull, CT 06611, 203-377-3971
   Pubs: *Pavor Nocturnus* (Washout Pub Co, 1979),
   *Yankee, Connecticut River Rev, Greenfield Rev, NYQ,
   Groundswell*

E. Ward Herlands 🎙   P
179 Fox Ridge Rd
Stamford, CT 06903, 203-322-3811
   Pubs: *Literature: Introduction to Poetry: Anth, Reading
   Fiction, Poetry, Drama & the Essay: Anth,* (McGraw-Hill,
   2000, 1998), *Prairie Schooner, Prose Poem: An Intl
   Jrnl, New York Times, Pittsburgh Qtly*

Pati Hill   P&W
20 Grand St
Stonington, CT 06378, 203-535-1747

Barbara Holder P
55 Gallow Hill Rd
Redding, CT 06896, 203-938-4043
  Pubs: *Literature 4th Ed.: Anth, Modern American Poets: Voices & Visions: Anth* (McGraw-Hill 1998, 1993), *Writing Through Literature: Anth* (Prentice Hall Bks, 1995), *Slow Dancer, Wind, Earth's Daughters, Footwork, Poetic Justice, Kentucky Poetry Rev*

David Holdt P
Watkinson School, 180 Bloomfield Ave, Hartford, CT 06105-1096, 860-236-5618
  Pubs: *In the Place of the Long River: Anth* (Blue Moon Pr, 1996), *River of Dreams: Anth* (Glover, 1990), *Northeast, Spitball, Stone Country, Amelia*

John Hollander ● ✈ P
Yale Univ, English Dept PO Box 208302, New Haven, CT 06520-8302, 203-432-2231
Internet: john.hollander@yale.edu
  Pubs: *Figurehead, Selected Poetry, Tesserae, Harp Lake* (Knopf, 1999, 1993, 1993, 1988), *Melodious Guile* (Yale U Pr, 1988), *Blue Wine* (Hopkins, 1979)

Donald Honig W
2322 Cromwell Gdns
Cromwell, CT 06416

Peyton Houston P
11 Indian Chase Dr
Greenwich, CT 06830
  Pubs: *The Changes/Orders/Becomings* (Jargon Society, 1990), *Paris Rev, Open Places, Hudson Rev*

Susan Howe P
115 New Quarry Rd
Guilford, CT 06437
  Pubs: *The Nonconformist's Memorial* (New Directions, 1993), *Singularities* (Wesleyan, 1990), *American Poetry Since 1950: Anth* (Marsilio, 1993)

Bob Jacob ● ✈ P
PO Box 1133
Farmington, CT 06034-1133, 860-677-0606
  Pubs: *The Day Seamus Heaney Kissed My Cheek in Dublin* (The Spirit That Moves Us Pr, 2000), *Café Rev*

Gray Jacobik ● ✈ P
Eastern Connecticut State Univ, English Dept, Willimantic, CT 06226, 860-963-0440
Internet: grayj@snet.net
  Pubs: *The Surface of Last Scattering* (Texas Rev Pr, 1999), *The Double Task* (U Mass Pr, 1998), *The Beach Book* (Sarabande, 1999), *The Best American Poetry: Anths* (Scribner, 1999, 1997), *Prairie Schooner, Ploughshares, Georgia Rev, NAR, Alaska Qtly Rev*

Sharon Ann Jaeger ● ✈ P
149 Water St #35
Norwalk, CT 06854
Internet: jaeger@goplay.com
  Pubs: *The Chain of Dead Desire, Filaments of Affinity* (Park Slope Edtns, 1990, 1989), *X-Connect*
Lang: German

Leland Jamieson, Jr. ● P
86 Ledgewood Rd
West Hartford, CT 06107-3734, 860-521-6359
Internet: leejamieson@erols.com
  Pubs: *Artword Qtly, Midwest Poetry Rev, Rattle, Sidewalks, Spillway, Wise Woman's Garden, Aurorean, Avocet, California Qtly, Coffee & Chicory, Inlet, Kansas*

John Jurkowski W
6 Walnut Ridge Rd
New Fairfield, CT 06812-0214, 203-746-7673
  Pubs: *New Yorker, Redbook, Shenandoah, QRL, NAR*

Susan A. Katz ● ✈ P
121 Painter Ridge Rd
Washington Depot, CT 06793-1710, 860-868-3549
  Pubs: *Two Halves of the Same Silence* (Confluence Pr, 1985), *Life on the Line: Anth* (Negative Capability Pr, 1992), *When I Am an Old Woman I Shall Wear Purple: Anth* (Papier-Mache Pr, 1991)
Groups: Teachers

Susan Baumann Kinsolving P
PO Box 175
Bridgewater, CT 06752-0175
  Pubs: *Dailies & Rushes* (Grove Pr, 1999), *Among Flowers* (Clarkson Potter/Random Hse, 1993), *Paris Rev, Grand Street, Kansas Qtly, Western Humanities Rev, New Republic, Nation, Harvard Mag, BPJ, Antioch Rev*

Binnie Klein P
142 E Rock Rd
New Haven, CT 06511, 203-781-8161
  Pubs: *Twilight Zones* (Co-author; U California Pr, 1997), *Sequoia, Dreamworks, Stone Country, Panache, Minnesota Rev, Confrontation, Center, Etcetera*

Kenneth M. Koprowski P
340 Bayberrie Dr
Stamford, CT 06902

Eileen Kostiner ● P
19 Thompson Rd
Storrs, CT 06268, 860-429-6983
  Pubs: *Love's Other Face, Poetry Like Bread: Anth* (Curbstone Pr, 1982, 1994), *MacGuffin, Nostalgia, SPR, Mediphors, Labyris, Creative Woman, Paintbrush, Embers*

Norman Kraeft   P
86 Bellamy Ln
Bethlehem, CT 06751-1203, 203-266-5113
  Pubs: *The Lyric, Sparrow, Orbis, Prairie Schooner,
  Connecticut River Rev, Bogg: An Anglo-American Jrnl,
  Pivot, Blue Unicorn*

Janet Krauss ♀   P
585 Gilman St
Bridgeport, CT 06605-3634, 203-333-7779
  Pubs: *A Pamphlet of Poems* (Palanquin Pr, 1995),
  *American Goat, Painted Hills, Green Hills Literary
  Lantern, Blue Buildings, Amaranth, California State
  Poetry Society, MacGuffin, Jabberwok, Rockhurst Rev,
  Dickinson Rev*
Groups: Children, Libraries

Philip Watson Kuepper   P&W
233 Bouton St W
Stamford, CT 06807-1322, 203-968-0165
  Pubs: *American Poetry Annual: Anth* (Amherst Soc,
  1997, 1996, 1995), *Connecticut Poets on AIDS: Anth*
  (Andrew Mountain Pr, 1996), *Currents*

Ken Kuhlken ♀ ✈   W
Donald Gastwirth & Associates, 265 College St, Suite
10-N,, New Haven, CT 06510
Internet: members.fortunecity.com/kenkuhlken
  Pubs: *The Angel Gang, The Venus Deal, The Loud
  Adios* (St. Martin's, 1994, 1992, 1991), *Midheaven*
  (Viking, 1980), *Crime Through Time: Anth* (Berkeley,
  1998), *Esquire, Puerto del Sol, Kansas Qtly, Colorado
  Rev, Mss.*

Helen Lawson   P&W
80 Wethersfield Ave, Apt 3
Hartford, CT 06114
  Pubs: *Live Me a River, Women As I Know Them* (Blue
  Spruce Pr, 1981, 1978), *Bronte Street, Caprice*

Rena Lee   P
179 Ledge Dr
Torrington, CT 06790
  Pubs: *Present Tense, Pulp, Bitterroot, Poet Lore, Shofar*

Ann Z. Leventhal ♀ ✈   P&W
19 Woodside Cir
Hartford, CT 06105-1120
Internet: azlhdl@ct2.nai.net
  Pubs: *Life-Lines* (Magic Circle Pr, 1986), *Publishers
  Weekly, Passages North, Cottonwood, Remark, Pacific
  Rev, Lake Effect, Georgia Rev, Other Voices, South
  Dakota Rev, Mississippi Rev*

Leonard C. Lewin   W
6 Long Hill Farm
Guilford, CT 06437
  Pubs: *Triage, Report from Iron Mountain* (Dial, 1972,
  1967), *Harper's, Nation, New York Times*

Pam Lewis   W
128 Courtyard Ln
Storrs Mansfield, CT 06250
  Pubs: *Wee Girls* (Spinifex, 1997), *New Yorker, Puerto
  del Sol, Intro 14*

David Low   W
276 Court St, #105
Middletown, CT 06457
  Pubs: *American Families: Anth* (NAL, 1989),
  Ploughshares

Rick Lyon   P
65 Main St, #17
Ivoryton, CT 06442, 860-767-0628
  Pubs: *Bell 8* (BOA Edtns, 1994), *Missouri Rev, Partisan
  Rev, Kansas Qtly, Agni, Massachusetts Rev, Nation,
  Tar River Poetry, APR, Ironwood, Colorado Rev*

Chopeta C. Lyons ♀   W
198 Jared Sparks Rd
West Willington, CT 06279-1406
  Pubs: *Northeast, Primavera, Negative Capability, Aura*

Robin Magowan ♀ ✈   P
PO Box 511
Salisbury, CT 06068, 860-435-9586
  Pubs: *Lilac Cigarette in a Wish Cathedral* (U South
  Carolina Pr, 1998), *Margin, Paris Rev, Yale Rev*

Saul Maloff   W
659-B Heritage Village
Southbury, CT 06488, 203-264-4885
  Pubs: *Heartland, Happy Families* (Scribner, 1973, 1969),
  New York Times Book Rev, Nation

Alice Mattison ♀ ✈   P&W
15 Anderson St
New Haven, CT 06511, 203-624-0332
  Pubs: *The Book Borrower, Men Giving Money, Women
  Yelling, Hilda & Pearl, The Flight of Andy Burns*
  (Morrow, 1999, 1997, 1995, 1993), *New Yorker, NER,
  NAR, Boston Rev, Shenandoah, Grand Street, Glimmer
  Train, Boulevard, Southern Humanities Rev*
I.D.: Jewish. Groups: College/Univ

Carole Spearin McCauley ♀ ✈   P&W
23 Buena Vista Dr
Greenwich, CT 06831-4210, 203-531-6192
Internet: mccaulea@concentric.net
  Pubs: *Cold Steal, Happenthing in Travel On* (Women's
  Pr, 1991, 1990), *Nightshade Reader: Anth* (Nightshade
  Pr, 1995), *Baba Yaga: Anth* (Woman of Wands, 1995),
  *Whispering Willows, Timber Creek Rev, Heaven Bone,
  Murderous Intent, Vermont, Ink*

J. D. McClatchy P
The Yale Review, Box 208243, New Haven, CT
06520-8243, 203-432-0499
   Pubs: *Ten Commandments, The Rest of the Way*
   (Knopf, 1998, 1990), *Stars Principal* (Macmillan, 1986),
   Scenes from Another Life (Braziller, 1981), *Vintage
   Book of Contemporary American Poetry: Anth* (Vintage,
   1990)

Kaye McDonough P
236 Santa Fe Ave
Hamden, CT 06517
   Pubs: *The Stiffest of the Corpse: An Exquisite Corpse
   Reader: Anth, City Lights Anth* (City Lights Bks, 1989,
   1974), *City Lights, Beatitude, Vagabond Press*

Rennie McQuilkin ♣ ✈ P
21 Goodrich Rd
Simsbury, CT 06070-1804, 860-658-1728
Internet: RMcQuil@juno.com
   Pubs: *We All Fall Down* (Swallow's Tale, 1988), *Poetry,
   Yale Rev, Southern Rev, Poetry NW, Hudson Rev,
   Atlantic*

Angela M. Mendez P
PO Box 26401
West Haven, CT 06516, 203-435-1157
   Pubs: *The Connecticut River Rev, Afterthoughts, Devil
   Blossoms, Lunar Offensive Pr*

Christopher Merrill ♣ ✈ P&W
PO Box 172
East Woodstock, CT 06244-0172, 860-963-2339
Internet: cmerrill@snet.net
   Pubs: *Watch Fire* (White Pine Pr, 1994), *The Grass of
   Another Country* (H Holt, 1993), *Paris Rev, Nation,
   Sierra, APR*

David L. Meth ♣ ✈ P
Writers' Productions, PO Box 630, Westport, CT
06881-0630, 203-227-8199
   Pubs: *American Pen, Confrontation, Poet Lore, Valley
   Views, Lake Superior Rev, Jeopardy*

Barbara Milton W
32 Elm St
Milford, CT 06460
   Pubs: *A Small Cartoon* (Wordbeat Pr, 1983), *Paris Rev,
   NAR, Apalachee Qtly*

Honor Moore ♣ ✈ P
PO Box 305
Kent, CT 06757-0305, 860-927-3418
Internet: honorm@aol.com
   Pubs: *The White Blackbird* (Penguin, 1997), *Memoir*
   (Chicory Blue, 1988), *A Formal Feeling Comes: Anth*
   (Story Line Pr, 1994), *New Yorker, Seneca Rev, Paris
   Rev, APR*
Groups: Women

H. L. Mountzoures W
29 Old Black Point Rd
Niantic, CT 06357-2815
   Pubs: *The Bridge, The Empire of Things* (Scribner,
   1972, 1968), *New Yorker, Yankee, Redbook, Atlantic*

Bryanne Nanfito ♣ ✈ P
4 S Broad St, Unit One
Meriden, CT 06450, 203-634-6675
   Pubs: *Greenfield Rev, NYQ, Kansas Qtly*

Peter Neill W
PO Box 3131
Stony Creek, CT 06405-1731, 203-488-3424
Internet: pneill@compuserve.com
   Pubs: *Acoma* (Leete's Island Bks, 1978), *Mock Turtle
   Soup* (Viking/Grossman, 1972), *A Time Piece*
   (Grossman, 1970)

Gunilla B. Norris P
PO Box 337
Mystic, CT 06355-0337, 203-264-6043
   Pubs: *Journeying in Place, Sharing Silence, Becoming
   Bread, Being Home* (Bell Tower Bks, 1994, 1994, 1992,
   1991), *Learning from the Angel* (Lotus, 1985)

Hugh Ogden ♣ ✈ P
331 Chestnut Hill Rd
Glastonbury, CT 06033, 203-657-3293
Internet: Hugh.Ogden@TrinColl.edu
   Pubs: *Gift, Two Roads & This Spring* (CRS OutLoud
   Bks, 1998, 1993), *Natural Things, Windfalls* (Andrew
   Mountain Pr, 1998, 1996), *New Letters, Poetry NW,
   North Dakota Qtly, Malahat Rev*

Jo Anna O'Keefe P
Knight St
Norwalk, CT 06856, 203-847-4543
   Pubs: *Come to the Garden* (C. R. Gibson Co, 1992),
   Christian Living

Maureen A. Owen ♣ ✈ P
109 Dunk Rock Rd
Guilford, CT 06437, 203-453-1921
Internet: pomowen@ix.netcom.com
   Pubs: *American Rush: Selected Poems, Moving
   Borders: Anth* (Talisman Hse Pub, 1998, 1998),
   Untapped Maps (Potes & Poets Pr, 1993), *Imaginary
   Income* (Hanging Loose Pr, 1992), *Five Fingers Rev,
   o.blek, Long News in the Short Century, NAW, 6ix,
   Hanging Loose*

Joan Pond W
277 Long Mtn
New Milford, CT 06776
   Pubs: *Reflections, Rose Garden* (Life-Link Bks, 1990,
   1989)

Joseph Raffa P
Box 414
Glastonbury, CT 06033, 203-659-3424
 Pubs: *No Archaeologist, Death Depends on Our Dark Silence* (John Brown Pr, 1987, 1986), *NYQ, Crosscurrents, Samisdat, Wisconsin Rev, Windless Orchard*

Charles Rafferty ♪ ✦ P
6 Longview Rd
Sandy Hook, CT 06482-1304, 203-270-3438
Internet: cmrafferty@usa.net
 Pubs: *The Man on the Tower* (U Arkansas Pr, 1995)
Groups: College/Univ

Kit Reed ♪ ✦ W
45 Lawn Ave
Middletown, CT 06457, 212-265-7330
Internet: www.focus-consulting.co.uk/kreed/reed.html
 Pubs: *@expectations* (Forge, 2000), *Seven for the Apocalypse, Weird Women, Wired Women* (Wesleyan U Pr, 1999, 1998), *J. Eden* (U Pr of New England, 1996), *Twice Burned, Gone* (Little, Brown, 1993, 1992), *Thief of Lives & Other Stories* (U Missouri Pr, 1992)

Dr. Nicholas M. Rinaldi ♪ ✦ P&W
Fairfield Univ, English Dept, Fairfield, CT 06430, 203-254-4000
Internet: nrinaldi01@snet.net
 Pubs: *The Jukebox Queen of Malta* (S&S, 1999), *Bridge Fall Down* (St. Martin's, 1985)

Becky Rodia ♪ P
PO Box 184
Trumbull, CT 06611-0164, 203-452-9652
Internet: brodyjean@aol.com
 Pubs: *Another Fire* (Adastra Pr, 1997), *Indiana Rev, Weber Studies, Laurel Rev, Cream City Rev, Poet Lore, Georgetown Rev*

Lawrence Russ ♪ ✦ P
33 Westford Dr
Southport, CT 06490-1444, 860-808-5090
Internet: lawrencer@snet.net
 Pubs: *Atlanta Rev, NYQ, Yankee, Nation, Image, Virginia Qtly Rev, Iowa Rev, Parabola, Chelsea*

Mark Saba P&W
144 Woodlawn St
Hamden, CT 06517, 203-230-8365
 Pubs: *Essential Love: Anth* (Poetworks, 2000), *Elvis in Oz: Anth* (U Pr Virginia, 1992), *Artemis, Connecticut River Rev, Confrontation, Jeopardy, Kentucky Poetry Rev, Larcom Rev, The Ledge, MacGuffin, Mildred, Permafrost, South Dakota Rev*

Domenic Sammarco P
54 Toquam Rd
New Canaan, CT 06840-3926, 203-866-3372
Internet: ticovismar@aol.com
 Pubs: *Wings* (Scholastic Bks, 1984), *Poem, The End of the Journey, American Scholar*

Maria Sassi ♪ ✦ P
11 Paxton Rd
West Hartford, CT 06107-3325, 860-521-2095
 Pubs: *Rooted in Stars* (Singular Speech Pr, 1998), *What I See* (Hanover Pr, 1997), *Trinity Rev, Connecticut River Rev, Padre, Italian-Americana, Blue Unicorn, Pivot*
Groups: Children, Seniors

Leslie Scalapino P
Wesleyan Univ Press, 110 Mt Vernon St, Middleton, CT 06459-0433
 Pubs: *The Return of Painting* (Talisman Hse Pub, 1997), *The Front Matter Dead Souls* (Wesleyan U Pr, 1996), *Crowd & Not Evening Or Light, What Is the Inside What Is Outside?: Anth* (O Bks, 1992, 1991), *How Phenomena Appear to Unfold* (Potes & Poets, 1990)

Jeffrey Schwartz P
289 Woodridge Ave
Fairfield, CT 06430
 Pubs: *Contending with the Dark* (Alice James Bks, 1978), *Pennsylvania Rev, Yankee, Connecticut Poetry Rev*

James R. Scrimgeour P
36 Caldwell Dr
New Milford, CT 06776
 Pubs: *Dikel, Your Hands* (Spoon River, 1979), *Margins, Wormwood Rev, Oyez, Cave, Aspect, Zahir*

Thalia Selz W
52 Coolidge St
Hartford, CT 06106-3720, 860-527-4141
 Pubs: *American Fiction 3: Anth* (Birch Lane, 1992), *Oktoberfest V: Anth* (Druid Pr, 1990), *Antaeus, Partisan Rev, Missouri Rev, New Letters, Chicago, Kansas Qtly*

Joan Shapiro P
17 Fairview Dr/Box 752
South Windsor, CT 06074, 203-644-2311
 Pubs: *The Puppet Lady: Poems, Coloring Book: Poems* (Blue Spruce, 1982, 1978)

Vivian Shipley ♪ ✦ P
Southern Connecticut Univ, 501 Crescent St, New Haven, CT 06515, 203-392-6737
 Pubs: *Fair Haven, Devil's Lane* (Negative Capability, 2000, 1996), *Echo & Anger, Still* (Louisiana Literature Pr, 2000), *Crazy Quilt* (Hanover Pr, 1999), *How Many Stories* (U South Carolina-Aiken, 1997), *American Scholar, Southern Rev, New Letters*

Joan Seliger Sidney 🎤 ✈ P
74 Lynwood Rd
Storrs, CT 06268-2012, 860-429-7271
Internet: jsidney@juno.com
    Pubs: *The Way the Past Comes Back* (Kutenai Pr,
1991), *Deep Between the Rocks* (Andrew Mountain Pr,
1985), *Beyond Lament: Anth* (Northwestern U Pr,
1998), *Her Face in the Mirror: Anth* (Beacon Pr, 1994),
Israel Horizons, Massachusetts Rev, Michigan Qtly Rev
Groups: Adults, Teenagers

Sharyn Jeanne Skeeter P&W
PO Box 16819
Stamford, CT 06905
    Pubs: *In Search of Color Everywhere: Anth* (Stewart,
Tabori & Chang, 1994), *Connecticut River Rev, Cafe
Rev, Obsidian, Callaloo, Greenfield Rev, Fiction*

Rod Steier P
39 Pheasant Hill Dr
West Hartford, CT 06107
    Pubs: *28 Days to Satori, Kevin* (Bartholomew's Cobble,
1976, 1975)

Jonathan Stolzenberg P
31 Woodland St #11R
Hartford, CT 06105, 860-246-8374
    Pubs: *Notre Dame Rev, Half Tones to Jubilee, Eureka
Literary Magazine, Licking River Rev, Louisville Rev,
Gulf Stream Magazine, Mangrove, Texas Rev*

William Styron W
Rucum Rd
Roxbury, CT 06783
    Pubs: *This Quiet Dust, Sophie's Choice* (Random Hse,
1982, 1979)

William Swarts P
27 Wright St
Westport, CT 06880-9113, 203-259-7566
    Pubs: *Treehouse of the Mind* (Andrew Mountain Pr,
1981), *Small Pond, Embers, Outerbridge, Poets On*

Wally Swist P
44 Capen St
Windsor, CT 06095-3109, 860-688-0174
    Pubs: *Veils of the Divine* (Hanover Pr, 2001), *The
White Rose* (Timberline Pr, 2000), *The New Life* (Plinth
Bks, 1998), *Intimate Kisses: Anth* (New World Library,
2001), *Stories from Where We Live: Anth* (Milkweed
Edtns, 2000)

Lisa C. Taylor 🎤 ✈ P
PO Box 484
Mansfield Center, CT 06250
Internet: taylor@neca.com
    Pubs: *Falling Open* (Alpha Beat Pr, 1994), *Written with
a Spoon: Anth* (Sherman Asher Publishing, 1995), *Cape
Rock, Connecticut River Rev, Midwest Rev, Xanadu*
Groups: Seniors, Children

Randeane Tetu 🎤 ✈ W
41 Old Turnpike Rd
Haddam, CT 06438, 860-345-4226
    Pubs: *Flying Horses, Secret Souls, Merle's & Marilyn's
Mink Ranch, When I Am an Old Woman I Shall Wear
Purple: Anth* (Papier-Mache Pr, 1997, 1991, 1987),
Massachusetts Rev, Minnesota Rev

Sue Ellen Thompson 🎤 ✈ P
PO Box 326
Mystic, CT 06355-0326, 860-536-0215
Internet: iambic@aol.com
    Pubs: *The Leaving: New & Selected* (Autumn Hse Pr,
2001), *The Wedding Boat* (Owl Creek Pr, 1995), *This
Body of Silk* (Northeastern U Pr, 1986)

Jessica Treat 🎤 ✈ W
PO Box 752
Lakeville, CT 06039, 860-435-1259
Internet: nw_treat@commnet.edu
    Pubs: *Not a Chance* (Fiction Collective 2, 2000), *A
Robber in the House* (Coffee Hse Pr, 1993), *Wildcards:
Anth* (Virago, 1999), *Green Mountains Rev, Ms., Epoch,
Black Warrior Rev, Qtly West, Seattle Rev, Dominion
Rev*
Lang: Spanish. Groups: Women, Teenagers

Edwina Trentham 🎤 ✈ P
Asnuntuck Community Colllege, 170 Elm St, Enfield, CT
06082, 860-253-3103
Internet: as_et@commnet.edu
    Pubs: *Atomic Ghost: Anth* (Coffee Hse Pr, 1995), *Pivot,
Yankee Mag, Massachusetts Rev, Sun, Embers,
Dickinson Rev, Harvard Mag, American Voice, New
Virginia Rev*

Peter J. Ulisse P
65 Rivercliff Dr
Devon, CT 06460-5025, 203-874-0618
    Pubs: *Wings & Roots* (Icarus Pr, 1985), *Poet, Poets
On, Poetry South, Wayfarers, Connecticut River Rev*

Katrina Van Tassel P
6 Broad St
Guilford, CT 06437, 203-453-2328
    Pubs: *Trundlewheel* (Andrew Mountain Pr, 1981),
*Yankee, Embers, Red Fox Rev, Stone Country,
Footworks*

Theresa C. Vara 🎤 P
56 Shane Dr
Southbury, CT 06488
    Pubs: *Poeti Italo-Americani/Italian-American Poets: Anth*
(Italbooks, 1992), *Reflections of a County: Anth* (White
Pond Center, 1982), *Earthwise, Beanfeast*
Groups: Christian, Women

Patricia Volk 🎤 ✈   W
Box 295
Sharon, CT 06069
    Pubs: *All It Takes* (Atheneum, 1990), *The Yellow
    Banana* (Word Beat, 1984), *Redbook, Playboy, New
    Yorker, Atlantic*
Groups: Prisoners

Marilyn Nelson Waniek   P
English Dept, U-25, Univ Connecticut, Storrs, CT 06268,
203-486-2141
    Pubs: *In Search of Color Everywhere: Anth* (Stewart,
    Tabori & Chang, 1994), *Every Shut Eye Ain't Asleep:
    Anth* (Little, Brown, 1994), *Southern Rev, Kenyon, APR*

Susan Watson   P
c/o W. Watson, 200 Bedford Rd, Greenwich, CT 06830,
203-869-1133
    Pubs: *Birds That Stay* (Arrow Graphics, 1983), *Alaska
    Qtly, Scratch Gravel Hills*

Katharine Weber 🎤 ✈   W
108 Beacon Rd
Bethany, CT 06524-3018, 203-393-1559
Internet: katweber@snet.net
    Pubs: *The Music Lesson* (Crown, 1999), *Objects in
    Mirror Are Closer Than They Appear* (Picador, 1996),
    New Yorker, Story, Redbook

David Wilk   P
Inland Book Company, PO Box 120261, East Haven, CT
06512, 800-243-0138
    Pubs: *Get Up Off Your Ass & Sing* (Membrane, 1985),
    Tree Taking Root (Truck, 1977), *Sixpack*

Max Wilk   W
29 Surf Rd
Westport, CT 06880, 203-226-7669
    Pubs: *They're Playing Our Song* (Da Capo, 1996), *OK!
    The Story of Oklahoma* (Grove-Atlantic, 1993)

Adrienne Wolfert 🎤 ✈   P&W
89 Skytop Dr
Fairfield, CT 06432-1216, 203-372-3802
Internet: wolfrite@aol.com
    Pubs: *Making Tracks* (Silver Moon Pr, 2000), *Blue
    Unicorn, Great River Rev, Greenfield Rev, NAR, Poem,
    Poetry Rev*
Groups: Seniors, Teenagers

Ann Yarmal   P
27 Northil St
Stamford, CT 06907, 203-322-5638
    Pubs: *The North Star & the Southern Cross, On This
    Crust of Earth: Anth of Fairfield County Poets* (Yuganta
    Pr, 1989, 1987), *Black Bear Rev*

Virginia Brady Young   P
44 Currier Pl
Cheshire, CT 06410, 203-272-2434
    Pubs: *The Way a Live Thing Moves* (Croton Rev Pr,
    1989), *Wind in the Long Grass: Anth* (S&S, 1993),
    *Frogpond Mag, Haiku Intl, Modern Haiku, Woodnotes
    Haiku Mag*

Sondra Zeidenstein 🎤 ✈   P
795 E St N
Goshen, CT 06756-1130, 860-491-2271
Internet: sondraz@compuserve.com
    Pubs: *A Detail in that Story, Late Afternoon Woman*
    (Chicory Blue Pr, 1998, 1992), *Passionate Lives: Anth*
    (Queen of Swords Pr, 1998), *Calliope, The Ledge,
    Mudfish, Lungfull, Lilith, Earth's Daughters, Black
    Buzzard Rev, Embers, Poet Lore, Rhino*
Groups: Seniors, Women

Feenie Ziner 🎤 ✈   W
182 Shore Dr
Branford, CT 06405-4857, 203-481-9095
    Pubs: *Within This Wilderness* (Akadine, 1999), *Squanto*
    (Shoe String Pr, 1988), *A Lively Oracle: Anth* (Larson
    Pub, 1999), *I Always Meant to Tell You: Anth* (Pocket
    Bks, 1997), *Na'amat Woman, Northeast*

DELAWARE

Fleda Brown Jackson   P
195 Starr Rd
Newark, DE 19711
    Pubs: *Do Not Feel the Birches, Fishing with Blood*
    (Purdue U Pr, 1993, 1988), *Poetry, Georgia Rev, Ariel,
    Midwest Qtly, Indiana Rev, Iowa Rev, SPR*

Bernard Kaplan   W
Univ Delaware, English Dept, Newark, DE 19711,
302-831-2361
    Pubs: *Obituaries, Prisoners of This World* (Grossman,
    1976, 1970)

Devon Miller-Duggan   P
213 Sypherd Dr
Newark, DE 19711-3626, 302-453-0564

Francis Poole 🎤 ✈   P
335 Paper Mill Rd
Newark, DE 19711-2254
    Pubs: *Gestures* (Anhinga, 1979), *Zero Zero* (Broken
    Arrow Pr, 1972), *Five Points, Rolling Stone, Lost &
    Found Times, Poetry East, Pearl, Blades, Exquisite
    Corpse, Poem*

Cruce Stark W
1316 N Clayton St
Wilmington, DE 19806, 302-658-9440
   Pubs: *Chasing Uncle Charley* (SMU Pr, 1992)

Z. Vance Wilson W
8 Phelps Ln
Newark, DE 19711-3512, 302-738-8755
   Pubs: *The Quick & the Dead* (Arbor Hse, 1986), *Jrnl of Short Story in English, Missouri Rev*

DISTRICT OF COLUMBIA

Jonetta Rose Barras P
PO Box 21232
Washington, DC 20009, 202-882-2838
   Pubs: *The Corner Is No Place for Hiding* (Bunny & The Crocodile Pr, 1996), *In Search of Color Everywhere* (Tabori & Chang, 1995), *New Republic*

Edward L. Beach W
1622 29th St NW
Washington, DC 20007-2901
   Pubs: *Keepers of the Sea* (USNI, 1983), *Cold Is the Sea* (HRW, 1978), *Proceedings, Naval History Mag, American Heritage, Reader's Digest, Bluebook*

Wayne Biddle W
2032 Belmont Rd NW, #210
Washington, DC 20009, 202-234-2868
   Pubs: *Barons of the Sky* (S&S, 1991), *Coming to Terms* (Viking, 1980), *The Nation*

Dale S. Brown P
4570 MacArthur Blv NW, #104
Washington, DC 20007, 202-338-7111
   Pubs: *I Know I Can Climb the Mountain* (Mountain Bks, 1995), *Challenging Voices: Anth* (Lowell Hse, 1995), *Speak Out, The Little Flower Mag, The Acher*

Rick Cannon P
c/o Gonzaga, 19 Eye St NW, Washington, DC 20001, 202-336-7159
   Pubs: *Xanadu, Sidewalks, Cumberland Poetry Rev, Slant, America, Iowa Rev, Verve, Whetstone, Midwest Qtly, Antietam Rev, Cimarron Rev, Folio, Mudfish*

Alan Cheuse W
3700 33rd Pl NW
Washington, DC 20008, 202-363-7799
   Pubs: *Lost & Old Rivers, The Light Possessed, The Grandmother's Club, The Tennessee Waltz* (SMU Pr, 1998, 1998, 1994, 1992)

Eric Cheyfitz P
English Dept, Georgetown Univ, Washington, DC 20057, 202-625-4949
   Pubs: *Bones & Ash* (Cymric Press, 1977), *Esquire, The New Rev, Times Literary Supplement*

Maxine Clair P&W
English Dept, George Washington Univ, Washington, DC 20052, 202-994-6180
   Pubs: *Rattlebone* (FSG, 1994), *October Brown* (Time Printers, 1992), *Coping with Gravity* (Washington Writers' Pub Hse, 1988)

William Claire P
Washington Resources, Inc, 1250 24th St NW, Ste 300, Washington, DC 20037, 202-463-0388
   Pubs: *Literature & Medicine: The Physician as Writer* (Johns Hopkins U Pr, 1985), *Delos, Horizon, American Scholar, Carleton Miscellany, Chelsea, Nation, Washingtonian*

Shirley Graves Cochrane P&W
127 Seventh St SE
Washington, DC 20003, 202-546-1020
   Pubs: *Letters to the Quick/Letters to the Dead, Everything That's All* (Signal Bks, 1998, 1991), *The Fair-haired Boy* (Word Works/Mica Pr, 1997), *Truths & Half Truths* (Washington Expatriates Pr, 1996), *Family & Other Strangers* (Word Works, 1986)

Maxine Combs 🎙 ✈ P&W
2216 King Pl NW
Washington, DC 20007
   Pubs: *The Inner Life of Objects* (Calyx, 2000), *Handbook of the Strange* (Signal Bks, 1996), *The Foam of Perilous Seas* (Slough Pr, 1990), *Swimming Out of the Collective Unconscious* (The Wineberry Pr, 1989)
I.D.: Jewish. Groups: Women

Noemi Escandell P&W
1525 Q St NW, #11
Washington, DC 20009-7802, 202-328-7197
   Pubs: *Palabras/Words, Cuadros* (SLUSA, 1986, 1982), *CPU Rev, Third Woman, Letras Femeninas, Plaza, Stone Country, Peregrine*

Laura Fargas P
621 Lexington Pl NE
Washington, DC 20002, 202-546-2347
   Pubs: *Strange Luck* (U California Pr, 1994), *Reflecting What Light We Can't Absorb* (Riverstone Pr, 1993), *Georgia Rev, Paris Rev, Atlantic, Poetry*

Julia Fields P
3636 16 St NW, #B-647
Washington, DC 20010
   Pubs: *A Summoning, A Shining* (Red Clay Pr, 1976), *East of Moonlight* (Poets' Pr, 1973)

Candida Fraze   P&W
3722 Harrison St NW
Washington, DC 20015
   Pubs: *Renifleur's Daughter* (H Holt, 1987), *Poet Lore*

Edward Gold   P
3702 Jenifer St NW
Washington, DC 20015, 202-966-5724
   Pubs: *Owl* (Scop Pub, 1983), *NYQ, Crab Creek Rev,
Red Cedar Rev, Gargoyle, Poet Lore, Kansas Qtly*

Patricia Gray ⚲ ✈   P&W
Library of Congress, 101 Independence Ave SE,
Washington, DC 20541-4912, 202-707-1308
Internet: pgray@loc.gov
   Pubs: *The Denny Poems* (Lincoln U Pr, 1996), *Old
Wounds, New Words: Anth* (Jesse Stuart Foundation,
1994), *MacGuffin, Poetry East, Shenandoah, Poet Lore,
Cider Press Rev*

Ron Green   P
Literature Dept, American Univ, Washington, DC 20016,
202-687-2450

Patricia Browning Griffith   W
1215 Geranium St NW
Washington, DC 20012
   Pubs: *Supporting the Sky, The World Around Midnight*
(Putnam, 1996, 1991), *Tennessee Blue* (Clarkson
Potter, 1981), *Harper's*

Anthony Hecht   P
4256 Nebraska Ave NW
Washington, DC 20016
   Pubs: *The Venetian Vespers, The Hard Hours*
(Atheneum, 1979, 1967)

Errol Hess ⚲ ✈   P
515 E Capitol St, SE
Washington, DC 20003, 202-543-5560
   Pubs: *Homeworks: Anth* (U Tennessee Pr, 1996), *A
Gathering at the Forks: Anth* (Vision Bks, 1993), *Sow's
Ear Rev, Friends Jrnl, Lactuca, Potato Eyes, Pegasus
Rev*
I.D.: Appalachian, Quakers

Anne Sue Hirshorn   PP
2039 37th St NW
Washington, DC 20007

David E. Hubler   W
Jenny Bent, Graybill & English, 1920 N St NW, #660,
Washington, DC 20036, 202-861-0106
   Pubs: *You Gotta Believe* (NAL/Signet, 1983), *McCall's,
American Way, Lifestyles*

Mark C. Huey   P
1515 Caroline St NW
Washington, DC 20009
   Pubs: *The Persistence of Red Dreams* (Alderman Pr,
1980), *Shenandoah, Virginia Literary Rev*

Gretchen Johnsen   P
3038 N St NW
Washington, DC 20007, 202-333-1544
   Pubs: *Journal: August 1978-August 1981* (Cumberland
Jrnl, 1981), *Paper Air, Aerial, Frank, Bogg*

Dan Johnson   P
1328 E Capitol St NE
Washington, DC 20003, 202-546-9865
   Pubs: *Come Looking* (Washington Writer's Pub Hse,
1995), *Suggestions from the Border* (State Street Pr,
1983), *Lullwater Rev, Dickinson Rev, Lip Service,
Virginia Mag*

Beth Baruch Joselow   P
2927 Tilden St NW
Washington, DC 20008, 202-966-5998
   Pubs: *Excontemporary, Broad Daylight* (Story Line Pr,
1989, 1989), *Mississippi Rev, APR*

Yala Korwin ⚲ ✈   P
c/o Holocaust Publications, U.S. Holocaust Memorial
Museum, Washington, DC 20024
   Pubs: *Voices of the Holocaust: Anth* (Perfection
Learning, 1999), *Beyond Lament: Anth* (Northwestern U
Pr, 1998), *Images from the Holocaust: Anth* (National
Textbook, 1996), *To Tell the Story, Poems of the
Holocaust* (Holocaust Pubs, 1987), *Poetry Digest*

David Kresh ⚲ ✈   P
601 N Carolina SE
Washington, DC 20003
   Pubs: *Sketches After "Pete's Beer"* (Stone Man, 1986),
Bloody Joy: Love Poems (Slow Dancer, 1981)

Kwelismith   PP
1820 Valley Terr SE
Washington, DC 20032
   Pubs: *Brown Girl in the Ring* (Washington Writer's
Publishing Hse, 1992), *Slavesong: The Art of Singing*
(Anacostia Repertory Co, 1989)

Kala Ladenheim   P
1707 Columbia Rd NW, #419
Washington, DC 20009
   Pubs: *Not Far from the Mountains of the Moon* (Dog
Ear Pr, 1982), *Kennebec, Maze, 4 Zoas, Glitch, Cafe
Rev, Frontiers, Maine Times*

Mary Ann Larkin 🎤 ✈ P
221 Channing St NE
Washington, DC 20002, 202-832-3978
   Pubs: *White Clapboard* (Carol Allen, 1988), *The Coil of
   the Skin* (WWPH, 1982), *Ireland in Poetry: Anth,
   America in Poetry: Anth* (Abrams, 1990, 1988), *Poetry
   Ireland, New Letters, Potato Eyes, Potomac Rev*

Joyce E. Latham 🎤 ✈ P
3001 Veazey NW
Washington, DC 20008, 202-966-2494
Internet: jlcomm@erols.com
   Pubs: *Circumference of Days: Anth* (Westmoreland PA
   Arts Center, 1999), *My Mama Always Said: Anth* (Faith
   Byrnie, 1998), *Poetry Motel, Sliver Quill, Allusive
   Images, Art Inspires Writing, Poet Mag, Federal Poet,
   Jrnl of Graduate Liberal Studies, Poetry Today*

Joanne Leedom-Ackerman 🎤 ✈ P&W
3229 R St NW
Washington, DC 20007
Internet: 100734.3553@compuserve.com
   Pubs: *The Dark Path to the River, No Marble Angels*
   (Saybrook Pub, 1988, 1987)

Kate Lehrer W
Ronald Goldfarb & Assoc., 918 16th St NW, Washington,
DC 20006
   Pubs: *Out of Eden, When They Took Away the Man in
   the Moon* (Harmony Bks, 1996, 1993), *Best Intentions*
   (Little, Brown, 1987)

Sharon Lerch W
1733 Riggs Pl NW
Washington, DC 20009-6114, 202-462-2511
   Pubs: *Virginia Qlty Rev, Kansas Qtly, Literary Rev,
   Black Warrior Rev*

Vladimir Levchev 🎤 ✈ P
5410 Connecticut Ave NW, Apt 516
Washington, DC 20015, 202-363-2297
Internet: www.vox-international.com
   Pubs: *Black Book of the Endangered Species* (Word
   Works, 1999), *Leaves from the Dry Tree* (CCC, 1996),
   *Anthology of Magazine Verse, Yearbook of American
   Poetry: Anth* (Monitor Bk Co, 1997)
I.D.: Bulgarian

Gregory Luce P
1421 Massachusetts Ave NW, #408
Washington, DC 20005, 202-483-2949
   Pubs: *Kansas Qtly, Iron, Cimarron Rev, Rikka, Dancing
   Shadow Rev, Shades of Gray*

C. M. Mayo 🎤 ✈ W
2700 Virginia Ave NW, #406
Washington, DC 20037
Internet: www.cmmayo.com
   Pubs: *Sky Over El Nido* (U Georgia Pr, 1999), *NW
   Rev, Rio Grande Rev, Natural Bridge, Witness, SW
   Rev, Paris Rev, The Qtly*

Richard McCann 🎤 ✈ P
1734 P St NW, #2
Washington, DC 20036, 202-885-2978
Internet: rmccann@american.edu
   Pubs: *Things Shaped in Passing* (Persea Bks, 1997),
   Ghost Letters (Alice James Bks, 1994), *Men on Men:
   Anth* (Dutton, 2000), *Gay Short Stories: Anth* (Penguin,
   1995), *The Nation, Atlantic, Esquire*
Groups: G/L/B/T, Medical Students

Terry McMillan W
c/o Speakers Worldwide, 5301 Wisconsin Ave NW, Ste
330, Washington, DC 20015, 202-686-3221
   Pubs: *How Stella Got Her Groove Back, Waiting to
   Exhale, Disappearing Acts, Breaking Ice: Anth* (Viking,
   1996, 1992, 1989, 1990), *Mama* (HM, 1987), *Essence,
   Esquire, Elle*

Larry McMurtry W
1209 31st St
Washington, DC 20007, 202-338-0366
   Pubs: *Buffalo Girls, All My Friends Are Going to Be
   Strangers, Anything for Billy* (Pocket Bks, 1995, 1992,
   1989), *Cadillac Jack* (S&S, 1982)

E. Ethelbert Miller 🎤 ✈ P
Howard Univ, PO Box 441, Washington, DC 20059,
202-291-1560
Internet: emiller698@aol.com
   Pubs: *Whispers, Secrets & Promises, First Light: New
   & Selected Poems* (Black Classic Pr, 1998, 1994), *In
   Search of Color Everywhere: Anth* (Stewart, Tabori &
   Chang, 1994)

Faye Moskowitz 🎤 ✈ P&W
3306 Highland Pl NW
Washington, DC 20008, 202-363-8628
   Pubs: *And the Bridge Is Love, Her Face in the Mirror:
   Anth* (Beacon Pr, 1991, 1994), *Calyx, Prairie Schooner,
   13th Moon, Woman's Day, Victoria Mag, Feminist
   Studies*
I.D.: Jewish. Groups: Jewish, Women

Jean Nordhaus 🎤 ✈ P
623 E Capitol St SE
Washington, DC 20003-1234, 202-543-1905
Internet: jean-nordhaus@worldnet.att.net
   Pubs: *A Purchase of Porcelain* (Kinloch Rivers
   Chapbks, 1998), *My Life in Hiding* (QRL, 1991), *A
   Bracelet of Lies* (WWPH, 1987), *Poetry, APR, Prairie
   Schooner, Hudson Rev, West Branch, Washington Rev*
I.D.: Jewish. Groups: Jewish

Michael Novak W
American Enterprise Institute, 1150 17th St NW, Rm 1200,
Washington, DC 20036
Pubs: *This Hemisphere of Liberty* (AEI, 1990)

Andrew Oerke P
2949 Macomb St NW
Washington, DC 20008, 202-966-8819

Alicia Partnoy W
PO Box 21425
Washington, DC 20009, 202-483-5549
Pubs: *Revenge of the Apple: Poems, The Little School*
(Cleis Pr, 1992, 1986)

Fred Rachford P
609 12th St NE
Washington, DC 20002

Dwaine Rieves 🎤 ✈ P
1907 New Hampshire Ave NW
Washington, DC 20009-3309, 301-827-5352
Internet: dcrieves@aol.com
Pubs: *Georgia Rev, DoubleTake, Chelsea, River Styx,
Sycamore Rev*

Elisavietta Ritchie 🎤 ✈ P&W
3207 Macomb St NW
Washington, DC 20008-3327, 202-363-8036
Internet: www.elisavietta.com
Pubs: *In Haste I Write You This Note* (Washington
Writers' Pub Hse, 2000), *Elegy for the Other Woman,
The Arc of the Storm, Flying Time* (Signal Bks, 1995,
1995, 1992), *Poetry, American Scholar, NYQ, Press,
Confrontation*
Groups: Seniors

Robert Sargent 🎤 ✈ P
815 A St NE, #2
Washington, DC 20002-6033, 202-543-1868
Pubs: *Stealthy Days* (Forest Woods Media Pr, 1998), *A
Woman from Memphis, Aspects of a Southern Story*
(Word Works, 1987, 1983), *Poetry, College English*

Mary McGowan Slappey P
National Writers Association, 4500 Chesapeake St NW,
Washington, DC 20016, 202-363-9082
Pubs: *Swiss Songs & Other Selected Poetry, Lafayette
& Harriet, Glory of Wooden Walls* (Interspace Bks,
1995, 1989, 1986)

Laurie Stroblas P
2500 Wisconsin Ave NW, #549
Washington, DC 20007, 202-333-1026
Pubs: *The First Yes: Poems About Communicating:
Anth* (Dryad Pr, 1997), *Hungry As We Are: Anth*
(Washington Writers Pub Hse, 1995), *George
Washington Rev, Poet Lore, Gargoyle, Calyx, Asha Jrnl,
Outerbridge*

Mary Swope P
3927 Idaho Ave NW
Washington, DC 20008, 212-363-1394
Pubs: *The Book of Falmouth: Anth* (Falmouth Historical
Commission, 1986), *Radcliffe Qtly*

Joseph Thackery P&W
4201 Harrison St NW
Washington, DC 20015, 202-363-7675
Pubs: *The Dark Above Mad River* (Washington Writers'
Pub Hse, 1992), *Evidence of Community* (Center for
Washington Area Studies, 1984)

Roberto H. Vargas P
1627 New Hampshire NW
Washington, DC 20009, 202-387-4371
Pubs: *Nicaragua, I Sing You Kisses, Bullets, Visions of
Liberty* (Pocho Che, 1979)

David Veronese 🎤 ✈ W
4200 Cathedral Ave NW, #907
Washington, DC 20016-4922, 202-234-0047
Internet: dveronese@aol.com
Pubs: *JANA* (Serpent's Tail, 1993), *Prism Intl, Club,
Mystery Scene, Blue Zebra*
Lang: Spanish. I.D.: Anarchists, A.A.U.W.. Groups:
Prisoners, Homeless

Hugh Walthall P
1603 Kearny St NE
Washington, DC 20018, 202-232-1876
Pubs: *Ladidah* (Ithaca Hse, 1978)

Edward Weismiller P&W
2400 Virginia Ave NW, #C1119
Washington, DC 20037-2664, 202-223-0333
Pubs: *The Branch of Fire* (Word Works, 1980), *The
Serpent Sleeping* (Putnam, 1962)

Faith Williams P
3768 McKinley St NW
Washington, DC 20015, 202-362-0189
Pubs: *Woman the Gatherer: Anth* (Yale U Pr, 1981),
*Bogg, Poet Lore, Earth's Daughters, The Bridge,
Nimrod, Kansas Qtly, Kalliope, Boston Literary Rev*

Joyce Winslow 🎤 ✈ W
2800 Wisconsin Ave NW, #403
Washington, DC 20007-4705, 202-686-1747
Pubs: *Best American Short Stories: Anth* (HM, 1969),
*New Virginia Rev, River City, Yankee, Washington Post,
Redbook, Town & Country, Mademoiselle*
Groups: Teenagers, Jewish

Mary Kay Zuravleff 🎤 ✈ W
3730 Jocelyn St NW
Washington, DC 20015-1808, 202-966-9535
Pubs: *The Frequency of Souls* (FSG, 1996), *Women's Glibber: Anth* (Crossing Pr, 1993), *Gila Rev, Gargoyle, Appearances, New Mexico Humanities Rev*

FLORIDA

Marnie K. Adler 🎤 P
266 W Casurina Pl
Beverly Hills, FL 34465, 352-746-0998
Pubs: *Florida State Poetry Society: Anths* (Florida State Poetry Society, 1995, 1994), *American Anthology of Southern Poetry* (Great Lakes Poetry Pr, 1987), *Bitterroot, Harpstrings, Voices Israel*

Eileen Annie P&W
PO Box 485
Eastpoint, FL 32328, 904-670-8518
Pubs: *Half the Bran Muffin Is Gone, Life on a Beanstalk* (Bench Pr, 1991, 1986), *LIQ, Confrontation*

Mark Ari P&W
943 Seashell Ln
Ponte Vedra Beach, FL 32082, 904-285-9477
Pubs: *The Shoemaker's Tale* (Zephyr Pr, 1994), *The Stroker Anthology* (Stroker, Papandrea, Schumann, 1995), *Lost Creek Letters, Home Planet News*

Mary Alice Ayers W
Univ Miami, 327 Ashe Bldg, English Dept, Coral Gables, FL 33124, 305-284-3090
Pubs: *Partisan Rev, Village Advocate, Newsday Mag, Florida Mag, Impact*

Mary Baron P
Dept of Language & Literature, Univ North Florida, 4567 St Johns Bluff Rd S, Jacksonville, FL 32216, 904-646-2580
Pubs: *Wheat Among Bones* (Sheep Meadow Pr, 1990), *Letters for the New England Dead* (Godine, 1974), *Southern Rev, Northward Jrnl*

Lynne Barrett 🎤 ✈ W
English Dept, Florida International Univ, 3000 NE 151st St, North Miami, FL 33181, 305-919-5506
Pubs: *The Secret Names of Women, The Land of Go* (Carnegie Mellon U Pr, 1999, 1988), *Mondo Barbie: Anth* (St. Martin's Pr, 1993), *Tampa Rev, Other Voices, Redbook, Ellery Queen's Mystery Mag*

Dina Ben-Lev 🎤 ✈ P
1232 Riverbreeze Blvd
Ormond Beach, FL 32176, 904-441-5636
Internet: dinabeach@cs.com
Pubs: *American Poetry: Anth* (Carnegie Mellon U Pr, 2000), *Broken Helix* (Mid-List Pr, 1997), *Sober on a Small Plane* (Wind Pub, 1995)
Groups: Seniors, Prisoners

Judith A. Berke P
5600 Collins Ave, #11P
Miami Beach, FL 33140-2411, 305-868-3302
Pubs: *Acting Problems* (Silverfish Rev Pr, 1993), *White Morning* (Wesleyan U Pr, 1989), *APR, Atlantic, Poetry, Field, Massachusetts Rev, Ohio Rev, Iowa Rev*

Wendy Bishop P
Florida State Univ, English Dept, Tallahassee, FL 32306, 850-893-1381
Pubs: *Working Words: The Process of Creative Writing* (Mayfield Pub, 1992), *Colors of a Different Horse: Anth* (Natl Council of Teachers of English, 1994)

Margaret Blaker P
210 Lake Howard Dr NW
Winter Haven, FL 33880-2302, 863-294-2226
Pubs: *Knowing Stones: Anth* (J.G. Burke, 2000), *Light Year: Anth* (Bits Pr, 1989), *Norton Book of Light Verse: Anth* (Norton, 1986), *Archaeology, Florida Rev*

Bocaccio PP
c/o Dewey, 1700 Glenhouse Dr, #406, Sarasota, FL 34241-6766

Barbara Boncek P
5220 Sydney St
Port Orange, FL 32127
Pubs: *Sunrust, Resoundings, Wide Open Mag, Stone Ridge Poetry, Oxalis, OutLoud, Echoes, Almanac*

Van K. Brock 🎤 ✈ P
1213 Lucy St
Tallahassee, FL 32308, 850-224-5078
Internet: vbrock@mailer.fsu.edu
Pubs: *Unspeakable Strangers* (Anhinga Pr, 1995), *The Window* (Chase Ave Pr, 1981), *The Made Thing: Anth* (U Arkansas Pr, 1999), *Holocaust Poetry: Anth* (St. Martin's Pr, 1995), *Ploughshares, NER, New Yorker, Sewanee Rev, Southern Rev*

Harry Brody 🎤 ✈ P
3033 Pinecrest St
Sarasota, FL 34239-7037, 941-923-5098
Pubs: *For We Are Constructing the Dwelling of Feeling* (Bluestone Pr, 1992), *Fields* (Ion Bks, 1987), *Chariton Rev, Carolina Qtly, Spirit That Moves Us*
Groups: Prisoners

Janet Burroway 🎤 ✈   P&W
English Dept, Florida State Univ, Tallahassee, FL 32306,
850-222-8272
Internet: jburroway@english.fsu.edu
    Pubs: *Cutting Stone* (HM, 1992), *Opening Nights*
    (Atheneum, 1986), *Prairie Schooner, New Letters, New
    Virginia Rev*

Howard Camner 🎤 ✈   P
10440 SW 76 St
Miami, FL 33173-2903, 305-412-0793
Internet: victorian.fortunecity.com/duchamp/546/index.html
    Pubs: *Brutal Delicacies, Bed of Nails, Jammed Zipper,
    Banned in Babylon, Stray Dog Wail* (Camelot Pub Co,
    1996, 1995, 1994, 1993, 1992), *Florida in Poetry: Anth*
    (Pineapple Pr, 1995), *Reporting to Hell, Without Halos,
    Security Blanket*

Rick Campbell   P
RR1, Box 209D
Quincy, FL 32351, 904-442-4146
    Pubs: *The Breathers at St. Marks* (Wellberry Pr, 1994),
    *Prairie Schooner, SPR, Missouri Rev, Georgia Rev,
    Puerto del Sol*

Eli Cantor   P&W
384 N Washington Dr
Sarasota, FL 34236
    Pubs: *Love Letters, Enemy in the Mirror* (Crown, 1979,
    1977), *Esquire, Story, Accent, Poetry Mag, Coronet,
    Saturday Rev*

Ella Cavis   P
1408 56th St W
Bradenton, FL 34209
    Pubs: *Florida Qtly, Sarasota Qtly, Mobius, Voices Intl,
    Tucumcari, Prophetic Voices, MPR, Slant, Orphic Lute,
    Old Hickory Rev, Parnassus*

Joanne Childers   P
3504 NW 7th Pl
Gainesville, FL 32607, 904-376-9773
    Pubs: *Moving Mother Out* (Florida Literary Fdn, 1992),
    Aisles of Flowers: Anth (Anhinga Pr, 1995),
    *Massachusetts Rev, Poet & Critic, Chattahoochee Rev,
    Kalliope, Kentucky Rev*

Elsa Colligan   P
3 Portside Dr
Ft Lauderdale, FL 33316
    Pubs: *The Aerialist* (Barlenmir Hse, 1979), *Harper's,
    NYQ, Chicago Rev, Poets On, BPJ, Footwork*

Kirby Congdon   P
715 Baker's Ln
Key West, FL 33040-6819, 305-294-6979
    Pubs: *Poems from Fire Island Pines & Key West*
    (Cycle Pr, 1999), *Party Train: North American Prose
    Poetry: Anth* (New Rivers Pr, 1996), *Gay Roots: Anth*
    (Gay Sunshine Pr, 1991), *Small Press Rev, Caprice,
    Cayo, Pivot*

John Charles Cooper   P&W
70 E Cahill Ct
Big Pine Key, FL 33043
    Pubs: *Cast a Single Shadow* (Northwest Pub Co,
    1996), *Vicki's Lake* (Harrodsburg Herald, 1989),
    *Christianity Today, Scripset, Time of Singing, Rant,
    Wind*

Patricia Corbus 🎤 ✈   P
PO Box 5601
Sarasota, FL 34277-5601, 941-349-0325
Internet: brcorbus@aol.com
    Pubs: *Green Mountains Rev, Folio, Antigonish Rev,
    Wallace Stevens Jrnl, Windsor Rev, Greensboro Rev,
    South Carolina Rev, Cream City Rev, Paris Rev,
    Antioch Rev, Georgia Rev, Iconoclast, Cincinnati Poetry
    Rev, Kestrel*

Harry Crews   W
English Dept, Univ Florida, Gainesville, FL 32601,
904-392-0777

Edwin Crusoe 🎤   P
2222 Middle Torch Rd
Summerland Key, FL 33042-5805, 305-872-9073
    Pubs: *Wanderings* (Rip Off Pr, 1971), *Key West Poetry
    Guild: Anth* (Key West Poetry Guild, 1999, 1989),
    Paradise: Anth (Florida Literary Fdtn Pr, 1995), *Hidden
    Path, Florida Keys Maritime Historical Jrnl, Key West
    Rev*
Lang: French, Spanish. I.D.: Euro-American, Muskogee
(Creek). Groups: Native American, Unitarian-Universalist

Ron De Maris   P
9621 SW 103 Pl
Miami, FL 33176
    Pubs: *APR, Nation, Sewanee Rev, Poetry NW, New
    Letters, New Orleans Rev, Carolina Qtly, Southern Rev,
    NER, Ploughshares, Gettysburg Rev, Atlanta Rev, New
    Republic*

Donna Decker   P
74 Westview
Panacea, FL 32346, 850-984-0151
    Pubs: *Three Thirds* (Word Banks Pr, 1984), *North of
    Wakulla: Anth* (Anhinga Pr, 1989), *American Voice,
    New Collage, Snake Nation Rev, Gulf Stream*

Leonardo DellaRocca 🎤 ✈   P
2800 Fiore Way #107
Delray Beach, FL 33445-4551, 561-278-4072
Internet: dellarocca@earthlink.net
    Pubs: *Having a Wonderful Time: Anth* (S&S, 1999),
*Wisconsin Rev, Nimrod, Poet Lore, Apalachee Qtly,
Sun Dog, Seattle Rev*

Matthew Diomede 🎤 ✈   P
125 Tenth St E
Tierra Verde, FL 33715-2206
    Pubs: *Apalachee Qtly, Riverside Qtly, Rolling Coulter,
Wisconsin Rev, Centennial Rev, Oyez Rev, Christianity
& Literature, The Viet Nam Generation, Big Book, Black
Buzzard Rev, Western Ohio Jrnl*
I.D.: Italian-American

Frances Driscoll   P
56 Seaplace, 901 Ocean Blvd, Atlantic Beach, FL 32233,
904-241-5075
    Pubs: *The Rape Poems* (Pleasure Boat Studio, 1997),
Talk to Me (Black River, 1987), *Pushcart Prize Anth
XIX* (Pushcart Pr, 1994), *Mudlark, Ploughshares*

Didi S. Dubelyew   P
PO Box 1330
Anthony, FL 32617-1330, 352-622-5802
    Pubs: *Just Remember, I Told You So...* (Whird Whirrx,
1985), *Monkey Part I: Liner Note* (Koch Jazz, 1996),
Rapscallion's Dream, Telephone

John Dufresne 🎤 ✈   P&W
Creative Writing Program, Florida International Univ, N
Miami Campus, North Miami, FL 33181, 305-919-4568
Internet: borzilleri@aol.com
    Pubs: *Love Warps the Mind a Little, Louisiana Power &
Light, The Way That Water Enters Stone* (Norton, 1997,
1994, 1991), *Mississippi Rev, Missouri Rev, Greensboro
Rev*

Page Edwards, Jr.   W
PO Box 1117
St Augustine, FL 32085-1117, 904-829-9341
    Pubs: *The Search for Kate DuVal, American Girl, The
Lake* (Marion Boyars Pub, 1996, 1990, 1986)

Sheila Natasha Simro Friedman   PP
15451 SW 67 Ct
Miami, FL 33157, 305-233-4280

Sue Gambill   W
509 Curtis Rd
Tallahassee, FL 32311, 904-942-6597
    Pubs: *Heartscape* (Naiad Pr, 1989), *Word of Mouth:
Anth* (Crossing Pr, 1990), *Moonseed*

Nola Garrett 🎤 ✈   P
2228 Orchard Park Dr
Spring Hill, FL 34608, 352-666-5867
Internet: ngarrett@atlantic.net
    Pubs: *The Pastor's Wife Considers Pinball* (Wordart,
1998), *The Muse Strikes Back: Anth* (Story Line, 1997),
Odd Angles of Heaven: Anth (Harold Shaw, 1994),
*Formalist, Georgia Rev, Cimarron Rev, Christian
Century, Poet Lore, Crab Orchard Rev, Yellow Silk*
Groups: Spiritual/Religious

Jim Gerard   P
1227 W Orange
Lake City, FL 32055, 904-752-6325

Stephen M. Gibson   P
119 Royal Pine Cir North
Royal Palm Beach, FL 33411, 407-793-6552
    Pubs: *Bodies in the Bog* (Texas Rev Pr, 1984), *Paris
Rev, NER, Poetry, Chelsea, Texas Rev, Boulevard*

Andrew Glaze 🎤 ✈   P
825 NW 14 Ct
Miami, FL 33125-3621, 305-649-6944
Internet: andrewglaze@juno.com
    Pubs: *Someone Will Go on Owing* (Black Belt Pr,
1998), *Reality Street* (St. Andrews Pr, 1991), *Atlantic,
Negative Capability, Pivot, NYQ, New Yorker*

Herman Gold   P
9420 W Bay Harbor Dr
Bay Harbor Island, FL 33154, 305-868-1039
    Pubs: *NYQ, Poetry Now, Confrontation, Tropic,
Wormwood Rev, Contact II, Samisdat*

Bonnie Gordon   W
2464 SW 19 Terr
Miami, FL 33145, 305-856-2776
    Pubs: *Childhood in Reno* (Street New York, 1982),
Songs from Unsung Worlds: Anth (Birkhauser, 1986)

Deborah Eve Grayson   P
The Center for Natural Health, 4227 W Commercial Blvd,
Tamarac, FL 33319, 305-739-5751
    Pubs: *Breath Marks in the Wind* (Breath Marks/IDF,
1988), *Journal of Poetry Therapy, Pudding Mag*

Daniel Green   P
1248 Belleflower St
Sarasota, FL 34232-1107, 941-366-6573
    Pubs: *All Told, Better Late, On Second Thought*
(Fithian Pr, 1997, 1994, 1992)

Debora Greger 🎤 ✈   P
Univ Florida, English Dept, PO Box 117310, Gainesville,
FL 32611-7310, 352-392-0777
Internet: dgreger@english.ufl.edu
    Pubs: *Desert Fathers, Uranium Daughters* (Penguin,
1996), *Norton Anthology of Poetry* (Norton, 1996), *New
Yorker, New York Times, New Republic, Nation, Yale
Rev*

Jack Gresham 🎤 ✈   P
5385 SW 83 Pl
Ocala, FL 34476-3799, 352-873-3976
    Pubs: *The Red Candle Treasury: Anth* (Red Candle Pr,
1999), *Kit-Cat Rev, American Poets & Poetry, Mobius,
Neovictorian/Cochlea, Satire, Tucumcari Literary Rev*
Groups: Unitarian-Universalist

Kelle Groom   P&W
1726 Gurtler Court #4
Orlando, FL 32804
    Pubs: *Florida Rev, Sun Dog, Chiron Rev, Flyway,
Slipstream*

Bob Grumman 🎤 ✈   P
1708 Hayworth Rd
Port Charlotte, FL 33952-4529, 813-629-8045
Internet: bobgrumman@nut-n-but.net
    Pubs: *Mathemaku 1-5* (Tel-Let, 1992), *The World of
Zines: Anth* (Penguin, 1992), *Score, Lost & Found
Times, Windless Orchard, Kaldron, The Experioddicist*

Jim Hall   P
English Dept, Florida International Univ, Miami, FL 33199
    Pubs: *False Statements, The Mating Reflex* (Carnegie
Mellon, 1985, 1980)

Barbara Hamby 🎤 ✈   P
1168 Seminole Dr
Tallahassee, FL 32301-4656, 850-877-7411
Internet: bhamby@nettally.com
    Pubs: *The Alphabet of Desire* (NYU Pr, 1999), *Delirium*
(U North Texas Pr, 1995), *Kenyon Rev, Harvard Rev,
Five Points, Southern Rev, Iowa Rev, Paris Rev*

Peter Hargitai   P&W
English Dept, Florida International Univ, Miami, FL 33199,
305-348-3405
    Pubs: *Magyar Tales* (U Massachusetts Intl Studies
Program, 1989), *Budapest to Bellevue, The Art of
Taxidermy* (Palmetto Pr, 1988, 1988)

Anne Haskins   P
4714 NW 57 Dr
Gainesville, FL 32606-4369
    Pubs: *The Earthquake on Ada Street: Anth* (Jupiter Pr,
1979), *Overtures, Mati, Ommation*

Lola Haskins 🎤 ✈   P
PO Box 18
LaCrosse, FL 32658-0018, 904-462-3117
    Pubs: *Desire Lines, Extranjera* (Story Line Pr, 2001,
1998), *Hunger* (U Iowa Pr/Story Line Pr, 1996), *BPJ,
Southern Rev, Georgia Rev, Atlantic, CSM*
Lang: Spanish. Groups: Teenagers, Rural Communities

Gerald Hausman 🎤 ✈   P&W
12699 Cristi Way
Bokeelia, FL 33922-3321
Internet: ghausman@compuserve.com
    Pubs: *The Jacob Ladder* (Orchard Bks, 2001), *Cats of
Myth, Tom Cringle* (S&S, 2000, 2000)

Hunt Hawkins 🎤 ✈   P
Florida State Univ, English Dept, Tallahassee, FL 32306,
850-644-0240
Internet: hhawkins@english.fsu.edu
    Pubs: *The Domestic Life* (U Pitt Pr, 1994), *A New
Geography of Poetry: Anth* (U Arkansas Pr, 1992),
*TriQtly, Southern Rev, Georgia Rev, Apalachee Qtly,
Poetry, Minnesota Rev*

Jonellen Heckler   W
5745 SW 75 St, PMB322
Gainesville, FL 32608, 352-332-1005
Internet: jonellenh@aol.com
    Pubs: *Final Tour, Circumstances Unknown* (Pocket Bks,
1994, 1993), *White Lies, A Fragile Peace, Safekeeping*
(Putnam, 1989, 1986, 1983)

Judith Hemschemeyer 🎤 ✈   P&W
436 Knowles Ave #2
Winter Park, FL 32789-3232, 407-644-9116
    Pubs: *Certain Animals* (Snake Nation Pr, 1998), *The
Harvest* (Pig Iron Pr, 1998), *The Ride Home* (Texas
Tech U Pr, 1987), *Very Close & Very Slow* (Wesleyan
U Pr, 1975), *Hudson Rev, Colorado Rev, Tampa Rev,
Dickinson Rev, Florida Rev*

Michael Hettich 🎤 ✈   P
561 NE 95 St
Miami Shores, FL 33138-2731, 305-237-3187
Internet: mhettich@mdcc.edu
    Pubs: *Sleeping with the Lights On* (Pudding Hse,
2000), *The Point of Touching* (LeBow, 2000), *Having a
Wonderful Time* (S&S, 1997), *Many Simple Things,
Immaculate Bright Rooms* (March Street Pr, 1997,
1994), *A Small Boat* (U Florida Pr, 1990), *Witness
Lierary Rev*

Patricia Higginbotham   P
3211 Swann Ave #310
Tampa, FL 33109-4685, 813-874-3498
Internet: higginp2@yahoo.com
    Pubs: *Conjure This* (WJM Pr, 1997), *Orbis, Tower
Poetry, ELF, Poetpourri, Lyric, The Formalist, Staple*

Rochelle Lynn Holt 🎤 ✈ P&W
15223 Coral Isle Ct
Ft Myers, FL 33919
  Pubs: *Caution: Child at Play* (Chiron Rev Pr, 2000),
  *Scars: A Novel, 360 Degrees, Mentor, Pilot, Gulf Coast
  Woman, Kalliope, Synesthesia, Chiron Rev, River King,
  The Pilot, Kalliope*
Groups: Seniors, G/L/B/T

Susan Hubbard 🎤 ✈ P&W
PO Box 4009
Winter Park, FL 32793-4009, 407-823-2212
Internet: shubbard@pegasus.cc.ucf.edu
  Pubs: *Blue Money, Walking on Ice & Other Stories* (U
  Missouri Pr, 1999, 1990), *NAR, Ploughshares,
  Passages North, Wooster Rev, Dickinson, Green
  Mountains Rev, TriQtly, Mississippi Rev*

John Kapsalis P
5776 Deauville Lake Cir, #308
Naples, FL 34112, 941-793-4530
Internet: johnathy@aol.com
  Pubs: *The Saga of Chrysodontis Pappas, Tales of
  Pergamos* (Aegina Pr, 1994, 1988), *Bitterroot, Dark
  Horse, Indigo, Joycean Lively Arts Guild Rev,
  Northeastern Jrnl, Nebraska Rev*

David A. Kaufelt W
PO Box 182
Key West, FL 33041, 305-292-1288
  Pubs: *The Winter Women Murders, The Fat Boy
  Murders* (Pocket Bks, 1994, 1993), *American Tropic*
  (Poseidon, 1987), *Cosmopolitan*

Marcia Gale Kester-Doyle P
516 NE 6 St
Pompano Beach, FL 33060, 954-943-0685
  Pubs: *Driving Through Nebraska* (Cooper Hse, 1991),
  The Healing Stone: Anth (Golden Apple Pr, 1998),
  *Baby's World, Green Hills Literary Lantern, SPR,
  Twinsworld, Bereavement, The Poet, Echoes*

Daniel Keyes 🎤 ✈ W
PMB 110, 7491 N Federal Hwy, Ste C-5
Boca Raton, FL 33487
Internet: dankeyes@usa.net
  Pubs: *Unveiling Claudia* (Bantam Bks, 1986), *The
  Minds of Billy Milligan* (Random Hse, 1981), *The Fifth
  Sally* (HM, 1980), *Flowers for Algernon* (HB, 1966)

David Kirby 🎤 ✈ P
1168 Seminole Dr
Tallahassee, FL 32301-4656, 850-877-7411
Internet: dkirby@english.fsu.edu
  Pubs: *Traveling Library* (Orchises, 2001), *House of Blue
  Light* (LSU Pr, 2000), *Five Points, Paris Rev,
  Parnassus, Kenyon Rev, Southern Rev, Ploughshares,
  NW Rev*

Smith Kirkpatrick W
English Dept, Univ Florida, Gainesville, FL 32601,
904-392-0777
  Pubs: *The Sun's Gold* (HM, 1974)

Jeffrey Knapp P
3457 Sheridan Ave
Miami Beach, FL 33140, 305-531-4309
  Pubs: *The Acupuncture of Heaven* (Do Something Pr,
  1989), *Palmetto Rev, Free Lunch, La Bete*

Nancy Roxbury Knutson P
9791 NW 10 St
Plantation, FL 33322-4880
  Pubs: *Nothing Shall Fall to Waste* (Arts Wayland Fdn,
  1983), *If I Had a Hammer: Anth* (Papier-Mache Pr,
  1990), *APR, Calyx, Iowa Rev, Nimrod, New Virginia
  Rev*

Sam Koperwas W
2701 NE 35 Dr
Ft Lauderdale, FL 33308
  Pubs: *Easy Money* (Morrow, 1983), *Hot Stuff* (Dutton,
  1978)

Steve Kronen 🎤 ✈ P
6871 SW 76 Terr
S Miami, FL 33143-4444, 305-662-1614
Internet: skronen@hotmail.com
  Pubs: *Empirical Evidence* (U Georgia Pr, 1992), *Isle of
  Flowers: Anth* (Anhinga Pr, 1995), *Poetry, Paris Rev,
  Southern Rev, Georgia Rev, Agni, Virginia Qtly Rev,
  New Republic*

Elsie Bowman Kurz P
Isle of Capri B50, Kings Point
Delray Beach, FL 33484, 407-498-2733
  Pubs: *Rhyming the Bible: Songs Your Mother Never
  Taught You, Endangered Species* (PPB Pr, 1996,
  1996), *We Speak for Peace: Anth* (KIT, 1993),
  Passager, Harp Strings, Poets Forum

Zilia L. Laje W
PO Box 45-1732 Shenandoah Station
Miami, FL 33245-1732, 305-856-9314
  Pubs: *The Sugar Cane Curtain* (Guarina Publishing,
  2000)

P. V. LeForge P&W
2037 W Pensacola St
Tallahassee, FL 32304, 904-576-7369
  Pubs: *The Secret Life of Moles* (Anhinga Pr, 1992),
  The Principle of Interchange (Paperback Rack Bks,
  1990), *Q Mag, Nightstallion, Mid-American Rev*

Edith Mize Lewis P
8919 Old Pine Rd
Boca Raton, FL 33433-3152
  Pubs: *Haiku is...A Feeling* (Pippin Bks, 1990)

Duane Locke 🎤 ✈   P
2716 Jefferson St
Tampa, FL 33602-1620, 813-223-5174
Internet: duanelocke@netzero.net
  Pubs: *Watching Wisteria* (Vida Pr, 1995), *Ghost Dance:
  Anth* (Whitston, 1994), *Black Moon, Bitter Oleander,
  Glass Cherry, APR, American Literary Rev, Nation*

William Logan 🎤   P
210 NE 7 St
Gainesville, FL 32601
Internet: wlogan@english.ufl.edu
  Pubs: *Night Battle, Vain Empires* (Penguin, 1999,
  1998), *Sullen Weedy Lakes* (Godine, 1988)

Jo Ann Lordahl 🎤 ✈   P
PO Box 6165
Bradenton, FL 34281-6165, 941-752-0016
Internet: www.targetpublish.com

Carol Mahler 🎤 ✈   P
168 Barre Dr
Port Charlotte, FL 33952, 813-494-5034
  Pubs: *When Life Mates Die: Stories of Love, Loss &
  Healing: Anth* (Fairview Pr, 1997), *Comstock Mag,
  Many Mountains Moving, Passages North, BPJ, Poets
  On, New Collage Mag, Negative Capability, Fan Mag,
  Red Brick Rev, Stone Country*
Groups: Seniors, Children

Michael Margolin   P
1801 S Ocean Dr, #837
Hallandale, FL 33009-4947
  Pubs: *NAR, Shenandoah, Carleton Miscellany, SPR,
  Smith, Epoch*

Dionisio D. Martinez 🎤 ✈   P
4509 N Lincoln Ave
Tampa, FL 33614-6631, 813-874-6747
Internet: http://members.aol.com/ddmartinez
  Pubs: *Climbing Back, Bad Alchemy* (Norton, 2000,
  1995), *History as a Second Language* (Ohio State U
  Pr, 1993), *New Republic, APR, Iowa Rev, Prairie
  Schooner, Virginia Qtly Rev, Georgia Rev, Denver Qtly,
  Kenyon Rev*
Lang: Spanish

Richard Mathews 🎤 ✈   P
Univ of Tampa, PO Box 19-F, Tampa, FL 33606,
813-253-6266
Internet: rmathews@alpha.utampa.edu
  Pubs: *Numbery* (Borgo Pr, 1995), *A Mummery*
  (Konglomerati, 1975), *SPR, Louisville Rev, Berkeley
  Rev*

Irma McClaurin 🎤 ✈   P
5128 NW 16 Pl
Gainesville, FL 32605-3302, 352-336-2154
Internet: i.mcclaurin@worldnet.att.net
  Pubs: *Pearl's Song* (Lotus Pr, 2000), African *American
  Literature: Anth* (Glencoe/McGraw-Hill, 2000), *A Rock
  Against the Wind: Anth* (Perigee, 1996), *Essence, Drum
  Rev, Obsidian II*
I.D.: African-American

Jane McClellan   P
2838 NE 14 Ave
Ocala, FL 34470-3700, 352-622-6145
Internet: doctorjmcc@aol.com
  Pubs: *Crucible, Poet Lore, Green Hills Literary Lantern,
  Callaloo, Ellipsis, RE:AL, Cumberland Poetry Rev,
  MacGuffin, Skylark, Westview, Centennial Rev, Cape
  Rock, Blue Unicorn*

Tom McDaniel   P
249 Lake Ave E
Longwood, FL 32750-5442
  Pubs: *Pulpsmith, Wind, Plains Poetry Jrnl, Blue
  Unicorn, Florida Rev, Kansas Qtly*

Kevin McGowin   P&W
PO Box 14806
Gainesville, FL 32604, 352-336-7178
  Pubs: *Eclectica Mag, Rosebud, Whiskey Island,
  Yemassee, National Forum*

Campbell McGrath   P
Florida International Univ, N Miami Campus, North Miami,
FL 33181, 305-919-5954
  Pubs: *Spring Comes to Chicago, American Noise* (Ecco
  Pr, 1996, 1994), *New Yorker, Antaeus, Paris Rev,
  Ploughshares, TriQtly, Ohio Rev*

Peter Meinke 🎤 ✈   P&W
147 Wildwood Ln SE
St Petersburg, FL 33705-3222, 727-896-1862
Internet: meinkep@acasun.eckerd.edu
  Pubs: *Zinc Fingers, Scars, Liquid Paper* (U Pitt Pr,
  2000, 1996, 1991), *Atlantic, New Yorker, Georgia Rev,
  Poetry*

A. McA Miller 🎤 ✈   P
New Collage Magazine, 5700 N Tamiami Trail, Sarasota,
FL 34243-2197, 813-359-4605
  Pubs: *BPJ, Epos, Gryphon, Negative Capability, Spirit
  That Moves Us, Tendril*

Karl F. Miller   P&W
1999 NW 83 Dr
Coral Springs, FL 33071-6274, 954-341-8672
  Pubs: *A Warning* (Merging Media, 1990), *Comstock
  Rev, Cold Mountain Rev, Galley Sail Rev, Portland
  Rev, Mudfish, Bad Haircut, Impetus, RE:AL, Glass
  Cherry*

Michael G. Minassian   P
1921 NW 93 Ave
Pembroke Pines, FL 33024, 305-431-2229
    Pubs: *Ararat, Wind, Western Poetry, Passaic Rev,*
    Pegasus Rev, San Fernando Poetry Jrnl

Susan Mitchell ♀ ✦   P
9287-C Boca Gardens Circle S
Boca Raton, FL 33496-1797, 561-451-4326
Internet: sunmil@aol.com
    Pubs: *Erotikon, Rapture* (HC, 2000, 1992), *Atlantic,*
    New Yorker, Yale Rev

Harry Morris   P
3940 W Kelly Rd
Tallahassee, FL 32301, 904-877-4307

Bridget Balthrop Morton ♀ ✦   P
736 Espanola Way
Melbourne, FL 32901-4140, 321-724-9636
Internet: bridgetbal@aol.com
    Pubs: *Florida in Poetry: Anth* (Pineapple Pr, 1995),
    Song for Occupations: Anth (Wayland Pr, 1991),
    America, Visions Intl, U.S. Air, Commonweal, Gulf
    Stream
I.D.: Literacy, Social Justice. Groups: Children, Schools

William Moseley   W
102 Highview Dr
Cocoa, FL 32922, 407-639-1538
    Pubs: *Earth Tones* (Vergin Pr, 1994), *People Around*
    You: Anth (Germany; Schoningh, 1997), *Polyphany:*
    Anth of Florida Poets (Panther Pr, 1989), *Kansas Rev,*
    Scripsit, Virginia Qtly Rev

Joseph M. Moxley   P&W
English Dept, Univ South Florida, Tampa, FL 33620,
813-974-2421
    Pubs: *Paragraph*

George E. Murphy, Jr. ♀ ✦   P
PO Box 2626
Key West, FL 33045-2626
    Pubs: *The Key West Reader* (Tortugas, 1990),
    Rounding Ballast Key (Ampersand Pr, 1987)

Patrick J. Murphy ♀ ✦   W
3612 Monmouth Ct
Tallahassee, FL 32308, 850-386-8698
    Pubs: *Way Below E* (White Pine Pr, 1994), *100% Pure*
    Florida Fiction: Anth (U Pr Florida, 2000), *Tampa Rev,*
    New Orleans Rev, Cream City Rev, Buffalo Spree,
    Sequoia

Patricia Muse   W
2118 Cochise Trail
Casselberry, FL 32707
    Pubs: *Eight Candles Glowing* (Ballantine Bks, 1976),
    The Belle Claudine (Avalon Bks, 1971)

Norman Nathan   P&W
Stratford Ct #219, 6343 Via de Sonrisa del Sur, Boca
Raton, FL 33433, 407-391-2716
    Pubs: *Prince William B* (Mouton, 1975), *Contemporary*
    American Satire: Anth (Exile Pr, 1988), *Poetry Event,*
    Wisconsin Rev, Chaminade, Fiction, Z Miscellaneous,
    Poem

Barbra Nightingale ♀ ✦   P
2231 N 52 Ave
Hollywood, FL 33021-3310, 954-961-7126
Internet: bnighting@aol.com
    Pubs: *Greatest Hits* (Pudding Hse, 2000), *Singing in*
    the Key of L (NFSPS Pr, 1999), *Lunar Equations* (East
    Coast Edtns, 1993), *Lovers Never Die* (Pteranodon Pr,
    1981), *Having a Wonderful Time: Anth* (HB, 1997),
    Florida in Poetry: Anth (Pineapple Pr, 1996)

Richard O'Connell   P
1147 Hillsboro Mile #907
Hillsboro Beach, FL 33062-1723, 954-428-0419
    Pubs: *The Bright Tower, Voyages, Retro Worlds:*
    Selected Poems (U Salzburg, 1997, 1995, 1993), *The*
    Caliban Poems (Atlantis Edtns, 1992), *New Yorker,*
    Paris Rev, The Atlantic

Sheila Ortiz-Taylor   P&W
Florida State Univ, English Dept, Tallahassee, FL
32306-1580, 850-644-5776
    Pubs: *Imaginary Parents, Coachella* (U New Mexico Pr,
    1998, 1996), *Faultline* (Naiad Pr, 1982), *Americas Rev,*
    Sinister Wisdom, Common Lives/Lesbian Lives,
    Innisfree, Apalachee

Joseph Papaleo   W
150 Cypress Pl
Oldsmar, FL 34677, 813-781-4605
    Pubs: *Picasso at Ninety One* (Seaport Bks, 1988),
    Unsettling America: Anth (Viking Penguin, 1994),
    Paterson Literary Rev, Paris Rev

Ricardo Pau-Llosa   P
South Campus English Dept, Miami-Dade Community
College, 11011 SW 104 St, Miami, FL 33176,
305-237-2510
    Pubs: *Cuba* (Carnegie Mellon Pr, 1993), *Bread of the*
    Imagined (Bilingual Pr, 1992), *Kenyon Rev, TriQtly,*
    APR, Denver Qtly, Missouri Rev, NER

Nola Perez ♀   P
2004 Vista Cove Rd
Saint Augustine, FL 32095-2620
    Pubs: *The Continent of Dreams* (Sulphur River Literary
    Review Pr, 2000), *Bay Area Poets Coalition Anth*
    (BAPC, 1994), *Bottomfish, Red Rock Rev, Outerbridge,*
    U Windsor Rev

Diane Marie Perrine   P
500 SW 33rd Ave, Apt 93-A
Ocala, FL 34474-1967
   Pubs: *Nexus, Icon, Writers Haven Jrnl, Silver Wings,
   Prickly Pear*

Robin Perry   W
541 Nightingale Dr
Indialantic, FL 32903, 407-777-3310
   Pubs: *Videography, Shadows of the Mind* (Writer's
   Digest Bks, 1985, 1981)

Mario A. Petaccia 🎤   P&W
762 Sailfish Dr
Fort Walton Beach, FL 32548, 850-244-5001
Internet: mpetaccia1@cs.com
   Pubs: *Walking on Water* (CCC, 1986), *Florida in
   Poetry: Anth* (Pineapple Pr, 1995), *Yankee, Poet, SPR,
   Apalachee Qtly, NYQ, Greenfield Rev, Poem Mag,
   Potomac Rev, Voices in Italian Americana*
Groups: Children, Disabled

Emmett Peter, Jr.   W
813 Rosemere Cir
Orlando, FL 32835-4474
   Pubs: *Florida Rev, Sunrust, Other Voices, Exile, Oasis,
   Carolina Qtly*

Allan Peterson 🎤 ✈   P
5397 Soundside Dr
Gulf Breeze, FL 32561-9530, 850-932-3077
Internet: aandf@pcola.gulf.net
   Pubs: *Small Charities* (Panhandler Pr, 1995), *Stars on
   a Wire* (Parallel Edtns, 1989), *Bellingham Rev,
   Pleiades, Agni, Gettysburg Rev, Willow Springs, River
   Styx, Epoch, Green Mountains Rev*

Geoffrey Philp   P&W
18558 NE 18 Ave, #103
North Miami Shores, FL 33179, 305-949-1708
   Pubs: *Hurricane Center, Uncle Obadiah & the Alien,
   Florida Bound* (Peepal Tree Pr, 1998, 1997, 1994),
   Florida in Poetry: Anth (Pineapple Pr, 1994), *Mississippi
   Rev, Compost, Caribbean Writer, Michigan Rev, Gulf
   Stream, Intl Qtly*

Padgett Powell   P&W
English 4008 TUR, Univ Florida, Gainesville, FL 32611,
904-392-0777
   Pubs: *A Woman Named Drown, Edisto* (FSG, 1987,
   1984)

Ilmars Purens 🎤 ✈   P
1244 Bel Aire Dr
Daytona Beach, FL 32118-3639, 904-255-6644
   Pubs: *The New Time, Kayak, Wisconsin Rev, Epoch,
   Poetry Now, Nation, The Little Rev*

Anne Giles Rimbey   P
6119 E 112 Ave
Tampa, FL 33617-3131, 813-989-1430
   Pubs: *Dusty Sandals* (Skin Drum Pr, 1992), *I Am
   Becoming the Woman I've Wanted: Anth* (Papier-Mache
   Pr, 1994), *Tampa Rev, Birmingham Poetry Rev,
   Kalliope, Press, Crosscurrents, The Alembic*

Andres Rivero   W
CSP Publications, PO Box 650909, Miami, FL 33265,
305-380-6833
   Pubs: *Cuentos Torvos, Nina Melancolia, Somos Como
   Somos, Recuerdos* (CSP Pub, 1998, 1993, 1982,
   1980), *El Nuevo Herald, Diario Las Americas, Spanish
   Today Mag*

David B. Robinson   P
PO Box 1414
Miami Shores, FL 33153-1414, 305-757-7405
   Pubs: *Simcoe Rev, The Writer's Lifeline, Black Creek
   Rev*

Marcia J. Roessler 🎤 ✈   P&W
966 Red Bay Terr NW
Murdock, FL 33948-3517
Internet: mroess7170@tnh.net
   Pubs: *Traveled Paths* (Haworth Society, 1998),
   Wordspinners: Anth (Burlington County, 1994), *Wide
   Open Mag, Feelings*
Groups: Children, Seniors

David Rosenberg   P
11121 SW 62 Ave
Miami, FL 33156-4003
   Pubs: *The Book of David* (Harmony Bks, 1997), *The
   Lost Book of Paradise, A Poet's Bible* (Hyperion, 1993,
   1991), *Five Fingers Rev, Harper's, APR, The Nation*

Sandra Russell   P&W
508 Simonton, #3
Key West, FL 33040
   Pubs: *Solares Hill, Ball State U Pr, Croton Rev, Forum,
   Aspen Anth, Amelia, Sunrust, Toad Highway*

Brian Salchert   P
3530 SW 24 Ave, Lot 41
Gainesville, FL 32608
   Pubs: *Teasings, First Pick* (Thinking Lizard, 1986,
   1982), *Rooted Sky* (Monday Morning Pr, 1972),
   Wisconsin Rev, Sou'wester, Saltillo, Studia Mystica

Nicholas Samaras 🎤 ✈   P
3823 Lancaster Court #101
Palm Harbor, FL 34685-4116
Internet: saddlemaker@ij.net
   Pubs: *Survivors of the Moving Earth* (U Salzburg Pr,
   1998), *Hands of the Saddlemaker* (Yale U Pr, 1992),
   *Paris Rev, Poetry, American Scholar, New Yorker, New
   Criterion, Poetry, Kenyon Rev*
Lang: Greek

Bonny Barry Sanders P
1411 E Blackhawk Trail
Jacksonville, FL 32225-2703, 904-744-3511
  Pubs: *New Voices: Anth* (Colorado State U, 1994),
  *Midwest Qtly, Avocet, CSM, Blueline, Skylark, Red
  Rock Rev, Hayden's Ferry Rev, Plainsongs,
  Puckerbrush Rev, CSM, George Washington Rev, South
  Dakota Rev, Kalliope, Negative Capability*

Christy Sheffield Sanford P&W
714 Northeast Blvd
Gainesville, FL 32601-4375, 352-375-7565
  Pubs: *Sur Les Pointes* (White Eagle Coffee Store,
  1995), *The H's: The Spasms of a Requiem* (Bloody
  Twin, 1994), *Coffeehouse: Writings from the Web: Anth*
  (Manning, 1997), *American Poets Say Goodbye to the
  20th Century: Anth* (4 Walls, 8 Windows, 1996)

Lin Schlossman P
4480 Deer Trail Blvd
Sarasota, FL 34238-5606
  Pubs: *Panhandler, Treasure House, Crazyquilt, Poem,
  Maryland Poetry Rev, Poetpourri, Birmingham Poetry
  Rev, Cincinnati Judaica Rev, Owen Wister Rev*

Peter Schmitt 🎤 ✈ P
Box 248145
Coral Gables, FL 33124, 305-284-4074
Internet: profpschmitt@gateway.net
  Pubs: *Hazard Duty, Country Airport* (Copper Beech Pr,
  1995, 1989), *The Nation, Paris Rev, Ploughshares,
  Poetry, Southern Rev, Hudson Rev*

Paul K. Shepherd P&W
117 Lasswade Dr
Tallahassee, FL 32312
  Pubs: *Other Testaments: Anth* (Other Testaments
  1998), *Folio, Maryland Rev, Portland Rev, Prairie
  Schooner, William & Mary Rev*

Rose Sher P
7135 Collins Ave, APt 1202
Miami Beach, FL 33141-3230
  Pubs: *Anthology Two* (Florida State Poets Assn, 1984),
  Euterpe Housetops, Earthwise, Newscribes

Edmund Skellings P
600 NE 2nd Pl
Dania, FL 33004, 954-929-3595
  Pubs: *Collected Poems 1958-1998, Selected Poems*
  (CD), *Living Proof, Showing My Age, Face Value* (U Pr
  Florida, 1998, 1997, 1987, 1978, 1977)

Elaine Campbell Smith W
5587 W Kelly Rd
Tallahassee, FL 32311
  Pubs: *A Wish Too Soon* (Silhouette, 1986), *Fantasy
  Lover* (Harlequin, 1984), *Southern Rev, Snap,
  Whispering Palms, Ellery Queen's Mystery Mag*

Patrick D. Smith W
1370 Island Dr
Merritt Island, FL 32952, 407-452-6590
  Pubs: *Angel City* (Valkyrie, 1991), *Forever Island* (Dell,
  1990), *A Land Remembered* (Pineapple Pr/Signet,
  1986)

Jim Sorcic P
2348 NW 98 Way
Coral Springs, FL 33065, 305-345-3662
  Pubs: *This Could Lead to Dancing, The Cost of Living,
  The Secret Oral Teachings of Jim the House* (Morgan
  Pr, 1991, 1980, 1971)

Les Standiford W
Creative Writing Program, Florida International Univ, N
Miami Campus, North Miami, FL 33181, 305-253-7053
  Pubs: *Black Mountain* (Putnam, 1999), *Presidential
  Deal, Done Deal* (HC, 1998, 1993), *Spill* (Atlantic
  Monthly Pr, 1991), *Confrontation, Kansas Qtly, BPJ,
  Image, Travel Holiday, Writer's Digest*

Thomas Starling W
PO Box 2222
Cocoa, FL 32923-2222, 407-639-3162
  Pubs: *Peter Paladine of the Great Heart, Jethrow's
  Cabin* (Spindrift Pr, 1995, 1982)

Suzi P
PO Box 7472
Ocala, FL 34472, 352-687-1321
  Pubs: *Rogue Scolars, Conspire, Recursive Angel,
  Mesechabe, Long Shot, The New Laurel Rev, New
  American Writing, Exquisite Corpse*

Millie Taylor P&W
PO Box 5001
Jacksonville, FL 32247-5001
  Pubs: *Thema, Kalliope, South Dakota Rev, Passager*

Sandra Thompson 🎤 ✈ W
3020 W Harbor View Ave
Tampa, FL 33611-1645, 813-831-3311
Internet: sandrachris@att.net
  Pubs: *Wild Bananas* (Atlantic Monthly Pr, 1985),
  Close-Ups (U Georgia Pr, 1984)

Linda Trice 🎤 ✈ P&W
Box 17933
Sarasota, FL 34276
Internet: joyandhappiness@hotmail.com
  Pubs: *Pockets, Small Pond, Mini Romance, Sun &
  Shade, Papyrus, INK, Sarasvati, Show & Tell,
  Colorlines, Candlelight Poetry Jrnl, Idiolect, Short
  Stories, Writer's Gazette, Papyrus*
I.D.: African-American. Groups: Minorities, Ethnic

Dorothy Twiss   P
5125 Soundside Dr
Gulf Breeze, FL 32561-8923, 850-932-5619
Internet: dottwiss@aol.com
  Pubs: *Mississippi Writers: Reflections of Childhood &
  Youth: Anth* (U Pr Mississippi, 1988)

Kathryn Vanspanckeren 🎤 ✈   P
Univ Tampa, English Dept, Tampa, FL 33606,
813-251-1914
Internet: kvanspackeren@alpha.utampa.edu
  Pubs: *Salt & Sweet Water, Mountains Hidden in
  Mountains* (Empty Window, 1993, 1992), *APR,
  Ploughshares, 13th Moon, Carolina Qtly, Contact II,
  Boundary 2*
I.D.: Women, Native American

Fanny Ventadour   P&W
PO Box 547067
Orlando, FL 32854-7067, 407-647-0418
  Pubs: *The Centre Holds, Blue Is Recessive As in Irises*
  (Two Cities Edtns, 1977, 1966), *Gryphon*

Bruce Wallace   P
PO Box 6614
Key West, FL 33041
  Pubs: *Poet Lore, Z Miscellaneous, Zone 3, Plainsongs,
  Rambunctious Rev, Poetpourri, Columbia*

Sterling Watson   W
Eckerd College, PO Box 12560/Letters Collegium, St
Petersburg, FL 33733, 813-864-8281
  Pubs: *Deadly Sweet* (S&S, 1994), *The Calling* (Dell,
  1989), *Blind Tongues* (Delacorte, 1989)

Herbert J. Waxman   P
3502 Bimini Ln, #H4
Coconut Creek, FL 33066, 954-979-4593
  Pubs: *Where the Worm Grows Fat* (Full Court Pr,
  1975), *NYQ, Speakeasy, Alive & Kicking*

Craig Weeden 🎤 ✈   P
5855 Midnight Pass Rd, #128
Siesta Key, FL 34242-2106, 941-349-4702
Internet: muzzles@kudos.net
  Pubs: *American Sports Poems: Anth* (Orchard, 1988),
  *Poetry Now, New Orleans Rev, Chowder Rev, SPR,
  Cimarron Rev, Calliope*

Sarah Brown Weitzman 🎤 ✈   P
555 SE Sixth Ave, Apt 2B
Delray Beach, Fl 33483-5252, 561-276-4464
  Pubs: *Poet Lore, CQ, Mid-American Rev, Kansas Qtly,
  Poet & Critic, Madison Rev, Croton Rev, Abraxas, New
  America*
Groups: Seniors, Teenagers

Alison Welsh 🎤 ✈   P
1305 N Atlantic Ave
New Smyrna Beach, FL 32169-2205, 904-426-5864
Internet: AceWelsh53@aol.com
  Pubs: *Isle of Flowers: Anth* (Anhinga Pr, 1995), *Florida
  in Poetry: Anth* (Pineapple Pr, 1995), *Poetry, Jama,
  Cream City Rev, Whetstone, Florida Rev, Kalliope*

Jean West   P
Box 2710, Rollins College
Winter Park, FL 32789-4499, 407-646-2666
  Pubs: *Holding the Chariot* (Open Hse, 1976), *Florida in
  Poetry: Anth* (Pineapple Pr, 1995), *Lullwater Rev,
  Kalliope, Confrontation, CSM*

William M. White   P&W
721 Navigator's Way
Edgewater, FL 32141, 904-423-8633
  Pubs: *Where I Stand* (Tudor Pubs, 1992)

Millie Mae Wicklund 🎤 ✈   P
3623 N Long Pine Point
Beverly Hills, FL 34465-3307
  Pubs: *Wallorvisions, Moving Paper, The History of My
  Parachute* (Ghost Dance, 1995, 1990, 1986), *American
  Writing, Altered State, Art/Life*

Joy Williams   W
8128 Midnight Pass Rd
Siesta Key, FL 33581
  Pubs: *Escapes* (Atlantic Monthly Pr, 1990), *Breaking &
  Entering* (Random Hse, 1988), *Granta*

Robley Wilson 🎤 ✈   P&W
PO Box 4009
Winter Park, FL 32793-4009
Internet: robley.wilson@uni.edu
  Pubs: *Everything Paid For* (U Pr of Florida, 1999), *The
  Victim's Daughter, Terrible Kisses* (S&S, 1991, 1989), *A
  Pleasure Tree* (U Pitt Pr, 1990), *Iowa Rev, Prairie
  Schooner, Epoch, Southern California Anth*

Norma Woodbridge   P
2606 Zoysia Ln
North Fort Myers, FL 33917-2476
  Pubs: *Poetry Norma Woodbridge* (International Poets,
  1995), *Graces* (Harper, 1994), *When God Speaks, Joy
  in the Morning, Meditations of a Modern Pilgrim,
  Resting Places* (Star Bks, 1991, 1990, 1989, 1988),
  Woman's World, Broken Streets

Fred W. Wright, Jr.   P
PO Box 86158
St Petersburg, FL 33738, 813-595-5004
  Pubs: *Fiddler Crab, Pegasus, Reiki Jrnl, Gryphon,
  Chattahoochee Rev, Sharing, Pudding*

Stephen Caldwell Wright   P
Seminole Community College, 100 Weldon Blvd, Sanford,
FL 32773-6199, 407-328-2063
    Pubs: *With Fortitude, The Chicago Collective,*
    Circumference, Talking to the Mountains
    (Christopherr-Burghardt, 1991, 1990, 1989, 1988)

Wyatt Wyatt   W
Univ Central Florida, English Dept, Orlando, FL 32816,
305-275-2212
    Pubs: *Deep in the Heart* (Atheneum, 1981), *Catching*
    Fire (Random Hse, 1977)

Jim Young   P
4811 NW 17 Pl
Gainesville, FL 32605, 904-378-4208
    Pubs: *Plains Poetry Jrnl, Light Year, Lyric, Wind, Stone*
    Country, Sunrust, Negative Capability

Iris M. Zavala   P
100 Kings Point Dr, #1707
Miami, FL 33160-4731
    Pubs: *Kiliagonia* (Mexico, 1980), *Que-Nadiemuera Sin*
    Amar El Mar (Spain, 1982), *Third Woman*

GEORGIA

Ken Anderson   P
Floyd College, 5198 Ross Rd, Acworth, GA 30102,
770-975-4150
    Pubs: *Smooth 'N' Sassy, The Intense Lover: A Suite of*
    Poems, (Star Bks, 1998, 1995), *Chattahoochee Rev,*
    Lullwater Rev, Connecticut Poetry Rev, James White
    Rev, Bay Windows, Beloit Poetry Rev

Joan Anson-Weber   P
Cherokee Publishing Co., 4331 Lake Chimney Ct, Roswell,
GA 30075, 770-587-3077
    Pubs: *Snuffles* (Cherokee Pub Co, 1995), *The Gate of*
    the Year (Kingham Pr, 1993), *Before the Trees Turn*
    Gray (Wings Pr, 1981), *Poets at Work, Creative Arts &*
    Science, Nashville Newsletter, Poets of Now, Ultimate
    Writer, Small Pond

Rebecca Baggett ♣ ✈   P
330 College Cir
Athens, GA 30605-3630, 706-548-0029
Internet: rbaggett@franklin.uga.edu
    Pubs: *Gold, Still Life with Children* (Pudding Hse Pub,
    2000, 1996), *A More Perfect Union: Anth* (St. Martin's
    Pr, 1998), *Claiming the Spirit Within: Anth* (Beacon,
    1996), *For She Is the Tree of Life: Anth* (Conari Pr,
    1994)
I.D.: Feminist, Episcopalian. Groups: Spiritual/Religious,
Women

Coleman Barks ♣ ✈   P
196 Westview Dr
Athens, GA 30606, 706-543-2148
    Pubs: *The Glance* (Viking, 1999), *The Essential Rumi*
    (Harper SF, 1995), *Gourd Seed* (Maypop, 1992),
    Georgia Rev, Kenyon Rev, NER

Ka Bowles   P
358 Oakland Ave SE
Alpharetta, GA 30312
    Pubs: *Poem, Lullwater Rev, Panhandler, Bellingham*
    Rev, Voices Intl, Cape Rock

Gloria G. Brame   P&W
PO Box 18552
Atlanta, GA 31126, 404-364-9968
    Pubs: *Elf, Thermopylae*

Roy Bush   W
Box 6
Colquitt, GA 31737, 912-758-3524

Lucas Carpenter ♣ ✈   P
Oxford College of Emory Univ, English Dept, Oxford, GA
30267, 404-784-8301
Internet: lcarpen@emory.edu
    Pubs: *John Gould Fletcher & Southern Modernism* (U
    Arkansas Pr, 1990), *Carolina Qtly, Minnesota Rev,*
    Crescent Rev, Kansas Rev, College English, The Jrnl,
    Southern Humanities Rev, South Carolina Rev

Turner Cassity   P
510 E Ponce De Leon Ave, Apt J
Decatur, GA 30030, 404-373-3514
    Pubs: *The Destructive Element* (Ohio U Pr, 1998),
    Between the Chains, Hurricane Lamp (U Chicago Pr,
    1991, 1986), *Poetry*

Mary Ann Coleman   P
205 Sherwood Dr
Athens, GA 30606
    Pubs: *Disappearances* (Anhinga Pr, 1978), *Kansas Qtly,*
    National Forum, Negative Capability, Literary Rev

Stephen Corey ♣ ✈   P&W
357 Parkway Dr
Athens, GA 30606-4951, 706-542-3481
Internet: scorey@arches.uga.edu
    Pubs: *Mortal Fathers & Daughters* (Palanquin Pr, 1999),
    All These Lands You Call One Country (U Missouri Pr,
    1992), *Shenandoah*

Gary Corseri   P&W
2455 Kingsland Dr
Atlanta, GA 30360, 404-396-8377
    Pubs: *Random Descent, North of Wakulla: Anth*
    (Anhinga Pr, 1989, 1989), *City Lights Rev, Redbook,*
    Georgia Rev, Poetry NW, Florida Rev

Doris Davenport   P&W
PO Box 135
Cornelia, GA 30531-0135, 704-535-3121
   Pubs: *Voodoo Chile/Slight Return* (Soque Street Pr,
   1991), *Eat Thunder & Drink Rain* (Self, 1982), *Melus,
   Mid-American Rev, Women's Rev of Bks, Lesbian
   Studies*

Cynde Gregory De Acevedo Jerez   P
2615 Ridge Brook Trail
Duluth, GA 30096, 770-797-9099
   Pubs: *Satori, Black Ice, Instructor Mag, BPJ, North
   Country Anth, Calyx*

Juni Dunklin   P&W
407 W Church St
Sandersville, GA 31082

Pam Durban   W
English Dept, Georgia State Univ, University Plaza,
Atlanta, GA 30303
   Pubs: *All Set About with Fever Trees* (Godine, 1985),
   Georgia Rev, The Reaper, TriQtly

John Ehrlichman   W
795 Hammond Dr #1607
Atlanta, GA 30328
   Pubs: *The China Card, Witness to Power* (S&S, 1986,
   1983), *Parade Mag, Texas Monthly, New York Mag*

Nadine Estroff   P
3134 Edinburgh Dr
Augusta, GA 30909-3316
   Pubs: *Hollins Critic, NYQ, Southern Rev, SW Rev,
   Carleton Miscellany, Texas Qtly, Kansas Qtly, Lyrical
   Voices*

Blanche Farley   P&W
1501 N Decatur Rd NE, #3
Atlanta, GA 30307-1042, 404-264-9811
   Pubs: *The Bedford Introduction to Literature: Anth* (St.
   Martin's Pr, 1990), *Southern Humanities Rev,
   Pilgrimage, Catalyst*

Richard Flynn 🎤 ✈   P
310 Savannah Ave
Statesboro, GA 30458-5259, 912-489-1913
   Pubs: *The Age of Reason* (Hawkhead Pr, 1993),
   Reaper, Washington Rev, lower limit speech

Starkey Flythe, Jr.   W
403 Telfair St
Augusta, GA 30901
   Pubs: *The American Story* (Curtis Pub, 1977), *Georgia
   Rev, Greensboro Rev, Ploughshares, Wind*

H. E. Francis   W
Frederic C. Beil, Publisher, 609 Whitaker St, Savannah,
GA 31401
   Pubs: *Sudden Fictions* (Peregrine Smith, 1986), *A
   Disturbance of Gulls* (Braziller, 1983), *Itinerary of
   Beggars* (Iowa, 1973), *Kenyon Rev, Alaska Qtly,
   Ontario Rev, Beloit Fiction, Literary Rev, Missouri Rev*

Walter Griffin 🎤 ✈   P
2518 Maple St
East Point, GA 30344-2432, 404-762-9196
   Pubs: *Nights of Noise & Light* (Skidrow Penthouse,
   1999), *Western Flyers* (U West Florida Pr, 1990),
   Georgia Voices: Anth (U Georgia Pr, 2000), *Atlantic,
   Evergreen, Paris Rev, Literary Rev, Southern Rev, New
   Criterion, Poetry, Harper's*
Groups: Schools, Prisoners

Gary D. Grossman   P
237 Highland Ave
Athens, GA 30606, 706-549-5897
   Pubs: *Mobius, Old Red Kimono, Brussels Sprout, In
   Your Face, Midwest Poetry Rev, Opus Literary Rev,
   Poetry Motel, Feh, The Acorn, Cotton Gin, Pearl, Lilliput
   Rev, Blood & Fire Rev*

Linda Lee Harper   P
3693 Inverness Way
Augusta, GA 30907, 706-860-1876
   Pubs: *Blue Flute* (Adastra Pr, 1998), *Toward Desire*
   (Word Works, 1996), *A Failure of Loveliness*
   (Nightshade Pr, 1994), *Anth of South Carolina Poets*
   (Ninety-Six Pr, 1994), *Georgia Rev, Massachusetts Rev,
   Illinois Rev, Kansas Qtly, Laurel Rev, Passages North*

Robert Hays   P
3360 Trickum Rd
Marietta, GA 30006-4683, 770-924-9228
Internet: haysr@aol.com
   Pubs: *Parnassus Literary Jrnl, Dekalb Literary Arts Jrnl,
   Reach of Song, Alura*

Katherine L. Hester   W
714 Woodland Ave SE
Atlanta, GA 30316
   Pubs: *Eggs for Young America* (Penguin, 1998),
   Ex-Files: New Stories About Old Flames: Anth (Context
   Bks, 2000), *Prize Stories 1994: The O. Henry Awards:
   Anth* (Anchor/Doubleday, 1995), *American Short Fiction,
   Cimarron Rev, Five Points, Indiana Rev*

Robert W. Hill   P
Kennesaw State College, 1000 Chastain Rd, Kennesaw,
GA 30144-5591, 404-423-6297
   Pubs: *Human Factors* (Poetry Atlanta Pr, 1989), *James
   Dickey* (G.K. Hall, 1983), *Southern Rev*

Robert Holland   P
140 Ridley Cir
Decatur, GA 30030, 404-378-2103
   Pubs: *Norton Introduction to Literature: Anth* (Norton,
   1978), *Georgia Rev, Midwest Qtly*

Emmett Jarrett   P
St. Michael and All Angels, Episcopal Church, 6740
Memorial Dr, Stone Mountain, GA 30083-2235
   Pubs: *To Heal the Sin-Sick Soul* (Episcopal Urban
   Caucus, 1996), *God's Body* (Hanging Loose Pr, 1975),
   Hanging Loose, Fellowship Papers, Jubilee Pubs

Greg Johnson 🎤 ✈   W
808 Amsterdam Ave
Atlanta, GA 30306, 770-423-6491
Internet: rjohn@aol.com
   Pubs: *Sticky Kisses* (Alyson Bks, 2001), *Distant Friends*
   (U Georgia Pr, 1997), *I Am Dangerous & Other Stories,
   A Friendly Deceit* (Johns Hopkins Pr, 1996, 1992),
   Pagan Babies (Dutton, 1993), *Distant Friends* (Ontario
   Rev Pr, 1990), *TriQtly, Georgia Rev*

Seaborn Jones 🎤 ✈   P
PO Box 469
Lizella, GA 31052-0469, 912-935-3659
   Pubs: *Lost Keys* (Snake Nation Pr, 1996), *X-Ray
   Movies* (Georgia Arts Council, 1988), *Drowning from the
   Inside Out* (Cherry Valley, 1983), *Georgia Voices: Anth*
   (U Georgia Pr, 2000), *NYQ, Atlanta Rev, Pearl, SPR,
   River Styx*

Anthony Kellman 🎤 ✈   P&W
796 Palatine Ave SE
Atlanta, GA 30316-2490
Internet: akellman@aol.com
   Pubs: *Wings of a Stranger, The Long Gap, The Coral
   Rooms, Watercourse* (Peepal Tree Pr, 2000, 1996,
   1994, 1990), *Chelsea, Callaloo*
I.D.: African-American, African-Caribbean. Groups:
Teenagers, Seniors

Gary Kerley 🎤 ✈   P
4720 Creek Wood Dr
Gainesville, GA 30507-8870, 770-532-3430
   Pubs: *From the Green Horseshoe: Anth* (U South
   Carolina Pr, 1987), *SPR, Yankee*

Robert S. King   P
RR1 Box 222
Carlton, GA 30627-9620, 706-743-3098
   Pubs: *Immortelles: Anth* (Xavier Rev Pr, 1995), *Kenyon
   Rev, Spoon River Poetry Rev, Visions Intl, California
   Qtly, Negative Capability, SPR*

Diane Kistner   P
738 Ormewood Ave SE
Atlanta, GA 30312
   Pubs: *Falling in Caves* (Bootlaig Pr, 1982), *Poem, Aura,
   Literary Arts Rev, North Carolina Sun*

Martin Lammon 🎤 ✈   P
Georgia College & State Univ, Arts & Letters, Campus
Box 89, Milledgeville, GA 31061, 478-445-1289
Internet: mlammon@mail.gcsu.edu
   Pubs: *News from Where I Live* (U Arkansas Pr, 1998),
   *Nimrod, Gettysburg Rev, Midwest Qtly Rev,
   Ploughshares*

M. Rosser Lunsford   P
456 Rockville Springs Dr
Eatonton, GA 31024, 404-485-3449
   Pubs: *Thoughts About Life* (Rainbow Bks, 1988),
   Sparrowgrass Anth (Washington U, 1998), *Reach of
   Song Anth* (Georgia Poetry Society, 1997), *Arizona
   Highways, Jean's Jrnl, Rhyme Time*

Marion Montgomery   P&W
Box 115
Crawford, GA 30630, 706-743-5359
   Pubs: *The Men I Have Chosen for Fathers* (U Missouri
   Pr, 1990), *The Trouble with You Innerleckchuls*
   (Christendom College Pr, 1988)

Janice Townley Moore   P
English Dept, Young Harris College, Young Harris, GA
30582, 828-389-6394
   Pubs: *The Bedford Intro to Literature: Anth* (St. Martin's
   Pr, 1996), *When I Am an Old Woman I Shall Wear
   Purple: Anth* (Papier-Mache Pr, 1987), *SPR, Georgia
   Rev, Atlanta Rev*

Cynthia A. Mortus   P
509 Cross Creek
Stone Mountain, GA 30087-5328, 770-879-9704
   Pubs: *Connecticut River Rev, Black Bear Rev, Poem,
   Cotton Boll, Spoon River Qtly, Encore, Earth's
   Daughters, Virginia Country*

Chuck Oliveros   P
1206 Lyndale Dr SE
Atlanta, GA 30316, 404-624-1524
   Pubs: *Bleeding from the Mouth, The Pterodactyl in the
   Wilderness* (Dead Angel, 1992, 1982), *Caliban*

Lee Passarella   P
1384 Township Dr
Lawrenceville, GA 30243, 404-995-9475
   Pubs: *Out of A/Maze: Anth* (Chiron Review Pr, 1996),
   *Sun, JAMA, Chelsea, Literary Rev, Formalist, Cream
   City Rev*

Phyllis E. Price   P
509 Cross Creek Pt
Stone Mountain, GA 30087, 404-841-5515
   Pubs: *Cotton Boll, Connecticut River Rev, Virginia
   Country Mag, Embers, Oxford, Appalachian Heritage,
   Poem*

Robert Earl Price   P&W
19 Ollie St NW
Atlanta, GA 30314, 404-753-3113
    Pubs: *Blues Blood* (CAC Pr, 1995), *Blood Elegy* (Poetry
    Atlanta Pr, 1987), *Blood Lines* (Togetherness Pr, 1984),
    Black Poetry of the '80s in the Deep South: Anth
    (Beans & Brown Rice Pub, 1990), *Snake Nation Rev,
    African American Rev, Atlanta Rev, Quest*

Rosetta Radtke   P&W
PO Box 2123
Savannah, GA 31402-2123
    Pubs: *Staten Island, Passages North, Blue Pitcher, Off
    Main Street, Wind, Pembroke, Poetry Now*

Barbara Ras   P
PO Box 82375
Athens, GA 30608, 706-552-3626
    Pubs: *Bite Every Sorrow* (Louisiana State U Pr, 1998),
    The New American Poets: Anth (U Pr of New England,
    2000), *Georgia Rev, Massachusetts Rev*

Paul Rice   P
Brunswick College, Altama at Fourth, Brunswick, GA
31523, 912-264-7357
    Pubs: *Georgia Rev, Chattahoochee Rev, Tar River Rev,
    Blue Unicorn, Barataria Rev, Mountain Rev*

William P. Robertson   P
PO Box 14532
Savannah, GA 31416
    Pubs: *Life After Sex Life* (Four Winds Pr, 1983)

Jalane Rogers   P
4461 Florence St
Tucker, GA 30084
    Pubs: *Broken Streets, Living Streams, Silver Wings,
    Parnassus, Red Pagoda, Archer Mag*

Larry Rubin   P
Box 15014, Druid Hills Branch
Atlanta, GA 30333
    Pubs: *All My Mirrors Lie* (Godine, 1975), *Lanced in
    Light* (HBJ, 1967), *Unanswered Calls: Anth*
    (Kendall/Hunt, 1997), *New Yorker, Harper's, Poetry,
    Yale Rev, Sewanee Rev, Kenyon Rev*

Esta Seaton 🎤   P
1200 Beech Valley Rd NE
Atlanta, GA 30306-3124, 404-874-0147

Bettie M. Sellers   P
PO Box 274
Young Harris, GA 30582
    Pubs: *Wild Ginger* (Imagery, 1988), *Liza's Monday &
    Other Poems* (Appalachian Consortium, 1986)

L. S. Shevshenko   P&W
4008 Kemper Ave
Macon, GA 31206-1826, 912-784-8260
Internet: www.shevshenko.com
    Pubs: *Rob Amsterdam, Ice House* (Moon Dog Pr, 1996,
    1996), *The Paper Moon* (Moon Calf Pr, 1995), *In Our
    Own Words II & I: Anths* (MW Enterprises, 2000,
    1999), *In the Wind, Expresso Poetry, Sounds of Poetry,
    Dream Intl Qtly, Deathrealm Mag, Poet's Rev*

Kristina Simms 🎤   P
710 Mason Terr, #40
Perry, GA 31069-2034, 912-988-8560
Internet: ktina@alltel.net
    Pubs: *Zone 3, Habersham Rev, Poem, Aura, Snake
    Nation Rev, Chattahoochee Rev*

Terrill Shepard Soules   P
1616 Piedmont Ave NE, #S-3
Atlanta, GA 30324, 404-881-1988
    Pubs: *Vacations, The Selectric Poems* (Pynyon Pr,
    1986, 1983), *Esquire, Kayak, San Jose Studies*

George E. Statham 🎤   P
699 McRidge Rd
Hiawassee, GA 30546, 706-896-5431
    Pubs: *Gunny's Rhymes, Poetic Injustice* (Fireside Pub,
    1996, 1996), *Potry Churg Mag, Writers Exchange,
    Parnassus Literary Jrnl, Laureate Letter Newsletter,
    Leatherneck Mag, Lines & Rhymes, Poetic Eloquence,
    Blind Man's Rainbow, Ultraflight Mag, Apostrophe*

Leon Stokesbury   P
English Dept, Georgia State Univ, Atlanta, GA 30303,
404-651-2900
    Pubs: *Autumn Rhythm, The Made Thing, The Drifting
    Away* (U Arkansas Pr, 1996, 1987, 1986), *New Yorker,
    Georgia Rev, Kenyon Rev*

John Stone 🎤 ✈   P
3983 Northlake Creek Ct
Tucker, GA 30084
    Pubs: *Where Water Begins, The Smell of Matches, In
    All This Rain* (LSU, 1998, 1988, 1980), *In the Country
    of Hearts* (Delacorte, 1992)

Eileen H. Stratidakis 🎤 ✈   P
PO Box 941954
Atlanta, GA 31141-0954, 770-270-9392
    Pubs: *Partisan Rev, Sycamore Rev, Cape Rock, Florida
    Qtly, Cottonwood, Lullwater Rev*
Groups: Children, Prisoners

Heather Tosteson   P&W
PO Box 2359
Decatur, GA 30031
    Pubs: *Nation, Pequod, Calyx, SPR, New Virginia Rev,
    Cottonwood Rev, Southern Rev, NW Rev*

Memye Curtis Tucker 🎤 ✈   P
184 Rhodes Dr
Marietta, GA 30068-3672, 770-971-1834
Internet: mctucker@avana.net
   Pubs: *The Watchers* (Ohio U Pr, 1998), *Admit One* (State Street Pr, 1998), *Storm Line* (Palanquin Pr, 1998), *Holding Patterns* (Poetry Atlanta Pr, 1988), *Buck & Wing: Anth* (Shenandoah, 2000), *What Have You Lost?: Anth* (Greenwillow Bks, 1999), *Georgia Rev*

Dan Veach 🎤 ✈   P
PO Box 8248
Atlanta, GA 31106, 404-636-0052
Internet: dan@atlantareview.com
   Pubs: *Annual Survey of American Poetry: Anth* (Roth, 1986), *Sotheby's Intl Poetry Competition: Anth* (Arvon 1982), *Irish Times, Sulphur Rev, CQ, Peabody Rev, Chattahoochie Rev, Pinchpenny*

James E. Warren, Jr.   P
St. Anne's Terrace, 3100 Northside Pkwy NW, #309,
Atlanta, GA 30327, 404-233-0712
   Pubs: *All Years Be Praised* (microPRINT, 1989), *Poems of Lovett* (The Lovett School, 1986), *Intl Poetry Rev, Lullwater Rev, Blue Unicorn*

Sharon Webb   W
Rt 2, Box 2600
Blairsville, GA 30512, 404-745-4454
   Pubs: *Pestis 18* (Tor/St. Martin's Pr, 1987), *Ram Song* (Bantam, 1985)

GUAM

Richard E. Mezo 🎤 ✈   P
PO Box 24814, GMF
Barrigada, GU 96923, 671-477-1961
Internet: remezo@netpci.com
   Pubs: *Mainstreeter, Penny Dreadful, Colorado Qtly, Nantucket Rev, Christianity & the Arts, Poetry Motel, CQ, Buffalo Bones, Riverrun, SPR, Buffalo Spree, South Dakota Rev, HVE, Kaleido, Graffiti, George & Mertie's, Haight-Ashbury Literary Jrnl, Kimera*

HAWAII

Nell Altizer   P
English Dept, Univ Hawaii, 1733 Donaghho Rd, Honolulu, HI 96822, 808-948-7619
   Pubs: *The Man Who Died En Route* (U Massachusetts Pr, 1989), *Hawaii Rev, Ploughshares, Chaminade Rev, Massachusetts Rev*

Laureen Ching   P
2930 Varsity Cir, #4
Honolulu, HI 96826
   Pubs: *Rosalind, Thea* (Fawcett, 1985, 1985), *Hawaii Rev, Mississippi Valley Rev, Dacotah Territory*

Eric E. Chock   P
95-1053 Kopalani St
Mililani, HI 96789
   Pubs: *Last Days Here* (Bamboo Ridge Pr, 1990), *The Open Boat, Poems of Asian America: Anth* (Anchor, 1993), *Seattle Rev, Zyzzyva, Jrnl of Ethnic Studies*

Kermit Coad 🎤 ✈   P
1802 Mokehana Pl
Kihei, HI 96753-7920, 808-879-1782
   Pubs: *Poetry Hawaii: Anth* (U Hawaii Pr, 1979), *Stoogism Anthology* (Scarecrow Bks, 1977), *The Spirit that Moves Us, Makali'i, Bamboo Ridge*

Reuel Denney   P
2957 Kalakaua Ave, #315
Honolulu, HI 96815-4647, 808-923-9618
   Pubs: *Feast of Strangers* (Greenwood Pr, 1999), *Conrad Aiken* (U Minnesota Pr, 1964), *The Astonished Muse, In Praise of Adam* (U Chicago Pr, 1989, 1961), *The Lonely Crowd* (w/D. Reisman & N. Glazer; Yale U Pr, 1950), *New Directions, Kaimana, Poetry, Chelsea*

Ray Freed 🎤 ✈   P
PO Box 2883
Kailua-Kona, HI 96745-2883, 808-326-1138
Internet: www.tropweb.com/indigo/poems.htm
   Pubs: *All Horses are Flowers, Much Cry Little Wool* (Street Pr, 1998, 1990), *The Juggler's Ball* (Hualalai Pr, 1996)

Rasma Haidri 🎤 ✈   P
84-4940 Keala o Keawe Rd
Captain Cook, HI 96704-8413, 808-328-9494
Internet: rasma@hialoha.net
   Pubs: *Essential Love: Anth* (Grayson Bks, 2000), *The Pocket Poetry Parenting Guide: Anth* (Pudding House Pr, 1999), *Earth's Daughters, Fine Madness, Fish Stories, Lullwater Rev, Passages North, Prairie Schooner*
Lang: Norwegian. Groups: Children, Schools

Joy Harjo   P
1140-D Alewa Dr
Honolulu, HI 96817-1562, 808-595-8549
Internet: katcvpoet@aol.com
   Pubs: *A Map to the Next World, Reinventing the Enemy's Language, The Woman Who Fell from the Sky* (Norton, 2000, 1997, 1994), *The Spiral of Memory* (U Michigan Pr, 1996), *In Mad Love & War* (Wesleyan, 1990)

Norman Hindley   P
46-049 Aliianela Pl, #1721
Kaneohe, HI 96744-3703, 808-236-2229
   Pubs: *A Good Man* (Fawcett, 1993), *Winter Eel*
(Petronium Pr, 1984), *Chaminade Literary Rev, Hawaii
Rev, Hawaii Literary Arts, Poetry*

Faye Kicknosway   P
English Dept, Univ Hawaii at Manoa, 412 Kuykendall,
Honolulu, HI 96822, 808-956-7619
   Pubs: *Listen to Me, The Violence of Potatoes*
(Ridgeway Pr, 1992, 1990), *All These Voices* (Coffee
Hse Pr, 1986)

Irina Kirk   W
475 Front St, #323
Lahaina, HI 96761, 808-661-4835
   Pubs: *Chekhov* (Twayne, 1980), *Profile in Russian
Resistance* (Quadrangle, 1975)

Jim Kraus   P
English Department, Chaminade Univ, 3140 Waialae Ave,
Honolulu, HI 96816, 808-735-4863
   Pubs: *Poetry Hawaii* (U Hawaii Pr, 1979), *Virginia Qtly
Rev, San Marcos Rev, Pequod, Hawaii Rev, Ramrod,
Kentucky Poetry Rev, Chaminade Literary Rev*

Patrick Leahy   W
c/o NOAA, 3651 Ahukini Rd, Lihue, HI 96766-9713
   Pubs: *Bachy, Rocky Mountain Rev, Pulp*

Darrell H. Y. Lum 🎤 ✈   W
990 Hahaione St
Honolulu, HI 96825-1036, 808-626-1481
Internet: darrel@hawaii.edu
   Pubs: *Pass On, No Pass Back!, The Best of Bamboo
Ridge: Anth* (Bamboo Ridge Pr, 1990, 1986), *Into the
Fire: Anth* (Greenfield Rev Pr, 1996), *Seattle Rev,
Manoa, Chaminade Rev*
I.D.: Chinese-American. Groups: Hawaii Creole English

Wing Tek Lum   P
80 N King St
Honolulu, HI 96817, 808-531-5200
   Pubs: *Expounding the Doubtful Points* (Bamboo Ridge,
1987)

Alan Decker McNarie   P&W
77 Mohouli St
Hilo, HI 96720, 808-935-7210
   Pubs: *Yeshua: The Gospel of St. Thomas* (Pushcart Pr,
1993), *Chaminade Literary Mag, Hawaii Pacific Rev,
Kaimana, Bamboo Ridge, Cape Rock, Poultry, Wind*

William J. Puette   P
3363-A Keanu St
Honolulu, HI 96816
   Pubs: *The Hilo Massacre* (U Hawaii Pr, 1988), *Guide
to the Tale of Genji* (Tuttle, 1983)

Tony Quagliano 🎤 ✈   P
509 University Ave #902
Honolulu, HI 96826-5002
   Pubs: *Poetry of Solitude: Anth* (Rizzoli, 1995), *Rolling
Stone, New Directions, NYQ, Harvard Rev, Exquisite
Corpse, Yankee, JAMA, Kaimana*

Robert Shapard   W
English Dept, Univ Hawaii-Manoa, 1733 Donaghho Rd,
Honolulu, HI 96822-2315, 808-956-3078
Internet: rshapard@hawaii.edu
   Pubs: *Stories in the Stepmother Tongue: Anth* (White
Pine Pr, 2000), *Sudden Fiction Continued: Anth,
Sudden Fiction Intl: Anth* (Norton, 1996, 1989), *Flaunt,
NER, Kenyon Rev, Literary Rev, Prism Intl,
Mid-American Rev, Cimarron Rev*

Stephen Shrader   P
41-945b Laumilo St
Waimanalo, HI 96795, 808-259-5692

Cathy Song   P
PO Box 27262
Honolulu, HI 96827, 808-626-1481
   Pubs: *School Figures* (U Pitt Pr, 1994), *Frameless
Windows, Squares of Light* (Norton, 1988), *Picture Bride*
(Yale U Pr, 1983), *Poetry, Shenandoah, Southern Rev,
Kenyon Rev, Michigan Qtly Rev, Carolina Qtly Rev,
Poetry Ireland, NER*

Joseph Stanton 🎤 ✈   P
Dept. of Art, University of Hawaii at Manoa,, Honolulu, HI
96822, 808-956-4050
Internet: jstanton@hawaii.edu
   Pubs: *Imaginary Museum* (Time Being Bks, 1999),
What the Kite Thinks (U Hawaii Pr, 1994), *Cortland
Rev, Ekphrasis, Poetry, Poetry East, Harvard Rev,
NYQ, Image*

Frank Stewart   P
Univ Hawaii, English Dept, Honolulu, HI 96822,
808-956-3064
   Pubs: *Flying the Red Eye, The Open Water* (Floating
Island, 1986, 1982), *Ploughshares, Zyzzyva, Ironwood,
Orion*

Jean Yamasaki Toyama   P
European Languages/Literature, Univ Hawaii, 1890
East-West Rd, Moore 485, Honolulu, HI 96822,
808-956-4185
   Pubs: *What the Kite Thinks: A Linked Poem* (U Hawaii
Pr, 1994), *The Forbidden Stitch: Anth* (Calyx, 1989),
*Illuminations, Kaimana, Caprice, Redneck Rev, Michigan
Qtly Rev*

Dorothy Winslow Wright   P&W
2119 Ahapii Pl
Honolulu, HI 96821, 808-734-0846
   Pubs: *Computer Legends, Lies, & Lore* (Ageless Pr,
   1994), *The Book Group Book: Anth* (Chicago Rev Pr,
   1993), *Poet, Mature Living, Blue Unicorn*

IDAHO

William C. Anderson   W
4857 Lake Shore Pl
Boise, ID 83703, 208-853-4812
   Pubs: *Please Don't Tailgate the Real Estate* (Trailer
   Life Bks, 1997), *Lady Bluebeard, Taming Mighty Alaska:
   An RV Odyssey* (Fred Pruett Pub, 1994, 1990),
   Reader's Digest

Dan Gerber   P&W
Michigan State Univ Press, PO Box 371, Driggs, ID 83422
   Pubs: *A Last Bridge Home, A Voice from the River,
   Grass Fires* (Clark City, 1992, 1990, 1989), *New
   Yorker, Nation, Georgia Rev*

Mark Geston   W
1829 Edgecliff Terr
Boise, ID 83702, 208-344-8535
   Pubs: *Mirror to the Sky* (Morrow, 1992), *Lords of the
   Starship* (Ace, 1967), *Amazing Stories, Fantasy & Sci
   Fi*

Gary Gildner 🎤 ✈   P&W
RR2, Box 219
Grangeville, ID 83530-9615, 208-983-1663
   Pubs: *The Birthday Party* (Limberlost Pr, 2000), *Blue
   Like the Heavens* (U Pitt Pr, 1984), *Bunker in the
   Parsley Fields, The Warsaw Sparks* (U Iowa Pr, 1997,
   1990), *Poetry, Georgia Rev, New Letters, Shenandoah,
   NAR, Poetry NW, Witness*

Janet Campbell Hale   P&W
799 Wildshoe Dr
Desmet, ID 83824, 208-274-2034
   Pubs: *The Owl's Song & Other Stories* (HC, 1995),
   Bloodlines (Random Hse, 1993)

Miriam Halliday-Borkowski   P
Pomulty Farm, PO Box 374, Bonners Ferry, ID 83805,
208-267-1120
   Pubs: *For the Beloved* (Handbuilt Bks/San Raphael,
   1996), *In Memoriam Jo Ann Yellow Bird*
   (Colouredpoetry/Handbuilt Bks, 1988), *Columbia,
   Beatitude, Kansas Qtly*

Janet Holmes 🎤 ✈   P
1304 N 26th St
Boise, ID 83702-2323
Internet: jholmes@boisestate.edu
   Pubs: *The Physicist at the Mall* (Anhinga Pr, 1994),
   The Green Tuxedo (U Notre Dame Pr, 1998),
   Paperback Romance (State Street Pr, 1984)

Daryl Jones   P
Boise State Univ, 1910 University Dr, Boise, ID 83725,
208-385-1202
   Pubs: *Someone Going Home Late* (Texas Tech U Pr,
   1990), *Sewanee Rev, TriQtly, New Orleans Rev*

Ron McFarland   P&W
857 E 8 St
Moscow, ID 83843, 208-882-0849
   Pubs: *The Haunting Familiarity of Things* (Singular
   Speech Pr, 1993), *Tumblewords: Writers Reading the
   West: Anth* (U Nevada Pr, 1995), *Poetry NW, American
   Literary Rev, Midwest Qtly, Willow Springs, Talking
   River Rev, Urbanus Mag*

Helen Olsen 🎤   P&W
23289 Homedale Rd
Wilder, ID 83676, 208-337-3469
   Pubs: *Afterthoughts, Bogg, Maverick Pr, New Era, New
   Writers, St. Anthony Messenger, St. Joseph's Mag,
   Time of Singing, Tree Spirit, Yankee Mag*

Lance Olsen   W
Bear Creek Cabin, 1490 Ailor Rd, Deary, ID 83823,
208-877-1422
   Pubs: *Time Famine, Tonguing the Zeitgeist* (Permeable
   Pr, 1996, 1994), *Scherzi, I Believe* (Wordcraft, 1994),
   *Fiction Intl, Mondo 2000, VLS, Black Ice, ACM,
   Gargoyle, Iowa Rev, Hudson Rev*

Joan Silva   P
PO Box 67
Emmett, ID 83617
   Pubs: *Attila* (Black Scarab Pr, 1976), *Slipstream,
   Tandava, Pteranadon, Contact II, Exquisite Corpse,
   Gryphon, Prickly Pear*

William Studebaker 🎤 ✈   P
2616 E 4000 N
Twin Falls, ID 83301, 208-733-8584
   Pubs: *Short of a Good Promise* (Washington State U
   Pr, 1999), *Travelers in an Antique Land* (U Idaho Pr,
   1997), *River Religion, The Rat Lady at the Company
   Dump* (Limberlost, 1997, 1990), *Dickinson Rev, Ohio
   Rev, High Country News, George Washington Rev*

Eberle Umbach   W
Box 172
McCall, ID 83638
   Pubs: *NW Rev, Timbuktu, Oh Idaho Mag, Whole Earth
   Rev*

Norman Weinstein P
730 E Bannock St
Boise, ID 83712, 208-345-8516
  Pubs: *A Night in Tunisia: Imaginings of Africa in Jazz*
  (Scarecrow Pr, 1992), *Village Voice, Sulfur, Io, Tree*

Robert Wrigley 🎤 ✈ P
RR1, Box 98W4
Lenore, ID 83541-9609, 208-836-5691
Internet: rwrigley@uidaho.edu
  Pubs: *Reign of Snakes, In the Bank of Beautiful Sins*
  (Penguin, 1999, 1995), *What My Father Believed, Moon
  in a Mason Jar* (U Illinois Pr, 1991, 1986)

Harald Wyndham 🎤 ✈ P
1849 Pebble Road
Inkom, ID 83245, 208-232-5118
  Pubs: *Tuscany* (Acid Pr, 2000), *The Christmas Sonnets,
  Heavenly Rhythm & Blues* (Blue Scarab Pr, 1996,
  1993)

ILLINOIS

Carol M. Adorjan 🎤 ✈ W
1667 Winnetka Rd
Glenview, IL 60025, 847-657-8502
Internet: http://members.aol.com/writenow4
  Pubs: *I Can! Can You?, WKID: Easy Radio Plays*
  (Albert Whitman, 1990, 1988), *NAR, Redbook, Denver
  Qtly, Woman's Day, Natl Radio Theatre*
Groups: Children

Michael A. Anania P&W
5755 Sunset Ave
La Grange, IL 60525
  Pubs: *Selected Poems* (Moyer Bell, 1994)

Arnold Aprill PP
2850 N Seminary
Chicago, IL 60657, 312-281-0927

Asa Baber W
247 E Chestnut
Chicago, IL 60611

Mary Shen Barnidge 🎤 P
1030 W Dakin St
Chicago, IL 60613-2912, 773-871-3904
  Pubs: *Detours* (Lonesome Traveler Pub, 1997), *Piano
  Player at the Dionysia* (Thompson Hill, 1984), *Power
  Lines: Anth* (Tia Chucha Pr, 1999), *Whetstone,
  Overtures, Leatherneck, Howling Dog, Kaleidoscope,
  DEROS*

Jill Barrie P
10S 272 Alma Ln
Naperville, IL 60564
  Pubs: *Calapooya Collage, Gulf Stream, American
  Literary Rev, Cimarron, New Virginia Rev, Calliope,
  Black River Rev, SPR, American Literary Rev*

Saul Bellow W
1126 E 59 St
Chicago, IL 60637
  Pubs: *The Dean's December* (H&R, 1982), *Herzog*
  (Viking, 1964)

Ronald Belluomini 🎤 ✈ P
1721 Juliet Ln
Libertyville, IL 60048, 847-367-4218
  Pubs: *The Thirteenth Labor* (Dragon's Teeth Pr, 1985),
  Rhino, FOC Rev, Menagerie

Brooke Bergan P
1150 N Lake Shore Dr #19F
Chicago, IL 60611-1025
  Pubs: *Storyville* (Moyer Bell, 1993), *Distant Topologies,
  Windowpane* (Wine Pr, 1976, 1974), *ACM, Oyez, Wire*

Susan Bergman 🎤 ✈ P&W
880 N Lake Shore Dr, #8AE
Chicago, IL 60611-1761, 888-408-7678
Internet: sbergman@previewport.com
  Pubs: *Anonymity* (FSG, 1994), *Martyrs: Anth* (HC,
  1996), *TriQtly, Ploughshares, Pequod*

Leslie Bertagnolli P
2800 Prudential Plaza
Chicago, IL 60601, 312-861-8617
  Pubs: *Family Photographs* (Red Herring Pr, 1979)

Leigh Buchanan Bienen W
639 Central St
Evanston, IL 60201-1732
  Pubs: *The Ways We Live Now: Anth* (Ontario Rev Pr,
  1986), *O. Henry Prize Stories 1983: Anth* (Doubleday,
  1983), *Descant, Ontario Rev*

James Bonk P
400 N Main St
Mt Prospect, IL 60056, 312-253-7673
  Pubs: *Poetry Connection – Dial a Poem Chicago Anth*
  (City of Chicago, 1991), *America, Minnesota Rev,
  Commonweal*

Walter L. Bradford P
932 E 50 St
Chicago, IL 60615, 312-373-2957

Ardyth Bradley ♣ ✈ P
514 Broadway
Libertyville, IL 60048, 708-362-4635
Internet: jbradley@enteract.com
  Pubs: *Inside the Bones Is Flesh* (Ithaca Hse, 1978),
  Benchmark Anth of Contemporary Illinois Poetry
  (Stormline Pr, 1988), *Three Winter Poems: Anth*
  (Penumbra Pr, 1986), *Poetry, Parting Gifts,*
  Shenandoah, Cutbank, Ironwood, Tendril, Chili Verde
  Rev

John M. Bradley ♣ ✈ P
504 Sycamore Rd
DeKalb, IL 60115, 815-756-1533
  Pubs: *To Dance with Uranium* (Lake Effect Pr, 1995),
  Beyond Lament: Anth (Northwestern, 1998), *Atomic*
  Ghost: Anth (Coffee Hse, 1995), *Prose Poem, Poetry*
  East, Another Chicago Mag, Sonora

Becky Bradway ♣ ✈ W
Millikin Univ, English Dept.
Decatur, IL 62522, 217-362-6465
Internet: bbradway@mail.millikin.edu
  Pubs: *ACM, American Fiction, Ascent, Beloit Fiction*
  Jrnl, Cream City Rev, Green Mountains Rev,
  Greensboro Rev, Laurel Rev, Literary Rev, NAR, Other
  Voices, River Styx, Third Coast, Troika, Writing on the
  Edge

Alice G. Brand P
1235 N. Astor St
Chicago, Il 60610, 312-664-4822
Internet: abrand@brockport.edu
  Pubs: *Studies on Zone* (BkMk Pr, 1989), *As It Happens*
  (Wampeter Pr, 1983), *Confrontation, River Styx, Nimrod,*
  Paintbrush, New Letters, Minnesota Rev

June Rachuy Brindel P&W
2740 Lincoln Ln
Wilmette, IL 60091, 847-251-9228
  Pubs: *Phaedra* (St. Martin's Pr, 1985), *Nobody Is Ever*
  Missing (Story Pr, 1984), *Sound of Writing, Other*
  Voices, Mss., Iowa Rev, Story Qtly, Cimarron Rev

Glen Brown P
100 S Brainard Ave
La Grange, IL 60525-2100, 708-579-6300
Internet: ghbrown@enc.k12.il.us
  Pubs: *Yes, No, Maybe* (Lake Shore Pub, 1995), *Don't*
  Ask Why (Thorntree Pr, 1994), *Illinois Rev, Oyez Rev,*
  Poetry, Poet & Critic, Negative Capability, Spoon River
  Poetry Rev

Rosellen Brown ♣ ✈ P&W
5421 S Cornell, #16
Chicago, IL 60615, 773-288-3349
  Pubs: *Half a Heart, Cora Fry's Pillow Book, Before &*
  After (FSG, 2000, 1994, 1992), *Rosellen Brown Reader*
  (U Pr of New England, 1992), *Street Games* (Milkweed,
  1991)
  I.D.: Jewish. Groups: Children, Seniors

Michael H. Brownstein ♣ ✈ P
PO Box 268805
Chicago, IL 60626-8805, 312-409-6762
Internet: garlic2222@aol.com
  Pubs: *The Principle of the Thing* (Tight Pr, 1994),
  Poems from the Body Bag (Ommation Pr, 1989),
  Always a Beautiful Answer: Anth (Kings Estate Pr,
  1999), *Samisdat, Cafe Rev, Rosewell Literary Rev,*
  Artisan, Wordwrights, Potpourri, Beyond Baroque

Debra Bruce ♣ ✈ P
English Dept, Northeastern Illinois Univ, 5500 N St Louis
Ave, Chicago, IL 60625
Internet: D-Bruce-kinnebrew@neiu.edu
  Pubs: *What Wind Will Do* (Miami U Pr, 1997), *Sudden*
  Hunger, Pure Daughter (U Arkansas Pr, 1987, 1984),
  APR, Kenyon Rev, Michigan Qtly Rev, Poetry, Virginia
  Qtly Rev, Atlantic

Rex Burwell P
1286 Robinwood Dr
Elgin, IL 60123
  Pubs: *Anti-History* (Smokeroot Pr, 1977), *Chicago Rev,*
  Shenandoah, Big Scream

Anne Calcagno ♣ ✈ W
English Dept, DePaul Univ, 802 W Belden, Chicago, IL
60614-3214, 773-325-1771
  Pubs: *Pray for Yourself, Fiction of the Eighties: Anth*
  (TriQtly Bks, 1993, 1990), *American Fiction: Anth* (Birch
  Lane Pr, 1991), *NAR, TriQtly, Epoch, Denver Qtly*
  I.D.: Italian-American

Paul Carroll P
Univ Illinois, PO Box 4348, English Dept, Chicago, IL
60680, 312-996-3260
  Pubs: *Poems* (Spoon River Poetry, 1988), *The Garden*
  of Earthly Delights (Chicago Public Library, 1986)

Ana Castillo P&W
3036 N Sawyer
Chicago, IL 60618
  Pubs: *The Mixquiahuala Letters* (Bilingual Rev Pr,
  1985), *Spoon River Qtly, River Styx, Maize*

George Chambers P&W
318 Sarah Barnewolt Dr
Peoria, IL 61604, 309-637-0454
  Pubs: *The Great Blue Sea* (Snowberries Pr, 1994), *The*
  Last Man Standing (Fiction Collective Two, 1990),
  Caprice, Situation, Iowa Rev, Prose Poem

Joan Colby ♣ ✈ P
10N226 Muirhead Rd
Elgin, IL 60123, 847-464-5250
Internet: joanmc@aol.com
  Pubs: *The Atrocity Book* (Lynx Hse, 1987), *The Lonely*
  Hearts Killers (Spoon River, 1986), *What Have You*
  Lost: Anth (Greenwillow Bks, 1999), *Poetry, Illinois Rev,*
  New Renaissance, Cream City Rev, Grand Street

Judith Cooper   W
6620 N Glenwood
Chicago, IL 60626
  Pubs: *Southern Rev, ACM, Whetstone, Black Warrior
  Rev, Louisville Rev, Nebraska Rev, MacGuffin,
  Permafrost*

Mark Costello   W
English Dept, Univ Illinois, Urbana, IL 61801

Patricia Cronin   W
414 Audubon Rd
Riverside, IL 60546, 708-442-5098
  Pubs: *Jane's Stories II: Anth* (Wild Dove Studio &
  Press, Inc, 2000), *Qtly West, Blue Skunk Companion,
  Workshirts Writing Center, Inc, Alabama Literary Rev*

Carlos Cumpian   P
March, Inc, PO Box 2890, Chicago, IL 60690,
312-935-6188
  Pubs: *Coyote Sun, Emergency Tacos* (March/Abrazo Pr,
  1990, 1989), *3rd World: Anth* (Pig Iron, 1989)

David Curry   P&W
2045 N Dayton
Chicago, IL 60614-4309
  Pubs: *Contending to Be the Dream, Here* (New Rivers
  Pr, 1979, 1970), *Crab Orchard Rev, Karamu*

Molly Daniels   W
Creative Writing School, 410 S Michigan Ave #720,
Chicago, IL 60605, 773-684-5985
  Pubs: *Father Gander Rhymes & Other Poems: Anth,
  The Clothesline Rev, No. 4: Anth* (Clothesline Review
  Pr, 1996, 1989), *Chicago Rev*

Nat David   P
1718 Sherman Ave #203
Evanston, IL 60201
  Pubs: *Heartdance* (Doublestar Pr, 1989), *Primal Voices,
  Strong Coffee, Hammers, Chaminade Literary Rev,
  Footwork: The Paterson Literary Rev*

Marjorie Carlson Davis   W
292 W Hurst St
Bushnell, IL 61422
  Pubs: *Baltimore Rev, Timber Creek Rev, Sidewalks,
  Thema, Many Mountains Moving*

Ronda Marie Davis   P
10454 S Calumet
Chicago, IL 60628, 312-955-2971

Connie Deanovich   P
c/o A. Denoyer, 5534 N Parkside, Chicago, IL 60630
  Pubs: *Watusi Titanic* (Timken, 1996), *Walk on the Wild
  Side: Contemporary Urban Poetry Anth* (Scribner, 1994),
  *Parnassus, Sulfur, Gertrude Stein Awards, New
  American Writing, Grand Street, Bomb, See*

Helen Degen Cohen   P
1166 Osterman
Deerfield, IL 60015, 847-945-0487
  Pubs: *Sarajevo Anth, Blood to Remember: Poets on
  the Holocaust: Anth* (Texas Tech U Pr, 1993, 1991),
  Partisan Rev, ACM, Stand, Outerbridge

Mary Krane Derr   P
6103 S Woodlawn, #1
Chicago, IL 60637, 773-288-2596
  Pubs: *Switched-on Gutenberg, Pudding, Sacred
  Journey, Lilliput Rev, Poet Mag, Psychopoetica, Jrnl of
  Poetry Therapy, Mobius*

John J. Desjarlais 🎙 ✈   W
934 Crest Ct
Byron, IL 61010
  Pubs: *Relics* (Thomas Nelson, 1993), *The Throne of
  Tara* (Crossway Bks, 1990)
Groups: Christian

John Dickson   P
2249 Sherman Ave
Evanston, IL 60201, 708-864-4793
  Pubs: *Waving at Trains* (Thorntree, 1986), *Victoria Hotel*
  (Chicago Rev Pr, 1979), *Poetry, TriQtly, American
  Scholar, Willow Rev, Wire, Whetstone*

George Drury 🎙 ✈   P
2674 N Burling St
Chicago, IL 60614-1514, 773-244-0095
  Pubs: *Massenmedien und Kommunikation, Pages,
  Strong Coffee, Big Scream*

Elizabeth Eddy   P
1050 W Jeffrey
Kankakee, IL 60901, 708-946-3167
  Pubs: *The Tie That Binds* (Papier-Mache Pr, 1988),
  Spoon River Qtly, Whetstone, Korone, New Poetry Jrnl

Cassie Edwards   P&W
RR#3, Box 60
Mattoon, IL 61938
  Pubs: *Savage Thunder, Savage Sunrise, Savage Winds*
  (Leisure Bks, 1994, 1993, 1993), *Wild Splendor, Wild
  Embrace, Wild Desire* (NAL, 1994, 1993, 1993)

Jim Elledge 🎙 ✈   P&W
Illinois State Univ, English Dept/4240, Normal, IL
61790-4240, 309-438-7705
Internet: jmelled@ilstu.edu
  Pubs: *The Chapters of Coming Forth by Day, Into the
  Arms of the Universe* (Stonewell, 2000, 1995), *Indiana
  Rev, Fiction Intl, Paris Rev*
I.D.: G/L/B/T. Groups: G/L/B/T

Charles Elwert ♦ ✈ P
681-A Katherine Ln
Addison, IL 60101-6401, 630-916-4876
Internet: 85corvette@compuserve.com
　Pubs: *Poetry Connection 1981-1991* (Hydra, 1991),
Paris Rev, Spoon River Qtly

Robert Klein Engler P
901 S Plymouth Apt 1801
Chicago, IL 60605, 312-922-9040
　Pubs: *Return to Alexandria* (i Universe.com, 1999),
Medicine Signs, Shore Line (Alphabeta Pr, 1997, 1999),
*Borderlands, Hyphen, Christopher Street, James White
Rev, Kansas Qtly, Fish Stories*

Pamela Erbe W
3608 N Pine Grove Ave, #B7
Chicago, IL 60613-4556
　Pubs: *American Fiction: Anth* (New Rivers Pr, 1995),
New Stories from the South: Anth (Algonquin Bks,
1994), *River Oak Rev, Antioch Rev, Columbia, NAR,
Ms.*

Dave Etter ♦ ✈ P
628 E Locust St
Lanark, IL 61046, 815-493-6778
　Pubs: *How High the Moon, Sunflower County* (Spoon
River, 1996, 1994), *I Want to Talk About You*
(Crossroads Pr, 1995)

H. R. Felgenhauer P&W
PO Box 146486
Chicago, IL 60614, 312-772-8686
　Pubs: *IAPT3, Insects Are People Two* (Puffn' Stuff
Productions, 1998, 1996), *Bouillabaisse, Gotta Write,
Mind in Motion, Fantasy Commentator*

Peter Fellowes P
3225 W Foster
Chicago, IL 60625
　Pubs: *Yale Rev, APR, Commonweal, Shenandoah,
Ontario Rev, Epoch, Poetry Now, TriQtly*

Calvin Forbes P
School of the Art Institute, 37 S Wabash Ave, Chicago, IL
60603, 312-899-5187
　Pubs: *From the Book of Shine* (Burning Deck, 1979),
Blue Monday (Wesleyan U Pr, 1974)

Phyllis Ford-Choyke P
23 Windsor Dr
Elmhurst, IL 60126-3971, 312-337-1482
　Pubs: *Apertures to Anywhere* (Harper Square Pr, 1979),
Poetry NW, Voices Israel, Rhino

Rich Foss ♦ ✈ P&W
19235 Plow Creek
Tiskilwa, IL 61368, 815-646-4264
Internet: richfoss@theramp.net
　Pubs: *Jonas & Sally* (Good Bks, 2000), *Poet's Page,
North Country, Christian Poetry Jrnl, Christianity &
Literature*

Alan Friedman W
English Dept, Box 4348, Univ Illinois, Chicago, IL 60680,
312-413-2200
　Pubs: *Hermaphrodeity* (Knopf, 1972), *The Turn of the
Novel* (Oxford U, 1966), *Raritan, Partisan Rev, Paris
Rev*

Paul Friedman W
310 W Illinois St
Urbana, IL 61801, 217-328-3247
　Pubs: *Serious Trouble, And If Defeated Allege Fraud* (U
Illinois Pr, 1986, 1971), *Mid-American Rev, Boulevard,
Cimarron Rev*

Richard Friedman P
5819 N Sacramento
Chicago, IL 60659, 312-275-7154
　Pubs: *Physical Culture* (Yellow Pr, 1979)

Paul Friedrich P
1130 E 59th St
Chicago, IL 60637-1539, 773-702-7004
　Pubs: *Speaking in Tongues: Anth* (Black Buzzard Pr,
1994), *Mutatis Mutandis, Mississippi Valley Rev, Blue
Unicorn, Flutter By Pr, Kansas Qtly*

Robert Fromberg W
734 N La Salle Dr, #1114
Chicago, IL 60610-3530, 312-440-9129
　Pubs: *Blue Skies* (Floating Island Pubs, 1992), *Indiana
Rev, Bellingham Rev, Tennessee Qtly, Salmon,
Colorado Rev, Northeast*

Al Gabor ♦ ✈ P&W
1630 Mulford
Evanston, IL 60202, 847-475-2483
Internet: a-gabor@northwestern.edu
　Pubs: *XY Files: Anth* (Sherman Asher, 1997), *ACM,
Cream City Rev, Ascent, Puerto del Sol, Great River
Rev, Mississippi Valley Rev, Chattahoochee Rev,
Plainsongs, Willow Rev*

Cynthia Gallaher ♦ ✈ P
PO Box A3604
Chicago, IL 60690, 773-330-6508
Internet: swimmer53@yahoo.com
　Pubs: *Earth Elegance, Night Ribbons* (Polar Bear Pr,
2000, 1990), *Swimmer's Prayer* (Missing Spoke Pr,
1999), *Private, On Purpose* (Mulberry Pr, 1993),
Boomer Girls: Anth (U Iowa Pr, 1999), *Power Lines:
Anth* (Tia Chucha, 1999), *Grrrrr: Anth* (Arctos Pr, 1999)
I.D.: Environmentalist, Performance. Groups: Children

Bruce M. Gans 🎤 ✈ W
5324 Hyde Park Blvd #1
Chicago, IL 60615, 773-643-8888
Internet: bmg1030@earthlink.net
    Pubs: *Here's the Story: Fiction with Heart: Anth* (Spirit
    That Moves Us Pr, 1986), *American Scholar, Hawaii
    Rev, Playboy, Mademoiselle, Kansas Qtly, Memphis
    State Rev*

Bill Garson P&W
PO Box 3126
Rockford, IL 61106-0126, 815-398-5414
    Pubs: *Where Are You Now, Boy Billie?* (Fithian Pr,
    1992), *Brother Earth* (Imagination Plus), *Hardboiled
    Detective, Grit, Sunshine*

Lucia C. Getsi P
English Dept, Illinois State Univ, Normal, IL 61790-4240,
309-438-7906
    Pubs: *Intensive Care* (New Rivers, 1995), *No One
    Taught This Filly to Dance* (Pikestaff Pr, 1989), *Many
    Mountains Moving, Women's Rev of Bks, Willow Rev*

Reginald Gibbons 🎤 ✈ P&W
English Dept, Northwestern Univ, 215 University Hall,
Evanston, IL 60208-2240, 847-491-7294
Internet: rgibbons@northwestern.edu
    Pubs: *Homage to Longshot O'Leary* (Holy Cow! Pr,
    1999), *Sparrow* (LSU Pr, 1997), *Sweetbitter* (Penguin,
    1996), *Maybe It Was So* (U Chicago, 1991), *Tikkun,
    APR, Harper's, Southern Rev, QRL, Atlantic*
Lang: Spanish. Groups: Literacy

Netta Gillespie 🎤 P
211 E Sherwin Dr
Urbana, IL 61802-7129, 217-328-7268
Internet: gillesp1@uiuc.edu
    Pubs: *Knowing Stones: Anth* (John Gordon Burke,
    2000), *Essential Love: Anth* (Grayson Bks/Poetworks,
    2000), *Spoon River Poetry Rev, Birmingham Poetry
    Rev, Snowbound, Wisconsin Rev, Karamu, Apocalypse*

Philip Graham P&W
605 W Vermont St
Urbana, IL 61801-4824, 217-337-6898
    Pubs: *Interior Design, How to Read an Unwritten
    Language* (Scribner, 1996, 1995), *New Yorker, NAR,
    Paris Rev, Fiction, Missouri Rev, Washington Post*

Cindy Guentherman 🎤 P
7721 Venus St
Loves Park, IL 61111-3142, 815-654-8491
Internet: haikupup@aol.com
    Pubs: *Korone, Acorn Whistle, Rockford Rev, Without
    Halos, Heart & Soul, Kumquat Meringue, Modern Haiku,
    Parnassus, Riverrun, Lynx, Impetus, American Poets &
    Poetry*

Lee Gurga 🎤 ✈ P
514 Pekin St
Lincoln, IL 62656, 217-732-8731
    Pubs: *Fresh Scent* (Brooks Bks, 1998), *In & Out of the
    Fog* (Press Here, 1997), *The Measure of Emptiness,*
    (Press Here, 1991), *Global Haiku: Anth* (Iron Pr, 2000),
    The Haiku Anthology (Norton, 1999), *Haiku World: Anth*
    (Kodansha International, 1996)

Mary Hanford P
c/o Jeanne McWherter, RR2, Box 78, Aledo, IL 61231
    Pubs: *Spoon River Qtly, Another Place to Publish,
    Brushfire, Spectrum, The Carillion*

Barbara Harr P
c/o Juanita M. N. Harr, 20 S Fremont St, Naperville, IL
60540-4329, 708-778-9528
    Pubs: *The Mortgaged Wife* (Swallow, 1970), *The
    Nation, Rough Edges, Choice, Womanspirit,
    Shenandoah*

Kent Haruf W
Southern Illinois Univ, English Dept, Carbondale, IL 62901,
618-453-6867
    Pubs: *Where You Once Belonged* (S&S, 1990), *Where
    Past Meets Present: Anth* (U Colorado Pr, 1994), *Best
    American Short Stories: Anth* (HM, 1987), *Grand Street*

M. M. M. Hayes W
431 Sheridan Rd
Kenilworth, IL 60043, 847-256-6998
    Pubs: *New Stories from the South: Anth* (Algonquin
    Bks, 1995), *Awards XVI: Katherine Anne Porter Award:
    Anth* (Nimrod, 1996), *NAR, Redbook, High Plains
    Literary Rev*

Robert R. Hellenga 🎤 ✈ W
Knox College, English Dept, Galesburg, IL 61401,
309-343-0112
Internet: rhelleng@knox.edu
    Pubs: *The Fall of a Sparrow* (Scribner, 1996), *The
    Sixteen Pleasures* (Dell, 1995), *Mississippi Valley Rev,
    Chicago Rev, Iowa Rev, California Qtly, Columbia,
    Ascent, Crazyhorse, TriQtly*

Greg Herriges W
c/o William Rainey, Harper College, 1200 Algonquin Rd,
Palatine, IL 60047
    Pubs: *The Winter Dance Party Murders* (Wordcraft,
    1998), *Secondary Attachment* (William Morrow, 1986),
    Some Place Safe (Avon, 1985)

Richard Holinger P&W
335 Colonial Cir
Geneva, IL 60134-3640, 630-232-9996
    Pubs: *Iowa Rev, Witness, Boulevard, Southern Rev,
    Chelsea, Ohio Rev, ACM, Hampden-Sydney Poetry
    Rev, Cream City Rev, New Renaissance, Writers'
    Bar-B-Q, Zone 3, Other Voices*

Barbara Savadge Horton   P
c/o V. Vedanta, 5423 S Hyde Park Blvd, Chicago, IL
60615, 773-667-8170
   Pubs: *The Verb to Love* (Silver Apples Pr, 1989), *Anth
   of Magazine Verse* (Monitor Bk Co, 1997), *Passages
   North, Poetry NW, Kansas Qtly, New Letters, SPR,
   ACM*

Jean Howard   PP&P
3404 N Troy
Chicago, IL 60618, 312-539-9744
   Pubs: *Dancing in Your Mother's Skin* (Tia Chucha Pr,
   1991), *Banyon Anth* (Banyon Pr, 1982), *Harper's,
   Spoon River Rev, ACM, Hammers, Harley & The Hill*

Dan Howell 🎤 ✈   P
738 W Aldine Ave, #1W
Chicago, IL 60657, 312-935-9244
   Pubs: *Lost Country* (U Massachusetts Pr, 1993)

Mary Gray Hughes   W
2610 Central Park Ave, #2
Evanston, IL 60201, 708-864-6082
   Pubs: *The Empty Lot* (Another Chicago Pr, 1992), *The
   Calling* (U Illinois, 1980), *Virginia Qtly Rev, Poetry,
   Sou'wester, Southern Rev, Descant, Puckerbrush Rev,
   American Literary Rev*

Christine Hume 🎤 ✈   P
5532 S Shore Dr #7E
Chicago, IL 60637, 773-752-5822
   Pubs: *Musca Domestica* (Beacon Pr, 2000), *American
   Poetry: The Next Generation: Anth* (Carnegie Mellon,
   2000), *Best American Poetry 1997: Anth* (Scribner,
   1997), *Boston Rev, The New Rep, Fence, Rhizome,
   New American Writing*

John Jacob 🎤 ✈   P&W
417 S Taylor Apt 3B
Oak Park, IL 60302-4300, 708-383-3167
   Pubs: *Every Day I Got the Blues* (Small Poetry Pr,
   1999), *Hungers* (Lake Shore Pub, 1995), *Long Ride
   Back* (Thunder's Mouth, 1988), *TriQtly, Partisan Rev,
   Poetry, Mississippi Rev, Chicago Mag*
Groups: Prisoners, HIV/AIDS

Phyllis Janik   P
805 W Chicago Ave
Hinsdale, IL 60521, 708-887-1674
   Pubs: *Fuse* (ACP Bks, 1989), *No Dancing/No Acts of
   Dancing* (BkMk Pr, 1982), *New Renaissance*

Curt Johnson   W
PO Box 302
Highland Park, IL 60035, 847-940-4122
   Pubs: *Thanksgiving in Vegas* (Bottlehouse Pr, 1995),
   The Mafia Manager (St. Martin's Pr, 1995), *Song for
   Three Voices* (Carpenter Pr, 1984)

Joyce Sandeen Johnson   P
6532 Spring Brook Rd #212
Rockford, IL 61114-8136, 815-654-0502
   Pubs: *Impressions Chapbook* (River City Pr, 1994),
   *Pegasus, Midwestern Poetry Rev, Oatmeal & Poetry,
   Rockford Rev, Quarter Moon, Jean's Jrnl, Lynx,
   Parnassus, Mobius, The Poet's Pen*

Allison Joseph 🎤 ✈   P
Southern Illinois Univ, English Dept, Faner Hall,
Carbondale, IL 62901, 618-453-5321
   Pubs: *In Every Seam* (U Pitt 1997), *Soul Train*
   (Carnegie Mellon U Pr, 1997), *What Keeps Us Here*
   (Ampersand Pr 1992), *The New Young American Poets:
   Anth* (SIU Pr, 2000), *Callaloo, Tamaqua*
I.D.: African-American, Women. Groups: African-American,
Women

Henry Kanabus   P
2925 N Kenneth Ave, Apt 1
Chicago, IL 60641, 312-725-3973
   Pubs: *Night Ministry & Other Stories* (Brigham Hse,
   1990), *Capillary Sun* (Lebensraum Pr, 1989)

David Michael Kaplan 🎤 ✈   P&W
4100 N Springfield
Chicago, IL 60618-1919, 773-509-0760
   Pubs: *Skating in the Dark* (Pantheon, 1991), *Comfort*
   (Viking, 1987), *Mississippi Rev, Ohio Rev, Atlantic,
   Fiction, Story, Playboy, Redbook, TriQtly, Mirabella*

Brigit Pegeen Kelly   P
506 W Main St
Urbana, IL 61801-2504, 217-384-6933
   Pubs: *Song* (BOA Limited Edtns, 1994), *In the Place of
   Trumpets* (Yale U Pr, 1988), *NER, Antioch Rev,
   Southern Rev, Yale Rev, Massachusetts Rev*

Kathryn Kerr   P
11947 Deer Run Rd
Marion, IL 62959, 618-964-1917
   Pubs: *I Feel a Little Jumpy Around You* (S&S, 1996),
   First Frost, Benchmark Anth (Stormline Pr, 1985, 1987),
   *ACM, Ascent, Thema, River Styx, Spoon River,
   Tamaqua, Karamu*

William Kir-Stimon   P
729 Emerson St
Evanston, IL 60201, 708-475-5548
   Pubs: *Inside the Open Cage* (Cooperfield, 1984),
   *Voices, Pilgrimage, NU ILR Jrnl, Jrnl of Poetry Therapy,
   CPU Rev, Midwest Rev*

Elizabeth Klein   P&W
610 S Chicago Ave
Champaign, IL 61821, 217-356-2683
   Pubs: *Reconciliations* (Berkley Bks, 1984), *Approaches*
   (Red Herring Pr, 1980), *ACM, Farmer's Market, Jewish
   Spectator, Shofar, Prairie Schooner*

John Knoepfle 🎤 ✈   P
1008 W Adams
Auburn, IL 62615-1036, 217-438-6079
  Pubs: *The Chinkapin Oak* (Rosehill Pr, 1996), *Begging an Amnesty* (Druid Pr, 1995), *Centennial Rev, Intl Qtly, Private Arts, New Letters, Crosscurrents*

Art Lange 🎤 ✈   P
6553 N Artesian
Chicago, IL 60645
Internet: alange@megsinet.net
  Pubs: *Needles at Midnight* (Z Pr, 1986), *Evidence* (Yellow Pr, 1981), *Postmodern American Poetry: Anth* (Norton, 1994), *New American Writing, Transfer, Partisan Rev, Washington Rev*

William Leahy   W
1929 W Waveland Ave, #2
Chicago, IL 60613, 312-871-3402
  Pubs: *Verb, Cyphurs, Nit & Wit Mag, Northwest Challenge, City, North Dakota Qtly*

Li-Young Lee   P
853 W Lawrence Ave
Chicago, IL 60640, 312-275-3054
  Pubs: *The City in Which I Love You, Rose* (BOA Edtns, 1990, 1986), *Grand Street, TriQtly*

Laurence Lieberman 🎤 ✈   P
Univ Illinois, 608 S Wright, 208 English Bldg, Urbana, IL 61801, 217-367-7186
  Pubs: *The Regatta in the Skies* (U Georgia Pr, 1998), *Compass of the Dying, Dark Songs* (U Arkansas Pr, 1998, 1996), *New & Selected Poems: 1962-1992* (U Illinois Pr, 1993), *Body Electric: Anth* (Norton, 2000), *Atlantic, APR, Sewanee Rev, Nation, Boulevard*

C. A. Lofton   P
c/o ALSP, Olive Harvey College, 10001 S Woodlawn Ave, Chicago, IL 60628
  Pubs: *Friends Jrnl, Audio Pubs*

Beth Lordan 🎤 ✈   W
Southern Illinois Univ, English Dept, Carbondale, IL 62901, 618-453-6849
  Pubs: *And Both Shall Row* (Picador USA, 1998), *August Heat* (Harper & Row, 1989), *Atlantic, Sycamore Rev, Farmer's Market, Gettysburg Rev*

William F. Love   W
940 Cleveland Rd
Hinsdale, IL 60521, 708-325-9097
  Pubs: *Bloody Ten, The Fundamentals of Murder, The Chartreuse Clue* (Donald I. Fine, 1992, 1991, 1990)

James M. Loverde   P
3719 N Southport Ave #219
Chicago, IL 60613-3756
  Pubs: *Mutated Viruses, FEH!, Haunted Jrnl, 'scapes, Wolf's Season, Silver Apple Branch, Art/Life*

Roslyn Rosen Lund 🎤   W
9220 E Prairie Rd, Apt #410
Evanston, IL 60203-1644
  Pubs: *Her Face in the Mirror: Anth* (Beacon Pr, 1995), *Loss of the Ground-Note: Anth* (Clothespin Fever Pr, 1992), *Prism Intl, Crosscurrents, Ascent, Descant, Other Voices*

Haki R. Madhubuti   P
PO Box 730
Chicago, IL 60619, 312-651-0700
  Pubs: *Black Men: Obsolete, Single, Dangerous?* (Third World Pr, 1990)

Michael Patrick Malone 🎤 ✈   W
VP Development & University Relations, Northern Illinois Univ, Dekalb, IL 60115, 815-753-6065
  Pubs: *PEN Short Story Collection: Anth* (Ballantine, 1986), *Kansas Qtly, New Letters, Ascent, Chicago Reader, U.S. Catholic, Mississippi Rev*
I.D.: Irish-American

Norma Marder 🎤 ✈   W
1009 W Church St
Champaign, IL 61821, 217-352-1824
  Pubs: *An Eye for Dark Places* (Little, Brown, 1993), *Georgia Rev, Gettysburg Rev*

Marion M. Markham 🎤 ✈   W
2415 Newport Rd
Northbrook, IL 60062
Internet: mmrbm@juno.com
  Pubs: *The St. Patrick's Day Shamrock Mystery, The April Fool's Day Mystery* (HM, 1995, 1991), *McCall's, House Beautiful, Alfred Hitchcock's Mystery, London Mystery, American Way, Buffalo Spree*
Groups: Children

Cris Mazza   W
English Dept M/C162, Univ of Illinois at Chicago, Chicago, IL 60607, 312-413-2200
  Pubs: *Former Virgin, Revelation Countdown* (FC2, 1997, 1993), *Dog People, Your Name Here:___, Exposed, How to Leave a Country* (Coffee Hse Pr, 1997, 1995, 1994, 1992), *Fiction Intl, High Plains Literary Rev*

James McGowan   P
410 E Walnut St
Bloomington, IL 61701, 309-828-0807

James McManus   P&W
School of the Art Institute, 37 S Wabash, Chicago, IL
60603-3017, 847-256-4109
   Pubs: *Going to the Sun, Great America* (HC, 1996,
   1993), *Out of the Blue, Ghost Waves, Chin Music*
   (Grove Pr, 1989, 1988, 1987), *Best American Poetry
   1994: Anth* (S&S, 1994), *Atlantic, American Poetry Rev,
   DoubleTake, Paris Rev, Poetry*

Erica Helm Meade 🎤 ✈   PP
Open Court Publishing Co., 332 S Michigan Ave, Ste
#2000, Chicago, IL 60604
   Pubs: *Tell It By Heart, Crossroads: Anth* (Open Court
   Pub, 1995, 1996), *Intimate Nature: Anth* (Ballantine,
   1998), *Goddess: Anth* (Stewart, Tabori & Chang, 1997),
   The Sun

Orlando Ricardo Menes   P
4947 N Harlem Ave Apt 1
Chicago, IL 60656, 773-763-5892
   Pubs: *Borderlands with Angels* (Bacchae Pr, 1995),
   *Indiana Rev, Negative Capability, Ploughshares, Antioch
   Rev, Callaloo, Chelsea*

Michael Mesic   P
2112 Orrington Ave
Evanston, IL 60201, 312-328-9147

Robin Metz 🎤 ✈   P&W
695 N Broad St
Galesburg, IL 61401, 309-343-6746
   Pubs: *Unbidden Angel* (CCC, 1999), *National Poetry
   Competition Anthology* (Chester H. Jones, 1996), *Abiko
   Qtly, Paris Rev, Epoch, Other Voices, Writers' Forum,
   Visions Intl, Intl Poetry Rev, Storytellers, December
   Mag, Medicinal Purposes*

Effie Mihopoulos   P
5548 N Sawyer
Chicago, IL 60625, 773-539-5745
   Pubs: *Languid Love Lyrics, The Moon Cycle* (Ommation
   Pr, 1993, 1991), *Tomorrow, Volume No, Lost & Found
   Times, Hammers, Perceptions, Hob-Nob*

Jordan Miller   P
334 Hawthorn Ave
Glencoe, IL 60022, 312-751-7302
   Pubs: *Bequest: Poems 1959-1979* (Academy Chicago
   Ltd, 1980), *Gallery Poets, Choice, Midwest*

Pamela Miller 🎤 ✈   P
7538 N Bell, #3A
Chicago, IL 60645-1962, 773-973-6690
Internet: pmiller@enteract.com
   Pubs: *Mysterious Coleslaw* (Ridgeway, 1993), *Fast Little
   Shoes* (Erie Street, 1986), *Feathers, Fins & Fur: Anth*
   (Outrider, 1999), *Dangerous Dames: Anth* (11th Hour,
   1998), *Freedom's Just Another Word: Anth* (Feminist
   Writers Guild, 1998), *Pudding, MacGuffin*
I.D.: Feminist

Patricia Monaghan 🎤 ✈   P
De Paul Univ, 25 E Jackson, Chicago, IL 60604,
312-362-6773
Internet: pmonagha@wppost.depaul.edu
   Pubs: *Seasons of the Witch* (Delphi Pr, 1992), *The
   Next Parish Over: Anth* (New Rivers Pr, 1994), *Creation
   Spirituality, Sou'wester, River Oak Rev, NAR*

Lisel Mueller 🎤 ✈   P
909 W Foster Ave #607
Chicago, IL 60640-2510
   Pubs: *Alive Together, Waving from Shore, Second
   Language* (LSU Pr, 1996, 1989, 1986), *Learning to
   Play By Ear* (Juniper Pr, 1990), *Paris Rev, Poetry*
Groups: German Lang & Lit

G. E. Murray   P
1401 Jackson
River Forest, IL 60305, 312-366-4144
   Pubs: *Oils of Evening* (Lake Shore Pr, 1996), *Walking
   the Blind Dog* (U Illinois Pr, 1992), *Repairs* (U Missouri
   Pr, 1979), *Poetry, Hudson Rev, Georgia Rev, TriQtly*

George Nelson   P
2304 Hastings Ave
Evanston, IL 60201, 847-475-7006
   Pubs: *NAW, Wire, ACM, Private, The Critic*

Richard L. Newby   P
1007 Porter Ln
Normal, IL 61761, 309-452-1726
   Pubs: *Ball State University Forum, Mississippi Rev,
   Gryphon, Descant, Small Pond*

Dwight Okita   P
426 W Surf, #111
Chicago, IL 60657, 312-883-5219
   Pubs: *Crossing with the Light* (Tia Chucha Pr, 1992),
   Unsettling America: Anth (Penguin, 1994), *ACM,
   Hyphen Mag, Asian Pacific American Jrnl, New City*

Elaine Fowler Palencia   W
1608 W Healey
Champaign, IL 61821, 217-356-3893
   Pubs: *Taking the Train* (Grex Pr, 1997), *Small
   Caucasian Woman* (U Missouri Pr, 1993), *Virginia Qtly
   Rev, Byline, Pegasus, Other Voices, Sow's Ear Poetry
   Rev, Iowa Woman, Willow Rev, Chattahoochee Rev,
   Appalachian Heritage*

Elise Paschen   P
2200 N Kenmore Ave, #3
Chicago, IL 60614, 773-871-6339
   Pubs: *Infidelities* (Story Line Pr, 1996), *New Yorker,
   Poetry, New Republic, The Nation*

Rob Patton   P
1142 S Euclid Ave
Oak Park, IL 60304
   Pubs: *Dare, Thirty-Seven Poems* (Ithaca Hse, 1977,
1971), *Greenfield Rev*

Mark Perlberg 🎤 ✈   P
612 Stratford Pl
Chicago, IL 60657-2632, 773-477-3287
Internet: perl@ripco.com
   Pubs: *The Impossible Toystore* (LSU Pr, 2000), *The
Feel of the Sun* (Ohio U/Swallow, 1982), *The Burning
Field* (Morrow, 1970), *New Yorker, Illinois Rev, Poetry
East, Poetry, Hudson Rev, Prairie Schooner*

Bob Perlongo 🎤 ✈   P&W
820 Reba Pl
Evanston, IL 60202-2691, 847-475-6645
Internet: xyzzo@aol.com
   Pubs: *All Hours of the Night* (Writers Workshop
Calcutta, 1998), *Boulevard, Reed, The Little Mag,
Massachusetts Rev, Playboy, Village Voice*

Karen Peterson   P&W
633 S Lombard
Oak Park, IL 60304, 708-848-8498
   Pubs: *American Fiction 2: Anth* (Birch Lane Pr, 1991),
*Poetry, Qtly West, Other Voices, West Branch, Spoon
River Qtly, Karamu*

Deborah Rebollar Pintonelli   P&W
c/o Lee Webster, 77 W Wacker Dr, Chicago, IL
60601-1696, 312-326-8803
   Pubs: *Ego Monkey* (Another Chicago Pr, 1991),
Unbearables: Anth (Autonomedia, 1995), *Jungles
D'Amerique: Anth* (Arbres a Cames, 1993)

James Plath 🎤 ✈   P&W
Illinois Wesleyan Univ, English Dept, Bloomington, IL
61702-2900, 309-556-3352
Internet: http://titan.iwu.edu/~jplath
   Pubs: *Courbet, On the Rocks* (White Eagle Coffee
Store Pr, 1994), *Men of Our Time: Anth* (U Georgia Pr,
1992), *The Caribbean Writer, Amelia, Salt Hill Jrnl, Gulf
Stream, Apalachee Qtly, Mississippi Valley Rev*

Frederik Pohl   W
855 S Harvard Dr
Palatine, IL 60067-7026, 847-991-6009
   Pubs: *O Pioneer* (Tor, 1998), *Stopping at Slowyear*
(Bantam Bks, 1992), *Mining the Oort* (Ballantine/Del
Rey, 1992), *The World at the End of Time* (Ballantine,
1990)

Enid Levinger Powell 🎤 ✈   W
1300 Lake Shore Dr, #21B
Chicago, IL 60610, 312-787-7451
Internet: enidbert@prodigy.net
   Pubs: *The Divorce Handbook* (Random Hse, 1984),
McCall's, Mississippi Valley Rev, Yankee
I.D.: Jewish. Groups: Children, Seniors

David Radavich 🎤 ✈   P
1832 Ashby Dr
Charleston, IL 61920-3217, 217-345-9280
Internet: cfdar@eiu.edu
   Pubs: *By the Way* (Buttonwood, 1998), *Slain Species*
(Court Poetry, 1980), *Die Weiten Horizonte: Anth*
(Pressler Verlag, 1985), *Orbis, Connecticut River Rev,
Intl Qtly, Kansas Qtly, Louisville Rev, Northwoods Jrnl*

Eugene B. Redmond 🎤 ✈   P
English Dept, Southern Illinois Univ, Box 1431,
Edwardsville, IL 62026-1431, 618-650-3991
   Pubs: *The Eye in the Ceiling* (Writers & Readers,
1991), *Furious Flowering: Anth* (U Pr Virginia, 1999),
Drumvoices Rev: Anth (Southern Illinois U Pr, 1999),
Trouble the Water: Anth (Mentor, 1997), *Spirit & Flame:
Anth* (Syracuse U Pr, 1997), *New Rain*

Rosemary Roberts   P
RR1, Box 89
Broughton, IL 62817-9754
   Pubs: *Let His Light Shine* (American Arts Assn, 1989),
Voices in Poetics: Anth (Yes Pr, 1986)

Carolyn M. Rodgers 🎤 ✈   P
PO Box 804271
Chicago, IL 60680-4104, 773-324-3003
   Pubs: *The Salt of the Earth, A Train Called Judah,
Chosen to Believe* (Eden Pr, 1999, 1996, 1996),
Daughters of Africa (Pantheon, 1993), *Poetry, Essence,
Nation, Black Scholar, Caprice, Nommo*
I.D.: African-American, Women. Groups: Schools

Paulette Roeske 🎤 ✈   P&W
1200 Harvard Terr
Evanston, IL 60202-3214, 847-475-5228
Internet: pauletteroeske@aol.com
   Pubs: *Anvil, Clock, & Last, Divine Attention,* (LSU Pr,
2001, 1995), *The Body Can Ascend No Higher* (Illinois
Writers, 1992), *Breathing Under Water* (Stormline,
1988), *Threepenny Rev, Indiana Rev, Virginia Qtly Rev,
Georgia Rev, Glimmer Train, Poetry*

Alane Rollings   P
5455 S Ridgewood Ct
Chicago, IL 60615, 773-947-0759
   Pubs: *The Logic of Opposites* (TriQtly Bks, 1998), *The
Struggle to Adore* (Story Line Pr, 1993), *In Your Own
Sweet Time* (Wesleyan, 1989), *Transparent Landscapes*
(Raccoon Bks, 1984)

Charles Rossiter 🎤 ✈   PP&P
705 S Gunderson Ave
Oak Park, IL 60304-1423, 708-660-9376
Internet: posey@juno.com
    Pubs: *What Men Talk About* (Pudding Hse, 2000),
    Identity Lessons: Anth (Penguin, 1999), *Passionate
    Hearts: Anth* (New World Lib, 1996), *Paterson Literary
    Rev, Maryland Poetry Rev, Lips, NPR, Nuyorican Poets
    Café, Green Mill*
I.D.: Liberal, Populist

Linda Roth 🎤 ✈   P
6207 Blomberg Rd
Cherry Valley, IL 61016-9760, 815-874-7131
Internet: lroth65@aol.com
    Pubs: *Grasslands Rev, Natural Bridge, Southern Rev,
    Massachusetts Rev, Midwest Qtly, Rockford Rev*

Charles Rowling 🎤 ✈   P&W
1636 W Thorndale
Chicago, IL 60660, 773-989-1859
    Pubs: *Hammers: Anth* (Doublestar Pr, 1995), *Hyphen*

Biff Russ   P
1517 W Fargo #2
Chicago, IL 60626-1822, 773-761-8762
Internet: bruss@21stcentury.net
    Pubs: *Black Method* (Helicon Nine Edtns, 1991),
    Fathers: Anth (St. Martin's Pr, 1997), *Prairie Schooner,
    Cream City Rev, Poetry East, Indiana Rev, Berkeley
    Poetry Rev, Passages North, Boulevard*
Groups: Seniors

Alice Ryerson Hayes 🎤   P
5550 S Shore Dr #615
Chicago, IL 60037-5032, 773-753-4395
    Pubs: *Journal of the Lake* (Open Bks, 1997), *Water
    Sheba's Story* (Bookwrights Pr, 1997), *New & Selected
    Poems* (Spoon River, 1987), *Do Not Disturb: Anth*
    (Writer's Digest Bks, 1989), *Spoon River Qtly, Prairie
    Schooner, Whetstone, Women's Rev of Bks*

R. Craig Sautter 🎤 ✈   P
School for New Learning, DePaul Univ, 243 S Wabash
Ave, Chicago, IL 60604, 312-262-5806
    Pubs: *Wicked City Chicago* (w/C. Johnson), *Express
    Lane Through the Inevitable City* (December Pr, 1994,
    1990), *Central Park, Assembling*

Whitney Scott 🎤 ✈   PP&P&W
Outrider Press, 937 Patricia Ln, Crete, IL 60417-1375,
708-672-6630
Internet: www.outriderpress.com
    Pubs: *Dancing to the End of the Shining Bar, Earth
    Beneath Sky Above: Anth, Feathers Fins & Fur: Anth,
    Freedom's Just Another Word: Anth, Prairie Hearts:
    Anth* (Outrider Pr, 1995, 2000, 1999, 1997, 1996),
    Dangerous Dames, Tomorrow, Wide Open, Obelisk
Groups: Seniors, G/L/B/T

Maureen Seaton 🎤 ✈   P
Columbia College of Chicago, 33 E Congress, 3rd Floor,
Chicago, IL 60605, 312-344-8139
Internet: mseaton@popmail.edu
    Pubs: *Furious Cooking* (U Iowa, 1996), *Fear of
    Subways* (Eighth Mountain, 1991), *Green Mountains
    Rev, Quarter After Eight, Paris Rev, Atlantic, Kenyon
    Rev*

Lynette Seator 🎤 ✈   P
1609 Mound Ave
Jacksonville, IL 62650-2257, 217-245-6427
Internet: lseator@csj.net
    Pubs: *Mississippi Valley Rev, Praxis, Pulpsmith, Melus,
    Lodestar, Open Places, Kalliope*
Lang: Spanish. Groups: Prisoners

Irene Sedeora 🎤 ✈   P&W
107 Cedar Ave
Morton, IL 61550-1007
Internet: sedeora@bwsys.net
    Pubs: *The Aurorean, Poetalk, The TMP Irregular, MM
    Rev, Ibbetson Street Pr, New Moon Rev, Stuff, Yet
    Another Small Mag, Downstate Story, Poetry Motel,
    Parting Gifts, The Artful Mind*

John Sennett   P
237 Park Trail Ct
Schaumburg, IL 60173, 847-517-1690
    Pubs: *Magic Changes, Mississippi Valley Rev, Washout
    Rev, Derby City News, Bloodroot*

Gregg Shapiro   P&W
5209 N Ashland
Chicago, IL 60640-2001, 773-784-8258
    Pubs: *Reclaiming the Heartland: Anth* (U Minnesota,
    1996), *Unsettling America: Anth* (Viking, 1994), *Mondo
    Barbie: Anth* (St. Martin's Pr, 1993), *Christopher Street,
    Columbia Poetry Rev, Modern Words, Faultline,
    Gargoyle, Illinois Rev*

Harry B. Sheftel   P
900 Coach Rd
Homewood, IL 60430-4143
    Pubs: *Quotations from My Questing, Of Truths &
    Wonderments, From Alpha to Omega* (Jesse Poet
    Pubs, 1991, 1991, 1991), *CSM, Now Mag, Modern
    Maturity*

Barry Silesky   P&W
3709 N Kenmore
Chicago, IL 60613-2905, 773-248-7665
Internet: btsds@aol.com
    Pubs: *One Thing That Can Save Us* (Coffee Hse Pr,
    1994), *Greatest Hits* (Pudding Hse Pr, 1999), *The New
    Tenants* (Eye of the Comet Pr, 1991), *Boulevard,
    Witness, NAW, Fiction, Poetry East, Poetry, The Prose
    Poem, Fiction Intl*

Brian Skinner   W
4044 N Avers
Chicago, IL 60618, 773-866-2610
  Pubs: *Liars, Tattlers & Weavers* (Monadnock Group
  Pubs, 1992), *Christmas Blues: Anth* (Amador Pubs,
  1995), *Other Voices, Magic Realism, Karamu, Atom
  Mind*

James Park Sloan   W
Univ Illinois, English Dept, Box 4348, Chicago, IL 60680,
312-996-3282
  Pubs: *The Last Cold-War Cowboy* (Morrow, 1987), *The
  Case History of Comrade U* (Avon, 1972)

Jared Smith ♪ ✦   P
409 N Vine St
Hinsdale, IL 60521-3321, 312-887-7338
  Pubs: *Walking the Perimeters of the Plate Glass
  Window Factory* (Birch Brook Pr, 2000), *Keeping the
  Outlaw Alive* (Erie Street Pr, 1988), *NYQ*
Groups: College/Univ, Environmentalist

Michael S. Smith   P
Rte 13, Box 219
Bloomington, IL 61704-8935, 309-828-0703
  Pubs: *XY Files: Poems on the Male Experience: Anth*
  (Sherman Asher Pub, 1997), *Passionate Hearts: Anth*
  (New World Library, 1996), *Writers' Forum, ELF, Hellas,
  Plainsongs, Thema, Roanoke Rev, Cathartic, Artworld
  Qtly, Comstock Rev, Spoon River*

Paul Andrew E. Smith   P&W
McHenry County Creative Comm, PO Box 354, Cary, IL
60013, 708-639-9200
  Pubs: *Scenes from the Postmodern Butler* (White Eagle
  Coffee Store Pr, 1992), *Postmodern Culture, Kalliope,
  Willow Rev, Hawaii Rev, Fly Rod & Reel, Whetstone,
  Alaska Qtly Rev, Carolina Qtly*

Sharon Solwitz   W
3709 N Kenmore
Chicago, IL 60613, 312-248-7665
  Pubs: *Blood & Milk* (Sarabande, 1997), *TriQtly,
  Ploughshares, American Short Fiction, Boulevard,
  Tikkun, Mademoiselle, Sassy*

Sheryl St. Germain   P
Knox College, English Dept, Box 66, Galesburg, IL
61407-4999, 309-343-3568
  Pubs: *The Journals of Scheherazade, How Heavy the
  Breath of God* (U North Texas Pr, 1996, 1994), *Making
  Bread at Midnight* (Slough Pr, 1992), *TriQtly, 5 A.M.,
  Calyx*

Scott Starbuck   P
955 4th St, Apt 7
Charleston, IL 61920, 217-345-4430
  Pubs: *Atom Mind, High Country News, Kerf, Awareness
  Jrnl, Going Down Swinging, Wild Earth, The Climbing
  Art, Calapooya Collage, Green Fuse, Moksha Jrnl, Dry
  Heat, Mandrake Poetry Rev*

Kevin Stein ♪ ✦   P
Bradley Univ, English Dept, Peoria, IL 61625,
309-677-2480
Internet: kstein@bradley.edu
  Pubs: *Chance Ransom, Bruised Paradise* (U Illinois Pr,
  2000, 1996), *A Circus of Want* (U Missouri Pr, 1992),
  Poetry, NAR

Richard Stern   W
Univ Chicago, English Dept, 1050 E 59 St, Chicago, IL
60637, 773-702-8536
  Pubs: *A Sistermony* (Donald I. Fine, 1995), *One Person
  & Another* (Baskerville, 1993), *Shares & Other Fictions*
  (Delphinium, 1992), *Noble Rot: Stories* (ACP, 1991), *A
  Father's Words* (Phoenix, 1990), *TriQtly, Paris Rev,
  Antioch Rev, Iowa Rev*

Anthony E. Stockanes   W
2201 E Vermont Ave
Urbana, IL 61801
  Pubs: *Ladies Who Knit for a Living* (U Illinois Pr,
  1981), *Sewanee Rev, Ascent, Chicago Magazine*

Lucien Stryk ♪ ✦   P
342 Delcy Dr
Dekalb, IL 60115-1906, 815-756-8817
  Pubs: *And Still Birds Sing, Of Pen & Ink & Paper
  Scraps* (Swallow/Ohio U Pr, 1998, 1989), *Where We
  Are: Selected Poems & Zen Translations* (England;
  Skoob Bks Ltd, 1997)

Walter Sublette ♪ ✦   P&W
English Dept, Aurora Univ, 347 S Gladstone, Aurora, IL
60506, 708-844-5407
Internet: wsublete@aurora.edu
  Pubs: *Naked Exlie* (U Michigan Pr, 1991), *The
  Resurrection on Friday Night* (U Ohio Pr, 1981), *Go
  Now in Darkness* (Baker Pr, 1965)

Jean Thompson   W
Univ Illinois, 608 S Wright St, English Dept, Urbana, IL
61801
  Pubs: *The Woman Driver, Little Face, My Wisdom*
  (Watts, 1985, 1984, 1982), *Mademoiselle, American
  Short Fiction, NER, Ploughshares, New Yorker*

Phyllis Alexander Tickle   P
c/o Joseph Durepos, 5114 1/2 Main St, Downers Grove,
IL 60515, 630-852-5298
  Pubs: *God-Talk in America, Re-Discovering the Sacred*
  (Crossroad Pub, 1997, 1996), *My Father's Prayer: A
  Remembrance* (Upper Room Bks, 1996)

Alpay K. Ulku 🎤 ✈   P
24494 Norelius
Round Lake, IL 60073, 847-546-6055
Internet: alpayulku@hotbot.com
    Pubs: *Meteorology* (Boa Edtns, 1999), *Ploughshares,*
    Witness, Gettysburg Rev, NW Rev, Black Warrior Rev,
    Malahat Rev

Martha M. Vertreace 🎤   P
c/o Dr. James Plath, Illinois Wesleyan Univ, PO Box
2900, Bloomington, IL 61702-2900, 773-363-0766
    Pubs: *Dragon Lady* (Riverstone Pr, 1999), *Second*
    Mourning, Light Caught Bending (Diehard Pr, 1998,
    1994), *Smokeless Flame* (Frith Pr, 1998), *Maafa: When*
    Night Becomes a Lion (Ion Bks, 1996), *Oracle Bones,*
    (White Eagle Coffee Store Pr, 1994)

Doris Vidaver   P&W
Professional Bldg 1106, Rush Univ, 600 S Paulina St,
Chicago, IL 60612, 312-942-2063
    Pubs: *Arch of a Circle* (Swallow, 1981), *Articulations:*
    Anth (U Iowa Pr, 1994), *Literary Rev, Illinois Rev,*
    ACM, Prairie Schooner, Poetry, American Scholar,
    Chelsea

Mary E. Weems   P
508 Louisiana Ave
Champaign, IL 61820
    Pubs: *White* (Wick Chapbook Kent State U Pr, 1997),
    Fembles (The Heartlands Today, 1996), *Blackeyed*
    (Burning Pr, 1994), *A Hole in the Ghetto: Anth* (CSU
    Poetry Ctr, 1995), *Pearl, The Listening Eye*

J. Weintraub 🎤 ✈   P&W
5442 E View Pk, #3
Chicago, IL 60615-5930
    Pubs: *Bite to Eat Place: Anth* (Redwood Coast Pr,
    1995), *Movieworks: Anth* (Little Theatre Pr, 1990), *New*
    Criterion, Formalist, Kansas Qtly, Chicago Reader

Bill West 🎤 ✈   P
666 W Irving Park Rd, I-2
Chicago, IL 60613-3125
    Pubs: *Aabye, Iota, Envoi, Mainichi, Asahi, Lynx, Tundra,*
    Blue Collar Rev, Parnassus, Tanka Jrnl, Poetry Chain,
    Poetry Today, Lotus, Borderlines, Poet's Podium,
    T.O.P.S, Heron Qtly, Azami, Presence, Poetry Church
    Anth, Point Judith Light, American Tanka

David Buffington Wham 🎤   W
860 Hinman Ave, #724
Evanston, IL 60202-2341, 847-733-8015
    Pubs: *CPU Rev, Pilgrimage, Maelstrom, The Fair,*
    Means, Charlatan, December, Woodwind

Eugene Wildman   W
2705 N Mildred
Chicago, IL 60614, 312-281-7167

Anne Winters 🎤 ✈   P
English Dept (MC 162), Univ of Illinois at Chicago, 601 S
Morgan St, Chicago, IL 60607
    Pubs: *The Key to the City* (U Chicago Pr, 1986),
    Salamander (Princeton U Pr, 1979), *Paris Rev, Yale*
    Rev, New Yorker

S. L. Wisenberg   W
1209 W Waveland Ave, #3W
Chicago, IL 60613-3803, 312-871-5361
    Pubs: *Nice Jewish Girls: Anth* (Plume-Penguin, 1996),
    Feminism 3: Anth (Westview Pr, 1996), *Tikkun, New*
    Yorker, NAR, Kenyon Rev, Wigwag, ACM, Calyx

David Wojahn   P
1542 W Norwood
Chicago, IL 60660, 812-855-7967
    Pubs: *The Falling Hour, Late Empire, Mystery Train* (U
    Pitt Pr, 1997, 1994, 1990), *Poetry, New Yorker, APR,*
    TriQtly, Ploughshares, Southern Rev

Gene Wolfe   W
PO Box 69
Barrington, IL 60011
    Pubs: *Castleview, Soldier of Arete, There Are Doors*
    (Tor, 1990, 1989, 1988)

Janet Wondra 🎤 ✈   P
School of Liberal Studies, Roosevelt Univ, 430 S Michigan
Ave, Chicago, IL 60605, 312-341-3710
Internet: jwondra@roosevelt.edu
    Pubs: *Long Division* (Holocene Pub, 1998), *The*
    Wandering Mother, Emerging Island Cultures: Anth
    (Emerging Island Cultures Pr, 1989, 1984), *Calyx,*
    Connecticut Rev, Southern Rev, Michigan Qtly Rev,
    Denver Qtly, Witness, New Orleans Rev, Berkeley
    Poetry Rev

Etta L. Worthington   P&W
233 N Taylor
Oak Park, IL 60302, 708-848-2184
    Pubs: *Emergence III: Anth* (Emergence Pr, 1996), *Farm*
    Wives & Other Iowa Stories: Anth (Mid-Prairie Pr,
    1995), *Jane's Stories: Anth* (Wild Dove Pr, 1994),
    Christian Century, Slipstream, Verve, Secret Alameda,
    Ariel

Joanne Zimmerman 🎤 ✈   W
18255 Perth Ave
Homewood, IL 60430-1615, 708-798-8136
    Pubs: *Family: The Possibility of Tradition: Anth* (Pig
    Iron Pr, 2001), *An Intricate Weave: Anth* (Iris Edtns,
    1997), *Shenandoah, Antioch Rev, Descant*

Yvonne Zipter 🎤 ✈   P
4710 W Hutchinson
Chicago, IL 60641-1607
Internet: yzipter@journals.uchicago.edu
    Pubs: *Contemporary Lesbian Love Poems: Anth*
    (Ballantine Bks, 1996), *The Poetry of Sex: Anth*
    (Banned Bks, 1992), *Spoon River Poetry Rev, Modern*
    Words, Columbia Poetry Rev
I.D.: G/L/B/T. Groups: College/Univ, G/L/B/T

INDIANA

Tony Ardizzone 🎤 ✈   P&W
Indiana Univ, Department of English, Bloomington, IN
47401
Internet: ardizzon@indiana.edu
    Pubs: *In the Garden of Papa Santuzzu* (Picador USA,
    2000), *Taking it Home* (U Illinois Pr, 1996), *Larabi's*
    Ox: Stories of Morocco (Milkweed Edtns, 1992),
    Georgia Rev, Prairie Schooner, Gettysburg Rev, TriQtly,
    Witness

Deborah Bacharach   P
1585 N Oakhill Dr
South Bend, IN 46637, 219-243-9853
    Pubs: *Kalliope, Bellowing Ark, College English, Atom*
    Mind, Stuff, Slipstream, South Coast Poetry Jnrl,
    Wellspring, Bridges, Soundings East, Paramour, Poet
    Lore

William Baer   P&W
320 Hunter Dr
Evansville, IN 47711, 812-479-2975
    Pubs: *The Unfortunates* (New Odyssey Pr, 1997),
    Ploughshares, Hudson Rev, Iowa Rev, Poetry, Southern
    Rev

B. E. Balog   P
264 N Lake St
Gary, IN 46403
    Pubs: *Loaves & Fishes Anth* (Free Writer's Pr, 1982),
    Alternatives, Indiannual, Skylark

Willis Barnstone   P
Comparative Literature Dept, Indiana Univ, Bloomington, IN
47405, 812-855-9780
    Pubs: *Selected Poems* (Sheep Meadow Pr, 1997), *The*
    Secret Reader: 501 Sonnets (U Pr of New England,
    1996), *Partisan Rev, New Yorker*

Marianne Boruch 🎤 ✈   P
415 Maple St
West Lafayette, IN 47906-3016, 765-743-1420
Internet: mboruch@purdue.edu
    Pubs: *A Stick That Breaks & Breaks, Moss Burning*
    (Oberlin College Pr, 1997, 1993), *Descendant*
    (Wesleyan, 1989), *New Yorker, APR, Iowa Rev, Field,*
    Georgia Rev, Denver Qtly

James H. Bowden   P&W
2078 Ball Diamond Hill Rd
Lanesville, IN 47136
    Pubs: *Peter De Vries* (G. K. Hall, 1983), *Shenandoah,*
    College English, Negative Capability

Catherine Bowman   P
Indiana Univ, 442 Ballantine Hall English Dept,
Bloomington, IN 47401, 812-855-1834
    Pubs: *Rock Farm, 1-800-HOT-RIBS* (Gibbs Smith, 1997,
    1993), *Best American Poetry: Anths* (Scribner, 1995,
    1994), *TriQtly, River Styx, Paris Rev*

Matthew Brennan 🎤 ✈   P
Indiana State Univ, English Dept, Terre Haute, IN 47809,
812-237-3277
    Pubs: *The Music of Exile* (Cloverdale Bks, 1994),
    Seeing in the Dark (Hawkhead Pr, 1993), *Good*
    Company: Anth (Grinnell College, 2000), *South Dakota*
    Rev, Blue Unicorn, Poem, Classical Outlook, Poetry
    Ireland Rev, Descant

Edward Byrne   P
Valparaiso Univ, English Dept, Valparaiso, IN 46383,
219-464-5278
    Pubs: *East of Omaha* (Pecan Grove Pr, 1996), *Words*
    Spoken, Words Unspoken (Chimney Hill Pr, 1995),
    Along the Dark Shore (BOA Edtns, 1977), *APR, Porch*

Jared Carter 🎤 ✈   P
1220 N State Ave
Indianapolis, IN 46201-1162, 317-638-8136
    Pubs: *Les Barricades Mysterieuses, Work, For the Night*
    Is Coming, After the Rain (Cleveland State U Poetry
    Ctr, 1999, 1995, 1993), *Poetry, New Yorker, Nation,*
    Iowa Rev, TriQtly, The Formalist, Kenyon Rev, New
    Letters

Richard Cecil 🎤 ✈   P
Indiana Univ, Ballantine Hall 442, English Dept,
Bloomington, IN 47405, 812-855-8224
    Pubs: *In Search of the Great Dead* (Southern Illinois U
    Pr, 1999), *Alcatraz* (Purdue U Pr, 1992), *Einstein's*
    Brain (Utah U Pr, 1986), *APR, Poetry, Crazyhorse,*
    NER, Ploughshares, American Scholar, Virginia Qtly,
    Georgia Rev

Elizabeth Christman   W
American Studies Department, Univ Notre Dame, Notre
Dame, IN 46556, 219-239-7316
    Pubs: *Ruined for Life* (Paulist Pr, 1987), *A Broken*
    Family (Morrow, 1981), *The Critic*

Stephen R. Clark   P&W
36 Walnut St
Indianapolis, IN 46227-5187
    Pubs: *The Godtouch: Poems* (Northwoods Pr, 1985),
    Christianity & Literature, Christian Herald, Encore,
    Face-to-Face, Alive Now!, Wellspring

Ruth Allison Coates   P&W
8140 Township Line Rd
Indianapolis, IN 46260, 317-824-9548
   Pubs: *Waiting for the Westbound* (Ocean Tree Bks,
   1992), *Great American Naturalists* (Lerner Pubs, 1974),
   Minnesota Rev, Boys' Life, Byline

Marilyn Durham   W
1508 Howard St
Evansville, IN 47713, 812-423-3342
   Pubs: *Flambard's Confession, Dutch Uncle, The Man
   Who Loved Cat Dancing* (HBJ, 1982, 1973, 1972)

Darlene M. Eddy   P
1409 W Cardinal St
Muncie, IN 47303, 317-285-8584
   Pubs: *Leaf Threads, Wind Rhymes* (Barnwood Pr,
   1986), *Alternatives: An American Poetry Anth* (Best
   Cellar, 1987), *Blue Unicorn, Pebble, Cottonwood, Calyx*

Leslie Edgerton 🎙 ✈   W
4941 Maple Ridge Dr
Fort Wayne, IN 46835-3930, 219-485-9207
Internet: edgertonl@cs.com
   Pubs: *Over Easy* (Random Hse, 1999), *Monday's Meal,
   The Death of Tarpons* (U North Texas Pr, 1997, 1996),
   *South Carolina Rev, Arkansas Qtly/Kansas Rev,
   Hopewell Rev, NAR, Breeze, Flyway Literary Rev, High
   Plains Literary Rev*
Groups: Prisoners

Douglas Eichhorn   P
208 W Main
Centerville, IN 47330, 317-855-3398
   Pubs: *Rituals: A Book of Poems* (Salt Mound Pr, 1968)

William C. Elkington   P
10433 Haverford Pl
Fort Wayne, IN 46845-6504
   Pubs: *Snowy Egret, Laurel Rev, Karamu, North
   Country, Denver Qtly, Aldebaran, Third Eye, Gravida*

Lenny Emmanuel   P
Indiana Univ Medical Center, 930 W Michigan St,
Indianapolis, IN 46223, 317-274-1744
   Pubs: *The Ice Cream Lady* (Ramparts, 1996), *The
   Cathartic, Descant, Poetry Rev, Outposts, Imago, Jrnl of
   Teaching Writing, Exquisite Corpse, Windless Orchard*

Mari Evans   P
PO Box 483
Indianapolis, IN 46206, 317-926-5229

Christine Farris   P
English Dept, Indiana Univ, Bloomington, IN 47405
   Pubs: *Mining the Beaches for Watches & Small
   Change* (Konglomerati Pr, 1981), *Some, Kairos*

Stephen Fredman   P
English Dept, Univ Notre Dame, Notre Dame, IN 46556,
219-631-7555
   Pubs: *Sagetrieb, Talisman, Boundary 2, o.ars, North
   Dakota Qtly, 20th Century Literature*

Alice Friman 🎙 ✈   P
6312 Central Ave
Indianapolis, IN 46220-1738, 317-257-2105
   Pubs: *Zoo* (U Arkansas Pr, 1999), *Inverted Fire* (BkMk
   Pr, 1997), *Driving for Jimmy Wonderland* (Barnwood Pr,
   1992), *Insomniac Heart* (Years Pr, 1990), *Poetry,
   Georgia Rev, Ohio Rev, Gettysburg Rev, Prairie
   Schooner, Poetry Rev* (U.K.), *Boulevard, Field*

Helen Frost 🎙 ✈   P
6108 Old Brook Dr
Fort Wayne, IN 46835-2438, 219-485-1785
Internet: frost-thompson@worldnet.att.net
   Pubs: *Skin of a Fish, Bones of a Bird* (Ampersand Pr,
   1993), *The Sacred Place: Anth* (U Utah Pr, 1996),
   Season of Dead Water: Anth (Breitenbush, 1990), *Ms.,
   Chile Verde, Antioch Rev, Calyx, Calliope, Malahat Rev*
Groups: Children, Teenagers

Sonia Gernes 🎙 ✈   P
Univ Notre Dame, 210 Decio Hall, Notre Dame, IN 46556,
219-631-5218
Internet: sonia.g.gernes.1@nd.edu
   Pubs: *A Breeze Called the Fremantle Doctor, Women
   at Forty* (U Notre Dame Pr, 1997, 1990), *Southern
   Rev, Poetry NW, Sewanee Rev, American Short Fiction,
   Georgia Rev, New Letters*

Paul E. Grabill   W
905 S Spring St
Evansville, IN 47714, 812-477-2584
   Pubs: *Youth's A Stuff Will Not Endure* (Avon, 1977),
   Bitterroot

Matthew Graham   P
Univ Southern Indiana, 8600 University Blvd, Evansville, IN
47712, 812-464-1953
   Pubs: *1946, New World Architecture* (Galileo, 1991,
   1985), *Indiana Rev, Harvard Rev*

Nancy Hagen   W
1133 Glenway St
West Lafayette, IN 47906, 765-497-1259
   Pubs: *Alternatives: Roads Less Travelled: Anth, Prairie
   Hearts: Women View the Midwest: Anth* (Outrider Pr,
   1997), *Mystery Time: Anth* (Hutton Pub, 1997)

Anne Haines 🎤 ✈   P
PO Box 2501
Bloomington, IN 47402-2501
Internet: php.indiana.edu/~ahaines
   Pubs: *NW Rev, Kansas Qtly, Sojourner, Prairie
   Schooner, Sidewalks, Common Lives/Lesbian Lives,
   New Zoo Poetry Rev, Sinister Wisdom*
I.D.: G/L/B/T, Feminist. Groups: Women, G/L/B/T

Patricia Henley   P&W
PO Box 259
Battle Ground, IN 47920, 765-567-2058
   Pubs: *The Secret of Cartwheels, Friday Night at Silver
   Star* (Graywolf, 1992, 1986), *Learning to Die* (Three
   Rivers, 1979), *Atlantic, Ploughshares*

Joe L. Hensley   W
2315 Blackmore
Madison, IN 47250, 812-273-1683
   Pubs: *Grim City* (St. Martin's Pr, 1994)

Marc Hudson   P
English Dept, Wabash College, Crawfordsville, IN 47933,
317-364-4232
   Pubs: *Journal for an Injured Son* (Lockhart Pr, 1991),
   *Kenyon Rev, Massachusetts Rev, Prairie Schooner,
   Poetry East, Fine Madness*

Karen I. Jaquish 🎤 ✈   P
4817 W Arlington Park Blvd
Fort Wayne, IN 46835-4311
Internet: kijaquish@prodigy.net
   Pubs: *Prairie Schooner, Notre Dame Rev, SPR,
   Plainsongs, Connecticut Poetry Rev, 11th Muse, Poet
   Lore, South Carolina Rev, Nation, Hopewell Rev, Free
   Songs, Flying Island, Denver Qtly*

George Kalamaras   P
1202 Illsley Pl
Fort Wayne, IN 46807, 219-456-3151
   Pubs: *Beneath the Breath* (Tilton Hse Pr, 1988), *Heart
   Without End* (Leaping Mountain Pr, 1986), *Best
   American Poetry: Anth* (S&S, 1997), *Chariton Rev,
   Epoch, Sulfur, New Letters, Iowa Rev*

Margaret Kingery 🎤 ✈   W
c/o Dimoplon, 4103 N Redding Rd, Muncie, IN
47304-1338, 317-289-5022
   Pubs: *Dark Horse* (Ball State U, 1997), *Willow Rev,
   Flying Island, South Dakota Rev, Hopewell Rev, Texas
   Rev, Confrontation, Kansas Qtly, Prairie Schooner,
   Earth's Daughters, Thema, Emrys Jrnl*

Terry Alan Kirts   P
1620 Central Ae #102
Indianapolis, IN 46202, 317-921-9416
   Pubs: *Third Coast, Green Mountains Rev, Sycamore
   Rev, Artful Dodge*

Tom Koontz 🎤 ✈   P
Ball State Univ
Muncie, IN 47306, 765-288-0145
Internet: www.bsu.edu/classes/koontz
   Pubs: *Rice Paper Sky* (Amelia, 2000), *In Such a Light*
   (Mississinewa Pr, 1996), *Black Fly Rev, Hopewell Rev,
   Birmingham Poetry Rev, Flying Island, PBQ*

Karen Kovacik 🎤 ✈   P
1325 N Central, #6
Indianapolis, IN 46202
Internet: kkovacik@inpui.edu
   Pubs: *Beyond the Velvet Curtain, Nixon & I, A
   Gathering of Poets: Anth* (Kent State U Pr, 1999, 1998,
   1992), *Return of the Prodigal* (Poetry Atlanta Pr, 1991),
   Salmagundi, BPJ, Confrontation

Marcia H. Kruchten   W
442 S Maple St
Orleans, IN 47452, 812-865-2663
   Pubs: *Skyborn* (Schoastic, 1989), *I Don't Want to Be
   Like Her, Too Many Parents, The Ghost in the Mirror*
   (Willowisp Pr, 1996, 1996, 1986), *Indianapolis Woman,
   Writer's Digest, Prim-Aid, Black Box*

D. E. Laczi   P
805 S 9th St
Lafayette, IN 47905-1430, 317-742-2539
Internet: midwayog@wcic.cioe.com
   Pubs: *Jrnl of Kentucky Studies, Flying Island, Tears in
   the Fence, Black Buzzard Rev, Oyez Rev, Maverick Pr,
   Phoebe, Sistersong, Kentucky Writing, Piedmont Literary
   Rev, Onion River Rev*

John Matthias 🎤 ✈   P
Univ Notre Dame, English Dept, Notre Dame, IN 46556,
219-239-7226
Internet: john.e.matthias.1@nd.edu
   Pubs: *Pages, Swimming at Midnight, Beltane at
   Aphelion* (Swallow Pr, 2000, 1995, 1995), *TriQtly,
   Salmagundi, ACM, Southern Rev, Stand*

Kathy A. Mayer   P
PO Box 1135
Lafayette, IN 47902, 765-423-1393
   Pubs: *Haraka Pr, Story Circle Jrnl, Moon Jrnl,
   L'Ouverture, Outrider Press, Flying Island, Earth's
   Daughters, Pike Creek Rev*

John A. McCluskey, Jr.   W
Afro-American Studies, Indiana Univ, Memorial Hall, #31,
Bloomington, IN 47401
   Pubs: *Mr. America's Last Season Blues* (LSU, 1983),
   Black American Literary Forum, Southern Rev, Callaloo

Joan McIntosh 🎤 ✈ P
213 Wakewa Ave
South Bend, IN 46617, 219-232-4502
Internet: robert.p.mcintosh.1@nd.edu
  Pubs: *Lake Michigan Shore, Branch & Shadow Branch*
  (Writer's Center of Indianapolis, 1997, 1982),
  *Cumberland Poetry Rev, Connecticut River Rev,
  Shenandoah*

Howard McMillen W
English Dept, Indiana State Univ, Terre Haute, IN 47809,
812-237-3168
  Pubs: *The Many Mansions of Sam Peeples* (Viking,
  1972), *Literary Mag Rev, Gambling Times, Win
  Magazine*

Margaret McMullan W
737 Norman Ave
Evansville, IN 47714-2121
  Pubs: *When Warhol Was Still Alive* (Crossing Pr,
  1994), *Catholic Girls & Boys: Anth* (Penguin/NAL,
  1994), *Greensboro Rev, New England Living*

Brent Michael P&W
1513 E Market St Apt 3
New Albany, IN 47150, 812-949-1963
  Pubs: *Chance Mag, Struggle, Twisted Savage, Mount
  Olive Rev, Atom Mind, Curmudgeon, Jefferson Rev,
  Appalachian Heritage*

Roger Mitchell 🎤 ✈ P
1010 E 1st St
Bloomington, IN 47401, 812-332-1045
  Pubs: *Braid* (The Figures, 1997), *The Word for
  Everything, Adirondack* (BkMk Pr, 1996, 1988),
  Clearpond (Syracuse U, 1991), *A Clear Space on a
  Cold Day* (Cleveland State U Pr, 1986), *Poetry Comes
  Up Where It Can: Anth* (U Utah Pr, 2000), *Tar River
  Rev, Pequod*

Neil Myers P
901 N Chauncey
West Lafayette, IN 47906
  Pubs: *The Blade of Manjusri* (Sun Moon Bear, 1989),
  All That, So Simple (Purdue U Pr, 1980)

Susan Neville W
Butler Univ, 4600 Sunset Ave, Box 135, Indianapolis, IN
46208, 317-940-9676
  Pubs: *Indiana Winter* (Indiana U Pr, 1999), *In the
  House of Blue Lights* (Notre Dame Pr, 1998), *Invention
  of Flight* (U Georgia Pr, 1984), *NAR, Boulevard,
  Georgia Rev, Sycamore Rev, Crazyhorse, Mid-American
  Rev*

William O'Rourke W
Univ Notre Dame, English Dept, Notre Dame, IN 46556,
219-631-7377
Internet: william.a.o'rourke.1@nd.edu
  Pubs: *Campaign America '96* (Notre Dame Pr, 2000),
  Notts (Marlowe & Co, 1996), *Signs of the Literary
  Times* (SUNY, 1993), *The Nation, ACM, Hopewell Rev*

Harry Mark Petrakis W
80 E Rd, Dune Acres
Chesterton, IN 46304, 219-787-8283
Internet: hmp80@hotmail.com
  Pubs: *Collected Stories* (Ravenswood, 1990), *Days of
  Vengeance* (Doubleday, 1983), *Atlantic, Saturday
  Evening Post, Harper's Bazaar*

Roger Pfingston 🎤 ✈ P
4020 Stoutes Creek Rd
Bloomington, IN 47404-1332, 812-339-2482
Internet: snapshot@bluemarble.net
  Pubs: *Something Iridescent* (Barnwood Pr, 1987), *The
  Party Train: Anth* (New Rivers Pr, 1996), *Inheriting the
  Land: Anth* (U Minnesota Pr, 1993), *Poet Lore, Laurel
  Rev, Yankee*

Richard Pflum 🎤 ✈ P
1473 Shannon Ave
Indianapolis, IN 46201-1758, 317-356-2048
Internet: drahcir@indy.net
  Pubs: *A Strange Juxtaposition of Parts* (Writers' Ctr Pr
  of Indiana, 1995), *A New Geography of Poets: Anth* (U
  Arkansas Pr, 1992), *Ploplop Mag, Poetry Tonight, Tears
  in the Fence, Flying Island, Hopewell Rev*

Michael Joseph Phillips P
238 N Smith Rd #25
Bloomington, IN 47408-3188, 812-336-2530
  Pubs: *Dreamgirls* (Cambric, 1989), *Selected Love
  Poems* (Wm. Hackett, 1980), *Massachusetts Rev, The
  Nation*

Donald Platt 🎤 ✈ P
Dept of English, Purdue Univ, 1356 Heavilon Hall, West
Lafayette, IN 47907-1356, 765-494-3740
  Pubs: *Leap Second at the Turn of the Millennium* (Ctr
  for Book Arts NY, 2000), *Fresh Peaches, Fireworks, &
  Guns* (Purdue U Pr, 1994), *Best American Poetry: Anth*
  (Scribner, 2000), *Kenyon Rev, Nimrod, New Republic,
  Paris Rev, Qtly West*

Fran Quinn P
599 W Westfield Blvd #38
Indianapolis, IN 46208, 317-259-9096
  Pubs: *The Goblet Crying for Wine* (Ally Pr, 1995), *At
  the Edge of the Worlds* (Presada Pr, 1994)

William Craig Rice   P
Liberty Fund, Inc, 8335 Allison Pointe Trail, Indianapolis,
IN 46250-1684, 800-368-7897
Internet: wcrice@libertyfund.org
   Pubs: *Sewanee, New Criterion, Sparrow, Harvard Rev,*
   Dog World

Scott Russell Sanders   W
1113 E Wylie St
Bloomington, IN 47401
   Pubs: *Writing from the Center* (Indiana U Pr, 1995),
   Staying Put, Secrets of the Universe (Beacon Pr, 1993,
   1991), *Harper's, Omni, Georgia Rev, NAR*

Valerie Sayers   W
English Dept, Univ Notre Dame, Notre Dame, IN 46617,
219-631-7160
   Pubs: *Brain Fever, The Distance Between Us, Who Do*
   You Love (Doubleday, 1996, 1996, 1991)

John Sherman 🎤 ✈   P
4175 Central Ave
Indianapolis, IN 46205-2604, 317-283-3330
Internet: shermco@earthlink.net
   Pubs: *Marjorie Main: Rural Documentary Poetry,*
   America Is a Negro Child: Race Poems (Mesa Verde
   Pr, 1999, 1981), *Touched by Adoption: Anth* (Green
   River Pr, 1999), *Dying: A Book of Comfort: Anth*
   (Doubleday, 1996), *Coe Rev, American Jones, Nebo,*
   MM Rev

Dennis Sipe   P
4897 W Watertower Rd
Austin, IN 47401, 812-794-2201
   Pubs: *My Days Are Stray Dogs That Won't Come*
   When I Call (LongRod Pr, 1993), *Black Fly Rev,*
   Louisville Rev, American Writing, Wind, Permafrost

R. E. Smith   W
520 Terry Ln
West Lafayette, IN 47906, 317-743-1074
   Pubs: *Unknown Texas: Anth* (Macmillan, 1988), *South*
   By Southwest: Anth (U Texas Pr, 1986), *Concho River*
   Rev, Chariton Rev, Descant, Texas Rev

Maura Stanton 🎤 ✈   P&W
Indiana Univ, Ballantine Hall 442, English Dept,
Bloomington, IN 47405, 812-855-1296
Internet: stanton@indiana.edu
   Pubs: *Life Among the Trolls* (Carnegie Mellon, 1998),
   Tales of the Supernatural (Godine, 1988), *The Country*
   I Come From (Milkweed Edtns, 1988), *Ploughshares,*
   Crazyhorse, APR, Southern Rev, Paris Rev, Crab
   Orchard Rev

Felix Stefanile 🎤 ✈   P
103 Waldron St
West Lafayette, IN 47906-2836, 765-743-0530
   Pubs: *The Country of Absence* (Bordighera Pr, 2000),
   The Dance at St. Gabriel's (Story Line Pr, 1995),
   Unsettling America: Anth (Penguin, 1994), *Sewanee*
   Rev, Hudson Rev, Formalist, Poetry

Leon Titche 🎤 ✈   P
510 Renard Rd
West Lafayette, IN 47906-9489, 765-743-1059
Internet: ljtitche@concentric.net
   Pubs: *Reflections from a Desert Pond* (Century Pr,
   1998)
Lang: German

Bronislava Volkova   P
926 Commons Dr
Bloomington, IN 47401, 812-339-3618
   Pubs: *Shattered Worlds* (Votobia, 1995), *Courage of the*
   Rainbow (Sheep Meadow, 1993), *The Deaf & Dumb*
   Hand (Pm D, 1993), *Metamorphoses, Visions, Poetry*
   East, Nimrod, Midwest Poetry Rev, Witness

Matt Wade   P
875 W 900 N
Fortville, IN 46040, 317-485-7579
   Pubs: *Black Dirt, Formalist, Mudfish, New Laurel Rev,*
   River Styx

Elizabeth Weber   P
4771 Stansbury Ln
Indianapolis, IN 46254
   Pubs: *Small Mercies* (Owl Creek, 1984), *Puerto del Sol,*
   Florida Rev, 6ix

Henry Weinfield 🎤 ✈   P
1113 N St Joseph
South Bend, IN 46617-1253, 219-288-7648
   Pubs: *The Sorrows of Eros & Other Poems* (U Notre
   Dame Pr, 1999), *Sonnets Elegiac & Satirical, In the*
   Sweetness of New Time (House of Keys, 1982, 1980),
   Pequod, Denver Qtly, Talisman

Joanna H. Wos 🎤 ✈   W
8148 Lieber Rd
Indianapolis, IN 46260-2839, 317-255-6086
Internet: jhwriter@indy.net
   Pubs: *A House of Butter* (Writers Center Pr, 1998),
   Loss of the Groundnote: Anth (Clothespin Fever Pr,
   1992), *Flash Fiction: Anth* (Norton, 1992), *Malahat Rev,*
   Kalliope, Permafrost, Webster Rev, MacGuffin, Qtly
   West
I.D.: Immigrants, Polish

Marguerite Young   P&W
2506 Knollwood Dr
Indianapolis, IN 46208-2188

IOWA

Nina Barragan W
c/o Weinstein, 3880 Owl Song Ln SE, Iowa City, IA
52240-9044, 319-351-4700
　　Pubs: *No Peace at Versailles, The House on Via
　　Gambito: Anth* (New Rivers Pr, 1991, 1991), *B'nai B'rith
　　Intl Jewish Monthly*

Marvin Bell P
1416 E College St
Iowa City, IA 52245, 319-337-5217
　　Pubs: *Wednesday: Selected Poems 1966-1997* (Ireland;
　　Salmon Pub, 1998), *Ardor: The Book of the Dead Man,
　　Vol 2, The Book of the Dead Man* (Copper Canyon,
　　1997, 1994), *A Marvin Bell Reader* (Middlebury/U Pr of
　　New England, 1994), *Poetry, New Yorker, APR*

Virginia Bensheimer P
Route 1, Box 68
Macedonia, IA 51549
　　Pubs: *Visions, Green's Mag, The Little Mag, Urthkin,
　　Long Pond Rev, Truely Fine*

Frederick Bock P
Embassy Manor Care Center, 200 S Eighth Ave E,
Newton, IA 50208
　　Pubs: *The Fountains of Regardlessness* (Macmillan,
　　1961), *Ascent, Poetry, Antaeus, Iowa Rev*

Michael Borich P
1308 Vermont St
Waterloo, IA 50702, 319-232-0275
　　Pubs: *Nana's Ark* (Thomas Nelson, 1984), *A Different
　　Kind of Love* (HR&W, 1984)

Jerry Bumpus W
619 Church St Suite 127
Ottumwa, IA 52501
　　Pubs: *The Civilized Tribes* (U Akron Pr, 1995), *Dawn of
　　the Flying Pigs* (Carpenter Pr, 1992), *Esquire, Paris
　　Rev, Partisan Rev, Yellow Silk, December Mag*

Dan Campion 🎤 ✈ P
1700 E Rochester Ave
Iowa City, IA 52245
　　Pubs: *Calypso* (Syncline, 1981), *ACM, College English,
　　English Jrnl, Midwest Qtly, Ascent, Borderlands, Light,
　　Poetry, Slant, Poet Lore*

Rick Christman W
6601 Lincoln Ave
Des Moines, IA 50322, 515-276-9317
　　Pubs: *Falling in Love at the End of the World, The
　　Party Train: Anth* (New Rivers Pr, 1998, 1996),
　　*Descant, River Oak Rev, Indiana Rev, River City, Red
　　Rock Rev, Permafrost, The Alembic*

Robert Dana P
1466 Westview Dr
Coralville, IA 52241, 319-354-2171
　　Pubs: *Hello Stranger: Beach Poems, Yes, Everything*
　　(Another Chicago Pr, 1996, 1994), *Kenyon Rev, Manoa,
　　Witness, Georgia Rev, High Plains Literary Rev*

Irma Dovey P
1224 13th St NW, #321
Cedar Rapids, IA 52405-2404, 319-363-1966
　　Pubs: *Long About Tuesday* (Dovey, 1989), *Lyrical Iowa:
　　Anths* (Iowa Poetry Association, 1995, 1994, 1990),
　　Midwest Chaparral, Thirteen, Quickenings, Story Friends

Jim Dunlap P
2830 Brattleboro #2
Des Moines, IA 50311-4008, 515-279-3540
　　Pubs: *Mobius, Dream Intl Qtly, Infinity Limited, Mind in
　　Motion, Prophetic Voices, Candelabrum, Plainsongs,
　　Stand Alone, Lyrical Iowa, Potpourri, Paris/Atlantic*

Gary Eller W
1243 24th St
Ames, IA 50010, 515-232-4654
　　Pubs: *Thin Ice & Other Risks* (New Rivers, 1994),
　　*Flyway, Other Voices, Crescent Rev, River City,
　　Sidewalks, New Press*

Jocelyn Emerson P
English Dept, Univ of Iowa, 308 EPB, Iowa City, IA 52242
　　Pubs: *Carolina Qtly, Colorado Rev, Common
　　Lives/Lesbian Lives, Cosmos, Denver Qtly, The Jrnl,
　　Seneca Rev, Sojourner, NAW*

William Ford P
1808 Morningside Dr
Iowa City, IA 52245
　　Pubs: *Poetry, Pennsylvania Rev, Three Rivers Poetry
　　Jrnl*

Phillip H. Hey P
2750 Malloy Rd
Sioux City, IA 51103, 712-277-2811
　　Pubs: *A Change of Clothes* (Celestial Light, 1989),
　　Voices on the Landscape: Anth (Loess Hills Pr, 1996),
　　Zone 3, Art/Life, Briar Cliff Rev

Jan D. Hodge 🎤 ✈ P
4920 Morningside Ave
Sioux City, IA 51106, 712-276-2999
Internet: jandhodge@aol.com
　　Pubs: *Poems to Be Traded for Baklava* (Onionhead,
　　1997), *Things Taking Shape* (Harold's Pr, 1992), *Voices
　　on the Landscape: Anth* (Loess Hills Pr, 1996), *South
　　Coast Poetry Rev, Black Bear Rev, BPJ, ELF, Defined
　　Providence*

Donald Justice   P
338 Rocky Shore Dr
Iowa City, IA 52246
    Pubs: *Orpheus Hesitated Beside the Black River* (Anvil
    Pr, 1998), *New & Selected Poems* (Knopf, 1995)

Juliet Yli-Mattila Kaufmann   P
428 Clark St
Iowa City, IA 52240
    Pubs: *Cold Pastoral* (Virgil Burnett & Robert Williams,
    1974), *Lake Effect, Chicago Rev, Rochester Rev*

Theodore Krieger   P
403 8th Ave
Charles City, IA 50616-2309, 515-228-2270
    Pubs: *Novitiate* (Unified Pub, 1987), *Bearing It Alone*
    (Ansuda, 1980), *Spoon River Qtly, Poetry Now,
    Sou'wester, Pteranodon, Pawn Rev*

Rustin Larson   P
501 N C St
Fairfield, IA 52556, 515-472-1370
    Pubs: *Voices on the Landscape: Anth* (Loess Hill Pr,
    1996), *Iowa Rev, Cimarron Rev, William & Mary Rev,
    Passages North, The New Yorker, Boundary 2, Poetry
    East, Indiana Rev, America*

Todd Lieber   W
789 Jesup St
Indianola, IA 50125, 515-961-7691
    Pubs: *Crazyhorse, Sycamore Rev, Nimrod, Mss.,
    Missouri Rev, Yale Rev*

Lucille Gripp Maharry 🎤 ✈   P
300 N Sumner Ave
Creston, IA 50801-2041
    Pubs: *Suddenly I Am Home* (Celestial Light, 1996),
    *Decision, Sunday Digest, Secret Place, Delta Kappa
    Gamma Bulletin, Bible Advocate, Evangel, Green's Mag,
    One Hundred Words, Minnesota Monthly, Poetpourri,
    Buffalo Spree*

Julie McDonald 🎤 ✈   W
2802 E Locust St
Davenport, IA 52803-3430, 319-355-7246
Internet: jmcdonad@saunix.sau.edu
    Pubs: *North of the Heart* (1st Bks, 2000), *My Brother,
    Grant Wood* (State Historical Society of Iowa, 1993),
    Young Rakes (East Hall Pr, 1991)

James McKean 🎤 ✈   P
1164 E Court St
Iowa City, IA 52240-3232, 319-338-3976
    Pubs: *Tree of Heaven* (U Iowa Pr, 1995), *Headlong* (U
    Utah Pr, 1987), *Georgia Rev, Poetry, Southern Rev,
    Ironwood, Poetry NW, Seneca Rev, Iowa Rev*

James McPherson 🎤 ✈   W
711 Rundell St
Iowa City, IA 52240, 319-338-3136
    Pubs: *A Region Not Home, Crabcakes* (S&S, 2000,
    1998), *Fathering Daughters: Anth* (Beacon Pr, 1998),
    DoubleTake, Iowa Rev, Center Eight

Gordon W. Mennenga   W
1805 Windsor Ct
Iowa City, IA 52245, 319-338-7255
    Pubs: *Oxford Mag, Folio, NAR, Foothills Qtly, Seems,
    Seven*

Chuck Miller   P
PO Box 2814
Iowa City, IA 52244, 319-335-9223
    Pubs: *How in the Morning* (Spirit That Moves Us Pr,
    1989), *From Oslo* (Friends Pr, 1988), *Harvestors*
    (Coffee Hse Pr, 1984)

Eleanora Miller   P
208 SW Church St
Leon, IA 50144-1349, 515-446-4401
    Pubs: *Lyrical Iowa: Anth* (Iowa Poetry Assn, 1999), *A
    Song of Myself: Anth* (CSS Pub, 1987), *Polestar,
    Sandcutters, Cats*

James Minor   P
1450 Alta Vista St
Dubuque, IA 52001-4327
    Pubs: *Against the Night, A Measure of Light* (Juniper
    Pr, 1986, 1984), *New Cicada, Northeast*

Nancy Price   P&W
English Language & Literature Dept., Univ Northern Iowa,
Cedar Falls, IA 50614, 319-273-2821
    Pubs: *Snake in the Blackberries, L'Incendiaire* (Presses
    de la Cité, 2000, 1998), *Night Woman* (Pocket Bks,
    1992), *Sleeping with the Enemy* (S&S, 1987), *An
    Accomplished Woman* (Coward McCann Geoghegan,
    1979), *A Natural Death* (Little, Brown, 1973)

John Quinn   P
PO Box 847
Cedar Falls, IA 50613-0847
    Pubs: *The Wolf Last Seen* (Pacific Hse Bks, 1987),
    Easy Pie (Buttonmaker, 1986), *Interim, College English,
    Laurel Rev, Hudson Rev, Puerto del Sol*

Keith Ratzlaff 🎤 ✈   P
306 Liberty
Pella, IA 50219-1753, 515-628-8466
Internet: ratzlaffk@central.edu
    Pubs: *Man Under a Pear Tree* (Anhinga Pr, 1997),
    Across the Known World (Loess Hills Pr, 1997), *New
    Winter Light* (Nightshade Pr, 1994), *Out Here* (State
    Street Pr, 1984), *Poetry NorthWest, Colorado Rev, Jrnl,
    Denver Qtly, Georgia Rev, NER, Three Penny Rev*

James Calvin Schaap 🎤 ✈   W
Dordt College, English Dept, Sioux Center, IA 51250,
712-722-6250
Internet: jschaap@dordt.edu
  Pubs: *Romey's Place, The Secrets of Barneveld
  Calvary, In the Silence There Are Ghosts* (Baker Bks,
  1999, 1997, 1995), *Called to Die* (Eerdmans, 1994),
  *Prairie Schooner, Other Side, Image, Wind, Poet &
  Critic*

Mary Helen Stefaniak 🎤 ✈   W
PO Box 2134
Iowa City, IA 52244-2134, 319-354-8515
Internet: mhs@creighton.edu
  Pubs: *Self Storage & Other Stories* (New Rivers Pr
  1997), *A Sweet Secret: Anth* (Toronto; Second Story
  Pr, 1997), *Antioch Rev, EPOCH, Iowa Rev, Nebraska
  Rev, NAR, Iowa Woman, Yale Rev, Calyx, Crescent
  Rev, Agni, Seattle Rev, Redbook*

Ann Struthers 🎤 ✈   P&W
503 Forest Dr SE
Cedar Rapids, IA 52403-4234, 319-362-3764
Internet: astruthe@coe.edu
  Pubs: *The Alcott Family Arrives* (Coe Rev Pr, 1993),
  Stoneboat & Other Poems (Pterodactyl Pr, 1988),
  *Calyx, The New Renaissance, Poetry, Hudson Rev,
  American Scholar, Iowa Woman*
Groups: Women, Middle-Eastern Communities

James Sutton   P
4324 Kingman Blvd
Des Moines, IA 50311-3418, 515-255-7031
  Pubs: *Minnesota Rev, Phi Delta Kappan, College
  English, Teacher, Stand Alone*

Jody Swilky   P
Drake Univ, 2707 University Ave, Des Moines, IA 50312,
515-271-2853
  Pubs: *A City of Fences* (La Huerta Pr, 1977), *NAR,
  Mid-American Rev, Chelsea, New Boston Rev, Yale
  Rev, Raccoon, Ohio Rev, Missouri Rev, Georgia Rev*

Thomas Swiss   P
Drake Univ, English Dept, Des Moines, IA 50311,
515-271-3777
  Pubs: *Measure* (U Alabama, 1986), *Ploughshares,
  American Scholar, Sewanee Rev*

Fred Truck   P
4225 University
Des Moines, IA 50311, 515-255-3552
  Pubs: *Art Engine Texts* (Electric Bank, 1989),
  Simulation Stimulation (Art Com Electronic, 1986)

Liz Waldner   P
Univ of Iowa Press, 100 Kohl House, Iowa City, IA 52242,
319-335-2000
  Pubs: *A Point Is That Which Has No Part* (U Iowa Pr,
  2000), *Call* (Meow Pr, 2000), *With the Tongues of
  Angels* (Owl Creek, 2000), *Homing Devices* (O Bks,
  1998)

Melvin Wilk   P
3013 Terrace Dr
Des Moines, IA 50312, 515-255-3346
  Pubs: *In Exile* (BkMk Pr, 1979), *Mss., New Yorker,
  Poetry, Massachusetts Rev*

Frederic Will   P
617 7 St, N
Mt Vernon, IA 52314

Valorie Broadhurst Woerdehoff   P
3246 St Anne Dr
Dubuque, IA 52001-3951, 319-556-3534
Internet: vwoerdeh@loras.edu
  Pubs: *Haiku World: Anth* (Kodansha America Inc,
  1996), *Haiku Moment: Anth* (C.E. Tuttle Co, 1993),
  Midwest Haiku: Anth (High/Coo Pr, 1992), *Modern
  Haiku, Frogpond, Cottonwood Rev, Spoon River, Iowa
  Woman, 100 Words, Cicada*
Groups: Children

Ray A. Young Bear   P
751 Meskwaki Rd
Tama, IA 52339
  Pubs: *Black Eagle Child, Remnants of the First Earth*
  (Grove, 1997, 1996), *The Invisible Musician* (Holy Cow!
  Pr, 1990), *Winter of the Salamander* (H&R, 1980), *The
  Best American Poetry: Anth* (Scribner, 1996),
  Ploughshares, Akwekon

KANSAS

Marie A. Asner 🎤 ✈   P
PO Box 4343
Overland Park, KS 66204-0343
  Pubs: *Tenebrae* (CSS Pubs, 2001), *3: An Interview of
  Poets, Man of Miracles II: The Followers* (New Spirit
  Pr, 1999, 1994), *Angels* (Maka, 1998), *The Tree of Life*
  (Kindred Spirit Pr, 1996), *An Inquiring Mind* (Green
  Meadow Pr, 1993)

Thomas Fox Averill 🎤 ✈   W
Washburn Univ, 1700 College, Topeka, KS 66621,
913-231-1010
Internet: zzaver@washburn.edu
  Pubs: *Seeing Mona Naked* (Watermark, 1989), *O.
  Henry Award: Anth* (Doubleday, 1991), *The Best of the
  West #4: Anth* (Norton, 1991), *NAR, Cimarron Rev,
  Cottonwood, DoubleTake, Greensboro Rev*

Gar Bethel P
212 N Iowa
Winfield, KS 67156, 316-221-0939
  Pubs: *Small Wonder, Dust, Rivers & Stars* (Point Riders Pr, 1996, 1992), *Fresh Eggs* (Wythe Hse Pr, 1992)

G. W. Clift W
English Dept, Kansas State Univ, Manhattan, KS 66506, 913-532-6716
  Pubs: *Bill Made Up a Point of History* (BkMk Pr, 1994), *Illinois Rev, Borderlands, Wind, Uncle, Vanderbilt Rev, Union Street Rev, Salad, Kansas Qtly, Fiction Rev, Bakunin*

Kay L. Closson P
2033 S Dellrose St
Wichita, KS 67218-5107, 316-681-3248
  Pubs: *Smith, Pulpsmith, Newsart, Taurus, Occasional Rev, Dog River Rev, Ms., Ghost Dance*

Marilyn Coffey ♒ ✈ P&W
305 W 15 St
Hays, KS 67601-3719, 785-623-2879
Internet: mcoffey65@hotmail.com
  Pubs: *Marcella: A Novel* (Quartet, 1976), *Eating Our Hearts Out: Anth* (Crossing Pr, 1993), *Voices of the Plains: Anth* (A Slow Tempo Pr, 1992), *NCB Qtly: Anth* (Nebraska Ctr for the Bk, 1991), *The Pushcart Prize: Anth* (Pushcart Pr, 1976)
Groups: Libraries

Victor Contoski P
4110 W 12 St
Lawrence, KS 66049, 913-842-5303
  Pubs: *A Kansas Sequence* (Cottonwood-Tellus, 1983), *Names* (New Rivers, 1979)

Marjorie Culver P
8027 W 113 St
Overland Park, KS 66210
  Pubs: *Turn West at Jefferson* (Potpourri Pub Co, 1993), *A Garden of Cucumbers* (Mid-America Pr, 1977), *Passager, Missouri Poets, DeKalb Literary Arts*

Celia A. Daniels ♒ ✈ P
1521 SW College Ave
Topeka, KS 66604-2759
Internet: cadaniel@ukans.edu
  Pubs: *Fissures* (Singular Speech Pr, 1993), *Great Plains Poets: Anth* (Midwest Qtly, 1995), *Common Journeys, Sunflower Petals, Midwest Qtly, Cottonwood Rev, Nebraska English Jrnl, Kansas Qtly, Spoon River Qtly, Inscape, Z-Misc*
Groups: Multicultural, Disabled

A. A. Dewey P
PO Box 154
Eudora, KS 66025-0154, 913-842-1782
  Pubs: *Heartland II: Poets of the Midwest: Anth* (Northern Illinois U Pr, 1975), *Hanging Loose*

Bryan D. Dietrich ♒ ✈ P
335 N Volutsia
Wichita, KS 67214, 316-683-7389
  Pubs: *Paris Rev, Nimrod, Chelsea, Midwest Qtly, Prairie Schooner, Western Humanities Rev, Bellingham Rev, NW Rev, Qtly Rev*
Groups: G/L/B/T, Prisoners

Elizabeth Dodd ♒ ✈ P
English Dept, Kansas State Univ, Manhattan, KS 66506, 785-532-0384
Internet: edodd@ksu.edu
  Pubs: *Archetypal Light* (U Nevada Pr, 2001), *Like Memory, Caverns* (NYU Pr, 1992), *Tar River Poetry, Seneca Rev, Ascent, Crab Orchard Rev, Crazyhorse, High Plains Literary Rev*

Carolyn Doty W
Univ Kansas, 1630 Barker, English Dept, Lawrence, KS 66044-3765, 785-843-6254
  Pubs: *Whisper* (Scribner, 1992), *What She Told Him, Fly Away Home, A Day Late* (Viking, 1985, 1982, 1980)

Harley Elliott P
328 E Beloit
Salina, KS 67401
  Pubs: *The Monkey of Mulberry Pass* (Woodley Pr, 1991), *The Citizen Game* (Basilisk Pr, 1988), *Darkness at Each Elbow* (Hanging Loose Pr, 1981)

James P. Girard W
11 Circle Dr
Newton, KS 67114, 316-283-1798
  Pubs: *The Late Man* (Atheneum, 1993), *A Killing in Kansas* (Fawcett, 1991), *Snake Nation Rev, Black Warrior Rev, Virginia Qtly Rev, Penthouse*

Albert Goldbarth P
English Dept, Wichita State Univ, Wichita, KS 67208, 316-683-6191
  Pubs: *Marriage, & Other Science Fiction* (Ohio State U Pr 1994), *Across the Layers: Poems Old & New* (U Georgia Pr, 1993), *New Yorker, Poetry, Paris Rev, Georgia Rev*

James Gunn ♒ ✈ W
2215 Orchard Ln
Lawrence, KS 66049, 913-864-3380
  Pubs: *Human Voices* (Henan People's Pub Hse, 1999), *The Joy Machine, The Mind Masters* (Pocket Bks, 1996, 1982), *Crisis!* (Tor, 1986), *The Unpublished Gunn, Part Two, Tiger! Tiger!* (Drumm, 1996, 1984), *Analog, Sci Fi*

Jeanine Hathaway 🎤 ✈ P&W
Wichita State Univ, Box 14, Wichita, KS 67260-0014,
316-978-3130
    Pubs: *Motherhouse* (Hyperion, 1993), *Best Spiritual
    Writing: Anth* (Harper SF, 2000), *Image, Georgia Rev,
    Ohio Rev, New Orleans Rev, Poetry NW*

Michael Hathaway 🎤 ✈ P
702 N Prairie
St John, KS 67576-1516, 316-549-6156
Internet: http://www.geocities.com/SoHo/Nook/1748
    Pubs: *Obsessed: A Flesh & the Word Collection of Gay
    Erotica: Anth* (Penguin, 1999), *A Day for a Lay: A
    Century of Gay Poetry: Anth* (Barricade, 1999), *Always
    the Beautiful Answer: A Prose Poem Primer: Anth*
    (King's Estate Press, 1999), *5 A.M., Pudding*
Groups: G/L/B/T

Stephen Hathaway W
English Dept, Wichita State Univ, Wichita, KS 67208,
316-689-3130
    Pubs: *A Kind of Redemption* (Louisiana State U, 1990),
    Accent on Fiction, Itinerary Four, Kansas Qtly

Steve F. Heller W
English Dept, Denison Hall, Kansas State Univ,
Manhattan, KS 66506, 913-532-6716
    Pubs: *The Automotive History of Lucky Kellerman*
    (Doubleday, 1989), *Chariton Rev*

Steven Hind P
Woodley Press, Washburn Univ, 1700 SW College,
Topeka, KS 66621
    Pubs: *In a Place with No Map* (Woodley Pr, 1997),
    That Trick of Silence (Ctr for Kansas Studies, 1990),
    *Anth of Magazine Verse & Yearbook of American
    Poetry* (Monitor, 1997)

Jonathan Holden 🎤 ✈ P
Kansas State Univ, Denison Hall, English Dept,
Manhattan, KS 66506, 785-532-0388
Internet: jonhold@ksu.edu
    Pubs: *Knowing: New & Selected Poems* (U Arkansas
    Pr, 2000), *The Sublime* (U Texas Pr, 1996), *American
    Gothic* (U Georgia Pr, 1992), *Against Paradise* (U Utah,
    1990), *The Name of the Rapids* (U Massachusetts,
    1985)

Robert B. Hutchinson P&W
Regency Health Care Center, 915 McNair, Halstead, KS
67056, 316-835-2276
    Pubs: *Standing Still* (Eakins, 1971), *Poetry, Harper's,
    Atlantic*

Kenneth Irby P
English Dept, Univ of Kansas, Lawrence, KS 66045,
913-864-3118
    Pubs: *Call Steps* (Station Hill/Tansy, 1992), *A Set,
    Catalpa* (Tansy, 1983, 1977), *Orexis* (Station Hill, 1981)

Michael L. Johnson P
1621 N 1st St
Baldwin City, KS 66006-6901, 785-594-4823
    Pubs: *XY Files: Poems on the Male Experience: Anth*
    (Sherman Asher, 1997), *Violence & Grace* (Cottonwood
    Pr, 1993), *Owen Wister Rev, Rhino, Oregon Rev,
    Chouteau Rev, Midwest Qtly, Sequoia, Roanoke Rev,
    The Literary Rev*

Ronald Johnson P
1422 Tyler
Topeka, KS 66612
    Pubs: *Ark* (drive he said pr, 1996), *Eyes & Objects*
    (Jargon Pr, 1976), *Conjunctions, Sulfur, Chicago Rev,
    Sagetrieb, Parnassus, Occident*

Denise Low 🎤 ✈ P
1916 Stratford Rd
Lawrence, KS 66044-4540, 913-841-5757
Internet: dlowweso@ross1.cc.haskell.edu
    Pubs: *Touching the Sky, Tulip Elegies* (Penthe, 1994,
    1993), *Vanishing Point* (Mulberry Pr, 1991), *Starwater*
    (Cottonwood Pr, 1988), *Connecticut Rev, Kestrel,
    Controlled Burn, Midwest Qtly, Chariton Rev, Stiletto*

Stephen Meats 🎤 ✈ P&W
2310 E 8 St
Pittsburg, KS 66762, 316-231-2998
Internet: smeats@pittstate.edu
    Pubs: *Looking for the Pale Eagle: Poems, Kansas
    Stories: Anth* (Woodley, 1994, 1989), *Hurakan, Leftbank
    Rev, The Qtly, Blue Unicorn, Poetry East, Tampa Rev*
Groups: Teenagers

W. R. Moses 🎤 P
314 Denison Ave
Manhattan, KS 66502, 785-537-1954
    Pubs: *Tu Fu Poems, Edges, Memoir, Double View*
    (Juniper Pr, 1996, 1994, 1992, 1984)

Michael Paul Novak 🎤 ✈ P
Saint Mary College
Leavenworth, KS 66048, 913-682-5151
Internet: novakm@smcks.edu
    Pubs: *From the Tower* (Forest of Peace, 1996),
    Whatever Flames Upon the Night (Potpourri, 1994), *A
    Story to Tell* (BkMk Pr, 1990), *Kenyon Rev,
    Confrontation, Hudson Rev, New Letters*

David Ohle W
911 Hilltop Dr
Lawrence, KS 66044, 913-842-3310
    Pubs: *Motorman* (Knopf, 1972), *Paris Rev, Esquire,
    Harper's, Caliban, Missouri Rev*

Emanuela O'Malley P
Box 279 Nazareth
Concordia, KS 66901, 913-243-2113
    Pubs: *Cloud of Darkness: The Pain of Apartheid*
    (Winston-Derek, 1990)

Tom Page 🎤 ✈   P
PO Box 4446
Wichita, KS 67204-0446, 316-775-5287
Internet: maudx@yahoo.com
    Pubs: *Going Places with the Kids, The Fort Scott
    Poems* (Free Soil Pr, 1997, 1994), *The Name of the
    Place* (John Brown Pr, 1989), *Minnesota Rev, Phoenix,
    Caprice, Viet Nam Generation, Blue Light, Pemmican,
    Galley Sail*
Lang: Portuguese

Cynthia S. Pederson 🎤 ✈   P
1521 SW College Ave
Topeka, KS 66604, 785-232-0332
    Pubs: *Fissures* (Singular Speech Pr, 1993), *Of Frogs &
    Toads: Anth* (Ione, 1998), *Climb Into My Lap: Anth,
    Call Down the Moon: Anth* (S&S, 1998, 1995), *Roll
    Along: Anth* (Macmillan, 1993), *Midwest Qtly, Poets On,
    Cottonwood, Great River Rev, Kansas Qtly*
Groups: Children, Teachers

Antonia Quintana Pigno   P
Modern Languages Dept, Kansas State Univ, Eisenhower
Hall, Manhattan, KS 66506, 785-532-1924
    Pubs: *Old Town Bridge, La Jornada* (Zauberberg Pr,
    1987, 1987), *Kenyon Rev, Kansas Qtly, Puerto del Sol,
    Cyphens, Writers' Forum, Ploughshares*

Trish Reeves 🎤 ✈   P
5307 W 51 St
Roeland Park, KS 66205-1242
    Pubs: *Returning the Question* (Cleveland State U Pr,
    1988), *New Letters, Ploughshares, Ironwood*

R. Stephen Russell   P
English Dept/Box 14, Wichita State Univ, Wichita, KS
67208, 316-689-3130
    Pubs: *Paris Rev, Carleton Miscellany, Denver Qtly,
    Kansas Qtly, Midwest Qtly, Impact*

Mark Scheel 🎤 ✈   P&W
5738 Maple Dr
Shawnee Mission, KS 66202-2723, 913-262-4281
Internet: markscheel@hotmail.com
    Pubs: *A Backward View* (5th Street Irregulars Pr &
    Leathers Pub, 1998), *Poet, Kansas Qtly, Cincinnati
    Poetry Rev, Facet, Telescope*
Groups: Seniors

Ann Slegman 🎤   P&W
6531 Overbrook
Shawnee Mission, KS 66208-1941, 913-362-7885
Internet: slegdog@aol.com
    Pubs: *Return to Sender, Spud Songs: Anth* (Helicon
    Nine Edtns, 1995, 1999), *Coal City Rev, New Letters,
    Helicon Nine, Kansas City Star*
I.D.: Jewish, Women

Roderick Townley 🎤 ✈   P&W
PO Box 13302
Shawnee Mission, KS 66282-4307, 913-381-1984
    Pubs: *The Great Good Thing* (Atheneum, 2001), *Final
    Approach* (Countryman Pr, 1986), *Minor Gods* (St.
    Martin's Pr, 1977), *Paris Rev, NAR, Yale Rev, New
    Letters, Western Humanities Rev*

Wyatt Townley 🎤 ✈   P
PO Box 13302
Shawnee Mission, KS 66282-4307, 913-381-1984
    Pubs: *Perfectly Normal* (The Smith, 1990), *Ravishing
    Disunities: Anth* (Wesleyan, 2000), *Prayers for a
    Thousand Years: Anth* (HC, 1999), *JM: A
    Remembrance: Anth* (Academy of American Poets,
    1996)

Donna Trussell 🎤 ✈   P&W
7520 Briar
Prairie Village, KS 66208, 913-648-1632
Internet: mensawhitetrash@aol.com
    Pubs: *Texas Bound Book II: Anth* (Southern Methodist
    U, 1998), *Growing Up Female: Anth* (Mentor/Penguin,
    1993), *New Stories from the South: Anth* (Algonquin
    Bks, 1990), *NAR, TriQtly, Poetry, Chicago Rev, Poetry
    NW*
Groups: Children, Prisoners

KENTUCKY

Rebecca Bailey 🎤 ✈   P&W
2465 Rock Fork Rd
Morehead, KY 40351, 606-783-1811
    Pubs: *A Wild Kentucky Garden* (Jesse Stuart Fdn,
    1998), *Reign of the Girl-King* (Esterling Pr, 1998),
    Three Women Alone in the Woods (Trillium, 1992),
    *Literal Latte, Jrnl of Kentucky Studies, Asheville Poetry
    Rev, Emrys Jrnl*
I.D.: Appalachian

Garry Barker   P&W
3375 CCC Trail
Morehead Morehead, KY 40351, 606-780-4343
    Pubs: *Notes from a Native Son, Appalachia Inside Out:
    Anth* (U Tennessee Pr, 1995, 1995), *Groundwater: Anth*
    (Lexington Pr, 1992), *Appalachian Heritage, Mountain
    Spirit.*

Joy Bale Boone   P
PO Box 188
Elkton, KY 42220-0188

Pat Carr   W
Western Kentucky Univ, English Dept, Bowling Green, KY
42101, 502-745-5998
   Pubs: *Sonahchi* (Cinco Puntos Pr, 1994), *Our Brother's
   War* (Sulgrave Pr, 1993), *Southern Rev, Southern Mag,
   Texas Monthly, Kansas Qtly, Arizona Qtly*

Rick Clewett   P
English Dept, Eastern Kentucky Univ, Lexington, KY
40475, 606-272-4247
   Pubs: *Salome, Encore, Bitterroot, Confrontation, Poetry
   Mag, Pudding, Samisdat, Microcosm*

Jenny Galloway Collins ♦ ✈   P&W
25 Wolfpen Dr
Thornton, KY 41855
   Pubs: *A Cave & a Cracker* (Elkhorn Pub, 1996),
   Blackberry Tea (Appalapple Productions, 1988),
   Appalachian Heritage, Back Home in Kentucky
I.D.: Appalachian. Groups: Children, Seniors

Guy Davenport   P&W
621 Sayre Ave
Lexington, KY 40508, 606-257-6972
   Pubs: *Charles Burchfield's Seasons* (Pomegranate Bks,
   1994), *A Table of Green Fields* (New Directions, 1993),
   Antaeus, New Criterion, Yale Rev

Judith DeGroote   P
Box 72, 2nd St
Corydon, KY 42406, 502-533-6753
   Pubs: *Visions Intl, Blue Unicorn, Phoenix, Birmingham
   Poetry Rev, South Florida Poetry Rev, Thema, Another
   Small Mag*

Kim Edwards   W
126 Arcadia Pk
Lexington, KY 40503

Normandi Ellis   W
2369 Sullivan Ln
Frankfort, KY 40601, 502-223-0402
   Pubs: *Voice Forms* (Watersign Pr, 1998), *Sorrowful
   Mysteries* (Arrowood Bks, 1991), *Agni Rev, Appalachian
   Heritage, Southern Humanities Rev, Between C & D,
   New Blood, Mediphors, Wind*

Jane Gentry   P
c/o Jane Gentry Vance, 340 Morgan St, Versailles, KY
40383, 606-873-5700
   Pubs: *A Garden in Kentucky* (LSU Pr, 1995), *Cries of
   the Spirit* (Beacon Pr, 1990), *Elvis in Oz: Hollins
   Writing Program Anth* (U Pr Virginia, 1992), *American
   Voice*

Sarah Gorham ♦ ✈   P
Sarabande Books, 2234 Dundee Rd, Ste 200, Louisville,
KY 40205, 502-458-4028
Internet: sarabandes@aol.com
   Pubs: *The Tension Zone* (Four Way Bks, 1996), *Don't
   Go Back to Sleep* (Galileo Pr, 1989), *Paris Rev,
   Antaeus, Nation, Poetry, Georgia Rev, Ohio Rev, Grand
   Street*

Jonathan Greene ♦ ✈   P
PO Box 475
Frankfort, KY 40602-0475, 502-223-1858
Internet: jgnomon@aol.com
   Pubs: *Incidents of Travel in Japan* (Bookgirl Pr, 1999),
   Of Moment, Inventions of Necessity (Gnomon Pr, 1998,
   1998), *Home: Anth* (Abrams, 1999), *What Book!?: Anth*
   (Parallax Pr, 1998), *American Voice*

Robert Gregory   P
404 Harrodswood Rd Apt 15
Frankfort, KY 40601, 502-227-5779
   Pubs: *Boy Picked Up the Wind* (Bluestem Pr, 1992),
   Interferences (Poltroon Pr, 1988), *Caliban, Oasis,
   Central Park, Exquisite Corpse, River Styx, ACM,
   Mississippi Mud, Willow Springs, Painted Bride, Poetry
   Flash, American Letters*

James Baker Hall   P&W
617 Dividing Ridge Rd S
Sadieville, KY 40370, 606-234-6481
   Pubs: *Fast Signing Mute* (Larkspur Pr, 1993), *Stopping
   on the Edge to Wave* (Wesleyan, 1988), *New Yorker,
   Poetry, Ploughshares, Hudson Rev, Paris Rev*

Wade Hall   P
1568 Cherokee Rd
Louisville, KY 40205, 502-451-5516
   Pubs: *Hell-Bent for Music: The Life of Pee Wee King,
   The Rest of the Dream: Black Odyssey of Lyman
   Johnson* (U Pr Kentucky, 1996, 1988), *Jefferson Rev*

Marcia L. Hurlow ♦ ✈   P
Asbury College, Wilmore, KY 40390-1198, 859-223-1579
Internet: marcia.hurlow@asbury.edu
   Pubs: *Dangers of Travel* (Riverstone, 1994), *Aliens Are
   Intercepting My Brain Waves* (State Street Pr, 1991),
   *Nimrod, Nebraska Rev, Poetry, Poetry NW, Poetry
   East, Poetry Wales, Chicago Rev, Another Chicago
   Magazine, Crab Creek Rev, Malahat Rev*
Lang: French. Groups: Teenagers, Prisoners

Ann Jonas ♦ ✈   P
2425 Ashwood Dr
Louisville, KY 40205-2439, 502-459-0701
   Pubs: *Writing Who We Are: Anth* (Western KY U Pr,
   1999), *Ipso Facto: Anth* (Hub Pub, 1975), *Louisville
   Rev, Chaffin Jrnl, American Voice, Poetry Rev, Orbis,
   KY Poetry Rev, Prism Intl, Quest, Southern Rev,
   Southern Humanities Rev, Colorado Qtly, Carolina Qtly*

Jane Wilson Joyce   P
Classics Dept, Centre College, Danville, KY 40422,
606-236-5211
    Pubs: *Appalachian Heritage, Sing Heavenly Muse!,
Laurel Rev, Appalachian Jrnl, Poet Lore

Kenneth King 🎤 ✈   P
PO Box 3222
Somerset, KY 42564, 606-423-3553
Internet: kenneth_e@eudoramail.com
    Pubs: *Poetry NW, College English, NW Rev, Kansas
Qtly, Appalachian Jrnl

Wallace E. Knight   W
819 16th St
Ashland, KY 41101, 606-324-0867
    Pubs: *Lightstruck* (Little, Brown, 1979), *The Literature of
the South* (Scribner, 1979), *Atlantic*

Karen S. Lee   P
12892 Hwy 42
Walton, KY 41094
    Pubs: *SPA's Finest: Anth* (Southern Poetry Assoc,
1992), *Riding on Golden Wings: Anth* (Geryon Pr,
1989), *Feelings, Kentucky Explorer, The Jrnl, Tucumcari
Literary Rev, Instructor Mag, Southern Poetry Assoc,
Rio Grande Pr, Poetry Only, Poetry Pr*

George Ella Lyon   P&W
913 Maywick Dr
Lexington, KY 40504, 606-278-3956
    Pubs: *Counting on the Woods, With a Hammer for My
Heart* (DK Ink, 1998, 1997), *Here & Then* (Orchard,
1994), *Catalpa* (Wind Pubs, 1993), *The United States
of Poetry: Anth* (Harry N. Abrams, 1996), *Mossy Creek
Reader, Booklinks, Louisville Mag*

Leah Maines 🎤 ✈   P
PO Box 76181
Highland Heights, KY 41076-0181
    Pubs: *Looking to the East with Western Eyes* (Finishing
Line Pr, 1998), *California Qtly, Flyway, Nebo, This: A
Serial Rev, A New Song, Upsouth, Licking River Rev,
Owen Wister Rev*
Lang: Japanese. I.D.: Native American, Latino/Latina

Davis McCombs 🎤 ✈   P
PO Box 1045
Munfordville, KY 42765-1045, 270-524-3593
Internet: dmmc69@aol.com
    Pubs: *Ultima Thule* (Yale U Pr, 2000)

Kristina McGrath   P&W
1214 Cherokee Rd
Louisville, KY 40204
    Pubs: *House Work* (Bridge Works, 1994), *Pushcart
Prize XIV: Anth* (Pushcart Pr, 1989), *Iowa Rev, Paris
Rev, Kenyon Rev, American Voice, Yale Rev, Harper's*

R. Meir Morton   P
3923 Central Ave
Louisville, KY 40218, 502-458-7396
    Pubs: *Pegasus, Reaching, Brentwood Bee*

Joseph Napora   P
2205 Moore St
Ashland, KY 41101, 606-324-1953
    Pubs: *The Walam Olum* (Greenfield Rev Pr, 1990),
Bloom Blood (Bottom Dogs Pr, 1988), *Texture, First
Intensity, Asheville Poetry Rev, Small Press Rev*

Alan Naslund 🎤 ✈   P&W
225-A Flirtation Walk
Louisville, KY 40219, 502-969-5511
    Pubs: *Silk Weather* (Fleur-de-lis Pr, 1999), *Pleiades,
Louisville Rev, Amelia, Jefferson Rev, Pegasus,
Calliope, River City Rev*
Groups: Rural Communities, Multicultural

Sena Jeter Naslund   W
English Dept, Univ Louisville, Louisville, KY 40208
    Pubs: *Ice Skating at the North Pole* (Ampersand, 1989),
Michigan Qtly Rev, Georgia Rev, American Voice

Gurney Norman   W
43 1/2 Richmond Ave
Lexington, KY 40502, 606-269-9594
    Pubs: *Divine Rights Trip, Kinfolks* (Gnoman Pr, 1990,
1990), *Crazy Quilt* (Larkspur, 1990)

Rose Orlich   P
1345 Knapp Ave
Morehead, KY 40351-1141, 606-784-6384
    Pubs: *The Rosewood Poems* (Small Poetry Pr, 1996),
Rose-Bloom at My Fingertips (Adams Pr, 1981), *Wind,
Catholic School Jrnl, Poet*

Phil Paradis   P
Northern Kentucky Univ, Literature & Language Dept,
Highland Heights, KY 41076, 606-572-6636
    Pubs: *Along the Path* (White Fields, 1996), *Something
of Ourselves* (Cedar Creek Pr, 1994), *Poetry, Cimarron
Rev, American Scholar, Poet & Critic, Tar River Poetry*

Lee Pennington   P&W
Univ Kentucky, PO Box 1036, Louisville, KY 40202,
502-584-0181
    Pubs: *Appalachian Quartet, The Scotian Women* (Arion
Pr, 1984, 1984), *Writer's Digest, Wind*

Nolan Porterfield   W
564 Boyce Fairview Rd
Alvaton, KY 42122-9648
    Pubs: *Country: The Music & the Musicians* (Abbeville
Pr, 1988), *Sewanee Rev, NAR, Harper's*

Bruce Rogers P
5615 Ridgecrest Rd
Louisville, KY 40218
  Pubs: *Starships* (Whippoorwill Pr, 1973), *Minnesota Rev, New Salt Creek Reader, Handsel, Dust*

Daryl Rogers ⚲ ✈ P
PO Box 24198
Lexington, KY 40524
Internet: river25rat@aol.com
  Pubs: *Blue Beat Jacket, Green's Mag, Chiron Rev, Parting Gifts, Clutch, Krax, Abbey, Atom Mind, Fuck!, Sepia, Dufus, Slipstream, Caprice, Poetry Motel, Graffiti Rag, Main Street Rag*

Jeffrey Skinner ⚲ ✈ P&W
Director of Creative Writing, Univ Louisville, College of Arts & Sciences, Louisville, KY 40292, 502-588-5920
Internet: jts120849@aol.com
  Pubs: *The Company of Heaven* (U Pitt Pr, 1992), *Real Toads in Imaginary Gardens* (Chicago Rev Pr, 1991), *Last Call: Anth* (Sarabande Bks, 1997), *Atlantic*

Frederick Smock P&W
Bellarmine College, 2001 Newburg Rd, Louisville, KY 40205, 502-452-8000
  Pubs: *Gardencourt: Poems* (Larkspur Pr, 1997), *Iowa Rev, Poetry, Intl Qtly, Poet & Critic*

Philip St. Clair ⚲ ✈ P
Ashland Community College, 1400 College Dr, Ashland, KY 41101, 606-326-2033
Internet: philip.stclair@kctcs.net
  Pubs: *Acid Creek* (Bottom Dog Pr, 1997), *Little-Dog-Of-Iron, At the Tent of Heaven* (Ahsahta Pr, 1985, 1984), *Harper's, Cincinnati Poetry Rev, Gettysburg Rev, Greensboro Rev, Minnesota Rev, Ploughshares, Black Warrior Rev, Chattahoochee Rev, Shenandoah*

Martha Bennett Stiles W
861 Hume-Bedford Rd
Paris, KY 40361, 606-987-4158
  Pubs: *Lonesome Road* (Gnomon Pr, 1998), *Kate of Still Waters, Sarah the Dragon Lady* (Macmillan, 1990, 1986), *Esquire, TriQtly, Georgia Rev, Virginia Qtly Rev, Missouri Rev, New Orleans Rev, Horsemen's Jrnl*

James Still P&W
Univ Press Kentucky, PO Box 865, Hindman, KY 41822, 606-785-0721
  Pubs: *An Appalachian Mother Goose, Sporty Creek, Jack & the Wonder Beans, The Wolfpen Notebooks, The Wolfpen Poems, Pattern of a Man, The Run for the Elbertas* (U Pr Kentucky Pr, 1998, 1998, 1996, 1991, 1986, 1976, 1953), *American Voice*

George Strange W
347 Wolf Gap Rd
Berea, KY 40403, 606-986-1257
  Pubs: *Lullwater Rev, Descant, Appalachian Heritage, Habersham Rev*

Jane Stuart P&W
1000 W-Hollow
Greenup, KY 41144
  Pubs: *Sestinas* (Cameo, 2000), *Journeys* (Summit Poetry Pr, 1998), *Moon Over Miami* (Poetry Forum Pr, 1995), *Passage Into Time* (Big Easy Pr, 1994), *Bloodroot: Anth* (U Kentucky Pr, 1998), *Byron Poetry Works, White River Qtly, Afterthoughts, Poet's Challenge*

Joe Survant ⚲ ✈ P
English Dept, Western Kentucky Univ, Bowling Green, KY 42101, 270-745-5709
Internet: joe.survant@wku.edu
  Pubs: *Anne & Alpheus, 1842-1882* (U Arkansas Pr, 1996), *We Will All Be Changed* (State Street Pr, 1995), *Ring of Words: Anth* (Sutton Pub Ltd, 1998), *American Voice, Nimrod, Cincinnati Poetry Rev*

Dorothy Sutton ⚲ ✈ P&W
Eastern Kentucky Univ, Dept of English, Richmond, KY 40475, 859-623-6071
Internet: d.sutton@eku.edu
  Pubs: *Startling Art* (Finishing Line Pr 1999), *DarwinL: Anth* (Norton, 2000), *Grolier Prize: Anth* (Grolier Bks, 1991), *Poetry, Hudson Rev, Poetry Ireland Rev, Southern Rev, Virginia Qtly Rev, Antioch Rev, Prairie Schooner*
I.D.: Appalachian, Farming

Lynne Taetzsch W
105 Country East
Morehead, KY 40351, 606-784-6905
  Pubs: *Hippo, Eotu, Pacific Rev, Asylum, Atticus Rev, Potato Eyes*

Richard Taylor P&W
335 Holt Ln
Frankfort, KY 40601, 502-223-5775
  Pubs: *Earth Bones* (Gnomon Pr, 1979), *Girty* (Turtle Island Foundation, 1977)

Jeff Worley P
136 Shawnee Pl
Lexington, KY 40503, 606-277-0257
  Pubs: *A Simple Human Motion* (Larkspur Pr, 2000), *The Only Time There Is* (Mid-List Pr, 1995), *Natural Selections* (w/Lance Olsen; Still Waters Pr, 1993), *New Virginia Rev, Missouri Rev, Boulevard, Yankee College English, Threepenny Rev, Poetry NW.*

LOUISIANA

Thomas Atkins   W
Univ New Orleans, Drama & Communications Dept, New
Orleans, LA 70148, 504-286-6345
    Pubs: *The Blue Man, The Fire Came By* (Doubleday,
    1978, 1976)

Fredrick Barton   W
63 Versailles Blvd
New Orleans, LA 70125, 504-861-1668
    Pubs: *With Extreme Prejudice* (Villard/Random Hse,
    1993), *The El Cholo Feeling Passes* (Dell, 1988),
    Xavier Rev, Louisiana Literature 99, Cresset

John Biguenet   P&W
Loyola Univ, Box 50, English Dept, New Orleans, LA
70118, 504-865-2474
    Pubs: *Foreign Fictions* (Vintage, 1978), *NAR, Witness,
    Ploughshares, Boulevard, Threepenny Rev, Georgia
    Rev, Granta, Story*

Thomas Bonner, Jr. 🎤 ✈   P&W
25 W Park Pl
New Orleans, LA 70124, 504-488-9014
    Pubs: *Xavier Rev, Poiesis, Potpourri, Maple Leaf Rag,
    New Laurel Rev, Negative Capability, Old Hickory Rev,
    Bluegrass Literary Rev, Louisiana English Jrnl*

Vance Bourjaily   W
c/o English Dept, Louisiana State Univ, Baton Rouge, LA
70803, 504-388-2862
    Pubs: *Old Soldier* (Donald I. Fine, 1990), *The Great
    Fake Book* (Wiedenfeld & Nicolson, 1987), *A Game
    Men Play* (Dial, 1980)

Catharine Savage Brosman 🎤 ✈   P
1550 2nd St #7-I
New Orleans, LA 70130, 504-899-6016
Internet: cbrosman@tcs.tulane.edu
    Pubs: *Places in Mind* (LSU Pr, 2000), *Passages,
    Journeying from Canyon de Chelly* (Louisiana State U,
    1996, 1990), *Abiding Winter* (R. L. Barth, 1983),
    *Sewanee Rev, Southern Rev, American Scholar, NER,
    SW Rev*
Lang: French

Robert Olen Butler   W
McNeese State Univ, Box 92012, Lake Charles, LA 70609
    Pubs: *The Deep Green Sea, They Whisper, A Good
    Scent from a Strange Mountain* (H Holt, 1998, 1994,
    1992), *Esquire, New Yorker, GQ, Paris Rev, Harper's,
    Sewanee Rev, Hudson Rev, Virginia Qtly Rev*

Maxine Cassin 🎤 ✈   P
2131 General Pershing St
New Orleans, LA 70115-5437, 504-891-3458
Internet: maxine_cassin@yahoo.com
    Pubs: *The Other Side of Sleep* (Portals Pr, 1995),
    Turnip's Blood (Sisters Grim Pr, 1985),
    Uncommonplace: Anth (LSU Pr, 1998), *Chicago Rev,
    New Republic, New York Times*
Groups: Seniors

Christopher Chambers   P&W
1224 Soniat
New Orleans, LA 70115, 504-865-2475
    Pubs: *This Is What I Hear* (Stillwater Pr, 1997), *BOMB
    Mag, Confrontation, Exquisite Corpse, Florida Rev,
    Hayden's Ferry Rev, Mid-American Rev, Mississippi
    Mud, New Delta Rev, New Orleans Rev, Quarter After
    Eight, Qtly West, Sonora Rev, Washington Rev*

Andrei Codrescu 🎤 ✈   P&W
Louisiana State Univ, English Dept, Baton Rouge, LA
70803-0001
    Pubs: *Messiah* (S&S, 1999), *A Bar in Brooklyn, Alien
    Candor* (Black Sparrow, 1999, 1998), *License to Carry
    a Gun* (Carnegie Mellon U Pr, 1998)

Carlos Colon 🎤 ✈   P
185 Lynn Ave
Shreveport, LA 71105-3523, 318-868-8932
Internet: ccolon@smlnet.sml.lib.la.us
    Pubs: *Haiku Compass* (Haiku Intl Society, 1994), *Thin
    Curve: Anth* (Red Moon Pr, 2000), *Haiku World: Anth*
    (Kodansha Intl, 1996), *Louisiana English Jrnl, Modern
    Haiku, Writer's Digest, Frogpond, Piedmont Literary Rev*
I.D.: Hispanic, Latino/Latina. Groups: College/Univ,
Teenagers

Peter Cooley 🎤 ✈   P
English Dept, Tulane Univ, New Orleans, LA 70118,
504-862-8174
Internet: pjcooley@msn.com
    Pubs: *Sacred Conversations, The Astonished Hours,
    The Van Gogh Notebook* (Carnegie Mellon, 1998, 1992,
    1987), *New Yorker, Atlantic, Poetry, Esquire, Nation,
    New Republic*

Pearl Garrett Crayton   P&W
1727 Harvard St
Alexandria, LA 71301, 318-449-1720
    Pubs: *Kente Cloth: Anth* (U North Texas Pr, 1997),
    Rites of Passage: Anth (Hyperion Bks, 1994), *Trials,
    Tribulations, & Celebrations: Anth* (Intercultural Pr,
    1992), *Out of Our Lives: Anth* (Howard U Pr, 1975),
    Reed Mag, Pudding Mag

Moira Crone 🎤 ✈   W
English Dept/Allen Hall, Louisiana State Univ, Baton
Rouge, LA 70808, 504-864-9976
Internet: moiracrone@aol.com
   Pubs: *Dream State* (U Pr Mississippi, 1995), *Period of
   Confinement* (Harper Torch, 1988), *Winnebago
   Mysteries* (Fiction Collective, 1985), *New Stories by
   Southern Women: Anth* (U South Carolina Pr, 1989),
   New Yorker, Louisiana Literature

Joel Dailey   P
3003 Ponce De Leon St
New Orleans, LA 70119, 504-943-5198
   Pubs: *Release Window* (Semiquasi Pr, 1998), *Audience,
   Ambience, Ambulance* (Blank Gun Silencer Pr, 1993),
   Doppler Effects (Shockbox Pr, 1993), *American Poets
   Say Goodbye to 20th Century: Anth* (Four Walls Eight
   Windows, 1996), *Exquisite Corpse*

Tom Dent   P
Box 50584
New Orleans, LA 70150, 504-944-2412
   Pubs: *Blue Lights & River Songs* (Lotus Pr, 1982),
   Magnolia Street (Edwards Publishing Co, 1976)

Jim Donahoe   P
1380 Sigur Ave
Metairie, LA 70005, 504-833-3893

Don Keck DuPree 🎤 ✈   P&W
PO Box 41188
Shreveport, LA 71134-1188
Internet: personal.centenary.edu/~ddupree
   Pubs: *Sewanee Rev, Chattahoochee Rev, Missouri Rev,
   Ploughshares, Southern Rev*

Charles East   W
1455 Knollwood Dr
Baton Rouge, LA 70808-8650, 225-926-3304
   Pubs: *Distant Friends & Intimate Strangers* (U Illinois
   Pr, 1996), *Where the Music Was* (HBJ, 1965),
   Sewanee Rev, Mademoiselle, Yale Rev, Southern Rev

Daniel Mark Fogel 🎤 ✈   P
English Dept, Louisiana State Univ, Allen Hall, Baton
Rouge, LA 70810, 504-388-3161
Internet: evcp@lsu.edu
   Pubs: *A Trick of Resilience* (Ithaca, 1975), *Southern
   Rev, National Forum, Western Humanities*

Ernest J. Gaines   W
Univ Southwestern Louisiana, PO Box 44691, Lafayette,
LA 70503, 318-232-2034
   Pubs: *A Lesson Before Dying, A Gathering of Old Men*
   (Knopf, 1993, 1984)

Timothy Martin Gautreaux   P&W
Southeastern Louisiana Univ, PO Box 889, Hammond, LA
70402, 504-549-5022
   Pubs: *The Next Step in the Dance, Same Place, Same
   Things* (Picador/St. Martin's, 1998, 1996), *New Stories
   from the South: Anth* (Algonquin Pr, 1996), *Harper's,
   Atlantic, GQ, Story, Massachusetts Rev, Virginia Qtly
   Rev*

Andrea Saunders Gereighty 🎤 ✈   P
257 Bonnabel Blvd
Metairie, LA 70005-3738, 504-835-3419
Internet: ager80@worldnet.att.net
   Pubs: *The Beat of the Forum* (Circasoft Pr, 2001),
   Restless for Cool Weather, The Season of the Crane
   (Gris Gris Pr, 2000, 1998), *Illusions & Other Realities*
   (Medusa Pr, 1974), *New Laurel Rev, Dalliance*

Norman German   P&W
108 McVay St
Lake Charles, LA 70605, 318-478-1285
   Pubs: *No Other World* (Blue Heron Pr, 1992), *The
   Liberation of Bonner Child* (Aegina, 1992), *Hawaii Rev,
   BPJ, Worcester Rev, Wisconsin Rev*

John Gery 🎤 ✈   P
English Dept, Univ New Orleans, New Orleans, LA
70148-2315, 504-280-6133
Internet: jgery@uno.edu
   Pubs: *American Ghost* (CCC, 1999), *The Enemies of
   Leisure* (Story Line Pr, 1995), *Three Poems* (Lestat Pr,
   1989), *The Burning of New Orleans* (Amelia Pr, 1988),
   *Iowa Rev, Kenyon Rev, Louisiana Literature, Paris Rev,
   Sparrow, West Branch*

Hedwig Irene Gorski   PP
327 Clinton St
Lafayette, LA 70501-8101, 318-261-0239
   Pubs: *Slow Paradise, Polish Gypsy with Ghost*
   (Shinebone Pr, 1998, 1998)

Claudia K. Grinnell   P&W
4507 Churchill Circle
Monroe, LA 71203, 318-345-4263
   Pubs: *The Alembic, CQ, Hayden's Ferry Rev, Phoebe,
   Bottomfish, The Comstock Rev, Princeton Arts Rev*

Lee Meitzen Grue   P
New Laurel Review, 828 Lesseps St, New Orleans, LA
70117, 504-947-6001
   Pubs: *Good Bye Silver, Silver Cloud* (Plain View Pr,
   1994), *Inheritance of Light: Anth* (U North Texas Pr,
   1996), *Ploughshares, Xavier Rev, Louisiana Literature,
   Quimera*

Nancy C. Harris ☙ P
8418 Freret St
New Orleans, LA 70118-1158, 504-861-7162
Internet: apewoman@poetic.com
    Pubs: *Mirror Wars, Maple Leaf Rag II: Anth* (Portals Pr,
    1999, 1994), *The Ape Woman Story* (Pirogue, 1989),
    From a Bend in the River: Anth (Runagate Pr, 1998),
    *Hawaii Rev, New Orleans Rev, Ellipsis, Negative
    Capability*

Ava Leavell Haymon ☙ ✈ P
672 Nelson Dr
Baton Rouge, LA 70808-5066, 225-766-4739
    Pubs: *Why the Groundhog Fears Her Shadow* (March
    Street Pr, 1995), *Staving Off Rapture* (Flume Pr, 1994),
    Built in Fear of Heat (Nightshade Pr, 1994)
Groups: Women, Art Therapy

Don A. Hoyt P
RR2 Box 107
Downsville, LA 71234, 318-644-2012
    Pubs: *A New Kerygma* (Bootleg Pr, 1993), *Crossroads,
    Redneck Rev, Avra, Florida Rev, Whiskey Island,
    Oxford Mag, Pacific Rev, Pannus Index, MacGuffin*

Joe C. Ireland P
410 Huntlee Dr
Algiers, LA 70131-3722, 504-394-8003
    Pubs: *Short Order* (New Orleans Poetry Forum, 1974),
    The Smith, Dust, Bouillabaisse, Kumquat Meringue, Oxy

Rodger Kamenetz P
1209 Pine St
New Orleans, LA 70118-5218
    Pubs: *The Jew in the Lotus* (Harper SF, 1994), *The
    Missing Jew: New & Selected Poems* (Time Being Bks,
    1992), *New Republic, Grand Street, Prairie Schooner,
    Ploughshares*

Julie Kane P
955 Laurie Ln, #1
St Gabriel, LA 70776, 504-642-5743
    Pubs: *The Bartender Poems* (Greville Pr, 1991), *Body
    & Soul* (Pirogue Pub, 1987), *London Mag, Feminist
    Studies, Epoch, Mademoiselle, Negative Capability,
    Thema*

Katherine Kane P
Dept. of Language & Communication, Northwestern State
Univ, 316 Kyser Hall, Natchitoches, LA 71497,
318-352-8002
    Pubs: *Ferry All the Way Up* (Porch, 1978), *Iowa Rev,
    Missouri Rev, Ontario Rev, Poetry Now, New Letters,
    Virginia Qtly Rev*

John Cantey Knight P
4440 W Esplanade
Metairie, LA 70006
    Pubs: *Lullwater Rev, Now & Then, Louisiana Literature,
    Pikeville Rev, Monocacy Valley Rev*

Pinkie Gordon Lane ☙ ✈ P
2738 77th Ave
Baton Rouge, LA 70807-5607, 225-356-3450
Internet: pinkieg@aol.com
    Pubs: *Elegy for Etheridge, Girl at the Window* (LSU Pr,
    2000, 1991), *Double Stitch: Anth* (Beacon Pr, 1991)

David Madden ☙ ✈ PP&P&W
LSU, English Dept, Baton Rouge, LA 70803-0001,
504-344-3630
Internet: dmadden@lsu.edu
    Pubs: *Cassandra Singing, Sharpshooter* (U Tennessee
    Pr, 1998, 1996), *Revising Fiction* (NAL, 1988), *Southern
    Rev, New Letters, Gettysburg Rev, Kenyon Rev,
    Playboy*

Carolyn Maisel P
English Dept, Univ New Orleans/Lakefront, New Orleans,
LA 70148
    Pubs: *Witnessing* (L'Epervier Pr, 1978), *NAR, New
    Yorker, Choice*

Leo Luke Marcello ☙ ✈ P&W
PO Box 5508
Lake Charles, LA 70606
    Pubs: *Nothing Grows in One Place Forever* (Time
    Being Bks, 1998), *The Secret Proximity of Everywhere*
    (Blue Heron Pr, 1994), *Blackrobe's Love Letters* (Xavier
    Rev Pr, 1994), *Paterson Literary Rev, America, Italian
    Americana, Voices in Italian Americana*

Martha McFerren ☙ ✈ P
2679 Verbena St
New Orleans, LA 70122-6037, 504-944-2707
    Pubs: *Women in Cars* (Helicon Nine Edtns, 1992),
    Contours for Ritual (LSU Pr, 1988), *Georgia Rev,
    Southern Rev, Shenandoah, New Laurel Rev, Louisiana
    Literature, Poetry NW*

Bryan T. McMahon P
PO Box 743
Ponchatoula, LA 70454, 504-386-2877
    Pubs: *Kree* (New Voices Pr, 1971), *The Ponchatoula
    Times*

Harold B. McSween P&W
PO Box 12907
Alexandria, LA 71315, 318-442-3215
    Pubs: *Hampden-Sydney Poetry Rev, South Carolina
    Rev, Virginia Qtly Rev, Poet & Critic, Sewanee Rev,
    Southern Rev*

Kay A. Murphy P&W
'F" St John Ct
New Orleans, LA 70119, 504-488-5552
    Pubs: *The Autopsy* (Spoon River Poetry Pr, 1985),
    Fiction Intl, St. Andrews Rev, Poetry

James Nolan 🎤 ✈ P
925 Dauphine St
New Orleans, LA 70116-3036, 504-522-5934
Pubs: *What Moves Is Not the Wind, Why I Live in the Forest* (Wesleyan, 1980, 1974), *Georgia Rev, City Lights Rev, Southern Rev, Exquisite Corpse, Poetry, New Letters*
Lang: Spanish. I.D.: Southern Writer. Groups: Hispanic, G/L/B/T

Brenda Marie Osbey P
c/o LSU Press, The French House, Baton Rouge, LA 70122
Pubs: *All Saints: New & Selected Poems* (LSU Pr, 1997), *Desperate Circumstance, Dangerous Woman* (Story Line, 1990), *In These Houses* (Wesleyan, 1988), *American Poetry Rev, Callaloo, American Voice, Georgia Rev, Southern Rev*

Sue Owen P
2015 General Cleburne Ave
Baton Rouge, LA 70810, 504-769-3449
Pubs: *My Doomsday Sampler* (Louisiana State U Pr, 1999), *The Book of Winter* (Ohio State U Pr, 1988), *Harvard Mag, Iowa Rev, Massachusetts Rev, Nation, Poetry, Southern Rev*

Burton Raffel 🎤 ✈ P&W
203 Mannering Ave S
Lafayette, LA 70508-4829, 337-232-4112
Internet: bnraffel@net-connect.net
Pubs: *Beethoven in Denver & Other Poems* (Conundrum Pr, 1999), *Founders Fury* (Pocket Bks, 1988), *Paris Rev*

Stan Rice P
1239 1st St
New Orleans, LA 70130, 504-566-1544
Pubs: *The Radiance of Pigs, Fear Itself, Singing Yet: New & Selected Poems* (Knopf, 1998, 1995, 1992), *Body of Work* (Lost Roads, 1983), *Some Lamb* (Figures, 1976), *Whiteboy* (Mudra, 1975)

Kenneth Robbins 🎤 ✈ W
Louisiana Tech Univ, School of the Performing Arts, Ruston, LA 71272-0001, 318-257-2711
Pubs: *The Baptism of Howie Cobb* (U South Dakota Pr, 1995), *Buttermilk Bottoms* (U Iowa Pr, 1987)

Kalamu ya Salaam P&W
Box 52723
New Orleans, LA 70152, 504-523-4443
Pubs: *What Is Life?* (Third World Pr, 1994), *Word Up: Black Poetry of the '80s from the Deep South: Anth* (Beans & Brown Rice, 1990), *African American Rev*

Dave Smith P&W
1430 Knollwood Dr
Baton Rouge, LA 70808, 504-923-0388
Pubs: *Fate's Kite* (Louisiana State U Pr, 1996), *Night Pleasures* (Bloodaxe Bks, 1992), *Cuba Night* (Morrow, 1992), *New Yorker, Atlantic, Yale Rev, Poetry, Georgia Rev*

Garland Strother 🎤 ✈ P
516 Hester Ave
River Ridge, LA 70123-1405, 504-737-1278
Internet: glstroth@bellsouth.net
Pubs: *Blue Cloud Qtly, Inscape, Louisiana Rev, National Library Literary Rev, North Dakota Qtly, Pontchartrain Rev, South Dakota, Southern Exposure*

Don Ray Thornton P
Thornton Publishing, 1504 Howard St, New Iberia, LA 70560, 318-364-2752
Pubs: *Ascending, Mentor* (Thornton Pub, 1993, 1993), *A Walk on Water* (Cajun Pub, 1985), *Catalyst, Slipstream, Muse*

Keith Veizer W
825 Gallier St
New Orleans, LA 70117
Pubs: *Intro, NAR, Sou'wester, Exquisite Corpse, Fell Swoop, Story Qtly, Pulpsmith*

Jan Villarrubia 🎤 ✈ P
38 Crane
New Orleans, LA 70124-4309, 504-288-0153
Pubs: *Odd Fellows Rest* (Xavier Rev Pr, 1996), *Miz Lena's Backyard* (Dramatic Pub Co, 1994), *Mississippi Valley Rev, Third Wind, Literary Rev, Negative Capability*

Bernice Webb W
159 Whittington Dr
Lafayette, LA 70503, 318-234-5397
Pubs: *Mating Dance, Spider Web* (Spider Pr, 1996, 1993), *Born to Be a Loser* (w/Johnnie Allan; Jadfel Pub Co, 1993), *Voices Intl*

Leilah Wendell P
5219 Magazine St
New Orleans, LA 70115-1858
Pubs: *The Necromantic Ritual Book, The Complete Books of Azrael, Shadows in the Half-Light* (Westgate Pr, 1994, 1992, 1989), *Carpe Noctem, Esoterra, Elegia*

Tom Whalen W
6109 Magazine St
New Orleans, LA 70118-5825, 504-895-5619
Pubs: *Newcomer's Guide to the Afterlife* (w/Daniel Quinn; Bantam Bks, 1997), *Roithamer's Universe* (Portals Pr, 1996), *Elongated Figures* (Red Dust, 1991), *Iowa Rev, Nebraska Rev, NW Rev, Fiction Intl, The Qtly, NAR*

Gail White 🎤 ✈   P
1017 Spanish Moss Ln
Breaux Bridge, LA 70517-6711
    Pubs: *Landscape with Women* (Singular Speech Pr,
    1998), *The Muse Strikes Back: Anth, A Formal Feeling
    Comes: Anth* (Story Line Pr, 1998, 1994), *The
    Formalist, Cape Rock, Cream City Rev, Hellas, Light,
    Midwest Qtly, Tennessee Qtly, The Lyric*

John Wood 🎤 ✈   P
McNeese State Univ
Lake Charles, LA 70609, 337-475-5326
    Pubs: *Selected Poems 1968-1998* (U Arkansas Pr,
    1999), *The Gates of the Elect Kingdom, In Primary
    Light* (U Iowa Pr, 1997, 1994)

Angus Woodward   W
1045 E River Oaks
Baton Rouge, LA 70815
    Pubs: *Dominion Rev, Laurel Rev, Innisfree, Soundings
    East, Habersham Rev, Gulf Stream, Louisiana Literature*

Yictove 🎤 ✈   P
2832 St Bernard Ave
New Orleans, LA 70119-2120
    Pubs: *D. J. Soliloquy* (Thrown Stone Pr, 1988), *Blue
    Print* (Portals Pr, 1997), *D.J. Soliloquy* (Thrown Stone
    Pr, 1988), *A Bend in the River: 100 New Orleans
    Poets: Anth* (Runagate Pr, 1998), *Identity Lessons: Anth*
    (Penguin, 1997), *Gathering of the Tribes*

Andy Young 🎤 ✈   P
935 Gov Nicholls, #4
New Orleans, LA 70116, 504-529-2634
    Pubs: *Mine* (Lavender Ink, 2000), *What Have You Lost:
    Anth* (Greenwillow Pr, 1999), *Exquisite Corpse, Stinging
    Fly, Pierogi Pr, mind the gap, Snow Apple, New Laurel
    Rev, Appalachian Heritage, Florida Rev, New Orleans
    Rev, Texas Observer, Mesechabe*
    Groups: Prisoners, Children

Ahmos Zu-Bolton, II   P
1616 Marigny St
New Orleans, LA 70117, 504-949-1648
    Pubs: *The Widow Paris: A Folklore of Marie Laveau*
    (Copastetic, 1986), *Marquee, Black Voices*

MAINE

Jonathan Aldrich   P
41 Oakhurst Rd
Cape Elizabeth, ME 04107, 207-799-6028
    Pubs: *The Death of Michelangelo* (Puckerbrush Pr,
    1985)

Kate Barnes   P
432 Appleton Ridge Rd
Appleton, ME 04862
    Pubs: *Where the Deer Were* (Godine, 1994), *Crossing
    the Field* (Blackberry Bks, 1992), *BPJ, Harper's, NER,
    Kenyon Rev, New Yorker*

Ingrid Bengis   W
Box 421
Stonington, ME 04681
    Pubs: *The Writer & Her Work* (Norton, 1980), *I Have
    Come Here to Be Alone* (S&S, 1977)

Steve Benson 🎤 ✈   P
RR1, Box 614
Surry, ME 04684
    Pubs: *Roaring Spring* (Zasterle Pr, 1998), *Reverse
    Order* (Potes & Poets, 1991), *Blue Book* (The Figures,
    1988), *Poetics Jrnl, Language, Aerial, Zyzzyva, o.blek,
    Avec, Crayon, This, Writing, Raddle Moon*

Jim Bishop   P
PO Box 1448
Bucksport, ME 04416-1448
    Pubs: *Mother Tongue* (Contraband Pr, 1976)

Alice Bolstridge 🎤 ✈   P&W
Maine School of Science & Mathematics, 77 High St,
Limestone, ME 04750, 207-325-3303
    Pubs: *An Intricate Weave: Anth* (Iris Edtns, 1997),
    *Nimrod, The Maine Scholar, Animus, Cimarron Rev,
    Mediphors, Cincinnati Poetry Rev, Slant, Kalliope,
    Passager, Magic Realism*
    Groups: Seniors, Mentally Ill

Philip Booth   P
95 Main St
Castine, ME 04421-0330, 207-326-4644
    Pubs: *Lifelines, Pairs, Selves, Relations: Poems
    1950-1985* (Penguin, 1999, 1994, 1990, 1986), *Trying
    to Say It* (U Michigan, 1996), *The Best American
    Poetry: Anth* (Scribner, 1999), *Georgia Rev, APR,
    DoubleTake, Poetry, Yale Rev, BPJ*

Myrna Bouchey   P
RR1, Box 2285
Jonesport, ME 04649-9717
    Pubs: *Malahat, Niagara, BPJ, Hard Pressed, Heirs,
    Maine Times, Kennebec, Lakes & Prairies*

Henry Braun 🎤 ✈   P
Box 84
Weld, ME 04285, 207-585-2218
Internet: braun@ctel.net
    Pubs: *The Body Electric* (Norton, 2000), *The Vergil
    Woods* (Atheneum, 1968), *Maine Speaks: Anth* (Maine
    Writers & Publishers, 1989), *Painted Bride Qtly, APR,
    Poetry, Massachusetts Rev*

William Carpenter P&W
Box 1297
Stockton Springs, ME 04981, 207-567-4172
Internet: carpenter@acadia.net
Pubs: *A Keeper of Sheep* (Milkweed Edtns, 1994),
Speaking Fire at Stones (Tilbury Hse, 1992), *Rain*
(Northeastern U Pr, 1985)

Erleen J. Christensen P&W
Rte 1, Box 2315
Unity, ME 04988
Pubs: *Kennebec, Amelia, Wind, Prairie Schooner,
Kansas Qtly, Cottonwood, Memphis State Rev*

Robert M. Chute ♠ ✈ P
85 Echo Cove Ln
Poland, ME 04274
Pubs: *Sweeping the Sky* (Cider Pr, 2000), *Androscoggin
Too, Woodshed on the Moon* (Nightshade Pr, 1997,
1991), *Barely Time to Study Jesus* (Cider Pr, 1996),
Samuel Sewall Sails for Home (Coyote Love Pr, 1986),
BPJ, Larcom Rev, Lucid Stone, BOMB

Roger L. Conover P
55 Lambert Rd
Freeport, ME 04032
Pubs: *The Last Lunar Baedeker* (Jargon Pr, 1982),
Shenandoah, Ironwood, Montemora, Epoch

Paul G. Corrigan, Jr. P
146 Denbow Rd
St Albans, ME 04971, 207-695-2100
Pubs: *At the Grave of the Unknown Riverdriver* (North
Country Pr, 1992)

H. R. Coursen P&W
Frog Prince Manor, 21 Toad's Landing, Brunswick, ME
04011, 207-725-2130
Pubs: *History Lessons, The Green of Spring* (Mad
River 1998, 1997), *The Search for Archerland, Graves
of the Poets* (EM Pr, 1994, 1993), *Tar River, Small
Pond, Literary Rev, Hollins Critic, South Carolina Rev,
Iconoclast*

Alfred DePew W
31 Pine St
Portland, ME 04102-3807
Pubs: *The Melancholy of Departure* (U Georgia Pr,
1991)

Kathleen Lignell Ellis P
9 Harris Rd
Orono, ME 04473-1522, 207-581-3825
Pubs: *Red Horses* (Northern Lights, 1991), *The
Eloquent Edge* (Acadia, 1989), *NER, Columbia, Antioch,
NAR, SW Rev, New Letters, BPJ*

Theodore Enslin ♠ ✈ P
RFD Box 289, Kansas Rd
Milbridge, ME 04658, 207-546-7636
Pubs: *Then, & Now* (Natl Poetry Fdtn, 1999),
Re-Soundings (Talisman Hse, 1999), *Sequentiae*
(London; Stop Pr, 1999), *Skeins* (Origin-Longhouse,
1998), *The House of the Golden Windows, Love &
Science* (Light & Dust Bks, 1993, 1990), *Conjunctions,
Talisman*

Christopher Fahy ♠ ✈ P&W
15 Mechanic St
Thomaston, ME 04861, 207-354-8191
Internet: fahy@mint.net
Pubs: *Limerock: Maine Stories* (Coastwise Pr, 1999),
The Fly Must Die (Washington Inst for Creative Activity,
1993), *Beyond Lament: Anth* (Northwestern U Pr,
1998), *The King Is Dead, Tales of Elvis: Anth* (Delta,
1994)

Tom Fallon ♠ ✈ P&W
226 Linden St
Rumford, ME 04276, 207-364-7237
Internet: http://www.aopoetry.com
Pubs: *The Man on the Moon* (Small-Small Pr, 1988),
Maine Speaks: Anth (MWPA, 1991), *Panhandler, Black
Fly Rev, Kennebec, Cafe Rev, Puckerbrush Rev, La
Riviere, Animus*

Rod Farmer P
10 Anson St
Farmington, ME 04938, 207-778-9298
Internet: farmer@maine.edu
Pubs: *Universal Essence* (Brunswick Pub Co, 1986),
*ELF, Phase & Cycle, Riverrun, Webster Rev, Thorny
Locust, Without Halos*

Robert Farnsworth ♠ ✈ P
19 Ware St
Lewiston, ME 04240, 207-784-0416
Pubs: *Honest Water, Three Or Four Hills & a Cloud*
(Wesleyan, 1989, 1982), *Southern Rev, NER, BPJ,
Hudson Rev, Seneca Rev*

Richard Flanagan W
179 Covell Rd
Fairfield, ME 04937, 617-239-4256
Pubs: *Last of the Hippies* (Paycock, 1984), *San Jose
Studies, Earth's Daughters*

Richard Foerster ♠ ✈ P
PO Box 1040
York Beach, ME 03910-1040, 207-363-8220
Pubs: *Trillium* (BOA Edtns, 1998), *Patterns of Descent,
Sudden Harbor* (Orchises Pr, 1993, 1992), *Kenyon Rev,
Southern Rev, Poetry, Gettysburg*

Elaine Ford   W
Univ Maine, 304 Neville, Orono, ME 04469, 207-581-3834
    Pubs: *Life Designs* (Zoland, 1997), *Monkey Bay, Ivory
    Bright* (Viking, 1989, 1986), *Missed Connections*
    (Random Hse, 1983)

M. Ekola Gerberick   P
999 High St
Bath, ME 04530
    Pubs: *Siirtolaisuus, Kansas Qtly, Passages North,
    Finnish Americana, BPJ, Gravida*

Paul Guernsey   W
1247 Middle Rd
Warren, ME 04864
    Pubs: *Angel Falls* (S&S, 1990), *Unhallowed Ground*
    (Morrow, 1986)

Gunnar Hansen   P
PO Box 268
Northeast Harbor, ME 04662
    Pubs: *True Coast* (Harpswell, 1991), *Mt. Desert: An
    Informal History* (Mt. Desert, 1989)

Anne Hazlewood-Brady   P
Box 534
Kennebunkport, ME 04046
    Pubs: *One to the Many* (Puckerbrush Pr, 1979), *The
    Cross, the Anchor & the Heart* (Victoria, 1976)

Nancy Heiser ⚲ ✈   W
25 Hemlock Rd
Brunswick, ME 04011, 207-725-4253
Internet: nheiser@blazenetme.net
    Pubs: *Nightshade Nightstand Reader: Anth* (Nightshade
    Pr, 1995), *Seattle Rev, Potpourri, Footwork, Out of the
    Cradle, Thema, Paterson Literary Rev, Alkali Flats*

Lucille Iverson   P&W
133 N Main St
Morrill, ME 04952-9750, 207-342-5792
    Pubs: *We Become New* (Bantam, 1975), *Outrage*
    (Know Inc, 1974), *Soho Weekly News, Connections,
    Sunbury*

James Koller   P&W
PO Box 629
Brunswick, ME 04011
    Pubs: *Et Nous Les Os* (La Main Courante, 1996), *Dans
    La Gueule Du Loup* (AIOU, 1995), *AIOU, Gate, Active
    in Airtime, Copice Biancaneve, Doc(k)s*

Sharon Kraus ⚲ ✈   P
c/o Alice James Books, 98 Main St, Farmington, ME
04938, 207-778-7071
    Pubs: *Generation* (Alice James Bks, 1997), *Georgia
    Rev, Massachusetts Rev, Qtly West, Agni, TriQtly,
    Prairie Schooner, Mississippi Rev, Columbia: A Jrnl of
    Literature & Art*

Diane Kruchkow ⚲ ✈   P
3 Saltmarsh Rd
New Sharon, ME 04955
Internet: kruch@exploremaine.com
    Pubs: *Green Isle in the Sea* (December, 1986), *Stony
    Hills, Small Press News*

Kris Larson   P
PO Box 189
East Machias, ME 04630, 207-255-6525
    Pubs: *Second Thoughts, Groundwork* (Salt-Works Pr,
    1976, 1974), *The Egg, Opinion, Downeast Coastal
    Press*

Gary Lawless   P
617 E Neck Rd
Nobleboro, ME 04555, 207-729-5083
    Pubs: *Caribouddhism, First Sight of Land* (Blackberry
    Bks, 1998, 1990), *Somewhere Inside the Shell Mound*
    (Bull Head, 1995), *Earth Prayers* (H&R, 1991), *Green
    Fuse, Wild Earth, Raise the Stakes, BPJ, Napalm
    Health Spa, Northern Forest Forum*

Denis Ledoux ⚲ ✈   W
Soleil Press, 95 Gould Rd, Lisbon Falls, ME 04252-9707,
207-353-5454
    Pubs: *What Became of Them & Other Stories from
    Franco-America, Lives in Translation: Anth* (Soleil Pr,
    1988, 1991), *Mountain Dance & Other Stories*
    (Coastwise Pr, 1990)

James Lewisohn   P
25 W St Ext Apt 2
Bar Harbor, ME 04609, 207-288-4078
    Pubs: *Finkel, New & Selected Poems* (Horizon Pr,
    1990), *New Yorker, NYQ, Sojourner*

Carl Little ⚲ ✈   P
PO Box 273
Mount Desert, ME 04660-0273, 207-288-5015
Internet: ckl@ecology.coa.edu
    Pubs: *3,000 Dreams Explained* (Nightshade Pr, 1992),
    Maine Times, Puckerbrush Rev

Leni Mancuso ⚲ ✈   P
Box 303
Castine, ME 04421, 207-326-9381
    Pubs: *In Rothko's Cave* (Puckerbrush Rev Portfolio #6,
    1998), *Trenton Rev, BPJ, CSM, Potato Eyes,
    Paideuma, Maine Times*

Katherine McAlpine ⚲ ✈   P
11 Mitchell St
Eastport, ME 04631
    Pubs: *Garlic & Sapphires: Selected Sonnets* (RL Barth,
    1999), *The Muse Strikes Back: Anth* (Story Line Pr,
    1997), *Literature: The Human Experience: Anth* (St.
    Martin's Pr, 1997), *The Best Contemporary Women's
    Humor: Anth* (Crossing Pr, 1994), *Formalist, Light*

James McKenna   P
5 Summer St
Augusta, ME 04330, 207-289-3661
    Pubs: *Zone 3, Potato Eyes, Negative Capability, The
    Ledge, Kennebec, Slant, WordWrights*

Wesley McNair 🎙 ✈   P
1 Chicken St
Mercer, ME 04957, 207-587-4681
    Pubs: *Fire, Mapping the Heart, Talking in the Dark,
    The Town of No & My Brother Running* (Godine, 2001,
    2000, 1998, 1997), *Atlantic, Poetry, Iowa Rev, Sewanee
    Rev, Ploughshares, Gettysburg Rev*

Mark Melnicove   P
132 Water St
Gardiner, ME 04345, 207-737-8116
    Pubs: *Uncensored Guide to Maine* (Lance Tapley,
    1984), *Advanced Memories* (Bern Porter, 1983),
    Kennebec, Cold-Drill, Puckerbrush Rev

Robin Morgan 🎙 ✈   P
c/o Edite Kroll, Edite Kroll Literary Agency, 12 Grayhurst
Park, Portland, ME 04102
    Pubs: *A Hot January: Poems 1996-1999, Upstairs in
    the Garden: Selected Poems* (Norton, 1999, 1991), *The
    Mer-Child: A New Legend* (CUNY Feminist Pr, 1991),
    Dry Your Smile (Doubleday, 1989)

Paul Nelson   P
HC 70, Box 1085
Machiasport, ME 04655
    Pubs: *The Hard Shapes of Paradise* (U Alabama Pr,
    1988), *Days Off* (U Pr Virginia, 1982)

Edward Nobles 🎙 ✈   P
139 Kenduskeag Ave
Bangor, ME 04401, 207-973-3331
    Pubs: *The Bluestone Walk, Through One Tear* (Persea,
    2000, 1997), *Tin House, Colorado Rev, Boulevard,
    Denver Qtly, Gettysburg Rev, Paris Rev, Volt, Witness,
    Kenyon Rev*

Patricia O'Donnell   W
Univ Maine, Roberts Learning Center, Farmington, ME
04938, 207-645-4872
    Pubs: *The Quotable Moose: Anth* (New England Pr,
    1994), *New Yorker, NAR, Agni, Short Story*

Carolyn Page   P
Rte 2, Box 2575
Troy, ME 04987, 207-948-3427
    Pubs: *Barn Flight, Life on the Line: Anth* (Negative
    Capability, 1995, 1992), *Troy Corner Poems*
    (Nightshade Pr, 1994), *Parnassus, Comstock Rev, Now
    & Then, Pembroke, Fiddlehead, Zone 3*

Arnold Perrin   P
PO Box 809
Union, ME 04862, 207-785-4355
    Pubs: *Noah* (East Coast Edtns, 1993), *View from Hill
    Cabin* (Northwoods Pr, 1979), *Puckerbrush Rev,
    Kennebec, Potato Eyes, Maine Life, CSM, The Sun*

Mary Peterson   W
148 Pepperrell Rd
Kittery Point, ME 03905, 207-439-1640
    Pubs: *Mercy Flights* (U Missouri Pr, 1985), *Story Qtly,
    South Dakota Rev, NAR, Ms.*

Judith Rachel Platz   P
5 Atwood Ln
Brunswick, ME 04011, 207-725-0018
    Pubs: *A Gathering of Poets: Anth* (Kent State U Pr,
    1992), *Cafe Rev, SlugFest, Maine Poets & Writers,
    Haight-Ashbury Literary Jrnl, Milkweed Chronicle, Long
    Shot*

J. A. Pollard   P&W
RFD #2, Eames Rd, Box 5115
Winslow, ME 04901-9661, 207-873-6443

Sylvester Pollet 🎙 ✈   P
963 Winkumpaugh Rd
Ellsworth, ME 04605-3030, 207-667-2255
Internet: pollet@maine.edu
    Pubs: *The Dandelion Sutras* (Backwoods Broadsides
    Chaplets, 1994), *Maine Speaks: Anth* (MWPA, 1989),
    Exquisite Corpse, Poetry NY, NYQ, Bullhead

Bern Porter 🎙 ✈   P&W
50 Salmond St
Belfast, ME 04915, 207-338-4303
    Pubs: *Symbols* (Spoon Pr, 1994), *Less Than
    Overweight* (Plaster Cramp, 1993), *Sounds That Arouse
    Me* (Tilbury, 1992), *Bern Porter's Pillow Book, The Best
    Period of My Life* (Roger Jackson, 1996, 1996),
    Numbers, Neverends (Runaway Spoon, 1989, 1988)

Patricia Smith Ranzoni 🎙 ✈   P
HCR 78, Box 173
Bucksport, ME 04416-9618
Internet: members.aol.com/pranzoni
    Pubs: *Settling, Claiming* (Puckerbrush Pr, 2000, 1995),
    Prayers to Protest: Anth (Pudding Hse, 1998), *CSM,
    Animist, Shearsman, Spoon River Poetry Rev, Yankee,
    Cafe Rev, Blueline, Green Fuse*
I.D.: Rural Communities, Working Class. Groups:
Multicultural, Disabled

Kenneth Rosen   P
English Dept, Univ Southern Maine, Portland, ME 04103,
207-780-4296
    Pubs: *Reptile Mind, Longfellow Square* (Ascenius Pr,
    1993, 1993), *Paris Rev, Ploughshares, Western
    Humanities Rev, Massachusetts Rev, Poetry*

John Rosenwald 🎤 ✈   P
c/o Granite Rose Farm, Box 389, South Andover, ME
04216-0389, 207-392-1872
Internet: rosey@beloit.edu
   Pubs: *Descant, Wisconsin Poets Calendar, BPJ,
Kennebec, Kansas Qtly, Literary Rev*
Lang: German, Chinese

Ira Sadoff 🎤 ✈   P&W
53 Middle St
Hallowell, ME 04347-1114
Internet: i_sadoff@colby.edu
   Pubs: *Grazing* (U Illinois Pr, 1998), *An Ira Sadoff
Reader* (U New England Pr, 1992), *Emotional Traffic*
(Godine, 1990), *APR, New Yorker, Antaeus, Paris Rev*

Lee Sharkey 🎤 ✈   P&W
RR1 Box 4122
Vienna, ME 04360-9500, 207-293-2390
Internet: sharkey@maine.edu
   Pubs: *To a Vanished World* (Puckerbrush Pr, 1995),
*Prarie Schooner, Marlboro Rev, Manhattan Rev, Green
Mountains Rev, Cream City Rev*
I.D.: Jewish

Betsy Sholl   P
24 Brentwood St
Portland, ME 04103, 207-774-9414
   Pubs: *The Red Line* (U Pitt Pr, 1992), *Pick a Card*
(Coyote/Bark Pub, 1991), *Rooms Overhead* (Alice
James Bks, 1986)

Alix Kates Shulman   W
Long Island, ME 04050
   Pubs: *In Every Woman's Life, On the Stroll, Burning
Questions* (Knopf, 1987, 1981, 1978)

Michael Smetzer   P&W
PO Box 3112
Portland, ME 04104-3112
   Pubs: *Teaching the Clergy to Dance* (Manic Monkey
Bks, 1996), *A Quiet Man* (Baggeboda Pr, 1988),
*George & Mertie's Place, Red Rock, Cottonwood, New
Letters, Poetry Motel, Kansas Qtly*

Pam Burr Smith   P&W
Star Rte 3, Box 365
Bath, ME 04530, 207-443-9390
   Pubs: *Air Fish* (Omega Cat Pr, 1993), *Black Fly Rev,
Kansas Qtly, Kennebec, Cafe Rev, Slow Dancer,
Coyote's Jrnl*

Karen South 🎤 ✈   P
PO Box 235
Matinicus Island, ME 04851-0235, 207-366-3425
   Pubs: *National Forum, Abraxas, Hampden-Sydney
Poetry Rev, Ploughshares, MPR*

Debra Spark   W
English Dept, Colby College, 5284 Mayflower Hill Dr,
Waterville, ME 04901-8852, 207-872-3257
   Pubs: *Coconuts for the Saint* (Faber & Faber, 1996),
On the Tail of the Dog Star (Chikuma Shobo, 1990),
Twenty Under Thirty: Anth (Scribner, 1996), *Passages
North, Boston Globe Mag, Epoch, Agni, NAR,
Ploughshares, Esquire, Yankee*

Martin Steingesser 🎤 ✈   PP&P
PO Box 7575
Portland, ME 04112-7575, 207-828-9937
Internet: msteings@maine.rr.com
   Pubs: *The Wildman, Speaking of New England* (North
Country Pr, 1998, 1993), *Poetry Comes Up Where It
Can: Anth* (U Utah Pr, 2000), *This Sporting Life: Anth*
(Milkweed Edtns, 1996), *Wherever Home Begins: Anth*
(Orchard Bks, 1995), *Progressive, American Voice*
Groups: Children, Advocacy

Linda Tatelbaum 🎤 ✈   P&W
1050 Guinea Ridge Rd
Appleton, ME 04862, 207-785-4634
Internet: www.colby.edu/personal/l_tateb
   Pubs: *Writer on the Rocks, Carrying Water As a Way
of Life* (About Time Pr, 2000, 1997), *Utne Reader,
Maine Times, Maine in Print*
I.D.: Jewish, Rural Communities. Groups: Writing Groups

Lewis Turco 🎤 ✈   P&W
Mathom Bookshop, 40 Blinn Hill Rd, Dresden Mills, ME
04342, 207-737-4512
Internet: mathom@gwi.net
   Pubs: *A Book of Fears* (Bordighera, 1998), *Bordello*
(Grey Heron Pr, 1996), *World Poetry: Anth* (Norton,
1998)

Carol Wainright   P
RR1, Box 449
Deer Isle, ME 04627, 207-348-2580
   Pubs: *Distant Mountain* (Wind Chimes Pr, 1985), *CSM*

David C. Walker 🎤 ✈   P
Box 82
Freedom, ME 04941-0082, 207-382-6267
Internet: dwalker@maine.edu
   Pubs: *Voiceprints* (Romulus Edtns, 1989), *The Maine
Reader: Anth* (HM, 1991), *Poetry, NW Rev, New
Yorker, Georgia Rev, Antioch Rev*
Groups: Teenagers, Seniors

Douglas "Woody" Woodsum   P
PO Box 265
Scarborough, ME 04070, 207-799-3425
   Pubs: *Antioch Rev, Southern Rev, Massachusetts Rev,
Prairie Schooner, Denver Qtly, Yankee, Webster Rev,
Exquisite Corpse, Sun Dog, Albany Rev*

Baron Wormser P
19 1/2 Pleasant St Pl
Hallowell, ME 04347, 207-622-7052
  Pubs: *When* (Sarabande Bks, 1997), *Atoms, Soul Music & Other Poems* (Paris Rev Edtns, 1989), *Harper's, New Republic, Paris Rev*

Helen Yglesias W
Bay Rd
North Brooklin, ME 04616, 207-359-8584
  Pubs: *How She Died, Isabel Bishop, The Saviors* (HM, 1992, 1989, 1987), *Sweetsir* (S&S, 1981)

Leroy Zarucchi 🎤 ✈ P
RR2, Box 2575
Troy, ME 04987, 207-948-3427
Internet: potatoeyes@uninets.net
  Pubs: *Gunner's Moon* (Cider Pr, 1996), *Sparse Rain* (Pygmy Forest Pr, 1996), *Spirit That Moves Us: Anth* (Spirit That Moves Us, 1993), *Onthebus, Pembroke Mag, Fiddlehead*

MARYLAND

Karren LaLonde Alenier 🎤 ✈ P&W
4601 North Ave, #301
Chevy Chase, MD 20815, 301-652-7638
Internet: karren77@aol.com
  Pubs: *Looking for Divine Transportation* (Bunny & Crocodile Pr, 1999), *Winners: The Washington Prize: Anth* (Word Works, 1999), *MacGuffin, Crescent Rev, Jrnl of Poetry Therapy, Poet Lore, Negative Capability, Mississippi Rev, Jewish Currents*

Indran Amirthanayagam P
4810 Mercury Dr
Rockville, MD 20853, 301-946-8085
  Pubs: *The Elephants of Reckoning* (Hanging Loose Pr, 1993), *Four Way Reader: Anth* (Four Way Bks, 1996), *United States of Poetry: Anth* (Abrams, 1996)

Ellen Argo W
63 Conduit St
Annapolis, MD 21401, 301-268-3151
  Pubs: *Yankee Girl, Crystal Star, Jewel of the Seas* (Putnam, 1981, 1979, 1977)

Barri Armitage P
13904 N Gate Dr
Silver Spring, MD 20906-2217, 301-871-6656
  Pubs: *Double Helix* (Washington Writers Pub Hse, 1993), *Prairie Schooner, Poet Lore, Bridge, Poetry, Georgia Rev, Ohio Rev*

Ed Baker P
8215 Flower Ave
Takoma Park, MD 20912-6858, 301-587-1875
  Pubs: *Shrike* (tel-let, 2000), *Nine Perfect Ensos, Okeanos Rhos, The City, Hexapoem I, II, & III, This Wood* (Red Ochre Pr, 2000, 1995, 1994, 1982), *Amelia, Frogpond, Modern Haiku, Persimmon, Black Bough, Tundra, Bongos of the Lord, Hummingbird*

Diane DeMichele Barkett P
5394 Annapolis Dr
Mount Airy, MD 21771-5709
  Pubs: *Tempest, Archer, Up Against the Wall Mother, San Fernando Poetry Jrnl, Piedmont Literary Rev*

John Barth W
c/o The Writing Seminar, Johns Hopkins Univ, Baltimore, MD 21218, 410-516-7562
  Pubs: *On with the Story, The Last Voyage of Somebody the Sailor* (Little, Brown, 1996, 1991)

Robin Bayne P&W
215 Treherne Rd
Lutherville, MD 21093-1244
Internet: http://nbayne.com/child.htm
  Pubs: *Charity's Prisoner, A Matter of Life* (BT Bks/Indigo, 2001, 2000), *The Will of Time* (New Concepts Pub, 1999), *His Brother's Child* (Mountain View Pub, 1999)

David Beaudouin P
2840 St Paul St
Baltimore, MD 21218-4311, 410-467-6292
  Pubs: *The American Night* (Blue Nude, 1992), *Catenae–Set 1* (Apathy Pr, 1988), *Open 24 Hours, Stony Run*

Geoffrey Becker W
15 West Mt. Vernon Pl
Baltimore, MD 21201
  Pubs: *Bluestown* (St. Martin's Pr, 1996), *Dangerous Men* (U Pitt Pr, 1995)

Madison Smartt Bell W
Goucher College, English Dept, Towson, MD 21204, 410-337-6282
  Pubs: *Ten Indians, All Soul's Rising* (Pantheon, 1996, 1995), *Doctor Sleep* (HBJ, 1991), *Barking Man* (Ticknor & Fields, 1990), *Harper's, Hudson Rev*

Donald Berger P
105 Hodges Ln
Takoma Park, MD 20912-4229
  Pubs: *Quality Hill* (Lost Roads, 1993)

David Bergman   P
3024 N Calvert St, #C5
Baltimore, MD 21218, 410-467-8070
    Pubs: *Heroic Measures, Cracking the Code* (Ohio State,
    1998, 1985), *Gaiety Transfigured* (U Wisconsin, 1991),
    *Poetry, New Republic, Raritan, Paris Rev, Kenyon Rev,
    New Criterion*

Cathy Drinkwater Better   P
119 Caraway Rd Apt B1
Reisterstown, MD 21136, 410-833-1537
    Pubs: *The Moon Tonight* (Los Hombres Pr, 1996),
    Don't Hit Your Brother with Your Mouth Full (Acme Pr,
    1995), *Writer's Digest, St. Anthony Messenger, Modern
    Haiku, American Cowboy Poet Mag, Silver Web,
    Humpty Dumpty Mag, Psychopoetica, Raw Nervz*

Jody Bolz 🎤 ✈   P
4004 Maryland Ave
Brookmont, MD 20816-2671, 301-229-6578
    Pubs: *Her Face in the Mirror: Anth* (Beacon Pr, 1994),
    *Gargoyle, Indiana Rev, SPR, River Styx, Women's Rev
    of Bks, Ascent, Poet Lore, Ploughshares*

Betty Booker   P
27826 Island Dr
Salisbury, MD 21801, 410-546-1712
    Pubs: *Plainsong, Croton Rev, Stone Country, Artemis,
    Christian Century, America, Poetry Now*

Alan Britt 🎤 ✈   P
233 Northway Rd
Reisterstown, MD 21136-2136, 410-833-9424
    Pubs: *Bodies of Lightning* (Cypress Bks, 1995), *Fathers:
    A Collection of Poems: Anth* (St. Martin's Pr, 1997),
    Rising Waters: Anth (Pekitanoui Pub, 1995), *Black
    Moon, Bitter Oleander, Chariton Rev, Exquisite Corpse,
    Borderlands: Texas Rev, New Letters*

Melvin Edward Brown   P
1311 Kitmore Rd
Baltimore, MD 21239, 410-323-3708

Barbara Browne   P
6120 Edmondson Ave
Catonsville, MD 21228, 301-747-1090
    Pubs: *Studia Mystica, Wind, Anima, Poet's Pride*

Marion Buchman 🎤   P
11 Slade Ave, #315
Baltimore, MD 21208, 410-764-3327
    Pubs: *In His Pavilion* (Haskell Hse Pub, 1986), *America*
    (Thornhill Pr, 1976), *Redbook, Stanza*

Lynn Buck   P
13801 York Rd, Apt K-10
Cockeysville, MD 21030-1899, 410-771-0916
    Pubs: *Two Minus One* (Birnham Wood, 1994), *Autumn
    Fires* (Red Creek Pr, 1989), *Crazyquilt, Live Poets,
    Long Pond Rev, LIQ, Heartland*

Roser Caminals-Heath   W
Hood College, 401 Rosemont Ave, Frederick, MD 21701,
301-696-3474
    Pubs: *Un Segle De Prodigis* (Spain; Columbia, 1995),
    Once Remembered, Twice Lived (Peter Lang Pub,
    1993), *Georgia Rev, American Book Rev*

Grant Carrington 🎤 ✈   W
Box 1120
Laurel, MD 20725-1120, 301-490-6142
Internet: gccarrington@hotmail.com
    Pubs: *Time's Fool* (Doubleday, 1981), *Amazing,
    Fantastic, Cavalier, Canadian Forum, Eternity, Isaac
    Asimov's SF Mag*

John Carter   P
332 Lincoln Ave
Takoma Park, MD 20912
    Pubs: *Impetus, Poetry USA, Poetry SF, The Pearl,
    Prisoners of the Night, Gargoyle, Lactuca*

Lucille Clifton 🎤 ✈   P
St. Mary's College, St Mary's City, MD 20686
    Pubs: *Blessing the Boats, Terrible Stories, Quilting*
    (BOA Edtns, 2000, 1996, 1991), *The Book of Light*
    (Copper Canyon Pr, 1994), *Ten Oxherding Poems*
    (Moving Parts Pr, 1988)

Michael Collier   P
111 Smithwood Ave
Catonsville, MD 21228-4945, 410-719-7312
Internet: mc33@umail.umd.edu
    Pubs: *The Ledge* (HM, 2000), *The Neighbor* (U
    Chicago, 1995), *The Folded Heart* (Wesleyan, 1989),
    Atlantic, New Yorker

Geraldine Connolly 🎤 ✈   P
5802 Nicholson Lane
Rockville, MD 20852
Internet: sconno996@aol.com
    Pubs: *Province of Fire* (Iris Press, 1998), *Food for the
    Winter* (Purdue U Pr, 1990), *Boomer Girls: Anth* (U
    Iowa Pr, 1999), *Antioch Rev, Poetry, Georgia Review,
    Connecticut Rev, West Branch, Shenandoah, Cream
    City Rev, Hayden's Ferry Rev*

Sarah Cotterill   P
9624 Evergreen St
Silver Spring, MD 20901, 301-588-8983
    Pubs: *In the Nocturnal Animal House* (Purdue U Pr,
    1991), *The Hive Burning* (Sleeping Bird Pr, 1983), *APR,
    Poetry NW, Ploughshares, Nimrod, Kansas Qtly*

Judith Speizer Crandell 🎤 ✈ W
12 Hilltop Rd
Silver Spring, MD 20910, 301-588-2538
    Pubs: *Hudson River Anthology, Cleveland Magazine, Allied Pub, Laughing Bear, Whiskey Island*

James Cross W
c/o Hugh J. Parry, 4814 Falstone Ave, Chevy Chase, MD 20815, 301-652-5665
    Pubs: *To Hell for Half a Crown* (Random Hse, 1968), *Maryland Poetry Rev*

Bruce V. J. Curley 🎤 ✈ P&W
11404 Brundidge Terr
Germantown, MD 20876-5578, 301-540-8323
Internet: http://home.infospace.cow/brucec1
    Pubs: *Under a Gull's Wing: Anth* (Down the Shore Pr, 1996), *Baltimore Rev, Pannus Index, Lynx Eye, Mad Poets Rev, Voices Israel, Potomac Rev, WordWrights*

Ann Darr P
4902 Falstone Ave
Chevy Chase, MD 20815, 301-652-4292
    Pubs: *Flying the Zuni Mountains* (Forest Woods Media Productions, 1994), *Hungry As We Are: Anth* (Washington Writers Pub Hse, 1995)

Robert Day W
The O'Neil Literary House, Washington College, 300 Washington Ave, Chestertown, MD 21620, 410-778-2800
    Pubs: *Speaking French in Kansas* (Cottonwood, 1989), *The Four Wheel Drive Quartet* (Galileo, 1986), *TriQtly*

Enoch Dillon 🎤 P
6310 Hollins Dr
Bethesda, MD 20817-2351, 301-530-7795
Internet: enochdillon@email.msn.com
    Pubs: *Love, From the Ends of the Earth, The Bicentennial Blues* (Fithian Pr, 1990, 1988), *America, Poet Lore, Visions, Light, Friends Jrnl, Deus Ex Machina, Mediphors*

Stephen Dixon 🎤 ✈ W
Johns Hopkins Univ, Writing Seminars Gilman 135, Baltimore, MD 21218, 410-825-8038
    Pubs: *Tisch* (Red Hen Pr, 2000), *30* (H Holt, 1999), *Sleep* (Coffee Hse Pr, 1999), *Gould, Interstate* (Owl Bks, 1998, 1997), *TriQtly, Boulevard, Harper's, Virginia Qtly Rev, DoubleTake, Speak, Fence*

Thomas A. Dorsett P
4408 Wickford Rd
Baltimore, MD 21210, 410-467-4316
    Pubs: *Dance Fire Dance* (Icarus Pr, 1992), *Confrontation, Descant, Verse, Paintbrush, America, Slant, International Poetry Rev*

Maura Eichner P
College of Notre Dame
Baltimore, MD 21210
    Pubs: *Hope Is a Blind Bard* (Harold Shaw Pub, 1989), *What We Women Know* (Sparrow, 1980)

Daniel Mark Epstein 🎤 ✈ P
843 W University Pkwy
Baltimore, MD 21210-2911
    Pubs: *The Traveler's Calendar* (The Overlook Pr, 2001), *The Boy in the Well, Spirits* (The Overlook Pr/Viking, 1995, 1987), *Sister Aimee* (HB, 1993), *Love's Compass* (Addison-Wesley, 1990), *New Yorker, Atlantic, New Republic, Paris Rev, Nation*

Michael Fallon P
3041 St Paul St
Baltimore, MD 21218-3943, 410-366-6850
    Pubs: *A History of the Color Black* (Dolphin Moon Pr, 1989), *The Salmon, Puerto del Sol, Poets On, Maryland Poetry Rev, Potomac Rev*

Diana J. Felts P
113 Byway Rd
Owings Mills, MD 21117, 301-356-6984
    Pubs: *Impetus, Up Against the Wall Mother, Piedmont Literary Mag, The Mountain Laurel, Proof Rock*

Roland Flint P
8605 Milford Ave
Silver Spring, MD 20910, 301-585-7685
    Pubs: *Pigeon in the Night* (Fakel Pr, 1994), *Stubborn* (U Illinois Pr, 1991), *Pigeon* (North Carolina Wesleyan College Pr, 1990)

Elizabeth Follin-Jones P&W
4896 Chevy Chase Blvd
Chevy Chase, MD 20815, 301-652-4346
    Pubs: *Bite to Eat Place* (Redwood Coast Pr, 1995), *One Flight from the Bottom* (Artscape, 1990), *Poet Lore, Maryland Poetry Rev, Embers, Free State*

Martin Galvin 🎤 ✈ P
Walt Whitman School, 7100 Whittier Blvd, Bethesda, MD 20817
    Pubs: *Appetites* (Bogg Pub, 2000), *Wild Card* (Washington Writer's Pub Hse, 1989), *Making Beds* (Sedwick Hse, 1989), *Best American Poetry: Anth* (Scribner, 1997), *Poetry, Atlantic, New Republic*

CJeanean Gibbs P
Palm Tree Enterprises, Inc, 1514 Roosevelt Ave, Landover, MD 20785, 301-322-5510
    Pubs: *Spirits of the Ancestors, Gurus & Griots* (Palm Tree Enterprises, 1993, 1987)

Michael S. Glaser 🎤 ✈   P
PO Box 1
Saint Mary's City, MD 20686-0001, 301-862-9676
Internet: msglaser@osprey.smcm.edu
    Pubs: *In the Men's Room & Other Poems* (Painted
    Bride Qtly, 1996), *A Lover's Eye* (Bunny & Crocodile
    Pr, 1989), *Light-Gathering Poems: Anth* (H Holt, 2000),
    Outsiders: Anth (Milkweed Edns, 1999), *Unsettling
    America: Anth* (Penguin, 1994), *CSM, New Letters, Sun*

Barbara Goldberg   P
6623 Fairfax Rd
Chevy Chase, MD 20815, 301-907-7994
    Pubs: *Marvelous Pursuits* (Snake Nation Pr, 1995),
    Cautionary Tales (Dryad Pr, 1990), *Paris Rev, Poetry,
    NER, American Scholar, Poet Lore*

Ivy Goodman 🎤 ✈   W
3911 Spring Meadow Dr
Ellicott City, MD 21042
    Pubs: *Heart Failure* (U Iowa Pr, 1983), *Gettysburg Rev,
    Confrontation, Epoch, DoubleTake, Witness, Michigan
    Qtly Rev, Ploughshares*

Jennifer Gostin   W
1 S Rolling Rd
Baltimore, MD 21228
    Pubs: *Peregrine's Rest* (Permanent Pr, 1996), *The
    Mage, North Shore Life, The Gamut, Whiskey Island,
    Byline, Monocacy Valley Rev*

Beatrice Greene   W
6418 Bannockburn Dr
Bethesda, MD 20817
    Pubs: *New Orleans Rev, Mississippi Rev, Panache, The
    Fiddlehead, Style, Calvert Rev*

Allen R. Grossman   P
English Dept, Johns Hopkins Univ, Baltimore, MD 21218
    Pubs: *The Ether Dome & Other Poems New &
    Selected 1979-1991, The Bright Nails Scattered on the
    Ground* (New Directions, 1991, 1986)

Greg Hannan   P
207 Hodge St
Takoma Park, MD 20912
    Pubs: *A Shout in the Street, The Poet Upstairs,
    Gargoyle, Cycloflame*

Jean Harmon   P&W
12813 Falmouth Dr
Silver Spring, MD 20904, 301-622-0442
    Pubs: *Thirteen, Z Misc, Popular Reality, Renegade,
    American Organist, Anathema Rev, 'Scapes, New
    Voices, Metropolitan, Opera Monthly, Neologisms, Verse
    Unto Us, Sacred Music News, Church Musician,
    Christianity & the Arts, Ancient Paths, Continuo Mag*

Reginald Harris 🎤 ✈   P&W
PO Box 7184
Baltimore, MD 21218, 410-889-8223
Internet: reginaldharris@africana.com
    Pubs: *Men on Men 7: Anth* (Plume, 1998), *His 3: Anth*
    (FSG, 1998), *The Road Before Us: Anth* (Galiens Pr,
    1991), *African-American Rev, The Pearl, Baltimore Rev,
    Harvard Gay & Lesbian Rev, Obsidian II*
I.D.: African-American, G/L/B/T. Groups: G/L/B/T

Clarinda Harriss 🎤 ✈   P
English Dept, Chair, Towson Univ, Towson, MD 21252,
401-830-2869
Internet: charris@towson.edu
    Pubs: *License Renewal for the Blind* (Cooper Hse,
    1994), *The Night Parrot* (Salmon Pub, 1989), *Forms of
    Verse* (Appleton-Century Croft, 1975), *The Bone Tree*
    (NPS, 1973), *Poetry, Southern Rev, Spoon River Anth*

John Hayes   P&W
1300K Scottsdale Rd
Bel Air, MD 21015, 410-420-7749
    Pubs: *Great Writers, Great Stories: Anth* (IM Pr, 1999),
    Fire on the Hills: Anth (Highlights for Children, 1995),
    *Lynx Eye, Bogg, Alabama Literary Rev, Thema,
    Rockford Rev, Onionhead, Fresh Ground, Implosion,
    Baltimore Rev, MacGuffin, Antipodean*

William Heath 🎤 ✈   P
Mount St Mary's College
Emmitsburg, MD 21727, 301-694-5365
Internet: heath@msmary.edu
    Pubs: *The Children Bob Moses Led* (Milkweed, 1997),
    The Walking Man (Icarus, 1994), *Kenyon Rev, Southern
    Rev, Massachusetts Rev, South Carolina Rev, Texas
    Rev, Monocacy Valley Rev, Cortland Rev*

David Hilton   P
413 Grinstead Rd
Severna Park, MD 21146
    Pubs: *No Relation to the Hotel* (Coffee Hse Pr, 1989),
    Huladance (Crossing Pr, 1976), *Poetry NW, BPJ,
    Exquisite Corpse, Poetry, Iowa Rev*

Geoffrey Himes   P
8 E 39 St
Baltimore, MD 21218-1801, 410-235-6627
    Pubs: *City Paper, Salt Lick, Columbia Flier, Maryland
    English Jrnl, Baltimore Sun, December*

Carol F. Hoover 🎤 ✈   W
4817 Tallahassee Ave
Rockville, MD 20853, 301-949-2514
    Pubs: *Story, Denver Qtly, Texas Qtly, Potomac Rev,
    Crescent Rev*

Gary Hotham 🎙 ✈ P
10460 Stansfield Rd
Laurel, MD 20723
   Pubs: *Breath Marks* (Canon Pr, 1999), *Footprints & Fingerprints* (Lilliput Rev Pr, 1999), *The Sky Stays Behind* (Juniper Pr, 2000), *Bare Feet* (Longhouse, 1998), *Modern Haiku, Northeast, BPJ, Paper Wasp, South By Southwest, Tundra, Puckerbrush Rev*

Josephine Jacobsen P&W
13801 York Rd #T-366
Cockeysville, MD 21030, 410-527-9472
   Pubs: *The Instant of Knowing* (U Michigan Pr, 1997), *What Goes Without Saying, In the Crevice of Time* (Johns Hopkins Pr, 1996, 1995), *Distances* (Bucknell U Fine Edtns, 1992), *On the Island* (Ontario Rev Pr, 1988), *Best American Poetry: Anth* (Scribner, 1993)

Philip K. Jason P
11500 Patriot Ln
Potomac, MD 20854, 301-299-4190
   Pubs: *The Separation* (Viet Nam Generation, 1995), *Creative Writer's Handbook* (Prentice Hall, 1990), *Near the Fire* (Dryad, 1983)

Eugene L. Jeffers 🎙 ✈ W
13412 Oriental Ct
Rockville, MD 20853, 301-460-0265
   Pubs: *A Rumor of Distant Tribes* (Ariadne Pr, 1994), *Pulpsmith, Crosscurrents, Orbis, Format: Art & the World, Virginia Country*

Rod Jellema P
4526 Avondale St, #4
Bethesda, MD 20814, 301-907-8824
   Pubs: *The Sound that Remains* (Eerdmans, 1990), *The Eighth Day* (Dryad Pr, 1985), *Field, Plum Rev*

Lane Jennings P
6373 Barefoot Boy
Columbia, MD 21045, 301-596-2943
   Pubs: *Open Secrets, White Lies* (Black Buzzard Pr, 1998, 1984), *Virtual Futures* (Other Worlds Pr, 1996), *White Lies, Visions, Amelia, Catalyst, Gargoyle, Starline, Treasure House*

Lynn Kanter W
3312 Camalier
Chevy Chase, MD 20815
   Pubs: *The Mayor of Heaven, On Lill Street* (Third Side Pr, 1997, 1992), *Breaking Up Is Hard to Do: Anth, The Time of Our Lives: Anth* (Crossing Pr, 1994, 1993)

Wayne Karlin 🎙 ✈ W
PO Box 239
St Mary's City, MD 20686-0239, 301-862-9871
Internet: waynek@csm.cc.md.us
   Pubs: *Prisoners, Rumors & Stones, The Other Side of Heaven: Anth* (Curbstone Pr, 1998, 1996, 1995), *Us, Lost Armies* (H Holt, 1993, 1988), *New Stories from the South, Prairie Schooner, Indiana Rev, Glimmer Train, Crab Orchard Rev*

Madeleine Keller P
4613 Wilmslow Rd
Baltimore, MD 21210
   Pubs: *Pearl, Stony Run, Tamarind, Telephone, Niagara, The Spirit That Moves Us, Knock-Knock*

Marta Knobloch 🎙 ✈ P
PO Box 48
Galena, MD 21635-0048, 410-648-5080
   Pubs: *The Room of Months/La Stanza dei Mesi* (Book Editore, 1995), *Sky Pond* (SCOP Pubs, 1992), *Beyond Lament: Anth* (Northwestern U Pr, 1998), *Leggere Donna, Maryland Poetry Rev, Lyric, Visions Intl, Delos, Poesie, Poetry Australia*

Ann B. Knox 🎙 ✈ P&W
PO Box 65
Hancock, MD 21750-0065, 717-294-3272
Internet: tinkerword@aol.com
   Pubs: *Staying Is Nowhere* (SCOP Pubs, 1996), *Late Summer Break* (Papier-Mache, 1995), *Poetry, Atlanta Rev, Plum Rev, Poets On, MacGuffin*

Susan Land W
7004 Exsair Rd
Bethesda, MD 20814, 301-652-4982
   Pubs: *Confrontation, Quarry West, West Branch, Other Voices, Wind, Kansas Qtly, Mississippi Rev, Alaska Qtly Rev*

Charles R. Larson W
3600 Underwood St
Chevy Chase, MD 20815, 301-656-9370
   Pubs: *Arthur Dimmesdale* (Avon, 1984), *The Insect Colony* (HRW, 1978)

Kevin J. Lavey 🎙 ✈ W
PO Box 1583
Baltimore, MD 21203-1583, 410-752-4708
Internet: kjlumb@earthlink.net
   Pubs: *Dan River Anth* (Dan River, 1995), *Slipstream, Z Miscellaneous, Licking River Rev*

Barbara F. Lefcowitz 🎤 ✈   P&W
4989 Battery Ln
Bethesda, MD 20814, 301-652-0835
  Pubs: *A Hand of Stars* (Dancing Moon Bks, 1999), *The
  Minarets of Vienna* (Chestnut Hills, 1996), *Red Lies &
  White Lies* (East Coast Bks, 1994), *Shadows &
  Goatbones* (SCOP Pubs, 1992), *Other Voices,
  Minnesota Rev*
I.D.: Jewish, College/Univ. Groups: Seniors

Harrison Edward Livingstone   W
PO Box 7149
Baltimore, MD 21218
  Pubs: *Baltimore, Harvard, John* (Conservatory Pr, 1988,
  1987), *The Wild Rose: A Novel of the Sea* (Word of
  Mouth Pr, 1980), *David Johnson Passed Through Here*
  (Little, Brown, 1971)

Kathy Auchincloss Lorr   P
302 Windsor St
Silver Spring, MD 20910, 301-585-7667
  Pubs: *Science 82, Poet Lore, Poets On, Dark Horse,
  Vision, Womanspirit, Gargoyle*

Kathy Mangan   P
3003 St Paul St
Baltimore, MD 21218, 410-243-0242
  Pubs: *Above the Tree Line* (Carnegie Mellon U Pr,
  1995), *Pushcart Prize XV: Anth* (Pushcart Pr, 1991),
  *Georgia Rev, Gettysburg Rev, Shenandoah, Southern
  Rev*

Sharon Bell Mathis   P&W
PO Box 44714
Fort Washington, MD 20744-7119
  Pubs: *Running Girl: The Diary of Ebonee Rose*
  (HB/Browndeer Pr, 1997), *Red Dog, Blue Fly: Football
  Poems* (Viking Penguin, 1991)

Lena Dale Matthews   P
4014 Roland Ave
Baltimore, MD 21211

John Mazur 🎤 ✈   P
247 S Ellwood Ave
Baltimore, MD 21224, 410-342-6843
  Pubs: *Lover's Lane: Anth, Ever Green & Sunsets Red:
  Anth, Little Verse, Big Thought: Anth* (Golden Apple Pr,
  1998, 1997, 1995), *Images of the Mind: Anth* (Modern
  Poetry Society, 1996), *eNteLechY*

Phillip McCaffrey 🎤 ✈   P
4121 Westview Rd
Baltimore, MD 21218
  Pubs: *Freud & Dora* (Rutgers U Pr, 1984), *Teaching
  the Door to Close* (Lame Johnny, 1983), *Poetry*

Jean McGarry   W
Johns Hopkins Univ, The Writing Seminars, Baltimore, MD
21218
  Pubs: *Gallagher's Travels, Home at Last, The Very
  Rich Hours* (Johns Hopkins U Pr, 1997, 1994, 1987),
  The Courage of Girls (Rutgers U Pr, 1992), *New
  Yorker, SW Rev, Boulevard, Yale Rev*

Ann Landis McLaughlin   W
6702 Maple Ave
Chevy Chase, MD 20815, 301-654-6877
  Pubs: *Maiden Voyage, Sunset at Rosalie, The
  Balancing Pole, Lightning in July* (John Daniel & Co,
  1999, 1996, 1991, 1989)

Margaret Meacham 🎤 ✈   W
Box 402, 10430 Falls Rd
Brooklandville, MD 21022, 410-337-0736
Internet: mmeac@aol.com
  Pubs: *Standing Up to Hammerhead* (Holiday Hse,
  2001), *Oyster Moon* (Tidewater, 1997), *Call Me Cathy*
  (Archway Pocket, 1995), *Vacation Blues, Love in Focus*
  (Berkley Pubs, 1985, 1983)

Carol A. Michalski   P
8601 Richmond Cir, Ste 204
Baltimore, MD 21234, 410-882-0834
  Pubs: *Don't Blame God* (Impact Christian Bks, 1995),
  Through the Years with Feelings: Anth (Andrea Poetry
  Pr, 1996), *Fauquier Poetry Jrnl, Perceptions, Feelings
  Poetry, Versus, Brobdingnagian Times*

Elizabeth J. Morris   W
8708 Ewing Dr
Bethesda, MD 20817, 301-530-3267
  Pubs: *Metropolitan, The Writing on the Wall, Gyst 6,
  Short Story, Crazyquilt*

Phyllis Reynolds Naylor   W
9910 Holmhurst Rd
Bethesda, MD 20817, 301-530-2340
  Pubs: *Achingly Alice, Sang Spell, The Fear Place, All
  But Alice, Shiloh, Send No Blessings* (Atheneum, 1998,
  1998, 1994, 1992, 1991, 1990)

Gloria Oden 🎤 ✈   P
Univ Maryland English Dept, 1000 Hilltop Circle, Baltimore,
MD 21250, 410-455-2384
  Pubs: *The Tie That Binds, Resurrections* (Olivant Pr,
  1980, 1978), *Ms., Saturday Rev, Nimrod*

Irene Orgel   W
6042 Green Meadow Pkwy
Baltimore, MD 21209
  Pubs: *The Odd Tales of Irene Orgel* (New York Eakins
  Pr, 1967), *Harper's, Mademoiselle*

Betty Parry P
4814 Falstone Ave
Chevy Chase, MD 20815, 301-652-5665
Pubs: *Shake the Parrot Cage* (New Poets Series, 1994), *Free State, A Harvest of Maryland Poets: Anth* (SCOP Prod, 1992), *Maryland Poetry Rev*

Linda Pastan 🎤 ✈ P
11710 Beall Mountain Rd
Potomac, MD 20854, 301-299-2362
Internet: lpastan@att.net
Pubs: *Carnival Evening: New & Selected Poems, An Early Afterlife, Heroes in Disguise, The Imperfect Paradise* (Norton, 1998, 1995, 1991, 1988), *Paris Rev, Kenyon Rev, Ohio Rev, Poetry, Gettysburg Rev, Georgia Rev*
I.D.: Jewish

Kathy Pearce-Lewis P
10501 Montrose Ave #102
Bethesda, MD 20814-4141, 301-530-4692
Internet: klew@erols.com
Pubs: *Waiting for You to Speak: Anth* (Mekler & Deahl, 1999), *Free State: Anth, The Cooke Book: A Seasoning of Poets: Anth* (SCOP Pub, 1989, 1987), *Taurus, Visions, Yet Another Small Mag, Bogg, Potomac Rev*

Lia Purpura 🎤 ✈ P
5116 Norwood Rd
Baltimore, MD 21212-4101
Internet: purpura@loyola.edu
Pubs: *Increase* (U Georgia Pr, 2000), *Stone Sky Lifting* (Ohio State U Pr, 2000), *The Brighter the Veil* (Orchises Pr, 1996)
Groups: Writing Groups

John Retallack P&W
4419 Ridge St
Chevy Chase, MD 20815, 301-656-8156
Pubs: *Circumstantial Evidence* (SOS, 1987), *The Best American Poetry: Anth* (Macmillan, 1990)

Marijane G. Ricketts 🎤 ✈ P
10203 Clearbrook Pl
Kensington, MD 20895-4121, 301-564-0852
Pubs: *Maryland Millennial Anth* (St Mary's College, 2000), *The Child Without, The Child Within: Anth* (Earth's Daughters, 1994), *Prose & Poetry: Anth* (Writers League of Washington, 1992), *Quirks, Washington Post, Montgomery Wkly, Maryland Clubwoman*

Phyllis Ringler 🎤 ✈ P&W
2306 Tucker Ln
Baltimore, MD 21207-6638, 410-448-2740
Pubs: *Nerval's Magic Alphabet* (Peter Lang Pub, 1989), *Catonsville Times, Arbutus Times, Baltimore Sun, Sub-Stance, Modern Language Notes, Minnesota Rev*

Doris Rochlin W
10100 Baldwin Ct
Bethesda, MD 20817, 301-581-0051
Pubs: *In the Spanish Ballroom* (Doubleday, 1991), *Frobisch's Angel* (Taplinger Pub Co, 1987)

Jean Rubin P
1227 Park Ave, #10
Baltimore, MD 21217-4135, 410-669-0344
Pubs: *Combinazioni III* (Theodore Presser, 1983), *The Ear's Chamber: Anth* (Metro, 1981), *le bayou, College Music Symposium, Notre Dame English Jrnl*

Peter Sacks P
Writing Seminars, Johns Hopkins Univ, 34th & N Charles St, Baltimore, MD 21218, 301-338-7564
Pubs: *Promised Lands* (Viking, 1990), *In These Mountains* (Macmillan, 1986)

Karen Sagstetter 🎤 ✈ P&W
6004 Madawaska Rd
Bethesda, MD 20816-3105, 301-229-2370
Pubs: *Ceremony* (State Street Pr, 1981), *New Stories from the South: Anth* (Algonquin Bks, 2000), *Antietam Rev, Glimmer Train, Poet Lore*
I.D.: Asian-American. Groups: Immigrants

Diane Scharper 🎤 P
Towson Univ, 8000 York Rd-Linthicum 219K, Towson, MD 21204-0001, 410-830-2868
Internet: dscharpe@towson.edu
Pubs: *Radiant* (Cathedral Fdn Pr, 1996), *The Laughing Ladies* (Dolphin Moon Pr, 1993), *Maryland Rev, City Paper, Saltimbanquers*

Steven Schutzman P&W
2903 Ailsa Ave
Baltimore, MD 21214-2524, 410-254-7870
Pubs: *Smoke the Burning Body Makes* (Panjandrum, 1978), *The History of Sleep* (Gallimaufry, 1976), *Sudden Fiction: Anth* (Gibbs Smith, 1986), *TriQtly*

Myra Sklarew P&W
6521 Marywood Rd
Bethesda, MD 20817, 202-885-2811
Pubs: *Lithuania: New & Selected Poems* (Azul Edtns, 1995), *Eating the White Earth* (Israel; Tag Pub, 1994), *Poetry, JAMA, Jerusalem Report*

Susan Sonde 🎤 ✈ P
2011 St Stephens Woods Dr
Crownsville, MD 21032-2200, 301-858-1528
Pubs: *In the Longboats with Others* (New Rivers, 1988), *Qtly West, Carolina Qtly, Cimarron, Conjunctions, NW Rev, Chelsea*

Elizabeth Spires ♀ ⟡   P
6208 Pinehurst Rd
Baltimore, MD 21212-2532, 410-532-9752
 Pubs: *The Mouse of Amherst* (FSG, 1999), *Worldling*
(Norton, 1995), *Annonciade* (Viking Penguin, 1989),
Swan's Island (H Holt, 1985)

Margaret Stavely   P
26096 Lambs Meadow Rd PO Box 8
Worton, MD 21678-0008, 410-348-2320
 Pubs: *Stopping the Sun* (Kent County Arts Council,
1982), *The Poets Domain: A Little Nonsense Vol 14:
Anth, The Poets Domain: Straightaway Dangerous: Anth*
(Road Pub, 1997, 1996), *Sun Mag, Little Balkans Rev,
Tapestry of the Mind, Maryland Poetry Rev*

Adele Steiner ♀ ⟡   P
6211 Wagner Ln
Bethesda, MD 20816-1028
Internet: beardog9@aol.com
 Pubs: *Refracted Love* (Bootleg Pr, 1993), *Lucid Stone,
Wordwrights, Black Buzzard Rev, M Mag, So to Speak,
Maryland Rev, Schmooze*
Groups: Teenagers

Elisabeth Stevens ♀ ⟡   P&W
6604 Walnutwood Cir
Baltimore, MD 21212-1213, 410-377-8338
 Pubs: *Household Words* (Three Conditions Pr, 2000), *In
Foreign Parts, The Night Lover* (Birch Brook, 1997,
1995), *Horse & Cart* (Wineberry, 1990), *Lower Than the
Angels: Anth* (Lite Circle, 1999), *In a Certain Place:
Anth* (SCOP, 1999), *Crosscurrents, Wind*

Joseph McNair Stover   P&W
20854 Sandstone St
Lexington Park, MD 20653-2439
 Pubs: *Commander Coatrack Returns* (HM, 1989), *South
Florida Poetry Rev, Florida Rev, The Cathartic,
Potomac Rev, Connections*

John Strausbaugh   P&W
3603 Elkader Rd
Baltimore, MD 21218
 Pubs: *Red Zone, Flying Fish* (Dolphin-Moon, 1988,
1986), *High Performance, Bartleby*

Ron Tanner   W
Loyola College, Writing & Media Dept, 4501 N Charles St,
Baltimore, MD 21210-2699, 410-617-2434
 Pubs: *Best of the West: Anth* (Norton, 1991), *The
Pushcart Prize XIV: Anth* (Pushcart Pr, 1990), *20 Under
30: Anth* (Scribner, 1986), *New Letters, Literary Rev,
Iowa Rev, Michigan Qtly Rev*

James Taylor ♀ ⟡   P
Dolphin-Moon Press, PO Box 22262, Baltimore, MD
21203, 410-444-7758
 Pubs: *Shocked & Amazed! On & Off the Midway,
Artifacture* (Dolphin-Moon Pr, 1995, 1989), *Puerto del
Sol, Lips*

Michelle M. Tokarczyk ♀ ⟡   P
Goucher College, English Dept, Baltimore, MD
21204-2753, 410-337-6165
 Pubs: *The House I'm Running From* (West End Pr,
1989), *For a Living: Poetry of Work: Anth* (U Illinois Pr,
1995), *College English, Minnesota Rev, Pearl, Poetry
NY*
Groups: Feminist, Labor Groups

Margot Treitel   P
5508 Mystic Ct
Columbia, MD 21044-1856, 410-730-8575
 Pubs: *The Inside Story* (Tropos Pr, 1987), *Chicago
Rev, Prairie Schooner, Literary Rev, NER, Carolina Qtly*

Mary M. Truitt   W
418 Duvall Ln
Annapolis, MD 21403, 410-268-8526
 Pubs: *1990 PEN Syndicated Fiction Project, Louisville
Rev, Gargoyle, Mississippi Mud*

Stacy Tuthill ♀ ⟡   P&W
713 Maiden Choice Ln, Apt 5303
Catonsville, MD 21228-3935, 410-536-1877
Internet: 102047.3727@compuserve.com
 Pubs: *House of Change* (Forest Woods Media, 1996),
Taste of Smoke (East Coast Bks, 1995), *Wisconsin
Rev, Hawaii Pacific Rev, Poet Lore, Emrys Jrnl, Poets
On*

Anne Tyler   W
222 Tunbridge Rd
Baltimore, MD 21212-3422
 Pubs: *A Patchwork Planet, Ladder of Years, Saint
Maybe, Breathing Lessons, The Accidental Tourist*
(Knopf, 1998, 1995, 1991, 1988, 1985)

Kevin Urick   W
114 Hutchins Ct
Havre de Grace, MD 21078, 410-939-7062
 Pubs: *Snow World, The Death of Colonel Jones* (White
Ewe, 1983, 1980)

Patricia Valdata ♀ ⟡   P&W
36 Gina Ct
Elkton, MD 21921-2300
Internet: pvaldata@dol.net
 Pubs: *Crosswind* (Wind Canyon Pub, 1996), *In Praise
of Pedagogy: Anth* (Calendar Island, 2000), *Boomer
Girls: Anth* (U Iowa, 1999), *Salt River Rev, Grasslands
Rev, Icarus*

Michael Waters 🎤 ✈   P
English Dept, Salisbury Univ, 1101 Camden Ave,
Salisbury, MD 21801-6860, 410-742-2559
Internet: mgwaters@ssu.edu
   Pubs: *Parthenopi: New & Selected Poems, Green Ash,
Red Maple, Black Gum* (BOA Edtns, 2001, 1997),
Bountiful, The Burden Lifters, Anniversary of the Air
(Carnegie Mellon, 1992, 1989, 1985)

Riggin Waugh 🎤 ✈   P&W
PO Box 5243
Takoma Park, MD 20913-5243, 301-891-3953
Internet: rigginwaugh@aol.com
   Pubs: *Dykes with Baggage: Anth* (Alyson Pubs, 2000),
Ex-Lover Weird Shit: Anth (TOOTS, 1994), *Women's
Glib: Anth, Word of Mouth: Anth* (Crossing Pr, 1991,
1991)
I.D.: G/L/B/T, Feminist. Groups: G/L/B/T, Feminist

Irving Weiss   P&W
319 Rosin Dr
Chestertown, MD 21620-2823, 410-778-2951
Internet: iweiss@washcoll.edu
   Pubs: *Number Poems, Visual Voices* (Runaway Spoon
Pr, 1997, 1994), *Score, Caliban, Context, Wordimage,
Lazy Bones Rev, Montserrat Rev, Synaesthetic, Ubu,
Rio Mag, Spilled Ink Forum, Abraxas*
Lang: French

Julia Wendell 🎤 ✈   P
3637 Blackrock Rd
Upperco, MD 21155-9322, 410-239-4662
Internet: jawendell@aol.com
   Pubs: *Wheeler Lane* (Igneous Pr, 1998), *An Otherwise
Perfect History* (Ithaca Hse, 1988), *Missouri Rev, Prairie
Schooner, Crazyhorse, The Jrnl*

John Milton Wesley   P
c/o Jamal A. Rahman, 3942 Resierstown Rd, Baltimore,
MD 21215, 410-578-8226
   Pubs: *The Soybean Field* (Wesley, 1985), *Black
Southern Voices: Anth* (NAL, 1985), *Metropolitan*

Philip Wexler   P
9208 Chanute Dr
Bethesda, MD 20814, 301-897-8367
   Pubs: *Slow Dancer, Kansas Qtly, Z Miscellaneous,
Painted Hills Rev, Mudfish, Jacaranda Rev, Monocacy
Valley Rev*

Reed Whittemore   P
4526 Albion Rd
College Park, MD 20740
   Pubs: *Six Literary Lives* (U Missouri Pr, 1993), *The
Past, the Future, the Present* (U Arkansas Pr, 1990)

Gary D. Wilson   W
5009 Falls Rd Terr
Baltimore, MD 21210, 410-323-9356
   Pubs: *Street Songs: New Voices in Fiction: Anth*
(Longstreet Pr, 1990), *Glimmer Train, Qtly West, City
Paper of Baltimore, Witness, Amelia*

Terence Winch   P
10113 Greeley Ave
Silver Spring, MD 20902, 301-681-8956
   Pubs: *Best American Poetry 1997: Anth* (Scribner,
1998), *The Great Indoors, Contenders* (Story Line Pr,
1995, 1989), *NAW, APR, New Republic, Western
Humanities Rev*

Marly Youmans 🎤 ✈   P&W
c/o Thomas F. Epley, Potomac Literary Agency, 19062
Mills Choice Rd, Ste #5, Gaithersburg, MD 20879,
301-208-0674
   Pubs: *Catherwood* (FSG, 1996), *Little Jordan* (David R.
Godine, 1995), *Carolina Qtly, South Carolina Rev,
Southern Humanities*

Winnie Zerne   P
731 Old Herald Harbor Rd
Crownsville, MD 21032-1524
   Pubs: *Maria, Daughter of Shadow* (Pacific Pr, 1976)

Maree Zukor-Cohen   P
4708 Roland Ave, #4
Baltimore, MD 21210, 410-243-8852
   Pubs: *New Oregon Rev, Hampden-Sydney Rev,
Sojourner, Sheba Rev, Vanderbilt Rev, Touchstone*

MASSACHUSETTS

Janet E. Aalfs 🎤 ✈   P&W
PO Box 1064
Easthampton, MA 01027, 413-586-6831
   Pubs: *Reach* (Perugia Pr, 1999), *Full Open* (Orogeny
Pr, 1996), *Sister/Stranger* (Sidewalk Revolution Pr,
1993), *And a Deer's Ear* (Cleis Pr, 1990), *Onion River
Rev, California State Poetry Qtly, Peregrine, Evergreen
Chronicles*

Jonathan Aaron   P
100 Larch Rd
Cambridge, MA 02138
   Pubs: *Corridor* (Wesleyan-New England, 1992), *Second
Sight* (Harper & Row, 1982), *The Best American
Poetry: Anths* (Scribner, 1992, 1991), *Partisan Rev*

Robert H. Abel 🎤 ✈   W
27 Stockwell Rd
North Hadley, MA 01035-9644, 413-584-6257
    Pubs: *Riding a Tiger* (Asia, 2000, 1997), *Ghost Traps*
    (U Georgia Pr, 1991), *Glimmer Train, Manoa, Writer's
    Forum, Colorado Rev*

Kathleen Aguero 🎤 ✈   P
3 Gladstone St
Cambridge, MA 02140
    Pubs: *The Real Weather* (Hanging Loose Pr, 1987),
    Thirsty Day (Alice James Bks, 1977), *Poetry, Sojourner*

Alan Albert 🎤 ✈   P
63 Indian Meadow Dr
Northboro, MA 01532-2437, 508-393-9014
Internet: aa1000@aol.com
    Pubs: *Worcester Rev, California Qtly, Mississippi Rev,
    Wisconsin Rev, APR, Madrona, SW Rev, Kansas Qtly,
    Obras Mag, New Infinity Rev*

Samuel Albert   P
1550 Worcester Rd, #102W
Framingham, MA 01701, 508-879-5113
    Pubs: *As Is* (Wampeter, 1983), *Hozannah The Home
    Run* (Little, Brown, 1972), *This Sporting Life: Anth*
    (Milkweed, 1987), *Atlantic, Hudson Rev, BPJ, Harvard
    Mag, Agni*

Francis Alix 🎤 ✈   P
226 The Jamaicaway
Boston, MA 02130, 617-522-9787
    Pubs: *Ordinary Time: Anth* (Daedalus Pr, 2000),
    *Aurorean, Ibbetson Street Pr, Affair of the Mind, Black
    Bear Rev, San Fernando Poetry Jrnl, Hawaii Pacific
    Rev, Bay Windows*
I.D.: G/L/B/T. Groups: G/L/B/T

Samuel W. Allen   P
145 Cliff Ave
Winthrop, MA 02152, 617-846-1996
    Pubs: *Every Round & Other Poems* (Lotus Pr, 1987),
    Paul Vesey's Ledger (Paul Breman Pr, 1975)

Keith Althaus 🎤 ✈   P
PO Box 163
North Truro, MA 02652-0163, 508-487-2557
    Pubs: *Tikkun, Rival Heavens* (Provincetown Arts Pr,
    1993), *APR, Agni, Virginia Qtly Rev, Seneca Rev,
    Provincetown Arts, Grand Street*

Peter Anastas 🎤 ✈   W
PO Box 211
Gloucester, MA 01931-0211, 978-283-4582
    Pubs: *Maximus to Gloucester* (Ten Pound Island Bk
    Co, 1992), *Larcom Rev, Mostly Maine, Split Shift, The
    Cafe Rev, Sulfur*

Frieda Arkin   W
6 Manning St
Ipswich, MA 01938-1922, 978-356-2128
    Pubs: *The Essential Kitchen Gardener* (H Holt, 1990),
    The Dorp (Dial, 1969), *Beyond Lament: Anth*
    (Northwestern U Pr, 1998), *McCall's, Georgia Rev, Yale
    Rev, Transatlantic Rev, California Qtly, Kenyon Rev*

Jeannine Atkins   W
PO Box 226
Whately, MA 01093
    Pubs: *Fiction Network, NAR, Pacific Rev, PEN
    Syndicated Fiction, Jam To-Day*

Robert Bagg   P
582 Pfersick Rd
Shelburne Falls, MA 01370-9590
    Pubs: *Body Blows: Poems New & Selected* (U
    Massachusetts, 1988), *The Scrawny Sonnets & Other
    Narratives* (Illinois U Pr, 1973), *Atlantic, Poetry, Boston
    Rev*

Carol Baker   P
2 Main St, PO Box 307
Montague, MA 01351-0307, 413-367-0367
    Pubs: *Sojourner, Ploughshares, NYQ, Mississippi Rev,
    Stand, Women's Rev of Bks, Massachusetts Rev, The
    Nation*

Donald W. Baker   P&W
61 Seaway
East Brewster, MA 02631, 508-896-7963
    Pubs: *Search Patterns, The Readiness* (Sugar
    Creek/Steppingstone, 1996, 1995), *The Day Before,
    Unposted Letters, Formal Application* (Barnwood Pr,
    1988, 1985, 1982)

Stanislaw Baranczak   P
Harvard Univ, 313 Boylston Hall, Cambridge, MA 02138
    Pubs: *Breathing Under Water, A Fugitive from Utopia*
    (Harvard U Pr, 1991, 1987), *Selected Poems: The
    Weight of the Body* (Another Chicago Pr, 1989)

R Bartkowech 🎤 ✈   W
54 Beach St
Woburn, MA 01801-3125, 781-937-0389
Internet: www.ziplink.net/~rayb
    Pubs: *Fiction Intl, Mississippi Rev, SPR, ACM,
    Greenfield Rev, APR*

Milton Bass   W
View Dr, Rte 49
Pittsfield, MA 01201, 413-698-2271
    Pubs: *The Broken-Hearted Detective, The Half-Hearted
    Detective* (Pocket Bks, 1994, 1993)

Guy R. Beining P
27A Franklin St
Lee, MA 01238
Pubs: *Too Far to Hear, Chapters XIV-XXVI* (Standing
Stones Pr, 1997), *Carved Erosion* (Elbow Pr, 1995),
The Ghost Dance Anthology (Whitston Pub Co, 1994),
*This, Kiosk, Private Arts, Ant, Yefief, Ozone, Chain,
Rio, Lost & Found, Juxta*

June Beisch P
19 Brown St
Cambridge, MA 02138, 617-497-2241
Pubs: *A Fatherless Woman* (Cape Women's Pr, 2000),
Take Notes (Epiphany Pubs, 1992), *Radcliffe Qtly,
Epiphany, North Essex Rev, Dialogue, Northland Qtly,
Literary Rev, Tendril, NE Corridor, Florida Rev, Cape
Women Mag*

Suzanne E. Berger P
23 Billingham St
Somerville, MA 02144, 617-625-3041
Pubs: *Legacies* (Alice James Pr, 1984), *These Rooms*
(Penmaen Pr, 1979), *Harvard Rev, New York Times,
We Animals, Texas Qtly Anth, Ploughshares, Sojourner*

Denise Bergman P
82 Elm St
Cambridge, MA 02139
Pubs: *City River of Voices: Anth* (West End Pr, 1992),
*Mudfish, Frontiers, Kalliope, Moving Out, 5 A.M.,
Sojourner, South Florida Poetry Rev, Sing Heavenly
Muse, Pig Iron, Nimrod, Oxford Rev*

Sylvia Berkman W
330 Broadway
Cambridge, MA 02139-1894, 617-876-1323
Pubs: *Blackberry Wilderness* (Doubleday, 1959),
Southern Rev, Harper's Bazaar, Botteghe Obscure

Anne Bernays W
16 Francis Ave
Cambridge, MA 02138, 617-354-2577
Pubs: *Professor Romeo* (Weidenfeld & Nicolson, 1989),
Growing Up Rich (Little, Brown, 1975), *Sports
Illustrated, New Woman, American Heritage, New
Republic, Sophisticated Traveler, Nation, Town &
Country*

MaryEllen Beveridge ♀ ✈ W
40 Linnaean St, #11
Cambridge, MA 02138-1566, 617-576-1720
Pubs: *Other Voices, Emrys Jrnl, Writers Mag, South
Carolina Rev, New Orleans Rev, New Renaissance,
Georgia Rev*

Frank Bidart ♀ ✈ P
63 Sparks St #3
Cambridge, MA 02138, 617-497-1226
Pubs: *Desire, In the Western Night: Collected Poems
1965-90* (FSG, 1997, 1990)

Barbara A. Blatner P
69 Oxford St, #1
Somerville, MA 02143, 617-629-2070
Pubs: *No Star Shines Sharper* (Baker's Plays, 1990),
The Pope in Space (Intertext Pr, 1986), *13th Moon,
Lift, Fireheart, NYQ, Mildred, Groundswell*

F. C. Blessington ♀ ✈ P
English Dept, Northeastern Univ, Boston, MA 02115,
617-437-2512
Pubs: *Wolf Howl* (BkMk Pr, 2000), *Lorenzo de Medici*
(U Pr America, 1992), *Lantskip* (Wm. L. Bauhan, 1987),
*Wind, Southern Rev, Piedmont Literary Rev,
Cumberland Poetry Rev, Harvard Mag*

Harold Bond P
11 Chestnut St
Melrose, MA 02176-5306, 781-662-7806
Pubs: *Articulations: The Body in Poetry: Anth* (U Iowa
Pr, 1994), *The Magical Pine Ring: Anth* (Wayne State
U Pr, 1992), *Ararat, Kaleidoscope, Raft*

Mary Bonina ♀ ✈ P
44 Thingvalla Ave
Cambridge, MA 02138, 617-491-6416
Pubs: *City River of Voices: Anth* (West End Pr 1992),
Noctiluca, Red Brick Rev, Hanging Loose, English Jrnl
Groups: Multicultural

Paula Bonnell P
44 Codman Hill Ave
Boston, MA 02124, 617-367-5990
Pubs: *Poet Lore, Blue Buildings, SPR, Manhattan
Poetry Rev, Blue Unicorn, Pulpsmith, Floating Island,
Invisible City*

Lisa Borders ♀ ✈ W
47 Avon St
Somerville, MA 02143-1601
Internet: borderslk@aol.com
Pubs: *NE Corridor, Crescent Rev, Iowa Woman,
Painted Bride Qtly, Agassiz Rev, Snake Nation Rev,
Black Warrior Rev, Bananafish, Washington Square*

Daniel Bosch ♀ ✈ P
Expository Writing, 8 Prescott St, Cambridge, MA
02138-3929, 617-496-8472
Internet: bosch@fas.harvard.edu
Pubs: *Agni, New Republic, Harvard Rev, Western
Humanities Rev, Denver Qtly, BPJ*

Laure-Anne Bosselaar ♀ ✈ P
21 Follen St
Cambridge, MA 02138, 617-576-2887
Internet: 103325,2023@compuserve.com
Pubs: *The Hour Between Dog & Wolf* (BOA Edtns,
1997), *Urban Nature: Anth, Outsiders: Anth, Night Out:
Anth, Drive They Said: Anth* (Milkweed Edtns, 2000,
1999, 1997, 1995), *Ploughshares, Harvard Rev,
Marlboro Rev, Massachusetts Rev, Crazyhorse, Luna*
Lang: French, Dutch. Groups: Prisoners, Seniors

Marguerite Guzman Bouvard   P
6 Brookfield Cir
Wellesley, MA 02181, 781-237-1340
    Pubs: *The Body's Burning Fields* (Wind Pub, 1997), *Of
    Light & Silence* (Zoland Bks, 1990), *With the Mothers
    of the Plaza de Mayo* (Igneus Pr, 1993), *Journeys Over
    Water, 50th Anniversary Anth* (QRL, 1980, 1994)

John Bovey   W
19 Chauncy St, #2A
Cambridge, MA 02138
    Pubs: *The Silent Meteor* (Bovey, 1988), *Desirable
    Aliens* (U Illinois Pr, 1980), *Virginia Qtly Rev, Canto,
    Literary Rev, NER, Confrontation, New Renaissance,
    Ploughshares*

William C. Bowie   P
30 Smith Rd
Ashfield, MA 01330
    Pubs: *The Conservator's Song* (U Arkansas Pr, 1993)

Sally Ryder Brady   W
Brady Literary Management, 267 Dudley Rd, Bedford, MA
01730, 617-275-1842
    Pubs: *Yankee Christmas* (Yankee Bks/Rodale Pr, 1993),
    Instar (Doubleday, 1976), *Good Housekeeping,
    Woman's Day, Catholic Digest*

Jeanne Braham   P
239 River Rd
Sunderland, MA 01375, 413-665-7857
    Pubs: *Starry, Starry Night* (Brookline Bks/Lumen Ed,
    1998), *Crucial Conversations* (Teachers College
    Pr/Columbia, 1995), *A Sort of Columbus* (U Georgia Pr,
    1984), *One Means of Telling Time* (Geryon Pr, 1981)

Melanie Braverman   P&W
PO Box 1404
Provincetown, MA 02657, 508-487-6576
    Pubs: *Welcome to Your Life: Anth* (Milkweed Edtns,
    1998), *East Justice* (Permanent Pr, 1996), *American
    Voice, Carolina Qtly, Provincetown Arts, APR*

Lucie Brock-Broido   P
Creative Writing Dept, Harvard Univ, 34 Kirkland St,
Cambridge, MA 02138
    Pubs: *A Hunger* (Knopf, 1988), *American Voice, Paris
    Rev, APR, New Republic, SW Rev, Ploughshares,
    Virginia Qtly, Mississippi Rev, Ironwood, Kenyon Rev*

Martin Broekhuysen   P
22 Traymore St
Cambridge, MA 02140, 617-492-4510
    Pubs: *The Nation, SPR, Niagara Mag, Nimrod,
    Miscellany*

Ben Brooks 🎤 ✈   W
PO Box 440387
West Somerville, MA 02144-0387, 617-623-3719
Internet: bbrooks@mos.org
    Pubs: *The Icebox* (Amelia Pr, 1987), *Seattle Rev,
    Sewanee Rev, Mississippi Rev, O. Henry Prize Stories,
    American Short Fiction, Alaska Qtly Rev, Confrontation*

Olga Broumas 🎤 ✈   P
162 Mill Pond Dr
Brewster, MA 02631, 508-896-6001
Internet: broumas@brandeis.edu
    Pubs: *Rave: Poems 1975-1999, Eros, Eros, Eros:
    Collected Translations of Odysseus Elytis, Sappho's
    Gymnasium* (w/T. Begley), *Perpetua* (Copper Canyon
    Pr, 1999, 1998, 1994, 1989), *APR, American Voice,
    Sonora Rev, Zyzzyva*

Kurt Brown 🎤 ✈   P
21 Follen St
Cambridge, MA 02138, 617-576-2887
Internet: kurt_brown@compuserve.com
    Pubs: *Return of the Prodigals* (Four Way Bks, 1999),
    Verse & Universe: Anth, Drive, They Said: Anth
    (Milkweed Edtns, 1999, 1994), *Harvard Rev,
    Crazyhorse, Indiana Rev, Ploughshares, SPR,
    Massachusetts Rev, Agni*

Robert Edward Brown   P
PO Box 442
Brimfield, MA 01010-0442
    Pubs: *Gathering The Light* (Red Hill Pr, 1976), *Altadena
    Rev, Bachy, Coast, Sunset Palms Hotel*

Steven Ford Brown   P
PO Box 2764
Boston, MA 02208
    Pubs: *Astonishing World* (Milkweed Edtns, 1993), *The
    Sky Is Guilty of an Oblique, Considered Music*
    (Harrington-Black, 1989), *Harvard Rev, Seneca Rev*

Sarah Browning 🎤 ✈   P
4 Old Leverett Rd
Montague, MA 01351-9603, 413-367-0180
    Pubs: *Flint Hills Rev, Permafrost, Alembic, Borderlands,
    Flyway, Hubbub, Larcom Rev, Literary Rev, Many
    Mountains Moving, Midwest Qtly, Mudfish, Natural
    Bridge, NYQ, Onionhead, Peregrine, Poet Lore, Seattle
    Rev, Sycamore Rev, Voices Intl, Whole Notes*
I.D.: Progressive, Feminist. Groups: Women, Teenagers

Jane Brox   P
1334 Broadway
Dracut, MA 01826
    Pubs: *Here & Nowhere Else* (Beacon Pr, 1995), *In
    Short: Anth* (Norton, 1996), *Georgia Rev, Gettysburg
    Rev, Salamander, NER, Hudson Rev*

Roy Bryan   P
Cross Place Rd
Washington, MA 01235, 413-623-6446
   Pubs: *Winter Lightning* (Wild Thistle Pr, 1979), *Poetry
   East, Home Planet News*

Ruth Buchman ♀   P
5 Mountain Ave
Somerville, MA 02143, 617-623-3874
   Pubs: *Sou'wester, Harvard Rev, Antioch Rev, Embers,
   Birmingham Poetry Rev, Cricket, Sojourner, Sing
   Heavenly Muse*

Claudia Buckholts ♀ ✈   P&W
15 Clarendon Ave
Somerville, MA 02144-1704, 617-666-9040
Internet: lanbuck@ix.netcom.com
   Pubs: *Prairie Schooner, Harvard Mag, Connecticut
   Poetry Rev, Minnesota Rev, Midwest Qtly, Kansas Qtly*

Julia Budenz ♀ ✈   P
1616 Massachusetts Ave, Apt 5
Cambridge, MA 02138, 617-868-4769
   Pubs: *From The Gardens of Flora Baum* (Wesleyan,
   1984), *A Formal Feeling Comes: Anth* (Storyline, 1994),
   *Rhino, YIP: Yale Italian Poetry, NEeuropa, Notre Dame
   Rev, American Voice, Sparrow*

Carol Burnes   P
Box 364
Weston, MA 02193, 781-899-7518
   Pubs: *An Episode of Buttons* (Flarestack Pub UK,
   1998), *Fine Lines* (Headland Pubs, 1992), *Roots &
   Wings* (Emerald Pr, 1986), *13th Moon, Little Mag, Pipe
   Works UK, Rhino, Sail, CSM, Connections, Connecticut
   Mag*

Gray Burr   P
7 Snows Rd, Box 575
Truro, MA 02666, 508-349-7327
   Pubs: *Afterlives* (Singular Speech Pr, 1996), *Sparrow,
   Northeast*

Teresa Cader   P
20 Clarke St
Lexington, MA 02173, 617-863-0166
   Pubs: *Guests* (Ohio State U Pr, 1991), *Touchstones:
   Anth* (U Pr of New England, 1996), *TriQtly, Harvard
   Mag, Ploughshares, Agni, Parnassus: Poetry in Rev*

Rafael Campo ♀ ✈   P
330 Brookline Ave
Boston, MA 02215, 617-667-1306
Internet: rcampo@caregroup.harvard.edu
   Pubs: *Diva, What the Body Told* (Duke U Pr, 1999,
   1996), *The Desire to Heal* (Norton, 1997), *The Other
   Man Was Me* (Arte Publico Pr, 1994), *Best American
   Poetry: Anth* (Scribner, 1995), *Beacon Best of 1999:
   Anth* (Beacon, 1999)
Lang: Spanish. I.D.: G/L/B/T, Latino/Latina. Groups:
Latino/Latina, G/L/B/T

Jeffrey A. Carver ♀ ✈   W
102 Melrose St
Arlington, MA 02474, 781-646-1375
Internet: http://starrigger.net
   Pubs: *Eternity's End, The Infinite Sea, Strange
   Attractors, Neptune Crossing Dragon Rigger, Dragons in
   the Stars* (Tor, 2000, 1996, 1995, 1994, 1993, 1992),
   From a Changeling Star (Bantam, 1989), *The Infinity
   Link* (Bluejay, 1984), *Science Fiction Age*

John Case   P&W
37A Prentiss St
Cambridge, MA 02140

Helen Marie Casey ♀ ✈   P
85 Pokonoket Ave
Sudbury, MA 01776, 978-443-4753
Internet: HMCasey@aol.com
   Pubs: *Ad Hoc Monadnock: Anth* (Monadnock Writers
   Group, 1995), *Larcom Rev, NE Corridor, Laurel Rev,
   Windhover, Worcester Rev, CSM, Passager*

Elena Castedo   P&W
Accent Media, 36 Lancaster St, Cambridge, MA
02140-2840, 617-492-6026
   Pubs: *Paradise* (Grove Pr, 1995), *El Paraiso* (Ediciones
   B, 1994), *Prairie Schooner, New Letters, Phoebe,
   Afro-Hispanic Rev, Listening to Ourselves, Iguana
   Dreams, Mirrored Garden*

Ed Cates ♀ ✈   P
72 Moreland St, 1st Fl
Somerville, MA 02145, 617-625-1945
   Pubs: *The Gypsy's Bible, Geopolitics* (Arm-in-Arm,
   1994, 1979), *Remember Your Dreams* (Olympic Music
   Pub, 1981), *Imagine, Z Misc, Moody Street Rev,
   Noctaluca, Boston Literary Rev, Door #3*
Groups: G/L/B/T

Karen Chase ♀ ✈   P&W
PO Box 634
Lenox, MA 01240, 413-637-0505
   Pubs: *Kazimierz Square* (Cavan Kerry Pr, 2000),
   *Introduction to Literature: Anth, Introduction to Poetry:
   Anth* (Norton, 1998, 1998), *Yellow Silk: Anth* (Crown,
   1990), *New Republic, Yale Rev, New Yorker,
   Gettysburg Rev*

Naomi Feigelson Chase   P
PO Box 1231, 66 Depot Rd
Truro, MA 02666-1231, 508-349-1991
   Pubs: *Stacked, Waiting for the Messiah in Somerville,
   Massachusetts* (Garden Street Pr, 1998, 1993),
   Listening for Water (Archival Pr, 1987), *Harvard Rev,
   South Coast Poetry Jrnl, Yankee, American Literary
   Rev, Prairie Schooner, Amaranth, ELF, Lowell Rev*

Polly Chase   P
17 Lovers Ln
Groton, MA 01450, 508-448-5093
    Pubs: *Cancelled Reservations* (Poet Pr, 1986), *Poet
    Lore, Driftwood East, Jean's Jrnl*

Helen Chasin   P
9 South St Ct
Rockport, MA 01966, 508-546-2937
    Pubs: *Casting Stones* (Little, Brown, 1975), *Coming
    Close* (Yale U Pr, 1968)

Laura Chester   P&W
25 Rose Hill
Alford, MA 01230, 413-528-0458
    Pubs: *The Story of the Lake* (Faber & Faber, 1995),
    Bitches Ride Alone (Black Sparrow, 1991), *The
    Unmade Bed: Anth* (HC, 1992)

James William Chichetto   P
PO Box 136
South Easton, MA 02375-0136
    Pubs: *Homage to Father Sorin* (Connecticut Poetry Rev
    Pr, 1993), *Blood to Remember: American Poets on the
    Holocaust: Anth* (Texas Tech U, 1991), *Poem, Colorado
    Rev, Boston Globe*

M. Riesa Clark   P
14 Windsor Rd
Beverly, MA 01915-2626, 978-524-0157
    Pubs: *Laurels: Anth* (Laurel Pr, 1994), *Parnassus, Night
    Roses, Moonstone Blue, World Order, The Poetry
    Peddler, Bitterroot*

John J. Clayton ⬤ ✈   W
English Dept, Univ Massachusetts, Amherst, MA 01003,
413-548-9645
Internet: jclayton@english.umass.edu
    Pubs: *Radiance* (OSU Pr, 1998), *Man I Never Wanted
    to Be* (Permanent Pr, 1998), *Bodies of the Rich* (U
    Illinois, 1984), *What Are Friends For?* (Little, Brown,
    1979), *Heath Intro to Fiction* (HM, 1999), *Esquire, Agni,
    Playboy, TriQtly, Georgia Rev*
I.D.: Jewish

Bradley Clompus   P
75 Brookings St
Medford, MA 02155
    Pubs: *Backwash, Outerbridge, Scape, Soundings/East,
    Cream City Rev, Police Beat, Pavement, Passages
    North, West Branch, Poet Lore, Amelia*

Dick Cluster   W
33 Jackson St
Cambridge, MA 02140-2424, 617-876-8464
Internet: dick.cluster@umb.edu
    Pubs: *Obligations of the Bone* (St. Martin's Pr, 1992),
    Return to Sender (Dutton, 1988)

Andrew Coburn   W
3 Farrwood Dr
Andover, MA 01810, 508-475-8701
    Pubs: *Birthright* (S&S, 1997), *Voices in the Dark, No
    Way Home* (Dutton, 1994, 1992), *Goldilocks* (Scribner,
    1989), *Love Nest, Sweetheart* (Macmillan, 1987, 1985),
    *A Woolf in Vita's Clothing, Lilacs, Charley Judd,
    Transatlantic Rev, Ellery Queen*

Judith Beth Cohen   W
Lesley College Graduate School, 29 Everett St,
Cambridge, MA 02138
    Pubs: *Seasons* (Permanent Pr, 1984), *High Plains
    Literary Rev, Rosebud, Rockford Rev, American Rev,
    New Letters*

Pat Lowery Collins   P&W
3 Wauketa Rd
Gloucester, MA 01930-1423, 978-283-2749
    Pubs: *Signs & Wonders* (HM, 1999), *The Quiet Woman
    Wakes Up Shouting* (Folly Cove Bks, 1998), *I Am an
    Artist* (Millbrook Pr, 1992), *Parting Gifts: Anth* (March
    Street Pr, 1994), *U.S. 1 Worksheets, CQ, Visions Intl,
    Wind, Small Pond, Yankee*

William Conelly   P&W
131 Montague Rd
Leverett, MA 01054, 413-548-9430
    Pubs: *Foothills, Nine Years After: Anth* (R. L. Barth,
    1987, 1989), *Tennessee Qtly, Dark Horse, Poets On,
    Pleiades, Epigrammatist, Sticks*

William Corbett   P
9 Columbus Sq
Boston, MA 02116, 617-266-5466
    Pubs: *City Nature III, On Blue Note* (Zoland Bks, 1991,
    1989), *o.blek, Lift, NAW, Talisman, Notus*

Christopher Jane Corkery   P
20 Kenwood St
Dorchester, MA 02124, 617-288-8512
    Pubs: *Blessing* (Princeton, 1985), *Boston Rev, Poetry,
    Ironwood, NER*

Bill Costley ⬤ ✈   P
One Sunset Rd
Wellesley, MA 02482, 781-431-1314
    Pubs: *Siciliconia* (Beehive Pr, 1995), *Terrazzo*
    (Malfunction Pr, 1993), *A(y)s(h)a, Rag(a)s* (Ghost
    Dance, 1988, 1978), *Ploughshares*

Steven Cramer ⬤ ✈   P
130 Bedford St
Lexington, MA 02420, 781-862-1704
    Pubs: *Dialogue for the Left & Right Hand* (Lumen
    Edtns, 1997), *The World Book* (Copper Beech, 1992),
    Atlantic, Nation, New Republic, Paris Rev, Poetry

Dean Crawford W
800 Northwest Hill Rd
Williamstown, MA 01267
Pubs: *Lay of the Land* (Viking, 1987), *Epoch, NER*

D. L. Crockett-Smith 🎙 ✈ P
131 Old State Rd
Berkshire, MA 01224, 413-499-9877
Pubs: *Civil Rites, Cowboy Amok* (Black Scholar Pr,
1996, 1987), *Black Scholar, Open Places, Minnesota
Rev, New Collage*
I.D.: African-American

George Cuomo P&W
276 Pelham Rd
Amherst, MA 01002, 413-253-0636
Pubs: *A Couple of Cops, Trial by Water* (Random Hse,
1995, 1993)

Siouxie D P
12 Wendell St #3
Cambridge, MA 02138, 617-491-8973
Pubs: *After Gary, It's Only Life* (Self/Aardvark
Enterprises, 1996, 1992), *Quest, Heartlight Jrnl, Poet's
Pen Qtly, Pagan America, Vision Seeker*

Ellen Darion W
335A Harvard St, Apt 12
Cambridge, MA 02139, 617-492-2793
Pubs: *Gettysburg Rev, Special Report: Fiction, Epoch*

Helene Davis P
19 Cherry St
Somerville, MA 02144, 617-864-1315

Hope Hale Davis W
1600 Massachusetts Ave, #704
Cambridge, MA 02138, 617-497-5988
Pubs: *Great Day Coming* (Steerforth Pr, 1994), *The
Dark Way to the Plaza* (Doubleday, 1968), *New Leader,
New Yorker, Radcliffe Qtly*

Peter Davison 🎙 ✈ P
70 River St
Boston, MA 02108-1125, 617-742-0342
Pubs: *Breathing Room: New Poems, The Poems of
Peter Davison 1957-1995* (Knopf, 2000, 1995), *The
Fading Smile: Poets in Boston 1955-1960: Anth*
(Norton, 1996), *Atlantic, Yale Rev, Frank, Nation, New
Republic, Five Points, DoubleTake, Poetry, APR*

Corinne Demas 🎙 ✈ W
Mount Holyoke College, English Dept, South Hadley, MA
01075, 413-538-2801
Pubs: *Eleven Stories High* (SUNY Pr, 2000), *What We
Save for Last* (HC, 2000), *The Disapppearing Island*
(S&S, 2000)
Groups: Children

Benjamin Demott W
English Dept, Amherst College, Amherst, MA 01002

Theodore Deppe P
30 High St
Florence, MA 01062, 860-535-4112
Pubs: *The Wanderer King, Children of the Air* (Alice
James Bks, 1996, 1990), *Kenyon, Harper's, Poetry,
Boulevard, Poetry NW, Crazyhorse*

Diana Der-Hovanessian P
2 Farrar St
Cambridge, MA 02138, 617-864-2224
Pubs: *Any Day Now, Circle Dancers, Selected Poems*
(Sheep Meadow Pr, 1999, 1997, 1994), *American
Scholar, Agni, Graham Hse, Partisan Rev, CSM,
Nation, Prairie Schooner, Yankee*

William Devoti P
Foley Rd
Sheffield, MA 01257, 413-229-8461
Pubs: *October Mountain* (Mountain Pr, 1991), *Coming
Out of It* (Hollow Springs, 1981), *Third Berkshire Anth*
(Berkshire Writers, 1982)

Richard Dey 🎙 ✈ P
178 Gardner St
Hingham, MA 02043, 617-740-2920
Pubs: *New Bequia Poems* (Offshore Pr, 1996), *The
Bequia Poems* (Caribbean; Macmillan, 1989), *Sail,
Poetry, Harvard Mag, Light, Caribbean Writer,
Caribbean Compass*

Gerard Dombrowski P
PO Box C
Somerville, MA 02143, 617-623-8017

David F. Donavel P
54 Pearl St
Amesbury, MA 01913, 508-388-2337
Pubs: *Cape Rock, Windless Orchard, Tendril, Snowy
Egret, Wind, Fireland Arts Rev, Kansas Qtly*

Susan Donnelly 🎙 ✈ P
32 Shepard St, #21
Cambridge, MA 02138, 617-491-4559
Internet: sedonne@aol.com
Pubs: *Tenderly Pressed* (Every Other Thursday Pr,
1993), *Eve Names The Animals* (Northeastern U Pr,
1985), *Norton Introduction to Poetry: Anth* (Norton,
1995), *Ploughshares, SPR, Poetry, Atlantic*
I.D.: Irish-American, Women

Susan Donovan P
Box 2662
Amherst, MA 01004-2662, 413-545-3897
Pubs: *White Lobster* (Blue Willow Inn, 1980), *Georgia
Rev, Massachusetts Rev, New Letters*

Mary Harris Driscoll P
206 W Main St
Milbury, MA 01527, 508-865-4242
    Pubs: *Soundings East: Anth* (Salem State College, 1985), *Skylark, Pegasus, Night Sun, Sounds of Poetry, Manhattan Poetry Rev, Embers, Riverwind, Potpourri, Prairie Dog, Green Mountains Rev, Black Fly Rev*

Amy Dryansky P
19 Hidden Ledge Dr
Conway, MA 01341
    Pubs: *How I Got Lost So Close to Home* (Alice James Bks, 1999), *Luna, DoubleTake, Bloomsbury Rev, SPR, Mudfish, Harvard Rev, NER, Marlboro Rev, Peregrine, Massachusetts Rev, Green Mountains Rev, Work, Eleventh Muse, Paragraph, Louisville Rev*

Andre Dubus, III W
24 Allen St
Newburyport, MA 01950-3002, 508-462-1010
    Pubs: *Bluesman* (Faber & Faber, 1993), *The Cage Keeper & Other Stories* (Dutton, 1989), *Playboy, Yankee, Crazyhorse, Epoch, Crescent Rev, Image*

Ann duCille P
Bridgewater State College, English Dept, Bridgewater, MA 02324, 617-697-1258
    Pubs: *For Neruda/For Chile: Anth* (Beacon Pr, 1975), *APR, Bridgewater Rev, Iowa Rev, New Letters*

Alan Dugan P
Box 97
Truro, MA 02666
    Pubs: *New & Collected Poems: 1961-1983* (Ecco Pr, 1983)

Susan Eisenberg P
9 Rockview St
Jamaica Plain, MA 02130
    Pubs: *Pioneering* (Cornell U Pr, 1998), *It's a Good Thing I'm Not Macho* (Whetstone, 1984), *If I Had My Life to Live Over: Anth* (Papier-Mache, 1992), *Prairie Schooner, Willow Springs, Mothering, Seattle Rev, Many Mountains Moving*

Craig Ellis ♣ ✈ P
40 Potter St
Concord, MA 01742, 978-369-5592
Internet: nlundy@ici.net
    Pubs: *Sparrow in the Supermarket* (Beehive Pr, 1997), *Aspect, Assembling, Gallimaufry, Intrepid, Nostoc, Wormwood Rev*

David Ely W
PO Box 1387
East Dennis, MA 02641
    Pubs: *A Journal of the Flood Year, Always Home & Other Stories* (Donald I. Fine, 1992, 1991), *Mr. Nicholas* (Putnam, 1974), *Walking Davis* (Charterhouse, 1972), *Poor Devils* (HM, 1970), *Time Out, The Tour* (Delacorte, 1968, 1967), *Trot, Seconds* (HM, 1963, 1963)

Leslie Epstein ♣ ✈ W
23 Parkman St
Brookline, MA 02146, 617-734-3896
Internet: leslieep@bu.edu
    Pubs: *Ice Fire Water: A Leib Goldkorn Cocktail, King of the Jews, Pinto & Sons* (Norton, 1999, 1992, 1992), *Goldkorn Tales* (SMU, 1998), *Pandaemonium* (St. Martin's, 1998), *Playboy, Georgia Rev, Harper's, Atlantic, TriQtly, Yale Rev, The Nation*

Martin Espada P
Univ Massachusetts, English Dept, Bartlett Hall, Amherst, MA 01003, 413-545-6594
    Pubs: *Imagine the Angels of Bread, City of Coughing & Dead Radiators* (Norton, 1996, 1993), *Rebellion Is the Circle of a Lover's Hands* (Curbstone, 1990)

Rhina P. Espaillat ♣ P
12 Charron Dr
Newburyport, MA 01950-3705, 508-462-9144
Internet: espmosk@juno.com
    Pubs: *Where Horizons Go* (New Odyssey Pr, 1998), *Lapsing to Grace* (Bennett & Kitchel, 1992), *Landscapes with Women: Anth* (Singular Speech Pr, 2000), *A Formal Feeling Comes: Anth* (Story Line Pr, 1994), *Poetry, Formalist, Pivot, Amer Scholar, Sparrow, Hellas*

Nancy Esposito ♣ ✈ P
34 Trowbridge St
Belmont, MA 02478-4002, 617-484-7479
Internet: nesposito@bentley.edu
    Pubs: *Changing Hands, QRL 50th Anniverary: Anth* (QRL, 1984, 1993), *Prairie Schooner, SW Rev, Indiana Rev, Nation, APR, Seattle Rev*

Howard Faerstein ♣ ✈ P
123 West St
Sandisfield, MA 01255-9792
Internet: hfaerstein@aol.com
    Pubs: *Play a Song on the Drums He Said* (Owl's Head Pr, 1977), *West Wind Rev, Poetry Motel, Airplane, Tuatara, Confrontation, Painted Bride Qtly, Touchstone, Berkshire Rev*
Groups: Prisoners, Disabled

Richard J. Fein 🎤 ✈   P
46 Irving St
Cambridge, MA 02138, 617-354-2785
  Pubs: *Ice Like Morsels, To Move into the House, At
  the Turkish Bath* (Chestnut Hills Pr, 1999, 1996, 1994),
  Kafka's Ear (The New Poets Series, 1990)
Lang: Yiddish

Alan Feldman 🎤 ✈   P&W
399 Belknap Rd
Framingham, MA 01701-2807, 508-877-4370
  Pubs: *Anniversary* (Chekhov & Co, 1992), *Lucy
  Mastermind* (Dutton, 1985), *Poetry, Virginia Qtly Rev,
  Denver Qtly*

Jyl Lynn Felman 🎤 ✈   W
8 High Meadow Rd
Northampton, MA 01060, 413-586-8080
  Pubs: *Cravings, Her Face in the Mirror: Anth, The
  Tribe of Dina: Anth* (Beacon, 1997, 1994, 1989) *Hot
  Chicken Wings* (Aunt Lute Bks, 1992)

William Ferguson   P&W
1 Tahanto Rd
Worcester, MA 01602, 508-757-1683
  Pubs: *Freedom & Other Fictions* (Knopf, 1984),
  Mississippi Rev, Fiction, Harper's, Paris Rev

Vincent Ferrini   P
126 E Main St
Gloucester, MA 01930, 978-283-5640
  Pubs: *Deluxe Daring* (Atelier, 1994), *Magdalene
  Silences, A Tale of Psyche* (Igneus, 1992, 1991), *Why,
  Atelier, First Intensity, House Organ, Left Curve*

David Ferry 🎤 ✈   P
8 Ellery St
Cambridge, MA 02138, 617-354-7327
Internet: david_ferry@hotmail.com
  Pubs: *Of No Country I Know, Dwelling Places: Poems
  & Translations* (U Chicago Pr, 1999, 1993), *The Odes
  of Horace, Gilgamesh: A New Rendering in English
  Verse* (FSG, 1997, 1992), *Raritan, Partisan Rev,
  Threepenny Rev, TriQtly, Arion, Agni*

Andrew Fetler   W
125 Amity St
Amherst, MA 01002-2202, 413-549-5056
  Pubs: *Norton Anth of Short Fiction* (Norton, 1994),
  Prize Stories: The O. Henry Awards Anth (Doubleday,
  1984), *Atlantic, TriQtly, New American Rev*

Thomas Filbin   W
104 Clear Pond Dr
Walpole, MA 02801
  Pubs: *William & Mary Rev, Cache Rev, Proof Rock,
  Mississippi Valley Rev, Boston Rev, New Renaissance*

Brent Filson   W
RFD White Oaks Rd
Williamstown, MA 01267, 413-458-5285
  Pubs: *Exploring with Lasers* (S&S, 1984), *The Puma*
  (Doubleday, 1984), *Yankee, Vermont Life*

Jack Flavin   P
634 Armory St
Springfield, MA 01104
  Pubs: *Atlantic, Massachusetts Rev, Epoch, Poetry NW,
  Plains Poetry Rev, Galley Sail Rev, Sonoma Mandala,
  Apalachee Qtly, Spoon River Poetry Rev, Midwest Qtly*

Ann Fletcher   P
PO Box 147
West Stockbridge, MA 01266-0147
  Pubs: *Qtly West, South Florida State Rev, Cimarron
  Rev, Prairie Schooner, Sing Heavenly Muse*

Marjorie Fletcher   P
36 Moon Hill Rd
Lexington, MA 02173, 617-861-9659
  Pubs: *33, Us: Women* (Alice James Bks, 1976, 1974)

Maria Flook   P&W
PO Box 2022
Truro, MA 02666, 508-487-7918
  Pubs: *You Have the Wrong Man, Open Water, Family
  Night* (Pantheon, 1996, 1995, 1993), *New Yorker, New
  Criterion, Ploughshares, Bomb*

Nick Flynn 🎤 ✈   P
Box 1341
Provincetown, MA 02657, 508-487-6950
  Pubs: *Some Ether* (Graywolf Pr, 2000), *New American
  Poets, A Bread Loaf Anth* (U Pr of New England,
  2000), *American Poetry: The Next Generation: Anth*
  (Carnegie Mellon U Pr, 2000), *Paris Rev*

Aaron Fogel 🎤 ✈   P
English Dept, Boston Univ, 236 Bay State Rd, Boston, MA
02215
Internet: amfogel@acs.bu.edu
  Pubs: *The Printer's Error* (Miami U Pr, 2001), *Best
  American Poetry: Anths* (Scribner, 1995, 1990), *The
  Stud Duck, Agni, Boulevard, American Poet*

Jack Ford   P&W
Box 6098
Newburyport, MA 01950
  Pubs: *12 Surrealist Fairy Tales* (Alphaville Bks, 1975),
  Chicago Rev, Small Press Rev, Aiieee Mag

Jan Frazier 🎤 ✈   P
183 Mt Hermon Rd
Northfield, MA 01360, 413-498-2952
Internet: janf@spire.com
  Pubs: *Our Mothers, Our Selves: Anth* (Bergin &
  Garvey, 1996), *Yankee Mag, Passages North, Plum
  Rev, High Plains Literary Rev, Artful Dodge, Kalliope,
  Calyx*

K. C. Frederick   W
68 Chestnut St, #1
West Newton, MA 02165-2549
  Pubs: *Country of Memory* (Permanent Pr, 1998),
  Sacred Ground (Milkweed Edtns, 1996), *Epoch,
  Shenandoah, Kansas Qtly, Fiction Intl, Ascent, Qtly
  West, Beloit Fiction Jrnl*

Jan Freeman 🎤 ✈   P
PO Box 487
Ashfield, MA 01330
  Pubs: *Simon Says* (Paris Pr, 2000), *Hyena* (Cleveland
  State U Poetry Ctr, 1993), *Autumn Sequence* (Paris Pr,
  1993), *Oxford Book of Women's Writing in the U.S.:
  Anth* (Oxford U Pr, 1995), *Chelsea, Massachusetts Rev,
  APR, American Voice*

Margaret Howe Freydberg   W
RR Box 21 Stonewall Pond
Chilmark, MA 02535, 508-645-2518
  Pubs: *Growing Up in Old Age* (Parnassus, 1998),
  Winter Concert (Countryman, 1985)

B. H. Friedman   W
c/o Gunther Stuhlmann, Box 276, Becket, MA 01223,
413-623-5170
  Pubs: *Between the Flags* (Fiction Collective, 1990), *The
  Polygamist* (Atlantic, 1981), *Epoch*

D. Dina Friedman 🎤 ✈   P
PO Box 1164
Northampton, MA 01061-1164, 413-586-2388
Internet: dina@frugal.fun.com
  Pubs: *Calyx, The Sun, Hurricane Alice, Paragraph,
  Black Bear Rev, Amelia, Oxalis, Worcester Rev,
  Permafrost, Pacific Poetry & Fiction Rev*

Barbara Friend 🎤 ✈   P
Atticus Books, 8 Main Street, Amherst, MA 01002,
413-542-2328
  Pubs: *Thirtieth Year to Heaven* (Jackpine Pr, 1980),
  *NEQ, Cumberland Rev, Commentary, Virginia Qtly Rev,
  Ms., Yankee*

Kenny Fries 🎤 ✈   P
42 Day Ave
Northampton, MA 01060-2353
  Pubs: *Anesthesia* (Avocado Pr, 1996), *The Healing
  Notebooks* (Open Bks, 1990), *Kenyon Rev, American
  Voice, Ploughshares, Progressive*
I.D.: Jewish. Groups: G/L/B/T, Disabled

Rocco Fumento   W
1100 Main St
Dalton, MA 01226-2202, 413-684-4006
  Pubs: *The Sea Wolf* (SLU Pr, 1998), *42nd Street* (U
  Wisconsin Pr, 1980), *Tree of Dark Reflection* (Knopf,
  1963), *Devil by the Tail* (McGraw-Hill, 1954), *Chicago,
  Ramparts*

Erica Funkhouser 🎤 ✈   P
179 Southern Ave
Essex, MA 01929
  Pubs: *The Actual World, Sure Shot* (HM, 1997, 1992),
  Natural Affinities (Alice James Bks, 1983), *Poetry,
  Ploughshares, Paris Rev, New Yorker, Atlantic*

Brendan Galvin 🎤 ✈   P
PO Box 383
Truro, MA 02666-0383, 508-349-6077
  Pubs: *The Strength of a Named Thing, Sky & Island
  Light, Saints in their Ox-Hide Boat, Wampanoag
  Traveler* (LSU Pr, 1999, 1997, 1992, 1989), *Hotel
  Malabar* (U Iowa Pr, 1998), *Great Blue: New &
  Selected Poems* (U Illinois Pr, 1990)

Kinereth Gensler   P
221 Mt Auburn St, #404
Cambridge, MA 02138, 617-576-7243
  Pubs: *Journey Fruit: Poems & a Memoir, Without Roof*
  (Alice James Bks, 1997, 1981), *Connection* (Teachers &
  Writers, 1978), *American Voice, The Bridge, Poetry,
  Ploughshares, Sou'wester, Massachusetts Rev*

David Giannini   P
PO Box 630
Otis, MA 01253-0630
  Pubs: *Keys* (Leave Bks, 1993), *Antonio & Clara*
  (Adastra Pr, 1992), *The Unmade Bed: Anth* (HC, 1992),
  Shadowplay, Sonora Rev, Tel-Let, Talisman

Celia Gilbert 🎤 ✈   P
15 Gray Gardens W
Cambridge, MA 02138, 617-864-8778
  Pubs: *An Ark of Sorts, Bonfire* (Alice James Bks, 1998,
  1983), *Queen of Darkness* (Viking, 1977), *Poetry, New
  Yorker, Grand Street*

Michael Gizzi   P
36 Cliffwood St
Lenox, MA 01240, 413-637-4215
  Pubs: *Continental Harmony* (Roof Bks, 1991), *Vers
  d'Aigrefin* (Les Cahiers de Royaumont, 1991), *TXT,
  Shiny, Talisman, Tyuonyi, Sulfur, Temblor*

Perry Glasser   W
Box 1913
Haverhill, MA 01831, 508-373-2687
  Pubs: *Singing on the Titanic* (U Illinois Pr, 1987),
  Suspicious Origins (New Rivers Pr, 1983), *Ms., NAW,
  TriQtly, Confrontation, Special Reports: Fiction*

James Glickman W
51 McGilpin Rd
Sturbridge, MA 01566-1230
  Pubs: *Sounding the Waters* (Crown, 1996), *Kansas Qtly, Redbook, Ladies Home Jrnl*

Louise Gluck 🎤 ✈ P
14 Ellsworth Park, #2
Cambridge, MA 02139-1011
  Pubs: *Vita Nova, Meadowlands, The Wild Iris, Ararat, The Triumph of Achilles* (Ecco, 1999, 1996, 1992, 1990, 1985), *New Yorker, APR, Threepenny Rev, Yale Rev, Tikkun*

Georgia Gojmerac-Leiner P
9 Union St
Natick, MA 01760-4709, 508-655-8073
  Pubs: *Whose Woods These Are: Anth* (Word Works, 1983), *96 Inc, Vermont Times, Onion River Rev, Embers, Green Mountains*

E. S. Goldman 🎤 ✈ P&W
PO Box 561
South Orleans, MA 02662-0561, 508-255-2312
  Pubs: *The Palmer Method, Big Chocolate Cookies* (John Daniel Co, 1995, 1988), *Earthly Justice* (TriQtly, 1990), *Atlantic, Missouri Rev, Cimarron*
Groups: Alzheimer's

Elizabeth Goldring P
383 Old Ayes Rd
Groton, MA 01450
  Pubs: *Laser Treatment* (Blue Giant Pr, 1983), *Without Warning* (Helicon Nine Edtns, 1995), *Asylum, Helicon Nine*

Susan Goldwitz P
9 Mendum St
Roslindale, MA 02131
  Pubs: *Dreams of the Hand* (Empty Bowl Pr, 1984), *Bellingham Rev, Eleven, Gargoyle, Dalmona*

Deborah Gorlin 🎤 ✈ P
20 Maplewood Dr
Amherst, MA 01002-1843, 413-549-4146
Internet: dgorlin@hampshire.edu
  Pubs: *Bodily Course* (White Pine Pr, 1997), *Best Spiritual Writing: Anth* (HM, 2000), *Bomb, APR, Connecticut Qtly, Massachusetts Rev, Poetry, Prairie Schooner, Crazy Horse, NER*

Tzivia Gover P&W
74 Ranney Corner Rd
Ashfield, MA 01330
  Pubs: *My Lover Is a Woman: Anth* (Ballantine Bks, 1996), *Peregrine, Malachite & Agate, Evergreen Chronicles, Sinister Wisdom, Japanophile, Sojourner, Amelia, Lesbian Short Fiction*

Jorie Graham P
Department of English, Harvard Univ, Barker Center, 12 Quincy St, Cambridge, MA 02138, 617-495-1189
  Pubs: *Swarm, The Errancy, The Dream of the Unified Field, Materialism, Region of Unlikeness, End of Beauty* (Ecco, 2000, 1997, 1996, 1990, 1987, 1983), *Erosion, Hybrids of Plants & of Ghosts* (Princeton, 1983, 1980)

Maria Grande-Conley P
724 Plymouth St
Holbrook, MA 02343
  Pubs: *The Rolling Coulter* (Missouri Western State College, 1990), *Anth of Italian American Poets* (Malefemmina Pr, 1993), *la bella figura*

Christina J. Green P
40 Ocean Ave
Salem, MA 01970-5406
  Pubs: *Up Against the Wall Mother, Poetalk, Wide Open Mag, Poetry Peddler, Free Focus, Jrnl of Poetry Therapy, The Pen, Poems of the World, Not Your Average Zine, Event*

Barbara L. Greenberg P&W
770 Boylston St, Apt 6-1
Boston, MA 02199-7705
  Pubs: *What Nell Knows* (Summer Hse/Snowberries Pr, 1997), *The Never-Not Sonnets* (U Pr Florida, 1989), *Fire Drills* (U Missouri Pr, 1982)

Bette Greene W
338 Clinton Rd
Brookline, MA 02146, 617-232-9855
  Pubs: *Them That Glitter* (Knopf, 1983), *Philip Hall Likes Me* (Dial, 1974)

Carole Gregory P
25 Custer St, Apt 5
Jamaica Plain, MA 02130-3130

Carolyn Gregory P
50 Green St, #106
Brookline, MA 02146
  Pubs: *Playing By Ear* (Green Street Pr, 1994), *Tour of Light: Anth* (Pressford, 1996), *Artword Qtly, Yankee, MacGuffin, Seattle Rev, Georgetown Rev*

Joe Haldeman 🎤 ✈ P&W
MIT, Writing Program, 14E-303, Cambridge, MA 02139
Internet: haldeman@mit.edu
  Pubs: *Forever Free, Forever Peace* (Berkley, 1999, 1997), *Saul's Death & Other Poems* (Anamnesis Pr, 1997), *None So Blind* (Avon, 1996), *1968, Worlds Enough & Time, Hemingway Hoax, Buying Time* (Morrow, 1995, 1992, 1990, 1989), *Worlds Apart* (Viking, 1983)

Anne Halley   P&W
244 Amity St
Amherst, MA 01002, 413-549-5083
    Pubs: *Rumors of the Turning Wheel* (Aife Pr, 1986),
    The Bearded Mother (U Massachusetts Pr, 1979)

Paul Hannigan   W
22 Fayette St, #2
Cambridge, MA 02139-1112
    Pubs: *Bringing Back Slavery* (Dolphin Edtns, 1976)

George Harrar ♐ ✈   W
10 Oxbow Rd
Wayland, MA 01778, 508-358-5071
    Pubs: *First Tiger* (Permanent Pr, 1999), *Best American
    Short Stories: Anth* (HM, 1999), *Dickinson Rev, Quarter
    After Eight, Rockford Rev, SideShow, Story Mag*
Groups: Teenagers, Health-Related

Jeffrey Harrison ♐ ✈   P
59 Highland Rd
Andover, MA 01810-2012
    Pubs: *Signs of Arrival* (Copper Beech Pr, 1996), *The
    Singing Underneath* (Dutton, 1988), *The Nation, Paris
    Rev, New Yorker, New Republic, Poetry*

Ken Harvey ♐ ✈   W
24 Slade St
Belmont, MA 02478-2228, 617-484-6089
    Pubs: *Baltimore Rev, Bananafish, Evergreen Chronicles,
    Green Mountains Rev, Gulf Stream, James White Rev,
    Laurel Rev, Massachusetts Rev, Nebraska Rev, Other
    Voices, River Styx, Worcester Rev*
Lang: Spanish. I.D.: G/L/B/T. Groups: G/L/B/T

James Haug ♐ ✈   P
15 Washington Ave
Northampton, MA 01060-2861, 413-584-0169
    Pubs: *Walking Liberty* (Northeastern, 1999), *Fox Luck*
    (Center for Book Arts, 1998), *The Stolen Car* (U
    Massachusetts Pr, 1989), *APR, Brilliant Corners,
    DoubleTake, Gettysburg Rev, Ploughshares,
    Massachusetts Rev, Crazyhorse*

Stratis Haviaras   P&W
Poetry Room, Harvard Univ, Cambridge, MA 02138,
617-495-2454
    Pubs: *The Heroic Age, When the Tree Sings* (S&S,
    1984, 1979), *Crossing the River Twice* (Cleveland State
    U Pr, 1976), *Harvard Rev, Iowa Rev, Columbia Rev*

Mary Hazzard ♐ ✈   W
452 Woodward St
Waban, MA 02468-1521, 617-332-6009
Internet: mdhazzard@juno.com
    Pubs: *Family Blood* (Ariadne Pr, 1999), *Sheltered Lives*
    (Pinnacle, 1981), *Idle & Disorderly Persons* (Madrona,
    1981), *Anyone Is Possible: Anth* (Red Hen Pr, 1997),
    Northern Rev, New England Writers Network, 96 Inc.

Judy Ann Heitzman   P
20 Old Barn Pathe
Marshfield, MA 02050
    Pubs: *Maybe Grace* (Sandstone Pub, 1994), *Intro to
    Literature: Anth* (Bedford Bks, 1993), *Agni, New Yorker,
    Sojourner, Yankee*

DeWitt Henry   W
33 Buick St
Watertown, MA 02172, 617-924-0012
    Pubs: *Fathering Daughters: Anth* (Beacon, 1998), *The
    Pushcart Prize XIV: Anth* (Pushcart Pr, 1989),
    *Boulevard, Texas Rev, Agni, Antioch Rev, Missouri
    Rev, Iowa Rev, Nebraska Rev, Colorado Rev, American
    Voice, Nerve*

Marcie Hershman ♐ ✈   W
46 Stanton Rd
Brookline, MA 02445-6839
Internet: mhershma@emerald.tufts.edu
    Pubs: *Safe in America, Tales of the Master Race* (HC,
    1995, 1991), *New York Times Mag, The Writer, Ms.,
    Tikkun, Ploughshares, Agni*

Alan V. Hewat   W
Thomas Hart Literary Agency, 20 Kenwood St, Dorchester,
MA 02124
    Pubs: *Lady's Time* (H&R, 1985), *Esquire, Ascent, Iowa
    Rev, New Boston Rev of the Arts, Massachusetts Rev*

Emily Hiestand   P
Palmer & Dodge Agency, 1 Beacon St, Boston, MA
02108, 617-573-0468
    Pubs: *Angela the Upside-Down Girl, The Very Rich
    Hours* (Beacon Pr, 1998, 1992), *Green the Witch-Hazel
    Wood* (Graywolf Pr, 1989), *New Yorker, Atlantic,
    Partisan Rev, Georgia Rev, Michigan Qtly Rev, Nation,
    Orion, SE Rev*

John Hildebidle ♐ ✈   P&W
MIT, 14N-434, Cambridge, MA 02139, 617-253-4452
    Pubs: *Defining Absence* (Ireland; Salmon Pub, 1999),
    One Sleep, One Waking (Wyndham Hall Pr, 1994), *The
    Errand of Keeping Alive: Anth* (Harvard U Pr, 1989),
    Yankee, Ploughshares, Poetry, Thema

Hollis Hodges   W
PO Box 436
Stockbridge, MA 01262, 413-298-4980
    Pubs: *Norman Rockwell's Greatest Painting* (Paul S.
    Eriksson, 1988)

Richard Hoffman   P
3 Gladstone St
Cambridge, MA 02140, 617-661-8043
    Pubs: *Half the House* (HB, 1995), *An Ear to the
    Ground: Anth* (U Georgia Pr, 1990), *Hudson Rev,
    Shenandoah, The Sun, American Rev*

William Holinger 🎤 ✈ W
20 Chapel St, #511-B
Brookline, MA 02446-5474
 Pubs: *The Football Wars, 21st Century Fox* (Scholastic, 1992, 1989), *Fence-Walker* (SUNY Pr, 1985), *Iowa Rev, Texas Rev, New Directions, Agni*

Lucy Honig 🎤 ✈ W
111 Dorchester St
Squantum, MA 02171
Internet: lhonig@bu.edu
 Pubs: *The Truly Needy & Other Stories* (U Pittsburgh Pr, 1999), *Prize Stories: O. Henry Awards: Anths* (Doubleday, 1996, 1992), *Best American Short Stories: Anth* (HM, 1988), *Gettysburg Rev, Witness, Georgia Rev, Fiction, Agni, DoubleTake, Ploughshares*

Shel Horowitz P
PO Box 1164
Northampton, MA 01061, 413-586-2388
 Pubs: *XY Files: Anth* (Sherman-Asher, 1997), *Breathe!* (Warthog Pr, 1980), *Against The Wall, Riverrun, Pudding, Home Planet News, North Country, Anvil*

William Hunt P
125 Christian Hill Rd
Great Barrington, MA 01230, 413-528-1639
 Pubs: *Oceans & Corridors of Orpheus* (Elpenor Pr, 1979), *Of the Map That Changes* (Swallow Pr, 1974), *APR, Paris Rev, TriQtly, Formations*

Barbara Helfgott Hyett 🎤 ✈ P
71 Mason Terr
Brookline, MA 02146-2602
Internet: bhelfgotthyett@msn.com
 Pubs: *The Tracks We Leave, The Double Reckoning of Christopher Columbus* (U Illinois Pr, 1996, 1992), *Hudson Rev, New Republic, Partisan Rev, Nation, Prairie Schooner, Agni*
Groups: Schools, Adults

Ruth Ice W
204 Aspinwall Ave
Brookline, MA 02146
 Pubs: *Epoch, Literary Rev, Kansas Qtly, Catholic Worker*

Mildred M. Jeffrey 🎤 ✈ P&W
Charles River Park, 9 Hawthorne Pl, Apt 5M, Boston, MA 02114
Internet: mimje@aol.com
 Pubs: *Detours & Intersections* (Pleasure Dome Pr, 1987), *In Autumn: Anth* (Birnham Wood Graphics, 1994), *American Land Forum, NAR, Live Poets, Xanadu*

Paul Jenkins P
40 Manning Rd
Conway, MA 01341
 Pubs: *Radio Tooth* (Four Way Bks, 1997), *Forget The Sky* (L'Epervier Pr, 1979), *New Yorker, Gettysburg Rev, Paris Rev, Kenyon, Prairie Schooner, Chelsea, Poetry NW, Malahat Rev*

Donald Junkins P
63 Hawks Rd
Deerfield, MA 01342, 413-774-3475
 Pubs: *Playing for Keeps* (Lynx Hse, 1991), *Crossing By Ferry* (U Massachusetts Pr, 1978), *APR, New Yorker, Atlantic, Sewanee Rev, Antioch Rev, Poetry*

Roberta Kalechofsky 🎤 ✈ W
Micah Publications, 255 Humphrey St, Marblehead, MA 01945-1645, 781-631-7601
Internet: www.micahbooks.com
 Pubs: *K'tia, A Savior of the Jewish People, Justice, My Brother, My Sister, Bodmin, 1349* (Micah Pubs, 1995, 1993, 1988)
I.D.: Jewish. Groups: Vegetarian

Mark Karlins P
88 Green St
Newburyport, MA 01951
 Pubs: *A Christmas Fable* (Atheneum, 1990), *Narrative of the Broken Winter* (North Atlantic Bks, 1988), *Origin, Sulfur*

Judy Katz-Levine 🎤 ✈ P
10 Hillshire Ln
Norwood, MA 02062-3009, 617-769-5931
 Pubs: *A Curious Architecture: Anth* (Stride Pr, 1996), *Diamonds Are a Girl's Best Friend: Anth* (Faber & Faber, 1994), *Bitter Oleander, Fence, 96 Inc, Salamander, Shadowplay, Hummingbird,*
I.D.: Jewish. Groups: Jewish, Children

William Kemmett P
PO Box 777
Bryantville, MA 02327-0777, 617-293-9915
 Pubs: *The Bradford Poems, Flesh of a New Moon* (Igneus Pr, 1995, 1991), *Faith of Stone* (Wampeter Pr, 1983), *Poetry East, Seattle Rev, Atelier*

X. J. Kennedy 🎤 ✈ P
22 Revere St
Lexington, MA 02420-4424
 Pubs: *Elympics* (Penguin Putnam, 1999), *Uncle Switch* (S&S, 1997), *Dark Horses: New Poems* (Johns Hopkins U Pr, 1992), *Best American Poetry: Anth* (Scribner, 1999)

Rod Kessler 🎤 ✈   W
Salem State College, English Dept, Salem, MA 01970,
978-542-6247
Internet: rkessler@salem.mass.edu
   Pubs: *Off in Zimbabwe* (U Missouri Pr, 1985),
   Outsiders: Anth (Milkweed Edtns, 1999), *Flash Fiction:
   Anth* (Norton, 1992), *North Shore Mag, Dudley Rev,
   Chariton Rev, Calliope, Harvard Rev, Radcliffe Qtly*

Claire Keyes 🎤 ✈   P
12 Higgins Rd
Marblehead, MA 01945-2122, 781-631-9454
Internet: ckeyes@erols.com
   Pubs: *Rising & Falling* (Foothills, 1999), *Onset Rev,
   Larcom Rev, Talking River Rev, Blueline, Fresh
   Ground, Vermont Literary Rev, Spoon River Poetry Rev,
   Earth's Daughters, Zone 3, Crania@digitaldaze.com,
   Eleventh Muse, Sojourner*
Groups: Seniors

Robert Lord Keyes   P
40 S Valley Rd
Amherst, MA 01002-9768, 413-253-2739
   Pubs: *Massachusetts Rev, Fresh Ground, Green Age,
   Spitball, Westwind Rev, Green Mountains Rev, Critical
   Times, Embers, The Fan, Wind, BPJ*

Rudy John Kikel 🎤 ✈   P
154 W Newton St
Boston, MA 02118, 617-421-6987
Internet: RudyK@aol.com
   Pubs: *Period Pieces* (Pride Imprints, 1997), *Long
   Division* (Writers Block Pub, 1993), *Lasting Relations*
   (Sea Horse, 1984), *Gents, Bad Boys & Barbarians:
   Anth* (Alyson Pub, 1995), *Kenyon Rev, Massachusetts
   Rev, Shenandoah*
I.D.: G/L/B/T. Groups: G/L/B/T

Richard E. Kim   W
59 Leverett Rd
Shutesbury, MA 01072
   Pubs: *In Search of Lost Years* (Korea; Suh Moon Pub,
   1985)

Norman Andrew Kirk   P
14 Bayfield Rd
Wayland, MA 01778
   Pubs: *Panda Zoo* (West of Boston, 1983), *Some
   Poems My Friends* (Four Zoas/Night Hse, 1981),
   Atlantic, Bitterroot, Poet Lore, Poem, Negative Capability

Stanley Koehler   P
54 Hills Rd
Amherst, MA 01002, 413-549-1505
   Pubs: *The Perfect Destroyers: Poems of WWII*
   (Stinehour Pr, 1995), *The Fact of Fall* (U
   Massachusetts Pr, 1969), *Sewanee Rev, Poetry, Yale
   Rev, Massachusetts Rev*

Norman Kotker   W
45 Lyman Rd
Northampton, MA 01060, 413-586-5207
   Pubs: *Billy in Love* (Zoland, 1996), *Learning About God*
   (H Holt, 1988), *Miss Rhode Island* (FSG, 1978)

Zane Kotker   W
160 Main St
Northampton, MA 01060-3134, 413-584-4597
   Pubs: *Try to Remember* (Random Hse, 1997), *White
   Rising, A Certain Man, Bodies in Motion* (Knopf, 1981,
   1976, 1972), *Mademoiselle*

Herbert Krohn   P
53 Centre St
Brookline, MA 02146, 617-232-6904
   Pubs: *Partisan Rev, Nation, New Yorker, Evergreen
   Rev, Boston Phoenix, Chelsea, Village Voice*

Joseph Langland   P
16 Morgan Cir
Amherst, MA 01002-1131, 413-549-6517
   Pubs: *Selected Poems* (APR, 1992), *Twelve Poems*
   (Adastra Pr, 1991), *A Dream of Love* (Pleiades Pr,
   1986), *New Yorker, Paris Rev, Massachusetts Rev, The
   Nation*

Jacqueline Lapidus   P
PO Box 902
Provincetown, MA 02657
   Pubs: *Ultimate Conspiracy* (Lynx Pubs, 1987), *Starting
   Over* (Out & Out, 1977), *Conditions, Sinister Wisdom,
   Hanging Loose, Women's Rev of Bks*

Joseph Lease   P
25 Story St, #1
South Boston, MA 02127, 617-268-6211
   Pubs: *Human Rights* (Zoland Bks, 1998), *Grand Street,
   Talisman, Paris Rev, Lingo, Colorado Rev, Denver Qtly,
   Pequod, Agni, NAW, Boston Rev*

Anne D. LeClaire 🎤 ✈   W
PO Box 656
South Chatham, MA 02659-1512, 508-432-6395
Internet: analee@capecod.net
   Pubs: *Sideshow* (Viking, 1994), *Grace Point* (Signet,
   1993), *Every Mother's Son, Land's End* (Bantam, 1987,
   1985), *I've Always Meant to Tell You: Anth* (Pocket
   Bks, 1997)

Jane LeCompte   W
PO Box 1393
Boston, MA 02117-1393
   Pubs: *Moon Passage* (H&R, 1989)

Jacob Leed   P
111 Gore St
Cambridge, MA 02141
  Pubs: *3x3* (Toucan Pr, 1986), *You Reading, Looking at
  Chinese Pictures* (Shelley's Pr, 1983, 1981)

Judith Leet   P
16 Gate House Rd
Chestnut Hill, MA 02167, 617-277-3857
  Pubs: *Flowering Trees & Shrubs: The Botanical
  Painting of Esther Heins* (H. Abrams, 1987), *Agni*

Brad Leithauser ♀ ✈   P&W
Mount Holyoke College, English Dept, South Hadley, MA
01075
  Pubs: *Hence* (Knopf, 1989)

Ruth Lepson ♀ ✈   P
49 Phillips St
Watertown, MA 02472-3917, 617-926-6990
  Pubs: *Dreaming in Color* (Alice James Bks, 1980),
  *POTEPOETZINE, Agni, Women's Rev of Bks,
  Ploughshares, Helicon Nine, Sojourner, Contact II,
  Harbor Rev, Poet Lore*
  I.D.: Jewish. Groups: Children, College/Univ

Kathleen Leverich   W
40 Rogers Ave
Somerville, MA 02144
  Pubs: *The New You* (Scholastic Pr, 2000), *Best
  Enemies Forever* (Greenwillow Bks, 1995), *Brigid the
  Bad, Brigid the Bewitched* (Random Hse, 1995, 1994),
  Ascent, Yankee, Mademoiselle, Cosmopolitan

Ruth Levin   P
221 Mt Auburn St, #307
Cambridge, MA 02138-4847, 617-491-7229
  Pubs: *Birthmark* (CCC, 1992), *To Whom it May
  Concern* (William L. Bouhan, 1986), *Southern Rev,
  Sewanee Rev, New Renaissance, Prairie Schooner, The
  Nation*

Miriam Levine   P
26-A Academy St
Arlington, MA 02174, 617-646-2618
  Pubs: *Devotion: A Memoir* (U Georgia Pr, 1993), *APR,
  Paris Rev, Kenyon Rev, Ploughshares, Boston Phoenix,
  Women's Rev of Books, American Voice*

Sharon Libera   P
139 Taylor St
Granby, MA 01033-9588
  Pubs: *Cries of the Spirit: Anth* (Beacon Pr, 1991),
  Ploughshares Poetry Reader: Anth (Ploughshares Bks,
  1986), *I Hear My Sisters Saying: Anth* (Thomas Y.
  Crowell, 1975), *Ploughshares, Poetry*

Karen Lindsey   P
33 Jefferson St
Cambridge, MA 02141
  Pubs: *A Company of Queens* (Bloody Mary Pr, 1977),
  Falling Off The Roof (Alice James Bks, 1975)

Margaret Lloyd   P
17 Lilly St
Florence, MA 01062, 413-584-2752
  Pubs: *This Particular Earthly Scene* (Alice James Bks,
  1993), *Poetry East, NER, The Jrnl, Willow Springs,
  Gettysburg Rev, American Voice, Planet*

Jayne Loader   W
292-Rear Whiting St
Hingham, MA 02043
  Pubs: *Wild America* (Grove-Weidenfeld, 1989), *Between
  Pictures* (Grove Pr, 1986), *The Met, Third Rave,
  WWWench, Positive, Panta, Marie-Claire, Details*

Edward Locke ♀ ✈   P
12 Flagstaff Hill Terr
Canton, MA 02021, 781-828-3978
  Pubs: *What Time Is It?, Names for the Self, Green
  Bank, Advancing Back* (Harlequinade Pr, 1998, 1997,
  1995, 1994), *Partisan Rev, Yale Rev, Poetry, Georgia
  Rev, Dalhousie Rev, BPJ, The Nation*

Edward Lodi ♀ ✈   W
41 Walnut St
Middleboro, MA 02346, 508-946-4738
  Pubs: *Northcote Anth of Short Stories* (Harold Shaw
  Pub, 1992), *Light, The Aurorean, Snowy Egret, Space
  & Time, Mediphors, New England Writers Network,
  Terminal Fright*
  I.D.: Italian-American

Gian S. Lombardo ♀ ✈   P
781 E Guinea Rd
Williamsburg, MA 01096-9736, 413-268-7012
Internet: lombardo@quale.com
  Pubs: *Sky Open Again, Standing Room, Between
  Islands,* (Dolphin-Moon, 1997, 1989, 1984), *Puerto del
  Sol, Lift, Denver Qtly, Talisman, Prose Poem, Iowa
  Rev, Agni, Quarter After Eight, Third Coast, Qtly West*

Dick Lourie   P
16 Alder-Sea, Prospect Hill
Somerville, MA 02143
  Pubs: *Anima* (Hanging Loose, 1977), *Stumbling*
  (Crossing, 1973), *The Sun, Cottonwood Rev, The
  Nation*

Steve Lowe   W
2 Laurie Ln
Natick, MA 01760, 508-655-8701
  Pubs: *Aurora* (Dodd, Mead, 1985)

Michael Lowenthal 🎤 ✈   W
11 Seaverns Ave #3F
Jamaica Plain, MA 02130-2873, 617-983-8772
Internet: maxfranz@aol.com
    Pubs: *The Same Embrace* (Dutton, 1998), *Neurotica:
    Anth* (Norton, 1999), *Best American Gay Fiction: Anth*
    (Litttle, Brown, 1996), *Men on Men 5: Anth*
    (Penguin/Plume, 1994), *Kenyon Rev, Crescent Rev,
    Other Voices, Yellow Silk*
Groups: Jewish, G/L/B/T

Betty Lowry   P
79 Moore Rd
Wayland, MA 01778, 508-358-4098
Internet: bettylowry@aol.com

Jean Lunn 🎤 ✈   P
25 Harvard St
Hyannis, MA 02601
    Pubs: *Yankee, Manhattan Poetry Rev, Sow's Ear,
    Hampden-Sydney Rev, Devil's Millhopper, Webster Rev*

Thomas Lux   P
52 Chester Ave
Waltham, MA 02154
    Pubs: *The Drowned River, Half Promised Land, Sunday*
    (HM, 1990, 1986, 1979), *Antaeus, Ploughshares*

David Lyon 🎤 ✈   P
6 Crawford St, #11
Cambridge, MA 02139, 617-864-0361
    Pubs: *The Sound of Horns* (L'Epervier Pr, 1984),
    Massachusetts Rev, NAR, BPJ

Daniel Lyons   W
34 Bartlett St, #1
Charlestown, MA 02129-2530
    Pubs: *The Last Good Man* (U Massachusetts Pr, 1992)

Jeanette C. Maes 🎤   P
64 Harrison Ave
Lynn, MA 01905, 781-599-1349
    Pubs: *The Way of Ignorance, Fantastic Confusions*
    (Sunlit Waters Pr, 1994, 1990)

Carol Magun 🎤 ✈   W
90 Marion Rd
Watertown, MA 02172-4708, 617-924-8874
    Pubs: *Circling Eden* (Academy Chicago Pub, 1995),
    *American Fiction, Artful Dodge, Jewish Women's
    Literary Annual*

Elissa Malcohn   P&W
PO Box 1764
Cambridge, MA 02238, 617-547-6533
    Pubs: *Full Spectrum: Anth* (Bantam, 1988), *Tales of the
    Unanticipated, Ice River, Diarist's Journal*

Karen A. Malley   W
North Village, #F23
Amherst, MA 01002, 413-546-4112
    Pubs: *Iowa Rev, Bottomfish, Sonora Rev, Kansas Qtly*

John Maloney 🎤 ✈   P
Allen Farm Rd
Chilmark, MA 02535, 508-645-9688
Internet: jmaloney@vineyard.net
    Pubs: *Proposal* (Zoland Bks, 1999), *Poetry, Poetry NW,
    Ploughshares, SPR, New York Times, North Atlantic*

Marvin Mandell   W
102 Anawan Ave
West Roxbury, MA 02132
    Pubs: *Best American Short Stories: Anth* (HM, 1972),
    Cape Cod Compass, English Jrnl, Offshore

Paul Mariani   P
PO Box M
Montague, MA 01351, 413-367-2820
    Pubs: *The Great Wheel, Salvage Operations: New &
    Selected Poems* (Norton, 1996, 1990), *Image, America,
    Poetry*

Paul Marion 🎤 ✈   P
Communications/Univ Massachusetts Lowell, 1 University
Ave, Lowell, MA 01854, 978-934-3107
Internet: Paul_Marion@uml.edu
    Pubs: *French Class* (Loom Pr, 1999), *For a Living:
    Anth* (U Illinois, 1995), *The Acre, Soundings East,
    Yankee, Salamander, Fan, CSM, River Rev, Bridge Rev*
I.D.: French-American

Ralph G. Martell   P
Foreign Language & Literature Dept, Westfield State
College, Westfield, MA 01086
    Pubs: *Palabras/Words, Cuadros, Ciclos* (Slusa, 1986,
    1982, 1982), *Peregrine, Stone Country*

Richard J. Martin 🎤 ✈   P
40 Searle Rd
West Roxbury, MA 02132-3014, 617-323-2547
Internet: dckmrtn@aol.com
    Pubs: *Modulations* (Asylum Arts, 1998), *Negation of
    Beautiful Words* (Igneus, 1996), *White Man Appears on
    Southern California Beach* (Bottom Fish Pr, 1991),
    American Poets Say Goodbye to the 20th Century
    (Four Walls Eight Windows, 1996), *Fell Swoop, ACM*

Valerie M. Martin   W
Houghton Mifflin Co., 222 Berkeley St, Boston, MA
02116-3764, 617-725-5000
    Pubs: *Alexandra, Set in Motion* (FSG, 1979, 1978)

Tara L. Masih   P&W
18 Dufton Rd
Andover, MA 01810-2716
    Pubs: *Essential Love: Anth* (Poetworks, 2000), *Two Worlds Walking: Anth* (New Rivers Pr, 1994), *Word of Mouth: Anth* (Crossing Pr, 1990), *Hayden's Ferry Rev, The Indian-American, Mind in Motion, New Millennium Writings, The Ledge, Pangolin Papers*
I.D.: Indian-American. Groups: Minorities

Suzanne Matson 🎤 ✈   P&W
English Dept, Boston College, Chestnut Hill, MA 02467, 617-552-3716
Internet: suzanne.matson@bc.edu
    Pubs: *A Trick of Nature, The Hunger Moon* (Norton, 2000, 1997), *Durable Goods, Sea Level* (Alice James Bks, 1993, 1990), *Harvard Rev, APR, Poetry, Indiana Rev, Shenandoah, Poetry NW, New York Times Mag*

Mary Mattfield   P
1 Emerson Pl, #5-Q
Boston, MA 02114
    Pubs: *Paintbrush, Poetry Now, Tendril, Descant, Panache, SPR, Harbinger, Folio, Graham House Rev, Webster Rev, Seattle Rev, Poetry East, Nimrod*

Mary Maxwell   P
PO Box 1120
Truro, MA 02666
    Pubs: *New Republic, Nation, Western Humanities Rev, Paris Rev, Salmagundi, Southern Rev, Pequod*

Ben Mazer   P
c/o Barbara Matteau Editions, PO Box 381280,
Cambridge, MA 02238-1280
    Pubs: *White Cities* (Barbara Matteau Edtns, 1995), *Verse, Harvard Mag, Lift, Atelier, Boston Phoenix, Poetry East, Dark Horse, Englynion, Stand, Compost*

Gail Mazur   P
5 Walnut Ave
Cambridge, MA 02140, 617-868-5753
    Pubs: *The Common* (U Chicago Pr, 1995), *The Pose of Happiness* (David Godine, 1986), *Atlantic, New Republic, Partisan Rev, Boulevard, Agni, Slate, Ploughshares, Poetry*

Grace Dane Mazur 🎤 ✈   W
35 Arlington St
Cambridge, MA 02140, 617-547-3895
Internet: gdm@math.harvard.edu
    Pubs: *Silk* (Brookline Bks, 1996), *Southern Rev, Harvard Rev, NER/BLQ, Story*

David R. McCann   P
Harvard Univ, EALC 2 Divinity Ave, Cambridge, MA 02138
    Pubs: *Form & Freedom in Korean Poetry* (E.J. Brill, 1988), *Winter Sky* (QRL, 1981)

Elizabeth McKim   P
108 Winthrop Rd
Brookline, MA 02146
    Pubs: *Boat of the Dream* (Troubadour, 1988), *Burning Through, Family Salt* (Wampeter, 1987, 1981), *To Stay Alive* (Audiotape; Talking Stone Pr, 1992)

Reginald McKnight   W
Christina Ward, PO Box 515, N Scituate, MA 02060, 781-545-1375
    Pubs: *White Boys* (H Holt, 1998), *The Kind of Light That Shines on Texas* (SMU Pr, 1996), *O. Henry Awards 1990: Anth* (Doubleday, 1990), *New Stories from the South: Anth* (Algonquin, 1990), *Kenyon Rev, Callaloo, Black American Literary Forum*

Anthony McNeill   P
CCEMBS Program, Univ Massachusetts, Amherst, MA 01002, 413-545-0031

Michael McWey   W
34 Sparks St
Cambridge, MA 02138, 617-876-1784
    Pubs: *Redbook, Seventeen, Special Report, YM, 'Teen, Apalachee Qtly, Crescent Rev, Sou'wester, Woman, Faith 'N Stuff, Rosebud, Satire, Guideposts for Kids*

Mameve Medwed 🎤 ✈   W
58 Washington Ave
Cambridge, MA 02140, 617-868-8805
    Pubs: *Host Family, Mail* (Warner Bks, 2000, 1997), *Ascent, Yankee, Redbook, Playgirl, Boston Globe, Missouri Rev*

Mark Mendel   PP&P
Box 343
Monterey, MA 01245, 413-528-4136

Ifeanyi Menkiti   P
8 Malvern Ave
Somerville, MA 02144, 617-666-2855
    Pubs: *The Jubilation of Falling Bodies* (Pomegranate, 1978), *Affirmations* (Third World, 1971)

Gary Metras   P
16 Reservation Rd
Easthampton, MA 01027, 413-527-3324
    Pubs: *Today's Lesson* (Bull Thistle Pr, 1997), *Seagull Beach* (Adastra Pr, 1995), *Atomic Ghost* (Coffee Hse, 1995), *American Voice, Poetry East, Potlatcxh, North Dakota Qtly*

Richard Michelson 🎤 ✈   P
PO Box 657
Amherst, MA 01004-0657, 413-586-3964
Internet: www.rmichelson.com
    Pubs: *Masks* (Gehenna Pr, 1999), *Animals That Ought
    to Be* (S&S, 1996), *Tap Dancing for the Relatives* (U
    Central Florida Pr, 1985), *Intro to Poetry: Anth* (Norton,
    1999)
I.D.: Jewish. Groups: Children, Libraries

Paul Milenski   W
PO Box 592
Dalton, MA 01227-0592, 413-684-2066
    Pubs: *Power Play: Individuals in Conflict: Anth* (Prentice
    Hall Regents, 1996), *Sudden Fiction Intl: Anth* (Norton,
    1989), *Witness, Wind Literary Jrnl, World of English,
    Berkshire Rev, Qtly West, Great River Rev*

Christopher Millis   P
290 Massachusetts Ave
Cambridge, MA 02139, 617-225-9608
    Pubs: *Impossible Mirrors* (Singular Speech Pr, 1995),
    On the Verge, Emerging Poets & Artists: Anth (Agni Pr,
    1993), *The Qtly, Intl Qtly, Harvard Rev, Seneca Rev*

Joan Millman   W
30 Ackers Ave, #1
Brookline, MA 02445-4160
Internet: joanmillmn@aol.com
    Pubs: *The Effigy & Other Stories* (U Missouri Pr, 1990),
    *Carolina Qtly, Virginia Qtly Rev, Ascent, Cimarron,
    Moment Mag*

Helena Minton   P
5 Random Ln
Andover, MA 01810, 508-475-6345
    Pubs: *The Canal Bed, Personal Effects* (Alice James
    Bks, 1985, 1976), *Poet & Critic, 5 A.M., Soundings
    East*

Wendy M. Mnookin 🎤 ✈   P
40 Woodchester Dr
Chestnut Hill, MA 02467-1033, 617-964-7759
Internet: jwmnookin@mediaone.net
    Pubs: *To Get Here* (BOA Edtns, 1999), *Guenever
    Speaks* (Round Table, 1991), *Urban Nature: Anth*
    (Milkwood, 2000), *Essential Love: Anth* (Grayson, 2000),
    Boomer Girls: Anth (Iowa, 1999)
Groups: Schools

Jean Monahan   P
121 Thorndike St
Cambridge, MA 02141, 617-661-9560
    Pubs: *Believe It Or Not* (Orchises Pr, 1999), *Hands*
    (Anhinga, 1992), *Shenandoah, Seneca, New Republic,
    Graham Hse, Chelsea, Webster Rev, Columbia, Nimrod*

Christine Palamidess Moore   W
35 Buena Vista
Cambridge, MA 02140, 617-491-6542
    Pubs: *The Virgin Knows* (St. Martin's Pr, 1995)

Richard Moore 🎤 ✈   P&W
81 Clark St
Belmont, MA 02478-2450, 617-489-0519
    Pubs: *The Naked Scarecrow* (Truman State U Pr,
    2000), *Pygmies & Pyramids, No More Bottom* (Orchises
    Pr, 1998, 1991), *The Mouse Whole* (Negative
    Capability, 1996), *The Investigator* (Story Line Pr,
    1991), *Poetry, Hudson Rev, APR, New Yorker, Harper's*

Andrea Moorhead 🎤 ✈   P
PO Box 297
Deerfield, MA 01342-0297
Internet: moorhead@k12s.phast.umass.edu
    Pubs: *From a Grove of Aspen* (U Salzburg Pr, 1997),
    *le vert est fragile, La Blancheur Absolue, le silence
    nous entoure* (Les Ecrits des Forges, 1999, 1995,
    1992), *Winter Light* (Oasis, 1994), *The Open Gate:
    Anth* (Deerfield Academy Pr, 2000), *Midwest Qtly*
Lang: French

Emma Morgan 🎤 ✈   P
491 Bridge Rd
Northampton, MA 01062
Internet: elmF85@hampshire.edu
    Pubs: *Staring Back: The Disability Experience from the
    Inside Out: Anth* (Plume, 1997), *Gooseflesh* (Clothespin
    Fever Pr, 1993), *Lucid Stone*
I.D.: Jewish, Disabled. Groups: G/L/B/T, Disabled

Rich Murphy 🎤   P
31 Eureka Ave
Swampscott, MA 01907
Internet: rmurphy277@aol.com
    Pubs: *E: Anth* (Universities West Pr, 1999), *Natural
    Bridge, Americas Rev, Icarus, Montserrat Rev, Spillway,
    Connecticut Poetry Rev, Grand Street, Slant, Seattle
    Rev, Blue Unicorn, International Poetry Rev, Sulphur
    River Rev*

Dennis Must 🎤 ✈   W
32 Estabrook Rd
Swampscott, MA 01907
Internet: must19@idt.net
    Pubs: *Banjo Grease* (Creative Arts Bk Co, 2000), *Blue
    Cathedral: Anth* (Red Hen Pr, 2000), *Salt Hill Jrnl,
    Writers' Forum, Crossconnect, Blue Moon Rev, Atom
    Mind, Sou'wester, RE:AL, Rosebud, SE Rev*

Mildred J. Nash   P
39 Sunset Dr
Burlington, MA 01803, 617-272-0206
    Pubs: *Beyond Their Dreams* (Pocahontas Pr, 1989),
    The Lyric, Formalist, Piedmont Literary Rev, Polyphon

Valery Nash P
12 Linwood Ave
Rockport, MA 01966, 978-546-2900
Pubs: *October Swimmer* (Folly Cove Bks, 1996), *The Narrows* (Cleveland State U, 1980), *Field, Poetry NW, Yankee, SPR, New Virginia Rev, The Bridge*

Tema Nason W
93 Longwood Ave, #4
Brookline, MA 02146
Pubs: *Ethel: Fictional Autobiography of Ethel Rosenberg* (Delacorte, 1990), *Crimson Tide: Anth* (Chicory Blue Pr, 1996), *Puckerbrush Rev, Brooklyn Literary Rev*

Judith Neeld 🎤 ✈ P
PO Box 132
Menemsha, MA 02552, 508-693-5832
Pubs: *To Fit Your Heart Into the Body* (Bright Hill Pr, 1999), *Naming the Island* (Thorntree Pr, 1988), *Sea Fire* (Adastra Pr, 1987), *Tar River Poetry, Texas Rev, Yarrow, Rhino, Massachusetts Rev*

Jay Neugeboren W
35 Harrison Ave
Northampton, MA 01060, 413-586-3732
Pubs: *Imagining Robert* (Morrow, 1997), *Don't Worry About the Kids* (U Massachusetts, 1997), *Poli: A Mexican Boy in Early Texas* (Corona, 1989), *Before My Life Began* (S&S, 1985)

Lesléa Newman 🎤 ✈ P&W
PO Box 815
Northampton, MA 01061-0815, 413-584-3865
Internet: www.lesleanewman.com
Pubs: *Runaway Dreidel* (H Holt, 2001), *Heather Has Two Mommies, Girls Will Be Girls* (Alyson, 2000, 2000), *Still Life with Buddy* (Pride Pubs, 1997), *Too Far Away to Touch* (Clarion, 1995), *Fat Chance* (Putnam, 1994), *A Letter to Harvey Milk* (Firebrand Pr, 1988)
I.D.: G/L/B/T, Jewish. Groups: G/L/B/T, Jewish

Philip Nikolayev P
334 Harvard St Apt D-2
Cambridge, MA 02139, 617-864-7874
Pubs: *Artery Lumen* (Barbara Matteau Edtns, 1996), *Verse, Grand Street, Culture Front, Exquisite Corpse*

Joan Norris P
1126 Broadway
Hanover, MA 02339-2705, 781-826-8931
Pubs: *Banquet* (Penmaen Pr, 1978), *Prairie Schooner, Nation, Ploughshares*

Marian Novick W
313 Brookline St
Needham, MA 02192-3523
Pubs: *At Her Age* (Scribner, 1985), *O. Henry Awards: Anth* (Doubleday, 1981), *Massachusetts Rev*

Nina Nyhart 🎤 P
185 Warren St
Brookline, MA 02445, 617-734-2698
Internet: nnyhart@aol.com
Pubs: *French for Soldiers, Openers* (Alice James Bks, 1987, 1979), *The Poetry Connection* (T&W, 1978), *Speaking for Yourself: Poems in Different Voices* (HC, 2000), *The Party Train: Anth* (New Rivers Pr, 1996)

Mary Oliver P
Molly Malone Cook Agency, Box 338, Provincetown, MA 02657, 508-487-1931
Pubs: *New & Selected Poems, House of Light* (Beacon, 1992, 1990), *Dream Work* (Atlantic Monthly Pr, 1986), *Paris Rev, Sierra, Southern Rev, Poetry*

David Olsen P
14 Vine Brook Rd
Westford, MA 01886-4212, 978-392-8617
Internet: davidolsen65@alum.calberkeley.org
Pubs: *The Gulf War: Many Perspectives: Anth* (Vergin Pr, 1992), *Homeless Not Helpless: Anth* (Canterbury Pr, 1991), *Larcom Rev, Poetry SF, Sunrust, Black Bear, Amelia, Poetry Connoisseur, Cicada, Bogg, Tomcat, Rockford Rev, Snakeskin, Common Touch*

Dzvinia Orlowsky P
Four Way Books, PO Box 607, Marshfield, MA 02050, 781-837-4887
Pubs: *Edge of House, A Handful of Bees* (Carnegie Mellon U Pr, 1999, 1994)

Rosalind Pace P
Box 687
Truro, MA 02666-0687, 508-349-2487
Internet: rpace@massed.net
Pubs: *Carnegie Mellon Anth of Poetry* (Carnegie Mellon U Pr, 1993), *APR, Ploughshares, Ontario Rev, Denver Qtly*

Pamela Painter 🎤 ✈ W
65 Marlborough St
Boston, MA 02116, 617-267-6799
Pubs: *The Long & Short of It* (Carnegie Mellon Pr, 1999), *Getting to Know the Weather* (U Illinois Pr, 1985), *Atlantic, Harper's, Story, Ploughshares, NAR, Harvard Rev*

Carol Ann Parikh W
54 Babcock St, #5
Brookline, MA 02146-3026, 617-731-2175
Pubs: *Side Show: Anths* (Somersault Pr, 1996, 1995), *Canto, Confrontation, Indiana Rev, The Jrnl, Literary Rev*

Ruth M. Parks P
1550 Beacon St, #11A
Brookline, MA 02246
Pubs: *Treacle on the Tongue* (Penrose Pub Co, 1994), *SPSM&H*, *The Lyric*, *Byline*, *Time of Singing*, *Coastal Forest Rev*, *Senior Times*

Marian Parry P
60 Martin St
Cambridge, MA 02138-1637, 617-876-0407
Pubs: *Margin*, *Shenandoah*, *Grand Street*, *2+2*, *Negative Capability*, *Antioch Rev*, *Carleton Miscellany*

Mark Pawlak 🎤 ✈ P
44 Thingvalla Ave
Cambridge, MA 02138, 617-491-6416
Internet: mark.pawlak@umb.edu
Pubs: *Special Handling: Newspaper Poems New & Selected*, *All the News* (Hanging Loose, 1993, 1985), *Abraxas*, *5 A.M.*, *Pig Iron*, *Transfer*, *Exquisite Corpse*, *Imagine*, *Bogg*, *Hanging Loose*, *Synaesthetic*

Peter Payack P
64 Highland Ave
Cambridge, MA 02139-1054, 617-492-2913
Pubs: *The Zen of America* (The Idea Works, 1992), *No Free Will in Tomatoes* (Zoland Bks, 1989), *Paris Review Anth* (Norton, 1990), *Asimov's Sci-Fi Mag*

Edith Pearlman W
21 Elba St
Brookline, MA 02146, 617-731-1387
Pubs: *Fiddlehead*, *Iowa Qtly*, *Alaska Qtly*, *NER*, *Other Voices*, *Boston Rev*, *Response*, *Tikkun*

Roland F. Pease, Jr. P
Zoland Books, Inc, 384 Huron Ave, Cambridge, MA 02138, 617-864-6252
Pubs: *Held Up for Answers* (Imaginary Pr, 1980), *Dreamworks*, *New York Times*, *Paris Rev*

Jean Pedrick P
48 Mt Vernon St
Boston, MA 02108, 617-227-9731
Pubs: *Mitteleuropa* (Small Poetry Pr, 1992), *An Ear to the Ground: Anth* (U Georgia Pr, 1989), *Yankee*, *Granite Rev*, *Compost*, *Antioch Rev*, *Southern Rev*, *Light*, *Press*, *Passager*

Joyce Peseroff 🎤 ✈ P
24 Balfour St
Lexington, MA 02421, 781-862-9333
Pubs: *Mortal Education*, *The Hardness Scale*, *A Dog in The Lifeboat* (Carnegie Mellon U, 2000, 2000, 1991), *Ploughshares*, *Agni*, *Kenyon Rev*, *Massachusetts Rev*

Stuart Peterfreund P
English Dept-406 HO, Northeastern Univ, 360 Huntington Ave, Boston, MA 02115-5096, 617-373-2512
Pubs: *Interstatements* (Curbstone, 1986), *Harder Than Rain* (Ithaca Hse, 1977), *Sow's Ear*, *New Rev*, *The Bridge*, *Wallace Stevens Jrnl*, *Abiko Qtly*, *Compost*

Michael Pettit P
217 W Pelham Rd
Shutesbury, MA 01072, 413-259-1602
Pubs: *Cardinal Points* (U Iowa Pr, 1988), *American Light* (U Georgia Pr, 1984), *Kenyon Rev*, *Gettysburg Rev*, *Southern Rev*, *Atlantic*

Steven J. Peyster 🎤 ✈ P
66 West St
New Salem, MA 01355-9721, 978-544-3887
Internet: speyster@mindspring.com
Pubs: *Alphabet for Zina* (Window Edtns, 1981), *City Lights Jrnl*, *River Styx*, *Telephone*, *Poets On*, *Home Planet News*, *National Poetry Mag of the Lower East Side*

Stephen Philbrick P
34 Shaw Rd
Windsor, MA 01270-9573
Pubs: *The Smith*, *Poetry Now*, *Chouteau Rev*, *Anyart Jrnl*, *Grub Street*, *Greensboro Rev*

Marge Piercy 🎤 ✈ P&W
Box 1473
Wellfleet, MA 02667-1473, 508-349-3163
Internet: www.capecod.net/~tmpiercy
Pubs: *Three Women* (Morrow, 1999), *Early Grrrl* (Leapfrog Pr, 1999), *The Art of Blessing the Day*, *What Are Big Girls Made Of*, *He, She, and It* (Knopf, 1999, 1997, 1991), *Storm Tide* (w/Ira Wood), *City of Darkness, City of Light* (Fawcett, 1998, 1996)

Ronald William Pies, M.D. P&W
PO Box 332
Bedford, MA 01730, 978-937-6028
Internet: ronpies@mass.med.org
Pubs: *Ethics of the Sages* (Jason Aronson, 2000), *Riding Down Dark* (Nightshade Pr, 1992), *Blood to Remember: Anth* (Texas Tech U Pr, 1991), *Vital Signs: Anth* (UCLA Med School, 1990), *Literary Rev*, *Oasis*

Helene Pilibosian 🎤 ✈ P
171 Maplewood St
Watertown, MA 02172-1324, 617-926-2602
Internet: rsarkiss@ultranet.com
Pubs: *At Quarter Past Reality*, *Carvings from an Heirloom* (Ohan Pr, 1998, 1983), *Half Tones to Jubilee*, *New Mexico Humanities Rev*, *Pacific Rev*, *Hawaii Rev*, *Cape Rock*, *Interim*, *Potpourri*, *Panhandler*

Robert Pinsky   P
Creative Writing Dept, Boston Univ, 236 Bay State Rd,
Boston, MA 02215, 617-353-2821
    Pubs: *The Figured Wheel, The Inferno of Dante* (FSG,
    1996, 1994), *The Want Bone* (Ecco Pr, 1990), *Agni,*
    New Yorker, Threepenny Rev

Susan Lyon Pope   W
PO Box 82
Monument Beach, MA 02553
    Pubs: *Catching the Light* (Viking, 1990), *Best of Wind:*
    Anth (Wind Pubs, 1994), *Northern New England Rev,*
    Calliope, The Writing Self

Linda Portnay   P
21 Robbins Rd
Lexington, MA 02173, 617-862-6004
    Pubs: *Wishing for the Worst* (Warthog Pr, 1993),
    Radcliffe Qtly, Northern Rev, Gulfstream, Thema,
    Kalliope, Sandscript, Slant, Worcester Rev, Wisconsin
    Rev

Carol Potter   P
27 Taylor Heights, PO Box 72
Montague, MA 01351
    Pubs: *Before We Were Born* (Alice James, 1990),
    Blueline, Massachusetts Rev, Sojourner, Iowa Rev,
    Out/Look, Field, APR, High Plains, Women's Rev of
    Bks, New Letters

Patricia Powell ♀ ✈   W
1 Dana St #11
Cambridge, MA 02138-5404
Internet: pepowell@fas.harvard.edu
    Pubs: *The Pagoda* (Knopf, 1998), *A Small Gathering of*
    Bones, Me Dying Trial (Heinemann, 1994, 1993)
I.D.: Afro-Caribbean. Groups: G/L/B/T, Communities of
Color

Stan Proper   P
Wentworth Institute, 550 Huntington Ave, #8-408, Boston,
MA 02115, 617-442-9010
    Pubs: *Portraits: Kith, Kin & Neighbors, Love Lyrics*
    (Poets' Pr, 1998, 1996), *Laurels: Anth* (E. Blanche,
    1994), *We Speak for Peace: Anth* (KIT, 1993)

Lawrence Raab ♀ ✈   P
139 Bulkley St
Williamstown, MA 01267-2020, 413-458-3870
Internet: lawrence.e.raab@williams.edu
    Pubs: *The Probable World, What We Don't Know About*
    Each Other (Penguin, 2000, 1993), *Other Children*
    (Carnegie Mellon, 1987)

Pat Rabby   P
23 Meriam St
Lexington, MA 02173, 617-861-0692
    Pubs: *Connecticut Poetry Rev, Lynx, Boston Today,*
    Glassworks, Women/Poems, The Bridge, Antigones

Richard F. Radford ♀ ✈   W
8 Juniper St, #29
Brookline, MA 02445-7112, 617-734-9893
    Pubs: *Drug Agent USA* (St. Martin's, 1991), *Trooper*
    (Quinlan, 1987), *New England Sampler, Alcoholism,*
    American Man, Pegasus, New Earth Rev, The Word
Groups: Prisoners, Seniors

David Raffeld   P
54 Henderson Rd
Williamstown, MA 01267, 413-458-4815
    Pubs: *The Ballad of Harmonica George & Other Poems*
    (Adastra Pr, 1989), *Poetry East, Phoebe, October*
    Mountain, Longhouse

Louise Rafkin   W
PO Box 1604
Provincetown, MA 02657, 508-487-4514
    Pubs: *Other People's Dirt* (Algonquin Bks, 1998), *Queer*
    & Pleasant Danger: Writing Out My Life, Different
    Mothers: Anth (Cleis Pr, 1992, 1991)

Edward Rayher   P
323 Pelham Rd
Amherst, MA 01002-1654, 413-256-8531
    Pubs: *Buffalo Spree, Antigonish Rev, Washout Rev,*
    Colorado Qtly

Monica E. Raymond   P
57 Brookline
Cambridge, MA 02139
    Pubs: *Sinister Wisdom, Iowa Rev, Heresies, Sojourner,*
    Village Voice, Light

Liam Rector ♀ ✈   P
183 Willow Ave
Somerville, MA 02144-2316, 617-623-2211
Internet: liamrector@aol.com
    Pubs: *American Prodigal* (Story Line, 1994), *The*
    Sorrow of Architecture (Dragon Gate, 1984),
    Ploughshares, Slate, Paris Rev, New Republic, APR,
    Agni

Jennifer Regan   P
992 Memorial Dr, #206
Cambridge, MA 02138-4872
    Pubs: *Cries of the Spirit: Anth* (Beacon Pr, 1991),
    Black Mountain Rev, Prairie Schooner, The Reaper,
    Ohio Rev, Confrontation, Hudson Rev, Chelsea

James S. Reinbold   W
44 School St
Rehoboth, MA 02769-2204

Steven Riel 🎤 ✈   P
PO Box 679
Natick, MA 01760-0006
    Pubs: *How to Dream* (Amherst Writers & Artists, 1992),
    Badboy Book of Erotic Poetry: Anth (Masquerade Bks,
    1995), *Art & Understanding, Minnesota Rev, Christopher
    Street*
I.D.: G/L/B/T, Latino/Latina. Groups: Franco-American,
G/L/B/T

David Rivard 🎤 ✈   P
72 Inman St, Apt A
Cambridge, MA 02139-1213, 617-661-6388
Internet: drivard@channel1.com
    Pubs: *Bewitched Playground, Wise Poison* (Graywolf,
    2000, 1996), *Torque* (U Pittsburgh Pr, 1988), *Poetry,
    Ploughshares, TriQtly, NAR, NER*

Laura Rodley 🎤 ✈   P
PO Box 63
Shelburne Falls, MA 01370-0063
    Pubs: *Massachusetts Rev, Prose Poem, Peregrine,
    Connecticut River Rev, Paragraph, Blueline, Earth's
    Daughters, Sanctuary, Zahara*

Tony Rogers 🎤 ✈   W
58 Larchmont Ave
Waban, MA 02468-2031, 617-965-5125
Internet: roge@med.mit.edu
    Pubs: *Larcom Rev, Painted Hills Rev, Outerbridge, Half
    Tones to Jubilee, Wooster Rev, Four Quarters, Boston
    Monthly, Oak Square, Wind, Thema*

John J. Ronan 🎤 ✈   P
Box 5524
Gloucester, MA 01930-0007, 978-525-2022
Internet: jronan@nscc.mass.edu
    Pubs: *John Ronan's Greatest Hits* (Pudding Hse, 2000),
    The Curable Corpse, The Catching Self (Folly Cove
    Bks, 1999, 1996), *Threepenny Rev, SPR, Folio,
    Greensboro Rev, NER, Yankee*
Lang: French. I.D.: Middle-Aged. Groups: College/Univ,
Women

Daniel Asa Rose   W
138 Bay State Rd
Rehoboth, MA 02769, 508-252-6315
    Pubs: *Small Family with Rooster, Flipping for It* (St.
    Martin's Pr, 1988, 1987), *Esquire, Playboy, Vanity Fair,
    New Yorker, GQ, New York Times Mag, Partisan Rev*

Jennifer Rose 🎤 ✈   P
94 Prospect St
Waltham, MA 02453-8501, 781-893-0361
Internet: jenr@tiac.net
    Pubs: *The Old Direction of Heaven* (Truman State U
    Pr, 2000)
Groups: G/L/B/T, Jewish

George H. Rosen   W
2 Barberry Heights Rd
Gloucester, MA 01930-1202, 978-281-3561
    Pubs: *Black Money* (Scarborough Hse, 1990), *Descant,
    NAR, Yale Rev, Harper's, A Matter of Crime, Ascent*

Karen Rosenberg   W
c/o Society of Fellows, Harvard Univ, 78 Mount Auburn
St, Cambridge, MA 02138, 617-495-2485
    Pubs: *Water Baby: Anth* (John Murray, 1995), *The
    Year's Best: Anth* (Tickled by Thunder, 1996), *Orbis,
    Metropolitan, Vigil, Potato Eyes, Oasis, Swansea Rev,
    Response, Prop*

Sarah Rossiter   W
72 Church St
Weston, MA 02193, 617-894-6184
    Pubs: *Beyond This Bitter Air* (U Illinois Pr, 1987), *The
    Human Season* (Little, Brown, 1987)

Eleanor Roth   W
131 Clarendon St
North Dartmouth, MA 02747-3269, 508-993-3328
Internet: ebroth@gis.net
    Pubs: *Female, Living, Herworld, The Humanist, Asia
    Mag, Asian Wall Street Jrnl, Green's Fiction Mag*

Lee Rudolph   P
Math Dept, Clark Univ, 950 Main St, Worcester, MA
01610
    Pubs: *Contemporary New England Poetry: Anth* (Texas
    Rev Pr, 1987), *New Yorker, Clark Now*

Marieve Rugo   P
31 Fayerweather St
Cambridge, MA 02138-3329, 617-969-6667
    Pubs: *Fields of Vision* (U Alabama Pr, 1983), *Kenyon
    Rev, Chelsea, Black Warrior, New Letters, SPR, North
    Dakota Qtly*

Hilary Russell   P
PO Box 578
Sheffield, MA 01257, 413-229-2549
    Pubs: *BPJ, Ploughshares, Carolina Qtly, Country Jrnl,
    Boulevard*

Catherine Sasanov 🎤 ✈   P
50 Follen St, Apt 101
Cambridge, MA 02138-3506, 617-661-7256
    Pubs: *Las Horas de Belén: A Book of Hours* (Mabou
    Mines, 1999), *Traditions of Bread & Violence* (Four
    Way Bks, 1996), *Field, Agni, Image*

Peter Saunders 🎤 ✈ P
Steppingstone, Box 327, Chatham, MA 02633,
508-945-5283
Internet: poetpeter@juno.com
  Pubs: *Ask Any Frog* (Steppingstone, 2000),
  *Provincetown Mag, CSM, Poetry In Your Face - P'town,
  WOMR-FM Poetry Corner, Steppingstone, Saltwind,
  Longfellow, Aurorean, Cape Codder, Cape Cod
  Chronicle*

Cheryl Savageau P&W
19 Walnut Hill Dr
Worcester, MA 01602, 508-752-3953
  Pubs: *Dirt Road Home, Poetry Like Bread: Anth*
  (Curbstone Pr, 1995, 1994), *Massachusetts Rev, Agni,
  River Styx, Indiana Rev, Nebraska English Jrnl, Boston
  Rev*

Mark Schafron W
6 Messenger St
Plainville, MA 02762-2206, 508-226-3519
  Pubs: *Raconteur, Atom Mind, Fresh! Mag, American
  Epitaph, Fiction Forum*

Randi Schalet 🎤 ✈ W
157 DeForest St
Boston, MA 02131-4907, 617-323-1942
Internet: rgschalet@cs.com
  Pubs: *Lunch* (Clothespin Fever Pr, 1994)
I.D.: G/L/B/T. Groups: Latino/Latina, G/L/B/T

Ada Jill Schneider 🎤 ✈ P
120 Friends Cove
Somerset, MA 02726-5900, 508-672-5989
Internet: adajillschneider@yahoo.com
  Pubs: *The Museum of My Mother, Fine Lines & Other
  Wrinkles* (Gratlau Pr, 1996, 1993), *Her Face in the
  Mirror: Anth* (Beacon Pr, 1994), *Nedge, Synaesthetic,
  Newport Rev, Crone's Nest, Mediphors, Everyday
  Epiphanies, Muddy River Poetry Rev*
Groups: Women

Nina Schneider W
Music St
West Tisbury, MA 02575, 508-693-5746
  Pubs: *The Woman Who Lived in a Prologue* (HM,
  1980), *Paris Rev*

Pat Schneider 🎤 ✈ P&W
PO Box 1076
Amherst, MA 01004, 413-253-3307
Internet: www.patschneider.com
  Pubs: *Olive Street Transfer* (Amherst Writers & Artists
  Pr, 1999), *Ms., Sewanee Rev, Chrysalis*

Ron Schreiber 🎤 ✈ P
9 Reed St
Cambridge, MA 02140-2413
  Pubs: *John* (Hanging Loose Pr/Calamus Bks, 1988),
  Tomorrow Will Really Be Sunday (Calamus, 1985)

Lloyd Schwartz 🎤 ✈ P
27 Pennsylvania Ave
Somerville, MA 02145-2217, 617-666-3233
Internet: lloyd.schwartz@umb.edu
  Pubs: *Cairo Traffic, Goodnight, Gracie* (U Chicago Pr,
  2000, 1992), *Handbook of Heartbreak: Anth* (Morrow,
  1998), *Best American Poetry 1994: Anth*
  (Scribner/Macmillan, 1994), *New Yorker, Paris Rev*

Elizabeth Searle 🎤 ✈ W
18 College Ave
Arlington, MA 02474-2253, 781-641-2906
Internet: jhodgkinson@mediaone.net
  Pubs: *Celebrities in Disgrace, A Four-Sided Bed*
  (Graywolf Pr, 2001, 1998), *My Body to You* (U Iowa
  Pr, 1993), *Lovers: Anth* (Crossing Pr, 1992), *Five
  Points, Ploughshares, Redbook, Kenyon Rev, Boulevard,
  Epoch, California Qtly, Agni*

Richard Seltzer 🎤 ✈ W
PO Box 161
West Roxbury, MA 02132
Internet: www.samizdat.com
  Pubs: *The Lizard of Oz* (B&R Samizdat Express, 1994),
  The Name of the Hero (J.P. Tarcher/HM, 1981), *Antic,
  Analog*

Richard C. Shaner 🎤 ✈ P
701 Nantascot Pl, 155 George Washington Blvd, Hull, MA
02045-3000, 617-925-2654
Internet: shaner@umbsky.cc.umb.edu
  Pubs: *A Nantucket Bestiary* (Poets Corner Pr, 1980),
  *College English, American Land Forum, Passages
  North, Waves, Hanging Loose*

Robert B. Shaw P
English Dept, Mount Holyoke College, South Hadley, MA
01075, 413-538-2444
Internet: rshaw@mtholyoke.edu
  Pubs: *Below the Surface, The Post Office Murals
  Restored* (Copper Beech Pr, 1999, 1994), *The Wonder
  of Seeing Double* (U Massachusetts Pr, 1988),
  Comforting the Wilderness (Wesleyan, 1977)

Beverly Shaw-Johnson P
217 Scudder Ave
Hyannis, MA 02601, 508-771-3471
  Pubs: *Massachusetts State Poetry Society Anth*
  (Massachusetts State Poetry Society, 1980), *Arizona
  Highways, Back Bay View, Worcester Rev, Itsblotto
  Karmics, Jlag Rev, Gargoyle*

Tom F. Sheehan 🎤 ✈ P
217 Central St
Saugus, MA 01906-2110, 617-233-5041
Internet: tomsheehan@mediaone.net
  Pubs: *A Gathering of Memories* (Millennium Assoc,
  2000), *Reflections from Vinegar Hill* (Slagpile Pr, 1999),
  Hummers, Knucklers & Slow Curves (U Illinois, 1991),
  The Best of Spitball: Anth (Pocket Bks, 1989),
  MacGuffin, Aethlon, Snowbound, Electric Acorn
I.D.: Environmentalist

Eve Shelnutt   P&W
College of Holy Cross, English Dept, One College St,
Worcester, MA 01610-2395, 614-593-2756
  Pubs: *First a Long Hesitation, Recital in a Private
  Room* (Carnegie Mellon, 1992, 1988), *The Writing
  Room* (Longstreet Pr, 1989)

Nancy Sherman   P
2 Brenda Ln
Belchertown, MA 01007-9758, 413-586-6151
  Pubs: *Ploughshares, Grolier Annual, Massachusetts
  Rev, Seneca Rev, Cream City Rev, AWP Chronicle*

Nina Silver   P&W
734 Huntington Rd
Worthington, MA 01098, 413-238-7769
  Pubs: *Birthing* (Woman In The Moon Pubs, 1996),
  Women's Glib: Anth (Crossing Pr, 1991), *Off Our
  Backs, New Internationalist, New Press, Jewish
  Currents*

Lazare Seymour Simckes   W
Williams College, 301 Stetson, Williamstown, MA 01267
  Pubs: *The Comatose Kids* (Fiction Collective, 1976),
  Seven Days of Morning (Random Hse, 1963)

Louise Simons   P
44 Arrowhead Rd
Weston, MA 02193, 781-891-1246
  Pubs: *Three Rivers Poetry Jrnl, 13th Moon, Caprice,
  Minnesota Rev, Painted Bride Qtly, Exquisite Corpse*

Jonathan Sisson   P
19 Barna Rd
Boston, MA 02124-4713, 617-825-5430
  Pubs: *Where Silkwood Walks* (Lake Street Rev Pr,
  1981), *Poetry, Paris Rev, Antaeus*

R. D. Skillings   W
730 Commercial St
Provincetown, MA 02657-1761, 508-487-3768
  Pubs: *Where the Time Goes* (U Pr of New England,
  1999), *In a Murderous Time, P-Town Stories*
  (Applewood Bks, 1984, 1980)

John Skoyles 🎤 ✈   P
PO Box 2022
Truro, MA 02666-2022, 508-487-7918
Internet: john_skoyles@emerson.edu
  Pubs: *Definition of the Soul, Permanent Change, A
  Little Faith* (Carnegie Mellon, 1998, 1990, 1981), *The
  Smoky Mountain Cage Bird Society* (Kodansha America,
  1997)

Tom Sleigh   P
1 Stinson Ct #3
Cambridge, MA 02139, 617-876-9002
  Pubs: *The Chain, Waking* (U Chicago Pr, 1996, 1990),
  After One (HM, 1983), *New Yorker, Poetry, Threepenny
  Rev, Partisan Rev, New Republic, Grand Street, Slate,
  TriQtly, Paris Rev*

Joel Sloman   P
82 Harvard Ave
Medford, MA 02155, 781-488-3788
  Pubs: *Stops* (Zoland Bks, 1997), *Virgil's Machines*
  (Norton, 1966)

William Jay Smith 🎤 ✈   P
63 Luther Shaw Rd
Cummington, MA 01026-9787, 413-634-5546
  Pubs: *The Cherokee Lottery* (Curbstone Pr, 2000)
  Around My Room, Laughing Time (FSG, 2000, 1990),
  The World Below the Window (Johns Hopkins U Pr,
  1998), *Here Is my Heart: Anth* (Little, Brown, 1999),
  New Criterion
Lang: French. I.D.: Native American. Groups: Children

Jacques Sollov   P
White Eagle Pub, PO Box 1332/Dept S-0111, Lowell, MA
01853, 603-881-5392
  Pubs: *Gold of the Stars, Reborn Again in the Kingdom*
  (White Eagle Pub, 1983, 1982)

Paul B. Solyn   P
35 Mt Hood Rd, #2
Brighton, MA 02146-1340
  Pubs: *Mistress Quickly's Garden* (Raintree Pr, 1978),
  New Letters, Minnesota Rev, Northeast

Stephen Sossaman 🎤 ✈   P
Westfield State College, English Dept, Westfield, MA
01086, 413-572-5335
Internet: s_sossaman@foma.wsc.ma.edu
  Pubs: *Bridge Traffic: Anth* (Tiny Poems Pr, 1999), *Viet
  Nam: Anth* (Bowling Green U Pr, 1987), *South Coast
  Poetry Rev, Southern Humanities Rev, Antigonish Rev,
  Ball State U Forum, Modern Haiku, Paris Rev,
  Formalist, Dalhousie Rev, Centennial Rev*

Kathleen (Drucker) Spivack 🎤 ✈   P&W
53 Spruce St
Watertown, MA 02472, 617-926-1637
Internet: kspivack@mac.com
  Pubs: *The Break-up Variations* (Zoland Bks, 2002), *The
  Honeymoon* (Graywolf Pr, 1986), *The Beds We Lie In*
  (Scarecrow Pr, 1986), *Kenyon Rev, New Letters,
  Harvard Rev, NAR, Poetry, Ploughshares, Agni, New
  Yorker*

Sue Standing 🎤 ✈   P
Wheaton College, English Dept, Norton, MA 02766
Internet: sstandin@wheatonma.edu
    Pubs: *Gravida* (Four Way Bks, 1995), *Deception Pass*
    (Alice James Bks, 1984), *APR, Iowa Rev, Nation,*
    Partisan Rev, Poetry NW, SW Rev

Judith W. Steinbergh 🎤 ✈   P
99 Evans Rd
Brookline, MA 02445-2117, 617-734-1416
Internet: judithst@aol.com
    Pubs: *Writing My Will, A Living Anytime* (Talking Stone
    Pr, 2000, 1988), *Winners: Washington Prize: Anth*
    (Word Works Pr, 1999), *Sojourner, Calyx*
I.D.: Jewish, Women. Groups: College/Univ, Seniors

Robert Steinem   P
40 Stranahan
Colrain, MA 01340, 413-624-3709
    Pubs: *This Wood Sang Out: Anth* (Literacy Project,
    1995), *Optimist, Poetry Motel, Sanctuary, ELF, Poems*
    for a Livable Planet, Written Arts, Peregrine, Folio

Harry Stessel   P
Westfield State College, Westfield, MA 01086,
413-568-3311
    Pubs: *American Studies* (Raindust Pr, 1975),
    Connecticut River Rev, SPR, Xanadu, Mss., Cottonwood
    Rev, Commonwealth Rev, Kansas Qtly

Jadene Felina Stevens   P
Salt Wind Poets, 12 Olde Homestead Way, East Harwich,
MA 02645, 508-432-6661
    Pubs: *The Original Trinity* (Stepping Stone Pr, 1994),
    Salt Wind Poets Anth (Blue Moon Pr, 1991), *Quilt,*
    Proof Rock, Transnational Perspectives, Sunrust

Susan Stinson 🎤 ✈   P&W
PO Box 1272
Northampton, MA 01061, 413-584-2736
Internet: sestinson@aol.com
    Pubs: *Martha Moody, Fat Girl Dances with Rocks*
    (Spinsters Ink, 1995, 1994), *Mammoth Book of Lesbian*
    Erotica: Anth (Robinson, 2000), *Diva, Curve, Kenyon*
    Rev, Sinister Wisdom, Heresies, Yellow Silk, Bay
    Windows
Groups: G/L/B/T, Women

Lewis Hammond Stone   P
PO Box 545
Mattapoisett, MA 02739
    Pubs: *The Nutritive & Therapeutic Uses of the Banana:*
    Anth (Church Hse, 1990), *Northeast Jrnl, Ararat, Green*
    Fuse, The Lowell Pearl, Temper, Chelsea

Jane Strete   P
106 Pleasant St, #2
Cambridge, MA 02139, 617-354-9487
    Pubs: *City River Voices* (West End Pr, 1992),
    Ourselves, Growing Older: Anth (S&S, 1987), *South*
    Coast Poetry Intl, Timbrel, Maine Times

Jonathan Strong 🎤 ✈   W
English Dept, Tufts Univ, Medford, MA 02155
    Pubs: *A Circle Around Her, The Old World, Offspring,*
    An Untold Tale, Companion Pieces, Secret Words
    (Zoland, 2000, 1997, 1995, 1993, 1993, 1992),
    Elsewhere (Ballantine, 1985)

Jack Sughrue   P
52 Heritage Dr
Whittinsville, MA 01588-2358
    Pubs: *The Book of Books, The Link* (Pakka Pr, 1993,
    1978), *Jlag Rev, Poets, Little Apple, The Lobe,*
    Gargoyle

James Sullivan 🎤 ✈   P
590A Sunrise Ave, PO Box 451
Barre, MA 01005-9519, 978-355-4389
    Pubs: *In Order of Appearance: 400 Poems* (Adams
    Printing Co, 1988), *America, Commonweal, Worcester*
    Rev
I.D.: Irish-Catholic

Stanley Sultan 🎤 ✈   W
1 Prospect Ave
Boston, MA 02131-3727, 617-325-1482
    Pubs: *Joyce's Becoming* (U Pr Florida, 2000), *Eliot,*
    Joyce & Company (Oxford U Pr, 1990), *Writing the*
    Culture: American Sephardic Authors: Anth (U Pr of
    New England, 1996), *Offshore*

John T.   P
7 Silverwood Terr
South Hadley, MA 01075

Cecilia M. Tan 🎤   W
Circlet Press Inc, 1770 Massachusetts Ave, #278,
Cambridge, MA 02140, 617-864-0492
Internet: ctan@circlet.com
    Pubs: *Black Feathers* (HC, 1998), *On a Bed of Rice*
    (Anchor Bks, 1995), *Isaac Asimov's Sci Fi Mag, Blithe*
    House Qtly, Herotica, Penthouse, Paramour, Looking for
    Mr. Preston, By Her Subdued, No Other Tribute, Dark
    Angels, Taste of Latex, Ms., Sojourner
I.D.: Asian-American. Groups: G/L/B/T, Science Fiction
Clubs

Stephen J. Tapscott   P
66 Martin St, #2
Cambridge, MA 02138, 617-876-6121
    Pubs: *From The Book of Changes* (Carcanet, 1996),
    Another Body (Cleveland State U Poetry Ctr, 1989),
    Mesopotamia (Wesleyan, 1975)

James Tate 🎤 ✈   P
16 Jones Rd
Amherst, MA 01002-9715
   Pubs: *Shroud of the Gnome, Worshipful Company of Fletchers* (Ecco Pr, 1997, 1994), *Distance from Loved Ones, Reckoner* (Wesleyan U, 1990, 1986), *APR, Poetry, Massachusetts Rev*

Janice Thaddeus   P
58 Garfield St
Cambridge, MA 02138, 617-547-7806
   Pubs: *Lot's Wife* (Saturday Pr, 1986), *Mountain Rev, Louisville Rev, Shenandoah, Cold*

Alexander Louis Theroux   W
Willow St
West Barnstable, MA 02668

Jessica Treadway   W
17 Old Colony Ln
Arlington, MA 02174-3205, 781-646-2748
   Pubs: *Absent Without Leave & Other Stories* (Delphinium Bks, 1993), *Ploughshares, Agni, Atlantic, Hudson Rev*

Florence Trefethen   P
23 Barberry Rd
Lexington, MA 02173, 617-862-0644
   Pubs: *The Little, Brown Reader: Anth* (HC, 1993), *Fairbank Remembered: Anth* (Harvard U Pr, 1992), *Bellingham Rev, Connecticut Rev, Negative Capability*

Jean Lorraine Tupper 🎤 ✈   P
165 Tilting Rock Rd
Wrentham, MA 02093-1360
   Pubs: *Castings: Anth* (Aubade Pr, 1991), *Thema, Tunxis Poetry Rev, Worcester Rev, Blue Unicorn, SPR, Connecticut River Rev, Piedmont Literary Rev, Voices Intl*

Gregoire Turgeon   P
5 Sherlock Ln
Westford, MA 01886
   Pubs: *Painted Bride Qtly, Poetry, Poetry NW, SPR, Louisville Rev*

Sondra Upham   P
37 Manters Pt
Plymouth, MA 02360
   Pubs: *Out of Season: Anth* (Amagansett Pr, 1993), *We Speak for Peace: Anth* (KIT, 1993), *Prairie Schooner, Phoebe, New Virginia Rev, Sojourner, Eclectic Literary Forum*

Cornelia Veenendaal   P
14 Wellesley Pk
Dorchester, MA 02124, 617-825-7262
   Pubs: *What Seas What Shores* (Rowan Tree Pr, 1984), *Arvon Fdn, Prairie Schooner, Sojourner, Soundings East, Ploughshares, Hanging Loose, Commonweal*

Peter Viereck   P
12 Silver St
South Hadley, MA 01075-1616, 413-534-5504
   Pubs: *Tide & Continuities* (U Arkansas Pr, 1995), *The Unadjusted Man* (Greenwood Pr, 1973), *New Yorker, Paris Rev, Parnassus, APR, New Republic*

Tino Villanueva 🎤 ✈   P
1112 Boylston St, Ste 270
Boston, MA 02215, 617-267-2592
   Pubs: *Chronicle of My Worst Years* (Northwestern U Pr, 1994), *Scene from the Movie "Giant"* (Curbstone Pr, 1993), *Bloomsbury Rev, Agni*
Lang: Spanish

Arturo Vivante 🎤 ✈   W
Box 3005
Wellfleet, MA 02667-3005, 508-349-6619
   Pubs: *The Tales of Arturo Vivante* (Sheep Meadow Pr, 1990), *Leopardi Poems, Italian Poetry: Anth* (Delphinium Pr, 1988, 1996), *New Yorker, Bostonia, Yankee, Italian Qtly*
Lang: Italian

Diane Wald   P
52 Paine St
Boston, MA 02131, 617-524-0072
   Pubs: *Double Mirror* (Runaway Spoon Pr, 1996), *My Hat That Was Dreaming* (Literary Renaissance, 1994), *Boston Literary Rev, APR, New Rev, Kayak, Missouri Rev*

William J. Walsh   P
298 Main St
Charlestown, MA 02129-2955
   Pubs: *Upsouth, Poetry Only, Amaranth Rev, Rainbow's End, Poetry Co-op, Perceptions, Manna*

Victor Walter 🎤 ✈   W
204 Aspinwall Ave
Brookline, MA 02446-6960, 617-566-2158
Internet: manush@bu.edu
   Pubs: *The Voice of Manush* (White Pine Pr, 1996), *A Ghost at Heart's Edge: Anth* (North Atlantic Bks, 1999), *Boston Globe Mag, Ellipsis, Short Story, Cimarron Rev, NER, Chaminade Rev, Magic Realism*
Groups: Music/Arts, Magic

Richard Waring ⏚ ✈   P
33 Chandler St
Belmont, MA 02478-5026, 617-489-1630
Internet: rwaring@nejm.org
   Pubs: *Listening to Stones, The Unitarian Universalist
Poets: Anth (Pudding Hse Pr, 1999, 1996), *Mothering,
Pine River Papers, Noctiluca, Dark Horse, Dragonfly,
Contact II, Zone*

Rosanna Warren   P
11 Robinwood Ave
Needham, MA 02192
   Pubs: *Stained Glass, Each Leaf Shines Separate*
(Norton, 1993, 1984)

Anne Sweeter Watson ⏚   P
105 Allen's Point
Marion, MA 02738-2301, 508-748-0674
Internet: oldsalt@compuserve.com
   Pubs: *Prisms of the Soul: Anth* (Morehouse Pub, 1996),
*The Living Church, Noetic Sciences Rev, Starting Point,
Time of Singing, Jrnl of Poetry Therapy, Human Quest,
Journeys, New England Writers Network*

Ellen Doré Watson   P
Manning Rd
Conway, MA 01341, 413-369-4414
   Pubs: *We Live in Bodies* (Alice James Bks, 1997),
Broken Railings (Owl Creek Pr, 1997), *Night Out: Anth*
(Milkweed Edtns, 1997), *New Yorker, Boulevard, APR,
Ploughshares, Prairie Schooner*

Nancy Dingman Watson ⏚ ✈   W
Box 32
Truro, MA 02666-0032, 508-349-2324
   Pubs: *Tommy's Mommy's Fish* (Viking, 1996),
Blueberries Lavender (Addison Wesley, 1977)

Afaa Michael Weaver   P&W
English Dept, Simmons College, 300 The Fenway, Boston,
MA 02115-5898, 617-521-2175
   Pubs: *Talisman* (Tia Chucha Pr, 1998), *Timber &
Prayer* (U Pitt Pr, 1995), *Stations in a Dream*
(Dolphin-Moon Pr, 1993), *Cream City Rev, Long Shot,
One Trick Pony, Plum Rev, Solo, Kenyon Rev,
Obsidian II, African-American Rev, Calliope, Pequod*

Suellen Wedmore   P
155 South St
Rockport, MA 01966, 978-546-3754
   Pubs: *Anthology of American Poetry* (Monitor Bks,
1997), *I Am Becoming the Woman I Wanted to Be:
Anth* (Papier-Mache Pr, 1994), *College English, Boston
Poet, Green Mountains Rev, Byline Mag, Teaching
Voices, Phoebe, Writer's Ink, The Artful Mind, Stuff
Mag*

Hannah Weiner   PP&P
64 Hillside Ave
West Newton, MA 02165
   Pubs: *Silent Teachers Remembered* (Tender Buttons Pr,
1993), *The Fast* (United Artists, 1992), *Raddle Moon,
Motel, Paper Air, Object, Grist, Writing*

Howard L. Weiner   W
114 Somerset Rd
Brookline, MA 02146, 617-738-5343
   Pubs: *The Children's Ward* (Putnam, 1980)

Chester Weinerman   P
20 Payson Rd
Brookline, MA 02167, 617-566-1611
   Pubs: *Poets for Life: Anth* (Crown, 1989), *Partisan Rev,
Bitterroot, SPR, Lips*

Ron Welburn ⏚ ✈   P&W
PO Box 420
Hadley, MA 01035-0420, 413-584-0419
Internet: rwelburn@english.umass.edu
   Pubs: *Coming Through Smoke & the Dreaming*
(Greenfield Rev Pr, 2000), *Council Decisions* (American
Native Pr Archives, 1991), *Returning the Gift: Anth* (U
Arizona Pr, 1995), *Durable Breath: Anth* (Salmon Run,
1994), *Red Owl, Cimarron Rev, Callaloo*
I.D.: Native American

Susan B. Weston   P&W
80 Park St #55
Brookline, MA 02146, 617-566-8672
   Pubs: *Children of the Light* (St. Martin's Pr, 1985),
*Other Voices, Kansas Qtly, Fiction Rev, Croton Rev,
Literal Latte, Press, Potpourri, Changes*

Dara Wier ⏚ ✈   P
504 Montague Rd
Amherst, MA 01002-1008
Internet: daraw@hfa.umass.edu
   Pubs: *Voyages in English, Our Master Plan, Blue for
the Plough, The Book of Knowledge* (Carnegie Mellon
U Pr, 2001, 1999, 1992, 1988), *Fence, Washington
Square, APR, Gettysburg Rev, Seattle Rev, Hollins
Critic, Conduit*

Richard Wilbur ⏚ ✈   P&W
87 Dodwells Rd
Cummington, MA 01026-9705
   Pubs: *Mayflies* (Harcourt, 2000), *More Opposites, New
& Collected Poems* (HBJ, 1991, 1988)

Bosley Wilder   P
121 Cold Hill
Granby, MA 01033, 413-467-3191
   Pubs: *You Once Had Wings* (China; Heilongjiang
People's Pub Hse, 1991), *The Wind Is Mine* (Academic
Bks, 1985), *Zuzu's Petals Qtly*

Mame Willey 🎤 ✈ P&W
33 Bay State Ave
Somerville, MA 02144-2132, 617-623-3611
Internet: mjjm@gis.net
Pubs: *Anthology of New England Writers* (New England Writers, 1998), *New Press Literary Qtly, Albany Rev, Hudson Rev, Colorado Qtly, Mississippi Rev, Hanging Loose, Blueline, U.S. 1 Worksheets*

Jane Williams W
19 Cottage St
Cambridge, MA 02139
Pubs: *Family Affairs* (H&R, 1977), *Harvard Mag, Boston Globe*

Irene Willis 🎤 ✈ P
2 Cornwall Dr
Great Barrington, MA 01230-1592, 413-528-1924
Pubs: *They Tell Me You Danced* (U Pr Florida, 1995), *Crazyhorse, Laurel Rev, NYQ, Kansas Qtly, Yankee, Florida Rev*
Groups: Seniors

Irene K. Wilson P
9 Foster Rd
Lexington, MA 02421-5505
Pubs: *The Cat's Meow!: Anth* (Maine Rhode Pubs, 1996), *Rosebud, Tucumcari Literary Rev, Redbook, Piedmont Literary Rev, Calapooya Collage, Poetry Nippon, Pegasus*

Joseph Wilson P
RFD #1, Irish Ln
Rutland, MA 01543, 617-886-6786

Joyce Wilson 🎤 ✈ P
158 Hollett St
Scituate, MA 02066-2037, 781-545-0731
Internet: www.poetryporch.com
Pubs: *Persephone: Anth* (U Pr of New England, 1999), *Descant, Poetry Ireland Rev, Antigonish Rev, Agni Rev*
Groups: Schools, Women

Ellen Wittlinger 🎤 ✈ P
47 Beach Ave
Swampscott, MA 01907-1765, 781-599-6951
Internet: pritchwitt@aol.com
Pubs: *What's in a Name, Hard Love* (S&S, 2000, 1999), *Noticing Paradise, Lombardo's Law* (HM, 1995, 1993), *Breakers* (Sheep Meadow Pr, 1979), *Iowa Rev, American Voice, Midwest Qtly, Ploughshares*

J. Barrett Wolf P
118 Captain Lijahs Rd
Centerville, MA 02632-1600
Pubs: *Old North Field & Other Poems* (Bear Pause Pubs, 1993), *Enchante Mag, Black Bear Rev, Fireheart*

Ira Wood W
Box 1473
Wellfleet, MA 02667, 508-349-1925
Pubs: *Storm Tide* (Fawcett-Columbine, 1998), *Going Public, The Kitchen Man* (Ballantine, 1992, 1987)

Douglas Worth 🎤 ✈ P
31 Maple Ave, #1
Cambridge, MA 02139-1115, 617-441-3983
Pubs: *Some Sense of Transcendence, Once Around Bullough's Pond* (William L. Bauhan, 1999, 1987), *From Dream, From Circumstance: New & Selected Poems 1963-1983* (Apple-Wood Bks, 1984)

Xiaodo Xiao W
135 Belchertown Rd
Amherst, MA 01002
Pubs: *DoubleTake, North Dakota Qtly, Confrontation, Antaeus, Atlantic*

Gene Zeiger 🎤 ✈ P
RFD 1, #274 Patten Hill Rd
Shelburne, MA 01370, 413-625-6113
Pubs: *Leaving Egypt* (White Pine Pr, 1994), *Sudden Dancing* (Amherst Writers & Artists Pr, 1988), *Georgia Rev, Tar River Poetry, Prose Poem, The Sun*
I.D.: Jewish, Women. Groups: Seniors

Tony Zizza P
13 Butterworth Rd
Beverly, MA 01915, 508-922-5704
Pubs: *The Magic of an Open Mind* (Readable Heart Pub, 1987)

Marilyn Zuckerman 🎤 ✈ P
153 Medford St
Arlington, MA 02174-3118, 617-643-8483
Internet: marizuck@aol.com
Pubs: *Poems of the Sixth Decade* (Garden Street Pr, 1993), *Claiming the Spirit Within: Anth* (Beacon Pr, 1996), *City River of Voices: Anth* (West End Pr, 1992), *Cedar Hill Rev, Rethinking Marxism, Karamu, Nimrod, The Little Mag*

MICHIGAN

Betsy Adams P
Chelsea Cats, Inc, PO Box 296, Dexter, MI 48130
Pubs: *The Dead Birth, Itself* (Paul Green/Spectacular Diseases, 1990)

Debra Allbery 🎤 ✈ P
161 Luella Ave
Ann Arbor, MI 48103, 734-668-4813
Pubs: *Walking Distance, The Pittsburgh Book of Contemporary American Poetry: Anth* (U Pitt Pr, 1991, 1993), *Poetry, Iowa Rev, TriQtly*

Alvin Aubert 🎤 ✈ P
18234 Parkside Ave
Detroit, MI 48221, 313-345-4790
Internet: ad8722@wayne.edu
    Pubs: *Harlem Wrestler* (Michigan State U Pr, 1995), *If Winter Come* (Carnegie Mellon U Pr, 1994), *African American Rev, Callaloo, Drumvoices*
I.D.: African-American

Sue A. Austin P
2211 Eastlawn Dr #7
Midland, MI 48642-5042
    Pubs: *The Three Moons of Earth, Not Your Usual Hearts & Flowers* (Curtis, 1991, 1990), *Lucidity, Bone & Flesh, Howling Dog, Cokefish, Color Wheel*

Carolyn Balducci W
Univ Michigan, Residential College, Ann Arbor, MI 48109-1245, 734-647-4388
    Pubs: *Earwax* (HM, 1972), *Alternative Rev, Sipario Intl, Antologia Nuova*

Ann Bardens P
English Dept, Central Michigan Univ, Mt Pleasant, MI 48859, 517-774-3101
    Pubs: *Stone & Water* (Canoe Pr, 1992), *MacGuffin, Mobius, Plainsongs, Kansas Qtly*

Michael J. Barney 🎤 ✈ P
27030 Havelock
Dearborn Heights,, MI 48127
Internet: mikeb@dhol.org
    Pubs: *True Life Adventures* (Budget Pr, 1998), *Silhouettes in the Electric Sky: Anth* (Newton's Baby, 1998), *Freefall, Midwest Poetry Rev, Wordwrights*
Groups: Children, Seniors

Jackie Bartley P
646 Pinecrest Dr
Holland, MI 49424, 616-392-6556
    Pubs: *The Terrible Boundaries of the Body* (White Eagle Coffee Store Pr, 1997), *When Prayer Is Far from Our Lips* (Franciscan U Pr, 1994), *For a Living: Anth* (U Illinois Pr, 1995), *West Branch, Calliope, Cincinnati Poetry Rev, Aileron, Blue Mesa Rev*

Charles Baxter P
1585 Woodland Dr
Ann Arbor, MI 48103, 313-769-0059
Internet: cbaxter@umich.edu
    Pubs: *The Feast of Love, Believers* (Pantheon, 2000, 1997), *Burning Down the House* (Graywolf, 1997), *Shadow Play, A Relative Stranger* (Norton, 1993, 1990)

Therese Becker P&W
2401 Eaton Gate Rd
Lake Orion, MI 48360, 248-391-1093
    Pubs: *Contemporary Michigan Poetry: Anth* (Wayne State U Pr, 1988), *Woman Poet, The Midwest: Anth* (Women in Literature, 1985), *Poetry East, Witness, NYQ*

Elinor Benedict 🎤 ✈ P&W
8627 S Lakeside Dr
Rapid River, MI 49878, 906-474-9273
Internet: elifax@aol.com
    Pubs: *All That Divides Us* (Utah State U Pr, 2000), *The Tree Between Us, Chinavision* (March Street Pr, 1997, 1995), *The Green Heart* (Illinois State U, 1994)

Terry Blackhawk P
16215 Warwick Rd
Detroit, MI 48219, 313-532-5763
    Pubs: *Body & Field* (Michigan State U Pr, 1999), *Trio: Voices from the Myths* (Ridgeway Press, 1998), *I Am Becoming the Woman I've Wanted: Anth* (Papier-Mache Pr, 1994), *Ekphrasis, Poet Lore, Visions Intl*

Norma Blair P
2025 McCann Rd
Hastings, MI 49058
    Pubs: *What's a Nice Girl Like You Doing in a Relationship Like This?: Anth* (Crossing Pr, 1992), *CityBook V: Sideshow Anth* (Flying Buffalo, 1991)

Shanda Hansma Blue 🎤 ✈ P
PO Box 20205
Kalamazoo, MI 49019-1205, 616-372-0481
Internet: shanda_blue@hotmail.com
    Pubs: *Southern Indiana Rev, Louisville Rev*
I.D.: Multicultural, Native American

Beth Brant P&W
18890 Reed
Melvindale, MI 48122, 313-381-3550
    Pubs: *Food & Spirits* (Firebrand Bks, 1991), *Kenyon Rev, American Voice, Turtle Qtly, Forum, Tiger Lily, Woman of Power*

Alfred J. Bruey P
201 S Grinnell St
Jackson, MI 49203, 517-784-1411
    Pubs: *Practising Insanity* (Pudding Hse Pub, 1987), *Wherever You Go, There You Are* (Suburban Wilderness Pr, 1985), *Pudding, Poetry Motel, Amelia, Attention Please*

Gary Bundy P
172 Jacaranda
Battle Creek, MI 49015
    Pubs: *CQ, Poetry Motel, Sell Outs Literary Mag, Without Halos, Chiron Rev, Spitball, Blue Light Rev, Birmingham Poetry Rev, Westering, Boar's Tusk*

Elizabeth Kane Buzzelli W
60185 Lamplight Ct
Washington, MI 48094
Pubs: *Gift of Evil* (Bantam, 1983)

Carol Carpenter 🎤 ✈ P&W
10005 Berwick
Livonia, MI 48150, 734-525-6586
Pubs: *Resourceful Woman* (Visible Ink Pr, 1994),
Generation to Generation: Anth (Papier-Mache Pr,
1998), *Hawaii Rev, Wisconsin Rev, Qtly West, Cape
Rock, Writers' Forum, Nit & Wit, Indiana Rev,
Confrontation, Iowa Woman, America, Carolina Qtly,
CSM*

John Carpenter P
1606 Granger Ave
Ann Arbor, MI 48104-4429, 734-996-4351
Internet: jcarpen172@aol.com
Pubs: *Paris Rev, Chicago Rev, Manhattan Rev, Slant,
Embers, New Yorker, NYRB, Kenyon Rev, Grand
Street, Michigan Qtly, Crosscurrents*

Andrew G. Carrigan P
212 W Henry St
Saline, MI 48176, 313-429-5868
Pubs: *To Read, To Read, The King, You Poems*
(Crowfoot Pr, 1981, 1981, 1979)

Patricia Clark P
Grand Valley State Univ, English Dept, Allendale, MI
49401, 616-895-3199
Pubs: *North of Wondering* (Women-In-Literature, 1998),
Worlds in Our Words: Anth (Blair/Prentice Hall, 1997),
*Seattle Rev, Mississippi Rev, New Criterion, CutBank,
NER, NAR, Nebraska Rev, Poetry*

Charles Cline P
9866 S Westnedge
Portage, MI 49024, 616-327-7135
Pubs: *Ultima Thule* (Tagore Inst of Creative Writing,
1984), *Riverrun, Poet, Aurag, Sou'wester*

Lyn Coffin P&W
2034 Norfolk
Ann Arbor, MI 48103, 734-663-1589
Pubs: *Crystals of the Unforseen* (Plain View Pr, 1998),
Poetry of Wickedness (Ithaca Hse, 1980), *Human
Trappings* (Abbattoir Edtn, 1980), *Wind Eyes: Anth*
(Plain View Pr, 1996), *Best American Short Stories:
Anth* (HM, 1969)

Margaret Jean Condon P
c/o Margaret Condon Taylor, 400 Maynard St, Ste 506,
Ann Arbor, MI 48104, 313-995-8627
Pubs: *Topographics* (Lame Johnny Pr, 1977)

Nicholas Delbanco 🎤 ✈ W
Univ Michigan, Hopwood Room, 1006 Angell Hall, Ann
Arbor, MI 48109, 734-764-6296
Pubs: *The Lost Suitcase* (Columbia U Pr, 2000), *What
Remains, Old Scores, In the Name of Mercy* (Warner
Bks, 2000, 1997, 1995), *Running in Place* (Atlantic
Monthly Pr, 1989)

Michael Delp P
Interlochen Arts Academy, PO Box 199, Interlochen, MI
49643, 616-276-9747
Pubs: *Under the Influence of Water, Over the Graves
of Horses* (Wayne State U Pr, 1992, 1988), *Playboy,
Poetry NW, Memphis State Rev*

Patricia Demetri P
11313 Rockland Ave
Redford, MI 48239
Pubs: *Manna, Alura, Iadr, Buselinesii, Jean's Journal,
Canadian Contingent Pr, Still Night Writings*

Pamela Ditchoff P&W
605 Butterfield
East Lansing, MI 48823
Pubs: *The Mirror of the Monsters & Prodigies* (Coffee
Hse Pr, 1995), *Lexigram Learns* (Interact Pr, 1994),
Home for The Holidays: Anth (Papier-Mache Pr, 1997),
Whose Woods These Are: Anth (Ecco Pr, 1993), *West*

Stephen Dunning 🎤 ✈ P&W
517 Oswego St
Ann Arbor, MI 48104, 734-668-7723
Internet: dunnings@umich.edu
Pubs: *Hunter's Park: 13 Stories, To the Beautiful
Women: Stories* (S. Russell, 1996, 1990), *Good Words*
(March Street Pr, 1991), *New Letters, Crescent Rev,
Synaesthesia, Fourth Genre*

Stuart Dybek 🎤 ✈ P&W
320 Monroe
Kalamazoo, MI 49006, 616-344-5590
Pubs: *The Coast of Chicago* (Knopf, 1990), *Childhood
& Other Neighborhoods* (Ecco, 1987), *Harper's, New
Yorker, Atlantic, DoubleTake, Poetry, Paris Rev*

Ed Engle, Jr. P
1 Birnwick
Adrian, MI 49221, 517-265-2035
Pubs: *Baking Catholic* (Summer Stream Pr, 1985), *Blue
Horse, Crab Creek Rev, New Collage Mag*

Gary James Erwin 🎤 ✈ W
529 S Edgeworth Ave
Royal Oak, MI 48067
Pubs: *PrePress Awards Vol II: Anth* (PrePress Pub
1995), *Driftwood Rev, Meat Whistle Qtly, Santa Fe
Literary Rev, Sun, MacGuffin, Red Cedar Rev*

Clayton Eshleman 🎤 ✈   P
210 Washtenaw Ave
Ypsilanti, MI 48197, 313-483-9787
    Pubs: *From Scratch, Under World Arrest* (Black
    Sparrow Pr, 1998, 1994), *Antiphonal Swing: Selected
    Prose 1962-87* (McPherson, 1988), *Terra Nova,
    Lusitania, Poesie* (Paris), *Hambone, Grand Street, Paris
    Rev*

Leslie D. Foster   P
Box 357
Marquette, MI 49855, 906-228-5131
    Pubs: *Myths for Dorothy* (Foster, 1992), *Northeast,
    Georgia Rev, Christian Century, Sisters Today, Interim,
    Anglican Theological Rev, Ariel*

Linda Nemec Foster 🎤 ✈   P
2024 Wilshire Dr SE
Grand Rapids, MI 49506-4014, 616-452-7204
Internet: mfapwgrr9@aol.com
    Pubs: *Amber Necklace from Gdansk* (LSU Pr, 2001),
    Living in the Fire Nest (Ridgeway Pr, 1996), *New
    Poems from the Third Coast: Anth* (Wayne State U Pr,
    1999), *Poet Lore, Atlanta Rev, Mid-American Rev,
    Georgia Rev, Indiana Rev, River Styx, Nimrod Qtly
    West*
Groups: Children, Seniors

Connie Fox   P&W
526 Forest
East Lansing, MI 48823, 515-351-5977
    Pubs: *Entre Nous* (Trout Creek Pr, 1992), *Our Lady of
    Laussel* (Spectacular Diseases, 1991)

Lucia Fox   P&W
Michigan State Univ, 546 Wells Hall, East Lansing, MI
48823, 517-332-5622
    Pubs: *Tales of an Indian Princess, Un Cierto Lugar*
    (Shambhala, 1979, 1978)

Berrien Fragos   PP
PO Box 455
Suttons Bay, MI 49682, 616-271-4089
    Pubs: *10 Field Notes by Berrien* (New York Jrnl of
    Folklore, 1987)

Randall R. Freisinger   P
Michigan Technological Univ, Humanities Dept, Houghton,
MI 49931, 906-487-3229
    Pubs: *Plato's Breath* (Utah State U Pr, 1997), *Hand
    Shadows* (Green Tower, 1988), *Runnin Patterns* (Flume,
    1985), *Tar River Poetry, Cream City Rev, Zone 3, New
    Letters, Tendril, Centennial Rev, Atlanta Rev*

Sonya Friedman   W
111 S Woodward, Ste 212B
Birmingham, MI 48009, 313-644-4794
    Pubs: *A Hero Is More Than Just a Sandwich* (Putnam,
    1986)

Alice Fulton   P&W
2370 LeForge Rd, RR#13
Ypsilanti, MI 48198-9638, 313-482-7197
    Pubs: *Sensual Math* (Norton, 1995), *Powers of
    Congress* (Godine, 1990), *Palladium* (U Illinois, 1986),
    *New Yorker, Parnassus, TriQtly, Pequod, American
    Voice*

Ken Gaertner   P&W
11447 Weiman Dr
Pinckney, MI 48169, 313-878-3711
    Pubs: *Koan Bread* (Survivor's Manual, 1977), *Christian
    Century, New Oxford Rev, America, Poem*

Laurence Goldstein 🎤 ✈   P
408 2nd St
Ann Arbor, MI 48103, 734-769-9899
    Pubs: *Cold Reading, The Three Gardens* (Copper
    Beech, 1995, 1987), *The Faber Book of Movie Verse:
    Anth* (F&F, 1994), *Iowa Rev, Ontario Rev, Poetry,
    Salmagundi, TriQtly*

Jaimy Gordon 🎤 ✈   P&W
Western Michigan Univ, English Dept, Kalamazoo, MI
49008, 616-381-6606
Internet: gordonj@wmich.edu
    Pubs: *Bogeywoman* (Sun & Moon Pr, 1999), *She Drove
    Without Stopping* (Algonquin, 1990), *Best American
    Short Stories: Anth* (HM, 1995), *Michigan Qtly Rev,
    Ploughshares, Missouri Rev, Gargoyle, Shankpainter*

Judith Goren   P
21525 W 13 Mile Rd
Beverly Hills, MI 48025
    Pubs: *Traveling Toward the Heart* (Ridgeway Pr, 1994),
    Contemporary Michigan Poetry: Anth (Wayne State U
    Pr, 1988), *Centennial Rev, Moving Out, Green River
    Rev, The Bridge*

Delcie Southall Gourdine 🎤 ✈   W
325 Yellow Creek Dr
St Joseph, MI 49085-9326, 616-429-8393
    Pubs: *Redbook, Obsidian, Green's Mag*

Linda Gregerson   P
4881 Hidden Brook Ln
Ann Arbor, MI 48105, 313-996-2702
    Pubs: *The Woman Who Died in Her Sleep: Anth* (HM,
    1996), *Fire in the Conservatory: Anth* (Dragon Gate,
    1982), *Atlantic, Poetry, TriQtly, Yale Rev*

Jim Gustafson   P
411 Pleasant
Birmingham, MI 48009, 313-642-1542
    Pubs: *Aloha Street* (Avatar Edtns, 1989), *Virtue &
    Annihilation* (The Alternative Pr, 1988)

Robert Haight 🎤 ✈   P
PO Box 744
Marcellus, MI 49067-0744, 616-372-5452
 Pubs: *Water Music* (Ridgeway Pr, 1993), *New Poems
 from the Third Coast: Anth* (Wayne State U Pr, 2000),
 Passages North: Anth (Milkweed Edtns, 1990),
 Contemporary Michigan Poetry: Anth (Wayne State U
 Pr, 1989), *Driftwood Rev, Controlled Burn, Northeast*

Charles Hanson   P
449 Moran Rd
Grosse Pointe Farm, MI 48236, 313-882-3627
 Pubs: *Poetry Ohio, Ego Flights, Anth of Mag Verse,
 White Rock Rev, Yellow Butterfly, BPJ, Stone Country,
 Crab Creek Rev*

Bill Harris   P
Univ Wayne State, 51 W Warren, Detroit, MI 48202
 Pubs: *The Ringmaster's Array* (Past Tents Pr, 1997),
 Yardbird Suite: Side One (Michigan State U Pr, 1997),
 Dispatch Detroit

Jim Harrison   P&W
PO Box 135
Lake Leelanau, MI 49653-0135
 Pubs: *Sundog* (Dutton, 1984), *Warlock, Legends*
 (Delacorte, 1981, 1979), *Farmer* (Viking, 1976)

Shayla Hawkins 🎤 ✈   P
20236 Redfern
Detroit, MI 48219-1269, 313-255-2698
Internet: Sahawkin@oakland.edu
 Pubs: *In Our Own Words: A Generation Defining Itself,
 Vol. 2: Anth* (MW Enterprises, 2000), *CQ, Afterthoughts,
 Maryland Rev, Obsidian II: Black Literature in Review,
 Paris/Atlantic*
Lang: French. I.D.: African-American, Christian. Groups:
African-American, Christian

Janet Ruth Heller 🎤 ✈   P
Western Michigan Univ, English Dept, Kalamazoo, MI
49008, 616-387-2572
Internet: janet.heller@wmich.edu
 Pubs: *Modern Poems on the Bible: Anth* (Jewish Pub
 Society, 1994), *Women's Glib: A Collection of Women's
 Humor: Anth* (Crossing Pr, 1991), *Anima*
I.D.: Jewish. Groups: Jewish, College/Univ

Conrad Hilberry 🎤 ✈   P
1601 Grand Ave
Kalamazoo, MI 49006, 616-345-5951
 Pubs: *Player Piano* (Louisiana State U, 1999), *Taking
 Notes* (Snowy Egret, 1999), *Sorting the Smoke* (U
 Iowa, 1990), *Luke Karamazov* (Wayne State U, 1987),
 *Tamaqua, Gettysburg Rev, Shenandoah, Virginia Qtly,
 Poetry*

Sheryl Morang Holmberg 🎤   P&W
45077 Custer
Utica, MI 48317-5701, 810-726-6615
Internet: sholmberg99@hotmail.com
 Pubs: *Driftwood Rev, Pike Creek Rev, Heron Qtly, Los,
 Indefinite Space, Ship of Fools, Eratica, Iconoclast,
 Cumberland Poetry Rev, SLUGfest, Ltd., Piedmont
 Literary Rev, Ever Dancing Muse, Cicada, black bough,
 Quantum Tao*

Patricia Hooper 🎤 ✈   P
616 Yarmouth Rd
Bloomfield Township, MI 48301
 Pubs: *At the Corner of the Eye* (Michigan State U Pr,
 1997), *The Flowering Trees* (State Street Pr, 1995),
 Other Lives (Elizabeth Street Pr, 1984), *Atlantic, New
 Criterion, Poetry, Hudson Rev, American Scholar*

Daniel Hughes   P
17524 3rd Ave, #104
Detroit, MI 48203, 313-345-5834
 Pubs: *You Are Not Stendhal* (Wayne State U Pr,
 1992), *Spirit Traps, Falling* (Copper Beech Pr, 1988,
 1979)

Deborah L. Hunt   W
PO Box 85960
Westland, MI 48185
 Pubs: *Mystic Fiction, Mythic Circle, New Authors Jrnl,
 Space & Time, Aberrations, Heliocentric Net, Mobius,
 New Altars, Outer Darkness, Perceptions*

David James   P
PO Box 721
Linden, MI 48451, 248-942-3214
Internet: jamesfam@internet4all.net
 Pubs: *Do Not Give Dogs What is Holy* (March Street
 Pr, 1994), *A Heart Out of This World* (Carnegie Mellon,
 1984), *Iowa Rev, Poem, Caliban, Kansas Qtly*

Arnold Johnston 🎤 ✈   P&W
471 W South St #102
Kalamazoo, MI 49008, 616-381-6316
Internet: arnie.johnston@wmich.edu
 Pubs: *What the Earth Taught Us* (March Street Pr,
 1996), *Third Coast: Anth* (Wayne State U Pr, 2000),
 *Embers, Rockford Rev, ELF, Malahat Rev, Colorado
 Qtly, Alabama Literary Rev, Indiana Rev, Cumberland
 Poetry Rev, Passages North, Hiram Poetry Rev*

Laura Kasischke   P
2997 S Fletcher Rd
Chelsea, MI 48118, 313-475-7485
 Pubs: *Suspicious River* (HM, 1996), *Housekeeping in a
 Dream* (Carnegie Mellon, 1995), *Wild Brides* (NYU Pr,
 1991), *Poetry*

Janet Kauffman   P&W
14671 W Cadmus Rd, Rte 1
Hudson, MI 49247, 517-448-4973
   Pubs: *The Body in Four Parts* (Graywolf, 1993),
   Obscene Gestures for Women (Knopf, 1989)

Josie Kearns   P
1111 Nielsen Apt 1
Ann Arbor, MI 48105, 313-995-5330
   Pubs: *New Numbers* (March Street Pr, 1998)

Elizabeth Kerlikowske ♪ ✈   P
2423 Russet Dr
Kalamazoo, MI 49008-4316, 616-343-4003
   Internet: mme642@aol.com
   Pubs: *The Seven, Her Bodies, Postcard* (March Street
   Pr, 1997, 1995, 1990), *Stand-Up Poetry: Anth* (U
   California Pr, 1993), *Parting Gifts, Visions Intl, Blue
   Violin, Mobius, Poetry Motel, Renegade, Iris, Creative
   Woman, Perhaps, Mediphors*

Judith Kerman   P
Dept of English, Saginaw Valley State Univ, 7400 Bay Rd,
University Center, MI 48710, 517-790-4063
   Pubs: *Mothering & Dream of Rain* (Ridgeway, 1997),
   Driving for Yellow Cab (Tout Pr, 1985), *Mothering*
   (Uroboros/Allegheny Mtn Pr, 1978), *Chelsea, Michigan
   Qtly Rev, Eastgate Qtly Rev, Controlled Burn, House
   Organ, Snowy Egret, Hiram Poetry Rev, Oxalis*

John Ketzer   W
Jayell Enterprises, Inc, PO Box 2616, Ft Dearborn Sta,
Dearborn, MI 48123
   Pubs: *My First Year Out* (Jayell Enterprises, 1984)

Lionel Bruce Kingery   P
947 Francis
Rochester Hills, MI 48307
   Pubs: *The Popular Songs of Bruce Kingery* (North
   American Mentor, 1980), *Arcadia Poetry Anth* (Arcadia
   Poetry Pr, 1992), *Verses, Voices Intl, Second Coming*

Margo LaGattuta   P
2134 W Gunn Rd
Rochester, MI 48306, 810-693-7227
   Pubs: *Embracing the Fall* (Plain View Pr, 1994), *The
   Dream Givers* (Lake Shore Pub, 1990), *Sun, Yankee,
   The Bridge, Passages North, Calliope, Woman Poet*

Christine Lahey   P
1540 Boulan Rd
Troy, MI 48084, 810-643-6525
   Pubs: *Blood to Remember: American Poets on the
   Holocaust: Anth* (Texas Tech U Pr, 1991), *All's Normal
   Here: Anth* (Ruddy Duck Pr, 1985), *Planet Detroit,
   Michigan Qtly Rev*

Betty Rita Gomez Lance   P&W
1562 Spruce Dr
Kalamazoo, MI 49008-2227, 616-345-0649
   Pubs: *Siete Cuerdas* (Ediciones Cardenoso, 1996), *Alas
   en el Alba* (Compotex, 1987), *Hoy Hacen Corro las
   Ardillas* (Editorial Papiro, 1985)

Douglas W. Lawder   P
Michigan State Univ, Morrill Hall, East Lansing, MI 48824
   Pubs: *Trolling* (Little, Brown, 1977), *The Nation, Poetry,
   Virginia Qtly Rev, The Seventies*

David Dodd Lee ♪ ✈   P
2627 Lorraine Ave
Kalamazoo, MI 49008, 616-373-6438
   Pubs: *Downsides of Fish Culture* (New Issues Pr,
   1997), *Green Mountains Rev, The Qtly, Worcester Rev,
   Willow Springs*
Groups: Mentally Ill

Stephen Leggett   P
PO Box 4551
Ann Arbor, MI 48106, 313-461-1574
   Pubs: *The Form It Takes* (Ridgeway Pr, 1988), *The
   All-Forest* (Waves, 1980)

Christopher Towne Leland   W
English Dept, Wayne State Univ, 51 W Warren, Detroit,
MI 48202, 313-577-2450
   Pubs: *The Professor of Aesthetics, Letting Loose: Anth*
   (Zoland, 1994, 1996), *The Book of Marvels* (Scribner,
   1990), *Mrs. Randall* (HM, 1987)

Kathleen Ripley Leo   P
42185 Baintree Cir
Northville, MI 48167-3447, 810-349-4827
   Pubs: *The Circle Is Assembled: Glass Poems, The Old
   Ways* (Sun Dog Pr, 1994, 1991), *Town One South,
   Northville Poems* (Northville Arts, 1988)

M. L. Liebler ♪ ✈   P&W
PO Box 120
Roseville, MI 48066, 313-577-7713
   Internet: mlliebler@aol.com
   Pubs: *Breaking the Voodoo* (Adastra Pr, 2001), *Written
   in Rain* (Tebot Bach Bks, 2000), *Stripping the Adult
   Century Bare* (Viet Nam Generation Pr, 1994), *Identity
   Lessons: Anth* (Viking, 1999), *Paterson Literary Rev,
   Hong Kong U Jrnl, Long Shot*
I.D.: Veterans, Working Class. Groups: Seniors, Schools

Judith Wood Lindenau   P
7707 Fouch Rd
Traverse City, MI 49684-9513, 616-947-9803

Thomas Lynch 🎤 ✈   P&W
328 E Liberty
Milford, MI 48381, 810-684-6645
Internet: thoslynch@aol.com
  Pubs: *Bodies in Motion & at Rest, Still Life in Milford,
  The Undertaking* (Norton 2000, 1998, 1997), *Grimalkin
  & Other Poems* (Cape/Random Hse, 1994), *New
  Yorker, Harper's, Poetry, London Rev of Bks, Paris
  Rev, New York Times Mag*

Naomi Long Madgett 🎤 ✈   P
18080 Santa Barbara Dr
Detroit, MI 48221-2531, 313-342-9174
Internet: nlmadgett@aol.com
  Pubs: *Remembrances of Spring* (Michigan State U Pr,
  1993), *Pink Ladies in the Afternoon* (Lotus Pr, 1990),
  Octavia & Other Poems (Third World Pr, 1988),
  *Witness, Essence, Obsidian, Michigan Qtly Rev, Sage,
  Black Scholar*
I.D.: African-American

Denise Martinson   P&W
Poetic Page, PO Box 71192, Madison Heights, MI
48071-0192
  Pubs: *Pieces of Eight: Anth* (Wordsmith Pub, 1992),
  Canto, Elk River Rev, Mobius, Metro Singles Lifestyle

Beverly Matherne   P
English Dept, Northern Michigan Univ, 1401 Presque Isle,
Marquette, MI 49855-1556, 906-227-1386
  Pubs: *La Grande Pointe* (CCC, 1995), *Two Worlds
  Walking: Anth* (New Rivers Pr, 1994), *Great River Rev,
  Kansas Qtly, Metamorphoses*

Kathleen McGookey 🎤 ✈   P
135 Lakeview Dr
Wayland, MI 49348, 616-792-6011
Internet: kathleen.mcgookey@wmich.edu
  Pubs: *Whatever Shines, The Party Train: Anth* (New
  Rivers Pr, 2001, 1996), *Boston Rev, Cimarron Rev,
  Seneca Rev, Epoch, Field*

Richard E. McMullen 🎤   P
128 Marvin St
Milan, MI 48160-1356, 313-439-7112
  Pubs: *Like Heaven* (Limited Mailing Pr, 1993), *Trying to
  Get Out* (Crowfoot Pr, 1981), *I Feel a Little Jumpy
  Around You: Anth* (S&S, 1996), *CSM, Commonweal,
  Epoch, Hanging Loose, Massachusetts Rev, New York
  Times, SPR, Wisconsin Rev*

Ken Mikolowski   P
1207 Henry St
Ann Arbor, MI 48104-4340, 313-662-1286
  Pubs: *Big Enigmas* (Past Tents Pr, 1991), *Little
  Mysteries* (Toothpaste Pr, 1979), *Re:view, Rolling Stock,
  Exquisite Corpse, Notus*

Sam Mills   P
116 W Maple St
Lansing, MI 48906, 517-482-4037
  Pubs: *Burning the Stratocaster* (Sleeping Buddha Pr,
  1992), *A Long Drink* (Poetry Centre, 1975), *In This
  Corner, Red Cedar Rev, Triage*

Ronald Milner   P
15865 Montevista
Detroit, MI 48238

Judith Minty 🎤 ✈   P
7113 S Scenic Dr
New Era, MI 49446-8005, 231-894-2121
Internet: judminty@aol.com
  Pubs: *Walking with the Bear* (MSU Pr, 2000), *Mad
  Painter Poems* (March Street Pr, 1996), *Yellow Dog
  Journal* (Parallax Pr, 1991), *Bloomsbury Rev, Poetry,
  Iowa Rev, Hawaii Rev, Prairie Schooner, Luna, Poetry
  Flash, Passages North, Controlled Burn*

Edward Morin 🎤 ✈   P
2112 Brockman Rd
Ann Arbor, MI 48104-4530, 734-668-7523
Internet: corso@umich.edu
  Pubs: *Labor Day at Walden Pond* (Ridgeway Pr, 1997),
  The Dust of Our City (Clover Pr, 1978), *Michigan Qtly
  Rev, New Letters, Windsor Rev, Hudson Rev,
  Ploughshares, TriQtly, Iowa Rev, River Styx*

Carol Morris   P
912 Rose Ave
Ann Arbor, MI 48104-4349, 313-761-5616
  Pubs: *Atomic Picnic* (Stellar Productions, 1995), *Sweet
  Uprisings* (Years Pr, 1990), *Slipstream, MacGuffin,
  Psychopoetica*

Julie Moulds 🎤 ✈   P
7546 S Crooked Lake Dr
Delton, MI 49046-8427, 616-623-3099
  Pubs: *Woman with a Cubed Head* (New Issues Pr,
  1998), *American Poetry: The Next Generation: Anth*
  (Carnegie Mellon U Pr, 2000), *Cream City Rev, Gulf
  Coast, Marlboro Rev, NYQ*
Groups: Feminist, Cancer Survivors

Calvin Murry   P&W
11714 Dyar St
Hamtramck, MI 48212
  Pubs: *My Brother's Keeper* (M. Datcher, 1992), *Prisoner
  Aboard S.S. Beagle, Light from Another Country*
  (Greenfield Review Pr, 1983, 1982), *Poetry, Art/Life*

Duane Niatum   P&W
Program in American Culture, Univ Michigan, 410 Mason
Hall, Ann Arbor, MI 48109, 313-763-1460
  Pubs: *Drawings of the Song Animals: New & Selected
  Poems* (Holy Cow! Pr, 1991), *North Dakota Qtly,
  Archae Mag, Seattle Rev, Michigan Qtly Rev, Chariton
  Rev*

William P. Osborn 🎤 ✈ W
145 Crestwood NW
Grand Rapids, MI 49504, 616-791-0049
Internet: osbornb@gvsu.edu
 Pubs: *Gettysburg Rev, ACM, Western Humanities Rev,
 Texas Rev, Carolina Qtly, Mississippi Rev, Faultline,
 Louisville Rev*

Charlene Noel Palmer P
2310 Calumet St
Flint, MI 48503-2811
 Pubs: *Anti-War Poem, Vol. II: Anth* (Stephen Gill,
 1986), *Voices for Peace: Anth* (Disarmament & Peace
 Task Force, 1983), *Peace or Perish: A Crisis Anth*
 (Poets for Peace, 1983), *Odyssey, Axios, Christian
 Century, Mediphors, December, Handmaiden*

David Palmer 🎤 ✈ P
2310 Calumet St
Flint, MI 48503-2811, 810-238-5919
 Pubs: *Quickly, Over the Wall* (Wake-Brook, 1966),
 Songs from Unsung Worlds: Anth (AAAS, 1985), *Peace
 or Perish: Anth* (Poets for Peace, 1983), *Beloit, Kayak,
 Passages North, Poets On, Immobius, Slipstream*

Miriam Pederson 🎤 P
Aquinas College, English Dept, 1607 Robinson Rd SE,
Grand Rapids, MI 49506-1705, 616-459-8281
Internet: pedermir@aquinas.edu
 Pubs: *Essential Love: Anth* (Poetworks, 2000), *New
 Poems from the Third Coast: Anth, The Third Coast:
 Anth* (Wayne State U Pr, 2000, 1990), *The Book of
 Birth Poetry: Anth* (Bantam Bks, 1995), *Passages North,
 MacGuffin, Sing Heavenly Muse*

William S. Penn 🎤 ✈ W
963 Lantern Hill Dr
East Lansing, MI 48823, 517-337-7313
Internet: penn@msu.edu
 Pubs: *Killing Time with Strangers* (U Arizona Pr, 2000),
 This Is the World (Michigan State U Pr, 2000), *The
 Absence of Angels* (Permanent Pr, 1994), *All My Sins
 Are Relative* (U Nebraska Pr, 1994), *Antaeus, Stand,
 Grain, Qtly West, Missouri Rev, Bananas*
I.D.: Native American

Rosalie Sanara Petrouske P
262 Whetstone Rd
Marquette, MI 49855, 906-225-8085
 Pubs: *The Geisha Box* (March Street Pr, 1996), *It's All
 the Rage: Anth* (Andrew Mountain Pr, 1997), *Poets On,
 Paintbrush, MacGuffin, Passages North, SPR, Seattle
 Rev, Parting Gifts, Rhino, Windless Orchard, Antigonish
 Rev*

Patricia Rachal P
2133 Ridge Rd
Kalamazoo, MI 49008, 616-345-3682

Dudley Randall P
12651 Old Mill Pl
Detroit, MI 48238, 313-935-1188
 Pubs: *Litany of Friends* (Lotus, 1981), *Black Poets:
 Anth* (Bantam, 1971)

Greg Rappleye P
Box 441
Grand Haven, MI 49417, 616-844-3335
 Pubs: *The PrePress Awards, 1992-1993: A Sampler of
 Emerging Michigan Writers: Anth* (PrePress Publishing
 of Michigan, 1993), *Mississippi Rev, Southern Rev,
 Prairie Schooner, Qtly West, Sky Books*

John R. Reed 🎤 ✈ P
English Dept, Wayne State Univ, 51 W Warren, Detroit,
MI 48202, 313-861-4298
Internet: john.reed@wayne.edu
 Pubs: *Life Sentences* (Wayne State U Pr, 1996), *Great
 Lake* (Ridgeway Pr, 1995), *Poetry, American Scholar,
 Michigan Qtly Rev, Ontario Rev, SW Rev, Partisan Rev*

Danny Rendleman 🎤 ✈ P
Univ Michigan, 326 Crob, Flint, MI 48502, 810-762-3388
Internet: dannyr@flint.umich.edu
 Pubs: *The Middle West, Victrola* (Ridgeway Pr, 1995,
 1994), *APR, Field, o.blek, Epoch, Passages North,
 Antigonish Rev*

Jack Ridl P
2309 Auburn Ave
Holland, MI 49424, 616-399-5925
 Pubs: *Approaching Poetry* (St. Martin's Pr, 1997),
 Poems from the Same Ghost & Between (Dawn Valley
 Pr, 1993), *For a Living: Poems of Work: Anth* (U
 Illinois, 1995), *Georgia Rev, The Jrnl, Artful Dodge,
 Poetry East, Ploughshares, Denver Qtly*

Daniel Rosochacki P
2223 Fremont
Grand Rapids, MI 49504

Gil Saenz 🎤 P
19211 Wall St
Melvindale, MI 48122-1876
 Pubs: *Dreaming of Love* (Pentland Pr, 1999)

William Schoenl 🎤 ✈ P
2643 Roseland
East Lansing, MI 48823-3870, 517-351-0456
 Pubs: *Big Two-Hearted, Alura Qtly, Riverrun, Parnassus*

Herbert Scott P
PO Box 2615
Kalamazoo, MI 49003, 616-342-5715
 Pubs: *The Wishing Heart* (Sutton Hoo Pr, 1999),
 Durations (LSU, 1984), *Groceries* (U Pittsburgh Pr,
 1976), *Poetry NW, Michigan Qtly Rev, Black Warrior
 Rev, Shenandoah, Kenyon Rev*

Heather Laurie Sellers 🎤 ✈ P&W
Hope College, 126 E 10 St, Holland, MI 49423-9000,
616-395-7116
Internet: sellers@hope.edu
Pubs: *Georgia Underwater* (Sarabande, 2001), *Your
Whole Life* (Panhandler, 1994), *William & Mary Rev,
Sonora Rev, The Sun, Five Points, New Virginia Rev,
Indiana Rev, Alaska Qtly Rev*

Diane Seuss 🎤 ✈ P
144 Monroe St
Kalamazoo, MI 49006-4475, 616-337-7038
Internet: dseussb@kzoo.edu
Pubs: *It Blows You Hollow* (New Issues Pr, 1998),
Boomer Girls: Anth (U Iowa Pr, 1999), *Poetry NW,
Alaska Qtly, Third Coast, Primavera, Indiana Rev,
Tamaqua, NW Rev, Cumberland Poetry Rev*

Maryl Shackett 🎤 P
323 Jefferson
Marine City, MI 48039-1620, 810-765-4383
Pubs: *Lucidity* (Bear House Pub, 2000), *This Is My
Beloved* (Anderie Poetry Pr, 1997), *Changes in the
Heart* (Lyre Loon, 1996), *The Seasons of Us,
Lovesounds* (Riverside-Popular, 1980, 1979), *Southill
Gazette*

Marc Sheehan P
15795 Peacock Rd
Haslett, MI 48840, 517-339-5985
Pubs: *Greatest Hits* (New Isues Pr, 1999), *Third Coast,
Sky, Controlled Burn, Burning World, Pannus Index,
Gulfstream, Parting Gifts*

Linda K. Nerva Sienkiewicz 🎤 P
520 W Third St
Rochester, MI 48307-1914, 248-652-3235
Internet: Fade2Blue@aol.com
Pubs: *Edge City Rev, Wayne Literary Rev, Heartlands
Today, Spoon River Poetry Rev, Maverick Pr, Thema,
Muddy River Poetry Rev, Touchstone Rev, Poetry Motel*

Anita Skeen 🎤 ✈ P
Michigan State Univ, 201 Morrill Hall, English Dept, East
Lansing, MI 48824, 517-355-7570
Internet: skeen@pilot.msu.edu
Pubs: *Outside the Fold, Outside the Frame* (MSU Pr,
1999), *Portraits* (Kida Pr, 1993), *Each Hand a Map*
(Naiad Pr, 1986), *Ploughshares, New Letters, Kansas
Qtly, Prairie Schooner, Ms., Nimrod*
Groups: Women, Adults

Elizabeth Anne Socolow P
Univ Ligget School, 1045 Cook Rd, Grosse Pte Woods,
MI 48236, 313-884-4444
Pubs: *Laughing at Gravity, Conversations with Isaac
Newton* (Beacon, 1988), *Bluestones & Salthay: Anth*
(Rutgers U Pr, 1990), *Michigan Qtly Rev*

Julie L. Stone P
1890 Carriage Rd #215
Muskegon, MI 49442, 616-773-0885
Pubs: *Playgirl, Berkeley Monthly, The Poet, The Hunter,
Scene, Vega, Hoosier Challenger*

Keith Taylor 🎤 ✈ P&W
1715 Dexter Ave
Ann Arbor, MI 48103-4007, 734-665-5341
Pubs: *Everything I Need* (March Street Pr, 1996), *Life
Science & Other Stories* (Hanging Loose Pr, 1995),
Detail from the Garden of Delights (Limited Mailing Pr,
1993), *Witness, Hanging Loose, Story, Pivot, Caliban,
Michigan Qtly Rev*

F. Richard Thomas 🎤 P
Dept of American Thought/Language, Michigan State Univ,
East Lansing, MI 48824-1033, 517-355-2400
Internet: thomasff@msu.edu
Pubs: *Death at Camp Pahoka, New Poems from the
Third Coast: Anth* (Michigan State U Pr, 2000, 2000),
Miracles (Canoe Pr, 1996), *Frog Praises Night*
(Southern Illinois U Pr, 1980)

Vonnie Thomas P
8757 Berridge Rd
Greenville, MI 48838, 616-754-8698
Pubs: *Gift of Time, Changing View* (Belding, 1992,
1990), *The View Beyond the Tree* (Greenville, 1981)

Ben Tibbs P
c/o R. Tibbs, 2127 Audley Dr NE, Grand Rapids, MI
49505, 616-349-2763
Pubs: *Graffiti Book, Italics Mine, Approaches* (Stovepipe
Pr, 1984, 1983, 1982), *Celery*

Richard Tillinghast 🎤 ✈ P&W
1317 Granger Ave
Ann Arbor, MI 48104-4480, 313-930-0532
Internet: rwtill@umich.edu
Pubs: *Six Mile Mountain* (Story Line Pr, 2000), *Today
in the Cafe Trieste* (Salmon/Dufour, 1997), *The
Stonecutter's Hand* (David R. Godine, 1995), *Our Flag
Was Still There* (Wesleyan U Pr, 1984), *Paris Rev,
New Yorker, Nation, Atlantic, New Criterion*

Eric Torgersen 🎤 ✈ P&W
8475 Chippewa Trail
Mount Pleasant, MI 48858-9488, 517-773-4559
Internet: eric.torgersen@cmich.edu
Pubs: *Inside Unity House, The Door to the Moon,*
(March Street Pr, 1999, 1993), *Dear Friend*
(Northwestern U Pr, 1998), *Good True Stories* (Lynx
Hse, 1994), *Hudson Rev, APR, Literary Rev,
Gettysburg Rev, River Styx*

Stephen H. Tudor   P
14447 Harbor Island
Detroit, MI 48215, 313-822-4895
    Pubs: *Haul-Out: New & Selected Poems, Hangdog
    Reef: Poems Sailing the Great Lakes* (Wayne State U,
    1996, 1989), *Michigan Qtly Rev, Bridge*

Christina-Marie Umscheid ⏺   P
149 Washington St
Petoskey, MI 49770-2948, 231-347-1775
Internet: christinu@voyager.net
    Pubs: *Images & Language* (Writers North, 1987),
    Voices of Michigan: Anth (Mackinac Jane Pub Co,
    1999), *At the Edge of Mirror Lake: Anth* (Plainview Pr,
    1999), *Poetry Tonight, Napalm Health Spa, Hiram
    Poetry Rev, MacGuffin, Caliban, Chicago Rev*
I.D.: Disabled, Breast Cancer Survivor

Robert Vandermolen ⏺ ⊀   P
2771 Glencairin Dr NW
Grand Rapids, MI 49504-2388, 616-453-7056
    Pubs: *Breath* (New Issues Pr, 2000), *Peaches* (Sky Pr,
    1998), *Night Weather* (Northern Lights Pr, 1991),
    *Mudfish, NAW, Artful Dodge, Exquisite Corpse, Caliban,
    Sulfur, Grand Street, House Organ, Epoch*

Diane Wakoski ⏺ ⊀   P
607 Division St
East Lansing, MI 48823-3428, 517-332-3385
Internet: wakoski@pilot.msu.edu
    Pubs: *Argonaut Rose, The Emerald City of Las Vegas,
    Jason the Sailor, Medea the Sorceress* (Black Sparrow
    Pr, 1998, 1995, 1993, 1990)

Sylvia Watanabe   W
145 Crestwood NW
Grand Rapids, MI 49504
    Pubs: *Talking to the Dead & Other Stories* (Doubleday,
    1992)

Barrett Watten ⏺ ⊀   P
English Dept, Wayne State University, Detroit, MI 48202,
313-577-3067
Internet: b.watten@wayne.edu
    Pubs: *Bad History* (Atelos Pr, 1998), *Frame,* (Sun &
    Moon Pr, 1997), *Under Erasure* (Zasterle Pr, 1991),
    Leningrad: American Writers in the Soviet Union (w/M.
    Davidson, et al; Mercury Hse, 1991), *Conduit* (Gaz,
    1986), *The World, Common Knowledge, Poetics Jrnl*

Ron Weber   P
2160 N County Line Rd
Watervliet, MI 49098-9535, 616-463-4049
    Pubs: *Bluff View from the Twin Cities: Poems from the
    West Bank* (Harbor Hse 1993), *Voices Intl, Tempo,
    Catalyst, Peninsula Poets, Poet, Analecta*

Robert E. Wegner   W
Alma College, Alma, MI 48801
    Pubs: *The Third Coast: Anth* (Wayne State, 1982),
    Short Story Intl, Karamu, SW Rev

Patricia Jabbeh Wesley ⏺ ⊀   P&W
English Department, Western Michigan Univ, Spau Tower,
Kalamazoo, MI 49008-5092, 616-387-2572
Internet: pjabbeh@juno.com
    Pubs: *Before the Palm Could Bloom* (New Issues Pr,
    1998), *Crab Orchard Rev, Michigan College English
    Association Jrnl, Institute for Liberian Studies Jrnl*
I.D.: African, Black. Groups: African-American, Multicultural

Gloria Whelan ⏺ ⊀   W
Oxbow, 9797 N Twin Lake Rd NE, Mancelona, MI 49659,
231-587-9501
    Pubs: *Homeless Bird, Return to the Island, Farewell to
    the Island* (HC, 2000, 2000, 1998), *Forgive the River,
    Forgive the Sky* (Eerdmans, 1998)

Carolyn White ⏺ ⊀   P&W
1661 Mt Vernon Ave
East Lansing, MI 48823-3740, 517-351-5866
    Pubs: *The Adventure of Lovey & Frank* (Greenwillow,
    2001), *Whuppity Stoorie* (Putnam, 1997), *The Tree
    House Children* (S&S, 1994), *Parabola, Magical Blend,
    Book of Contemporary Myth, Michigan Qtly Rev, Studia
    Mystica*
Groups: Children

Laurie Anne Whitt   P
PO Box 195
Chassell, MI 49916, 906-523-4566
    Pubs: *Icarus 95: Anth* (Kenan Pr, 1995), *New Voices:
    Anth* (Mosaic Pr, 1984), *Spoon River Poetry Rev,
    Puerto del Sol, Wisconsin Rev, Cottonwood, Hawaii
    Rev, Malahat Rev, Prism Intl*

Margaret Willey   P&W
431 Grant St
Grand Haven, MI 49417-1834, 616-846-1759
    Pubs: *Facing the Music, The Melinda Zone, Saving
    Lenny* (Bantam, 1996, 1993, 1990), *If Not for You,
    Finding David Dolores* (H&R, 1988, 1986), *Hungry Mind
    Rev, New Moon Network, Calyx, Passages North,
    Redbook, Qtly West*

Willie Williams   P
3836 Courville
Detroit, MI 48224, 313-824-4086
    Pubs: *Spillway, Way Station Mag, Red Cedar Rev,
    Howling Dog, Graffiti Rag, Triage*

Thomas Wiloch 🎤 ✈   P&W
PMB #226, 42015 Ford Rd
Canton, MI 48187
Internet: mssunltd@postmark.net
    Pubs: *Neon Trance, Decoded Factories of the Heart*
    (Runaway Spoon Pr, 1997, 1994), *Mr. Templeton's*
    Toyshop (Wordcraft, 1995), *Bitter Oleander, Small Pr*
    Rev, Winedark Sea, Publishers Weekly, Carpe Noctem,
    Bloomsbury Rev
I.D.: Euro-American

Melinda Wolf   P
1761 Oxford Rd SE
Grand Rapids, MI 49506, 616-956-9105
    Pubs: *Anth of Mag Verse & Yearbook of American*
    Poetry, NYQ, Mudfish, American Literary Rev, Cape
    Rock, Kalliope, Outerbridge, Intro, Pig Iron, South Coast
    Poetry Rev

Anne Ohman Youngs   P
5171 Hwy M35
Escanaba, MI 49829, 906-789-1934
    Pubs: *A Bracelet of Mouse Hands* (Frank Cat Pr,
    1995), *Markers* (Andrew Mountain Pr, 1988), *Prose*
    Poem, Cream City Rev, Mid-American Rev, Midwest
    Qtly, Tar River

Janice Zerfas 🎤 ✈   P
English Dept, Lake Michigan College, 2755 E Napier Ave,
Benton Harbor, MI 49022-1899, 616-927-3571
Internet: zerfas@lmc.cc.mi.es
    Pubs: *Parting Gifts, The Way In, MacGuffin, Indiana*
    Rev, Sky, Paterson Lit Rev, Graffiti Rag
Groups: Seniors

Jack Zucker   P
14050 Vernon St
Oak Park, MI 48237
    Pubs: *From Manhattan* (Pointe Pr, 1989), *Beginnings*
    (Katydid Pr, 1982), *The Bridge, Poetry NW, Esquire,*
    Literary Rev

MINNESOTA

C. Abartis   W
English Dept, St. Cloud State Univ, St Cloud, MN 56301,
612-255-3061
    Pubs: *Twilight Zone Mag, Lady's Circle, The Qtly, Beloit*
    Fiction Jrnl

Harold Adams 🎤   W
12916 Greenwood Rd
Minnetonka, MN 55343, 612-938-6426
    Pubs: *Lead, So I Can Follow, No Badge, No Gun, The*
    Icepick Artist, The Hatchet Job, The Ditched Blonde, A
    Way with Widows, A Prfctly Prpr Mrdr, The Mn Who
    Was Tllr Thn God (Walker, 1999, 1998, 1997, 1996,
    1995, 1994, 1993, 1992)

Jonis Agee   P&W
English Dept, College of St Catherine, 2004 Randolph, St
Paul, MN 55105
    Pubs: *South of Resurrection* (Viking, 1997), *Strange*
    Angels, Sweet Eyes (HC, 1994, 1992), *.38 Special & a*
    Broken Heart, Bend This Heart (Coffee Hse Pr, 1995,
    1989)

Paulette Bates Alden   W
4900 Washburn Ave S
Minneapolis, MN 55410, 612-920-1896
    Pubs: *Crossing the Moon* (Hungry Mind Pr, 1996),
    Feeding the Eagles (Graywolf Pr, 1988), *Ploughshares,*
    Mississippi Rev, Antioch Rev, New York Times Mag,
    First

Floyce Alexander   P&W
1211 Beltrami Ave NW
Bemidji, MN 56601-2826, 218-751-7382
    Pubs: *Memory of the Future* (Red Dragonfly Pr, 1998),
    Red Deer (L'Epervier, 1982), *Bottom Falling Out of the*
    Dream (Lynx Hse Pr, 1976), *The Nation, TriQtly,*
    Greenfield Rev, Contact II, Colorado Rev

Daniel Bachhuber 🎤 ✈   P
1288 Osceola Ave
St Paul, MN 55105, 612-699-1560
    Pubs: *Mozart's Carriage, Party Train: Anth* (New Rivers
    Pr, 2001, 1996), *Atlanta Rev, Visions Intl, SPR, Green*
    Hills Literary Lantern, Iowa Rev

Patricia Barone 🎤 ✈   P
686 Kimball St NE
Fridley, MN 55432-1643, 612-784-3386
Internet: baronel@juno.com
    Pubs: *Handmade Paper, The Wind, The Talking of*
    Hands: Anth, One Parrish Over: Anth (New Rivers Pr,
    1994, 1987, 1998, 1995), *American Voices: Anth*
    (Merrill, 1998), *Bless Me Father: Anth* (Penguin, 1994),
    Visions Intl, And Rev, Pleiades

David Bengtson 🎤 ✈   P
626 Oak Ct S
Long Prairie, MN 56347-1629, 320-732-6297
Internet: david_bengston@mail.lpge.k12.mn.us
    Pubs: *Open Windows* (Juniper Pr, 1990), *26 Minnesota*
    Writers: Anth (Nodin Pr, 1995), *Biggy's Candy Store:*
    Anth (The Loft, 1992), *Ascent, New Letters, NER,*
    Northeast, Sidewalks, Lake County Jrnl

Sigrid Bergie   P
1000 W Franklin Ave, Apt 120
Minneapolis, MN 55405
    Pubs: *Turning Out the Lights* (New Rivers Pr, 1988)

Candace Black 🎤 ✈ P
824 Baker Ave
Mankato, MN 56001, 507-625-6104
  Pubs: *The Decade Dance: Anth* (Sandhills Pr, 1991),
  Sport Literate, Passages North, Folio, Conscience,
  Milkweed Chronicle, Iowa Woman, Pennsylvania Rev,
  Seattle Rev, Gulf Stream Mag

Carol Bly W
1668 Juno Ave
St Paul, MN 55116-1415, 612-699-5427
  Pubs: *Changing the Bully Who Rules the World: Anth*
  (Milkweed Edtns, 1996), *New Yorker, TriQtly, Laurel*
  Rev, Iowa Rev

Robert Bly P
1904 Girard Ave S
Minneapolis, MN 55403-2945, 612-377-9817
  Pubs: *Eating the Honey of Words: New & Selected*
  Poems, Morning Poems, Meditations on the Insatiable
  Soul, What Have I Ever Lost by Dying? (HC, 1999,
  1997, 1994, 1993), *Nation, The Sun, Kenyon Rev,*
  Common Boundary

William Borden 🎤 ✈ P&W
Route 6, Box 284
Bemidji, MN 56601-8635, 218-586-2765
Internet: www.williamborden.com
  Pubs: *Turtle Island Blues* (Listening Winds, 2000),
  Eurydice's Song (St. Andrews, 1999), *Superstoe* (Orloff,
  1996), *Slow Step & Dance* (Loonfeather Pr, 1991),
  Minnesota Poetry Calendar: Anth (Black Hat, 2000),
  Sweat: Anth (OTSA Pr, 2000), *Rattle*

Jonathan Brannen P&W
7 Circle Pines St
Morris, MN 56267-2103
  Pubs: *Thing Is the Anagram of Night* (Texture Pr,
  1996), *Nothing Doing Never Again* (Score Pr, 1995),
  Black Ice, Situation, Fiction Intl, Asylum Annual, 6ix

Jill Breckenridge P
708 N 1st St, #534
Minneapolis, MN 55401-1152
  Pubs: *How to Be Lucky* (Blue Stem Pr, 1990), *Civil*
  Blood (Milkweed Edtns, 1986), *Noeva: 3 Women Poets:*
  Anth (Dakota Pr, 1975)

Kerri R. Brostrom P
2512 E 125 St
Burnsville, MN 55337-3139, 612-728-0053
  Pubs: *Oregon East, Pointed Circle, Ellipsis, Pearl, Old*
  Red Kimono, Alura, Cape Rock, Maryland Poetry Rev,
  Black River Rev, Rattle, Madison Rev

Michael Dennis Browne 🎤 ✈ P
English Dept, Univ Minnesota, Lind Hall, 207 Church St,
Minneapolis, MN 55455, 612-626-9555
  Pubs: *Selected Poems 1965-1995, You Won't*
  Remember This, Smoke from the Fires, The Sun
  Fetcher (Carnegie Mellon, 1997, 1992, 1985, 1978),
  APR, TriQtly
Groups: Children, Prisoners

Emilie Buchwald P&W
Milkweed Editions, 430 First Ave N, Ste 400, Minneapolis,
MN 55406, 612-332-3192
  Pubs: *The Sporting Life: Anth, The Poet Dreaming in*
  the Artist's House: Anth, Transforming a Rape Culture:
  Anth (Milkweed Edtns, 1987, 1984, 1993)

Alan Burns W
English Dept, 207 Lind Hall, Univ Minnesota, 207 Church
St SE, Minneapolis, MN 55455, 612-625-3363
  Pubs: *Revolutions of the Night* (Schocken, 1987), *The*
  Day Daddy Died (Allison & Busby, 1981)

John Caddy P
8870 202nd St N
Forest Lake, MN 55025, 612-464-6684
  Pubs: *The Color of Mesabi Bones, Eating the Sting*
  (Milkweed Edtns, 1989, 1986), *Dacotah Territory*

Katherine Carlson W
2912 34th Ave S, #2
Minneapolis, MN 55406, 612-296-6605
  Pubs: *Casualties* (New Rivers, 1982), *Minneapolis/St.*
  Paul Mag, New Directions for Women, In These Times,
  VIA, Minnesota Women's Pr, Spirit

Barry Casselman 🎤 ✈ P
1414 S 3rd St, #102
Minneapolis, MN 55454-1172, 612-321-9044
Internet: barcass@mr.net
  Pubs: *The Boat of the Blue Rose, Among Dreams*
  (Kraken Pr, 2000, 1985), *Language Is Not Words*
  (Lingua Pr, 1980), *APR, ACM, Calcutta 2000, Kansas*
  Qtly, North Stone Rev

Nadia Christensen P
1545 Fulham St
St Paul, MN 55108
  Pubs: *Turkestan* (w/Kling; France; Chene, 1991), *Action,*
  Reflection, Celebration (ARC, 1988)

Kathleen Coskran 🎤 ✈ W
152 Bank St SE
Minneapolis, MN 55414-1033
  Pubs: *The High Price of Everything, Tanzania on*
  Tuesday: Anth (New Rivers Pr, 1988, 1997), *Living on*
  the Edge: Anth (Curbstone Pr, 1999), *Going Up*
  Country: Anth (Scribner, 1994)

Jeanette M. Cox   P&W
Rte 4, Box 4
McGregor, MN 55760, 218-768-3851
    Pubs: *Variations in Time & Tempo* (Zigzag Pr, 1993),
    Dust & Fire: An Anth of Women's Writing (Bemidji
    State U, 1994), *Minnesota Women's Pr, North Woods
    Patchwork*

Florence Chard Dacey   P
Box 31
Cottonwood, MN 56229, 507-423-6652
    Pubs: *The Necklace* (Midwest Villages & Voices, 1988),
    The Swoon (Minnesota Writers Pub Hse, 1979)

Philip Dacey ⚲ ✈   P
English Dept, Southwest State Univ, Marshall, MN 56258,
507-537-7155
Internet: dacey@ssu.southwest.msus.edu
    Pubs: *The Deathbed Playboy* (Eastern Washington U
    Pr, 1999), *What's Empty Weighs the Most* (Black Dirt
    Pr, 1997), *Night Shift at the Crucifix Factory* (U Iowa
    Pr, 1991), *The Nation, Hudson Rev, Poetry, Georgia
    Rev, Paris Rev, Partisan Rev*

John D'Agata   P
c/o Graywolf Press, 2402 University Ave, Suite 203, St.
Paul, MN 55114, 651-641-0077
    Pubs: *Halls of Fame* (Graywolf Press, 2001), *Witness,
    Paris Rev, Colorado Rev, The Jrnl, Ploughshares*

Alan Davis   P&W
Moorhead State Univ, PO Box 229, Moorhead, MN 56563,
218-236-4681
    Pubs: *American Fiction, Rumors from the Lost World*
    (New Rivers, 1996, 1995), *The Qtly, Hudson Rev,
    North Dakota Qtly, South Dakota Rev, Chattahoochee
    Rev, Image*

Emilio DeGrazia ⚲ ✈   W
211 W 7 St
Winona, MN 55987, 507-454-6564
    Pubs: *A Canticle for Bread & Stones, Seventeen
    Grams Worth of Soul* (Lone Oak Pr, 1997, 1994), *Billy
    Brazil* (New Rivers Pr, 1992)
I.D.: Italian-American. Groups: Children, Italian-American

Leigh Donaldson   P&W
c/o North East Arts, PO Box 94, Kittery, MN 03904
    Pubs: *City River of Voices, Cafe Rev, Shooting Star
    Rev, Atelier, Art & Understanding, World Poetry 1998,
    Catalyst Mag, Intl Poetry Rev, Potato Eyes, Manhattan
    Poetry Rev, Portfolio Mag, Hawaii Rev, Obsidian II, AIM
    Qtly, Art Times, Minnesota Ink*

Scott Edelstein   W
4445 Vincent Ave S, #2
Minneapolis, MN 55410-1527, 612-823-5838
    Pubs: *Ellery Queen's Mystery Mag, Artist's Mag,
    Writer's Yearbook, Artlines, New Worlds, City Miner*

John Engman   P
1916 Colfax Ave S
Minneapolis, MN 55403, 612-874-9097
    Pubs: *Keeping Still, Mountain* (Galileo Pr, 1983), *New
    American Poets of the Nineties: Anth* (Godine, 1992),
    *Prairie Schooner, Virginia Qtly Rev, Iowa Rev, Poetry
    NW*

Barbara Juster Esbensen   P
5602 Dalrymple Rd
Edina, MN 55424, 612-929-2065
    Pubs: *Echoes for the Eye, Dance with Me, Who
    Shrank My Grandmother's House?* (HC, 1996, 1995,
    1992)

Michael Finley   P
1814 Dayton Ave
St Paul, MN 55104, 651-644-4540
    Pubs: *Looking for China* (Kraken Pr, 1994), *Pushcart
    Prize XI: Anth* (Pushcart Pr, 1986), *Paris Rev, New
    American & Canadian Poetry, Great River Rev*

Kevin FitzPatrick   P
3740 48th Ave, S
Minneapolis, MN 55406, 612-721-1499
    Pubs: *Rush Hour, Down on the Corner* (Midwest
    Villages & Voices, 1997, 1987)

Dee Fonville   P
2636 Freemont Ave S, #106
Minneapolis, MN 55408, 612-374-4160
    Pubs: *Iris: A Jrnl About Women, Caprice, New Letters,
    Poetry NW, Intro, Carolina Qtly, Memphis State Rev,
    Squeezebox Mag*

David J. Fraher   P
c/o Arts Midwest, Hennepin Center for the Arts, 528
Hennepin Ave, Ste 310, Minneapolis, MN 55403
    Pubs: *Western Humanities Rev, American Poetry Rev,
    New Letters, Slackwater Rev*

Mary Gardner ⚲ ✈   W
235 Arundel St, #5
St Paul, MN 55102, 651-291-8722
    Pubs: *Boat People* (Norton, 1995), *Milkweed*
    (Papier-Mache 1994), *Keeping Warm* (Atheneum 1987)
Lang: German

Terry A. Garey   P
3149 Park Ave S
Minneapolis, MN 55407, 612-824-5157
    Pubs: *Time Frames: Anth of Speculative Poetry* (Rune
    Pr, 1991), *Raw Sacks: Anth* (Bag Person Pr, 1991),
    Hurricane Alice, Weird Tales, Star*Line, AntiDog

Diane Glancy ♪ ✈   P
Macalester College, 1600 Grand, St Paul, MN 55105,
651-696-6516
Internet: www.macalester.edu/~glancy
   Pubs: *The Relief of America* (Tia Chucha Pr, 2000),
The Voice That Was in Travel (U Oklahoma, 1999),
Fuller Man, Flutie (Moyer Bell, 1999, 1998), *The West
Pole* (U Minnesota Pr, 1997), *Pushing the Bear* (HB,
1996)

Kate Green   P&W
c/o Lazear Agency, 430 1st Ave N, Ste 416, Minneapolis,
MN 55401, 612-332-8640
   Pubs: *Shooting Star* (HC, 1992), *The Fossil Family
Tales* (Creative Education, 1992), *Night Angel*
(Delacorte, 1989), *APR, Hungry Mind Rev*

Alvin Greenberg   P&W
1113 Lincoln Ave
St Paul, MN 55105, 612-290-9732
   Pubs: *How the Dead Live* (Graywolf Pr, 1998), *Why
We Live with Animals, The Man in the Cardboard Mask*
(Coffee Hse, 1990, 1985), *Heavy Wings* (Ohio Rev Pr,
1988), *NAR, Gettysburg Rev, Georgia Rev, Chelsea,
American Literary Rev*

Keith Gunderson   P
1212 Lakeview Ave S
Minneapolis, MN 55416, 612-374-4339
   Pubs: *A Continual Interest in the Sun & Sea & Inland
Missing the Sea* (Nodin, 1977), *Milkweed, North Stone
Rev, Baja Jrnl*

Patricia Hampl ♪ ✈   P
286 Laurel Ave
St Paul, MN 55102-2122
Internet: hampl@umn.edu
   Pubs: *I Could Tell You Stories* (Norton, 1999), *A
Romantic Education* (HM, 1992), *Virgin Time* (FSG,
1992), *Spillville* (Milkweed Edtns, 1987), *New Yorker,
Antaeus, Paris Rev*

Joanne Hart   P
Box 356
Grand Portage, MN 55605
   Pubs: *Minnesota Poetry Calendar: Anth* (Black Hat Pr,
1998), *The Women's Great Lakes Reader: Anth* (Holy
Cow! Pr, 1998), *Inheriting the Land: Anth* (U Minnesota
Pr, 1993), *Mixed Voices: Anth* (Milkweed Edtns, 1991),
North Coast Rev

Margaret M. Hasse   P
1698 Lincoln Ave
St Paul, MN 55105, 612-699-9138
   Pubs: *In a Sheep's Eye, Darling* (Milkweed Edtns,
1988), *Sisters of the Earth: Anth* (Vintage, 1991),
Tendril, Primavera, Milkweed Chronicle

Susan Carol Hauser ♪ ✈   P
Rt 1, Box 81
Puposky, MN 56667-9723, 218-243-2402
Internet: schauser@paulbunyan.net
   Pubs: *Redpoll on a Broken Branch* (Same Name Pr,
1992), *Girl to Woman* (Astarte Shell Pr, 1992), *Midwest
Qtly, Poetry Motel, North Coast Rev*

Ellen Hawley ♪ ✈   W
3223 36th Ave S
Minneapolis, MN 55406-2128, 612-729-8813
Internet: ellenhawley@yahoo.com
   Pubs: *Trip Sheets* (Milkweed Edtns, 1998), *Hers 3:
Anth* (Faber & Faber, 1999)
I.D.: G/L/B/T, Jewish. Groups: G/L/B/T

Robert Hedin   P
PO Box 59
Frontenac, MN 55026, 612-388-6103
   Pubs: *Tornadoes* (Ion Bks, 1990), *Alaska: Reflections
on Land & Spirit* (U Arizona Pr, 1989)

Donal Heffernan ♪ ✈   P
8570 Jewel Ave North
Stillwater, MN 55082, 651-426-9571
Internet: donal@msn.com
   Pubs: *Hillsides* (Anvil, 1990), *Orion* (Lone Oak Pr,
1994), *Artword, CPU Rev, Crisp Pine, Fan, Minnesota
Poetry Calendar, Paintbrush*

Scott Helmes ♪ ✈   P
862 Tuscarora
St Paul, MN 55102-3706, 612-339-9260
Internet: skaadenhelmes@compuserve.com
   Pubs: *Non Additive Postulations* (Runaway Spoon Pr,
2000), *Poems 1972-1997, Seven Poet/ms: Anth, Our
Bodies Our Icons: Anth* (Helmes, 1997, 1996, 1994),
Art Postale: Anth (AAA Edizioni, 1999), *Dictionary of
the Avant-Gardes: Anth* (Schirmer, 2000)
Groups: Children

Mary Ann Henn   P
104 Chapel Ln
St Joseph, MN 56374-0220, 320-363-7061
   Pubs: *Nu-N-Human, Nun-Plus* (Fig Pr, 1993, 1990),
*Time of Singing, Upsouth, Poets at Work, Parnassus,
Explorer, Smiles, Silver Wings, Simply Words, San
Fernando Poetry Jrnl, Waterways, Reflect*

Stephen Hesla   W
c/o Alma Hesla, #8 Lincoln Ln, Northfield, MN 55057
   Pubs: *The Hawthorn Conspiracy* (Dembner Bks, 1984)

Rolando Hinojosa   W
Univ Minnesota, 224 Church St SE/493 Ford Hall,
Minneapolis, MN 55455, 612-373-9707

H. Edgar Hix   P
5144 45th Ave South
Minneapolis, MN 55417-1625, 612-724-4362
  Pubs: *God's Special Book* (Concordia Pub, 1980),
  *Impetus, Waterways, Time of Singing, Midland Rev,
  Lilliput Rev, South Coast Poetry Jrnl, Burning Light,
  Untitled*

Richard D. Houff   P
604 Hawthorne Ave East
St Paul, MN 55101, 612-690-2615
  Pubs: *Exit(s), Used Shoes* (Roving Anvil Pr, 1996,
  1995), *Earthquake School: Anth* (Many Beaches Pr,
  1998), *Definitive Guide to the Twin Cities: Anth* (Spout
  Pr, 1997), *Riverrun, Gryphon, Psychopoetica, Krax,
  Brooklyn Rev, Clare, Gas, Rattle*

Alyce Ingram   W
Mears Park Place, 401 Sibley St #622, St Paul, MN
55101
  Pubs: *Best of Wind: Anth* (Wind Pub, 1994), *Sexual
  Harassment* (Crossing Pr, 1992), *Nightshade Short
  Story Reader: Anth* (Nightshade Pr, 1991), *Small Pond,
  Slate, Happy, Peep, Knocked, Potato Eyes, Pittsburgh
  Qtly, ELF, Briar Cliff Rev, Potpourri, Q Rev*

Dale Jacobson   P
810 1st Ave NE
East Grand Forks, MN 56721, 218-773-9226
  Pubs: *Shouting at Midnight* (Spirit Horse Pr, 1986),
  Poems for Goya's Disparates (Jazz Pr, 1980), *APR,
  Forkroads, Lilliput Rev, Pemmican, Prairie Volcano*

Louis Jenkins 🎤 ✈   P
101 Clover St
Duluth, MN 55812-1103, 218-724-6382
Internet: louis@skypoint.com
  Pubs: *Just Above Water, Nice Fish* (Holy Cow! Pr,
  1997, 1995), *All Tangled Up with the Living* (Nineties
  Pr, 1991)

Jim Johnson   P
New Rivers Press, 420 N 5 St, Ste 910, Minneapolis, MN
55401, 612-339-7114
  Pubs: *Wolves* (New Rivers Pr, 1993), *A Field Guide to
  Blueberries, Finns in Minnesota Midwinter* (North Star
  Pr, 1992, 1986)

Deborah Keenan 🎤 ✈   P
1168 Laurel Ave
St Paul, MN 55104, 612-647-0276
  Pubs: *Happiness* (Coffee Hse Pr, 1995), *Looking for
  Home: Anth* (Milkweed Edtns, 1990), *Santa Monica
  Rev, Shenandoah*

Garrison Keillor   W
Minnesota Public Radio, 45 E 7th St, St Paul, MN 55101

N. M. Kelby 🎤 ✈   W
553 Selby Ave
St. Paul, MN 55102-1728, 651-298-8544
  Pubs: *In the Company of Angels* (Hyperion Pr, 2001),
  Mississippi Rev

Patricia Kirkpatrick 🎤 ✈   P
1256 Osceola
St Paul, MN 55105, 612-690-0089
  Pubs: *What Have You Lost?: Anth* (S&S, 2000), *The
  Writing Path: Anth* (U Iowa Pr, 1995), *Minnesota
  Writers: Poetry Anth* (Milkweed Edtns, 1987), *Antioch
  Rev, Hungry Mind Rev*
Groups: Children, Teachers

Allan Kornblum   P
Coffee House Press, 27 N 4 St, Ste 400, Minneapolis,
MN 55401, 612-338-0125
  Pubs: *Awkward Song* (Toothpaste Pr, 1980), *The Salad
  Bushes* (Seamark Pr, 1975)

Cinda Kornblum   P
Coffee House Press, 27 N 4 St, Ste 400, Minneapolis,
MN 55401
  Pubs: *Bandwagon* (Toothpaste Pr, 1976), *The Actualist
  Anth* (The Spirit That Moves Us, 1977)

Jack Kreitzer   P
1031 Prior Ave S
Saint Paul, MN 55116
  Pubs: *Dark Moon* (Bald Mountain Pr, 1979), *Through
  Fire & Deep Water* (RVK Publishing, 1976)

J. L. Kubicek 🎤 ✈   P
16757-512 Lane, Rt 1, Box 167
Lake Crystal, MN 56055-9757, 507-546-3775
  Pubs: *Blood to Remember: Anth* (Texas Tech U Pr,
  1990), *Czech-American Writing: Anth* (New Rivers,
  1990), *Ariel, The Classical Outlook, Green's Mag,
  Midstream, New Hope Intl, Queen's Qtly, Prism Intl,
  Voices Israel*

Brett Laidlaw   W
2087 Princeton Ave
St Paul, MN 51105, 612-646-2472
  Pubs: *Blue Bel Air* (Norton, 1993), *Three Nights in the
  Heart of the Earth* (NAL, 1989), *Elvis in Oz: Anth* (U
  Virginia, 1992)

Roseann Lloyd   P
1146 Randolph Ave, #7
Saint Paul, MN 55105-2974, 612-699-1543
  Pubs: *War Baby Express* (Holy Cow! Pr, 1996), *She
  Who Was Lost Is Remembered* (Seal Pr, 1992),
  Looking for Home: Anth (Milkweed Edtns, 1991)

Diane Lunde   P
4105 E 34 St
Minneapolis, MN 55406-2827
   Pubs: *North Country: Anth* (Greenfield Rev, 1986),
   *Kentucky Rev, Visions, Midnight Lamp, 13th Moon,
   Sycamore Rev, St. Andrews Rev, Poetry NW*

Joseph Maiolo   W
English Dept, Univ Minnesota, Duluth, MN 55812,
218-726-8226
   Pubs: *Ploughshares, Sewanee, Shenandoah, Texas
   Rev, New Virginia Rev*

Freya Manfred 🎤 ✈   P
5595 Christmas Lake Point
Shorewood, MN 55331-9299, 952-470-0435
Internet: Thompope@aol.com
   Pubs: *American Roads* (Viking, 1985), *APR, New
   Letters, Antioch Rev, Minnesota Rev, Michigan Qtly Rev*
Groups: Children

Galen Martini   P
104 Chapel Ln
St. Joseph, MN 56374
   Pubs: *Fuel* (BOA Edtns, 1998), *Words Under the
   Words* (Far Corner Bks, 1995), *Atlantic, Five Points,
   Atlanta Rev, Georgia Rev, Tampa Rev, Indiana Rev*

Ken McCullough   P&W
372 Center St
Winona, MN 55987
   Pubs: *Sycamore Oriole* (Ahsahta Pr, 1991), *Travelling
   Light* (Thunder's Mouth Pr, 1987)

Bill Meissner   P&W
618 6th Ave N
St Cloud, MN 56303
   Pubs: *Hitting Into the Wind* (SMU Pr, 1997), *Twin Sons
   of Different Mirrors* (w/Jack Driscoll; Milkweed Edtns,
   1989)

Leslie Adrienne Miller 🎤 ✈   P
English Dept, Mail 30F, Univ St. Thomas, 2115 Summit
Ave, St Paul, MN 55105-1096, 651-962-5604
Internet: lamiller@stthomas.edu
   Pubs: *Yesterday Had a Man in It, Ungodliness, Staying
   Up for Love* (Carnegie Mellon U Pr, 1998, 1994, 1990),
   *APR, Kenyon Rev, NER, Georgia Rev, Ploughshares,
   Nimrod*

John Minczeski 🎤 ✈   P
1300 Dayton
St Paul, MN 55104, 651-646-9434
Internet: lyublinz@aol.com
   Pubs: *Gravity* (Texas Tech U Pr, 1991), *The
   Reconstruction of Light* (New Rivers Pr, 1987), *Agni,
   Meridian, Marlboro Rev, Pleiades, Crania, Free Lunch,
   Midwest Qtly, Cape Rock, Cream City Rev, Spoon
   River Poetry Rev, Pemmican*

Valerie Miner   W
English Dept, Univ Minnesota, Minneapolis, MN 55455,
612-625-3363
   Pubs: *A Walking Fire* (SUNY Pr, 1994), *Rumors from
   the Cauldron* (U Michigan Pr, 1992), *VLS, Michigan
   Qtly Rev, Ploughshares, Nation, Virginia Qtly Rev*

David R. Moffatt   P
Rte 3, Box 228
Pine City, MN 55063, 612-629-2816
   Pubs: *The Folded Paper Dream* (Tiger Moon Pr, 1992),
   *Riverrun, Verve, Poetic Knight, Star Triad, Shawnee
   Silhouette, The Archer*

James Moore 🎤 ✈   P
438 Laurel Ave, #5
St Paul, MN 55102-2049, 651-227-0047
Internet: laurel438@aol.com
   Pubs: *The Long Experience of Love, The Freedom of
   History* (Milkweed Edtns, 1995, 1988), *APR, Paris Rev,
   Nation, Kenyon Rev, Antioch Rev, Threepenny Rev*

Michael Moos   P
2223 Dayton Ave
St Paul, MN 55104, 612-642-0181
   Pubs: *Great River Review Anth* (Great River Rev,
   1989), *Minnesota Writers: Anth* (Milkweed, 1987)

David Mura 🎤 ✈   P
1920 E River Terr
Minneapolis, MN 55414-3672
Internet: davsus@aol.com
   Pubs: *The Colors of Desire* (Anchor, 1995), *After We
   Lost Our Way* (Carnegie Mellon U Pr, 1989), *APR,
   NER, New Republic, Conjunctions, Mother Jones, New
   York Times*
I.D.: Asian-American, Japanese-American

James Naiden 🎤 ✈   P
The North Stone Review, Box 14098, Minneapolis, MN
55414-0098, 612-721-8011
Internet: jack123904@aol.com
   Pubs: *Asphyxiations #1-40* (Metron Pr, 2001), *The
   Orange Notebook* (Metron Pr, 1973), *ShortStory.org,
   Poetry, Eire-Ireland, Nantucket Rev, New Hibernia Rev,
   Willow Avenue Rev, Wolf Head Qtly*

Josip Novakovich   W
Graywolf Press, 2402 University Ave, Ste 203, St. Paul,
MN 55114, 612-641-0007
   Pubs: *Salvation & Other Disasters* (Graywolf, 1995),
   Antaeus, Paris Rev, Ploughshares

W. Scott Olsen 🎤 ✈   W
443 42nd Ave
Moorhead, MN 56560-6719, 218-236-7037
Internet: olsen@cord.edu
  Pubs: *The Sacred Place* (U Utah Pr, 1996), *Acts of
  Illumination* (St. Mary's U Pr, 1996), *Meeting the
  Neighbors* (North Star Pr, 1993), *Just This Side of
  Fargo* (Ironwood Pr, 1992), *Ascent, Kenyon Rev, Willow
  Springs, North Dakota Qtly, Weber Studies*

Lon Otto   P&W
270 MacKubin St
St Paul, MN 55102, 612-227-7883
  Pubs: *Cover Me, Water Bodies* (Coffee Hse, 1988,
  1986), *A Nest of Hooks* (U Iowa Pr, 1978)

Tom Peacock   P
1507 Lockling Rd
Cloquet, MN 55720, 218-879-7326

Mary Ellis Peterson   P
13887 85th Pl N
Maple Grove, MN 55369-9237, 612-427-3168
  Pubs: *Journey Into Motherhood* (Riverhead Bks, 1996),
  Motherpoet (Mothering Pub, 1984), *And I Shall Be Your
  Ancestor* (Guild Pr, 1980)

Wang Ping   P&W
Lerner Publications, 241 1st Ave N, Minneapolis, MN
55410, 612-332-3344
  Pubs: *Of Flesh & Spirit, Foreign Devil, American Visa*
  (Coffee Hse Pr, 1998, 1996, 1994), *Sulfur, The World,
  Talisman, Manoa, Chicago Rev, River City, Asylum,
  Literary Rev, Westcoast Line*

Joan Wolf Prefontaine   P
18562 Nokay Lake Rd
Deerwood, MN 56444
Internet: prewolf@emily.net
  Pubs: *The Divided Sphere* (Floating Island Pr, 1985),
  *Prose Poem, Southern Humanities Rev, Christianity &
  the Arts*

Sister Bernetta Quinn   P
Sisters of St. Francis, Box #4900, Rochester, MN 55903,
507-282-7441
  Pubs: *Dancing in Stillness* (St. Andrews, 1983),
  Sewanee Rev, Yale Rev, America, English Jrnl, Sign

Thomas Dillon Redshaw   P
1944 Carroll Ave
St Paul, MN 55104, 612-645-7669
  Pubs: *The Floating World* (Truck Pr, 1979), *Sewanee
  Rev, Antioch Rev, Carleton Miscellany*

John Calvin Rezmerski 🎤 ✈   P
Box 202
Eagle Lake, MN 56024-0202, 507-257-3491
Internet: rez@gac.edu
  Pubs: *What Do I Know?* (Holy Cow! Pr, 2000), *One &
  Twenty Poems by Grace Lord Stoke* (Bootless Pub,
  1999), *Growing Down* (Minnesota Writers Pub Hse,
  1982)
Groups: Seniors, Professional Associations

Linda Lightsey Rice   W
1270 Goose Lake Rd
White Bear Lake, MN 55110, 612-429-7464
  Pubs: *Spectacle* (Pachanga Pr, 1998), *Southern
  Exposure* (Doubleday, 1991), *Home Works: Anth*
  (Tennessee Arts Commission, 1996), *Southern Literary
  Rev, Missouri Women's Pr, A View from the Loft, The
  Pheonix*

Melanie Richards   P
16570 22nd St S
St Mary's Point, MN 55043, 612-436-1666
  Pubs: *26 Minnesota Writers: Anth* (Nodin, 1996),
  *Harvard Rev, Yankee, Kalliope, Shenandoah, Negative
  Capability, Passages North*

Richard Robbins 🎤 ✈   P
Minnesota State Univ, 230 Armstrong Hall, Mankato, MN
56001, 507-389-1354
Internet: richard.robbins@mankato.msus.edu
  Pubs: *Famous Persons We Have Known* (Eastern
  Washington U Pr, 2000), *The Invisible Wedding* (U
  Missouri Pr, 1984), *NAR, Nation, Poetry NW*

George Roberts   P
1022 Sheridan Ave N
Minneapolis, MN 55411, 612-588-3723
  Pubs: *Scrut* (Holy Cow! Pr, 1983), *Night Visits to a
  Wolf's Howl* (Oyster Pr, 1979)

Mordecai M. Roshwald   W
Univ Minnesota, 314 Ford Hall, Minneapolis, MN 55455,
612-521-7955
  Pubs: *A Small Armageddon, Level 7* (NAL, 1976,
  1961), *Judaism, The Nation*

Ruth Roston   P
Parkshore Pl, 3663 Park Center Blvd, #501, Minneapolis,
MN 55416, 612-926-7132
  Pubs: *The Poet Dreaming in the Artist's House*
  (Milkweed Edtns, 1984)

CarolAnn Russell   P
English Dept, Bemidji State Univ, 1530 Birchmont Dr NE,
Bemidji, MN 56601, 218-755-2880
  Pubs: *Silver Dollar* (West End Pr, 1995), *Feast*
  (Loonfeather Pr, 1993), *Verse, Pemmican, Midwest Qtly,
  Hurakan, Puerto del Sol, Great River Rev*

Mark Ryan 🎤 ✈ W
5604 Upton Ave S
Minneapolis, MN 55410-2623, 612-926-6095
Internet: markdryan@aol.com
 Pubs: *Things That Fall from The Sky: Anth* (The Loft,
1994), *Pinehurst Jrnl, Alabama Literary Rev*

John M. Solensten P&W
500 E Larpenteur #102
St Paul, MN 55117
 Pubs: *Good Thunder* (SUNY Pr, 1983), *There Lies a
Fair Land: Anth* (New Rivers Pr, 1985)

Sally Jo Sorensen P
PO Box 611
Dassel, MN 55325, 320-275-3922
 Pubs: *A Turban Lily* (State Street, 1990), *Zone 3,
Laurel Rev, Sycamore Rev, Painted Bride Qtly, Poet &
Critic, Yarrow, West Branch, Amaranth, Nebraska Qtly,
Poem, Poet Lore*

Robert T. Sorrells 🎤 W
529 5th St SW
Rochester, MN 55902-3280, 507-289-0997
Internet: sorrelli@aol.com
 Pubs: *The Blacktop Champion of Ickey Honey & Other
Stories* (U Arkansas Pr, 1988), *Full Court: Anth, Tennis
& the Meaning of Life: Anth* (Breakaway Pr, 1996,
1995), *Pudding Mag*

Madelon Sprengnether 🎤 ✈ P
Univ Minnesota, 207 Church St, English Dept,
Minneapolis, MN 55455
Internet: spren001@tc.umn.edu
 Pubs: *La Belle et La Bête* (Sarasota Poetry Theater Pr,
1999), *Rivers, Stories, Houses, Dreams, The Normal
Heart, The House on Via Gambito: Anth* (New Rivers
Pr, 1983, 1981, 1990)

Francine Sterle 🎤 ✈ P
4023 River Rd
Iron, MN 55751-8044, 218-262-2503
Internet: fmsterle@uslink.net
 Pubs: *The White Bridge* (Poetry Harbor, 1999), *Great
River Rev, Midwest Qtly, NAR, Nimrod, BPJ, CutBank,
Zone 3, Birmingham Poetry Rev, Atlanta Rev*

Barton Sutter 🎤 ✈ P&W
1611 Lake Ave South
Duluth, MN 55802-2449, 218-720-6043
 Pubs: *My Father's War* (U Minnesota Pr, 2000), *Book
of Names* (BOA Edtns, 1993), *Pine Creek Parish Hall
& Other Poems* (Sandhills, 1985), *Sequoyah* (Ox Head,
1983), *Poetry*

Steve Swanson P
910 St Olaf Ave
Northfield, MN 55057, 507-645-6017
 Pubs: *The First Fall: Ytterboe Hall, 1946* (Nine Ten Pr,
1997), *Moving Out on Your Own, Is There Life After
High School?* (Augsburg, 1994, 1991)

Susan Marie Swanson 🎤 ✈ P
818 Seal St
St Paul, MN 55114
 Pubs: *Letter to the Lake, Getting Used to the Dark* (DK
Ink, 1998, 1997), *Primavera, How(ever), Ironwood,
Hungry Mind Rev, APR, Minnesota Writes, Cricket*
Groups: Children

Marcella B. Taylor P
English Dept, St. Olaf College, Northfield, MN 55057,
507-646-2222
 Pubs: *The Lost Daughter* (Renaissance Pr, 1985), *The
Butterfly Tree: Anth* (New Rivers Pr, 1991), *Poetry,
Tampa Bay Rev*

Richard Terrill 🎤 ✈ P
English Dept, Minnesota State Univ, Mankato, MN 56001,
507-389-5500
Internet: richard.terrill@mankato.msus.edu
 Pubs: *Fakebook* (Limelight Edtns, 2000), *The Cross &
the Red Star* (Asian Pacific Fdn, 1994), *Saturday Night
in Baoding: A China Memoir* (U Arkansas, 1990), *New
Letters, NAR, Mid-American Rev, Iowa Rev, Michigan
Qtly, Trafika*

Susan Allen Toth W
4820 Penn Ave S
Minneapolis, MN 55409, 612-927-0594
 Pubs: *My Love Affair with England* (Ballantine, 1993), *A
House of One's Own* (Potter, 1991), *Blooming* (Little,
Brown, 1981)

C. W. Truesdale P&W
New Rivers Press, 420 N 5th St, #910, Minneapolis, MN
55401, 612-339-7114
 Pubs: *Doctor Vertigo* (Wyrd Pr, 1976), *Cold Harbors*
(Latitudes Pr, 1974)

Mark Vinz 🎤 ✈ P&W
510 5th Ave S
Moorhead, MN 56560-2723, 218-236-5226
Internet: vinz@mnstate.edu
 Pubs: *Affinities* (Dacotah Territory, 1998), *Late Night
Calls* (New Rivers Pr, 1992), *Minnesota Gothic*
(Milkweed Edtns, 1992), *Mixed Blessings* (Spoon River
Poetry Pr, 1989)

Charles K. Waterman P
PO Box 473
St Peter, MN 56082, 507-931-6239
 Pubs: *Talking Animals* (Juniper Pr, 1978), *The Place*
(Minnesota Writers' Pub, 1977), *A Geography of Poets:
Anth* (Bantam, 1979), *Permafrost, Steelhead*

Susan Steger Welsh   P
181 Vernon St
St. Paul, MN 55105-1921, 651-699-2318
    Pubs: *Rafting on the Water Table* (New Rivers Pr,
    2000), *Essential Love: Anth* (Grayson Bks, 2000), *A
    Definitive Guide to the Twin Cities: Anth* (Spout Pr,
    1997), *Black Hat Pr, Wolf Head Qtly*

Jay P. White 🎤 ✈   P
4616 W 56 St
Minneapolis, MN 55424-1557, 612-925-0616
    Pubs: *The Salt Hour* (U Illinois Pr, 2001), *The
    Pomegranate Tree Speaks from the Dictator's Garden*
    (Holy Cow Pr, 1988)

Roberta Hill Whiteman   P
6539 Golden Valley Rd #101
Minneapolis, MN 55427-4656
    Pubs: *Talking Leaves: An Anth of Contemporary Native
    American Fiction* (Bantam-Dell, 1991), *New Voices from
    the Longhouse: Anth* (Greenfield Review Pr, 1989)

Warren Woessner   P
34 W Minnehaha Pkwy
Minneapolis, MN 55419-1365, 612-822-7848
Internet: wwoessner@slwk.com
    Pubs: *Iris Rising* (BkMk Pr of UMKC, 1998), *Clear to
    Chukchi* (Poetry Harbor Pr, 1995), *Storm Lines* (New
    Rivers Pr, 1987)

Karen Tei Yamashita 🎤 ✈   W
Coffee House Press, 27 N 4th St, Ste 400, Minneapolis,
MN 55401, 612-338-0125
    Pubs: *Tropic of Orange, Brazil-Maru, Through the Arc
    of the Rain Forest* (Coffee Hse Pr, 1997, 1992, 1990),
    Los Angeles Times, Amerasia Jrnl
Lang: Portuguese. I.D.: Asian-American, Brazilian. Groups:
Asian-American

MISSISSIPPI

Angela Ball   P
Box 5037, Southern Sta
Hattiesburg, MS 39406-5037, 601-266-4321
    Pubs: *The Museum of the Revolution, Quartet*
    (Carnegie Mellon, 1999, 1995), *Possession* (Valentine
    Pub Group, 1996), *NAR, Field, Southern Rev, Denver
    Qtly, New Yorker, Ploughshares*

D. C. Berry 🎤 ✈   P
306 Washington Ave
Ocean Springs, MS 39564-4628, 601-872-1927
Internet: david3berry@aol.com
    Pubs: *Divorce Boxing* (Eastern Washington Pr, 1998),
    Jawbone (Thunder City Pr, 1978), *Saigon Cemetery* (U
    Georgia Pr, 1972), *Poetry, Chicago Rev*

Price Caldwell   W
Mississippi State Univ, English Dept, Drawer E, Mississippi
State, MS 39762, 601-325-3644
    Pubs: *Mississippi Writers: Reflections of Childhood &
    Youth: Anth* (U Mississippi Pr, 1985), *Best American
    Short Stories 1977: Anth* (HM, 1978), *Carleton
    Miscellany, Georgia Rev, Image, Mississippi Rev, New
    Orleans Rev*

Carol Cox   P
PO Box 188
Tougaloo, MS 39174-0188, 601-956-2610
    Pubs: *The Water in the Pearl* (Hanging Loose Pr,
    1982), *Mississippi Writers: Anth* (U Pr Mississippi, 1988)

David Galef 🎤 ✈   W
Univ Mississippi, English Dept, University, MS 38677,
662-915-7439
Internet: dgalef@olemiss.edu
    Pubs: *Even a Stone Buddha Can Talk* (Tuttle, 2000),
    Turning Japanese (Permanent Pr, 1998), *Tracks*
    (Morrow, 1996), *Flesh* (Permanent Pr, 1995), *North
    Dakota Qtly, Gettysburg Rev, Crossroads, Grain,
    Pulpsmith, Chiron Rev, South Carolina Rev,
    Shenandoah*

Patricia Minter Grierson 🎤 ✈   P
PO Box 55808
Jackson, MS 39296, 601-982-3674
    Pubs: *Boston U Jrnl, Kansas Qtly, Mississippi Rev,
    Poem, Florida Qtly, Researcher*

Barry Hannah   W
1413 Van Buren Ave
Oxford, MS 38655, 601-234-2453
    Pubs: *Never Die, Boomerang* (Seymour Lawrence/HM,
    1991, 1989), *Esquire, The Qtly, Southern Rev, Chicago
    Rev, Harper's, Georgia Rev*

Charles Henley   W
426 11th Ave NW, #5
Magee, MS 39111-3365, 601-371-7827
    Pubs: *The Smith, The Phoenix, Intro, Mississippi Rev,
    Carolina Qtly*

John Horvath, Jr.   P
222 Melrose Dr
Jackson, MS 39211
    Pubs: *Critical Qtly, Aura, Poem, Dekalb Literary Arts
    Jrnl, Poet & Critic, Nimrod, Dalhousie Rev*

Gary Myers   P
English Dept, Mississippi State Univ, Drawer E, Mississippi
State, MS 39762, 601-325-3644
    Pubs: *Lifetime Possessions* (Riverstone Pr, 1997),
    World Effects (Nevertheless Pr, 1990), *New Yorker,
    Poetry, Indiana Rev, Kansas Qtly, Louisville Rev,
    Bitterroot*

Helon Howell Raines 🎤 ✈ W
2330 Kelly Ave
Gulfport, MS 39501, 228-822-2961
    Pubs: *Denver Qtly, Mississippi Rev, Outerbridge, Earth's Daughters, Worksheet, Wind Singers*

William Russell W
PO Box 35
Tunica, MS 38676, 601-363-2196
    Pubs: *Berlin Embassy* (Macfadden Bks, 1962), *A Wind Is Rising* (Scribner, 1950)

Larry Marshall Sams W
339 W Monroe Ave
Greenwood, MS 38930
    Pubs: *Dekalb Literary Arts Jrnl, Sucarnochee Rev, Wind, Pendragon, Dreamshore*

Glenn Robert Swetman P
PO Box 146
Biloxi, MS 39533-0146
    Pubs: *Concerning Carpenters* (Pterodactyl Pr, 1979), *Deka #2* (Paon Pr, 1979), *Texas Qtly*

Margaret Walker W
2205 Guynes Ave
Jackson, MS 39213

Jerry W. Ward, Jr. P
1872 Lincolnshire Blvd
Ridgeland, MS 39157-1213, 601-957-5062
    Pubs: *Trouble the Water: 250 Years of African-American Poetry: Anth* (Mentor, 1997), *Black Southern Voices: Anth* (NAL, 1992), *Callaloo, ADE Bulletin, Obsidian II, Open Places, Mississippi Qtly, Southern Qtly, Callaloo, Black American Literary Forum*

Eudora Welty W
1119 Pinehurst St
Jackson, MS 39202

Claude Wilkinson 🎤 ✈ P
2895 Lester Rd
Nesbit, MS 38651-9190, 662-429-4935
    Pubs: *Reading the Earth* (Michigan State U Pr, 1998), *Atlanta Rev, Blue Mesa Rev, CQ, A New Song, Poem, Southern Rev, Xavier Rev*
    Groups: College/Univ

Benjamin J. Williams P
3004 29th St
Gulfport, MS 39501, 601-864-6911
    Pubs: *Obsidian, Negro History Bulletin, Phylon, Black Scholar, Callaloo, Kitabu Cha Jua, Jrnl of Black Poetry, Afro American Qtly, Sphinx*

Joan Williams W
908 Old Taylor Rd
Oxford, MS 38655-4619
    Pubs: *Pay the Piper* (Dutton, 1988), *Pariah & Other Stories* (Atlantic Monthly Pr, 1983), *Esquire, Southern Accents*

Austin Wilson P&W
English Dept, Millsaps College, Jackson, MS 39210, 601-974-1305
    Pubs: *From the Green Horseshoe: Anth* (U South Carolina Pr, 1987), *Mississippi Writers: Reflections: Anth* (U Pr Mississippi, 1985), *New Orleans Rev, Hiram Poetry Rev, Southern Humanities Rev, Descant, Mississippi Rev, Roanoke Rev*

Steve Yates W
875 William Blvd, #412
Ridgeland, MS 39157-1519
    Pubs: *Arkansas Rev/Kansas Qtly, Ontario Rev, Missouri Rev, Nebraska Rev, Turnstile, Western Humanities Rev, Chariton Rev, Red Cedar Rev, Texas Rev, Laurel Rev, South Carolina Rev*

MISSOURI

Rosa M. Arenas P
7731 Gannon, #1 E
St Louis, MO 63130, 314-726-1145
    Pubs: *She Said Yes* (Fallen Angel Pr, 1981), *Kenyon Rev, Calyx, River Styx, Blue Mesa Rev, Americas Rev, Sycamore Rev*

Mary Jo Bang 🎤 ✈ P
Department of English, c/o Washington Univ, Box 1122, One Brookings Dr, St. Louis, MO 63130-4899, 314-935-5190
    Pubs: *The Downstream Extremity of the Isle of Swans* (U Georgia Pr, 2001), *Louise in Love* (Grove Pr, 2001), *Apology for Want, The New American Poets: A Bread Loaf Anthology* (U Pr of New England, 1997, 2000), *KGB Bar Book of Poems: Anth* (Morrow, 2000), *Verse*

Stanley E. Banks 🎤 ✈ P
7120 Indiana
Kansas City, MO 64132, 816-333-8705
Internet: banksse@mail.avila.edu
    Pubs: *Coming from a Funky Time & Place* (Georgia AB Pr, 1988), *On 10th Alley Way* (BkMk Pr, 1980)
I.D.: African-American

Walter Bargen 🎙 ✈   P
PO Box 19
Ashland, MO 65010, 573-657-2636
Internet: bargenw@missouri.edu
    Pubs: *Water Breathing Air, The Vertical River*
    (Timberline Pr, 1999, 1995), *Mysteries in the Public
    Domain* (BkMk Pr, 1990), *Georgia Rev, New Letters,
    Intl Qtly, Sycamore Rev*

Jim Barnes 🎙 ✈   P
The Chariton Review, Truman State Univ, Kirksville, MO
63501, 660-785-4499
Internet: jbarnes@truman.edu
    Pubs: *Paris, The Sawdust War* (U Illinois Pr, 1997,
    1992), *La Plata Cantata* (Purdue U Pr, 1989), *The
    Nation, Sewanee Rev, Kenyon Rev, NAR, SW Rev,
    TriQtly*

Ben Bennani 🎙 ✈   P
1103 Cherry Ln
Kirksville, MO 63501-2097, 660-665-1103
Internet: www.paintbrush.org
    Pubs: *Psalms for Palestine* (Three Continents Pr, 1993),
    Bread, Hashish & Moon (Unicorn Pr, 1982), *A Bowl of
    Sorrow* (Greenfield Rev Pr, 1977)
Lang: Arabic. I.D.: Arab-American

Edward Boccia   P
600 Harper Ave
Webster Groves, MO 63119, 314-962-5081
    Pubs: *No Matter How Good the Light Is* (Time Being
    Bks, 1998), *Moving the Still Life* (Pudding Hse, 1993),
    Against the Grain: Anth (CSS Pubs, 1988), *Blue
    Unicorn, California Qtly, Black Mullet Rev, Atlantic Rev,
    Poet Mag, River King Poetry Pr, Rockhurst Rev*

James J. Bogan 🎙 ✈   P
Univ Missouri, Philosophy & Liberal Arts Dept, Rolla, MO
65409-0670, 573-341-4755
Internet: www.umr.edu/~jbogan
    Pubs: *Ozark Meandering* (Timberline Pr, 1999), *Sparks
    of Fire* (North Atlantic Pr, 1982), *Exquisite Corpse,
    River Styx, Walking Mag, Latin American Lit Rev*

Michelle Boisseau 🎙 ✈   P
English Dept, Univ of Missouri–KC, 5100 Rockhill Rd,
Kansas City, MO 64110-2499, 816-235-2561
Internet: boisseaum@umkc.edu
    Pubs: *Understory* (Northeastern U Pr, 1996), *No Private
    Life* (Vanderbilt U, 1990), *Poetry, Agni, Ploughshares,
    Ohio Rev, Crazyhorse, Southern Rev, Georgia Rev,
    Gettysburg Rev*

Louis Daniel Brodsky   P
10411 Clayton Rd, Ste 201-203
St Louis, MO 63131, 314-432-1771
    Pubs: *Paper-Whites for Lady-Jane, Disappearing in
    Mississippi Latitudes, The Capital Cafe, Gestapo Crows*
    (Time Being Bks, 1995, 1994, 1993, 1992)

Catherine Browder 🎙 ✈   W
3611 Gladstone Blvd
Kansas City, MO 64123-1145, 816-483-8949
    Pubs: *The Heart: A Story* (Helicon Nine Edtns, 1995),
    The Clay That Breathes: Stories (Milkweed Edtns,
    1991), *The Broken Bridge: Anth* (Stone Bridge Pr,
    1997), *Kansas City Star, Shenandoah, New Letters,
    Prairie Schooner, Kansas Qtly*

R. A. Burns 🎙 ✈   P
English Dept, Southeast Missouri State Univ, Cape
Girardeau, MO 63701
Internet: raburns@semovm.semo.edu
    Pubs: *Black Dirt, Potpourri, River King Poetry
    Supplement, American Poets & Poetry, Satire, Poetry
    Now, College Composition & Communication*

Anthony Butts   P
107 Tate Hall
Columbia, MO 65211, 573-882-0681
    Pubs: *Evolution* (Sutton Hoo Pr, 1998), *Fifth Season*
    (New Issues Pr, 1997), *Yemassee, Crab Orchard Rev,
    MacGuffin, The Yalobusha Rev*

Marcus Cafagña 🎙 ✈   P
English Dept, 209C Pummill Hall, 901 S National Ave,
Springfield, MO 65804, 417-836-4793
Internet: msc607f@mail.smsu.edu
    Pubs: *The Broken World* (U Illinois Pr, 1996), *The
    Beacon Best of 1999: Anth* (Beacon Pr, 1999),
    *American Poetry Rev, Boulevard, DoubleTake, Field,
    Poetry, Southern Rev, Threepenny Rev, TriQtly*

David Carkeet   W
9307 Old Bonhomme Rd
St Louis, MO 63132, 314-994-7532
    Pubs: *The Error of Our Ways* (H Holt, 1997), *The Full
    Catastrophe* (S&S, 1990), *Carolina Qtly, Kansas Qtly,
    NAR, Village Voice, Oxford American*

Jan Garden Castro 🎙 ✈   P
7420 Cornell
St Louis, MO 63130, 314-725-0602
    Pubs: *Memories & Memoirs ... by Missouri Authors:
    Anth* (Sheba Review Publishing, 2000), *New Letters,
    Eclectic Press, Missouri Rev, River Styx, Wind,
    Southwinds, Greenfield Rev, Exquisite Corpse, Abraxas,
    Focus Midwest, Sheba Rev, Telephone, Roof*

Michael Castro 🎙 ✈   P
8368 Richard Ave
St Louis, MO 63132, 314-432-0236
    Pubs: *The Man Who Looked into Coltrane's Horn*
    (Caliban Pr, 1998), *(US)* (Ridgeway Pr, 1991),
    Interpreting the Indian (U Oklahoma Pr, 1991), *Drum
    Voices Rev, Mississippi Valley Rev, Tampa Rev, Edge,
    Printed Matter, Long Shot, Nexus, Many Moons, Grist*

David Clewell   P
Webster Univ, English Dept, 470 E Lockwood, St Louis,
MO 63119, 314-968-7170
 Pubs: *Jack Ruby's America, The Conspiracy Quartet*
 (Garlic Pr, 2000, 1997), *Now We're Getting Somewhere*
 (U Wisconsin Pr, 1994), *Blessings in Disguise* (Viking,
 1991), *Poetry, Georgia Rev, Kenyon Rev, Harper's,
 Ontario Rev, NER*

Carole Knipp Cohen ♀   P
911 Craig Dr
St. Louis, MO 63122, 314-965-4780
Internet: carcoh@juno.com
 Pubs: *Memories & Memoirs: Anth* (Mid-America Pr,
 2000), *Sou'wester, Cape Rock, Madison Rev, Prism,
 Ascent, Spoon River*

Gene Doty ♀ ✈   P
Univ Missouri, English Dept, Rolla, MO 65401,
573-364-5322
Internet: gdoty@umr.edu
 Pubs: *Nose to Nose* (Brooks Bks, 1998), *Zero: 30
 Ghazals* (AHA Bks Online, 1998), *Wind Five-Folded*
 (AHA Bks, 1994), *Uncommon Places: Anth* (Mayapple
 Pr, 2000), *Midwest Haiku Anth* (High/Coo Pr, 1992),
 Rolling Coulter, Lynx, Phase & Cycle, Woodnotes

Jon Dressel   P
376 Walton Row
St Louis, MO 63108, 314-361-3478
 Pubs: *Face to Face, The Road to Shiloh* (Gomer Pr,
 1997, 1994), *Out of Wales* (Alun Bks, 1985), *Prairie
 Schooner, Epoch, Poetry Wales, Counter-Measures,
 New Welsh Rev, Planet*

Debra L. Edwards ♀ ✈   P
3406 Arlington Ave
St. Louis, MO 63120
 Pubs: *Black Rose* (Upstream Productions, 1977), *Home
 Planet News, Natl Poetry Mag of the Lower East Side,
 Poetry NY, Limelight, Gulf Times, Cover, Barefoot
 Grass Jrnl, Quarter Horse*

Donald Finkel   P
2051 Park Ave #D
St Louis, MO 63104, 314-241-4426
 Pubs: *The Question of Seeing* (U Arkansas Pr, 1998),
 The Wake of the Electron, Selected Shorter Poems
 (Atheneum, 1987, 1987), *Yale Rev, SW Rev, Paris
 Rev, Kenyon Rev, Denver Qtly*

Robert A. Frauenglas   P&W
2624 Roseland Terr, #19
St. Louis, MO 63143-2328, 314-647-9002
 Pubs: *The Eclectic Musings of a Brooklyn Bum* (Somrie
 Pr, 1980), *Blood to Remember: Anth* (Texas Tech U
 Pr, 1991), *Scottish Book Collector, Cups, Waterways*

William H. Gass   W
6304 Westminster Pl
St Louis, MO 63130, 314-725-0317
 Pubs: *Cartesian Sonata, Finding a Form, The Tunnel*
 (Knopf, 1998, 1996, 1995), *On Being Blue* (Godine,
 1975), *New Republic, Harper's, Conjunction, Salmagundi*

Paul Gianoli   P
2600 S 14 Ave
Ozark, MO 65721, 417-581-0895
 Pubs: *Blueprint, Focus: Midwest, Wisconsin Rev,
 Mississippi Rev*

John F. Gilgun ♀ ✈   W
PO Box 7152
St Joseph, MO 64507-7152, 816-233-8374
Internet: gilgun@griffon.mwsc.edu
 Pubs: *The Dooley Poems* (Robin Price, 1991), *From
 the Inside Out* (3-Phase, 1991), *Music I Never
 Dreamed Of* (Amethyst, 1989)
I.D.: G/L/B/T. Groups: G/L/B/T

Galen Green   P&W
201 Westport Rd
Kansas City, MO 64111-2239
 Pubs: *World-Weary Polka* (Fireweed Pr, 1977), *NYQ,
 Poetry Now, West Coast Rev*

Charles Guenther ♀ ✈   P
9877 Allendale Dr
St Louis, MO 63123-6450, 314-544-0563
 Pubs: *Moving the Seasons* (BkMk Pr, 1994),
 Phrase-Paraphrase (Prairie Pr, 1970), *APR, Kenyon
 Rev, Literary Rev, Formalist, Black Mountain Rev, Critic*

Frank Higgins   P
12500 E 53 Terr
Kansas City, MO 64133, 816-353-4529
 Pubs: *Eating Blowfish* (Raindust Pr, 1996), *Starting from
 Ellis Island* (BkMk Pr, 1981), *New Letters, Dacotah
 Territory, Kansas Qtly, Chariton Rev, Poetry Now*

Peter Daniel Hilty   P
632 Bellevue
Cape Girardeau, MO 63701, 314-335-8332
 Pubs: *Thomas Crook's Shoebox, How Far Is Far?*
 (Southeast Missouri State U Pr, 1996, 1990)

Jane Hoogestraat   P
English Dept, Southwest Missouri State Univ, 901 S
National, Springfield, MO 65802, 417-836-6613
 Pubs: *Poetry, Southern Rev, Iowa Woman, High Plains
 Literary Rev, Poem, SPR*

Jane Ellen Ibur   P
3536 Victor St
St Louis, MO 63104, 314-771-7661
   Pubs: *If I Had a Hammer: Women & Work* Anth
   (Papier-Mache Pr, 1990), *Webster Rev, Slipstream,*
   Crazyquilt, Literati Internationale, Spitball, Pastiche

Donn Irving 🎤 ✈   W
Fletcher's Fold, 707 NW 100 Rd
Centerview, MO 64019, 660-656-3832
   Pubs: *III Novellas* (Woodley Pr, 1993), *Jazz, Theatre &*
   a Prayer (Potpourri Pubs, 1993), *These & Other Lands*
   (Westphalia Pr, 1986), *American Literary Rev, New*
   Letters, Crescent Rev, Habersham Rev

Jeanne Lebow   P
Northeast Missouri State Univ, Division of Language &
Literature, Kirksville, MO 63501, 816-785-5677
   Pubs: *The Outlaw James Copeland & the*
   Champion-Belted Empress (U Georgia Pr, 1991),
   Nimrod, Sun Dog

Thomas John Lochhaas   W
2349 S 11 St
St Louis, MO 63104, 314-771-7923
   Pubs: *Chicago Rev, Writers' Forum, Subject to Change,*
   Sawtooth, Slackwater Rev

Barbara Loots 🎤 ✈   P
7943 Charlotte
Kansas City, MO 64131, 816-361-3844
Internet: bkloots@earthlink.net
   Pubs: *Sibyl & Sphinx* (Rockhill Pr, 1988), *Landscapes*
   with Women: Anth (Singular Speech Pr, 1999), *The*
   Muse Strikes Back: Anth (Story Line Pr, 1997),
   Random House Treasury of Light Verse: Anth (Random
   Hse, 1995), *Lyric, Christian Century, Sparrow*

James McKinley   W
Professional Writing Program, Univ Missouri, 5100 Rockhill
Rd, Kansas City, MO 64110, 816-235-1120
   Pubs: *The Fickleman Suite & Other Stories* (U
   Arkansas Pr, 1993), *Acts of Love* (Breitenbush Bks,
   1987)

Ronald W. McReynolds   P
High Field, RR#5
Warrensburg, MO 64093, 816-747-8810
   Pubs: *The Blooding & Other Missouri Poems*
   (Mid-America Pr, 1979), *Chariton Rev*

Jerred Metz   P
2318 Albion Pl
St Louis, MO 63104
   Pubs: *Halley's Comet, 1910: Fire in the Sky* (Singing
   Bone, 1985)

Philip Miller   P
1841 Pendleton
Kansas City, MO 64124, 816-842-5872
   Pubs: *Dork* (Mulberry Pr, 1991), *Boulevard, College*
   English, Literary Rev, Confrontation, Mudfish, New
   Letters, Kansas Qtly, Puerto del Sol

Michael Murphy   W
4304 McCausland
St Louis, MO 63109, 314-647-4363
   Pubs: *AKA Ormand Sacker* (Norfolk-Hall, 1984),
   Hemingsteen (Autolycus Pr, 1978), *Esquire, Life*

Martin Musick   P
1661 Vassier Ave
St Louis, MO 63133, 314-389-2354
   Pubs: *Para*phrase, Midwest Poetry Rev*

Bob Myers   W
16503 3rd St N
Independence, MO 64056
   Pubs: *Kill the Fine Young Dreamers* (Abiding Mystery
   Pr, 1998), *Good Old Hillmont High* (Crescent, 1979),
   Mystery Forum Mag

Robert Nazarene   P
111 Hilltown Village Ctr, Suite 207
Chesterfield, MO 63017
Internet: wilsonland@aol.com
   Pubs: *5 AM, Atlanta Rev, Callaloo, Green Mountains*
   Rev, Indiana Rev, Nimrod, Pleiades, Ploughshares,
   Spoon River Poetry Rev, Washington Rev, Willow Rev

Christina V. Pacosz 🎤 ✈   P&W
2003 NE Russell Rd #102
Kansas City, MO 64116-2423, 816-452-4503
Internet: pacosz@earthlink.net
   Pubs: *One River* (Pudding Hse, 2000), *This Is Not a*
   Place to Sing (West End, 1987), *Some Winded, Wild*
   Beast (Black & Red, 1985), *Midwest Qtly, Calyx, Sing*
   Heavenly Muse, Pig Iron, Exquisite Corpse, Permafrost
I.D.: Polish-American. Groups: Teenagers, Prisoners

Tom Padgett 🎤 ✈   P
523 N Park Pl
Bolivar, MO 65613-1576, 417-326-5406
Internet: tpadgett@sbuniv.edu
   Pubs: *Barking Barkwards, The Magpie, The Weasel,*
   Prodigal Poet, Pets, Second Tuesday: Anth (Barnowl,
   1998, 1997, 1997, 1995, 1990, 1999), *Encore: Anths*
   (NFSPS, 1997, 1996), *By-Line, Lucidity,*
   Hampden-Sydney Rev, Verses, Rockford Rev, Penwood
   Rev

Michelle Paulsen 🎤 ✈   P
HC83, Box 64
Salem, MO 65560-8404, 573-743-6848
Internet: paulsens@yahoo.com
  Pubs: *Sixteen Voices: Anth* (Mariposa, 1994), *Weber
  Studies, Sink Full of Dishes, Perceptions, Midland Rev,
  Howling Dog, Recursive Angel, Fox Cry*

William Peden   W
603 Rollins CT
Columbia, MO 65205, 314-442-1228
  Pubs: *Fragments & Fictions: Work Books of an
  Obscure Writer* (Watermark Pr, 1991), *Twilight at
  Monticello* (HM, 1975)

David Perkins   P
Box 10016
Kansas City, MO 64111, 816-756-1744
  Pubs: *Wrapped Mind & Other Essays* (Woods Colt Pr,
  1988), *License to Kill* (BkMk Pr, 1974)

Carl Phillips   P
English Dept, Box 1122, One Brookings Dr, St. Louis, MO
63130, 314-935-7133
  Pubs: *Pastoral, From the Devotions, Cortege* (Graywolf,
  2000, 1998, 1995), *In the Blood* (Northeastern U Pr,
  1992)

Carol Poster   P&W
Univ Missouri, 107 Tate Hall, English Dept, Columbia, MO
65211, 314-449-0765
  Pubs: *Surrounded by Dangerous Things* (Singular
  Speech Pr, 1994), *Deceiving the Worms* (Sleeping
  Lizard Pr, 1984), *Poetry East, Formalist, Ploughshares*

Martin Quigley   W
4400 Lindell Blvd, #5B
St Louis, MO 63108
  Pubs: *The Original Colored House of David* (HM,
  1981), *Today's Game* (Viking, 1965), *Winners & Losers,
  The Secret Project of Sigurd O'Leary, A Tent on
  Corsica* (Lippincott, 1961, 1959, 1949)

Cathleen Quirk   P
c/o Dr. Thomas Quirk, 418-A N Clay St, Kirkwood, MO
63122, 314-909-1562
  Pubs: *Rue & Grace* (Crossing Pr, 1987), *Burden &
  Other Poems* (Orpheum Pr, 1980), *Ploughshares Poetry
  Reader: Anth* (Ploughshares Bks, 1994)

Carol Lee Sanchez 🎤 ✈   P
13918 Longwood Rd
Hughesville, MO 65334-2217, 660-827-5261
Internet: carolee@sockets.net
  Pubs: *Rainbow Visions & Earth Ways* (U Osnabrueck,
  1998), *From Spirit to Matter* (Taurean Horn Pr, 1997),
  She Poems, Crimson Edge: Anth (Chicory Blue Pr,
  1995, 2000), *Reinventing the Enemy: Anth* (Norton,
  1997)
I.D.: Multicultural. Groups: Seniors, Schools

Jo Sapp 🎤 ✈   W
1025 Hickory Hill Dr
Columbia, MO 65203-2322, 573-443-8964
Internet: djsapp@attglobal.net
  Pubs: *Fiction 100: Anth* (Prentice Hall, 2000), *Norton
  Anth of Short Fiction, Flash Fiction: Anth* (Norton, 1995,
  1992), *NAR, Intro, Epoch, Washington Rev, Kansas
  Qtly, Long Pond*
Groups: Libraries

Howard Schwartz   P&W
14 Hill N Dale Lane
St Louis, MO 63132, 314-997-4553
Internet: hschwartz@umsl.edu
  Pubs: *The Four Who Entered Paradise* (Jason Aronson
  Inc, 1995), *Gabriel's Palace* (Oxford U Pr, 1993),
  Sleepwalking Beneath the Stars (BkMk Pr, 1992)

Jory Sherman   P
3044 Shepherd Hill Expy, #642
Branson, MO 65616-8168
  Pubs: *Grass Kingdom, Trapper's Moon* (Tor/Forge,
  1994, 1994), *The Medicine Horn* (Tor Bks, 1991)

Peter L. Simpson   P
5261 Westminster Pl
St Louis, MO 63108, 314-361-5342
  Pubs: *Press Box & City Room, Stealing Home* (BkMk
  Pr, 1988, 1985), *Choice, New Letters*

Roland E. Sodowsky   W
Southwest Missouri State Univ, English Dept, Springfield,
MO 65804, 417-882-5791
  Pubs: *Interim in the Desert* (TCU Pr, 1990), *Un-Due
  West* (Corona, 1990), *Things We Lose* (U Missouri Pr,
  1989), *Concho River Rev, Atlantic*

Evelyn Somers   W
1201 6th St
Boonville, MO 65233
  Pubs: *Descant, Crazyhorse, Many Mountains Moving*

Arnold Stead   P&W
Univ Missouri, Tate Hall, Rm 1, Columbia, MO 65202,
314-882-0681
  Pubs: *The Blood of This Need* (Kawabata Pr, 1987),
  Woodrose, Sepia, Loonfeather, Lake Street Rev

Marjorie Stelmach   P
708 Carman Oaks Ct
Ballwin, MO 63021
  Pubs: *Night Drawings* (Helicon Nine Pr, 1995), *Kenyon
  Rev, Tampa Rev, The Jrnl, Chelsea, Ascent, River
  Styx, New Letters*

Robert Stewart 🎤 ✈   P
7714 Summit St
Kansas City, MO 64114-1742, 816-444-6870
    Pubs: *Letter from the Living* (Borderline Pubs, 1992),
    Plumbers (BkMk Pr, 1988), *Stand, Denver Qtly, Poetry
    NW, Nimrod*

Anthony J. Summers   W
1825 Bender Ln
Arnold, MO 63010, 314-752-3703
    Pubs: *Moving* (The Smith, 1981), *Metamorphosis*
    (Cornerstone Pr, 1979)

William L. Sutherland   W
654 W Bethel Dr
Columbia, MO 65203, 314-442-7241
    Pubs: *News from Fort God* (Midlist Pr, 1992)

Gladys Swan 🎤 ✈   W
2601 Lynnwood Dr
Columbia, MO 65203-2936, 573-442-9129
    Pubs: *News from the Volcano, A Visit to Strangers, Do
    You Believe in Cabeza de Vaca?* (U Missouri Pr, 2000,
    1996, 1991), *Ghost Dance: A Play of Voices, Of
    Memory & Desire* (LSU Pr, 1992, 1989)
Lang: Spanish. Groups: Prisoners

Marilyn R. Tatlow 🎤 ✈   W
1507 Keegan Ct
Columbia, MO 65203-6251
Internet: marilynt@gte.net
    Pubs: *Paradise* (Florida Literary Fdn, 1994), *Memories
    & Memoirs: Anth* (Mid-America Pr, 2000), *Missouri
    Women Writers: Anth* (Sheba Rev, 1987), *Prism,
    Slugfest, Pleiades, Poets' Edge, Palo Alto Rev*

Brian Taylor 🎤 ✈   P
4376 Maryland Ave, #A-4
St Louis, MO 63108-4101, 314-531-1437
    Pubs: *Transit* (London Mag Edtns, 1986), *River Styx,
    Antioch Rev, Missouri Rev, London Mag, The Listener,
    NER/BLQ, Sewanee Rev, Paris Rev, Stand*

Julius Eric Thompson   P
Black Studies Program, Univ Missouri, 313 Gentry Hall,
Columbia, MO 65211, 573-814-1592
    Pubs: *Blues Said: Walk On* (Energy, Earth Comm,
    1977), *Hopes Tied Up in Promises* (Dorrance & Co,
    1970), *Trouble with the Water: 250 Years of African
    American Poetry: Anth* (Penguin, 1997), *Freedomways,
    Phylon, Black Creation, Callaloo*

William Trowbridge 🎤 ✈   P
907 S Dunn St
Maryville, MO 64468, 660-582-3961
    Pubs: *Flickers, O Paradise, Enter Dark Stranger* (U
    Arkansas Pr, 2000, 1995, 1989), *Georgia Rev,
    Gettysburg Rev, Poetry, Colorado Rev, New Letters*

Mary Troy 🎤 ✈   W
Univ of Missouri/English Dept, 8001 Natural Bridge, St
Louis, MO 63121-4401, 314-516-6845
Internet: marytroy@umsl.edu
    Pubs: *Joe Baker Is Dead* (U Missouri Pr, 1998),
    *Chicago Tribune, Amer Fiction, Boulevard, River Styx,
    Ascent, ALR*

Mona Van Duyn   P
7505 Teasdale Ave
St Louis, MO 63130, 314-863-1943
    Pubs: *Firefall, If It Be Not I, Near Changes* (Knopf,
    1993, 1993, 1990), *Merciful Disguises* (Atheneum, 1982)

Gloria Vando 🎤 ✈   P
Helicon Nine Editions, The Writers Place, 3607
Pennsylvania, Kansas City, MO 64111, 816-753-1095
Internet: helicon9@aol.com
    Pubs: *Promesas* (Arte Publico Pr, 1993), *American
    Diaspora: Anth, 9MM: Anth* (U Iowa Pr, 2000, 2000),
    Verse & Universe: Anth (Milkweed, 1998), *Touching the
    Fire: Anth* (Anchor Bks, 1998), *River Styx, Western
    Humanities Rev, Kenyon Rev, New Letters*
Lang: Spanish. I.D.: Latino/Latina. Groups: Seniors

Maryfrances Wagner 🎤 ✈   P
5021 Tierney Dr
Independence, MO 64055-6930
Internet: zinnia@planetkc.com
    Pubs: *Red Silk, Tonight Cicadas Sing* (Mid-America Pr,
    1999, 1984), *Salvatore's Daughter* (BkMk Pr, 1995),
    Unsettling America: Anth (Penguin, 1994), *Birmingham
    Poetry Rev, Laurel Rev, New Letters, Nebraska Rev,
    Midwest Qtly*
I.D.: Italian-American

Morrie Warshawski   P
6364 Forsyth Blvd
St Louis, MO 63105, 314-727-7880
    Pubs: *Out of Nowhere* (Press-22, 1985), *Indiana Rev,
    Apalachee Qtly, Hayden's Ferry Rev, Exquisite Corpse,
    Modern Poetry Studies, NYQ*

Richard Watson   W
756 Harvard Ave
St Louis, MO 63130, 314-862-7646
    Pubs: *The Philosopher's Demise* (U Missouri Pr, 1995),
    Niagara (Coffee Hse Pr, 1993)

Jane O. Wayne 🎤 ✈   P
6376 Washington Ave
St Louis, MO 63130-4705, 314-725-6291
Internet: jowayne@inlink.com
    Pubs: *A Strange Heart* (Helicon Nine Edtns, 1996),
    Looking Both Ways (U Missouri Pr, 1985), *Poetry, Iowa
    Rev, Ploughshares, American Scholar, Massachusetts
    Rev, Michigan Qtly*

Susan Whitmore P
The Writers Place, 3607 Pennsylvania, Kansas City, MO
64111, 816-753-1090
    Pubs: *The Invisible Women* (Singular Speech Pr, 1991)

Rebecca M. Wright P
2011 Rutger St #A
St Louis, MO 63104, 314-231-0441
    Pubs: *Ciao Manhattan* (Telephone Bks, 1976), *Brief
Lives* (Ant's Forefoot, 1974)

Joan Yeagley ⬤ ✈ P
Rte 1, Box 1306
Stella, MO 64867-9623, 417-435-2341
Internet: hayeagley@juno.com
    Pubs: *The Studs of McDonald County, In the Middle:
Midwestern Women Poets: Anth* (BkMk Pr, 1987, 1985)

MONTANA

Sandra Alcosser ⬤ ✈ P
5791 W County Line Rd
Florence, MT 59833-6056, 406-273-0560
Internet: alcosser@mail.sdsu.edu
    Pubs: *Except By Nature* (Graywolf, 1998), *Sleeping
Inside the Glacier* (Brighton, 1997), *A Fish to Feed All
Hunger* (U Pr Virginia, 1986), *APR, New Yorker, Paris
Rev, Poetry*

Minerva Allen P
Box 5270 HC63
Dodson, MT 59524, 406-673-3596
    Pubs: *Winter Smoke, Thematic Approach Curriculum:
Anth* (Flores Hill County Printing Havremt, 1996, 1996),
The *Last Place: A Centennial Anth* (Montana Historical
Society, 1988), *Montana Mag of Western History*

Margaret Bridwell-Jones W
135 Village Ln
Bigfork, MT 59911, 406-837-0248
    Pubs: *Northwood Jrnl, Calliope, Green's Mag,
Colorado-North Rev, Hob-Nob*

Ed Chaberek ⬤ ✈ P
PO Box 424
Superior, MT 59872-0424, 406-822-4962
Internet: gchaberek@hotmail.com
    Pubs: *The Berkshire Polish Bar* (Ibbetson Street Pr,
1999), *Types, Vol. I* (Superior Poetry Pr, 1998), *And
What Rough Beast: Anth* (Ashland Poetry Pr, 1999),
*Ibbetson Street Rev, Spare Change, Midwest Qtly, Blue
Collar Rev, Plainsongs, Superior Poetry News*
Groups: Children

Barbara Corcoran W
PO Box 4394
Missoula, MT 59806-4394
    Pubs: *Wolf at the Door, Family Secrets, Stay Tuned*
(Atheneum, 1993, 1992, 1991)

James Crumley W
PO Box 9278
Missoula, MT 59807, 406-728-8602
    Pubs: *Dancing Bear, The Last Good Kiss, The Wrong
Case* (Random Hse, 1983, 1978, 1975)

Art Cuelho, Jr. P&W
PO Box 249
Big Timber, MT 59011
    Pubs: *Fiction 100* (Macmillan, 1994), *As Far As I Can
See* (Windflower Pr, 1989), *California Childhood*
(Creative Arts Bks, 1989)

David Dale ⬤ ✈ P
PO Box 257
Big Arm, MT 59910, 406-849-5702
    Pubs: *Skating Backwards, Montana Primer, The Way a
Bear Is* (Big Mountain Pub, 1999, 1996, 1994), *What
We Call Our Own* (Wright Impressions, 1991), *Bellowing
Ark, Camphorweed, Comstock Rev, CutBank,
Kinnikinnik, Kinesis, Midwest Qtly, Northern Journeys*
Groups: Children

Martha Elizabeth P&W
Once Only Productions, Box 9444, Missoula, MT 59807,
406-728-8602
    Pubs: *The Return of Pleasure* (Confluence Pr, 1996),
Basics of the Dance, Inheritance of Light: Anth (U
North Texas Pr, 1990, 1996), *Grow Old Along with Me:
Anth* (Papier-Mache Pr, 1996), *Georgia Rev, NER, New
Virginia Rev*

Pete Fromm ⬤ ✈ W
2908 3rd Ave N
Great Falls, MT 59401
    Pubs: *How All This Started, Night Swimming* (Picador
2000, 1999), *Blood Knot, Dry Rain, Indian Creek
Chronicles* (Lyons Pr, 1998, 1997, 1993), *Monkey Tag*
(Scholastic, 1994), *The Tall Uncut* (John Daniel & Co,
1992), *Glimmer Train*

Marilyn Kay Giuliani P
716 S 6th W
Missoula, MT 59801
    Pubs: *Poetic Eloquence, Dreambuilding Crusade Idea
Company, Capper's*

Patricia Goedicke 🎤 ✈   P
310 McLeod Ave
Missoula, MT 59801-4302, 406-549-0343
    Pubs: *As Earth Begins to End* (Copper Canyon, 2000),
Invisible Horses, Paul Bunyan's Bearskin (Milkweed,
1996, 1992), *Hudson Rev, Kenyon Rev, Prairie
Schooner, NER, BPJ, Manhattan Rev, Hubbub,
Gettysburg Rev*
Groups: Seniors

John Haines 🎤 ✈   P
509 Hollins Ave
Helena, MT 59601-2816, 406-449-7848
Internet: haines@mcn.net
    Pubs: *A Guide to the Four-Chambered Heart* (Larkspur
Pr, 1996), *Where the Twilight Never Ends* (Limberlost
Pr, 1994), *Ohio Rev, Sewanee Rev, Manoa, ELF,
Nimrod, Temenos Academy Rev, Atlantic*

Valerie Harms   W
PO Box 1123
Bozeman, MT 59771-1123, 406-587-3356
    Pubs: *The Inner Lover* (Aslan, 1999), *The Ecology of
Everyday Life* (Putnam, 1994)

John Holbrook   P
328 S 5th W
Missoula, MT 59801, 406-728-6223
    Pubs: *Clear Water on the Swan* (Falcon Pr, 1992),
*Hubbub, SPR, Poetry NW, Camas, Kinesis, Rain City,
Wisconsin Rev, Tamarack, Carolina Qtly, Mississippi
Rev, Nebraska Rev, Florida Rev, Green Hills Literary
Lantern, Northern Journeys, Bellowing Ark*

Lowell Jaeger   P
E Lake Shore
Bigfork, MT 59911, 406-982-3269
    Pubs: *Hope Against Hope, War on War* (Utah State U
Pr, 1990, 1988), *CutBank, High Plains Literary Rev,
Poetry NW*

William Kittredge   W
143 S 5th E
Missoula, MT 59801, 406-549-6605
    Pubs: *Who Owns the West* (Mercury Hse, 1996), *Hole
in the Sky* (Vintage, 1993), *The Last Best Place: Anth*
(Montana Historical Society Pr, 1988), *Paris Rev*

King D. Kuka   P
907 Ave C NW
Great Falls, MT 59404, 406-452-4449

David Long   W
820 3rd Ave E
Kalispell, MT 59901, 406-755-8490
    Pubs: *The Falling Boy, Blue Spruce* (Scribner, 1997,
1995), *The Flood of '64* (Ecco, 1987), *New Yorker, GQ,
Story, Sewanee Rev, Antaeus*

Maria R. Maris   P
2332 Ash
Billings, MT 59101, 406-259-1977
    Pubs: *Plains Poetry Jrnl, The Lyric, Poet Lore,
Piedmont Literary Rev, Wind, Kansas Qtly, Z
Miscellaneous*

Ruth McLaughlin   W
2506 1st Ave N
Great Falls, MT 59401
    Pubs: *Best American Short Stories: Anth* (HM, 1979),
California State Poetry Qtly

Thomas McNamee   P
West Boulder Ranch, Box 65, McLeod, MT 59052
    Pubs: *A Story of Deep Delight* (Viking, 1990), *The
Grizzly Bear* (Penguin, 1990)

Elsie Pankowski 🎤   P
1404 11 Ave S
Great Falls, MT 59405-4632, 406-452-0127
    Pubs: *Leaning Into the Wind* (HM, 1997), *Bellowing
Ark, Midwest Qtly, Thema, Midland Rev, Birdwatcher's
Digest, Manhattan Poetry Rev, Yankee*

Greg Pape 🎤 ✈   P
English Dept, Univ Montana, Missoula, MT 59812,
406-243-5231
    Pubs: *Sunflower Facing the Sun* (U Iowa Pr, 1992),
Storm Pattern, Black Branches, Border Crossings (U
Pitt Pr, 1992, 1984, 1978), *Atlantic, DoubleTake, Poetry*

Marnie Prange   P&W
231 Eagle's Pt
Stevensville, MT 59870, 406-777-5689
    Pubs: *Dangerous Neighborhoods* (Cleveland State
Poetry Ctr, 1994)

Lloyd Van Brunt 🎤 ✈   P&W
31 Hillside, PO Box 161, Basin, MT 59631-0161,
406-225-3577
Internet: lvb@mcn.net
    Pubs: *Poems New & Selected 1962-1992, Working
Firewood for the Night* (The Smith, 1993, 1990),
*Exquisite Corpse, The Generalist Papers, Re-Publish,
APR*
I.D.: Native American. Groups: Children, Health-Related

James Welch   P
2321 Wylie St
Missoula, MT 59802, 406-549-6713

Ivon W. White, Jr. 🎤 ✈   P
PO Box 637
Billings, MT 59103-0637, 406-245-6875
    Pubs: *Gates Left Open: Anth* (Montana Institute of the
Arts, 1989), *Portable Wall, Alkali Flats, Thomas Wolfe
Rev, The Villager, Art Times*
I.D.: Disabled, Seniors

Paul Zarzyski   P
PO Box 258
Augusta, MT 59410, 406-562-3860
  Pubs: *All This Way for the Short Ride* (Museum of
  New Mexico Pr, 1996), *I Am Not a Cowboy* (Dry Crik
  Pr, 1995), *Poetry, Prairie Schooner, Northern Lights,
  CutBank*

NEBRASKA

Susan Aizenberg   P
Creative Writing Program, Univ Nebraska, Omaha, NE
68182-0324, 402-493-6746
  Pubs: *Peru* (Graywolf Pr, 1997), *Prairie Schooner,
  Connecticut Rev, Devil's Millhopper, Iowa Woman, Third
  Coast, Agni, Spoon River Rev, Sun Dog, Kalliope, The
  Jrnl*

Grace Bauer 🎤 ✈   P
Univ of Nebraska English Dept, 202 Andrews, PO Box
880333, Lincoln, NE 68588-0333, 402-472-0993
Internet: gbauer@unlinfo.unl.edu
  Pubs: *Field Guide to the Ineffable* (Snail's Pace Pr,
  2000), *Women at the Well* (Portals Pr, 1998), *Where
  You've Seen Her* (Pennywhistle Pr, 1993), *House
  Where I've Never Lived* (Anabiosis Pr, 1993),
  *DoubleTake, Onthebus, Georgia Rev, American Literary
  Rev*

Stephen Behrendt 🎤 ✈   P
English Dept, Univ of Nebraska, Lincoln, NE 68588-0333,
402-472-1806
Internet: sbehrendt1@unl.edu
  Pubs: *A Step in the Dark, Instruments of the Bones*
  (Mid-List Pr, 1996, 1992), *Sewanee Rev, Hudson Rev,
  Texas Rev, Midwest Qtly*

Miriam Ben-Yaacov   P&W
1870 Mayfair Dr
Omaha, NE 68144, 402-333-1115
  Pubs: *Nexus, Short Story Intl, Nebraska English Jrnl,
  The Long Story, Smackwarm, Trans-Missouri Art View,
  Metropolitan*

J. V. Brummels 🎤 ✈   P
Two Cow
Winside, NE 68790, 402-286-4891
  Pubs: *Cheyenne Line* (Backwaters Pr, 2000), *Clay Hills*
  (Nosila Pr, 1996), *Sunday's Child* (Basfal Bks, 1994),
  Deus Ex Machina (Bantam Bks, 1989), *614 Pearl*
  (Abattoir Edtns, 1986), *Ellipsis, Chariton Rev, Puerto del
  Sol, Prairie Schooner*

Joanne M. Casullo   P
6300 N 7th St
Lincoln, NE 68521-8936
  Pubs: *All My Grandmothers Could Sing* (Free Rein Pr,
  1984), *Prairie Schooner, Kansas Qtly, South Dakota
  Rev*

Marilyn Dorf   P
4149 "E" St
Lincoln, NE 68510, 402-489-3104
  Pubs: *Kansas Qtly, Northeast, Midwest Poetry Rev,
  Bitterroot, Whole Notes, Mankato Poetry Rev,
  Plainsongs*

Lorraine Duggin 🎤 ✈   P&W
932 N 74 Ave
Omaha, NE 68114-3114, 402-397-6153
  Pubs: *The Heartlands Today* (Firelands Writing Ctr,
  1995), *In a New Land* (Natl Textbook Co, 1992),
  Nebraska Poets' Calendar (Black Star Pr, 2000),
  Boundaries of Twilight: Anth (New Rivers Pr, 1991),
  Kosmas: Czech & Euro Jrnl, Heartlands Today
I.D.: Czech-American

Richard Duggin   W
Writer's Workshop, Univ Nebraska, Fine Arts 223, Omaha,
NE 68182, 402-554-4801
  Pubs: *The Music Box Treaty* (Abbatoir Edtns, 1982),
  *Kansas Qtly, Laurel Rev, Playboy, Pulpsmith, NAR,
  Fiction Jrnl, American Literary Rev, BPJ, The Sun*

Charles Fort 🎤 ✈   P
Univ of Nebraska, English Dept, Kearney, NE 68849-1320,
308-865-8164
Internet: fortc@unk.edu
  Pubs: *Darvil* (St. Andrews, 1993), *The Town Clock
  Burning, Carnegie Mellon Anth of Poetry* (Carnegie
  Mellon U Pr, 1991, 1993), *Best American Poetry: Anth*
  (Scribner, 2000), *A New Geography of Poets: Anth* (U
  Arkansas Pr, 1992), *APR, Georgia Rev*

Mark Edwin Fuehrer   P
Imperial, NE 69033, 308-882-4219

Patrick Worth Gray   P
1109 Kingston Ave
Bellevue, NE 68005, 402-292-1908
  Pubs: *Spring Comes Again to Arnett* (Mr. Cogito Pr,
  1987), *Disappearances* (U Nebraska Pr, 1978)

Twyla Hansen 🎤 ✈   P
4140 N 42 St Cir
Lincoln, NE 68504-1210, 402-466-5839
Internet: twylahansen@alltel.net
  Pubs: *In Our Very Bones* (A Slow Tempo Pr, 1997),
  How to Live in the Heartland (Flatwater Edtns, 1992),
  Leaning Into the Wind (HM, 1997), *Inheriting the Land:
  Anth* (U Minnesota Pr, 1993), *Laurel Rev, Prairie
  Schooner, North Dakota Qtly, Crab Orchard Rev*

Arthur Homer   P&W
Univ Nebraska/Omaha, Writers Workshop, FAEB 221,
Omaha, NE 68182-0324, 402-556-4691
    Pubs: *The Drownt Boy: An Ozark Tale* (U Missouri Pr,
    1994), *Skies of Such Valuable Glass* (Owl Creek Pr,
    1990), *Georgia Rev, NAR, The Sun, Green Mountains
    Rev, Southern Rev*

Robert W. King   P
1930 Dakota St
Lincoln, NE 68502, 402-421-9215
    Pubs: *A Circle of Land* (Dacotah Territory Pr, 1990),
    Standing Around Outside (Bloodroot, 1979), *Ascent,
    NER, Midwest Qtly, Poetry, Massachusetts Rev*

William Kloefkorn   P
2502 N 63
Lincoln, NE 68507, 402-466-1032

Ted Kooser ⚲ ✈   P
1820 Branched Oak Rd
Garland, NE 68360-9303, 402-588-2272
Internet: kr84428@navix.net
    Pubs: *Winter Morning Walks; 100 Postcards to Jim
    Harrison* (Carnegie Mellon Pr, 2000), *Weather Central,
    One World at a Time* (U Pitt Pr, 1994, 1985),
    *Shenandoah, Atlantic, Ohio Rev, Georgia Rev, Kenyon
    Rev, Hudson Rev, Poetry*

Greg Kosmicki ⚲ ✈   P
Backwaters Press, 3502 N 52nd St, Omaha, NE
68104-3506, 402-451-4052
Internet: Gkosm62735@aol.com
    Pubs: *tables, chairs, wall, window, For My Son in a
    Motel Room* (Sandhills Pr, 2000, 1999), *nobody lives
    here who saw this sky* (Missing Spoke Pr, 1998), *How
    Things Happen* (bradypress, 1997), *Paris Rev, New
    Letters, Whole Notes, Lilliput Rev, Cimarron Rev*
Groups: Prisoners, Seniors

Greg Kuzma   P
English Dept, Univ Nebraska, Lincoln, NE 68588
    Pubs: *Good News* (Carnegie Mellon, 1994), *Wind Rain
    & Stars & the Grass Growing* (Orchises, 1993), *TriQtly,
    Crazyhorse, Harvard Rev, Virginia Qtly, Massachusetts
    Rev*

Wopashitwe Mondo Eye Langa   P
PO Box 2500
Lincoln, NE 68542-2500
    Pubs: *Morning of the Bright Bird* (Third World Pr,
    1992), *Shooting Star Qtly Rev, Nebraska Humanities,
    Obsidian, Black Scholar, Nantucket Rev, Pacifica Rev,
    Argo*

James Magorian   P
1225 N 46 St
Lincoln, NE 68503
    Pubs: *Hearts of Gold* (Acme Pr, 1996), *The Hideout of
    the Sigmund Freud Gang* (Black Oak Pr, 1987),
    *Plainsongs, Nebraska Rev, River Styx, Sewanee Rev,
    Atlanta Rev, SPR*

Mordecai Marcus   P
822 Mulder Dr
Lincoln, NE 68510-4032, 402-488-7831
    Pubs: *Pursuing the Lost* (Whole Notes Pr, 1993), *Poet
    Lore, Tar River Poetry, Poet & Critic, Cats Mag, South
    Dakota Rev, Santa Barbara Rev*

Nancy McCleery ⚲ ✈   P
3025 P St
Lincoln, NE 68503-3434, 402-477-8363
    Pubs: *Polar Lights* (Transient Pr, 1994), *Staying the
    Winter* (Cummington Pr, 1987), *Many Mountains
    Moving, Cafe Solo, Whole Notes, Hyperion, Portland
    Rev, Calyx*
Groups: Schools

Hilda Raz ⚲ ✈   P
Univ of Nebraska, 201 Andrews Hall, Lincoln, NE
68588-0334, 402-472-1812
Internet: hraz1@unl.edu
    Pubs: *Divine Honors* (Wesleyan, 1997), *The Bone Dish*
    (State Street Pr, 1989), *Cancer in the Voices of Ten
    Women: Anth* (Pandora/HC, 1997), *Second Helping:
    Anth* (Pleasant Dale Pr, 1996), *Kalliope, Southern Rev,
    Women's Rev of Bks, Ploughshares*

James Reed ⚲ ✈   W
1009 Hickory St
Omaha, NE 68108-3617, 402-345-3711
Internet: jpreed@radiks.net
    Pubs: *West Branch, Whetstone, Talking River Rev,
    Flash!Point, Apalachee Qtly, Tennessee Qtly, Aura
    Literary/Arts Rev, Carolina Qtly, Buffalo Spree, William
    & Mary Rev, River Styx, Brilliant Corners*

Roy Scheele ⚲ ✈   P
2020 S 25th St
Lincoln, NE 68502-3017, 402-477-1102
Internet: rcheele@doane.edu
    Pubs: *Keeping the Horses* (Windflower Pr, 1998), *Short
    Suite* (Main-Traveled Roads, 1997), *To See How It
    Tallies* (Whole Notes Pr, 1995), *The Voice We Call
    Human* (Juniper Pr, 1991), *American Scholar, Pivot,
    Poetry, Northeast, Southern Rev, Verse*

Michael Skau ⚲ ✈   P
Univ Nebraska, 60th & Dodge, English Dept, Omaha, NE
68182, 402-554-3314
Internet: micahel_skau@unomaha.edu
    Pubs: *Me & God Poems* (Bradypress, 1990),
    *Paintbrush, Kansas Qtly, Passaic Rev, Sequoia,
    Carolina Qtly, NW Rev, Cumberland Poetry Rev,
    Midland Rev*

James Solheim 🎤 ✈ P&W
3707 S 97th St
Omaha, NE 68124-3740, 402-393-6108
Internet: jamessolheim.com
Pubs: *It's Disgusting...and We Ate It* (Scholastic, 1999),
Pushcart Prize XV: Anth (Pushcart Pr, 1991), *ACM,
Poetry, Kenyon Rev, Iowa Rev, NW Rev, Chicago Rev,
Missouri Rev, Cimarron Rev*
Groups: Children

Brent Spencer 🎤 ✈ P&W
Creighton Univ, English Dept, Omaha, NE 68178,
402-280-2192
Internet: spencr@creighton.edu
Pubs: *Are We Not Men?*, *Lost Son* (Arcade, 1996,
1995), *GQ, Glimmer Train, Antioch Rev, Missouri Rev,
Atlantic*

Don Welch P
611 W 27 St
Kearney, NE 68847, 308-237-3861
Pubs: *Carved by Obadiah Verity* (Colorado College Pr,
1993), *Inheriting the Land: Anth* (U Minnesota Pr,
1993), *Prairie Schooner, Georgia Rev, Laurel Rev,
Nimrod, Aethlon*

Hargis Westerfield W
2914 Ave B
Kearney, NE 68847, 308-237-7107
Pubs: *The Forty-First Division* (Turner Pub Co, 1993),
SW Rev, Christian Century, Saturday Rev, Trains

Nancy G. Westerfield P
505 W 22 St, #2
Kearney, NE 68847, 308-237-7107
Pubs: *The Morning of the Marys* (Contemporary Drama
Service, 1986), *Welded Women* (Kearney State College
Pr, 1983), *Prairie Schooner, Poem, Trains, Grain*

Fredrick Zydek 🎤 ✈ P&W
5002 Decatur St
Omaha, NE 68104-5023, 402-551-0343
Internet: zydek007@aol.com
Pubs: *The Abbey Poems* (Lone Willow Pr, 1998),
Ending the Fast (Yellow Barn Pr, 1984), *Poetry,
Antioch, NER, Nimrod, Poetry NW, Prairie Schooner,
SW Rev*

NEVADA

Aliki Barnstone 🎤 ✈ P
University of Nevada, Las Vegas, Department of English,
Las Vegas, NV 89154-5011, 702-895-4341
Internet: www.barnstone.com
Pubs: *Wild with It* (Sheep Meadow Pr, 2001), *Voices of
Light: Anth* (Shambhala, 2000), *Madly in Love, Bright
Snow* (Carnegie Mellon U Pr, 1997, 1997), *A Book of
Women Poets from Antiquity to Now: Anth* (Random
Hse, 1992), *Agni, Antioch Rev, Poetry*
I.D.: Greek-American/Greek, Jewish

Charles H. Crump P
11 Condor Cir
Carson City, NV 89701, 702-883-6380
Pubs: *Desert Wood* (U Nevada Pr, 1991), *Piedmont
Literary Rev, Redneck Rev, Poultry, Manna, Silver State
Quill, Bellowing Ark*

Elaine Dallman P
PO Box 60550
Reno, NV 89506, 702-972-1671
Pubs: *A Parallel Cut of Air* (Medallion Guild, 1996),
Woman Poet: The West (Women in Literature, 1994),
Black Buzzard Rev, Flat Tired, Northern Contours

John H. Irsfeld W
Professor of English, Univ Nevada, 4505 Maryland Pkwy,
Las Vegas, NV 89154, 702-895-4877
Pubs: *Little Kingdom* (SMU, 1989), *Rats Alley* (U
Nevada, 1987), *New Texas '91: Anth* (U North Texas
Pr, 1991), *American Literary Rev, Kansas Qtly, The
Writer*

Stephen Shu Ning Liu 🎤 ✈ P
4024 Deerfield Ave
Las Vegas, NV 89117-4542, 702-871-5987
Pubs: *My Father's Martial Art* (U Nevada Pr, 1999),
Dream Journeys to China (New World Pr, 1982)

Melanie Perish 🎤 ✈ P
Univ Nevada, College of Engineering, MS256, Reno, NV
89557, 775-784-6433
Internet: mperish@equinox.unr.edu
Pubs: *Traveling the Distance* (Rising Tide, 1981), *Notes
of a Daughter from the Old Country* (Motherroot, 1978),
Calyx, Sinister Wisdom, Desert Wood, eNVee
Groups: Children, Seniors

Elizabeth Perry P
PO Box 61324
Boulder City, NV 89006, 702-294-0021
Internet: peg_pub@ix.netcom.com
Pubs: *Desert Wood* (U Nevada Pr, 1991), *Gathered
Echoes* (Pegasus Pr, 1991), *Interim, Midwest Poetry
Rev*

Kirk Robertson P
PO Box 1047
Fallon, NV 89407, 702-423-1440
Pubs: *Just Past Labor Day: New & Selected Poems* (U
Nevada Pr, 1996), *Music: A Suite & 13 Songs* (Floating
Island Pr, 1995), *Driving to Vegas: Poems 1969-1987*
(Sun/Gemini Pr, 1989), *New Directions*

G. J. Scrimgeour W
PO Box 2809
Reno, NV 89505, 702-786-1442
Pubs: *A Woman of Her Times* (Putnam, 1982)

NEW HAMPSHIRE

Allan Block   P
RFD Quarry Rd
Francestown, NH 03043, 603-547-2934
    Pubs: *In Noah's Wake* (William L. Bauhan, 1972), *The Nation, Massachusetts Rev, Prairie Schooner*

W. E. Butts 🎤 ✈   P
827 State St #5
Portsmouth, NH 03801-4330, 603-427-6963
    Pubs: *The Required Dance* (Igneus Pr, 1990), *Magazine Verse: Anth* (Monitor Bks, 1997), *Atlanta Rev, Contemporary Rev, Spillway, Mid-American Rev, Poet Lore, Calliope, Cimarron Rev, Defined Providence*

Martha Carlson-Bradley 🎤 ✈   P
18 Summer St
Hillsborough, NH 03244, 603-464-4033
Internet: nhwp@nh.ultranet.com
    Pubs: *Each Nest Full of Cries* (Adastra, 2000), *Anth of Mag Verse & Yearbook of American Poetry* (Monitor Bk Co, 1997), *BPJ, Poetry East, Carolina Qtly, Calliope, Chattahoochee Rev, Poets On, NER, Marlboro Rev*

Dan Carr   P
PO Box 111/30 Main St
Ashuelot Village, NH 03441, 603-239-6830
    Pubs: *Intersection* (Golgonooza Letter Foundry & Pr, 1990), *Mysteries of the Palaces of Water* (Four Zoas Night Hse, 1985), *Connecticut Poetry Rev*

Carolyn C. Carrara   P
HCR 58, Box 254
East Hebron, NH 03232, 603-744-5101
    Pubs: *Sojourner, Stuff, Phoebe, Onion River Rev, Mockingbird, Soundings East, Sandscript, Lucid Stone, Live Poets Society, Pebbles*

Jeannine Dobbs   P
PO Box 1076
Merrimack, NH 03054
    Pubs: *Threesome Poems* (Alice James Bks, 1976), *Ohio Rev, Midwest Qtly, Shenandoah, Amicus Jrnl, Merrimack*

William Doreski 🎤 ✈   P
79 Murphy Rd
Peterborough, NH 03458, 603-924-7987
    Pubs: *Suburban Light* (Cedar Hill, 1999), *Sublime of the North* (Frith Pr, 1998), *Pianos in the Woods* (Pygmy Forest Pr, 1998), *Ghost Train* (Nightshade Pr, 1991), *Cimarron Rev, Swamproot, Colorado Rev, Harvard Rev, Atlanta Rev*

Christopher Dornin   P
1 Appleton St
Concord, NH 03301-5942
    Pubs: *Contemporary Religious Poetry: Anth* (Paulist Pr, 1987), *Nimrod, Plains Poetry Rev, Gamut, Mudfish, Amelia, Blue Unicorn, Soundings East, Lucky Star*

Merle Drown 🎤 ✈   W
60 W Parish Rd
Concord, NH 03301, 603-224-7985
Internet: drown@mediaone.net
    Pubs: *The Suburbs of Heaven* (Soho Pr, 2000), *Plowing Up a Snake* (The Dial Pr, 1982), *New Hampshire College Jrnl, Other Voices*

Robert Dunn 🎤 ✈   P
53 Whidden St
Portsmouth, NH 03801
    Pubs: *Quo, Musa, Tendis* (Peter Randall, 1983), *Under the Legislature of Stars: Anth* (Oyster River Pr, 1999), *Larcom Rev, Black & White, Trayfull of Lab Mice, Aspect, Bellowing Ark, CSM, Crow, Portsmouth Art Annual*

Patricia Fargnoli 🎤 ✈   P
24 Beaver St
Keene, NH 03431
Internet: arielpf123@aol.com
    Pubs: *Necessary Light* (Utah State U Pr, 1999), *SPR, Laurel Rev, Indiana Rev, Poetry NW, Poet Lore, Seattle Rev, Spoon River Rev, Negative Capability, Midwest Qtly, Poetry, Green Mountains Rev, Ploughshares, Cimarron, Prairie Schooner*
Groups: Teenagers, Seniors

Alice B. Fogel   P
PO Box 25
Acworth, NH 03601, 603-835-6783
    Pubs: *I Love this Dark World, Elemental* (Zoland Bks, 1996, 1993)

Richard Frede   W
58 Concord St
Peterborough, NH 03458-1511, 603-924-6609
    Pubs: *The Boy, The Devil, And Divorce* (Pocket Bks, 1993), *The Nurses* (NAL, 1986), *Harper's, McCall's, Short Story Intl, Poetry, Fantasy & Sci Fi*

Jeff Friedman 🎤 ✈   P
PO Box 187
Hanover, NH 03755-0187, 603-643-8255
    Pubs: *Scattering the Ashes* (Carnegie Mellon Pr, 1998), *The Record-Breaking Heat Wave* (BkMk Pr, 1986), *American Poetry Rev, Missouri Rev, NER, Poetry, Press, Manoa, Boulevard, Antioch Rev, 5 A.M.*

Barbara Gibbs   P
c/o Barbara Gibbs Golffing, 272 Middle Hancock Rd,
Peterborough, NH 03458, 603-924-3487
    Pubs: *Possibility* (w/Francis Golffing; Peter Lang, 1991),
The Meeting Place of the Colors (Cummington Pr,
1972), *New Yorker, Yankee, Helicon 9*

Donald Hall 🎤 ✈   P&W
Eagle Pond Farm
Danbury, NH 03230
    Pubs: *Without, Old & New Poems* (HM, 1998, 1990),
*New Yorker, Atlantic, Nation, New Republic, Gettysburg
Rev, Iowa Rev*

Marie Harris 🎤 ✈   P
PO Box 203
Barrington, NH 03825, 603-664-7654
    Pubs: *Your Sun, Manny* (New Rivers, 1999), *Weasel in
the Turkey Pen* (Hanging Loose Pr, 1992), *The Party
Train, A Collection of North American Prose Poetry:
Anth* (New Rivers, 1996), *Granite Rev*

Hugh Hennedy   P
456 Lincoln Ave
Portsmouth, NH 03801, 603-431-2829
    Pubs: *Halcyon Time* (Oyster River Pr, 1993), *Tar River
Poetry, Hawaii Rev, James Joyce Qtly, Lilliput Rev,
Brownstone Rev*

Elizabeth Hodges   P
30 Graham Rd
Concord, NH 03301-6900
    Pubs: *A Green Place: Anth* (Delacorte Pr, 1982), *NAR,
Connecticut River Rev, Greenfield Rev*

Cynthia Huntington   P
60 Lyme Rd
Hanover, NH 03755, 603-646-2321
    Pubs: *We Have Gone to the Beach* (Alice James Bks,
1996), *The Fish-Wife* (U Hawaii Pr, 1986), *Kenyon Rev,
NER, Ploughshares, Agni*

J. Kates 🎤 ✈   P
PO Box 221
Fitzwilliam, NH 03447
    Pubs: *Under the Legislature of Stars* (Oyster River,
1999), *XY Files: Anth* (Sherman Asher, 1997), *The
Gospels in Our Image: Anth* (HB, 1995), *Larcom Rev,
Cream City Rev, Cyphers, Florida Rev, Mississippi Rev,
Denver Qtly*

Dolores Kendrick   P
Phillips Exeter Academy, Exeter, NH 03833
    Pubs: *The Women of Plums* (PEA Pr, 1991), *Columbia,
Ms.*

Lawrence Kinsman 🎤 ✈   P&W
PO Box 305
Manchester, NH 03105-0305
    Pubs: *Water from the Moon, A Well-Ordered Life*
(Abelard, 1998, 1995), *Kentucky Poetry Rev, MacGuffin,
Pacific Rev, New Laurel Rev*

Maxine Kumin 🎤 ✈   P&W
40 Harriman Ln
Warner, NH 03278-4300, 603-456-3709
    Pubs: *Quit Monks or Die!* (Story Line Pr, 1999),
*Selected Poems 1960-1990, Connecting the Dots,
Women, Animals & Vegetables* (Norton, 1997, 1996,
1994)

Ron Kurz   W
PO Box 164
Antrim, NH 03440, 603-588-3323
    Pubs: *Black Rococo, Lethal Gas* (M. Evans, 1976,
1974)

Nancy Lagomarsino 🎤 ✈   P
6 Brook Rd
Hanover, NH 03755, 603-643-3959
    Pubs: *The Secretary Parables, Sleep Handbook* (Alice
James Bks, 1991, 1987)
Groups: Teenagers

Esther M. Leiper   P
Box 87
Jefferson, NH 03583, 603-586-4505
    Pubs: *The Wars of Faery* (Amelia, 1994), *Stone
Country* (Caro-Lynn Pub, 1993), *Writer's Jrnl, North
Country Weekly, The Answer*

P. H. Liotta   P&W
2 Coach Rd
Exeter, NH 03833
    Pubs: *Rules of Engagement* (Cleveland State U Poetry
Ctr, 1991)

Ruth Doan MacDougall 🎤 ✈   W
285 Range Rd
Center Sandwich, NH 03227, 603-284-6451
Internet: www.ruthdoanmacdougall.com
    Pubs: *The Cheerleader* (Frigate Bks, 1998), *Snowy* (St.
Martin's Pr, 1993), *A Lovely Time Was Had By All*
(Atheneum, 1982)

Rodger Martin   P&W
Goosebrook, RR2 Box 72A
Peterborough, NH 03458, 603-924-7342
    Pubs: *The Nemo Poems* (Goosebrook, 1992), *Selected
Poems of Contemporary European & American Poets:
Anth* (Spring Breeze Pub, 1989), *Granite Rev,
Appalachia*

Cleopatra Mathis   P
13 E Wheelock St
Hanover, NH 03755-2137, 603-643-8781
  Pubs: *Guardian, The Center for Cold Weather, The
  Bottom Land, Aerial View of Louisiana* (Sheep Meadow
  Pr, 1995, 1990, 1983, 1980)

Bridget Mazur   W
Lebanon College, 1 Court St, Lebanon, NH 03766
  Pubs: *Iowa Rev, Shenandoah, Beloit Fiction Jrnl,
  Buffalo Spree, Apalachee Qtly, Cimarron, Buffalo
  Magazine*

Mekeel McBride   P
Univ New Hampshire, English Dept, Hamilton Smith,
Durham, NH 03824, 603-862-4216
  Pubs: *Red Letter Days, The Going Under of the
  Evening Land* (Carnegie Mellon U Pr, 1988, 1983)

Rollande Merz   P
Province Rd, Box 70A
Strafford, NH 03884
  Pubs: *Pictures: Life & Still Life* (Andrew Mountain Pr,
  1984), *Calliope, Bitterroot*

Edith Milton   W
PO Box 237
Francestown, NH 03043-0237
  Pubs: *Best American Short Stories: Anth* (HM, 1988),
  *Ploughshares, Tikkun, Witness, Yale Rev, Prairie
  Schooner*

Deborah Navas 🎤   W
1-H Bass St
Newmarket, NH 03857-1151
  Pubs: *Murdered By His Wife* (U Mass Pr, 2000),
  Things We Lost, Gave Away, Bought High & Sold Low
  (SMU Pr, 1992), *New Fiction from New England: Anth*
  (Yankee Bks, 1986), *PEN Syndicated Fiction*

Julia Older 🎤 ✈   P&W
PO Box 174
Hancock, NH 03449-0174
  Pubs: *Hermaphroditus in America, The Island Queen:
  Celia Thaxter of the Isles of Shoals, Higher Latitudes*
  (Appledore Bks, 2000, 1998, 1995), *Legislature of the
  Stars: 62 New Hampshire Poets* (Oyster River Pr,
  1999), *New Yorker, Nimrod, Yankee*

John Robinson 🎤 ✈   W
131 Jones Ave
Portsmouth, NH 03801-5515
Internet: jrobiz@aol.com
  Pubs: *Legends of the Lost* (Northland, 1989), *January's
  Dream* (Green Street Pr, 1985), *Ploughshares*

Rebecca Rule   W
178 Mountain Ave
Northwood, NH 03261, 603-942-8174
  Pubs: *The Best Revenge* (U Pr of New England, 1995),
  Creating The Story (w/Susan Wheeler; Heinemann,
  1993), *Yankee, Echoes, Whetstone, Northern Rev*

Steve Sherman   W
PO Box 174
Hancock, NH 03449-0174, 603-525-3581
  Pubs: *Primary Crime, Highboy, The Maple Sugar
  Murders* (Appledore, 2000, 2000, 1998), *The Hangtree*
  (Major Bks, 1977), *Ellery Queen*

Charles Simic   P&W
PO Box 192
Strafford, NH 03884-0192
  Pubs: *Orphan Factory* (Michigan U, 1997), *Walking the
  Black Cat, A Wedding in Hell, The Book of Gods &
  Devils* (HB, 1996, 1994, 1990), *Selected Poems*
  (Braziller, 1990)

Mark Smith   W
English Dept, Univ New Hampshire, Hamilton-Smith,
Durham, NH 03824, 603-862-1313
  Pubs: *Smoke Street, Doctor Blues* (Morrow, 1984,
  1983), *The Delphinium Girl* (H&R, 1980)

Sidney L. Surface   P&W
17 Old Milford Rd
Brookline, NH 03033, 603-673-4943
  Pubs: *Small Town Tales, What We Will Give Each
  Other* (Hobblebush Bks, 1997, 1993), *Dog Music: Anth*
  (St. Martin's, 1996), *L.A. Times Book Rev, Graham
  House Rev, Chattahoochee Rev, California Qtly, Hollins
  Critic, Midwest Qtly*

Parker Towle 🎤 ✈   P
836 Easton Valley Rd
Franconia, NH 03580-5407, 603-823-8157
Internet: parker.a.towle@hitchcock.org
  Pubs: *Our Places* (Andrew Mountain Pr, 1998),
  Handwork (Nightshade Pr, 1991), *Search for Doubloons*
  (Wings Pr, 1984), *Appalachia, Blueline, Cape Rock,
  Calliope, Great River Rev, Galley Sail Rev*

Donald Wellman 🎤 ✈   P
21 Rockland Rd
Weare, NH 03281-4725, 603-529-1060
Internet: soaring@ma.ultranet.com
  Pubs: *Fields* (Light & Dust, 1995), *Frames, Fields,
  Meanings* (O.ars, 1993), *Generator, Tyuonyi, Room,
  Puckerbrush Rev, O.ars, Boundary 2*

W. D. Wetherell 🎤 ✈   W
PO Box 84
Lyme, NH 03768-0084
  Pubs: *Morning* (Pantheon, 2001), *Chekhov's Sister*
  (Little, Brown, 1990)

Marc Widershien   P
Dawn Christensen, Managing Editor, Four Arts, Main St,
PO Box 641, Wilton, NH 03086
  Pubs: *Essays #0-11* (Four Arts, 1994), *Middle Journeys*
(Northwoods Pr, 1994), *Atelier, Small Press Rev,
Library Jrnl, New Directions, Small Mag Rev*

NEW JERSEY

Marion Arenas 🎤 ✈   P
694 Birchwood Dr
Wyckoff, NJ 07481-1007, 201-891-1051
  Pubs: *The U-U Poets: Anth* (Pudding Hse, 1996), *Life
on the Line: Anth* (Negative Capability Pr, 1992), *NYQ,
Jrnl of New Jersey Poets, Lyric*

Sylvia Argow   P
33 Osborne ST
Bloomfield, NJ 07003-2714
  Pubs: *Poet, Bitterroot*

Renee Ashley 🎤 ✈   P&W
210 Skylands Rd
Ringwood, NJ 07456, 973-962-1142
Internet: reneea@bellatlantic.net
  Pubs: *The Various Reasons of Light* (Avocet Pr, 1998),
Salt (U Wisconsin Pr, 1991), *Writing Poems: Anth* (HC,
1996), *Breaking Up Is Hard to Do: Anth* (Crossing Pr,
1993), *Harvard Rev, American Voice, Kenyon Rev,
Antioch Rev, Colorado Rev, 5 A.M., Indiana Rev*

Jay Stuart Auslander 🎤 ✈   P
270 Briarcliffe Rd
Teaneck, NJ 07666-3001, 201-837-1294
Internet: auslander@whafh.com
  Pubs: *A New Majority* (Broncho Pr, 1987), *Uncharted
Lines: Anth* (Boaz Pub, 1999), *MacGuffin, Orphic Lute,
Lucky Star, Blow, Connecticut River Rev, Jrnl of
American Medical Assoc., Sonoma Mandala*

Beth Bahler   P&W
201 S Livingston, #2F
Livingston, NJ 07039
  Pubs: *Parting Gifts, Footwork, New York Times,
Pinehurst Jrnl, Lilliput, Highlights for Children*

Neil Baldwin   P
17 Burnside St
Upper Montclair, NJ 07043, 201-783-1008

Benjamin R. Barber   W
c/o Political Science Dept, Rutgers Univ, New Brunswick,
NJ 08903
  Pubs: *Marriage Voices* (S&S, 1981), *Harper's,
Salmagundi*

Jan Barry 🎤 ✈   P
109 N Mountain Ave
Montclair, NJ 07042-2339, 973-746-5941
  Pubs: *From Both Sides Now: Anth* (Scribner, 1998),
Radical Visions: Anth (U Georgia Pr, 1994), *Carrying
the Darkness: Anth* (Texas Tech U Pr, 1989), *Paterson
Literary Rev, Jrnl of American Culture, Young Citizen*

Ronald D. Bascombe   P
39 Green Village Rd #102
Madison, NJ 07940-2588, 201-377-1597
  Pubs: *Black Creation, 360 Degrees of Blackness
Comin' at You, The Universal Black Writer*

Carol Becker   P&W
37 Sayre Dr
Princeton, NJ 08540, 609-987-0282
  Pubs: *Harvard Mag, College English, Redstart Plus,
Yankee, American Voice, Small Pond Mag*

Ahn Behrens   P
295 Grove St
Jersey City, NJ 07302-3602, 201-451-1074
  Pubs: *Movieworks Movieworks* (Little Theatre Pr, 1990),
*What's a Nice Girl Like You Doing In a Relationship
Like This?: Anth* (Crossing Pr, 1992), *Stet Mag, Pan,
McCall's, Hoboken Terminal, Buffalo News*

Emily Trafford Berges 🎤   W
English Dept, New Jersey City Univ, 2039 Kennedy Blvd,
Jersey City, NJ 07305, 201-200-3100
Internet: eberges@njcu.edu
  Pubs: *The Flying Circus* (Morrow, 1985)

Laura Boss 🎤 ✈   P
Lips, PO Box 1345, Montclair, NJ 07042, 201-662-1303
  Pubs: *Arms: New & Selected Poems* (Guernica, 1999),
Reports from the Front (CCC, 1995), *Outsiders: Anth*
(Milkweed, 1999), *Identity Lessons: Anth* (Penguin,
1999), *Unsettling America: Anth* (Viking/Penguin, 1995),
Abraxas, Greenfield Rev, New York Times
I.D.: Jewish. Groups: Seniors

Claude Brown   W
381 Broad St, #1605
Newark, NJ 07104

Sal St. John Buttaci 🎤   P
PO Box 887
Saddle Brook, NJ 07663-0887
Internet: sambpoet@yahoo.com
  Pubs: *The Writer, PoetryMagazine.com, Bereavement
Mag, Anemone, Black Mountain, CSM, Thirteen,
Pudding*
I.D.: Italian-American

Kevin O. Byrne 🎤 ✈   P
24 Dogwood Ln
New Providence, NJ 07974-1402, 908-464-2711
    Pubs: *The Panhandler, Poet & Critic, Bitterroot, CQ,
    Cottonwood, Concerning Poetry, Wisconsin Rev*

Richard Carboni   P
38 Marion Rd
Montclair, NJ 07043, 973-783-0598

Rafael Catala   P&W
Ometeca Institute, PO Box 38, New Brunswick, NJ
08903-0038, 908-435-0152
    Pubs: *Escobas De Milo* (Ometeca Institute & Ventura
    One, 1998), *Cuban Poets in New York: Anth* (Betania
    Madrid, 1988), *Ometeca, Trasimagen, Paterson Literary
    Rev, Realidad Aparte, Poesia De Venezuela*

Roberta Chester   P
234 Passaic Ave
Passaic, NJ 07055-3603
    Pubs: *The Eloquent Edge: Anth of Maine Women
    Writers* (Acadia Pr, 1989), *Tar River Poetry*

Donna L. Clovis 🎤 ✈   P&W
PO Box 0741
Princeton Junction, NJ 08550-0741
    Pubs: *Locket of Dreams* (Books for Black Children,
    2000), *Sound* (Addison-Wesley, 1998), *Native American
    Storybook* (Cherubic Pr, 1998), *Struggles for Freedom*
    (Dillon Pub, 1994), *Survival Through These Hard Times,
    Metamorphosis* (Northwoods Pr, 1991, 1988)
Lang: Spanish. Groups: Children, College/Univ

Peter Cole   P
46 Basswood Terr
Wayne, NJ 07470, 201-839-7472
    Pubs: *Rift* (Station Hill Pr, 1990), *Tel Aviv Rev, Agni
    Rev, Conjunctions, Scripsi, Partisan Rev*

Robert J. Conley 🎤 ✈   P
Cherry Weiner Literary Agency, 28 Kipling Way,
Manalapan, NJ 07726, 732-446-2096
Internet: cherry8486@aol.com
    Pubs: *Cherokee Dragon, War Woman* (St. Martin's Pr,
    2000, 1997), *Barjack, Brass* (Dorchester Pub, 2000,
    1999), *The Meade Solution* (U Pr Colorado, 1998),
    Mountain Windsong (U Oklahoma Pr, 1992), *Nickajack*
    (Doubleday, 1992), *True West*
I.D.: Cherokee

Edmund Conti 🎤 ✈   P
79 Tulip St
Summit, NJ 07901, 908-273-7632
    Pubs: *The Ed C. Scrolls, Eddies* (Runaway Spoon Pr,
    1996, 1994), *Light, Light Year, Abbey, Lyric, Studies in
    Contemporary Satire, Bogg, S.L.U.G.fest*

David Cope ✈   P
c/o Humana Press, 999 Riverview Dr, Ste #2, Totowa, NJ
07512, 201-256-1699
Internet: dcope@yahoo.com
    Pubs: *Silences for Love, Coming Home, Fragments
    from the Stars, On the Bridge, Quiet Lives* (Humana
    Pr, 1997, 1993, 1990, 1986, 1983), *Sierra, Lame Duck,
    Napalm Health Spa, Heaven Bone*

Steven Corbin   W
168 3rd St
Jersey City, NJ 07302-2514
    Pubs: *Fragments That Remain* (GMP Ltd, 1992), *No
    Easy Place to Be* (S&S, 1989), *Breaking Ice, More Like
    Minds, Passport 3*

Louie Crew 🎤 ✈   P
377 S Harrison St, 12D
East Orange, NJ 07018-1225, 973-395-1068
Internet: http://newark.rutgers.edu/~lcrew
    Pubs: *Book of Revelations* (Integrity, 1991), *From
    Queen Lutibelle's Pew* (Dragon Disks, 1990), *Midnight
    Lessons* (Samisdat, 1987)
I.D.: G/L/B/T, Episcopalian. Groups: G/L/B/T, Christian

Paula Bramsen Cullen 🎤 ✈   P
980 Stuart Rd
Princeton, NJ 08540, 609-924-9128
    Pubs: *Journey of Storms* (Millstone River Pr, 1994),
    *Cimarron Rev, Kansas Qtly, Connecticut Fireside &
    Book Rev, Poem*

Walter Cummins   W
English Dept, Fairleigh Dickinson Univ, 285 Madison Ave,
Madison, NJ 07940, 973-443-8564
Internet: wcummins@worldnet.att.net
    Pubs: *Where We Live* (Lynx Hse Pr, 1983), *Witness*
    (Samisdat, 1975), *Virginia Qtly Rev, Other Voices,
    Laurel Rev, Confrontation, North Atlantic Rev,
    Connecticut Rev*

Anne E. Cusack   P
975 Garrison Ave
Teaneck, NJ 07666, 201-836-4790
    Pubs: *Chelsea, Northeast Jrnl, 13th Moon, Open Places*

Mona Da Vinci   P&W
65 Spruce St
Bloomfield, NJ 07003, 201-748-6275
    Pubs: *Out of This World, Unnatural Acts, The Herald*

Suzanne Dale   P
501 Monument Rd
Pine Beach, NJ 08741

Melody Davis   P&W
24 Childsworth Ave
Bernardsville, NJ 07924, 908-630-0572
    Pubs: *The Center of Distance* (Nightshade Pr, 1992),
    *Chelsea, Brooklyn Rev, Poetry, BPJ, West Branch,
    Poetry NW, Verse, Sing Heavenly Muse!*

Elaine Denholtz   W
13 Birchwood Dr
Livingston, NJ 07039, 973-992-5480
    Pubs: *Playing for High Stakes* (Freundlich, 1986),
    Having it Both Ways (Stein & Day, 1981), *New Jersey,
    Woman, New Woman, Daily Record*

Emanuel Di Pasquale   P
392 Ocean Ave, #1G
Long Branch, NJ 07740, 908-222-6313
    Pubs: *Genesis* (Jostro, 1997), *Literature* (HC, 1993),
    Men of Our Time (Georgia U Pr, 1991), *APR, Sewanee
    Rev, Nation, NYQ, New York Times*

Constance Mary Diana   P
PO Box 474
East Brunswick, NJ 08816
    Pubs: *Is That You My God* (Zinnia Bks, 1997)

George-Therese Dickenson   P
125 Rock Lodge Rd
Stockholm, NJ 07460-1148
    Pubs: *Candles Burn in Memory Town* (Segue, 1988),
    Transducing (Roof, 1985), *Tricycle, Big Allis, Assassin,
    Amsterdam News, The World, Annoi*

Juditha Dowd   P
179 Old Turnpike Rd
Califon, NJ 07830, 908-439-2144
    Pubs: *Earth's Daughters, Black Fly Rev, California Qtly,
    Jrnl of New Jersey Poets, U.S. 1 Worksheets,
    Footwork, Kelsey Rev, Exit 13*

John Drexel 🎤 ✈   P
42 Edgewood Rd
Glen Ridge, NJ 07028, 973-680-8834
Internet: castlepoet@altavista.com
    Pubs: *Where Icarus Falls: Anth* (Santa Barbara Rev,
    1998), *Paris Rev, Acumen, Verse, Hampden-Sydney
    Poetry Rev, Seneca Rev, Illuminations, Oxford Poetry,
    Southern Rev, Hudson Rev, Outposts, Image,
    Salmagundi, First Things*

Rosalyn Drexler 🎤 ✈   P&W
60 Union St #1S
Newark, NJ 07105-1430
Internet: wrestlerarm@msn.com
    Pubs: *Art Does "Not!" Exist* (Fiction Collective 2, 1996)
Lang: Yiddish. Groups: College/Univ, Seniors

Sandra R. Duguid   P
114 Forest Ave
West Caldwell, NJ 07006, 201-226-1096
    Pubs: *Jrnl of New Jersey Poets, Anglican Theological
    Rev, Earth's Daughters, Modern Poetry Studies, West
    Branch, Connecticut Writer*

Lora Dunetz 🎤   P
PO Box 113
Whiting, NJ 08759, 732-350-9236
    Pubs: *To Guard Your Sleep & Other Poems* (Icarus,
    1987), *Anth of American Mag Verse 1997, Hellas,
    Without Halos, Blue Unicorn, Ararat, Amelia, Baltimore
    Rev, New Renaissance, Arkansas Rev*
Groups: Children, Christian

Stephen Dunn 🎤 ✈   P
445 Chestnut Neck Rd
Port Republic, NJ 08241, 609-652-1456
Internet: sdunn55643@aol.com
    Pubs: *Different Hours, Riffs & Reciprocities, Loosestrife,
    New & Selected Poems: 1974-1994, Landscape at the
    End of the Century, Between Angels* (Norton, 2000,
    1998, 1996, 1994, 1991, 1989)

Wendy Einhorn   P
234 Passaic Ave
Passaic, NJ 07055
    Pubs: *Do Not Say That She Is Happy Being Crazy*
    (Einhorn, 1975), *New Maine Writing, Kennebec*

K. S. Ernst   P
13 Yard Ave
Farmingdale, NJ 07727, 908-938-4297
    Pubs: *Sequencing* (Xerox Sutra Edtns, 1984), *Interstate,
    Earth's Daughters, Lost & Found Times*

Karen Ethelsdattar   P
229 Ogden Ave
Jersey City, NJ 07307, 201-653-3523
    Pubs: *The Spiral Dance* (H&R, 1979), *At Our Core:
    Women Writing About Power: Anth, If I Had My Life to
    Live Over I Would Pick More Daisies: Anth*
    (Papier-Mache Pr, 1998, 1992), *Christmas Blues:
    Beyond the Holiday Mask: Anth* (Amador Pub, 1995),
    CSM, Enchante

Prescott Evarts, Jr.   P
19 Linden Ave
West Long Branch, NJ 07764, 201-222-4205
    Pubs: *Harvard Mag, Hudson Rev, Cimarron Rev,
    Nebraska Rev, BPJ, Kansas Qtly*

Firth Haring Fabend   W
54 Elston Rd
Upper Montclair, NJ 07043, 201-746-5336
    Pubs: *A Dutch Family in the Middle Colonies,
    1660-1800* (Rutgers U, 1991)

John L. Falk 🎤 ✈ P
8 Fieldston Rd
Princeton, NJ 08540-6416, 609-452-1977
Internet: jfalk@rci.rutgers.edu
    Pubs: *Snow & Other Guises* (Guernica Edtns, 2000),
Antigonish Rev, Osiris, Prism Intl, Visions Intl

Sean-Thomas Farragher P
PO Box 1903
Cliffside Park, NJ 07010-1903, 201-840-9122
    Pubs: *Modern Rivers, Taxi Murders Sextet Vol. V
Christina* (Hudson River Pr, 1998, 1997), *Bluestones &
Salthay: Anth* (Rutgers U Pr, 1990), *Home Planet
News, Dublin Mag, Journal of New Jersey Poets,
Hipnosis, BPJ*

Patricia Fillingham P
29 S Valley Rd
West Orange, NJ 07052, 201-731-9269
    Pubs: *Report to the Interim Shareholders, John Calvin*
(Warthog Pr, 1991, 1988)

Bernadine Fillmore PP
8 Vincent Court #1A
Newark, NJ 07105, 973-465-1694
    Pubs: *Safe Haven Community Center, House of
Bishops, Mental Health Association, Here Come the
Poets*

Frank Finale 🎤 ✈ P
19 Quail Run
Bayville, NJ 08721-1376, 732-237-0776
Internet: ffinale@aol.com
    Pubs: *To the Shore Once More* (Jersey Shore Pubs,
1999), *Identity Lessons: Anth* (Penguin, 1999), *Shore
Stories: Anth, Under a Gull's Wing: Anth* (Down the
Shore Pub, 1998, 1996), *Sensations Mag, New
Renaissance, Lips, Press, Paterson Literary Rev*
I.D.: Italian-American

Patricia Ellen Flinn W
PO Box 2
Gillette, NJ 07933
    Pubs: *Loss of the Ground-Note: Anth* (Clothespin Fever
Pr, 1992), *Lynx Eye, Lullwater Rev, Alabama Literary
Rev, Mind in Motion, Portable Wall, Portland Rev*

Nancy Flynn P&W
c/o Paul Reese, 115 Mine Hill Rd, Hackettstown, NJ
07840, 201-852-5912
    Pubs: *Room, Because You Talk, Gallery Works,
Minotaur, Anthropology of Work Rev, Center*

Edward Foster P
Talisman House Publishers, PO Box 3157, Jersey City, NJ
07303-3157, 201-938-0698
    Pubs: *The Boy in The Key of E* (Goats & Compasses,
1998), *All Acts Are Simply Acts* (Rodent Pr, 1995), *The
Understanding* (Texture Pr, 1994), *Boston Book Rev,
River City, Bombay Gin, Five Fingers Rev, Boxkite,
American Letters & Commentary*

Hanna Fox W
Fox Associates, 175 Hamilton Ave, Princeton, NJ
08540-3857, 609-924-2990
    Pubs: *Transatlantic Rev, Jewish Frontier, Jewish Roots,
Kelsey Rev*

Sheldon Frank W
221 Jackson St, #9J
Hoboken, NJ 07030, 201-653-7534

Thomas Friedmann W
The Writer's Workbench, PO Box 117, Marlboro, NJ
07746
    Pubs: *Skills in Sequence* (St. Martin's Pr, 1988),
Damaged Goods (Permanent Pr, 1984), *Footworks*

Sondra Gash P
82 Martins Ln
Berkeley Heights, NJ 07922, 908-464-6780
    Pubs: *Silk Elegy* (Cavankerry Press, 2001), *Calyx, U.S.
1 Worksheets, Paterson Literary Rev*

Paul Genega P
Bloomfield College, Bloomfield, NJ 07003
    Pubs: *Striking Water* (Ireland; Salmon, 1989), *Seagirt* (A
Musty Bone, 1988), *The Nation, Epoch*

Dan Georgakas P&W
Smyra Press, PO Box 1151, Union City, NJ 07087-1151
    Pubs: *New to North America* (Burning Bush, 1997),
Solidarity Forever (Lake View Pr, 1985), *Greece in
Print, Greek American, Greek Star, Mr. Cogito, Odyssey
Mag*

Emery George 🎤 ✈ P
16 Buckingham Ave
Trenton, NJ 08618-3312, 609-984-8375
    Pubs: *A Year in Poetry: Anth* (Crown Pubs, 1995),
Contemporary East European Poetry: Anth (Oxford U
Pr, 1993), *Blue Unicorn, Denver Qtly, Partisan Rev, Jrnl
of New Jersey Poets*
Lang: German, Hungarian. Groups: Children, Prisoners

Richard Gessner P&W
PO Box 661
Montclair, NJ 07042-0661, 201-744-1744
    Pubs: *Excerpts from the Diary of a Neanderthal
Dilettante & the Man in the Couch* (Bombshelter, 1991),
Air Fish: Anth (Cat's Eye Bks, 1993), *Happy, The
Pannus Index, Java Snob, Devil Blossoms, Raw Vision*

Janet Frances Gibbs 🎤 ✈   P&W
39 Tiffany Dr
East Hanover, NJ 07936-2517, 973-386-8987
Internet: coner5039@aol.com
    Pubs: *Past & Promise: Women of New Jersey: Anth*
    (Scarecrow Pr, 1990), *Bitterroot, Sandsounds, Footworks*

Maria Mazziotti Gillan 🎤 ✈   P
40 Post Ave
Hawthorne, NJ 07506, 201-423-2921
Internet: www.pccc.cc.nj.us/Poetry
    Pubs: *Things My Mother Told Me, Where I Come From*
    (Guernica Edtns, 1999, 1995), *Identity Lessons: Anth,*
    Growing Up Ethnic in America: Anth (Penguin/Putnam,
    1999, 1999), *Unsettling America: Anth* (Viking, 1994),
    New Myths, Borderlands
I.D.: Italian-American

Martin Golan 🎤 ✈   P&W
196 Inwood Ave
Upper Montclair, NJ 07043-1947
Internet: mgolan@softhome.net
    Pubs: *My Wife's Last Lover* (Creative Arts, 2000),
    Bitterroot, Poet Lore, Literary Rev

Lester Goldberg   W
18 Woods Hole Rd
Cranford, NJ 07016, 908-276-4020
    Pubs: *In Siberia It Is Very Cold* (Dembner Bks, 1987),
    One More River (U Illinois Pr, 1978), *Ascent, Wind,*
    Literary Rev, Epoch, Iowa Rev, Cimarron Rev

Edward M. Goldman 🎤   P
43 W 32 St
Bayonne, NJ 07002, 201-436-4796
    Pubs: *Emes Mit Poemes* (Chortelach Pr, 1992), *Frost in*
    Spring: Anth, Celebrating T.S. Eliot: Anth (Wyndham
    Hall Pr, 1989, 1988)

Marion Goldstein   P
84 Highland Ave
Montclair, NJ 07042-1910, 973-746-0726
Internet: miggold@aol.com
    Pubs: *The Tie That Binds: Anth* (Papier-Mache Pr,
    1988), *CSM, Pivot, Croton Rev*

Bonnie Gordon   W
1001 N Kings Hwy #410
Cherry Hill, NJ 08034, 609-321-1363
    Pubs: *Thus May Be Figured in Numberless Ways*
    (Swamp Pr, 1985), *Sapiens, ADZ, Sarcophagus, Tracks*

Roger Granet 🎤 ✈   P
261 James St, Ste 2E
Morristown, NJ 07960-6348, 973-540-9490
Internet: RBG@aol.com
    Pubs: *Museum of Dreams* (Ross-Hunt Pub, 1999), *The*
    World's a Small Town (Negative Capability Pr, 1993)

Max Greenberg   P
127 Aycrigg Ave
Passaic, NJ 07055, 201-778-0937
    Pubs: *Country of the Old* (Chrysalis Pr, 1982), *Present*
    Tense

Patricia Celley Groth 🎤 ✈   P
Tree House Press, Inc, PO Box 268, Ringoes, NJ 08551,
908-806-3446
Internet: 102741.11611@compuserve.com
    Pubs: *The Gods' Eyes, Different Latitude: Anth* (DVP,
    1998, 1998), *Before the Beginning* (Belle Pr, 1987),
    U.S. 1 Worksheets, Jrnl of New Jersey Poets, Paterson
    Literary Rev, Encore, Stone Country
Groups: Seniors

James Haba   P
436 E Mountain Rd
Belle Mead, NJ 08502, 908-874-6209
    Pubs: *Ten Love Poems* (Ally Pr, 1981), *Jrnl of New*
    Jersey Poets, Paterson Literary Rev, U.S. 1
    Worksheets, Sunrust, George Washington Rev

Daniel Halpern   P
100 W Broad St
Hopewell, NJ 08525
    Pubs: *Selected Poems, Foreign Neon* (Knopf, 1994,
    1991), *Tango, Seasonal Rights, The Art of the Tale:*
    Anth (Viking, 1987, 1982, 1986)

Alfred Starr Hamilton   P
41 S Willow St
Montclair, NJ 07042
    Pubs: *The Big Parade* (Best Cellar Pr, 1982), *APR*

Patrick Hammer, Jr.   P
400 Fairview Ave, #3E
Fort Lee, NJ 07024, 201-585-0435
    Pubs: *Elements* (North River Pr, 1993), *The Yank: Irish*
    Poems, Coming to Light (Sub Rosa Pr, 1989, 1987),
    Poet, North River Rev

Joan Cusack Handler 🎤 ✈   P
6 Horizon Rd
Fort Lee, NJ 07024-6652, 201-224-9653
Internet: cavankerry@mindspring.com
    Pubs: *Westview, Southern Humanities Rev, Poetry East,*
    Agni, Painted Bride Qtly, Feminist Studies,
    Confrontation, Kalliope, Madison Rev, Negative
    Capability, Jrnl of New Jersey Poets

Jon Hansen   P
111 Loring Ave
Edison, NJ 08817
    Pubs: *SPR, Poetry Now, Intro II, Chicago Rev,*
    Cottonwood, Ironwood, Calliope

Terri Hardin   P
19 Morford Pl, Apt 3B
Red Bank, NJ 07701-1042, 908-530-6490
Pubs: *Nimue* (Guignol Bks, 1984), *Cuz I & II, Dyslexia*

Y. L. Harris   W
23 Topeka Pass
Willingboro, NJ 08046, 609-871-5168
Pubs: *Hindu-Kush* (Ashley Bks, 1990)

Lois Marie Harrod 🎤 ✈   P
111 Taylor Terr
Hopewell, NJ 08525, 609-466-1945
Pubs: *Spelling the World Backwards, This Is a Story
You Already Know, Part of the Deeper Sea* (Palaquin
U Pr of South Carolina, 2000, 1999, 1997), *Crazy
Alice, Every Twinge a Verdict* (Belle Mead Pr, 1991,
1987), *Zone 3, Literary Rev*

Elizabeth Hartman   P
127 Westmont Ave
Haddonfield, NJ 08033-2318, 856-354-9061
Internet: r.b.hartman@worldnet.att.net
Pubs: *Iconoclast, Nomad's Choir, Muse of Fire, Jersey
Woman, Poetry Scope, Midwest Poetry Rev, Encore,
Day Tonight/Night Today, Bitterroot*

Sheila Hellman   P
100 High St
Leonia, NJ 07605, 201-947-5534
Pubs: *In the Outbook: A Dreaming* (March Street Pr,
1999)

David Sten Herrstrom 🎤 ✈   P
P.O. Box 219, 15 Farm Ln, Roosevelt, NJ 08555
Pubs: *Appearing by Daylight* (Aegina Pr, 1993), *The
Disappearance of Jonah* (Ambrosia Pr, 1989), *Footwork,
Nimrod, U.S. 1 Worksheets, Stone Country, Columbia,
New River*

Mark Hillringhouse 🎤 ✈   P
428 Mountain View Rd
Englewood, NJ 07631, 201-816-1588
Internet: m.hillringhouse@worldnet.att.net
Pubs: *Chester H. Jones Natl Poetry Winners: Anth*
(Chester H. Jones Fdn, 1996), *Bluestones & Salthay:
Anth* (Rutgers U Pr, 1991), *Hanging Loose, New Jersey
Monthly, Literary Rev, Blade, APR, Kshanti Literary Rev*

Madeline Hoffer 🎤 ✈   P&W
5 Woodview Dr
Cranbury, NJ 08512, 609-655-2774
Internet: ProfrHofr@aol.com
Pubs: *Classical Outlook, Thema, Kelsey Rev,
Conservative Rev, Exit 13, Encodings, California Qtly,
This Broken Shore, Everdancing Muse, Hammers*
I.D.: Latino/Latina. Groups: Feminist, Seniors

Jean Hollander   P
592 Provinceline Rd
Hopewell, NJ 08525
Pubs: *Moondog* (QRL, 1996), *Crushed Into Honey*
(Saturday Pr, 1986), *Sewanee Rev, American Scholar,
Poem, Southern Humanities Rev*

Lew Holzman   P
95 Hillside Ave
Tenafly, NJ 07670
Pubs: *Men's Bodies, Men's Selves* (Deta, 1979), *Neo
Neo Dodo, Riverrun, Film Library Qtly*

Deborah L. Humphreys 🎤 ✈   P
55 Barbara St
Newark, NJ 07105, 973-589-0625
Pubs: *Conventional Wisdom* (Salmon Poetry, 2000),
Affilia, Christianity & the Arts, U.S. 1 Worksheets
Lang: Spanish, Irish. I.D.: Irish-American. Groups: Women,
Spiritual/Religious

Susan G. Jackson 🎤 ✈   P
16 Smoke Rise Ln
Bedminster, NJ 07921, 908-781-2747
Pubs: *South Mountain: Anth* (Millburn Free Public
Library, 1993), *Between Two Rivers: Anth* (From Here
Press, 1980), *Nimrod, Paterson Literary Rev*
Lang: French

Judah Jacobowitz 🎤 ✈   P
206 Cleveland La
Princeton, NJ 08540-9513, 732-329-6306
Pubs: *A Taste of Bonaparte* (Golden Quill Pr, 1990),
*Massachusetts Rev, River City, Small Pond, Green
Mountains Rev, Touchstone, Crab Creek Rev*
I.D.: Jewish, Seniors

Dana Andrew Jennings   W
34 Godfrey Rd
Montclair, NJ 07043-1330
Pubs: *Woman of Granite* (HBJ, 1992), *Mosquito Games*
(Ticknor & Fields, 1989)

Maynard Johnson   P
1907 Sunset Ave
Surf City, NJ 08008, 609-361-9630
Pubs: *National Poetry Jrnl, Black Bear Rev, Lehigh
Valley Anth, Chester Country Anth*

Morris A. Kalmus   P
c/o Yares, 227 Sandringham Rd, Cherry Hill, NJ 08003
Pubs: *Prophetic Voices, Heartland Jrnl, Reflect,
Common Ground, Poets Corner*

Edward Kaplan 🎤 ✈   P
213 Deland Ave
Cherry Hill, NJ 08034, 609-429-1836
　　Pubs: *Mechos* (Scotland; Glennifer Pr, 1983),
　　Pancratium (Swamp Pr, 1978), *Adz, Sapiens, Sulfur,*
　　Menu, Black Box, Red Handbook II

Milton Kaplan   P
554 Summit Ave
Oradell, NJ 07649
　　Pubs: *In a Time Between Wars* (Norton, 1973), *Radio*
　　& Poetry (Columbia, 1949)

Jaleelah Karriem   P
6907 Sussex Ave, #6907
East Orange, NJ 07018, 201-672-5205
　　Pubs: *a gathering of hands...tryin' to keep time & tryin'*
　　to make a difference (Ngoma's Gourd, 1991),
　　blackbooksbulletin (Third World, 1991), *Essence*

Adele Kenny 🎤 ✈   P
207 Coriell Ave
Fanwood, NJ 07023-1613, 908-889-7223
Internet: amkenny@worldnet.att.net
　　Pubs: *At the Edge of the Woods, Castles & Dragons*
　　(Yorkshire Hse Bks/Muse-Pie Pr, 1997, 1990), *Road to*
　　the Interior: Anth (Charles E. Tuttle, 1997), *Paterson*
　　Literary Rev, Sing Heavenly Muse, Black Swan Rev

M. Deiter Keyishian   P&W
English Dept, Fairleigh Dickinson Univ, 285 Madison Ave,
Madison, NJ 07940, 973-267-7901
　　Pubs: *Literary Rev, Ararat, Laurel Rev, Arts Mag,*
　　Fiction, Massachusetts Rev

Kathryn Kilgore   P
20 Nassau St, Ste 226
Princeton, NJ 08542, 212-865-5657
　　Pubs: *Something for Nothing* (Seaview Bks, 1982)

Burt Kimmelman 🎤 ✈   P
9 Lancaster Ave
Maplewood, NJ 07040, 973-763-8761
Internet: kimmelman@njit.edu
　　Pubs: *First Life* (Jensen/Daniels, 2000), *Musaics*
　　(Spuyten Duyvil Pr, 1992), *Natural Process* (Hill &
　　Wang, 1970), *Mudfish, First Intensity, Pequod, Poetry*
　　NY, Sagetrieb, Talisman, House Organ, Lo Straniero

Kinni Kinnict   P
113 Clover St
Mt Holly, NJ 08060
　　Pubs: *Crosscurrents, Archer, The Poet, Touchstone,*
　　San Fernando Poetry Jrnl, Undinal Songs

Nicholas Kolumban 🎤 ✈   P
150 W Summit St
Somerville, NJ 08876, 201-526-0682
　　Pubs: *Flares at Dusk* (Szephalom Pr, 2001), *The*
　　Science of In-Between, Surgery on My Soul (Box Turtle
　　Pr, 1999, 1996), *Antioch Rev, Artful Dodge, Chariton*
　　Rev, Mudfish, Onthebus, Poetry East, North Dakota
　　Qtly

Yusef Komunyakaa   P
185 Nassau St
Princeton, NJ 08544
　　Pubs: *Thieves of Paradise, Magic City, Dien Cai Dau*
　　(Wesleyan, 1998, 1992, 1988), *Kenyon Rev, Vox,*
　　Ploughshares, Threepenny Rev, Callaloo, Colorado Rev,
　　Iowa Rev

Donna Walters Kozberg   W
45 Dug Way
Watchung, NJ 07060, 908-226-1178
　　Pubs: *Forms, Cream City Rev, Junction, Wind Literary*
　　Jrnl, Parachute, For Art's Sake

Erlinda V. Kravetz 🎤 ✈   W
403 Hill Ln
Leonardo, NJ 07737-1802, 732-872-1749
Internet: ekravetz@earthlink.net
　　Pubs: *Philippine American Short Stories: Anth* (Giraffe
　　Bks, 1997), *Americas Rev, Chiricu, Maryland Rev,*
　　Rosebud, Taproot Literary Rev
I.D.: Asian-American

T. R. LaGreca   P
788 Winding Way
River Vale, NJ 07675
　　Pubs: *Cover/Arts New York, Ellipsis, Albany Rev,*
　　Wisconsin Rev, Parting Gifts, Jrnl of New Jersey Poets

Shirley Warren Lake   P
459 S Willow Ave
Absecon, NJ 08201-4633
　　Pubs: *The Bottomfeeders, Somewhere Between, Oyster*
　　Creek Icebreak (Still Waters Pr, 1995, 1991, 1989), *Jrnl*
　　of New Jersey Poets, Georgia Rev, American Writing,
　　Cream City Rev

Michael Lally 🎤 ✈   P&W
1 Oakland Rd
Maplewood, NJ 07040
Internet: lallyjmf@aol.com
　　Pubs: *It's Not Nostalgia* (Black Sparrow Pr, 1999), *Of*
　　(Quiet Liou Pr, 1999), *Can't Be Wrong* (Coffee Hse Pr,
　　1996), *Catch My Breath* (Salt Lick Pr, 1995), *Identity*
　　Lessons: Anth (Penguin Pr, 1999), *Forkroads, XY, Rain*
　　City Rev

Donald Lawder   P
Route 4, Box 4105
Hammonton, NJ 08037
   Pubs: *American Scholar, Nation, Kansas Qtly, New
   Yorker, Crazyhorse, BPJ*

Curt Leviant 🎤 ✈   W
PO Box 1266
Edison, NJ 08818
   Pubs: *Partita in Venice* (Livingston Pr, 1999), *The Man
   Who Thought He Was Messiah* (Jewish Publishing
   Society, 1990), *Zoetrope, Chariton Rev, Writers' Forum*

Joel Lewis   P
635 Washington St
Hoboken, NJ 07030
   Pubs: *North Jersey Gutter Helmet* (Oasis, 1997), *House
   Rent Boogie* (Yellow Pr, 1992), *Palookas of the Ozone*
   (e.g. Pr, 1991), *APR, NAW*

Antoinette Libro 🎤   P
College of Communication, Rowan Univ, Mullica Hill Rd,
Glassboro, NJ 08028, 609-256-4290
Internet: libro@rowan.edu
   Pubs: *The House at the Shore* (Lincoln Springs Pr,
   1997), *Women Without Wings* (Blackbird Pr, 1993),
   Weight of Light: Anth (Press Here, 1999), *Identity
   Lessons: Anth* (Penguin Putnam, 1999), *Modern Haiku,
   Jrnl of New Jersey Poets, Atlantic City Pr*

Deena Linett 🎤 ✈   P&W
English Dept, Montclair State Univ, Upper Montclair, NJ
07043, 973-655-7320
Internet: linettd@mail.montclair.edu
   Pubs: *Rare Earths: Poems* (BOA Edtns, 2001), *The
   Slow Mirror & Other Stories* (U.K., 5 Leaves Pr, 1996),
   The Translator's Wife (Humanities & Arts Pr, 1986), *On
   Common Ground* (SUNY Pr, 1983), *Her Face in the
   Mirror: Anth* (Beacon Pr, 1994), *Harvard Mag*

Timothy Liu 🎤 ✈   P
William Paterson Univ, 300 Pompton Rd, Wayne, NJ
07470, 973-720-3567
Internet: liut@wpunj.edu
   Pubs: *Say Goodnight, Burnt Offerings* (Copper Canyon
   Pr, 1998, 1995), *Vox Angelica* (Alice James Bks, 1992),
   Word of Mouth: Anth (Talisman Hse, 2000), *Grand
   Street, Nation, Sulfur, Volt, Ploughshares, TriQtly, Paris
   Rev, Poetry*
Groups: G/L/B/T, Asian-American

Diane Lockward 🎤 ✈   P
4 Midvale Ave
West Caldwell, NJ 07006-8006, 973-226-0807
Internet: dslockward@aol.com
   Pubs: *Against Perfection* (Poets Forum, 1998),
   *Rattapallax, BPJ, Confluence, Cumberland Poetry Rev,
   Free Lunch, Kalliope, Literary Rev, Negative Capability,
   Poet Lore, Rattle, Spoon River, Wind*

Doughtry "Doc" Long   P
67 Garfield Ave
Trenton, NJ 08609, 609-695-8462
   Pubs: *Deliberations: Fire, Eros, Ascension & Earth*
   (Third World, 1994), *A Rock Against the Wind: Anth*
   (Perigee Bks, 1996), *Painted Bride Qtly, Obsidian*

Joyce Greenberg Lott 🎤 ✈   P
5 Toth Ln
Rocky Hill, NJ 08553, 609-921-2492
Internet: lottofjoy@aol.com
   Pubs: *A Teacher's Stories* (Boynton/Cook/Heinemann,
   1994), *Kalliope, Writing for Our Lives, Ms., U.S. 1
   Worksheets, English Jrnl, Jrnl of New Jersey Poets,
   Footwork: Paterson Literary Rev*

Valerie Loveland 🎤 ✈   P
98 Oak St #1414
Lindenwold, NJ 08021-2423
Internet: corvash@home.com
   Pubs: *Mad Poet's Rev, Maelstrom, Pegasus, RE:AL,
   Thema, Third Coast, Thorny Locust*

Joe L. Malone   P&W
169 Prospect St
Leonia, NJ 07605, 201-944-7104
   Pubs: *Carmina Gaiana, Above the Salty Bay* (Linear
   Arts, 2000, 1998), *Wings, Iconoclast, Brooklyn Literary
   Rev, Jrnl of New Jersey Poets, Hellas, New Press*

Pamela Malone 🎤 ✈   P&W
169 Prospect St
Leonia, NJ 07605, 201-944-7104
   Pubs: *That Heaven Once Was My Hell* (Linear Arts,
   2000), *Anth of Contemporary American Poetry*
   (Finishing Line Pr, 1999), *Hungry Poets Cookbook: Anth*
   (Applezaba Pr, 1987), *The Sun, Chelsea, Belletrist Rev,
   Bellowing Ark, West Branch, Blue Unicorn*

Charlotte Mandel 🎤 ✈   P&W
60 Pine Dr
Cedar Grove, NJ 07009, 973-256-5053
   Pubs: *Sight Lines* (Midmarch Arts Pr, 1998), *The
   Marriages of Jacob* (Micah Pubs, 1991), *The Life of
   Mary* (Saturday Pr, 1988), *Indiana Rev, Mississippi
   Valley Rev, Nimrod, Seneca Rev, Raccoon, New
   Millennium Writings*
Groups: Women

Stanley Marcus   P
658 Valley Rd I-3
Upper Montclair, NJ 07043, 201-783-7353
   Pubs: *For a Living: The Poetry of Work: Anth* (U Illinois
   Pr, 1995), *Virginia Qtly Rev, Literary Rev, Denver Qtly,
   Prairie Schooner, Minnesota Rev, North Dakota Qtly*

David Matthew 🎤 ✈ P&W
East Rutherford, NJ, 201-438-1658
Internet: daopen@yahoo.com
 Pubs: *New Press, Rag Shock, Up Front News, Pagan Place, Open Moments, Pinched Nerves, The Rift*
I.D.: Anti-poet

Cathy Mayo P
33 W Paul Ave
Trenton, NJ 08638-4513
 Pubs: *Her Soul Beneath the Bone: Anth* (U Illinois Pr, 1988), *Up Against the Wall Mother, Plainsongs, Tsunami, Bogg, Connecticut River Rev*

James T. McCartin W
Lincoln Springs Press, PO Box 269, Franklin Lakes, NJ 07417, 718-833-2036
 Pubs: *The Crazy Aunt & Other Stories* (Lincoln Springs Pr, 1988), *Arizona Qtly, Footwork, Descant*

Florence McGinn 🎤 ✈ P
46 Featherbed Ln
Flemington, NJ 08822-5638, 908-782-0894
 Pubs: *Blood Trail* (Pennywhistle Pr, 2000), *Midwest Poetry Rev, Parnassus, Poetry Flash, Modern Haiku, Cicada, Eclectic Literary Forum*
I.D.: Asian-American. Groups: Teachers

Pablo Medina P&W
318 Claremont Ave
Montclair, NJ 07042, 973-509-0222
 Pubs: *The Marks of Birth* (FS&G, 1994), *Arching Into the Afterlife* (Bilingual Pr, 1991), *APR, Antioch Rev, Poetry, Pivot*

Rochelle Hope Mehr P
5 Silver Spring Rd
West Orange, NJ 07052-4317, 973-731-0433
Internet: rochellemehr@hotmail.com
 Pubs: *Aabye, Anthology, Nedge, Offerta Speciale, Adobe Abalone, Pegasus, Ibbetson Street Pr, Pennine Ink, Panda, Way Station Mag, Poetalk, The Iconoclast, Lilliput Rev, Psychopoetica, CER*BER*US, Concho River Rev, Bogg, Art Times, Neovictorian/Cochlea*

Judy Rowe Michaels P
336 Hopewell-Amwell Rd
Hopewell, NJ 08525, 609-466-1932
 Pubs: *Nimrod, River Styx, Columbia, Georgetown Rev, Yankee, Poetry NW*

Yvette Mintzer P
159 Cedar Ln
Princeton, NJ 08540, 609-430-9245
 Pubs: *Dreamline Express* (Inwood Pr, 1975)

Marilyn Mohr 🎤 ✈ P
109 Rynda Rd
South Orange, NJ 07079, 201-762-5403
Internet: MMohr@klezpoets.com
 Pubs: *Satchel* (CCC, 1992), *Blood to Remember: Anth* (Texas Tech U, 1991), *Sarah's Daughters Sing: Anth* (KTAV Pub, 1990), *Medicinal Purposes, Jewish Women's Literary Annual, Lips, Noctiluca, Home Planet News*

Rory Morse P
53 Parlin Ln
Watchung, NJ 07060, 908-769-0780
 Pubs: *Golden Retriever World, Arulo, Vega, CSP World News, Hob-Nob, Wings, Night Writers, True Romance, Robin's Nest, Retriever's Qtly, Dog Song, Red Owl*

Peter E. Murphy 🎤 ✈ P
18 N Richards Ave
Ventnor, NJ 08406-2136, 609-823-5076
Internet: www.murphywriting.com
 Pubs: *Yellow Silk: Anth* (Harmony Bks, 1990), *Cortland Rev, Atlanta Rev, Commonweal, Many Mountains Moving, Spelunker Flophouse, Witness, BPJ, NYQ, Painted Bride Qtly*

Walter Dean Myers W
2543 Kennedy Blvd
Jersey City, NJ 07304
 Pubs: *Me, Mop, & the Moondance Kid* (Delacorte Pr, 1988), *Black World, Essence, Espionage*

Murat Nemet-Nejat 🎤 ✈ P
1122 Bloomfield St
Hoboken, NJ 07030-5304, 201-420-7790
Internet: muratnn@aol.com
 Pubs: *A Blind Cat Black & Orthodoxies* (Sun & Moon Pr, 1997), *I, Orhan Veli* (Hanging Loose, 1989), *The Bridge* (Martin Brian & O'Keeffe, 1978), *Thus Spake the Corpse: Anth* (Black Sparrow Pr, 1999), *Talisman, World, Little Mag, Transfer*

Joyce Carol Oates P&W
9 Honeybrook Dr
Princeton, NJ 08540
 Pubs: *My Heart Laid Bare, Man Crazy, We Were the Mulvaneys, A Bloodsmoor Romance* (Dutton, 1998, 1998, 1997, 1982), *Invisible Woman* (Ontario Rev Pr, 1982)

Vanessa L. Ochs W
57 Fairmount Ave
Morristown, NJ 07960, 201-984-3913
 Pubs: *Words on Fire: One Woman's Journey Into the Sacred* (HBJ, 1990)

Dawn O'Leary   P
47 Oakwood Ave
Upper Montclair, NJ 07043, 201-783-6729
    Pubs: *Antioch Rev, Poetry NW, New Letters,
    Commonweal, NW Rev*

Alicia Ostriker ♦ ✈   P
33 Philip Dr
Princeton, NJ 08540, 609-924-5737
Internet: ostriker@rci.rutgers.edu
    Pubs: *The Little Space: New & Selected Poems, The
    Crack in Everything* (U Pitt Pr, 1998, 1996), *The
    Nakedness of the Fathers* (Rutgers U Pr, 1994), *Paris
    Rev, APR, Kenyon Rev, New Yorker, TriQtly*
I.D.: Jewish

Christopher Parker ♦ ✈   P
PO Box 43206
Upper Montclair, NJ 07043, 973-509-0523
Internet: parkerc@mail.montclair.edu
    Pubs: *Newshole, Poetry NW, Jrnl of New Jersey Poets,
    New Jersey Poetry, Waterways, Spirit, Calliope,
    Footwork, Phoenix, Crazyquilt*
Groups: Children

George Pereny   P
134 Van Ave
Pompton Lakes, NJ 07442, 201-831-7411
    Pubs: *New Worlds Unlimited: Anth* (Sal Buttaci, 1985),
    English Jrnl, Slant, Footwork, Black Belt

Alfred "Sonny" Piccoli   PP
41 James St
Bloomfield, NJ 07003, 973-748-9856
    Pubs: *Phenomenal Lives* (1st Bks, 1997), *Municipal
    Access TV, NewArk Writers Collective, Franklin School,
    Christian Faith Center, First Congregational Church,
    Nuyorican Poets Cafe, Barnes & Noble*

Stanley Plumly   P
Ecco Press, 100 W Broad St, Hopewell, NJ 08525
    Pubs: *The Marriage in the Trees, Boy on the Step,
    Summer Celestial, Out-of-the-Body Travel* (Ecco/Norton,
    1996, 1989, 1983, 1978)

Minnie Bruce Pratt ♦ ✈   P
PO Box 8212
Jersey City, NJ 07308, 201-659-2326
Internet: www.mbpratt.org
    Pubs: *Walking Back Up Depot Street* (U Pitt Pr, 1999),
    S/HE, Crime Against Nature (Firebrand Bks, 1995,
    1990), *Ploughshares, NER, Progressive, American
    Voice, Village Voice, Out/Look, TriQtly, Hungry Mind
    Rev*
Groups: G/L/B/T

Norman Henry Pritchard, II   P
45-A Phelps Ave
New Brunswick, NJ 08901-3712
    Pubs: *Eecchhooeess* (NYU Pr, 1971), *The Matrix:
    Poems 1960-1970* (Doubleday, 1970), *The Chronicle of
    the Horse*

Rich Quatrone   P
c/o Millennium Editions, PO Box 732, Spring Lake, NJ
07762
    Pubs: *Lucia's Rain* (Passaic Rev Pr, 1989), *Beehive,
    Aquarian, Lips, Footwork, Jrnl of New Jersey Poets,
    Long Shot, Steppingstones, Passaic Review, New
    Leaves, Phatitude, Lucid Moon, Alphabeat Soup*

Doris Radin   P
116 Hawthorne Ave
Glen Ridge, NJ 07028, 973-748-0895
    Pubs: *There Are Talismans* (Saturday Pr, 1991), *Prairie
    Schooner, Helicon Nine, Nation, Massachusetts Rev,
    New Letters, Chelsea*

Jan Emily Ramjerdi   P&W
c/o Boonstra, 56 Oakwood Dr, Wayne, NJ 07470,
973-694-8197
    Pubs: *RE.LA.VIR, Degenerative Prose: Anth* (Black
    Ice/FC2, 1999, 1995), *Tasting Life Twice: Anth* (Avon,
    1995), *Qtly West, Fiction Intl, Black Ice, The Little Mag,
    13th Moon, Mid-American Rev, Denver Qtly*

Thomas Reiter ♦ ✈   P
105 Sycamore St
Neptune, NJ 07753-3933, 732-922-3437
    Pubs: *Pearly Everlasting* (LSU Pr, 2000), *A Good Man:
    Fathers & Sons: Anth* (Fawcett Columbine, 1993),
    Poetry, Georgia Rev, Gettysburg Rev, NER, Ohio Rev

Robert R. Reldan   P
Box 861-62212
Trenton, NJ 08625-0861, 201-894-1927
    Pubs: *Paterson Lit Rev, Climbing the Walls, U.S. 1
    Worksheets, Kelsey Rev*

James Richardson ♦ ✈   P
Creative Writing Program, Princeton Univ, 185 Nassau St,
Princeton, NJ 08544-2095, 609-258-4712
Internet: jrich@princeton.edu
    Pubs: *How Things Are* (Carnegie Mellon, 2000), *A
    Suite for Lucretians* (QRL, 1999), *As If* (National Poetry
    Series, 1992), *Ploughshares, Slate, Yale Rev, Georgia
    Rev*

Ruby Riemer   P
Box 210, Village Rd
Green Village, NJ 07935
    Pubs: *Jrnl of New Jersey Poets, Multicultural Rev,
    Exquisite Corpse, Belles Lettres, SPR, Nation, American
    Book Rev, APR, Poet Lore, Anth of Mag Verse*

Ed Roberson 🎤 ✈   P
9 Edgeworth Pl
New Brunswick, NJ 08901-3021, 732-220-2920
Internet: roberson@aesop.rutgers.edu
   Pubs: *Atmosphere Conditions* (Sun & Moon Pr, 1999),
Just In/Word of Navigational Challenges (Talisman Hse,
1998), *Voices Cast Out to Talk to Us In* (U Iowa Pr,
1996)
I.D.: African-American

Sarah Rodgers   P
44 Wiggins St
Princeton, NJ 08540, 609-924-9448
   Pubs: *Croton Rev, Day Tonight/Night Today, Impact,
Dark Horse, Chelsea, Second Coming, Urthkin*

Wilhelm Hermann Röhrs 🎤   P
Dunhill & Clark of New York, 82 Jacoby St, Maplewood,
NJ 07040-3052
   Pubs: *Tears of Time, The Zeneida Cycle, Against the
Tide* (Small Poetry Pr, 1998, 1996, 1994), *Mortal Truth*
(Dunhill & Clark, 1987), *New Yorker, Staatszeltung,
Maplewood-S Orange News Record, NAR, Cambridge
Collection, Independent Rev, New Jersey Free Pr*
Lang: German

Martin C. Rosner 🎤 ✈   P
234 Vivien Ct
Paramus, NJ 07652-4615, 201-262-7749
Internet: roscape@aol.com
   Pubs: *Pilgrim at Sunset* (Research Triangle Pub, 1994),
Hormones & Hyacinths (Libra Pub, 1981), *Cape
Codder, Voices Intl, Ararat, New Jersey Poetry Monthly,
Essence, New York Times*
Groups: Hospitals, Jewish

Diana Kwiatkowski Rubin 🎤 ✈   P
The Cognitive Overload Press, PO Box 398, Piscataway,
NJ 08855-0398
   Pubs: *A Gathered Meadow* (Prospect Pr, 2000), *Visions
of Enchantment* (JVC Bks, 1991), *Poet, Touchstone,
Fox Cry, Minetta Rev, Antigonish Rev, Amelia*

Frank Rubino   P&W
76 High St
Bloomfield, NJ 07003, 201-667-9162
   Pubs: *Toy of the Evil Genie* (New Observations Pr,
1983), *The World*

Dorothy Rudy 🎤 ✈   P
161 W Clinton Ave
Tenafly, NJ 07670-1916, 201-569-7771
   Pubs: *Voices Through Time & Distant Places* (Willdor
Pr, 1993), *Knightscapes, Poem, Laurel Rev, Write
Connection, Bergen Poets, Footnotes, Lips, Connection
Collection*
I.D.: Seniors, Women. Groups: College/Univ, Adults

James Ruffini   P
20 E Elro Dr
Oak Ridge, NJ 07438, 973-208-7250
   Pubs: *Against Suburbia* (Ocean Size Pr, 1991), *Busy
Signals from the Holy City* (Sub Rosa, 1988), *Earth
Bound, Poetry Motel, Cicada, Blank Gun Silencer*

Dorothy Ryan 🎤   P
3 N Bridge Dr
Long Valley, NJ 07853-3205, 973-584-7028
   Pubs: *Paterson Literary Rev, Black-Bough, CSM,
Catbird Seat, Frogpond, Visions*
I.D.: Irish-American. Groups: Disabled, Seniors

Mark SaFranko 🎤 ✈   W
205 Hudson St, #1011
Hoboken, NJ 07030-5824, 201-653-1750
   Pubs: *Ellery Queen's Mystery Mag, Hawaii Rev, Green
Hills Literary Lantern, Wind, Sulphur River Literary Rev,
MacGuffin, Footwork, NAR, New Orleans Rev,
Soundings East, Art Times, Cimarron Rev, Pig Iron,
The Panhandler, South Carolina Rev*

Penelope Scambly Schott 🎤 ✈   P
Box 215
Rocky Hill, NJ 08553-0215, 609-924-8993
   Pubs: *Penelope: The Story of the Half-Scalped Woman*
(U Pr Florida, 1999), *The Perfect Mother* (Snake Nation
Pr, 1994), *These Are My Same Hands* (State Street Pr,
1989), *A Little Ignorance* (Potter, 1986), *Lear's,
American Voice, Georgia Rev*

Barry Seiler   P
321 Bloomfield St, #3
Hoboken, NJ 07030, 201-653-3612
   Pubs: *Black Leaf, The Waters of Forgetting* (U Akron
Pr, 1997, 1994), *Retaining Wall* (L'Epervier Pr, 1979),
NER/BLQ, The Qtly

Sylvia Semel   P
109 Oakland Ave
Somerset, NJ 08873
   Pubs: *Possession* (For Poets Only, 1988), *Innisfree,
Modern Haiku*

Robbie Clipper Sethi   P&W
English Dept, Rider Univ, 2083 Lawrenceville Rd,
Lawrenceville, NJ 08648-3099, 609-895-5578
   Pubs: *The Bride Wore Red* (Picador, 1997), *Atlantic,
Philadelphia Inquirer Mag, Massachusetts Rev,
California Qtly, Wind, Ascent, Alaska Qtly Rev,
Crescent Rev, Mademoiselle, Boulevard, Literary Rev*

Fatima Shaik 🎤 ✈   W
English Dept, St. Peter's College, 121 Glenwood Ave,
Jersey City, NJ 07306, 201-915-9325
Internet: shaik_f@spcvxa.spc.edu
    Pubs: *Melitte* (Puffin, 2000), *On Mardi Gras Day, Jazz
    of Our Street,* (Dial Bks, 1999, 1998), *Breaking Ice:
    Anth* (Viking Penguin, 1990), *Southern Rev, Tribes, Rev
    of Contemporary Fiction, Double Dealer Redux, Xavier
    Rev, Callaloo*
    I.D.: African-American. Groups: Children, Teenagers

Harry S. Shapiro   PP
530 Upper Mountain Ave
Upper Montclair, NJ 07043, 973-783-6009
    Pubs: *Journey to Harmony* (Rachel Pub, 1984),
    Spaceships Are Too Slow, Seeds of the Universe (Intl
    Printing, 1973, 1971), *Dream Shop*

Norma Voorhees Sheard   P
14 Fawn Dr
Flemington, NJ 08822-2602
    Pubs: *NYQ, Maryland Rev, Black Fly Rev, Nimrod,
    Footworks, U.S. 1 Worksheets, Dragonfly, Jrnl of New
    Jersey Poets, Paterson Literary Rev, Cape Rock Rev*

Barry Sheinkopf 🎤 ✈   W
601 Palisade Ave
Englewood Cliffs, NJ 07632-1802, 201-567-4017
Internet: 102100.1065@compuserve.com
    Pubs: *The Ivory Kitten, The Longest Odds* (Lynx Bks,
    1990, 1989)

William Sherman 🎤 ✈   P
9300 Atlantic Ave, #218
Margate, NJ 08402-2340, 609-822-7050
    Pubs: *From the South Seas* (Roman F. Garbacik,
    1997), *A Tale for Tusitala* (Branch Redd, 1993),
    Tahitian Journals (Hearing Eye, 1990), *Exquisite
    Corpse, Fire*

Herschel Silverman   P
47 E 33 St, #1
Bayonne, NJ 07002, 201-339-3880
    Pubs: *High on the Beat* (Water Run, 2000), *Poems
    Forged in a Forest of Words* (JVC, 1999), *15 Poems
    for Allen Ginsberg* (Blue Jacket Pr, 1997), *Outlaw Bible
    of Amer Poetry: Anth* (Thunder's Mouth Pr, 2000), *Long
    Shot, Talisman, Blue Beat Jacket, Connections*

Diane Simmons   W
9 Lancaster Ave
Maplewood, NJ 07040, 201-763-8761
    Pubs: *Dreams Like Thunder* (Story Line Pr, 1992), *Let
    the Bastards Freeze in the Dark* (S&S, 1980), *Green
    Mountains Rev, NW Rev, Whetstone*

Carol Sturm Smith 🎤 ✈   W
41 Aunt Molly Rd
Hopewell, NJ 08525, 609-466-8229
Internet: cssbeaumont@compuserve.com
    Pubs: *Cosmic Clowns* (Subscription Edns, 1999), *Only
    a Dream, Partners, Renewal* (Ballantine, 1984, 1982,
    1982)

Ed Smith 🎤 ✈   P
1413 Winesap Dr
Manasquan, NJ 08736-4020
Internet: manlib@bellatlantic.net
    Pubs: *Under a Gull's Wing: Anth* (Down the Shore,
    1996), *Bluestones & Salthay: Anth* (Rutgers U Pr,
    1990), *Talisman, Footwork, The World*
    I.D.: Italian-American. Groups: Seniors, Libraries

Mark Sonnenfeld 🎤 ✈   P
45-08 Old Mill Stone Dr
East Windsor, NJ 08520-4674, 609-443-0646
Internet: www.experimentalpoet.com
    Pubs: *Sky, Washington Rev, Bathtub Gin, De'Pressed
    Intl, Lost Continent Rev, Neologisms, Suffusion,
    Quicksilver*

Sharon Spencer   W
72 Watchung Ave, 2nd Fl
Upper Montclair, NJ 07043, 973-655-5151
    Pubs: *Dance of the Ariadnes* (Sky Blue Pr, 1998), *Wire
    Rims* (Heinemann Bks, 1995), *Crosscurrents, Calyx,
    Amelia, Mississippi Rev, Paintbrush, Innovation*

Donna Baier Stein   P&W
15 Main St, PO Box 659
Peapack, NJ 07977-0659, 908-781-7849
    Pubs: *I Always Meant to Tell You: Letters from Women
    Writers to Their Mothers: Anth* (S&S, 1997), *Whiskey
    Island Mag, The Literary Rev, Alembic, Westview,
    Florida Rev, Poet Lore*

Toby Stein   W
45 Church St
Montclair, NJ 07042
    Pubs: *Only the Best* (Arbor Hse, 1984), *Getting
    Together* (Atheneum, 1980), *Moment, Reconstructionist*

Gerald Stern 🎤 ✈   P
89 Clinton St
Lambertville, NJ 08530-1912, 609-397-2562
    Pubs: *Last Blue, This Time, Odd Mercy, Bread Without
    Sugar* (Norton, 2000, 1998, 1995, 1992)

Shane Stevens   W
PO Box 1927
Hoboken, NJ 07030
    Pubs: *Hot Tickets, Jersey Tomatoes* (Arbor Hse, 1987,
    1986), *The Anvil Chorus* (Delacorte, 1985)

D. E. Steward 🎤 ✈   P&W
PO Box 1239
Princeton, NJ 08542-1239
   Pubs: *A Letter to a Writer Down the Line* (Oasis,
   1987), *Contact Inhibition* (Avant, 1985), *NAR, Hawaii
   Rev, Chicago Rev, Epoch, Sulfur, Conjunctions,
   Temblor, Chelsea, SW Rev, Denver Qtly, Fiction Intl,
   NW Rev*

Carole Stone 🎤 ✈   P
16 Howard St
Verona, NJ 07044-1412, 973-655-7312
Internet: stonec@mail.montclair.edu
   Pubs: *Lime & Salt* (Carriage Hse Pr, 1997), *Orphan in
   the Movie House, Giving Each Other Up* (Andrew
   Mountain Pr, 1997, 1985), *Anthology of Father Poems*
   (St. Martin's Pr, 1997), *BPJ, Devil's Millhopper, Contact
   II, Heresies*

Adam Szyper   P
12 Winant Rd
Kendall Park, NJ 08824, 908-297-9069
   Pubs: *And Suddenly Spring* (CCC, 1992), *The Current,
   New Hope Intl Writing*

Marcia Tager   W
193 Elm St
Tenafly, NJ 07670
   Pubs: *Shaking Eve's Tree: Anth* (Jewish Pub, 1990),
   *The Literary Rev, North Dakota Qtly, Confrontation,
   Wind, Ascent*

Madeline Tiger 🎤 ✈   P
126 Beverly Rd
Bloomfield, NJ 07003
   Pubs: *White Owl* (Spuyten Duyvil, 2000), *Water Has No
   Color* (New Spirit Pr, 1992), *Mary of Migdal* (Still
   Waters Pr, 1991), *My Father's Harmonica* (Nightshade
   Pr, 1991), *Word Thursdays II: Anth* (Bright Hill Pr,
   1999), *Sow's Ear, One Trick Pony, New Moon Rev*
I.D.: Jewish, Seniors. Groups: Seniors, Teachers

Inge Trachtenberg   W
288 Oakwood Rd
Englewood, NJ 07631
   Pubs: *An Arranged Marriage, So Slow the Dawning*
   (Norton, 1977, 1973)

Steve Troyanovich 🎤 ✈   P
1 Pelle Ct
Florence, NJ 08518-1615, 609-499-3878
   Pubs: *Dream Dealers & Other Shadows* (Triton, 1978),
   *Quarry, Argonaut, Yellow Butterfly, Abraxas, Moody
   Street Irregulars, Eric Burdon Connection*

Robert Blake Truscott   P
88 Guilden St
New Brunswick, NJ 08901, 201-846-3767
   Pubs: *Cumberland Poetry Rev, Literary Rev, Virginia
   Qtly Rev, Stone Country*

Rod Tulloss   P
PO Box 57
Roosevelt, NJ 08555-0057, 609-448-5096
   Pubs: *The Machine Shuts Down* (Berkeley Poets Pr,
   1982), *Bluestones & Salthay: Anth* (Rutgers U Pr,
   1990), *Archae, U.S. 1 Worksheets, Exquisite Corpse,
   Nimrod*

Lois Van Houten   P
16 Harlow Cres
Fairlawn, NJ 07410
   Pubs: *Korone Women's Voices: Anth* (Womanspace Inc,
   1996), *Women & Death: Anth* (Ground Torpedo Pr,
   1994), *Footwork, Stone Country, Jrnl of New Jersey
   Poets*

Lourdes Vázquez 🎤 ✈   P&W
Alexander Library, Rutgers Univ, 169 College Ave, New
Brunswick, NJ 08901-1063
   Pubs: *Historias de Pulgarcito* (Cultural, 1999), *La Rosa
   Mecánica* (Huracan, 1991), *Sortilegio de Tifinagh: Anth*
   (Alcance, 1998), *Tertuliando/Hanging Out: Anth* (Santo
   Domingo; Comision Permanente de la Feria del Libro,
   1997), *Revista Casa de las Americas*
Lang: Spanish. I.D.: Latino/Latina

Patrick Walsh   P
321 Witherspoon St
Princeton, NJ 08540
   Pubs: *College Green, Hudson Rev, Press, The
   Recorder, The Shop, U.S. 1*

William John Watkins   P&W
The Sand Agency, 1406 Garven Ave, Ocean, NJ 07712,
201-988-2287
   Pubs: *Cosmic Thunder* (Avon Bks, 1996), *Tracker: The
   Story of Tom Brown, Jr.* (Prentice-Hall, 1978),
   *Commonweal, Asimov's, Rhino, Hellas, MacGuffin,
   Satire*

Daniel J. Weeks 🎤 ✈   P
905 Norwood Ave
Elberon, NJ 07740-4546, 908-222-3858
   Pubs: *Ancestral Songs* (Libra Pubs, 1992), *X Poems*
   (Blast Pr, 1991), *Cimarron Rev, Mudfish, Slant, Fennel
   Stalk*

Richard K. Weems 🎤 ✈   W
101 E Gibbsboro Rd #511
Clementon, NJ 08021-1912, 856-782-0006
Internet: richardweems@hotmail.com
   Pubs: *Best of Pif Mag Off-Line: Anth* (Fusion Pr, 1999),
   *Story Bytes, Eratica, Sparks, Papyrus, New Works Rev,
   Wired Hearts, Southern Ocean Rev, Barcelona Rev, La
   Petite Zine, Oval, Beloit Fiction Jrnl, Bluff City,
   Mississippi Rev, Eclectica, Crescent Rev*

Theodore Weiss   P
26 Haslet Ave
Princeton, NJ 08540, 609-921-6976
    Pubs: *Selected Poems* (TriQtly Bks, 1995), *A Sum of Destructions* (LSU Pr, 1994), *New Republic, Poetry, APR, Paris Rev, New Criterion, Partisan Rev*

Alix Weisz   P
PO Box 4205
Clifton, NJ 07012-4205, 973-779-4710
Internet: cetaitmoi@aol.com
    Pubs: *Lobotomy, Alix Poems Weisz* (New Broom Pr, 1993, 1992), *Do You Sense an Angel: Anth* (Ashby Lane Pr, 1993), *Fenice, Phoenix Sheets, Pegasus Rev, Iota, Whisper*

Debbie Lee Wesselmann   W
19 Elm St
Hopewell, NJ 08525, 609-466-8868
    Pubs: *The Earth & the Sky* (SMU Pr, 1998), *Trutor & the Balloonist* (MacMurray & Beck, 1997), *Literary Rev, Ascent, Folio, Gulf Stream Mag, Beloit Fiction Jrnl, Pennsylvania English, NAR, Florida Rev, Fiction, Philadelphia Inquirer*

John A. Williams   P&W
693 Forest Ave
Teaneck, NJ 07666
    Pubs: *Captain Blackman* (Coffee Hse Pr, 2000), *Clifford's Blues* (Coffee Hse Pr, 1999), *Sons of Darkness, Sons of Light,* (Northeastern U Pr, 1999), *Click Song, The Man Who Cried I Am* (Thunder's Mouth Pr, 1987, 1985)

Meredith Sue Willis 🎤 ✈   W
311 Prospect St
South Orange, NJ 07079-1806, 973-378-8361
Internet: msuewillis@aol.com
    Pubs: *Trespassers* (Hamilton Stone Edtns, 1997), *Marco's Monster* (HC, 1996), *In The Mountains of America* (Mercury Hse, 1994), *Quilt Pieces* (Gnomon, 1991)
    I.D.: Appalachian

Ted Wilson   P
342 Warwick Ave
South Orange, NJ 07079, 973-763-9550
    Pubs: *In Defense of Mumia: Anth* (Writers & Readers, 1996), *Amiri Baraka: The Kaleidoscope Torch: Anth* (Steppingstone Pr, 1985), *Nobo, Drumvoices, Essence, Callaloo, Black Nation*

Barbara Wind   P
10 Londonderry Way
Summit, NJ 07901, 908-608-1748
    Pubs: *Jacob's Angels* (Emmet Pr, 1998), *South Mountain: Anth* (Milburn Public Library, 1993), *Poetry Works: Anth* (NewArk Writers Collective, 1993), *JAMA, Footwork, Whiskey Island, Negative Capability, Pleiades, Philae, Paterson Literary Rev*

Holly Woodward 🎤 ✈   W
76 Jackson St
Hoboken, NJ 07030-6054
Internet: artictfox@aol.com
    Pubs: *Story Mag, Rag Mag, New Letters, American Voice, Chicago Rev*
Groups: Children

Ruth Zimmerman   P
7 Marianna Pl
Morristown, NJ 07960-2708
Internet: rewritez@aol.com
    Pubs: *Thema, Messages from the Heart, Dream Intl Qtly, Passages North, Jrnl of New Jersey Poets, Embers, Without Halos, Mary Jane, Yet Another Small Mag, The Ledge, Mediphors, Buffalo Bones, Sensations, Nostalgia, Art Factory*

Sander Zulauf 🎤 ✈   P
County College of Morris, 214 Center Grove Rd, Randolph, NJ 07869, 201-328-5471
Internet: szulauf@ccm.edu
    Pubs: *Succasunna New Jersey* (Breaking Point Inc, 1987), *The Art & Craft of Poetry: Anth* (Writer's Digest, 1994), *Sewanee Rev, Lips, Editor's Choice III, CSM, Negative Capability, Ometeca*

NEW MEXICO

Anya Achtenberg 🎤 ✈   P&W
1313 La Poblana NW
Albuquerque, NM 87107
Internet: aachtenberg@earthlink.net
    Pubs: *I Know What the Small Girl Knew* (Holy Cow! Pr, 1983), *A Pocketful of Prose: Anth* (HRW, 1991), *ACM, Paterson Literary Rev, Blue Mesa Rev, New Letters*
Groups: Women, Working Class

Rudolfo Anaya 🎤 ✈   W
5324 Canada Vista NW
Albuquerque, NM 87120-2412
    Pubs: *Elegy on the Death of Cesar Chavez* (Cinco Puntos Pr, 2000), *Farolitos for Abuelo, The Farolitos of Christmas* (Hyperion, 2000, 1995), *My Land Sings* (HC, 1999), *Shaman Winter, Rio Grande Fall, Zia Summer, Bless Me Ultima* (Warner)

Rudy S. Apodaca   W
829 Canterbury Arc
Las Cruces, NM 88005-3715, 505-525-8421
Internet: xqx@prodigy.net
    Pubs: *The Waxen Image* (Titan Publishing Co, 1977)

Aztatl 🎤 ✈   P&W
PO Box 173
Cedar Crest, NM 87008-0173
   Pubs: *Next Exit* (Chichimecatl Pr, 1999), *Todo Nada*
   (Red Age Unlimited Pr, 1998), *Masks, Folk Dances & a*
   Whole Bunch More (Ridgeway Pr, 1989), *Callaloo,*
   California Qtly, Black Bear Rev, Poetry East, Gatherings
I.D.: Chichimeca Coahuila, Mexican. Groups: Native
American, Latino/Latina

Lee Bartlett   P
Box 250, Star Rte
Placitas, NM 87043, 505-867-4891
   Pubs: *The Greenhouse Effect* (Lords of Language,
   1994), *Sagetrieb*

Sabra Basler   P
1920 Gold SE
Albuquerque, NM 87106, 505-243-7687
   Pubs: *Coyote's Jrnl, Quercus, Cold Drill, Windchimes,*
   Modern Haiku, Aero-Zero

Laura Beheler 🎤   P&W
3 Placita Rafaela
Santa Fe, NM 87501-2845, 505-983-9166
   Pubs: *The Snow Moon* (Pentland, Ltd, 1986), *Phone*
   Calls Late at Night to God (Four Winds, 1983)
Groups: Children

Charles Greenleaf Bell   P&W
1260 Canyon Rd
Santa Fe, NM 87501-6128, 505-983-6035
   Pubs: *Five Chambered Heart* (Persea, 1985), *New*
   Yorker, Atlantic, Harper's

Forest Stirling Bell   P
#36 Country Club Gdns
Santa Fe, NM 87501
   Pubs: *Seer Ox, WPA, Sun, Tweed, Astral Projection,*
   Haiku, West, Cinema News, Reversal

David Benedetti   P
222 Richmond SE
Albuquerque, NM 87106, 505-256-0003
   Pubs: *Telling Remark* (The Lost Fdn, 1992), *Defense*
   Mechanism (Deposed Innocence, 1986), *Poetics Jrnl,*
   American Poetry, Impulsive Living, Telephone, Hills

Carol Berge   P&W
2070 Calle Contento
Santa Fe, NM 87505-5406, 505-438-3979
   Pubs: *Zebras* (Tribal Center Pr, 1991), *Thus Spake the*
   Corpse: Anth (Black Sparrow Pr, 1999), *A Secret*
   Location on the Lower East Side: Anth (NYPL, 1998),
   Literature: Anth (St.Martin's Pr, 1998), *Art & Antiques,*
   Fiction Intl, TriQtly, Poetry Chicago
I.D.: Seniors

Stanley Berne 🎤 ✈   P&W
American-Canadian Pub, Inc, PO Box 4595, Santa Fe,
NM 87502-4595, 505-983-8484
   Pubs: *Swimming to Significance, Gravity Drag, To Hell*
   with Optimism, Every Person's Little Book of
   P-L-U-T-O-N-I-U-M (Rising Tide, 2000, 1999, 1996,
   1992), *Living Underground: Anth* (Whitston Pr, 1999)

Mei-mei Berssenbrugge   P
PO Box 831
Abiquiu, NM 87510-0831
   Pubs: *Four Year Old Girl, Sphericity* (Kelsey Street Pr,
   1998, 1993), *Empathy* (Station Hill Pr, 1988)

Sallie Bingham 🎤 ✈   W
369 Montezuma, #316
Santa Fe, NM 87501-2626, 505-989-1205
Internet: sabingham@aol.com
   Pubs: *Straight Man, Matron of Honor, Small Victories*
   (Zoland Bks, 1996, 1994, 1992), *Upstate* (Permanent
   Pr, 1993), *Passion & Prejudice* (Knopf, 1989), *SW Rev,*
   New Woman/New Fiction, Amicus Jrnl

Robert Boswell   W
New Mexico State Univ, English Dept, Box 3E, Las
Cruces, NM 88003, 505-527-2335
   Pubs: *Living to Be a Hundred, Mystery Ride, The*
   Geography of Desire (Knopf, 1994, 1993, 1989), *Iowa*
   Rev, New Yorker

John Brandi 🎤 ✈   P&W
56 Priestly Pl
Corrales, NM 87048
   Pubs: *Reflections in the Lizard's Eye* (Western Edge,
   2000), *Visits to the City of Light* (Milk Pr, 2000), *Stone*
   Garland (Tooth of Time, 2000), *Weeding the Cosmos*
   (La Alameda, 1998), *Heartbeat Geography* (White Pine,
   1995)

Michael Breslow   W
103 Catron, #8
Santa Fe, NM 87501
   Pubs: *Lifeline* (Viking Pr, 1978)

Paul Bufis 🎤 ✈   P
123 1/2 Martinez St
Santa Fe, NM 87501-2219, 505-983-1951
Internet: zeebufi@interserve.com
   Pubs: *XY Files: Anth* (Sherman Asher Pub, 1997),
   Saludos Poemas De Nuevo Mexico/Poems of New
   Mexico: Anth (Pennywhistle Pr, 1995), *SPR, River Styx,*
   Visions, Blue Unicorn, Permafrost, Rhino, Wind,
   Phantasm

Barney Bush 🎤 ✈   PP&P
Box 22779
Santa Fe, NM 87502-2779
　　Pubs: *Redemption of the Serpent* (Paris; Albin Michelle
　　Pr, 2000), *A Sense of Journey, Left for Dead, Remake
　　of the American Dream, Oyate* (CD; Paris; Nato
　　Records, 1996, 1995, 1994, 1989)
I.D.: Native American. Groups: Schools

Laura Calvert   P
1029 Guadalupe del Predo NW
Albuquerque, NM 87107, 505-345-7064
　　Pubs: *Discurso Literario, Studia Mystica, The
　　Backwoodsman, Southern Rev, North Dakota Rev*

Nash Candelaria 🎤 ✈   W
111 E San Mateo Rd
Santa Fe, NM 87505-4721, 505-983-0795
Internet: nashcan@aol.com
　　Pubs: *Uncivil Rights & Other Stories, Leonor Park*
　　(Bilingual Pr, 1998, 1991), *Growing Up Ethnic in
　　America: Anth* (Penguin, 1999), *Americas Rev, De
　　Colores, Imagine, Puerto del Sol, Bilingual Rev,
　　Riversedge*

Alvaro Cardona-Hine 🎤 ✈   P
PO Box 326
Truchas, NM 87578-0326
　　Pubs: *Thirteen Tangos for Stravinsky, A History of Light*
　　(Sherman Asher Pub, 1999, 1997), *A Garden of Sound*
　　(Pemmican Pr, 1996), *When I Was a Father* (New
　　Rivers Pr, 1982), *The Half-Eaten Angel* (Nodin Pr,
　　1981), *American Writing, Chelsea*
Lang: Spanish

Ioanna Carlsen 🎤 ✈   P&W
PO Box 307
Tesuque, NM 87574, 505-983-6910
　　Pubs: *Saludos Poemas De Nuevo Mexico/Poems of
　　New Mexico: Anth* (Pennywhistle Pr, 1995),
　　*Ploughshares, Field, Marlboro Rev, The Qtly, Poetry,
　　Cafe Solo, Nimrod, Chelsea, Blue Mesa Rev*
I.D.: Greek-American/Greek

Christine Cassidy   P
369 Montezuma, Suite 158
Santa Fe, NM 87501, 212-727-0531
Internet: cccassidy@aol.com
　　Pubs: *First Time Ever: Anth* (Naiad Pr, 1995),
　　Persistent Desire: Anth (Alyson, 1992), *Lambda Book
　　Report, Mudfish, BPJ, Chalk Circle*

Susan Chapman   P
5801 Lowell St NE, #5A
Albuquerque, NM 87111
　　Pubs: *Conversations with Dracaena* (Word Merchant Pr,
　　1982), *The Spirit That Wants Me: Anth* (Duff, 1991),
　　Haiku Qtly, Pudding Mag, Frogpond

James Colbert   W
Dept of English Language and Literature, Univ New
Mexico, Humanities Bldg 217, Albuquerque, NM
87131-1106, 505-277-6347
　　Pubs: *God Bless the Child, All I Have Is Blue, Skinny
　　Man* (MacMillan, 1993, 1992, 1990), *No Special Hurry,
　　Profit & Sheen* (HM, 1988, 1986)

Jane Candia Coleman 🎤 ✈   P&W
PO Box 40
Rodeo, NM 88056-0040, 520-558-2367
　　Pubs: *The O'Keefe Empire, Doc Holliday's Gone, I,
　　Pearl Hart* (Thorndike 5-Star, 1999, 1999, 1998),
　　Moving On (Leisure Bks, 1999), *Doc Holliday's Woman*
　　(Warner Bks, 1995), *Discovering Eve, Stories from
　　Mesa Country* (Ohio U Pr/Swallow Pr, 1993, 1991)

Joseph L. Concha   P
c/o Mr. & Mrs. Alex Concha, Box 1184, Taos, NM 87571

Michele Connelly   P
PO Box 28
Coyote, NM 87012
　　Pubs: *Rebirth of Power: Anth* (Mother Courage, 1987),
　　*Hudson Valley Writers' Ctr River Anth, Reed Mag, High
　　Country News, Sinister Wisdom, Swamproot*

Gina Covina   W
PO Box 226
Vallecitos, NM 87581, 505-582-4226
　　Pubs: *The City of Hermits* (Barn Owl Bks, 1983),
　　Yellow Silk, Berkeley Works, New Age

Sheila Cowing 🎤 ✈   P
5 Bonito Rd
Santa Fe, NM 87505-8793, 505-466-4163
　　Pubs: *Stronger in the Broken Places* (Sherman Asher,
　　1999), *Living in Storms: Anth* (Purdue U Pr, 2000),
　　Saludasi: Anth (Pennywhistle, 1996), *Chattahoochee
　　Rev, Warren Wilson Rev, Georgia Rev, Dalhousie Rev,
　　Mid-American Rev, New Laurel Rev, MacGuffin*

Stanley Crawford 🎤 ✈   W
PO Box 56
Dixon, NM 87527-0056, 505-579-4288
Internet: scrawford@newmexico.com
　　Pubs: *A Garlic Testament* (HC, 1992), *Mayordomo* (U
　　New Mexico Pr, 1988), *Some Instructions* (Knopf, 1978)

Judson Crews   W
2323 Kathryn SE, #531
Albuquerque, NM 87106-3456, 505-266-2938
　　Pubs: *The Brave Wild Coast* (Dumont Pr, 1997), *The
　　Clock of Moss* (Ahsahta Pr, 1983), *Wormwood Rev,
　　New York Rev, Xib, Burning World, Zen Tattoo, Atom
　　Mind*

Richard Currey   W
160 Washington SE, #185
Albuquerque, NM 87108, 505-255-9801
   Pubs: *Lost Highway, Fatal Light* (HM, 1997, 1997), *The Wars of Heaven* (Vintage, 1991), *Witness, NAR, Utne Reader*

Pierre Delattre   W
PO Box 190
Dixon, NM 87527
   Pubs: *Walking on Air* (HM, 1980), *Atlantic, Playboy, Texas Qtly, Antioch Rev*

R. P. Dickey 🎤 ✈   P&W
PO Box 87
Ranchos de Taos, NM 87557-0087, 505-758-4898
   Pubs: *Collected Poems, The Way of Eternal Recurrence* (21st Century Pr, 1999, 1994), *The Little Book on Racism & Politics* (Mohualu Pr, 1990), *New Yorker, Atlantic, Poetry*

G. J. Dubovik   W
9201 Preston Trail NE
Albuquerque, NM 87111
   Pubs: *I, Woman* (Lintel, 1990), *Southwest Writers, Albuquerque Gazette*

Thomas Fitzsimmons   P
1 Balsa Rd
Santa Fe, NM 87505, 505-466-9909
   Pubs: *The Dream Machine* (Pennywhistle Pr, 1996), *Water Ground Stone* (Katydid Bks/U Hawaii Pr, 1992)

Phillip Foss   P
PO Box 1322
San Juan Pueblo, NM 87566-1322
   Pubs: *Venaculture* (Jensen/Daniels, 1999), *Chromatic Defacement* (Chax Pr, 1998), *Courtesan of Seizure, The Excesses, The Caprices* (Light & Dust Bks, 1993, 1990), *Tyuonyi, Conjunctions, Avec, Sulfur, Hambone*

Gene Frumkin 🎤 ✈   P&W
3721 Mesa Verde NE
Albuquerque, NM 87110-7723, 505-266-1319
   Pubs: *The Old Man Who Swam Away & Left Only His Wet Feet* (La Alameda Pr, 1998) *Saturn Is Mostly Weather* (Cinco Puntos Pr, 1992), *Comma in the Ear* (Living Batch, 1990), *Paris Rev, Manoa, Prairie Schooner*

Carl Ginsburg   P
3212 Monte Vista NE
Albuquerque, NM 87106, 505-266-6699
   Pubs: *Medicine Journeys: Ten Stories* (Center Pr, 1991), *The Spirit That Wants Me: A New Mexico Anth* (Duff, 1991), *Southwest Discovery*

Larry Goodell   PP&P
PO Box 571
Placitas, NM 87043, 505-867-5877
   Pubs: *From Here on Earth: A Book of Sonnets* (Alameda Pr, 1996), *Out of Secrecy* (YooHoo Pr, 1992), *New Mexico Poetry Renaissance: Anth* (Red Crane, 1994)

MacDonnell Gordon   P
1026 Governor Dempsey
Santa Fe, NM 87501
   Pubs: *Loon, Road Apple Rev, Greenfield Rev, Alembic, Hard Pressed, Cedar Rock, Blue Buildings*

Becky Hagenston   W
2510 S Espina St #4B
Las Cruces, NM 88001, 505-541-9313
   Pubs: *A Gram of Mars* (Sarabande Bks, 1999), *Prize Stories: Anth* (Doubleday, 1996), *Shenandoah, Crescent Rev, Press, Antietam Rev, Carolina Qtly, Folio, TriQtly, Witness, Southern Rev*

Nancy Harrison   PW
PO Box 227
Ocate, NM 87734, 505-666-2519
   Pubs: *Powers of Desire: Anth* (Monthly Rev Pr, 1983), *Fiction & Poetry by Texas Women: Anth* (Texas Center for Writers Pr, 1975), *Feminary, Sinister Wisdom, Kalliope*

Penny Harter 🎤 ✈   P&W
PO Box 2740
Santa Fe, NM 87504-2740, 505-438-3249
Internet: handh@att.net
   Pubs: *Lizard Light: Poems from the Earth* (Sherman Asher Pub, 1998), *Turtle Blessing* (La Alameda Pr, 1996), *Stages & Views* (Katydid Bks, 1994), *American Nature Writing: Anth* (Oregon State U Pr, 2000)

Nancy Peters Hastings   P
PO Box 1374
Las Cruces, NM 88004, 505-382-7446
   Pubs: *A Quiet I Carry with Me* (A Slow Tempo Pr, 1994), *The Spirit That Wants Me: Anth* (Duff, 1988), *Kansas Qtly, Poetry, Prairie Schooner, Connecticut River Rev*

Laura Hendrie   W
Box 202
Dixon, NM 87527-0202
   Pubs: *Remember Me* (Picador, 2000), *Stygo* (MacMurray & Beck, 2000), *Walking on Air* (U Alabama, 1996), *Best of the West III: Anth* (Gibbs Smith, 1990), *Missouri Rev, Taos Rev, Writers' Forum, Outside, Life*

Mary Rising Higgins 🎤 ✈   P
801 Malachite Dr SW
Albuquerque, NM 87121, 505-831-9254
　　Pubs: *Red Table* (La Alameda Pr, 1999), *O'Clock*
(Potes & Poets Pr, 2000), *No Roses Rev, O.ars,
Tyuoni, Denver Qtly, Big ALLIS, Hambone, Central Park*
Groups: Prisoners, G/L/B/T

William J. Higginson 🎤 ✈   P&W
From Here Press, PO Box 2740, Santa Fe, NM
87504-2740, 505-438-3249
Internet: handh@att.net
　　Pubs: *Red Fuji* (From Here Pr, 1997), *Met on the
Road* (Press Here, 1993), *Wind in the Long Grass*
(S&S, 1991), *Haiku World: Anth* (Kodansha Intl, 1996),
Center, Edge, Frogpond, Modern Haiku, Still, Albatross

Judyth Hill 🎤 ✈   P
HC 69 Box 20-H
Sapello, NM 87745-9602, 505-454-9628
Internet: rockmirth@prodigy.net
　　Pubs: *Black Hollyhock, First Light* (La Alameda Pr,
2000), *Men Need Space, A Presence of Angels*
(Sherman Asher Pubs, 1996, 1995), *Altar of the
Ordinary* (Ya-Hoo Pr, 1993), *Goddess Cafe* (Fish Drum,
1990)
I.D.: Jewish. Groups: Nature/Environment, Children

Tony Hoagland   P
English Dept, New Mexico State Univ, Las Cruces, NM
88011, 505-646-2247
　　Pubs: *Donkey Gospel, Sweet Ruin* (Graywolf, 1998,
1992), *History of Desire* (Moon Pony Pr, 1990), *Talking
to Stay Warm* (Coffee Cup Pr, 1986), *A Change in
Plans* (San Pedro, 1985)

Suzanne Marie Hobbs   P
4805 Downey St NE
Albuquerque, NM 87109, 505-296-4662

Phyllis Hoge   P
213 Dartmouth Dr SE
Albuquerque, NM 87106, 505-265-2042
　　Pubs: *The Ghosts of Who We Were* (U Illinois Pr,
1986), *What the Land Gave* (QRL, 1981), *Hudson Rev,
QRL, Manoa, Shenandoah*

J. R. Humphreys   W
Box 5461
Santa Fe, NM 87502, 505-983-5685
　　Pubs: *Maya Red* (Cane Hill, 1989), *Timeless Towns &
Haunted Places* (St. Martin's, 1989), *Chelsea*

David Johnson   P
1025 Summit NE
Albuquerque, NM 87106, 505-266-9960
　　Pubs: *Fire in the Fields* (Writers on the Plains, 1996),
Western Literature in a World Context: Anth (St.
Martin's Pr, 1995), *Puerto del Sol, Cafe Solo*

Stanley Kiesel   P&W
8 Betatkin PT
Placitas, NM 87043
　　Pubs: *The War Between the Pitiful Teachers & the
Splendid Kids, Skinny Malinky Leads the War for
Kidness* (Avon, 1994, 1985)

Don Kurtz   W
PO Box 4182
Las Cruces, NM 88003, 505-521-4832
　　Pubs: *South of the Big Four* (Avon, 1996), *O. Henry
Festival Stories: Anth* (Trans-Verse Pr, 1987), *Iowa
Rev, Puerto del Sol, Epoch*

Elizabeth Searle Lamb   P
970 Acequia Madre
Santa Fe, NM 87501-2819, 505-982-8890
　　Pubs: *Across the Windharp* (La Alameda Pr, 1999),
Casting Into a Cloud (From Here Pr, 1985), *New
Mexico Poetry Renaissance: Anth* (Red Crane Bks,
1994), *Modern Haiku, Frogpond*

Dana Levin   P
Creative Writing Program, College of Santa Fe, 1600 St
Michael's Dr, Santa Fe, NM 87505
　　Pubs: *In the Surgical Theatre* (APR, 1999), *Influence &
Mastery: Anth* (Paul Dry Bks, 2001), *American Poetry:
Next Generation: Anth* (Carnegie Mellon U Pr, 2000),
Pushcart Prize XXII: Anth (Pushcart Pr, 1998), *Volt,
Third Coast, Marlboro Rev, Ploughshares*
I.D.: Jewish, Women. Groups: Women, Health-Related

Robert Lloyd   P
English Dept, Univ New Mexico, 217 Humanities Bldg,
Box 132, Albuquerque, NM 87131

Joan Logghe 🎤 ✈   P&W
12C Eckard's Way
Espanola, NM 87532, 505-753-3174
Internet: jlogghe@espanola.com
　　Pubs: *Sofía, Twenty Years in Bed with the Same Man*
(La Alameda Pr, 1999, 1995), *Blessed Resistance*
(Mariposa, 1999), *Another Desert: Anth* (Sherman
Asher, 1998), *Catch Our Breath: Anth* (Mariposa, 1996),
Frank, Women's Review of Books, Puerto Del Sol
I.D.: Jewish. Groups: Jewish, Prisoners

Robert Longoni   P
HC61 Box 750
Ramah, NM 87321
　　Pubs: *Woodpiles* (Moon Pony Pr, 1997), *Poetry of the
Desert Southwest: Anth* (Baleen Pr, 1973), *Earthcare*

Sandra Lynn   P
1814 Hermosa Dr NE
Albuquerque, NM 87110-4924, 505-255-0410
　　Pubs: *Where Rainbows Wait for Rain* (Tangram, 1989),
Inheritance of Light: Anth (U North Texas Pr, 1996),
Three Texas Poets: Anth (Prickly Pear, 1986)

Hank Malone 🎤 ✈   P
1220-J Nakomis NE
Albuquerque, NM 87112
Internet: hanksharon@aol.com
    Pubs: *Experiencing New Mexico: Lyrical & Critical
    Essays, New Mexico Haiku* (Poetic License Pr, 1998,
    1996), *Footstrikes & Spondees* (Parkville Pr, 1993), *The
    Maverick Poets: Anth* (Gorilla Pr, 1988)

E. A. Mares 🎤 ✈   P
202 Edith NE
Albuquerque, NM 87102-3526, 505-248-0946
Internet: www.rt66.com/~sfpoetry/mares.html
    Pubs: *The Unicorn Poem & Flowers & Songs of
    Sorrow* (U New Mexico Pr, 1992), *Paper Dance: Anth*
    (Persea Bks, 1995), *Santa Fe Poetry Broadside, Prairie
    Schooner, Blue Mesa Rev, Blanco Movil, Century Mag,
    Cafe Solo, San Marcos Rev*
Lang: Spanish. Groups: Schools, Seniors

Margueritte   P
PO Box 318
Rodeo, NM 88056-0318
    Pubs: *Kimstar* (Pinched Nerves Pr, 1992), *Apostrophe,
    Talisman, Poetry*

Barbara McCauley   P
PO Box 326
Truchas, NM 87578
    Pubs: *Small Mercies, Written with a Spoon* (Sherman
    Asher Pub, 1998, 1996), *Drug-Related Diseases*
    (Franklin Watts, 1986), *Finding the Balance* (Red Hill,
    1977), *The Nation*

Karen Quelle McKinnon 🎤 ✈   P
PO Box 508
Sandia Park, NM 87047-0508, 505-281-9856
Internet: karennrich@aol.com
    Pubs: *Coming True* (Solo Pr, 2000), *Saludos Poemas
    De Nuevo Mexico/Poems of New Mexico: Anth*
    (Pennywhistle Pr, 1995), *Queen Anne's Lace: Anth*
    (Wildflowers Pr, 1994), *Blue Mesa Rev, Puerto del Sol*

Emerson Blackhorse Mitchell   P
Box #204
Shiprock, NM 87420

Carol Moldaw 🎤 ✈   P
RR5, Box 231
Santa Fe, NM 87501-9300, 505-455-3074
    Pubs: *Chalkmarks on Stone* (La Alameda Pr, 1998),
    Taken from the River (Alef Bks, 1993), *New Mexico
    Poetry Renaissance: Anth* (Red Crane Bks, 1994),
    *Manoa, Threepenny Rev, TriQtly, SW Rev, Kenyon
    Rev, New Republic, New Yorker, Orion*

N. Scott Momaday   P&W
PO Box 6
Jemez Springs, NM 87025-0006

Linda Monacelli-Johnson 🎤 ✈   P
308 W Houghton
Santa Fe, NM 87501-4349, 505-988-4569
    Pubs: *Campanile* (Drummer Pr, 1999), *Weathered*
    (Sunstone Pr, 1986), *Lacing the Moon* (Cleveland State
    U Poetry Ctr, 1978), *Zeta, CSM, Rio Grande Writers
    Qtly, South Florida Poetry Rev, Pembroke Mag,
    Tributaries*
I.D.: Italian-American

Frank D. Moore 🎤 ✈   P
4 Glorieta Rd
Santa Fe, NM 87505-2257, 505-466-0226
Internet: framoore@ix.netcom.com
    Pubs: *Literary Rev, Painted Bride Qtly, Passages North,
    Sou'wester, Four Quarters, Piedmont Literary Rev*

Todd Moore 🎤 ✈   P
3216 San Pedro Dr NE
Albuquerque, NM 87110-2634, 505-837-1167
Internet: moorebt@aol.com
    Pubs: *The Corpse Is Dreaming* (Lummox Pr, 2000),
    Working on My Duende (Kings Estate Pr, 1998),
    Dillinger: Book II (Primal Pub, 1992), *Outlaw Bible: Anth*
    (Thunder's Mouth Pr, 1999), *Chiron Rev, Nerve
    Cowboy, Sin Fronteras, NYQ*

Barbara Beasley Murphy   W
Casa Esteban, 486 Circle Dr, Santa Fe, NM 87501,
505-983-9607
    Pubs: *Fly Like an Eagle, Join In* (Delacorte, 1994,
    1993), *Ace Hits It Big* (Bantam, 1992)

Tessa Nelson-Humphries 🎤 ✈   P&W
3228 Jupiter Rd, 4 Hills
Las Cruces, NM 88012-7742
    Pubs: *Envoi: Summer Anth* (Poets Pubs, 1990), *Array,
    New Frontiers New Mexico, Negative Capability,
    Alaskan Poetry Jrnl, Confrontations, Animal Cavalcade
    Appalachian Heritage, Blue Unicorn, Cobblestones*
Lang: Spanish. Groups: Children, College/Univ

Antonya Nelson   W
English Dept, Box 3E, New Mexico State Univ, Las
Cruces, NM 88003, 505-646-3536
    Pubs: *Nobody's Girl, Talking in Bed* (Scribner, 1998,
    1997), *Family Terrorists* (HM, 1994), *In the Land of
    Men* (Avon, 1993), *New Yorker, Story, Redbook,
    TriQtly, Esquire, Antioch Rev*

Kathleen Neuer   P
PO Box 2409
Taos, NM 87571-2409, 505-758-2994
    Pubs: *Prairie Schooner, Texas Rev, Pennsylvania Rev,
    Malahat, Black Warrior, Threepenny Rev*

Stanley Noyes 🎤 ✈   P&W
634 E Garcia
Santa Fe, NM 87501-2858, 505-982-4067
   Pubs: *Commander of Dead Leaves* (Tooth of Time,
   1984), *Saludos Poemas De Nuevo Mexico/Poems of
   New Mexico: Anth* (Pennywhistle Pr, 1995), *Sin
   Fronteras, High Plains, Blue Unicorn*

Antony Oldknow   P
PO Box 1091
Portales, NM 88130, 505-359-0901
   Pubs: *Ten Small Songs* (Paraiso Pr, 1985), *Consolation
   for Beggars* (Song Pr, 1978), *Antaeus*

Bill Pearlman 🎤 ✈   P
Box 613
Placitas, NM 87043-0613
Internet: b2pearl@juno.com
   Pubs: *Flareup of Twosomes* (La Alameda Pr, 1996)
Lang: Spanish, Portuguese. Groups: Seniors, Prisoners

V. B. Price 🎤 ✈   P
PO Box 6175
Albuquerque, NM 87197-6175
Internet: vbp@swcp.com
   Pubs: *Chaco Trilogy* (La Alameda Pr, 1998), *Saludos
   Poemas De Nuevo Mexico/Poems of New Mexico: Anth*
   (Pennywhistle Pr, 1995), *New Mexico Poetry
   Renaissance: Anth* (Red Crane Bks, 1994)

Sheila Raeschild 🎤 ✈   P&W
1303 Bartlet Court
Santa Fe, NM 87501-1643, 505-982-7280
Internet: child@cybermesa.com
   Pubs: *Earth Songs* (NAL, 1984), *The Defiant* (Dell,
   1982), *Trolley Song* (Zebra, 1981), *Spectral Line: Anth*
   (IAIA, 2000), *Redbook*

Margaret Randall   P
50 Cedar Hill Rd NE
Albuquerque, NM 87122-1928, 505-856-6543
   Pubs: *Hunger's Table* (Papier-Mache Pr, 1997),
   Sandino's Daughters Revisited (Rutgers U Pr, 1994),
   Gathering Rage (Monthly Review Pr, 1992), *American
   Voice, Ms., Ikon, Calyx, Berkeley Poetry Rev, Blue
   Mesa Rev*

Harvena Richter   P&W
1932 Candelaria Rd NW
Albuquerque, NM 87107-2855, 505-344-6766
   Pubs: *Innocent Island* (Puckerbrush Pr, 1999), *Green
   Girls, The Yaddo Elegies* (North Valley Pr, 1996, 1995),
   The Human Shore (Little, Brown, 1959), *South Dakota
   Rev, Blue Mesa Rev*

Janet Rodney   P
PO Box 8187
Santa Fe, NM 87504
   Pubs: *Orphydice* (Salt Works Pr, 1986), *Crystals* (North
   Atlantic Bks, 1979), *Conjunctions, Sulfur*

Leo Romero   P&W
34 Calle de Gancho
Santa Fe, NM 87501, 505-473-7151
   Pubs: *Rita & Los Angeles* (Bilingual Review Pr, 1994),
   Going Home Away Indian (Ahsahta Pr, 1990), *Fish
   Drum, The Magazine, L'Ozio, Mid-American Rev, Yefief,
   Bilingual Rev/Revista Bilingue, Americas Rev*

Sharman Apt Russell 🎤 ✈   W
1113 West St
Silver City, NM 88061-4633, 505-538-6345
Internet: sharman@zianet.com
   Pubs: *Last Matriarch* (U New Mexico Pr, 2000), *When
   the Land Was Young, Kill the Cowboy, Songs of the
   Fluteplayer* (Addison-Wesley, 1996, 1993, 1991), *The
   Humpbacked Fluteplayer* (Knopf, 1994)

Miriam Sagan   P
626 Kathryn Ave
Santa Fe, NM 87501
   Pubs: *Coastal Lives* (Center Pr, 1991), *True Body*
   (Parallax, 1991), *Fish Drum, Hayden's Ferry, Agni, Blue
   Mesa, APR, Ploughshares, Family Circle*

Jim Sagel   P
PO Box 942
Espanola, NM 87532, 505-753-6357
   Pubs: *Mas Que No Love It* (West End Pr, 1991), *El
   Santo Queso/The Holy Cheese* (Ediciones del Norte,
   1990)

Scott Patrick Sanders   P
English Dept, Univ New Mexico, Albuquerque, NM 87131,
505-277-4437
   Pubs: *Mr. Cogito, Rocky Mountain Rev of Language &
   Literature, Chiaroscuro, Spoon River Qtly, Weber
   Studies*

Roberto Sandoval   P
137 Romero St
Santa Fe, NM 87501, 505-982-9605

Lorna D. Saunders 🎤 ✈   P
Kralor Press, PO Box 1867, Magdalena, NM 87825-1867
   Pubs: *The Elsewhere* (Kralor Pr, 2000), *Wild Outdoor
   World, Poet Lore, Bitterroot, Apprentice, Bloodroot,
   Planet X*
Groups: Children

Ken Saville   P
Box 4662
Albuquerque, NM 87196, 505-268-0265
   Pubs: *20 Postcards* (Transient Pr, 1979)

Rebecca Seiferle 🎤 ✈   P
5602 Tarry Terr
Farmington, NM 87402-8261, 505-325-6145
Internet: seiferle@yahoo.com
  Pubs: *The Music We Dance To, The Ripped-Out Seam,
  Trilce* (Sheep Meadow Pr, 1999, 1993, 1992), *Best
  American Poetry: Anth* (Scribner, 2000), *Calyx, TriQtly,
  Indiana Rev, APR, Harvard Rev, Blue Mesa Rev*

Jeanne Shannon 🎤 ✈   P&W
The Wildflower Press, PO Box 4757, Albuquerque, NM
87196-4757, 505-296-0691
Internet: jspoetry@aol.com
  Pubs: *Sometimes the Light* (Wildflower Pr, 2000), *The
  House on Afternoon Street* (Penhaligon Page, 2000),
  Learning By Heart: Anth (U Iowa Pr, 1999), *In Good
  Company: Anth* (Live Wire Pr, 1999), *The Party Train:
  Anth* (New Rivers Pr, 1996), *Quarter After Eight*
Groups: Seniors

Sherri Silverman   P
PO Box 66
Santa Fe, NM 87504-0066, 505-984-0327
  Pubs: *Crosswinds, Santa Fe Spirit Mag, Studia Mystica,
  Cicada, Sackbut Rev, Manna, Reconstructionist, Salome*

Katie Singer 🎤 ✈   W
PO Box 6574
Santa Fe, NM 87502-6574, 505-820-0773
Internet: www.KatieSinger.com
  Pubs: *The Wholeness of a Broken Heart* (Riverhead
  Bks, 1999), *Heresies, Sojourner, Lilith*
I.D.: Jewish

Florentin Smarandache 🎤 ✈   P&W
Univ New Mexico, 200 College Rd, Gallup, NM
87301-5603
Internet: www.gallup.unm.edu/~smarandache
  Pubs: *Leitmotives, Destiny, In Seven Languages,
  Deformed Writings, Non Novel* (Aius, 2000, 2000, 2000,
  1997, 1993), *Non Poems* (Xiquan Pub Hse, 1990),
  *Dorul, Rivista Internationale, Revista Divaagacao
  Cultural, Poet, Poetry Nippon, Art Et Poesie De
  Touraine*
Lang: French, Romanian

Linda Wasmer Smith   P
12017 Kashmir St NE
Albuquerque, NM 87111, 505-296-3095
  Pubs: *Second Aid* (Fish Down Pr, 1993), *If I Had My
  Life to Live Over I Would Pick More Daisies: Anth*
  (Papier-Mache Pr, 1992), *Defined Providence*

Maryhelen Snyder   P
422 Camino Del Bosque NW
Albuquerque, NM 87114, 505-898-7047
  Pubs: *Enough* (Solo Pr, 1979), *The Practice of Peace:
  Anth* (Sherman Asher Pr, 1998), *Blue Mesa Rev,
  Puerto del Sol, New America, Southwestern
  Discoveries, Slant, Cafe Solo, New Laurel Rev, Tulsa
  Poetry Qtly*

Anthony Sobin   P
22 Alcalde Rd
Santa Fe, NM 87505
  Pubs: *The Sunday Naturalist* (Ohio U Pr, 1982), *Poetry,
  Poetry NW, BPJ*

Jane Somerville   P
2442 Cerillos Rd, Ste 455
Sante Fe, NM 87505-3262
  Pubs: *The Only Blessing* (Greenhouse Review Pr,
  1992), *Making the Light Come* (Wayne State U Pr,
  1990), *APR, Gettysburg Rev, Kansas Qtly, Ohio Rev*

Joseph Somoza 🎤 ✈   P
1725 Hamiel Dr
Las Cruces, NM 88001-5222, 505-522-1119
Internet: josomoza@nmsu.edu
  Pubs: *Sojourner, So to Speak* (La Alameda Pr, 1997),
  Out of This World (Cinco Puntos Pr, 1990), *New
  Mexico Poetry Renaissance: Anth* (Red Crane Bks,
  1994), *Convolvulus, Maryland Poetry Rev*

Marcia Southwick   P
1001 Camino Pinones
Santa Fe, NM 87505, 505-989-8781
  Pubs: *A Saturday Night at the Flying Dog* (Field Pr,
  1998), *Why the River Disappears* (Carnegie Mellon U,
  1990), *The Night Won't Save Anyone* (U Georgia,
  1980), *APR, Harvard Rev, Field, Prairie Schooner,
  Antaeus, Poetry, Iowa Rev*

Arlene Stone   P&W
PO Box 2880
Sante Fe, NM 87504-2880
  Pubs: *Son Sonnets* (Emmanuel Pr, 1994), *The Double
  Pipes of Pan* (North Atlantic Bks, 1983), *Harper's,
  Yellow Silk, Contact II*

Mary Swander   P
Univ New Mexico, English Dept, Humanities Bldg 217,
Albuquerque, NM 87131-1106
  Pubs: *Out of This World* (Viking, 1995),
  Heaven-and-Earth House, Driving the Body Back
  (Knopf, 1994, 1986), *New Republic, CSM, Nation, New
  Yorker, Poetry*

George Swaney   P
1825 Meadow Ln
Las Cruces, NM 88005
  Pubs: *Iowa Rev, Poetry East, Georgetown Rev, Gulf
  Stream, Mudfish, Rastown Rev, Antietam Rev,
  Haight-Ashbury Jrnl, Jacaranda Rev, Sou'wester,
  Pittsburgh Qtly*

Arthur Sze 🎤 ✈   P
PO Box 457
Santa Fe, NM 87504-0457, 505-455-3074
  Pubs: *The Redshifting Web, Archipelago* (Copper
  Canyon Pr, 1998, 1995), *River River* (Lost Roads,
  1987), *APR, Paris Rev, Manoa, Conjunctions, Kenyon
  Rev, Orion*

Nathaniel Tarn 🎤 ✈   P
PO Box 871
Tesuque, NM 87574-0871, 505-982-3990
  Pubs: *The Architextures* (Chax Pr, 2000), *Selected
  Poems: 1950-2000* (Wesleyan U Pr, 2000), *Seeing
  America First* (Coffee Hse Pr, 1989), *Jacket, Sulfur,
  Conjunctions, First Intensity*
Lang: Spanish, French

John Tritica 🎤 ✈   P
4931 Palo Alto SE
Albuquerque, NM 87108, 505-265-2856
  Pubs: *How Rain Records Its Alphabet* (La Alameda Pr,
  1998), *Central Park, Talisman*
Lang: Swedish, German. Groups: Disabled, Prisoners

Paul Edward Trujillo   P
Box 396
Peralta, NM 87042, 505-864-0307
  Pubs: *Bilingual Rev, Ceremony of Brotherhood, Poetry
  Now, Writers' Forum*

Sharon Oard Warner 🎤 ✈   W
English Language & Literature, Univ New Mexico,
Humanities Bldg 217, Albuquerque, NM 87131-1106,
505-277-6248
Internet: swarner@unm.edu
  Pubs: *Deep in the Heart* (Dial Pr, 2000), *Learning to
  Dance & Other Stories* (New Rivers Pr, 1992), *Other
  Voices, Iowa Woman, Long Story, Gamut, Prairie
  Schooner, Green Mountains Rev, Sonora Rev, AWP
  Chronicle, Studies in Short Fiction*

Mark Weber   P
725 Van Buren Pl SE
Albuquerque, NM 87108, 505-255-3012
  Pubs: *Existential Hum* (Pearl Special Edtns, 1996),
  Swindler's Harmonica Siesta, Drunk City (Zerx Pr, 1994,
  1991), *Pearl, Wormwood Rev, Caprice, Chiron*

Joel Weishaus   P
401 14th St SW #11
Albuquerque, NM 87102-2871
  Pubs: *Woods, Shore, Desert: 1968 Notebook of
  Thomas Merton* (Museum of New Mexico Pr, 1983),
  Artspace

Kathleene West 🎤 ✈   P
New Mexico State Univ, PO Box 30001, English Dept,
Las Cruces, NM 88003-8001
Internet: kwest@nmsu.edu
  Pubs: *Death of a Regional Poet* (Hurakin Pr, 1998),
  The Farmer's Daughter (Sandhills, 1990), *Water
  Witching, Gift of Tongues: Anth* (Copper Canyon, 1984,
  1996), *TriQtly, Kenyon Rev, Prairie Schooner*

Keith Wilson 🎤 ✈   P
1500 S Locust #C-21
Las Cruces, NM 88001-5356, 505-522-8389
Internet: kewilson@nmsu.edu
  Pubs: *Bosque Redondo* (Penny Whistle Pr, 2000),
  Graves Registry (Clark City Pr, 1992)

Herta Wittgenstein   W
c/o B. J. Harris, PO Box 9848, Santa Fe, NM 87504,
505-984-1154
  Pubs: *Watching A Field of Zebras* (Demarais Studio Pr,
  1992)

Arlene Zekowski 🎤 ✈   P&W
Pamela Tree, PO Box 6136, Santa Fe, NM 87502,
505-983-8484
  Pubs: *Against the Disappearance of Literature, The
  Living Underground: Anth* (Whitston Pr, 1998, 1999),
  Every Person's Little Book of P-L-U-T-O-N-I-U-M (Rising
  Tide Pr, 1992), *Dictionary of the Avant-Gardes: Anth* (A
  Cappella Pr, 1994), *Tyuonyi, Margins*

NEW YORK

Sam Abrams 🎤 ✈   P
Rochester Inst Technology, College of Liberal Arts,
Rochester, NY 14623, 716-475-2444
Internet: sxagsl@rit.edu
  Pubs: *The Old Pothead Poems* (Backwoods Broadsides,
  1999), *Jazz Poetry: Anth* (Indiana U Pr, 1991), *Out of
  this World: Anth* (Crown, 1991), *Up Late: Anth* (4 Walls
  8 Windows, 1987), *Talisman, Mesechabe, Exquisite
  Corpse, Napalm Health Spa Report, Alcatraz*

Ally Acker 🎤 ✈   P
8 Hayloft Ln
Roslyn Heights, NY 11577
Internet: www.reelwomen.com
  Pubs: *Waiting for the Beloved* (Red Hen Pr, 1999),
  Surviving Desire (Garden Street Pr, 1994), *American
  Voice, Poetry Kanto, Ploughshares*

Barbara Adams 🎤 ✈   P&W
59 Coach Ln
Newburgh, NY 12550-3818, 914-564-3499
Internet: bbadams@fsinter.net
    Pubs: *The Muse Strikes Back: Anth* (Storyline Pr,
1997), *When a Lifemate Dies: Anth* (Fairview Pr, 1997),
*Texas Rev, Free Associations, Psychoanalytic Rev,
Humanist, Breakfast All Day, Belles Lettres*
I.D.: Irish-American, Jewish. Groups: Women, Book Clubs

Jeanette Adams   P
208 Old Country Rd
Elmsford, NY 10523
    Pubs: *Poetry in Performance 19* (CUNY, 1991),
Parallels Artists Poets: Anth (Midmarch Arts, 1993),
Drumvoices Revue: Anth (U Southern Illinois, 1992)

Joan Albarella 🎤 ✈   P&W
3574 Clinton St
Buffalo, NY 14224-1401
Internet: jkea@juno.com
    Pubs: *Called to Kill, Agenda for Murder* (Rising Tide Pr,
2000, 1999), *Spirit & Joy* (Alpha Pr, 1993), *Women,
Flowers, Fantasy* (Textile Bridge Pr, 1987)
I.D.: Italian-American. Groups: Seniors, G/L/B/T

Joan Alden   W
242 Main St
Catskill, NY 12414, 518-943-5526
    Pubs: *Before Our Eyes, Letting in the Night* (Firebrand
Bks, 1993, 1989), *A Boy's Best Friend* (Alyson Pubs,
1992)

Linda Allardt 🎤 ✈   P
2 Ann Lynn Rd
Pittsford, NY 14534-3910, 716-248-5223
    Pubs: *River Effect, Seeing for You* (State St Pr, 1998,
1981), *The Names of the Survivors* (Ithaca Hse, 1979),
The Bridge, BPJ, West Branch

John Allman 🎤 ✈   P&W
28 Frances Dr
Katonah, NY 10536-3212, 914-232-3835
Internet: allmanej@cs.com
    Pubs: *Inhabited World* (Wallace Stevens Society Pr,
1995), *Descending Fire & Other Stories* (New
Directions, 1994), *Poetry, Pivot, The Qtly, BPJ, Poetry
NW*

Karen Alpha 🎤 ✈   W
106 Welch Rd
Corning, NY 14830, 607-936-6576
    Pubs: *Redbook, NAR, Blueline, North Dakota Qtly*

Lynne Alvarez   P
RR1, PO Box 27
Cooperstown, NY 13326-9801
    Pubs: *On New Ground* (TCG, 1987), *Living with
Numbers, The Dreaming Man* (Waterfront, 1987, 1984)

Kath M. Anderson 🎤 ✈   P
28 Arlington St
Rochester, NY 14607
Internet: dempander@earthlink.net
    Pubs: *An Abbreviated History of Water* (State St Pr,
1996), *Hauling Water* (Jumping Cholla Pr), *Poetry, Qtly
West, Georgia Rev, Carolina Qtly, Ploughshares,
Sonora Rev, Orion*

Lori Anderson   P
English Dept, SUNY Albany, Albany, NY 12222,
518-442-4500
    Pubs: *Cultivating Excess* (Eighth Mtn Pr, 1992), *Walking
the Dead* (Heaven Bone Pr, 1991), *Seeds*

Marjorie Appleman 🎤 ✈   P&W
PO Box 39
Sagaponack, NY 11962-0039, 631-537-1741
    Pubs: *Against Time* (Birnham Wood, 1994),
*Confrontation, LIQ, Poetry Pilot, Poetry Rev, Wind,
Kentucky Poetry Rev, Sojourner*

Philip Appleman 🎤 ✈   P&W
PO Box 39
Sagaponack, NY 11962-0039, 631-537-1741
    Pubs: *New & Selected Poems* (U Arkansas Pr, 1996),
Let There Be Light (HC, 1991), *Darwin's Ark* (Indiana U
Pr, 1984), *Poetry, Partisan Rev, Yale Rev, Nation,
Paris Rev*
Groups: Humanists

Sondra Audin Armer 🎤 ✈   P
1 Everett Ave
Ossining, NY 10562-5503, 914-941-0648
Internet: ssaphd@aol.com
    Pubs: *Moonsnap: Anth* (Amarantus Pr, 1998), *Dog
Music: Anth* (St. Martin's Pr, 1996), *Sparrow, Amelia,
Western Humanities Rev, Apalachee Qtly, Negative
Capability, Home Planet News*

Deborah Artman 🎤 ✈   P&W
9 Hill 99
Woodstock, NY 12498-1424
    Pubs: *Bite to Eat Place* (Redwood Coast Pr, 1995),
*Puerto del Sol, Fish Stories, American Short Fiction,
Carolina Qtly, Cottonwood, Seattle Rev, Ironwood,
Appearances*

Linda Ashear   P
92 Paulding Ave
Tarrytown, NY 10591-5708
    Pubs: *The Rowers, the Swimmers & the Drowned*
(Morris Pr, 1996), *Toward the Light* (Croton Rev Pr,
1989), *MacGuffin, Santa Barbara Rev, Without Halos*

Rilla Askew   W
PO Box 324
Kauneonga Lake, NY 12749
    Pubs: *The Mercy Seat* (Viking, 1997), *Strange Business*
    (Viking Penguin, 1992), *Prize Stories 1993: O. Henry
    Awards Anth* (Doubleday, 1993), *Nimrod, Puerto del
    Sol, Carolina Qtly*

Katharine Assante   P
22 Armand's Way
Highland Mills, NY 10930-9801, 914-534-8522
    Pubs: *A Delicate Blue Veil, October's Child* (Assante,
    1994, 1990), *Algonquin Qtly, On Course, Critical Mass*

Susan Astor ⎇ ✈   P
32 Jefferson Ave
Mineola, NY 11501-2928, 516-873-2547
    Pubs: *Vital Signs* (U Wisconsin Pr, 1989), *Dame* (U
    Georgia Pr, 1980), *Paris Rev, Partisan Rev, Poet Lore,
    Kansas Qtly, Confrontation, Croton Rev*
Groups: Children, Mentally Ill

Brett Axel   P
11 Wickham Ave, Apt 1
Middletown, NY 10940, 914-343-1377
    Pubs: *First on the Fire* (Genesis/Fly by Night Pr, 1999)
    The Spastic Grandson, Twenty-six Different Poems
    (Heaven Bone Pr, 1998, 1998), *Diner Eucharist: Anth*
    (Orange County Arts Council, 1997), *Princeton Arts
    Rev, Unknown Writer, Algonquin Qtly*

David B. Axelrod ⎇ ✈   P
233 Mooney Pond Rd, PO Box 2344, Selden, NY 11784,
631-451-0478
Internet: axelrodthepoet@yahoo.com
    Pubs: *Intro to Literature: Anth* (HC, 1998), *The Chi of
    Poetry: New & Selected Poems, 1960-2000* (Birnham
    Wood, TK), *LIQ, Shi Kahn, Kansas Qtly, Nasa Kniga,
    North Carolina Qtly*
Lang: Yiddish, French

J. C. Axelrod   P&W
25C Nymph Rd
Rocky Point, NY 11778, 516-744-7058
    Pubs: *Facts of Life, Entrances to Nowhere* (CCC, 1987,
    1976), *West Hills Rev, New Letters, Greenfield Rev*

Donald Everett Axinn ⎇   P&W
131 Jericho Turnpike
Jericho, NY 11753-1024, 516-333-8500
    Pubs: *The Ego Makers* (Arcade, 1998), *The Latest
    Illusion, Spin* (Arcade, 1995, 1994), *Dawn Patrol* (CCC,
    1992), *The Colors of Infinity* (Blue Moon Bks, 1990),
    Antaeus, NER, NYQ, Confrontation

Anna Ruth Ediger Baehr   P
218 Brompton Rd
Garden City, NY 11530
    Pubs: *Moonflowers at Dusk* (Birnham Wood, 1996),
    *American Scholar, Long Island Poetry Rev, Xanadu,
    Mennonite Life, Choice Mag Listening*

George Bailin ⎇ ✈   P
Sacred Orchard, PO Box 298, Harriman, NY 10926-0298,
914-783-8154
Internet: www.sacredorchard.org
    Pubs: *Sage of Ananda, First Strike* (Seaport Poets &
    Writers Pr, 1993, 1988), *Dead Reckoning*
    (Dragonsbreath Pr, 1984), *Evening News Report* (Court
    Poetry Pr, 1984), *Meditators Newsletter*
Groups: Spirituai/Religious

Ansie Baird   P
17 Tudor Pl
Buffalo, NY 14222, 716-882-0979
    Pubs: *Paris Rev, Poetry NW, Denver Qtly, Poetry Now,
    Vassar Qtly, The Qtly, Earth's Daughters, Southern
    Rev, South Dakota Rev, Green River Rev*

Peter Balakian ⎇ ✈   P
Colgate Univ, English Dept, Hamilton, NY 13346
    Pubs: *June-tree* (HC, 2001), *Reply from Wilderness
    Island, Sad Days of Light* (Sheep Meadow Pr, 1988,
    1983), *Poetry*

Harry Barba   W
Harian Creative Books, PO Box 189, Clifton Park, NY
12065, 518-885-6699
    Pubs: *Mona Lisa Smiles, Round Trip to Byzantium,
    Gospel According to Everyman* (Harian Creative Bks,
    1993, 1985, 1981)

Stanley H. Barkan ⎇ ✈   P
239 Wynsum Ave
Merrick, NY 11566-4725, 516-868-5635
Internet: cccpoetry@aol.com
    Pubs: *Unsettling America: Anth* (Viking, 1994), *Modern
    Poems on the Bible: Anth* (JPS, 1994), *On Prejudice:
    Anth* (Doubleday, 1993), *Confrontation, Visions,
    Forward, Lips, Shabdaguchha*
Lang: Italian. I.D.: Jewish. Groups: Jewish, Italian-American

Mildred Barker   W
229 Main St
Kingston, NY 12401
    Pubs: *Speaking the Words* (Word Thursdays/Bright Hill
    Pr, 1994), *If I Had a Hammer: Women's Work: Anth*
    (Papier-Mache Pr, 1990), *Oxalis Literary Qtly, Almanac,
    Nimrod, Reporter*

Nancy Barnes P
Erie Community College, 121 Ellicott St, Buffalo, NY
14203, 716-851-1018
    Pubs: *Pure Light, Earth's Daughters, Black Mountain
    Rev, Centrum Jrnl, Fine China: Twenty Years of Earth's
    Daughters: Anth* (Springhouse Edtns, 1993)

Helen Barolini ♦ ✈ P&W
86 Maple Ave
Hastings-on-Hudson, NY 10706, 914-478-5774
    Pubs: *Umbertina, a novel* (Feminist Pr, 1998),
    Chiaroscuro: Essays of Identity (Bordighera, 1997),
    Aldus & His Dream Book (Italica Pr, 1991), *The Dream
    Book: Anth* (Syracuse U Pr, 2000), *SW Rev, Virginia
    Qtly Rev, New Letters*

Linda Michelle Baron PP
Panache Inc, PO Box 4051, Hempstead, NY 11551-4051
    Pubs: *The Sun Is On, Rhythm & Dues* (Harlin Jacque,
    1981, 1981)

Marylin Lytle Barr ♦ ✈ P
PO Box 75
Grahamsville, NY 12740, 914-985-7337
    Pubs: *Unexpected Light* (Essex Pr, 1999), *Concrete
    Considerations* (Sweetwater Pub, 1993), *Drawn from the
    Shadows* (Egret Pr, 1991), *Alchemist 8: Anth* (Alchemy
    Club, 1995), *Poetry Page, Oxalis, Zephyr, Outloud,
    Piedmont Qtly, Alchemist, Touchstone*
Groups: Children, Seniors

Jack Barry ♦ ✈ P
121 North Way
Camillus, NY 13031-1254, 315-488-3566
    Pubs: *Hints & Hunches* (Garlic Pr, 1974), *New Letters,
    APR, Notre Dame Rev, Poetpourri, Syracuse Rev*

Jill Bart P&W
80 Pauls Ln
Water Mill, NY 11976, 516-537-1163
    Pubs: *The Naked & the Nude* (Birnham Wood, 1993),
    First Light (Paumanok Pr, 1988), *Negative Capability,
    Blue Unicorn, Long Pond Rev, Poetry East, LIQ, Ms.*

Michael Basinski ♦ ✈ PP&P
Poetry/Rare Books Collection, SUNY Buffalo, 420 Capen
Hall, Buffalo, NY 14260-2200, 716-645-2917
Internet: basinski@acsu.buffalo.edu
    Pubs: *By* (Hse Pr, 1999), *Heebee-Jeebees, Cnyttan*
    (Meow Pr, 1996, 1993), *SleVep* (Tailspin Pr, 1995),
    Abacus, Lung, Boxkite

John Batki P&W
211 Lockwood Rd
Syracuse, NY 13214, 315-445-0137

M. Garrett Bauman ♦ ✈ W
Monroe Community College, English Dept, Rochester, NY
14623, 716-292-2000
Internet: garrettbauman@cs.com
    Pubs: *Ideas & Details* (HB, 2001), *Story, Yankee,
    Greensboro Rev, Chrysalis*
Groups: Nature/Environment

E. R. Baxter, III P
2709 Braley Rd
Ransomville, NY 14131, 716-791-4611
    Pubs: *Looking for Niagara, What I Want* (Slipstream
    Pub, 1993, 1993), *Albany Rev, Black Mountain Rev,
    Earth's Daughters, Pig Iron*

Michael Benedikt P&W
315 W 98 St, #6-A
New York, NY, 212-865-4538
    Pubs: *The Badminton at Great Barrington* (U Pitt Pr,
    1980), *Night Cries* (Wesleyan U Pr, 1976)

Bruce Bennett ♦ ✈ P
PO Box 145
Aurora, NY 13026, 315-364-3228
    Pubs: *Navigating the Distances: Poems New &
    Selected* (Orchises, 1999), *It's Hard to Get the Angle
    Right* (Greentower Press, 1997), *I Never Danced with
    Mary Beth* (FootHills Pub, 1991), *Harvard Rev, The
    Qtly, Laurel Rev, Tar River Poetry*

Sally Bennett ♦ P&W
846 Ostrom Ave
Syracuse, NY 13210-2902, 315-478-7129
    Pubs: *American Fiction: Anth* (Birch Lane Pr, 1990),
    *Anth of Magazine Verse & Yearbook of American
    Poetry* (Monitor Bks, 1987), *Pangolin Papers, The
    Distillery, Poetry, Seneca Rev, Gulf Stream Mag,
    Syracuse Scholar, Sycamore Rev*

Saul Bennett ♦ ✈ P
115 Broadview
Woodstock, NY 12498
    Pubs: *Harpo Marx at Prayer, New Fields & Other
    Stones/On a Child's Death* (Archer Bks, 2000, 1998),
    Jesus Matinees & Other Poems (Pudding Hse, 1998),
    *Amelia, Christian Century, ELF, First Things, Peregrine,
    Pudding Mag*
I.D.: Jewish

Robert Bensen ♦ ✈ P
14 Harrison Ave
Oneonta, NY 13820-1107, 607-431-4902
Internet: bensenr@hartwick.edu
    Pubs: *Scriptures of Venus* (Swamp Pr, 2000), *Agni,
    River Styx, Caribbean Writer, Paris Rev, Partisan Rev,
    Antioch Rev, Akwe:kon Jrnl, Cumberland Poetry Rev,
    Poetry Wales, Ploughshares, Cimarron Rev, Yankee*

Kimberly Berg 🎤 ✈   P
489 East Rd
Cadyville, NY 12918-2037
Internet: moontree@worldnet.att.net
    Pubs: *Amerikua!, Phoebus, Hummingbird, Minkhill Jrnl,
Colorwheel, Visions, High Rock Rev, Negative
Capability, CSM*

Frank Bergon 🎤 ✈   W
Vassar College, Box 94, Poughkeepsie, NY 12604-0094,
914-437-5663
Internet: bergon@vassar.edu
    Pubs: *Wild Game, The Temptations of St. Ed & Brother
S* (U Nevada Pr, 1995, 1993), *Shoshone Mike* (Viking
Penguin, 1987)

Bruce Berlind 🎤 ✈   P
PO Box 237
Hamilton, NY 13346, 315-893-7078
    Pubs: *Charon's Ferry* (Northwestern U Pr, 2000), *Otto
Orban's The Journey of Barbarus* (Passegiatta Pr,
1997), *When You Became She* (Xenos Bks, 1994),
Birds & Other Relations (Princeton U Pr, 1987),
Partisan Rev, Kenyon Rev, Grand Street, Poetry, APR

Cassia Berman 🎤 ✈   P
11 1/2 Tannery Brook Rd
Woodstock, NY 12498, 914-679-9457
Internet: cassia@netstep.net
    Pubs: *Divine Mother Within Me, Divine Mother Poems*
(Divine Mother Communications, 1995, 1993), *Her
Words: An Anth of Poetry About the Great Goddess*
(Shambhala, 1999), *APR, Chelsea, Northeast Jrnl, The
Falcon, Poetry Studies, Collaboration*
I.D.: Jewish. Groups: Spiritual/Religious, Women

Charles Bernstein   P
Poetics Program, SUNY, English Dept, 438 Clemens Hall,
Buffalo, NY 14260, 716-645-3810
    Pubs: *My Way: Speeches & Poems* (U Chicago Pr,
1998), *Republics of Reality: Poems 1975-1995* (Sun &
Moon Pr, 1998), *A Poetics* (Harvard U Pr, 1992),
*Chain, L=A=N=G=U=A=G=E, Sulfur, Avec, West Coast
Line*

Holly Beye   P&W
PO Box 1043
Woodstock, NY 12498, 914-679-2820
    Pubs: *Out of the Catskills & Beyond: Anth* (Bertha
Rogers, 1997), *In the City of Sorrowing Clouds* (Print
Workshop, 1953), *Oxalis, New Directions Annual*

Harvey Bialy   P
81 W Market St
Red Hook, NY 12571
    Pubs: *The Broken Pot, Babalon 156* (Sandollar, 1975,
1970)

Rand Bishop   P
SUNY Oswego, English Dept, Oswego, NY 13126,
315-341-2616
    Pubs: *Black Warrior Rev, Sou'wester, Florida Rev, Red
Cedar Rev, Galley Sail Rev, Kansas Qtly*

Celia Bland 🎤 ✈   P
6 Friendship St
Tivoli, NY 12583
    Pubs: *Too Darn Hot: Anth* (Global City Rev/Persea Bks,
1998), *Alembic, Mudfish, 13th Moon, Snake Nation Rev,
Chain, Poet Lore, Pequod, Columbia Mag, Verse,
Pavement, New Poetry from Oxford, Washington Rev,
Madison Rev, Apalachee Qtly*

Pamela Wharton Blanpied   W
19 Pinnard St
Rochester, NY 14610, 716-473-5483
    Pubs: *Dragons: An Introduction to the Modern
Infestation* (Warner Bks, 1981)

Sarah W. Bliumis   P
8 Pheasant Dr
Armonk, NY 10504, 914-273-8324
    Pubs: *Spoon River Qtly, Ceilioh, Whetstone*

Janet Bloom   P
The Barn Mt Airy, 1 Hale Hollow Rd #3A,
Croton-on-Hudson, NY 10520, 914-271-0091
    Pubs: *APR, Poetry Now, NYQ, Parnassus, Teachers &
Writers Mag, Imagery Today*

Etta Blum   P
c/o Shrier, 397 Spruce Ln, East Meadow, NY 11554
    Pubs: *Poems* (Golden Eagle Pr, 1937), *Poetry, Paris
Rev, Nation, New Republic, Open Places*

(Bonnie Hoag) Bonnielizabethoag 🎤 ✈   PP
Dionondehowa Wildlife Sanctuary/School, 148 Stanton Rd,
Shushan, NY 12873-3215, 518-854-7764
    Pubs: *WRPI 91.5FM* (Troy, NY, 2000), *Interview with a
Young Crone* (Orion Pr, 1996), *Sand Paintings* (Muse
Room, 1995)

Audrey Borenstein 🎤 ✈   W
4 Henry Ct
New Paltz, NY 12561-3000
    Pubs: *Women of the 14th Moon* (Crossing Pr, 1991),
Paradise: Anth (Florida Fdn, 1994), *Messages from the
Heart, Medicinal Purposes Literary Rev, Oxalis, Albany
Rev, MacGuffin, North Dakota Qtly, Kansas Qtly,
Arkansas Rev, Albany Rev*

Emily Borenstein   P
189 Highland Ave
Middletown, NY 10940, 914-343-3796
  Pubs: *Night of the Broken Glass* (Timberline Pr, 1981),
Cancer Queen (Barlenmir Hse, 1979), *Aura Literary/Arts
Rev, Home Planet News, Pivot, Poet Lore, Response,
Webster Rev*

Martin Boris   W
Ghame Writing Corp, 1019 Northfield Ave, Woodmere, NY
11598, 516-374-2058
  Pubs: *Brief Candle* (Crown, 1990), *Woodridge, 1946*
(Ace, 1981), *Two & Two* (Ballantine, 1980)

Megan Boyd   P
PO Box 27
Sag Harbor, NY 11963, 516-725-9220
  Pubs: *Gathering to Deep Water* (Quay Bks, 1988), *New
Voices: Anth* (Acad of American Poets, 1984)

Maureen Brady 🎙 ✈   W
135 Winnie Rd
Mt Tremper, NY 12457
Internet: meb4444@prodigy.net
  Pubs: *Mom* (Alyson, 1998), *Daybreak* (Harper SF,
1991), *The Question She Put to Herself, Folly*
(Crossing Pr, 1987, 1982), *Pillow Talk 2: Anth* (Alyson,
2000), *Cabbage & Bones: Irish-American Women's
Fiction: Anth* (H Holt, 1997), *Feminary, Ikon*
Groups: G/L/B/T, Women

Anthony Brandt   P&W
54 High St
Sag Harbor, NY 11963, 516-725-1937
  Pubs: *The People Along the Sand: Three Stories, Six
Poems & a Memoir* (Canio's Edtns, 1992), *Prairie
Schooner, NYQ, Boulevard, TLS*

Kate Braverman   P&W
PO Box 794
Alfred, NY 14802
  Pubs: *Small Craft Warnings* (U Nevada Pr, 1998),
Wonders of the West, Squandering the Blue (Ballantine,
1993, 1990), *Postcard from August, Hurricane Warnings*
(Illuminati, 1990, 1987), *Palm Latitudes* (S&S, 1988)

Susan Breen   W
1 Riverview Ct
Irvington, NY 10533, 914-591-7841
  Pubs: *Kinesis, Kansas Qtly/Arkansas Rev, American
Literary Rev, North Dakota Qtly, Chattahoochee, New
Delta*

Wendy Brenner   W
150 Capen Rd
Brockport, NY 14420, 716-395-9159
  Pubs: *Large Animals in Everyday Life* (U Georgia Pr,
1996), *New Stories from the South: Anth* (Algonquin,
1995), *Ploughshares, Southern Exposure, Puerto del
Sol*

William Bronk   P
57 Pearl St
Hudson Falls, NY 12839
  Pubs: *Selected Poems* (New Directions, 1995),
Ourselves, The Mild Day (Talisman Hse, 1995, 1993),
Living Instead (North Point Pr, 1991)

Joseph E. Bruchac, III 🎙 ✈   P&W
PO Box 308
Greenfield Center, NY 12833-0308, 518-584-1728
Internet: nudatlog@earthlink.net
  Pubs: *Sacajawea, Between Earth & Sky* (HB, 2000,
1996), *No Borders* (Holy Cow Pr, 1999), *Dawn Land*
(Fulcrum Pub, 1993), *Green Mountains Rev, Kestrel,
Parabola, Gatherings, Puerto del Sol, Bullhead*
I.D.: Native American

Judith Bruder   W
132 Wagon Rd
Roslyn Heights, NY 11577
  Pubs: *Convergence* (Doubleday, 1993), *Going to
Jerusalem* (S&S, 1979)

Ira Beryl Brukner   P
123 Fayette St
Ithaca, NY 14850, 607-256-2114
  Pubs: *Questions, Short Poems, Water & Air* (Junction
Pr, 1998)

Felice Buckvar   W
43 Juneau Blvd
Woodbury, NY 11797, 516-692-5485
  Pubs: *Dangerous Dream* (Royal Fireworks Pr, 1998),
Ten Miles High (Morrow, 1981), *Happily Ever After*
(Zebra Bks, 1980), *Family Circle, Woman's Day,
Reader's Digest, Real People*

Frederick Henderson Buell 🎙 ✈   P
72 Amity Rd
Warwick, NY 10990, 914-258-6076
  Pubs: *Full Summer* (Wesleyan, 1979), *Theseus & Other
Poems* (Ithaca Hse, 1971), *Poetry, Hudson Rev, NER,
Little Mag, Kansas Qtly, Pembroke Mag, Southern Rev,
SW Rev*

Brio Burgess 🎙 ✈   PP&P
c/o Gail Tolley, 5 Cuyler St, Albany, NY 12202,
518-447-7448
  Pubs: *The Butcher's Block Volume 1: Anth*
(Butchershop Pr, 2000), *Street Kids & Other Plays:
Anth* (Angel Enterprises, 1995), *Outlaw Blues: Anth*
(Tawanna L. Brace Knowles, 1992), *Bay Area Poets
Anth, Poetalk, Open Mic, Bay Area Poets Coalition*
I.D.: Jewish, African-American. Groups: Hedonist, Adults

Michael Burkard P
313 E Hamilton Ave
Sherrill, NY 13461, 315-361-4822
    Pubs: *Entire Dilemma* (Sarabande Bks, 1998), *My Secret Boat* (Norton, 1990), *The Fires They Kept* (Metro Bk Co, 1986), *Paris Rev, APR, Epoch, Denver Qtly, Exquisite Corpse, Central Park, Salt Hill Jrnl, Volt, Plum Rev, Zone 3*

Gabrielle Burton 🎤 ✈ P&W
211 Le Brun Rd
Eggertsville, NY 14226, 716-835-5062
    Pubs: *Heartbreak Hotel* (Dalkey Archive Pr, 1999)

Frederick Busch 🎤 ✈ W
839 Turnpike Rd
Sherburne, NY 13460, 607-847-8646
Internet: fbusch@mail.colgate.edu
    Pubs: *The Night Inspector* (Ballantine, 2000), *Don't Tell Anyone* (Norton, 2000), *Girls* (Fawcett, 1998), *A Dangerous Profession* (St. Martin's, 1998), *The Children in the Woods* (Fawcett/Columbine, 1994)

Rebecca Busselle W
RR2, PO Box 270
Millerton, NY 12546, 518-789-3413
    Pubs: *An Exposure of the Heart* (Norton, 1999), *A Frog's-Eye View, Bathing Ugly* (Orchard Bks, 1990, 1989)

Don Byrd P
English Dept, SUNY Albany, 1400 Washington, Albany, NY 12222, 518-442-4055
    Pubs: *The Great Dimestore* (Station Hill Pr, 1986), *Technics of Travel* (Tansy-Zelot, 1984)

Charles Calitri W
30 Gristmill Ln
Halesite, NY 11743
    Pubs: *The Goliath Head, Father, Strike Heaven on the Face* (Crown, 1974, 1962, 1958)

Jimmie Gilliam Canfield P&W
Erie Community College/City Campus, 121 Ellicott St, Buffalo, NY 14203, 716-842-8676
    Pubs: *Pieces of Bread* (White Pine Pr, 1986), *Black Mountain 2 Rev, Earth's Daughters*

Joe Cardillo P
Hudson Valley Comm College, MRV 214, Troy, NY 12180, 518-270-7577
    Pubs: *Karate Lessons, Pulse* (Dutton/Penguin, 2000, 1996), *The Rock N' Roll Journals, No Surrender* (Stone Buzzard Pr, 1996, 1993), *Fine Madness, Crab Creek Rev, Sierra Madre Rev, Footwork, Lactuca*

Michael Carrino P
19 Guy Way, Apt B
Plattsburgh, NY 12901, 518-564-2134
    Pubs: *Some Rescues* (New Poets Series, 1994), *Green Mountains Rev, Hudson Rev, Poetry East, Slant, Calliope, Hayden's Ferry Rev*

Hayden Carruth P
RD 1, PO Box 128
Munnsville, NY 13409, 315-495-6665
    Pubs: *Collected Shorter Poems, 1946-1991* (Copper Canyon, 1992), *Tell Me Again How the White Heron Rises & Flies Across the Nacreous River at Twilight Toward the Distant Islands* (New Directions, 1991)

Shari Elaine Carter 🎤 ✈ PP
4677 N St Rd
Marcellus, NY 13108-9724, 315-673-1789
Groups: Women, Mentally Ill

Fran Castan 🎤 ✈ P
PO Box 1923
Amagansett, NY 11930, 631-267-8646
Internet: waters.edge@hamptons.com
    Pubs: *What Have You Lost* (Green Willow/Morrow, 1999), *The Widow's Quilt* (Canio's Edtns, 1996), *From Both Sides Now: Poetry of Vietnam: Anth* (Scribner, 1998), *The Seasons of Women: Anth* (Norton, 1995), *The Doll House Anth* (Pushcart, 1995), *Ms., Poetry Mag*

Alan Catlin 🎤 ✈ P
143 Furman St
Schenectady, NY 12304-1113, 518-372-5016
    Pubs: *Hair of the Dog That Bit Me, Killer Cocktails* (Four Sep Pub, 2000, 1997), *Celtic Twilight* (JVC Bks, 1999), *Shelley & the Romantics* (Adastra, 1994), *NYQ, Happy, Lucid Stone, Press, Poet Lore, Literary Rev, Pleiades*

Siv Cedering P&W
PO Box 800
Amagansett, NY 11930-0800, 516-267-8030
    Pubs: *Letters from an Observatory* (Karma Dog Edtns, 1998), *Letters from the Floating World* (U Pitt Pr, 1984), *The Blue Horse* (Clarion Bks, 1979), *Harper's, Ms., Georgia Rev, Paris Rev, Antaeus*

Elaine Rollwagen Chamberlain P
97 Springville Ave
Amherst, NY 14226, 716-837-0475
    Pubs: *Pictures from the Bee House* (White Pine Pr, 1978)

Lena London Charney P
PO Box 145
Mohegan Lake, NY 10547-0145, 914-528-5162
   Pubs: *Beyond Lament: Anth* (Northwestern U Pr, 1998),
   A Celebration of Poets: Anth (Poetry Guild, 1998), *The
   Color of Gold: Anth* (Golden Apple Pr, 1995), *We
   Speak for Peace: Anth* (KIT Pub, 1993), *Westchester
   Writer, Lucid Stone, Raconteur, Robin's Nest*

Robert Chatain P&W
PO Box 1770
Amagansett, NY 11930
   Pubs: *Touring Nam: The Viet Nam War Reader*
   (Morrow, 1985), *Best of TriQtly: Anth* (Washington Sq
   Pr, 1982)

Sanford Chernoff W
3 Laurel Ave
Glen Cove, NY 11542
   Pubs: *All Our Secrets Are the Same* (Norton, 1977),
   New Directions, The Qtly, Partisan Rev, Epoch

L. John Cieslinski ♀ ✈ P
8 Close Hollow Dr
Hamlin, NY 14464-9302, 716-964-2868
   Internet: johnmore@concentric.net
   Pubs: *Amelia, Pearl, Stone Country, Karamu, Negative
   Capability, Magical Blend, Black Bear Rev, Voices Intl,
   Sore Dove, Piedmont Literary Rev*

Josephine Clare P
435 Exchange St
Geneva, NY 14456, 315-789-9517
   Pubs: *Mammatocumulus* (Ocotillo Pr, 1977),
   Deutschland & Other Poems (North Atlantic Bks, 1974)

Barbara Moore Clarkson P
26 N Helderberg Pkwy
Slingerlands, NY 12159-9260, 315-474-3533
   Pubs: *The Flame Tree* (Basfal Bks, 1996), *Farewell to
   the Body* (The Word Works, 1991), *APR, Georgia Rev,
   Massachusetts Rev, Poetry, Salmagundi, NER*

Mickey Clement W
14 Bay Crest
Huntington Bay, NY 11743, 516-427-8316
   Pubs: *The Irish Princess* (Putnam, 1994)

Vince Clemente ♀ ✈ P
25 Cornell Rd
Sag Harbor, NY 11963, 516-725-8905
   Internet: clemente.ppc@yahoo.com
   Pubs: *Watergate along the Thames, The Shining Place*
   (Birnham Wood, 1999, 1992), *Place for Lost Children,
   Girl in the Yellow Caboose* (Karma Dog, 1996, 1992),
   American Lit Rev, South Carolina Rev
   I.D.: Italian-American

Arthur L. Clements P
English Dept, SUNY Binghamton, Binghamton, NY
13902-6000, 607-777-2168
   Pubs: *Dream of Flying* (Endless Mountains, 1994),
   Poetry of Contemplation (SUNY Pr, 1990), *Common
   Blessings* (Lincoln Springs, 1987), *Bellingham Rev,
   LIPS, Paterson Literary Rev, Poet, Poet Lore, Ruah*

Robert Cline W
Echo Ridge, Lake Lonely
Saratoga Springs, NY 12866, 518-584-5817
   Pubs: *The Tattooed Innocent & the Raunchy
   Grandmother* (Argos Hse, 1983)

Stephen Clorfeine ♀ ✈ PP
63 Cooper St
Accord, NY 12404-6200, 845-626-3096
   Internet: goldsun@ulster.net
   Pubs: *Beginning Again* (The Advocate Pr, 1994), *Out of
   the Catskills: Anth* (Bright Hill Pr, 1999), *Parabola,
   Shambhala Sun*
   I.D.: Jewish, Buddhist. Groups: Children, Seniors

Steven Coffman ♀ ✈ W
1874 Dombroski Rd
Dundee, NY 14837, 607-243-7561

Joan Cofrancesco P
306 Kasson Rd
Camillus, NY 13031, 315-487-5338
   Pubs: *Cat Bones in the Tree* (Hail Mary Pr, 1998),
   Walpurgis Night (San Diego Poets Pr, 1993), *Sinister
   Wisdom, Kalliope, Common Lives/Lesbian Lives, Aurora,
   Thesmophoria, Amazon Qtly, 13th Moon, Amelia, Poetry
   Flash*

Arlene Greenwald Cohen ♀ ✈ P
36 Colonial Ln
Bellport, NY 11713-2906, 631-286-5752
   Internet: agc55@earthlink.net
   Pubs: *PPA Lit Rev, Pen Woman, Electric Umbrella,
   Island Poets, LIQ, Taproot Jrnl, Oxalis, Wordworks, Live
   Poets Society, Pegasus*

Jonathan Cohen ♀ ✈ P
101-75 Sylvan Ave
Miller Place, NY 11764-2425, 631-331-9178
   Pubs: *Countersong to Walt Whitman* (Azul, 1993), *With
   Walker in Nicaragua* (Wesleyan U, 1984), *American
   Voice, Agni, City Lights Rev*

Jim Cohn P
Birdsfoot Farm, Star Rte, Box 138, Canton, NY 13617,
315-386-4852
   Pubs: *Prairie Falcon* (North Atlantic Bks, 1989), *Nada
   Poems: Anth* (Nada Pr, 1988), *Big Scream, Hanging
   Loose, Heaven Bone, Brief, Colorado North Rev,
   Exquisite Corpse*

Arthur Coleman   W
C. W. Post College, Greenvale, NY 11548
    Pubs: *A Case in Point, Petals on a Wet Black Bough*
(Watermill, 1979, 1973)

Zena Collier ♪ ✈   W
83 Berkeley St
Rochester, NY 14607-2207, 716-442-6941
Internet: zenacollier@juno.com
    Pubs: *Ghost Note* (Grove Weidenfeld, 1992), *A Cooler
Climate* (British American, 1990), *New Letters, SW Rev,
Southern Humanities Rev*

Billy Collins ♪ ✈   P
RD #2, Route 202
Somers, NY 10589-9802, 914-248-6613
    Pubs: *Picnic, Lightning, The Art of Drowning* (U
Pittsburgh Pr, 1998, 1995), *Questions About Angels*
(Morrow, 1991), *New Yorker, Paris Rev, Poetry*

Kathleen Collins ♪ ✈   W
19 Victory Knoll Path
Miller Place, NY 11764-1748, 631-331-8876
Internet: andercoll@aol.com
    Pubs: *The Romantic Naiad, Lovers in the Present
Afternoon* (Naiad Pr, 1993, 1984), *The Mountain, The
Stone* (Puckerbrush Pr, 1978)
Groups: G/L/B/T, Women

Frank Conaway   P&W
PO Box 257
Unionville, NY 10988
    Pubs: *Beloit, Tennessee Qtly, Chicago Rev, West
Branch, Poet & Critic, JAMA, Cumberland Poetry Rev,
Wordsmith, Gray's Sporting Jrnl*

Brenda Connor-Bey   PP
501 Old Kensico Rd, #2R
White Plains, NY 10603-3118, 914-686-8187
    Pubs: *Thoughts of an Everyday Woman—An Unfinished
Urban Folk Tail, New Rain 6 & 7* (Blind Beggar Pr,
1995, 1991), *Phatitude—Asian African Diaspora: Anth*
(Phatitude Literary Mag, 1998), *Essence*

Clark Coolidge   P
PO Box 420
New Lebanon, NY 12125
    Pubs: *Research* (Tuumba, 1982), *Mine: The One That
Enters the Stories* (The Figures, 1982)

Helen Cooper   P
English Dept, SUNY, Stony Brook, NY 11794,
516-632-7400
    Pubs: *13th Moon, City, Xanadu, Jrnl of New Jersey
Poets, U.S. 1, Gravida, 19th Century Fiction*

James Finn Cotter ♪ ✈   P
Mount Saint Mary College, Newburgh, NY 12550-3612,
914-561-0800
Internet: cotter@msmc.edu
    Pubs: *Hudson Rev, America, Commonweal, Thought*

Jack Coulehan ♪ ✈   P
4 Townsend Ct
Setauket, NY 11733, 516-689-6958
Internet: jcouleh@prevmed.som.sunysb.edu
    Pubs: *First Photographs of Heaven, The Knitted Glove*
(Nightshade Pr, 1994, 1991), *Blood & Bone: Poems By
Physicians: Anth* (U Iowa Pr, 1998), *JAMA, Kansas
Qtly, Prairie Schooner, Negative Capability, Wisconsin
Rev, Lancet*
Groups: Hospitals

Nancy Vieira Couto ♪ ✈   P
508 Turner Pl
Ithaca, NY 14850-5630, 607-273-8559
Internet: nvcouto@hotmail.com
    Pubs: *The Face in the Water, Pittsburgh Bk of
Contemporary Poetry: Anth* (U Pittsburgh Pr, 1990,
1993), *Second Word Thursdays: Anth* (Bright Hill Pr,
1999), *American Voice, Black Warrior Rev, Gettysburg
Rev, Salamander, Epoch*

Joseph Cowley ♪ ✈   W
69430 Main Rd
Greenport, NY 11944-2801, 516-477-8719
Internet: JoeCowley@cs.com
    Pubs: *Dust Be My Destiny* (Denlinger's, 2000), *Three
Novellas* (Morris, 1998), *The Chrysanthemum Garden*
(S&S, 1981), *Ohio Short Fiction: Anth* (Northmont Pub
Inc, 1995), *Prairie Schooner, Maryland Rev, New Story,
Facet, New Generation*

Timothy Craig   P
RR Box 150, Tug Hollow Farm
Shushan, NY 12873, 518-854-7601
    Pubs: *Advice to the Rain* (Grey Walls Pr, 1990), *Knots
& Fans* (Tamara, 1985), *London Mag, Pale Fire,
Xanadu*

Jack Crawford, Jr.   P
54 Joy Rd
Woodstock, NY 12498
    Pubs: *Poetry, Poetry NW, Virginia Qtly Rev,
Massachusetts Rev, Prairie Schooner, Chelsea*

Linda Crawford   W
PO Box 1814
Southold, NY 11971, 212-777-8439
    Pubs: *Vanishing Acts* (Putnam, 1983), *Something to
Make Us Happy* (S&S, 1978)

Robert Creeley 🎤 ✈   P&W
64 Amherst St
Buffalo, NY 14207, 7166452575 1018
Internet: creeley@acsu.buffalo.edu
    Pubs: *So There: Poems 1976-83, Life & Death* (New
    Directions, 1998, 1998), *Selected Poems* (U California
    Pr, 1991)

James Crenner   P
English Dept, Hobart & Wm. Smith Colleges, Geneva, NY
14456, 315-781-3361
    Pubs: *My Hat Flies on Again* (L'Epervier Pr, 1979), *The
    Airplane Burial Ground* (Hoffstadt, 1976)

Ida Maria Cruzkatz   P
24 Fairlawn Ave
Dobbs Ferry, NY 10522, 914-693-4473
    Pubs: *Bitterroot, New Collage, Tempest, MPR, Windless
    Orchard, Samisdat*

E. J. Cullen   P&W
23 Glen Washington Rd
Bronxville, NY 10708
    Pubs: *Our War & How We Won It* (Viking, 1987), *NAR,
    Western Humanities Rev, The Qtly*

Jack Curtis 🎤   P&W
Mildred Marmur Assoc LTC, 2005 Palmer Ave, Ste 127,
Larchmont, NY 10538, 408-667-2440
    Pubs: *Dawn Waters* (Spring Creek Pr, 1998), *Christmas
    in Calico* (Daybreak Pr, 1998), *Mercy Shot, Pepper
    Tree Rider* (Walker & Co, 1995, 1994), *The Fight for
    San Bernardo, Jury on Smoky Hill, Sheriff Kill* (Pocket
    Bks, 1993, 1992, 1991)

Michele Cusumano   P
Box 117
New Suffolk, NY 11956, 516-734-6090
    Pubs: *Just as the Boy Dreams of White Thighs Under
    Flowered Skirts* (Street Pr, 1981), *Zephyr*

Vincent T. Dacquino   W
38 Curry Rd
Mahopac, NY 10541, 914-628-9092
    Pubs: *Sybil Ludington: The Call to Arms* (Purple
    Mountain Pr, 2000), *Kiss the Candy Days Good-Bye*
    (Dell, 1983)

Kate Dahlstedt   P
10 Winthrop Ave
Albany, NY 12203, 518-438-1062
    Pubs: *Outpost, Brussels Sprout, Groundswell, Mildred,
    Voices*

Beatrice G. Davis 🎤 ✈   P
105 Ludwig Ln
East Williston, NY 11596
    Pubs: *Looking Out with an Inner Eye* (Small Poetry Pr,
    2000), *Mother of the Groom: Anth* (Distinctive Pub,
    1996), *Reflections of Life* (EPS Pub, 1996), *Taproot,
    Common Ground, Just Write, Remembrance, Pocket
    Inspirations, Writers Exchange*

George Davis   W
327 Claremont Ave
Mount Vernon, NY 10552
    Pubs: *Love, Black Love* (Doubleday, 1978), *Coming
    Home* (Random Hse, 1972), *Essence, Black World*

Marjorie De Fazio   P
254 Burrows Rd
Unadilla, NY 13849, 607-988-6358
    Pubs: *A Quiet Noise* (The Poet's Pr, 1972), *Out of the
    Catskills & Just Beyond: Anth* (Bright Hill Pr, 1997),
    Omen, Aphra, Michael's

Tatiana de la Tierra 🎤 ✈   P&W
PMB 104, 266 Elmwood Ave, Buffalo, NY 14222
    Pubs: *Pillow Talk II: Anth* (Alyson, 2000), *Latino
    Heretics: Anth* (Black Ice/FC 2, 1999), *Women on the
    Verge: Anth; Gay & Lesbian Poetry in Our Time: Anth*
    (St Martins Pr, 2000; 1988), *Mid-American Rev,
    Cimarron Rev, Tropic/Miami Herald Sunday Mag*
Lang: Spanish. I.D.: Hedonist, Latino/Latina. Groups:
Latino/Latina, G/L/B/T

Beltran De Quiros   W
PO Box 6134
Syracuse, NY 13217, 315-476-8994
    Pubs: *Narrativa y Libertad: Anth, La Otra Cara De La
    Moneda* (Ediciones Universal, 1996, 1984), *Los Unos,
    Los Otros y El Seibo '71*

Edward De Roo   W
7 Bacon St
St. James, NY 11780, 516-862-9397
    Pubs: *Rumble in the Housing Project* (Ace Bks, 1944),
    Nassau Qtly Rev, New Mexico Qtly

Regina deCormier   P&W
34 Sparkling Ridge
New Paltz, NY 12561
    Pubs: *Claiming the Spirits Within* (Beacon Pr, 1996),
    Two Worlds Walking (New Rivers Pr, 1994), *Hoofbeats
    on the Door* (Helicon Nine Edtns, 1993), *APR, Nation,
    Salmagundi, Poetry East, Nimrod*

Constance Dejong   W
131 S Broadway, #3
Nyack, NY 10960
    Pubs: *I.T.I.L.O.E.* (Top Stories, 1984), *Satyagraha*
    (Tianam Pr, 1983)

Samuel R. Delany   W
c/o Henry Morrison Inc, PO Box 235, Bedford Hills, NY
10507, 914-666-3500

Louise Budde DeLaurentis 🎤   P&W
983 Cayuga Heights Rd
Ithaca, NY 14850
    Pubs: *Outerbridge, Kalliope, Farm Jrnl, Plainswoman,
Frontiers*
I.D.: Women

Bruce D. Delmont   W
443 Wendel Ave
Buffalo, NY 14223-2211
    Pubs: *Art Voice, MDA Chronicle, The Villager, Buffalo
Mag, Poetry Forum Short Stories*

Robert DeMaria 🎤 ✈   W
106 Vineyard Pl
Port Jefferson, NY 11777, 631-928-3460
Internet: rdemaria@portjeff.net
    Pubs: *The White Road* (Permanent Pr, 2000), *That
Kennedy Girl* (Vineyard Pr, 1999), *Stone of Destiny*
(Ballantine, 1985), *New Letters, Antaeus, Florida Rev*

Mary Russo Demetrick   P&W
345 Buckingham Ave
Syracuse, NY 13210-3313, 315-476-9876
    Pubs: *Italian Notebook, First Pressing* (Hale Mary Pr,
1995, 1994), *Hey!: Anth* (Durland Alternative Pr, 1998),
Malachite & Agate: Anth (Grove Pr, 1997), *Word of
Mouth: Anth* (Crossing Pr, 1990), *Asheville Poetry Rev,
Footwork*

Carl Dennis   P
49 Ashland Ave
Buffalo, NY 14222, 716-886-1331
    Pubs: *Ranking the Wishes, Meetings with Time*
(Penguin, 1997, 1992), *The Outskirts of Troy, The Near
World* (Morrow, 1988, 1985)

Mark Dery   P&W
19 White Ave
Nyack, NY 10960
    Pubs: *Two Men Meet on a Beach* (Broadside; Atticus
Pr, 1982), *EFQ, Frank, Red Light Blue Light*

Rachel Guido deVries   P
PO Box 228
Cazenovia, NY 13035-0228, 315-655-8020
    Pubs: *How to Sing to a Dago, The Voices We Carry:
Anth* (Guernica Edtns, 1996, 1994), *Tender Warriors*
(Firebrand Bks, 1986), *Voices in Italian Americana,
Frontiers, Yellow Silk*

Robb Forman Dew   W
Miriam Altschuler Literary Agency, 5 Old Post Rd, Red
Hook, NY 12571, 914-758-9408
    Pubs: *The Family Heart* (Addison-Wesley, 1994), *The
Time of Her Life* (Morrow, 1984), *Dale Loves Sophie to
Death* (FS&G, 1982)

Katherine Dewart   P
333 Ellis Hollow Creek Rd
Ithaca, NY 14850, 607-272-8548

Bob Dial   P
15 Callaghan Blvd
Ballston Lake, NY 12019-2641
    Pubs: *Gulf Coast, Ledge, MacGuffin, Chiron Rev,
Writer, Plastic Tower*

Anthony DiFranco   W
Suffolk Community College, 533 College Rd, English Dept,
Selden, NY 11784, 516-451-4159
    Pubs: *Ardent Spring* (Bantam, 1986), *Prize Stories: O.
Henry Awards: Anth* (Doubleday, 1986), *Four Quarters,
NAR*

Arthur Dobrin   P
613 Dartmouth St
Westbury, NY 11590, 516-997-8545
    Pubs: *Angles & Chambers* (CCC, 1990), *Out of Place*
(Backstreet, 1982)

Anthony J. Dolan   P&W
69 Sheryl Cres
Smithtown, NY 11787, 516-724-1859

Lynn Domina   P
RR2 Box 21
Delhi, NY 13753, 607-746-7857
    Pubs: *Corporal Works* (Four Way Bks, 1995), *Marlboro
Rev, Carolina Qtly, Indiana Rev, Poetry NW, Prairie
Schooner, SPR*

George Drew 🎤 ✈   P
PO Box 298
Poestenkill, NY 12140, 518-283-1339
    Pubs: *So Many Bones* (Rarus Pr, 1997), *Toads in a
Poisoned Tank* (Tamarack, 1986), *Poetry NW, Qtly
West, Salmagundi, The Qtly, Texas Rev*

Joseph Duemer   P
School of Liberal Arts, Clarkson Univ, Potsdam, NY
13699, 315-262-2466
    Pubs: *Static* (Owl Creek Pr, 1996), *Customs* (U Georgia
Pr, 1987), *APR, Iowa Rev, NER, Boulevard, Mss.,
Tampa Rev, Tar River Poetry*

Peter Kane Dufault 🎤 ✈   P
56 Hickory Hill Rd
Hillsdale, NY 12529, 518-672-4897
Internet: www.webjogger.net/poetrydufault
  Pubs: *Looking in All Directions* (Worple Pr, 2000),
  *Memorandum to the Age of Reason, New Things Come
  Into the World* (Lindisfarne, 1993, 1989), *Norton Anth of
  Poetry* (Norton, 1996), *New Yorker, New Republic,
  Atlantic, Spectator*
Groups: Adults

T. Dunn   P&W
PO Box 4853
Ithaca, NY 14852
  Pubs: *Range of Motion* (Squeaky Wheel Pr, 1993),
  *Asylum Annual, Black Buzzard Rev, Voices Intl, Snail's
  Pace Rev, Synaesthetic, Tight, Nixon*

Mary Durham 🎤   P
PO Box 2856
Poughkeepsie, NY 12603-8856, 914-473-0405
  Pubs: *Crazy Ladies, Wise Women: Anth* (Crazy Ladies
  Pr, 1999), *Almanac, Outloud, Poetry Peddler, Home
  Planet News, Kaatskill Life*
Groups: Seniors

M. D. Elevitch 🎤 ✈   W
Box 604
Palisades, NY 10964, 914-365-3772
  Pubs: *New Directions 33: Anth* (New Directions, 1976),
  Green Eternal Go (Foolscap Pr, 1991), *Americans at
  Home* (First Person, 1976), *Chelsea, Transatlantic Rev,
  TriQtly, Chicago Rev, Audience, Pacific Coast Jrnl,
  Trace, Oasis*

Richard Elman   W
PO Box 216
Stony Brook, NY 11790-0216
  Pubs: *Tar Beach* (Sun & Moon Pr, 1991), *Disco Frito*
  (Peregrine Smith, 1988), *Tikkun, Raritan, Antaeus,
  Georgia Rev, Newsday, Exquisite Corpse*

Virginia Elson   P
Smith Pond Rd, RD 2
Avoca, NY 14809, 607-566-8355
  Pubs: *And Echoes for Direction, Where in the Sun to
  Stand* (State St Pr, 1987, 1982), *Atlantic, Literary Rev,
  Prairie Schooner, Poetry NW, Yankee*

P. A. Engebrecht   W
112 Cliffside Dr
Canandaigua, NY 14424-8808, 716-396-2166
  Pubs: *Promise of Moonstone* (Beaufort, 1983), *Under
  the Haystack* (Thomas Nelson, 1973), *Yankee*

Judith Sue Epstein   P
1859 Slaterville Rd
Ithaca, NY 14850, 607-277-4205
  Pubs: *Keeping Score* (Ithaca Hse, 1975), *Epoch,
  Hanging Loose, The Trojan Horse, The Grapevine*

Amelia Etlinger   PP
44 Barney Rd
Clifton Park, NY 12065

Graham Everett 🎤 ✈   P
PO Box 772
Sound Beach, NY 11789-0772
Internet: everett@adelphi.edu
  Pubs: *Corps Calleux* (Street, 2000), *The Doc Fayth
  Poems* (Mongrel, 1998), *Minus Green Plus*
  (Breeze/Street, 1995), *Minus Green* (Yank This Pr,
  1992), *Caprice, LIQ, 4x4, Exquisite Corpse*

Pat Falk   P
Nassau Community College, English Dept, Garden City,
NY 11530-6793, 516-572-7185
  Pubs: *In the Shape of a Woman* (Canios Edtns, 1995),
  13th Moon, Poets On, LIQ, Thema, Wordsmith

John Fandel   P
609 Palmer Rd, Apt 2-L
Yonkers, NY 10701
  Pubs: *Ranging & Arranging* (Roth, 1990), *A Morning
  Answer* (Forward Movement Pub, 1988)

Patricia Farewell 🎤 ✈   P
PO Box 198
Pleasantville, NY 10570-0198, 914-769-7228
  Pubs: *Waltzing on Water: Anth* (Dell, 1989), *Desire:
  Anth* (St. Martin's Pr, 1980), *Chelsea, Green Mountains
  Rev, Formalist*

Raymond Federman   P&W
46 Four Seasons W
Buffalo, NY 14226, 716-835-9611
  Pubs: *The Twofold Vibration, Smiles on Washington
  Square* (Sun & Moon, 1998, 1995), *To Whom It May
  Concern* (Fiction Collective 2, 1990)

Eric Felderman   P&W
PO Box 194
Pelham, NY 10803
  Pubs: *Two Men & a Kangaroo Go Into a Bar*
  (Portmanteau Edtns, 1990)

Irving Feldman 🎤 ✈   P
SUNY Buffalo, English Dept, Buffalo, NY 14260,
716-885-4122
Internet: feldman@acsu.buffalo.edu
  Pubs: *Beautiful False Things* (Grove, 2000), *The Life &
  Letters* (U Chicago, 1994), *All of Us Here, Teach Me
  Dear Sister, New & Selected Poems* (Viking Penguin,
  1986, 1983, 1979)
Lang: Spanish

Jim Feraca   W
1428 Midland Ave
Bronxville, NY 10708
    Pubs: *Light Year Anth* (Bits Pr, 1985), *Green Hse,*
    Rapport, Transatlantic Rev

Mary Ferrari   P
288 Weaver St
Larchmont, NY 10538, 914-834-2132
    Pubs: *The Poet Exposed: Anth* (St. James, 1986),
    Aphros, B-City 3, New Nation

Anne Lathrop Fessenden ♀ ✈   P
PO Box 35
Willow, NY 12495-0035
    Pubs: *Newark Rev, Woodstock Times*

Sally A. Fiedler   P
154 Morris Ave
Buffalo, NY 14214-1610
    Pubs: *Eleanor Mooseheart* (Weird Sisters Pr, 1992), *To*
    Illinois, With Love (Tyler School of Art, 1975), *APR*

Jeanne Finley ♀ ✈   P&W
46 Pinewood Ave
Albany, NY 12208-2712, 518-438-8728
    Pubs: *Anth of Mag Verse & Yearbook of American*
    Poetry (Monitor, 1988), *North Country: Anth* (Greenfield
    Rev Pr, 1986), *New Myths, Little Mag, Visions Intl*
Groups: Adults, Libraries

Mike Finn   P
930 Comfort Rd
Spencer, NY 14883, 607-277-2345
    Pubs: *And Death Is Watching, A Man Mistaking His*
    Mother for His Ego (Poortree Bks, 1996, 1992),
    Mothering, Audit/Poetry, Choice, Second Growth, Not
    Man Apart

Adam D. Fisher ♀ ✈   P
11 Media Ln
Stony Brook, NY 11790-2811, 631-751-6606
Internet: adfisher@erols.com
    Pubs: *God's Garden* (Behrman Hse, 1999), *Dancing*
    Alone (Birnham Wood, 1993), *An Everlasting Name*
    (Behrman Hse, 1992), *LIQ, West Hills Rev, MPR, NAR,*
    CCAR Jrnl
Groups: Jewish

Harrison Fisher   P
91 N Pine Ave, #3
Albany, NY 12203, 518-482-2402
    Pubs: *Rhomboid Hairdo* (Frank Doom Bks, 1990),
    World Prefix (Edge Bks, 1989), *Room 5, o.blek*

Lou Fisher ♀   W
12 Julie Dr
Hopewell Junction, NY 12533
    Pubs: *The Blue Ice Pilot* (Warner Bks, 1986), *Suntop 8*
    (Dell, 1978), *Mississippi Rev, Other Voices, Crescent*
    Rev, Florida Rev, MacGuffin

Charles Fishman ♀ ✈   P
2956 Kent Rd E
Wantagh, NY 11793-2435, 516-826-4964
Internet: charllzz@optonline.net
    Pubs: *The Firewalkers* (Avisson Pr, 1996), *The Death*
    Mazurka, Blood to Remember: Anth (Texas Tech U Pr,
    1989, 1991), *Georgia Rev, Southern California Anth,*
    New Letters, NER, Country of Memory (Rattapallax Pr,
    2001)
I.D.: Jewish

Gregory Fitz Gerald   P&W
32 Cherry Dr
Brockport, NY 14420, 716-637-9372
    Pubs: *October Blood & Other Stories* (Spectrum Pr,
    1993), *The Hidden Quantum* (Hobaugh Pubs, 1993),
    The Druze Document (Cliffhanger Pr, 1987), *Galaxy,*
    Aberrations, Red Herring, Fantastic Worlds, Show &
    Tell

Jane Flanders   P
1 Hazen St
Pelham, NY 10803-2408, 914-738-3776
    Pubs: *Timepiece* (U Pitt, 1988), *The Students of Snow*
    (U Massachusetts Pr, 1982), *Prairie Schooner, New*
    Yorker, Paris Rev, Nation, New Republic, Poetry

Peggy Flanders ♀ ✈   P
4956 St John Dr
Syracuse, NY 13215-1245, 315-488-8077
    Pubs: *Comstock Rev, Queen's Qtly, Radiology,*
    Poetpourri, Voices Intl, Open Window, Pegasus, Poets
    On, South Florida Rev

Lisa Fleck   P
18 Glendale Rd
Ossining, NY 10562
    Pubs: *Musical Chairs in the Garden* (1st East Coast
    Theatre & Publishing Co, 1987)

Sheldon Flory ♀ ✈   P
6981 Rte 21
Naples, NY 14512
    Pubs: *A Winter's Journey* (Copper Beech, 1979), *Arvon*
    Intl Poetry Competition Anth (Arvon, 1990),
    Puckerbrush, Graffiti Rag, Ekphrasis, Natl Prison
    Reform Association News, New Yorker, Poetry, Iowa
    Rev, Seneca Rev, Mangrove, Zone 3, Gulf Coast
Lang: Spanish, French

Jim Flosdorf 🎤 ✈   P
18 Lillian Ln
Troy, NY 12180-4700, 518-272-6210
Internet: flosdj@sage.edu
   Pubs: *My Father Was Shiva* (Ablex, 1994), *North
   Country: Anth* (Greenfield Rev Pr, 1986), *Groundswell,
   Voices*

Gertrude Ford   W
3 Midwood Cross
Roslyn, NY 11576-2414
   Pubs: *81 Sheriff Street* (Frederick Fell, 1981)

Joan Elizabeth Ford   P
151 Woodward Ave
Buffalo, NY 14214, 716-886-7136
   Pubs: *Intrepid, Moody Street Irregulars, Swift Kick,
   Earth's Daughters*

Peter Fortunato 🎤 ✈   P
172 Pearsall Pl
Ithaca, NY 14850
Internet: www.lightlink.com/fortuna
   Pubs: *Letters to Tiohero* (Grapevine Pr, 1979), *A Bell
   or a Hook* (Ithaca Hse, 1977), *Nimrod, Seneca Rev,
   Yellow Silk, Voices in Italian Americana*
I.D.: Italian-American. Groups: Spiritual/Religious

Walt Franklin   P
1205 County, Rte 60
Rexville, NY 14877, 607-225-4592
   Pubs: *The Singing Groves* (Timberline Pr, 1996),
   Uplands Haunted by the Sea (Great Elm Pr, 1992),
   The Wild Trout (Nightshade Pr, 1991), *Poem, Grain,
   Pig*

Darren Franz 🎤   P&W
733 Stowe Ave
Baldwin, NY 11510, 516-377-1479
   Pubs: *Crimson, Gathering Darkness, Nightmares, Outer
   Darkness*

Mary Lamb Freeman   P
182 Oxford Ave
Amherst, NY 14226
   Pubs: *Ripples, Crowdancing, Midwest Poetry Rev,
   Room of Our Own, Green Feather, Dream Intl Qtly*

Emanuel Fried   W
1064 Amherst St
Buffalo, NY 14216-3606, 716-873-4131
   Pubs: *The Un-American* (Springhouse Edtns, 1992), *Big
   Ben Hood, Elegy for Stanley Gorski* (Labor Arts Bks,
   1988, 1986), *Dramatists Qtly*

Bruce Jay Friedman   W
PO Box 746, Holly Ln
Watermill, NY 11976, 212-691-8077
   Pubs: *The Current Climate, About Harry Towns, Stern*
   (Atlantic Monthly Pr, 1989, 1989, 1989)

Lee Frisbee   P
91 Bev Ln
Brockport, NY 14420-1236, 716-637-5672
   Pubs: *Driftwood East, Encore, English Jrnl, Fiesta, New
   Infinity Rev, Rufus*

Carol Frost 🎤 ✈   P
959 County Hwy 7
Otego, NY 13825, 607-988-7170
Internet: frostc@hartwick.edu
   Pubs: *Love & Scorn, Venus & Don Juan, Pure* (TriQtly
   Bks, 2000, 1996, 1994), *Chimera* (Peregrine Smith,
   1990), *Day of the Body* (Ion Bks, 1986), *APR, Atlantic,
   NER, TriQtly, Partisan Rev, Ploughshares, Kenyon Rev,
   Shenandoah, Southern Rev, Volt*

Richard Frost   P
959 Co Hwy 7
Otego, NY 13825, 607-988-7170
   Pubs: *Neighbor Blood* (Sarabande Bks, 1996), *The
   Family Way* (Devil's Millhopper Pr, 1994), *Jazz for Kirby*
   (State St Pr, 1990), *Paris Rev, Poetry, Georgia Rev*

Gerard Furey   W
HGHS 70 Roaring Brook Rd
Chappaqua, NY 10514, 914-238-3911
   Pubs: *Pittsburgh Mag, St. Anthony Messenger, Ambit*

Enid Futterman 🎤 ✈   W
661 Rte 23
Craryville, NY 12521, 518-851-6340
Internet: EnidF@aol.com
   Pubs: *Bittersweet Journey* (Viking, 1998)
I.D.: Jewish. Groups: Women

Judith Gaberman   W
PO Box 135
South Salem, NY 10590
   Pubs: *In Summertime It's Tuffy* (Bradbury Pr, 1977)

Elizabeth Gaffney   P
English Dept, Westchester Community College, 75
Grasslands Rd, Valhalla, NY 10595, 914-785-6194
   Pubs: *SPR, College English, Wordsmith, Descant, Wind,
   New Voices, The Smith, Dark Horse*

Diane Gallo 🎤 ✈   P&W
846 County Rd 37
Mount Upton, NY 13809, 607-764-8139
Internet: gallod@norwich.net
   Pubs: *Point of Departure* (Pudding Hse Pr, 2000), *The
   Neighbor's Dog Howls* (Madwoman's Daughter Pr,
   1996), *Creating the Literature Portfolio: Anth* (NTC Pub
   Group, 1996), *Asheville Poetry Rev, Phoebe*
Groups: Abuse Victims, Women

Beatrice Ganley 🎤 ✈   P
4095 East Ave
Rochester, NY 14618-3732, 716-586-1000
Internet: bganley@ssjrochester.org
   Pubs: *The Sea of Connection* (Heirloom Pub, 1996),
   *Sisters Today, Broomstick, Lake Effect, Wyoming,
   Verity, Muse Reader*
Groups: Children, Seniors

Eric Gansworth 🎤 ✈   P&W
Niagara County Community College, 3111 Saunders
Settlement Rd, Sanborn, NY 14132, 716-614-6715
Internet: onondaga@localnet.com
   Pubs: *Nickel Eclipse: Iroquois Moon, Indian Summers*
   (Michigan St U Pr, 2000, 1998), *Nothing But the Truth:
   Anth* (Prentice Hall, 2000), *Children of the Dragonfly* (U
   Arizona Pr, 2000), *Word Thursdays II: Anth* (Bright Hill,
   1999)

Eugene K. Garber 🎤 ✈   W
13 Empire Circle
Rensselaer, NY 12144-9319, 518-434-3294
Internet: egarber1@nycap.rr.com
   Pubs: *The Historian* (Milkweed Edtns, 1994), *Norton
   Anth of Contemporary Fiction* (Norton, 1989, 1988),
   Paris Rev

Lewis Gardner   P
16 Cedar Way
Woodstock, NY 12498, 914-679-4090
   Pubs: *Columbia, Firewood, U.S. 1 Worksheets, Ethical
   Society*

Sandra Gardner 🎤 ✈   P
16 Cedar Way
Woodstock, NY 12498
   Pubs: *Mutant Mule Rev: Anth* (Finishing Line Pr, 1999),
   Freedom's Just Another Word: Anth (Outrider Pr, 1998),
   Bobbe Meisehs by Shayneh Maidelehs: Anth (Herbooks,
   1989), *I Name Myself Daughter & It Is Good: Anth*
   (Sophia Bks, 1981), *Dark Horse, U.S. 1 Worksheets*

Beatrix Gates   P
PO Box 28
Greenport, NY 11944, 516-477-0729
   Pubs: *Shooting at Night* (Granite Pr, 1980), *Naming the
   Waves: Anth* (Crossing Pr, 1990), *Kenyon Rev, North
   Dakota Qtly, Nation, Women's Rev of Bks, CutBank,
   Nimrod*

Thomas Gavin   W
Univ Rochester, English Dept, Rochester, NY 14627,
716-244-8052
   Pubs: *Breathing Water* (Arcade, 1994), *The Last Film of
   Emile Vico* (Viking, 1986), *Kingkill* (Random Hse, 1977),
   Icarus, Prairie Schooner, Georgia Rev, TriQtly

Ruth Geller   W
270 Potomac Ave
Buffalo, NY 14213, 716-881-5391
   Pubs: *Triangles, Nice Jewish Girls: Anth* (Crossing Pr,
   1984, 1984), *Ms., Sojourner*

Willard Gellis   P&W
57 Seafield Ln
Bay Shore, NY 11706
   Pubs: *Die Metal* (Big Easy Pr, 1996), *Bronco Junky*
   (Wild Strawberry Pr, 1994), *Penny Dreadful Rev, Beast
   Qtly, Erotica, Meta-4, LIQ, UFO*

Kathleen Gemmell 🎤 ✈   P
209 1/2 Pleasant St
Ithaca, NY 14850-5603, 607-273-6511
Internet: ksg3@cornell.edu
   Pubs: *A Common Bond* (Allegheny Pr, 1976),
   *Bookpress, Bitterroot, Blackbird Circle, Pembroke Mag,
   Poet Lore, South Carolina Rev, Voices Intl*

William Gifford   W
English Dept, Vassar College, Box 344, Poughkeepsie, NY
12604-0344, 914-471-5132
   Pubs: *Colorado Qtly, QRL, Apalachee Qtly, Peregrine,
   Open City*

Mary Gilliland 🎤 ✈   P
Writing Program, Cornell Univ, 172 Pearsall Pl, Ithaca, NY
14850, 607-273-6637
Internet: mg24@cornell.edu
   Pubs: *Gathering Fire* (Ithaca Hse, 1982), *Poetry,
   Southern California Anthology, Nimrod, Seneca Rev,
   Spoon River Qtly, Yellow Silk, Seattle Rev*

Dugan Gilman   P
201 Berkeley Dr
Syracuse, NY 13210, 315-472-0484

Gail Godwin   W
7 Laura Ln
Woodstock, NY 12498

Rebecca T. Godwin   W
PO Box 211
Poestenkill, NY 12140-0211
   Pubs: *Keeper of the House* (St. Martin's Pr, 1994),
   Private Parts (Longstreet Pr, 1991), *Paris Rev, Iris: A
   Jrnl about Women, Crescent Rev, South Carolina Rev*

Myra Goldberg W
Sarah Lawrence College, Writing Program, Bronxville, NY
10708, 914-337-0700
    Pubs: *Whistling & Other Stories* (Zoland Bks, 1993),
Representations of Motherhood: Anth (Yale U Pr, 1994),
Ploughshares, NER, Tikkun, Feminist Studies

Gail Kadison Golden 🎤 ✈ P
18 Zabella Dr
New City, NY 10956
Internet: peacepoet@aol.com
    Pubs: *Visions, Korone, Embers, Footwork, Karamu,
Outerbridge, Milieu*
I.D.: Jewish, Feminist

Barry Goldensohn 🎤 ✈ P
11 Seward St
Saratoga Springs, NY 12866, 518-584-7962
    Pubs: *Dance Music* (Cummington Pr, 1992), *The
Marrano* (Natl Poetry Fdn, 1988), *Poetry, Yale Rev,
Agenda, Salmagundi, Agni*

Lorrie Goldensohn 🎤 ✈ P
11 Seward St
Saratoga Springs, NY 12866
    Pubs: *East Long Pond* (Cummington Pr, 1997), *The
Tether* (L'Epervier, 1982), *Dreamwork* (Porch, 1980),
Salmagundi, Ploughshares, Poetry

Cynthia R. Golderman P
5 Edison Ave
Albany, NY 12208, 518-438-7360
    Pubs: *Oh, That We Would, At This Last Breach...The
Facility* (Cerulean Pr, 1986, 1986)

Barbara Goldowsky 🎤 ✈ P&W
PO Box 663
Southampton, NY 11969-0663, 631-283-2044
Internet: Goldowsky@aol.com
    Pubs: *Restless Spirits, Ferry to Nirvana & New Poems*
(Amereon Ltd, 1992, 1991), *Whelks Walk Rev, Fiction
Rev, Embers, Confrontation, The Round Table,
Brookspring '92, Caprice*

Gloria Goldreich 🎤 ✈ W
356 Marbledale Rd
Tuckahoe, NY 10707-1716, 914-961-2688
    Pubs: *That Year of Our War, Years of Dreams,
Mothers* (Little, Brown, 1994, 1992, 1989), *Commentary,
Midstream, Redbook, McCall's, Moment*
Lang: Hebrew. I.D.: Jewish

Ann Goldsmith P
494 Woodward Ave
Buffalo, NY 14214, 716-833-1879
    Pubs: *Scarecrow Poetry* (Ashland Poetry Pr, 1994),
Child's Blue Wall (Orchard Pr, 1982), *Poets at Work:
Anth* (Just Buffalo Literary Center, 1995), *The Qtly,
Helicon Nine, Earth's Daughters, Pembroke Mag*

Catherine Gonick P
48 Fair St #C4
Cold Spring, NY 10516-3009, 914-265-2775
Internet: gm@highlands.com
    Pubs: *Pivot, Plain Dealer Mag, New Boston Rev, Zone,
City, Mothering*

Stephen Goodwin W
PO Box 47
Bedford, NY 10506-0047
    Pubs: *The Blood of Paradise* (Dutton, 1979), *Kin* (H&R,
1975), *Country Jrnl, Yankee*

Marea Gordett P
1 Hunter's Run Blvd
Cohoes, NY 12047
    Pubs: *Freeze Tag* (Wesleyan U Pr 1984), *The Pushcart
Prize V: Anth* (Pushcart Pr, 1980), *Georgia Rev,
Ploughshares, Antioch Rev*

Fred Gordon W
35 Carriage Rd
Great Neck, NY 11024
    Pubs: *Benjamin Grabbed His Glicken & Ran* (H&R,
1971)

Kirpal Gordon P
c/o Steven Hirsch, Heaven Bone Pr, PO Box 486,
Chester, NY 10918, 718-797-3321
    Pubs: *Dear Empire State Building, This Ain't No
Ballgame* (Heaven Bone Pr, 1990, 1988)

Darcy Gottlieb 🎤 P
67 Orchard Beach Blvd
Port Washington, NY 11050-1427
    Pubs: *Matters of Contention* (Aesopus, 1979), *No
Witness But Ourselves* (U Missouri Pr, 1973), *Beyond
Lament: Anth* (Northwestern U Pr, 1998), *For Neruda,
for Chile: Anth* (Beacon Pr Bks, 1975)

C. D. Grant 🎤 ✈ P
24 Bowbell Rd
White Plains, NY 10607-1106, 914-683-6792
Internet: 71211.3721@compuserve.com
    Pubs: *Images in a Shaded Light, Keeping Time, New
Rain Vol. 9: Anth* (Blind Beggar Pr, 1986, 1981, 1999),
Black Masks Mag, Suburban Styles, Mentor, Essence
I.D.: African-American

Marcia Grant P
15 Miller Hill Dr
La Grangeville, NY 12540
    Pubs: *Connecticut River Rev, Oxalis, Z Misc, Bitterroot,
Alura Poetry Qtly, Midwest Poetry Rev, Archer*

Jerome Greenfield   W
English Dept, SUNY New Paltz, New Paltz, NY 12561,
914-257-2720
   Pubs: *Wilhelm Reich vs. the USA* (Norton, 1974), *The
   Chalk Line* (Chilton Bks, 1963), *Midstream*

Linda Greenwald 🎤 ✈   P&W
47 Elm St
Cobleskill, NY 12043-1021, 518-234-7162
Internet: greenwl@cobleskill.edu
   Pubs: *Word Thursdays II: Anth* (Bright Hill Pr, 1999),
   Heart Music: Anth (the unmade bed, 1988), *The Stories
   We Hold Secret: Anth* (Greenfield Rev Pr, 1986),
   Comstock Rev

Eamon Grennan 🎤 ✈   P
Vassar College, Box 352, Poughkeepsie, NY 12604-0352,
914-437-5655
   Pubs: *Relations: New & Selected Poems, So It Goes,
   As If It Matters* (Graywolf, 1998, 1995, 1992), *What
   Light There Is & Other Poems* (North Point Pr, 1989),
   New Yorker, Kenyon Rev, Poetry

Ronald Gross   P
17 Myrtle Dr
Great Neck, NY 11021, 516-487-0235

Susan Anne Gubernat 🎤 ✈   P
English Dept Dr, Nassau Community College, One
Education, Garden City, NY 11530, 516-572-7185
Internet: guberns@sunynassau.edu
   Pubs: *Flesh* (Helicon Nine Ednts, 1999)

Jorge Guitart 🎤 ✈   P
Univ Buffalo, 910 Clemens Hall, Buffalo, NY 14260-4620,
716-645-2191
Internet: guitart@acsu.buffalo.edu
   Pubs: *Film Blanc* (Meow Pr, 1996), *Foreigner's
   Notebook* (Shuffaloff Bks, 1993), *Exquisite Corpse, First
   Intensity, Tin Fish, Kiosk*
Lang: Spanish. I.D.: Latino/Latina, Cuban. Groups: Children

Robert Guzikowski   P
900 Pratt Dr
Vestal, NY 13850-3843
   Pubs: *Letters, Grub Street, Tightrope*

Jennie Hair   P
10 Oxford St
Northport, NY 11768-1952, 516-261-4924
   Pubs: *An Old Century: A New Testament* (Birnham
   Wood, 1996), *A Sisterhood of Songs* (Canio Edtns,
   1994), *LIQ*

Joan Halperin   P
23 Hastings Landing
Hastings-On-Hudson, NY 10706
   Pubs: *Connecticut River Rev, Poet Lore, Modern
   Images, Pudding, Goblets, Confrontation, NYQ, Echoes,
   Southern Poetry Jrnl, Tar River Poetry, Cimarron Rev*

Janet Hamill 🎤 ✈   P
24 Chaucer Ct
Middletown, NY 10941, 914-692-7263
   Pubs: *Lost Ceilings* (Telephone Bks, 1999), *Nostalgia of
   the Infinite* (Ocean View Bks, 1992), *Will Work for
   Peace: Anth* (zeropanik pr, 1999), *Living with the
   Animals: Anth* (Faber & Faber, 1994), *Longshot,
   Gargoyle, A Gathering of the Tribes*

Jill Hammer   P&W
108 Mt View Rd
Fishkill, NY 12524
   Pubs: *Response, Encodings, Harp-Strings, Writing for
   Our Lives, Jewish Spectactor, Glass Cherry, Snowy
   Egret, Lilith*

Louis Hammer 🎤 ✈   P&W
PO Box 9
Old Chatham, NY 12136-0009, 518-794-8327
   Pubs: *Poetry at the End of the Mind & Postmodern
   Poems* (Sachem Pr, 1992), *The Mirror Dances*
   (Intertext, 1986)

Mac Hammond   P
314 Highland Ave
Buffalo, NY 14222, 716-882-1642
   Pubs: *Mappamundi, New & Selected Poems* (Bellevue,
   1989), *Cold Turkey* (Swallow, 1969), *The Horse Opera*
   (Ohio State, 1966)

Emily Hanlon   W
RD 1, Chapman Rd
Yorktown, NY 10598
   Pubs: *Petersburg* (Putnam, 1988), *Love Is No Excuse*
   (Bradbury Pr, 1981)

Gail Hanlon 🎤 ✈   P
100 Edge of Woods
Southampton, NY 11968
Internet: gailhanlon@aol.com
   Pubs: *Best American Poetry: Anth* (Scribner, 1996),
   Iowa Rev, Poetry Flash, Calyx, Poet Lore

Tom Hanna   P
210 Eddy St
Ithaca, NY 14850, 607-255-3001
   Pubs: *New Letters Reader 2: Anth* (U Missouri, 1984),
   From A to Z: Anth (Swallow, 1981), *Epoch, New
   Letters, West Coast Rev, The Stone, Latitudes*

Lisa A. Harris P&W
5111 Perry City Rd
Trumansburg, NY 14886, 607-387-6977
  Pubs: *Low County Stories* (Bright Hill Pr, 1997), *Flight*
  (Words & Spaces Pr, 1995), *Feminism 3: Anth* (HC,
  1996), *Karamu, Fennel Stalk*

Muriel Harris Weinstein 🎤 P&W
644 Pauley Dr
West Hempstead, NY 11552-2225
  Pubs: *Sidewalks: Anth* (Sidewalks, 1996), *Listening Eye,
  Nassau Rev, Outerbridge, Voices Intl, Ethereal Dances,
  Nexus, The Cape Rock*
I.D.: Health-Related. Groups: Seniors, Children

Gayle Ellen Harvey 🎤 ✈ P
11 Shaw St
Utica, NY 13502, 315-735-4194
Internet: gaylelen1@juno.com
  Pubs: *White Light of Trees* (Permafrost, 1995),
  Flower-Of-Turning-Away (Geryon Pr, 1992), *Working the
  Air* (Winter Creek Pr, 1991), *Painted Hills, Yellow Silk,
  Poetry NW, Zone 3, Atlanta Rev, Intl Qtly, Exquisite
  Corpse, Bitter Oleander*
Groups: Prisoners

William Hathaway P
243 Maple Ave
Saratoga Springs, NY 12866
  Pubs: *Churlsgrace, Look Into the Heart* (U Central
  Florida, 1992, 1988), *Gettysburg Rev, Southern Rev,
  NAR*

Brooks Haxton P
21 Bloomingdale Rd
White Plains, NY 10605, 914-949-7123
  Pubs: *Traveling Company* (Knopf, 1989), *Dead
  Reckoning* (Story Line Pr, 1989), *APR, NER, Paris Rev*

Deborah C. Hecht 🎤 ✈ W
114 Burr's Ln
Dix Hills, NY 11746-6030, 516-491-3042
Internet: hecht@tourolaw.edu
  Pubs: *A More Perfect Union: Anth* (St. Martin's Pr,
  1998), *in*tense, Fine Print, American Scholar, Good
  Housekeeping, Women's World, Colorado North,
  Nantucket Rev, The Writer*
Groups: Seniors, Lawyers

Safiya Henderson-Holmes P&W
438 Columbus Ave, #1
Syracuse, NY 13210
  Pubs: *Madness & a Bit of Hope* (Harlem River Pr,
  1990), *Confirmation* (Quill Pr, 1985), *Ikon*

William C. Henderson 🎤 ✈ W
PO Box 380
Wainscott, NY 11975-0380, 631-324-9300
  Pubs: *Tower* (FSG, 2000), *Her Father* (Faber & Faber,
  1995), *The Kid That Could* (Chipps & Co, 1990), *His
  Son* (Norton, 1981)

Rick Henry W
Dept of English, SUNY Potsdam, Potsdam, NY 13676,
315-267-2043
  Pubs: *Airfish: Anth* (Catseye Bks, 1993), *Between C&D:
  Anth* (Pemguine Bks, 1998), *Short Story, Acorn,
  Raconteur, Salthouse*

Lance Henson P
c/o Joseph Bruchac, 2 Middle Grove Rd, Greenfield
Center, NY 12833
  Pubs: *A Motion of Sudden Aloneness* (American Native
  Pr Archives, 1991), *Another Distance* (Point Rider's Pr,
  1991), *Poetry East, Pig Iron, Tamaqua*

William Herrick W
36 Dunham Hollow Rd
East Nassau, NY 12062
  Pubs: *Bradovich, That's Life, Kill Memory* (New
  Directions, 1990, 1985, 1983), *Hermanos* (Second
  Chance Pr, 1969), *Hudson Valley Mag, The New
  Leader,*

Bill Herron P&W
c/o Joel Herron, Pine Ridge Dr, Wappingers Falls, NY
12590
  Pubs: *Rituals of Our Time* (Carolina Wren, 1980),
  Couvade Notebooks (Salthouse, 1980)

William Heyen 🎤 ✈ P
142 Frazier St
Brockport, NY 14420, 716-637-3867
  Pubs: *Crazy Horse in Stillness* (BOA Edtns, 1996), *The
  Host: Selected Poems 1965-1990* (Time Being Bks,
  1990), *Contemporary American Poets* (HM, 2000),
  TriQtly, Ontario Rev, Southern Rev

Catherine Hiller W
528 Munro Ave
Mamaroneck, NY 10543, 914-698-5328
  Pubs: *Skin: Sensual Tales* (Carroll & Graf, 1997),
  California Time, 17 Morton Street (St. Martin's Pr, 1993,
  1990), *Redbook, Penthouse, State Mag*

Michael Thomas Hinkemeyer W
35 Cove Dr
Manhasset, NY 11030, 516-365-8761
  Pubs: *The Order of the Arrow* (TOR, 1993), *The
  Substitute Teacher* (Pocket, 1993), *Soulcatchers*
  (Warner, 1990)

Edward D. Hoch   W
2941 Lake Ave
Rochester, NY 14612, 716-865-1179
   Pubs: *The Ripper of Storyville, Diagnosis: Impossible*
   (Crippen & Landru, 1997, 1996), *Year's Best Mystery &*
   Suspense Stories: Anth (Walker, 1995), *Ellery Queen*
   Mystery Mag, Antaeus

Barbara Hoffman   P&W
1330 1st St
W Babylon, NY 11704
   Pubs: *Each in Her Own Way: Anth* (Queen of Swords
   Pr, 1994), *Catholic Girls: Anth* (Penguin, 1992), *Poets*
   On, BPJ, Gryphon, Aura, Minnesota Rev

Roald Hoffmann 🎤 ✈   P
Chemistry Dept, Cornell Univ, Baker Laboratory, Ithaca,
NY 14853-1301, 607-255-3419
Internet: rh34@cornell.edu
   Pubs: *Memory Effects* (Calhoun Pr, 1999), *Gaps &*
   Verges, The Metamict State (U Central Florida Pr,
   1990, 1987), *Paris Rev, Prairie Schooner, Yale Rev,*
   Chelsea, Grand Street, Raritan

Kay Hogan   W
154 East Ave
Saratoga Springs, NY 12866-2636
   Pubs: *North Country* (Greenfield Pr, 1986), *Library*
   Bound: Anth (Saratoga Springs Library, 1996), *Bless*
   Me, Father: Anth, Catholic Girls: Anth (Penguin, 1995,
   1993), *Spiritual Life, Complete Woman, Descant, Jrnl of*
   Irish Literature, Long Pond Rev

Susan Holahan   P&W
370 Mulberry St
Rochester, NY 14620-2514, 716-244-8052
   Pubs: *Sister Betty Reads the Whole You* (Gibbs Smith,
   1998), *Bitches & Sad Ladies: Anth* (Harper's, 1975),
   Crazyhorse, Seneca Rev, American Letters, Spoon
   River Rev, Women's Rev of Bks, Central Park

Barbara D. Holender   P
263 Brantwood Rd
Snyder, NY 14226
   Pubs: *Is This the Way to Athens?* (QRL, 1996), *Ladies*
   of Genesis (Jewish Women's Resource Ctr, 1991),
   Helicon 9, Prairie Schooner, Literary Rev

Dennis Tilden Holzman   P
13 Cherry Ave
Delmar, NY 12054, 518-463-8173
   Pubs: *Greenfield Rev, Berkeley Poets Cooperative,*
   Washout Rev

George J. Honecker   P
453 Mineola Blvd
Williston Park, NY 11596, 516-746-3120
   Pubs: *Glass Bottom Boat* (John Street Pr, 1987),
   Rampike, Fiction Intl, Sun & Moon, Little Mag

Akua Lezli Hope 🎤 ✈   P
PO Box 33
Corning, NY 14830, 607-936-8367
Internet: artfarm@servtech.com
   Pubs: *Embouchure Poems on Jazz & Other Musics*
   (Artfarm Pr, 1995), *Dark Matter: Anth* (Warner Bks,
   2000), *Bluelight Corner: Anth* (Three Rivers Pr, 1998),
   Sisterfire: Anth (HC, 1994), *Obsidian, Eyeball, Bluecage,*
   Hambone, African American Rev
I.D.: African-American, Women

Michael F. Hopkins   P
18 Stanislaus St
Buffalo, NY 14212, 716-895-9749
   Pubs: *A Kind of Twilight* (Smiling Cat Pub, 1995), *The*
   Fourth Man (Textile Bridge Pr, 1981)

Mikhail Horowitz 🎤 ✈   P
PO Box 3443
Kingston, NY 12402, 914-246-7441
Internet: mhorowitz@totalsports.net
   Pubs: *The Opus of Everything in Nothing Flat*
   (Outloud/Red Hill, 1993), *Big League Poets* (City Lights,
   1978), *Outlaw Bible of American Poetry: Anth*
   (Thunder's Mouth Pr, 1999), *Elysian Fields Qtly*

Nat Hough   P&W
306 Lake Ave
Ithaca, NY 14850
   Pubs: *Ithaca Women's Anthology* (NYSCA, 1992), *About*
   Chickadees: Anth (Raspberry Pr, 1982), *Willow Springs,*
   High Rock Rev

Tom House 🎤 ✈   W
PO Box 856
Wainscott, NY 11975-0856, 631-907-0071
Internet: tomhouse1@aol.com
   Pubs: *Men on Men: Anth* (Plume, 2000), *Best American*
   Gay Fiction: Anth (Little, Brown, 1998, 1997), *NAR,*
   Harper's, Chicago Rev, Gettysburg Rev, Western
   Humanities Rev, Puerto del Sol, Other Voices,
   Christopher Street
I.D.: G/L/B/T. Groups: G/L/B/T

Ben Howard   P
English Division, Alfred Univ, Alfred, NY 14802,
607-871-2256
   Pubs: *Midcentury* (Ireland; Salmon Pub, 1997), *The*
   Pressed Melodeon (Story Line Pr, 1996), *The Other*
   Shore (Passim Edtns, 1991), *Lenten Anniversaries:*
   Poems 1982-89 (Cummington Pr, 1990), *Poetry,*
   Sewanee Rev, Iowa Rev, Chelsea, New Hibernia Rev,
   Seneca Rev

Eric Machan Howd   P
106 Fayette St
Ithaca, NY 14850-5261
   Pubs: *Origami* (Sometimes Y Pubs, 1993), *Blaming*
   Icarus (Crane Pr, 1992), *Yankee, Calapooya Collage,*
   Sun Dog, Chaminade Lit Rev, Round Table

Edward Hower 🎙 ✈ W
1409 Hanshaw Rd
Ithaca, NY 14850
Internet: edwardhower@hotmail.com
   Pubs: *Queen of the Silver Dollar, Night Train Blues*
   (Permanent Pr, 1997, 1996), *The Pomegranate Princess*
   (Wayne State U Pr, 1991), *Southern Rev, Epoch,*
   Transition
Groups: Prisoners

Joan Howlett P
14 High St
Norwood, NY 13668, 315-353-2713
   Pubs: *Variations of White, Against the Grain: Anth, A*
   Song of Myself: Anth (CSS, 1986, 1988, 1987)

Paul Humphrey 🎙 ✈ P
2329 S Union St
Spencerport, NY 14559-2229, 716-352-4421
   Pubs: *Bedford Intro to Lit: Anth* (St. Martin's Pr, 1998),
   Ladies First: Anth (Tow Path Bks, 1996), *Saturday*
   Evening Post, Cosmopolitan, Good Housekeeping,
   Ladies Home Jrnl, True Love
Groups: College/Univ

William Humphrey W
RD #1, Box 139
Hudson, NY 12534

Johanna Hurwitz 🎙 ✈ W
10 Spruce Pl
Great Neck, NY 11021, 516-829-6205
   Pubs: *Peewee's Tale* (North South, 2000), *One Small*
   Dog (HC, 2000), *Faraway Summer, Spring Break, Even*
   Stephen, A Llama in the Family, School Spirit, Ali Baba
   Bernstein (Morrow Junior Bks, 1998, 1997, 1996, 1994,
   1994, 1992)

Rose Graubart Ignatow W
PO Box 1458
East Hampton, NY 11937-0995
   Pubs: *Surplus Love & Other Stories, Down the*
   American River (Copper Beech Pr, 1985, 1979)

Suzanne Potter Ironbiter P
7 Fay Ln
South Salem, NY 10590
   Pubs: *Devi* (Yuganta Pr, 1987), *Cumberland Poetry*
   Rev, Puerto del Sol

Charles F. Itzin 🎙 ✈ P
PO Box 159
Fairhaven, NY 13064-0159, 315-947-5522
Internet: itzinhouse@redcreek.net
   Pubs: *New Letters, Visions, Greenfield Rev, NW Rev,*
   Little Mag, Nimrod, Phoenix

Anita Jacobs W
3641 Regent Ln
Wantagh, NY 11793, 516-731-8188
Internet: caasi3641@aol.com
   Pubs: *Where Has Deedie Wooster Been All These*
   Years (Delacorte Pr, 1981)

Karoniaktatie Alex Jacobs P
RFD 1, Box 116
Bombay, NY 12914-9718, 518-358-4460
   Pubs: *New Voices from the Longhouse: Anth*
   (Greenfield Rev, 1988), *Returning the Gift: Anth* (Sun
   Tracks, 1995), *Akwesasne Notes, Semiotext(e), Tribes*

Robert Jagoda W
547 Lucas Ave Ext
Kingston, NY 12401-8215, 914-331-5473
   Pubs: *Nobody Wants My Resume: Anth* (McGraw-Hill,
   1979), *A Friend in Deed: Anth* (Norton, 1976)

Phyllis Janowitz P
English Dept, Cornell Univ, Goldwin Smith Hall, Ithaca, NY
14853, 607-257-3279
   Pubs: *Temporary Dwellings* (U Pitt Pr, 1988), *Visiting*
   Rites (Princeton, 1982), *Epoch, Free Lunch, Verve,*
   River Styx, The Qtly, The Bridge, Ithaca Women's Anth

Joachim W
c/o Costas Parpas, 23 Cullen Dr, East Northport, NY
11731, 516-758-7647

Polly Joan P
604 Taylor Pl
Ithaca, NY 14850, 607-277-3738
   Pubs: *The Living Alternative* (Human Sciences Pr,
   1985), *No Apologies* (Women Writing Pr, 1975)

Bobby Johnson P
110 Normandy Ave
Rochester, NY 14619, 716-436-5929
   Pubs: *Mr. Parker Songbook, Clarissa Street Project*
   (Johnson, 1991, 1985)

Bonnie L. Johnson P
2316 Shadagee Rd
Eden, NY 14057
   Pubs: *The Jungle Book* (Textile Bridge Pr, 1983), *Fine*
   China, Twenty Years of Earth's Daughters: Anth
   (Springhouse Edtns, 1993), *Room of Our Own,*
   Serendipity Pr

Darren Johnson 🎙 ✈ P&W
PO Box 672
Water Mill, NY 11976-0672, 631-369-0518
Internet: rocketusa@delphi.com
   Pubs: *Jazz Poems* (So It Goes/U Pitt, 1996), *I Do Not*
   Prefer to Have Sex (NPI, 1994), *Hampton Shorts, LIQ,*
   U-Direct, Plastic Tower, Impetus

Kate K. Johnson 🎤   P
Sarah Lawrence College, Bronxville, NY 10708,
914-666-5274
    Pubs: *Wind Somewhere, & Shade, This Perfect Life*
    (Miami U Pr, 2001, 1993), *When Orchids Were Flowers*
    (Dragon Gate, 1986), *Ploughshares, The Sun, Salt Jrnl,*
    Luna, Bloomsbury Rev, Decade, Poetry, Ironwood,
    Tendril, One Meadway

Nora Johnson   W
2 Villa Ln
Larchmont, NY 10538-1227, 914-834-1682
    Pubs: *Perfect Together* (Dutton/Wm. Abrahams, 1991),
    Uncharted Places, Tender Offer (S&S, 1988, 1985)

Ina Jones   P&W
12 Cleveland Ave
Cobleskill, NY 12043
    Pubs: *Womenstory: Memoir: Anth* (Sing Heavenly
    Muse!, 1997), *Out of the Catskills & Just Beyond: Anth,*
    Word Thursdays: Anth (Bright Hill Pr, 1997, 1995),
    West Branch, Cape Rock

Barbara Jordan 🎤 ✈   P
5149 Old West Lake Rd
Honeoye, NY 14471, 716-229-4365
Internet: micaamber@aol.com
    Pubs: *Trace Elements* (Penguin, 1998), *Channel*
    (Beacon Pr, 1990), *Atlantic, Sulfur, Agni, New Yorker,*
    Paris Rev

Susan Jordan   P
39 Beaufort St
Rochester, NY 14620, 716-271-1589
    Pubs: *Crystal Spirit* (Snakesisters Pr, 1988), *Benzene*
    (Truck Pr, 1977), *Ikon, And*

Pierre Joris 🎤 ✈   P
English Dept, SUNY Albany, Albany, NY 12202,
518-442-4085
    Pubs: *Poasis* (Wesleyan U Pr, 2001), *Breccia* (Edtns
    Phi/Station Hill, 1987)
Lang: French, German

Laurence Josephs   P
c/o Wilolea Farm, 992 Locust Grove Rd, Greenfield
Center, NY 12833
    Pubs: *New & Selected Poems* (Copley Pub Group,
    1988), *Salmagundi, St. Johns Rev, Southern Rev*

Frank Judge   P
Syndicated News Service, 232 Post Ave, Rochester, NY
14619-1398, 716-328-2144
    Pubs: *The Flickering Dark* (Exit Pr, 1994), *24*
    Exposures (Writers & Bks, 1988), *The Spy's Handbook,*
    Two Voices (Center Pr, 1987, 1985)

Franz Kamin   W
c/o Station Hill Press, Station Hill Rd, Barrytown, NY
12507, 612-227-0225
    Pubs: *Scribble Death* (Station Hill Pr, 1986), *Hotel*
    (Prospect Bks, 1986)

Paul Kane 🎤 ✈   P
8 Big Island
Warwick, NY 10990-2408, 914-986-8522
Internet: kane@vassar.edu
    Pubs: *Drowned Lands* (U South Carolina Pr, 2000),
    The Farther Shore (George Braziller, 1989), *Paris Rev,*
    New Republic, Grand Street, Sewanee Rev, Western
    Humanities Rev, Shenandoah, Poetry

Ro'ee Bob Kaplan 🎤 ✈   P
774 Greenbelt Pkwy W
Holbrook, NY 11741-4213, 631-472-3416
    Pubs: *Poetry Today, New Thought Jrnl, Rosemaryes,*
    All Pocket Poetry, Creations

Mary Karr 🎤 ✈   P&W
English Dept, Syracuse Univ, Syracuse, NY 13244,
315-443-2173
    Pubs: *Viper Rum, The Devil's Tour* (New Directions,
    1998, 1993), *Abacus* (Wesleyan U Pr, 1987), *Seneca*
    Rev, Poetry, Parnassus, Willow Springs, Ploughshares,
    Columbia

Peter Katopes   P&W
c/o Univ College, Adelphi Univ, Garden City, NY 11530
    Pubs: *The Vietnam Reader: Anth, The Human*
    Condition in the Modern Age: Anth (Kendall/Hunt, 1991,
    1991)

Miriam Polli Katsikis   P&W
200 E Bayberry Rd
Islip, NY 11751
    Pubs: *St. Anthony Messenger, Primavera, Buffalo*
    Spree, Playgirl, Plainswoman, Echoes, Earthwise Poetry
    Jrnl, Anemone, Cimarron, Ripples

Rita Katz   P
8 Greentree Rd
Mineola, NY 11501, 516-742-4320
    Pubs: *Breaking In: New Writer's Series: Anth* (New
    Writer's Series Pubs, 1993), *The Alembic, Piedmont Lit*
    Rev, LIQ, Midwest Poetry Rev

Merilee Kaufman   P
3256 Elliott Blvd
Oceanside, NY 11572
    Pubs: *Sarah's Daughters Sing: Anth* (K'Tav Pub Hse,
    1990), *Confrontation, Nassau Rev, Slugfest, Live Poets,*
    Messages from the Heart

Stuart Kaufman P
English Dept, Nassau Community College, 1 Education Dr,
Garden City, NY 11530, 516-572-7185
   Pubs: *Fast Friends* (Minerva Pr, 1996), *The Ultimate
   Cigar & Other Poems* (First East Coast Pubs, 1984),
   Verse, Mudfish, Poetry, Privates, Kingfisher

Tim Keane W
305 Rich Ave
Mt Vernon, NY 10552
   Pubs: *Qtly West, NW Rev, First Intensity, American
   Writing, William & Mary Rev*

Terrance Keenan ♀ ✈ P
305 DeForest Rd
Syracuse, NY 13214-2002, 315-446-0612
Internet: txkeenan@library.syr.edu
   Pubs: *St. Nadie in Winter* (Charles Tuttle Pubs, 2001),
   Practicing Eternity (Basfal Bks, 1996), *Herbal* (Great
   Elm Pr, 1988), *Georgia Rev, Poetry Now, Epoch,
   Ironwood*
I.D.: Zen Buddhist. Groups: Prisoners, Recovering Addicts

Bill Keith P
Howland Public Library, 313 Main St, Beacon, NY 12508,
914-831-1134
   Pubs: *Pictographs* (Left Hand Pr, 1996), *Wingdom*
   (Runaway Spoon Pr, 1992), *Writers Forum, African
   American Rev, Poems*

Emily Keller P
9354 Rivershore Dr
Niagara Falls, NY 14304-4449, 716-283-0606
   Pubs: *Anth of Mag Verse & Yearbook of American
   Poetry* (Monitor Bks, 1984), *Kansas Qtly, Hollins Critic,
   Confrontation, Piedmont Lit Rev, McCall's, San Jose
   Studies, Poetry Now, Images*

Dave Kelly P
PO Box 53
Geneseo, NY 14454, 716-243-0987
   Pubs: *The Sumal Reader* (MSU Pr, 1996), *Talking to
   Myself* (State Street Pr, 1994), *Northern Letter*
   (Nebraska Rev Pr, 1980), *The Paris Rev Anth* (Norton,
   1990)

Robert Kelly P&W
Bard College, Annandale-on-Hudson, NY 12504,
914-758-6549
   Pubs: *Red Actions: Selected Poems 1960-93* (Black
   Sparrow Pr, 1995), *Queen of Terrors* (McPherson &
   Co, 1994), *Conjunctions, Notus, Ashen Meal, Grand
   Street*

Sylvia Kelly W
PO Box 53
Geneseo, NY 14454, 716-243-0987
   Pubs: *Conjunctions: 14* (Collier-Macmillan, 1989),
   MacGuffin, Redstart Plus, Transpacific

Maurice Kenny ♀ ✈ P
PO Box 1029, 55 Riverside Dr
Saranac Lake, NY 12983, 518-891-5865
   Pubs: *Tortured Skins & Other Fictions* (MSU Pr, 2000),
   Backward to Forward, Tekonwatonti (White Pine Pr,
   1997, 1992), *Wooster Rev, House Organ, River Styx,
   Cimarron, Adirondack Life, Amicus*

Milton Kessler P
25 Lincoln Ave
Binghamton, NY 13905, 607-772-1217
   Pubs: *The Grand Concourse* (Mss., 1993), *Riding First
   Car* (Sulfur 31, 1993), *On Prejudice: Anth* (Doubleday,
   1993), *Poems on the Underground, Walt Whitman Qtly*

Siri Narayan Kaur Khalsa ♀ ✈ P&W
460 Ashland Ave
Buffalo, NY 14222-1502, 716-881-5504
Internet: siri_naray@aol.com
   Pubs: *Dancing with the Guru* (White Lion Pr, 1996),
   Unconditional Love, Life Junkies: Anth (Textile Bridge,
   1992, 1991)

Robert Kimm ♀ ✈ P
RR2
Marcellus, NY 13108-9623
   Pubs: *Goin' Nowhere Sunday* (Bull Thistle Pr, 1996),
   *Nerve Cowboy, Rhino, Apocalypse, Camellia, Fat
   Tuesday, Plastic Tower, Hiram Poetry Rev, Connecticut
   Poetry Rev, Prairie Schooner*
Lang: German

Joan Payne Kincaid P
132 Du Bois Ave
Sea Cliff, NY 11579-1826, 516-671-2375
Internet: jpaynekincaid@juno.com
   Pubs: *Skinny Dipping* (Bogg Pubs, 1998),
   Understanding the Water (Kings Estate Pr, 1997), *Art of
   Haiku: Anth* (New Hope Intl, 2000), *Confrontation: Anth*
   (Long Island U Pr, 2000), *The Qtly: Anth* (Random
   Hse, 1990), *Crosscurrents, Oyez, Black River Qtly*

Judith Kitchen P
35 College St
Brockport, NY 14420, 716-637-0023
   Pubs: *In Short* (Norton, 1996), *Perennials* (Anhinga,
   1986), *Georgia Rev, Gettysburg Rev, Prairie Schooner,
   Seneca Rev*

Jon Klimo P
82 Main Ave
Sea Cliff, NY 11579, 516-671-5480

Henry Korn W
Guild Hall of East Hampton, 158 Main St, East Hampton,
NY 11937
   Pubs: *Marc Chagall* (Artists Ltd Edtns, 1985), *Brooklyn
   College Rev, Unmuzzled Ox, Congress Monthly, Staten
   Island Advance, Connoisseur*

Allen Kovler   P
90 Grandview Ave Ext
Catskill, NY 12414, 518-943-9479
  Pubs: *Prairie Smoke: Anth* (Pueblo Poetry Project,
  1990), *Groundswell, Look Quick*

David Kowalczyk   P&W
716 Lafayette Ave
Buffalo, NY 14222-1448
Internet: sladeadamsson23@yahoo.com
  Pubs: *Stealing the Sky* (Last Peso Pr, 1999), *Bless Me,
  Father: Anth* (Penguin/Plume, 1994), *A Gentle
  Metamorphosis* (Full Court Pr, 1993), *Entelechy, Oxalis,
  Maryland Rev, Albany Rev, Crazyquilt, Buffalo News,
  Cold Mountain Rev, riversedge*

Lynn Kozma   P
165 W Islip Rd
West Islip, NY 11795, 516-587-6479
  Pubs: *Catching the Light* (Pocahontas Pr, 1989),
  *Phases of the Moon, If I Had My Life to Live Over:
  Anth, When I Am an Old Woman: Anth* (Papier-Mache,
  1994, 1992, 1991), *Dumb Beautiful Ministers: Anth*
  (Birnham Wood, 1997), *Color Wheel, Xanadu*

Eric Kraft   W
PO Box 1830
Sag Harbor, NY 11963
  Pubs: *Leaving Small's Hotel* (Picador, 1998), *At Home
  with the Glynns, What a Piece of Work I Am, Where
  Do You Stop, Little Follies, Herb 'N' Lorna* (Crown,
  1995, 1994, 1992, 1992, 1988)

Thomas Krampf   P
4611 Gile Hollow Rd
Hinsdale, NY 14743, 716-557-2518
  Pubs: *Shadow Poems, Satori West* (Ischua Bks, 1997,
  1987), *Subway Prayer & Other Poems* (Morning Star
  Pr, 1976)

Norbert Krapf 🎤 ✈   P
134 Willow St
Roslyn Heights, NY 11577-1216, 516-299-2391
Internet: www.krapfpoetry.com
  Pubs: *Bittersweet Along the Expressway* (Waterline Bks,
  2000), *Somewhere in Southern Indiana, Blue-Eyed
  Grass* (Time Being Bks, 1997, 1993), *Poetry, American
  Scholar, Ontario Rev*

Nancy Kress   W
50 Sweden Hill Rd
Brockport, NY 14420, 716-637-2339
  Pubs: *Oaths & Miracles* (St. Martin's Pr, 1996),
  Beggars & Choosers (TOR, 1994), *Omni, Asimov's Sci
  Fi, Analog, Writer's Digest*

Gary Krist   W
166 Colabaugh Pond Rd
Croton-on-Hudson, NY 10520
  Pubs: *Bone by Bone* (Harcourt Brace, 1994), *The
  Garden State* (Vintage, 1989), *Boulevard, Tikkun, The
  Qtly, Hudson Rev, Ladies' Home Jrnl*

Mindy Kronenberg   P
9 Garden Ave
Miller Place, NY 11764, 516-331-4118
  Pubs: *Dismantling the Playground* (Birnham Wood,
  1994), *I Am Becoming the Woman I've Wanted: Anth*
  (Papier-Mache Pr, 1994), *MPR, Hawaii Rev, LIQ, North
  Atlantic Rev, Confrontation*

Lawrence Kucharz   P
International Audiochrome, PO Box 1068, Rye, NY 10580
Internet: intaudiocr@aol.com
  Pubs: *Poesie Sonore Internationale* (Edtns Jean-Michel
  Place, 1979), *Dramatika, Assemblings, Against Infinity*

Lesley Kuhn   P
58 18th Ave
Sea Cliff, NY 11579
  Pubs: *West Wind Rev, Innisfree, Footwork, Waterways,
  Black Buzzard Rev, Poets On, Metis, North Shore,
  Women's Newspaper*

Carol Scarvalone Kushner 🎤 ✈   W
4 Lore Ln
Red Hook, NY 12571-2310, 914-758-2014
  Pubs: *Crazyquilt Qtly, Passages North, Esprit,
  Italian-Americana*

A. LaFaye   W
PO Box 262
Chazy, NY 12921, 518-846-8761
  Pubs: *The Year of the Sawdust Man, Strawberry Hill,
  Nissa's Place, Dad?,* (S&S, 1999), *Edith Shay* (Viking,
  1998)

Billy Lamont   PP&P
Other Perspective Management, PO Box 284, Northport,
NY 11702
  Pubs: *Into the 21st Century* (CD), *The Gallery of Light*
  (National Post Modern Pubs, 1998, 1994)

Pedro M. Lastra   P
Dept of Hispanic Languages, SUNY Stony Brook, Stony
Brook, NY 11794-3371
  Pubs: *Noticias Del Extranjero* (Chile; Editorial Univ,
  1992), *Travel Notes/Notas de Viaje* (La Yapa Editores,
  1991)

Lynn Lauber   W
112 Paradise Ave
Piermont, NY 10968, 914-359-4382
  Pubs: *21 Sugar Street* (Norton, 1993), *White Girls*
  (Vintage Contemporaries, 1991)

Ann Lauterbach P
Ruth & David Schwab Prof of Literature, Bard College, Annandale-on-Hudson, NY 12504
Pubs: *Clamor* (Viking/Penguin, 1991), *How Things Bear Their Telling* (France; Collective Generation, 1990), *Conjunctions, o.blek, Ploughshares*

Denize Lauture 🎤 ✈ P
St. Thomas Aquinas College, Rte 340, Sparkill, NY 10976, 914-398-4132
Pubs: *Running the Road to ABC* (S&S, 1996), *Father & Son* (Putnam/Grosset Group, 1993), *Caribbean Connections: Anth* (Networks of Educators, 1998), *Litté Réalité* (Etudes Francaises, 1998), *Callaloo, Litoral, Presence Africaine, Black American Literary Forum*
Lang: French, Spanish. Groups: Children, Haitian

Dorianne Laux 🎤 ✈ P
BOA Editions, 260 East Ave, Rochester, NY 14604
Internet: dlaux@darkwing.uoregon.edu
Pubs: *Smoke, What We Carry* (BOA Edtns, 2000, 1994), *Kenyon Rev, Southern Rev, DoubleTake, Zyzzyva, APR, American Voice*
I.D.: Women

Patrick Lawler P&W
College of Environmental Science, Writing Project, Moon LLRC, Syracuse, NY 13210, 315-451-3161
Pubs: *A Drowning Man Is Never Tall Enough* (U Georgia, 1990), *Passages North, Southern Humanities Rev, Central Park, APR, Iowa Rev, Ironwood, Nimrod*

Beverly Lawn P
Adelphi Univ, Garden City, NY 11530, 516-877-4020
Pubs: *Throat of Feathers* (Pleasure Dome Pr, 1979), *New Letters, Xanadu, Poetry Rev, Live Poets #4*

Naomi Lazard P
61 Pantigo Rd
East Hampton, NY 11937, 516-324-6104
Pubs: *Lives Through Literature* (Macmillan, 1990), *The True Subject* (Princeton U Pr, 1987), *Ordinances* (Owl Creek Pr, 1984), *A Book of Luminous Things: Anth* (HB, 1996), *New Yorker, Harper's, Frank, Solo*

John Leax P
Houghton College, Houghton, NY 14744, 716-567-9464
Pubs: *Standing Ground, Country Labors, Nightwatch* (Zondervan, 1991, 1991, 1989), *Nimrod*

Julia Lebentritt P
PO Box 1357
Troy, NY 12181-1357, 518-274-6713
Internet: jlcunas@cs.com
Pubs: *The Kooken* (H Holt, 1992), *Universal Lullabies* (Song Bank, 1990), *Cultural Connections, New York Folklore*

Adam LeFevre 🎤 ✈ P
2 Hummel Rd
New Paltz, NY 12561, 914-255-9275
Pubs: *Everything All at Once* (Wesleyan, 1978), *Vital Signs: Anth* (U Wisconsin Pr, 1989), *APR, Ploughshares, Paris Rev, Nation, Grand Street*

Christine Lehner W
271 S Broadway
Hastings-On-Hudson, NY 10706-2906
Pubs: *Expecting* (New Directions, 1982), *Agni, NAR, Chelsea*

Barbara Lekatsas P
Comparative Literature Dept, Hofstra Univ, Hempstead, NY 11550, 516-463-6553
Pubs: *Demeter in the Deep North, Persephone* (CCC, 1994, 1986), *Artists & Influence*

Naton Leslie P&W
31 McMaster St
Ballston Spa, NY 12020-1907, 518-885-3819
Pubs: *75 Readings: Anth* (McGraw-Hill, 1998), *Best American Essays: 1997: Anth* (HM, 1997), *Agincourt Irregular, Riverwind, Massachusetts Rev, Chariton Rev, Prairie Schooner, Yarrow, Puerto del Sol, Pikeville Rev, West Branch, Intl Poetry Rev*

Louise Landes Levi 🎤 ✈ P
c/o Barrytown GPO
Barrytown, NY 12507, 212-614-1810
Internet: lllevi32@hotmail.com
Pubs: *Guru Punk* (Cool Grove Pr, 2000), *Extinction* (Left Hand Bks, 1990)
Lang: French, Hindi. Groups: Prisoners, Hospitals

Marvin Levine P
Dept of Psychology, SUNY Stonybrook, Stonybrook, NY 11794, 516-632-7804
Pubs: *Look Down from Clouds* (Writers Ink Pr, 1997)

Stephen Lewandowski 🎤 ✈ P
PO Box 943
Canandaigua, NY 14424-9502, 716-374-5473
Pubs: *Artesia* (Foothills Pub, 1989), *Poacher* (White Pine Pr, 1986), *Earth First!, Country Jrnl*

F. R. Lewis 🎤 ✈ W
PO Box 12093
Albany, NY 12212-2093, 518-869-9317
Internet: writing_frl@yahoo.com
Pubs: *Each in Her Own Way* (Queen of Swords, 1994), *Mother of the Groom: Anth* (Distinctive Pr, 1996), *13th Moon, Alaska Qtly Rev, Tampa Rev, Kinesis, William & Mary Rev*

George Liaskos 🎤 ✈   P
PO Box 11-481
Loudonville, NY 12211-1481
    Pubs: *Library Bound: Anth* (Saratoga Springs Public
    Library, 1996), *Saratogian, Mill Hunk Herald, MacGuffin,*
    Poetalk, Ormfaer

Lyn Lifshin 🎤 ✈   P&W
2142 Appletree Ln
Niskayuna, NY 12309, 703-242-3829
Internet: onyxvelvet@aol.com
    Pubs: *Before It's Light, Cold Comfort* (Black Sparrow
    Pr, 1999, 1997), *Blue Tattoo* (Event Horizon, 1995),
    Marilyn Monroe Poems (Quiet Lion, 1994), *Reading*
    Lips (Morgan Pr, 1992), *The Doctor Poems* (Applezaba
    Pr, 1991), *American Scholar, Press, Ploughshares*

Leatrice Lifshitz 🎤 ✈   P
PO Box 615
Pomona, NY 10970-0615, 914-354-2507
Internet: leatty@aol.com
    Pubs: *Only Morning in Her Shoes: Anth* (Utah State U
    Pr, 1990), *Kalliope, Modern Haiku, Slant, Poets On,*
    Sing Heavenly Muse!, Stone Country

Ray Lindquist   P
Craig Rd
Pavilion, NY 14525, 716-584-3307
    Pubs: *By-Products* (Crossing Pr, 1972), *Mother Jones,*
    West End

Romulus Linney   W
289 Dales Bridge Rd
Germantown, NY 12526
    Pubs: *Sand Mountain, A Woman Without a Name*
    (Dramatists Play Service, 1986, 1985)

Geri Lipschultz 🎤 ✈   PP
487 Old Country Rd
Huntington Station, NY 11746, 631-423-8050
Internet: www.alpswriters.org/bios/lipschultz.shtml
    Pubs: *Black Warrior Rev*
Groups: Children

Mike Lipstock   W
132 Hazelwood Dr
Jericho, NY 11753, 516-681-0171
    Pubs: *Chicken Soup for the Soul: Anth* (Health
    Communications Inc, 1998, 1997), *Gifts of Our Fathers:*
    Anth (Crossing Pr, 1994), *A Loving Voice: Anth*
    (Charles Pr, 1994), *Rosebud, Evansville Rev, Nassau*
    Rev, Mediphors, Palo Alto Rev, Midstream, Potpourri
Groups: Seniors

Robert Long 🎤 ✈   P&W
313A Three Mile Harbor, Hog Creek Rd, East Hampton,
NY 11937-2014
Internet: rtlong@mindspring.com
    Pubs: *Blue* (Canios Edtns, 2000), *The Sonnets*
    (Illuminati, 1994), *What Happens* (Galileo Pr, 1988),
    New Yorker, Partisan Rev, Poetry, New American Poets
    of the '90s

James Longstaff 🎤 ✈   P
8944 Syracuse Rd
Cazenovia, NY 13035, 315-655-1090
Internet: jflongst@aol.com
    Pubs: *River Poems: Anth* (Slapering Hol Pr, 1992),
    South Dakota Rev, Green Hills Lit Lantern, Chaminade
    Lit Rev, North Stone Rev, Pike Creek Rev

Michael Lopes   P
260 Jay St
Katonah, NY 10536, 914-232-4584
    Pubs: *Mr. & Mrs. Mephistopheles & Son* (Dustbooks,
    1975), *Poets West, Hanging Loose, Kansas Qtly*

Barbara Lucas   P
6 Briarcliff Ln
Glen Cove, NY 11542, 516-676-7686
    Pubs: *Confrontation, Xanadu, Nassau Rev, Dodeca,*
    Sharing, BPJ, Hiram Poetry Rev

Dennis Lucas   P&W
PO Box 263
Hunter, NY 12442, 518-263-4865
    Pubs: *Thirteen Ways of Looking at Crows, Poetic*
    License: Anth (Left Hand Bks, 1992, 1997), *Amelia,*
    Zone 3, Black River Rev, Outloud, Satori, Flipside,
    Ploplop, Shockbox, Creatum Sinistra

Sister Mary Lucina   P
Mount Mercy Convent, 625 Abbott Rd, Buffalo, NY 14220,
716-826-6192
    Pubs: *Webster Rev, Zone 3, Nimrod, Florida Rev, River*
    City, Greensboro Rev, Mid-American Rev, Sun Dog,
    Nebraska Rev, Slant, National Forum

Jack Ludwig   W
PO Box A-2028
Setauket, NY 11733
    Pubs: *The Great American Spectaculars* (Doubleday,
    1976), *A Woman of Her Age* (McClelland & Stewart,
    1973), *Above Ground* (Little, Brown, 1968), *Atlantic,*
    Partisan Rev, London Mag, Qtly Rev

Susan Lukas   W
85 Rockland Rd
Sparkill, NY 10976
    Pubs: *Morgana's Fault* (Putnam, 1980), *Stereopticon,*
    Fat Emily (Stein & Day, 1975, 1974)

David Lunde 🎤 ✈ P&W
252 King Rd
Forestville, NY 14062-9746, 716-934-4199
Internet: davelunde@prodigy.net
Pubs: *Nightfishing in Great Sky River* (Anamnesis Pr,
1999), *Blues for Port City, Uncommon Places: Anth*
(Mayapple Pr, 1995, 2000), *Asimov's Sci Fi Mag,
Renditions, Literary Rev*

Alan Lupack 🎤 ✈ P&W
375 Oakdale Dr
Rochester, NY 14618
Pubs: *The Dream of Camelot* (Green Chapel, 1990),
Pig Iron, Aileron

Alison Lurie W
English Dept, Cornell Univ, Ithaca, NY 14853
Pubs: *Women & Ghosts* (Doubleday, 1994), *Don't Tell
the Grownups, The Truth About Lorin Jones* (Little,
Brown, 1990, 1988)

Dennis Lynds W
c/o Henry Morrison, PO Box 235, Bedford Hills, NY 10507
Pubs: *The Cadillac Cowboy* (DIF-Penguin, 1995),
Talking to the World (John Daniel & Co, 1995),
Cassandra in Red (Donald I. Fine, 1992), *South
Carolina Rev, Cimarron Rev*

Ali MacDonald 🎤 ✈ P&W
PO Box 33
St. Johnsville, NY 13452-0033, 518-568-7447
Internet: alijohn@klink.net
Pubs: *Phoebe, LIQ*
I.D.: Native American, British. Groups: Children, Native
American

Katharyn Howd Machan 🎤 ✈ P&W
PO Box 456
Ithaca, NY 14851-0456, 607-273-3744
Internet: machan@ithaca.edu
Pubs: *Delilah's Veils* (Sometimes Y Pubs, 1999),
Bedford Intro to Lit: Anth, Literature: Anth (St. Martin's
Pr, 2001, 2000), *Beloit, Seneca Rev, Louisiana Lit,
Yankee, Nimrod*
Groups: Feminist, Historical Societies

Jennifer B. MacPherson 🎤 ✈ P
907 Comstock Ave
Syracuse, NY 13210-2813, 315-475-0339
Internet: jennymac@dreamscape.com
Pubs: *As They Burn the Theater Down* (Hale Mary Pr,
1998), *Another Use for Husbands* (Saltfire Pr, 1990),
*Taproot, Primavera, Listening Eye, Ship of Fools,
Mobius, Hampden-Sydney Poetry Rev, Maryland Rev,
Comstock Rev, Lyric, Kalliope*

Kathleen A. Magill P
33 Linwood Ave
Buffalo, NY 14209
Pubs: *Just Buffalo Pr, Deros, Common Ground, Up
Against the Wall Mother*

Mary Makofske P&W
32 Maple Ave
Florida, NY 10921-1309, 914-651-7723
Pubs: *The Disappearance of Gargoyles* (Thorntree,
1988), *Tangled Vines: Anth* (HBJ, 1992), *Lullwater Rev,
Cream City Rev, Calyx, Cumberland Poetry Rev, Iris*

Dennis Maloney P
White Pine Press, 76 Center St, Fredonia, NY 14063,
716-672-5743
Pubs: *Between This Floating Mist* (Spring Hse Edtns,
1992), *The Map Is Not the Territory: Poems &
Translations* (Unicorn Pr, 1990)

Bridget Manney P
165 E Dover St
Valley Stream, NY 11580
Pubs: *Twigs, Unicorn, Hyacinths & Biscuits*

Laura Marello W
62 Woodlake Rd, Apt 12
Albany, NY 12203-4160
Pubs: *The Voices We Carry: Italian-American Women's
Fiction Anth* (Guernica Pr, 1994), *The Qtly, Mississippi
Rev, New Directions, Sonora Rev, Shankpainter,
Colorado North Rev*

George Maritime P
44 Cherwing Rd
Yonkers, NY 10701, 914-963-4971
Pubs: *Noble Deeds, The Rap* (The New Pr, 1991,
1986), *Rose Colored Glasses: Anth* (ABC No Rio,
1985)

Wallace Markfield W
15 Vista Way
Port Washington, NY 11050

Grace B. Martin P&W
898 Richmond Ave
Buffalo, NY 14222-1118, 716-884-6942
Pubs: *Grannies: 101* (Slipstream, 1992), *Buffalo News,
Today, Forward*

Janette Martin P
The Writer's Center @ Chautauqua, 953 Forest Ave Ext,
Jamestown, NY 14701, 716-483-0381
Pubs: *Connecticut River Rev, Pudding, Bitterroot,
Crazyquilt, Anemone, Harbinger*

Patricia Martin   P&W
PO Box 773
New Paltz, NY 12561, 914-255-1664
    Pubs: *The Bombay Tree* (Phantom Pr, 1991), *Bitterroot,
    Wide Open Mag, Oxalis, Parnassus, Amelia, Maryland
    Poetry Rev, George Washington Rev, Art Times*

Paul Martin   W
135 Parkwood Dr
Snyder, NY 14226
    Pubs: *The Floating World Cycle Poems* (Great Raven
    Pr, 1979), *Greenfield Rev, Contact II*

Anne Marx   P
315 The Colony
Hartsdale, NY 10530
    Pubs: *Love in Late Season* (Wm. H. Bauhan, 1992),
    The Courage to Grow Old: Anth (Ballantine Bks, 1989),
    *CSM, Amelia, Lyric, Good Housekeeping, Modern
    Maturity, South Florida Poetry Rev*

Dan Masterson ♦ ✈   P
41 Fisher Ave
Pearl River, NY 10965, 914-735-5815
Internet: www.poetrymaster.com
    Pubs: *All Things, Seen & Unseen, World Without End,
    Those Who Trespass* (U Arkansas Pr, 1997, 1991,
    1985), *Southern Rev, Prairie Schooner, NYQ, Ontario
    Rev, Gettysburg Rev, Poetry NW, Georgia Rev,
    Sewanee Rev, Paris Rev*
Groups: College/Univ, Prisoners

Debby Mayer   W
PO Box C-25
Hollowville, NY 12530
    Pubs: *Sisters* (Berkley, 1985), *New Yorker, Redbook,
    Fiction Intl, Plainswoman*

Harry Mazer   W
7626 Brown Gulf Rd
Jamesville, NY 13078, 315-682-6799

Jerome Mazzaro ♦ ✈   P
147 Capen Blvd
Buffalo, NY 14226-3052, 716-835-3269
    Pubs: *Rubbings* (Quiet Hills, 1985), *The Caves of Love*
    (Jazz Pr, 1985), *From the Margin: Anth* (Purdue U Pr,
    1990), *Accent, SW Rev, Colorado Rev, New Republic,
    Nation, Hudson Rev, Poetry, Sewanee Rev, Salmagundi*

Gerald McCarthy   P
St. Thomas Aquinas College, Rte 340, Sparkill, NY 10976,
914-359-9500
    Pubs: *Shoetown* (Cloverdale Library, 1992), *War Story*
    (Crossing Pr, 1977), *Mid-American Rev, New Letters,
    And Rev, America, Cloverdale Rev, Poet Lore*

Kenneth Anderson McClane ♦ ✈   P
English Dept, Cornell Univ, 343 Rockefeller Hall, Ithaca,
NY 14853, 607-277-3497
    Pubs: *Take Five: Collected Poems* (Greenwood, 1988),
    A Tree Beyond Telling (Black Scholar, 1983)
I.D.: African-American

James McConkey ♦ ✈   W
402 Aiken Rd
Trumansburg, NY 14886, 607-387-9830
    Pubs: *Stories from My Life with the Other Animals,
    Court of Memory* (Godine, 1993, 1993), *Anatomy of
    Memory: Anth* (Oxford U Pr, 1996), *Hudson Rev*

James McCorkle ♦ ✈   P
790 S Main St
Geneva, NY 14456-3235, 315-789-2139
Internet: mccorkle@epix.net
    Pubs: *Best American Poetry: Anth* (Collier Bks, 1992),
    *Kenyon Rev, Partisan Rev, Colorado Rev, Bomb, NER,
    Poetry, SW Rev, Verse, Green Mountains Rev, Manoa,
    Pequod, Turnstile, Boulevard, Plum Rev, Ontario Rev*

Maureen McCoy   W
Cornell Univ, Goldwin Smith 250, Ithaca, NY 14850
    Pubs: *Divining Blood, Summertime, Walking After
    Midnight* (Poseidon, 1992, 1987, 1985)

Bryan McHugh   P
Station Hill Rd
Barrytown, NY 12507
    Pubs: *Public Enemy, Wolf's Clothing, Rillo: Finders
    Keepers, Rillo: Hymns* (Left Hand Bks, 1996, 1994,
    1993, 1992), *Vamos, Varmint* (Texture Pr, 1995),
    Creacion

Sandy McIntosh ♦ ✈   P
2823 Rockaway Ave
Oceanside, NY 11572-1018, 516-766-1891
Internet: amcintos@optoline.net
    Pubs: *Endless Staircase* (Street Pr, 1991), *Sleepers
    Awake, Monsters of the Antipodes* (Survival Manual
    Bks, 1989, 1989)

Robert T. McLaughlin   W
24 Goodrich St
Williston Park, NY 11596

Gary McLouth   P&W
490 Waterbury Rd
Nassau, NY 12123-9412, 518-766-4385
    Pubs: *North Country: Anth* (Greenfield Rev Pr, 1986),
    *Art Times, Writers, Adirondack Life, Blueline, Voices,
    Groundswell*

Susan Merrill   P
340 Grand St
Croton-on-Hudson, NY 10520, 914-271-3893
    Pubs: *Croton Rev, Kansas Qtly, Footwork, Pudding,
NYQ, Purchase Poetry Rev, Pomegranate Series

Bart Midwood 🎤 ✈   W
64 Meadow St
Garden City, NY 11530, 516-747-6239
Internet: bamidwood@imcnyc.com
    Pubs: *The World in Pieces* (Permanent Pr, 1999),
Bennett's Angel (British-American Paris Rev Edtns,
1989), *The Nativity* (Bel Esprit, 1981), *Phantoms*
(Dutton, 1970), *Bodkin* (Random Hse, 1967)

Carol Miller   P
30 Grace St
Oyster Bay, NY 11771, 516-922-0067
Internet: carol_m_11771@yahoo.com
    Pubs: *Life on the Line* (Negative Capability Pr, 1992),
*Cape Rock, Wisconsin Rev, Oregon East, Buffalo
Spree, New Infinity Rev, Calapooya Collage, Albatross,
Confrontation*

Deborah Miller   W
31 Milo St
Hudson, NY 12534, 518-828-3493
    Pubs: *Alaska Qtly Rev, Antioch Rev, Cottonwood,
Ascent, PEN Fiction Project '87*

Edmund Miller 🎤 ✈   P
English Dept, Long Island Univ, C W Post Campus,
Brookville, NY 11548-1300, 516-299-2391
Internet: edmundmiller@liu.edu
    Pubs: *Nighttimes* (Prowler, 2000), *Leavings* (Birnham
Wood, 1995), *Fucking Animals* (Florida Lit Fdn, 1994),
Pleasures of the Flesh: Anth (Starbooks, 1999),
Flashpoint: Gay Male Sexual Writing: Anth (Richard
Kasak, 1996), *Vice, LIQ*
I.D.: G/L/B/T. Groups: G/L/B/T

Thomas Milligan   P
9 King St
Homer, NY 13077, 607-748-3368
    Pubs: *Virginia Qtly Rev, New Mexico Humanities Rev,
Georgia Rev, Jeopardy, West Branch*

Marianne Milton   P
6558 4 Section Rd, #149
Brockport, NY 14420-2472
    Pubs: *Coal-Slit Dawn* (Bone & Flesh, 1997), *Practice of
Peace: Anth* (Sherman Asher, 1998), *Spoon River
Poetry Rev, Apalachee Qtly*

Phil Mintz   P
c/o Newsday, Melville, NY 11747, 516-843-2754
    Pubs: *Nation, Village Voice, Xanadu, The Smith*

Eugene Mirabelli   W
29 Bennett Terr
Delmar, NY 12054, 518-439-5978
Internet: mirabelli@global2000.net
    Pubs: *The Language Nobody Speaks* (Spring Harbor
Pr, 1999), *The World at Noon* (Guernica Edtns, 1994),
No Resting Place (Viking, 1972), *Metroland, Third
Coast, Via, Michigan Qtly, APR, Grand Street*

Jo Mish   P
10 Main St
Laurens, NY 13796, 607-432-2990

Eileen Moeller 🎤 ✈   P
20 Marvin St
Clinton, NY 13323, 315-853-4295
Internet: eimoell@banet.net
    Pubs: *Cries of the Spirit: Anth, Claiming the Spirit
Within: Anth* (Beacon Pr, 2000, 1995), *The Nerve:
Writing Women 1998: Anth* (Virago Pr, 1998), *Fine
China: Twenty Years of Earth's Daughters: Anth*
(Springhouse Edtns, 1993), *Kalliope, Feminist Studies*
I.D.: Feminist

Ann Mohin 🎤 ✈   P&W
338 Pike Rd
McDonough, NY 13801-0083, 607-647-5643
Internet: anchor@clarityconnect.com
    Pubs: *The Farm She Was: A Novel* (Bridge Works
Pub, 2000)

Daniel Thomas Moran 🎤 ✈   P
PO Box 2008
Shelter Island, NY 11964, 631-749-2595
    Pubs: *In Praise of August* (Canio's Edtns, 1999), *LIQ,
Confrontation, Nassau Rev, Inky Blue, New Pr, Sulfur
River, Pannus Index*
I.D.: Irish-American. Groups: Seniors, Schools

Carole Morgan   W
45 Old Roaring Brook Rd
Mt Kisco, NY 10549, 914-241-0936
    Pubs: *Heirlooms* (Macmillan, 1981)

Robert Morgan   P&W
427 Ferguson Rd
Freeville, NY 13068, 607-844-4538
    Pubs: *The Hinterlands* (Algonquin Bks, 1994), *The
Mountain Won't Remember Us & Other Stories*
(Peachtree Pubs, 1992)

Mark Morganstern   P&W
PO Box 279
Rosendale, NY 12472, 914-658-3511
    Pubs: *Crescent Rev, New Southern Lit Messenger,
Espresso, Tilt, Piedmont Lit Rev, Tempest*

David Morrell   W
Henry Morrison, Inc, PO Box 235, Bedford Hills, NY
10507, 914-666-3500
  Pubs: *Double Image, Desperate Measures, Assumed
Identity, Covenant of the Flame, Fifth Profession*
(Warner Bks, 1998, 1994, 1993, 1991, 1990)

William L. Morris   P
414 Elmwood Ave
Buffalo, NY 14222
  Pubs: *Chicago Rev, Poetry NW, Yale Lit, Third Eye,
Buckle*

Sylvia Moss 🎤 ✈   P
462 Weaver St
Larchmont, NY 10538-1307, 914-834-2724
Internet: sylviasmoss@aol.com
  Pubs: *Cities in Motion* (U Illinois, 1987), *Six Poets:
Anth* (Russia: Abel, 1999), *Foreign Lit, New Letters,
New Laurel Rev, Helicon Nine*

William Mulvihill   W
PO Box 204
Sag Harbor, NY 11963
  Pubs: *Serengeti, God Is Blind* (Brickiln Pr, 1996, 1996),
Night of the Axe (HM, 1972)

Christopher Munford   P
PO Box 161
Warwick, NY 10990-0161
  Pubs: *Sermons in Stone* (Birch Brook Pr, 1993), *River
Night* (Sub Rosa Pr, 1989), *Make Room for Dada,
Home Planet News, Outerbridge, Sub Rosa*

Fred Muratori 🎤 ✈   P
John M Olin Library, Cornell Univ, Ithaca, NY 14853,
607-255-6662
Internet: fmm1@cornell.edu
  Pubs: *Despite Repeated Warnings* (Basfal Bks, 1994),
The Possible (State Street Pr, 1988), *Best American
Poetry: Anth* (Scribner, 1994), *Denver Qtly, Talisman,
ACM*

Joan Murray 🎤 ✈   P
PO Box 214/Albany Turnpike
Old Chatham, NY 12136, 518-794-9722
  Pubs: *Queen of the Mist* (Beacon, 1999), *Looking for
the Parade* (Norton, 1999), *The Same Water*
(Wesleyan, 1990), *Hudson Rev, Paris Rev, Ontario
Rev, Nation, Atlantic, APR*

Robert T. Natello   PP
2 West
Lake George, NY 12845, 518-668-3048
  Pubs: *Bohemian Cafe* (Passages Pr, 1998), *Rude Poets
& Polite Musicians* (Back Door Cafe, 1996), *Tropic
Cafe, Botanical Gardens, Old Courthouse Cafe, Full
Moon Cafe, Cafe Dolce, Cafe Lena*

Mark Neider   P&W
4 Chestnut Ridge Way
Dobbs Ferry, NY 10522, 914-693-1237
  Pubs: *Mudfish, Cumberland Poetry Rev, Judaism, Cross
Roads, Everyman, Medicinal Purposes, Lilliput Rev,
Mediphors, Iconoclast, Hollins Critic, Magic Realism,
Decade, Pacific, New Mexico Qtly*

Howard Nelson 🎤 ✈   P
3617 Keesee Rd
Moravia, NY 13118, 315-364-8536
Internet: nelsonH33@hotmail.com
  Pubs: *Prayers for a Thousand Years* (Harper SF,
1999), *Bone Music* (Nightshade Pr, 1997), *Gorilla
Blessing* (Falling Tree Pr, 1993), *The Rag & Bone
Shop of the Heart: Anth* (HC, 1992), *Green Fuse,
Poetry East, West Branch, Whole Terrain, CSM*

Shirley Nelson   W
122 Lancaster St
Albany, NY 12210, 518-432-5163
  Pubs: *Fair, Clear, & Terrible* (British American, 1989),
The Last Year of the War (Harold Shaw, 1989), *Image:
A Jrnl of the Arts*

Mark Nepo   P
48 Willett St, #2
Albany, NY 12210-1104
  Pubs: *Acre of Light* (Ithaca Hse, 1994), *Fire Without
Witness* (British American, 1988), *Antaeus, Kenyon Rev,
Chelsea, Sewanee Rev, Voices, Pilgrimage*

Tam Lin Neville   P
PO Box 673
Keene Valley, NY 12943-0673
  Pubs: *Journey Cake* (BkMk Pr/U Kansas City, 1998),
*Indiana Rev, APR, Ironwood, Crazyhorse,
Massachusetts Rev*

Ben Nightingale 🎤 ✈   W
14 Soundview Ave, #C5-28
White Plains, NY 10606-3327, 914-428-5991
  Pubs: *Mendocino Rev, Network Africa, Obsidian*
I.D.: Jewish, Black

David Michael Nixon 🎤 ✈   P
140-1 Lake Vista Court
Rochester, NY 14612-5332, 716-865-0965
  Pubs: *Season of the Totem* (Linear Arts, 1999), *Hunting
the World* (FootHills Pub, 1989), *Blue Water Line Blues*
(Mott Calligraphy, 1988), *Blueline, Waterways, Black
Buzzard Rev, Cocodrilo, Gypsy, Home Planet News,
Hazmat Rev, Potato Eyes, Comstock Rev*
Groups: Social Justice

Sharyn November   P
81 Salem Rd
East Hills, NY 11577
  Pubs: *Poetry, NAR, Poetry Miscellany, Small Pond,
New Infinity Rev*

Beatrice O'Brien 🎤 ✈ P
RD 2, Box 155
Cohocton, NY 14826
Internet: bobrien4@juno.com
Pubs: *Loon Lake Jrnl* (H&H Pr, 2000), *One Track*
(Mozart Park Pr, 1995), *From the Wings* (Rainbow Pr,
1990), *Lake Effect, Time of Singing*
I.D.: Irish-American. Groups: Seniors, Veterans

Mary Beth O'Connor 🎤 ✈ P&W
Ithaca College, The Writing Dept, Ithaca, NY 14850,
607-274-1576
Internet: moconner@ithaca.edu
Pubs: *Life on the Line: Reflections on Words & Healing*
(Negative Capability Pr, 1992), *Blithe Hse Qtly,
Concourse 7, Ithaca Women's Anth, Nimrod*

Toni Ortner P
PO Box 213, Bell Hollow Rd
Putnam Valley, NY 10579
Pubs: *Requiem, American Poetry Confronts the 1990s:
Anth* (Black Tie Pr, 1991, 1990), *Mudfish, Lit Rev,
Canadian Forum, Kansas City Rev*

Lawrence Osgood W
PO Box 575
Germantown, NY 12526-0575, 212-673-5232
Pubs: *Canadian Fiction Mag, Carleton Miscellany,
London Mag*

Ron Overton 🎤 ✈ P
16 Renown St
Lake Grove, NY 11755-2014, 516-585-8032
Pubs: *Hotel Me* (Hanging Loose Pr, 1994), *Poetry,
Hanging Loose, Downbeat, Minnesota Rev, Poetry NW,
Commonweal, Salmagundi, Massachusetts Rev, Kayak*
Groups: Children

Kent Jorgensen Ozarow P
4 Edgewood Pl
Great Neck, NY 11024, 516-466-0976
Pubs: *Poetry Now, Confrontation, Croton Rev, Xanadu,
Paris Rev, West Hills Rev, Alura, Yankee*

Jim Papa P&W
26 Awixa Ave
Bay Shore, NY 11706, 516-968-6947
Pubs: *In Autumn: Anth* (Birnham Wood, 1994),
*Petroglyph, Isle, Fire Island Tide, NAR, LIQ, College
English, Wordsmith, Plainsong, Panhandler, Madison
Rev*

Ned Pastor 🎤 ✈ P
1200 Midland Ave
Bronxville, NY 10708-6412, 914-337-4214
Pubs: *Lighten Up: Anth* (Meadowbrook Pr, 1999, 1998),
Golf: Anth (Meadowbrook Pr, 1996), *Treasury of Light
Verse: Anth* (Random Hse, 1995), *Sometime the Cow
Kick Your Head: Anth* (Bits Pr, 1988), *Pennsylvania
Poetry Society Prize Poems, Amelia, Light*

William B. Patrick 🎤 ✈ P
2 The Crossways
Troy, NY 12180-7263, 518-272-1446
Pubs: *We Didn't Come Here for This, These Upraised
Hands, Roxa: Voices of the Culver Family* (BOA Edtns,
1999, 1995, 1989), *Southern Rev, North Dakota Rev,
Kansas Qtly, Carolina Qtly, Epoch*

Raymond R. Patterson 🎤 ✈ P
2 Lee Ct
Merrick, NY 11566, 516-868-3874
Pubs: *Elemental Blues* (CCC, 1982), *Best American
Poetry: Anth* (Scribner, 1996), *Every Shut Eye Ain't
Asleep: Anth* (Little, Brown, 1994), *Drumvoices*

Elizabeth Patton P
5273 Kingston Rd, PO Box 427
Elbridge, NY 13060, 315-689-9782

Nita Penfold 🎤 ✈ P&W
c/o Penfold, 11385 Big Tree Rd, East Aurora, NY 14052,
617-846-5445
Internet: penfold5@hotmail.com
Pubs: *Woman with the Wild-Grown Hair* (Pudding Hse
Pub, 1998), *Family Celebrations: Anth* (Andrews
McMeel Pubs, 1999), *At Our Core: Women Writing
About Power: Anth* (Papier-Mache Pr, 1998), *Claiming
the Spirit Within: Anth* (Beacon Pr, 1996), *Maryland
Rev*
I.D.: Feminist, Spiritual/Religious

Simon Perchik 🎤 ✈ P
10 Whitby Ln
East Hampton, NY 11937, 631-324-2834
Pubs: *Letters to the Dead* (St. Andrews Pr, 1994),
Redeeming the Wings (Dusty Dog Pr, 1991), *Partisan
Rev, New Yorker, New Letters*

Michael Perkins 🎤 ✈ P&W
750 Ohayo Mountain Rd
Glenford, NY 12433, 914-657-6439
Pubs: *Dark Games* (Thunder's Mouth, 2000), *Night
Moves* (Robinson, 2000), *Dark Matter* (Titan Bks, 1996),
The Good Parts (R. Kasak Bks, 1994), *Out of the
Catskills: Anth* (Bright Hill, 1997), *The Stiffest of the
Corpse: Anth* (City Lights, 1988), *Notre Dame Rev*

John Niels Perlman 🎤 ✈ P
38 Ferris Pl
Ossining, NY 10562, 914-762-1978
Internet: johnperl@aol.com
Pubs: *Edward John* (Tel-Let Pr, 1998), *Natural History
of Trees* (Texture Pr, 1995), *Anacoustic* (Standing
Stone Pr, 1993), *Talisman, O.ars, Tel-Let, Shearsman,
Juxta, Texture, Key Satch(el), Origin*

Ellen Perreault   P
34 Danker Ave
Albany, NY 12206, 518-459-2795
   Pubs: *Greenfield Rev, Hollow Springs Rev, Washout
   Rev, Laurel Rev, Three Sisters*

Marion Perry   P
Word Worth, PO Box 221, East Aurora, NY 14052,
716-851-1712
   Pubs: *Dishes, Establishing Intimacy* (Textile Bridge,
   1989, 1982), *Hiram Poetry Rev, Footwork, Esprit, Black
   Mountain Rev, Buckle, Earth's Daughters, Intrepid*

Kathrin Perutz   W
16 Avalon Rd
Great Neck, NY 11021, 516-482-0804
   Pubs: *Writing for Love & Money* (U Arkansas Pr,
   1991), *Faces* (Pseudonym: Joanna Kingsley; Bantam,
   1987)

Joan Peternel   P&W
65 Bay Ave
Hampton Bays, NY 11946-2507, 516-723-0425
   Pubs: *Howl & Hosanna* (Whelks Walk Pr, 1997), *Anth
   of Magazine Verse* (Monitor Bk Co, 1997), *James
   Joyce Qtly, Small Press Rev, Mandrake Poetry Rev,
   LIQ*

Donald Petersen   P
12 Grand St
Oneonta, NY 13820, 607-432-8308
   Pubs: *The Spectral Boy* (Wesleyan U Pr, 1964), *New
   Criterion*

Anthony Piccione   P
Crow Hill Farm, Box 295
Prattsburgh, NY 14873, 607-522-3289
   Pubs: *For the Kingdom, Seeing It Was So* (BOA Edtns
   Ltd, 1995, 1987), *APR, Choice, Iowa Rev, Chicago
   Rev, Literary Rev, Painted Bride Qtly*

Paul Pines   P&W
55 Garfield St
Glens Falls, NY 12801-2660, 518-798-2858
   Pubs: *Pines Songs* (Ikon Pr, 1992), *Hotel Madden
   Poems* (Contact II, 1991), *The Tin Angel* (Morrow,
   1983), *New Directions, Global City Rev, First Intensity*

Joseph Pintauro   P&W
PO Box 531
Sag Harbor, NY 11963, 516-725-4141
   Pubs: *State of Grace* (Times Bks, 1983), *Cold Hands*
   (Signet, 1980)

Allen Planz   P
PO Box 212
East Hampton, NY 11937, 516-725-1667
   Pubs: *A Night for Rioting* (Swallow, 1990), *Wild Craft*
   (Living Ports Pr, 1976), *Chonderhara Street Pr*

Mariquita Platov   P
Rte 1, Box 4
Tannersville, NY 12485, 518-589-0135
   Pubs: *Banana Girl* (Peace Creativity, 1988), *One
   Moment* (Plowshare Pr, 1961), *Groundswell, Fellowship,
   Concern, Imprints Qtly, Inward Light, The Word*

Charles Plymell 🎤 ✈   P&W
PO Box 303
Cherry Valley, NY 13320-0303, 607-264-3707
Internet: www.buchenroth.com/cplymell.html
   Pubs: *Hand on the Doorknob* (Water Row Bks, 2000),
   Forever Wider (Scarecrow Pr, 1985), *Trashing of
   America* (Kulchur Fdn, 1975), *Outlaw Bible of American
   Poetry: Anth* (Thunder's Mouth Pr, 1999)

Kathryn Poppino   P
1027 Hickory Rd
Schenectady, NY 12309
   Pubs: *The Smith, Tightrope, Yellow Brick Road,
   Chicago Rev, Hanging Loose*

Richard Posner 🎤 ✈   W
Henry Morrison, Inc, PO Box 235, Bedford Hills, NY
10507
   Pubs: *Sweet Sixteen & Never Been Killed, Can You
   Hear Me Scream?* (Pocket Bks, 1994, 1994)

Cally Pourakis   P
11 Nortema Ct
New Hyde Park, NY 11040-2031, 516-437-9511
   Pubs: *Thirteen Poetry Mag, Haiku Zasshi Zo, Salome,
   Bitterroot, Calli's Tales, Hoosier Challenger*

Shirley Powell   P&W
229 Main St
Kingston, NY 12401, 845-340-1567
   Pubs: *Bridges* (Springtown Pr, 1997), *Other Rooms,
   Villages & Towns, Alternate Lives* (Poets' Pr, 1997,
   1993, 1990), *Home Planet News, True West, Oxalis,
   Green's Mag, Ball State Forum, Art Times*

Prem Nagpal Prasad   P&W
7 Roberta Ave
Farmingville, NY 11738, 516-698-0512
   Pubs: *Padmavati* (Birnham Wood, 1994), *We Speak for
   Peace: Anth* (Knowledge, Ideas & Trends Inc, 1993),
   LIQ, Bharti, Willow, Massachusetts Rev

Elaine Preston 🎤 ✈   P
Suffolk Community College-West, Sagtikos Bldg, Rm 202,
Brentwood, NY 11717, 516-851-6788
Internet: epwingz@aol.com
   Pubs: *Fishing Underground* (H&H Pr, 1997), *Look for a
   Field to Land* (Bridge Works Pub, 1994), *Always the
   Beautiful Answer: Anth* (King's Estate Pr, 1999),
   *Confrontation, Jrnl of Poetry Therapy, Poet Lore,
   Comstock Rev, Passager, Peregrine, NYQ*
Groups: Abuse Victims

Dan Propper 🎤 ✈   P
PO Box 346
Bearsville, NY 12409-0346
   Pubs: *For Kerouac in Heaven, Fable of the Final Hour*
(Energy Pr, 1980, 1958), *Tale of the Amazing Tramp*
(Cherry Valley Edtns, 1976), *Maverick Poets: Anth*
(Gorilla Pr, 1988), *The Beats: Anth* (Gold Medal, 1960),
Hunger, Woodstock Seasoner, Love Lights
I.D.: Post-Beat

William Pruitt 🎤 ✈   P
294 Sagamore Dr
Irondequoit, NY 14617-2406, 716-467-9510
Internet: c21pruitt@earthlink.net
   Pubs: *Ravine Street* (White Pine, 1977), *Editor's
Choice: Anth* (The Spirit That Moves Us Pr, 1980),
Potato Eyes, Blueline, Ploughshares, Poetry Now

George Quasha   P
Station Hill Rd
Barrytown, NY 12507, 914-758-5291
   Pubs: *In No Time, Giving the Lily Back Her Hands*
(Station Hill, 1988, 1979)

Stuart P. Radowitz   P
2484 Kayron Ln
North Bellmore, NY 11710, 516-826-3278
   Pubs: *Steppenwolf, Fragments, Crazyhorse, Aspen
Leaves, Process, Syracuse Poems, Star Web Rev*

Diana Ramirez-De-Arellano   P
23 Harbor Cir
Centerport, NY 11721, 516-757-3498
   Pubs: *Adelfazar, Tree at Vespers/Arbol en Visperas*
(Spain; Editorial Torremozas, 1995, 1987),

Larry Rapant 🎤 ✈   P
35 School Rd
Voorheesville, NY 12186-9615, 518-765-3471
Internet: lrapant@sescva.esc.edu
   Pubs: *Alpha Beat Soup, Modern Haiku, Cotyledon,
Passages North, Slugfest, Mildred, Mati, Knocked, Lynx
Eye, Potpourri*
I.D.: Performance, Music/Arts

Nefretete S. Rasheed 🎤 ✈   P
65 McKinley Ave, Ste C3-4
White Plains, NY 10606
Internet: rasheedn@prodigy.net
   Pubs: *Theatre: Anth* (NTC/Contemporary Pub Grp,
1999), *Three Thirds: Anth* (Wordbanks Pr, 1984),
Phoebe, Plum Rev, Salome
I.D.: African-American

Regina Reibstein   P
26 Oxford Blvd
Great Neck, NY 11023, 516-487-6839
   Pubs: *Midstream, SW Rev, California Qtly, Poem,
Skylark Qtly, Judaism, Pale Fire Rev*

Edward V. Reiff   P
18 Baker Hill Rd
Great Neck, NY 11023
   Pubs: *Visions Harbor Mag*

Robert L. Reiff 🎤 ✈   P&W
8 Dover Dr
Latham, NY 12110, 518-783-8271
Internet: rlr47@aol.com
   Pubs: *MacGuffin, Proof Rock, Gargoyle, Antigonish Rev,
Schenectady Rev, Deros, Skylark, Alura, Augusta
Spectator*

Samuel Reifler 🎤 ✈   W
PO Box 299
Clinton Corners, NY 12514-0299, 914-266-5186
Internet: rhinebeckrecords@compuserve.com
   Pubs: *Esquire, New Directions, TriQtly, Denver Qtly,
Mid-Atlantic Rev*

Donna Reis 🎤   P
201 Jessup Rd
Warwick, NY 10990-2543, 914-987-8179
Internet: dreis@warwick.net
   Pubs: *Dog Shows & Church, Incantations* (Eurydice Pr,
2000, 1995), *Beyond Lament: Anth* (Northwestern U Pr,
1998), *Women & Death: Anth* (Ground Torpedo Pr,
1994), *Promethean, Lullwater Rev, Zone 3, Cumberland
Poetry Rev, A Gathering of the Tribes*

Rose Reitter   P
25 Forest Ave
Hastings-On-Hudson, NY 10706, 914-478-3077
   Pubs: *The Pomegranate Series, Voices Intl, Attention
Please*

Elliot Richman 🎤 ✈   P
159 Oak St
Plattsburgh, NY 12901-1624, 518-562-1838
Internet: comrado@together.net
   Pubs: *Franz Kafka's Daughter Meets the Evil Nazi
Empire!!!, Honorable Manhood, The World Dancer*
(Asylum Arts, 1999, 1994, 1993), *Walk on Trooper* (Viet
Nam Generation Pr, 1994)
I.D.: Jewish, Holocaust. Groups: Prisoners

Frances Bragan Richman   P
237 Circle Ln
Webster, NY 14580, 716-671-6165
   Pubs: *Yellow Butterfly, Saturday Evening Post, Ladies
Home Jrnl*

Arthur Rifkin   P
7 Fourth Rd
Great Neck, NY 11021
   Pubs: *Lake Superior Rev, Bitterroot, Encore, Poet Lore,
Dodeca*

Jean Rikhoff   W
42 Sherman Ave
Glens Falls, NY 12801
    Pubs: *David Smith, I Remember* (The Loft Pr, 1985),
    Where Were You in '76?, *The Sweetwater*, *One of the
    Raymonds* (Dial Pr, 1978, 1976, 1974)

Mary Ann Malinchak Rishel   W
Ithaca College, Writing Dept, 204 Williams Hall, Ithaca, NY
14850, 607-274-3324
Internet: rishel@ithaca.edu
    Pubs: *Shankpainter*, *Scrivener*, *Red Cedar Rev*, *Hudson
    Rev*, *Cornell Rev*

Helen Morrissey Rizzuto   P&W
548 E Bay Dr
Long Beach, NY 11561, 516-431-5263
    Pubs: *A Bird in Flight*, *Evening Sky on a Japanese
    Screen* (Lintel, 1986, 1978), *Birmingham Poetry Rev*,
    America, *Crazyquilt*

Sheryl Robbins   P
369 Maryland St
Buffalo, NY 14201, 716-885-0804
    Pubs: *Or, The Whale* (Shuffaloff Bks, 1993), *Snapshots
    of Paradise* (Just Buffalo Pr, 1981), *Denver Qtly*, *Works
    & Days, Inc #2*, *Earth's Daughters*

Mary Elsie Robertson   W
3238 Brick Schoolhouse Rd
Hamlin, NY 14464, 716-964-8683
    Pubs: *Family Life* (Atheneum, 1987), *What I Have to
    Tell You* (Doubleday, 1989), *Literary Outtakes: Anth*
    (Ballantine, 1990), *Ascent*, *Mississippi Rev*, *Nebraska
    Rev*, *NER*, *New Virginia Rev*, *Outerbridge*, *Phoebe*,
    Seattle Rev, *Stand*, *Virginia Qtly*

Anthony Robinson   W
153 Huguenot St
New Paltz, NY 12561, 914-255-8040
    Pubs: *Home Again, Home Again* (Morrow, 1970), *The
    Easy Way* (S&S, 1963)

Bruce Robinson ♦ ✈   P
PO Box 26
Albany, NY 12201-8026
Internet: wrobinso@mail.nysed.gov
    Pubs: *Weber Studies*, *Xavier Rev*, *Sow's Ear*, *Spoon
    River*, *Greenfield Rev*, *Opera Jrnl*, *Paragraph*, *Fiction*

Bertha Rogers ♦ ✈   P
Bright Hill Farm, RR1, Box 545, Delhi, NY 13753-9739,
607-746-7306
Internet: bkrogers@catskill.net
    Pubs: *Beowulf* (Birch Bk Pr, 2000), *A House of Corners*
    (Three Conditions Pr, 2000), *Aurora* (Bull Thistle, 1991),
    For the Girl Buried in the Peat Bog: Anth (Six Swans,
    1999), *Second Word Thursdays: Anth* (Bright Hill Pr,
    1999), *Many Mountains Moving*

Jay Rogoff ♦ ✈   P
35 Pinewood Ave
Saratoga Springs, NY 12866-2622, 518-584-0912
Internet: jrogoff@skidmore.edu
    Pubs: *First Hand* (Mica Pr, 1997), *The Cutoff: A
    Sequence* (The Word Works, 1995), *Georgia Rev*,
    DoubleTake, *Kenyon Rev*, *Paris Rev*, *Partisan Rev*,
    Prairie Schooner, *Shenandoah*

Ginny Rorby   W
c/o Barbara Kouts, Barbara Kouts Agency, Box 560,
Bellport, NY 11715
    Pubs: *Dolphin Sky* (Putnam, 1996)

Marina L. Roscher   P&W
4571 Merrick Rd
Massapequa, NY 11758, 516-798-2829
    Pubs: *Catlives* (Texas Tech U Pr, 1992), *NYQ*,
    Apalachee Qtly, *Madison Rev*, *Buffalo Spree*,
    Rohwedder, *Gaia*, *Prism Intl*

Liz Rosenberg   P&W
English Dept, SUNY Binghamton, Binghamton, NY 13901,
607-777-2168
Internet: lrosenb@binghampton.edu
    Pubs: *The Fire Music* (U Pitt Pr, 1985), *The Angel
    Poems* (State Street Pr, 1984), *Harper's*

William Rosenfeld   W
Hamilton College, Clinton, NY 13323, 315-859-4462

M. L. Rosenthal   P
17 Bayard Ln
Suffern, NY 10901, 914-357-0856
    Pubs: *Running to Paradise*, *As for Love: Poems &
    Translations* (Oxford U Pr, 1994, 1987), *Southern Rev*,
    Ploughshares, *Nation*, *Exile*, *Pequod*

Geri Rosenzweig ♦ ✈   P
63 Mystic Dr
Ossining, NY 10562-1965, 914-762-7025
    Pubs: *Half the Story* (March Street Pr, 1997), *Under a
    Jasmine Moon* (HMS Pr, 1993), *Lullwater Rev*, *Poet &
    Critic*, *River City*, *Greensboro Rev*, *Verse*

Gary Earl Ross   P&W
PO Box 1261
Buffalo, NY 14215, 716-838-9786
    Pubs: *Sideshow 1995: Anth* (Somersault Pr, 1994),
    Artisans Anth of Fiction (Marienhelz Artisans, 1994),
    Artvoice, *Buffalo Mag*, *Buffalo Spree*, *ELF*

Henry H. Roth   W
288 Piermont Ave
South Nyack, NY 10960, 914-358-2399
    Pubs: *In Empty Rooms* (December Pr, 1980), *Kansas
    Qtly*, *South Carolina Rev*, *Confrontation*

Paul B. Roth 🎤 ✈　　　　　　　　　　　　**P**
4983 Tall Oaks Dr
Fayetteville, NY 13066-9776, 315-637-3047
Internet: bones44@ix.netcom.com
　　Pubs: *Nothing Out There* (Vida Pr, 1996), *Half-Said*
　　(Bitter Oleander Pr, 1977), *Immanentist: Anth* (The
　　Smith, 1973), *Higginsville Reader, Glass Cherry, Black*
　　Moon, Bitter Oleander, Yefief, Comstock Rev

Chuck Rothman 🎤 ✈　　　　　　　　　　　**W**
2012 Pyle Rd
Schenectady, NY 12303-3071, 518-356-4205
Internet: www.sff.net.people/rothman
　　Pubs: *Staroamer's Fate* (Warner/Questar Bks, 1986),
　　Blood Muse: Anth (Donald I. Fine, 1995), *Fantasy &*
　　Sci Fi Mag, Aboriginal Sci Fi, Galaxy, VB Tech Mag,
　　Realms of Fantasy, Tomorrow Sci Fi

Berton Roueche　　　　　　　　　　　　　**W**
PO Box 693
Amagansett, NY 11930, 516-267-3822

Ann Rower　　　　　　　　　　　　　　　　**W**
60-82 60 Dr
Maspeth, NY 11378-3536, 212-966-6737
　　Pubs: *If You're a Girl* (Semiotext(e), *1990*)

Stan Sanvel Rubin 🎤 ✈　　　　　　　　　　**P**
The Writers Forum, SUNY Brockport, Brockport, NY
14420, 716-395-5713
Internet: srubin@brockport.edu
　　Pubs: *Midnight* (State Street Pr, 1985), *Chelsea,*
　　Virginia Qtly Rev, Georgia Rev, Poetry NW, Tar River
　　Poetry, Laurel Rev, Ohio Rev, Kenyon Rev

Helen Ruggieri 🎤 ✈　　　　　　　　　　　**P**
111 N 10 St
Olean, NY 14760-2101, 716-372-0935
Internet: ruggieri@localnet.com
　　Pubs: *Glimmergirls* (Mayapple Pr, 1999), *The Poetess*
　　(Allegheny Mountain Pr, 1981), *Under A Gull's Wing:*
　　Anth (Down the Shore, 1996), *Flutes of Power: Anth*
　　(Great Elm Pr, 1995), *Coal Seam: Anth* (U Scranton
　　Pr, 1993), *Heartlands Today, Poet Lore, MacGuffin*

Michael Rumaker　　　　　　　　　　　　**P&W**
139 S Broadway
South Nyack, NY 10960
　　Pubs: *To Kill a Cardinal* (Arthur Mann Kaye Pub,
　　1992), *Gringos & Other Stories* (North Carolina
　　Wesleyan College Pr, 1991)

Paul Russell 🎤 ✈　　　　　　　　　　　　**W**
Vassar College, English Dept, Poughkeepsie, NY 12604,
914-437-5645
Internet: russell@vassar.edu
　　Pubs: *The Coming Storm* (St. Martin's Pr, 1999), *Sea*
　　of Tranquility, Boys of Life (Dutton, 1994, 1991)

Michael Rutherford　　　　　　　　　　　　**P**
Alternative Literary Programs, RD 1, Box 147, Indian
Ledge Rd, Voorheesville, NY 12186, 518-765-2613

Sarah Ryder　　　　　　　　　　　　　　　**P**
1588 Hereford Rd
Hewlett, NY 11557

Natalie Safir　　　　　　　　　　　　　　**P**
PO Box 602
Rhinebeck, NY 12572-0602, 914-876-7666
　　Pubs: *Made Visible* (Singular Speech Pr, 1998), *To*
　　Face the Inscription (La Jolla Poets, 1987), *McGraw-Hill*
　　Book of Poetry: Anth (McGraw-Hill, 1993), *Reading*
　　Poetry: Anth (Random Hse, 1989), *Slant, Pivot, Roh*
　　Wedder, Poets On, MacGuffin, West Hills Rev

Kenneth Salzmann 🎤 ✈　　　　　　　　　**P**
156 Second St 1B
Troy, NY 12180, 518-272-6562
Internet: ksalzmann@theartscenter.cc
　　Pubs: *Peninsula Rev, Spillway, Piedmont Literary Rev,*
　　Poetry Motel, CQ, SYZYGY, Medicinal Purposes,
　　Musing Mag, Rattle, Afterthoughts, Sheila-na-gig
Groups: Jewish

Edward Sanders 🎤 ✈　　　　　　　　　　**P&W**
PO Box 729
Woodstock, NY 12498-0729, 914-679-6556
　　Pubs: *America, A History in Verse, Vols 1& 2; 1968, A*
　　History in Verse; Chekhov: A Biography in Verse; Hymn
　　to the Rebel Cafe: Poems 1987-1991 (Black Sparrow,
　　2000, 2000, 1997, 1995, 1992)

Pamela Sargent　　　　　　　　　　　　　**W**
15 Crannell Ave
Delmar, NY 12054-1535
Internet: sarzeb@compuserve.com
　　Pubs: *Climb the Wind* (Harper Prism, 1999), *Women of*
　　Wonder (HB, 1995), *Ruler of the Sky* (Crown, 1993),
　　Alien Child (H&R, 1988), *Venus of Shadows*
　　(Doubleday, 1988), *Amazing Stories, Sci Fi Rev,*
　　Asimov's Sci Fi Mag

Judith Saunders 🎤　　　　　　　　　　　**P**
Marist College, Humanities Division, Poughkeepsie, NY
12601, 914-575-3000
　　Pubs: *Check-Out Counter Suite* (Panhandler/U West
　　Florida Pr, 1992), *Poetry USA, Potpourri, NAR, CSM,*
　　Aura, Art Times, Folio, Concho River Rev, Bay
　　Windows, CQ

Joan Sauro 🎤 ✈　　　　　　　　　　　　**P&W**
315 Herkimer St
Syracuse, NY 13204-1609
　　Pubs: *U.S. Catholic, Critic, America, Commonweal, New*
　　Catholic World
Groups: Adults

Robert J. Savino 🎤   P
363 Oak Neck Rd
West Islip, NY 11795-3616, 631-422-6934
Internet: dynsus@aol.com
    Pubs: *Urban Beat, In My Shoes, Angel Flesh, Wooden
    Head Rev, Surreal Underground, Conflict of Interest,
    Incoming, Tantra Pr, The Equinox, Avenging Spirit,
    Ellipsis, Axe Factory, Babylon Rev*

Lynne Savitt   P
2646A Riverside Dr
Wantagh, NY 11793, 516-221-7182
    Pubs: *The Burial of Longing Beneath the Blue Neon
    Moon* (Ye Olde Fonte Shoppe, 1999), *Sleeping
    Retrospect of Desire* (Konocti Bks, 1993), *A New
    Geography of Poets* (Arkansas, 1992), *NYQ, Chiron
    Rev, Painted Bride Qtly, Caprice*

Boria Sax 🎤 ✈   P
25 Franklin Ave, #2F
White Plains, NY 10601-3819, 914-946-6735
Internet: vogelgreif@aol.com
    Pubs: *Apples Until the End of Time, I Am That Snow
    Flake* (The Poet's Pr, 2000, 1990), *Rhineland Market*
    (Textile Bridge Pr, 1985), *Storytelling, Poésie Europe,
    Poet & Critic, Greenprints, Gegengift, Parabola*

Susan Schefflein 🎤 ✈   P&W
16 Partridge Ln
Putnam Valley, NY 10579-2800, 914-528-6338
    Pubs: *Each in Her Own Way* (Queen of Swords Pr,
    1994), *Birmingham Rev of Poetry, Forum, Touchstone,
    Live Writers!, Prophetic Voices, Wind, Pandora*

Geraldine Schmitz   W
81 Campbell St
New Hyde Park, NY 11040-1758
    Pubs: *Four Quarters, Zantia, More Womanspace*

Budd Schulberg   W
Miriam Altschuler Literary Agency, RR#1, Box 5, Old Post
Rd, Red Hook, NY 12571
    Pubs: *Love, Action, Laughter & Other Sad Tales, What
    Makes Sammy Run?* (Random Hse, 1990, 1990)

Philip Schultz 🎤 ✈   P&W
880 Osborne Ln
East Hampton, NY 11937, 631-329-3151
Internet: gusandbenya@earthlink.net
    Pubs: *Deep Within the Ravine, Like Wings* (Viking,
    1984, 1978), *New American Poets of the '90s: Anth*
    (Godine, 1991), *New Yorker, Poetry Chicago, Nation*

Doris E. Schuyler   W
Canal Side Publishers, PO Box 137, RFD #3, Frankfort,
NY 13340, 315-895-7535
    Pubs: *Adirondack Princess 2* (Canal Side Pubs, 1990),
    Butlersbury (LED Pr, 1985), *Aunt Cad, Adirondack
    Princess* (Worden Pr, 1984, 1982)

Patricia Roth Schwartz 🎤 ✈   P&W
Weeping Willow Farm, 1212 Birdsey Rd, Waterloo, NY
13165-9422, 315-539-0948
Internet: prschwartz@juno.com
    Pubs: *The Names of the Moons of Mars* (New Victoria,
    1989), *Sojourner, Beloit Fiction Jrnl*
I.D.: Feminist. Groups: Prisoners, Children

Sheila Schwartz   W
SUNY New Paltz, New Paltz, NY 12561, 914-255-0097
    Pubs: *The Most Popular Girl, Bigger Is Better*
    (Crosswinds, 1987, 1987), *Sorority* (Warner, 1987)

Joanna Scott 🎤 ✈   W
Univ Rochester, English Dept, Rochester, NY 14616,
716-275-4092
    Pubs: *Make Believe* (Little, Brown, 2000), *The Manikin,
    Various Antidotes* (H Holt, 1997, 1994), *Arrogance*
    (S&S, 1990), *The Closest Possible Union* (Ticknor &
    Fields, 1988)

Dee Rossi Script   P&W
887 W Ferry St
Buffalo, NY 14209, 716-884-6393
    Pubs: *About the World of Sherlock Holmes: Jrnl* (Bruce
    Aikin, 1997), *The Formidable Scrapbook of Baker
    Street: Anth* (Sherlockian Pubs, 1996), *ELF, Baker
    Street Jrnl*

Ralph W. Seager   P
311 Keuka St
Penn Yan, NY 14527-1153
    Pubs: *My Folks & the One-Room Schoolhouse* (Capper
    Pr, 1993), *Parnassus of World Poets: Anth* (Ramasamy
    Devaraj, 1995), *Ideals Country, Time of Singing*

Hollis Rowan Seamon 🎤 ✈   W
College of Saint Rose, English Dept, Albany, NY 12203,
518-454-5207
Internet: seamonh@mail.strose.edu
    Pubs: *Body Work* (Spring Harbor Pr, 2000), *A Line of
    Cutting Women: Anth* (Calyx Pr, 1998), *Sacred Ground:
    Anth* (Milkweed Edtns, 1996), *Hudson Rev, McCall's,
    Crosscurrents, American Voice, Creative Woman, Calyx,
    Chicago Rev, 13th Moon*

G. J. Searles 🎤 ✈   P
Humanities Dept, Mohawk Valley Comm College, 1101
Sherman Dr, Utica, NY 13501, 315-792-5439
    Pubs: *Mudville Diaries: Anth* (Avon Bks, 1996),
    *Rockhurst Rev, Greenfield Rev, The Bridge, Light,
    Footwork, Lynx Eye, Yet Another Small Mag, Asbury
    Park Pr, Main Street Rag, Wings, Artword Qtly*

Christopher Seid   P
83 Tappan Landing Rd
Tarrytown, NY 10591
    Pubs: *Prayers to the Other Life* (Helicon Nine Edtns
    1997)

Joanne Seltzer 🎤 ✈   P&W
2481 McGovern Dr
Schenectady, NY 12309-2433, 518-377-9049
Internet: sseltzer1@juno.com
    Pubs: *Inside Invisible Walls* (Bard Pr, 1989), *Suburban
    Landscape* (MAF Pr, 1988), *The Muse Strikes Back:
    Anth* (Story Line Pr, 1997), *When I Am an Old Woman
    I Shall Wear Purple: Anth* (Papier-Mache Pr, 1987),
    Sistersong, Karamu, Nebo, Hadassah Mag
I.D.: Jewish, Feminist. Groups: Seniors, Women

Dee Shapiro   P&W
28 Clover Dr
Great Neck, NY 11021-1819
Internet: betiren1@aol.com
    Pubs: *Blueline, Small Pond Mag of Lit, Black Bear Rev,
    Chiron Rev, New Press Lit Qtly*

Wilfrid Sheed   W
Stock Farm Ln/New Haven
Sag Harbor, NY 11963, 516-725-3797

Marilyn Pocius Shelton 🎤 ✈   P
13 Sunset Terr
Baldwinsville, NY 13027-1111, 315-638-4068
Internet: marp123@aol.com
    Pubs: *Bedside Prayers: Anth* (Harper SF, 1997),
    *Mudfish, Bitter Oleander, Blue Mesa Rev, Poetry Motel,
    Seasons, Green Hills Lit Lantern*
I.D.: Lithuanian-American. Groups: Teenagers

Reginald Shepherd 🎤 ✈   P
411 Second St, Apt 2
Ithaca, NY 14850-3511, 607-272-5076
Internet: rshepherd@worldnet.att.net
    Pubs: *Wrong, Angel, Interrupted, Some Are Drowning*
    (U Pitt Pr, 1999, 1996, 1994), *Best American Poetry:
    Anth* (S&S, 1996, 1995), *Nation, Poetry, Paris Rev*
I.D.: G/L/B/T, African-American. Groups: G/L/B/T

Alana Sherman   P
Alms House Press, PO Box 217, Pearl River, NY 10965
    Pubs: *Home Ground* (Alms Hse Pr, 1994), *Everything
    Is Gates* (Willamette River Bks, 1991)

Carol Sherman 🎤 ✈   P
PO Box 2083
Bridgehampton, NY 11932-2083, 631-537-7006
    Pubs: *Swimming in Lavender* (Fieldside Pr, 1998),
    *Women Under Assault, The Old Judge Stories, In
    Autumn: Anth* (Birnham Wood, 1995, 1993, 1994),
    Celebrating Gaia: Anth, Olden Times: Anth (Sweet
    Annie & Sweet Pea Rev, 2000, 1999)

Edith Shiffert   P
c/o Dennis Maloney, White Pine Press, 76 Center St,
Fredonia, NY 14063, 310-540-1880
    Pubs: *The Light Comes Slowly* (Katsura Pr, 1997),
    *When on the Edge, Touching the Point, New &
    Selected Poems* (White Pine Pr, 1991, 1990, 1979),
    Forest House with Cat (Japan; Unio Corp, 1991), *New
    Yorker, CSM, Kyoto Jrnl*

Dan Sicoli 🎤 ✈   P
Slipstream, PO Box 2071, New Market Stn, Niagara Falls,
NY 14301, 716-282-2616
    Pubs: *Sweet Nothings: Anth* (Indiana U Pr, 1994), *A
    Choice: Anth* (Malafemmina Pr, 1993), *A New
    Geography of Poets: Anth* (U Arkansas Pr, 1992), *ZZZ
    ZYNE, Zero City, Slipstream, Pearl, Sheila-Na-Gig*

Weslea Sidon   P
84 Hillside Ave
Roslyn Heights, NY 11577, 516-621-5117
    Pubs: *In Autumn* (Birnham Wood, 1994), *This Is Where
    I Live* (Shooting Star, 1981), *LIQ, Gulf Stream, Xanadu,
    Confrontation, Risings*

Peter Siedlecki 🎤 ✈   P
249 Winspear Ave
Buffalo, NY 14215-1035, 716-837-2863
Internet: psiedlec@daemen.edu
    Pubs: *Waterbirds* (Uprising Pr, 1994), *2 River View,
    Terra Poetica, Escarpment, New Kent Qtly, Stone
    Country, Slant, Nantucket Rev, Red Cedar, Buffalo Jrnl*
Groups: Children, Prisoners

Joan I. Siegel 🎤 ✈   P&W
PO Box 99
Blooming Grove, NY 10914-0099, 914-496-9784
    Pubs: *Beyond Lament: Anth* (Northwestern U Pr, 1998),
    American Visions: Anth (Mayfield Pub, 1994), *Calyx,
    Hawaii Pacific Rev, CSM, American Scholar, New
    Letters, Nightsun, Commonweal, Literary Rev, Yankee,
    Amicus Jrnl, River Oak Rev, Free Lunch*

Roberta Silman 🎤 ✈   W
18 Larchmont St
Ardsley, NY 10502-2327, 914-693-2816
    Pubs: *Beginning the World Again* (Viking, 1990), *The
    Dream Dredger* (Persea, 1986), *New England Stories:
    Anth* (Globe-Pequot Pr, 1992), *Voices Louder Than
    Words: Anth* (Vintage, 1991), *Virginia Qtly Rev,
    McCall's*
I.D.: Jewish

Maxine Silverman   P
224 Foss Dr
Upper Nyack, NY 10960, 914-353-4106
    Pubs: *Saturday's Women* (Saturday Pr, 1982), *Pushcart
    Prize III, Greenfield Rev*

Louis Simpson P&W
PO Box 119
Setauket, NY 11733, 516-689-0498
  Pubs: *There You Are* (Story Line Pr, 1995), *Jamaica Poems* (Pr of Appletree Alley, 1993), *Hudson Rev, Southern Rev, APR, Five Points*

Nancy Simpson 🎤 ✈ P
State Street Press, Brockport, NY 28904, 828-389-6497
  Pubs: *Night Student, Across Water* (State Street Pr, 1985, 1983), *Word & Witness: Anth* (Carolina Academic Pr, 1999), *Georgia Rev, Prairie Schooner, Indiana Rev, Florida Rev, New Virginia Rev, SPR, Confrontation*

Susan Sindall 🎤 ✈ P&W
PO Box 527
Shady, NY 12409, 914-679-7490
  Pubs: *Confluence, Passager, Kenyon Rev, Prairie Schooner, Pivot, 13th Moon, Salamander, Fiddlehead*
Groups: Children, Seniors

Marcia Slatkin P&W
PO Box 663
Shoreham, NY 11786-0663, 516-744-5023
  Pubs: *Poems 1974-81* (Backstreet Pr, 1982), *Paris Rev, San Francisco Chronicle, Earth's Daughters, Xanadu, Bellingham Rev, Sycamore Rev*

John C. Smedley W
14 Oakdale Dr
Hastings-On-Hudson, NY 10706
  Pubs: *The Villager, St. Andrews Rev, Phantasm*

Barbara Leavell Smith P
359 56 Rd, RD 1
Petersburg, NY 12138
  Pubs: *Appalachia, Waterways, Pegasus Rev, Footwork, Black Willow*

Bill Smith P&W
RFD 1, Box 280
Colton, NY 13625, 315-262-2436
  Pubs: *Adirondack Memories* (Tape; Northern Roads Productions, 1992), *I Always Tell the Truth: Anth* (Greenfield Rev Pr, 1990)

Jordan Smith 🎤 ✈ P
English Dept, Union College, Schenectady, NY 12308, 518-383-0775
Internet: smithj@union.edu
  Pubs: *The Household of Continuance* (Copper Beech, 1992), *Lucky Seven* (Wesleyan, 1988), *Agni, American Short Fiction, Antaeus, NER, Yale Rev*

Mason Smith P
N Point Rd
Long Lake, NY 12847, 518-624-6398
  Pubs: *Everybody Knows & Nobody Cares* (Knopf, 1971), *Blue Line*

W. D. Snodgrass 🎤 ✈ P
RD 1, Box 51
Erieville, NY 13061-9801, 315-684-3752
  Pubs: *The Fuehrer Bunker* (BOA Edtns, 1995), *Selected Poems 1957-1987* (Soho Pr, 1991, 1987)

Bonnie Snow PP
41 Ft Putnam St
Highland Falls, NY 10928
  Pubs: *Milkweed Chronicle, Playing for Free* (Wartsenall Records, 1988)

Miriam Solan P
1 Dolma Rd
Scarsdale, NY 10583, 914-725-1041
  Pubs: *Woman Combing* (Hard Pr, 1997), *For a Living: Anth* (U Illinois Pr, 1996), *Lingo, The World, Poetry NY*

J. R. Solonche 🎤 P
English Dept, Orange County Community College, 115 South St, Middletown, NY 10940-6404, 914-341-4021
  Pubs: *Anth of Mag Verse* (Monitor, 1997), *Blood to Remember: Anth* (Texas Tech U Pr, 1991), *Mixed Voices: Anth* (Milkweed Edtns, 1991), *Poet & Critic, New Criterion, Poetry NW, American Scholar, Literary Rev, Cumberland Poetry Rev, Yankee*

Ted Solotaroff W
19 Beachland Ave
East Quogue, NY 11942-4940, 514-728-7340
  Pubs: *A Few Good Voices in My Head* (H&R, 1988), *The Red Hot Vacuum* (Godine, 1980)

Donna Spector 🎤 ✈ P&W
115 Blooms Corners Rd
Warwick, NY 10990-2305, 914-986-7718
Internet: dspector@warwick.net
  Pubs: *At Our Core: Anth* (Papier-Mache Pr, 1998), *XY Files: Anth* (Sherman Asher Pub, 1997), *Sycamore Rev, Greensboro Rev, Poet & Critic, Poet Lore, Paterson Literary Rev, Bellingham Rev, Hiram Poetry Rev*

Susan Fantl Spivack 🎤 ✈ P
RD 1, PO Box 528
Cobleskill, NY 12043-9745, 518-234-3840
Internet: spivack@telenet.net
  Pubs: *Times River 2: Anth* (Singing Frog Pr, 1999), *Word Thursdays 2: Anth, Out of the Catskills & Just Beyond: Anth* (Bright Hill Pr, 1999, 1997), *Sunlight on the Moon: Anth* (Carpenter Gothic, 1998), *Calyx, Kalliope, Earth's Daughters*

B. A. St. Andrews 🎤 ✈ P
Upstate Medical Univ - SUNY, Bioethics & Medical Humanities, Syracuse, NY 13210, 315-464-6920
Internet: standreb@vax.cs.hscsyr.edu
  Pubs: *The Healing Muse* (Silverman Pr, 1999), *Stealing the Light* (Sous Pr, 1992), *Forbidden Fruit* (Whitston Pub, 1986), *Paris Rev, New Yorker, Commonweal, Gettysburg Rev, CSM, Carolina Qtly*

Megan Staffel W
4635 East Valley
Andover, NY 14806, 607-478-8178
Pubs: *The Notebook of Lost Things* (Soho Pr, 1999),
She Wanted Something Else (North Point Pr, 1987), *A
Length of Wire & Other Stories* (Pym Randall Pr,
1983), *Ploughshares, Kansas State Qtly*

Alice P. Stein P
166 Kingsbury Ln
Tonawanda, NY 14150
Pubs: *Lyric, California State Poetry Qtly, Erewhon,
Pastiche, Snippets, Light Year '87, Light, Pearl*

Charles Stein P
Station Hill Rd
Barrytown, NY 12507-5005, 914-758-3214
Pubs: *The Hat Rack Tree, Selected Poems from
Theforestforthetrees* (Station Hill Pr, 1994), *A Night of
Thought* (St. Lazaire, 1987), *Little Mag*

Alan L. Steinberg P
English Dept, Potsdam College, Potsdam, NY 13676,
315-267-2008
Pubs: *Cry of the Leopard* (St. Martin's Pr, 1997),
Divided (Aegina Pr, 1996), *The Road to Corinth*
(Players Pr, 1984), *Carolina Qtly, William & Mary Rev,
New Rev, Louisville Rev, Poem, Wisconsin Rev,
Blueline*

Russell Steinke P
109 Matthews Rd
Oakdale, NY 11769, 516-589-4164
Pubs: *Confrontation, Poetry Miscellany, Pembroke Mag,
Charleton Rev, John O'Hara Jrnl*

Eugene L. Stelzig P
6892 Bailey Rd
Groveland, NY 14462, 716-245-5273
Pubs: *Poetpourri, A Shout in the Street, Crab Creek
Rev, Greenfield Rev, Literary Rev, Sou'wester,
Desperate Act*

Jody T. Sterling P
76 Esopus Ave
Ulster Park, NY 12487
Pubs: *Bitterroot, Sunrust, Echoes, Art Times, Esprit*

Steve Stern W
42 Bryan St
Saratoga Springs, NY 12866, 518-583-1026
Pubs: *The Wedding Jester* (Graywolf, 1999), *A Plague
of Dreamers,* (Scribner, 1993), *Harry Kaplan's
Adventures* (Underground, 1990), *Lazer Malkin Enters
Heaven* (Viking, 1986), *The Moon & Ruben Shein*
(August Hse, 1984)

Lou Stevens PP
PO Box 2524
East Hampton, NY 11937-0246
Pubs: *Fine Art Photography, The Personal Peace
Program* (Perf; PPP Prod, 1998, 1993), *Anamiles* (Perf;
Clone Pub, 1992)

Edward William Stever P&W
Writers Edge, Box 284, Ridge, NY 11961, 516-924-7463
Pubs: *Propulsion, Transparency* (Writers Ink Pr, 1992,
1990), *LIQ, Chiron Rev, Poets On, Pearl, Live Poets,
Long Islander*

Margo Stever P
157 Millard Ave
Sleepy Hollow, NY 10591, 914-332-4469
Pubs: *Reading the Night Sky* (Riverstone Pr, 1996),
Imperiled Landscapes Endangered Legends: Anth
(Rizzoli Intl Pub, 1997), *Minnesota Rev, Ironwood,
Chelsea, NER, West Branch, Webster Rev, Seattle Rev*

Ellen Greene Stewart P
4 Roosevelt Ave
Roxbury, NY 12474-9778, 607-326-4340
Pubs: *Prose & Poet Tastery: Anth* (Integrity Pr, 1999),
*Catskill Mountains News, Ailanthus, Up Against the Wall
Mother, Archer, Encore, Pudding*

Ken Stone P
PO Box 392
Portlandville, NY 13834, 607-286-7500
Pubs: *A Lust in My Bones* (MAF Pr, 1990), *A Man
Holds a Tree* (Pygmy Forest Pr, 1989), *Jrnl of Poetry
Therapy, Piedmont Lit Rev, Lilliput, Innisfree*

Ruth Stone P
97 Mitchell Ave, Apt 2B
Binghamton, NY 13903-3245
Pubs: *Mother Stone's Nursery Rhymes* (MBIRA, 1992),
Who Is the Widow's Muse, Second Hand Coat (Yellow
Moon Pr, 1991, 1991), *Boulevard, American Voice, APR*

Marc J. Straus P
707 Westchester Ave
White Plains, NY 10604, 914-328-9696
Pubs: *Scarlet Crown* (Aureole Pr, 1994), *One Word*
(TriQtly Pr, 1994), *Field, Ploughshares, Kenyon Rev,
Passages North, Exquisite Corpse, Poetry East, TriQtly,
Virginia Qtly Rev*

David Levi Strauss P
244 Rock Hill Rd
High Falls, NY 12440-5412, 914-687-7914
Pubs: *Manoeuvres* (Aleph Pr/Eidolon Edtns, 1980),
49+1: Nouveaux Poètes Americains (Edtns Royaumont,
1991), *Apex of the M, Intent, Five Fingers Rev,
Hambone*

Julia P. Suarez ♀ ⊀   P
19 Tilton Ave
Oneonta, NY 13820-2619
Internet: suarezj@hartwick.edu
    Pubs: *The Lesser Light* (Swamp Pr, 1979), *Second
    Word Thursdays: Anth, Word Thursdays: Anth* (Bright
    Hill Pr, 1999, 1997), *Phoebe, Wordsmith, Salmagundi,
    Tightrope*

Robyn Supraner ♀ ⊀   P&W
420 Bryant Ave
Roslyn Harbor, NY 11576-1125, 516-621-1779
    Pubs: *Sam Sunday & the Mystery at the Ocean Beach
    Hotel* (Viking, 1996), *Under Open Sky: Poets on Wm.
    Cullen Bryant: Anth* (Fordham U Pr, 1986), *Berkeley
    Poetry Rev, Massachusetts Rev, BPJ, Prairie Schooner,
    Ploughshares, Confrontation*

Shulamith Surnamer ♀ ⊀   P&W
27 W Penn St
Long Beach, NY 11561, 516-889-7163
Internet: judith27@aol.com
    Pubs: *From Adam to Zipporah* (Judi-isms, 1991),
    *Filtered Images: Women Remembering Their
    Grandmothers: Anth* (Vintage '45 Pr, 1992), *Caprice,
    Vulcan's Lyre, Midnight Zines Café, LitvakSIG Poetry
    Page*

Hariette Surovell   W
c/o Henry Morrison, Henry Morrison, Inc, PO Box 235,
Bedford Hills, NY 10507, 914-666-3500
    Pubs: *The Stiffest of the Corpse: Anth* (City Lights Pub,
    1989), *Glamour, New York Woman, Seven Days,
    Playgirl*

Harriet Susskind ♀ ⊀   P
670 Pittsford-Mendon Rd
Pittsford, NY 14534, 716-381-3436
    Pubs: *To See the Speech of Trees* (Amygdala Pr,
    1995), *Denver Qtly, Prairie Schooner, Seneca Rev,
    Nimrod, Georgia Rev, Ohio Rev*

Lois Swann   W
22 Sagamore Rd, #5D
Bronxville, NY 10708, 914-961-8104
    Pubs: *Torn Covenants, The Mists of Manittoo* (Scribner,
    1981, 1976)

Phillip P. Sweeney   PP
137 Shamrock Pl, #2
Harpursville, NY 13787, 607-693-4138
    Pubs: *Wail* (Beverly Arts Council, 1991), *Fell Swoop:
    Big Horror Reader: Anth* (J. Daily, 1989)

Bruce Sweet ♀ ⊀   P&W
34 Hannahs Terr
Rochester, NY 14612-4909, 716-581-0998
    Pubs: *Mixed Voices* (Milkweed Edtns, 1991), *Yankee,
    Minnesota Monthly, Blueline, Commonweal*

David Swickard   P
PO Box 800
Amagansett, NY 11930
    Pubs: *Confrontation, Nimrod, Bluefish, Poet Lore,
    Mid-American Rev, CutBank, Panhandler*

Aaron Syl   P
English Dept, Dowling College, Oakdale, NY 11769,
516-567-4758
    Pubs: *Indigo & Other Poems, A Century of Yiddish
    Poetry: Anth* (Cornwall Bks, 1991, 1989), *Cumberland
    Poetry Jrnl, Kenyon Rev, NER, Writers' Forum*

William Sylvester ♀ ⊀   P&W
411 Parkside Ave
Buffalo, NY 14216-3404, 716-838-6780
Internet: sylvester@acsu.buffalo.edu
    Pubs: *War & Lechery, Fever Spreading Into Light,
    Heavy Metal from Pliny, Scarecrow Poetry: Anth*
    (Ashland Poetry Pr, 1995, 1992, 1992, 1994), *Acre, No
    Exit, House Organ, Exquisite Corpse, Chelsea, Poetry*

Mary Vigliante Szydlowski ♀ ⊀   W
37 Normanside Dr
Albany, NY 12208-1018, 518-453-3613
Internet: maszyd@aol.com
    Pubs: *Worship the Night, Silent Song* (Back In Print,
    2000, 2000), *I Can't Talk, I've Got Farbles in My
    Mouth* (Greene Bark Pr, 1995), *Worship the Night*
    (Leisure Bks, 1985), *Show & Tell, ESC! Mag, Star
    Light Star Bright, The Hand of My Enemy*

Deborah Tall   P
Hobart & Wm Smith Colleges, Geneva, NY 14456,
315-781-3364
    Pubs: *The Poet's Notebook* (Norton, 1995), *From
    Where We Stand* (Knopf, 1993), *Come Wind, Come
    Weather* (State Street Pr, 1988)

Patti Tana ♀ ⊀   P&W
462 W Beech St
Long Beach, NY 11561-3126, 516-432-3362
    Pubs: *When the Light Falls Short of the Dream* (Eighth
    Moon Pr, 1998), *Wetlands* (Papier-Mache Pr, 1993),
    Ask the Dreamer Where Night Begins (Kendall/Hunt,
    1986), *Hiram Poetry Rev, Anth of Magazine Verse,
    Nassau Rev*
Groups: Jewish, Women

Barry Targan ♀ ⊀   P&W
259 Mahaffey Rd
Greenwich, NY 12834, 518-692-9409
    Pubs: *Ark of the Marindor* (MacMurray & Beck, 1998),
    Tangerine Tango Equation (Thunder's Mouth, 1991),
    Falling Free (U Illinois Pr, 1989), *Kingdoms* (SUNY Pr,
    1981), *NAR, Yankee, Sewanee Rev, Confrontations*

Ann R. Taylor P
91 Acacia Ave
Hempstead, NY 11550, 516-485-9206
  Pubs: *Feel 'N' Good* (Delar Pub Co, 1986), *Hopes & Dreams* (Panache Enterprises, 1986)

Ted Taylor P
82 Eleanor Dr
Mahopac, NY 10541, 914-628-6307
  Pubs: *Whetstone, Atlanta Rev, The Bridge, Slugfest, No Exit, Pebbles, Amaranth, Wolf Head Qtly, Kit-Cat Rev*

Gayl Teller 🎤 ✈ P
1 Florence Ln
Plainview, NY 11803-3903, 516-931-5876
  Pubs: *At the Intersection of Everything You Have Ever Loved* (San Diego Poets Pr, 1989), *Sow's Ear Poetry Rev, MacGuffin, Crone's Nest, Phoebe, Halftones to Jubilee, Dominion Rev, Spring, Hudson Valley Echoes*

Silvia Tennenbaum W
763 Fireplace Rd
East Hampton, NY 11937, 516-324-9618
  Pubs: *Yesterday's Streets* (Random Hse, 1981), *Best American Short Stories 1978, American Rev*

Kathleen M. Tenpas 🎤 P
7549 Rte 474 N Clymer
Panama, NY 14767, 716-355-4176
Internet: hillfarm@cecomet.net
  Pubs: *Hill Farm* (Arachne, 1985), *Seedbed to Harvest: Anth* (Seven Buffalos, 1985), *Artifacts, Chadakoin Rev*
I.D.: Rural Communities, Farming

Virginia R. Terris 🎤 ✈ P
84 N Bayview Ave
Freeport, NY 11520-1938, 516-378-3481
  Pubs: *Folding/Unfolding,* (Birnham Wood, 1992), *Hanging Loose, LIQ, Confrontation, SPR, Hampden-Sydney Rev*

Holly Thompson W
46 Grand St
Croton-on-Hudson, NY 10520, 914-271-9242
  Pubs: *Potato Eyes, Dominion Rev, Thema, Printed Matter, Wingspan*

Ed Tick P
10 Winthrop Ave
Albany, NY 12203, 518-438-3779
  Pubs: *Healing a Generation* (Guilford, 1991), *Sacred Mountain: Encounters with the Viet Nam Beast* (Moon Bear, 1989), *Voices, Key West Rev*

Ellen Tifft 🎤 ✈ P&W
45 Crane Rd
Elmira, NY 14901-9240, 607-732-4756
Internet: www.xenosbooks.com
  Pubs: *Moon, Moon, Tell Me True* (Xenos Bks, 1996), *Yale Rev, New Yorker, Poetry, New Letters, Laurel Rev, Transatlantic Rev*
I.D.: Middle-Aged. Groups: Seniors, Quakers

Carl Tiktin W
87 Alta Ave
Yonkers, NY 10705, 914-968-3655
  Pubs: *Ron, The Hourglass Man* (Arbor Hse, 1979, 1978)

Martin Tucker 🎤 ✈ P&W
English Dept, Long Island Univ, CW Post College,
Brookville, NY 11548, 516-299-2391
  Pubs: *Attention Spans* (Potpourri Pub, 1997), *Homes of Locks & Mysteries* (Dovetail Pr, 1982), *Fathers: Anth* (St. Martin's Pr, 1999), *Confrontation, Boulevard, Sarasota Poetry Rev, Northern Centinel, Choice, Literary Rev, Collages & Bricolages*

Chase Twichell 🎤 ✈ P
Ausable Press, HCR 1, PO Box 46, Keene, NY
12942-9717, 518-576-9273
Internet: editor@ausablepress.com
  Pubs: *The Snow Watcher, The Ghost of Eden* (Ontario Rev Pr, 1998, 1995), *Perdido* (FSG, 1991), *The Odds, Northern Spy* (U Pitt Pr, 1986, 1981)

Jim Tyack 🎤 ✈ P
326 Echo Lake Rd
New Hampton, NY 10958-3522, 914-374-6042
Internet: moho@orn.net
  Pubs: *Tundra, A Limousine to Nowhere* (Street Pr, 1997, 1994), *Thus Spake the Corpse: Anth* (Black Sparrow Pr, 1999), *McGraw-Hill Book of Poetry: Anth* (McGraw-Hill, 1994), *Exquisite Corpse, Rain City Rev, Prairie Schooner*

Barbara Unger 🎤 ✈ P&W
101 Parkside Dr
Suffern, NY 10901, 914-357-1683
  Pubs: *Two Worlds Walking* (New Rivers Pr, 1994), *Bronx Accent: A Literary & Pictorial History of the Borough: Anth* (Rutgers U Pr, 2000), *Massachusetts Rev, Nation, NYQ, Denver Qtly, Carolina Qtly*
Groups: Seniors, Schools

Sonia Usatch 🎤 ✈ PP
371 S Ocean Ave #2
Patchogue, NY 11772-3729, 631-289-9631
Internet: susatch@suffolk.lib.ny.us
  Pubs: *Noodle Kugel & Life's Other Meichels* (Writers Ink Pr, 1989), *Journal of Poetry Therapy*
Groups: Hospitals, Singles

Desire Vail 🎤   P
6136 Unionville Rd
Bath, NY 14810-8164, 607-776-9157
  Pubs: *In the Fold of a Hill, First Shine of Dawn, See
  How Wet the Street Sounds* (FootHills Pub, 2000,
  1996, 1992)

Frank Van Zant 🎤 ✈   P
11 Metcale Ln
E Northport, NY 11731-4419, 516-368-6306
Internet: veezee@staffordnet.com
  Pubs: *The Lives of the Two-Headed Baseball Siren*
  (Kings Estate Pr, 2000), *Climbing Daddy Mountain*
  (Pudding Hse, 2000), *What's Become of Eden?*
  (Slapering Hol Pr, 1994), *Our Mothers, Our Selves:
  Anth* (Greenwood, 1996), *Yankee, Context South*

Janine Pommy Vega 🎤 ✈   P
PO Box 162
Bearsville, NY 12409-0162, 914-688-7068
  Pubs: *Mad Dogs of Trieste* (Black Sparrow Pr, 2000),
  Tracking the Serpent (City Lights Bks, 1997), *Women
  of the Beat Generation: Anth* (Conari Pr, 1996), *What
  We Know So Far: Anth* (St Martin's Pr, 1995), *Nexus,
  Luna Luna*
Lang: Spanish

John Vernon 🎤 ✈   P&W
English Dept, Binghamton Univ, Box 6000, Binghamton,
NY 13902-6000, 607-777-2750
Internet: fac026@binghamton.edu
  Pubs: *The Great Unknown, A Book of Reasons* (HM,
  2001, 1999), *All for Love* (S&S, 1995), *Peter Doyle*
  (Random Hse, 1991), *Lindbergh's Son* (Viking, 1987),
  The Book of Love: Anth (Norton, 1998), *APR, Paris
  Rev, Poetry, Harper's*

Janine M. Veto 🎤 ✈   P&W
92 Crescent St
Sag Harbor, NY 11963
Internet: jmveto@aol.com
  Pubs: *The Dream Book* (Schocken, 1988), *Iris* (Alyson,
  1983), *la bella figura, Cedar Rock*

Paul Violi   P
23 Cedar Ledges
Putnam Valley, NY 10579-2133, 914-526-3392
  Pubs: *Breakers* (Coffee Hse Pr, 2000), *Fracas, The
  Curious Builder, Likewise* (Hanging Loose Pr, 1998,
  1992, 1988), *Splurge* (Sun Pr, 1982), *Kenyon Rev,
  Partisan Rev, Harper's, NAW*

Helena Maria Viramontes   W
Cornell Univ, Dept of English
Ithaca, NY 14853, 607-255-6800
  Pubs: *Under the Feet of Jesus* (Dutton/Penguin 1995),
  The Moths & Other Stories (Arte Publico Pr 1985)

Anneliese Wagner 🎤 ✈   P
36 Shaw Pl
Hartsdale, NY 10530-1015, 914-761-5874
  Pubs: *Murderous Music* (Chicory Blue Pr, 1995), *Fish
  Magic* (Black Swan Pr, 1989), *NW Rev, West Branch,
  Paris Rev, Prairie Schooner, Chelsea, Kenyon Rev,
  Ploughshares, Threepenny Rev*

Eliot Wagner   W
651 Sheffield Rd
Ithaca, NY 14850-9253, 212-362-0609
  Pubs: *My America!* (Kenan, 1980), *Better Occasions*
  (Crowell, 1974), *Grand Concourse* (Bobbs Merrill, 1964),
  Antioch Rev

Phil Wagner 🎤 ✈   W
1675 Amazon Rd
Mohegan Lake, NY 10547-1804
  Pubs: *Marlowe in the South Seas* (Cove View, 2001),
  *Iconoclast, Libido, Reality & Meaning, Mediphors,
  Objectivity, Common Journeys, Samisdat*

Kathleen Wakefield   P
1840 Baird Rd
Penfield, NY 14526-1046, 716-586-1368
  Pubs: *Notations on the Visible World* (Anhinga Pr,
  2000), *There & Back* (State Street Pr, 1993), *Georgia
  Rev, Kenyon Rev, Image, The Jnl, Poetry*

Charlotte Zoe Walker 🎤 ✈   W
Hummingbird House, PO Box 14, Gilbertsville, NY
13776-0014, 607-783-2278
Internet: walkercz@oneonta.edu
  Pubs: *Condor & Hummingbird* (Women's Pr, 1987),
  Intimate Nature (Anth (Ballantine, 1998), *Storming
  Heaven's Gate: Anth* (Penguin, 1997), *O. Henry
  Awards: Anth* (Doubleday, 1991), *Ms., Georgia Rev*

Lois V. Walker 🎤 ✈   P
149 Harbor S
Amityville, NY 11701-3820, 516-691-2376
Internet: lvwalkerappts@earthlink.net
  Pubs: *You & You & Me* (Studio, 1993), *Saturday's
  Women: Anth* (Saturday Pr, 1982), *Xanadu, Helicon 9,
  New Letters, Sojourner, Poets On*

George Wallace   P
Long Islander, 313 Main St, Huntington, NY 11743,
516-427-7000
  Pubs: *Tales of a Yuppie Dropout* (Writers Ink, 1992),
  The Milking Jug (CCC, 1989), *Lips, Rialto, South
  Florida Poetry Rev*

Thom Ward 🎤 ✈ P
1054 Stafford Rd
Palmyra, NY 14522-9561, 315-597-1155
Internet: boaedit@frontiernet.net
Pubs: *Small Boat with Oars of Different Size* (Carnegie Mellon, 1999), *Tumblekid* (Devil's Millhopper Pr, 1999) *Anth of Magazine Verse* (Anth of Mag Verse, 1997), *Atlantic, Poetry NW, Tar River Poetry*

David S. Warren W
514 Edgewood Pl
Ithaca, NY 14850, 607-273-1283
Pubs: *Natural Bone, The World According to Two-Feathers* (Ithaca Hse, 1979, 1973)

Burton D. Wasserman 🎤 P
191 Winding Brook Rd
New Rochelle, NY 10804-1920, 914-235-2256
Pubs: *The XY Files: Anth* (Sherman Asher Pub, 1997), *Images of the Holocaust: Anth* (NTC Pub Group, 1996), *Blood to Remember: Anth* (Texas Tech U Pr, 1991), *Atlanta Rev, California Qtly, Mediphors, Black River Rev, Dickinson Rev, Potpourri, Fox Cry*

Rosanne Wasserman P
PO Box 704
Hudson, NY 12534, 516-767-8503
Pubs: *No Archive on Earth, The Lacemakers* (Gnosis Pr, 1995, 1992), *Sultur, Joe Soap's Canoe, Boulevard, Broadway, Caprice, Lingo*

Angus M. Watkins P
106 Pullman Ave
Kenmore, NY 14217-1516, 716-877-0963
Pubs: *Gathered at the River* (White Wolf Edtns, 1993), *River Poems: Anth* (Hudson Valley Writers Ctr, 1992), *Poetic Space, Blue Unicorn, Rolling Coulter*

R. B. Weber P
Humanities Dept, Southampton College, Southampton, NY 11968, 516-283-4000
Pubs: *The Fishing-Print Poems, Poems from the Xenia Hotel* (Street Pr, 1984, 1980), *Oxalis*

James L. Weil P
103 Van Etten Blvd
New Rochelle, NY 10804-2319, 914-636-7569
Pubs: *Washday, & Others* (Kelly-Winterton Pr, 1999), *Founding Fathers* (Origin Pr, 1997), *Hummingbird, Harvard Mag, Potlatch, Notre Dame Rev, Shearsman, Tel-Let*

Gregg Thomas Weinlein P&W
35 Albany Pl
East Greenbush, NY 12061, 518-479-7221
Pubs: *In the Mirror of Departures* (Claddagh Pr, 1992), *The Avenue of Tears* (Kelly Colm Pr, 1986), *Albany Rev, American Family*

Paul Weinman P
79 Cottage Ave
Albany, NY 12203, 518-482-3003
Pubs: *Tongue-Dancing* (Concrete Block Pr, 1993), *Suck My Cock, White Boy* (Drew Blood Pr, 1992), *Shattered Wig, Lost & Found Times, Pink Pages, NYQ*

Sigmund Weiss P
7 Neil Dr
Lake Grove, NY 11755-2608, 516-751-3309
Pubs: *Survivor in Limbo* (JVC Bks, 1990), *Impetus, Thirteen, San Fernando Poetry Jrnl, Orphic Lute, Omnific, Cerberus*

Beverley Wiggins Wells P
Black Belles-Lettres, PO Box 2019, Sag Harbor, NY 11963-0058, 516-725-9128
Pubs: *Simply Black* (Canio's Edtns, 1993), *A Rock Against the Wind: Anth* (Putnam Berkley Group, 1996), *Essence, Dickinson Rev, Texas Jrnl of Women & Law*

Bill Wertheim P
100 Sycamore Ave
Mount Vernon, NY 10553, 914-664-5452
Pubs: *Building a New Home* (First Issue Pr, 1977)

Paul West 🎤 ✈ W
126 Texas Ln
Ithaca, NY 14850-1755
Pubs: *O.K.* (Scribner, 2000), *The Dry Danube* (New Directions, 2000), *Conjunctions, Yale Rev, Parnassus, ArtForum, Witness*

William Wetmore W
Cascade Mountain Vineyards, Flint Hill Rd, Amenia, NY 12501, 914-373-9021
Pubs: *Here Comes Jamie* (Little, Brown, 1972), *All the Right People* (Doubleday, 1964)

Maxwell Corydon Wheat, Jr. 🎤 ✈ P
333 Bedell St
Freeport, NY 11520-5131, 516-623-5530
Pubs: *Christian Century, Friends Jrnl, Bird Watcher's Digest, Appalachia, Confrontation, Nassau Rev*
Groups: Nature/Environment

Claire Nicolas White 🎤 ✈ P&W
Moriches Rd, Box 5, RFD 1
St James, NY 11780, 516-584-5736
Pubs: *Riding at Anchor* (Waterline Bks, 1994), *Fragments of Stained Glass* (Mercury Hse, 1981), *World Poetry: Anth* (Norton, 1998), *Critic, Partisan Rev, Confrontation, Primavera, New Yorker*
Lang: French, Dutch. Groups: Children, Seniors

Sea-Flower White Cloud Dawson 🎤 ✈   P
203 Concord Ln
Middletown, NY 10940, 914-342-6982
  Pubs: *Planetary Action* (CT Robinson, 1971),
  Akwesasne Notes
I.D.: Native American. Groups: College/Univ

Marsha White   P
Mohawk Valley Community College, Floyd Ave, Rome, NY
13440
  Pubs: *The Mother Tongue* (Outland Pr, 1975),
  Ironwood, New American Rev, New Jersey Poetry Jrnl

Steven F. White 🎤 ✈   P
St. Lawrence Univ, Modern Languages Dept, Canton, NY
13617, 315-379-5160
Internet: swhite@stlawu.edu
  Pubs: *Fire that Engenders Fire* (Verbum, 2000), *From
  the Country of Thunder, For the Unborn, Burning the
  Old Year* (Unicorn, 1990, 1986, 1984), *Ayahuasca
  Reader: Anth* (Synergetic, 2000)
Lang: Spanish

Gary J. Whitehead   P
34-A Wawayanda Rd
Wawrek, NY 10990, 914-986-8089
  Pubs: *Walking Back to Providence* (Sow's Ear Pr
  1997), *Voices on the Landscape: Contemporary Iowa
  Poets: Anth* (Loess Hills Pr, 1996), *What's Become of
  Eden: Poems of Family at Century's End: Anth*
  (Slapering Hol Pr, 1994), *DoubleTake, BPJ, Poet Lore*

Max Wickert   PW
Dept of English, 306 Clemens, Univ of Buffalo, Amherst,
NY 14260, 7136452575x1032
  Pubs: *Pat Sonnets* (Street Pr, 2000), *All the Weight of
  the Still Midnight* (Outriders, 1972), *Poetry, Shenandoah,
  Sewanee Rev, APR, Chicago Rev, Choice, The Lyric,
  Xanadu, Pequod*

Patricia Wilcox   P&W
27 Chestnut St
Binghamton, NY 13905, 607-772-8750
  Pubs: *An Exile from Silence* (Alembic Pr, 1981), *A
  Public & Private Hearth* (Bellevue, 1978), *New Republic,
  Missouri Rev, Mss., Denver Qtly, Emory U Qtly, Spirit*

Nancy Willard 🎤 ✈   P
Vassar College, Poughkeepsie, NY 12604
  Pubs: *Swimming Lessons, Sister Water* (Knopf, 1998,
  1994), *Telling Time: Angels, Ancestors, & Stories* (HB,
  1993)

Gil Williams   P
60 Schubert St
Binghamton, NY 13905, 607-771-6800
  Pubs: *Moving on* (Bellevue Pr, 1969), *Dear Winter:
  Anth* (Northwoods Pr, 1984), *Aspect, Shocks*

Russ Williams 🎤 ✈   P
Greemantle, 12 S Helderberg Pkwy, Slingerlands, NY
12159-9262, 518-439-3260
Internet: lrpleader@aol.com
  Pubs: *Gates to the City* (Albany Tricentennial, 1986),
  North Country: Anth (Greenfield Rev Pr, 1986), *Blueline,
  Bullet, Glens Falls Rev*

Robin Kay Willoughby   P
1711 Amherst St
Buffalo, NY 14214, 716-837-7778
  Pubs: *Not a Poem* (Press Me Close, 1983), *Earth's
  Daughters, Contact II, Place Stamp Here*

Pearl Mary Wilshaw   P
59 S Ocean Ave
Center Moriches, NY 11934-3332
  Pubs: *Plainsongs, Midwest Poetry Rev, Ginger Hill,
  Twilight Ending, Poetry Depth Qtly, Tucumacari Lit Rev,
  Mobius, Nomad's Choir*

Howard Winn 🎤 ✈   P
22A Sheldon Dr
Poughkeepsie, NY 12603-4818, 914-462-1604
Internet: ohwinn@banet.net
  Pubs: *Bridges* (Springtown Pr, 1988), *Four Picture
  Sequence* (Front Street Pub, 1978), *MacGuffin, Pearl,
  Slant, Small Pond, Kansas Qtly*

Janet B. Winn   W
22A Sheldon Dr
Poughkeepsie, NY 12603-4818, 914-462-1604
Internet: ohwinn@banet.net
  Pubs: *The Open Mind* (Peter Lang, 1989), *Connecticut
  Low* (HM, 1980), *Sucarnochee Rev, MacGuffin*

Stephen Wolf   W
103 Willis Ave
Port Jefferson, NY 11777-2076
  Pubs: *American Families* (NAL, 1989), *Playboy*

Daniel Wolff   P
12 Castle Heights
Upper Nyack, NY 10960
  Pubs: *You Send Me* (Morrow, 1995), *Danny Lyon
  Photo Film* (Edtns Braus, 1991), *The Real World* (Sons
  of Leisure, 1981), *Partisan Rev, Musician, Paris Rev,
  Threepenny Rev, Sulfur, DoubleTake*

Amy An Mei Wong   P&W
2089 Kodma Pl
East Meadow, NY 11554-2519, 516-794-9587
  Pubs: *55 to the Nth Possibilities* (Turn of River Pr,
  1991), *Long Island Chinese Center Jrnl*

Wendy Wood   P
PO Box 127
Cuddebackville, NY 12729
  Pubs: *Mudfish, Alabama Lit Rev*

Karen Wunsch 🎤   W
93 Glenwood Ave
New Rochelle, NY 10801-3127, 914-654-0354
    Pubs: *Living & Learning* (Avon, 1972), *Press, North Dakota Qtly, Confrontation, Epoch*

Bettie Wysor   W
70 Cove Hollow Rd
East Hampton, NY 11937, 516-324-8664
    Pubs: *Echos, A Stranger's Eyes* (Jove, 1983, 1981), *To Remember Tina* (Stein & Day, 1975)

Carolyn Yalkut   P&W
Director, Journalism Program, SUNY Albany, English Dept, Albany, NY 12222, 518-442-4065
    Pubs: *Northeast Jrnl, West Hills Rev, Webster Rev, Poet & Critic, Tales*

Jose Yaryura-Tobias   P&W
935 Northern Blvd, #102
Great Neck, NY 11021
    Pubs: *El Ser Humano Integral* (Mexico; Diana, 1992), *The Integral Being* (H Holt, 1987), *Circular* (Botella al Mar, 1983)

R. H. Yodice   P&W
PO Box 534
Hurley, NY 12443-0534
    Pubs: *Voices in the Wind* (DocWat, 1999), *Oxalis, Writer's World, Byline, Writers' Haven Jrnl, Mage, Orphic Lute*

Christoper A. Zackey   P&W
19 Chenango Ave S, #3
Clinton, NY 13323-1661, 315-853-3112
    Pubs: *New Hope Intl, Piedmont Lit Rev, Slant, Minas Tirith Evening-Star, Lost Worlds, Mythic Circle*

Jane Breskin Zalben 🎤 ✈   P&W
70 South Rd
Port Washington, NY 11050-2601, 516-944-8590
Internet: janezalben@hotmail.com
    Pubs: *To Every Season, Unfinished Dreams* (S&S, 1999, 1996), *Beni's Family Treasury, Beni's Family Cookbook* (H Holt, 1999, 1996), *New York Times, Newsday*
    Groups: Children, Spiritual/Religious

Leah Zazulyer   P
450 Rugby Ave
Rochester, NY 14619, 716-436-5035
    Pubs: *The Word Is a Wedding* (FootHills Pub, 1993), *Round Trip Year: A Book of Days* (Vick-Witte, 1992), *Literal Latte, Bridges, Ontario Rev, Georgia Rev, South Coast Poetry Jrnl, Negative Capability*

David Zeiger 🎤 ✈   P
9 Fourth Rd
Great Neck, NY 11021-1505, 516-466-2977
    Pubs: *Life on My Breath* (Sarna Pr, 1995), *We Speak for Peace: Anth* (KIT, 1993), *Mixed Voices: Anth* (Milkweed Edtns, 1991), *Wordsmith, Verve, Minnesota Rev, Midstream, Slant*

Lila Zeiger 🎤 ✈   P
PO Box 4518
Great Neck, NY 11023, 516-466-2977
    Pubs: *The Way to Castle Garden* (State Street Pr, 1982), *Paris Rev, Georgia Rev, New Republic*

James A. Zoller 🎤 ✈   P&W
9800 Seymour St
Houghton, NY 14744-8703, 716-567-9465
Internet: jzoller@houghton.edu
    Pubs: *Literature: Anth* (McGraw-Hill, 1994), *Christian Century, Prose Poem, Laurel Rev, Red Dancefloor*

Carol Zuravleff   P
RD 2, Box 73
Otego, NY 13825, 607-988-7170
    Pubs: *Venus & Don Juan, Pure* (TriQtly Bks, 1996, 1994), *Chimera* (Peregrine Smith Bks, 1990), *Day of the Body* (Ion Bks, 1986), *APR, Atlantic, NER, TriQtly, Partisan Rev, Ploughshares, Kenyon Rev, Shenandoah, Southern Rev, Volt*

NEW YORK CITY

Stephen Abbott   P
164 E 81 St
New York, NY 10028-1804
    Pubs: *Holy Terror* (Crossing Pr, 1989), *Skinny Trip to a Far Place* (e.g. Pr, 1988)

Walter Abish   P&W
PO Box 485 Cooper Sta
New York, NY 10276, 212-982-3074
    Pubs: *Eclipse Fever* (Knopf, 1993), *99: The New Meaning* (Burning Deck, 1990), *How German Is It* (New Directions, 1980)

William Abrahams   W
Holt, Rinehart & Winston, 383 Madison Ave, New York, NY 10017, 212-688-9100

Linsey Abrams W
c/o Laurie E. Liss, Harvey Klinger Inc., 301 W 53 St, Ste 13B, New York, NY 10019, 212-581-7068
Pubs: *Our History in New York* (Great Marsh Pr/Umbrella Pubs, 1998), *The Reading Room: Writing of the Moment: Anth* (Great Marsh Pr, 2000), *Glimmer Train, Central Park, Colorado Rev, Seattle Rev, New Directions Annual, 13th Moon*
Groups: G/L/B/T

Richard S. Abrons W
812 Park Ave, #4E
New York, NY 10021, 212-517-4230
Pubs: *Nebraska Rev, MacGuffin, Sou'wester, Columbia, NAR, Cosmopolitan, Fiction Network, Other Voices*

Diane Ackerman P
Random House, 201 E 50 St, New York, NY 10022
Pubs: *I Praise My Destroyer, The Rarest of the Rare, Jaguar of Sweet Laughter: New & Selected Poems* (Random Hse, 1998, 1995, 1991)

Alice Adams W
c/o Amanda Urban, ICM, 40 W 57 St, New York, NY 10019, 212-556-5600
Pubs: *Almost Perfect, Caroline's Daughters, After You've Gone* (Knopf, 1993, 1991, 1989)

Anna Adams P
Doug Treem, Agent, 217 E 22 St, #5, New York, NY 10010, 212-889-0462
Pubs: *The Ratio of One to a Stone* (First East Coast Theatre & Pub Co, 1982), *NYQ, QRL, Poetry, Best Poems of 1957*

Elizabeth Adams W
Philip Spitzer Literary Agency, 788 9th Ave, New York, NY 10019, 212-265-6003
Pubs: *Phoebe, Caprice, Chicago Rev, Alaska Qtly Rev, NAR, Groundswell, Intro 10, The Raddle Moon, Massachusetts Rev*

Glenda Adams W
Goodman Assoc, 500 W End Ave, New York, NY 10024
Pubs: *The Tempest of Clemenza* (Faber & Faber, 1996), *Longleg* (Cane Hill, 1992), *TriQtly, Village Voice, Hanging Loose, Seattle Rev*

Lloyd E. Addison 🎤 P
1704 St Johns Pl, #7F
Brooklyn, NY 11233, 718-771-2778
Pubs: *Mystery of the Invention of Doublecross Baseball* (Private Pubs, 1981), *Drum Voices Revue*

C. S. Adler W
Avon Books, 1350 Ave of the Americas, New York, NY 10019
Pubs: *Courtyard Cat* (Clarion, 1995), *Youn Hee & Me* (HB, 1995)

Joel Agee W
Donadio & Olson, Inc, 121 W 27 St, Ste 704, New York, NY 10001, 212-691-8077
Pubs: *Twelve Years—An American Boyhood in East Germany* (FSG, 1981), *New Yorker, Harper's*

Jack Agueros P&W
212 W 14 St
New York, NY 10011, 212-243-2270
Pubs: *Dominoes & Other Stories* (Curbstone Pr, 1993), *Sonnets from the Puerto Rican* (Hanging Loose Pr, 1996), *Parnassus, Callaloo, Agni*

Ellen Akins W
Charlotte Sheedy Literary Agency, 65 Bleecker St, New York, NY 10012, 212-780-9800
Pubs: *Hometown Brew* (Knopf, 1998), *Public Life* (HC, 1993), *World Like a Knife* (John Hopkins U Pr, 1991), *Georgia Rev, Southern Rev, SW Rev, Missouri Rev*

Viki Akiwumi 🎤 ✈ PP&P
61 E 8th St, #180
New York, NY 10003-6450, 212-459-4540
Pubs: *Sister Fire* (HC, 1994), *In the Tradition* (Harlem River Pr, 1993), *Ancient Youth & Elders Reborn* (Universal Black Writers Pr, 1985), *Essence, Testimony, Presstime*
I.D.: African-American

Daisy Aldan P&W
260 W 52 St, #5-L
New York, NY 10019
Pubs: *Day of the Wounded Eagle* (The LeMay Co, 1991), *In Passage* (Folder Edtns, 1990), *Anais Nin: A Book of Mirrors: Anth* (Sky Blue Pr, 1996), *Caprice, Threefold Rev*

Charlotte Alexander P
112 E 10 St, #2
New York, NY 10003
Pubs: *Outerbridge, Mid-American Rev, Earth's Daughters, Three Gray Geese Anth, Tide Turning Anth, The Dolphin's Arc Anth*

Elena Alexander P&W
198 Broadway, Rm 903
New York, NY 10038-2515, 212-693-0405
Pubs: *Second Word Thursdays: Anth* (Bright Hill Pr 1999), *Aloud: Voices from the Nuyorican Poets Cafe: Anth* (H Holt, 1994), *Hanging Loose, LUNGFULL!, Minnesota Rev, Bomb, Hotel Series*

Meena Alexander 🎤 ✈ P&W
c/o English Dept, Hunter College, CUNY, 695 Park Ave, New York, NY 10021, 212-772-5200
Internet: MAlexander@gc.cuny.edu
Pubs: *Manhattan Music* (Mercury Hse, 1997), *River & Bridge* (Toronto Rev Pr, 1996), *Shock of Arrival* (Southend Pr, 1996), *Fault Lines* (Feminist Pr, 1993), *Grand Street, Poetry Rev*
Lang: Malayalam, Hindi. I.D.: Asian-American. Groups: Women, Asian-American

Austin M. Alexis 🎤 ✈ P&W
58 E 4 St, #9
New York, NY 10003-8914, 212-260-7525
Internet: amalexisjj@yahoo.com
Pubs: *NE Corridor, The Jrnl, Obsidian II, Barrow St, Mixed Media, Connecticut River Rev, James White Rev*
I.D.: African-American. Groups: G/L/B/T, Performance

Donna Allegra P&W
60 E 4 St, #3
New York, NY 10003-8916, 212-477-1109
Pubs: *Does Your Mama Know?: Anth* (Redbone Pr, 1997), *Hers 2: Brilliant New Fiction by Lesbians: Anth* (Faber & Faber, 1997), *Best Lesbian Erotica: Anth* (Cleis Pr, 1997), *Close Calls: Anth, SportsDykes: Anth* (St. Martin's, 1996, 1994)

Deborah Allen 🎤 P
PO Box 1452, Stuyvesant Sta
New York, NY 10009
Pubs: *Yellow Leaves* (A Musty Bone, 1990), *Three Mile Harbor, Salmon, Painted Bride Qtly, South Dakota Rev, BPJ, Blue Unicorn, Ledge*

Edward Allen W
c/o Irene Skolnick, Curtis Brown Ltd., 10 Astor Pl, New York, NY 10003-6935, 212-473-5400
Pubs: *Straight Through the Night* (Soho Pr, 1989), *Best American Short Stories 1990: Anth, GQ, New Yorker*

Paula Gunn Allen P
Sanford J. Greenburger Assoc., 55 Fifth Ave, New York, NY 10003-4301, 212-206-5600
Pubs: *The Sacred Hoop* (Beacon Pr, 1992), *The Voice of the Turtle: Anth* (Ballantine Pr, 1994), *Chicago, Yefief, Global Rev, Transpersonal Rev*

Roberta Allen 🎤 ✈ W
c/o DeAnna Heindel, Georges Borchardt Inc., 136 E 57 St, New York, NY 10022
Pubs: *The Daughter, The Travelling Woman* (Painted Leaf Pr, 2000, 2000), *Certain People* (Coffee Hse Pr, 1997), *Amazon Dream* (City Lights Bks, 1993), *Open City, Epoch, Bomb, American Voice*

Mindy Aloff P
708 Eighth Ave, #4L
Brooklyn, NY 11215
Pubs: *Night Lights* (Prescott Street Pr, 1979), *APR, Choice, St. Andrews Rev*

Julia Alvarez 🎤 ✈ P&W
S. Bergholz Literary Services, 17 W 10 St, #5, New York, NY 10011, 212-387-0545
Pubs: *In the Name of Salome, Something to Declare, Yo!, In the Time of the Butterflies, How the Garcia Girls Lost Their Accents* (Algonquin Bks, 2000, 1998, 1997, 1994, 1991), *New Yorker, Ploughshares*

Mark Ameen 🎤 ✈ P&W
235 E 4 St #5A
New York, NY 10009-7231
Internet: markjameen@aol.com
Pubs: *The Buried Body* (Amethyst, 1990), *A Circle of Sirens* (Seahorse Pr, 1985), *James White Rev, Between C&D*
I.D.: G/L/B/T. Groups: G/L/B/T, Performance

Beth Anderson 🎤 ✈ PP&P
135 Eastern Pkwy Apt 4D
Brooklyn, NY 11238, 718-636-6010
Internet: www.interport.net/~beand/
Pubs: *Text-Sound Texts, Dramatika Mag, Poetry Mailing List, Assemblings, Flash Art, Ear Mag*
Groups: Women

Jack Anderson 🎤 ✈ P
40 E 10 St, #1H
New York, NY 10003-6221, 212-677-7698
Pubs: *Traffic* (New Rivers Pr, 1998), *Field Trips on the Rapid Transit* (Hanging Loose Pr, 1990), *Selected Poems* (Release Pr, 1983), *Poetry, Paris Rev, Caliban, Hanging Loose, Chelsea*

Poul Anderson W
Scovil-Chichak-Galen Literary Agency, 381 Park Ave S, #1112, New York, NY 10016, 212-679-8686
Pubs: *The Stars Are Also Fire, Harvest of Stars* (Tor, 1994, 1993), *Orion Shall Rise* (Timescape, 1983)

Michael Andre 🎤 ✈ P
Unmuzzled Ox, 105 Hudson St, #311, New York, NY 10013, 212-226-7170
Pubs: *Experiments in Banal Living* (Empyreal Pr, 1998), *It as It* (Money for Food Pr, 1990), *Letters Home* (Vehicle, 1981), *Mudfish, O.ars, Exquisite Corpse, Coves, Small Pr Rev*

Marianne Andrea P&W
250 Cabrini Blvd, #2C
New York, NY 10033
Pubs: *The 5th Corner* (Mohansic Pr, 1976), *Atlanta Rev, Helicon Nine, Crosscurrents, Queens Qtly*

Bruce Andrews P
41 W 96 St, #10D
New York, NY 10025
Pubs: *I Don't Have Any Paper So Shut Up, Give Em Enough Rope* (Sun & Moon Pr, 1990, 1987)

Victoria Andreyeva P&W
PO Box 42, Prince St Sta
New York, NY 10012
Pubs: *Dream of the Firmament* (Gnosis Pr, 1989), *Lit Rev, The Unknown Terra, Spring, Voskreshenie*

Lucy Angeleri   PP
71-34 Harrow St
Forest Hills, NY 11375, 718-544-2877
    Pubs: *Tidings #2* (Four Facet Pr, 1992), *Tidings* (Print
    Center, 1974), *Lake Effect, Oread, Z Misc, Nomad,
    Slipstream, American Lit Rev, Slant, Croton Rev*

Roger Angell   P&W
The New Yorker, 20 W 43 St, New York, NY 10036
    Pubs: *Once More Around the Park* (Ballantine, 1991),
    Season Ticket (HM, 1988), *New Yorker*

Allan Appel   P&W
332 E 84 St, #5A
New York, NY 10028, 212-737-1946
    Pubs: *High Holiday Sutra* (Coffee Hse Pr, 1997), *The
    Rabbi of Casino Boulevard* (St. Martin's Pr, 1986), *A
    Pocket Apocalypse: Anth* (Riverhead Bks, 1997), *Nation,
    National Lampoon*

Jacob M. Appel   W
140 Claremont Ave, Apt 30
New York, NY 10027, 212-663-3643
    Pubs: *Cimarron Rev, South Dakota Rev, Real, Writers'
    Forum, Green Mountains Rev, Boston Rev, Fugue,
    Buffalo Spree*

Ron Arias   W
People Magazine, Time & Life Bldg, Rockefeller Ctr, New
York, NY 10020, 212-522-2711
    Pubs: *Five Against the Sea* (NAL, 1989), *The Road to
    Tamazunchale* (Bilingual Pr, 1984)

Linda Arking   W
110 Thompson St
New York, NY 10012

Richard R. Armijo   P
PO Box 477, 128 E Broadway
New York, NY 10002, 212-228-3033
    Pubs: *Wishing on a Star* (American Idealism Rag,
    1990), *Suburban Ambush* (Johns Hopkins U Pr, 1989),
    *A Gathering of the Tribes, New Leaves Rev, Zien,
    Blast*

Emily Arnold   W
3 Washington Sq Village, #16-I
New York, NY 10012-1809, 212-260-2246
    Pubs: *Life Drawing* (Delacorte, 1986), *A Craving* (Dell,
    1986)

Katherine Arnoldi   W
Sterling Lord Literistic, 65 Bleecker, New York, NY 10012,
212-673-4602
    Pubs: *The Amazing True Story of a Teenage Single
    Mom* (Hyperion, 1998), *The Qtly: Anths* (Vintage, 1991,
    1990, 1989), *Room of One's Own, Fiction, World, The
    Qtly, Onthebus, Red Tape, A Gathering of the Tribes,
    New Observations*

Maria Arrillaga ♀ ✈   P&W
140 Charles St #8E
New York, NY 10014, 212-929-4046
Internet: mariajoe@banet.net
    Pubs: *Manana Valentina* (Room of One's Own, 1995),
    These Are Not Sweet Girls (White Pine Pr, 1994),
    Cascada de Sol (Inst of Puerto Rican Culture, 1977),
    Yo Soy Fili Mele: Anth (U PR Pr, 1999), *Festa Da
    Palabra, Cupey, Tercer Milenio, Confrontation, PEN Intl*
Lang: Spanish. I.D.: Puerto-Rican. Groups: Women,
Latino/Latina

Elizabeth Arthur ♀ ✈   W
Sterling Lord Literistic, 65 Bleecker St 12th Fl, New York,
NY 10012
Internet: www.elizabetharthur.org
    Pubs: *Antarctic Navigation, Looking for the Klondike
    Stone* (Knopf, 1995, 1993)

Carol Ascher   W
158 W 23 St #5
New York, NY 10011
    Pubs: *The Flood* (Curbstone Pr, 1996), *Hard Lessons:
    Public Schools & Privatization* (Twentieth Century Fund,
    1996), *Between Women* (Routledge, 1993), *Kenyon
    Rev, Shenandoah, Virginia Qtly Rev, Boulevard, Literary
    Rev, Ms., Witness, ACM*

Sheila Ascher   PP&P&W
PO Box 176
Rockaway Park, NY 11694-0176, 718-474-6547
    Pubs: *ABC Street* (Green Interger, 2001), *The Menaced
    Assassin, The Other Planet, Red Moon/Red Lake*
    (McPherson, 1989, 1988, 1988), *Central Park,
    Confrontation, NAW*

Baron James Ashanti ♀ ✈   P&PP
274 West 140 St #45
New York, NY 10030
Internet: brilancefactory@aol.com
    Pubs: *Nova* (Harlem River Pr, 1990), *Nubiana II*
    (Shamal, 1979), *Essence, Eye Ball Mag, Greenfield
    Rev, Race Today, Pan African Jrnl, Telephone Bar,
    Southern University, Howard University*
I.D.: A.A.U.W., Cherokee. Groups: College/Univ, Teenagers

John Ashbery ♀ ✈   P
Georges Borchardt Inc., 136 E 57 St, New York, NY
10022, 212-753-5785
    Pubs: *Girls on the Run, Wakefulness, And the Stars
    Were Shining* (FSG, 1999, 1998, 1994), *Hotel
    Lautreamont* (Knopf, 1992)

Gary Aspenberg   P
323-A E 89 St, #1W
New York, NY 10128
    Pubs: *Bus Poems* (Broken Moon Pr, 1993)

James Atlas   P
The New York Times, 229 W 43 St, New York, NY 10036
   Pubs: *The Great Pretender* (Atheneum, 1986), *New Republic, Atlantic*

Louis Auchincloss   W
1111 Park Ave
New York, NY 10028, 212-348-3723

Jean M. Auel   W
Jean V. Naggar Literary Agency, 216 E 75 St, Ste 1E,
New York, NY 10021, 212-794-1082
   Pubs: *The Plains of Passage, The Mammoth Hunters, The Valley of Horses, The Clan of the Cave Bear* (Crown, 1990, 1985, 1982, 1980)

Jane Augustine 🎤 ✈   P
PO Box 1289, Stuyvesant Sta
New York, NY 10009, 212-533-1928
Internet: AugustineJane@cs.com
   Pubs: *French Windows* (Poetry NY, 1998), *Journeys* (Pig Pr, 1985), *Beneath a Single Moon: Anth* (Shambhala, 1991)
Groups: Women, Seniors

Paul Auster   P
c/o Carol Mann, Carol Mann Agency, 55 Fifth Ave, New York, NY 10003
   Pubs: *Mr. Vertigo, Leviathan* (Viking, 1994, 1992)

DorisJean Austin   W
3657 Broadway #9G
New York, NY 10031
   Pubs: *After the Garden* (NAL, 1988), *Streetlights: Illuminating Tales of the Urban Black Experience: Anth* (Viking, 1995), *Essence, Ms., Emerge*

Kofi Awoonor   W
Harold Ober Assoc, 425 Madison Ave, New York, NY 10017, 212-759-8600
   Pubs: *Until the Morning After* (Greenfield Rev Pr, 1987)

Elizabeth Ayres 🎤 ✈   P
E Ayres Ctr for Creative Writing, 155 E 31 St, Ste 4R, New York, NY 10016, 212-689-4692
   Pubs: *Writing the Wave* (Putnam, 1999), *Fresh Paint: Anth* (Ailanthus Pr, 1978), *Malahat Rev, Aspect, Hanging Loose, Encore, Bitterroot*

Jody Azzouni 🎤 ✈   P&W
301 Hicks St
Brooklyn, NY 11201, 718-852-6282
Internet: jody@azzouni.com
   Pubs: *The Lust for Blueprints* (Poet's Pr, 1999), *Artful Dodge, Bitter Oleander, Spillway, Hiram Poetry Rev, Alaska Qtly Rev, Poetry NY*

Virginia Bagliore   P
PO Box 244, Ryder St Sta
Brooklyn, NY 11234
   Pubs: *Oracles of Light* (Pella Pub, 1986), *The Inkling, Z Misc, Bitterroot, Eve's Legacy*

Alison Baker   W
Gail Hochman, Brandt & Brandt Literary Agents, Inc, 1501 Broadway, New York, NY 10036
   Pubs: *Thousands Live!* (Helianthus Pr, 1996), *Loving Wander Beaver: Novella & Stories, How I Came West, & Why I Stayed: Stories* (Chronicle Bks, 1995, 1993)

Julius Balbin 🎤 ✈   P
945 W End Ave, #9A
New York, NY 10025, 212-666-6526
   Pubs: *Inter Vivo Kaj Morto, Damnejoj* (Edistudio, 1996, 1992), *Imperio De L'Koroj: Esperanto Poetry* (Italy; Estudio, 1989)

Jean Balderston 🎤   P
1225 Park Ave, #8C
New York, NY 10128-1758, 212-876-4111
   Pubs: *Visiting Emily* (U Iowa Pr, 2001), *A More Perfect Union: Anth* (St Martin's Pr, 1998), *Poetry from A to Z: Anth* (Bradbury Pr, 1994), *NYQ, Wormwood Rev, Light, Poets On, Mudfish, Sing Heavenly Muse!*

J. G. Ballard   W
Robin Straus Agency, 229 E 79 St, New York, NY 10021, 212-472-3282

Robert Joseph Banfelder   W
53-38 195 St
Fresh Meadows, NY 11365, 718-357-7330
   Pubs: *No Stranger Than I* (Hudson View Pr, 1991)

William Henry Banks, Jr.   W
PO Box 2268
New York, NY 10163-2268, 203-562-7940
   Pubs: *A Love So Fine* (Pyramid Bks, 1974)

Russell Banks 🎤 ✈   P&W
Ellen Levine Literary Agency, 15 E 26 St, Ste 1801, New York, NY 10010, 212-889-0620
   Pubs: *Angel on the Roof, Cloudsplitter, Rule of the Bone, Sweet Hereafter* (HC, 2000, 1998, 1995, 1991)

Barbara Baracks   P
427 15 St, #4B
Brooklyn, NY 11215, 718-783-2881
   Pubs: *Poems Out of Place* (Language, 1978), *No Sleep* (Tuumba Pr, 1977), *Village Voice, Ms.*

Amiri Baraka 🎤 ✈   P
Sterling Lord Literistic, 65 Bleecker St, New York, NY
10012, 212-780-6050
  Pubs: *The Fiction of LeRoi Jones/Amiri Baraka*
  (Lawrence Hill Bks, 1999), *Eulogies, Transbluesency*
  (Marsilio, 1997, 1995), *Funklore* (Litoral, 1996),
  Y's/Why's/Wise: The Griot's Song (Third World Pr,
  1995)

Barbara Barg   P&W
520 E 14 St, #26
New York, NY 10009, 212-529-8751
  Pubs: *Origin of the Species* (Semiotext(e), *1994),
  Obeying the Chemicals* (Hard Pr, 1984), *Playboy, High
  Times, Short Qtly, Language Anthology*

Jane Barnes 🎤 ✈   P&W
300 8 Ave, Apt 2-0
Brooklyn, NY 11215, 718-832-7298
Internet: dalgordal@aol.com
  Pubs: *Extremes* (Blue Giant Pr, 1981), *Secret Sisters:
  Anth* (Alyson Pub, 2000), *Gay & Lesbian Poetry in Our
  Time: Anth* (St. Martin's Pr, 1989), *Chapel Hill
  Advocate, River Styx, Hanging Loose, Ploughshares,
  Sojourner, Brooklyn Rev, Harvard Mag*
  Lang: Spanish. I.D.: Bisexual, Lyricist/Librettist. Groups:
  G/L/B/T, Working Class

Suze Baron   PP&P
549 E 34 St
Brooklyn, NY 11203, 718-282-7159
  Pubs: *When Black People Pray* (Self, 1990), *The P.S.
  269 Fivers* (P.S. 269, 1988), *Raven Chronicles, Z Misc,
  NYQ, Calapooya Collage, New Press, Pegasus Rev*

Andrea Barrett   W
Wendy Weil Agency Inc, 232 Madison Ave, Ste 1300,
New York, NY 10016, 212-685-0030
  Pubs: *Ship Fever & Other Stories* (Norton, 1996), *The
  Forms of Water* (Pocket Bks, 1993), *Story, Missouri
  Rev, Southern Rev, NER*

Marvin Barrett   W
115 E 67 St, #3B
New York, NY 10021-5901

Fran Barst 🎤 ✈   P&W
115 E 9 St #11B
New York, NY 10003-5419, 212-677-8934
  Pubs: *The Death Gods* (Intl Poetry & Fiction Pr, 1991),
  *Bitter Oleander, Negative Capability, Korone, Carolina
  Qtly, Indian American, Denver Qtly*

Douglas Bauer   W
c/o Al Lowman, 19 W 44 St, Ste 1602, New York, NY
10036
  Pubs: *Book of Famous Iowans* (HHolt, 1997), *The Very
  Air* (Morrow, 1993), *Dexterity* (S&S, 1989), *Prairie City,
  Iowa* (Putnam, 1979), *Atlantic, Esquire*

Tricia Bauer 🎤 ✈   P&W
Susan Gleason, Literary Agent, 325 Riverside Dr, New
York, NY 10025, 212-662-3876
  Pubs: *Shelterbelt* (St Martin's Pr, 2000), *Hollywood &
  Hardwood, Boondocking, Working Women & Other
  Stories* (Bridge Works Pub, 1999, 1997, 1995)

Jonathan Baumbach   W
English Dept, Brooklyn College, Brooklyn, NY 11210,
718-856-6501
  Pubs: *Separate Hours, The Life & Times of Major
  Fiction* (Fiction Collective, 1990, 1987)

Judith Baumel   P
3530 Henry Hudson Pkwy, #12M
Bronx, NY 10463, 718-548-3053
  Pubs: *Now* (Miami U Pr, 1996), *The Weight of
  Numbers* (Wesleyan, 1988)

Ann Beattie   W
c/o Lynn Nesbit, Janklow & Nesbit Assoc, 598 Madison
Ave, New York, NY 10022-1614, 212-421-1700
  Pubs: *What Was Mine, Picturing Will* (Random Hse,
  1991, 1990)

Jeanne Marie Beaumont 🎤 ✈   P
120 W 70 St, #2D
New York, NY 10023-4444
Internet: bobbyjeanne@.att.net
  Pubs: *Placebo Effects* (Norton, 1997), *Mondo Marilyn:
  Anth* (St. Martin's Pr, 1995), *Boston Rev, Verse, Nation,
  NAW, Denver Qtly, Volt, Harper's, Poetry*

Mary Ann Beban   P
22 Jones St, #3F
New York, NY 10014, 212-929-2511
  Pubs: *Lips Unsealed: Anth* (Capra Pr, 1990),
  *Slipstream, Connecticut River Rev, Blueline, The
  Writer's Eye*

Stephen Becker   W
Russell & Volkening, Inc, 50 W 29 St, New York, NY
10001, 212-684-6050
  Pubs: *A Rendezvous in Haiti* (Norton, 1987), *Blue Eyed
  Shan, Dog Tags* (Random Hse, 1982, 1973)

Joshua Saul Beckman   P
182 Franklin St, Apt E16
Brooklyn, NY 11222, 718-383-0042
  Pubs: *Things Are Happening* (APR/Copper Canyon Pr,
  1998), *There Is an Ocean* (WSW, 1997), *Blue
  Paradise, At the News of Your Death* (Permeable Pr,
  1997, 1995), *ACM, APR, Gulf Coast, Response*

Madeleine D. Beckman 🎤 ✈   P&W
131 Thompson St, #3A
New York, NY 10012, 212-533-2033
Internet: www.echonyc.com/~madi
   Pubs: *Dead Boyfriends* (Linear Arts Bks 1998),
Contact/II: Anth (Contact II), *Fetishes, Skidrow
Penthouse, Salonika Qtly, Happy, Confrontations, SPR,
Jewish Frontier, Reflections, NYQ, Response, Barrow
Street, Tempus*
Groups: Seniors, Hospitals

Louis Begley   W
Georges Borchardt Inc., 136 E 57 St, New York, NY
10022, 212-753-5785
   Pubs: *The Man Who Was Late, Wartime Lies* (Knopf,
1993, 1991)

Judith Bell 🎤 ✈   W
Witherspoon Assoc, Inc, 235 E 31 St, New York, NY
10016, 212-889-8626
Internet: psbeagle@juno.com
   Pubs: *Generation to Generation, Grow Old Along with
Me: Anth* (Papier-Mache Pr, 1998, 1996), *Farm Wives
& Other Iowa Stories: Anth* (Mid- Prairie Bks, 1995),
*Washington Rev, First, Short Fiction By Women, Snake
Nation Rev, Parting Gifts, ALR, Potomac Rev*

Bruce Benderson 🎤 ✈   W
257 E 7 St, #7
New York, NY 10009, 212-228-3114
Internet: bruxe@aol.com
   Pubs: *User* (Dutton/Plume, 1996), *Pretending to Say No*
(L'incertain, 1992; NAL, 1990), *Men on Men 3: Anth*
(Dutton, 1990), *Central Park, Lit Rev, Outweek, NYQ,
Advocate*
Lang: French

Frances Bendix 🎤 ✈   PP
2676 Grand Concourse, #3H
Bronx, NY 10458-4939, 718-295-2697
   Pubs: *Resonance, Modern Images, Ararat, NY Poets
Qtly, Poetry Jrnl, Bronx Arts, Words & Image, Slug
Fest, Visions*

Helen Benedict 🎤 ✈   W
Richard Parks Literary Agency, 138 E 16 St, New York,
NY 10003
   Pubs: *The Sailor's Wife* (Zoland, 2000), *Bad Angel, A
World Like This* (Dutton, 1996, 1990), *Ontario Rev,
Antioch Rev*

Ruth Benjamin   P&W
1158 Fifth Ave, #5D
New York, NY 10029, 212-348-6624
   Pubs: *Naked at Forty* (Horizon Pr, 1984), *Albany Rev*

Hal Bennett   W
William Morris Agency, 1325 Ave of the Americas, New
York, NY 10019, 212-586-5100

Nathan Bergenfeld   P
2632 W 2 St
Brooklyn, NY 11223, 718-769-6773
   Pubs: *Life Spirals, Garden Gleanings* (NYC Dept of
Parks, 1987, 1986)

Rachel Berghash 🎤   P
7 E 20 St
New York, NY 10003-1106, 212-533-1541
   Pubs: *Chicago Rev, Anima, Waterways, Pulp, Jewish
Frontier, Bitterroot, Blue Unicorn, Israel Horizons, West
Wind Rev, Poetpourri*
Lang: Hebrew. I.D.: Jewish

Eleanor Bergstein   W
210 Central Park S, Ste 14C
New York, NY 10019, 212-245-4313
   Pubs: *Ex-Lover* (Random Hse, 1989), *Advancing Paul
Newman* (Viking Pr, 1973)

Nancy Berke   P
164 Sterling Pl, #3D
Brooklyn, NY 11217
   Pubs: *Alternative Poetry & Fiction, Footwork, Pig Iron,
Slipstream, Central Park, New Voices*

Constance E. Berkley   P
Fordham Univ, Lincoln Center, Rm 414, New York, NY
10023

Howard Berland   PP
3044 Kingsbridge Ave, #26
Bronx, NY 10463, 212-593-7552

Carol W. Berman 🎤   W
866 UN Plaza #473
New York, NY 10017-1822, 212-758-2901
   Pubs: *Aphrodite Gone Berserk, Caprice, Challenging
Destiny, Fetishes*
I.D.: Jewish, Women. Groups: Mentally Ill, Animal Rights

Kenneth Bernard 🎤   P&W
800 Riverside Dr, #8H
New York, NY 10032, 212-927-8851
   Pubs: *The Qui Parle Play & Poems, The Baboon in
the Night Club* (Asylum Arts Pub, 1999, 1994), *Clown
at Wall* (Confrontation Pr, 1996), *From the District File*
(Fiction Collective 2, 1992), *Chelsea, Fiction Intl,
Salmagundi, Contre-Vox, Collages & Bricolages*

Louise Bernikow 🎤 ✈   P
318 W 105 St, #4A
New York, NY 10025, 212-662-6307
Internet: weezieman@aol.com
   Pubs: *Alone in America, Among Women* (H&R, 1985,
1982)
I.D.: Women, Jewish. Groups: Women

Burton Bernstein   P&W
Donadio & Olson, Inc, 121 W 27 St, Ste 704, New York,
NY 10001, 212-691-8077
    Pubs: *Plane Crazy* (Ticknor & Fields, 1985), *Family
    Matters* (Summit, 1982), *New Yorker, Esquire*

Daniel Berrigan   P
220 W 98 St, #11-L
New York, NY 10025, 212-662-6358
    Pubs: *Whereon to Stand, Sorrow Built a Bridge:
    Friendship & AIDS* (Fortcamp Pr, 1991, 1990)

Eliot Berry   W
c/o Carl Brandt, Brandt & Brandt Literary Agents, 1501
Broadway, New York, NY 10036
    Pubs: *Tough Draw* (H Holt/John MacRae Bks, 1992),
    Four Quarters Make a Season (Berkley Pr, 1973)

Lebert Bethune   P&W
110 W 96 St, #16C
New York, NY 10025, 212-866-8059

Marcia Biederman   W
41 2nd St, #3
Brooklyn, NY 11231
    Pubs: *Post No Bonds* (Scribner, 1988), *Sisters in Crime
    3: Anth* (Berkley Pub, 1990)

Rachelle Bijou   P
300 W 23 St, #2E
New York, NY 10011
    Pubs: *Entrance to the City* (Buffalo Pr, 1978), *Out of
    This World: Anth* (Crown, 1992), *Telephone, The World,
    Response, Transfer*

Sarah Bird   W
c/o Kristine Dahl, ICM, 40 W 57 St, New York, NY
10019, 212-556-5600
    Pubs: *Virgin of the Rodeo, The Mommy Club*
    (Doubleday, 1993, 1991), *Mademoiselle, Texas
    Observer, Cosmopolitan*

Ann Birstein 🎤 ✈   W
1623 3rd Ave, #27-J W
New York, NY 10128-3642, 212-289-0346
Internet: abirstein@aol.com
    Pubs: *The Last of the True Believers* (Norton, 1988),
    The Rabbi on 47th Street (Dial Pr, 1982), *McCall's,
    New Yorker, Confrontation*

Ellen Marie Bissert   P
735 Kappock St, #9A/F
Riverdale, NY 10463
    Pubs: *The Immaculate Conception of the Blessed Virgin
    Dyke* (13th Moon, 1977), *Beyond Baroque, 13th Moon*

Isaac J. Black   P
119-10 225 St
Cambria Heights, NY 11411, 718-723-5148
    Pubs: *Obsidian, Callaloo, Hoodoo, First World, BPJ,
    Black World*

Sophie Cabot Black 🎤 ✈   P
PO Box 528
New York, NY 10024
    Pubs: *The Misunderstanding of Nature* (Graywolf Pr,
    1994), *Atlantic, Antaeus, Partisan Rev, APR*
Groups: G/L/B/T, Women

Star Black   P
111 E 36 St
New York, NY 10016, 212-683-6127
    Pubs: *October for Idas* (Painted Leaf Pr, 1997),
    Waterworn (Tribes Bks, 1995), *Doubletime* (Groundwater
    Pr, 1995)

Nicole Blackman 🎤 ✈   PP&P
PO Box 534
New York, NY 10156
Internet: www.nicole-blackman.com
    Pubs: *Blood Sugar* (Incommunicado Bks, 2000), *Poetry
    Nation: Anth* (Vehicule Pr, 1999), *Will Work for Peace:
    Anth* (zeropanik pr, 1999), *Revival: Anth* (Manic D Pr,
    1995), *Aloud: Anth* (H Holt, 1994), *Oculus, Flexible
    Head, Gargoyle, Barrow Street*
Groups: Teenagers, Women

George Blagowidow   W
Hippocrene Books, 171 Madison Ave, New York, NY
10016, 212-685-4371
    Pubs: *In Search of the Lady Lion Tamer* (HBJ, 1987)

Lucienne S. Bloch   W
1111 Park Ave
New York, NY 10128
    Pubs: *Finders Keepers* (HM, 1982), *On the Great-Circle
    Route* (S&S, 1979)

Lawrence Block   W
c/o Knox Burger, 39 1/2 Washington Sq S, New York, NY
10012
    Pubs: *A Walk Among the Tombstones, A Dance at the
    Slaughterhouse* (Morrow, 1992, 1991), *Playboy,
    American Heritage*

Amy Bloom   W
c/o Phyllis Wender, Rosenstone/Wender, 3 E 48 St, New
York, NY 10077, 212-832-8330
    Pubs: *Come to Me* (HC, 1993), *Best American Short
    Stories: Anths* (HM, 1992, 1991), *New Yorker*

Laurel Blossom 🎤 ✈ P
920 Park Ave, #2B
New York, NY 10028-0208, 212-628-0239
Internet: lbaines920@aol.com
 Pubs: *The Papers Said* (Greenhouse Rev Pr, 1993),
Lights, Camera, Poetry: Anth (HB, 1996), *Paris Rev,
Poetry, Pequod, Confrontation, APR, Lips, Many
Mountains Moving*

Bonnie Bluh 🎤 ✈ W
55 Bethune St, #1007A
New York, NY 10014, 212-255-3322
Internet: bbluh@aol.com
 Pubs: *The Eleanor Roosevelt Girls* (LyreBird Bks,
1999), *The Old Speak Out* (Horizon, 1979), *Banana*
(Macmillan, 1976), *Woman to Woman* (Starogubski,
1974)
Groups: Women, Prisoners

Victor Bockris P
106 Perry St
New York, NY 10014

Richard Bodtke P
175 W 93 St, #5A
New York, NY 10025
 Pubs: *Tragedy & the Jacobean Temper* (U Salzburg,
1972), *World of Undisguise* (Nauset, 1968)

Karen Iris Bogen P
c/o Letitia Lee, Ann Elmo Literary Agency, 60 E 42 St,
New York, NY 10165, 212-661-2883
 Pubs: *Will the Circle Be Unbroken: Anth* (Spinsters/Aunt
Lute Pr, 1986), *SPR*

Nancy Bogen 🎤 ✈ W
31 Jane St, #17B
New York, NY 10014-1982, 212-741-2417
 Pubs: *Klytaimnestra Who Stayed at Home, Bagatelle
Guinevere, Bobe Mayse: A Tale of Washington Square*
(Twinkenham Pr, 1998, 1995, 1993)
Groups: Jewish, G/L/B/T

Magda Bogin P&W
425 Riverside Dr
New York, NY 10025, 212-662-9434
 Pubs: *Natalya, God's Messenger* (Scribner, 1994)

Portia Bohn 🎤 ✈ W
49 W 12 St Apt 5G
New York, NY 10011-8531, 646-486-6736
 Pubs: *Confrontation, Carolina Qtly, Short Story Intl,
Massachusetts Rev, Other Voices, Kalliope*

Thomas Bolt P
110 Suffolk St, #6B
New York, NY 10002
 Pubs: *Out of the Woods* (Yale U Pr, 1989)

Roger Bonair-Agard 🎤 ✈ PP&P
748 Madison St. #2
Brooklyn, NY 11221, 718-455-3412
Internet: bonairpoet@aol.com
 Pubs: *and chaos congealed* (Fly By Night Pr, 2000),
Burning Down the House (w/Colman, et al; Soft Skull
Pr, 2000), *360: A Revolution of Black Poets: Anth*
(Black Words Pr, 1998), *Phati'tude, 13 Bar/Lounge,
Nuyorican Poets Cafe, Spy, Antioch College*

Gina Angeline Bonati P
607 E 11 St, #10
New York, NY 10009, 212-473-1950
 Pubs: *Resurrection* (Venom Pr, 1993), *The Weight of a
Place* (Enemy Loose Pub, 1990), *A Different Drummer,
Curare, Village Voice, Resister*

Rafael Bordao P
Arcas, PO Box 023617, Brooklyn, NY 11202-3617
 Pubs: *Libro De Las Interferencias, Escurridduras De La
Soledad* (Editorial Palmar, 1995, 1995), *Diario Las
Americas, Cuzcatlan, Latino Stuff Rev, El Diario*

David Bottoms P&W
Maria Carvainis Literary Agency, 235 W End Ave, New
York, NY 10023, 212-580-1559
 Pubs: *Armored Hearts: New & Selected Poems* (Copper
Canyon Pr, 1995), *Easter Weekend* (HM, 1990), *Under
the Vulture-Tree, In a U-Haul North of Damascus*
(Morrow, 1987, 1983), *Atlantic, New Yorker, Paris Rev,
Harper's, Poetry, APR*

Matthew S. Boyd W
Little, Brown & Company, 1271 Ave of the Americas, New
York, NY 10020, 212-522-8000
 Pubs: *The Art of Breaking Glass* (Little, Brown, 1997),
Nightmare Logic (Bantam, 1989)

T. Coraghessan Boyle 🎤 ✈ W
Georges Borchardt Inc., 136 E 57 St, New York, NY
10022, 212-753-5785
 Pubs: *A Friend of the Earth, Riven Rock, T.C. Boyle
Stories, The Tortilla Curtain, The Road to Wellville,
East Is East, If the River Was Whiskey, World's End*
(Viking, 2000, 1998, 1998, 1995, 1993, 1990, 1989,
1987)

David Bradley W
Wendy Weil Agency Inc, 232 Madison Ave, Ste 1300,
New York, NY 10016, 212-685-0030
 Pubs: *The Chaneysville Incident* (H&R, 1990), *South
Street* (Scribner, 1986), *Esquire, New Yorker,
Philadelphia, Harper's*

Kathleen Brady W
305 E 72 St
New York, NY 10021
 Pubs: *Ida Tarbell: Portrait of a Muckraker* (U Pittsburgh,
1989), *Inside Out* (Norton, 1979)

Perry Brass 🎤 ✈   P&W
2501 Palisade Ave, #A1
Bronx, NY 10463-6104, 718-884-6606
Internet: www.perrybrass.com
   Pubs: *Angel Lust, The Lover of My Soul, The Harvest,
   Albert, or, The Book of Man, Sex-Charge* (Belhue Pr,
   2000, 1998, 1997, 1995, 1991), *Columbia Anth of Gay
   Literature* (Columbia U Pr, 1998), *James White Rev,
   Christopher Street*
I.D.: G/L/B/T, Jewish. Groups: G/L/B/T, Jewish

Kamau Brathwaite   P
37 Washington Sq W, #4B
New York, NY 10011
   Pubs: *Sunpoem, The Arrivants* (Oup, 1982, 1973),
   Savacou: Jrnl of the Caribbean Artists

Brian Breger   P
179 E 3 St, #33
New York, NY 10009
   Pubs: *Journeys to the Center of the Earth* (Piecework
   Pr, 1986), *Mojave* (# Pr, 1980), *Mulch*

Betty Bressi 🎤   P
74 Claradon Ln
Staten Island, NY 10305, 718-273-1793
   Pubs: *Letternet I, Letternet II, Letters from Italy*
   (Glassworks Pr, 1998, 1990), *Poeti Italo Americani:
   Anth* (Alfonsi, 1985), *Small Pond, Box 749, Contact II,
   Jam Today*

Peter Bricklebank   W
1803 Riverside Dr, #2J
New York, NY 10034, 212-567-3686
   Pubs: *American Voice, Crescent Rev, Mid-American
   Rev, Kansas Qtly, Carolina Qtly, Confrontation*

Richard P. Brickner   W
Lantz-Harris Literary Agency, 156 Fifth Ave, Ste 617, New
York, NY 10010, 212-924-6269
   Pubs: *After She Left* (H Holt, 1988), *Tickets* (S&S,
   1981)

Les Bridges   P
313 E 10 St, #4
New York, NY 10009, 212-677-2799
   Pubs: *Read 'em & Weep, Fractured Snapshots*
   (LynDawn, 1993, 1992), *The Literature of Work* (U
   Phoenix Pr, 1991)

Stewart Brisby   P
463 West St, #G113
New York, NY 10014-2010, 212-633-1642
   Pubs: *A Death in America* (Wolverine Pr, 1986),
   Caprice, Greenfield Rev, Berkeley Barb, Margins

Jean Brody   W
Jean V. Naggar Literary Agency, 216 E 75 St, Ste 1E,
New York, NY 10021, 212-794-1082
   Pubs: *A Coven of Women* (Atheneum, 1987), *Gideon's
   House* (Putnam, 1984), *Special Report, Lear's*

Janet Brof 🎤 ✈   P&W
380 Riverside Dr, #2F
New York, NY 10025-1801, 212-663-6254
   Pubs: *Through a Half-Open Door* (Catkin Pr, 1988),
   *Kansas Qtly, Poets On, Negative Capability, Stone
   Country, Mid-Stream, Mss*

E. M. Broner   W
Charlotte Sheedy Literary Agency, 65 Bleecker St, New
York, NY 10012, 212-780-9800
   Pubs: *Mornings & Mournings, The Telling* (HC, 1994,
   1993), *A Weave of Women, Her Mothers* (HR&W,
   1978, 1975)

Donna Brook 🎤 ✈   P
231 Wyckoff St
Brooklyn, NY 11217-2208, 718-643-9559
   Pubs: *A More Human Face, What Being Responsible
   Means to Me, Notes on Space/Time* (Hanging Loose
   Pr, 1998, 1988, 1977), *Without Child: Anth* (Feminist
   Pr, 1999), *Verse, Hanging Loose, Telephone, Alternative
   Pr, B'way II, River Styx, The World*

Terry Brooks   W
Ballantine Books/Del Rey Fantasy, 201 E 50 St, New
York, NY 10022
   Pubs: *The Wishsong of Shannara, The Elfstones of
   Shannara* (Del Rey/Ballantine Bks, 1985, 1982)

P. R. Brostowin 🎤 ✈   P
88-38 74 Ave
Glendale, NY 11385-7924, 718-997-0227
   Pubs: *In Other Words* (Alfalfa, 1976), *Kansas Qtly,
   Smith, Blue Unicorn, Windless Orchard*

Millicent Brower 🎤 ✈   P&W
484 W 43 St, #10-F
New York, NY 10036, 212-239-1881
   Pubs: *Young Performers* (Julian Messner, 1985), *I Am
   Going Nowhere* (Putnam, 1972), *Ingenue* (Ballantine,
   1959), *Language Arts, Cricket*

Andrea Carter Brown 🎤 ✈   P
355 S End Ave Apt 5A1
New York, NY 10280-1060, 212-321-2928
   Pubs: *Girls: An Anthology* (Global City Pr, 1997),
   *Phoebe, Barnabe Mountain Rev, River Oak Rev,
   Sandhills Rev, Mississippi Rev, Gettysburg Rev,
   Marlboro Rev, Talking River Rev, Borderlands*

Kenneth H. Brown 🎤 ✈   P&W
150 74th St
Brooklyn, NY 11209
    Pubs: *You'd Never Know It from the Way I Talk*
(Ashland Poetry Pr, 1990), *The Narrows* (Dial Pr,
1971), *The Brig* (Hill & Wang, 1965), *Gallery Mag, City
Lights*

Rita Mae Brown   P&W
Wendy Weil Agency Inc, 232 Madison Ave, Ste 1300,
New York, NY 10016
    Pubs: *Rest in Pieces, Wish You Were Here* (w/S.P.
Brown), *Bingo* (Bantam, 1992, 1990, 1988), *Southern
Discomfort* (H&R, 1982)

Michael Brownstein 🎤 ✈   P&W
21 E 2 St, #3
New York, NY 10003, 212-260-0109
    Pubs: *Self-Reliance* (Coffee Hse Pr, 1994), *The Touch*
(Autonomedia, 1993), *New Yorker, Open City*

Anne-Marie Brumm 🎤 ✈   P&W
175 W 13 St #8A
New York, NY 10011-7869, 212-255-5030
    Pubs: *Last Exit to Peace, Come Drink Coffee with Me*
(Widener & Lewis, 2000, 1994), *Confrontation, SW Rev,
Response, Abiko Qtly, Prospice, Paterson Lit Rev,
Nexus, Global City Rev, Urban Affairs, Intl Poetry Rev,
Queen's Qtly, Karam*
I.D.: Jewish, Academic. Groups: Seniors, Singles

C. D. B. Bryan   W
c/o Lynn Nesbit, Janklow & Nesbit Assoc, 598 Madison
Ave, New York, NY 10022-1614, 212-421-1700
    Pubs: *Beautiful Women, Ugly Scenes* (Doubleday,
1983), *Friendly Fire* (Putnam, 1976)

Frederick Buechner   W
Harriet Wasserman Agency, 137 E 36 St, New York, NY
10016, 212-689-3257
    Pubs: *Godric, Whistling in the Dark* (Harper, 1988,
1980)

Melvin Jules Bukiet 🎤 ✈   W
c/o Jennifer Lyons, The Writers House, 21 W 26 St, New
York, NY 10010, 212-685-2663
    Pubs: *Signs & Wonders* (Picador, 1999), *After* (St.
Martin's Pr, 1996), *While the Messiah Tarries* (HB,
1995), *Stories of an Imaginary Childhood* (Northwestern
U Pr, 1992), *Antaeus, Paris Rev*

Aaron E. Bulman   P
15 Magaw Pl, #1B
New York, NY 10033, 212-781-5498
    Pubs: *Plum Rev, Jewish Currents, Partisan Rev, Home
Planet News, Small Pond Rev, Images, Paris Rev,
Jewish Spectator*

Michelina Buonocore   P
2141 Crotona Ave, #13G
Bronx, NY 10457, 212-733-5946
    Pubs: *The Last Portrait* (Dragon's Teeth Pr, 1987),
Bicentennial Hymn (Edward James, 1979)

France Burke   P&W
170 Ave C, #21D
New York, NY 10009
    Pubs: *Women in Search of Utopia: Anth* (Schocken
Bks, 1984), *Paris Rev, Confrontation, Panache,
Dramatist Guild Qtly*

Kathe Burkhart 🎤 ✈   PP&P&W
47 S 5 St, 3rd Fl
Brooklyn, NY 11211-5106, 718-486-7383
    Pubs: *Velvet Revolution* (Italy; Galleria in Arco, 1993),
Red Tape: Anth (M. Carter, 1993), *Best of the
Underground: Anth* (Masquerade, 1998), *From Under
the 8-Ball: Anth* (Line, 1985), *Williamsburg Observer,
Purple Fiction, Meaning, Flash Art, Peep*
Groups: Prisoners, Abuse Victims

Herbert Burkholz   W
Georges Borchardt Inc., 136 E 57 St, New York, NY
10022, 212-753-5785
    Pubs: *The FDA Follies* (Basic Bks, 1994), *Brain
Damage* (Atheneum, 1992), *Writer-in-Residence*
(Permanent Pr, 1992), *New Republic, Longevity*

Brian Burland   P&W
W W Norton, 500 5 Ave, New York, NY 10110
    Pubs: *A Few Flowers for St. George, Love Is a
Durable Fire, Fall from Aloft* (Grafton/Collins, 1987,
1987, 1987), *New Letters*

Diane Burns   P
46 E 1st St, #4B
New York, NY 10003, 212-475-5680
    Pubs: *Riding the One-Eyed Ford* (Contact/II Pr, 1981),
Aloud: Voices from the Nuyorican Poets Cafe: Anth
(New Worlds of Literature, 1994), *Greenfield Rev, A
Gathering of the Tribes, Akwesasne Notes, Anishinabe
Aki, LAC Court Oreilles Jrnl*

Stanley Burnshaw   P&W
250 W 89 St, #PH2G
New York, NY 10024, 212-595-7907
    Pubs: *The Seamless Web* (Braziller, 1991), *A Stanley
Burnshaw Reader* (U Georgia Pr, 1990), *Atlantic,
Sewanee Rev, Poetry, Saturday Rev, Nouvelle Rev*

Anne Kelleher Bush   W
Donald Maass Literary Agency, 157 W 57 St, Ste 1003,
New York, NY 10019
    Pubs: *The Misbegotten King, Children of Enchantment*
(Warner Bks, 1997, 1996)

Naomi Bushman   P
716 Broadway
New York, NY 10013, 212-421-1637
    Pubs: *West End, Trellis Two, Hanging Loose*

Peter Bushyeager 🎤 ✈   P
9 Stuyvesant Oval, #5F
New York, NY 10009, 212-995-8102
    Pubs: *Vital Wires* (Unimproved Edtns Pr, 1986),
    Synergism Anth (Boshi Pr, 1995), *Unbearables Anth,
    Talisman, The World, NAW, Painted Bride Qtly,
    Nostalgia, Pagan Place*

Edward Butscher   P&W
84-01 Main St
Briarwood, NY 11435, 718-441-9766
    Pubs: *Child in the House: Poems* (Canio's Bks, 1995),
    Eros Descending: A Selection (Dusty Dog Pr, 1992)

Christopher Butters 🎤 ✈   P
488 12th St
Brooklyn, NY 11215-5205, 718-768-1724
    Pubs: *Americas* (Viet Nam Generation, 1996), *The
    Propaganda of a Seed* (Cardinal Pr, 1990), *Split Shift,
    Blue Collar Rev*

Cheryl Byron   PP&P
Something Positive, 225 E 89 St, Box 20, New York, NY
10128, 212-289-3785
    Pubs: *Womantalk* (Heartbeat Records, 1986),
    Womanrise (Shamal Bks, 1978)

Luis Cabalquinto   P&W
PO Box 618, Stuyvesant Sta
New York, NY 10009-0618, 212-254-4514
    Pubs: *Dreamwanderer, The Dog-Eater & Other Poems*
    (Kalikasan Pr, 1992, 1989), *APR, Prairie Schooner,
    Manoa, Trafika, Poetry Australia, River Styx*

Regie Cabico   PP
Emerald Garden #136 577 2nd Ave
New York, NY 10016, 718-388-5216
    Pubs: *The Trick, I Saw Your Ex-Lover Behind the
    Starbucks Counter* (Bigfat Pr, 2000, 1997), *The Outlaw
    Bible of American Poetry* (Thunder's Mouth, 1999),
    Onomatopoeia & a 1/4 Life Crisis (Here Theater, 1999),
    The Gene Pool (Dixon Place 1999)

Olga Cabral   P&W
463 West St, #H-523
New York, NY 10014, 212-691-4855
    Pubs: *Voice/Over: Selected Poems* (West End Pr,
    1993), *American Visions: Anth* (Mayfield Pub, 1994),
    Cream City Rev, Signal Intl, Pemmican

Rosalie Calabrese 🎤 ✈   P
700 Columbus Ave, #16D
New York, NY 10025-6680, 212-663-6620
Internet: rcmgt@yahoo.com
    Pubs: *Anth of American Verse & Yearbook of American
    Poetry* (Monitor, 1997), *Full Circle: Anth* (Pittenbruach
    Pr, 1997), *Caprice, Byline, Thirteen, New Laurel Rev,
    Up Front Muse Intl Rev, And Then, Jewish Currents*
I.D.: Jewish

Justin Caldwell   P
410 W 24 St, #2A
New York, NY 10011, 212-675-3931
    Pubs: *The Sleeping Porch* (Lost Roads Pr, 1979),
    Southern Rev, Poetry Now, Ironwood

Hortense Calisher   W
Donadio & Olson, Inc, 121 W 27 St, Ste 704, New York,
NY 10001, 212-691-8077
    Pubs: *In the Slammer with Carol Smith* (Marion Boyars,
    1997), *The Novellas of Hortense Calisher, In the
    Palace of the Movie King* (Random Hse, 1997, 1993),
    Kissing Cousins, Age (Weidenfeld, 1988)

Paulette Callen 🎤 ✈   W
215 W 83 St #1F
New York, NY 10024
    Pubs: *Beyond Lament: Poets of the World Bearing
    Witness to the Holocaust: Anth* (Northwestern U Pr,
    1998), *Vanity, Charity* (S&S, 1998, 1997), *Negative
    Capability*
Groups: G/L/B/T, Spiritual/Religious

James Camp   P
365 W End Ave, #7C
New York, NY 10024
    Pubs: *Paris Rev Anth* (Norton, 1990), *Light Year: Anth*
    (Bits Pr, 1989), *Cincinnati Rev, Poetry NY, Sagetrieb*

Tina Cane 🎤 ✈   P
178 Frost St
Brooklyn, NY 11211, 718-383-1629
    Pubs: *Girls: An Anthology* (Global City Pr, 1998),
    Laisse de Mer: Anth (Francoforum, 1999), *New Press
    Lit Qtly, Hanging Loose, Salt Hill Jrnl*

Ethan Canin   W
Maxine Groffsky Literary Agency, 853 Broadway, Ste 708,
New York, NY 10003, 212-979-1500
    Pubs: *For Kings & Planets, The Palace Thief* (Random
    Hse, 1998, 1994), *Blue River, Emperor of the Air* (HM,
    1991, 1988)

Steve Cannon   W
285 E 3 St, 3rd Fl
New York, NY 10009, 212-674-8262
    Pubs: *Groove, Bang & Jive Around* (Olympia Pr, 1968),
    American Rag, Sunbury 9, Pulp

Robert Canzoneri P&W
c/o Roberta Pryor, 24 W 55 St, New York, NY 10019,
212-245-0420
  Pubs: *Potboiler: An Amateur's Affair with La Cuisine*
  (North Point, 1989), *Story, Chariton Rev, Modern
  Maturity*

Phyllis Capello P&W
495 16th St
Brooklyn, NY 11215-5913
  Pubs: *Journey into Motherhood* (Riverhead Putnam,
  1996), *Voices in Italian Americana: Anth* (Purdue U Pr,
  1997), *The Voices We Carry: Anth* (Guernica Edtns,
  1993), *Footwork, Literary Mag, NYQ, Downtown Mag*

Alberto O. Cappas 🎤 ✈ P
85 Fourth Ave, Apt 3JJ
New York, NY 10003-5206, 212-353-9114
Internet: cappas@aol.com
  Pubs: *The Pledge, Roots to Reality, Disintegration of
  the Puerto Ricans* (Don Pedro Enterprises, 1998, 1998,
  1997), *Echolalia, Verse & Vibration of Alberto O.
  Cappas* (Carlton Pr, 1988), *Black Men Still Singing:
  Anth* (Guild Pr, 1990), *Primal Voices*

Nick Carbo P
36-09 21 Ave
Astoria, NY 11105, 212-274-9357
  Pubs: *El Grupo McDonald's* (Tia Chucha Pr, 1995),
  Poetry, TriQtly, Poet Lore

Peter Carey 🎤 ✈ W
c/o Amanda Urban, ICM, 40 W 57 St, New York, NY
10019, 212-556-5600
  Pubs: *True History of the Kelly Gang, Jack Maggs, The
  Unusual Life of Tristan Smith, The Tax Inspector*
  (Knopf, 2001, 1997, 1995, 1992), *Oscar & Lucinda,
  Illywhacker, Bliss* (H&R, 1988, 1986, 1982), *The Fat
  Man in History* (Random Hse, 1980)

Don Carpenter W
E. P. Dutton & Co., 375 Hudson St, New York, NY
10014, 212-366-2000

Julie A. Carr 🎤 ✈ P
11 Schermerhorn St #5FE
Brooklyn, NY 11201, 718-935-0935
  Pubs: *Epoch, Greensboro Rev, NER, Pequod, Poet
  Lore, Salamander, TriQtly*
Groups: Children

Mary Anne Cartelli P
122 Spring St, #4S
New York, NY 10012, 212-334-5229
  Pubs: *The Little Mag, Bomb, Joe Soap's Canoe, World,
  Field, Luna Tack, Berkeley Poetry Rev*

Charlotte Carter W
c/o Faith Childs, Charlotte Sheedy Literary Agency, 65
Bleecker St, New York, NY 10012, 212-780-9800
  Pubs: *Personal Effects* (United Artists, 1990), *Transfer*

Mary Casanova W
Hyperion, 114 5th Ave, New York, NY 10011
  Pubs: *Stealing Thunder, Wolf Shadows, Riot, Moose
  Tracks* (Hyperion Bks, 1997, 1997, 1996, 1995),
  Cricket, Once Upon a Time, Highlights, Loonfeather

John Casey 🎤 ✈ W
Michael Carlisle, 24 E 64 St, New York, NY 10026,
212-813-1881
  Pubs: *The Halflife of Happiness* (Knopf, 1998), *Spartina*
  (Vintage, 1998), *Testimony & Demeanor, An American
  Romance* (Avon, 1991, 1991), *New Yorker, L.A. Times*

Maud Casey W
253 Cumberland St, Apt #605
Brooklyn, NY 11205, 718-260-8912
  Pubs: *Drastic, The Shape of Things to Come* (Morrow,
  2002, 2001), *Confrontation, Georgia Rev, Beloit Fiction
  Jrnl, Threepenny Rev*

Kay Cassill W
c/o Elise Goodman, Goodman Assoc, 500 W End Ave,
New York, NY 10024, 212-873-4806
  Pubs: *Twins: Nature's Amazing Mystery* (Atheneum,
  1982), *The Twins Letter*

R. V. Cassill W
Donadio & Olson, Inc, 121 W 27 St, Ste 704, New York,
NY 10001
  Pubs: *Late Stories, The Unknown Soldier* (Texas Center
  for Writers, 1995, 1991), *The Man Who Bought
  Magnitogorsk* (The London Co, 1994)

J. N. Catanach W
560 Riverside Dr, #20-F
New York, NY 10027
  Pubs: *The Last Rite of Hugo T* (St. Martin's Pr, 1992),
  Brideprice, White Is the Color of Death (The
  Countryman Pr, 1989, 1988)

Thomas M. Catterson 🎤 ✈ P
86-37, 120th St
Richmond Hill, NY 11418
  Pubs: *This Pot has Pepper* (Cross-Cultural Lit Edtn,
  1998)

Anita Mirenberg Caylor 🎤 ✈ PP&P
437 E 118 St
New York, NY 10035, 212-534-2764
  Pubs: *BPJ, East Coast Writers Anth, Bronx Roots*

Marisha Chamberlain   P
Bill Craver/Writers & Artists, 19 W 44 St, Ste #1000, New
York, NY 10036, 212-391-1112
  Pubs: *A Line of Cutting Women* (Calyx Jrnll, 1998),
  Scheherazade (Dramatists Play Service, 1985), *Powers*
  (New Rivers Pr, 1983), *Minneapolis Rev of Baseball,
  City Pages, Hungry Mind Rev*

Clovr Chango   PP
631 E 11 St #24
New York, NY 10009

Laura Chapman   W
c/o Hruska, 1148 Fifth Ave, New York, NY 10128
  Pubs: *Multiple Choice* (Doubleday, 1978), *Legal
  Relations* (Dutton, 1977)

Steve Chappell   W
Ellen Levine Literary Agency, 15 E 26 St, Ste 1801, New
York, NY 10010, 212-889-0620
  Pubs: *Outlaws in Babylon* (S&S, 1984), *Don't Mind
  Dying* (Doubleday, 1980), *Los Angeles Times*

Suzy McKee Charnas 🎤 ✈   W
c/o Jennifer Lyons, The Writers House, 21 W 26 St, New
York, NY 10010, 212-685-2663
  Pubs: *The Slave & the Free, Conqueror's Child, Ruby
  Tear, Furies* (Tor Bks, 1999, 1999, 1997, 1995),
  Vampire Tapestry (U New Mexico Pr, 1993), *Kingdom
  of Kevin Malone* (HB, 1993), *Golden Thread, Silver
  Glove* (Bantam, 1989, 1988)

Jerome Charyn   W
302 W 12 St, #10C
New York, NY 10014, 212-691-2879
  Pubs: *Elsinore, The Good Policeman* (Mysterious Pr,
  1991, 1990), *Movieland, Metropolis* (Putnam, 1989,
  1986)

Peter Cherches   W
195 Garfield Pl, #3E
Brooklyn, NY 11215
  Pubs: *Between a Dream & a Cup of Coffee* (Red Dust,
  1987), *Condensed Book* (Benzene Edtns, 1986)

Edith Chevat 🎤 ✈   W
395 S End Ave, #19J
New York, NY 10280, 212-321-2524
Internet: 1chevat@aol.com
  Pubs: *Writers As World Witnesses* (Pen & Brush,
  2000), *Love Lesson* (Valon Bks, 1998), *Girls: An Anth*
  (Global City Pr, 1997), *The One You Call Sister: Anth*
  (Cleis Pr, 1989), *Bridges, Global City Rev, Sojourner,
  Other Voices, Home Planet News*

Fay Chiang   P
60 E 4 St, #20
New York, NY 10003
  Pubs: *Voci Dal Silenzio* (I Canguri/Feltrinelli, 1996),
  Miwa's Song, In the City of Contradictions (Sunbury Pr,
  1982, 1979), *Girls: An Anth* (Global City Pr, 1997)

Evans Chigounis   P
224 E 18 St, #3A
New York, NY 10003
  Pubs: *Secret Lives* (Wesleyan U Pr, 1972)

China   P&W
44 Hamilton Terr #4FL
New York, NY 10031-6403
  Pubs: *Voices of Color* (Applause, 1993), *Feelings of
  Love Not Yet Expressed* (Folkways, 1978), *Essence,
  Yardbird Reader, Bergen Sun, Velvet Glove*

Sri Chinmoy   P
c/o Dr. V. Bennett, 85-38 151st St, Jamaica, NY 11432,
718-523-3826
  Pubs: *My Lord's Lotus-Feet, Seventy-Seven Thousand
  Service-Trees, Today, My Morning Begins* (Agni Pr,
  1998, 1998, 1996, 1996), *War: Man's Abysmal
  Abyss-Plunge* (Aum Pubs, 1991)

Kathleen Chodor   P
148 W 23 St
New York, NY 10011

Sonja Christina   P
PO Box 142 Lenox Hill
New York City, NY 10021, 212-737-7691
  Pubs: *The Great Adventure* (ART Pr, 1997)

Pamela Christman   W
5 Peter Cooper Rd, #7A
New York, NY 10010, 212-982-1971
  Pubs: *Bluff City, Amaranth Rev, Parting Gifts, Sassy,
  Housewife-Writer's Forum, GW Rev*

Nicholas Christopher 🎤 ✈   P&W
Janklow & Nesbit Assoc, 445 Park Ave, New York, NY
10022-2606, 212-421-1700
  Pubs: *A Trip to the Stars, Veronica* (Dial, 2000, 1996),
  *Atomic Field: Two Poems, The Creation of the Night
  Sky* (HB, 2000, 1998), *5 Degrees & Other Poems, In
  the Year of the Comet* (Viking, 1995, 1992)

Jane Ciabattari 🎤 ✈   W
36 W 75 St #5A
New York, NY 10023
  Pubs: *Winning Moves* (Penguin, 1990), *Redbook, NAR,
  Denver Qtly, Blueline, Caprice, Hampton Shorts, East
  Hampton Star*

Jill Ciment W
254 E 7 St, #15-16
New York, NY 10009
  Pubs: *Half a Life* (Crown, 1996), *The Law of Falling
  Bodies* (Poseidon Pr, 1993), *Michigan Rev, CQ, South
  Carolina Rev*

Vivina Ciolli ♀ P
PO Box 620797
Little Neck, NY 11362-0797, 718-279-4988
  Pubs: *Bitter Larder* (New Spirit Pr, 1994), *Negative
  Capability, Maryland Poetry Rev, Poets On, LIQ,
  Sistersong, Earth's Daughters*
Groups: Women

Sandra Cisneros P&W
S. Bergholz Literary Services, 17 W 10 St, #5, New York,
NY 10011, 212-387-0545
  Pubs: *Woman Hollering Creek* (Random Hse/Vintage,
  1991), *The House on Mango Street* (Vintage, 1991), *My
  Wicked, Wicked Ways* (Third Woman Pr, 1987)

Jean Clark W
Harold Ober Assoc, 425 Madison Ave, New York, NY
10017, 212-759-8600
  Pubs: *The Marriage Bed* (Putnam, 1983), *Untie the
  Winds* (Macmillan, 1976)

Jan Clausen ♀ ✈ P&W
132 Maple St
Brooklyn, NY 11225
  Pubs: *Apples & Oranges* (HM, 1999), *Books & Life*
  (Ohio State U, 1989), *The Prosperine Papers, Sinking,
  Stealing* (Crossing Pr, 1988, 1985), *Kenyon Rev, 13th
  Moon, ACM, Out/Look, Feminist Studies, The Women's
  Review of Books, Luna, The Progressive*

Russell Clay P
585 W End Ave, #7E
New York, NY 10024, 212-877-4808
Internet: www.cowell-clay.com
  Pubs: *Father Poems, From Ghost Through Bone to
  Man, Half-Life Poems* (West End Poetry Pr, 1998,
  1997, 1997), *Georgia Jrnl, Poetry Jrnl, Share, Sow's
  Ear, Poetry Motel, Talking River Rev, Lucid Stone,
  Mediphors Jrnl*

Carol Clemeau W
Bobbe Siegel, Literary Agent, 41 W 83 St, New York, NY
10024, 212-877-4985
  Pubs: *The Ariadne Clue* (Scribner, 1982), *Ellery
  Queen's Mag*

Francois Clemmons ♀ ✈ P
4 W 101 St, #35
New York, NY 10025

Michelle Cliff W
c/o Faith Childs, Faith Childs Literary Agency, 915
Broadway, Ste 1009, New York, NY 10010, 212-995-9600
  Pubs: *The Store of a Million Items: Short Stories, Best
  American Short Stories: Anth* (HM, 1998, 1997), *Free
  Enterprise, No Telephone to Heaven* (Dutton, 1993,
  1987), *VLS, Parnassus, American Voice, Ms., Kenyon
  Rev, Nation, Agni, TriQtly*

William Leo Coakley ♀ ✈ P
120 W 71 St
New York, NY 10023, 212-873-6884
  Pubs: *Humor in America: Anth* (Open Places, 1984),
  Sotheby's Poetry Competition Anth (Arvon Fdn, 1984),
  *NYQ, Harvard Gay & Lesbian Rev, Paris Rev, Nation,
  Christopher Street, Aquarius*
I.D.: Irish-American, G/L/B/T. Groups: G/L/B/T

Judith Ortiz Cofer ♀ ✈ P&W
c/o Jane Pasanen, Chelsea Forum, 377 Rector Pl, New
York, NY 10280, 212-945-3100
Internet: parallel.park.uga.edu/~jcofer
  Pubs: *An Island Like You* (Penguin, 1997), *The Latin
  Deli* (Norton, 1995), *Silent Dancing* (Arte Publico Pr,
  1990), *The Line of the Sun* (U Georgia Pr, 1989),
  *Georgia Rev, Kenyon Rev, Southern Rev, Prairie
  Schooner, Parnassus*

Alice Eve Cohen PP
250 W 77 St, #103
New York, NY 10024
  Pubs: *Book of Truth, Book of Lies* (Baltimore Museum
  of Art, 1989), *Goliath on 74th Street vs. The Woman
  Who Loved Vegetables* (Manhattan Punchline, 1989)

Esther Cohen P&W
66 W 77 St
New York, NY 10024, 212-595-0122
  Pubs: *No Charge for Looking* (Schocken Bks, 1985)

Gerald Cohen P&W
English Dept, BMCC, CUNY, 199 Chambers St, New
York, NY 10007, 717-646-2858
  Pubs: *Fire Readings/Tumbleweed: Anth* (Paris;
  Shakespeare & Co, 1996), *Chicago Rev, Lit Rev, NER,
  Confrontation, Poetry NW, Kansas Qtly*

Ira Cohen P
c/o Faye Cohen, 225 W 106 St, New York, NY 10025,
212-222-4068
  Pubs: *The Majoon Traveller* (CD; Sub Rosa, 1994),
  Ratio: (Media Shamans, 1991), *First Intensity, Third
  Rail, Exquisite Corpse*

Marc Cohen 🎤 ✈   P
1 University Pl, #3E
New York, NY 10003-4514, 212-228-6781
Internet: marc_cohen@schindler.com
　　Pubs: *Mecox Road, On Maplewood Time* (Groundwater
　　Pr, 1996, 1989), *KGB Bar Book of Poems: Anth*
　　(Perennial, 2000), *Best American Poetry: Anth* (Scribner,
　　1993, 1991), *NAW, Paris Rev, Columbia, APR*

Marty Cohen 🎤 ✈   P
600 W 246 St, #810
Bronx, NY 10471
Internet: mcohen@workinamerica.org
　　Pubs: *A Traveler's Alphabet* (Prescott Str Pr, 1979),
　　Parnassus, Northern Rev, Abraxas

Marvin Cohen 🎤 ✈   P&W
PO Box 460, Stuyvesant Sta
New York, NY 10009, 212-677-2040
　　Pubs: *Aesthetics in Art & Life* (Gull Bks, 1982), *The
　　Inconvenience of Living* (Urizen Bks, 1977), *Nation,
　　Antaeus, Hudson Rev, Sun & Moon, Chelsea*

Michael Cohen 🎤 ✈   P
59 Livingston St #3D
Brooklyn, NY 11201-4834, 718-797-9649
Internet: mcohen@arcllc.com
　　Pubs: *In This Sea* (New School Pets Series, 1997)

William Cole   P
201 W 54 St, #6A
New York, NY 10019
　　Pubs: *A Zooful of Animals* (HM, 1992), *A Boy Named
　　Mary Jane* (Franklin Watts, 1977), *New Yorker,
　　Saturday Rev*

Judith Woolcock Columbo   W
DC 37 Education Fund, Rm 202, 125 Barclay St, New
York, NY 10007-2179
　　Pubs: *The Fablesinger* (Crossing Pr, 1989)

Tram Combs   P
5 Spring St #14
New York, NY 10012
　　Pubs: *Art in America, Arts Mag, Noticias de Arte*

Brad Conard   W
Donadio & Olson, Inc, 121 W 27 St, Ste 704, New York,
NY 10001
　　Pubs: *Southern Rev, Yale Rev, Virginia Qtly Rev, SW
　　Rev*

Elizabeth Cook-Lynn   P&W
c/o Regula Noetzli, Charlotte Sheedy Literary Agency, 65
Bleecker St, New York, NY 10012, 212-780-9800
　　Pubs: *I Remember the Fallen Trees* (Eastern
　　Washington U Pr, 1998), *Woyake Kinikiya Vol II, Vol I:
　　Anths* (Oak Lake Writers Pr, 1995, 1994), *Talking Up a
　　Storm: Anth* (U Nebraska Pr, 1994), *The Writer's
　　Perspective: Anth* (Prentice Hall, 1994), *Indian Artist*

Bernard Cooper 🎤 ✈   P&W
c/o Sloan Harris, ICM, 40 W 57 St, New York, NY 10019,
212-556-5600
Internet: bcooper635@aol.com
　　Pubs: *Guess Again* (S&S, 2000), *Truth Serum* (HM,
　　1996), *A Year of Rhymes* (Viking Penguin, 1993),
　　Harper's, Paris Rev
Groups: G/L/B/T

David Cooper 🎤 ✈   P
1149 Prospect Ave, #1R
Brooklyn, NY 11218, 718-965-9337
Internet: dfc5715@hotmail.com
　　Pubs: *XY Files: Poems on the Male Experience: Anth*
　　(Sherman Asher Pub, 1997), *Green Mountains Rev,
　　Archipelago, New Works Rev, Synaesthetic, Kinesis,
　　Response, Pudding, Davka, Literary Rev, Massachusetts
　　Rev, Passages North, Painted Bride Qtly*
Lang: Hebrew. I.D.: Jewish. Groups: Children, Seniors

Jane Cooper 🎤   P
545 W 111 St, #8K
New York, NY 10025, 212-663-3934
　　Pubs: *The Flashboat: Poems Collected & Reclaimed*
　　(Norton, 1999), *Green Notebook, Winter Road,
　　Scaffolding: Selected Poems* (Tilbury Hse, 1994, 1993),
　　*APR, Field, New Yorker, Paris Rev, Kenyon Rev, New
　　Yorker, American Voice, Iowa Rev*

Claire Cooperstein   P&W
Rhoda Weyr Literary Agency, 151 Bergen St, Brooklyn,
NY 11217, 718-522-0410
　　Pubs: *Johanna—Novel of Van Gogh Family*
　　(Scribner/S&S, 1995), *Counting Keepsakes* (Andrew
　　Mountain Poetry Pr, 1989), *Ko—Japanese Haiku,
　　Frogpond*

Mark Coovelis   W
Sterling Lord Literistic, 65 Bleecker St, New York, NY
10012, 212-780-6050
　　Pubs: *Gloria* (S&S, 1994), *American Voice, California
　　Qtly, Short Story Rev, City Lights Rev*

Robert Coover   W
Georges Borchardt Inc., 136 E 57 St, New York, NY
10022, 212-753-5785
　　Pubs: *John's Wife, Pinocchio in Venice, A Night at the
　　Movies, Whatever Happened to Gloomy Gus of the
　　Chicago Bears?* (S&S, 1996, 1991, 1987, 1987)

Alfred Corn   P&W
720 Fort Washington Ave, Apt 6V
New York, NY 10040, 212-928-6177
  Pubs: *Part of his Story* (Mid-List Pr, 1997), *Present*
  (Counterpoint, 1997), *Autobiographies, The West Door*
  (Viking Penguin, 1992, 1988), *Notes from a Child of
  Paradise* (Viking, 1984), *A Call in the Midst of a Crowd*
  (Viking, 1978)

Gregory Corso   P
Roger Richards Rare Books, 26 Horatio St, #24, New
York, NY 10014

Jayne Cortez   P
PO Box 96, Village Sta
New York, NY 10014, 212-431-5067
  Pubs: *Somewhere in Advance of Nowhere* (Serpent's
  Tail/High Risk Bks, 1996), *Poetic Magnetic, Everywhere
  Drums* (CD) (Bola Pr, 1991, 1991)

Angela Costa 🎤 ✈   PP
PO Box 1356, Canal St Station
New York, NY 10013-0877
Internet: http://www.AngelaCosta.com
  Pubs: *1000 Reasons* (Pride Pub, 1997), *Penis Is As
  Penis Does* (Little Black Bks, 2000), *Nuyorican Poets
  Cafe, Knitting Factory, Living Theater, Mona's, St.
  Mark's Poetry Project*

Jonathan Cott   P
247 E 33 St, #6A
New York, NY 10016
  Pubs: *Wandering Ghost: The Odyssey of Lafcadio
  Hearn* (Knopf, 1991), *The Search for Omm Sety*
  (Warner Bks, 1989)

Cynthia Cotts   W
59 E 7 St, #2
New York, NY 10003
  Pubs: *Art & Artists, Columbus Dispatch, Appearances,
  Gargoyle, Telescope*

Linda Cousins   P
The Universal Black Writer Pr, PO Box 5, Radio City Sta,
New York, NY 10101, 718-398-8941
  Pubs: *The Mystical Experiences of Harriet Tubman,
  Black & in Brooklyn* (Universal Black Writer Pr, 1992,
  1983), *Cottonwood* (U Kansas Pr, 1986)

Stephanie Amy Cowell 🎤 ✈   W
585 W End Ave
New York, NY 10024, 212-877-4808
Internet: stephanie@cowell-clay.com
  Pubs: *The Players, The Physician of London, Nicholas
  Cooke* (Norton, 1997, 1995, 1993)

Douglas Crase   P
470 W 24 St
New York, NY 10011
  Pubs: *The Revisionist* (Little, Brown, 1981)

Gwyneth Cravens   W
c/o Amanda Urban, ICM, 40 W 57 St, New York, NY
10019, 212-556-5600
  Pubs: *The Gates of Paradise* (Ticknor & Fields, 1991),
  Heart's Desire, Love & Work (Knopf, 1986, 1982), *New
  Yorker, Nation, Harper's*

Marc Crawford   W
360 W 21 St, #4-M
New York, NY 10011, 212-675-7197
  Pubs: *The Lincoln Brigade* (Atheneum, 1989), *Emerge,
  Freedomways, Time Capsule*

Tad Crawford 🎤 ✈   W
10 E 23 St, Ste 400
New York, NY 10010
  Pubs: *Confrontation, Central Park, Phantasm*

Jennifer Crewe   P
285 Riverside Dr #3B
New York, NY 10025-5226, 212-865-6254
  Pubs: *Pequod, Tar River Poetry, The American Muse,
  Poet & Critic, Ploughshares, Piedmont Lit Rev*

William Cullen, Jr. 🎤   P
910 Albemarle Rd
Brooklyn, NY 11218, 718-287-7507
Internet: billcu@aol.com
  Pubs: *Frogpond, Gryphon, St. Anthony Messenger,
  Home Planet News, Parnassus, Plainsong, Modern
  Haiku*

Elizabeth Cullinan   W
463 West St Apt 817-D
New York, NY 10014
  Pubs: *A Change of Scene* (Norton, 1982), *House of
  Gold* (HM, 1969), *Shenandoah, Colorado Rev, Irish Lit
  Supplement, Threshold, New Yorker*

Lorraine Rainie Currelley   P
PO Box 562, College Sta
New York, NY 10030-0562
  Pubs: *Gaptooth Girlfriends The Third Act* (Gaptooth
  Girlfriends The Third Act, 1994)

David Curzon 🎤 ✈   P
254 W 82 St, #2B
New York, NY 10024-5450, 212-874-3989
  Pubs: *Dovichik* (Penguin Bks, 1996), *The View from
  Jacob's Ladder, Modern Poems on the Bible: Anth
  (Jewish Pub Soc, 1996, 1994), *The Gospels in Our
  Image: Anth* (HB, 1995), *Poetry, Antaeus, New
  Republic, Sewanee Rev, Formalist, Tikkun*

Susan Daitch   W
c/o Miriam Altshuler, 50 W 29 St, New York, NY 10001,
212-684-6050
  Pubs: *Storytown* (Dalkey Archive Pr, 1996), *Avant Pop
  Anthology* (Viking Penguin, 1995), *Top Stories, Rev of
  Contemporary Fiction, Bomb, Fiction Intl, VLS*

Vinni Marie D'Ambrosio   P
11 5 Ave, #3N
New York, NY 10003, 212-673-5875
  Pubs: *Mexican Gothic: A Frieda Kahlo Narrative* (Blue
  Heron Pr, 1996), Life *of Touching Mouths* (NYU Pr,
  1971), *McGraw-Hill Book of Poetry: Anth* (McGraw-Hill,
  1993), *Italo American Poets: Anth* (A. Carello, 1985)

Enid Dame 🎤 ✈   P&W
3047 Brighton First Pl
Brooklyn, NY 11235-7419, 718-769-2854
Internet: dame@admin.njit.edu
  Pubs: *Anything You Don't See* (West End, 1992), *Lilith
  & Her Demons* (CCC, 1989), *One Trick Pony, Jews,
  Many Mountains Moving, Davka, Bridges, NYQ, Tikkun,
  American Voice, Phoebe*
I.D.: Jewish, Feminist. Groups: Women, Jewish

Rosemary Daniell   P&W
Wendy Weil Agency Inc, 232 Madison Ave, Ste 1300,
New York, NY 10016, 212-685-0030
  Pubs: *The Woman Who Spilled Words All Over Herself*
  (Faber & Faber, 1997), *The Hurricane Season* (Morrow,
  1992), *Fort Bragg & Other Points South, Sleeping with
  Soldiers* (H Holt, 1988, 1984), *American Voice,
  Chattahoochee Rev*

Kathryn Daniels   P&W
35-45 78 St, Apt #2
Jackson Heights, NY 11372
  Pubs: *If I Had a Hammer: Anth* (Papier-Mache Pr,
  1990), *Chrysanthemum, Earth's Daughters, Korone*

Jack Dann   W
c/o Merrilee Heifetz, The Writers House, 21 W 26 St,
New York, NY 10010, 212-691-4575
  Pubs: *The Man Who Melted* (H C Australia, 1998), *The
  Silent, The Memory Cathedral* (Bantam Bks, 1998,
  1995), *Nebula Awards 32: Anth* (HB, 1998), *High Steel*
  (w/J.C. Haldema; Tor, 1993), *Playboy, Twilight Zone
  Mag*

Ruth Danon   P
NYU/ADSD, 225 Shimkin Hall, 50 W 4 St, New York, NY
10003
  Pubs: *Triangulation from a Known Point* (North Star
  Line/Blue Moon Bks, 1990), *Bomb, Paris Rev*

Ann Darby 🎤 ✈   W
245 W 104 St, #2D
New York, NY 10025-4279
Internet: darbann@aol.com
  Pubs: *The Orphan Game* (Morrow, 1999), *The
  American Story: The Best of Story Qtly: Anth* (Cane Hill
  Pr, 1990), *NW Rev, Blue Light/Red Light, Story Qtly,
  Organica, Malahat Rev*
Groups: Teenagers

Alice Elliott Dark 🎤   W
Henry Dunow Literary Agency, 22 W 23rd St, New York,
NY 10010
Internet: aedark@aol.com
  Pubs: *In the Gloaming* (S&S, 2000), *Naked to the
  Waist, Best American Short Stories: Anth* (HM, 1991,
  19999), *Harper's, New Yorker*

Eric Darton 🎤 ✈   P&W
315 8th Ave, #20F
New York, NY 10001, 212-242-0579
  Pubs: *Free City* (Norton, 1996), *Radio Tirane*
  (Conjunctions, 1991), *Conjunctions 17 Anth* (Bard,
  1991), *NER, Confrontation, American Letters &
  Commentary, Central Park, Metropolis, Culturefront,
  Leonardo, Fiction Intl*

Kiana Davenport 🎤 ✈   W
Henry Dunow Literary Agency, 22 W 23 St, 5th Fl, New
York, NY 10010, 212-645-7606
  Pubs: *Song of the Exile* (Ballantine, 2000), *Shark
  Dialogues* (Plume, 1995), *Charlie Chan Is Dead: Anth*
  (Penguin, 1993), *Story, Hawaii Pacific Rev, Seattle Rev,
  Ikon, Honolulu Mag, New Letters*
Groups: Women, Multicultural

Richard Davidson   P
200 W 94 St, #3E
New York, NY 10025, 212-749-0870
  Pubs: *Tower Nine* (Ann Salazar, 1986), *The Gentleman
  from Hyde Park* (Bard, 1982), *Jewish Affairs, Home
  Planet News, People's Weekly World, Arts Muse*

Bradley B. Davis   P
1235 Park Ave
New York, NY 10028, 212-876-1609

Christopher Davis   W
c/o Clyde Taylor, Curtis Brown Ltd., 10 Astor Pl, New
York, NY 10003-6935, 212-473-5400
  Pubs: *Dog Horse Rat* (Viking, 1990), *A Peep Into the
  20th Century* (Arbor Hse, 1985), *Waiting for It* (H&R,
  1980)

Annabel Davis-Goff   W
c/o Jennifer Hengen, Sterling Lord Literistic, 65 Bleecker
St, New York, NY 10012, 212-780-6050
  Pubs: *The Dower House* (St. Martin's, 1998), *Walled
  Gardens* (Knopf, 1989), *Tail Spin, Night Tennis* (Coward
  McCann, 1981, 1978), *Lear's*

L. J. Davis 🎤 ✈ W
138A Dean St
Brooklyn, NY 11217, 718-625-3365
  Pubs: *Billionaire Shell Game* (Doubleday, 1998)

Lydia Davis 🎤 ✈ W
c/o Denise Shannon, ICM, 40 W 57 St, New York, NY
10019, 212-556-6727
Internet: dshannon@icmtalent.com
  Pubs: *Almost No Memory, The End of the Story, Break
  it Down* (FSG, 1997, 1995, 1986), *Best American
  Poetry: Anth* (Scribner, 1999), *KGB Bar Reader: Anth*
  (Morrow, 1998), *Granta, Harper's, Grand Street, Paris
  Rev, Conjunctions*

Thulani Davis P
Grove Weidenfeld Press, 841 Broadway, New York, NY
10003
  Pubs: *Playing the Changes* (Wesleyan U Pr, 1985), *All
  the Renegade Ghosts Rise* (Anemone, 1978)

Cecil Dawkins W
Charlotte Sheedy Literary Agency, 65 Bleecker St, New
York, NY 10012, 212-780-9800
  Pubs: *The Quiet Enemy, Charleyhorse* (Viking Penguin,
  1986, 1985), *The Live Goat* (H&R, 1971), *Paris Rev,
  SW Rev, Sewanee Rev, McCall's, Redbook*

Fielding Dawson W
49 E 19 St
New York, NY 10003, 212-254-4076
  Pubs: *Moment's Notice* (Coffee Hse, 1993), *Out of This
  World* (Crown, 1991), *The Trick* (Black Sparrow, 1991),
  Ploughshares, Exquisite Corpse, Ontario Rev

Storm De Hirsch P
1760 3rd Ave, #721B
New York, NY 10029

James De Jongh W
6 Fordham Hill Oval, #9D
Bronx, NY 10468, 212-933-6131
  Pubs: *Vicious Modernism: Black Harlem & the Literary
  Imagination* (Cambridge U Pr, 1990)

Irma Del Valle 🎤 P
96-07 42nd Ave
Corona, NY 11368-2146
  Pubs: *Polvo Poetico, Senderos Contigo, Ilusiones*
  (Archer Bks, 1990, 1974, 1966)
Lang: Spanish

Don DeLillo W
Wallace Literary Agency, 177 E 70 St, New York, NY
10021
  Pubs: *Underworld* (Scribner, 1997), *Mao II, Libra, White
  Noise* (Viking, 1991, 1988, 1985), *The Names* (Knopf,
  1982)

Jane DeLynn 🎤 ✈ W
Promethean Artists Management, 1133 Broadway, New
York, NY 10010, 212-219-9038
  Pubs: *Don Juan in the Village* (Pantheon, 1990), *Real
  Estate* (Poseidon/S&S, 1988), *Bad Sex Is Good: Anth,
  New York Sex: Stories: Anth* (Painted Leaf Pr, 1998,
  1998), *The Mammoth Book of Modern Lesbian Short
  Stories* (Robinson Pr, XXXX), *Paris Rev, Harper's*
I.D.: Jewish. Groups: G/L/B/T

Arto DeMirjian, Jr. W
311 W 24 St, Apt 20-G
New York, NY 10011, 212-989-4967
  Pubs: *Not a Clue* (Popular Pr, 1974), *Ararat Qtly*

Alice Denham 🎤 ✈ W
Claudia Menza Literary Agency, 1170 Broadway, Ste 807,
New York, NY 10001, 212-889-6850
  Pubs: *AMO* (Putnam, 1975), *My Darling from the Lions*
  (Bobbs-Merrill, 1967), *Great Tales of City Dwellers*
  (Pyramid & Lion, 1965), *Best of the Missouri Rev: Anth*
  (U Missouri Pr, 1991), *Confrontation, Playboy,
  Discovery, Nation, San Miguel Writer*

Alma Denny P
353 W 56 St, #3B
New York, NY 10019, 212-757-4648
  Pubs: *Blinkies: Funny Poems to Read in a Blink*
  (Spectacle Lane Pr, 1992), *Lyric, Cosmopolitan, Ladies
  Home Jrnl, Good Housekeeping, Light Qtly*

Shira Dentz 🎤 ✈ P
333 5th Ave
Brooklyn, NY 11215-2808, 718-369-6218
  Pubs: *Salt Hill Jrnl, Phoebe, Cimarron Rev, Illuminators,
  Barrow Street, No Exit, WV, 6ix, 13th Moon, So to
  Speak, Evergreen Chronicles, Salamander, Paragraph,
  Modern Words*
I.D.: Feminist. Groups: Children, Prisoners

Ed Depasquale P
59 Christopher St
New York, NY 10014, 212-675-0833
  Pubs: *Ally, Poems in Captivity, Velvet Wings, Helen
  Rev, Mati, Contact II, Poetry*

Nan DeVincent-Hayes Ph.D 🎤 ✈ W
c/o Ivy Fischer Stone, Fifi Oscard Literary & Talent
Agency, 24 W 40 St 17th Fl, New York, NY 10018,
212-764-1100
  Pubs: *Jacob's Trouble, Thy Brother's Reaper*
  (Renaissance Alliance Pub, 2001, 2000), *22 Friar Street*
  (Flower Valley Pr, 2000), *Grit, Mature Years, Redbook,
  Slipstream, Sojourner*
Groups: Christian

Graham Diamond   W
2320 Parsons Blvd
Whitestone, NY 11357-3442
   Pubs: *Forest Wars* (Lion Pr, 1994), *Black Midnight*
   (Zeba Bks, 1989)

Joan Didion   W
Janklow & Nesbit Assoc, 598 Madison Ave, New York,
NY 10022-1614, 212-421-1700

David Diefendorf   W
789 W End Ave, #5D
New York, NY 10025, 212-663-4932

May Dikeman 🎤 ✈   W
70 Irving Pl
New York, NY 10003, 212-475-4533
   Pubs: *The Devil We Know, The Angelica* (Atlantic/Little,
   Brown, 1973, 1971), *Atlantic, Harper's*

Annie Dillard   P&W
c/o Timothy Seldes, Russell & Volkening, Inc, 50 W 29
St, New York, NY 10001
   Pubs: *For the Time Being* (Knopf, 1999), The *Living*
   (HC, 1992), *An American Childhood, Pilgrim at Tinker
   Creek* (H&R, 1987, 1974)

Carol Dine 🎤 ✈   P
c/o Peter Rubie, Perkins/Rubie & Assoc, 240 W 35 St,
Ste 500, New York, NY 10001
Internet: cdine@acad.suffolk.edu
   Pubs: *Trying to Understand the Lunar Eclipse* (Erie
   Street Pr, 1992), *Naming the Sky* (Golden Quill, 1989),
   Living on the Margins: Anth (Persea Bks, 1999), *A Map
   of Hope: Anth* (Rutgers U Pr, 1999), *Women's Rev of
   Books, Prairie Schooner*

Susan Grathwohl Dingle 🎤 ✈   P
166 E 96 St
New York, NY 10128
Internet: dingle0925@aol.com
   Pubs: *For Neruda, for Chile: Anth*: (Beacon, 1975), *US
   Submarine Veterans Reporter, Island Submariner, Mock
   Turtle, Parents Mag, APR, Partisan Rev, Ohio Rev*

Ray DiPalma 🎤 ✈   P
301 W 108 St #6B
New York, NY 10025, 212-663-1686
   Pubs: *Letters* (Littoral Pr, 1998), *Motion of the Cypher*
   (Roof Bks, 1995), *Provocations* (Potes & Poets Pr,
   1994), *APR, First Intensity, Verse, Quaderno, Fence, La
   Polygraphe, Chicago Rev, To Mag, Revue Pretexte,
   Five Fingers, Iowa Rev, Rhizome, Arshile*

Thomas M. Disch   P&W
Karpfinger Agency, 357 W 20 St, New York, NY
10011-3379, 212-691-2690
   Pubs: *Dark Verses & Light, Yes, Let's: New & Selected
   Poems* (Johns Hopkins U Pr, 1991, 1989), *The M.D.: A
   Horror Story* (Knopf, 1991), *Poetry*

Stephen Dobyns   P&W
Henry Holt & Co., 115 W 18 St, New York, NY 10011
   Pubs: *Cemetery Nights, A Boat Off the Coast* (Viking,
   1987, 1987)

E. L. Doctorow   W
c/o Amanda Urban, ICM, 40 W 57 St, New York, NY
10019, 212-556-5600

J. D. Dolan   W
c/o Amanda Urban, ICM, 40 W 57 St, New York, NY
10019, 212-556-5764
   Pubs: *New Stories from the South: Anth* (Algonquin,
   1996), *Esquire, Antioch Rev, Mississippi Rev,
   Shenandoah, Nation*

Sharon Dolin   P
600 W 111 St, #11D
New York, NY 10025
   Pubs: *Climbing Mount Sinai* (Dim Gray Bar Pr, 1996),
   Heart Work (Sheep Meadow Pr, 1995), *Poetry,
   Boulevard, Kenyon Rev, Ploughshares, Salamander,
   American Voice*

Bob Dombrowski 🎤 ✈   PP
805 6 Ave
New York, NY 10001, 212-741-2525
   Pubs: *Run, Highway #17,* (The Cycle) *Ravings from the
   Periphery* (Dombrowski/Petruska Productions, 1994,
   1992, 1991)

Jack Donahue   P
50-19 Bell Blvd
Bayside, NY 11364, 718-225-7992
   Pubs: *Midwestern U Qtly, Yet Another Small Mag,
   Cedar Rock, Snowy Egret, Gnosis, Dekalb Lit Arts Jrnl*

Stephen R. Donaldson 🎤 ✈   W
Howard Morhaim Agency, 175 Fifth Ave, #709, New York,
NY 10010, 212-529-4433
   Pubs: *Reave the Just & Other Tales, This Day All
   Gods Die, Forbidden Knowledge, The Real Story*
   (Bantam/Spectra, 1999, 1996, 1991, 1991), *Lord Foul's
   Bane* (Del Rey/Ballantine, 1977)

Alfred Dorn 🎤 ✈   P
PO Box 580174, Station A
Flushing, NY 11358-0174
   Pubs: *Voices from Rooms, from Cells to Mindspace*
   (Somers Rocks Pr, 1997, 1997), *Hudson Rev, New
   Criterion, Formalist, Orbis, Light Year, The Lyric,
   Amelia, Pivot, Sparrow, Light*

Ellen Douglas W
RLR Assoc, 7 W 51 St, New York, NY 10017
  Pubs: *Can't Quit You, Baby* (Viking Penguin, 1989),
  Black Cloud, White Cloud (U Pr Mississippi, 1989)

Michael Drinkard W
c/o Cynthia Cannell, Janklow & Nesbit Assoc, 598
Madison Ave, New York, NY 10022-1614, 212-421-1700
  Pubs: *Disobedience* (Norton, 1993), *Green Bananas*
  (Knopf, 1989)

Sally Ann Drucker 🎤 ✈ P
PO Box 7888
New York, NY 10116-7888
  Pubs: *Walking the Desert Lion* (Ena, 1984), *Words on
  the Page, The World in Your Hands: Anth* (H&R,
  1990), *Bitterroot, Buckle, Epos, Pig Iron, Womanspirit*
I.D.: Jewish

Nancy du Plessis 🎤 ✈ PP&P
150 W 80 St
New York, NY 10024
  Pubs: *Notes des Cahiers Marocaine/Notes from the
  Moroccan Journals, Art New York* (Paris; L'Harmattan,
  1995), *Home Planet News*
Lang: French. Groups: Women, Seniors

Helen Duberstein P&W
463 West St, #904D
New York, NY 10014
  Pubs: *Shadow Self & Other Tales, The Shameless Old
  Lady* (Ghost Dance Pr, 1996, 1995), *The Radical
  Theatre Notebook* (Applause, 1994), *Signal Network Intl*

Maggie Dubris 🎤 ✈ P&W
27 1st Ave, #14
New York, NY 10003, 212-673-1583
  Pubs: *Willieworld* (Cuz Bks, 1998), *Ladies, Start Your
  Engines: Anth* (Faber & Faber, 1996), *Out of This
  World: Anth* (Crown, 1991), *Cybercorpse 3, Big Bridge,
  Koff, Cuz 2, Tribes, Exquisite Corpse, Tamarind,
  $lavery, Minimus*

Denise Duhamel P
36-09 21 Ave
Astoria, NY 11105
  Pubs: *The Star-Spangled Banner* (Southern Illinois U
  Pr, 1999), *Kinky* (Orchises Pr, 1997), *Girl Soldier*
  (Garden Street, 1996), *The Woman with Two Vaginas*
  (Salmon Run, 1994), *Global City Rev, Third Coast,
  Urbanus, Salt Hill Rev, APR, Ontario Rev, Chelsea*

Margaret Mitchell Dukore W
Bobbe Siegel Literary Agency, 41 W 83 St, New York, NY
10024
  Pubs: *Bloom, Survival of the Fittest* (Franklin Watts,
  1985, 1985), *Rev of Contemporary Fiction*

Harris Dulany W
273 Warren St
Brooklyn, NY 11201
  Pubs: *One Kiss Led to Another* (H C 1994), *Falling*
  (Saturday Rev Pr, 1971)

Gerald Dumas P
King Features Syndicate, 235 E 45 St, New York, NY
10017
  Pubs: *An Afternoon in Waterloo Park* (Wayne State U
  Pr, 1988), *Rabbits Rafferty* (Avon Camelot, 1985),
  Atlantic, Smithsonian

Erika Duncan W
463 West St, #933B
New York, NY 10014, 212-691-0539
  Pubs: *Those Giants: Let Them Rise, Unless Soul Clap
  Its Hands* (Schocken, 1985, 1985)

Pearl Duncan 🎤 ✈ W
PO Box 1274, Church St Sta
New York, NY 10008-1274, 212-962-3944
Internet: pearl@pearlduncan.com
  Pubs: *A Rock Against the Wind: African-American
  Poems* (Berkley/Perigee, 1996), *Water Dancing* (Aegina
  Pr, 1991), *Essence, Black Enterprise, Sailing, Sail*

Robert Dunn 🎤 ✈ W
Brandt & Brandt Literary Agents, 1501 Broadway, New
York, NY 10036, 212-840-5760
  Pubs: *The Stingrays* (Election Pr, 2000), *New Yorker,
  Fiction Network, Atlantic, Sewanee Rev, Mother Jones*

Robert Dunn 🎤 ✈ P
75-05 210 St, #6N
Bayside, NY 11364, 718-776-8853
  Pubs: *Guilty as Charged, Zen Yentas in Bondage*
  (Cross-Cultural Lit Edtn 1999, 1997)
Groups: Children, Seniors

Roger Duvernoy P
70 Riverside Dr, #3E
New York, NY 10024, 212-721-5402
  Pubs: *Ripples, Numbers, Circle, Poetry North Rev, Star,
  Cathartic*

Martin S. Dworkin P&W
c/o Brian Cave, 245 Park Ave, New York, NY
10167-0002, 212-254-2960
  Pubs: *Northern Perspective, The World & I, Zymergy,
  Contemporary Rev, Transnational Perspectives, ACM,
  Poetry Ireland Rev, Takahe, Laurel Rev, Nutshell*

Miriam Dyak P
82 Garfield Pl
Brooklyn, NY 11215
  Pubs: *Dying, Fire Under Water* (New Victoria Pubs,
  1979, 1978)

Bru Dye   P
164 Hall St
Brooklyn, NY 11205
    Pubs: *Yellow Silk, Exquisite Corpse, Central Park,*
    James White Rev, Amethyst, Slow Motion Mag

Joan Eades   P&W
484 W 43 St, #28C
New York, NY 10036, 212-592-1834
    Pubs: *Kansas Qtly, North Dakota Qtly, Plainswoman,*
    Louisville Rev, Random Hse Audio Bks

Cornelius Robert Eady   P
39 Jane St #GB
New York, NY 10014, 212-242-8646
    Pubs: *The Gathering of My Name* (Carnegie Mellon,
    1990), *Seneca Rev, Ploughshares*

Patricia Eakins ♀ ✈   P&W
1200 Broadway, #4C
New York, NY 10001, 212-679-7413
Internet: www.fabulara.com
    Pubs: *The Marvelous Adventures of Pierre Baptiste,*
    Father & Mother, First & Last (NYU Pr, 1999), *The*
    Hungry Girls (Cadmus, 1988), *Oono* (I-74 Pr, 1982),
    Sources, Parnassus, Iowa Rev, Conjunctions, Central
    Park, Storia, Paris Rev, Hotwired

Elaine Edelman ♀ ✈   P
444 E 86 St #27B
New York, NY 10028-6464, 212-535-7066
    Pubs: *Boom-de-Boom* (Pantheon, 1980), *Noeva: Three*
    Women Poets: Anth (U South Dakota Pr, 1990),
    Mudfish, APR, Frontiers, Prairie Schooner, Malahat Rev,
    The Cape Rock
I.D.: Jewish. Groups: Seniors, Women

John Ehle   W
Donadio & Olson, Inc, 121 W 27 St, Ste 704, New York,
NY 10001, 212-691-8077
    Pubs: *The Widow's Trial, The Winter People* (H&R,
    1989, 1984), *Trail of Tears* (Anchor, 1988)

Gretel Ehrlich   P
Darhansoff & Verrill Agency, 179 Franklin St, 4th Fl, New
York, NY 10013
    Pubs: *Drinking Dry Clouds, Wyoming Stories* (Capra Pr,
    1991, 1986), *Islands, The Universe, Home, Heart*
    Mountain (Viking, 1991, 1988)

Janice Eidus ♀ ✈   W
77 Seventh Ave, #14G
New York, NY 10011-6632, 212-924-3018
    Pubs: *Urban Bliss, The Celibacy Club, Vito Loves*
    Geraldine (City Lights, 1998, 1996, 1990), *SW Rev,*
    Village Voice, Witness, Asylum Arts

J. Eigo ♀ ✈   W
182 Ave A, #1B
New York, NY 10009, 212-533-2769
Internet: jimeigo@aol.com
    Pubs: *Quickies 2: Anth* (Arsenal Pulp Pr, 1999), *Best*
    American Gay Fiction 3: Anth (Little, Brown 1998), *Best*
    Gay Erotica 1997: Anth (Cleis Pr, 1997), *Butch Boys:*
    Anth (Bad Boy/Kasak Bks, 1997), *Stallions: Anth* (PDA
    Pr, 1995)
I.D.: G/L/B/T. Groups: G/L/B/T

Bernard Lionel Einbond   P
PO Box 307, Ft George Sta
New York, NY 10040, 718-960-8361
    Pubs: *The Tree As It Is* (Brander O'Neill Pr, 1996),
    The Coming Indoors (Charles E. Tuttle, 1979), *Bogg,*
    Wordsmith, Modern Haiku, Frogpond

Barbara Einzig ♀ ✈   P
375 S End Ave, #27-N
New York, NY 10280, 212-912-1303
    Pubs: *Distance Without Distance* (Kelsey Street Pr,
    1994), *Life Moves Outside* (Burning Deck Pr, 1987),
    Five Fingers Rev, Chelsea, Conjunctions, VLS, Fence,
    APR
Groups: Teenagers, Nature/Environment

Deborah Eisenberg   W
c/o Lynn Nesbit, Janklow & Nesbit Assoc, 598 Madison
Ave, New York, NY 10022-1614, 212-421-1700
    Pubs: *The Stories (So Far)* (Noonday, 1997), *All*
    Around Atlantis, Under the 82nd Airborne (FSG, 1997,
    1992), *Transactions in a Foreign Currency* (Knopf,
    1987)

Kim Elizabeth   P&W
c/o John Habermas, PO Box 120036, Staten Island, NY
10312-0036, 718-317-6110
    Pubs: *Netherworld* (Ghost Girl Graphix, 1995),
    Darkworld Vampires (Millennium Pubs, 1995), *Dead of*
    Night, The Tome, Haunted Sun, Ghastly, Scream in the
    Dark

Kate Ferguson Ellis   P
240 W 102 St
New York, NY 10025, 212-662-6232
    Pubs: *The Contested Castle* (U Illinois Pr, 1989), *Ms.,*
    Feminist Studies, Chrysalis, Salamander, Telephone,
    Marxist Perspectives

Harlan Ellison   W
Richard Curtis Associates, Inc, 171 E 74 St, New York,
NY 10021
    Pubs: *Slippage* (HM, 1997), *Edgeworks 3 & 4,*
    Edgeworks: Volume I (White Wolf, 1997, 1996), *Mefisto*
    in Onyx (Mark V. Ziesing Bks, 1993), *Mag of Fantasy*
    & Sci Fi, Buzz Mag, Playboy, Ohio Writer

Patricia Elmore W
Marcia Amsterdam Agency, 41 W 82 St, New York, NY
10024
Pubs: *Susannah & the Purple Mongoose Mystery*
(Dutton, 1992), *Susannah & the Blue House Mystery*
(Scholastic Apple, 1990)

Barbara Elovic P
586 Henry St
Brooklyn, NY 11231-2721, 718-834-0291
Pubs: *Time Out* (Amity Street Pr, 1996), *Walk on the
Wild Side: Anth* (Scribner, 1994), *Poetry, Pivot,
Exquisite Corpse, Mss., Sonora Rev, Onthebus*

W. R. Elton P
PhD Program in English, City Univ New York, 33 W 42
St, Box 510, New York, NY 10036, 212-642-2206

Carol Emshwiller 🎤 ✈ W
210 E 15 St, #12E
New York, NY 10003-3938, 212-982-5779
Internet: cemsh@aol.com
Pubs: *Leaping Man Hill, Ledoyt* (Mercury Hse, 1998,
1995), *Love Stories for the Rest of Us: Anth, Pushcart
Prize XXII: Anth* (Pushcart Pr, 1995, 1989), *Omni,
TriQtly, Wild Women, Women of Wonder*

Helen Engelhardt P
805 E 21 St
Brooklyn, NY 11210, 718-859-5440
Pubs: *Latitude 30'18', Intl Poetry Rev, Bitterroot, Dark
Horse, Mixed Voices*

Russell Epprecht W
PO Box 734, Stuyvesant Sta
New York, NY 10009, 212-254-1004
Pubs: *Yardstick, Further* (Domesday Bks, 1984, 1983),
Redtape, Homeless Catalogue

Seymour Epstein W
750 Kappock St #608
Bronx, NY 10463-4616, 212-796-0091
Pubs: *Light* (H Holt, 1989), *September Faces, A
Special Destiny* (Donald I. Fine, 1987, 1986)

Elaine Equi P
298 Mulberry St, #3L
New York, NY 10012, 212-941-8724
Pubs: *Decoy, Surface Tension* (Coffee Hse Pr, 1994,
1989), *Conjunctions, APR, Sulfur, Chelsea, NAW,
Caliban, Paris Rev*

Nancy Watson Erikson P&W
c/o Writers Group, West Side Arts Coalition, PO Box 527,
Cathedral Sta, New York, NY 10025
Pubs: *Splinters of Fear* (Avon, 1960), *This Singing
Earth: Anth* (Round Table, 1959), *Stories*

John Eskow P
247 W 87 St, #23-F
New York, NY 10024, 212-662-5766

Eurydice P&W
c/o Gear, 450 W 15 St, 5th Fl, New York, NY 10011,
212-771-7000
Pubs: *F/32: The Second Coming* (Virago Pr, 1993),
F/32 (Kasak Bks, 1993), *Barebreasted* (Greece; Fosti
Edtns, 1980), *Iowa Rev, Black Ice, Cups, Texture,
Open End, Spin, Gear, Harper's, George*

Bill Evans 🎤 ✈ P
99 E 4 St #3F
New York, NY 10003-9074, 212-982-5462
Pubs: *Monologues from the Road: Anth, Elvis
Monologues: Anth* (Heinemann Bks, 1999, 1998), *Puerto
del Sol, Quarry West, Antioch Rev, Mudfish, Exquisite
Corpse*
Groups: Teenagers, Children

RobertOh Faber 🎤 P
160 Claremont Ave
New York, NY 10027-4635, 212-864-6151
Pubs: *NYQtly, Light, Clown War, Poets, Kauri,
Wormwood Rev, Daily World*

Arnold E. Falleder 🎤 ✈ P
160 W 87 St, #7B
New York, NY 10024-2951, 212-724-4712
Pubs: *Midrash for Macbeth, The God-Shed* (Runaway
Spoon Pr, 2000, 1992), *William Said, Generator 9: Anth*
(Generator Pr, 1996, 1999), *Cover, The Poet, Christian
Century, Onthebus, Stone Country, Purple, Rattle,
Fiddlehead*

Louis Falstein W
2571 Hubbard St
Brooklyn, NY 11235
Pubs: *Sole Survivor* (Dell, 1954), *Chicago Jewish
Forum*

Margot Farrington 🎤 ✈ PP&P
118 N 9 St
Brooklyn, NY 11211-1915, 718-388-2184
Pubs: *Rising & Falling* (Warthog Pr, 1985), *Out of the
Catskills & Just Beyond: Anth, Word Thursday Anth of
Poetry & Fiction, Speaking the Words: Anth* (Bright Hill
Pr, 1997, 1995, 1994), *Poetry Wales Intl, California
Qtly, Phoebe, ALR*

Irvin Faust 🎤 ✈ W
417 Riverside Dr
New York, NY 10025-7928, 212-864-5410
Pubs: *Jim Dandy* (Carroll & Graf, 1994), *Contemporary
Atlantic: Anth* (Atlantic Monthly, 1988), *Year of the Hot
Jock* (Dutton, 1984), *Newsreel* (HBJ, 1980), *O. Henry
Prize Stories 1986: Anth, Michigan Qtly Rev, Esquire,
Confrontation, Lit Rev, Paris Rev*
Groups: College/Univ, Jewish

Naomi F. Faust 🎤 ✈   P
112-01 175 St
Jamaica, NY 11433-4135, 718-291-5338
 Pubs: *And I Travel by Rhythms & Words, All Beautiful
 Things* (Lotus Pr, 1990, 1983)
I.D.: African-American

Susan C. Fawcett   P
67 Riverside Dr, #9B
New York, NY 10024
 Pubs: *Abandoned House* (Silver Apples Pr, 1988),
 Michigan Qtly Rev, Nation, Montana Rev, Nimrod

Cheri Fein 🎤 ✈   P&W
8 Stuyvesant Oval, #8F
New York, NY 10009, 212-995-5486
 Pubs: *Home Before Light* (Ridgeway Pr, 1991), *Pequod,
 Bomb, Ploughshares, Partisan Rev, Nimrod, Between
 C&D*

Frederick Feirstein   P
c/o Egon Dumler, 575 Madison Ave, New York, NY 10028
 Pubs: *New & Selected Poems, City Life* (Story Line Pr,
 1998, 1991), *Ending the 20th Century, Family History*
 (QRL, 1994, 1991)

Annette B. Feldmann   P
Shelley Society of New York, 77-07 138 St, #2F, Flushing,
NY 11367, 718-969-7010
 Pubs: *The Carousel* (Diamond Hitch Pr, 1992), *The
 Scarab Beetle Speaks* (Iota Pr, 1993), *New Rev,
 Hellas, Mew Pr, Poetry Digest*

Daniel Fernandez   P
119 Payson Ave #3E
New York, NY 10034
 Pubs: *Apples from Hesperides* (Pegasus Pubs, 1971),
 *Intl Poetry Rev, The Lyric, Plains Poetry Jrnl, Christian
 Century, New Laurel Rev*

Jean Fiedler   W
69-23 Bell Blvd
Bayside, NY 11364-2532
 Pubs: *When a Sparrow Falls, Sisters in Crime: Anth*
 (Berkley, 1992, 1991), *The Year the World Was Out of
 Step with Jancy Fried* (HBJ, 1981)

Edward Field 🎤 ✈   P
463 West St, #A-323
New York, NY 10014
Internet: fieldinski@yahoo.com
 Pubs: *A Frieze for a Temple of Love, Counting Myself
 Lucky, Selected Poems 1963-1992* (Black Sparrow Pr,
 1998, 1992), *APR, Exquisite Corpse*

Jennie Fields 🎤 ✈   W
452 8th St
Brooklyn, NY 11215-3616, 718-965-9335
 Pubs: *Crossing Brooklyn Ferry* (Avon, 1998), *Lily Beach*
 (Warner, 1994)

Elliot Figman 🎤 ✈   P
484 13 St, 2nd Fl
Brooklyn, NY 11215
 Pubs: *TriQtly, The American Voice, Poetry, Ironwood,
 Choice, Pequod, Lips, Confrontation*

Jose-Angel Figueroa   P
258 Nassau Ave
Brooklyn, NY 11222, 718-383-5564
 Pubs: *Hypocrisy Held Hostage* (Noo Jork Pub, 1987),
 La Patria (Arts Partners, 1984), *Nuestro*

Marlene Rosen Fine 🎤 ✈   P
490 W End Ave, #7E
New York, NY 10024-4331, 212-874-6671
 Pubs: *Clouds Fire the Smell of Wood* (Author, 1981),
 Ordinary Women: Anth (Common Differences Pr, 1985),
 Green Mountains Rev, Helen Rev, Atlantic, Connections
I.D.: Jewish

Miriam Finkelstein   W
680 W End Ave
New York, NY 10025
 Pubs: *Domestic Affairs* (H M, 1982), *Ascent, Arizona
 Qtly, Commonweal, Hanging Loose, Kalliope, Atlanta
 Rev, Kayak, Letters*

Cheryl Fish   P&W
40 Harrison St #23D
New York, NY 10013-2726
 Pubs: *My City Flies By* (e.g. Pr, 1986),
 African-American Travel Writing: Anth (Beacon Pr,
 1998), *Ladies, Start Your Engines: Anth* (Faber &
 Faber, 1998), *NAW, Long News, Response, Poetry NY,
 Talisman, Santa Monica Rev, Between C&D, B City*

Sally Fisher 🎤 ✈   P
98 Riverside Dr, #16C
New York, NY 10024
Internet: sallyxfish@aol.com
 Pubs: *Field, Chelsea, Poetry East, New Directions, Tar
 River Poetry, The Sun*

Robert Fitterman   P
1 Washington Sq, Village #16-0
New York, NY 10012, 212-533-8030
 Pubs: *Metropolis 1-15, Gertrude Stein Awards: Anth*
 (Sun & Moon Pr, 2000, 1996), *Metropolis 16-20* (Edge
 Bks, 1998), *Ameresque* (Buck Downs Bks, 1996),
 Leases (Periphery Pr, 1989)

Jack Flam   W
Georges Borchardt Inc., 136 E 57 St, New York, NY
10022, 212-753-5785
    Pubs: *Bread & Butter* (Viking, 1977), *Zoltan Gorency*
(Hodder & Stoughton, 1974)

Bernice Fleisher 🎤   P
350 1st Ave, #4C
New York, NY 10010
    Pubs: *Poet Dreaming in Artist's House: Anth* (Milkweed
Edtns, 1988), *East West: A Poetry Annual, Nostalgia,
Leading Edge, Nimrod, Jam Today, Love Lyrics, Voices
for Peace*

Eugene C. Flinn   W
Stewart H Benedict Literary Agency, 27 Washington Sq N,
New York, NY 10011-9165, 212-228-1440
    Pubs: *Strictly Fiction II: Anth* (Potpourri Pubs, 1995),
Best of Spitball: Anth (Pocket Bks, 1988), *Thalia, Lynx
Eye, Eclectic Literary Forum, Monocacy Valley Rev,
Thin Ice, Small Pond Mag*

George Flynn   P
303 W 66 St, Apt 8CE
New York, NY 10023, 212-496-7658
    Pubs: *Zingers* (Letter Pr, 1978), *Kansas Qtly, Wisconsin
Rev, Folio, Florida Qtly*

Helen Fogarassy   W
58 W 36 St, #2A
New York, NY 10018, 212-947-6913
    Pubs: *Mix Bender* (Quality Pubs, 1987), *Queen's Qtly,
Our Town, Greenfeather, Gypsy, Sidewinder, Mildred,
Home Planet News, Innisfree, Echoes, Nostalgia*

Dorothy Swartz Foley   P
81-48 169 St
Jamaica, NY 11432, 718-380-4134
    Pubs: *Bitterroot, Orphic Lute, Artist's Mag, Saturday
Evening Post*

Montserrat Fontes   W
W W Norton, 500 5th Ave, New York, NY 10110,
800-223-2584
    Pubs: *Dreams of the Centaur, First Confession* (Norton,
1996, 1991), *High Contrast* (Naiad Pr, 1987), *Westways*

Charles Henri Ford   P
1 W 72 St, #103
New York, NY 10023
    Pubs: *Water from a Bucket, I Will Be What I Am* (U
Southern Illinois Pr, 1993, 1992), *Out of the Labyrinth:
Selected Poems* (City Lights, 1986), *Arshile*

Richard Ford   W
c/o Amanda Urban, ICM, 40 W 57 St, New York, NY
10019, 212-556-5600
    Pubs: *Women with Men: Stories, Independence Day*
(Knopf, 1997, 1995), *New Yorker, Esquire, Harper's,
Granta*

Vic Fortezza   W
2546 E 13th St, #B-12
Brooklyn, NY 11235
    Pubs: *HELLP!, Neologisms, L'Ouverture, Forbidden
Lines, Blue Lady*

Elizabeth Fox 🎤 ✈   P&W
61 Eastern Pkwy #3-C
Brooklyn, NY 11238, 718-789-3640
    Pubs: *Limousine Kids on the Ground* (Rocky Ledge
Cottage Edtns, 1983), *Asylum Annual 1994: Anth*
(Asylum Arts Pub, 1994), *The World, Transfer, Bombay
Gin, Sugar Mule*

Geoffrey Edmund Fox 🎤 ✈   W
14 E 4 St, #812
New York, NY 10012, 212-505-2615
Internet: gefox@post.harvard.edu
    Pubs: *Welcome to My Contri* (Lintel, 1988), *Yellow Silk
Erotic Arts & Letters: Anth* (Harmony Bks, 1990),
Threepenny Rev, Fiction Intl, Yellow Silk, Central Park
Lang: Spanish

Paula Fox   W
c/o Robert Lesher, 47 E 19 St, New York, NY 10003,
212-529-1790
    Pubs: *The Eagle Kite, Western Wind, Monkey Island,
The Village by the Sea* (Orchard Bks, 1995, 1993,
1991, 1988), *The God of Nightmares* (North Point Pr,
1990)

Patricia Weaver Francisco 🎤 ✈   W
Ellen Levine Literary Agency, 15 E 26 St, Ste 1801, New
York, NY 10010
    Pubs: *Village Without Mirrors* (Milkweed Edtns, 1989),
Cold Feet (S&S, 1988)
Groups: Women, Abuse Victims

Jeffrey Frank   W
235 W 71 St, #62
New York, NY 10023-3737
    Pubs: *The Creep* (FSG, 1969)

Don Frankel 🎤 ✈   W
3411 Wayne Ave, Apt 5E
Bronx, NY 10467, 718-405-9683
Internet: dfabmd@aol.com
    Pubs: *The Newscribes, Fan Mag, Steppingstones Pr*

J. E. Franklin P
PO Box 517
New York, NY 10031-0517, 212-926-5974
   Pubs: *Black Girl from Genesis–Revelations* (Howard U, 1977), *Voices of Color: Anth* (Applause Bks, 1992), *Black Short Story Anth* (NAL, 1972), *Black Scholar*

Jonathan Franzen W
c/o Susan Golomb, 35 E 9 St, #90, New York, NY 10003, 212-505-7330
   Pubs: *Strong Motion, The Twenty-Seventh City* (FSG, 1992, 1988), *Fiction Intl, Grand Street, Icarus*

Lynn Freed ♀ ✈ W
The Writers Shop, 101 5th Ave, 11th Fl, New York, NY 10003, 212-255-6515
   Pubs: *Friends of the Family, The Bungalow, Home Ground* (Story Line Pr, 2000, 1999, 1998) *The Mirror* (Ballantine, 1999), *New Yorker, Atlantic, SW Rev, Harper's, Threepenny Rev*

Mathias B. Freese ♀ ✈ W
9050 Union Turnpike, #1M
Glendale, NY 11385, 718-805-2420
   Pubs: *i* (Freese Pub, 1997), *Confessions of Two Twigs* (Brett Jordan Pub, 1996), *Pilgrimage, Skywriters, Voices, Global Stamp News*
I.D.: Jewish. Groups: Jewish, Teenagers

Joan French P
427 E 73 St
New York, NY 10021, 212-840-1234
   Pubs: *Voices Intl, Green's Mag, Intrepid, Modularist Rev, Lake Superior Rev*

Mike Frenkel P
71-57 162 St
Fresh Meadows, NY 11365, 718-380-7599
   Pubs: *Beyond Lament: Poets of the World Bearing Witness on the Holocaust* (Northwestern U Pr, 1998), *Blood to Remember: American Poets on the Holocaust* (Texas Tech U Pr, 1991), *Bone & Flesh, Fan Mag, New Press Lit Qtly*

Philip Fried ♀ ✈ P
440 Riverside Dr, #38
New York, NY 10027
Internet: phfried@aol.com
   Pubs: *Quantum Genesis* (Zohar Pr, 1997), *Mutual Trespasses* (Ion, 1988), *Acquainted with the Night: Anth* (Rizzoli, 1997), *Partisan, Paris Rev, Massachusetts Rev, BPJ, Maryland Poetry Rev, Cream City Rev, Chelsea, Tin House*

Dorothy Friedman P
582 E 2 St
Brooklyn, NY 11218, 718-633-1503
   Pubs: *Family Album, The Liberty Years* (Rio Edtns, 1989, 1987), *Partisan Rev, California Qtly, Kayak, Ms.*

Nancy Bengis Friedman ♀ ✈ P
551 4th St #2
Brooklyn, NY 11215, 718-499-8383
   Pubs: *Fine China: Anth* (Springhouse Edtns, 1993), *The Tie that Binds: Anth* (Papier-Mache Pr, 1992), *Natl Poetry Mag of the Lower East Side, Lips, New Pr, Eleven*

Norman Friedman ♀ ✈ P
33-54 164 St
Flushing, NY 11358-1442, 718-353-3631
   Pubs: *The Magic Badge: Poems 1953-1984* (Slough Pr, 1984), *Intl Poetry Rev, Centennial Rev, BPJ, New Mexico Qtly, New Voices, Georgia Rev, Nation, Texas Qtly*

Sanford Friedman W
37 W 12 St, #10F
New York, NY 10011
   Pubs: *Rip Van Winkle* (Atheneum, 1980), *Still Life, A Haunted Woman, Totempole* (Dutton, 1975, 1968, 1965)

Celestine Frost P
PO Box 6877, Yorkville Sta
New York, NY 10128, 212-722-0446
   Pubs: *I Gathered My Ear from the Green Field* (Logo-Daedalus, 1996), *An Imagined Experience Over the Entrance* (Dusty Dog, 1993), *Camellia, Epoch*

Abby Frucht ♀ ✈ W
Gelfman Schneider Literary Agents, Inc, 250 W 57 St, New York, NY 10107, 212-245-1993
   Pubs: *Polly's Ghost, Life Before Death* (Scribner, 2000, 1997), *Are You Mine?* (Grove Pr, 1993), *Licorice* (Graywolf, 1990), *Fruit of the Month* (U Iowa Pr, 1987)

Lewis Burke Frumkes W
c/o The Writing Center, Marymount Manhattan College, 221 E 71 St, New York, NY 10021, 212-734-3073
   Pubs: *The Logophile's Orgy* (Delacorte, 1995), *Metapunctuation* (Dell, 1993), *How to Raise Your IQ By Eating Gifted Children* (McGraw-Hill, 1983), *Harper's, Punch, Reader's Digest*

Peter Fusco P
58 Stratford Rd
Brooklyn, NY 11218-2704
   Pubs: *Electric Messiah Anth* (Iota Pr, 1993), *Kiosk, Brooklyn Rev, Home Planet News, Light, Through the Cracks*

Daniel Gabriel ♀ P
211 Sixth Ave, #3A
Brooklyn, NY 11215-1220, 718-857-5669
   Pubs: *Columbus* (Spuyten Duyvil, 1996), *Sacco & Vanzetti* (Gull Bks, 1983), *Poetry NY, Home Planet News, APR, City, Gnosis*

Roger Gaess P
47 Jane St, #16
New York, NY 10014, 212-691-8352
    Pubs: *Leaving the Bough* (International, 1982)

Jonathan Galassi P
FSG, 19 Union Sq W, New York, NY 10003,
212-741-6900
    Pubs: *Morning Run* (Paris Rev Edtns, 1988)

Tess Gallagher P&W
c/o Amanda Urban, ICM, 40 W 57 St, New York, NY
10019, 212-556-5600
    Pubs: *At the Owl Woman Saloon* (Scribner, 1997),
    Portable Kisses, My Black Horse (Bloodaxe Pr, 1996,
    1995), *Portable Kisses Expanded* (Capra Pr, 1994),
    *Zyzzyva, Glimmer Train, Sycamore Rev, Ploughshares,
    Indiana Rev, Atlantic, APR, Michigan Qtly Rev*

James Gallant 🎤 ✈ W
c/o Noah Lukeman, Lukeman Literary Management, 249
W 34 St, New York, NY 10001
Internet: Noah@Lukeman.com
    Pubs: *Press, Exquisite Corpse, Raritan, Rhino, Georgia
    Rev, Epoch, Kansas Qtly, Mississippi Rev, NAR,
    Massachusetts Rev, Story Qtly*

Mavis Gallant W
Georges Borchardt Inc., 136 E 57 St, New York, NY
10022, 212-753-5785

Kenneth Gangemi 🎤 ✈ P&W
211 E 5 St
New York, NY 10003, 212-777-4795
    Pubs: *The Volcanoes from Puebla, Olt, The Interceptor
    Pilot* (Marion Boyars, 1989, 1984, 1982)

Suzanne Gardinier P&W
110 W 96 St, #8C
New York, NY 10025-6474
    Pubs: *A World That Will Hold All the People* (U
    Michigan Pr, 1996), *The New World* (U Pitt Pr, 1993),
    USAHN: Ten Poems & a Story (Grand Street Bks,
    1990), *Best American Poetry: Anth* (Scribner, 1990)

Nancy Bruff Gardner P&W
200 E 66 St, #D803
New York, NY 10021, 212-752-8774
    Pubs: *The Mist Maiden* (Dell, 1975), *My Talon in Your
    Heart* (Dutton, 1946)

Johanna Garfield W
200 E 94 St, #1517
New York, NY 10128, 212-996-2568
    Pubs: *Cousins* (Donald I. Fine, 1990), *The Life of a
    Real Girl* (St. Martin's Pr, 1986), *Ms., Reader's Digest,
    McCall's, Art & Antiques, Paris Rev, American Art*

Peggy Garrison 🎤 ✈ P&W
74 E 7 St
New York, NY 10003-8417, 212-533-1996
    Pubs: *Ding the Bell* (Poetry NY, 1999), *Charing Cross
    Bridge* (P&Q Pr, 1998), *Beloit Fiction, South Dakota
    Rev, Poetry Now, The Smith, Ball State U Forum,
    Images, Literary Rev, Slant, Global City Rev, Mudfish*
Lang: French

Ellen Gruber Garvey 🎤 ✈ P&W
202 St Marks Ave, #3
Brooklyn, NY 11238
Internet: egarvey@nscu.edu
    Pubs: *Tales of Magic Realism By Women: Anth,
    Speaking for Ourselves: Anth* (Crossing Pr, 1990,
    1990), *If I Had a Hammer: Anth* (Papier-Mache, 1990),
    The Tribe of Dina: Anth (Beacon Pr, 1989), *Minnesota
    Rev, Feminist Studies, Paragraph, Bridges*
I.D.: G/L/B/T. Groups: G/L/B/T, Seniors

Serge Gavronsky P
525 W End Ave, #12H
New York, NY 10024, 212-787-7068
    Pubs: *Talisman, Lingo, Bitter Oleander, Action Poetique,
    Interstice, Raddle Moon, Pequod, Nioques*

Joan Austin Geier P
39-91 48 St
Sunnyside Garden, NY 11104-1021, 718-899-5919
    Pubs: *A Formal Feeling Comes* (Story Line Pr, 1994),
    Mother of Tribes (Four Circles Pr, 1987), *The Lyric,
    Potomac Rev, New Rev, U Portland Rev, Northern
    Spirit, Amelia, Negative Capability, Visions, Poets On*

Barrie Gellis P
43-06 159 St, #D-2
Flushing, NY 11358, 718-961-3521
    Pubs: *We Speak for Peace: Anth* (KIT Inc, 1993),
    *Forum, Pandemonium, Athena, Long Shot, Yellow Silk,
    Inside-Outside, Poets on Photography, Genesis*

Sally George W
715 Carroll St
Brooklyn, NY 11215
    Pubs: *Frog Salad* (Scribner, 1981), *Ms., Redbook, NAR,
    Conditions, Heresies, Massachusetts Rev*

Corinne Gerson W
101 W 12 St, #2N
New York, NY 10011
    Pubs: *Cyberdog* (Royal Fireworks Pr, 1998),
    Rendez-Vous Au Zoo (Rageout-Editeur, 1992), *My
    Grandfather the Spy* (Walker, 1990)

Peter Gethers W
Villard Books, 201 E 50 St, New York, NY 10022
    Pubs: *The Cat Who Went to Paris* (Crown, 1991),
    Getting Blue, Rotisserie League Baseball (Dell, 1989,
    1989)

Andrew Gettler   P
2663 Heath Ave #6D
Bronx, NY 10463-7520, 718-884-1316
   Pubs: *A Condition, Not an Event* (New Spirit Pr, 1992),
   Footsteps of a Ghost (Iniquity Pr, 1991), *Boston Lit
   Rev, Excursus, Confrontation, Santa Clara Rev*

P. J. Gibson   PP
400 W 43 St, #14L
New York, NY 10036

Dagoberto Gilb ♦ ✈   W
c/o Grove Press, 841 Broadway, New York, NY 10003
   Pubs: *The Woodcuts of Women, The Last Known
   Residence of Mickey Acuna, The Magic of Blood*
   (Grove Pr, 2001, 1994, 1993), *Threepenny Rev, New
   Yorker, DoubleTake, Ploughshares, Texas Observer*

Ilsa Gilbert ♦ ✈   P
203 Bleecker St, #9
New York, NY 10012-1456, 212-254-5289
   Pubs: *The Poet of Bleecker Street II* (Downtown Music
   Prod, 1994), *Survivors & Other New York Poems* (Bard
   Pr, 1991), *And Then, Poet Lore, Quartet, Waterways,
   Landscapes, St. Clements Qtly, Voices, New Press*
I.D.: Women. Groups: Seniors, Teenagers

Frank D. Gilroy   W
Gilbert Parker-William Morris Agency, 1325 Ave of the
Americas, New York, NY 10019, 213-586-5100
   Pubs: *I Wake Up Screening* (Southern Illinois U Pr,
   1973), *Private* (HB, 1970)

Estelle Gilson   W
7 Sigma Pl
Bronx, NY 10471, 718-549-3979
   Pubs: *Present Tense, Midstream, Moment, Columbia,
   Salome, New Renaissance, Quarto, Other Voices, Wind,
   Congress Monthly*

Saul B. Gilson   P
7 Sigma Pl
Bronx, NY 10421, 718-601-3105
   Pubs: *Basilisic* (Cross Cultural Lit Edtns, 1996), *New
   Renaissance, Annals of Internal Medicine*

John Giorno ♦ ✈   PP&P
222 Bowery
New York, NY 10012-4216, 212-925-6372
Internet: giornopoetry@attglobal.net
   Pubs: *You Got to Burn to Shine* (High Risk, 1994),
   Grasping at Emptiness, Balling Buddha (Kulchur Fdn,
   1985, 1970), *Shit, Piss, Blood, Pus & Brains* (Painted
   Bride, 1978)

Daniela Gioseffi ♦ ✈   PP&P&W
57 Montague St #8G
Brooklyn, NY 11201, 718-624-2165
Internet: daniela@garden.net
   Pubs: *Going On: Poems, Word Wounds & Water
   Flowers* (Via/Purdue U, 2000, 1996), *In Bed with the
   Exotic Enemy: stories & novella* (Avisson, 1997), *Paris
   Rev, Nation, American Book Rev, Ms., Hungry Mind
   Rev, Prairie Schooner, Poetry East*

Nikki Giovanni   P
William Morrow & Co., 105 Madison Ave, New York, NY
10016

Todd Gitlin ♦ ✈   P
New York Univ, Dept of Culture & Communication, 239
Greene St, Rm 735, New York, NY 10003
   Pubs: *Sacrifice* (Metropolitan/Holt, 1999), *The Murder of
   Albert Einstein* (Bantam, 1994), *Nation, Civilization,
   Dissent*

Julia Glass   W
137 W 12 St
New York, NY 10011
   Pubs: *Amer Short Fiction, Bellingham Rev, Chicago
   Tribune*

Eleanor Glaze   W
Ellen Levine Literary Agency, 15 E 26 St, Ste 1801, New
York, NY 10010, 212-889-0620
   Pubs: *Jaiyavara* (Peachtree, 1988), *Homeworks* (U
   Tennessee Pr, 1986), *Atlantic, New Yorker, Redbook,
   The Sun*

Judith Gleason   W
26 E 91 St #6B
New York, NY 10128, 212-534-2019
   Pubs: *Oya: In Praise of the Goddess* (Shambhala,
   1987), *Leaf & Bone* (Viking, 1980)

Karen Glenn ♦ ✈   W
301 E 66 St, #15H
New York, NY 10021, 212-249-7198
Internet: prahu@aol.com
   Pubs: *Some Kind of Hero* (Viking, 1997), *Poetry NW,
   NYQ, Cream City Rev, Water-stone, Chattahoochie Rev,
   National Forum, Tar River Poetry, Portland Rev,
   Southern Humanities Rev, Scholastic Scope, Denver
   Qtly, Dekalb Literary Arts Jrnl*
Groups: Children

Adele Glimm ♦ ✈   W
120 E 81 St #16E
New York, NY 10028-1423
   Pubs: *Epoch, Redbook, Cosmopolitan, McCall's,
   Southern Humanities Rev, Good Housekeeping, Ellery
   Queen's Mystery Mag*

Tony Gloeggler 🎤 ✈   P
83-45 116 St, #2B
Richmond Hill, NY 11418, 718-441-8195
    Pubs: *One on One* (Pearl Edtns, 1999), *Full Court: A
    Literary Anth of Basketball* (Breakaway Bks, 1996),
    *Puerto Del Sol, Mangrove, West Branch, Rattle, The
    Ledge, Graffiti Rag, NYQ, Chiron Rev, Rhino, Black
    Bear Rev, Mudfish, Yellow Silk*

Tereze Gluck   W
333 E 69 St #4J
New York, NY 10021, 212-535-5417
    Pubs: *Chelsea, Antioch Rev, Malahat Rev, Ascent,
    Epoch, Fiction, Alaska Qtly, Threepenny Rev, Story,
    Columbia*

John Godfrey   P
437 E 12 St, #32
New York, NY 10009, 212-475-6532
    Pubs: *Dabble: Poems 1966-1980* (Full Court Pr, 1982),
    From the Other Side of the Century: Anth (Sun &
    Moon Pr, 1994), *Lingo, Poetry NY, World, o.blek*

Ulf Goebel   P&W
25 W 87 St, #5F
New York, NY 10024, 212-724-3722
    Pubs: *After Caligula* (Ulf Goebel, 1981), *Webster Rev,
    Cumberland Poetry Rev, Agni, Aspect*

Ivan Gold   W
Mary Yost Assoc, 59 E 54 St, New York, NY 10022,
212-980-4988
    Pubs: *Sams in a Dry Season, Nickel Miseries, Sick
    Friends* (Washington Square Pr, 1992, 1992, 1992)

Gerald Jay Goldberg   W
Georges Borchardt Inc., 136 E 57 St, New York, NY
10022, 212-753-5785
    Pubs: *Heart Payments* (Viking, 1982), *The Lynching of
    Orin Newfield* (Dial, 1970)

Isaac Goldemberg   P&W
4555 Henry Hudson Pkwy, #703
Bronx, NY 10471-3844
    Pubs: *La Vida al Contado* (Ediciones Del Norte, 1992),
    Play By Play (Persea Bks, 1985)

Mike Golden   P&W
Black Market Press, 400 W 43 St, Ste 37K, New York,
NY 10036
    Pubs: *The Buddhist 3rd Class Junk Mail Oracle* (Seven
    Stories Pr, 1999), *Crimes of the Beats, Unbearables:
    Anth* (Autonomedia, 1998, 1995), *Vibe, Creative
    Screenwriting, Curio, Pink Pages, Paris Rev, Beet,
    Exquisite Corpse, Code*

Lloyd Goldman   P
448 2nd St
Brooklyn, NY 11215-2503

Michael Goldman   P
425 Riverside Dr
New York, NY 10025

William Goldman   W
c/o Urban del Rey, Ballantine Books, 201 E 50 St, New
York, NY 10022
    Pubs: *Control, Tinsel* (Delacorte, 1982, 1979), *The
    Princess Bride* (Ballantine, 1977)

Barbara Goldsmith   W
c/o Lynn Nesbit, Janklow & Nesbit Assoc, 1021 Park Ave,
New York, NY 10028, 212-534-3637
    Pubs: *The Straw Man* (FSG, 1975), *Vanity Fair, New
    Yorker*

Howard Goldsmith   W
41-07 Bowne St, #6B
Flushing, NY 11355-5629, 718-886-5819
    Pubs: *Science Through Stories* (McGraw-Hill, 1999),
    *The Twiddle Twins' Amusement Park Mystery, The
    Twiddle Twins' Single Footprint Mystery* (Mondo Pub,
    1998, 1998), *Scholastic Storyworks, Short Story Intl,
    London Mystery, Disney Adventures*

Jeanette Erlbaum Goldsmith 🎤 ✈   W
1483 E 34 St
Brooklyn, NY 11234, 718-253-3484
    Pubs: *Confrontation* (Long Island U, 1987), *Each in Her
    Own Way* (Queen of Swords Pr, 1994), *Whetstone,
    Hawaii Rev, Antioch Rev, Commentary, Malahat Rev,
    Mid-American Rev*

Jewelle Gomez   P&W
Michele Karlsberg Publicity, 47 Dongan Hills Ave, Staten
Island, NY 10306, 718-980-4262
    Pubs: *Don't Explain, Oral Tradition, The Gilda Stories*
    (Firebrand Bks, 1998, 1996, 1991), *Essence, Ms., Black
    Scholar, Advocate, Qtly Black Rev, Zyzzyva, Curve*

Guy LeCharles Gonzalez 🎤 ✈   PP&P
c/o 13 Bar Lounge, 35 E 13 St
New York, NY 10003, 201-662-5560
Internet: www.geocities.com/loudpoet
    Pubs: *Burning Down the House* (w/R. Bonair-Agard, et
    al: Soft Skull, 2000), *di-verse-city 2000: Anth* (AIPF,
    2000), *Will Work for Peace: Anth* (zeropanik pr, 1999),
    Austin Intl Poetry Festival (2000, 1999), *National Poetry
    Slam* (1999, 1998), *SoUPFest* (1999)
    I.D.: Multicultural

Brad Gooch   P
Joy Harris Literary Agency, 156 Fith Ave, Ste 617, New
York, NY 10010, 212-924-6269
    Pubs: *Scary Kisses* (Putnam, 1988), *Jailbait & Other
    Stories* (Sea Horse Pr, 1984), *Paris Rev, Partisan Rev,
    Bomb, Between C&D, Shiny, Christopher Street*

Melinda Goodman   P
45 E 1 St, #4
New York, NY 10003
    Pubs: *Middle Sister* (MSG Pr, 1988), *My Lover Is a
    Woman: Anth* (Ballantine Bks, 1996), *The Arch of Love:
    Lesbian Love Poems: Anth* (Scribner, 1996), *Sinister
    Wisdom, Conditions, Heresies*

Coco Gordon 🎤 ✈   P
138 Duane St, #5SW
New York, NY 10013-3854, 212-285-1609
Internet: cocogord@mindspring.com
    Pubs: *Knee* (Ginocchio) (Porto Dei Santi Pr, 2000),
    Tikysk: Permaculture Getting to Know You (Foot Square
    Space, 1997), *Superskywoman* (Leonardi V-Idea, 1995),
    Oreste 2: Anth (Venice Biennale, 2000), *Pig Iron, New
    Observations, Aquaterra, Eternal Network*
Lang: Italian. I.D.: Holocaust. Groups: Nature/Environment

Mary Gordon   W
Sterling Lord Literistic, 65 Bleecker St, New York, NY
10012, 212-780-6050
    Pubs: *Spending* (Scribner, 1998), *Men & Angels, The
    Company of Women, Final Payments* (Random Hse,
    1985, 1981, 1978)

hattie gossett   P&W
775 Riverside Dr, #6J
New York, NY 10032
    Pubs: *presenting ... sister noblues* (Firebrand Bks,
    1988), *Seeing Jazz: Anth* (Smithsonian/Chronicle Bks,
    1998), *Conditions, Heresies, Sinister Wisdom, Essence,
    Womanews, Between Ourselves, Playbill*

Amy Gottlieb   W
2465 Palisade Ave
Riverdale, NY 10463
    Pubs: *Midstream, Other Voices, Puerto del Sol*

Lois Gould 🎤 ✈   W
Charlotte Sheedy Literary Agency, 65 Bleecker St, New
York, NY 10012, 212-780-9800
    Pubs: *No Brakes* (H Holt, 1997), *Medusa's Gift* (Knopf,
    1992), *Subject to Change* (FSG, 1988), *La Presidenta,
    A Sea-Change* (S&S, 1981, 1976)

Roberta Gould 🎤 ✈   P
315 E 18 St, #4R
New York, NY 10003, 212-982-6818
Internet: nobertag@ulster.net
    Pubs: *In Houses with Ladders, Not by Blood Alone*
    (Lince/Waterside NY Pr, 2000, 1990), *Three Windows*
    (Reservoir Pr, 1997), *Only Rock* (Folder Edtns, 1985),
    *Rio On Line, Bridges, Stet, Home Planet, Confrontation,
    Green Mountains Rev, Downtown*
Lang: Spanish. Groups: Prisoners

Pascale Gousseland   P
Poet Tree, 6234 138 St #6F, Kew Gardens, NY 11435,
212-472-6881
    Pubs: *Second Glance, Medicinal Purpos, Poems that
    Thump in the Dark, Nomad's Choir, Albatross, Thirteen,
    New Press*

E. J. Graff 🎤 ✈   W
c/o Louise Quayle, Ellen Levine Literary Agency, 15 E 26
St, Ste 1801, New York, NY 10010
    Pubs: *What Is Marriage For?* (Beacon Pr, 1999),
    Tasting Life Twice: Anth (Avon Morrow, 1995), *Voices
    of the X-iled: Anth* (Doubleday, 1994), *Iowa Rev,
    Kenyon Rev, Nation*
I.D.: Jewish, G/L/B/T. Groups: G/L/B/T

Ignatius Graffeo   P
82-34 138 St, #6F
Kew Gardens, NY 11435, 718-847-1482
    Pubs: *She Came with the Magazine, Xanthus* (New
    Spirit Pr, 1995, 1993), *We Speak for Peace: Anth* (Kit
    Pubs, 1994), *Poetry Digest, Maryland Poetry Rev*

James Graham   P
PO Box 605, Cooper Sq Sta
New York, NY 10276
    Pubs: *Search Engine: Difficult Path, One Skin*
    (Machete, 1998, 1994), *Small Hours of the Night*
    (Curbstone Pr, 1996), *Found Body* (Soncino Bks, 1993),
    *Hungry Mind Rev, Rev: Latin America, Nexus, Cover,
    Machete, The Sun, Nexus, Harper's*

Shirley Ann Grau 🎤 ✈   W
JCA, 27 W 20 St, New York, NY 10011, 212-807-0888
    Pubs: *The Black Prince, The Roadwalkers, Keepers of
    the House* (Knopf, 1996, 1994, 1965)

Elizabeth Graver   W
Richard Parks Literary Agency, 138 E 16 St, New York,
NY 10003, 212-228-1786
    Pubs: *Unravelling* (Hyperion, 1997), *Have You Seen
    Me?* (Ecco Pr, 1993), *O. Henry Prize Stories: Anths*
    (Anchor, 1996, 1994), *Best American Essays, Best
    American Short Stories, Tikkun, Boulevard, Story*

Dorothy Randall Gray   P&W
328 Flatbush Ave, Ste 148
Brooklyn, NY 11238, 718-638-6415
    Pubs: *Soul Between the Lines* (Avon Bks, 1998),
    *Woman, A Taste of Tamarindo, The Passion Collective,
    Muse Blues* (Polaris Pr, 1996, 1994, 1991, 1990),
    Frontiers, Binnewater Tides

Francine du Plessix Gray   W
Georges Borchardt Inc., 136 E 57 St, New York, NY
10022, 212-753-5785
    Pubs: *Adam & Eve & the City, October Blood* (S&S,
    1987, 1985), *New Yorker, Yale Rev, Harper's*

Mayo L. Gray W
15 W 72 St #8T
New York, NY 10023
 Pubs: *The Savage Season* (Fawcett, 1978), *Washington Times, The Poet Anth, Scimitar & Song*

Richard Grayson W
Linda Konner Literary Agency, 10 W 15 St, Ste 1918,
New York, NY 10011-6829
 Pubs: *I Survived Caracas Traffic* (Avisson Pr, 1996), *I Brake for Delmore Schwartz* (Zephyr, 1983)

Stephen Greco P
134 Henry St
Brooklyn, NY 11201, 718-855-8759
 Pubs: *Penguin Book of Gay Short Stories: Anth* (Viking Penguin, 1994), *Flesh & the Word: Anth* (Dutton, 1992), *Interview, 7 Days*

Hannah Green W
52 Barrow St
New York, NY 10014, 212-243-3070

Jessica Greenbaum 🎤 ✈ P
404 Vanderbilt Ave
Brooklyn, NY 11238-1505, 718-398-4242
 Pubs: *Inventing Difficulty* (Silverfish Rev Pr, 2000)
I.D.: Brooklyn

Harry Greenberg P
321 W 94 St, #6-NE
New York, NY 10025, 212-866-3242
 Pubs: *Handbook of Poetic Forms: Anth, The Point: Anth* (Teachers & Writers, 1987, 1983), *Agni*

Joanne Greenberg W
Wallace Literary Agency, 177 E 70 St, New York, NY
10021, 212-570-9090
 Pubs: *Where the Road Goes, No Reck'ning Made, In This Sign* (H Holt, 1998, 1993, 1970), *Literature: Anth* (Prentice Hall, 1998), *High Fantastic: Anth* (Ocean View Bks, 1995), *Hadassah, Hudson Rev, Redbook, Denver Qtly*

Henry L. Greene P
58-27 212 St
Bayside, NY 11364
 Pubs: *Modern Images, A Different Drummer, Spoon River Qtly*

Ted Greenwald P
206 E 17 St, #4-D
New York, NY 10003
 Pubs: *Word of Mouth* (Sun & Moon Pr, 1986), *Exit the Face* (w/R. Bosman; MOMA, 1982)

Arthur Gregor P
250 W 94 St, #6J
New York, NY 10025, 212-666-5031
 Pubs: *The River Serpent, Secret Citizen* (Sheep Meadow Pr, 1995, 1989), *Boulevard, Ploughshares, Nation, Hudson Rev*

Kathleen C. Griffin 🎤 ✈ P
6425 Broadway
Riverdale, NY 10471, 718-549-8405
Internet: kathleengriffin@gobi.com
 Pubs: *Newsletter, Waterways, Home Planet News*

Tom Grimes 🎤 ✈ W
Henry Dunow Literary Agency, 22 W 23 St, 5th Fl, New
York, NY 10010
Internet: tg02@swt.edu
 Pubs: *A Stone of the Heart* (Southern Methodist U Pr, 1997), *City of God* (Picador, 1996), *Season's End* (Bison Bks, 1996)

Gwendolen Gross P&W
Elaine Koster Literary Agency, 55 Central Pk W Ste 6,
New York, NY 10023
 Pubs: *Amelia, Cold Mountain Rev, Fresh Ground, Global City Rev, Hubbub, Laurel Rev, MacGuffin, Madison Rev, Prism Intl, Red Cedar Rev, Salt Hill Jrnl, Santa Barbara Rev, Seattle Rev, Southern Humanities Rev, Wind Mag*

Brian J. Groth P
139-40 Caney Ln
Jamaica, NY 11422
 Pubs: *San Fernando Jrnl, Weirdbook, Wide Open, Journal of Regional Criticism, Calliope's Corner*

Doris Grumbach W
c/o Timothy Seldes, Russell & Volkening, Inc, 50 W 29
St, New York, NY 10001, 212-684-6050
 Pubs: *The Pleasure of Their Company, The Presence of Absence, Life in a Day, Fifty Days of Solitude* (Beacon, 2000, 1998, 1996, 1994), *Extra Innings, Coming into the End Zone* (Norton, 1993, 1991)

Barbara Guest P
49 W 16 St
New York, NY 10011
 Pubs: *Defensive Rapture, Fair Realism* (Sun & Moon Pr, 1993, 1989), *Conjunctions, Sulfur, NAW*

Amy Guggenheim 🎤 ✈ PP
Pratt Institute, 200 Willoughby Ave, Brooklyn, NY 11215,
718-963-1977
Internet: agenheim@cs.com
 Pubs: *Havana Intl Theater Festival, HERE, Pratt Institute, Home Theatre for Contemporary Art & Performance, La Mama, Casa Del Lago, Cleveland Performance Open, Performance Mix/DIA Art Fdn, American Letters & Commentary*

Joanna Gunderson 🎙 ✈   P
1148 5th Ave, #12B
New York, NY 10128, 212-348-4388
Internet: reddustjg@aol.com
  Pubs: *Kaleidoscape 1969* (Spuyten Duyvil, 2000), *The
  Field, Sights* (Red Dust, 1999, 1963), *Midland Rev,
  Rampike, How(ever), Frank, Northeast Jrnl*

Allan Gurganus   W
c/o Amanda Urban, ICM, 40 W 57 St, New York, NY
10019, 212-556-5600
  Pubs: *The Practical Heart, Plays Well with Others,
  White People, Oldest Living Confederate Widow Tells
  All* (Knopf, 2000, 1997, 1992, 1989), *New Yorker,
  Antaeus, Harper's, Granta, Atlantic, Yale Rev, Paris
  Rev*

C. W. Gusewelle   W
Harvey Klinger, Inc, 301 W 53 St, New York, NY 10019
  Pubs: *The Rufus Chronicle: Another Autumn* (Ballantine
  Bks, 1998), *A Paris Notebook* (Lowell Pr, 1995), *Far
  from Any Coast: Pieces of America's Heartland* (U
  Missouri Pr, 1989), *American Heritage, Antioch Rev,
  Virginia Qtly Rev, Audience, Harper's*

Rosa Guy   W
Ellen Levine Literary Agency, 15 E 26 St, Ste 1801, New
York, NY 10010, 212-889-0620
  Pubs: *The Sun, The Sea, A Touch of the Wind*
  (Dutton, 1995) *The Ups & Downs of Carl Davis III,
  Paris, Pee Wee & Big Dog* (Delacorte, 1989, 1984), *My
  Love, My Love, or the Peasant Girl* (H Holt, 1985)

Gabor G. Gyukics   P
PO Box 023061
Brooklyn, NY 11202, 718-365-3416
  Pubs: *Apache Qtly, Nexus, Northwoods Jrnl, Phati'tude,
  Medicinal Purposes, Poetry in Motion, Big Spoon, Rain
  City Rev, Corde*

Charles Hackenberry   W
M. Evans & Co, Inc, 216 E 49 St, New York, NY 10017

Marilyn Hacker 🎙 ✈   P
230 W 105 St #10A
New York, NY 10025, 212-678-1074
  Pubs: *Squares & Courtyards, Winter Numbers, Selected
  Poems* (Norton, 2000, 1994, 1994), *Going Back to the
  River* (Random Hse, 1990), *Paris Rev, TriQtly, Prairie
  Schooner, American Voice*

Pamela White Hadas   P
210 E 17 St, #3B
New York, NY 10003
  Pubs: *Beside Herself, Designing Women* (Knopf, 1983,
  1979)

Rachel Hadas 🎙 ✈   P
838 W End Ave, #3A
New York, NY 10025, 212-666-4482
  Pubs: *Merrill, Cavafy, Poems & Dreams* (Michigan,
  2000), *Halfway Down the Hall, The Empty Bed*
  (Wesleyan U Pr, 1998, 1995), *The Double Legacy*
  (Faber & Faber, 1995), *New Yorker, Threepenny Rev,
  Paris Rev, Yale Rev, New Republic*

Jessica Hagedorn   PP&W
Harold Schmidt Literary Agency, 343 W 12 St, #1B, New
York, NY 10014, 212-727-7473
  Pubs: *The Gangster of Love, Dogeaters, Charlie Chan
  Is Dead: Anth* (Penguin, 1996, 1991, 1993)

Hannelore Hahn   P
PO Box 810, Gracie Sta
New York, NY 10028, 212-737-7536
  Pubs: *Places, On the Way to Feed the Swans* (Tenth
  Hse Enterprises, 1990, 1982), *To Jump Or Not Jump:
  Anth* (Traveler's Tales Guides, 1998), *Network*

Kimiko Hahn   P
421 3rd St #1
Brooklyn, NY 11215
  Pubs: *The Unbearable Heart* (Kaya Pr, 1995), *Earshot,
  Air Pocket* (Hanging Loose, 1992, 1990), *Bomb, Manoa,
  American Voice, Ikon, River Styx, Mudfish, Tyuonyi*

Isidore Haiblum   W
160 W 77 St
New York, NY 10024
  Pubs: *Crystalworld, Specterworld* (Avon, 1992, 1991),
  Bad Neighbors (St. Martin's, 1990), *Out of Sync* (Del
  Ray, 1990)

Jana Haimsohn   PP
530 Canal St, #3-E
New York, NY 10013, 212-925-4071
  Pubs: *Collective Consciousness: Art Performances in
  the '70s Anth* (Performing Arts Journal Pubs, 1981)

Victoria Hallerman   P
65 Fort Hill Cir
Staten Island, NY 10301
  Pubs: *The Night Market, The Woman in the Magic
  Show* (Firm Ground Pr, 1998, 1995), *Poetry, Nation,
  SPR, Indiana Rev, Global City Rev, Pivot*

Nancy Hallinan 🎙 ✈   W
276 Riverside Dr, #2D
New York, NY 10025, 212-222-6936
  Pubs: *Sasakawa: Global Philanthropist* (Pergamon Pr,
  1981), *Night Swimmers, Rough Winds of May* (H&R,
  1976, 1955), *Voice from the Wings* (Knopf, 1965), *O.
  Henry Prize Stories Anth, Harper's, Cosmopolitan,
  Pulpsmith, American Vanguard, Cornhill, Touchstone*

Mary Stewart Hammond 🎤 ✈   P
1095 Park Ave, #4A
New York, NY 10128, 212-289-6264
    Pubs: *Out of Canaan* (Norton, 1991), *Atlantic, APR,
    New Yorker, New Criterion, Paris Rev, Yale Rev*

Jim Handlin   P
Brooklyn Friends School, 375 Pearl St, Brooklyn, NY
11201, 718-852-1029
    Pubs: *Editors' Choice III: Anth* (The Spirit That Moves
    Us Pr, 1992), *Bluestones & Salthay: Anth* (Rutgers
    1990), *The Haiku Anth* (S&S, 1986)

William Hanley   W
575 W End Ave
New York, NY 10024

Edward Hannibal   W
601 E 20 St, #11D
New York, NY 10010
    Pubs: *A Trace of Red* (Dial Pr, 1982), *Chocolate Days
    Popsicle Weeks* (HM, 1970)

Barbara Hantman 🎤   P
15-17 Utopia Pkwy
Whitestone, NY 11357, 718-352-2098
    Pubs: *Pegasus Rev, Sunday Suitor Poetry Rev,
    Troubadour*
Lang: Spanish. I.D.: Humanists. Groups: Jewish, Seniors

Rob Hardin   P&W
PO Box 2214, Stuyvesant Sta
New York, NY 10009, 212-477-1066
    Pubs: *Distorture* (BIB/FC2, 1997), *Forbidden Acts: Anth*
    (Avon, 1995), *Avant Pop: Anth* (Black Ice Bks, 1993),
    Michigan Rev, Sensitive Skin

Nancy Harding   W
Meredith Bernstein Literary Agency, 2112 Broadway, Ste
503A, New York, NY 10023
    Pubs: *Wind Child, The Silver Land* (Pocket Bks, 1990,
    1989)

Enid Harlow 🎤   W
175 Riverside Dr, #12L
New York, NY 10024
    Pubs: *A Better Man* (Van Neste Bks, 2000), *Love's
    Shadow* (Crossing Pr, 1993), *American Fiction 4: Anth*
    (Birchlane Pr, 1993), *Mediphors, TriQtly*

Curtis Harnack   W
205 W 57 St
New York, NY 10019, 212-757-9235
    Pubs: *We Have All Gone Away* (Iowa State U Pr,
    1987), *American Short Fiction, Confrontation, Nation*

Joseph Harris   P&W
Ann Elmo Literary Agency, 60 E 42 St, New York, NY
10165, 212-661-2880
    Pubs: *Seriously Meeting Karl Shapiro, Life on the Line*
    (Negative Capability Pr, 1993, 1992), *Georgia Rev,
    Prairie Schooner*

Stephanie Hart   W
Fashion Institute of Technology, 227 W 27 St, New York,
NY 10011, 212-760-7994
    Pubs: *Mondo James Dean: Anth* (St. Martin's, 1996), *Is
    There Any Way Out of Sixth Grade* (Coward, McCann
    & Geoghegan, 1978), *Caprice*

Steven Hartman   P
1610 Ave P, #6B
Brooklyn, NY 11229
    Pubs: *Pinched Nerves* (CCC, 1992), *Coffeehouse
    Poetry Anth* (Bottom Dog Pr, 1996)

Yukihide Maeshima Hartman   P
200 W 83 St, #2N
New York, NY 10024, 212-595-3092
    Pubs: *A Coloring Book* (Hanging Loose Pr, 1996), *New
    Poems* (Empyreal Pr, 1991), *New Directions, Hanging
    Loose, Telephone, Zymerzy, The World*

George Egon Hatvary   W
61 Jane St, #3B
New York, NY 10014
    Pubs: *The Murder of Edgar Allan Poe* (Carroll & Graf,
    1997), *The Suitor* (Avon, 1981), *Hawaii Rev, Hawaii
    Pacific Rev, Hudson Rev, U Kansas City Rev, Short
    Story Intl*

Helen Haukeness   W
100 Bank St
New York, NY 10014
    Pubs: *Novel Writing: Anth* (Writer's Digest Bks, 1992),
    Los Angeles Times, CSM, NAR

Marianne Hauser   W
Curtis Brown Ltd., 10 Astor Pl, New York, NY 10003-6935
    Pubs: *Me & My Mom, Prince Ishmael* (Sun & Moon Pr,
    1993, 1989), *Fiction Intl, Parnassus*

Michael Hawley   W
642 E 14 St, #11
New York, NY 10009-3384, 212-673-4549
    Pubs: *New Yorker, Boston Rev, Sun Dog*

Annette Hayn 🎤 ✈   P
225-23 88 Ave
Queens Village, NY 11427, 718-465-8214
    Pubs: *Enemy on the Way to School, Calendar House*
    (Poet's Pr, 1994, 1990), *Caprice, Wind, Antenna,
    Telephone, Painted Bride Qtly*

Shirley Hazzard   W
200 E 66 St, #C-1705
New York, NY 10021
    Pubs: *Countenance of Truth, The Transit of Venus*
    (Viking Penguin, 1990, 1980), *New Yorker*

Carol Hebald 🎤 ✈   P&W
463 West St, #H660
New York, NY 10014-2036
Internet: chebald@aol.com
    Pubs: *Three Blind Mice & Clara Kleinschmidt* (Unicorn,
    1989), *Whelks Walk Rev, Humanist, Antioch Rev,
    Caprice, Confrontation, PEN Intl, Massachusetts Rev,
    Intl Poetry Rev*

Ursula Hegi   W
Brandt & Brandt Literary Agents, 1501 Broadway, New
York, NY 10036
    Pubs: *Stones from the River, Floating in My Mother's
    Palm, Unearned Pleasures* (Poseidon, 1994, 1990,
    1998)

Larry Heinemann   W
Ellen Levine Literary Agency, 15 E 26 St, New York, NY
10010, 212-889-0620
    Pubs: *Cooler By the Lake, Paco's Story* (FSG, 1992,
    1986), *Harper's, Penthouse, Playboy, TriQtly, Van Nghe,
    Atlantic*

George Held 🎤 ✈   P&W
285 W 4 St
New York, NY 10014-2222, 212-989-2591
    Pubs: *Beyond Renewal* (Cedar Hill, 2000), *Open &
    Shut, Salamander Love & Others* (Talent Hse Pr, 1999,
    1998), *Winged* (Birnham Wood, 1995), *And What
    Rough Beast: Anth* (Ashland Poetry Pr, 1999),
    *Confrontation, Chariton Rev, American Writing,
    Plainsongs*

Richard Hell   P&W
437 E 12 St, #25
New York, NY 10009
    Pubs: *Artifact* (Hanuman, 1990), *Penguin Book of Rock
    & Roll Writing: Anth* (Viking, 1992), *The World, Cuz,
    Verbal Abuse, Portable Lower East Side*

Joseph Heller   W
390 W End Ave
New York, NY 10024
    Pubs: *Picture This* (Putnam, 1988), *Something
    Happened* (Dell, 1985), *Good As Gold* (PB, 1980)

Michael Heller 🎤 ✈   P&W
PO Box 1289, Stuyvesant Sta
New York, NY 10009-8953, 212-533-1928
Internet: mh7@is2.nyu.edu
    Pubs: *Wordflow* (Talisman, 1997), *In the Builded Place*
    (Coffee Hse Pr, 1989), *Paris Rev, Conjunctions, Tel
    Aviv Rev, Ohio Rev, Parnassus*

J. V. Hellew   P
318 W 100 St, #7-A
New York, NY 10025-5372
    Pubs: *NYQ, Diarist's Jrnl, The Little Mag, Hollins Critic,
    Portland Rev, Voices Intl, Avenue*

Bob Heman 🎤 ✈   P
PO Box 2165, Church St Sta
New York, NY 10008-2165
    Pubs: *Some Footnotes for the Future* (Luna Bisonte,
    1986), *15 Structures* (Incurve Pr, 1986), *Yefief, First
    Intensity, Caliban, Prose Poem, Artful Dodge,
    Ant-E-Nym, Juxta, Key Satch(el)*

David Henderson   P
PO Box 1158, Cooper Sta
New York, NY 10276, 212-978-3901
    Pubs: *The Low East* (North Atlantic Bks, 1981), *Rap &
    Hip Hop Voices* (Pantheon, 1992)

Geoffrey Hendricks   PP
486 Greenwich St
New York, NY 10013
    Pubs: *Sky Anatomy* (Rainer Verlag, 1985), *White Walls*

Donna Henes 🎤 ✈   PP&P
PO Box 380403
Brooklyn, NY 11238-0403, 718-857-2247
Internet: cityshaman@aol.com
    Pubs: *Reverence to Her, Pt I* (CD; Io Prods, 1998),
    Celestially Auspicious Occasions (Perigee, 1996),
    Dressing Our Wounds in Warm Clothes (Astro Artz,
    1982), *Isis Rising: Anth* (Isium Pr, 2000), *Free Spirit,
    New Visions, Catalyst, Changes*
I.D.: Spiritual/Religious, Nature/Environment

Eileen Hennessy 🎤 ✈   P
PO Box 1470
New York, NY 10185-1470, 212-661-7445
    Pubs: *The Best of Writers at Work: Anth* (Pecan Grove
    Pr, 1995), *The Next Parish Over: A Collection of
    Irish-American Writing* (New Rivers Pr, 1993), *Artful
    Dodge, Prairie Schooner, Cream City Rev, Nimrod,
    Confluence, Lullwater Rev, SPR, Cimarron Rev*

Barbara Henning   P
English Dept, Long Island Univ, University Plaza, Brooklyn,
NY 11201, 718-488-1050
    Pubs: *Love Makes Thinking Dark, Smoking in the
    Twilight Bar* (United Artists, 1995, 1988), *Lingo, Poet
    Intl, Paris Rev, Poetry NY, Talisman, Chain, Trois, The
    World, Fiction Intl, Lacanian Ink*

Carol Henry   P
129 E 106 St
New York, NY 10029-4614
    Pubs: *Caprice, Footwork*

Gerrit Henry   P
70 Seventh Ave, #5A
New York, NY 10011-6606
Pubs: *The Mirrored Clubs of Hell* (Little, Brown, 1991),
The Lecturer's Aria (Groundwater Pr, 1989), *Ecstatic
Occasions, Expedient Forms: Anth* (Collier Bks, 1987),
*Art News, Art in America, Arts, Poetry, Paris Rev,
Chelsea, Brooklyn Rev, NAW*

James Leo Herlihy   W
c/o Jay Garon, 415 Central Pk W, New York, NY 10025

Grace Herman   P
370 1st Ave #9C
New York, NY 10010, 212-982-7197
Pubs: *Set Against Darkness* (Natl Council of Jewish
Women, 1992), *Blood & Bone: Poems By Physicians:
Anth* (U Iowa Pr, 1998), *Anthology #19* (Bay Area
Poets Coalition, 1997), *Lilith Anth* (Jewish Women's
Research Ctr, 1994), *Poetalk, Comstock Rev*

Joanna Herman   🎤 ✈   P&W
370 Riverside Dr, #10C
New York, NY 10025, 212-866-8817
Internet: jclapps@worldnet.att.net
Pubs: *Massachusetts Rev, Kalliope, Crescent Rev,
Critic, Paterson Lit Rev, VIA, Italian Americana, Earth's
Daughters, Woman's Day*

Calvin Hernton   P&W
Marie Brown Assoc Inc, 625 Broadway, New York, NY
10012
Pubs: *The Sexual Mountain & Black Women Writers*
(Doubleday/Anchor, 1987)

Ruth Herschberger   P
463 West St
New York, NY 10014-2010, 212-645-6050
Internet: www.poets.org/poets/
Pubs: *Adam's Rib* (H&R, 1970), *Nature & Love Poems*
(Eakins Pr, 1969), *Botteghe Oscure, Kenyon Rev,
Nation, NYQ, Poetry*

Stella K. Hershan   W
2 Fifth Ave
New York, NY 10011, 212-533-9759
Pubs: *The Naked Angel* (Pinnacle Bks, 1977), *Talent,
Pirquet Mag*

Robert Hershon   🎤 ✈   P
231 Wyckoff St
Brooklyn, NY 11217-2208, 718-643-9559
Internet: print225@aol.com
Pubs: *The German Lunatic, Into a Punchline: Poems
1984-1994* (Hanging Loose Pr, 2000, 1994), *How to
Ride on the Woodlawn Express* (Sun, 1986), *The
World, Poetry NW*

Frank Hertle   P
401 E 74 St
New York, NY 10021, 212-861-7446
Pubs: *Cicada, Blue Unicorn, Gravida, Lake Superior
Rev, Voices Intl*

Carol Hill   🎤 ✈   W
2 Fifth Ave, #19-U
New York, NY 10011
Pubs: *Henry James' Midnight Song* (Poseidon Pr,
1993), *The Eleven Million Mile High Dancer* (HHolt,
1985), *Let's Fall in Love, Jeremiah 8:20* (Random Hse,
1981, 1970)
Groups: Prisoners

Donna Hill   🎤 ✈   W
530 E 23 St, #6B
New York, NY 10010-5029
Pubs: *Shipwreck Season* (Clarion Bks, 1998), *Eerie
Animals: Seven Stories* (Newfield, 1997), *More Stories
to Dream on: Anth* (HM, 1993), *Murder Uptown* (Carroll
& Graf, 1992), *First Your Penny* (Atheneum, 1985),
Alfred Hitchcock's Mystery

Kathleen Hill   W
106 Morningside Dr
New York, NY 10027, 212-662-0055
Pubs: *Scent of Water* (TriQtly Bks, 1999), *Yale Rev,
Hudson Rev, Kenyon Rev, Prairie Schooner, Arizona
Qtly*

Rebecca Hill   W
The Writers Shop, 101 5th Ave, Ste 11-F, New York, NY
10003, 212-255-6515
Pubs: *Killing Time in St. Cloud* (Delacorte, 1988),
Among Birches, Blue Rise (Morrow, 1986, 1983)

Daryl Hine   🎤 ✈   P&W
Alfred A Knopf, Inc, 201 E 50 St, New York, NY 10022,
212-751-2600
Pubs: *Ovid's Heroines* (Yale U Pr, 1991), *Postscripts*
(Knopf, 1991)

Alan Hines   W
Sterling Lord Literistic, 65 Bleecker St, New York, NY
10012
Pubs: *Square Dance* (H&R, 1984), *St. Andrews Rev,
Texas Qtly, Junction*

Douglas Hobbie   🎤 ✈   W
Donadio & Olson, Inc, 121 W 27 St, Ste 704, New York,
NY 10011, 212-691-8077
Pubs: *This Time Last Year, Being Brett, The Day,
Boomfell* (H Holt, 1998, 1996, 1993, 1991)

Rolaine Hochstein W
c/o Emilie Jacobson, Curtis Brown Ltd., 10 Astor Pl, New York, NY 10003-6935
Pubs: *Table 47* (Doubleday, 1983), *Stepping Out* (Norton, 1977), *O. Henry Prize Stories, Pushcart Prize, Atlantic, NAR, Massachusetts Rev, Antioch, Nacyvilag Jrnl of Intl Fiction*

Jill Hoffman P&W
184 Franklin St, Ground Fl
New York, NY 10013, 212-219-9278
Pubs: *Jilted* (S&S, 1993), *Mink Coat* (HRW, 1973), *New Yorker, New Republic, Mudfish, NW Rev, Now This, Helicon Nine*

William Hoffman W
Curtis Brown Ltd., 10 Astor Pl, New York, NY 10003-6935, 212-473-5400
Pubs: *Tidewater Blood* (Algonquin, 1998), *Follow Me Home, Furors Die* (LSU Pr, 1994, 1990), *O. Henry Prize Stories: Anth* (Doubleday, 1996), *Sewanee Rev, Virginia Qtly Rev, Shenandoah*

William M. Hoffman P
c/o Mitch Douglas, ICM, 40 W 57 St, New York, NY 10019, 212-556-5600
Pubs: *As Is* (Vintage/Random Hse, 1985), *Gay Plays* (Avon, 1979)

Cliff Hogan 🎤 ✈ PP
89-32 88 St
Woodhaven, NY 11421-2529, 718-849-5576
Pubs: *Waterfalls* (Muse Federation Ink Poets, 1987)
Groups: Children, Prisoners

Kam Holifield P
2086 2nd Ave, #20A
New York, NY 10029
Pubs: *Workshop Poems* (Big Apple Pub, 1989), *Haiku Anth* (Norton, 1999), *Pink Bulldozer: Anth* (Spring St Haiku Group, 1999), *Timepieces: Anth* (Cloverleaf Bks, 1995), *Haiku Headlines, Frogpond, Vitis Vine, New Press Lit Qtly*

Amy Holman 🎤 ✈ P&W
233 Smith St, #1
Brooklyn, NY 11231
Internet: Snowies63@gateway.net
Pubs: *Tissue & Bone* (Linear Arts, 1998,), *Best American Poetry 1999: Anth* (Scribner, 1999), *Second Word Thursdays Anth* (Bright Hill Pr, 1999), *Whole Notes, Literal Latte, CrossConnect, Mystic River Rev, Poet Lore, 4th Street, Failbetter, Clean Sheets*

Bob Holman 🎤 ✈ P
173 Duane St, #2
New York, NY 10013, 212-334-6414
Internet: holman@bard.edu
Pubs: *Beach Simplifies Horizon* (Grenfell Pr, 1999), *In with the Out Crowd* (Mouth Almighty/Mercury, 1998), *Bob Holman's Collect Call of the Wild* (H Holt, 1995), *KGB Bar Book of Poems: Anth* (Perennial, 2000), *Chrysanthemum, Exquisite Corpse, Bomb, Talisman*

Darryl Holmes P
The Afrikan Poetry Theatre, 176-03 Jamaica Ave, Jamaica, NY 11432, 718-528-3392
Pubs: *Wings Will Not Be Broken* (Third World Pr, 1990), *Catalyst Mag*

Doloris Holmes 🎤 PP&P
Director, White Mask Theatre/Press, 22 W 30 St, New York, NY 10001, 212-683-9332
Internet: janaiseast@aol.com
Pubs: *Soul Poems, Upbeat Triangles of Pastime, Poems on the Brain & Red Feet Too, Lady of the Grape Arbor* (White Mask Pr, 1999, 1997, 1996, 1991), *Upfront Muse Intl Jrnl*

Spencer Holst 🎤 ✈ P&W
55 Bethune St, #313-C
New York, NY 10014, 212-929-5770
Pubs: *Brilliant Silence: A Book of Paragraphs & Sentences & 13 Very, Very Short Stories, The Zebra Storyteller: Collected Stories, Something to Read to Someone* (Station Hill Pr, 2000, 1993, 1980)

A. M. Homes W
The Wylie Agency, 250 W 57 St, #2106, New York, NY 10107, 212-246-0069
Pubs: *The End of Alice* (Scribner, 1996), *In a Country of Mothers* (Knopf, 1993), *The Safety of Objects* (Norton, 1990), *Jack* (Vintage, 1990), *New Yorker*

Peter Hood P
15 Greenway Terr
Forest Hills, NY 11375, 718-263-9640

William Hooker PP
444 W 52 St, #E
New York, NY 10019
Pubs: *New Observations*

Susan Hoover 🎤 ✈ P
211 W 10 St #6D
New York, NY 10014, 212-924-3765
Internet: misterborges@yahoo.com
Pubs: *The Magnet & the Target* (New School Chapbook Series, 1995), *Taxi Dancer* (Exotic Beauties Pr, 1977), *U Colorado Lit Mag, Granite, Cold Mountain Rev, Isinglass Rev, Cover/Arts New York*

Doug Hornig W
Jane Dystel Literary Management, 1 Union Sq W, New
York, NY 10003, 212-627-9100
  Pubs: *Stinger, Virus* (NAL, 1990, 1989), *Deep Dive,
Waterman (Mysterious Pr, 1988, 1987)

Israel Horovitz P&W
c/o Biff Liff, William Morris Agency, 1325 Ave of the
Americas, New York, NY 10019, 212-586-5100
  Pubs: *Horovitz: Collected Works* (Smith & Kraus, 1994),
Three Gloucester Plays (Doubleday/Fireside, 1993),
L'Avant-Scene

Richard Howard P
23 Waverly Pl
New York, NY 10003, 212-228-6689
  Pubs: *Like Most Revelations* (Pantheon, 1994),
Trappings (Counterpoint, 1998), *No Traveller, Lining Up*
(Atheneum 1987, 1983), *Paris Rev, Yale Rev*

Thomas J. Hubschman ♀ W
473 17 St, #6
Brooklyn, NY 11215-6226
Internet: www.gowanusbooks.com/resume2.htm
  Pubs: *Billy Boy* (Crossroads Pub, 2000), *Space Ark*
(Tower, 1981), *Alpha-II* (Manor, 1980), *BBC World
Service, Blue Penny Qtly, New York Pr, In Vivo, Morpo
Rev, Kudzu, Blue Moon Rev*

Ingrid Hughes ♀ P&W
311 E 9 St, #6
New York, NY 10003-7742, 212-254-0635
  Pubs: *All the Trees in the Ocean* (Pink Granite Pr,
2000), *Women in the Midrash: Anth* (Jason Aronson,
1996), *Birmingham Rev, Negative Capability, Blue Light
Rev, West Branch, Mudfish, Bad Henry, MPR,
Massachusetts Rev*

Sophie Hughes P
49 W 12 St #2H
New York, NY 10011, 212-255-8144
  Pubs: *We Speak for Peace: Anth* (KIT, 1993), *Hollins
Critic, Interim, Potato Eyes, Poet's Edge,
NeoVictorian/Cochlea, Poem, Confrontation, Panhandler,
Sidewalks, Echoes, Writers' Forum, ProCreation*

Josephine Humphreys W
Harriet Wasserman Agency, 137 E 36 St, New York, NY
10016
  Pubs: *The Fireman's Fair, Rich in Love, Dreams of
Sleep* (Viking, 1991, 1987, 1984)

Christian X. Hunter P&W
166 Suffolk St #C
New York, NY 10002, 212-228-7864
  Pubs: *Crimes of the Beats: Anth* (Autonomedia, 1998),
Verses That Hurt: Anth (St. Martin's Pr, 1997), *Ikon,
Red Tape, The World, Portable Lower East Side,
Sensitive Skin, New York Pr*

Evan Hunter ♀ ✈ W
c/o Jane Gelfman, Gelfman Schneider Literary Agents, Inc,
250 W 57 St, New York, NY 10107, 212-245-1993
  Pubs: *The Last Dance, Big Bad City, Blackboard
Jungle* (S&S, 2000, 1999, 1954), *Privileged
Conversation* (Warner Bks, 1996)

Jerrie W. Hurd ♀ ✈ W
Jane Chelius Literary Agency, 548 2 St, Brooklyn, NY
11215, 718-499-0236
Internet: jchelius@worldnet.att.net
  Pubs: *RavenEyed, HoopSnaked, Lady Pinkerton Gets
Her Man, Kate Bourke Shoots the Old West, Miss
Ellie's Purple Sage Saloon* (Pocket Bks, 2002, 2001,
1998, 1997, 1995), *Kansas Qtly, Antioch Rev*

Eleanor Hyde W
343 E 74 St, #12L
New York, NY 10021, 212-861-2116
  Pubs: *Animal Instincts, In Murder We Trust* (Fawcett
Bks, 1996, 1995), *Arizona Qtly, Cosmopolitan, Satire*

Colette Inez ♀ ✈ P
5 W 86 St
New York, NY 10024, 212-874-2009
  Pubs: *Clemency* (Carnegie Mellon U Pr, 1998), *Getting
Underway: New & Selected Poetry, Family Life* (Story
Line Pr, 1993, 1992), *Hudson Rev, Partisan Rev, Ohio
Rev, Iowa Rev, Ploughshares, Prairie Schooner*

Elizabeth Inness-Brown ♀ ✈ W
Carlisle & Co., 24 E 64 St, New York, NY 10021,
212-813-1881
Internet: mvc@carlisleco.com
  Pubs: *Burning Marguerite* (Knopf, 2001), *Here* (LSU,
1994), *Satin Palms* (Fiction Intl Pr, 1981), *New Yorker,
Glimmer Train, Boulevard, NAR, Cream City Rev,
Mississippi Rev, Sycamore Rev*

Carole Ione ♀ ✈ P
Melanie Jackson Agency, 250 W 57 St, New York, NY
10107, 212-582-8585
Internet: www.deeplistening.org/ione
  Pubs: *Piramida Negra, Selected Poems* (Live Letters
Pr, 1991), *The Night Train to Aswan: Anth* (Neterv
Edtns, 1998), *Spirits of the Passage: Anth* (S&S, 1997),
*Hot Flashes, Women Writers on the Change of Life:
Anth* (Faber & Faber, 1995)
Lang: French

Ivor S. Irwin W
c/o Geri Thoma, Elaine Markson Literary Agency, 44
Greenwich Ave, New York, NY 10011, 212-243-8480
  Pubs: *A Peacock or a Crow* (Willes e-Pr, 1998), *Cape
Discoveries: Anth* (Sheep Meadow Pr, 1996), *Street
Songs: Anth* (Longstreet Pr, 1990), *Sycamore Rev,
Playboy, North Carolina Literary Rev, Mangrove,
Crushed Cigarette Pr, Emrys Jrnl, No Roses Rev, The
Sun*

Susan Isaacs   W
c/o Owen Laster, William Morris Agency, 1325 Ave of the
Americas, New York, NY 10019, 212-586-5100
  Pubs: *Shining Through, Almost Paradise* (H&R, 1988,
  1984)

Rashidah Ismaili   P
1851 Adam Clayton Powell Blvd
New York, NY 10026, 212-222-8631
  Pubs: *Missing in Action & Presumed Dead* (Africa
  World Pr, 1992), *Oniybo* (Shamal, 1986)

Peter Israel   W
Georges Borchardt Inc., 136 E 57 St, New York, NY
10022, 212-753-5785

Philip Israel   W
257 Beach 130 St
Belle Harbor, NY 11694, 718-945-0680
  Pubs: *Me & Brenda* (Norton, 1990), *Carlton Miscellany,
  Transatlantic Rev*

Beverly Jablons 🎤   W
63 E 9 St, #9K
New York, NY 10003-6334
  Pubs: *Dance Time* (Berkley, 1981), *Midstream, NAR*

Gale P. Jackson   P&W
180 Prospect Park W
Brooklyn, NY 11215
  Pubs: *Khoisan Tale of Beginnings & Ends, Bridge
  Suite: Narrative Poems* (Storm Imprints, 1998, 1998),
  Poets at Work: Anth (Just Buffalo Lit Ctr, 1996),
  *American Voice, Ploughshares, Ikon Mag, Callaloo,
  Black American Lit, Kenyon Rev*

Mae Jackson   P
165 Clinton Ave, #2G
Brooklyn, NY 11205, 718-237-0762
  Pubs: *Can I Poet with You* (Broadside Pr, 1970), *Black
  Scholar, Essence, Encore, Nimrod*

Sheila Cathryn Jackson   PP&P
PO Box 7554, FDR Sta
New York, NY 10150
  Pubs: *WomanStuff* (La Mama La Galleria, 1993),
  Letters from Texas (New Works Project, 1993),
  Manhattan Class Co Theatre, Playwrights' Ctr

Bev Jafek   W
24-08 24 Ave
Astoria, NY 11102-2832
  Pubs: *The Man Who Took a Bite Out of His Wife*
  (Overlook Pr, 1995), *Best American Short Stories: Anth*
  (HM, 1985), *Columbia, Yellow Silk, Missouri Rev*

Louise Jaffe 🎤 ✈   P
2411 E 3 St, #3E
Brooklyn, NY 11223, 718-998-0038
  Pubs: *Wisdom Revisited* (Adams Pr, 1987), *Which Lilith:
  Anth* (Jason Aronson, 1998), *American Poets & Poetry,
  Sunday Suitor, New Press Lit Qtly, Poetry Digest,
  Frontiers*

John Jakes   W
Rembar & Curtis Attorneys, 19 W 44 St, New York, NY
10036
Internet: www.johnjakes.com
  Pubs: *On Secret Service, American Dreams* (Dutton,
  2000, 1998), *Homeland* (Doubleday, 1993), *In the Big
  Country: The Best Western Stories of John Jakes*
  (Bantam, 1993), *Parade Mag*

Kelvin Christopher James 🎤 ✈   W
1295 5th Ave, #32F
New York, NY 10029
  Pubs: *A Fling with a Demon Lover* (HC, 1996),
  Secrets, Jumping Ship & Other Stories (Villard Bks,
  1993, 1992), *Leave to Stay: Anth* (Virago, 1996),
  Children of the Night: Anth (Little, Brown, 1995), *Low
  Rent: Anth* (Grove Pr, 1994)
I.D.: Caribbean-American

Elizabeth Janeway   W
350 E 79 St #8D
New York, NY 10021-9204

Ronald Wiley Janoff 🎤 ✈   P
1 Washington Sq Village, #15A
New York, NY 10012-1610, 212-995-8791
Internet: rwj1@nyu.edu
  Pubs: *Choice, Modern Poetry Studies, Abraxas,
  Hanging Loose, First Issue, Purchase Poetry Rev*

Tama Janowitz   W
c/o Amanda Urban, ICM, 40 W 57 St, New York, NY
10019, 212-556-5600
  Pubs: *By the Shores of Gitchi Gumee, The Male
  Cross-Dresser Support Group* (Crown, 1996, 1992),
  New Yorker

Lisa Jarnot   P
PO Box 185, Stuyvesant Sta
New York, NY 10009, 718-802-9575
  Pubs: *screens & tasted parallels, Black Bread, o.blek*

Gish Jen   W
Maxine Groffsky Literary Agency, 853 Broadway Ste 708,
New York, NY 10003
  Pubs: *Who's Irish* (Knopf 1999), *Mona in the Promised
  Land* (Knopf 1996), *Typical American* (HM 1991)

Ruth Prawer Jhabvala   W
400 E 52 St #7G
New York, NY 10022
   Pubs: *Three Continents, Out of India, In Search of Love & Beauty* (Morrow, 1987, 1986, 1983)

Vita Marie Jimenez   P
567 81 St
Brooklyn, NY 11209, 718-630-5440
   Pubs: *To Grow Grapes, The Courtship of Mickey & Minnie* (A Little Pr, 1998, 1990), *Crunchy, Munchy Cookies* (Newbridge Comm, 1993), *The World, Poetry Project Newsletter, Hanging Loose*

Carlos Johnson   W
30-98 Crescent St, #2B
Astoria, NY 11102, 718-956-3240
   Pubs: *Entre Nosotros, Centerpoint, Revista Chicano-Riquena, Chasqui, Linden Lane Mag, Inti*

Fenton Johnson   W
Malaga Baldi Literary Agency, PO Box 591, Radio City Sta, New York, NY 10101-5078, 212-222-1221
   Pubs: *Geography of the Heart* (Scribner, 1996), *Scissors, Paper, Rock* (Washington Sq Pr, 1996), *Virginia Qtly Rev, Mother Jones, Sewanee Rev*

Halvard Johnson 🎤 ✈   P
55 Bethune St, #610C
New York, NY 10014, 212-691-2764
Internet: halvard@earthlink.net
   Pubs: *Mixed Voices, This Sporting Life* (Milkweed Edtns, 1991, 1987), *Blue Moon Rev, CrossConnect, Poetry NY, Salt River Rev, Crania, Synaesthetic, Gargoyle, Pares Cum Parebus, RealPoetik, Ironwood, Puerto del Sol, Mudfish, St. Andrews Rev, Gulf Stream*

J. Chester Johnson 🎤 ✈   P
315 E 86 St, #16GE
New York, NY 10028-4780, 212-831-5063
   Pubs: *Curate's Chorus, Lazarus* (Juliet Pr, 1998, 1993), *NY Times, SPR, Parnassus*
Groups: Spiritual/Religious, College/Univ

Jacqueline Joan Johnson   P
Marie Brown Assoc Inc, 625 Broadway, New York, NY 10012, 718-574-4475
   Pubs: *A Gathering of Mother Tongues* (White Pine Pr, 1998), *Beyond the Frontier* (Black Classical Pr, 1998), *Drum Voices* (U St. Louis Pr, 1994), *Streetlights: Illuminating Tales of the Urban Black Experience: Anth* (Viking Penguin, 1996), *River Styx*

Joe Johnson   P&W
215 W 92 St, #11E
New York, NY 10025, 212-877-7619
   Pubs: *Tight* (Lee/Lucas Press, 1978)

Judith E. Johnson   PP&P&W
890 W End Ave, #1A
New York, NY 10025, 212-866-2639
   Pubs: *The Ice Lizard* (Sheep Meadow Pr, 1992), *The Waste Trilogy* (Countryman Pr, 1979), *Partisan Rev, New Yorker, Little Mag, Hudson Rev, Caprice, Frontiers*

Nicholas Johnson 🎤 ✈   P
141 Huntington St
Brooklyn, NY 11231, 718-624-7305
   Pubs: *Second Word Thursdays Anth* (Bright Hill Pr, 1999), *Anth of Magazine Verse & Yearbook of American Poetry* (Monitor Bk Co, 1997), *Men of Our Time: Anth* (U Georgia Pr, 1992), *APR, Rattle, Rattapallax, The Jrnl, Pivot, Poetry Wales, Troubadour, AL&C*
I.D.: Greek-American/Greek. Groups: College/Univ, Irish-American

Tom Johnson   P
Two-Eighteen Press, PO Box 218, Village Sta, New York, NY 10014-0218
   Pubs: *The Voice of New Music* (Het Apollohuis, 1989), *Imaginary Music: Anth* (Two-Eighteen Pr, 1976), *Unmuzzled Ox, Black Box*

Gary Johnston 🎤 ✈   P
Blind Beggar Press, PO Box 437, Williamsbridge Sta, Bronx, NY 10467
   Pubs: *Crossings, Two* (Blind Beggar Pr, 1995, 1994), *New Rain, African Voices, Black Nation*

Gerald Jonas   P
70 W 95 St, #5H
New York, NY 10025, 212-864-3949
   Pubs: *Dancing* (Harry Abrams, 1992), *Poetry*

Hettie Jones 🎤 ✈   W
27 Cooper Sq
New York, NY 10003, 212-473-5193
   Pubs: *Drive* (Hanging Loose Pr, 1998), *How I Became Hettie Jones* (Grove Pr, 1996), *Big Star Fallin' Mama* (Viking, 1995), *Hanging Loose, Ploughshares, Global City Rev*

J. E. M. Jones 🎤   P&W
The Picture Poet, PO Box 23144, Hollis, NY 11423
   Pubs: *Veiled Truths, Travelin on Faith/Travelin on Credit* (Jones, 1992, 1982), *The Nubian Gallery: A Poetry Anth* (Blacfax, 2000), *Blacfax Mag*

Kaylie Jones 🎤 ✈   W
Lantz-Harris Literary Agency, 156 5th Ave, Ste 617, New York, NY 10010, 212-924-6269
Internet: kayliej@mindspring.com
   Pubs: *Celeste Ascending, A Soldier's Daughter Never Cries* (HC, 2000, 1998), *Quite the Other Way* (Doubleday, 1989)
Lang: French. Groups: Children

Larry Jones 🎤 ✈   P
101 Ave A
New York, NY 10009-6103, 212-529-2336
   Pubs: *we become a picnic* (Venom Pr, 1994),
   Downtown Poets 1999: Anth (Montclair Takilma, 1999),
   *Hart Mag, Ikon, Curare, Tamarind, Olivetree Rev, Fag
   Rag, Provincetown Poets, Downtown, Zone*
I.D.: G/L/B/T. Groups: G/L/B/T

Patricia Spears Jones 🎤 ✈   P
426 Sterling Pl, #1C
Brooklyn, NY 11238, 718-399-2356
   Pubs: *Blood & Tears* (Painted Leaf Pr, 1999), *The
   Weather That Kills* (Coffee Hse Pr, 1995), *Best
   American Poetry: Anth* (Scribner, 2000), *Sing the Sun
   Up: Anth* (Teachers & Writers, 1998), *Aloud: Voices
   from the Nuyorican Cafe: Anth* (H Holt, 1994), *Agni*
I.D.: African-American, Women

Erica Mann Jong   P&W
c/o K. D. Burrows, 425 Park Ave, New York, NY
10022-5739, 212-980-6922
   Pubs: *Fear of Fifty, Becoming Light* (HC, 1994, 1991)

Joanne Joseph 🎤 ✈   P
770 Amsterdam Ave, #4N
New York, NY 10025, 212-840-1234
Internet: joannejoseph@juno.com
   Pubs: *NYQ, Dirty Goat*
I.D.: Women. Groups: College/Univ, Performance

Lawrence Joseph 🎤 ✈   P
St. John's Univ Law School, Jamaica, NY 11439,
718-990-6014
   Pubs: *Lawyerland, Before Our Eyes,* (FS&G, 1997,
   1993), *Curriculum Vitae, Shouting at No One* (U Pitt Pr,
   1988, 1983)

Stephen M. Joseph   W
270 1st Ave, #8E
New York, NY 10009, 212-254-5078
   Pubs: *Children in Fear* (HR&W, 1974), *The Me Nobody
   Knows* (Avon, 1969)

Ellen Kahaner   W
79-10 34 Ave #4Y
Jackson Heights, NY 11372
   Pubs: *Fourth Grade Loser* (Troll, Inc, 1992),
   Motorcycles (Capstone Pr, 1991), *Growing Up Female*
   (Rosen Pubs, 1991)

Anna Kainen   P
689 Columbus Ave, #14B
New York, NY 10025
   Pubs: *Whispers* (New York Poetry Fdn, 1986), *I Am
   Woman* (Anna Kainen, 1983), *Plowman, The Qtly*

Layding Kaliba   P
60 E 135 St, Apt 7C
New York, NY 10037, 212-690-2472
   Pubs: *The Moon Is My Witness, Up on the Down Side*
   (Single Action Prod, 1988, 1982)

Robert Kalich   W
240 Central Pk S
New York, NY 10019-1413
   Pubs: *The Handicapper* (Crown, 1981)

Laura Kalpakian   W
c/o Meg Ruley, Jane Rotrosen Agency, 318 E 51 St, New
York, NY 10022, 212-592-4330
   Pubs: *Dark Continent & Other Stories* (Viking/Penguin,
   1990), *Crescendo* (Times Bks, 1987)

Marc Kaminsky   P
291 11th St
Brooklyn, NY 11215, 718-788-0250
   Pubs: *Target Populations* (Central Park Edtns, 1991),
   The Road from Hiroshima (S&S, 1984), *Sun*

Linda Kampley   P
407 W 50 St, #3
New York, NY 10019
   Pubs: *Widener Rev, Soundings East, Connecticut River
   Rev, Panhandler, Voices Intl, Cream City Rev*

Alan Kapelner   W
40 King St, #1A
New York, NY 10014, 212-242-7496
   Pubs: *All the Naked Heroes* (Braziller, 1965), *Lonely
   Boy Blues* (Scribner, 1950), *New Voices*

Allan Kaplan   P
45 Christopher St, #16G
New York, NY 10014
   Pubs: *Paper Airplane* (H&R, 1972), *Free Lunch, GW
   Rev, Folio, Fine Madness, Green Hills Lit Lantern,
   Wind, Apalachee Qtly, Hubbub, Gulf Stream,
   Panhandler, Half Tones to Jubilee*

Johanna Kaplan 🎤   W
411 W End Ave, #11E
New York, NY 10024-5722
   Pubs: *O My America!* (Syracuse U Pr, 1995), *Other
   People's Lives* (Knopf, 1975), *Commentary*
Groups: Jewish

Robert Kaplan   P&W
300 W 23 St #14D
New York, NY 10011, 212-242-8687
   Pubs: *A Loving Testimonial: Remembering Loved Ones
   Lost to AIDS: Anth* (Crossing Pr, 1995), *Beyond
   Definition: Anth* (Manic D Pr, 1994), *Evergreen
   Chronicles, Modern Words, Anemone, Amethyst, RFD:
   A Country Jrnl for Gay Men Everywhere, New Leaves
   Rev*

Arno Karlen   P&W
350 Bleecker St, #1P
New York, NY 10014
   Pubs: *New Letters, Antioch Rev*

Mollyne Karnofsky 🎤 ✈   PP
515 E 88 St, #1D
New York, NY 10128-7743, 212-517-8607
Internet: mkarnart@aol.com
   Pubs: *Collide: A Scope* (Performance; Chuck Levitan
   Art Gallery, 1998), *Elemental Sounds/Equinox Life Line*
   (Performance; Anth Film Archives, 1996), *Spanish
   Moss, Dear Sun, Uncle Mike* (Performance; Med Art
   Intl, 1992)
   I.D.: Visual Arts

Vickie Karp 🎤 ✈   P
Thirteen/WNET, 450 W 33 St, New York, NY 10001,
212-560-3123
Internet: karp@thirteen.org
   Pubs: *A Taxi to the Flame* (U South Carolina, 1999),
   KGB Bar Reader: Anth (HC, 2000), *Best American
   Poetry: Anth* (Macmillan, 1991, 1989), *New Yorker, New
   Republic, New York Rev, Yale Rev, Paris Rev*

Jean Karsavina   W
c/o Knox Burger, 39 1/2 Washington Sq S, New York, NY
10012, 212-289-2368
   Pubs: *White Eagle, Dark Skies* (Scribner, 1975), *Tree
   By the Waters* (Young World Bks, 1949)

Ben Katchor   W
PO Box 2024 Cathedral Sta
New York, NY 10025, 212-665-8913
   Pubs: *The Jew of New York* (Pantheon, 1999), *Julius
   Knipl, Real Estate Photographer* (Little, Brown, 1996),
   Cheap Novelties (Penguin, 1991), *D.C. City Paper,
   Forward, San Francisco Weekly, Chicago New City,
   Metropolis Mag, River Front Times*

Eliot Katz 🎤 ✈   P
Old Chelsea Stn, PO Box 1621, New York, NY
10113-0879
Internet: ekatz@panix.com
   Pubs: *Unlocking the Exits* (Coffee Hse Pr, 1999),
   *Space & Other Poems for Love, Laughs, & Social
   Transformation* (Northern Lights, 1990), *Poems for the
   Nation: Anth* (Seven Stories.Pr, 2000)

Leandro Katz   PP
25 E 4 St
New York, NY 10003, 212-260-4254
   Pubs: *Death Trip* (Turt, 1990), *27 Windmills* (Viper's
   Tongue, 1986)

Vincent Katz 🎤 ✈   P
211 W 19 St, 5 Fl
New York, NY 10011-4001
   Pubs: *Pearl* (PowerHouse Bks, 1998), *Boulevard
   Transportation* (Tibor de Nagy Edtns, 1997), *Cabal of
   Zealots* (Hanuman, 1988), *Carnegie Intl 1999/2000
   Artists' Reader, Bomb, Exquisite Corpse, New
   Censorship, Little More, The World, The Fred, Ars
   Electronica*

Andrew Kaufman   P
585 Isham St #4E
New York, NY 10034, 212-304-8657
   Pubs: *Cinnamon Bay Sonnets* (Center for Book Arts,
   1996), *Anth of Mag Verse & Yearbook of American
   Poetry, Massachusetts Rev, College English, Spoon
   River Poetry Rev, BPJ, Carolina Qtly, Crazyhorse*

Bel Kaufman   W
1020 Park Ave, #20-A
New York, NY 10028, 212-288-8783
   Pubs: *Up the Down Staircase* (HC, 1991), *Love, Etc.*
   (Prentice Hall, 1981), *Esquire, McCall's, Commonweal,
   New Choices, Ladies' Home Jrnl, Saturday Rev of Lit,
   Today's Education*

Rebecca Kavaler 🎤 ✈   W
425 Riverside Dr
New York, NY 10025, 212-865-4632
   Pubs: *Tigers in the Wood* (U Illinois Pr, 1986),
   Doubting Castle (Schocken, 1984), *The Further
   Adventures of Brunhild* (U Missouri Pr, 1978), *Carolina
   Qtly*

Marvin Kaye   W
c/o Donald C. Maass, Donald Maass Literary Agency, 157
W 57 St, Ste 1003, New York, NY 10019, 212-757-7755
   Pubs: *Fantastique* (St. Martin's Pr, 1993), *Ghosts of
   Night & Morning, A Cold Blue Light* (Berkley, 1987,
   1983)

Melanie Kaye/Kantrowitz   P&W
922 8th Ave #3B
Brooklyn, NY 11215, 718-788-5333
   Pubs: *My Jewish Face & Other Stories* (Aunt Lute,
   1990), *Sinister Wisdom, Calyx, Bridges, Tikkun,
   Sojourner, Women's Rev of Bks, Gay Community
   News, Village Voice*

Meg Kearney   P
National Book Fdn, 260 5th Ave Rm 904, New York, NY
10001, 212-685-0261
   Pubs: *An Unkindness of Ravens* (BOA Edtns, 2001),
   *Milkweed, Santa Barbara Rev, Mind the Gap, Black
   Warrior Rev, Pivto, Free Lunch, Passages North,
   Berkshire Rev, Synaesthetic*

Celine Keating   W
697 W End Ave, #5D
New York, NY 10025-6823, 212-666-9174
   Pubs: *North Stone Rev, Emry's Jrnl, Appearances,*
   Echoes, Prairie Schooner, Santa Clara Rev

John Keeble 🎤 ✈   W
c/o Denise Shannon, ICM, 40 W 57 St, New York, NY
10019, 212-556-6727
Internet: jkeeble@mail.ewu.edu
   Pubs: *Out of the Channel* (HC, 1991), *Broken Ground*
   (H&R, 1987), *Outside*

Edmund Keeley 🎤 ✈   P&W
Georges Borchardt Inc., 136 E 57 St, New York, NY
10022, 212-753-5785
Internet: keeley@princeton.edu
   Pubs: *School for Pagan Lovers* (Rutgers U Pr, 1993),
   A Wilderness Called Peace (S&S, 1985), *Antaeus,*
   Harvard Rev, Mediterraneans, Intl Qtly, Passager,
   TriQtly, Ontario Rev, Seattle Rev
Groups: Translation

Joyce Keener   W
Sarah Lazin Books, 126 5th Ave, Ste 300, New York, NY
10011, 212-989-5757
   Pubs: *Limits of Eden, Borderline* (Ace Bks, 1981,
   1979), *Womanblood: Anth* (Continuing Saga, 1981)

Johanna Beale Keller   P&W
116 Pinehurst Ave, Hudson View Gardens A-64, New
York, NY 10033-1755, 212-781-3500
   Pubs: *The Skull* (Colorado College Pr, 1998), *SW Rev,*
   Chelsea, Nimrod, Connecticut Rev, Dark Horse, Voices
   Israel, Plum Rev, Pivot, New Plains Rev, Jean Rhys
   Rev

Tsipi Edith Keller   P&W
333 E 14 St
New York, NY 10003, 212-674-1076
   Pubs: *Vintage Book of Contemporary Poetry: Anth*
   (Vintage Bks, 1996), *Anthology of Magazine Verse,*
   Partisan Rev, Seneca Rev, Prairie Schooner, Between
   C&D, Minetta Rev, MPR, Mildred, George Washington
   Rev, Present Tense, Jewish Pr, Cream City Rev

William Melvin Kelley   W
c/o The Wisdom Shop, PO Box 2658, New York, NY
10027
   Pubs: *A Different Drummer* (Doubleday, 1973)

Raymond Kennedy   W
English Dept/Lewisohn Hall 615, Columbia Univ, New
York, NY 10027
   Pubs: *The Bittersweet Age, Ride a Cockhorse* (Ticknor
   & Fields, 1994, 1991), *Lulu Incognito* (Vintage, 1988),
   The Flower of the Republic (Knopf, 1983)

William Kennedy   W
Darhansoff & Verrill Agency, 1220 Park Ave, New York,
NY 10128, 212-534-2479
   Pubs: *Very Old Bones, Quinn's Book, Ironweed* (Viking,
   1992, 1988, 1983)

Bliem Kern   P
230 Riverside Dr, #15CC
New York, NY 10025-6172
   Pubs: *Temple of Sound, Hail Jupiter* (La Maison de la
   Bleame, 1995, 1995), *Spiritual Unity of Nations, Ingress,*
   Ararita

Sarah Kernochan   W
William Morris Agency, 1325 Ave of the Americas, New
York, NY 10019, 212-586-5100

Katharine Kidde 🎤 ✈   P
335 E 51 St, #1G
New York, NY 10022, 212-755-9461
   Pubs: *Sounding for Light* (Linear Arts, 1998), *Home*
   Light: Along the Shore (North Atlantic Rev, 1994),
   Context South, LIQ, Pegasus, Maryland Poetry Rev,
   Whelks Walk Rev, Whole Notes

Jamaica Kincaid   W
FSG, 19 Union Sq W, New York, NY 10003
   Pubs: *My Brother, A Small Place, At the Bottom of the*
   River (FSG, 1997, 1988, 1983), *Lucy, Annie John*
   (NAL, 1991, 1986)

Basil King 🎤 ✈   P&W
326-A 4 St
Brooklyn, NY 11215, 718-788-7927
   Pubs: *Identity, Ward Spasm* (Spuyten Duyvil, 2000,
   2000), *The Complete Miniatures, Devotions* (Stop Pr,
   1997), *Split Peas* (Zealot Pr, 1986), *Poetry NY,*
   Synaesthetic, First Intensity, Box Kite

Martha King 🎤 ✈   P
326-A 4 St
Brooklyn, NY 11215, 718-788-7927
   Pubs: *Little Tales of Family & War* (Spuyten Duyvil,
   2000), *Seventeen Walking Sticks* (Stop Pr, 1998), *The*
   Taking of Hands: Anth (New Rivers Pr, 1999), *House*
   Organ, Poetry Project Newsletter, NAW, Bomb, Salt
   Lick, Carbuncle

Gloria Devidas Kirchheimer 🎤 ✈   W
210 W 101 St, #15G
New York, NY 10025
   Pubs: *Goodbye, Evil Eye* (Holmes & Meier, 2000), *We*
   Were So Beloved: Autobiography of a German Jewish
   Community (U Pitt, 1997), *Sephardic-American Voices:*
   Anth, Follow My Footprints: Anth (U Pr of New
   England, 1997, 1993), *Kansas Qtly, Carolina Qtly, NAR*

Karl Kirchwey P
54 Morningside Dr, #43
New York, NY 10025-1760, 212-316-0130
  Pubs: *The Engrafted Word* (H Holt, 1998), *Those I Guard* (HB, 1993), *A Wandering Island* (Princeton U Pr, 1990), *Best of the Best American Poetry 1988-1997: Anth* (Scribner, 1998), *New Yorker, New Republic, Nation, Poetry, Paris Rev, Kenyon Rev*

Binnie Kirshenbaum 🎤 ✈ W
84 Charles St, #18
New York, NY 10014
Internet: Binniex@aol.com
  Pubs: *Pure Poetry* (S&S, 2000), *A Disturbance in One Place, On Mermaid Avenue* (Fromm Intl, 1994, 1993), *NER, BLQ, Mid-American Rev, Indiana Rev*

Natalie Kirstein W
140-21 Burden Cres, #602
Jamaica, NY 11435
  Pubs: *Revista/Review Interamericana, Midstream, New Letters*

William Kistler P
101 W 79 St, #22C
New York, NY 10024, 212-874-6150
  Pubs: *Notes Drawn from the River of Ecstasy, America February, The Elizabeth Sequence* (Council Oak Bks, 1996, 1991, 1989), *Poems of the Known World* (Arcade Pubs, 1995), *APR, Antaeus, Poetry Flash, Poetry Intl, New Criterion, New Directions Annual, Harper's*

Myra Klahr 🎤 ✈ P
40 E 9 St, #12L
New York, NY 10003-6421, 212-505-2606
Internet: lingosmart@earthlink.net
  Pubs: *The Waiting Room* (Fiddlehead Pr, 1972), *Caprice, Sesheta, Unicorn, Hanging Loose, Squeezebox*
Groups: Children, Seniors

Irena Klepfisz P
155 Atlantic Ave
Brooklyn, NY 11201, 718-855-2905
  Pubs: *A Few Words in the Mother Tongue: Poems Selected & New* (Eighth Mountain Pr, 1990), *The Tribe of Dina: A Jewish Women's Anth* (Beacon, 1989), *Bridges, Ms.*

Nancy Kline 🎤 ✈ W
540 Prospect Ave
Brooklyn, NY 11215
  Pubs: *The Faithful* (Morrow, 1968), *Fiction 1986: Anth* (Exile Pr, 1986), *Ascent, Playgirl, Boston Globe Sunday Mag, Nantucket Rev, Colorado Qtly, Weber Studies*
Lang: French. Groups: Prisoners, Seniors

Jay Klokker P
311 E 9 St
New York, NY 10003
  Pubs: *Devil's Millhopper, BPJ, Bellingham Rev, Hanging Loose, State St Rev*

Alison Knowles PP&P
122 Spring St
New York, NY 10012, 212-226-5703
  Pubs: *Event Scores* (Left Hand Bks, 1992), *A Bean Concordance* (Printed Edtns, 1983), *Aperture, New Wilderness Letter 11*

John Knowles W
Curtis Brown Ltd., 10 Astor Pl, New York, NY 10003-6935, 212-473-5400
  Pubs: *A Stolen Past* (HRW, 1983), *Spreading Fires* (Random Hse, 1974), *A Separate Peace* (Macmillan, 1960), *Playboy, Esquire*

Kenneth Koch P&W
25 Claremont Ave, #2B
New York, NY 10027, 212-854-4015
  Pubs: *Straits, One Train* (Knopf, 1998, 1994), *Poetry, New York Rev of Books, APR, Artes, Arshile, The World*

Stephen Koch 🎤 ✈ W
Carlisle & Co., 24 E 64 St, New York, NY 10021, 212-813-1881
Internet: stephenkoch@dellnet.com
  Pubs: *The Bachelor's Bride* (Marion Boyars, 1986)

Ronald Koertge 🎤 ✈ P
c/o William Reiss, John Hawkins & Assoc, 71 W 23 St, Ste 1600, New York, NY 10010, 212-807-7040
Internet: ronkoe@earthlink.net
  Pubs: *Geography of the Forehead, Making Love to Roget's Wife* (U Arkansas Pr, 2000, 1997), *The Heart of the City, Confess-O-Rama, Tiger, Tiger Burning Bright* (Orchard Bks, 1998, 1996, 1994), *The Harmony Arms, Mariposa Blues* (Little, Brown, 1992, 1991)

Wayne Koestenbaum 🎤 ✈ P
c/o Faith Hamlin, Sanford J. Greenburger Assoc., 55 Fifth Ave, New York, NY 10003
  Pubs: *The Milk of Inquiry, Rhapsodies of a Repeat Offender, Ode to Anna Moffo & Other Poems* (Persea, 2000, 1994, 1990), *New Yorker, Paris Rev, APR, Yale Rev*

Sybil Kollar 🎤 ✈ P
10 Clinton St, #12M
Brooklyn, NY 11201-2708, 718-858-4749
Internet: sybkollar@aol.com
  Pubs: *In Rooms We Come & Go* (Somers Rocks Pr, 1998), *Party Train: Anth* (New Rivers Pr, 1996), *Coumbia, American Voice, Pivot, Lit Rev*

Ron Kolm 🎤 ✈   P&W
30-73 47 St, #3F
Long Island City, NY 11103, 718-721-0946
    Pubs: *Outlaw Bible of American Poetry: Anth* (Thunder's
    Mouth Pr, 1999), *Crimes of the Beats: Anth,
    Unbearables: Anth* (Autonomedia, 1998, 1995), *New
    Observations, Redtape, Pink Pages, Public Illumination
    Mag, Gargoyle*

Todd Alan Komarnicki   W
The Writers Shop, 101 5th Ave, 11 Fl, New York, NY
10003, 212-255-6515
    Pubs: *Free* (Doubleday, 1993)

Edith Konecky   W
511 E 20 St, #9G
New York, NY 10010, 212-228-2253
    Pubs: *A Place at the Table* (Ballantine, 1990), *Allegra
    Maud Goldman* (The Feminist Pr, 1990)

Hans Koning   W
Sterling Lord Literistic, 65 Bleecker St, New York, NY
10012, 212-780-6050
    Pubs: *Pursuit of a Woman on the Hinge of History*
    (Brookline Bks, 1998), *The Conquest of America*
    (Monthly Rev Pr, 1994), *Acts of Faith* (H Holt, 1988),
    New Yorker, Harper's, Atlantic

Jean Hanff Korelitz 🎤 ✈   P&W
Pam Bernstein & Assoc., 790 Madison Ave, Ste 310, New
York, NY 10021, 212-288-1700
    Pubs: *The Sabbathday River* (FSG, 1999), *A Jury of
    Her Peers* (Crown, 1996), *The Properties of Breath*
    (Bloodaxe/Dufour, 1988)

Nina Kossman   P&W
30-11 49 St
Long Island City, NY 11103
    Pubs: *Behind the Border* (Morrow, 1994), *The Gospels
    in Our Image: Anth* (HB, 1995), *Southern Humanities
    Rev, Qtly West, Connecticut Poetry Rev, Prairie
    Schooner, Columbia, Threepenny Rev*

Richard Kostelanetz   PP&P&W
PO Box 444, Prince St Sta
New York, NY 10012-0008, 212-982-3099
    Pubs: *Wordworks: Poems Selected & New* (BOA Edtns,
    1993), *The New Poetries & Some Old* (Southern
    Illinois, 1991)

Dean Kostos 🎤 ✈   P&W
211 W 21 St, #5-W
New York, NY 10011-3144, 212-255-6860
    Pubs: *The Sentence That Ends with a Comma, Blood
    & Tears: Anth* (Painted Leaf, 1999, 1999), *Celestial
    Rust* (Red Dust, 1994), *SW Rev, Boulevard, James
    White Rev, Poetry NY, Barrow Street, Chiron Rev*
I.D.: G/L/B/T, Greek-American/Greek. Groups: Children,
Seniors

Robert Kotlowitz 🎤 ✈   W
54 Riverside Dr
New York, NY 10024-6509, 212-787-0239
    Pubs: *Before Their Time, His Master's Voice, Boardwalk*
    (Knopf, 1997, 1992, 1976), *Sea Changes* (North Point
    Pr, 1986), *Somewhere Else* (Charterhouse, 1972)

Jose Kozer   P
10933 71 Rd, #5F
Forest Hills, NY 11375-4816
    Pubs: *Projimos/Intimates* (Spain; Carrer Ausias, 1991),
    De Donde Oscilan Los Seres en Sus Proporciones (El
    Guerrero Encendido, 1990)

Elaine Kraf   W
7226 Manse St
Forest Hills, NY 11375-6728
    Pubs: *The Princess of 72nd Street* (New Directions,
    1979), *Find Him!* (Fiction Collective, 1977)

Daniel Krakauer   P
346 E 10 St #6
New York, NY 10009, 212-533-8537
    Pubs: *Poems for the Whole Family* (United Artists,
    1994), *Out of This World: Anth* (Crown, 1991), *Transfer,
    Tamarind, Mag City, Downtown, The World, Cover*

Cynthia Kraman 🎤 ✈   P
16 Charles St
New York, NY 10014, 212-675-7435
    Pubs: *The Mexican Murals* (E.G. Pr, 1986), *Taking on
    the Local Color* (Wesleyan U Pr, 1977), *Antaeus, Paris
    Rev, Poetry Flash, Southern Rev*
Groups: Women, Prisoners

Larry Kramer   W
2 Fith Ave, #32
New York, NY 10011

Robert Kramer 🎤 ✈   P
Manhattan College, Language Dept, Riverdale, NY 10471,
718-862-7401
    Pubs: *From Action to Dynamic Silence* (Charles
    Schlacks, 1991), *Rattapallax, Home Planet News, Pivot,
    Poets, Night Sun, Quarry West, Apocalypse*
Groups: Translation

David Kranes   W
Harold Matson Co, Inc, 276 Fifth Ave, New York, NY
10001, 212-679-4490

Christine Kraus   P
151 2nd Ave, #2A
New York, NY 10003, 212-982-5603

Rochelle Kraut P
334 E 11 St, #16
New York, NY 10003
  Pubs: *Art in America* (Little Light Bks, 1984), *Little Light, The World, Mag City, Rocky Ledge*

Steven M. Krauzer W
c/o Ginger Barber, The Writers Shop, 101 5th Ave, Ste 11-F, New York, NY 10003, 212-255-6515
  Pubs: *Frame Work* (Bantam, 1989)

Ann Kregal P
24 Riverside Dr, 1F
New York, NY 10023
  Pubs: *Gyro, Home Planet News, Telephone*

Nancy Kricorian ♣ ✦ P
Witherspoon Assoc, Inc, 235 E 31 St, New York, NY 10016
  Pubs: *Zabelle: A Novel* (Atlantic Monthly Pr, 1998), *River Styx, Ararat, Literary Rev, Mississippi Rev, Witness, Graham House Rev, Ikon, Caliban, Heresies, Parnassus*
I.D.: Armenian-American. Groups: Children, Women

Leonard Kriegel W
355 8th Ave, #19F
New York, NY 10001-4838, 212-243-7832
  Pubs: *Flying Solo* (Beacon, 1998), *Falling into Life* (North Point Pr, 1991), *Quitting Time* (Pantheon, 1982)

Jill Kroesen P
15 E 17 St, #5
New York, NY 10003
  Pubs: *Disposable Art* (D-Cup Dog Pr, 1975), *High Performance, Ear Mag, Art Rite, Criteria*

Frank Kuenstler P
670 W End Ave
New York, NY 10025, 212-362-1691
  Pubs: *In Which* (Cairn Edtns, 1994), *13 1/2 Poems* (SZ Pr, 1984), *Empire* (Archive Pr, 1976)

Stanley Kunitz P
37 W 12 St, #2J
New York, NY 10011-8503, 212-924-9155
  Pubs: *The Collected Poems, Passing Through: The Later Poems* (Norton, 2000, 1995) *Next to Last Things* (Atlantic, 1985)

Daniela Kuper ♣ ✦ W
c/o Sally Wofford-Girard, Elaine Markson Literary Agency, 44 Greenwich Ave, New York, NY 10011
Internet: daniela@acadia.net
  Pubs: *Cherries in the Snow* (Picador USA, 1999), *Storming Heaven's Gate: Anth* (Penguin, 1996), *Many Mountains Moving, The Sun, Cream City Rev, Coe Rev, Amaranth Rev, Mobius, Lilith, Poetry Forum, Black Warrior Rev*

Tuli Kupferberg ♣ ✦ W
160 6th Ave
New York, NY 10013, 212-925-3823
Internet: tuli@escape.com
  Pubs: *Teach Yourself Fucking* (Autonomedia, 2000), *Don't Make Trouble* (Strolling Dog Pr, 1991), *Portable Beat Reader: Anth* (Viking Penguin, 1992), *Home Planet News, NY Press, Revolting News, MNN, Fugs, Against the Current, Shadow*

Bill Kushner ♣ ✦ P
319 W 22 St, #2A
New York, NY 10011-2675, 212-691-7276
  Pubs: *Pen Upside Down* (Rattapallax Pr, 2000), *That April* (United Artists Bks, 2000), *In Our Time: Anth* (St Martin's Pr, 1989)
Groups: G/L/B/T

Paul Kuttner W
Dawnwood Press, 387 Park Ave S, 5th Fl, New York, NY 10016-8810
  Pubs: *The Iron Virgin, Absolute Proof, Condemned,* (Dawnwood Pr, 1987, 1984, 1983), *The Man Who Lost Everything* (Sterling Pub, 1976)

Michael La Bombarda P
89-04 172 St
Jamaica, NY 11432, 718-526-5826
  Pubs: *Five Plus Five* (Low Tech Pub, 1984), *Appearances*

Mary La Chapelle W
Robin Rue, Anita Diamant Agency, 310 Madison Ave, New York, NY 10017
  Pubs: *House of Heroes* (Vintage, 1990), *Sing Heavenly Muse!, Warm Jrnl, Northern Lit Qtly*

Tom LaBar W
436 W Broadway
New York, NY 10012

Martha J. LaBare ♣ ✦ P
1 Old Fulton St
Brooklyn, NY 11201, 718-855-2896
Internet: martha_labare@bloomfield.edu
  Pubs: *Shooting Star & Other Poems* (Swollen Magpie Pr, 1982), *Footwork, Roof, Telephone, World, Poet & Critic*

Oliver Lake P
163 Adelphi St
Brooklyn, NY 11205

Wally Lamb 🎤 ✈   W
Linda Chester Literary Agency, 630 5th Ave Ste 2662,
New York, NY 10111, 212-218-3350
    Pubs: *I Know This Much Is True* (Regan Bks/HC,
1998), *She's Come Undone* (Pocket Bks/S&S, 1992),
Best of the Missouri Review: Fiction 1978-1990: Anth
(U Missouri Pr, 1991), *Pushcart Prize XV Anth 1990*

Annette Henkin Landau 🎤 ✈   W
301 E 66 St, #16K
New York, NY 10021-6219, 212-861-7425
Internet: jwrcncjw@aol.com
    Pubs: *Best of Moment Mag: Anth* (Jason Aronson,
1987), *Confrontation, Commentary, Tikkun, Other
Voices, Moment, Vignette, Jewish Women's Lit Annual*
I.D.: Jewish, Feminist

Sandy Landsman   W
43-57 Union St, #6C
Flushing, NY 11355, 516-921-0808
    Pubs: *Castaways on Chimp Island, The Gadget Factor*
(Atheneum, 1986, 1984)

Marcia Lane   PP
462 Amsterdam Ave
New York, NY 10024, 212-799-1196
    Pubs: *Christoph Wants a Party* (Kane-Miller Bks, 1995),
Picturing the Rose (H.W. Wilson, 1993), *National
Storytelling Lit Jrnl, Creative Classroom*

George Lanning   W
c/o Tony Outhwaite, JCR, Inc, 27 W 20 St, Ste 1103,
New York, NY 10011

Joan Larkin 🎤 ✈   P
813 Eighth Ave
Brooklyn, NY 11215-4116, 718-499-1629
Internet: larkin7@aol.com
    Pubs: *Cold River* (Painted Leaf Pr, 1997), *A Long
Sound* (Granite Pr, 1986), *Gay & Lesbian Poetry in Our
Time: Anth* (St. Martin's Pr, 1988), *APR, Global City
Rev, Hanging Loose, Out Mag, Sing Heavenly Muse*
I.D.: G/L/B/T

Wendy Wilder Larsen 🎤 ✈   P
439 E 51 St
New York, NY 10022-6473
    Pubs: *Braided Lives* (Minnesota Humanities
Commission, 1991), *The KGB Bar Book of Poems:
Anth* (HC, 2000), *Outsiders: Anth, Night Out: Anth*
(Milkweed Edtns, 1999, 1997), *A Year in Poetry: Anth*
(Crown, 1995), *After the Storm: Anth* (Maisonneuve,
1992)

Pam Laskin 🎤 ✈   P&W
414 5th St
Brooklyn, NY 11215
    Pubs: *Dear Hades* (New Spirit Pr, 1994), *In a Glass
Ball* (Green Meadow Pr, 1992), *The Buried Treasure,
Heroic Horses* (McGraw-Hill, 1998, 1998), *A Wish Upon
Star* (Magination, 1991), *Music from the Heart* (Bantam,
1990), *Sassy, Sidewalks,*
I.D.: Jewish. Groups: Children, Seniors

Michael Lassell   P&W
114 Horatio St, #512
New York, NY 10014-1579, 212-206-7339
    Pubs: *A Flame for the Touch That Matters* (Painted
Leaf Pr, 1998), *The Hard Way* (Richard Kasak Bks,
1995), *Decade Dance* (Alyson, 1990), *City Lights Rev,
Portable Lower East Side, Excursus, Central Park,
Zyzzyva, Global City Rev, Hanging Loose*

Charles Keeling Lassiter   P
1382 1st Ave, #19
New York, NY 10021-9526, 212-535-6075
    Pubs: *C.K. Lassiter: Drawings & Writing, 1957-1990*
(Switzerland; Sylvia Acatos, 1990)

Kristin Hunter Lattany 🎤   W
Jane Dystel Literary Management, 1 Union Sq W, New
York, NY 10003, 212-627-9100
    Pubs: *Do Unto Others, Kinfolks* (Ballantine, 2000,
1996), *God Bless the Child* (Howard U Pr, 1986),
*Philadelphia Inquirer, Essence, Seventeen, Callaloo,
Nation*
I.D.: African-American. Groups: Seniors, Children

Lynne Lawner   P
Georges Borchardt Inc., 136 E 57 St, New York, NY
10022, 212-737-5619
    Pubs: *Lives of the Courtesans* (Rizzoli, 1987), *Paris
Rev, Radcliffe Qtly, Confrontation, Chelsea, Georgia
Rev, The Bridge*

Kathleen Rockwell Lawrence   W
510 E 23 St, #13-B
New York, NY 10010-, 212-533-7563
    Pubs: *The Boys I Didn't Kiss* (British-American, 1990),
The Last Room in Manhattan, Maud Gone (Atheneum,
1989, 1986)

Jane Lazarre   W
Wendy Weil Agency Inc, 232 Madison Ave, Ste 1300,
New York, NY 10016, 212-685-0300
    Pubs: *Worlds Beyond My Control* (Dutton/NAL, 1991),
The Powers of Charlotte (Crossing Pr, 1988), *The
Mother Knot* (Beacon Pr, 1985)

Cynthia LeClaire   P&W
Philosophy Dept, St. Francis College, 180 Remsen St,
Brooklyn, NY 11201, 718-522-2300
    Pubs: *The Rape of Persephone* (New Spirit Pr, 1993),
Homage to the Light (Black Swan Pr, 1985)

Jeanne Lee　　　　　　　　　　　　　PP
c/o Hillegas, JMLF Productions, 525 Hudson St, #3RN,
New York, NY 10014, 212-860-4209
　　Pubs: *Natural Affinities* (CD; Owl, 1992), *Songposts*
　　(CD; Word of Mouth, 1991)

Marie G. Lee　　　　　　　　　　　　W
c/o Wendy Schmalz, Harold Ober Assoc, 425 Madison
Ave, New York, NY 10017, 212-759-8600
　　Pubs: *Necessary Roughness* (HC, 1996), *Finding My
　　Voice* (HM, 1992), *Kenyon, American Voice, Asian
　　Pacific American Jrnl*

Roland Legiardi-Laura　　　　　　　P
295 E 8 St
New York, NY 10009, 212-529-9327
　　Pubs: *Bomb, Appearances, The World 40, Telephone
　　19, Lumen/Avenue A, Main Trend, Sunbury 9*

David Lehman　　　　　　　　　　　P
104 MacDougal St, #1
New York, NY 10012
　　Pubs: *Valentine Place* (Scribner, 1996), *Operation
　　Memory, An Alternative to Speech* (Princeton, 1990,
　　1986)

Eric Gabriel Lehman 🎤 ✈　　　　　W
Malaga Baldi Literary Agency, 204 W 84 St, Ste 3C, New
York, NY 10024, 212-579-5075
　　Pubs: *Summer's House* (St. Martin's Pr, 2000),
　　Quaspeck, Waterboys (Mercury Hse, 1993, 1989), *Best
　　American Gay Fiction 3: Anth* (Back Bay Bks, 1998),
　　James White Rev, New Letters, Modern Words
Lang: German. Groups: G/L/B/T

Alan Lelchuk　　　　　　　　　　　W
Georges Borchardt Inc., 136 E 57 St, New York, NY
10022, 212-573-5785
　　Pubs: *Playing the Game* (Baskerville Pubs, 1995),
　　Brooklyn Boy, Miriam at Thirty-Four (McGraw-Hill, 1990,
　　1989), *American Mischief* (FSG, 1974), *Atlantic, New
　　American Rev, New Republic*

Gabrielle LeMay 🎤　　　　　　　　P
250 W 99 St #7A
New York, NY 10025
Internet: LeMayNYC@aol.com
　　Pubs: *Ravishing DisUnities: Real Ghazals in English:
　　Anth* (Wesleyan, 2000), *Jrnl of New Jersey Poets,
　　Thema, Paterson Lit Rev, Confrontation, River Oak
　　Rev, Poets Ou: Coping, Mudfish*

John Leonard　　　　　　　　　　　W
Curtis Brown Ltd., 10 Astor Pl, New York, NY
10003-6935, 212-473-5400

Estelle Leontief　　　　　　　　　　P
37 Washington Sq W, #16B
New York, NY 10011
　　Pubs: *Sellie & Dee: A Friendship* (Chicory Blue Pr,
　　1993), *Genia & Wassily: A Russian American Memoir*
　　(Zephyr Pr, 1987), *Sojourner, Florida Rev*

Eleanor Lerman　　　　　　　　　　P
10460 Queens Blvd, #20H
Flushing, NY 11375-7325
　　Pubs: *Come the Sweet By & By* (U Massachusetts Pr,
　　1975), *Armed Love* (Wesleyan U Pr, 1973)

Rhoda Lerman　　　　　　　　　　　W
c/o Owen Laster, William Morris Agency, 1325 Ave of the
Americas, New York, NY 10019, 212-586-5100
　　Pubs: *In the Company of Newfies, Animal Acts, God's
　　Ear, Book of the Night, Eleanor* (H Holt, 1997, 1994,
　　1989, 1984, 1979)

Linda Lerner 🎤 ✈　　　　　　　　P
PO Box 020292
Brooklyn, NY 11202-0007, 212-766-4109
　　Pubs: *No Earthly Sense Gets It Right* (Lummox Pr,
　　2000), *Anytimeblues, New & Selected Poems, She's
　　Back* (Ye Olde Font Shoppe Pr, 1999, 1998, 1996),
　　Ragged Lion: Anth (Vagabond/Smith, 1999), *Rattle,
　　Chiron Rev, Nexus, Home Planet Rev, Haight-Ashbury
　　Lit Jrnl*

Rika Lesser 🎤 ✈　　　　　　　　　P
133 Henry St, #5
Brooklyn, NY 11201-2550, 718-852-1163
Internet: rika.lesser.mc.74@aya.yale.edu
　　Pubs: *Growing Back* (U South Carolina Pr, 1997), *All
　　We Need of Hell* (U North Texas Pr, 1995), *Etruscan
　　Things* (Braziller, 1983), *Paris Rev, New Yorker,
　　Partisan, Poetry, Nation*

Donald Lev 🎤 ✈　　　　　　　　　P
3047 Brighton First Pl
Brooklyn, NY 11235-7419, 718-769-2854
　　Pubs: *Twilight* (CRS Outloud Bks, 1995), *A New
　　Geography of Poets: Anth* (U Arkansas Pr, 1992),
　　*Caprice, Jews, And Then, Long Shot, Ikon, Home
　　Planet News*

Jan Heller Levi 🎤 ✈　　　　　　　P&W
244 Waverly Pl, #2B
New York, NY 10014-2246, 212-929-1951
　　Pubs: *Once I Gazed at You in Wonder* (LSU Pr, 1999),
　　*TriQtly, Graham Hse Rev, Poetry East, Ploughshares,
　　Pequod, Antioch Rev, River Styx, BPJ*
Groups: Children

Toni Mergentime Levi 🎙 ✈   P
105 W 73 St #4D
New York, NY 10023, 212-362-5481
Internet: tonimerg@cs.com
    Pubs: *For a Dancing Bear* (Three Mile Harbor, 1995),
*Prairie Schooner, California Qtly, Manhattan Poetry Rev,
Negative Capability, Crosscurrents, Texas Rev, Kansas
Qtly, Confrontation*
I.D.: Jewish

Phillis Levin   P
128 W 13 St, #42
New York, NY 10011-7822, 212-741-1977
    Pubs: *Mercury, The Penguin Book of the Sonnet: Anth*
(Penguin/Putnam, 2001, 2001), *The Afterimage* (Copper
Beech Pr, 1995), *Temples & Fields* (U Georgia Pr,
1988), *Atlantic, New Yorker, Paris Rev, New Republic,
Poetry, Partisan Rev, Nation*

Anne-Marie Levine 🎙 ✈   P
156 E 89 St
New York, NY 10128
Internet: stinpilot@aol.com
    Pubs: *With Sophie* (Peapod Pr, 1999), *Euphorbia*
(Provincetown Arts Pr, 1994), *Tin House, Salamander,
American Letters & Commentary, Parnassus,
Ploughshares, Provincetown Arts, Pequod, BPJ*

Howard Levy 🎙 ✈   P
70 E 96 St, #12B
New York, NY 10128
    Pubs: *A Day This Lit* (Cavankerry Pr, 2000), *Poetry,
Paris Rev, Threepenny Rev, Gettysburg Rev, APR,
Georgia Rev, Massachusetts Rev, Columbia*

Owen Levy   W
217 Central Pk N
New York, NY 10026
    Pubs: *A Brother's Touch* (Pinnacle Bks, 1982)

Robert J. Levy   P
595 W End Ave #4A
New York, NY 10024-1727, 212-799-6836
    Pubs: *Chefs at Twilight* (Bacchae Pr, 1996), *The
Perfection of Standing Aside* (South Coast Pr, 1993),
Paris Rev, Poetry, Georgia Rev, Southern Rev

Stephen Levy   P
106 W 13 St, #11
New York, NY 10011, 212-691-0442
    Pubs: *Many Hands* (Firefly Pr, 1982), *Israel Horizons,
Genesis 2, Reconstructionist, And Then*

Harry Lewis   P
115 Barrow St #4B
New York, NY 10014, 212-243-1393
    Pubs: *Two for One, Silly 1-14* (Little Rootie Tootie/Ikon
Pr, 1994, 1992), *Ikon, Sun, Number, Mulch, Transfer*

Marilyn Jaye Lewis   W
777 W End Ave
New York, NY 10025
    Pubs: *Swingers, Safeway, Neptune & Surf, I Like Boys*
(Masquerade Bks, 1998, 1998, 1999), *Frighten the
Horses, Bad Attitude, Masquerade Erotic Jrnl*

Owen Lewis   PP
24 E 82 St
New York, NY 10028
    Pubs: *New Pictures at an Exhibition* (Alexander Browde,
1977), *Princeton Spectrum*

Richard Lewis 🎙 ✈   P
141 E 88 St, #3E
New York, NY 10028-1323, 212-831-7717
Internet: alewis212@aol.com
    Pubs: *Each Sky Has Its Words* (Touchstone Ctr Pub,
2000), *Living By Wonder* (Parabola Bks, 1998), *Poets
at Work* (Just Buffalo Lit Ctr, 1995), *When Thought Is
Young* (New Rivers Pr, 1992), *Asheville Poetry Rev*

Leslie Li 🎙 ✈   W
Witherspoon Assoc, Inc, 235 E 31 St, New York, NY
10016
    Pubs: *Bittersweet* (Charles Tuttle, 1992), *American
Identities: Anth* (U Pr of New England, 1994)
I.D.: Asian-American

Herbert Lieberman   W
Georges Borchardt Inc., 136 E 57 St, New York, NY
10022, 212-753-5785
    Pubs: *Sandman, Sleep* (St. Martin's Pr, 1992), *Shadow
Dancers* (Little, Brown, 1989), *The Climate of Hell, City
of the Dead* (S&S, 1978, 1976) *Crawlspace* (David
McKay, 1971), *Redbook*

Herbert Liebman   W
College of Staten Island, 2800 Victory Blvd, Staten Island,
NY 10314, 212-242-1909
    Pubs: *Confrontation, Chelsea, PEN Syndicated Fiction,
Paris Transcontinental, Midstream*

Kate Light   P
225 W 106 St, #3M
New York, NY 10025, 212-222-9620
    Pubs: *The Laws of Falling Bodies* (Story Line Pr,
1997), *Paris Rev, Sparrow, Western Humanities Rev,
Feminist Studies, Wisconsin Rev, Janus*

Frank Lima   P
147-20 35 Ave, #11-B
Flushing, NY 11354-3706, 718-961-0301
    Pubs: *Angel* (Liveright, 1976), *Underground with the
Oriole* (Dutton, 1971)

Nancy Linde   P
20 Cliff St #8E
Staten Island, NY 10305, 718-876-9293
    Pubs: *The Orange Cat Bistro* (Kensington, 1996),
*Buckle, Symposium, Sojourner, 13th Moon, Promethean,
Endymion*

Don Linder   P&W
243 Riverside Dr, #604
New York, NY 10025, 212-866-9001
    Pubs: *West Side Spirit, Other Voices, Mss., Beacon
Rev, Stardancer, Inprint*

Elinor Lipman   W
The Writers Shop, 101 5th Ave, New York, NY 10003
    Pubs: *The Inn at Lake Devine* (Random Hse, 1998),
Isabel's Bed (Pocket Bks, 1995), *The Way Men Act,
Then She Found Me* (Washington Square Pr, 1993,
1991)

Rhoda Marilyn Lippel   P
365 W 28 St, #20E
New York, NY 10001-7919, 212-691-3925
    Pubs: *Curious West, Write Technique, Downtown,
Journal of the e. e. cummings Society, Clinton
Chronicle*

Marcia Lipson 🎤 ✈   P
900 W End Ave 16D
New York, NY 10025, 212-666-8853
    Pubs: *bite to eat place: Anth* (Redwood Coast Pr,
1995), *Stories from Where We Live: Anth* (Milkweed
Edtns, 2001), *Appalachia, Cream City Rev, Barrow
Street, Bridge, Gargoyle, Jewish Women's Lit Annual,
Kerem, Paterson Lit Rev, Plum Rev, Yankee*

Gordon Lish   W
Four Walls Eight Windows, 39 W 14 St, New York, NY
10011, 212-206-4769
    Pubs: *Peru, The Mourner at the Door, Epigraph, Dear
Mr. Capote, What I Know So Far* (Four Walls Eight
Windows, 1997, 1997, 1996, 1996, 1996)

Olga Litowinsky 🎤 ✈   W
Curtis Brown Ltd., 10 Astor Pl, New York, NY 10003-6935
    Pubs: *Boats for Bedtime* (Clarion, 2000), *The Pawloined
Paper* (Big Red Chair Bks, 1998), *Oliver's High Flying
Adventure* (as M. McBrier; Troll, 1986), *The High
Voyage* (Viking, 1977)

Iris Litt 🎤 ✈   P
252 W 11 St
New York, NY 10014
    Pubs: *Word Love* (Cosmic Trend, 1996), *Love's
Shadow: Anth* (Crossing Pr, 1993), *Icarus, Travellers'
Tales, Pacific Coast Jrnl, Onthebus, Lactuca, Earth's
Daughters, Poetry Now, Central Park, Pearl*

Larry Litt 🎤 ✈   PP&W
3515 84th St. #3D
Jackson Heights, NY 11372, 718-478-2929
Internet: humornet@aol.com
    Pubs: *Aesop's America* (Oralit Pr, 1995), *eine DATA
base* (Germany; Edition Cantz, 1993), *Art 20/21 The
Turn of the Century* (S. Korea; Taejon Pr, 1993),
Downtown, Street News, The Fugue
I.D.: Fluxus, Advocacy. Groups: Prisoners, Teenagers

Susan Litwack   P
752 W End Ave, #6F
New York, NY 10025, 212-663-1379
    Pubs: *Mudfish, SPR, Outerbridge, Puerto del Sol,
Cincinnati Poetry Rev, Zone 3*

Tsaurah Litzky 🎤 ✈   P
1 Old Fulton St
Brooklyn, NY 11201-6908, 718-875-1107
Internet: tsaurah@mindspring.com
    Pubs: *Kamikaze Lover* (Appearances, 1999), *Blessing
Poems* (Synaethesia Pr, 1996), *Blue Bird Buddha of No
Regrets* (Apathy Pr, 1994), *Best American Erotica: Anth*
(S&S, 2001, 1999, 1997, 1995), *Unmade Bed: Anth*
(Borders, 1999), *Long Shot, Rant, Pink Pages*

Jay Liveson 🎤 ✈   P
3671 Hudson Manor Terr
Riverdale, NY 10463, 718-796-3750
Internet: jliveson@pol.net
    Pubs: *What Counts* (Fithian Pr, 2000), *Atlanta Rev,
Mediphors, Judaism, New England Jrnl of Medicine,
Modern Haiku, JAMA, Riverrun, Western Jrnl of
Medicine, Einstein Qtly, Hollins Critic, Plainsongs*
Lang: Hebrew

Bernard Livingston 🎤 ✈   W
235 W End Ave, #3E
New York, NY 10023, 212-873-8571
    Pubs: *Closet Red* (Waverly, 1985), *Papa's Burlesque
House* (Pyramid, 1971)

Zelda Lockhart 🎤 ✈   P&W
Sally Wofford-Girand, Elaine Markson Literary Agency, 44
Greenwich Ave, New York, NY 10011, 212-243-8480
    Pubs: *Sojourner, Wordwrights, Sinister Wisdom, Calyx*
I.D.: African-American, G/L/B/T. Groups: African-American,
G/L/B/T

Katinka Loeser   W
Watkins Loomis Agency, Inc, 133 E 35 St, Ste 1, New
York, NY 10016
    Pubs: *The Archers at Home, Tomorrow Will Be Monday*
(Atheneum, 1968, 1964), *New Yorker, McCall's*

Eloise Loftin   P
77 Eastern Pkwy #5B
Brooklyn, NY 11238, 718-783-7062

Robert Emmet Long   W
c/o Ruth Nathan, 80 Fifth Ave, #705, New York, NY
10011

Sabra Loomis   P
136 Waverly Pl, Apt 6E
New York, NY 10014, 212-645-5131
   Pubs: *Travelling on Blue* (Firm Ground Pr, 1998),
   Rosetree (Alice James Bks, 1989), *APR, American
   Voice, Poetry Ireland Rev, Cyphers, Salt Hill Jrnl,
   Salamander, Cincinnati Poetry Rev, Negative Capability*

Phillip Lopate 🎤 ✈   P&W
402 Sackett St
Brooklyn, NY 11231
Internet: plopate@aol.com
   Pubs: *Portrait of My Body* (Anchor, 1996), *Against Joie
   de Vivre* (Poseidon, 1989), *The Rug Merchant* (Viking,
   1987), *Paris Rev, Harper's, Threepenny Rev, SW Rev,
   Parnassus, Boulevard*

Judy Lopatin   W
925 Union St, #6C
Brooklyn, NY 11215, 718-399-7903
   Pubs: *Modern Romances* (Fiction Collective, 1986), *AM
   Lit: Anth* (Edtn Druckhaus, 1992), *Lone Star Lit Qtly,
   VLS, Between C&D, Witness, Europe*

Barry Lopez   W
c/o Peter Matson, Sterling Lord Literistic, 65 Bleecker St,
New York, NY 10012, 212-780-6050
   Pubs: *Light Action in the Caribbean, Field Notes*
   (Knopf, 2000, 1994), *Crow & Weasel* (North Point Pr,
   1990), *Winter Count* (Scribner, 1981), *Georgia Rev,
   Paris Rev, Story, Esquire, American Short Fiction,
   Manoa*

Eileen Lottman   W
Karpfinger Agency, 357 W 20 St, New York, NY
10011-3379, 212-691-2690
   Pubs: *She & I* (Morrow, 1991), *After the Wind* (Dell,
   1979)

Richard L. Loughlin   P
83-57 118 St #4D
Kew Gardens, NY 11415-2366
   Pubs: *Verses Vice Verses, Harian Creative Awards
   Anth* (Harian Creative Pr, 1980, 1981)

Esther Louise 🎤 ✈   P
568-3 Louisiana Ave
Brooklyn, NY 11239, 718-942-3001
Internet: elm@con2.com
   Pubs: *Confirmations Anth* (Quill, 1983), *Essence, City,
   Obsidian, American Rag, Bopp, Freshtones*

Cortnie A. Lowe   PP&P
172 St Marks Ave
Brooklyn, NY 11238
   Pubs: *Hexagram* (Poets Union Pr, 1977), *Partisan Rev*

Marilyn Lowen   P
286 South St, #16A
New York, NY 10002, 212-227-5364
   Pubs: *Vague* (Fire Sign Pr, 1983), *Reflections: Anth*
   (Diana Pr, 1971), *City, The New Women*

Bruce Lowery   W
Georges Borchardt Inc., 136 E 57 St, New York, NY
10022, 212-753-5785

Carmen D. Lucca 🎤 ✈   PP
3131 Grand Concourse
Bronx, NY 10468, 718-367-0780
   Pubs: *Maboiti, Carver of Birds, Bilingual Edtn,
   Brushstrokes & Landscapes* (Poets' Refuge, 2000,
   1990), *Latino Mothers: Anth* (Lee & Low Bks, 2000),
   *Puerto Rico's Ateneo 1992, Brujula-Compass, Ashland
   Poetry Pr*
Lang: Spanish. Groups: Children, Seniors

Thomas Luhrmann   P
468 Riverside Dr, #82A
New York, NY 10027, 212-663-3372
   Pubs: *The Objects in the Garden* (Wesleyan U Pr,
   1982)

K. Curtis Lyle   P
132-11 Foch Blvd
South Ozone Park, NY 11420, 718-659-4776
   Pubs: *Fifteen Predestination Weather Reports* (Beyond
   Baroque, 1976)

Charles H. Lynch 🎤 ✈   P
263 Eastern Pkwy, #5B
Brooklyn, NY 11238-6335, 718-638-3047
   Pubs: *New Rain: The Men's Issue: Anth* (Blind Beggar
   Pr, 1999), *Rattapallax, Way Station, Black American Lit
   Forum, World Order, Black Scholar, Chelsea, Hanging
   Loose, Crab Orchard Rev, Obsidian,*
Groups: African-American, Teenagers

Ellen Windy Aug Lytle   P&W
80 N Moore St, #9B
New York, NY 10013, 212-571-6774
   Pubs: *Factory Fish: Selected Short Fiction, MSS* (Linear
   Arts Pr, 1998, 1998), *Lettuce After Moon* (Ikon Pr,
   1993), *Down Under Manhattan Bridge: Anth* (Dan
   Freeman, 1996), *Global City Rev, And Then,
   Crossroads, Downtown, Lowell Rev, Mind the Gap*

Jackson Mac Low 🎤 ✈   PP&P
42 N Moore St, #6
New York, NY 10013-2468, 212-226-3346
Internet: tarmac@pipeline.com
   Pubs: *20 Forties* (Zasterle, 1999), *Barnesbook* (Sun &
   Moon Pr, 1996), *42 Merzgedichte in Memoriam Kurt
   Schwitters* (Station Hill, 1994), *Sulfur, Talisman,
   Conjunctions, Crayon, Chain*

Norman MacAfee 🎤 ✈   P
55 W 11 St #8D
New York, NY 10011-8692, 212-924-8247
Internet: idt.net/~miguelc/forest.html
   Pubs: *A New Requiem* (Cheap Rev Pr, 1988), *Hanging
   Loose, The World, Rouge*

James MacGuire   P&W
412 E 55 St, Apt 3H
New York, NY 10022, 212-838-0651
   Pubs: *Dusk on Lake Tanganyika* (Fermanagh Pr, 1999),
   Ironwood, Southern Rev, America, Kansas Qtly

Ginny MacKenzie   P&W
66 Grand St
New York, NY 10013, 212-966-5643
   Pubs: *By Morning* (Coyote Pr, 1984), *Boulevard, Iowa
   Rev, Agni, New Letters, Pequod, Ploughshares*

Elizabeth Macklin   P
207 W 14 St, #5F
New York, NY 10011
   Pubs: *A Woman Kneeling in the Big City* (Norton,
   1992), *Best American Poetry: Anth* (Scribner, 1993),
   *Paris Rev, Nation, Threepenny Rev, SW Rev, New
   Yorker, Lyra*

Phillip Mahony   P
PO Box 947
New York, NY 10021
   Pubs: *Supreme, Catching Bodies* (North Atlantic Bks,
   1989, 1986)

Norman Mailer   W
ICM, 40 W 57 St, New York, NY 10019, 212-556-5600

Gerard Malanga   P
221 Mott St, #8
New York, NY 10012
   Pubs: *Mythologies of the Heart* (Black Sparrow Pr,
   1996), *Night Errands: Anth* (U Pitt Pr, 1998), *Purple*

Michael Malinowitz   P
41 John St #2A
New York, NY 10038-3715, 212-473-5144
   Pubs: *Michael's Ear* (Groundwater Pr, 1993), *Best
   American Poetry: Anth* (Scribner, 1988), *Private, Poetry
   Motel, Bad Henry Rev, Brooklyn Rev*

George Malko   W
36 W 84 St
New York, NY 10024
   Pubs: *Luna* (Pan Bks Ltd 1980), *Take What You Will*
   (Pyramid Bks 1975), *Inkwell, Red Rock Rev, North
   Dakota Qtly, Riversedge, Licking River Rev, Distillery,
   Pleiades*

Michael Malone   W
c/o Owen Laster, William Morris Agency, 1325 Ave of the
Americas, New York, NY 10019, 212-586-5100
   Pubs: *Handling Sin, Foolscap, Uncivil Seasons, Time's
   Witness* (Washington Sq Bks, 1992, 1992, 1991, 1990),
   Playboy, Nation, Partisan Rev

Carolina Mancuso 🎤 ✈   W
c/o PSC, 123 7th Ave, Brooklyn, NY 11215
Internet: caro50@aol.com
   Pubs: *Word of Mouth, Vols II, I: Anth, Love, Struggle &
   Change: Anth* (Crossing Pr, 1991, 1990, 1988), *Amelia,
   Ikon*
Groups: Prisoners, G/L/B/T

Allen Mandelbaum   P
CUNY Graduate Center, 33 W 42 St, New York, NY
10036, 212-879-6076
   Pubs: *A Lied of Letter Press* (Pennyroyal, 1980),
   Chelmaxioms (Godine, 1978), *Denver Qtly, Poetry*

Norman Manea   W
201 W 70 St, #10-I
New York, NY 10023
   Pubs: *The Black Envelope* (FSG, 1996), *On Clowns:
   The Dictator & the Artist* (Grove Pr, 1992), *TriQtly,
   Partisan, New Republic, Paris Rev, Salmagundi*

Peggy Mann   W
46 W 94 St
New York, NY 10025
   Pubs: *Reader's Digest, McCall's, Good Housekeeping*

D. Keith Mano   W
392 Central Pk W, #6P
New York, NY 10025
   Pubs: *The Fergus Dialogues* (Intnl Scholars Pub, 1998),
   Take Five (Dalkey Archive Pr, 1998), *Topless* (Random
   Hse, 1991), *Playboy, National Rev*

Jaime Manrique 🎤 ✈   P&W
33 Bank St, #5
New York, NY 10014, 212-929-4960
Internet: jmardila@aol.com
   Pubs: *Eminent Maricones: Arenas, Lorca, Puig, & Me*
   (U Wisconsin Pr, 1999), *Colombian Gold* (Painted Leaf
   Pr, 1998), *Twilight at the Equator* (Faber & Faber,
   1997), *My Night with Federico Garcia Lorca*
   (Groundwater Pr, 1995)
Lang: Spanish. I.D.: Latino/Latina. Groups: G/L/B/T,
Latino/Latina

Jan Marino   W
c/o Dorothy Markinko, McIntosh & Otis, Inc, 310 Madison
Ave, New York, NY 10017
    Pubs: *Searching for Atticus* (S&S, 1997), *The Day That
Elvis Came to Town* (Little, Brown, 1991)

Wendy Mark   P
2 W 67 St #9D
New York, NY 10023
    Pubs: *Prairie Schooner, Literary Cupboard, Res Gestae*

Sol Markoff   P
13 W 13 St, #3CS
New York, NY 10011, 212-243-8663
    Pubs: *Anthology of World Haiku* (Kubota Pr, 1979),
Seventeen Grains of Sand (Print Center, 1976)

David Markson 🎤   W
215 W 10 St, #3E
New York, NY 10014-2913, 212-243-8688
    Pubs: *Reader's Block, Wittgenstein's Mistress* (Dalkey
Archive Pr, 1996, 1988)

Julia Markus   W
Harriet Wasserman Agency, 137 E 36 St, New York, NY
10016
    Pubs: *A Change of Luck* (Viking/Penguin, 1991),
American Rose, Friends Along the Way, Uncle (Dell,
1990, 1986, 1986)

Regina Marler   W
Maia Gregory Assoc, 311 E 72 St, New York, NY 10021,
212-288-0310
    Pubs: *Carolina Qtly, Chattahoochee Rev, NAR, NW
Rev*

Elizabeth Marraffino   P
75 Bank St, #6H
New York, NY 10014, 212-691-9806
    Pubs: *Blue Moon for Ruby Tuesday* (Contact II Pub,
1981), *Choice, Sun, The Dream Book, Nation*

Paule Marshall   W
Faith Childs Literary Agency, 275 W 96 St, New York, NY
10025, 212-662-1232
    Pubs: *Brown Girl, Brownstones* (Feminist Pr, 1996), *The
Chosen Place, The Timeless People* (Vintage Pr, 1992),
Daughters (Atheneum, 1991), *Praisesong for the Widow*
(Putnam, 1983)

Charles Martin   P
116 Pinehurst Ave, Hudson View Gardens A-64, New
York, NY 10033-1755, 212-781-3500
    Pubs: *What the Darkness Proposes, Steal the Bacon*
(Johns Hopkins U Pr, 1996, 1987), *Boulevard, Hellas,
The Formalist, Threepenny Rev, Tennessee Qtly*

Paula Martinac 🎤   W
237 E 26 St #2-E
New York, NY 10010-1952
Internet: pmartinac@aol.com
    Pubs: *Chicken* (Alyson Pub, 1997), *Home Movies, Out
of Time, Voyages Out* (Seal Pr, 1993, 1990, 1989), *Art
& Understanding, Queer City, Conditions, Sinister
Wisdom, Blithe Hse Qtly*
Groups: G/L/B/T

Andrew Marum   W
3640 Johnson Ave, Apt 7F
Bronx, NY 10463, 212-601-3748
    Pubs: *Follies & Foibles* (Facts On File, 1984)

Donna Masini   P&W
PO Box 5, Prince St Sta
New York, NY 10012, 212-260-0496
    Pubs: *About Yvonne* (Norton, 1997), *The Kind of
Danger* (Beacon Pr, 1994), *Georgia Rev, Paris Rev,
Parnassus, Boulevard, VLS*

Carole Maso   W
Georges Borchardt Inc., 136 E 57 St, New York, NY
10022, 212-753-5785
    Pubs: *Defiance* (Dutton, 1998), *The American Woman
in the Chinese Hat* (Plume, 1995), *Ghost Dance* (Ecco
Pr, 1995), *APR, Common Knowledge, Rev of
Contemporary Fiction, Bomb, Nerve, Conjunctions*

Bobbie Ann Mason 🎤 ✈   W
c/o Amanda Urban, ICM, 40 W 57 St, New York, NY
10019, 212-556-5764
    Pubs: *Clear Springs* (Random Hse, 1999), *Feather
Crowns, Shiloh* (HC, 1993, 1982), *Love Life, In Country*
(H&R, 1989, 1985), *Southern Rev, DoubleTake,
Harper's, Story, New Yorker, Atlantic, Paris Rev*

Greg Masters 🎤 ✈   P&W
437 E 12 St, #26
New York, NY 10009-4042, 212-777-2714
Internet: www.artomatic.com/~gmasters
    Pubs: *The Poem & Other Poems* (Skylab Pr, 2000), *My
Women & Men, Part 2* (Crony Bks, 1980), *Nuyorican
Poetry Anth* (H Holt, 1994)

Harry Mathews 🎤 ✈   P&W
Maxine Groffsky Literary Agency, 2 Fifth Ave, New York,
NY 10011, 212-473-0004
    Pubs: *Oulipo Compendium* (Atlas Pr, 1998), *The
Journalist, Singular Pleasures* (Dalkey Archive Pr, 1997,
1993), *Out of Bounds* (Burning Deck Pr, 1989), *The
Orchard* (Bamberge Bks, 1988), *Yale Rev, Brick: A
Literary Jrnl, Paris Rev*

Mindy Matijasevic P&W
2877 Grand Concourse, #2J
Bronx, NY 10468, 718-933-9209
  Pubs: *Lynx Eye, Anna's House, Howling Dog, Portable Wall, Free Focus, Kana, Impetus, Rebirth of Artemis, A Taste of Summer, Amazon*

Peter Matthiessen W
Donadio & Olson, Inc, 121 W 27 St, Ste 704, New York, NY 10001, 212-691-8077

Sharon Mattlin P
60 E 4 St, #21
New York, NY 10003, 212-475-7110
  Pubs: *The Big House: A Collection of Poets' Prose: Anth* (Ailanthus Pr, 1978), *Telephone, Dragonfly*

Susan Maurer 🎤 ✈ P
210 E 15 St, #9P
New York, NY 10003
  Pubs: *By the Blue Light of the Morning Glory* (Linear Arts, 1997), *Self Help: Anth* (Semiotext(e), 2001), *Cafe Nico Anth* (Venom Pr, 1996), *Gare du Nord, Virginia Qtly Rev, Crazyhorse, Brooklyn Rev, American Voice, Orbis, Prisoners of the Night*

Bernadette Mayer P&W
172 E 4 St, #9B
New York, NY 10009, 212-254-5308
  Pubs: *The Formal Field of Kissing* (Catchword Papers, 1990), *Sonnets* (Tender Buttons, 1990)

Jane Mayhall P&W
15 W 67 St, #6MW
New York, NY 10023-6226
  Pubs: *Treasury of American Short Stories: Anth* (Dell, 1994), *Best of Wind Literary Mag: Anth* (Wind Pubs, 1994), *Confrontation, Partisan Rev, New Renaissance, Hudson Rev, New Yorker, New Letters, Shenandoah*

Norma Fox Mazer W
Elaine Markson Literary Agency, 44 Greenwich Ave, New York, NY 10011, 212-243-8480
  Pubs: *When She Was Good* (Arthur Levine/Scholastic, 1997), *Missing Pieces, Silver, After the Rain* (Morrow, 1995, 1988, 1987), *Heartbeat* (Bantam, 1989), *English Jrnl*

Charles McCarry W
c/o Owen Laster, William Morris Agency, 1325 Ave of the Americas, New York, NY 10019, 212-586-5100
  Pubs: *The Better Angels, The Secret Lovers* (Dutton, 1979, 1977)

Robbie McCauley PP
223 E 4 St, #4
New York, NY 10009, 212-473-1801

Rebecca McClanahan 🎤 ✈ P&W
244 W 54 St #800
New York, NY 10019, 212-245-3619
Internet: mcclanmuse@aol.com
  Pubs: *Naked As Eve, The Intersection of X & Y* (Copper Beech Pr, 2000, 1996), *One Word Deep* (Ashland Poetry Pr, 1993), *Best American Poetry: Anth* (Scribner, 1998), *Southern Rev, Shenandoah, Kenyon Rev, Gettysburg Rev*

Michael McClure P&W
New Directions, 80 8th Ave, New York, NY 10011
  Pubs: *Three Poems* (Penguin, 1995), *Simple Eyes, Rebel Lions* (New Directions, 1994, 1991), *Testa Coda* (Rizzoli Bks, 1991), *Love Lion* (Video; Mystic Fire Video, 1991)

Suzanne McConnell 🎤 ✈ W
133 W 24 St, 5th Fl
New York, NY 10011-1936, 212-620-4196
Internet: smcconnell2@mindspring.com
  Pubs: *Personal Fiction Writing: Anth* (Teachers & Writers, 1984), *Kalliope, Earth's Daughters, Fiddlehead, Green Mountains Rev, Calyx, Little Mag, Olive Tree Rev, Dreamworks, Appearances*
Groups: Prisoners, Teenagers

Mary Joneve McCormick P
427 W 51 St, #4E
New York, NY 10019
Internet: http://www.quicklink.com/~joneve
  Pubs: *Small Bird Bones: Anth* (New Pr, 1993), *Single Flower, Japanophile, Soul to Soul, New Pr, Golden Isis, Smoke Signals, Nomad's Choir, Standard, Sisyphus*

James McCourt W
c/o Vincent Virga, 145 E 22 St, New York, NY 10003
  Pubs: *Kaye Wayfaring in "Avenged"* (Knopf, 1984), *Mawrdew Czgowchwz* (FSG, 1975), *New Yorker*

Sharyn McCrumb W
Dominick Abel Literary Agency, 146 W 82 St, New York, NY 10024, 212-877-0710
  Pubs: *The Ballad of Frankie Silver, The Rosewood Casket* (Dutton, 1998, 1996), *She Walks These Hills, Hangman's Beautiful Daughter* (Scribner, 1994, 1992), *Appalachian Heritage, Writer's Digest*

Alice McDermott W
Harriet Wasserman Agency, 137 E 36 St, New York, NY 10016
  Pubs: *Charming Billy, At Weddings & Wakes, That Night* (FSG, 1998, 1992, 1987), *A Bigamist's Daughter* (Random Hse, 1982), *Ms., Mademoiselle*

Joyce McDonald 🎤 ✈ W
McIntosh & Otis, Inc, 353 Lexington Ave, New York, NY 10016
Internet: jmcdonald@nac.net
    Pubs: *Shadow People, Swallowing Stones, Comfort Creek* (Delacorte, 2000, 1997, 1996), *Homebody, Mail-Order Kid* (Putnam 1991, 1988)
Groups: Children, Teenagers

Joseph McElroy W
Melanie Jackson Agency, 250 W 57 St, #1119, New York, NY 10107
    Pubs: *The Letter Left to Me* (Knopf, 1988), *Fathers & Sons: Anth* (Grove Pr, 1992)

Gardner McFall 🎤 ✈ P
924 W End Ave, #101
New York, NY 10025-3544, 212-678-1595
    Pubs: *The Pilot's Daughter* (Time Being Bks, 1996), *Naming the Animals* (Viking, 1994), *New Criterion, Nation, Ploughshares, Paris Rev, New Yorker*
Groups: Children

Thomas McGuane W
FSG, 19 Union Sq W, New York, NY 10003, 212-741-6900

Arona McHugh W
224 Davis Ave
Staten Island, NY 10310, 718-448-9089
    Pubs: *A Banner with a Strange Device* (Dell, 1965)

Brian McInerney P
200 W 81 St, #56
New York, NY 10024, 212-496-9084
    Pubs: *All My Life* (James L. Weil, 1985), *The Photographs Are Still Here* (Smoot Pr, 1984), *Origin*

Taylor Mead PP&P&W
163 Ludlow St
New York, NY 10002
    Pubs: *Excerpts from Son of Andy Warhol* (Hanuman Bks, 1990), *Living with the Animals: Anth* (Faber & Faber, 1995), *Outlook, Boss*

Rosemari Mealy P
WBAI Radio, 505 8th Ave, New York, NY 10018, 212-279-0707
    Pubs: *Confirmations* (Morrow/Quill, 1983), *Mickle Street Rev, Shooting Star, Sunbury*

James Mechem 🎤 W
420 E 54 St #3E
New York, NY 10022-5180, 212-888-1392
    Pubs: *Welcome to Bangkok* (Fell Swoop, 1997), *Della* (The Fault Pr, 1976), *Women Without Qualities* (Cafe Solo, 1973), *A Diary of Women* (Winter Hse Pr, 1970), *Joyful Noise: Anth* (Kings Estate, 1996)

Tony Medina P
PO Box 335
New York, NY 10026, 212-982-3158
    Pubs: *No Noose Is Good Noose* (Harlem River Pr, 1996), *Identity Lessons: Anth* (Viking Penguin, 1998), *Catch the Fire: Anth* (Riverhead Bks, 1998), *Long Shot, Vibe, African Voices, Paterson Lit Rev, Catalyst, Third World Viewpoints*

Susie Mee P
349 W 22 St
New York, NY 10011, 212-989-0405

Joshua Mehigan P
647 President St #2B
Brooklyn, NY 11215
    Pubs: *Confusing Weather* (Black Cat Pr, 1998), *Ploughshares, Verse, Poetry, Sewanee Rev, Pequod*

Ved Parkash Mehta W
The Wylie Agency, 250 W 57 St, Ste 2114, New York, NY 10107
    Pubs: *Three Stories of the Raj* (Scolar Pr, 1986), *Delinquent Chacha* (H&R, 1967), *Observer, Harper's, Statesman, New Yorker, Atlantic, Spectator*

Richard Meier P
16 Tompkins Pl
Brooklyn, NY 11231, 718-855-3683
    Pubs: *New Voices, 1984-1988: Anth* (Acad of American Poets, 1989), *APR, Chelsea, Mudfish, Phoebe, Graham Hse Rev, o.blek, Prairie Schooner*

Jesus Papoleto Melendez 🎤 ✈ P
PO Box 268
New York, NY 10029-0260, 212-828-5814
Internet: www.papoleto.com
    Pubs: *Concertos on Market Street* (Kemetic Images, 1993), *Street Poetry* (Barlenmir Hse, 1972), *In Defense of Mumia: Anth* (Writers & Readers, 1996), *Centro*
I.D.: Puerto-Rican, Post-Beat. Groups: Latino/Latina, Teenagers

D. H. Melhem 🎤 ✈ P&W
250 W 94 St, #2H
New York, NY 10025-6954, 212-865-9216
Internet: www.dhmelhemhome.att.net
    Pubs: *Country: An Organic Poem* (CCC, 1998), *Rest in Love* (Confrontation Mag Pr, 1995), *Blight* (Riverrun Pr, 1995), *Confrontation, Ararat, Home Planet News, New Pr, Paintbrush, Medicinal Purposes, Graffiti Rag*
I.D.: Arab-American

Daniel Meltzer W
251 W 74 St, #3D
New York, NY 10023, 212-362-4116
  Pubs: *The Square Root of Love* (Samuel French,
  1979), *The Pushcart Prize Anth* (Pushcart Pr, 1997), *A
  Contemporary Reader for Creative Writing: Anth* (HB,
  1994), *Prize Stories 1992: The O. Henry Awards: Anth*
  (Doubleday, 1992), *Vignette*

Samuel Menashe P
75 Thompson St #15
New York, NY 10012, 212-925-4105
  Pubs: *Collected Poems* (National Poetry Fdn, 1986),
  Penguin Modern Poets, Vol. 7: Anth (Penguin U.K.,
  1996), *An Introduction to Poetry: Anth* (HC, 1994),
  *Partisan Rev, New Yorker, Sunday Times London,
  Tundra*

Douglas A. Mendini P&W
403 W 54 St, #1D
New York, NY 10019, 212-541-6328
  Pubs: *Country Living, MacGuffin, Modernsense, Real
  Fiction, No, Clock Radio, Lactuca, Pudding, Details*

Claudia Menza 🎤 ✈ P
Claudia Menza Literary Agency, 1170 Broadway, New
York, NY 10001, 212-889-6850
  Pubs: *The Lunatics Ball, Cage of Wild Cries* (Mosaic
  Pr, 1994, 1990), *The Dream Book: Anth* (Schocken Pr,
  1985), *L.A. Times, Ploughshares*

Louise Meriwether 🎤 ✈ W
Ellen Levine Literary Agency, 15 E 26 St, Ste 801, New
York, NY 10010, 212-725-4501
  Pubs: *Shadow Dancing* (Ballantine, 2000), *Fragments of
  the Ark* (Pocket Bks, 1994), *Daddy Was a Number
  Runner* (Feminist Pr, 1984), *Essence, Icarus, Black
  Scholar, Harbor Rev*
I.D.: African-American

Daphne Merkin W
c/o Owen Laster, William Morris Agency, 1325 Ave of the
Americas, New York, NY 10019, 212-586-5100
  Pubs: *Enchantment* (HBJ, 1986), *Out of the Garden:
  Women Writing on the Bible: Anth* (Ballantine, 1994),
  New Yorker, Partisan Rev, Esquire

Susan Mernit P&W
164 Sterling Pl #1D
Brooklyn, NY 11217, 718-789-1396
  Pubs: *Moving to a New School* (Blackbird Pr, 1993),
  Tree Climbing (Membrane Pr, 1981), *Harper's, Agenda,
  Georgia Rev*

W. S. Merwin P&W
Alfred A Knopf, Inc, 201 E 50 St, New York, NY 10022,
212-751-2600
  Pubs: *Travels: Poems, The Lost Upland, The Rain in
  the Trees* (Knopf, 1993, 1992, 1998), *New Yorker*

Robin Messing P
660 Vanderbilt St
Brooklyn, NY 11218, 718-435-2696
  Pubs: *From Temporary Worker* (Lee-Lucas Pr, 1979), *#
  Mag, Dodeca, Telephone, Negative Capability, The
  Sycamore Rev, Brooklyn Rev*

Shelley Messing P&W
582 2nd St, #4C
Brooklyn, NY 11215, 718-768-2453
  Pubs: *Making Contact* (Voyage Out, 1978), *Women: A
  Journal of Liberation, Moving Out, Sojourner*

Mike Metz P
150 E 56 St, PHA
New York, NY 10022, 212-421-5443
  Pubs: *Street Fighting at Wall & Broad* (Macmillan,
  1982)

Claire Michaels P
35-50 82 St #6E
Jackson Heights, NY 11372, 718-672-7889
  Pubs: *Making Contact* (Willow Bee, 1989), *We Speak
  for Peace: Anth* (KIT, 1993), *Poetpourri, Aurora,
  Pudding, Parnassus, Wyoming: Hub of the Wheel*

Frank Michel 🎤 W
333 E 80 St, #3-I
New York, NY 10021-0664, 212-861-8258
Internet: fearstone@cs.com
  Pubs: *Witness, Bilingual Rev, American Writing,
  Gettysburg Rev, Indiana Rev, Glimmer Train, Crescent
  Rev, Alaska Qtly Rev, Qtly West*

Robert William Middlemiss W
Jonathan Dolger Agency, 49 E 96 St, #9B, New York, NY
10128, 212-427-1853
  Pubs: *Cormorant Documents* (Pageant Bks, 1989), *The
  Pelican's Clock* (Fawcett, 1981)

Betty Miles W
c/o Library Marketing, Random House, 225 Park Ave S,
New York, NY 10003, 212-254-1600
  Pubs: *The Sky Is Falling, The Tortoise & the Hare*
  (S&S, 1998, 1998), *Hey! I'm Reading, Save the Earth,
  Sink or Swim, I Would If I Could, Maudie & Me* (Knopf,
  1995, 1991, 1986, 1982, 1980)

Arthur Miller W
c/o Bridget Ashenberg, ICM, 40 W 57 St, New York, NY
10019, 212-556-5600
  Pubs: *The Creation of the World & Other Business,
  The Crucible, Death of a Salesman* (Viking Penguin,
  1973, 1953, 1949)

Ellen Miller W
c/o Jennifer Rodolph Walsh, The Writers Shop, 101 5th
Ave, 11th Floor, New York, NY 10003, 212-255-6515
  Pubs: *Like Being Killed* (Dutton, 1998)

Shelley Miller   P
299 W 12 St, #17H
New York, NY 10014
   Pubs: *World, Natl Poetry Mag of the Lower East Side,
   Tone, Cover, SoHo Arts Weekly, Inner Harvest, Arts
   New York*

Stephen Paul Miller   P
60 E 8 St, #6P
New York, NY 10003, 212-677-6739
   Pubs: *Art Is Boring for the Same Reason We Stayed
   in Viet Nam* (Domestic Pr, 1992), *Best American
   Poetry: Anth* (S&S, 1994), *Talisman*

Walter James Miller 🎙 ✈   P
100 Bleecker St #17-E
New York, NY 10012-2205, 212-674-1466
   Pubs: *Making An Angel* (Pylon, 1977),
   Hampden-Sydney Poetry Rev Anth (Hampden-Sydney,
   1990), *Croton Rev, Lit Rev, NYQ, Artemis, Poet Lore*

Joyce Milton   P
60 Plaza St, #6B
Brooklyn, NY 11238, 718-636-4471
   Pubs: *Save the Loonies* (Four Winds Pr, 1983), *The
   Rosenberg File* (HR&W, 1983)

Mark Mirsky   W
English Dept, CCNY, Convent Ave & 138 St, New York,
NY 10031, 212-650-5408
   Pubs: *The Red Adam* (Sun & Moon, 1990), *The Secret
   Table* (Macmillan, 1977), *The Qtly, Fiction, TriQtly,
   Mississippi Rev, Ways of Knowing, Partisan Rev,
   Massachusetts Rev*

Julia Mishkin   P
330 W 85 St, #1G
New York, NY 10024
   Pubs: *Cruel Duet* (QRL Poetry Series, 1986), *Poetry,
   Georgia Rev, Paris Rev, Nation, Iowa Rev*

Tom Mitchelson   PP&W
524 W 143 St, #3
New York, NY 10032, 212-690-5040
   Pubs: *Untold Lies As Love Tales* (WBAI, 1994), *Street
   Lights: Illuminating Tales of the Urban Black
   Experience: Anth* (Viking Penguin, 1995)

Charles Molesworth   P
109-23 71 Rd
Forest Hills, NY 11375, 718-268-8024
   Pubs: *Words to That Effect* (Seven Woods, 1981),
   Salmagundi

Ursule Molinaro   W
65 E 2 St
New York, NY 10003, 212-982-2204
   Pubs: *Power Dreamers* (McPherson, 1994), *Fat
   Skeletons* (Serif London, 1993), *Obsession: Anth*
   (Serpent's Tail, 1995), *Caprice, Manoa*

Timothy Monaghan 🎙   P
78-44 80 St
Glendale, NY 11385-7659
   Pubs: *5 A.M., Slipstream, Long Shot, NYQ, Negative
   Capability, Mudfish, Chiron Rev, Sulphur River, The
   Ledge, Poet Lore, Rattle, Birmingham Poetry Rev*

Susan Montez   P
875 W 181 St, #1E
New York, NY 10033, 212-781-5433
   Pubs: *Radio Free Queens* (Braziller, 1994), *NYQ, 13th
   Moon, Artful Dodge, Cream City Rev, Hampden-Sydney
   Poetry Rev, Long Shot, Puerto del Sol, Asylum*

Lorrie Moore   W
Melanie Jackson Agency, 250 W 57 St, Ste 1119, New
York, NY 10107
   Pubs: *Birds of America, Who Will Run the Frog
   Hospital?, Like Life, Anagrams* (Knopf, 1998, 1994,
   1990, 1986), *Forgotten Helper* (Kipling, 1987), *New
   Yorker, Paris Rev*

Susanna Moore   W
c/o Andrew Wylie, The Wylie Agency, 250 W 57 St, New
York, NY 10107, 212-246-0069
   Pubs: *In the Cut, Sleeping Beauties* (Knopf, 1995,
   1993), *The Whiteness of Bones* (Doubleday, 1989), *My
   Old Sweetheart* (HM, 1983)

Speer Morgan   W
c/o Esther Newberg, ICM, 40 W 57 St, New York, NY
10019, 573-882-4460
Internet: morganr@missouri.edu
   Pubs: *The Freshour Cylinders* (MacMurray & Beck,
   1998), *The Whipping Boy* (HM, 1994), *The Assemblers*
   (Dutton, 1986), *Brother Enemy* (Little, Brown, 1981),
   Belle Starr (Atlantic, 1979), *Harper's, Atlantic, Prairie
   Schooner, Iowa Rev*

Kyoko Mori   P&W
Ann Rittenberg Agency, 14 Montgomery Pl, Brooklyn, NY
11215, 212-886-9317
   Pubs: *Polite Lies, The Dream of Water, Shizuko's
   Daughter* (H Holt, 1998, 1996, 1993), *Prairie Schooner,
   Missouri Rev, Kenyon Rev, American Scholar,
   Crosscurrents, Denver Qtly, Paterson Rev*

John Morressy 🎤 ✈ W
William Morris Agency, 1325 Ave of the Americas, New York, NY 10019
  Pubs: *Mammoth Book of Comic Fantasy II: Anth* (Carroll & Graf, 1999), *Mladý Kedrigern A Pátráni Po Minulosti, Trocha Prace Bzneseneho Druhu* (Polaris, 1999, 1995), *The Juggler* (H Holt, 1996), *A Remembrance for Kedrigern* (Ace, 1990), *Sci Fi Age*
I.D.: Irish-American. Groups: College/Univ

James Cliftonne Morris P&W
Rivercross Publishing, 127 E 59 St, New York, NY 10022, 800-451-4522
  Pubs: *Potpourri from a Black Pen* (Rivercross Pr, 1995), *Poem of Love in the Long Run* (Professional Pr, 1994), *Phylon, Freedomways*

Mary Morris 🎤 ✈ P&W
Ellen Levine Literary Agency, 15 E 26 St, New York, NY 10010, 212-889-0620
  Pubs: *Acts of God* (Picador, 2000), *House Arrest, A Mother's Love, The Waiting Room* (Doubleday, 1996, 1993, 1989), *Ontario Rev, Paris Rev, Boulevard, Epoch, Crosscurrents*

Julia Morrison ✈ P
Seagate Music, 595 Columbus Ave, #9P, New York, NY 10024-1930
  Pubs: *Smile Right to the Bone* (Seagate, 1989), *New World Writing, Accent, Poetry, Prism Intl*
Groups: Prisoners, Libraries

Lillian Morrison 🎤 P
116 Pinehurst Ave, #F42
New York, NY 10033, 212-928-2662
  Pubs: *Slam Dunk* (Hyperion Bks, 1995), *Whistling the Morning In* (Boyds Mills Pr, 1992), *I Scream; You Scream: Anth* (August Hse, 1997), *Confrontation, American Writing, Poets On, Fan, Light, Aethlon*

Toni Morrison W
Janklow & Nesbit Assoc, 598 Madison Ave, New York, NY 10022-1614
  Pubs: *Paradise, Jazz, Tar Baby, Song of Solomon, Sula* (Knopf, 1998, 1992, 1981, 1977, 1974), *Beloved* (Random Hse, 1987)

Bradford Morrow W
21 E 10 St Apt 3E
New York, NY 10003
  Pubs: *Trinity Fields* (Viking Penguin, 1995), *The New Gothic* (Random Hse/Vintage, 1993), *The Almanac Branch* (Linden Pr/S&S, 1991), *Conjunctions, VLS*

Charlie Morrow PP&P
365 W End Ave
New York, NY 10024, 212-799-0636
  Pubs: *Exiled in the Word: Anth* (Copper Canyon Pr, 1989), *Ear Collective, Raven, Unmuzzled Ox*

Carl Morse 🎤 ✈ P
460 W 24 St, #17B
New York, NY 10011
  Pubs: *Columbia Anth of Gay Literature* (Columbia U Pr, 1998), *The Badboy Book of Erotic Poetry: Anth* (Masquerade Bks, 1995), *Gay & Lesbian Poetry in Our Time: Anth* (St. Martin's Pr, 1988), *3 New York Poets: Anth* (Gay Men's Pr, 1987), *Poetry London*

Jo-Ann Mort P
40 Prospect Pk W, Apt 3C
Brooklyn, NY 11215, 718-499-6261
  Pubs: *Without a Single Answer: Poems on Contemporary Israel: Anth* (Magnes Museum, 1990), *Social Text, Stand, Jewish Qtly, Pequod, Midstream*

Bette Ann Moskowitz W
Jonathan Dolger Agency, 49 E 96 St, New York, NY 10028, 212-427-1853
  Pubs: *Leaving Barney* (H Holt, 1988), *Appearances*

Stanley Moss P
Sheep Meadow Press, PO Box 1345,
Riverdale-On-Hudson, NY 10471
  Pubs: *The Intelligence of Clouds* (HBJ, 1989), *Skull of Adam* (Horizon Pr, 1979), *Poetry*

Elaine Mott P
80-31 210 St
Hollis Hills, NY 11427, 718-776-8450
  Pubs: *Blood to Remember: American Poets on the Holocaust Anth* (Texas Tech U Pr, 1991), *Anth of Magazine Verse & Yearbook of American Poetry* (Monitor Bk Co, 1989)

Marnie Mueller P&W
119 W 77 St #5
New York, NY 10024
  Pubs: *The Climate of the Country, Green Fires* (Curbstone Pr, 1999, 1994), *Home to Stay, Asian-American Fiction by Women: Anth* (Greenfield Pr, 1990), *VLS, River Styx, Qtly West, Laurel Rev, Clinton Street, Five Fingers Rev*

Maureen Mulhern 🎤 ✈ P
440 E 88 St
New York, NY 10128-6688, 212-369-8791
Internet: maureen@juniperrecords.com
  Pubs: *Parallax* (Wesleyan, 1986), *Poetry, Crazyhorse, Phoebe, Prairie Schooner, Indiana Rev, Denver Qtly*

Hester Mundis W
Harold Ober Assoc, 425 Madison Ave, New York, NY 10017, 212-759-8600
  Pubs: *Just Humor Me* (Random Hse, 1996), *101 Ways to Avoid Reincarnation* (Workman Pub, 1989)

Jerrold Mundis   W
c/o Merrilee Heifetz, The Writers House, 21 W 26 St,
New York, NY 10010, 212-685-2605
    Pubs: *The Dogs* (Berkley, 1988), *The Retreat* (Warner,
    1985)

Carole Murray   P
214 Riverside Dr, #207
New York, NY 10025, 212-666-5967
    Pubs: *NAR, Driftwood East, Milkweed, Amelia, Cedar
    Rock, Womanchild*

William Murray   W
Helen Brann Agency, 157 W 57 St, New York, NY 10019,
212-247-3511
    Pubs: *Tip on a Dead Crab* (Viking, 1984), *New Yorker,
    Geo, Playboy, Esquire, Cosmopolitan*

Eileen Myles   P
86 E 3 St, #3C
New York, NY 10003, 212-982-4703
    Pubs: *Maxfield Parrish: Early & New Poems, Chelsea
    Girls* (Black Sparrow Pr, 1995, 1994), *APR, Denver
    Qtly, Valentine, Jejeune, XXXFruit, Zing*

Zakee Nadir   P
159 Ashford St
Brooklyn, NY 11207, 718-277-3916
    Pubs: *Don't Run, Listen* (Poet Tential Unltd, 1979)

Robert Nathan   W
350 Central Pk W
New York, NY 10025
    Pubs: *The White Tiger* (S&S, 1987), *Rising Higher*
    (Dial, 1981), *Harper's, New Republic, New York*

Elinor Nauen 🎤 ✈   P
27 1st Ave, #9
New York, NY 10003-9447, 212-677-3792
Internet: enauen@aol.com
    Pubs: *American Guys* (Hanging Loose Pr, 1997),
    *Ladies, Start Your Engines: Anth, Diamonds Are a
    Girl's Best Friend: Anth* (Faber & Faber, 1997, 1994),
    *The World, Exquisite Corpse, Long Shot, Fiction, Gas,
    Koff, NAW*
Groups: Prisoners, Children

Gloria Naylor 🎤 ✈   W
Sterling Lord Literistic, 65 Bleecker St, New York, NY
10012, 212-780-6050
    Pubs: *The Men of Brewster Place* (Hyperion, 1998),
    Bailey's Cafe (HBJ, 1992), *Children of the Night: The
    Best Short Stories By Black Writers: Anth* (Little, Brown,
    1996)

Shelley Neiderbach   P
39 Remsen St, #4B
Brooklyn, NY 11201, 718-875-5862
    Pubs: *Invisible Wounds* (Haworth Pr, 1985)

Stanley Nelson   P
454 37 St
Brooklyn, NY 11232, 718-788-6088
    Pubs: *Immigrant: Books III, II, I* (Birch Brook Pr, 1995,
    1993, 1990), *Long Shot, The Smith, Pinched Nerve,
    Kansas Qtly, Confrontation, For Now*

Vernita Nemec   PP
361 Canal St
New York, NY 10013, 212-925-4419

Cindy Nemser   W
41 Montgomery Pl
Brooklyn, NY 11215, 718-857-9456
    Pubs: *Eve's Delight* (Pinnacle, 1982), *Feminist Art Jrnl,
    Women: A Jrnl of Liberation, The Free Press*

Joan Nestle 🎤 ✈   P&W
215 W 92 St, #13A
New York, NY 10025, 212-873-3765
Internet: joannestle@aol.com
    Pubs: *A Fragile Union* (Cleis Pr, 1998), *A Restricted
    Country* (Pandora, 1996), Vintage *Bk of Intl Lesbian
    Fiction* (Vintage, 1999), *Women on Women 3: Anth*
    (Plume, 1996), *Sister & Brother: Anth* (Harper SF,
    1994)
I.D.: Jewish. Groups: G/L/B/T

Amos Neufeld   P
65 W 90 St, #9E
New York, NY 10024, 212-496-0683
    Pubs: *Blood to Remember: American Poets on the
    Holocaust: Anth* (Texas Tech U Pr, 1991), *Ghosts of
    the Holocaust: Anth* (Wayne State U Pr, 1989),
    Response

Joachim Neugroschel   P
447 Beach 136 St
Belle Harbor, NY 11694, 718-318-2147
    Pubs: *Extensions, Just Before Sailing*

Lucia Nevai 🎤   W
251 Central Pk W
New York, NY 10024
    Pubs: *Normal* (Algonquin, 1997), *Star Game* (U Iowa
    Pr, 1987), *Zoetrope: All Story: Anth* (HB, 2000),
    American Fiction: Anth (Birch Lane Pr, 1993), *NAR,
    North Dakota Qtly, Iowa Rev, NER, New Yorker, ACM,
    Gulf Coast, Literary Rev, atlantic unbound*

Leslie Newman   W
Georges Borchardt Inc., 136 E 57 St, New York, NY
10022, 212-753-5785
Groups: G/L/B/T, Jewish

Wade Newman 🎤 ✈   P
505 E 14 St, #9C
New York, NY 10009, 212-598-9483
   Pubs: *Testaments* (Somers Rocks Pr, 1996), *Edge City
   Rev, Pivot, Amer Arts Qtly, Kenyon Rev, Croton Rev,
   Cumberland Poetry Rev, Crosscurrents, Nebo, Nimrod,
   Confrontation*

Fae Myenne Ng   W
Donadio & Olson, Inc, 121 W 27 St, Ste 704, New York,
NY 10001
   Pubs: *Bone* (Hyperion, 1993), *Charlie Chan Is Dead:
   Anth* (Penguin, 1994), *Harper's, Pushcart Prize XII*

Joan Kane Nichols   W
165 Bennett Ave, #4D
New York, NY 10040, 212-702-4251
   Pubs: *All But the Right Folks* (Stemmer Hse, 1986)

M. M. Nichols   P
311 E 50 St, #5H
New York, NY 10022-7941, 212-759-8733
   Pubs: *Haiku World: Anth* (Kodansha Intl 1996),
   Timepieces: Anth (Cloverleaf Bks 1993), *Wind in the
   Long Grass: Anth* (S&S, 1991), *Salamander,
   Waterways, Modern Haiku, Frogpond*

Nina daVinci Nichols 🎤 ✈   W
305 W 13 St, #5H
New York, NY 10014, 212-924-1423
   Pubs: *Pirandello & Film* (U Nebraska Pr, 1996),
   Ariadne's Lives (Fairleigh Dickinson U Pr, 1995), *Child
   of the Night* (Bantam, 1985), *Behind the Veil: Anth*
   (Eden Pr, 1982), *Stages, American Bk Rev,
   Shakespeare Bulletin*

Richard Nickson   P
205 W 19 St
New York, NY 10011, 212-989-7833
   Pubs: *Stones: A Book of Epigrams* (Lithic Pr, 1998),
   Cause at Heart (w/Junius Scales; U Georgia Pr, 1987),
   Staves (Moretus Pr, 1977)

Hugh Nissenson   W
411 W End Ave
New York, NY 10024, 212-873-5193

Kathryn Nocerino 🎤 ✈   P
139 W 19 St, #2B
New York, NY 10011
   Pubs: *Death of the Plankton Bar & Grill, Wax Lips*
   (New Rivers Pr, 1987, 1980), *Candles in the Daytime*
   (Warthog Pr, 1986)

Suzanne Noguere 🎤 ✈   P
27 W 96 St #12B
New York, NY 10025, 212-865-1045
   Pubs: *Whirling Round the Sun* (Midmarch Arts Pr,
   1996), *A Formal Feeling Comes: Anth* (Story Line Pr,
   1994), *Poetry, Nation, Lit Rev, Sparrow*

James Nordlund   P
318 Third Ave, Apt 553
New York City, NY 10010
   Pubs: *Serendipity, Jones Av, Pink Cadillac, Poets
   Fantasy*

Constance Norgren   P
303A 16 St
Brooklyn, NY 11215-5504
   Pubs: *Yankee, Northland Qtly, Minnesota Rev, Tendril,
   Louisville Rev, Poetry Rev, Confrontation*

Charles North   P
c/o English Dept., Pace Univ, 1 Pace Plaza, New York,
NY 10038, 212-346-1410
   Pubs: *New & Selected Poems* (Sun & Moon Pr, 1999),
   The Year of the Olive Oil (Hanging Loose Pr, 1989),
   Leap Year (Kulchur Fdn, 1978)

Jenifer Nostrand 🎤   P
11 Waverly Pl E
New York, NY 10003
   Pubs: *Bless the Day: Anth* (Kodansha America, 1998),
   *Cumberland Poetry Rev, Kansas Qtly, Louisville Rev,
   Birmingham Poetry Rev, Hiram Poetry Rev, Greensboro
   Rev, Bridge*

Craig Nova 🎤 ✈   W
Peter Matson, Sterling Lord Literistic, 65 Bleecker St, New
York, NY 10012, 212-780-6050
   Pubs: *Universal Donor, Book of Dreams* (HM, 1998,
   1994), *Trombone* (Grove, 1992), *Esquire, Paris Rev*

Barbara Novack 🎤 ✈   P
134-18 228 St
Laurelton, NY 11413-2441, 718-527-3674
   Pubs: *On a Sea of Sighs, A Rainbow in the Sand, Still
   Life* (Michael Gaily Bks, 1999, 1999, 1999), *CQ, LIQ,
   South Coast Poetry Jrnl, Cape Rock, Alms House
   Sampler, Verve, Nassau Rev*

Minda Novek   PP
226 W 47 St, 2nd Fl
New York, NY 10036-1413, 212-921-9040
   Pubs: *Daily News Sunday Supplement, Adamant Jrnl,
   Seaport Mag*

D. Nurkse 🎤 ✈   P
598 17 St, #1
Brooklyn, NY 11218, 718-788-0024
Internet: Dnurkse@hotmail.com
  Pubs: *Leaving Xaia, Voices Over Water* (Four Way
  Bks, 2000, 1996), *Staggered Lights* (Owl Creek Pr,
  1990), *Shadow Wars* (Hanging Loose, 1988), *APR,
  Poetry, Kenyon Rev, Hudson Rev, New Yorker,
  Hanging Loose*
Lang: French, Spanish. Groups: Prisoners, Seniors

Michael O'Brien   P
400 W 23 St, #6L
New York, NY 10011
Internet: michaelobrien@mindspring.com
  Pubs: *Sills: Selected Poems of Michael O'Brien* (Zoland
  Bks, 2000), *The Floor & the Breath, Veil, Hard Rain*
  (Cairn Edtns, 1994, 1986), *Blue Springs* (Sun, 1976)

Francis V. O'Connor 🎤 ✈   P
250 E 73 St, #11C
New York, NY 10021-4310, 212-988-8927
Internet: http://members.aol.com/FVOC
  Pubs: *Twelve Sonnets fro the Abstract Expressionists*
  (Art Jrnl, 1988), *And What Rough Beast: Anth* (Ashland
  Poetry Pr, 1999), *Whelks Walk Rev*

Stephen O'Connor   P&W
Witherspoon Assoc, Inc, 235 E 31 St, New York, NY
10016, 212-889-8626
  Pubs: *Rescue* (Harmony Bks, 1989), *Columbia,
  Massachusetts Rev, The Qtly, Fiction Intl, Partisan Rev,
  Hubbub*

Sidney Offit 🎤 ✈   W
23 E 69 St
New York, NY 10021, 212-737-5144
  Pubs: *He Had It Made* (Beckham Classic Reprint,
  1999), *The Bookie's Son, A Memoir* (St. Martin's Pr,
  1995), *What Kind of Guy Do You Think I Am?*
  (Lippincott, 1970)
Groups: Children, Seniors

Ned O'Gorman   P
2 Lincoln Sq
New York, NY 10023, 212-799-0806

Jennifer O'Grady 🎤 ✈   P
250 W 94 St, #6D
New York, NY 10025-6954
  Pubs: *White* (Mid-List Pr, 1999), *American Poetry: Anth*
  (Carnegie Mellon, 2000), *Yale Rev, Kalliope, Colorado
  Rev, Antioch Rev, Georgia Rev, Poetry, Poetry East,
  Seneca Rev, Southern Rev, Harper's, 13th Moon,
  Western Humanities Rev, SW Rev, Kenyon Rev*

Valery Oisteanu   P
170 2nd Ave, #2A
New York, NY 10003, 212-777-3597
  Pubs: *Zen-Dada Meditations for the 3rd Millennium*
  (Linear Arts Pr, 1998), *Planet Dada, Temporary
  Immortality, King of Penguins, Moons of Venus* (Pass
  Pr, 1996, 1995, 1992, 1990), *Anth of American Poetry*
  (Vrshatz-Belgrade-Library Pr, 1997), *New Observations*

Adrian Oktenberg 🎤 ✈   P
c/o Ellen Yaroshevsky, CLC, 55 5th Ave, Rm 1116, New
York, NY 10003-4301, 212-790-0410
  Pubs: *The Bosnia Elegies* (Paris Pr, 1997), *Drawing in
  the Dirt* (Malachite & Agate, 1997), *Luna, Qtly West,
  Prairie Schooner, Provincetown Arts, Salamander, WRB,
  American Voice*
Groups: G/L/B/T, Political Groups

Sharon Olds   P
Alfred A Knopf, Inc, 201 E 50 St, New York, NY 10022,
212-751-2600
  Pubs: *The Gold Cell, The Dead & the Living* (Knopf,
  1987, 1984), *Satan Says* (U Pitt Pr, 1980)

Sharon Olinka 🎤 ✈   P
23-38 28 St
Astoria, NY 11105, 718-267-1792
Internet: sazibree@aol.com
  Pubs: *A Face Not My Own* (West End Pr, 1995)
Groups: Children, Seniors

Sondra Spatt Olsen   W
201 W 16 St, #10A
New York, NY 10011
  Pubs: *Traps* (U Iowa Pr, 1991), *Yale Rev, Ontario Rev,
  New Yorker, Iowa Rev, Boulevard, Redbook, Mississippi
  Rev, Confrontation, Qtly West*

Gregory Orfalea   P&W
Tom Wallace, The Wallace Literary Agency, 177 E 70 St,
New York, NY 10021, 212-570-9090
  Pubs: *Messengers of the Lost Battalion* (The Free Pr,
  1995), *Before the Flames* (U Texas Pr, 1988), *Antioch
  Rev, TriQtly, CSM, Epoch*

Peter Orlovsky   P
PO Box 582, Stuyvesant Sta
New York, NY 10009
  Pubs: *Straight Hearts' Delight* (w/Allen Ginsberg; Gay
  Sunshine Pr, 1980), *Clean Asshole Poems & Smiling
  Vegetable Songs* (City Lights Bks, 1978)

Miguel A. Ortiz   P
516 Seventh St
Brooklyn, NY 11215

Susan Osterman 🎤 ✈   P
610 W 115 St #94
New York, NY 10025, 212-678-1115
   Pubs: *A Head of Her Time* (Theo, 1996), *Strip Mining* (Cambric Pr, 1987), *Village Voice, Cover, Downtown*

Suzanne Ostro 🎤   P&W
321 W 94 St, #2W
New York, NY 10025
Internet: pombooks@aol.com
   Pubs: *Dream of the Whale* (Toothpaste Pr, 1982), *Demolition Zone* (New Rivers Pr, 1975), *River Styx, Exquisite Corpse, Paris Rev, Partisan Rev, Open Places, Yardbird*

Iris Owens   W
c/o Arlene Donovan, ICM, 40 W 57 St, New York, NY 10019, 212-556-5600

Cynthia Ozick   W
c/o Theron Raines, Raines & Raines, 71 Park Ave, New York, NY 10016
   Pubs: *Quarrel & Quandary, Fame & Folly* (Knopf, 2000, 1996), *The Puttermesser Papers* (Vintage, 1998), *A Cynthia Ozick Reader* (Indiana U Pr, 1996)

Richard Pa   P
210 E 15 St, #14K
New York, NY 10003, 212-420-1854
   Pubs: *Landscape of Skin & Single Rooms* (Monday Morning Pr, 1973), *Chester H. Jones Anth* (Chester H. Jones Fdn, 1997), *Prairie Schooner, Paris Rev, Windless Orchard*

William Packard   P&W
232 W 14 St, #2A
New York, NY 10011, 212-255-8531
   Pubs: *Art of Poetry Writing* (St. Martin's Pr, 1990), *The Poet's Dictionary* (H&R, 1989)

Eve Packer 🎤 ✈   P&PP
78 Bank St, #17
New York, NY 10014-2102, 212-243-3496
Internet: evebpacker@aol.com
   Pubs: *west frm 42nd* (CD; Altsax Records, 1998), *Showworld* (Kango Pub, 1996), *skulls head samba* (fly-by-night pr, 1994), *Hart, Jrnl, Café Rev, Ikon, Long Shot, Verve, Peau Sensible, Red Tape, What Happens Next, No Roses Rev, Excursus, Lungfull, Paramour*
Lang: Spanish

Ron Padgett   P&W
342 E 13 St, #6
New York, NY 10003-5811, 212-477-4472
   Pubs: *New & Selected Poems* (Godine, 1995), *Great Balls of Fire* (Coffee Hse Pr, 1990), *The Big Something* (The Figures, 1990)

Maggie Paley 🎤   W
c/o Jane Gelfman, Gelfman Schneider Literary Agents, Inc, 250 W 57 St, #2515, New York, NY 10107
   Pubs: *Elephant* (Groundwater Pr, 1990), *Bad Manners* (Clarkson Potter, 1986), *Mudfish, New Observations*

Marion Palm 🎤 ✈   P
705 41 St, #17
Brooklyn, NY 11232
   Pubs: *Islands of the Blest* (Print Ctr, 1993), *Nightingale Day Songs* (Wingate Pr, 1984), *Working Mother, Big Apple, Minneapolis Star & Tribune*
Lang: Swedish. Groups: Schools, Libraries

Bruce Palmer   W
Elaine Markson Literary Agency, 44 Greenwich Ave, New York, NY 10011, 212-243-8480
   Pubs: *The Karma Charmer* (Harmony Bks, 1994)

Anne Paolucci   P&W
166-25 Powells Cove Blvd
Beechhurst, NY 11357, 718-767-8380
   Pubs: *Terminal Degrees* (Novella, 1997), *Queensboro Bridge & Other Poems* (Potpourri Pubs, 1995), *Three Short Plays* (Griffon Hse Pubs, 1995), *The World & I, Pirandello Society Annual, Choice*

Helen Papell 🎤   P
720 W End Ave
New York, NY 10025-6299, 212-316-5821
   Pubs: *Talking with Eve Leah Hagar Miriam* (Jewish Women's Resource Ctr, 1996), *Lilith: Anth* (Jason Aronson, 1999), *Sarah's Daughters Sing: Anth* (KTAV, 1990), *Verve, Metis, Mildred, Negative Capability, Prairie Schooner, Jewish Women's Lit*
I.D.: Jewish, Seniors. Groups: Jewish, Seniors

Matthew Paris   P&W
645 E 14 St, Apt 9E
New York, NY 10009, 212-995-0299
   Pubs: *The Holy City* (Carpenter Pr, 1979), *Mystery* (Avon Bks, 1973), *Home Planet News, Generalist Papers, The Phoenix, Downtown, New Worlds, Brooklyn Lit Rev, Bright Hill*

Gwendolyn M. Parker   W
Marie Brown Assoc Inc, 625 Broadway, New York, NY 10012, 212-533-5534
   Pubs: *Trespassing: My Sojourn in the Halls of Privilege, These Same Long Bones* (HM, 1997, 1994)

Beth Passaro   W
514 W 110 St, #21
New York, NY 10025, 212-662-6224
   Pubs: *Columbia, NW Rev*

Vincent Passaro   W
Georges Borchardt Inc., 136 E 57 St, New York, NY
10022, 212-753-5785
    Pubs: *Lust, Violence, Sin, Magic: Esquire Anth* (Atlantic
Monthly Pr, 1993), *Best of the West: Anth* (Norton,
1992), *Harper's, Story, Willow Springs, NAW*

Ben Passikoff 🎤 ✈   P
73-07 164 St
Flushing, NY 11366
    Pubs: *Qtly Rev of Lit, Poetry Intl, Sarah Lawrence Rev,
Small Pond Mag, Verve, Connecticut River Rev,
Madison Rev, Painted Bride Qtly, Interim, Literal Latte*

Ann Patchett   W
c/o Lisa Bankoff, ICM, 40 W 57 St, New York, NY 10019,
212-556-5600
    Pubs: *Taft, The Patron Saint of Liars* (HM, 1994, 1992)

Kathryn Paulsen 🎤 ✈   W
340 W 28 St, #16E
New York, NY 10011-4764
    Pubs: *New Letters, West Branch, Sundog, Cottonwood
Rev, New Constellations*

Basil Payne   P
c/o Keating, 43-30 46 St, #4B, Sunnyside, NY 11104,
718-388-2184

Molly Peacock 🎤 ✈   P&W
505 E 14 St, #3-G
New York, NY 10009, 212-677-3535
Internet: peacockmol@aol.com
    Pubs: *Original Love* (Norton, 1995), *Take Heart, Raw
Heaven* (Random Hse, 1989, 1984), *And Live Apart* (U
Missouri Pr, 1980)
I.D.: Women

Pamela Manche Pearce   P&W
92 Grove St
New York, NY 10014, 212-691-4537
    Pubs: *Straight Ahead Intl, Samba, Brooklyn Rev,
Hellenic Times*

Gerry Gomez Pearlberg   P&W
418 Bergen St
Brooklyn, NY 11217, 718-638-1233
    Pubs: *Marianne Faithfull's Cigarette, Queer Dog:
Homo/Pup/Poetry: Anth* (Cleis Pr, 1998, 1997), *The
Best American Erotica: Anth* (Macmillan, 1994), *Women
on Women 2: Anth* (Plume, 1993), *Chelsea, BPJ,
Apalachee Qtly, Lesbian Rev of Bks, Plazm, Pucker Up*

Fredda S. Pearlson 🎤 ✈   P
350 Bleecker St
New York, NY 10014-2602
    Pubs: *The Dolphin's Arc: Anth* (SCOP, 1989),
*Wisconsin Rev, Helicon Nine, Stone Country, Chrysalis,
Little Mag, Centennial Rev, California Qtly*

Deborah Pease   P&W
c/o Roland Pease, 45 E 72 St, New York, NY 10021
    Pubs: *Into the Amazement* (Puckerbrush Pr, 1993),
Real Life (Norton, 1971), *New Yorker, Paris Rev, Agni,
Gettysburg Rev, Grand Street, Antioch Rev*

Robert Pease   W
500 E 77 St, #1017
New York, NY 10021
    Pubs: *The Associate Professor* (S&S, 1967)

Richard Peck   P&W
c/o Delacorte Press, 245 E 47 St, New York, NY 10017
    Pubs: *Remembering the Good Times, This Family of
Women* (Delacorte, 1985, 1983)

Sylvia Peck   W
136 W 75 St, #3C
New York, NY 10023
    Pubs: *Kelsey's Raven, Seal Child* (Morrow Junior, 1992,
1989)

Anca Pedvis   P
625 Main St #1233
New York, NY 10044, 212-319-5339
    Pubs: *Romanian Writers in New York: Anth* (Vestala
Press, 1998), *Cartea Romaneasca, Romania Literara,
Pen & Brush Club*

Ted Pejovich   W
233 W 99 St, #6E
New York, NY 10025-5017, 212-663-7621
    Pubs: *The State of California* (Knopf, 1989), *The Qtly,
Kenyon Rev, Story Qtly*

Derek Pell   P&W
Donadio & Olson, Inc, 121 W 27 St, Ste 704, New York,
NY 10001
    Pubs: *Morbid Curiosities* (Jonathan Cape, 1983),
Expurgations (Hyena, 1981), *Playboy, Benzene*

Michael M. Pendragon   P&W
407 W 50 St, #16
New York, NY 10019
    Pubs: *Poetry Motel, Afterthoughts, Portal, Maverick Pr,
Clinton Chronicles, Grim Commander Fright Library,
Barefoot Grass Jrnl, Terror Tales, Blue Lady, Pluto's
Orchard, Visionary Tongue, Nasty Piece of Work*

Edmund Pennant   P
2902 210 St
Bayside, NY 11360, 718-229-6104
    Pubs: *Askance & Strangely: New & Selected Poems,
The Wildebeest of Carmine Street* (Orchises Pr, 1993,
1990), *Confrontation, Shenandoah, American Scholar,
Pivot, NER, Madison Rev*

Willie Perdomo 🎤 ✈   PP&P
PO Box 1363
New York, NY 10113
    Pubs: *Where a Nickel Costs a Dime* (Norton, 1996),
    Listen Up!: Anth (One World, 1999), *Boricuas: Anth*
    (Ballantine, 1996), *Aloud: Anth* (H Holt, 1994),
    Nuyorican Poets Cafe, Aaron Davis Hall, Lincoln Center

Victor Perera   W
Watkins Loomis Agency, Inc, 133 E 35 St, Ste 1, New
York, NY 10016, 212-532-0080
    Pubs: *Rites: A Guatemalan Boyhood* (HBJ, 1986),
    Atlantic, New Yorker, Harper's, Nation

Deborah Perlberg   W
305 E 6 St #7
New York, NY 10003, 212-228-4154
    Pubs: *Cliff House* (M. Evans, 1990), *Heartaches High
    School, Heartaches* (Fawcett/Ballantine, 1987, 1983)

John Perreault   P
54 E 7 St
New York, NY 10003, 212-677-3504
    Pubs: *Hotel Death & Other Tales* (Sun & Moon Pr,
    1989), *Harry* (Coach Hse, 1974)

Joan K. Peters   W
c/o Susan Ginsberg, The Writers House, 21 W 26 St,
New York, NY 10010, 212-929-1583
    Pubs: *Manny & Rose* (St. Martin's Pr, 1985), *Global
    City Rev, Family Life*

Keith Peterson   W
Deborah Schneider, Agent, 250 W 57 St, #1007, New
York, NY 10107, 212-941-8050
    Pubs: *The Scarred Man* (Doubleday, 1990), *Rough
    Justice* (Bantam, 1989), *Ellery Queen*

Ann Petry   P&W
Russell & Volkening, Inc, 50 W 29 St, New York, NY
10001, 212-684-6050
    Pubs: *Miss Muriel, The Narrows, The Street* (HM, 1971,
    1953, 1946), *New Yorker*

Simon Pettet   P
437 E 12 St #6
New York, NY 10009
    Pubs: *Selected Poems* (Talisman Hse, 1996), *Talking
    Pictures* (w/Rudy Burckhardt; Zoland, 1994), *Twenty
    One Love* (Microbrigade, 1990)

D. F. Petteys   P
90 Bank St
New York, NY 10014, 212-989-4528
    Pubs: *Against Infinity* (Primary Pr, 1979), *Lying Awake*
    (Lillian Pr, 1977)

Richard Pevear   P
313 W 107 St
New York, NY 10025, 212-662-7190
    Pubs: *Exchanges* (Spuyten Duyvil, 1982), *Night Talk*
    (Princeton U Pr, 1977), *Hudson Rev, Occident*

Tom Phelan 🎤 ✈   W
Four Walls Eight Windows, 39 W 14 St, New York, NY
10011
    Pubs: *Derrycloney, Brandon Book of Irish Short Stories:
    Anth, Iscariot* (Brandon, 1999, 1998, 1995), *In the
    Season of the Daisies* (Four Walls, Eight Windows,
    1996)
I.D.: Irish-American

Betty Phillips   W
309 E 87 St #2-O
New York, NY 10128
    Pubs: *Lit Rev, Denver Rev, Women, Confrontation,
    Barat Rev, Dekalb Lit Arts Jrnl*

Louis Phillips 🎤 ✈   P&W
375 Riverside Dr, #14-C
New York, NY 10025, 212-866-9643
    Pubs: *Bus to the Moon* (Fort Schuyler Pr, 2000), *A
    Dream of Countries Where No One Dare Live* (SMU
    Pr, 1993), *Hot Corner: Baseball Writings* (Livingston U
    Pr, 1996), *Georgia Rev, Massachusetts Rev, Epoch*

Robert Phillips 🎤 ✈   P&W
Wieser & Wieser, Inc, 25 E 21 St, 6th Fl, New York, NY
10010, 212-260-0860
    Pubs: *Spinach Days, Breakdown Lane* (Johns Hopkins
    U Pr, 2000, 1994), *Public Landing Revisited* (Story Line
    Pr, 1992), *Personal Accounts* (Ontario Rev Pr, 1986),
    Paris Rev, Hudson Rev, New Yorker, Poetry, Nation
Groups: College/Univ

Wanda Phipps 🎤 ✈   P
470 State St
Brooklyn, NY 11217, 718-852-1722
Internet: wanda@interport.net
    Pubs: *Verses That Hurt: Pleasure & Pain from the
    Poemfone Poets* (St. Martin's Pr, 1997), *Writing from
    the New Coast: Anth* (o.blek edtns, 1994), *Agni, The
    World, Owen Wister Rev, Exquisite Corpse*
I.D.: African-American

Bruce Piasecki   P
c/o Lettie Lee, Ann Elmo Literary Agency, 60 E 42 St,
New York, NY 10017, 212-661-2880
    Pubs: *In Search of Environmental Excellence* (S&S,
    1990), *America's Future* (Greenwood, 1988)

Pedro Juan Pietri   P
400 W 43 St, #38E
New York, NY 10036, 212-244-4270
    Pubs: *An Alternate* (Hayden Bk Co, 1980), *The Blue &
    the Gray* (Cherry Valley Edtns, 1975)

Sonia Pilcer   W
172 W 79 St, #19A
New York, NY 10024
  Pubs: *I-Land, Little Darlings* (Ballantine, 1987, 1983),
  Maiden Rites (Viking, 1982), *Visions of America: Anth*
  (Persea Bks, 1993), *L.A. Times, Seven Days*

Kevin Pilkington   P
New School for Social Research, 66 W 12 St, New York,
NY 10011, 212-741-5690
  Pubs: *Reading Stone* (Jeanne Duval Edtns, 1988),
  Poetry, Ploughshares, NYQ, Alaska Rev, Yankee

Thomas Pinnock   PP
265 Bainbridge St
Brooklyn, NY 11233, 718-467-0563
  Pubs: *Essence, Everybody's*

Beverly Pion   P
58-19 251 St
Little Neck, NY 11362, 718-225-3019
  Pubs: *Sunlight on the Moon: Anth* (Carpenter Gothic,
  2000), *LIQ: Anth* (Birnam Wood, 1997), *Eve's Legacy,
  Crone's Nest: Wisdom of the Elderwoman, Taproot, Lit
  Rev*

Belva Plain   W
Janklow & Nesbit Assoc, 598 Madison Ave, New York,
NY 10022-1614, 212-421-1700
  Pubs: *Daybreak, Whispers* (Dell, 1994, 1993),
  Treasures, Harvest, Blessings (Delacorte, 1992, 1990,
  1989)

Susan Pliner 🎤 ✈   P
2501 Palisade Ave, #E-1
Bronx, NY 10463-6104, 718-796-2885
  Pubs: *Paris Rev, Pivot, APR, Greenfield Rev, Kenyon
  Rev*

Tamra Plotnick 🎤 ✈   P&W
397 16 St #1
Brooklyn, NY 11215, 718-499-5774
Internet: tplotnick@pace.edu
  Pubs: *Poetry Project Newsletter, Caprice, Curare, A
  Gathering of the Tribes*
Lang: Spanish

Eileen Pollack   W
c/o Maria Massie, Witherspoon Assoc, Inc, 235 E 31 St,
New York, NY 10016, 212-889-8626
  Pubs: *Paradise, New York* (Temple U Pr, 1998), *The
  Rabbi in the Attic & Other Stories* (Delphinium, 1991),
  Pushcart Prize XX, XVI: Anths (Pushcart Pr, 1996,
  1992), *NER, Ploughshares, Prairie Schooner, Michigan
  Qtly Rev, Agni, Literary Rev*

Shirley B. Pollan-Cohen 🎤   PP&P
2939 Grand Concourse #4C
Bronx, NY 10468-1708, 718-289-5679
  Pubs: *Connections, Grub Street, Bronx Roots, Garland,
  Jewish Currents, Hieroglyphics Pr*

Elizabeth Pollet   W
463 West St, #D-817
New York, NY 10014
  Pubs: *A Family Romance* (NAL, 1951)

Katha Pollitt   P
317 W 93 St
New York, NY 10025
  Pubs: *Antarctic Traveller* (Knopf, 1982), *The Best
  American Poetry: Anth* (Scribner, 1991), *New Yorker,
  Antaeus, Atlantic, Nation, Poetry*

Edward Pomerantz 🎤 ✈   W
351 W 24 St #10F
New York, NY 10011-1517, 212-255-6277
Internet: ejp20@columbia.edu
  Pubs: *Brisburial Play* (Magic Circle Pr, 1981), *Into It*
  (Dial Pr, 1972), *Tyuonyi*

Marie Ponsot   P
340 E 93 St, #2J
New York, NY 10128
  Pubs: *The Bird Catcher, The Green Dark, Admit
  Impediment* (Knopf, 1998, 1988, 1981), *Commonweal,
  The Jrnl, New Yorker, Paris Rev, Ploughshares, Gulf
  Coast, Kenyon Rev*

Melinda Camber Porter   P
c/o Faith Hamlin, Sanford J. Greenburger Assoc., 55 5th
Ave, New York, NY 10003, 212-206-5600
  Pubs: *Badlands, The Art of Love* (Writers & Readers,
  1996, 1993)

Penelope Prentice   W
Garland Publishing, Inc, 717 Fifth Ave, New York, NY
10022-8101, 212-308-9399
  Pubs: *The Pinter Aesthetic: The Erotic Aesthetic*
  (Garland Pub, 1994), *Boundary II, 20th Century Literary
  Tales, Wisconsin Rev, Spree, Cithara, Paper Curtain*

Richard Price   W
Janklow & Nesbit Assoc, 598 Madison Ave, New York,
NY 10022-1614
  Pubs: *Freedomland* (Broadway Bks, 1998), *Clockers,
  Ladies Man, Bloodbrothers* (HM, 1992, 1978, 1976),
  The Breaks (S&S, 1984)

Ron Price 🎤 ✈ P
210 E 15 St, #14A
New York, NY 10003-3939, 212-353-3993
Internet: Ronprice@julliard.edu
Pubs: *A Crucible for the Left Hand* (Wubbie
Productions for Exoterica, 1998), *Full Circle* (Charlotte
Poetry Project, 1995), *Downtown Poets: Anth*
(Downtown, 1998), *Rattapallax, Northeast Corridor,
Poetry*

William Price W
292 Clermont Ave
Brooklyn, NY 11205
Pubs: *The Potlatch Run* (Dutton, 1971), *Evergreen Rev,
Saturday Evening*

Robert Prochaska 🎤 ✈ P
39-72 52 St
Woodside, NY 11377-3257, 718-457-3432
Pubs: *Fourfront* (Bearstone, 1982), *Pipe Dream,
Exquisite Corpse, Louisville Rev, Slipstream, Woodrose,
Rhode Island Rev, Moody Street Irregulars*
Groups: College/Univ, Disabled

Wayne Providence P
2960 Decatur Ave #6G
Bronx, NY 10458-2334, 718-329-2470
Pubs: *Long Journey Home: Anth* (Meta Pr, 1985), *New
City Voices: Anth* (Metamorphosis, 1980), *American
Rag, New York City Public Art Fund*

James Purdy P&W
236 Henry St
Brooklyn, NY 11201, 718-858-0015
Pubs: *Out with the Stars* (Peter Owen Ltd, 1992), *63:
Dream Palace, Collected Stories 1956-1986* (Black
Sparrow Pr, 1991)

Thomas Pynchon W
c/o Ray Roberts, Henry Holt & Co, Inc, 115 W 18 St,
New York, NY 10011
Pubs: *Mason & Dixon* (H Holt, 1997), *Vineland* (Little,
Brown, 1990), *Gravity's Rainbow* (Penguin, 1987), *V.*
(H&R, 1986)

David Quintavalle 🎤 ✈ P
36 Commerce St
New York, NY 10014-3755
Pubs: *Global City Rev, Gulfstream Mag, Mudfish 11,
Slant*
Groups: G/L/B/T

Margo Rabb 🎤 ✈ W
1498 3rd Ave #5
New York, NY 10028
Pubs: *New Stories from the South: Anth* (Algonquin
Bks, 2000), *Best New American Voices: Anth* (HB,
2000), *Atlantic, Zoetrope, Seventeen, Glimmer Train,
The Sun*

Anna Rabinowitz 🎤 P
850 Park Ave
New York, NY 10021-1845, 212-734-2233
Internet: rabanna@aol.com
Pubs: *At the Site of Inside Out* (U Massachusetts Pr,
1997), *KGB Bar Book of Poems: Anth* (Harper, 2000),
Best American Poetry: Anth (Scribner, 1989), *Atlantic,
SW Rev, Paris Rev, NAW, Sonora Rev, Cream City
Rev, Colorado Rev, Sulfur, Denver Qtly*

Nahid Rachlin W
300 E 93 St, Apt 43-D
New York, NY 10128, 212-996-3478
Pubs: *Heart's Desire, Married to a Stranger, Veils* (City
Lights, 1995, 1994, 1993), *Foreigner* (Norton, 1979),
*Fiction, Shenandoah, Ararat, Redbook, Literary Rev,
Columbia, Confrontation, Natural History*

Dotson Rader W
Janklow & Nesbit Assoc, 598 Madison Ave, New York,
NY 10022, 212-421-1700
Pubs: *Tennessee: Cry of the Heart* (Doubleday, 1985),
Beau Monde (Random Hse, 1980), *Esquire, Paris Rev*

Keith Rahmmings P&W
PO Box 371
Brooklyn, NY 11230
Pubs: *Lost & Found Times, Qwertyuiop, Glassworks, So
& So, NRG, Star-Web-Paper, Assembling*

Heidi Rain P
402 4th St
Brooklyn, NY 11215, 718-499-0502
Pubs: *Mirrors of the Soul* (Modern Poetry Society,
1995), *Seasons: Anth* (Poets Under Glass, 1994), *Rag
Shock, Saturn Series, Copulation: Erotic Lit, Salonika,
Medicinal Purposes, New Press Lit Qtly, Nomad's
Choir, Wings*

Diane Raintree P
360 W 21 St
New York, NY 10011-3305, 212-242-2387
Pubs: *The Wind in Our Sails* (Midnight Sun, 1982),
*Global City Rev, Slow Motion Mag, Tamarind, Helen
Rev, NYQ*

Alice Ramirez W
Donald MacCampbell, Inc, PO Box 20191, New York, NY
10025-1518
Pubs: *Bright Glows the Dawn* (Pseudonym: Santa
Arroyo; Leisure Historical Romance, 1984)

Peter Rand W
Wendy Weil Agency Inc, 232 Madison Ave, Ste 1300,
New York, NY 10016
Pubs: *China Hands* (S&S, 1995), *Gold from Heaven,
The Private Rich* (Crown, 1988, 1984), *Firestorm*
(Doubleday, 1969)

Victor Rangel-Ribeiro 🎤 ✈   W
172-28 83 Ave
Jamaica, NY 11432-2104, 718-658-7064
Internet: vrangelrib@aol.com
    Pubs: *Tivolem* (Milkweed Edtns, 1998), *Ferry Crossings:
    Anth* (India; Penguin, 1999), *Iowa Rev, NAR, Lit Rev*
I.D.: Indian-American, Asian-American. Groups:
College/Univ

Claudia Rankine   P
c/o Grove/Atlantic, 841 Broadway, New York, NY 10003
    Pubs: *The End of the Alphabet* (Grove Pr, 1998),
    Nothing in Nature Is Private (Cleveland Poetry Pr 1994)

Carolyn Raphael   P
Queensborough Community College, English Dept,
Springfield Blvd, Bayside, NY 11364, 718-631-6303
    Pubs: *Diagrams of Bittersweet* (Rocks Pr, 1997),
    *Cumberland Poetry Rev, Pivot, The Lyric, Edge City
    Rev, Orbis, Poetry Digest*

Phyllis Raphael 🎤 ✈   W
Writing Program, Columbia Univ, 612 Lewisohn Hall, New
York, NY 10027, 212-595-5286
Internet: pr4@columbia.edu
    Pubs: *They Got What They Wanted* (Norton, 1972),
    Seasons of Women: Anth (Norton/BOMC, 1995),
    Boulevard, PEN Syndicated Fiction

Rebecca Rass   W
54 W 16 St, #14C
New York, NY 10011, 212-627-9122
    Pubs: *From A-Z* (Proza, 1985), *The Mountain, The
    Fairy Tales of My Mind* (Lintel, 1982, 1978), *Solo:
    Women on Woman Alone* (Dell, 1977), *Moznaim, Zero
    Mag, Seven Days*

Carter Ratcliff 🎤   P
26 Beaver St
New York, NY 10004-2311, 212-825-9012
    Pubs: *Give Me Tomorrow* (Vehicle, 1983), *Fever Coast*
    (Kulchur Pr, 1973), *KGB Bar Book of Poems: Anth*
    (Harper, 2000), *Out of this World: Anth* (Crown, 1991),
    The World Anth (Bobbs-Merrill, 1969)

Rochelle Ratner 🎤 ✈   P&W
609 Columbus Ave, #16F
New York, NY 10024-1433, 212-769-0498
Internet: rratner@idt.net
    Pubs: *Zodiac Arrest* (Ridgeway Pr, 1995), *Lion's Share*
    (Coffee Hse Pr, 1992), *Someday Songs: Poems Toward
    a Personal History* (BkMk Pr, 1992), *Bearing Life: Anth*
    (Feminist Pr, 2000), *Antaeus, Nation, Hanging Loose,
    First Intensity, Caprice*
Groups: Seniors, Hospitals

John Rechy   W
Georges Borchardt Inc., 136 E 57 St, New York, NY
10022, 212-753-5785
    Pubs: *Our Lady of Babylon, The Miraculous Day of
    Amalia Gomez* (Arcade, 1996, 1991), *Marilyn's
    Daughter, Bodies & Soul* (Carroll & Graf, 1988, 1983)

Victoria Redel 🎤 ✈   P&W
90 Riverside Dr #12A
New York, NY 10024-5318, 212-873-2502
Internet: vredel@aol.com
    Pubs: *Where the Road Bottoms Out* (Knopf, 1995),
    Already the World (Kent State U Pr, 1995), *Antioch
    Rev, Missouri Rev, Bomb, The Qtly, Epoch*
I.D.: Jewish. Groups: Women

Gomer Rees   P
325 Riverside Dr, #3
New York, NY 10025, 212-865-7035
    Pubs: *Loves, Etc, Choice, NYQ, Chelsea, Purchase
    Poetry Rev, Studies in Contemporary Satire*

Gail Regier   W
c/o Matthew Bialer, William Morris Agency, 1325 Ave of
the Americas, New York, NY 10019, 212-586-5100
    Pubs: *Laurel Rev, New Virginia Rev, Greensboro Rev,
    Zone 3, Emrys Jrnl, Yarrow, Atlantic*

Barbara Reid   W
138 W 11 St
New York, NY 10011, 212-924-4967
    Pubs: *The Tears of San Lorenzo* (Apple-Wood Pr,
    1977), *Prize Stories 1981: The O. Henry Awards: Anth*
    (Doubleday, 1981), *Pulpsmith*

Barbara Eve Reiss   P
1290 Madison Ave, #2N
New York, NY 10128, 212-369-8663
    Pubs: *Family Mirrors* (HM, 1991), *Tangled Vines: Anth*
    (HBJ, 1992), *Antaeus, Agni, Nation, Virginia Qtly Rev*

Gertrude Reiss 🎤 ✈   P&W
74 Beaumont St
Brooklyn, NY 11235-4104, 718-615-0327
    Pubs: *The Perceptive I* (NTC Pub Group, 1997),
    Legacies (HC, 1993), *The New Press, Jewish Currents,
    Outloud, Oxalis, Riverrun, Pumpkin Stories*
I.D.: Jewish. Groups: Children, Seniors

Sally Renfro   P
401 E 64 St, #2D
New York, NY 10021-7590
    Pubs: *13th Moon, Atlantic, Texas Qtly*

Vittoria repetto 🎤 ✈   P
24 Mulberry St, #4R
New York, NY 10013-4360, 212-267-1434
   Pubs: *Head for the Van Wyck* (Monkey Cat Pr, 1994),
Unsettling America: Anth (Penguin, 1994), *Paterson Lit
Rev, Voices in Italian Americana, Mudfish, Lips*
I.D.: G/L/B/T, Italian-American. Groups: G/L/B/T, Italian-
American

Naomi Replansky 🎤   P
711 Amsterdam Ave, #8E
New York, NY 10025-6916, 212-666-1233
   Pubs: *The Dangerous World: New & Selected Poems*
(Another Chicago Pr, 1994), *Ring Song* (Scribner,
1952), *Ploughshares, Feminist Studies, NYQ*

A. Wanjiku H. Reynolds   P
Ngoma's Gourd, Inc, PO Box 24, W Farms Sq Sta,
Bronx, NY 10460
   Pubs: *Cognac & Collard Greens* (Single Action
Productions, 1986), *A Gathering of Hands: Anth*
(Ngoma's Gourd, 1991)

Martha Rhodes   P
80 N Moore St, #33J
New York, NY 10013, 212-571-4683
   Pubs: *At the Gate* (Provincetown Arts Pr, 1995), *Agni,
Boston Rev, Harvard Rev, Ploughshares, Virginia Rev*

Richard Rhodes   W
Janklow & Nesbit Assoc, 598 Madison Ave, New York,
NY 10022-1614, 212-421-1700
   Pubs: *Deadly Feasts, A Hole in the World, Farm, The
Making of the Atomic Bomb* (S&S, 1997, 1990, 1989,
1986)

M. Z. Ribalow 🎤 ✈   P
431 E 20 St, #4C
New York, NY 10010-7507, 212-777-3538
   Pubs: *Fishdrum, NYQ, Paris Rev, Literary Rev*

Anne Rice   W
ICM, 40 W 57 St, New York, NY 10019, 212-556-5600
   Pubs: *The Vampire Armand* (Knopf, 1998), *Violin, The
Witching Hour* (Ballantine, 1998, 1993), *Belinda, Exit to
Eden* (Arbor Hse, 1986, 1985), *The Vampire Lestat*
(Knopf, 1985)

Adrienne Rich   P
W W Norton, 500 5 Ave, New York, NY 10110,
212-354-5500
   Pubs: *Midnight Salvage, What Is Found There, An
Atlas of the Difficult World* (Norton, 1999, 1993, 1991),
Kenyon Rev, APR, Sulfur

Mindy Rinkewich   P&W
290 9th Ave #5F
New York, NY 10001, 212-242-4445
   Pubs: *The White Beyond the Forest* (CCC, 1992), *Lips,
Schmate, Bitterroot, Poet Lore*

Edward Rivera   W
321 W 100 St, #6
New York, NY 10025
   Pubs: *Family Installments* (Morrow, 1982), *New
American Rev, Bilingual Rev, New York Mag*

Louis Reyes Rivera 🎤 ✈   P
Shamal Books, Inc, GPO Box 16, New York, NY
10116-0016, 718-622-4426
   Pubs: *Scattered Scripture, This One for You, Who Pays
the Cost* (Shamal Bks, 1997, 1984, 1977), *Blind
Beggar, Sunbury*
I.D.: Puerto-Rican, Caribbean-American

Agnes Robertson   P
3100 Brighton 2nd St, #6J
Brooklyn, NY 11235, 718-934-3018
   Pubs: *The Me Inside of Me, The Chestnut Tree* (Gull
Bks, 1987, 1987)

Corinne Robins 🎤 ✈   W
83 Wooster St
New York, NY 10012-4376, 212-925-3714
   Pubs: *Marble Goddesses with Technicolor Skins*
(Segue, 2000), *Facing It* (Pratt, 1996), *The Pluralist Era*
(H&R, 1984), *American Book Rev, ACM, NAW, Caprice,
Poetry NY, Confrontation, Situation*

Natalie Robins 🎤 ✈   P
c/o Lynn Nesbit, Janklow & Nesbit Assoc, 445 Park Ave,
New York, NY 10022, 212-421-1700
Internet: nrobins@escape.com
   Pubs: *Eclipse* (Swallow Pr, 1981)

Jeremy Robinson   P
275 Central Pk W, #12E
New York, NY 10024, 212-362-0574

Jill Robinson   W
c/o Lynn Nesbit, Janklow & Nesbit Assoc, 445 Park Ave,
New York, NY 10022, 212-421-1700
   Pubs: *Perdido* (Knopf, 1978), *Bed/Time/Story* (Random
Hse, 1974)

Bruce Holland Rogers   P&W
c/o Shawna McCarthy, 381 Park Ave S, Ste 1020, New
York, NY 10016, 212-679-8686
   Pubs: *Sudden Fiction: Anth* (Norton, 1996), *Year's Best
Mystery & Suspense Stories: Anth* (Walker & Co,
1994), *The Qtly, Fantasy & Science Fiction, Qtly West*

Michael Rogers   W
c/o Gail Hochman, Brandt & Brandt Literary Agents, 1501
Broadway, New York, NY 10036, 212-840-5760
    Pubs: *Forbidden Sequence* (Bantam, 1988), *Silicon
    Valley* (S&S, 1982), *Esquire, Playboy, West, Manhattan
    Inc.*

Gilbert Rogin   W
Sports Illustrated, Time-Life Building, New York, NY
10020, 212-556-3123

Marcus Rome 🎤 ✈   P
2727 Palisade Ave
Riverdale, NY 10463-1018, 718-548-7330
    Pubs: *Repercussions, Abreactions* (Birch Brook Pr,
    2000, 1989), *Visual Eyes* (Ziggurat Pr, 1997), *Red Owl,
    Wordsmith, The Bridge, Vincent Brothers Rev, Pacific
    Coast Jrnl*

Cheryl Romney-Brown   P
c/o Philippa Brophy, Sterling Lord Literistic, 65 Bleecker
St, New York, NY 10012, 212-780-6050
    Pubs: *Circling Home* (Scripta Humanistica, 1989),
    American Beauties: Anth (Abrams, 1993)

Rose Rosberg   P
880 W 181 St #4-I
New York, NY 10033, 212-928-7089
    Pubs: *Chrysalis* (Swedenborg Fdn, 1995), *The Country
    of Connections* (University Edtns, 1993), *Breathe In,
    Breathe Out* (Singular Speech Pr, 1992), *Pacific Coast
    Jrnl, Poetry Digest, Skylark, American Poets & Poetry,
    Lyric, Neovictorian, Comstock Rev*

Joel Rose   W
156 Waverly Pl
New York, NY 10014-3852, 212-206-8331
    Pubs: *Kill Kill Faster Faster* (Crown, 1997), *Kill the
    Poor* (Atlantic Monthly Pr, 1988), *Love Is Strange: Anth*
    (Norton, 1993), *Between C&D: Anth* (Penguin, 1988)

Norma Rosen 🎤   W
c/o Gloria Loomis, Watkins Loomis Agency, Inc, 133 E 35
St, New York, NY 10016, 212-532-0080
    Pubs: *Biblical Women Unbound,* (JPS, 1997), *John &
    Anzia, At the Center* (Syracuse U Pr, 1997, 1996),
    Accidents of Influence (SUNY Pr, 1992), *Tikkun, Lilith*

Alice Rosenblitt 🎤 ✈   P
47-25 43 St, #1F
Woodside, NY 11377-6229, 718-937-2891
    Pubs: *Celebrating Women: 20 Years of Co-Education:
    Anth* (Yale Women's Ctr, 1990), *Long Shot, Natl Poetry
    Mag of the Lower East Side, La Mia Ink, Pome*

Linda Rosenkrantz   W
Howard Morhaim Agency, 841 Broadway, Ste 604, New
York, NY 10003, 212-529-4433
    Pubs: *SoHo, Gone Hollywood* (Co-author; Doubleday,
    1981, 1979)

Ira Rosenstein   P
PO Box 3102
Long Island City, NY 11103
    Pubs: *Twenty-two Sonnets, Left on the Field to Die*
    (Starlight Pr, 1986, 1984)

Barbara Rosenthal 🎤 ✈   PP&P&W
The Media Loft, 463 West St #A-628, New York, NY
10014-2035, 212-924-4893
    Pubs: *Soul & Psyche, Homo Futurus, Sensations, Clues
    to Myself* (Visual Studies Wkshp, 1998, 1986, 1986,
    1980), *Cradle & All: Anth* (Faber & Faber, 1990),
    *Parting Gifts, Kopy Kultur, Spit, Feelings, Afterimage,
    Umbrella, MacGuffin Rdr, Bohemian Chronicle*
I.D.: Jewish, Women

Bob Rosenthal   P
334 E 11 St, #16
New York, NY 10003, 212-777-6786
    Pubs: *Rude Awakenings* (Yellow Pr, 1982), *Lies About
    the Flesh* (Frontward Bks, 1977), *Mag City*

Carole Rosenthal   W
37 1/2 St Marks Pl, #B2
New York, NY 10003, 212-228-4289
    Pubs: *Best of the Underground: Anth* (Rhinoceros Mass
    Market Edtns, 1998), *Powers of Desire: Anth* (Monthly
    Rev Pr, 1983), *Dreamworks, Confrontation, Minnesota
    Rev, Mother Jones, Ellery Queen's Mystery Mag, Other
    Voices, Cream City Rev*

Martha Rosler   W
143 McGuinness Blvd
Brooklyn, NY 11222, 718-383-2277
    Pubs: *3 Works* (Nova Scotia, 1981), *Service* (Printed
    Matter, 1978), *Heresies*

Elizabeth Rosner 🎤 ✈   P&W
Joelle Delbourgo, 450 7th Ave, Ste 3004, New York, NY
10123, 212-279-9027
Internet: joelle@delbourgo.com
    Pubs: *The Solitaire Bird* (Ballantine, 2001), *Gravity*
    (Small Poetry Pr, 1998), *SPR, Faultline, Blue Mesa
    Rev, Poetry East, ACM, Cream City Rev*
I.D.: Jewish

David Ross   P
33 Riverside Dr, #5A
New York, NY 10023-8025
    Pubs: *Three Ages of Lake Light* (Macmillan, 1962), *The
    New Yorker Book of Poems: Anth* (Viking, 1969),
    Nation, Poetry, New Yorker, Transatlantic Rev

Terrence Ross W
8 Spring St, #4RW
New York, NY 10012, 212-226-0520
Pubs: *Bitter Graces* (Avon, 1980)

Judith Rossner W
Wendy Weil Agency Inc, 232 Madison Ave, Ste 1300,
New York, NY 10016, 212-685-0030
Pubs: *Perfidia* (Talese/Doubleday, 1997), *Olivia* (Crown,
1994), *His Little Women* (Summit, 1990), *August* (HM,
1983), *Emmeline, Attachments, Looking for Mr. Goodbar*
(S&S, 1980, 1977, 1975), *Any Minute I Can Split*
(McGraw Hill, 1972)

Beatrice Roth PP
86 Horatio St
New York, NY 10014
Pubs: *Out from Under: Anth* (TCG, 1990),
Massachusetts Rev

Philip Roth W
FSG, 19 Union Sq W, New York, NY 10003

Joyce Andrea Rothenberg 🎤 ✈ PP&P
PO Box 6041, FDR Sta
New York, NY 10150-6041
Pubs: *The Symphony Is Barely Audible* (Symphony Pr,
1991)

Earl Rovit W
309 W 109 St, #6G
New York, NY 10025
Pubs: *Crossings, A Far Cry, The Player King* (HBJ,
1973, 1967, 1965)

Arkady Rovner W
PO Box 42, Prince St Sta
New York, NY 10012
Pubs: *Guests from the Province* (Moscow Worker Pr,
1992), *Kalalatsy* (Moscow; Timan Pr, 1991), *The King's
Visit* (Gnosis, 1988), *Central Park, Lit Rev, Alea*

Peter Rubie W
1781 Riverside Dr
New York, NY 10034
Pubs: *Werewolf* (Longmeadow Pr, 1992), *Mindbender*
(Lynx Bks, 1989)

Kathryn Ruby P
180 Cabrini Blvd, #71
New York, NY 10033, 212-781-3833
Pubs: *Twentieth Century Views* (Prentice-Hall, 1979),
We Become New (Bantam, 1975), *Rio*

Mark Rudman P
817 W End Ave, #4A
New York, NY 10025, 212-666-3648
Pubs: *Rider* (Wesleyan U Pr, 1994), *Diverse Voices*
(Story Line Pr, 1993), *The Nowhere Steps* (Sheep
Meadow Pr, 1990), *APR, Harper's, Paris Rev, New
Yorker*

Raphael Rudnik P
66 Garfield Pl, #3S
Brooklyn, NY 11215-1923
Pubs: *Frank 207* (Ohio U Pr, 1982), *Pequod, Kentucky
Rev*

Frazier Russell P&W
240 Carroll St
Brooklyn, NY 11231, 718-237-9816
Pubs: *How We Are Spared, Four Way Books Reader:
Anth* (Four Way Bks, 2000, 1996), *Fweivel: The Day
Will Come* (Ridgeway Pr, 1996), *Ploughshares, Global
City Rev, American Voice, Marlboro Rev, Phoebe*

Suzanne Ruta 🎤 ✈ W
55 Bethune St, Apt B647
New York, NY 10014-2010, 212-675-5170
Pubs: *Stalin in the Bronx & Other Stories* (Grove Pr,
1987), *Wigwag, VLS, Grand Street*
Lang: Spanish, French. Groups: Immigrants, Latino/Latina

Thaddeus Rutkowski 🎤 ✈ W
PO Box 187, Cooper Sta
New York, NY 10276-0187, 212-387-0056
Internet: thadrand@earthlink.net
Pubs: *Roughhouse* (Kaya, 1999), *Basic Training* (March
Street Pr, 1996), *Outlaw Bible of Amer Poetry: Anth*
(Thunder's Mouth Pr, 1999), *Will Work for Peace: Anth,
Zeropanik, 1999), Crimes of the Beats: Anth*
(Autonomedia, 1998), *Cutbank, Faultline, Mudfish*

Lester Rutsky P
2930 W 5 St
Brooklyn, NY 11224

Reba Ruttel P
231 W 18 St
New York, NY 10011-4598
Pubs: *Poetry Peddler, Innisfree, Catharsis, Pincushion
Poetry, Poetry Motel, Old Hickory Rev*

Margaret Ryan 🎤 ✈ P
250 W 104 St #63
New York, NY 10025-4282, 212-666-2591
Pubs: *Black Raspberries* (Parsonage Pr, 1986), *Filling
Out a Life* (Front Street, 1981), *Nation, Poetry,
Confrontation, Kansas Qtly, BPJ*
I.D.: Irish-American. Groups: Children, Seniors

Elizabeth-Ann Sachs W
c/o Anne Borchardt, Georges Borchardt Inc., 136 E 57 St, New York, NY 10022, 212-753-5785
Pubs: *Mountain Bike Madness, The Boy Who Ate Dog Biscuits* (Random Hse, 1994, 1989), *Just Like Always* (Aladdin Bks, 1991)

Howard Sage 🎤 ✈ P
720 Greenwich St, #4H
New York, NY 10014-2574, 212-627-8959
Internet: hs15@is.nyu.edu
Pubs: *Fictional Flights: Anth* (Heinle & Heinle, 1993), *Folio, New Voices*

Raymond Saint-Pierre 🎤 ✈ P
Street Editions, 25 Cumming St, #3B, New York, NY 10034, 212-304-2265
Internet: streeteditions@juno.com
Pubs: *Orgasms of Light* (Gay Sunshine Pr, 1976), *Hell's Kitchen: Anth* (Public Pr, 1999), *One Teacher in Ten: Anth* (Alyson Pub, 1994), *Breakfast All Day, Bay Windows, Prophetic Voices, Amherst Rev, Boston Lit Rev, Connecticut River Rev, Real, Oyez Rev*
Lang: Spanish. I.D.: Native American, G/L/B/T. Groups: G/L/B/T

Jerome Sala P
298 Mulberry St, #3L
New York, NY 10012, 212-941-8724
Pubs: *Raw Deal: New & Selected Poems* (Another Chicago Pr, 1994), *The Trip* (Highlander Pr, 1987), *Aerial, Exquisite Corpse, NAW, Onthebus, Ploughshares*

Joseph S. Salemi P
3222 61 St
Woodside, NY 11377-2030, 718-932-5351
Pubs: *Masquerade, Nonsense Couplets, Formal Complaints* (Somers Rocks Pr, 2000, 1999, 1997), *Ekphrasis, Light, Piedmont Lit Rev, Carolina Qtly, Hellas, Cumberland Poetry Rev, Blue Unicorn, Formalist, Satire, Sparrow, Edge City Rev, Maledicta*

J. D. Salinger W
Harold Ober Assoc, 425 Madison Ave, New York, NY 10017, 212-759-8600

James Salter W
c/o Peter Matson, Sterling Lord Literistic, 65 Bleecker St, New York, NY 10012, 212-780-6050
Pubs: *Dusk & Other Stories, Light Years, A Sport & a Pastime* (North Point Pr, 1988, 1982, 1980), *Esquire*

Thomas Sanchez W
c/o Esther Newberg, ICM, 40 W 57 St, New York, NY 10019, 212-556-5600
Pubs: *Mile Zero, Rabbit Boss* (Knopf/Vintage, 1990, 1989)

Ronni Sandroff W
Elaine Markson Literary Agency, 44 Greenwich Ave, New York, NY 10011
Pubs: *Fighting Back* (Jove, 1979), *Party, Party/Girlfriends* (Knopf, 1975)

Myro Sandunes W
The Dramatists Guild, 234 W 44 St, New York, NY 10036, 212-398-9366
Pubs: *The Go-Between, Placebo* (Albatross Pub, 1983, 1983)

Reuben Sandwich PP
PO Box 020841
Brooklyn, NY 11202
Pubs: *The Shredder*

Rosemarie Santini 🎤 W
Donald Maass Literary Agency, 157 West 57 St, Ste 703, New York, NY 10019, 212-751-7755
Internet: dmla@mindspring.com
Pubs: *Blood Sisters, Private Lives* (Pocket Bks, 1990, 1989), *The Disenchanted Diva, A Swell Style of Murder* (St. Martin's, 1988, 1986), *Music Lesson, Movie Murder, Sins of the Father, New Mystery Mag*

Sapphire 🎤 ✈ W
521 41 St #D-4
Brooklyn, NY 11232
Internet: sapphire11000@aol.com
Pubs: *Black Wings & Blind Angels, Push* (Knopf, 1999, 1996), *American Dreams* (High Risk Bks, 1994), *Wann bitte findet das Leben statt?: Anth* (Germany; Rowohlt, 1998), *Black Scholar, New Yorker, Bomb*
I.D.: African-American, Women

Helen Saslow P
3626 Kings Hwy #5L
Brooklyn, NY 11234-2751
Pubs: *Arctic Summer* (Barlenmir Hse, 1974), *The Villanelle: The Evolution of a Poetic Form: Anth* (U Idaho Pr, 1987), *NYQ, Glassworks, Confrontation, Hellcoal Annual, Hanging Loose, Small Pond*

Steven Sater P
c/o Mike Lubin, William Morris Agency, 1325 Ave of the Americas, New York, NY 10019, 212-586-5100
Pubs: *Take Ten: Anth* (Vintage, 1997), *Portland Rev, Poems & Plays, Confrontation, Rockford Rev, Hawaii Rev, MacGuffin*

Tom Savage 🎤 ✈ P
622 E 11 St, #14
New York, NY 10009-4140, 212-533-3893
Internet: tomshantideva@hotmail.com
Pubs: *Brain Surgery Poems* (Linear Arts, 1998), *Political Conditions/Physical States, 1993), Out of This World* (Crown, 1991), *Lungfull, The World, Synaesthetic, Tamarind, Hanging Loose, Talisman, Long Shot*
I.D.: G/L/B/T, Disabled. Groups: G/L/B/T, Disabled

Sally Savic P&W
Melanie Jackson Agency, 250 W 57 St, #1119, New York,
NY 10107
  Pubs: *Elysian Fields* (Scribner, 1988), *Cosmopolitan*,
Intro

Lynwood Sawyer 🎤 ✈ W
85 State St, #5
Brooklyn, NY 11201-5534, 718-237-2296
Internet: uncertain@altavista.com
  Pubs: *Uncertain Currency* (Avocet Pr, 2000), *Hawaii
Pacific Rev, Art Access, Pembroke Rev, Just Pulp, St.
Andrews Rev, Ellery Queen's Mystery Mag*

Ann Scaglione P
244-23 73 Ave
Douglaston, NY 11362, 718-523-8839
  Pubs: *Vega, Arulo, Modern Images*

Hindy Lauer Schachter 🎤 W
420 E 64 St
New York, NY 10021-7853
  Pubs: *Intl Poetry Rev, Response, Jewish Frontier*

Sandy Rochelle Schachter 🎤 ✈ PP
438 W 23 St #A
New York, NY 10011-2165, 212-929-6245
Internet: chelsea438@aol.com
  Pubs: *Poems from the Heart* (The Plowman, 1992),
Connecticut River Rev, Visions Intl

Susan Fromberg Schaeffer P&W
c/o Morton L. Janklow, Janklow & Nesbit Assoc, 598
Madison Ave, New York, NY 10022-1614, 212-421-1700
  Pubs: *The Golden Rope, First Nights, Buffalo Afternoon*
(Knopf, 1996, 1993, 1989), *The Injured Party* (St.
Martin's Pr, 1987)

Lorraine Schein 🎤 P&W
41-30 46 St, #5A
Sunnyside, NY 11104-1829
  Pubs: *The Raw Brunettes: Anth* (Wordcraft of Oregon,
1995), *Wild Women: Anth* (Overlook Pr, 1994),
*Exquisite Corpse, Semiotext(e), Poetry NY, Brooklyn
Rev*

Jeanne Schinto W
c/o Faith Hamlin, Sanford J. Greenburger Assoc., 55 5th
Ave, New York, NY 10003, 212-206-5600
  Pubs: *Children of Men* (Persea Bks, 1991), *Shadow
Bands* (Ontario Rev Pr, 1988), *The Literary Dog: Anth*
(Atlantic Monthly Pr, 1990), *Virginia Qtly Rev, Yale Rev*

Robert Schirmer W
24 1st St
Brooklyn, NY 11231-5002
  Pubs: *Living with Strangers* (NYU Pr, 1991), *NER,
Indiana Rev, Greensboro Rev, New Letters*

Murray Schisgal W
275 Central Pk W
New York, NY 10024-3015
  Pubs: *Days & Nights of a French Horn Player* (Little,
Brown, 1980), *Luv & Other Plays* (Dodd, Mead, 1983)

Peter Schjeldahl P
53 St Marks Pl
New York, NY 10003, 212-674-5889
  Pubs: *Since 1964: New & Selected Poems* (Sun Pr,
1978)

Tobias Schneebaum W
463 West St, #410A
New York, NY 10014, 212-691-0022
  Pubs: *Embodied Spirits* (Peabody Museum of Salem,
1990), *Where the Spirits Dwell, Keep the River on Your
Right* (Grove, 1988, 1969)

Elio Schneeman P
29 St Marks Pl
New York, NY 10003, 212-982-7682
  Pubs: *Along the Rails* (United Artists, 1991), *In
February I Think* (C Pr, 1978), *Poetry NY, World,
Hanging Loose, Long News, Flatiron News, Shiny*

Carolee Schneemann 🎤 ✈ PP&P
114 W 29 St
New York, NY 10001
Internet: caroleel2@aol.com
  Pubs: *Imaging Her Erotics* (MIT Pr, 2000), *More Than
Meat Joy* (McPherson & Co, 1996), *A Book of the
Book; Vulva's Morphia* (Granary Bks, 2000; 1997),
Deep Down (Faber & Faber, 1988), *Parts of a Body
House Book* (U.K.; Beau Geste Pr, 1972), *White Walls
Jrnl*

Bart Schneider 🎤 ✈ P
c/o Gloria Loomis, Watkins Loomis Agency, Inc, 133 E 35
St, New York, NY 10016, 212-532-0080
  Pubs: *Secret Love, Blue Bossa* (Viking, 2001, 1998),
Race (Crown, 1997), *Seasons of the Game* (Elysian
Fields, 1992), *Water for a Stranger* (Blue Teal Pr,
1979), *Teachers & Writers Mag*
Groups: Jewish, Seniors

Elizabeth Lynn Schneider P
480 2nd St
Brooklyn, NY 11215, 718-768-6296

L. J. Schneiderman W
Marcia Amsterdam Agency, 41 W 82 St, New York, NY
10024-5613, 212-873-4945
  Pubs: *The Appointment* (S&S, 1991), *Sea Nymphs by
the Hour* (Bobbs-Merrill, 1972), *Confrontation, Ascent,
Kansas Qtly, Chouteau Rev, Black Warrior Rev*

Lynda Schor 🎤 ✈   W
463 West St, #610C
New York, NY 10014
  Pubs: *True Love & Real Romance* (Coward, McCann &
  Geoghegan, 1979), *Appetites* (Warner, 1976), *Playboy,
  Mademoiselle, Redbook, GQ, Confrontation, Ms.*

Roni Schotter   W
c/o Susan Cohen, The Writers House, 21 W 26 St, New
York, NY 10010, 914-478-3231
  Pubs: *Purim Play, Passover Magic, A Fruit & Vegetable
  Man* (Little Brown, 1998, 1995, 1993), *Nothing Ever
  Happens on 90th Street, Dreamland* (Orchard Bks,
  1997, 1996), *When Crocodiles Clean Up* (Macmillan,
  1993)

Peninnah Schram   PP&P&W
525 W End Ave, #8C
New York, NY 10024, 212-787-0626
  Pubs: *Tales of Elijah the Prophet, Jewish Stories One
  Generation Tells Another* (Jason Aronson, 1991, 1987)

Susan Schreibman   P
372 5th Ave #4N
New York, NY 10018, 212-695-2947
  Pubs: *Poetry Ireland, Footwork, Atlanta Rev, Poet Lore,
  Dreamworks, Wind, Crazyquilt, Amelia*

Grace Schulman 🎤 ✈   P
1 University Pl, #14-F
New York, NY 10003-4519, 212-533-0235
  Pubs: *The Paintings of Our Lives* (HM, 2001), *For That
  Day Only, Hemispheres* (Sheep Meadow Pr, 1994,
  1984), *New Yorker, Paris Rev, Boulevard, Pequod,
  Kenyon Rev, Poetry*

Helen Schulman   W
782 W End Ave #73
New York, NY 10025-5401
  Pubs: *Out of Time* (Atheneum, 1991), *Not a Free Show*
  (Knopf, 1988), *Antioch Rev, NAR, Story Qtly, The Qtly,
  Arete*

Sarah Schulman   W
406 E 9 St, #20
New York, NY 10009-4972, 212-982-1033
  Pubs: *Shimmer* (Avon, 1998), *Rat Bohemia* (E.P.
  Dutton, 1995), *Empathy* (Plume, 1993)

David Schultz 🎤 ✈   P&W
162-31 9th Ave #4A
Whitestone, NY 11357-2010, 718-767-7455
  Pubs: *Liquid Pony Ink, Somniloquy, Poesie USA,
  Footwork, Horizontes, Transition, Ambrosia, The Haven,
  Tin Wreath, Italian-Americana*
Lang: Spanish, Yiddish

Beatrice Schuman   W
3604 Skillman Ave
Long Island City, NY 11101
  Pubs: *It's Not Easy to Marry an Elephant, Am I Greedy
  if I Want More* (Fred Fell, 1982, 1979)

Elaine Schwager 🎤 ✈   P
228 W 22 St
New York, NY 10011-2701, 212-807-1225
Internet: esschwager@aol.com
  Pubs: *I Want Your Chair* (Rattapallax Pr, 2000), *It Is
  the Poem Singing in Your Eyes: Anth* (Harper, 1971),
  City in all Directions: Anth (Macmillan, 1969),
  Rattapallax, Literal Latte, Writ, Armadillo
Groups: Jewish, Seniors

Leonard Schwartz   P
120 Cabrini Blvd, #96
New York, NY 10033
  Pubs: *Flicker at the Edge of Things* (Spuyten Duyvil,
  1998), *New & Selected Poems: Words Before the
  Articulate* (Talisman Hse, 1997), *Gnostic Blessing*
  (Goats & Compasses Pr, 1992), *First Intensity, Five
  Fingers Rev, Talisman, Poetry NY, Pequod*

Lynne Sharon Schwartz   W
50 Morningside Dr, #31
New York, NY 10025
  Pubs: *Ruined by Reading* (Beacon, 1996), *The Fatigue
  Artist* (Scribner, 1995), *Leaving Brooklyn* (HM, 1989)

Marian Schwartz   W
c/o Emilie Jacobson, Curtis Brown Ltd., 10 Astor Pl, New
York, NY 10003-6935
  Pubs: *Realities* (St. Martin's Pr, 1981)

Doris Schwerin   W
317 W 83 St, #4W
New York, NY 10024
  Pubs: *Cat & I* (H&R, 1990), *Leanna, Diary of a Pigeon
  Watcher* (Morrow, 1978, 1976), *Rainbow Walkers*
  (Villard/Random Hse, 1986), *The Tomorrow Book*
  (Pantheon, 1984)

Armand Schwerner   PP&P
20 Bay St Landing, #B-3C
Staten Island, NY 10301, 718-442-3784
  Pubs: *The Tablets I-XXVI* (National Poetry Fdn, 1998),
  Poems for the Millennium: Anth (U California Pr, 1996),
  Conjunctions, Sulfur, Tyuonyi, Talisman

Virginia Scott   P
255 Fieldston Terr, #3A
Bronx, NY 10471
  Pubs: *Toward Appomattox, The Witness Box*
  (Motherroot Pubs, 1985), *Prairie Schooner, Antigonish
  Rev, American Voice*

Peter Seaton P
229 E 25 St, #3A
New York, NY 10010, 212-683-1449
Pubs: *Crisis Intervention* (Tuumba Pr, 1983), *The Son Master* (Roof Bks, 1982), *Paris Rev, This*

Edith Segal P
60 Plaza St, #3A
Brooklyn, NY 11238, 718-638-8372
Pubs: *Tributes & Trumpets, A Time to Thunder* (Philmark Pr, 1986, 1982)

Lore Segal 🎤 ✈ W
280 Riverside Dr, #12K
New York, NY 10025-9031
Internet: lsegal70@aol.com
Pubs: *Her First American* (Knopf, 1994), *The Story of King Saul & King David* (Schocken, 1991), *The Book of Adam to Moses* (Pantheon, 1989), *Best American Short Stories: Anth* (HM, 1990), *Congregation: Anth* (HB, 1987), *Social Research, Harper's*

Frederick Seidel P
FSG, 19 Union Sq W, New York, NY 10003,
212-741-6900
Pubs: *Going Fast, My Tokyo* (FSG, 1998, 1991), *Poems 1959-1979, These Days* (Knopf, 1989, 1989), *Sunrise* (Viking Penguin, 1980)

Hugh Seidman 🎤 ✈ P
463 West St, #H822
New York, NY 10014-2038, 212-255-5847
Pubs: *Selected Poems: 1965-1995; People Live, They Have Lives* (Miami U Pr, 1995, 1992)

Robert J. Seidman 🎤 ✈ W
Harvey Klinger, Inc, 301 W 53 St, New York, NY 10019
Internet: seidman@ix.netcom.com
Pubs: *Bucks County Idyll* (S&S, 1980), *One Smart Indian* (Overlook Pr, 1979)

Bernice Selden W
808 W End Ave, #507
New York, NY 10025, 212-222-5819
Pubs: *The Mill Girls* (Atheneum, 1983), *Music in My Heart* (Dutton, 1982)

Robyn Selman P
62 W 11 St, #3F
New York, NY 10011
Pubs: *Directions to My House* (U Pittsburgh Pr, 1995), *Best American Poetry: Anths* (Macmillan, 1995, 1991), *Paris Rev, Prairie Schooner, American Voice, Puerto del Sol, Ploughshares, Kenyon Rev, APR*

Joseph Semenovich P
2610 Glenwood Rd, #6E
Brooklyn, NY 11210, 718-859-2991
Pubs: *The Peter Poems* (Trout Creek Pr, 1984), *Prothalamion* (Textile Bridge Pr, 1982), *Webster Rev, Dog River Rev, Slipstream, Rain City Rev*

Jacques Servin W
PO Box 464, Prince St Sta
New York, NY 10012-0464, 212-875-7780
Pubs: *Mermaids for Attila* (Fiction Collective Two, 1991)

Vikram Seth P&W
c/o Irene Skolnick, Curtis Brown Ltd., 10 Astor Pl, New York, NY 10003-6935, 212-473-5400
Pubs: *All You Who Sleep Tonight* (Knopf, 1990), *The Golden Gate* (Random Hse, 1986)

Elizabeth Sewell P&W
Harold Ober Assoc, 425 Madison Ave, New York, NY 10017
Pubs: *Acquist* (Acorn, 1984), *An Idea* (Mercer U Pr, 1983), *To Be a True Poem* (Hunter Pub, 1979), *Soundings*

Bob Shacochis W
c/o Gail Hochman, Brandt & Brandt Literary Agents, 1501 Broadway, New York, NY 10036, 212-840-5760
Pubs: *Swimming in the Volcano* (Scribner, 1993), *Easy in the Islands* (Crown, 1985), *Paris Rev, Harper's, Esquire, Outside*

R. L. Shafner W
100 W 92 St, #8A
New York, NY 10025, 212-496-0979
Pubs: *Stop Me if You've Heard This* (Signet, 1986), *Formations, TriQtly, Shankpainter*

David Shapiro P
3001 Henry Hudson Pkwy #3B
Riverdale, NY 10463, 718-601-3425
Pubs: *After a Lost Original, House Blown Apart, To an Idea* (Overlook, 1994, 1988, 1984), *Lingo, NAW, Boulevard, New Yorker, Paris Rev*

Harvey Shapiro 🎤 ✈ P
43 Pierrepont St
Brooklyn, NY 11201-3362, 718-858-3765
Pubs: *Selected Poems* (Wesleyan, 1997), *A Day's Portion* (Hanging Loose Pr, 1994)
I.D.: Jewish

Myra Shapiro 🎤 ✈ P
111 4th Ave, #12I
New York, NY 10003-5243, 212-995-0659
Pubs: *I'll See You Thursday* (Blue Sofa Pr, 1996), *Best Amer Poetry: Anth* (Scribner, 1999), *Harvard Rev, Pearl, Ploughshares, Ohio Rev, River Styx, Calyx Jrnl*

Peter Sharpe   P
Wagner College, 1 Campus Rd, Staten Island, NY 10301,
718-390-3370
  Pubs: *Lost Goods & Stray Beasts* (Rowan Tree Pr,
  1983), *Massachusetts Rev, Tendril, Harbor Rev,
  Southern Rev, Davidson Miscellany, Poet Lore*

Brenda Shaughnessy   P
FSG, 19 Union Sq W, New York, NY 10003,
212-741-6900
  Pubs: *Interview with Sudden Joy* (FSG, 1999), *Paris
  Rev, Yale Rev, Chelsea*

Don Shea   W
102 E 22 St #5G
New York, NY 10010
  Pubs: *New York Sex: Anth* (Painted Leaf Pr, 1998),
  Fast Fiction: Anth (Story Pr, 1997), *Flash Fiction: Anth*
  (Norton, 1992), *NAR, Gettysburg Rev, The Lit Rev, The
  Qtly, Confrontation, High Plains Lit Rev, Crescent Rev,
  Onthebus, Descant*

Laurie Sheck   P
303 Mercer St, Apt A-502
New York, NY 10003
Internet: jlpeck1098@aol.com
  Pubs: *Io at Night, The Willow Grove: Anth* (Knopf,
  1990, 1996), *Amaranth* (U Georgia Pr, 1981), *Best
  American Poetry: Anths* (MacMillan, 2000, 1991), *New
  Yorker, Poetry, Iowa Rev*

Evelyn Shefner   W
230 E 15 St, #5N
New York, NY 10003-3943, 212-242-5810
  Pubs: *Common Body, Royal Bones* (Coffee Hse Pr,
  1987), *O. Henry Prize Stories: Anth* (Doubleday, 1979),
  Southern Rev, Negative Capability, The Bridge

Susan Sherman 🎤 ✈   P
305 E 6 St #3
New York, NY 10003
Internet: shermansu@aol.com
  Pubs: *The Color of the Heart* (Curbstone Pr, 1990), *We
  Stand Our Ground* (Ikon Bks, 1988), *A Gathering of the
  Tribes, Long Shot, Heresies, Poetry, APR*
  Groups: Women, G/L/B/T

James Sherry   P&W
300 Bowery
New York, NY 10012, 212-353-0555
  Pubs: *Our Nuclear Heritage* (Sun & Moon Pr, 1991),
  The Word I Like White Paint Considered (Awede,
  1986), *Popular Fiction* (Roof Bks, 1985)

David Shetzline   W
ICM, 40 W 57 St, New York, NY 10019, 212-556-5600

David Shields   W
Witherspoon Assoc, Inc, 235 E 31 St, New York, NY
10016, 212-889-8626
  Pubs: *Remote, Dead Languages* (Knopf, 1996, 1989),
  Harper's, Village Voice, Utne Reader

Ann Allen Shockley 🎤 ✈   W
Carole Abel Literary Agent, 160 W 87 St, #7D, New York,
NY 10024, 212-724-1168
  Pubs: *Loving Her* (Northeastern U Pr, 1997),
  Homeworks: Anth (U Tenn Pr, 1996), *Women in the
  Trees: Anth* (Beacon Pr, 1996), *Revolutionary Tales:
  Anth* (Dell, 1995), *Centers of the Self: Anth* (Hill &
  Wang, 1994), *Calling the Wind: Anth* (Harper, 1993)
I.D.: African-American

Enid Shomer 🎤 ✈   P&W
173 Riverside Dr, #2Y
New York, NY 10024-1615, 212-580-4207
Internet: enidshomer@aol.com
  Pubs: *Black Drum, This Close to the Earth* (U
  Arkansas Pr, 1997, 1992), *Imaginary Men* (U Iowa Pr,
  1993), *New Yorker, Atlantic, Paris Rev, Poetry, New
  Criterion, Georgia Rev, Modern Maturity*

Susan Richards Shreve   W
Russell & Volkening, Inc, 50 W 29 St, New York, NY
10001, 212-684-6050
  Pubs: *Plum & Jaggers* (FSG, 2000), *The Visiting
  Physician, The Train Home, Daughters of the New
  World* (Doubleday, 1996, 1993, 1992), *A Country of
  Strangers* (S&S, 1989)

Kenneth Siegelman   P
2225 W 5 St
Brooklyn, NY 11223
  Pubs: *Urbania, American Imprints, Through Global
  Currents* (Modern Images Pr, 1996, 1994, 1993),
  Parnassus, Poet

Eleni Sikelianos 🎤 ✈   P
106 Ridge St, #2D
New York, NY 10002
Internet: sikelianos@aol.com
  Pubs: *Of Sun, Of History, Of Seeing* (Coffee Hse,
  2001), *Book of Tendons* (Post-Apollo Pr, 1997), *To
  Speak While Dreaming* (Selva Edtns, 1993), *New
  American Poets: Anth* (Talisman, 1999), *The World,
  Grand Street, Verse, Sulfur, Skanky Possum*
I.D.: Greek-American/Greek. Groups: Children, Homeless

Joan Silber 🎤 ✈   W
43 Bond St
New York, NY 10012-2463, 212-228-9728
Internet: jksilber@earthlink.net
  Pubs: *In My Other Life* (Sarabande, 2000), *In the City,
  Household Words* (Viking, 1987, 1980), *Pushcart Prize
  XXV: Anth* (Pushcart Pr, 2000), *An Inn Near Kyoto:
  Anth* (New Rivers Pr, 1998), *Ploughshares, VLS, New
  Yorker, Paris Rev*

Layle Silbert 🎤   P&W
Seven Stories Press, 140 Watts St, New York, NY 10013,
212-226-8760
Internet: www.sevenstories.com
  Pubs: *The Free Thinkers* (Seven Stories Pr, 2000),
  New York, New York (St. Andrews Pr, 1996), *Burkah &
  Other Stories* (Host Pubs, 1992), *Imaginary People &
  Other Strangers* (Exile Pr, 1985), *Denver Qtly,
  Salmagundi, Michigan Qtly Rev, Confrontation*

Lari Field Siler   W
361 E 50 St
New York, NY 10022, 212-759-7364
  Pubs: *Adrienne's House* (HR&W, 1979), *Epicure, True
  Love, Teens Today*

Christopher Silver   W
300 Central Pk W
New York, NY 10024, 413-238-7769

Ruth M. Silver   P
374 Eastern Pkwy
Brooklyn, NY 11225
  Pubs: *Brooklyn Book Fair: Anth* (Somrie Pr, 1984),
  Brooklyn College Lit Rev

Mike Silverton 🎤 ✈   P
459 12 St, #2C
Brooklyn, NY 11215-5153, 718-788-0805
Internet: hensteeth@aol.com
  Pubs: *Battery Park* (Thing Pr, 1966)

Shirley J. Simmons   P
JAF Box 7496, GPO
New York, NY 10116
  Pubs: *Song of Circe* (Art & Oxygen, 1988), *Liberation*
  (Platen Pub, 1986), *Up Against the Wall*

Laura Simms   PP&P
814 Broadway, #3
New York, NY 10003, 212-674-3479
  Pubs: *Moon & Otter & Frog* (Hyperion, 1995), *Chosen
  Tales: Anth* (Rosen, 1995), *Revisioning the Myth of
  Demeter & Persephone: Anth* (Shambala, 1994)

Ana Maria Simo   W
New Dramatists, 424 W 44 St, New York, NY 10036

Jane Simon   P
145 Central Pk W
New York, NY 10023, 212-877-3566
  Pubs: *Incisions* (Croton Rev Pr, 1989), *UCLA Poet
  Physician Anth* (UCLA Pr, 1990), *Poet, Black Buzzard
  Rev, New Voices*

Mona Simpson   P&W
c/o Amanda Urban, ICM, 40 W 57 St, New York, NY
10019, 212-556-5600
  Pubs: *Anywhere But Here* (Knopf, 1987)

Abiola Sinclair   PP&P
Black History Magazine, 2565 Broadway MBE 262, New
York, NY 10025, 212-662-2942
Internet: www.blackhistorymag.com
  Pubs: *Black History Mag, Charleston Chronicle, New
  York Beacon, Daily Challenge, Black Mask, Big Red,
  Amsterdam News*

Davida Singer   P
223 W 105 St, #3FW
New York, NY 10025-3968, 212-663-3937
  Pubs: *Khupe* (CD; Recording, 1997), *Shelter Island
  Poems* (Canio's Edtns, 1995), *Ignite, Response, Little
  Mag, Passager, Caprice, Sinister Wisdom*

Frieda Singer 🎤   P
161-08 Jewel Ave, #1-C
Flushing, NY 11365, 718-591-2288
  Pubs: *Voices of the Holocaust: Anth* (Perfection
  Learning, 2000), *Which Lilith: Anth* (Jason Aronson,
  1999), *Blood to Remember: Anth* (Texas Tech U Pr,
  1992), *Poetpourri, The Formalist, South Florida Poetry
  Rev, Negative Capability*

Ravi Singh   P
225 E 5 St, #4D
New York, NY 10003, 212-475-0212
  Pubs: *Long Song to the One I Love* (White Lion,
  1986), *Another World: Anth* (Crown, 1992), *Grand
  Union, Exquisite Corpse, Cover*

Harriet Sirof 🎤   W
792 E 21 St
Brooklyn, NY 11210-1042, 718-859-3296
Internet: hsirof@aol.com
  Pubs: *Bring Back Yesterday, Because She's My Friend*
  (Atheneum, 1996, 1993)
Groups: Children

Hal Sirowitz   P
144-45 Sanford Ave, #2C
Flushing, NY 11355, 718-461-7892
  Pubs: *My Therapist Said, Mother Said* (Crown, 1998,
  1996), *Poetry in Motion: Anth* (Norton, 1996), *Chelsea,
  The Ledge, ACM, Speak*

Denis Sivack 🎤 ✈   P
1165 E 54 St, #4-F
Brooklyn, NY 11234-2426
  Pubs: *Gargoyle, Weber Studies, Esprit*

Arnold Skemer   W
58-09 205 St
Bayside, NY 11364-1712, 718-428-9368
  Pubs: *Investigations of the Cyberneticist, The Ruins of
  the City, Momus, B* (Phrygian Pr, 1999, 1998, 1997,
  1996), *Lost & Found Times, Transmoog, Drop Forge,
  Meat Epoch, Generator, New Surrealism*

Morty Sklar 🎤 ✈   P
35-50 85 St, Apt 8E
Jackson Heights, NY 11372-5540, 718-426-8788
Internet: msklar@mindspring.com
    Pubs: *To the White Lady* (The Spirit That Moves Us
    Pr, 1999), *The Night We Stood the First Poem*
    (Snapper Pr, 1987), *From A to Z: Anth* (Swallow Pr,
    1980), *Up for Our Rights* (Toothpaste Pr, 1977), *New
    Letters, NYQ, World Letter, Smiling Dog, Pearl*
I.D.: Editor. Groups: Teenagers, Recovering Addicts

Bob Slaymaker 🎤 ✈   P&W
415 W 24 St #4F
New York, NY 10011, 212-989-3212
Internet: bobslaymaker@mindspring.com
    Pubs: *Callaloo, CSM, Essence, Gargoyle, Natl Catholic
    Rptr, NYQ, Orbis, Press, River Styx, Weber Studies,
    Writers' Forum, Zuzu's Petals Qtly*

Henry Slesar   W
125 E 72 St, #12-A
New York, NY 10021, 212-628-1741
    Pubs: *Death on Television* (U Illinois Pr, 1989), *Murders
    Most Macabre* (Avon Bks, 1986), *Ellery Queen's
    Mystery Mag, Alfred Hitchcock's Mystery*

Barbara Smith 🎤 ✈   P&W
Charlotte Sheedy Literary Agency, 65 Bleecker St, 12th Fl,
New York, NY 10012
    Pubs: *Yours in Struggle* (Firebrand Bks, 1984), *Home
    Girls: Black Feminist Anth* (Kitchen Table, 1983), *Ms.,
    The Guardian, American Voice, Black Scholar, Village
    Voice*

C. W. Smith   W
Elaine Markson Literary Agency, 44 Greenwich Ave, New
York, NY 10011, 212-243-8480
    Pubs: *Thin Men of Haddam* (Texas Christian U Pr,
    1990), *Uncle Dad* (Berkley Bks, 1989), *Buffalo Nickel*
    (Poseidon, 1989), *Esquire, Quartet*

Charlie Smith 🎤 ✈   P&W
Maria Carvainis Literary Agency, 235 W End Ave, New
York, NY 10023, 212-580-1559
    Pubs: *Heroin, Before & After* (Norton, 2000, 1995),
    Shine Hawk (U Georgia Pr, 1998), *Cheap Ticket to
    Heaven,* (H Holt, 1996), *New Yorker, Paris Rev, Fence,
    Open City, Poetry, APR, New Republic*

Dinitia Smith   W
210 W 101 St, #3J
New York, NY 10025, 212-864-3866
    Pubs: *Remember This* (H Holt, 1989), *The Hard Rain*
    (Dial Pr, 1980), *Hudson Rev, Pequod*

Harry Smith 🎤 ✈   P
69 Joralemon St
Brooklyn, NY 11201-4003, 718-834-1212
    Pubs: *Two Friends II* (w/Menke Katz), *Ballads for the
    Possessed* (Birch Brook Pr, 1988, 1987)

Leora Skolkin Smith   W
61 Lexington Ave, #4G
New York, NY 10010
    Pubs: *Hystera* (Persea Bks, 1979), *Sarah Lawrence
    Rev*

Patti Smith   P
c/o Ina Lea Meibach, Meibach Epstein Reiss & Regis, 680
Fifth Ave, Ste 500, New York, NY 10019

Phil Demise Smith 🎤 ✈   P
421 Hudson St, #220
New York, NY 10014-3647, 212-989-7845
Internet: philsmith@waresforart.com
    Pubs: *Constant Variations, The Lost Supper/The Last
    Generation* (w/Gunter Temech) (Gegenshein, 1993,
    1990)

Robert L. Smith   P
271 E 78 St
New York, NY 10021, 212-734-3474
    Pubs: *Refractions* (Dragon's Teeth, 1979), *Galley Sail
    Rev, Roanoke Rev, Orbis, Long Pond Rev*

John J. Soldo   P
1627 81 St
Brooklyn, NY 11214-2107, 718-259-8016
    Pubs: *Sonnets for Our Risorgimento, In the Indies*
    (Brunswick Pub, 1993, 1991), *High Plains Scenarios*
    (Earthwise Pub, 1992), *Encore, Parnassus, Omnific*

Stacey Sollfrey   P
1117 E 86 St, Downstairs
Brooklyn, NY 11236, 718-209-9840
    Pubs: *Feeling the Roof of a Mouth That Hangs Open*
    (w/Sheila Murphy; Luna Bisonte Prod, 1991), *Lost &
    Found Times, Impetus, Fine Madness*

Barbara Probst Solomon 🎤   W
c/o Jennifer Lyons, The Writers House, 21 W 26 St, New
York, NY 10010, 212-961-0636
    Pubs: *Arriving Where We Started, The Beat of Life*
    (Great Marsh Pr, 1999, 1999), *Smart Hearts in the City*
    (HB, 1992), *Horse Trading & Ecstasy* (Northpoint,
    1989), *Short Flights* (Viking Pr, 1983)

Susan Sontag   W
The Wylie Agency, 250 W 57 St, New York, NY 10107
    Pubs: *In America, The Volcano Lover, A Susan Sontag
    Reader, Under the Sign of Saturn, I, Etcetera* (FSG,
    1999, 1992, 1982, 1981, 1978)

Gilbert Sorrentino   W
c/o Mel Berger, William Morris Agency, 1325 Ave of the
Americas, New York, NY 10019
    Pubs: *Pack of Lies, Under the Shadow, Misterioso,
    Rose Theatre* (Dalkey Archive, 1997, 1991, 1989,
    1987), *Red the Fiend* (Fromm Intl, 1995), *Odd Number*
    (North Point, 1985)

Peter Sourian   W
30 E 70 St
New York, NY 10021
   Pubs: *At the French Embassy in Sofia* (Ashod Pr,
   1992), *Drawing, Annandale, Ararat, The Nation*

Ellease Southerland   P&W
Marie Brown Assoc Inc, 625 Broadway, New York, NY
10012, 917-863-6528
Internet: www.ebeleoseye.com
   Pubs: *A Feast of Fools* (Africana Legacy Pr, 1998), *Let
   the Lion Eat Straw* (Scribner, 1979), *Calling the Wind:
   Anth* (Harper Perennial, 1993), *Breaking Ice: Anth*
   (Penguin, 1990), *Massachusetts Rev, Poet Lore*

Tom Spanbauer   W
Donadio & Olson, Inc, 121 W 27 St, Ste 704, New York,
NY 10001, 212-691-8077
   Pubs: *Les Chiens de L'Enfer* (Gallimard, 1989),
   Faraway Places (Putnam, 1988), *Mississippi Mud*

Muriel Spanier   W
c/o Amanda Urban, ICM, 40 W 57 St, New York, NY
10019, 212-556-5600
   Pubs: *Staying Afloat* (Random Hse, 1985), *Redbook,
   Sewanee Rev, QRL, Colorado Qtly*

Al Spector   P
69-31 222 St
Bayside, NY 11364, 718-224-8950
   Pubs: *Whispers of Spring* (The Plowman, 1994), *Bogg,
   Midwest Poetry Rev, Wind, Orphic Lute, Chicago St*

Scott Spencer   W
Alfred A Knopf, Inc, 201 E 50 St, New York, NY 10022,
212-751-2600
   Pubs: *The Rich Man's Table, Men in Black, Secret
   Anniversaries* (Knopf, 1998, 1995, 1990)

Katia Spiegelman   W
392 Sackett St, 2nd Fl
Brooklyn, NY 11231, 718-858-1404
   Pubs: *Peculiar Politics, Soul Catcher* (Marion Boyars
   Pub, 1993, 1990)

Peter Spielberg   W
321 W 24 S, Apt 13F
New York, NY 10011, 212-989-4298
   Pubs: *Hearsay* (Fiction Collective Two, 1992),
   Crash-Landing (Fiction Collective, 1985), *Fiction Intl,
   Europe, Mississippi Rev*

Norman Spinrad   W
c/o Jane Rotrosen, 318 E 51 St, New York, NY 10022,
212-752-1038

Peter Spiro   W
925 Union St
Brooklyn, NY 11215, 718-789-9020
   Pubs: *The United States of Poetry: Anth* (Abrams,
   1996), *Aloud: Voices from the Nuyorican Poets Cafe:
   Anth* (H Holt, 1994), *Poetry NY, Outerbridge, Flex,
   Maryland Rev*

Nancy Springer   W
Jean V. Naggar Literary Agency, 216 E 75 St, Ste 1E,
New York, NY 10021
   Pubs: *I Am Mordred* (Philomel, 1998), *Fair Peril, Larque
   on the Wing* (Avon, 1996, 1994), *Alfred Hitchcock's
   Mystery, Mag of Fantasy & Sci-Fi, Cricket, Boys Life,
   Pirate Writings*

Tricia Springstubb   W
c/o Elizabeth Kaplan, Ellen Levine Literary Agency, 15 E
26 St, Ste 1801, New York, NY 10010, 212-889-0620
   Pubs: *Two Plus One Goes Ape, Two Plus One Makes
   Trouble* (Scholastic, 1995, 1991)

Helen Leslie St. Aubin   P
900 W 190 St, #8-O
New York, NY 10040, 212-795-9209
   Pubs: *Poetry Rev, Confrontation, California State Poetry
   Qtly, Poet Lore, Poetry, Canada Rev, Wind*
Groups: G/L/B/T

Stephen Stark   W
c/o Lisa Ross, Spieler Agency, 154 W 57 St, New York,
NY 10019, 212-757-4439
   Pubs: *Second Son* (H Holt, 1992), *The Outskirts*
   (Algonquin Bks, 1988), *New Yorker, The Jrnl*

Robert Steiner   W
Georges Borchardt Inc., 136 E 57 St, New York, NY
10022, 212-753-5785
   Pubs: *Toward a Grammar of Abstraction* (Pennsylvania
   State Pr, 1993), *Broadway Melody of 1999, Matinee*
   (Fiction Collective Two, 1993, 1991)

Stephen Stepanchev 🎙 ✈   P
140-60 Beech Ave, #3C
Flushing, NY 11355-2831, 718-539-4463
   Pubs: *Seven Horizons* (Orchises Pr, 1997), *Descent*
   (Stone Hse Pr, 1988), *Poetry, New Yorker, New
   Criterion, Commonweal, Interim, NYQ*

Jack Stephens   P&W
51 7th Ave S, #5C
New York, NY 10014-6705
   Pubs: *Vector Love* (Haw River Bks, 1990), *Triangulation*
   (Crown, 1990), *Prairie Schooner, APR*

Michael Stephens   P&W
520 W 110 St, #5C
New York, NY 10025
　　Pubs: *The Brooklyn Book of the Dead* (Dalkey Archive,
　　1994), *Green Dreams* (U Georgia Pr, 1994), *Fiction,
　　Ontario Rev, Pequod*

Daniel Stern   W
Georges Borchardt Inc., 136 E 57 St, New York, NY
10022
　　Pubs: *Twice Upon a Time: Stories* (Norton, 1992),
　　Twice-Told Tales (Paris Rev Edtns, 1989), *An Urban
　　Affair* (S&S, 1980), *Paris Rev, Raritan, Columbia*

Phyllis Stern 🎤 ✈   P
167 W 71 St, Apt 9
New York, NY 10023-3833, 212-799-4365
Internet: s6mkjphyllis@netscape.com
　　Pubs: *Making Contact: Anth* (Voyage Out Pr, 1978),
　　Lilith, Womanews, Home Planet News
I.D.: G/L/B/T, Health-Related. Groups: Seniors, Prisoners

Margaret Stetler 🎤 ✈   P
189-49 45th Dr
Flushing, NY 11358-3412, 718-353-2185
Internet: mastetler@aol.com
　　Pubs: *The Naming of the Soul* (Four Zoas, 1980), *West
　　Wind Rev, Womanchild, Small Pond Rev, Kosmos,
　　Pegasus Dreaming, Telephone*

Nikki Stiller   P&W
341 E 65 St
New York, NY 10021, 212-472-1522
　　Pubs: *Notes of a Jewish Nun* (CCC, 1992), *Poetry NY,
　　Shaking Eve's Tree, Response, Primavera, Midstream,
　　Jewish Currents*

William R. Stimson   W
333 W 21 St, Apt 2FW
New York, NY 10011, 212-675-1213
　　Pubs: *Parting Gifts, Snowy Egret, New Thought Jrnl*

B. E. Stock 🎤 ✈   P
c/o Dolan, 28 Vesey St, PMB 2143, New York, NY
10007-2906
　　Pubs: *We Speak for Peace: Anth* (KIT Pr, 1993), *Orbis,
　　Blue Unicorn, Lyric, New Pr, Spring, Array, Karamu,
　　Skylark, Poems That Jump in the Dark, Piedmont Lit
　　Rev, Edge City Rev*

Norman Stock 🎤 ✈   P
77-11 35 Ave #2P
Jackson Heights, NY 11372-4633, 718-898-1762
Internet: stockn@mail.montclair.edu
　　Pubs: *Buying Breakfast for My Kamikaze Pilot* (Gibbs
　　Smith, 1994), *Verse, New Republic, College English,
　　NYQ, Denver Qtly, NER, Asylum*

Bob Stokes   W
PO Box 905
New York, NY 10039, 212-681-2966
　　Pubs: *The Circle Inside* (Nambati Pr, 1988), *Words to
　　Go* (Cultural Council Fdn, 1980)

Carolyn Stoloff   P
32 Union Sq E, Rm 911
New York, NY 10003, 212-473-0256
　　Pubs: *You Came to Meet Someone Else* (Asylum Arts
　　Pr, 1993), *A Year in Poetry: Anth* (Crown Pub, 1995),
　　New Yorker, Partisan Rev, Southern Rev, Yankee

Alison J. Stone 🎤 ✈   P
230 E 15 St, #7F
New York, NY 10003-3944
Internet: nygoddess@aol.com
　　Pubs: *Sweet Nothings: Rock & Roll in American Poetry:
　　Anth* (Indiana U Pr, 1994), *Catholic Girls: Anth* (Plume,
　　1992), *Paris Rev, Poetry, Ploughshares, NYQ, Artful
　　Dodge, Witness, Many Mountains Moving*

Alma Stone   W
523 W 112 St
New York, NY 10025

Laurie Stone 🎤 ✈   W
808 W End Ave
New York, NY 10025-5369, 212-663-7011
Internet: lstonehere@aol.com
　　Pubs: *Close to the Bone* (Grove, 1997), *Laughing in
　　the Dark* (Ecco, 1997), *Starting with Serge* (Doubleday,
　　1990), *TriQtly, New Letters, VLS, Nation, New Yorker*

Robert Stone   W
c/o Candida Donadio, Donadio & Olson, Inc, 121 W 27
St, Ste 704, New York, NY 10001, 212-691-8077
　　Pubs: *Outerbridge Reach* (Ticknor & Fields, 1992),
　　Children of Light, A Flag for Sunrise (Knopf, 1986,
　　1981)

James Story 🎤 ✈   P
500 9th St, #3F
Brooklyn, NY 11215-4112, 718-768-6919
　　Pubs: *Paper Boat, Berkeley Poetry Rev, Home Planet
　　News, Karamu, Now, Poets*

Mark Strand   P&W
c/o Harry Ford, Alfred A Knopf, Inc, 201 E 50 St, New
York, NY 10022, 212-751-2600
　　Pubs: *Dark Harbor* (Knopf, 1993), *Hopper: Anth* (Ecco
　　Pr, 1994)

Dennis Straus PP&P&W
PO Box 176
Rockaway Park, NY 11694-0176, 718-474-6547
   Pubs: *ABC Street* (Green Integer, 2001), *The Menaced Assassin, The Other Planet, Red Moon/Red Lake* (McPherson, 1989, 1988, 1988), *NAW, Central Park, Confrontation, Exile*

Brad Strickland W
Richard Curtis Associates, Inc, 171 E 74 St, New York, NY 10021, 212-772-7393
   Pubs: *Stowaways* (Pocket, 1994), *Ghost in the Mirror* (w/J. Bellairs; Dial, 1993), *Dragon's Plunder* (Atheneum, 1992), *Mag of Fantasy & Sci Fi*

Stephanie Strickland 🎤 ✈ P
220 E 70 St, #14C
New York, NY 10021-5421, 212-472-5502
   Pubs: *True North Hypertext* (Eastgate Systems, 1998), *True North* (U Notre Dame Pr, 1997), *The Red Virgin: A Poem of Simone Weil* (U Wisconsin Pr, 1993), *Give the Body Back* (U Missouri Pr, 1991), *Paris Rev*
Groups: Women, New Media

Vicki Stringer 🎤 P
5614 Netherland Ave, #1G
Riverdale, NY 10471
Internet: vicrvdl@aol.com
   Pubs: *Still Waters: Anth* (Poetry Today, 1997), *Troubadour, Amelia, American Poets & Poetry, Light, Lucidity, Nostalgia*

Chris Stroffolino P
331 13 St, Apt 4L
Brooklyn, NY 11215-5022, 201-459-9245
   Pubs: *Oops* (Pavement Saw Pr, 1994), *APR, Lift, First Intensity, o.blek, Lingo, Painted Bride Qtly, Talisman, Caliban, Sulfur*

Mark Sullivan P
630 Ft Washington Ave, Apt 2J
New York, NY 10040, 212-740-0013
   Pubs: *Willow Springs, Orion, BOMB*

Victoria Sullivan 🎤 ✈ P
620 W 116 St, #21
New York, NY 10027-7044, 212-749-7685
   Pubs: *The Divided Bed* (Hatch-Billops, 1982), *When a Lifemate Dies: Anth* (Fairview Pr, 1997), *Medicinal Purposes, NE Corridor, Chadakoin Rev, Pivot, Manhattan Poetry Rev, 13th Moon, Cape Rock, Artist & Influence, Poetry in Performance*
Groups: Women, College/Univ

Sekou Sundiata PP
910 Grand Concourse #7K
Bronx, NY 10451, 718-588-1205
   Pubs: *Longstoryshort* (CD; Righteous Babe, 2000), *The Blue Oneness of Dreams* (CD; Mouth Almighty, 1997), *Are & Be* (CD; Nommo Records, 1982), *Spirit & Flame: Anth* (Syracuse U Pr, 1997), *Essence, Black Nation, Blasted Allegories, New Museum*

David Surface W
81 St James Pl
Brooklyn, NY 11238
   Pubs: *Four Minute Fictions: Anth* (Word Beat Pr, 1987), *DoubleTake, Artful Dodge, Fiction, Crazyhorse, Willow Springs*

Linda Svendsen 🎤 ✈ W
Robin Straus Agency, 229 E 79 St, New York, NY 10021, 212-472-3282
   Pubs: *Marine Life* (FSG, 1992), *Oxford Book of Stories by Canadian Women* (Oxford, 1999), *Penguin Bk of Stories by Canadian Women* (Penguin, 1998)

Terese Svoboda 🎤 ✈ P
56 Ludlow St
New York, NY 10002
   Pubs: *Trailer Girl, A Drink Called Paradise* (Conterpoint Pr, 2001, 2000), *Mere Mortals, All Aberration* (U Georgia Pr, 1995, 1985), *Cannibal* (NYU Pr, 1994), *Laughing Africa* (U Iowa Pr, 1990), *Cleaned the Crocodile's Teeth* (Greenfield Rev Pr, 1985)

Brian Swann P
Faculty of Humanities, The Cooper Union, 41 Cooper Sq, New York, NY 10003, 212-353-4279
   Pubs: *Wearing the Morning Star* (Random Hse, 1996), *Song of the Sky* (U Massachusetts Pr, 1993), *The Plot of the Mice* (Capra Pr, 1986)

Roberta M. Swann 🎤 ✈ P&W
19 Stuyvesant Oval, #8B
New York, NY 10009-2027, 212-533-8705
Internet: swann@cooper.edu
   Pubs: *Yellow Silk* (Crown, 1990), *Everything Happens Suddenly, The Model Life* (Ancient Mariner Pr, 1989, 1988), *Indiana Rev, Kenyon Rev, Queen's Qtly, American Voice, New Letters, NAR, Ploughshares*
Groups: Seniors

Burton Swartz 🎤 ✈ PP
235 W 107 St, #234
New York, NY 10025-3020, 212-866-0118
   Pubs: *Grasshoppers* (Amer Theatre of Actors, NYC, 1999), *Eastside Roulette* (Homegrown Theatre, NYC, 1999), *The Hidden, Once Upon a Deal* (Riant Theatre, 1998, 1996), *Downbeat, Columbia Spectator, College Times, Show Business, National Star Chronicle*

Karen Swenson 🎙 ✈   P
25 W 54 St, #12E
New York, NY 10019-5404, 212-586-8507
Internet: karswen@aol.com
    Pubs: *A Daughter's Latitude, The Landlady in Bangkok*
    (Copper Canyon, 1999, 1994), *A Sense of Direction*
    (The Smith, 1990), *Attic of Ideals* (Doubleday, 1974),
    New Yorker, Saturday Rev

Janet Sylvester   P
W W Norton, 500 5th Ave, New York, NY 10110,
212-354-5500
    Pubs: *The Mark of Flesh* (Norton, 1997), *That Mulberry*
    Wine (Wesleyan, 1985), *Best American Poetry: Anth*
    (Scribner, 1994), *Boulevard, TriQtly, Shenandoah*

Ryder Syvertsen   W
c/o Robin Rue, The Writers House, 21 W 26 St, New
York, NY 10010
    Pubs: *C.A.D.S. #1-8* (Pinnacle Bks, 1990, 1985), *Mystic*
    Rebel, Doomsday Warrior (Zebra Bks, 1989, 1986),
    Psychic Spawn (Popular Library, 1987)

Sherri Szeman 🎙 ✈   P&W
c/o Jennifer Hengen, Sterling Lord Literistic, 65 Bleecker
St, New York, NY 10012, 212-780-6050
    Pubs: *Only with the Heart, Kommandant's Mistress*
    (Arcade, 2000), *Writer, Chicago Rev, Kenyon Rev,*
    Centennial Rev
Groups: Jewish, Alzheimer's

Marilynn Talal 🎙 ✈   P
308 E 79 St, #4E
New York, NY 10021-0906
    Pubs: *Our Own Clues: Poets of the Lake 2: Anth* (Our
    Lady of the Lake U Pr, 1993), *Blood to Remember:*
    Anth (Texas Tech U Pr, 1991), *Western Humanities*
    Rev, Poetry, New Republic, The Qtly
Groups: Children, Prisoners

Amy Tan   W
G P Putnam's Sons, 375 Hudson St, New York, NY
10014
    Pubs: *The Hundred Secret Senses* (Ivy Bks, 1996), *The*
    Kitchen God's Wife, The Joy Luck Club (Putnam, 1991,
    1989), *Atlantic, SF Focus, Seventeen*

Herbert Tarr   W
Scott Meredith Literary Agency, 845 3rd Ave, New York,
NY 10022, 212-245-5500
    Pubs: *A Woman of Spirit* (Donald I. Fine, 1989), *So*
    Help Me God! (Times Bks, 1981)

Ronald Tavel   P
c/o Mary Lou Aleskie, Helen Merrill Agency, 435 W 23 St,
#1A, New York, NY 10011, 212-691-5326
    Pubs: *Street of Stairs* (Olympia Pr, 1968), *Night Mag,*
    Unmuzzled Ox, Brooklyn Literary Rev

Meredith Tax   W
532 W 111 St, #75
New York, NY 10025
    Pubs: *Union Square, Rivington St* (Morrow, 1988,
    1982), *Rising of Women* (Monthly Rev, 1980), *Nation*

Conciere Taylor   P
67-08 Parsons Blvd, #6B
Flushing, NY 11365-2955
    Pubs: *In Concert: Anth, Shock Treatment: Anth* (Peak
    Output, 1989, 1988), *Rapunzel, Rapunzel: Anth* (Kathryn
    Machan Aal, 1979), *Earth's Daughters, Scapes,*
    Whetstone, Slugfest, Calliope

Laurie Taylor   W
Rodell-Collin Literary Agency, 110 W 40 St, New York,
NY 10018
    Pubs: *A Murder Waiting to Happen, Poetic Justice*
    (Walker & Co, 1989, 1988), *Analog, Alfred Hitchcock's*
    Mystery, Great River Rev

Theodore Taylor   W
c/o Gloria Loomis, Watkins Loomis Agency, Inc, 133 E 35
St, Ste 1, New York, NY 10016, 212-532-0080
    Pubs: *Rogue Wave, The Bomb, To Kill the Leopard,*
    Timothy of the Cay (HB, 1996, 1995, 1993, 1993)

Richard Tayson   P
86-75 Midland Parkway, Apt 4N
Jamaica Estates, NY 11432, 718-523-0370
    Pubs: *Pushcart Prize XXI: Anth* (Pushcart Pr, 1997),
    Things Shaped in Passing: Anth (Persea Bks, 1997),
    American Poetry: Next Generation: Anth (Carnegie
    Mellon, 2000), *The World in Us: Lesbian & Gay Poetry*
    of the Next Wave: Anth (St. Martin's Pr, 2000)

Nathan Teitel   P&W
365 W 25 St
New York, NY 10001, 212-255-9376
    Pubs: *In Time of Tide* (Lintel, 1990), *The Conscious*
    Reader: Anth (Macmillan, 1991), *Midstream*

Eleanor Wong Telemaque   W
230 E 88 St, #6G
New York, NY 10128-3383, 212-722-8828
    Pubs: *It's Crazy to Stay Chinese in Minnesota* (Thomas
    Nelson, 1995), *Haiti Through Its Holidays* (Blyden Pr,
    1990)

Fiona Templeton 🎙 ✈   PP&P
100 St Marks Pl, #7
New York, NY 10009-5822
    Pubs: *Delirium of Interpretations* (Green Integer, 2000),
    oops the join (rempress, 1997), *Hi Cowboy*
    (Mainstream, 1997), *Cells of Release, You–The City*
    (Roof Bks, 1997, 1990), *London* (Sun & Moon Pr,
    1984)

Megan Terry 🎤 ✈   P
E. Marton Agency, 1 Union Sq W Rm 612, New York, NY
10003-3303, 212-255-1908
    Pubs: *Right Brain Vacation Photos* (Omaha Magic
    Theatre Pr, 1991), *Fireworks: Anth* (Smith & Kraus,
    1995)

Nadja Tesich   W
855 W End Ave, #7A
New York, NY 10025
    Pubs: *Shadow Partisan, American Fiction: Anth* (New
    Rivers Pr, 1989, 1995), *Mademoiselle, Kenyon Rev,
    Confrontation, ACM, City Lights Rev, Nation, 13th Moon*

Catherine Texier   W
255 E 7 St
New York, NY 10009, 212-677-4748
    Pubs: *Panic Blood, Love Me Tender* (Viking, 1990,
    1987), *New Observations, Bomb, Heresies*

Marcelle Thiebaux   W
305 W 86 St, #11A
New York, NY 10024, 212-362-9906
    Pubs: *Literal Latte, Cream City Rev, Karamu, Twisted,
    El Gato Tuerto/The One-Eyed Cat*

James Alexander Thom   W
c/o Mitch Douglas, ICM, 40 W 57 St, New York, NY
10019
    Pubs: *The Children of First Man, Follow the River*
    (Ballantine, 1994, 1981)

Abigail Thomas 🎤 ✈   P&W
395 Riverside Dr
New York, NY 10025-1859, 212-864-6867
    Pubs: *Herb's Pajamas, An Actual Life, Getting Over
    Tom* (Algonquin, 1998, 1996, 1994), *DoubleTake,
    Missouri Rev, Paris Rev, Nation*

Charles Columbus Thomas   P
1245 Park Ave, #11K
New York, NY 10028, 212-876-9464

Joyce Carol Thomas   P
c/o Mitch Douglas, ICM, 40 W 57 St, New York, NY
10019
    Pubs: *Journey, The Golden Pasture* (Scholastic, 1988,
    1986), *Watergirl* (Avon, 1986)

Barbara Thompson   W
205 W 57 St
New York, NY 10019, 212-581-5448
    Pubs: *The Pushcart Prize Anthology, Shenandoah,
    McCall's, Paris Rev*

John A. Thompson   P&W
418 Central Pk W
New York, NY 10025, 212-749-1256
    Pubs: *The Founding of English Metre* (Columbia U Pr,
    1988)

Sharon Thompson   W
PO Box 20739, Tompkins Sq Sta
New York, NY 10009
    Pubs: *Powers of Desire* (Monthly Rev Pr, 1983), *Village
    Voice, Heresies, Feminist Studies*

Newton Thornburg   W
Don Congdon Assoc Inc., 156 5th Ave, Ste 625, New
York, NY 10010-7002, 212-645-1229
    Pubs: *Beautiful Kate, Valhalla, Black Angus* (Little,
    Brown, 1982, 1980, 1978)

Judith Thurman   P
445 E 86 St, #15D
New York, NY 10028
    Pubs: *Magic Lantern, Flashlight & Other Poems*
    (Atheneum, 1978, 1976)

Irene Tiersten   W
JET Literary Assoc, 124 E 84 St, New York, NY 10028,
212-879-2578
    Pubs: *One Big Happy Family* (The Reader Project,
    1990), *Among Friends* (St. Martin's, 1982), *Mediphors,
    First for Women, New Directions*

Gioia Timpanelli 🎤 ✈   PP
c/o Ira Silverberg, Donadio & Olson, Inc, 121 W 27 St,
Ste 704, New York, NY 10001, 212-691-8077
    Pubs: *Sometimes the Soul* (Vintage Pr, 2000)
Lang: Italian

Arthur Tobias   P
229 W 97 St, Apt 4J
New York, NY 10025-5611, 212-665-2962
    Pubs: *The View from Cold Mountain* (White Pine,
    1982), *Choice, Epoch, Ironwood, White Pine Jrnl*

James Tolan 🎤 ✈   P
110 Bement Ave
Staten Island, NY 10310-1500, 718-273-9447
Internet: jimtolan@mindspring.com
    Pubs: *Coffeehouse Poetry Anth* (Bottom Dog Pr, 1996),
    What Have You Lost: Anth (Greenwillow, 1999),
    *American Lit Rev, Atlanta Rev, The Baffler, Indiana
    Rev, Intl Qtly, Luna, The Qtly, Salt Hill Jrnl, Wisconsin
    Rev*
Groups: Children, Seniors

Vincent J. Tomeo 🎙 ✈   P
PO Box 52-7203
Flushing, NY 11352-7203, 718-961-6208
Internet: Mmin2@aol.com
   Pubs: *Poetry in Braille* (Intl Lighthouse Pr, 1999) *The
   American Dissident: Anth* (ContraOstrich Pr, 1999)
   Queens Times, US Korean Rev,

Lydia Tomkiw   P
85 E 3 St, #A3
New York, NY 10003-9040, 212-982-7256
   Pubs: *Unbearables: Anth* (Autonomedia, 1995), *Walk on
   the Wild Side: Anth* (Macmillan, 1994), *Aerial, B-City,
   Joe Soap's Canoe, Brooklyn Rev*

Yasunao Tone   PP
307 W Broadway, 3rd Fl
New York, NY 10013, 212-966-0945
   Pubs: *Solo for Wounded* (CD; Tzadik, 1997), *Musica
   Iconologos, Trio for a Flute Player & Lyrictron in Upper
   Air Observation* (CDs; Lovely Music, 1994, 1991),
   Conjunctions, Music

Mike Topp 🎙 ✈   P
8 Stuyvesant Oval #8H
New York, NY 10009, 212-673-2766
Internet: mike_topp@hotmail.com
   Pubs: *McSweeny's, Exquisite Corpse, LUNGFULL!,
   Long Shot, RealPoetik, Big Bridge, Tricyle, Mudfish,
   Brooklyn Rev, Poetry Project Newsletter, Columbia,
   Talisman*

Juanita Torrence-Thompson 🎙 ✈   P&W
Dept of Communications & Media, Fordham Univ, GSAS,
441 E Fordham Rd, Bronx, NY 10458, 718-817-4850
Internet: jtth@aol.com
   Pubs: *Paterson Lit Rev, Montserrat Rev, Snail's Pace
   Rev, San Fernando Poetry Jrnl, Chaminade Lit Rev,
   CQ, Green Hills Lit Lantern, Yefief, AIM, Caprice,
   Tucumcari, Appearances, Array Mag, Women's Work*
I.D.: African-American

Robert Towers   W
English Dept, Queens College, Flushing, NY 11367,
718-520-7480
   Pubs: *The Monkey Watcher, The Necklace of Kali*
   (HBJ, 1964, 1960)

Tony Towle   P
Tyler Productions, 75 Hudson St, New York, NY 10013,
212-285-0922
   Pubs: *Some Musical Episodes, Broadway 2: Anth*
   (Hanging Loose Pr, 1992, 1989), *New & Selected
   Poems 1963-1983* (Kulchur, 1983), *Postmodern
   American Poetry: Anth* (Norton, 1994), *Arshile, Otis
   Run, Hanging Loose, The World, Blade, Notas*

Peter Trachtenberg   W
c/o Gloria Loomis, Watkins Loomis Agency, Inc, 133 E 35
St, Ste 1, New York, NY 10016, 212-532-0080
   Pubs: *The Casanova Complex* (S&S, 1988),
   Mademoiselle, Der Stern, Chicago

Patricia Traxler 🎙 ✈   P&W
Brandt & Brandt Literary Agents, 1501 Broadway, New
York, NY 10036
   Pubs: *Blood* (St Martin's Pr, 2001), *Forbidden Words* (U
   Missouri Pr, 1994), *Best American Poetry: Anth*
   (Scribner, 1994), *Kenyon Rev, Ploughshares, Nation,
   Glimmer Train, Ms., Agni*

Calvin Trillin   W
12 Grove St
New York, NY 10014, 212-243-3455

David Trinidad 🎙 ✈   P
401 W Broadway, #1
New York, NY 10012, 212-274-9529
Internet: david_trinidad@hotmail.com
   Pubs: *Plasticville* (Turtle Point Pr, 2000), *Answer Song*
   (High Risk/Serpent's Tail, 1994), *Hand Over Heart:
   Poems 1981-1988* (Amethyst Pr, 1991)

Frederic Tuten 🎙 ✈   W
Watkins Loomis Agency, Inc, 133 E 35 St, Ste 1, New
York, NY 10016, 212-532-0080
   Pubs: *Van Gogh's Bad Cafe, Tintin in the New World*
   (Morrow, 1997, 1993), *Tallien* (FSG, 1988), *TriQtly,
   Fiction, Global City Rev*

David Unger   P
340 W 72 St, #4B
New York, NY 10023-2645
   Pubs: *Tropical Synagogues: Latin American Jewish
   Writing Anth* (Holmes & Meiers, 1994), *Neither
   Caterpillar Nor Butterfly* (Es Que Somos Muy Pobres
   Pr, 1986)

John Updike   P&W
Alfred A Knopf, Inc, 201 E 50 St, New York, NY 10022,
212-751-2600
   Pubs: *Trust Me, Roger's Version, The Witches of
   Eastwick* (Knopf, 1987, 1987, 1984), *New Yorker*

Robert Upton   W
419 W 22 St
New York, NY 10011, 212-989-5349
   Pubs: *A Killing in Real Estate, The Faberge Egg*
   (Dutton, 1990, 1988), *Dead on the Stick* (Viking, 1986)

Jean Valentine 🎤 ✈   P
527 W 110 St, #81
New York, NY 10025-2082, 212-866-9740
   Pubs: *Cradle of Real Life* (Wesleyan U Pr, 2000),
Growing Darkness, Growing Light (Carnegie Mellon,
1997), *The River at Wolf, Home Deep Blue* (Alice
James Bks, 1992, 1989), *Field, New Yorker, APR*

Anthony Valerio   W
106 Charles St, #14
New York, NY 10014-2695, 212-675-4685
   Pubs: *Paris Rev, Paris Transcontinental*

Nicholas Valinotti   P
448 Bergen St, #4C
Brooklyn, NY 11217
   Pubs: *Brooklyn Rev, Cathartic, Galley Sail Rev, Home
Planet News, Cottonwood, The Archer, Ailanthus,
Cover, Mudfish*

Carmen Valle   P&W
71 E 4 St, #6A
New York, NY 10003, 212-673-7824
   Pubs: *Entre la Vigilia y el Sueno de las Fieras, Desde
Marruecos Te Escribo* (Instituto de Cultura
Puertorriqena, 1994, 1992), *Trasimagen, Balcon*

Henry Van Dyke   W
40 Waterside Plaza, #16-L
New York, NY 10010, 212-683-5587
   Pubs: *Lunacy & Caprice* (Ballantine, 1987),
Afro-American Short Story Anth (HC, 1993), *Antioch
Rev, Story Qtly*

Ronald Vance   W
10 W 18 St
New York, NY 10011
   Pubs: *Interstate, O.ars, Benzene, Clown War, Sun &
Moon*

Herminio Vargas   P
Brooklyn College, Bedford Ave & Ave H, Brooklyn, NY
11210

Susan Varon 🎤 ✈   P
136 E 76th St, #3D
New York, NY 10021-2830, 212-744-1564
Internet: susanvaron@juno.com
   Pubs: *Slant, Spillway, Outerbridge, South Coast Poetry
Jrnl, Snail's Pace Rev, Sow's Ear Poetry Rev,
Passager, Defined Providence, Passages North, Third
Coast, Green Mountains Rev, Rattle*

Ed Vega   W
S. Bergholz Literary Services, 17 W 10 St, #5, New York,
NY 10011, 212-387-0545
   Pubs: *Casualty Report, Mendoza's Dreams, The
Comeback* (Arte Publico Pr, 1991, 1987, 1985),
Portable Lower East Side, MBM

Richard Vetere 🎤 ✈   P&W
53-40 62 St
Maspeth, NY 11378-1208, 718-939-9398
   Pubs: *The Third Miracle* (S&S, 1998), *A Dream of
Angels* (Northwoods Pr, 1984), *Memories of Human
Hands* (Manyland Bks, 1976), *Poets On, Dreamworks,
Cobweb, Orbis, Hybrid, Abraxas*

Gore Vidal   W
William Morris Agency, 1325 Ave of the Americas, New
York, NY 10019, 212-586-5100

Joseph Viertel   W
c/o Owen Laster, William Morris Agency, 1325 Ave of the
Americas, New York, NY 10019, 212-586-5100
   Pubs: *Lifelines, Monkey on a String* (S&S, 1982, 1968),
To Love &Corrupt (Random Hse, 1962)

David Vigoda   W
Ann Elmo Literary Agency, 60 E 42 St, New York, NY
10017
   Pubs: *Nucleus* (Baronet Publishing, 1980)

Michael Villanueva   P
437 E 12 St, #17
New York, NY 10009, 212-673-1671
   Pubs: *Nice to See You: Homage to Ted Berrigan: Anth*
(Coffee Hse, 1988), *Transfer, Cover, Gandhabba*

Vincent Virga 🎤 ✈   W
Elaine Markson Literary Agency, 44 Greenwich Ave, New
York, NY 10011, 212-243-8480
   Pubs: *Vadriel Vail, Gaywyck* (Alyson, 2001, 2000), *A
Comfortable Corner* (Avon, 1982)
Groups: G/L/B/T

Tricia Vita   W
42 Perry St
New York, NY 10014-7307
   Pubs: *Yankee, Boston Rev, Provincetown Arts, Ms.,
Games Mag, Shocked & Amazed!*

Susan Volchok 🎤 ✈   W
303 W 66 St
New York, NY 10024-6305, 212-787-4262
Internet: suzev@aol.com
   Pubs: *Virginia Qtly Rev, New Novel Rev, 13th Moon,
Paris Transcontinental, Kenyon Rev, Asylum Annual,
Confrontation, Hayden's Ferry Rev*
Lang: Dutch, French. I.D.: Jewish, Martial Arts. Groups:
Children, Seniors

Lenore Von Stein 🎤 ✈   PP
29 Charles St
New York, NY 10014
Internet: vonstein@earthlink.net
   Pubs: *Tolerating Ambition, Blind Love = Porno?, Love
Is Dead* (CD: 1687, Inc, 1999, 1996, 1993)

Dina von Zweck   P&W
80 Beekman St
New York, NY 10038-1879, 212-732-1020
    Pubs: *Halloween & Other Poems, Sam Shepard's Dog*
    (White Deer Bks, 1985, 1984), *Helicon 9, Modularist
    Rev, Berkshire Rev, New Letters*

Kurt Vonnegut   W
Donald C Farber, Hartman & Craven LLP, 460 Park Ave,
11 Fl, New York, NY 10022-1906
    Pubs: *God Bless You, Dr. Kevorkian* (Seven Stories Pr,
    2000), *Timequake, Hocus Pocus, Bluebeard* (Putnam,
    1997, 1990, 1987)

Susan Vreeland 🎤 ✈   W
Barbara Braun Assoc, 115 W 18 St, 5th Fl, New York,
NY 10011, 212-604-9023
Internet: http://users.funtv.com/~igray/susanvreeland.html
    Pubs: *Artemesia, Girl in Hyacinth Blue* (Viking, 2001,
    2000), *What Love Sees* (Thorndike/S&S, 1996), *NER,
    New Millennium, Dominion Rev, Missouri Rev,
    Confrontation, Manoa, Alaska Qtly Rev, Crescent Rev*

Chuck Wachtel   P&W
337 E 5 St #5FW
New York, NY 10003, 212-673-1511
    Pubs: *Because We Are Here: Stories & Novellas, The
    Gates* (Viking/Penguin 1996, 1993), *Joe the Engineer*
    (Morrow, 1983), *The World, Sun, Hanging Loose,
    Nation, Village Voice, Witness, Pequod*

Dan Wakefield   W
Helen Brann Agency, 157 W 57 St, New York, NY 10019
    Pubs: *Home Free* (Delacorte, 1977)

Derek Walcott   P
FSG, 19 Union Sq W, New York, NY 10003
    Pubs: *Tiepolo's Hound, Bounty* (FSG, 2000, 1997)

William Walden   P
30 E 9 St, #4K
New York, NY 10003
    Pubs: *New Yorker, Atlantic, Georgia Rev,
    Massachusetts Rev, Light, Punch*

Mel Waldman   P&W
1660 E 13 St, #D2
Brooklyn, NY 11229, 718-375-1474
    Pubs: *Festina Lente* (Somrie Pr, 1982), *The Saint,
    Espionage Mag, Pulpsmith, Prelude to Fantasy*

Alice Walker   P&W
Wendy Weil Agency Inc, 232 Madison Ave, Ste 1300,
New York, NY 10016, 212-685-0030
    Pubs: *Possessing the Secret of Joy, Her Blue Body
    Everything We Know: Earthing Poems 1965-1991,
    Finding the Green Stone* (HBJ, 1992, 1991, 1991)

Pamela Walker   W
239 W 256 St
Bronx, NY 10471
    Pubs: *World in Our Words* (Blair Pr/Prentice Hall,
    1997), *Twyla* (Prentice-Hall/Berkley, 1976), *The Whole
    Story: Anth* (Bench Pr, 1995), *Hawaii Rev, Iowa
    Woman*

Wendy Walker   W
855 W End Ave, #6A
New York, NY 10025-4995
    Pubs: *Stories Out of Omarie, The Secret Service* (Sun
    & Moon Pr, 1995, 1992), *Conjunctions, Fiction Intl,
    Parnassus*

Barry Wallenstein 🎤 ✈   P
340 Riverside Dr, #7B
New York, NY 10025-3436, 212-222-2556
    Pubs: *A Measure of Conduct, The Short Life of the
    Five Minute Dancer* (Ridgeway Pr, 1999, 1993), *Love &
    Crush* (Persea, 1991), *Poetry Wales, Pequod,
    Ploughshares, Laurel Rev*

Rhoda Waller 🎤 ✈   P
370 W 11 St, #4
New York, NY 10014-6246
    Pubs: *Sea Sky Light* (Private, 1999), *Between Worlds,
    Plumed Horn, Black Maria, Cummington Rev, Ikon*
Groups: Seniors

Irene Wanner 🎤 ✈   W
Donadio & Olson, Inc, 121 W 27 St, Ste 704, New York,
NY 10001, 212-691-8077
Internet: iwanner@u.washington.edu
    Pubs: *Sailing to Corinth* (Owl Creek Pr, 1988), *Circle of
    Women: Anth* (Penguin, 1994), *Antaeus, Antioch Rev,
    Ploughshares, NW Rev, Blue Mesa Rev, New Orphic
    Rev*

Constance Warloe   W
Linda Chester Literary Agency, 630 5th Ave, Rockefeller
Ctr, New York, NY 10111, 212-439-0881
    Pubs: *The Legend of Olivia Cosmos Montevideo*
    (Atlantic Monthly Pr, 1994)

Larkin Warren   P
315 W 23 St, #11-B
New York, NY 10011
    Pubs: *Old Sheets* (Alice James Bks, 1979), *Yankee,
    Mississippi Rev, Tendril, Mid-American Rev, Akros*

Lewis Warsh   P
701 President St, #1
Brooklyn, NY 11215, 718-857-5974
    Pubs: *Money Under the Table* (Trip Street Pr, 1997),
    Avenue of Escape (Long News, 1995), *A Free Man*
    (Sun & Moon, 1991)

Chocolate Waters   PP&P&W
415 W 44 St, #7
New York, NY 10036, 212-581-6820
Pubs: *Mom: Candid Memories* (Alyson Pubs, 1998),
Coffeehouse Poetry Anth (Bottom Dog Pr, 1996), *My
Lover Is a Woman: Anth* (Ballantine, 1996), *Medicinal
Purposes, Libido, Poetry Cafe, Mudfish, Zero City,
Westerly*

Gordon R. Watkins   P
675 Water St, #19D
New York, NY 10002

D. Rahim Watson   PP&P
250 W 54 St, Ste 811
New York, NY 10019, 212-541-7600
Pubs: *Lovers, Friends & Enemies, Survival '80s, Things
We Do to Each Other* (1st Cousins, 1982)

Vivienne Wechter ⊈ ⊀   P
Artist in Residence, Fordham Univ, FMH 230, Bronx, NY
10458, 718-817-4898
Pubs: *A View from the Ark* (Barlenmir Hse, 1975), *Arts
Interaction, Other Voices*

Jerome Weidman   W
1230 Park Ave #10C
New York, NY 10128-1728

Bibi Wein ⊈ ⊀   W
210 W 101 St, #9-A
New York, NY 10025-5035
Pubs: *Yes* (HBJ, 1969), *Ariadne's Thread: Anth* (H&R,
1982), *Kalliope, Mademoiselle, Iris, Permafrost, Other
Voices, American Letters & Commentary*
I.D.: Rural Communities, Prisoners. Groups: Prisoners,
Seniors

Jeff Weinstein   W
54 E 7 St
New York, NY 10003, 212-677-3504
Pubs: *Life in San Diego* (Sun & Moon, 1982), *Pushcart
Prize IV Anth, Crawl Out Your Window*

R. Weis   PP
516 E 6 St, #2
New York, NY 10009, 212-677-9093
Pubs: *Friday Evening at La Galleria: New Voices New
Works* (La Mama, 1988), *Lyra, In Fashion*

Marjorie Welish ⊈ ⊀   P
225 W 10 St #2C
New York, NY 10014-2974
Pubs: *The Annotated "Here"* (Coffee Hse Pr, 2000),
Begetting Textile (Equipage, 2000), *Else, in Substance*
(Paradigm Pr, 1999), *Casting Sequences* (U Georgia
Pr, 1993), *Moving Borders: Anth* (Talisman Hse, 1998)
Groups: College/Univ

Sheila Weller   W
39 Jane St, #5A
New York, NY 10014, 212-741-0042
Pubs: *Hansel & Gretel in Beverly Hills* (Morrow, 1978),
Ms., Redbook

Mac Wellman ⊈ ⊀   P
c/o Buddy Thomas, ICM, 40 W 57 St, New York, NY
10019, 212-556-5720
Pubs: *Annie Salem, The Land Beyond the Forest, The
Fortuneteller, A Shelf in Woop's Clothing* (Sun & Moon
Pr, 1996, 1995, 1991, 1990)

Rebecca Wells   W
Jonathan Dolger Agency, 49 E 96 St, #9B, New York, NY
10128, 212-427-1853
Pubs: *Divine Secrets of the Ya-Ya Sisterhood, Little
Altars Everywhere* (HC, 1996), *Mississippi Rev*

Kate Wenner   W
Elaine Markson Literary Agency, 44 Greenwich Ave, New
York, NY 10011, 212-243-8480
Pubs: *Shamba Letu* (HM 1970)

Eliot Werbner   P
1150 E 22 St
Brooklyn, NY 11210-3620
Pubs: *Prelude* (The Four Seas, 1930), *Blue Unicorn,
The Lyric, Western Poetry, The Archer*

Judith Werner   P
3987 Saxon Ave
Bronx, NY 10463, 718-796-4548
Pubs: *Sixteen Voices: Anth* (Mariposa Pub, 1994),
*South Dakota Rev, Visions Intl, Bridges, The Lyric,
ELF, Yankee, Four Quarters, Slant, Sow's Ear*

Evelyn Wexler ⊈ ⊀   P
5550 Fieldston Rd, #7D
Bronx, NY 10471-2522, 718-549-4636
Internet: evwex@aol.com
Pubs: *Occupied Territory, The Geisha House* (Mayapple
Pr, 1994, 1992), *Beyond Lament :Anth* (Northwestern U
Pr, 1998), *ACM, Nimrod, Negative Capability, Classical
Outlook*
Lang: Hungarian

Kate Wheeler   W
Witherspoon Assoc, Inc, 235 E 31 St, New York, NY
10016
Pubs: *Not Where I Started From* (HM, 1993), *O. Henry
Awards: Anth* (Doubleday, 1992), *Threepenny Rev,
Black Warrior Rev, Gettysburg Rev*

Susan Wheeler 🎤 ✈   P
37 Washington Sq W, #10A
New York, NY 10011-9100, 212-254-3984
Internet: susanwheeler@earthlink.net
    Pubs: *Source Codes* (SALT, 2000), *Smokes* (Four Way
    Bks, 1998), *Bag o' Diamonds* (U Georgia Pr, 1993),
    Best American Poetry: Anth (Macmillan, 1996), *New
    Yorker, Paris Rev*

Clark Whelton   W
39 1/2 Washington Sq S
New York, NY 10002

Edgar White   P&W
New Dramatists, 424 W 44 St, New York, NY 10036,
212-757-6960
    Pubs: *The Rising* (Marion Boyars Pub, 1990)

Edmund White   W
313 W 22 St, #2D
New York, NY 10011, 212-989-7084
    Pubs: *The Married Man* (Knopf, 2000), *A Boy's Own
    Story, States of Desire* (Dutton, 1982, 1980)

Wendy White-Ring 🎤 ✈   W
Literary Dept, William Morris Agency, 1325 Ave of the
Americas, New York, NY 10019
Internet: whitering@uswest.net
    Pubs: *Micro Fiction: Anth* (Norton, 1996), *Breaking Up
    Is Hard to Do: Anth* (Crossing Pr, 1994), *NAR,
    American Lit Rev, Sun Dog, SE Rev, Great Stream
    Rev*
Groups: Children, Seniors

Anne Whitehouse 🎤 ✈   P
340 Riverside Dr
New York, NY 10024-3423, 212-749-5377
    Pubs: *The Surveyor's Hand* (Compton Pr, 1981),
    Boulevard, American Voice, Buffalo Spree

Nathan Whiting 🎤 ✈   P
105 Buckingham Rd, #6D
Brooklyn, NY 11226-4330, 718-856-6248
    Pubs: *Contemplations* (MAF Pr, 1987), *Light Talks a
    Lot* (Agni, 1983)

George Whitmore   P
10 Downing St, #5T
New York, NY 10014, 212-675-4594
    Pubs: *The Confessions of Danny Slocum* (St. Martin's,
    1980), *On the Line: Anth* (Crossing Pr, 1981)

Frances Whyatt   P
61 Jane St #9G
New York, NY 10014, 212-255-7378
    Pubs: *A Real Man & Other Stories* (British
    American/Paris Rev Edtns, 1990), *McCall's*

Mildred Wiackley   P
PO Box 82, Stuyvesant Sta
New York, NY 10009, 718-386-3283
    Pubs: *Ante, Apercu, Eidon, Graffiti, Format*

Leo Wiener 🎤   P
PO Box 610233
Bayside, NY 11361-0233, 718-225-3523
Internet: leopo@juno.com
    Pubs: *Out of Season: Anth* (Amangansett Pr, 1993),
    *Vega, DeKalb Lit Jrnl, Sonoma Mandala, Proof Rock,
    Plowman, Quickenings, Work Technique, JVC, Thirteen,
    Hob-Nob*
I.D.: Seniors

Brooke Wiese   P
230 E 97 St, Apt 4W
New York, NY 10029, 212-427-4691
    Pubs: *At the Edge of the World* (Ledge Pr, 2000), *My
    Lover Is a Woman: Anth* (Ballantine Bks, 1996),
    *American Tanka, Atlanta Rev, Brooklyn Rev,
    Confluence, Flyway, Hawai'i Rev, Laurel Rev, Ledge,
    Plainsongs, Pleiades, Poetry Motel, Tucumcari Lit Rev*

Elie Wiesel   W
Georges Borchardt Inc., 136 E 57 St, New York, NY
10022, 212-753-5785
    Pubs: *Night, The Forgotten, All Rivers Run to the Sea*
    (Knopf, 1995, 1995, 1995)

Roslyn Willett 🎤 ✈   W
441 W End Ave, #15A
New York, NY 10024, 212-787-6060
    Pubs: *Papyrus, Short Stories Bimonthly, Art &
    Understanding, Timber Creek Rev, Words of Wisdom*
Lang: French

C. K. Williams 🎤 ✈   P
c/o Jonathan Galassi, FSG, 19 Union Sq W, New York,
NY 10003
Internet: ckwilliams@compuserve.com
    Pubs: *Misgivings, Repair, The Vigil, Selected Poems, A
    Dream of Mind, Flesh & Blood* (FSG, 2000, 1999,
    1997, 1994, 1992, 1987), *Tar* (Random Hse, 1983),
    New Yorker, APR

Edward F. Williams 🎤 ✈   PP
1633 Sterling Pl, #4H
Brooklyn, NY 11233-4970, 718-735-6153
    Pubs: *E. F. Williams, Urban Poet* (CD; Libra
    Productions, 1999)
Groups: Prisoners, Spiritual/Religious

Gary Williams   P
36 E 4 St, Apt 2
New York, NY 10003, 212-982-7602
    Pubs: *Waterways, Pan Arts Mag, Jane, Manhattan
    Poetry Rev, Home Planet News*

Regina E. Williams   P
132-11 Foch Blvd
South Ozone Park, NY 11420, 718-322-9550
  Pubs: *Our Work & God's World* (Presbyterian Pub Hse,
  1988), *New Rain: Anth* (Blind Beggar, 1988)

J. N. Williamson   W
Kay McCauley, Pimlico Literary Agency, Box 20447, 1539
1st Ave, New York, NY 10028, 212-628-9720
  Pubs: *Bloodlines, The Book of Webster's* (Longmeadow
  Pr, 1994, 1993), *Don't Take Away the Light* (Zebra
  Bks, 1993), *Pulphouse, Nightworld*

Leigh Allison Wilson   W
c/o Elizabeth McKee, Harold Matson Co, Inc, 276 5th
Ave, New York, NY 10001
  Pubs: *Wind: Stories* (Morrow, 1989), *From the Bottom
  Up* (Penguin, 1984), *Harper's, Grand St*

Martha Wilson   PP&W
112 Franklin St
New York, NY 10013, 212-925-4671

Paul Hastings Wilson   W
314 E 84 St
New York, NY 10028
  Pubs: *Turning Islands* (Avon, 1977), *Center*

William S. Wilson   W
458 W 25 St
New York, NY 10001-6502, 212-989-2229
  Pubs: *Birthplace* (North Point Pr, 1982), *Why I Don't
  Write Like Franz Kafka* (Ecco/Norton, 1977)

Fran Winant   P
PO Box 398, Stuyvesant Sta
New York, NY 10009
  Pubs: *Goddess of Lesbian Dreams, Dyke Jacket,
  Looking at Women* (Violet Pr, 1980, 1976, 1971)

Ronna Wineberg (Blaser) 🎤 ✈   W
11 Washington Mews
New York, NY 10003
Internet: ronnagroup@aol.com
  Pubs: *A Tennessee Landscape, People & Places: Anth*
  (Cool Springs Pr, 1996), *South Dakota Rev, Crone's
  Nest, American Way, Midstream, Colorado Rev,
  Colorado Daily*
Groups: Jewish, Prisoners

David Winn   W
English Dept, Hunter College, 695 Park Ave, New York,
NY 10021
Internet: dwinn@hejira.hunter.cuny.edu
  Pubs: *Gangland* (Knopf, 1982)

Mary Winters 🎤 ✈   P
434 E 52 St, #4E
New York, NY 10022-6402, 212-753-3320
  Pubs: *A Pocket History of the World* (Nightshade Pr,
  1996), *Anth of Mag Verse & Yearbook of American
  Poetry: Anth* (Monitor Bk Co, 1997), *Qtly West,
  Commonweal, Press, Poetry East, Poet Lore, Gulf
  Coast*
I.D.: Women. Groups: Women, Children

Elizabeth Winthrop 🎤 ✈   W
250 W 90 St #6A
New York, NY 10024-1123
Internet: www.absolute-sway.com/winthrop
  Pubs: *Promises,* (Clarion, 2000), *Island Justice* (Morrow,
  1998), *The Battle for the Castle* (Holiday Hse, 1993),
  Best American Short Stories: Anth (HM, 1992)
Groups: Children, Emerging Writers

William Wiser   W
c/o Emilie Jacobson, Curtis Brown Ltd., 10 Astor Pl, New
York, NY 10003-6935, 212-473-5400

Ellen Wisoff   P
1782 E 19 St
Brooklyn, NY 11229, 718-375-2355
  Pubs: *Partisan Rev, Denver Qtly, Sun & Moon, NY Arts
  Jrnl, Zone, City*

Francine Witte   P
PO Box 6694, Yorkville Sta
New York, NY 10128, 212-289-3034
  Pubs: *Calliope, Poet & Critic, Connecticut River Rev,
  Florida Rev, Bellingham Rev, Tar River Poetry,
  Outerbridge*

Larry Woiwode 🎤 ✈   P&W
Donadio & Olson, Inc, 121 W 27 St, New York, NY
10001, 212-691-8077
Internet: woiwode@ctctel.com
  Pubs: *Beyond the Bedroom Wall* (Graywolf, 1997),
  Silent Passengers (Atheneum, 1993), *Acts* (Harper SF,
  1993), *New Yorker, Paris Rev, Image, Atlantic, Harper's*

Michele Wolf 🎤 ✈   P
407 E 88 St, #4A
New York, NY 10128-6661, 212-876-0710
  Pubs: *Conversations During Sleep* (Anhinga Pr, 1998),
  The Keeper of Light (Painted Bride Qtly, 1995), *When I
  Am an Old Woman I Shall Wear Purple: Anth*
  (Papier-Mache Pr, 1987), *Poetry, Hudson Rev,
  Boulevard, Antioch Rev, SPR, Poet Lore*

Linda Wolfe   W
c/o Lynn Nesbit, Janklow & Nesbit Assoc, 598 Madison
Ave, New York, NY 10022-1614, 212-421-1700
  Pubs: *Love Me to Death* (Pocket Bks, 1998), *Professor
  & the Prostitute* (HM, 1986), *Private Practices* (S&S,
  1980), *Cosmopolitan, Woman, Ladies' Home Jrnl*

Eunice Wolfgram   P
c/o Raymond Ross, 47 E Houston St, #3, New York, NY
10012, 212-966-0897
    Pubs: *Three Hundred Chinese & Other Events* (Home
    Planet Pub, 1975)

Hilma Wolitzer   W
500 E 85 St, #18H
New York, NY 10028-7456, 212-861-8062
    Pubs: *Tunnel of Love* (HC, 1994), *Silver, In the
    Palomar Arms, Hearts* (FSG, 1988, 1983, 1980), *In the
    Flesh* (Morrow, 1977)

Meg Wolitzer   W
c/o Peter Matson, Sterling Lord Literistic, 65 Bleecker St,
New York, NY 10012, 212-780-6050
    Pubs: *This Is Your Life* (Crown, 1988), *Hidden Pictures*
    (HM, 1986)

Diane Wolkstein   PP&P
10 Patchin Pl, 1 Fl
New York, NY 10011
    Pubs: *DreamSongs, Abulafia, Part of My Heart*
    (Cloudstone Pr, 1992), *The First Love Stories* (H&R,
    1991), *Oom Razoom* (Morrow, 1991)

Janet S. Wong 🎤 ✈   P
c/o Margaret McElderry, S&S, 1230 Ave of the Americas,
New York, NY 10020-1586
Internet: www.janetwong.com
    Pubs: *Night Garden, The Rainbow Hand, Behind the
    Wheel, A Suitcase of Seaweed & Other Poems* (S&S,
    2000, 1999, 1999, 1996), *Good Luck Gold & Other
    Poems* (Macmillan, 1994)
I.D.: Asian-American. Groups: Children, Teachers

Jacqueline Woodson   W
Charlotte Sheedy Literary Agency, 65 Bleecker St, New
York, NY 10012, 212-780-9800
    Pubs: *Autobiography of a Family Photo* (Dutton, 1995),
    I Hadn't Meant to Tell You This (Delacorte, 1994),
    Kenyon Rev, American Voice

Dale Worsley   W
150 Lafayette Ave #1
Brooklyn, NY 11238, 718-789-3640
    Pubs: *The Focus Changes of August Previco*
    (Vanguard, 1980), *Hoy* (NPR Broadcast, 1992)

Charles S. Wright   W
FSG, 19 Union Sq W, New York, NY 10003,
212-741-6900
    Pubs: *The Wig, The Messenger* (FSG, 1966, 1963)

Jeffrey Cyphers Wright   P
632 E 14 St, #18
New York, NY 10009, 212-673-1152
    Pubs: *Out Loud: Nuyorican Poets Cafe Anth* (H Holt,
    1995), *Out of this World: Anth* (Crown, 1991), *Up Late:
    Anth* (Four Walls, Eight Windows, 1987), *Exquisite
    Corpse*

K. C. Wright   W
c/o D. Kossow, Becker & London, 400 E 56 St #10B,
New York, NY 10022
    Pubs: *Everyman's Dream* (Carlyle Pr, 1978)

Sarah Elizabeth Wright   P&W
780 W End Ave, #1D
New York, NY 10025
    Pubs: *A Philip Randolph* (S&S/Silver Burdett, 1990),
    This Child's Gonna Live (Feminist Pr, 1986), *Black
    Scholar*

Stephen Wright   W
PO Box 1341, FDR Sta
New York, NY 10150, 212-213-4382
    Pubs: *The Adventures of Sandy West, Private Eye*
    (Mystery Notebook Edtns, 1986)

Susan Yankowitz 🎤 ✈   W
c/o Mary Harden, Harden-Curtis Assoc, 850 Seventh Ave,
New York, NY 10024, 212-977-8502
Internet: syankowitz@aol.com
    Pubs: *Silent Witness* (Knopf, 1976), *Excavators: Anth*
    (Gnosis Pr, 1993), *Taking The Fall: Anth* (Parnassus,
    1986), *QRL, Parnassus, Gnosis, Solo, Heresies,
    Performing Arts Jrnl, Yale Theatre, Poetry in Rev*

Camille D. Yarbrough   PP&P
246 W 137 St
New York, NY 10030, 212-491-9503
    Pubs: *Tamika & the Wisdom Rings* (Random Hse,
    1994), *The Shimmershine Queens* (Putnam-Paperstar,
    1989), *The Little Tree Growin in the Shade, Cornrows*
    (Coward, McCann, 1985, 1979), *Black Collegian*

John Yau   P
PO Box 1910, Canal St Sta
New York, NY 10013
    Pubs: *Radiant Silhouette: New & Selected Works* (Black
    Sparrow Pr, 1989), *APR, Sulfur, Sun*

Rafael Yglesias   W
c/o Lynn Nesbit, Janklow & Nesbit Assoc, 598 Madison
Ave, New York, NY 10022-1614
    Pubs: *Dr. Neruda's Cure for Evil, Fearless* (Warner
    Bks, 1996, 1993), *The Murderer Next Door* (Crown,
    1990), *Only Children* (Ballantine, 1989)

Michael T. Young   P
442 W 22 St, Apt 20
New York, NY 10011
    Pubs: *Because the Wind Has Questions* (Somers Rocks Pr, 1997), *Pivot, Red Jacket, The Lyric, The Hiram Poetry Rev, Birmingham Rev, Inkshed*

Bill Zavatsky 🎤 ✈   P
100 W 92 St, #9D
New York, NY 10025-7503, 212-496-2956
Internet: bzav@earthlink.net
    Pubs: *For Steve Royal & Other Poems* (COPE, 1985), *Theories of Rain & Other Poems* (Sun, 1975), *Out of This World: Anth* (Crown, 1991)

George Zebrowski 🎤 ✈   W
Richard Curtis Associates, Inc, 171 E 74 St, New York, NY 10021, 518-439-1994
    Pubs: *Cave of Stars* (Harper, 2000), *Brute Orbits* (Harper Prism, 1998), *The Sunspacers Trilogy* (White Wolf, 1996), *The Killing Star* (Avon-Morrow, 1995), *Stranger Suns* (Bantam, 1991), *The Monadic Universe* (Ace, 1985)

Kip Zegers   P
English Dept, Hunter College High School, 71 E 94 St, New York, NY 10128, 212-884-3011
    Pubs: *The American Floor* (Mayapple Pr, 1996), *The Promise Is* (Humana Pr, 1985)

Lisa Zeidner   P&W
Denise Shannon, ICM, 40 W 57 St, New York, NY 10019, 212-556-6727
    Pubs: *Layover* (Random Hse, 1999), *Limited Partnerships* (North Point Pr, 1989), *Pocket Sundial* (U Wisconsin Pr, 1988)

Roger Zelazny   W
c/o Kirby McCauley, Pimlico Literary Agency, Box 20477, 1534 1st Ave, New York, NY 10028, 212-683-7561
    Pubs: *Knight of Shadows, Frost & Fire* (Morrow, 1989, 1989), *A Dark Traveling* (Avon, 1989)

Joel Zeltzer   P
407 W 50 St, #3
New York, NY 10019
    Pubs: *Shadows in Light* (Poets Pr, 1985), *Daring Poetry Qtly, Green Feather Mag, MacGuffin*

Patricia Zelver   W
Wallace Literary Agency, 177 E 70 St, New York, NY 10021, 212-772-9090
    Pubs: *The Wonderful Towers of Watts* (Morrow, 1995), *The Wedding of Don Otavio* (Tambourine Bks, 1993), *A Man of Middle Age* (H Holt, 1974), *Ascent, Ohio Rev, Shenandoah, Atlantic, Virginia Qtly, Esquire, Redbook, Cosmopolitan*

Elizabeth Zelvin 🎤 ✈   P
115 W 86 St
New York, NY 10024-3410, 212-724-0494
Internet: lizzelvin@aol.com
    Pubs: *Gifts & Secrets: Poems of the Therapeutic Relationship, I Am the Daughter* (New Rivers, 1999, 1981), *Sarah's Daughters Sing: Anth* (KTAV Pub Hse, 1990), *Caprice, Home Planet News, Jewish Women's Lit Annual*

Alan Ziegler   P&W
45 Sutton Pl S
New York, NY 10022, 212-751-6244
    Pubs: *The Green Grass of Flatbush* (Word Beat Pr, 1986), *So Much to Do* (Release Pr, 1981), *New Yorker, Paris Rev*

Bette Ziegler   W
425 E 58 St
New York, NY 10022
    Pubs: *Older Women/Younger Men* (Doubleday, 1979), *An Affair for Tomorrow* (HBJ, 1978)

Edra Ziesk   W
444 E 85 St, #4B
New York, NY 10028, 212-861-9131
    Pubs: *Acceptable Losses* (SMU Pr, 1996), *Alaska Qtly Rev, Arkansas Rev, Turnstile, Folio, Other Voices, Blueline, Playgirl, Salmon*

Thomas Zigal 🎤 ✈   W
c/o Esther Newberg, ICM, 40 W 57th St, New York, NY 10019
Internet: tzigal@mail.utexas.edu
    Pubs: *Pariah, Hardrock Stiff, Into Thin Air* (Dell Paperback, 2000, 1997, 1996), *Playland* (Thorp Springs, 1982), *Western Edge* (Calliope Pr, 1982), *New Letters, Texas Qtly*

Evan Zimroth 🎤 ✈   P
Lydia Wills Artists Agency, 230 W 55 St, New York, NY 10019
    Pubs: *Gangsters* (Crown, 1996), *Giselle Considers Her Future* (Carnegie Mellon U Pr, 1996), *Dead, Dinner, or Naked* (TriQtly, 1993)
Groups: Jewish

Harriet Zinnes 🎤 ✈   P&W
25 W 54 St, #6A
New York, NY 10019-5404, 212-582-8315
Internet: hzinnes@aol.com
    Pubs: *The Radiant Absurdity of Desire* (Avisson Pr, 1998), *My, Haven't the Flowers Been?* (Magic Circle Pr, 1995), *Lover* (Coffee Hse Pr, 1989), *Ravishing Disunities: Anth* (Wesleyan, 2000), *Raintree, ABR, NY Arts Mag, Onthebus, Poetry NY, Chelsea*

Nonyaniso Zinza   P
c/o DuEwa, 630108 Spuyten Duyvil St, Bronx, NY 10463,
212-796-3070
  Pubs: *Affirmations, Declarations & Blues* (DuEwa, Inc,
  1988)

Larry Zirlin ♪ ✈   P
411 Clinton St, #5
Brooklyn, NY 11231-3544, 718-858-6229
Internet: larryz@worldnet.att.net
  Pubs: *Under the Tongue* (Hanging Loose Pr, 1992),
  Awake for No Reason (Cross Country Pr, 1979), *The
  World, Paris Rev, Hanging Loose, Transfer*

Harriet Zoltok-Seltzer   PP
Bronx Poets & Writers Alliance, The Bronx Council, 1738
Hone Ave, #4B, Bronx, NY 10461, 212-295-1779
  Pubs: *Alan Ball* (Grub St, 1979), *Bronx Roots III,
  American Mosaic, Bronx Poets*

Edward Zuckrow   P
303 Marcy Ave
Brooklyn, NY 11211, 718-782-3616
  Pubs: *Slowly, Out of Stones* (The Horizon, 1980), *The
  Death of Horn & Hardart* (Smith, 1971)

Ellen Zweig   P
93 E 3 St
Brooklyn, NY 11218, 718-972-7290
  Pubs: *Impressions of Africa* (e.g. Pr, 1986), *Women &
  Performance, De Zaak, Unsound, Moving Letters,
  Assembling*

NORTH CAROLINA

Beth Adamour   W
1804 W Friendly Ave
Greensboro, NC 27403
  Pubs: *Kansas Qtly, West Branch, Nimrod, Mid-American
  Rev, Crescent Rev*

Betty Adcock ♪ ✈   P
817 Runnymede Rd
Raleigh, NC 27607, 919-787-2407
  Pubs: *Intervale: New & Selected Poems* (LSU, 2000),
  The Difficult Wheel, Beholdings (LSU Pr, 1995, 1988),
  *Georgia Rev, Southern Rev, TriQtly, Gettysburg Rev,
  Kenyon Rev, Tar River Poetry*

Maya Angelou   P
3240 Valley Rd
Winston-Salem, NC 27106

James Applewhite   P
606 November Dr
Durham, NC 27712, 919-383-7734
  Pubs: *Daytime & Starlight, A History of the River* (LSU
  Pr, 1997, 1993), *River Writing: An Eno Journal*
  (Princeton U Pr, 1988), *Antaeus, APR, Atlantic, Poetry,
  Southern Rev, Esquire*

Jacqueline Ariail   W
1018 Monmouth Ave
Durham, NC 27701, 919-682-7809
  Pubs: *Fever: Erotic Writing By Women: Anth* (HC,
  1994), *Redbook*

Daphne Athas   P&W
English Dept 435 Greenlaw Hall, Univ North Carolina,
Chapel Hill, NC 27514, 919-962-5481
  Pubs: *Entering Ephesus* (Second Chance, 1991),
  Crumbs for the Bogeyman (St. Andrews Pr, 1991),
  Cora (Viking, 1978), *Southern Rev, Black Warrior Rev,
  Spectator, Carolina Qtly, Solo, Shenandoah*

Ellyn Bache   W
2314 Waverly Dr
Wilmington, NC 28403
  Pubs: *The Activist's Daughter* (Spinsters Ink, 1997),
  Safe Passage (Bantam, 1994), *The Value of Kindness*
  (Helicon Nine Edtns, 1993), *Festival in Fire Season*
  (August Hse, 1992)

John Balaban ♪ ✈   P&W
Dept of English, North Carolina State Univ, Campus Box
8105, Raleigh, NC 27695, 919-515-1836
Internet: tbalaban@msn.com
  Pubs: *Locusts at the Edge of Summer, Words for My
  Daughter* (Copper Canyon Pr, 1997, 1991), *Coming
  Down Again* (S&S, 1989), *Blue Mountain* (Unicorn,
  1982), *Harper's, TriQtly, Ploughshares*
Lang: Vietnamese. Groups: Vietnamese

Ronald H. Bayes ♪ ✈   P
St. Andrews Presbyterian College, Dogwood Mile,
Laurinburg, NC 28352, 919-277-5000
Internet: www.sapc.edu
  Pubs: *Chainsong for the Muse* (Northern Lights, 1993),
  Prescott St Reader: Anth (Prescott St Pr, 1995),
  *Goulash, Pembroke Mag, Prairie Schooner, NW Rev,
  TriQtly, Prism Intl*

Jeffrey Beam ♪ ✈   P
Golgonooza at Frog Level, 3212 Arthur Minnis Rd,
Hillsborough, NC 27278, 919-967-2470
Internet: jeffbeam@email.unc.edu
  Pubs: *Visions of Dame Kind* (The Jargon Society,
  1995), *The Fountain* (North Carolina Wesleyan, 1992),
  *Carolina Qtly, Worcester Rev, North Carolina Lit Rev,
  Yellow Silk, James White Rev, Modern Words*
I.D.: G/L/B/T. Groups: G/L/B/T

Doris Betts W
Alumni Distinguished Prof, English Dept, UNC-Chapel Hill, 230 Greenlaw Hall, CB#3520, Chapel Hill, NC 27599-3520, 919-962-4006
Pubs: *Beasts of the Southern Wild* (Scribner, 1998), *The Sharp Teeth of Love, Souls Raised from the Dead, Heading West* (Knopf, 1997, 1994, 1982)

Robert Bixby 🎤 ✈ P&W
3413 Wilshire
Greensboro, NC 27408
Pubs: *Omni, Sow's Ear, Passages North, Celery, Lactuca, Gypsy, Greensboro Rev, Oxalis*

Patrick Bizzaro 🎤 ✈ P
East Carolina Univ, Dept of English, Greenville, NC 27858, 919-328-6751
Pubs: *Fear of the Coming Drought* (Mount Olive College Pr, 2000), *Undressing the Mannequin* (Third Lung Pr, 1989), *Violence* (Tamarack Edtns, 1978), *NYQ, Poetry Now, Tar River Poetry, River City, Asheville Poetry Rev, SPR*

James Breeden 🎤 ✈ P&W
610 Wendy Way
Durham, NC 27712-9246, 919-471-7000
Pubs: *Xavier Rev, Pig Iron, Wind Literary Jrnl, Next Exit, Modern Haiku, S.L.U.G.fest, Wellspring, Piedmont Lit Rev, Arts Line*

Sue Ellen Bridgers W
PO Box 248
Sylva, NC 28779-0248, 704-586-6271
Pubs: *All We Know of Heaven* (Banks Channel Bks, 1996), *Keeping Christina* (HC, 1993)

Bill Brittain W
17 Wisteria Dr
Asheville, NC 28804, 704-252-7104
Pubs: *Shape-Changer, The Ghost from Beneath the Sea, Wings, Professor Popkin's Prodigious Polish* (HC, 1994, 1992, 1991, 1990)

Sally Buckner 🎤 ✈ P
3231 Birnamwood Rd
Raleigh, NC 27607, 919-782-3636
Pubs: *Strawberry Harvest* (St. Andrews Pr, 1986), *Word Witness: 100 Years of North Carolina Poetry: Anth, Our Words, Our Ways: Anth* (Carolina Academic Pr, 1999 1995), *Pembroke Mag, Crab Creek Rev, Christian Century*

Kathryn Stripling Byer 🎤 ✈ P
PO Box 489
Cullowhee, NC 28723, 828-293-5695
Pubs: *Black Shawl, Wildwood Flower* (LSU Pr, 1998, 1992), *The Girl in the Midst of the Harvest* (Texas Tech Pr, 1986), *Southern Rev, Georgia Rev, Greensboro Rev, SPR, Shenandoah, Carolina Qtly, Asheville Poetry Rev*

Dean Cadle W
135 Fulton Dr
Hendersonville, NC 28792, 704-696-9667
Pubs: *Yale Rev, SW Rev, Short Story Intl, Appalachian Jrnl, Contemporary Lit Criticism*

Mary Belle Campbell P
53 Pine Lake Dr
Whispering Pines, NC 28327-9388, 910-949-3993
Pubs: *Light from Dark Tombs: Mysteries of the Ancient Maya* (Persephone Pr, 1991), *Anima, Intl Poetry Rev, Pembroke, St. Andrews Rev, Stone Country*

Joan L. Cannon 🎤 P&W
207 B Ridgeside Terr
Morganton, NC 28655-2656, 828-439-8339
Pubs: *Elf, Expressions, Grit, Odessa Poetry Rev, Pulpsmith, Seacoast Life, Modern Woodman, Thema, Cappers*

Fred Chappell 🎤 ✈ P&W
305 Kensington Rd
Greensboro, NC 27403, 910-275-8851
Pubs: *Look Back All the Green Valley, Farewell, I'm Bound to Leave You* (Picador, 1999, 1996), *The Fred Chappell Reader* (St. Martin's, 1991), *Saturday Evening Post, Harper's, Georgia Rev, Poetry*

Richard Chess 🎤 ✈ P
Univ of North Carolina Asheville, Dept of Literature & Language CPO#2130, Asheville, NC 28804, 828-251-6576
Pubs: *Tekiah* (Georgia Pr, 1994), *Telling & Remembering: Anth* (Beacon Pr, 1997), *Ascent, Tampa Rev*
I.D.: Jewish. Groups: Jewish

Avery Grenfell Church P
2749 Park Oak Dr
Clemmons, NC 27012, 336-766-7737
Pubs: *Rainbows of the Mind* (Modern Images, 1982), *Dakota: Plains & Fancy: Anth* (Vermilion Lit Project, English Dept., U South Dakota, 1989), *San Fernando Poetry Jrnl, Bardic Echoes, Orphic Lute, Poets' Paper, American Bard, Parnassus Lit Jrnl*

Jim Clark 🎤 ✈ P&W
4706 Quaker Rd
Wilson, NC 27893, 252-243-9736
Internet: www2.coastalnet.com/~cn3368
Pubs: *Handiwork* (St. Andrews Pr, 1998), *Dancing on Canaan's Ruins* (Eternal Delight Pub, 1997), *Witnessing Earth: Anth* (Catamount Pr, 1994), *Cross Roads, Denver Qtly, SPR, Georgia Rev, Prairie Schooner, Greensboro Rev, Appalachian Heritage*

Kent Cooper   W
1124 Woodburn Rd
Durham, NC 27705-5738
    Pubs: *Fame & Fortune* (Playboy Bks, 1981), *The Harp
    Styles of Sonny Terry* (Oak Pub, 1975), *Below Houston
    Street, The Minnesota Strip* (Manor Bks, 1978, 1978),
    Paterson Lit Rev, Living Blues

Helen M. Copeland   W
1850 Maryland Ave
Charlotte, NC 28209, 704-375-3022
    Pubs: *Endangered Specimen & Other Poems from a
    Lay Naturalist* (St. Andrews, 1988)

Robert Cumming 🎤   P&W
PO Box 1047
Davidson, NC 28036-1047, 704-896-3479
Internet: rdgcumming@mindspring.com
    Pubs: *45/96: Anth* (Ninety-Six Pr, 1994), *Contemporary
    Thai Verse: Anth* (Amarin Pr, 1985), *Chattahoochee
    Rev, SPR*

Christopher Davis   P
English Dept, Univ North Carolina, Charlotte, NC 28223,
704-547-2296
    Pubs: *The Tyrant of the Past & the Slave of the
    Future* (Texas Tech U Pr, 1989), *Sonora Rev, Black
    Warrior Rev, Ploughshares, Denver Qtly, American
    Voice*

Angela Davis-Gardner 🎤 ✈   W
English Dept, Box 8105, North Carolina State Univ,
Raleigh, NC 27695-8105, 919-515-4173
Internet: agardner@unity.ncsu.edu
    Pubs: *Forms of Shelter* (Ticknor & Fields, 1991), *Felice*
    (Random Hse, 1982), *Close to Home: Anth* (John F.
    Blair, 1998), *A Few Thousand Words About Love: Anth*
    (St. Martin's, 1998), *Between Friends: Anth* (HM, 1994),
    Shenandoah, Crescent Rev, Greensboro Rev

Thadious M. Davis   P
English Dept, Univ North Carolina, Chapel Hill, NC 27514,
919-967-3778
    Pubs: *Black Scholar, Obsidian, South & West, Black
    American Lit Forum*

Irene Dayton   P
209 S Hillandale Dr
East Flat Rock, NC 28726-2609, 828-693-4014
    Pubs: *In Oxbow of Time's River, Seven Times the
    Wind* (Windy Row, 1978, 1977), *North Stone Rev,
    Women Artist News, Literary Rev*

Ann Deagon 🎤 ✈   P&W
802 Woodbrook Dr
Greensboro, NC 27410-3278, 336-292-5273
Internet: anndeagon@worldnet.att.net
    Pubs: *The Polo Poems* (U Nebraska-Omaha, 1990),
    The Diver's Tomb (St. Martin's/Marek, 1985)

Stuart Dischell 🎤 ✈   P
1614 W End Pl
Greensboro, NC 27403-1758, 336-334-4695
Internet: dischell@uncg.edu
    Pubs: *Evenings & Avenues* (Penguin, 1996), *Good
    Hope Road* (VikingPenguin, 1993)

Julia Nunnally Duncan   P&W
Rte 4, Box 981, Paxton Creek Rd
Marion, NC 28752, 704-724-9278
    Pubs: *Only Morning in Her Shoes* (Utah State U Pr,
    1990), *Writers' Forum, Potato Eyes, Appalachian
    Heritage, Birmingham Poetry Rev, Georgia Jrnl, The
    Lyricist*

Charles Edward Eaton   P&W
808 Greenwood Rd
Chapel Hill, NC 27514-3908, 919-942-4775
    Pubs: *The Jogger by the Sea, The Scout in Summer,
    The Country of the Blue, New & Selected Stories
    1959-1989* (Cornwall, 2000, 1998, 1994, 1989),
    *Sewanee Rev, Salmagundi, New Letters, Antioch Rev,
    Hollins Critic, Centennial Rev*

Julie Fay 🎤 ✈   P
158 Kingfisher Dr
Blounts Creek, NC 27814-9802, 252-975-6709
Internet: fayj@mail.ecu.edu
    Pubs: *The Woman Behind You* (U Pitt Pr, 1999),
    Portraits of Women (Ahsahta, 1991), *Images of Women
    in Literature* (HM, 1990), *In Every Mirror* (Owl Creek,
    1985), *New American Poets: Anth* (Hardscrabble, 2000),
    A Formal Feeling Comes: Anth (Story Line Pr, 1994),
    APR
Lang: French. Groups: Prisoners, Women

Thomas Feeny   P
306 Chamberlain St
Raleigh, NC 27607-7312, 919-515-9281
    Pubs: *The Paternal Orientation of Ramon Perez de
    Ayala* (Spain; Albatros-Hispanofila, 1985), *Puerto del
    Sol, Poets On, Hiram Poetry Rev, Cape Rock, Verve,
    Comstock Rev, Sulphur, Timber Creek Rev, Mankato
    Poetry Rev, GW Rev, RE:AL*

Candace Flynt 🎤 ✈   W
2005 Madison Ave
Greensboro, NC 27403-1511, 336-373-1025
    Pubs: *Mother Love* (FSG, 1987), *Sins of Omission*
    (Random Hse, 1984), *Chasing Dad* (Dial, 1980)

Marita Garin   P
PO Box 503
Black Mountain, NC 28711-0503, 828-669-7819
    Pubs: *Verse, Tar River Poetry, Oxford Mag, Kansas
    Qtly, Cumberland Poetry Rev, Kenyon Rev*

Philip Gerard 🎤 ✈ W
6231 Tortoise Ln
Wilmington, NC 28409
Internet: http://philipgerard.com
    Pubs: *Desert Kill* (Morrow, 1994), *Cape Fear Rising,
    Hatteras Light* (John F Blair, 1994, 1987), *Carolina
    Style, NER, Puerto del Sol, Hawaii Rev*

Grace Evelyn Loving Gibson P
709 McLean St
Laurinburg, NC 28352, 919-276-1769
    Pubs: *Frayed Edges, Drake's Branch, Home in Time*
    (St. Andrews Pr, 1995, 1982, 1977)

Marie Gilbert 🎤 ✈ P
2 St Simons Sq
Greensboro, NC 27408-3833, 336-288-3051
Internet: Ragmrg@worldnet.att.net
    Pubs: *Brookgreen Oaks* (Downhome Pr, 1999), *Word &
    Witness: 100 Years of NC Poetry: Anth* (Carolina
    Academic Pr, 1999), *Connexions, Myrtle Beach Back
    When* (St. Andrews, 1994, 1990)

Marianne Gingher 🎤 ✈ W
Univ North Carolina, Dept of English, CB#3520, Chapel
Hill, NC 27599, 919-962-0468
    Pubs: *How to Have a Happy Childhood* (John F Blair,
    2000), *Teen Angel, Bobby Rex's Greatest Hit*
    (Atheneum, 1988, 1986), *New Virginia Rev, NAR,
    Redbook, Southern Rev*

Judy Goldman 🎤 ✈ P
1121 Scotland Ave
Charlotte, NC 28207-2572, 704-334-6868
Internet: judygoldman@earthlink.net
    Pubs: *The Slow Way Back* (Morrow, 1999), *Wanting to
    Know the End* (Silverfish Rev Pr, 1993), *Holding Back
    Winter* (St Andrews Pr, 1987), *Ohio Rev, Kenyon Rev,
    Southern Rev, Crazyhorse, Shenandoah, Prairie
    Schooner, Gettysburg Rev*
Groups: Jewish, Writing Groups

Robert Waters Grey 🎤 ✈ P
647 Wilshire Ave SW
Concord, NC 28027-6403, 704-795-0920
    Pubs: *Saving the Dead* (Briarpatch Pr, 1992), *Poet &
    Critic, Black Warrior Rev, Sycamore Rev, Kansas Qtly,
    Hollins Critic, Willow Springs*

Frank Borden Hanes W
1057 W Kent Rd
Winston-Salem, NC 27104
    Pubs: *The Seeds of Ares* (Briarpatch Pr, 1977), *The
    Fleet Rabble* (Popular Library, 1967), *Jackknife John*
    (Naylor, 1964), *The Bat Brothers, Abel Anders* (Farrar
    Straus & Young, 1953, 1951)

Suzan Shown Harjo P
99 Pressley Rd
Asheville, NC 28805-1345

William Harmon 🎤 ✈ P
Univ North Carolina, English Dept, CB #3520, Chapel Hill,
NC 27599-3520
Internet: wharmon03@mindspring.com
    Pubs: *Mutatis Mutandis* (Wesleyan U Pr, 1985), *One
    Long Poem* (LSU Pr, 1982), *Carolina Qtly, Agni,
    Sewanee Rev, Poetry, Partisan Rev, Free Lunch*

Rabiul Hasan P
2609 MacGregor Downs Rd, #17
Greenville, NC 27834, 252-752-5556
    Pubs: *Mississippi Writers: Reflections of Childhood &
    Youth Anth* (Jackson & London/U Pr Mississippi, 1988),
    New Earth Rev, Aura Literary/Arts Rev, Piddiddle

Ardis Messick Hatch P
414 Oakridge Rd
Cary, NC 27511-4544
    Pubs: *The Illusion of Water* (St. Andrews Pr, 1980), *To
    Defend a Form* (Teachers & Writers, 1978)

Tom Hawkins P&W
5020 Oak Park Rd
Raleigh, NC 27612-3025, 919-782-3009
    Pubs: *Paper Crown* (BkMk Pr, 1989), *Flash Fiction:
    Anth* (Norton, 1992), *Greensboro Rev, Kansas Qtly,
    Sequoia Rev, Carolina Qtly, South Carolina Rev,
    Ploughshares*

Carol Bessent Hayman P
618 Ann St
Beaufort, NC 28516-2204, 252-728-7088
    Pubs: *A Garden of Virtues* (Abingdon Pr, 1996), *Images
    & Echoes of Beaufort-By-The-Sea* (Mt. Olive College Pr,
    1993), *Ideals, Listen, Marriage & Family Living, Mature
    Living, Our State, Down Home in North Carolina,
    Carolina Country*

Robert R. Hentz P&W
415 Chunns Cove Rd, 900A
Asheville, NC 28805, 704-252-9064
    Pubs: *Cape Rock, Hellas, Riverrun, Silhouette, Poem,
    Cold Mountain Rev, Sonoma Mandala, The Panhandler*

M. L. Hester 🎤 ✈ P
Avisson Press, PO Box 38816, Greensboro, NC 27438,
336-288-6989
    Pubs: *Another Jackie Robinson, With Crockett at the
    Alamo* (Tudor Pubs, 1996, 1995), *Poetry Now,
    American Scholar, Minnesota Rev*

Lonnie Hodge 🎤 ✈ P
179 Hoover Ave
Concord, NC 28025, 704-782-7423
    Pubs: *Unrisen Son* (Sandstone Pr, 2000), *Fishing for
    the Moon* (Sandstone Pr, 1994), *Shadow of the Peaks*
    (Crossroads, 1985), *America, Bridge, Passages North,
    Fujimi, Kansas Qtly, Alabama Lit Rev, Colorado North
    Qtly, Appalachia, Sulphur River Rev*
Lang: Japanese. Groups: Adults, Prisoners

Judy Hogan   P
PO Box 84
Saxapahaw, NC 27340-0084, 919-376-8152
   Pubs: *Light Food* (Latitudes Pr, 1989), *Small Press,
   Arts Jrnl, Pembroke, SPR, The Smith, Crucible, Literary
   Kostroma*

David Brendan Hopes ♀ ✈   P&W
Literature Dept, Univ North Carolina, 1 University Heights,
Asheville, NC 28804-3251, 828-254-6057
Internet: davehopes@aol.com
   Pubs: *Bird Songs of the Mesozoic, A Sense of the
   Morning* (Milkweed Edtns, 2000, 1999), *A Childhood in
   the Milky Way* (U Akron Pr, 1998), *Blood Rose*
   (Urthona Pr, 1996), *The Sacred Place* (U Utah Pr,
   1996), *Atlanta Rev, Cafe Bellas Artes, Salmon*

Maria Ingram   P
111 Stratford Rd
Winston-Salem, NC 27104, 919-722-7271
   Pubs: *Thirtieth Year to Heaven* (Jackpine Pr, 1980),
   Maria (Red Clay Bks, 1976)

Susan S. Kelly   W
522 Woodland Dr
Greensboro, NC 27408, 336-275-5499
   Pubs: *How Close We Come* (Warner Bks, 1999), *Iowa
   Woman, Crescent Rev*

Carol Klein   W
1-103 Carolina Meadows
Chapel Hill, NC 27514
   Pubs: *Prairie Schooner, Southern Humanities Rev,
   Roanoke Rev, St. Andrews Rev, Northland, Toyon*

Stephen Knauth   P
805 E Worthington Ave
Charlotte, NC 28203
   Pubs: *The River I Know You By, Twenty Shadows*
   (Four Way Bks, 1998, 1995), *The Pine Figures*
   (Dooryard Pr, 1986), *Virginia Qlty Rev, Prairie
   Schooner, Pacific Rev, Puerto del Sol, Alaska Qlty Rev,
   Ironwood, Kansas Qlty, MPR, NAR*

Carrie Knowles ♀ ✈   P&W
315 S Boylan Ave
Raleigh, NC 27603-1907, 919-833-6022
Internet: cwriter@bellsouth.net
   Pubs: *Cardinal: Anth* (Jacan Pr, 1986), *The Sun,
   TasteFull, Mothers Today, Beyond Baroque, Carolina
   Qtly, Glimmer Train*

Howard D. Koenig   P
3306 Middle Sound Rd
Wilmington, NC 28405
   Pubs: *Profiles in Leadership* (Quest, 1981), *Lyrical
   Iowa, American Poet, A Different Drummer*

Mary Kratt ♀ ✈   P
7001 Sardis Rd
Charlotte, NC 28270-6057, 704-366-0297
   Pubs: *Valley* (Sow's Ear Pr, 2000), *Small Potatoes* (St
   Andrew's Coll Pr, 1999), *On the Steep Side* (Briarpatch
   Pr, 1993), *The Only Thing I Fear Is a Cow & a
   Drunken Man* (Carolina Wren Pr, 1991), *Yankee, Tar
   River, Spoon River Qtly, Texas Rev, Shenandoah*

Richard Krawiec ♀ ✈   P&W
319 Wilmot Dr
Raleigh, NC 27602, 919-859-9297
   Pubs: *And Fools of God, Faith in What?, Voices from
   Home: The North Carolina Anth* (Avisson Pr, 2000,
   1997, 1998), *Time Sharing* (Viking Penguin, 1987),
   *Shenandoah, Witness, Cream City Rev, The Qtly, Many
   Mountains Moving, The Other Side*
I.D.: Polish-American, Irish-American. Groups: Homeless,
Literacy

Sandra Lake Lassen   P
1499 Lakeside Dr
West Jefferson, NC 28694-7291
   Pubs: *Womanwrit* (Miller, 1982), *Amaranth Rev,
   Wordart, Touchstone, American Scholar, Chiron Rev*

Brenda Kay Ledford ♀ ✈   P
450 Swaims Rd
Hayesville, NC 28904
   Pubs: *Writers Cramp, Roswell Lit Rev, The Aurorean,
   The Lyricist, The River's Edge, Pembroke Mag, New
   Thought Jrnl, Mobius, Asheville Poetry Rev,
   Appalachian Heritage*
Groups: Children

Lou Lipsitz ♀ ✈   P
168 Lake Ellen Dr
Chapel Hill, NC 27514-1937, 919-942-9574
Internet: loulipsitz@earthlink.net
   Pubs: *Seeking the Hook* (Signal Bks, 1998), *American
   Democracy* (St Martin's Pr, 1993), *Reflections on
   Samson* (Kayak, 1977), *NW Rev, New Letters, New
   Republic, The Sun, Witness, Southern Rev*
Groups: Schools, Men's Groups

Don Mager   P
Johnson C. Smith Univ, English Dept, Charlotte, NC
28216, 704-378-3593
   Pubs: *That Which Is Owed to Death* (Main St Rag Pr,
   1998), *Glosses* (St. Andrews Pr, 1992), *To Track the
   Wounded One* (Ridgeway, 1988), *River Styx, Lyricist,
   St. Andrews Rev, Sun Dog, Western Humanities Rev,
   North Dakota Qtly, Cape Rock, Main Street Rag*

E. T. Malone, Jr.   P
PO Box 18124
Raleigh, NC 27619, 919-269-0010
   Pubs: *The View from Wrightsville Beach* (Literary
   Lantern Pr, 1988), *Pembroke, St. Andrews Rev,
   Communicant*

Harry A. Maxson　　　　　　　　　　　　P
66 Hardy Rd
Wendell, NC 27591-8355, 919-365-0608
　　Pubs: *The Curley Poems* (Frank Cat Pr, 1994), *Walker
in the Storm* (K.M. Gentile Pub, 1981), *Turning the
Wood* (Cedar Creek Pr, 1976), *Kansas Qtly, Cimarron
Rev, New Rev, The Ledge, Nation*

Barbara J. Mayer 🎤 ✈　　　　　　　　P&W
805 Heatherly Rd
Mooresville, NC 28115-2778, 704-663-7593
　　Pubs: *I Am Becoming the Woman I've Wanted: Anth*
(Papier-Mache Pr, 1994), *Filtered Images: Anth* (Vintage
'45 Pr, 1992), *Atlanta Rev*
Groups: Seniors, Children

Jean McCamy　　　　　　　　　　　　P
145 W Sycamore Ave
Wake Forest, NC 27587, 919-556-5342
　　Pubs: *Uwharrie Rev, Davidson Miscellany, SPR, St.
Andrews Rev*

Michael McFee 🎤 ✈　　　　　　　　　P
English Dept, UNC-Chapel Hill, Greenlaw Hall CB# 3520,
Chapel Hill, NC 27599-3520, 919-962-3461
Internet: mcfee@email.unc.edu
　　Pubs: *Colander* (Carnegie Mellon U Pr, 1996), *The
Language They Speak Is Things to Eat: Anth* (UNC Pr,
1994), *Poetry, Hudson Rev, Southern Rev*

Jane Mead　　　　　　　　　　　　　P
English Dept, Wake Forest Univ, Box 7387, Reynolda
Station, Winston-Salem, NC 27109, 910-759-5383
　　Pubs: *The Lord & the General Din of the World*
(Sarabande Bks, 1996)

Thomas Meyer 🎤 ✈　　　　　　　　　P
PO Box 10
Highlands, NC 28741-0010, 828-526-4461
Internet: meyer@jargonbooks.com
　　Pubs: *At Dusk Iridescent* (Jargon Society, 2000),
Monotypes & Tracings (Enitharmon Pr, 1994),
Conjunctions, First Intensity, Oyster Boy Rev

Shirley Moody　　　　　　　　　　　P
1424 Laughridge Dr
Cary, NC 27511, 919-469-1314
　　Pubs: *Charmers, Four North Carolina Women Poets:
Anth* (St. Andrews Pr, 1990, 1982), *SPR, Crucible*

Lenard D. Moore 🎤 ✈　　　　　　　　P
North Carolina State Univ, English Dept, Tompkins Hall,
Raleigh, NC 27695, 919-515-4127
　　Pubs: *Forever Home* (St. Andrews Pr, 1996), *The
Garden Thrives* (HC, 1996), *Soulfires* (Penguin, 1996),
*African American Rev, Callaloo, North Carolina Lit Rev,
Black Scholar, Colorado Rev, North Dakota Qtly, Crab
Orchard Rev*

Ruth Moose 🎤 ✈　　　　　　　　　P&W
14 Matchwood
Pittsboro, NC 27312, 919-929-0376
　　Pubs: *Smith Grove* (Sow's Ear Pr, 1997), *Dreams in
Color* (August Hse, 1989), *The Wreath Ribbon & Other
Stories* (St. Andrews, 1986), *12 Christmas Stories By
North Carolina Writers: Anth* (Down Home Pr, 1997),
Southern Exposure, Cities & Roads

Jack Nestor　　　　　　　　　　　P&W
119 Leslie Dr
Chapel Hill, NC 27516
　　Pubs: *Love Is Ageless* (Serala Pr, 1987), *Stone
Country, Slow Motion Mag, Laurel Rev, Open Mag,
Wittenberg Rev, Ascent, Columbia, Jrnl of New Jersey
Poets*

P. B. Newman　　　　　　　　　　　P
Queens College, Charlotte, NC 28274, 704-332-7121
　　Pubs: *The George Washington Poems* (Briarpatch Pr,
1986), *Tar River Poetry, River City, Kennebec,
Apalachee Qtly, Carolina Qtly, SPR, Sun*

Suzanne Newton　　　　　　　　　　W
829-A Barringer Dr
Raleigh, NC 27606, 919-851-4710
　　Pubs: *Where Are You When I Need You?, A Place
Between, An End to Perfect* (Viking, 1991, 1986, 1984)

Claudio Oswald Niedworok　　　　　PP
Vision Era Concepts, PO Box 718, Broadway, NC
27505-0718, 919-499-2565
　　Pubs: *Seafarers* (Vision Era Concepts, 1996)

Valerie Nieman　　　　　　　　　　P&W
1313 Hawthorne Ave
Reidsville, NC 27320-5904
　　Pubs: *How We Live* (State St Pr, 1996), *Slipping Out
of Old Eve* (Sing Heavenly Muse, 1988), *Modern
Arthurian Literature: Anth* (Garland Pub, 1992), *Poetry,
New Letters, West Branch, Kenyon Rev, Antietam Rev*

Sallie Nixon 🎤　　　　　　　　　　P
Covenant Village, 1351 Robinwood Rd, #A-8, Gastonia,
NC 28054-1671
　　Pubs: *Spiraling* (Persephone Pr, 1990), *Second Grace*
(Moore Pub Co, 1977), *Pembroke Mag, Crucible,
Sandhills Rev*
Groups: Teenagers

Linda Orr　　　　　　　　　　　　P
Romance Languages Dept, Duke Univ, Durham, NC
27706, 919-684-3706
　　Pubs: *A Certain X* (L'Epervier Pr, 1980), *Antioch Rev,
Paris Rev, Pequod, Agni*

Sallie Page   W
PO Box 64
Lynn, NC 28750
    Pubs: *Grab-a-nickel, Potato Eyes, Lonzie's, Pine Mtn Sand & Gravel, Art/Life, St. Andrews Rev, Spindrift, Aura, Mountain Rev*

Leslie Parker 🎤 ✈   P
5004 Hiddenbrook Ct
McLeansville, NC 27301-9775, 336-621-7316
    Pubs: *A Turn in Time: Anth* (TransVerse Pr, 1999), *Cold Mtn Rev, Half Tones to Jubilee, Bay Leaves, Hawaii Rev, Black Buzzard Rev, Infinity Ltd, Byline, Elk River Rev, Panhandler, Poetpourri, Cape Rock*
Groups: Children

Peggy Payne   W
512 St Mary's St
Raleigh, NC 27605, 919-833-8021
    Pubs: *Revelation* (S&S, 1988), *New Stories from the South: Anth* (Algonquin, 1987), *Cosmopolitan, Ms., McCall's, Family Circle, Travel & Leisure*

Gail J. Peck   P
250 King Owen Ct
Charlotte, NC 28211, 704-364-1944
    Pubs: *Drop Zone* (Texas Rev, 1995), *New River* (Harper, 1993), *Uncommonplace: Anth* (Louisiana State Pr, 1998), *Southern Rev, Cimarron Rev, Carolina Qtly, High Plains Literary Rev, Southern Poetry, Malahat, Mangrove, Greensboro Rev, Cape Rock*

George Perreault   P
803 Willow St
Greenville, NC 27858, 252-328-1096
    Pubs: *Trying to Be Round* (Singular Speech Pr, 1994), *Curved Like an Eye* (Ahsahta Pr, 1994), *Jrnl of American Culture, Shenandoah, High Plains Literary Rev, NW Rev, The Lyric, Blue Mesa Rev*

Catherine Petroski 🎤 ✈   W
2528 Wrightwood Ave
Durham, NC 27705-5830, 919-489-9416
Internet: petroski@mindspring.com
    Pubs: *A Bride's Passage* (Northeastern U Pr, 1997), *The Summer That Lasted Forever* (HM, 1984), *I Know Some Things: Anth* (Faber & Faber, 1993), *Virginia Qtly Rev, NAR*

Henry Petroski   P
2528 Wrightwood Ave
Durham, NC 27705-5830, 919-489-9416
    Pubs: *Remaking the World* (Knopf, 1997), *Invention by Design* (Harvard U Pr, 1996), *Engineers of Dreams* (Knopf, 1995), *Design Paradigms* (Cambridge U Pr, 1994), *Virginia Qtly Rev, American Scientist*

Diana Pinckney 🎤 ✈   P
2215 Malvern Rd
Charlotte, NC 28207-2625, 704-377-6159
Internet: pinckpat@aol.com
    Pubs: *White Linen* (Nightshade Pr, 1998), *Fishing with Tall Women* (Persephone Pr, 1996), *Word & Witness: Anth* (Carolina Academic Pr, 1999), *SPR, Tar River, Sandhills Rev, Chattahoochee Rev, Pembroke, Cream City Rev*

Deborah Pope 🎤 ✈   P
Dept. of English, Duke Univ, Durham, NC 27708, 919-684-2741
    Pubs: *Falling Out of the Sky, Mortal World, Fanatic Heart* (LSU Pr, 1999, 1995, 1992), *Poetry, Georgia Rev, Southern Rev, Shenandoah, Poetry NW, Threepenny Rev*

Joe Ashby Porter   W
2411 W Club Blvd
Durham, NC 27705, 919-286-7075
Internet: japorter@acpub.duke.edu
    Pubs: *Resident Aliens* (New Amsterdam, 2000), *Lithuania: Short Stories, The Kentucky Stories* (Johns Hopkins U, 1990, 1983), *Yale Rev, Harper's, TriQtly, Fiction, Raritan, Antaeus, Iowa Rev*

Dannye Romine Powell 🎤 ✈   P
700 E Park Ave
Charlotte, NC 28203-5146, 704-334-0902
Internet: dannye700@aol.com
    Pubs: *At Every Wedding Someone Stays Home* (U Arkansas Pr, 1994), *America's Foremost Writers on Libraries: Anth* (Doubleday, 1989), *New Republic, Georgia Rev, Gettysburg Rev, Prairie Schooner, Poetry, Paris Rev, Crazyhorse*

Charles F. Powers 🎤 ✈   W
1412 Rock Creek Ln
Cary, NC 27511, 919-467-2629
Internet: moyesmax@aol.com
    Pubs: *A Matter of Honor* (First East Coast Theatre & Publishing Co, 1982)

Reynolds Price   P&W
PO Box 99014
Durham, NC 27708-9014
    Pubs: *Private Contentment, Vital Provisions, The Source of Light* (Atheneum, 1984, 1982, 1981)

Glenis Redmond 🎤 ✈   PP&P
PO Box 4142
Asheville, NC 28803, 800-476-6240
Internet: poetic.home.mindspring.com
    Pubs: *Back Bone* (Undergrouind Epics, 2000), *360 A Revolution of Black Poets: Anth* (Black Words, 1998), *Catch the Fire: Anth* (Riverhead Bks 1998), *Obsidian II*
I.D.: African-American. Groups: At-Risk Youth, Women

Tony Reevy   P&W
The Libraries, Campus Box 7111, North Carolina State U,
Raleigh, NC 27695-7111, 919-515-3339
    Pubs: *Now & Then, Charlotte Poetry Rev, Piedmont
Pedlar, Asheville Poetry Rev, Bath Avenue Newsletter*

Jonathan K. Rice   P
PO Box 18548
Charlotte, NC 28218-0548, 704-595-9526
    Pubs: *Slipstream, Bogg, Parting Gifts, Red Owl Mag,
Blue Collar Rev, Main St Rag, Wellspring, Cold
Mountain Rev, The Comstock Rev*

David Rigsbee   P
315 Oakwood Ave
Raleigh, NC 27601, 919-821-9851
    Pubs: *A Skeptic's Notebook: Longer Poems* (St.
Andrews Pr, 1997), *Your Heart Will Fly Away* (The
Smith, 1992), *Stamping Ground* (Ardis, 1976), *APR,
New Yorker, Iowa Rev, Ironwood, Southern Rev,
Georgia Rev, Ohio Rev, Willow Springs*

Eliot Schain   P&W
35 Maxwell Rd
Chapel Hill, NC 27514
    Pubs: *American Romance* (Zeitgeist, 1989), *APR,
Ploughshares, ACM, Mothering, Stone Country*

E. M. Schorb 🎤 ✈   P&W
PO Box 1461
Mooresville, NC 28115-9504, 704-660-5453
Internet: paschorb@aol.com
    Pubs: *Scenario for Scorsese* (Denlinger's Pub, 2000),
Murderer's Day (Purdue U Pr, 1998), *50 Poems* (Hill
Hse, 1986), *The Poor Boy* (Dragon's Teeth Pr, 1975),
American Scholar, Southern Rev, Yale Rev

James Seay   P
127 Windsor Cir
Chapel Hill, NC 27516, 919-929-9094
    Pubs: *Open Field, Understory: New & Selected Poems*
(LSU Pr, 1997), *The Light As They Found It* (Morrow,
1990)

Mabelle M. Segrest   P
811 Onslow St
Durham, NC 27705-4244
    Pubs: *My Mama's Dead Squirrel* (Firebrand Bks, 1985),
Southern Exposure, Feminary, Conditions

Rudy P. Shackelford 🎤 ✈   P
4156 Lattice Rd
Wilson, NC 27893
    Pubs: *Dreamers Wine, Poems, A Visual Diary &
Poems, Gathering Voices, Bamboo Harp, Rosewood,
Ascend the Hill*
Groups: Schools

Alan Shapiro   P
U North Carolina
Chapel Hill, NC 27599, 919-962-1994
    Pubs: *The Dead Alive & Busy, Mixed Company,
Covenant* (U Chicago Pr 2000, 1997, 1996), *In Praise
of the Impure* (Northwestern U Pr 1992), *Happy Hour,
The Courtesy* (U Chicago 1987, 1983), *After the
Digging* (Elpenor Bks 1981)

Bynum Shaw   W
2700 Speas Rd
Winston-Salem, NC 27106, 336-924-1644
    Pubs: *Oh, Promised Land!* (Stratford Bks, 1992), *Days
of Power, Nights of Fear* (St. Martin's, 1980), *The Nazi
Hunter* (Norton, 1969)

Janet Beeler Shaw   P&W
46 Newcross N
Asheville, NC 28805-9213, 704-298-8999
    Pubs: *Taking Leave* (Viking, 1987), *Dowry* (U Missouri
Pr, 1978), *Atlantic, Redbook, TriQtly, Shenandoah, SW
Rev, Esquire*

Benjamin Sloan   P
9700 Mary Alexander Rd, Apt I
Charlotte, NC 28213, 704-549-1648
    Pubs: *La-Bas, Bird Effort, Out There, Mouth of the
Dragon*

Lee Smith   W
219 N Churton St
Hillsborough, NC 27278
    Pubs: *Fair & Tender Ladies, Oral History* (Putnam,
1988, 1981), *Atlantic, Southern Exposure, New York
Times*

John Thom Spach   W
PO Box 11408
Winston-Salem, NC 27116-1408, 336-724-6774
    Pubs: *Time Out from Texas* (John F. Blair, 1970),
Great Commanders in Action: Anth (Cowles Enthusiast
Media, 1996), *Augusta Spectator, The State, Military
History, Cowboy, American Civil War, Retired Officer,
Saturday Evening Post, Grit, Reader's Digest*

Elizabeth Spencer   W
402 Longleaf Dr
Chapel Hill, NC 27514, 919-929-2115
    Pubs: *Landscapes of the Heart* (Random Hse, 1998),
The Light in the Piazza, The Snare (U Pr Mississippi,
1996, 1993), *The Voice at the Back Door* (LSU Pr,
1994), *Boulevard, Southern Rev, Story, Antaeus, New
Yorker, Atlantic*

Max Steele   W
English Dept, U North Carolina, Chapel Hill, NC 27514,
919-962-5481
    Pubs: *The Hat of My Mother* (Algonquin Bks, 1988),
Story, Paris Rev

Shelby Stephenson   P
UNC Pembroke, Pembroke Magazine, Box 1510,
Pembroke, NC 28372-1510, 919-521-4214
  Pubs: *Poor People, The Persimmon Tree Carol*
  (Nightshade Pr, 1998, 1990), *Plankhouse* (North
  Carolina Wesleyan College Pr, 1993), *Poetry NW,
  Hudson Rev, New Virginia Rev, Bits, Carolina Qtly*

John Stokes   P
124 Windemere Rd
Wilmington, NC 28405
  Pubs: *Texas Qtly, Voices Intl, The Poet, Pembroke
  Mag, Crucible*

Julie Suk ♀ ✈   P
845 Greentree Dr
Charlotte, NC 28211-2731, 704-366-8956
  Pubs: *The Angel of Obsession* (U Arkansas Pr, 1992),
  Heartwood (Briarpatch Pr, 1991), *Poetry, Shenandoah,
  Cream City Rev, American Lit Rev, River Styx, Georgia
  Rev*

Chuck Sullivan   P
1100 E 34 St
Charlotte, NC 28205, 704-334-3496
  Pubs: *Alphabet of Grace: New & Selected Poems*
  (Sandstone Pr, 1995), *Longing for the Harmonies* (St.
  Andrews Pr, 1992), *The Juggler on the Radio*
  (Briarpatch Pr, 1987), *The Catechism of Hearts* (Red
  Clay Bks, 1979)

Charleen Whisnant Swansea   P
404 Deming Dr
Chapel Hill, NC 27514
  Pubs: *Mindworks* (South Carolina Educational TV,
  1990), *Word Magic* (Doubleday, 1976), *SPR*

Nancy McFadden Tilly ♀ ✈   W
628 Kensington Dr
Chapel Hill, NC 27514-6731, 919-929-8880
  Pubs: *Golden Girl* (FSG, 1985), *Potato Eyes, Writer to
  Writer, Pembroke Mag, Raleigh News & Observer,
  Carolina Qtly, Cotton Boll, Writer's Choice, Albany Rev*

Stephanie S. Tolan ♀   P&W
4511 Eagle Lake Dr N
Charlotte, NC 28217-3001
Internet: steft@aol.com
  Pubs: *Ordinary Miracles, The Face in the Mirror,
  Welcome to the Ark, Who's There?, Save Halloween!*
  (Morrow, 1999, 1998, 1996, 1994, 1993)
Groups: Children, Teenagers

Kermit Turner   W
Lenoir-Rhyne College, Box 418, Hickory, NC 28601,
704-328-1741
  Pubs: *These Rebel Powers* (Frederick Warne & Co,
  1979), *Greensboro Rev, Roanoke Rev, Phylon*

Thomas N. Walters   P
5211 Melbourne Rd
Raleigh, NC 27606, 919-851-4899
  Pubs: *Always Next August, Seeing in the Dark* (Moore
  Pub Co, 1976, 1972)

Robert Watson ♀   P&W
9-D Fountain Manor Dr
Greensboro, NC 27405-8032, 336-274-9962
  Pubs: *The Pendulum: New & Selected Poems* (LSU Pr,
  1995), *Night Blooming Cactus* (Atheneum, 1980),
  *Poetry, Harper's, New Yorker, Georgia Rev,
  Shenandoah*

Susan C. Weinberg   W
English Dept, Appalachian State Univ, Boone, NC 28608,
704-262-2871
  Pubs: *Voices from Home: North Carolina Prose Anth*
  (Avisson Pr, 1997), *Gettysburg Rev, Other Voices,
  Gargoyle, Indiana Rev, MacGuffin, Third Coast,
  Washington Rev, Mississippi Rev*

John Foster West   P&W
157 West Ln
Boone, NC 28607-8605, 828-295-7704
  Pubs: *Lift Up Your Head, Tom Dooley* (Down Home Pr,
  1993), *The Summer People* (Appalachian Consortium
  Pr, 1988), *Wry Wine* (John F. Blair Pub, 1977), *Time
  Was* (Random Hse, 1965), *Southern Rev, Atlantic, SW
  Rev, Cold Mountain Rev, Crucible*

Nina A. Wicker   P
2356 Minter School Rd
Sanford, NC 27330
  Pubs: *Winter & Wild Roses* (Persephone Pr, 1989),
  October Rain on My Window (Honeybrook Pr, 1984),
  Heiwa: Anth (U Hawaii Pr, 1996), *Haiku Moment: Anth*
  (Charles E. Tuttle, 1993), *The Haiku Hundred: Anth*
  (Iron Pr, 1992), *Modern Haiku, Woodnotes, Frogpond*

Carol Lynn Wilkinson   P
PO Box 19312
Raleigh, NC 27609
  Pubs: *Taste of Remembered Wine* (North Carolina Rev
  Pr, 1975), *Wind, Miscellany*

Jonathan Williams ♀ ✈   P
PO Box 10
Highlands, NC 28741-0010, 828-526-4461
Internet: jwms@jargonbooks.com
  Pubs: *Blackbird Dust* (Turtle Pt Pr, 2000), *A Palpable
  Elysium* (D.R. Godine Pub, 2000), *Quote, Unquote* (Ten
  Speed Pr, 1989)

Dede Wilson 🎤 ✈ P
2409 Knollwood Rd
Charlotte, NC 28211-2707, 704-365-6846
    Pubs: *Glass* (Scots Plaid Pr, 1998), *Here's to the Land:
    Anth* (North Carolina Poetry Soc, 1992), *New Orleans
    Poetry Rev, SPR, Iowa Woman, Cream City Rev,
    Painted Bride Qtly, Flyway, Carolina Qtly, Tar River
    Poetry Rev*

Emily Herring Wilson P
3381 Timberlake Ln
Winston-Salem, NC 27106, 910-759-2309
    Pubs: *Hope & Dignity* (Temple U Pr, 1983)

Nancy Leffel Wilson 🎤 ✈ P&W
226 W Main St
Brevard, NC 28712, 828-966-4662
Internet: nmtnannie@citicom.net
    Pubs: *Pilgrimage, Onionhead, Saturday Evening Post,
    The Panhandler*

Lee Zacharias W
U North Carolina, English Dept, Greensboro, NC 27412,
336-334-4695
    Pubs: *Lessons* (HM, 1981), *Helping Muriel Make It
    Through the Night* (LSU Pr, 1976), *Southern Qtly, New
    Virginia Rev, Southern California Anth, New Territory,
    Redbook, Kansas Qtly*

NORTH DAKOTA

Carol Blair 🎤 ✈ P
1114 N 39 St, Apt 5
Grand Forks, ND 58203-2805, 701-775-7795
    Pubs: *Nobody Gets off the Bus* (Viet Nam Generation,
    1994), *The Color of Grief & Morning Glories* (Wolfe D.
    T. Pub, 1991), *New Press Lit Qtly*

Madelyn Camrud P
815 40 Ave, Apt 121F
Grand Forks, ND 58201, 701-772-2828
    Pubs: *Prairie Volcano* (Dacotah Territory & St. Ives,
    1995), *This House Is Filled with Cracks* (New Rivers
    Pr, 1994), *North Dakota Qtly, Kalliope, Nebraska Rev*

Rita Johnson P
PO Box 877
Stanley, ND 58784
    Pubs: *Plainswoman, Georgia Rev, Great River Rev,
    DeKalb Literary Arts Journal, Oxygen*

David Martinson P
English Dept, North Dakota State Univ, Minard 322 F,
University Sta, Fargo, ND 58105
    Pubs: *A Little Primer of Tom McGrath* (Shining Times,
    1998), *Hinges* (Aluminum Canoe, 1996), *Nation,
    Dacotah Territory, Pemmican, Minnesota Monthly,
    Floating Island, Another Chicago Mag*

Jay Meek 🎤 ✈ P
English Dept, Univ North Dakota, Box 7209, University
Stn, Grand Forks, ND 58203, 701-777-3321
    Pubs: *Memphis Letters, Headlands, Windows* (Carnegie
    Mellon U Pr, 2001, 1997, 1994), *BPJ, Crazyhorse,
    Great River Rev, Ohio Rev, Prose Poem*

Martha George Meek P
English Dept, Univ North Dakota, Box 8237, University
Sta, Grand Forks, ND 58202, 701-777-6391
    Pubs: *Rude Noises* (Dacotah Territory Pr, 1995),
    Preludes: Anth (Mount Holyoke College, 1973)

Susan Yuzna P
Univ North Dakota, English Dept, Grand Forks, ND
58202-7209, 701-777-4306
    Pubs: *Her Slender Dress* (U Akron Pr, 1996), *Burning
    the Fake Woman* (Green Tower Pr, 1996)

OHIO

Lee K. Abbott 🎤 ✈ W
4536 Carriage Hill Ln
Upper Arlington, OH 43220, 614-459-0197
Internet: abbott.4@osu.edu
    Pubs: *Wet Places at Noon* (U Iowa Pr, 1997), *Living
    After Midnight, Dreams of Distant Lives* (Putnam, 1991,
    1989), *Atlantic, Harper's, Georgia Rev, Kenyon Rev*

Steve Abbott P
91 E Duncan St
Columbus, OH 43202, 614-268-5006
    Pubs: *A Short History of the Word* (Pudding Hse,
    1996), *Coffeehouse Poetry Anth* (Bottom Dog Pr, 1996),
    *Pudding Hse, Wind, Birmingham Poetry Rev, Heartlands
    Today*

Laura Albrecht P
6217 Carmin Ave
Dayton, OH 45427-2058
    Pubs: *Skid* (WSU Prod, 1994), *Poetry Gumball*
    (Voicebox Pubs, 1993), *CQ, Coe Rev, Maverick Pr,
    Ohio Poetry Rev, Steam Ticket, Work*

Pamela Alexander P
Creative Writing Program, Rice Hall, Oberlin College,
Oberlin, OH 44074, 440-775-6567
 Pubs: *Inland* (Iowa U Pr, 1997), *Commonwealth of
 Wings* (Wesleyan, 1991), *Navigable Waterways* (Yale U
 Pr, 1985), *Atlantic, New Yorker, Michigan Qtly Rev,
 Shankpainter, Field, Margin*

Raman Nancy Ancrom P
PO Box 1913
Cincinnati, OH 45201-1913, 513-621-0531
 Pubs: *Still News* (Raman Arts, 1997), *A Fair Straight
 Ahead* (Window Edtns, 1981), *Willow Springs, Oxalis,
 Worc, Smoke Signals, Downtown, Nation, Poetry Mag
 of the Lower East Side, Telephone, Evil Dog, Black
 River Rev*

Julian Anderson ⏚ W
159 Riverview Park
Columbus, OH 43214
 Pubs: *Empire Under Glass* (Faber & Faber, 1996),
 Pushcart Prize XXIV: Anth (Pushcart Pr, 1999), *Kenyon
 Rev, Southern Rev, Cleveland Plain Dealer, la fontana,
 The Jrnl*
I.D.: Quakers, Scandinavian-American

Maggie Anderson ⏚ ✈ P
Wick Poetry Program, English Dept, Kent State Univ, PO
Box 5190, Kent, OH 44242, 330-672-2067
Internet: manders0@kent.edu
 Pubs: *Windfall, A Space Filled with Moving, Cold
 Comfort* (U Pitt Pr, 2000, 1992, 1986), *Years That
 Answer* (H&R, 1980), *Poetry East, APR, Ohio Rev,
 Third Coast*
I.D.: G/L/B/T, Appalachian. Groups: Children, Teachers

Tom Andrews W
English Dept, Ohio Univ, Athens, OH 45701-2979,
614-593-2756
 Pubs: *The Hemophiliac's Motorcycle* (U Iowa Pr, 1994),
 The Brother's Country (Persea Bks, 1990), *Poetry, Paris
 Rev, Kenyon Rev, Field, Virginia Qtly Rev*

Nuala Archer P
English Dept, Cleveland State Univ, Cleveland, OH 44115
 Pubs: *Two Women, Two Shores* (w/Medbh McGuckian;
 New Poets Series, 1989), *Epoch, Poetry Australia*

Rane Arroyo ⏚ ✈ P
PO Box 8254
Toledo, OH 43605, 419-243-2048
Internet: rarroyo@pop3.utoledo.edu
 Pubs: *Pale Ramon* (Zoland Bks, 1998), *The Singing
 Shark* (Bilingual Pr, 1996), *Death Cab for Cutie* (New
 Sins Pr, 1991), *Nimrod, Kenyon Rev, Spoon River Qtly,
 Americas Rev, Ploughshares, Many Mountains Moving,
 ACM, Callaloo, Ohio Rev, Poems & Plays*

Russell Atkins P
6005 Grand Ave
Cleveland, OH 44104, 216-431-7116
 Pubs: *The Garden Thrives: Anth* (HC, 1996), *Voices of
 Cleveland: Anth* (Cleveland State U, 1996), *Beyond the
 Reef* (Houghton, 1991), *Letters to America: Anth*
 (Wayne State U Pr, 1995), *Scarecrow Poetry: Anth*
 (Ashland Poetry Pr, 1994), *Splitcity*

David Baker ⏚ ✈ P
135 Granview Rd
Granville, OH 43023, 740-587-1269
 Pubs: *Truth About Small Towns, After the Reunion,
 Sweet Home, Saturday Night* (U Arkansas Pr, 1998,
 1994, 1991), *Haunts* (Cleveland State U Pr, 1985),
 *Atlantic, New Yorker, Poetry, Nation, Yale Rev, Kenyon
 Rev*

David Baratier ⏚ ✈ P
PO Box 6291
Columbus, OH 43206, 614-263-7115
Internet: www.pavementsaw.org
 Pubs: *In It What's in It* (Spuyten Duyvil, 2000), *The
 Fall of Because* (Pudding Hse, 1999), *A Run of Letter*
 (Poetry NY, 1998), *American Poetry: Anth* (Carnegie
 Mellon, 2000), *Clockpunchers: Anth* (Partisan Pr, 2000),
 5 AM, Denver Qtly, Fourteen Hills

Panos D. Bardis P&W
2533 Orkney Dr
Toledo, OH 43606
 Pubs: *A Cosmic Whirl of Melodies* (Literary Endeavor,
 1985), *Ivan & Artemis* (Pageant Pr, 1957), *Abira Digest,
 Poetry Project Four, Hellenic Times*

Steven Bauer ⏚ ✈ P&W
Miami Univ, English Dept, Oxford, OH 45056,
765-732-3768
Internet: bauersa@casmail.muohio.edu
 Pubs: *Cat of a Different Color* (Delacorte, 2000),
 Strange & Wonderful Tale of RBT McDoodle (S&S,
 1999), *Daylight Savings* (Peregrine Smith, 1989), *My
 Poor Elephant: Anth* (Longstreet Pr, 1992), *Hopewell
 Rev, Missouri Rev, Indiana Rev, High Plains Lit Rev*

Gail Bellamy ⏚ ✈ P
3422 E Scarborough Rd
Cleveland Heights, OH 44118-3412
Internet: gbellamy@worldnet.att.net
 Pubs: *Food Poems: Anth* (Bottom Dog Pr, 1998),
 Detours: Anth (Lonesome Traveler Pub, 1997), *Earth's
 Daughters, Cosmopolitan, Rolling Stone, Byline, New
 Mexico Humanities Rev*

John M. Bennett ♠ ✈   P
Luna Bisonte Prods, 137 Leland Ave, Columbus, OH
43214, 614-846-4126
Internet: bennet.23@osu.edu
  Pubs: *rOlling COMBers* (Potes & Poets Pr, 2000),
Mailer Leaves Ham (Pantograph Pr, 1999), *Know Other*
(Luna Bisonte Prods, 1998), *Seasons* (Spectacular
Diseases, 1997), *Door Door* (Juxta/3300 Pr, 1997),
Prime Sway (Texture Pr, 1996), *Caliban, DOC*(K)S,
Texture
Lang: Spanish

Paul Bennett ♠   P&W
Poet in Residence, Denison Univ, Granville, OH 43023,
614-587-6688
  Pubs: *Max: the Tale of a Waggish Dog* (Mayhaven
Pub, 1998), *Appalachian Mettle* (Savage Pr, 1997),
Follow the River (Orchard Bks, 1987), *Building a House*
(Limekiln Pr, 1986), *Agni, CSM, Delmar*

S. W. Bliss   P
128 Tionda S
Vandalia, OH 45377, 513-898-8966
  Pubs: *Images, Nexus, Daring Poetry Qtly, Green
Feather, Ohio Jrnl, Vincent Brothers Rev, Flights*

Maureen Bloomfield   P
1555 Donaldson Pl
Cincinnati, OH 45223-1713, 513-681-0037
  Pubs: *Error & Angels* (U South Carolina Pr, 1997),
*Ploughshares, Southern Rev, Cincinnati Poetry Rev,
New Republic, Poetry, Shenandoah*

Don Bogen ♠ ✈   P
362 Terrace Ave
Cincinnati, OH 45220, 513-221-2699
  Pubs: *The Known World, After the Splendid Display*
(Wesleyan, 1997, 1986), *Nation, New Republic, Yale
Rev, Paris Rev, Poetry, Partisan Rev*
Lang: French, German

Phil Boiarski   P
839 Lakefield Dr
Galloway, OH 43119, 614-870-6623
  Pubs: *Cornered* (Logan Elm Pr, 1990), *Coal & Ice*
(Yellow Pages Pr, 1980), *Paris Rev, California Qtly,
Rocky Mtn Rev, Green House, Ohio Jrnl, Handbook*

Imogene L. Bolls ♠ ✈   P
Wittenberg Univ, Box 720, English Dept, Springfield, OH
45501, 513-390-2176
  Pubs: *Advice for the Climb, Earthbound* (Bottom Dog,
1999, 1989), *Glass Walker* (Cleveland State U, 1983),
*Antioch Rev, Georgia Rev, Ohio Rev, SPR, South
Dakota Rev, Texas Rev*
Groups: Children, Seniors

Jennifer Bosveld ♠ ✈   P
Pudding Hse Writers Resource Ctr, 60 N Main St,
Johnstown, OH 43031, 740-967-6060
Internet: http://www.puddinghouse.com
  Pubs: *Prayers to Protest: Poems That Center & Bless:
Anth, Unitarian Universalist Poets: Anth* (Pudding Hse
Pub, 1998, 1996), *Coffeehouse Poetry Anth* (Bottom
Dog Pr, 1996), *Bottomfish, Heaven Bone, Chiron Rev,
Negative Capability, Psychopoetica, The Sun*
Groups: Spiritual/Religious

Daniel Bourne ♠ ✈   P
College of Wooster, English Dept, Wooster, OH 44691,
216-263-2577
Internet: dbourne@acu.wooster.edu
  Pubs: *The Household Gods* (Cleveland State U Pr,
1994), *APR, Shenandoah, Prairie Schooner, Field,
Poetry NW, Salmagundi*
Lang: Polish

Philip Brady   P
Youngstown State Univ, English Dept, Youngstown, OH
44555-3415, 216-742-1952
  Pubs: *Forged Correspondences* (New Myths, 1996),
Plague Country (Mbira Pr, 1990), *College English,
Poetry NW, Massachusetts Rev, Honest Ulsterman,
Centennial Rev*

David Breithaupt ♠ ✈   P&W
22900 Caves Rd
Gambier, OH 43022, 740-427-4170
Internet: breithau@kenyon.edu
  Pubs: *Thus Spake the Corpse, Vol. 2: Anth* (Black
Sparrow Pr, 2000), *Exquisite Corpse, Kumquat
Merinque, Beet, The Krellullin, Rant*

Denise Brennan Watson ♠ ✈   P&W
PO Box 68081
Cincinnati, OH 45206-0081
Internet: brennan7@earthlink.net
  Pubs: *Food-And Other Enemies* (Essex Pr, 2000), *The
Undertow of Hunger* (Finishing Line Pr, 1999),
Revelations II: Anth (U Cincinnati Pr, 1999), *Lucid
Stone*
Groups: Women

Robert L. Brimm ♠ ✈   P
1120 Carlisle Ave
Dayton, OH 45420-1917, 937-254-5165
Internet: rbrimm@aol.com
  Pubs: *Palo Alto Rev, Poetry Motel, Poem, Potpourri,
Midwest Poetry Rev, Riverrun, Sisters Today, American
Scholar, Silhouette*

Michael J. Bugeja   P&W
Special Assistant to the President, Ohio Univ, Cutler Hall
110, Athens, OH 45701, 740-593-2329
  Pubs: *Millennium's End* (Archer Pr, 1999), *Talk*
(Arkansas Pr, 1998), *Flight from Valhalla* (Livingston U
Pr, 1993), *Platonic Love* (Orchises Pr, 1991), *Poetry,
Harper's, TriQtly, Georgia Rev, Kenyon Rev*

Grace Butcher 🎤 ✈   P
PO Box 274
Chardon, OH 44024, 440-286-3840
Internet: graceb@geocities.com
    Pubs: *Child, House, World* (Hiram Poetry Rev, 1991),
    Rumors of Ecstasy (Barnwood, 1981), *Before I Go Out
    on the Road* (Cleveland State U Pr, 1979)

Catherine A. Callaghan 🎤 ✈   PP&P
Ohio State Univ, 222 Oxley Hall, 1712 Neil Ave,
Columbus, OH 43210-1298, 614-292-5880
    Pubs: *Other Worlds: Poems on Prints by M.C. Escher*
    (Pudding Hse, 1999), *Haiku Poems: Anth* (Bottom Dog
    Pr, 1999), *The Poet's Job: To Go Too Far: Anth, I
    Name Myself Daughter & It Is Good: Anth* (Sophia Bks,
    1985, 1981), *Pudding Mag, Dragonfly, Timber Creek*

Neil Carpathios 🎤 ✈   P
376 49th St NW
Canton, OH 44709, 330-499-7768
Internet: CantonCarp@aol.com
    Pubs: *The Weight of the Heart* (Blue Light Pr, 2000),
    Intimate Kisses: Anth (New World Library, 2001), *Our
    Mothers, Our Selves: Anth* (Bergin & Garvey, 1996), *I
    The Father* (Millennium Pr, 1993), *Georgia Rev, SPR,
    College English, Poetry*
I.D.: Greek-American/Greek. Groups: Children, Hospitals

Ellin Carter 🎤 ✈   P
414 Arcadia Ave
Columbus, OH 43202-2406, 614-267-8798
Internet: carter.3@osu.edu
    Pubs: *What This Is & Why* (Richmond Waters Pr,
    1992), *Kalliope, GW Rev, Earth's Daughters, Caprice,
    Prose Poem*
Groups: Seniors

Hale Chatfield 🎤 ✈   P&W
PO Box 115
Hiram, OH 44234, 440-632-5447
Internet: www.poetrypower.com
    Pubs: *Hale Chatfield Gold* (Pudding Hse Pr, 2000),
    Vox, Episodes, North Star, The Sotto Voce Massacres
    (North Star Pr, 1995, 1993, 1992, 1990)

David Citino 🎤 ✈   P
English Dept, Denney Hall, Ohio State Univ, 164 W 17
Ave, Columbus, OH 43210, 614-292-4856
    Pubs: *The Book of Appassionata: Collected Poems,
    The Discipline: New & Selected Poems, 1980-1992*
    (Ohio State U Pr, 1998, 1992), *Antioch Rev, Poetry,
    Kenyon Rev, Yale Rev, Salmagundi, NER, Georgia
    Rev, Ohio Rev*

Marian Clover   P&W
611 Yaronia Dr S
Columbus, OH 43214, 614-267-9201
    Pubs: *NAR, Kansas Qtly, Essence, Review 76, Review
    74*

E. R. Cole   P
274 E 214 St
Cleveland, OH 44123
    Pubs: *songpoems/poemsongs* (Weyburne, 1988),
    Uneasy Camber (Greystone Pr, 1986), *Northland Qtly*

Joan C. Connor 🎤 ✈   W
Ohio Univ, 327 Ellis Hall, English Dept, Athens, OH
45701, 740-593-2754
Internet: connor@oak.cats.ohiou.edu
    Pubs: *We Who Live Apart, Here on Old Rte. 7* (U
    Missouri Pr, 2000, 1997), *Matter of the Heart* (13th
    Moon, 2000), *Tiller & Pen: Anth* (Eighth Moon Pr,
    1994), *Kenyon Rev, TriQtly, Gettysburg Rev,
    Shenandoah, Southern Rev, NAR, Manoa*

David Craig   P&W
690 Overlook Dr N
Wintersville, OH 43953, 740-282-6950
    Pubs: *The Roof of Heaven* (Franciscan U Pr, 1998),
    The Cheese Stands Alone (CMJ Pub, 1997), *Only One
    Face* (White Eagle Coffee Store Pr, 1994), *The Odd
    Angles of Heaven: Anth* (Harold Shaw Pubs, 1994),
    Heartlands Today, Hiram Poetry Rev, Image

James Cummins 🎤 ✈   P
ML-#0033, Univ Cincinnati, Elliston Poetry Collection,
Cincinnati, OH 45221-0033, 513-556-1570
Internet: james.cummins@uc.edu
    Pubs: *Portrait in a Spoon* (U South Carolina Pr, 1997),
    The Whole Truth (North Point, 1986), *Paris Rev,
    Ploughshares, Shenandoah, New Republic*

Kent H. Dixon   W
Wittenberg Univ, PO Box 720, Springfield, OH 45501,
937-327-7069
    Pubs: *Kansas Qtly, Arkansas Rev, Grand Tour,
    Gettysburg Rev, Georgia Rev, TriQtly, Shenandoah,
    Iowa Rev, American Prospect, Libido*

Wayne Dodd   P
Ohio Univ, 209-C Ellis Hall, English Dept, Athens, OH
45701, 614-593-1900
    Pubs: *Of Desire & Disorder* (Carnegie Mellon Pr, 1994),
    Toward the End of the Century (U Iowa, 1992),
    Gettysburg Rev, Iowa Rev, Antioch, Georgia Rev

Cyril A. Dostal   P
3283 Dellwood Rd
Cleveland, OH 44118, 216-752-3008
    Pubs: *Emergency Exit* (Cleveland State U Pr, 1977),
    BPJ, Gamut Mag

John Drury 🎤 ✈ P
2824 Werk Rd
Cincinnati, OH 45211, 513-389-0303
Internet: John.Drury@uc.edu
Pubs: *The Disappearing Town* (Miami U Pr, 2000) *The Stray Ghost* (State St, 1987), *APR, Lit Rev, New Republic, Paris Rev, Poetry NW, Southern Rev, Verse, Western Humanities Rev*

Dennis S. Edwards P
7410 Avon Dr
Mentor, OH 44060, 216-953-1167
Pubs: *Parnassus, Green Feather, Rag Mag, Manna, Ripples, Hob-Nob, Calliope's Corner, Gryphon*

Leatrice Joy W. Emeruwa P
PO Box 21755
Cleveland, OH 44121, 216-381-3027
Internet: lemeruwa@aol.com
Pubs: *A Jazzzzzzz Poem* (Burning Pr, 1997), *Voices of Cleveland: Anth* (Cleveland State U Pr, 1996)

John Engle 🎤 ✈ P
1127 Neeld Dr
Xenia, OH 45385
Pubs: *Tree People, Laugh Lightly II* (Engle's Angle, 1990, 1989), *Writer's Digest, Lake Effect, Poetpourri, Byline, Science of Mind, Unity*

Angie Estes 🎤 ✈ P
242 N Liberty St
Delaware, OH 43015-1647, 614-292-0270
Internet: aestes@calpoly.edu
Pubs: *The Uses of Passion* (Peregrine Smith Bks, 1995), *Boarding Pass* (Solo Pr, 1990), *Geography of Home: Anth* (Heyday Bks, 1999), *Queer Dog: Anth* (Cleis Pr, 1997), *Shenandoah, Mid-American Rev, Gulf Coast, Agni, The Jrnl, Antioch Rev*

Kathy Fagan 🎤 ✈ P
English Dept, Ohio State Univ, 164 W 17 Ave, Columbus, OH 43210, 614-292-0270
Internet: fagan.3@osu.edu
Pubs: *MOVING & ST RAGE* (UNT, 1999), *The Raft* (Dutton, 1985), *Paris Rev, Missouri Rev, Ploughshares, Shenandoah, New Republic, Kenyon Rev*

Laurence S. Fallis P&W
4457 Woodglen St, Apt D
Kent, OH 44240-6954, 216-296-3765
Pubs: *Arizona Qtly, Woodrider, Texas Qtly, Blue Cloud Qtly, Orion, Middle Way, Invisible City*

Ross Feld P&W
6934 Miami Ave Room 23
Cincinnati, OH 45243, 513-271-3405
Pubs: *Shapes Mistaken, Only Shorter* (North Point, 1989, 1982), *Harper's, Parnassus*

B. Felton P&W
17102 Ridgeton Dr
Cleveland, OH 44128, 216-991-9245
Pubs: *Conclusions* (B. Felton, 1971)

Barbara Fialkowski P
Creative Writing Program, Bowling Green State Univ, Hannah Hall, Bowling Green, OH 43403, 419-372-8370
Pubs: *Framing* (Croissant Pr, 1978), *New Virginia Rev, NAR, Abraxas, Poetry Now*

Annie Finch 🎤 ✈ P
376 Howell Ave
Cincinnati, OH 45220-2015, 513-961-4982
Internet: www.muohio.edu/~finchar
Pubs: *Marie Moving, Eve* (Story Line Pr, 2002, 1997), *The Ghost of Meter, Exaltation of Forms: Anth* (U Michigan Pr, 1994, 2000), *Book of the Sonnet: Anth* (Penguin, 2000), *Ravishing DisUnities: Anth* (Wesleyan, 2000), *Kenyon Rev, Paris Rev, SW Rev, AGNI*
I.D.: Women

Norman M. Finkelstein 🎤 ✈ P
Xavier Univ, English Dept, 3800 Victory Pkwy, Cincinnati, OH 45207-4446, 513-745-2041
Internet: finkelst@xavier.xu.edu
Pubs: *Track* (Spuyten Duyvil, 1999), *The Ritual of New Creation* (SUNY Pr, 1992), *Restless Messengers* (U Georgia Pr, 1992), *Denver Qtly, Salmagundi, Peqoud, Hambone, Talisman, Notre Dame Rev, Colorado Rev*
I.D.: Jewish

Robert Flanagan 🎤 ✈ P&W
181 N Liberty St
Delaware, OH 43015-1642, 740-369-4820
Internet: rjflanag@cc.owu.edu
Pubs: *Getting By, In Buckeye Country, Loving Power* (Bottom Dog, 1996, 1994, 1990), *Norton Bk of American Short Stories: Anth* (Norton, 1988), *Civic Arts Rev, Illinois Qtly, Chicago, Fiction, Kansas Qtly, NW Rev, Ohio Rev*

Deborah Fleming P
2525 CR 775
Perrysville, OH 44864, 419-938-7305
Pubs: *Learning the Trade* (Locust Hill, 1992), *Hiram Poetry Rev, Pennsylvania Rev, Green River Rev, The Jrnl, Crosscurrents, Sucarnochee Rev, Organization & Environment, Pike Creek Rev, Ibis*

Robert R. Fox 🎤 ✈ P&W
Ohio Arts Council, 727 E Main St, Columbus, OH 43205-1796, 614-466-2613
Pubs: *Columbia Companion to the 20th Century Short Story: Anth* (Columbia U Pr, 2000), *Jrnl of Appalachian Studies, Pine Mountain Sand & Gravel, 5 a.m.*
Groups: Children, Seniors

Christopher Franke   P
c/o Deciduous, 1456 W 54 St, Cleveland, OH 44102,
216-651-7725
   Pubs: *Paren's Thesis* (Burning Pr, 1997),
frankeana/miscellangy (deciduous/worded print, 1996),
=5 (Wm. Busta Gallery, 1994), *Artcrimes, SplitCity,
Listening Eye, Coffeehouse Poetry Anth*

Stuart Friebert   P
172 Elm
Oberlin, OH 44074, 216-774-2302
   Pubs: *Funeral Pie* (Four Way Bks, 1996), *The
Darmstadt Orchids* (BkMk Pr, 1993), *Paris Rev, The
Qtly, Iowa Rev, Paterson Rev*

Diane Furtney 🎤 ✈   P
297 E Deshler
Columbus, OH 43206-2710, 614-444-1812
   Pubs: *Murder in the New Age* (as D.J.H. Jones; U
New Mexico Pr, 2000), *Murder at the MLA* (as D.J.H.
Jones; U Georgia Pr, 1993), *Destination Rooms*
(Riverstone Pr, 1980), *Chicago Rev, Kenyon Rev, Iowa
Rev*

Zona Gale   P
3877 Indian Rd
Toledo, OH 43606
   Pubs: *Her Soul Beneath the Bone* (U Illinois Pr, 1988),
Spirits & Seasons (Heatherdown Pr, 1982)

David Lee Garrison   P
Dept of Modern Languages, Wright State Univ, Dayton,
OH 45435, 937-293-8699
   Pubs: *Inside the Sound of Rain* (Vincent Brothers Co,
1997), *Blue Oboe* (Wyndham Hall Pr, 1984), *Pegasus,
Wind, Poetpourri, Whiskey Island Mag, Kansas Qtly,
Orphic Lute, Bitterroot, Comstock Rev, Denver Qtly,
Laurel Rev, Plains Poetry Jrnl, Vincent Brothers*

John Gerlach   P
140 Meadowhill Ln
Moreland Hills, OH 44022
   Pubs: *NAR, Ohio Rev, Prairie Schooner*

Elton Glaser 🎤 ✈   P
Univ Akron, English Dept, Akron, OH 44325-1906,
330-836-3388
Internet: eglaser@uakron.edu
   Pubs: *Winter Amnesties* (Southern Illinois U Pr, 2000),
Color Photographs of the Ruins (U Pitt Pr, 1992),
Tropical Depressions (U Iowa Pr, 1988), *Georgia Rev,
Parnassus, Poetry NW, Poetry*

William Greenway 🎤 ✈   P
English Dept, Youngstown State Univ, Youngstown, OH
44555, 330-742-3418
Internet: WillGreenway@aol.com
   Pubs: *Simmer Dim, How the Dead Bury the Dead* (U
Akron, 1999, 1994), *Father Dreams* (State St Pr, 1994),
Where We've Been (Breitenbush Bks, 1987), *Poetry,
APR, Southern Rev, Poetry NW, Prairie Schooner,
Shenandoah*

Gordon Grigsby   P
625 Edgecliff Dr
Columbus, OH 43235, 614-847-1780
   Pubs: *Mid-Ohio Elegies* (Logan Elm Pr, 1985), *West
Coast Rev, SPR, Mickle St Rev*

Jeff Gundy   P
Bluffton College, English Dept, Bluffton, OH 45817-1196,
419-358-3283
   Pubs: *A Community of Memory* (U Illinois Pr, 1996),
Flatlands (Cleveland State U Pr, 1995), *Antioch Rev,
Georgia Rev, Crazyhorse, Exquisite Corpse, Laurel Rev*

Mark Halliday 🎤 ✈   P
English Dept, Ohio Univ, Athens, OH 45705, 740-593-2758
Internet: hallidam@ohio.edu
   Pubs: *Selfwolf* (U Chicago Pr, 1999), *Tasker St* (U
Massachusetts Pr, 1992), *Little Star* (Morrow, 1987)

Yvonne Moore Hardenbrook   P
1757 Willow Way Cir N
Columbus, OH 43220, 614-459-4339
   Pubs: *Out of Season: Anth* (Amagansett Pr, 1993), *A
Gathering of Poets: Anth* (Kent State U Pr, 1992),
Amelia, Brussels Sprout, Frogpond, Modern Haiku

Donald M. Hassler 🎤 ✈   P
1226 Woodhill Dr
Kent, OH 44240, 330-672-2676
Internet: extrap@kent.edu
   Pubs: *Comic Tones in Science Fiction* (Greenwood,
1982), *A Gathering of Poets: Anth* (Kent State U Pr,
1992), *Extrapolation, Hellas, Tar River Poetry,
Onionhead, Above the Bridge, Hiram Poetry Rev,
Descant*

Laurie Henry   P
2824 Werk Rd
Cincinnati, OH 45211, 513-389-0303
Internet: henrylj@email.uc.edu
   Pubs: *Restoring the Chateau of the Marquis de Sade*
(Silverfish Rev Pr, 1985), *APR, Poetry NW*

Michelle Herman   W
English Dept, Ohio State Univ, 164 W 17 Ave, Columbus,
OH 43210, 614-292-5767
   Pubs: *A New & Glorious Life* (Carnegie Mellon U Pr,
1998), *Missing* (Ohio State U, 1990), *Twenty Under
Thirty: Anth* (Scribner, 1986)

Terry Hermsen   P
25 Weber Rd
Columbus, OH 43202
  Pubs: *Child Aloft in Ohio Theatre, 36 Spokes: The Bicycle Poems* (Bottom Dog Pr, 1995, 1985), *Images, Kansas Qtly, The Plough, The Jrnl, Nimrod, Antigonish, Confluence, Outerbridge, Hiram Poetry Rev, South Dakota Rev, Descant*

Garrison L. Hilliard   P&W
PO Box 25102
Cincinnati, OH 45225, 513-251-3747
  Pubs: *This Is a Romance* (?) (QCB Pr, 1994), *Minotaur, Aim, Leatherneck, Small Pond, Innisfree*

Gretchen Houser   W
6119 Denison Blvd
Parma Heights, OH 44130, 440-888-8587
  Pubs: *Concho River Rev, Writers' Jrnl, Midwest Characters & Voices, Plain Dealer Publishing Company, Leaves of Grass, Plain Brown Wrapper, Writers' Report*

Andrew Hudgins   P
Dept of English & Comparative Lit, Univ Cincinnati, 248-249 McMicken Hall (ML 69), Cincinnati, OH 45221, 513-556-5924
  Pubs: *The Glass Hammer: A Southern Childhood, The Never-Ending* (HM, 1994, 1991)

Robert Hudzik 🎤 ✈   P
403 Miami Ave
Terrace Park, OH 45174-1146, 513-248-2965
  Pubs: *From the Tree* (Alms Hse Pr, 1995), *Poetry, Poet Lore, Cincinnati Poetry Rev, Slow Loris Reader, Hiram Poetry Rev, Poetry NW*

Lynne Hugo 🎤 ✈   P&W
PO Box 454
Oxford, OH 45056, 513-523-4774
Internet: lynnephugo@aol.com
  Pubs: *Baby's Breath* (Synergistic Pr, 2000), *Swimming Lessons* (w/A.T. Villegas; Morrow, 1998), *A Progress of Miracles* (San Diego Poets Pr, 1993), *The Time Change* (Ampersand Pr, 1992), *The Qtly, Prairie Schooner, Cincinnati Poetry Rev, Mid American Rev*

Bonnie Jacobson 🎤 ✈   P
24395 Shaker Blvd
Cleveland, OH 44122-2346, 216-831-1916
  Pubs: *In Joanna's House* (Cleveland State U Poetry Center, 1998), *Stopping for Time* (GreenTower Pr, 1989), *Laurel Rev, Negative Capability, Prairie Schooner, Gettysburg Rev, Iowa Rev, Tar River Poetry*

jinni jovel   PP&P
Creative Freelance Channel, Box #913, Worthington, OH 43085-0913, 614-218-4976
  Pubs: *Galley Sail Rev*

Jack R. Justice   P
9023 Shadetree Dr
Cincinnati, OH 45242, 513-793-1969
  Pubs: *Blue Unicorn, Sou'wester, Hampden-Sydney, Kentucky Poetry Rev, Stone Country, Wind, Samisdat*

Bella Briansky Kalter   W
5 Lenox Ln
Cincinnati, OH 45229
  Pubs: *Ohio's Heritage, American Israelite, U Kansas City Rev, St. Anthony Messenger, Backbone*

Daniel Kaminsky   P
7116 Deveny Ave
Cleveland, OH 44105, 216-883-3683
  Pubs: *Snout to Snout, Voices of Cleveland: Anth* (Cleveland State U Pr, 1974, 1996), *Pig Iron*

J. Patrick Kelly 🎤   P
7336 Blue Boar Ct
Cincinnati, OH 45230-2181, 513-232-8962
  Pubs: *Touchstone, Son of Fat Tuesday, Ellipsis, Sierra Nevada Rev, Voices Intl, Bellowing Ark, Licking River Rev, Ascent, Mississippi Valley Rev, Louisville Rev*

Diane Kendig 🎤 ✈   P
235 Lexington Ave
Findlay, OH 45840-3709, 419-424-5965
Internet: kendig@mail.findlay.edu
  Pubs: *Tunnel of Flute Song* (Cleveland State U Pr, 1980), *Grrrrr: Anth* (Arctos, 2000), *U.S. 1 Worksheet, Minnesota Rev, Cincinnati Poetry Rev, Kalliope*
Groups: Prisoners, Children

Laura Ballard Kennelly 🎤 ✈   P
PO Box 626
Berea, OH 44017-0626, 216-243-4842
Internet: lkennelly@aol.com
  Pubs: *A Certain Attitude, A Measured Response* (Pecan Grove Pr, 1995, 1993), *Passage of Mrs. Jung* (Norton Coker Pr, 1990), *Redneck Rev, New Texas '92, La Carta De Oliver, San Jose Studies, Faultline, Ohio Writer*

Harley King   P
875 Maple St
Perrysburg, OH 43551
  Pubs: *Mother Don't Lock Me in that Closet* (Keller U Pr, 1989), *Empty Playground* (K&K Communications, 1980)

Robert Kinsley 🎤 ✈   P
6 Old Peach Ridge Rd
Athens, OH 45701-1342
  Pubs: *Field Stones, Endangered Species* (Orchises Pr, 1997, 1989), *Yankee Mag, Tar River Poetry*

Leonard Kress P
306 E Boundary
Perrysburg, OH 43551, 419-872-0398
 Pubs: *The Centralia Mine Fire* (Flume, 1987), *From the Life & Death of Chopin* (Lalka, 1976), *APR, Missouri Rev, New Letters, Massachusetts Rev, Commonweal*

Lolette Beth Kuby P
English Dept, Cleveland State Univ, E 22 & Euclid Ave, Cleveland, OH 44115, 216-932-4842
 Pubs: *The Mama Stories* (Bottom Dog Pr, 1995), *In Enormous Water* (Cleveland State U Pr, 1981), *Midwest Qtly, American Scholar, Proteus, Caesura, Nightsun, The Long Story*

Wayne Kvam P
Kent State Univ, English Dept, Kent, OH 44242, 216-672-2676
 Pubs: *Centennial Rev, Exile: A Literary Qtly*

Denise Reynolds Laubacher P
422 East St
Minerva, OH 44657, 216-868-3808
 Pubs: *Collective Works 1983-1987, Incognito* (Adams, 1987, 1985), *Whiskey Island, Touchstone*

Edward Lense P
673 Slate Hollow Ct
Powell, OH 43065
 Pubs: *Buried Voices* (Logan Elm Pr, 1982), *The Spirit That Moves Us, Greenfield Rev, Antioch Rev, Cimarron Rev, AWP Chronicle*

Kenneth Leonhardt P&W
321 Glen Oaks Dr
Cincinnati, OH 45238
 Pubs: *Goners* (University Edtns, 1996), *Sex Scells* (Fithian Pr, 1994), *Light, Bogg, Iconoclast, Abbey, Lilliput Rev, Higginsville Reader*

Joel A. Lipman P
English Dept, Univ Toledo, Toledo, OH 43606-3390, 419-841-3733
 Pubs: *The Real Ideal* (Luna Bisonte, 1996), *Machete Chemistry/Panades Physics* (Cubola New Art, 1994), *Fiction Intl, Generator, Exquisite Corpse*

Ernest Lockridge W
143 W South St
Worthington, OH 43085, 614-885-8964
 Pubs: *Flying Elbows, Prince Elmo's Fire* (Stein & Day, 1975, 1974), *New Jrnl, Ohio Jrnl*

Sandra Love W
898 E Hyde Rd
Yellow Springs, OH 45387-2700, 937-767-2700
 Pubs: *Dive for the Sun* (HM, 1982), *Life on the Line: Anth* (Negative Capability Pr, 1992), *Iowa Woman, South Dakota Rev, Kansas Qtly*

R. Nikolas Macioci 🎤 ✈ P
1506 Frebis Ave
Columbus, OH 43206-3721
 Pubs: *Why Dance?* (Singular Speech Pr, 1997), *Cafes of Childhood* (Event Horizon Pr, 1992), *Owen Wister Rev, Zone 3, Tampa Rev, Appalachee Qtly, Green Hills Lit Lantern, Crazyquilt, Fox Cry Rev*

James Magner, Jr. P
John Carroll Univ, English Dept, Cleveland, OH 44118, 216-397-4221
 Pubs: *Rose of My Flowering Night, Till No Light Leaps* (Golden Quill Pr, 1985, 1981), *America*

Doug Martin P
English Dept, Bowling Green State Univ, Bowling Green, OH 43403, 419-352-2822
 Pubs: *RE:AL, James White Rev, Riverrun, B City, Wormwood, Soundings: A Jrnl of the Living Arts, Malcontent, Eidos*

Herbert Woodward Martin P
English Dept, Univ of Dayton, 300 College Park Dr, #707, Dayton, OH 45469, 513-229-3439
 Pubs: *A Rock Against the Wind* (Berkley Pub Group, 1996), *Grand St, Ploughshares, Chaminade Rev, Poetry, Crone's Nest*

Jack Matthews W
Ohio Univ, English Dept, Athens, OH 45701, 614-593-2757
 Pubs: *Ghostly Populations, Booking in the Heartland* (Johns Hopkins U Pr, 1986, 1986), *Kenyon Rev*

Wendell Mayo 🎤 ✈ W
English Dept, Bowling Green State Univ, Bowling Green, OH 43403, 419-372-7399
 Pubs: *B. Horror & Other Stories* (Livingston, 1999), *In Lithuanian Wood,* (White Pine 1999), *Centaur of the North* (Arte Publico Pr, 1996), *Harvard Rev, Indiana Rev, Lit Rev, Missouri Rev, New Letters, Yale Rev*
I.D.: Latino/Latina. Groups: College/Univ

Howard McCord 🎤 ✈ P&W
15431 Sand Ridge Rd
Bowling Green, OH 43402, 419-352-5549
 Pubs: *Bone/Hueso* (Russell McKnight, 2000), *The Wisdom of Silenus* (St. Andrews Pr, 1996), *The Man Who Walked to the Moon* (McPherson & Co, 1997), *Thus Spake the Corpse, Vol. 2: Anth* (Black Sparrow Pr, 2000), *Skanky Possum, Exquisite Corpse, Die Young*
Lang: Spanish

Robert E. McDonough 🎤 ✈ P
3639 Harvey Rd
Cleveland Heights, OH 44118-2215
Internet: remcd@oh.verio.com
 Pubs: *No Other World* (Cleveland St U Pr, 1988), *Mississippi Valley Rev, Windless Orchard, Cornfield Rev, West Branch*

Robert McGovern 🎤 ✈   P
935 CR 1754
Ashland, OH 44805, 419-289-0499
Internet: rgovern@ashland.edu
   Pubs: *Selected Poems, Scarecrow Poetry, A Feast of Flesh & Other Occasions* (Ashland Poetry Pr, 2000, 1994, 1971), *Nation, Kansas Qtly, Hiram Poetry Rev, New Laurel Rev, Hollins Critic, Christian Century, Blue Unicorn*

Erin McGraw 🎤 ✈   W
English Dept, ML 69, Univ Cincinnati, Cincinnati, OH 45221-0069, 513-556-0923
   Pubs: *Lies of the Saints* (Chronicle Bks, 1996), *Bodies at Sea* (U Illinois Pr, 1989), *Georgia Rev, Southern Rev, Ascent, Kenyon Rev, Atlantic*

Joseph McLaughlin 🎤 ✈   P&W
433 Fair Ave NE
New Philadelphia, OH 44663, 330-343-1602
Internet: JosephMcL@aol.com
   Pubs: *Memory, In Your Country, Zen in the Art of Golf* (Pale Horse Pr, 1995, 1991), *The Listening Eye, The Formalist, SPR, Hiram Poetry Rev*

William McLaughlin   P
20865 Chagrin Blvd, #1
Cleveland, OH 44122, 216-752-8330
   Pubs: *At Rest in the Midwest* (Cleveland State U Pr, 1982), *Amherst Rev, Black Fly Rev, Cape Rock, Oxford Mag, Inlet, Nebo, Kansas Qtly*

William McMillen   P
824 Oak Knoll Dr
Perrysburg, OH 43551, 419-874-1596
   Pubs: *NAR, Prairie Schooner, Black Warrior Rev, Ohio Jrnl*

Roberta Mendel 🎤   P
The Pin Prick Press, 2664 S Green Rd, Shaker Heights, OH 44122-1536, 216-932-2173
   Pubs: *Ritter's Writers are Blossoming: Anth* (Ritter Public Library, 2000), *Indicting God: Anth* (Academic & Arts Pr, 1999), *Travels Through Time: Anth* (Creative With Words Pub, 1998), *Mushroom Dreams, Writer's Ink, Mandrake, Etcetera*

Larry Michaels 🎤   P
548 Robindale Ave
Toledo, OH 43616, 419-697-5550
Internet: michaelsOH@aol.com
   Pubs: *Poetry Today, Prophetic Voices, Aileron, Piedmont Lit Rev, Wind, Orphic Lute, Lyric*

John N. Miller 🎤 ✈   P
428 W College St
Granville, OH 43023, 740-587-4432
   Pubs: *In the Western World* (Spoon River Poetry, 1979), *Articles of War: Anth* (U Arkansas Pr, 1990), *Bellowing Ark, Atlanta Rev, Passages North, Hawaii Rev, Tar River Poetry, Birmingham Rev, Chariton Rev, American Poetry Monthly*
Lang: German

Lloyd L. Mills   P
English Dept, Kent State Univ, Kent, OH 44242, 330-673-6826
   Pubs: *Unreconciled Passions, Dry with a Twist: Anth* (Poets League of Greater Cleveland, 1993, 1997), *Laughter & Dry Mockery* (Commercial Pr, 1988), *Sics, New Laurel Rev, Louisiana Rev, Blue Unicorn*

Robert Miltner 🎤 ✈   P&W
English Dept, Kent State Univ Stark Campus, 6000 Frank Rd NW, Canton, OH 44720, 330-499-9600
Internet: rmiltner@stark.kent.edu
   Pubs: *On the Off-Ramp* (Implosion Pr, 1996), *Against the Simple* (Kent State U Pr, 1995), *The Seamless Serial Hour* (Pudding Hse Pub, 1993), *Cattle Bones & Coke Machines: Anth* (Smiling Dog Pr, 1995), *Barrow St, Prose Poem, Chiron Rev, CrossConnect, NYQ*

Judith Moffett   W
6908 Thorndike Rd
Cincinnati, OH 45227, 513-271-9349
   Pubs: *Homestead Year* (Lyons & Burford, 1995), *Time, Like an Ever-Rolling Stream, The Ragged World* (St. Martin's Pr, 1992, 1991), *Pennterra* (Congdon & Weed, 1987), *Kenyon Rev, New Yorker, Poetry, Asimov's Sci Fi, Georgia Rev*

Richard Morgan   P
Ohio Dominican College, English Dept, 1216 Sunbury Rd, Columbus, OH 43219, 614-846-0917
   Pubs: *Love & Anger* (ARN, 1982), *Tiger in the Air* (Blue Dog, 1979), *West Coast Rev, Rocky Mountain Rev*

Scott H. Mulrane   P
26 E 2 Ave, #20
Columbus, OH 43201-6500
   Pubs: *Cincinnati Poetry Rev, Oxford Mag, Cream City Rev, Sequoia, Galley Sail, Mudfish*

George Myers, Jr.   W
The Columbus Dispatch, 34 S 3rd St, Columbus, OH 43215, 614-461-5265
   Pubs: *Jump Hope* (Cumberland, 1992), *Worlds Without End* (Another Chicago Pr, 1990), *The Literary Rev, Seattle Rev, Ploughshares, The Qtly, Gargoyle, NAW*

Alan Napier　　　　　　　　　　　　　　P
3799 Olmsby Dr
Brimfield, OH 44240, 330-678-1686
　　Pubs: *Atomic Ghost* (Coffee Hse Pr, 1995), *Fathers: A Collection of Poems: Anth* (St. Martin's Pr, 1997), *Hiram Poetry Rev, SPR, Negative Capability, Colorado Rev, Key West Rev, Chelsea*

James R. Nichols　　　　　　　　　　　W
Muskingum College, English Dept, New Concord, OH 43762, 614-826-8265
　　Pubs: *Afterwords* (Intl U Pr, 1987), *Children of the Sea* (Blair, 1977), *Phoebe, Bitterroot, Encore*

Bea Opengart　　　　　　　　　　　　　P
1511 Chase Ave, Apt A
Cincinnati, OH 45223, 513-681-0729
　　Pubs: *Erotica* (Owl Creek Pr, 1995), *American Voice, Iowa Rev, Apalachee Qtly, The Jrnl, Shenandoah, Southern Humanities Rev*

Gary Bernard Pacernick　🎤　✈　　　　P
English Dept, Wright State Univ, Dayton, OH 45409-2345, 513-873-3136
　　Pubs: *The Jewish Poems* (Wright St U Pr, 1985), *Wanderers* (Prasada Pr, 1985), *Poetry East, APR, Ohio Rev, Tikkun, NAR, Poetry Now*

Frankie Paino　　　　　　　　　　　　　P
4196 W 212 St
Fairview Park, OH 44126
　　Pubs: *The Rapture of Matter* (Cleveland State U, 1991), *New American Poets of the '90s: Anth* (Godine, 1991), *Gettysburg Rev, Amer Voice, Antioch Rev*

Janis L. Pallister　🎤　　　　　　　　P
1249 Brownwood Dr
Bowling Green, OH 43402-3535, 419-353-9513
　　Pubs: *Shadows of Madness, At the Eighth Station, Sursum Corda* (Geryon, 1991, 1983, 1982), *Practices of the Wind: Anth* (Nicolas Kogon, 1997)

James Parlett　　　　　　　　　　　　　P
6878 Solon Blvd
Solon, OH 44139
　　Pubs: *News of the Assassin* (Raincrow, 1978), *Atlantic, Poetry NW, Cape Rock, En Passant*

Nancy Pelletier　　　　　　　　　　　　W
c/o Pansing, 624 5th St, Marietta, OH 45750-1910
　　Pubs: *Happy Families* (Collins, 1986), *The Rearrangement* (Paperback-Paperbooks, 1986), *Twigs*

Jane Piirto　🎤　✈　　　　　　　　　　P&W
233 W Walnut St
Ashland, OH 44805-3148, 419-281-6516
Internet: jpiirto@ashland.edu
　　Pubs: *A Location in the Upper Peninsula* (Sampo Pub, 1994), *The Three-Week Trance Diet* (Carpenter Pr, 1986), *South Dakota Rev, Denver Qtly*
Groups: Children, Teachers

Frank Polite　　　　　　　　　　　　　P
2537 Ohio Ave
Youngstown, OH 44504, 216-746-3955
　　Pubs: *Flamingo* (Pangborn Bks, 1990), *Letters of Transit* (City Miner, 1979), *Harper's, Nation, Free Lunch, New Yorker, Exquisite Corpse, Ohio Rev*

Lynn Powell　🎤　✈　　　　　　　　　P
171 E College St
Oberlin, OH 44074-1770, 440-775-2276
Internet: lynn@physics.oberlin.edu
　　Pubs: *Old & New Testaments* (U Wisconsin Pr, 1995), *Image, Seneca Rev, Poetry, Gettysburg Rev, Paris Rev*

Robert Pringle　🎤　✈　　　　　　　　P
11210 Gorsuch Rd
Galena, OH 43021, 614-965-4158
　　Pubs: *Cold Front* (Pudding Hse Pr, 1998), *Here's to Humanity: Anth* (The People's Pr, 2000), *Afterthoughts, Orbis, Psychopoetica, Pegasus Rev, Pudding Mag, Onionhead, Dream Intl Qtly, Poetry Motel, Envoi, Green's Mag, Paris/Atlantic, Vol. No.*
Groups: College/Univ

James S. Proffitt　　　　　　　　　　　P
7816 Foxtrot Dr
North Bend, OH 45052, 513-941-0835
　　Pubs: *Echoes Mag, Blue Ink Pr, Main St Rag, New Lifestyles, Bylines, Rockford Rev, The Oval, Ambergris*

Rose Mary Prosen　　　　　　　　　　　P
2300 Overlook Rd, #506
Cleveland Heights, OH 44106, 216-791-6145
　　Pubs: *Ethnic Literature & Culture in the U.S.A.: Anth* (Peter Lang, 1996), *Voices of Cleveland: Anth* (Cleveland State U, 1996), *Whiskey Island, Dry with a Twist, Writing Our Lives*

Nicholas Ranson　🎤　✈　　　　　　　　P
Univ Akron, English Dept, Akron, OH 44325-0001, 330-972-7606
Internet: nickranson@uakron.edu
　　Pubs: *Track Made Good* (Bits Pr, 1977), *Mississippi Rev, Lake Superior Rev, Wind*

James Reiss 🎤 ✈   P
English Dept, Miami Univ, Bachelor Hall, Oxford, OH
45056-3414, 513-529-5110
  Pubs: *Ten Thousand Good Mornings, The Parable of
  Fire* (Carnegie Mellon, 2002, 1996), *The Breathers*
  (Ecco Pr, 1974), *Atlantic, New Yorker, Poetry, Nation,
  New Republic, Paris Rev*
Lang: Spanish. Groups: Latino/Latina

Don Rice   W
5610 Blue Lagoon Ln
Hilliard, OH 43026-9033
  Pubs: *Fishes, Reptiles & Amphibians* (Van Nostrand,
  1981), *Providence Rev, Taedium*

Peter Roberts 🎤 ✈   P
1205 Laurelwood Rd
Mansfield, OH 44907-2328, 419-756-1460
Internet: www.geocities.com/peterroberts.geo/personal.html
  Pubs: *William & Mary Rev, Small Pond, Star*Line,
  NYQ, Confrontation, Beyond Baroque, Abbey, Frisson*

Linda Goodman Robiner   P&W
2648 S Belvoir Blvd
Cleveland, OH 44118-4661, 216-397-9473
  Pubs: *Reverse Fairy Tale* (Pudding Hse Pub, 1997),
  *North Atlantic Rev, Graham House Rev, Whiskey Island
  Mag, Black River Rev, Flights, Fine Lines, William &
  Mary Rev, CQ, Neovictorian*

Marge Rogers 🎤 ✈   P
5340 Silverdome Dr
Dayton, OH 45414-3648, 937-233-4822
Internet: Homeward5@juno.com
  Pubs: *Once Upon a Rhyme, Vol. 2* (Bear Hse Pubs,
  1999) *Common Threads, Poets at Work, Our Journey,
  Poetry in Motion, Byline Mag, Writers Block*
Groups: Teenagers, Seniors

Bill Roorbach 🎤 ✈   P
English Dept, Ohio State Univ, 164 W 17 Ave, Columbus,
OH 43215-1326, 614-292-0648
  Pubs: *Harper's, Granta, Iowa Rev, Witness*

Lynne Carol Rose 🎤 ✈   P
3911 Tamara Dr
Grove City, OH 43123-2832, 614-871-5840
  Pubs: *Child of the Washed World* (American Studies
  Pr, 1984), *Kingdom of Three* (Green River, 1980)
Groups: Children, Seniors

J. Allyn Rosser 🎤 ✈   P
12750 Rich Ln
Athens, OH 45701-9011
Internet: rosserj@oak.cats.ohiou.edu
  Pubs: *Bright Moves* (Northeastern U Pr, 1990),
  *Ploughshares, Alaska Qtly Rev, Poetry, Paris Rev,
  Hudson Rev, Georgia Rev, Denver Qtly, Ontario Rev,
  Crazyhorse, Gettysburg Rev*

Carol Rubenstein   P
Ohio Univ Press, Scott Quadrangle 220, Athens, OH
45701
  Pubs: *The Honey Tree Song: Poems & Chants of
  Sarawak Dayaks* (Ohio U Pr, 1985), *Ms.*

Joel Rudinger   P
6039 Zenobia Rd
Wakeman, OH 44889, 419-929-8767
  Pubs: *Lovers & Celebrations* (Dearborn Pr, 1984), *First
  Edition: 40 Poems* (Gull Pr, 1975)

Timothy Russell 🎤 ✈   W
202 Daniels St
Toronto, OH 43964-1340
  Pubs: *Adversaria* (TriQtly Bks/Northwestern U Pr, 1993),
  *Artful Dodge, Cincinnati Poetry Rev, Hiram Poetry Rev,
  Kestrel, Poetry, West Branch*

David Schloss 🎤 ✈   P
358 Bryant Ave, #1
Cincinnati, OH 45220-1628, 513-281-3551
Internet: schlosd@muohio.edu
  Pubs: *Sex Lives of the Poor & Obscure* (Carnegie
  Mellon Pr, 2002), *Legends* (Windmill Pr, 1976), *The
  Beloved* (Ashland Poetry Pr, 1973), *Poetry, Paris Rev,
  Western Humanities Rev, Iowa Rev, Antaeus*

Amy Jo Schoonover 🎤 ✈   P
3520 State Rte 56
Mechanicsburg, OH 43044-9714, 937-834-2666
  Pubs: *New & Used Poems* (Lake Shore Pub, 1988),
  *Kansas Qtly, Hiram Poetry Rev, U Portland Rev, Cape
  Rock, Negative Capability, Western Ohio Jrnl, Lyric,
  Pivot*
Groups: Seniors, Prisoners

Pearl Bloch Segall 🎤   P
425 Hunters Hollow SE
Warren, OH 44484-2367, 330-856-5565
  Pubs: *Amelia, Poetpourri, Pinehurst Jrnl*

Marilyn Weymouth Seguin 🎤 ✈   W
1830 Highbridge Rd
Cuyahoga Falls, OH 44223-1827, 330-928-6907
Internet: mseguin@kent.edu
  Pubs: *Where Duty Calls, Dogs of War, Silver Ribbon
  Skinny, The Bell Keeper, Song of Courage, Song of
  Freedom* (Branden Bks, 1999, 1997, 1996, 1995, 1993)

Tim Shay   W
7227 Scottwood Ave
Cincinnati, OH 45237-3128
  Pubs: *Short Stuff Mag, Prolific Writer, Fiction, Valley
  Views, Live Writers, Fiction Cincinnati*

Glenn Sheldon 🎤 ✈   P
PO Box 8254
Toledo, OH 43605, 419-243-2048
Internet: gsheldo@utnet.utoledo.edu
    Pubs: *Eagle or Beak* (Seffron Pub, 1995), *Wolves in
    Brown Wedding Gowns* (New Sins Pr, 1991), *Janus
    Head, Café Rev, Puerto del Sol, Rio Grande Rev,
    Mudfish, Marquee, Spoon River Qtly, Limestone*

David Shevin 🎤 ✈   P
142 1/2 N Washington St
Tiffin, OH 44883-1523, 419-447-2911
Internet: shevin@compuserve.com
    Pubs: *Needles & Needs, Dunbar: Suns & Dominions:
    Anth* (Bottom Dog, 1994, 1999), *Growl & Other Poems:
    Anth* (Carpenter Pr, 1990), *Confluence, The Crisis,
    Exquisite Corpse, Tikkun, Descant, The Jrnl*

Kay Sloan   P&W
English Dept, Miami Univ, Oxford, OH 45056,
513-529-2227
    Pubs: *Worry Beads* (Louisiana State U Pr, 1991),
    *Southern Exposure, Oxford Mag, Southern Rev,
    Pudding*

Francis J. Smith   P
John Carroll Univ, 20700 N Park Blvd, Rodman Hall,
University Heights, OH 44118, 216-397-4546
    Pubs: *All Is a Prize* (Pterodactyl Pr, 1989), *First
    Prelude* (Loyola U Pr, 1981), *America, Light, College
    English, Aethlon*

Larry Smith   P&W
Firelands College of BGSU, English Dept, Huron, OH
44839, 419-433-5560
    Pubs: *Beyond Rust* (Bottom Dog Pr, 1995), *Steel
    Valley: Postcards & Letters* (Pig Iron Pr, 1993),
    Parabola, Heartlands Today, Humanist

Monica E. Smith 🎤 ✈   P
8990 SR 287
West Liberty, OH 43357
Internet: sfsmes@foryou.net
    Pubs: *Romance: Anth* (Wings of Dawn, 2000),
    Questions: Anth (Poetfest, 2000), *Lummox, Sunday
    Suitor, The Poet's Paper, Syncopated City, Roswell Lit
    Rev, Oatmeal & Poetry, Medicinal Purposes, Lucidity*

John Stickney   P
4545 W 214
Cleveland, OH 44126
    Pubs: *Rampike, Caliban, Generator, Mississippi Rev,
    NYQ, Semiotext(e), Exquisite Corpse, Atticus Rev*

Gloria Still   P
1439 Alameda Ave
Lakewood, OH 44107-4920
    Pubs: *Free Songs* (Writers' Center Pr, 1992), *Indiana
    Rev, Hopewell Rev, Woman Poet, Arts Indiana Literary
    Supplement, Passages in Nonviolence*

Terry Stokes   P
PO Box 19359
Cincinnati, OH 45219, 513-651-3659
    Pubs: *Sportin' News* (Raccoon Bks, 1985), *Issuing of
    Scars* (Bartholomew's Cobble, 1981)

Lorraine J. Sutton   P
914 Franklin Ave
Columbus, OH 43205
    Pubs: *Saycred Laydy* (Sunbury Pr, 1975), *Ms., Latin
    New York, Conditions, West End*

Robert L. Tener 🎤   P
PO Box 182
Rootstown, OH 44272-0182
    Pubs: *A Dialogue of Marriage* (Plowman, 1989),
    Laughter & Dry Mockery (Kent, 1988), *Blue Unicorn,
    Green's Mag, Studies in Contemporary Satire*

James Thomas 🎤 ✈   W
802 Green St
Yellow Springs, OH 45387-1409, 937-767-9445
Internet: green802@aol.com
    Pubs: *Pictures, Moving* (Dragon Gate, 1986), *Flash
    Fiction: Anth, Sudden Fiction: Anth* (Norton, 1996,
    1994), *Carolina Qtly, Esquire, Cimarron, Epoch,
    Mississippi Rev, Crazyhorse*

John Thorndike 🎤 ✈   W
13034 McDougal Rd
Athens, OH 45701-9731
Internet: johnthorndike@compuserve.com
    Pubs: *Another Way Home* (Crown, 1996), *The Potato
    Baron* (Villard, 1989), *Anna Delaney's Child* (Macmillan,
    1986)

Caroline Totten   W
140 Santa Clara NW
Canton, OH 44709, 330-493-0913
    Pubs: *Montage* (Media Turf Prod, 1997), *Best of 1995
    Ohio Poetry: Anth* (Ohio Poetry Day Assn, 1995),
    Collage, Insight, Remington Rev, New Writers

Ann Townsend 🎤 ✈   P
Denison Univ, English Dept, Granville, OH 43023,
740-587-6331
Internet: townsend@cc.denison.edu
    Pubs: *Dime Store Erotics* (Silverfish Rev Pr, 1998),
    Modern Love (Bottom Dog Pr, 1994), *New American
    Poets: Anth* (U Pr of New England, 2000), *New Young
    American Poets: Anth* (Southern Illinois U Pr, 2000),
    Pushcart Prize XX: Anth (Pushcart Pr, 1995), *Nation*

Leonard Trawick 🎤 ✈   P
Cleveland State Univ, English Dept, Cleveland, OH 44115,
216-687-3971
Internet: l.trawick@csuohio.edu
    Pubs: *Beastmorfs* (Cleveland State U Poetry Ctr, 1994),
    Sometime the Cow Kick Your Head: Anth (Bits Pr,
    1988), *Laurel Rev, Poetry, BPJ, Phase & Cycle*

Alberta T. Turner   P
482 Caskey Ct
Oberlin, OH 44074, 440-775-7844
    Pubs: *Beginning with And: New & Selected Poems*
    (Bottom Dog Pr, 1994), *Responses to Poetry* (Longman,
    1990), *Stand, The Jrnl, South Carolina Rev, American
    Lit Rev*

Jim Villani   P&W
Pig Iron Press, PO Box 237, Youngstown, OH 44501,
216-783-1269
    Pubs: *Moment in Bronze, Stars on Lake* (Fantome Pr,
    1990, 1989), *Cincinnati Poetry Rev, Salome*

Diane Vreuls   W
131 Sycamore
Oberlin, OH 44074, 216-774-1737
    Pubs: *Let Us Know* (Viking, 1986), *Are We There Yet?*
    (Avon, 1976), *New Yorker, Paris Rev, Massachusetts
    Rev*

F. Keith Wahle   P
3357 Citrus Ln
Cincinnati, OH 45239, 513-923-3136
    Pubs: *A Choice of Killers* (Morgan Pr, 1998), *Almost
    Happy* (Rumba Train, 1980), *The Qtly, Yellow Silk,
    Cincinnati Poetry Rev*

Robert Wallace   P
English Dept, Case Western Reserve Univ, Cleveland, OH
44106, 216-795-2810
    Pubs: *The Common Summer: New & Selected Poems*
    (Carnegie Mellon, 1989)

Etta Ruth Weigl   P
56 Kendal Dr
Oberlin, OH 44074, 216-774-6101
    Pubs: *Seventh Age, Meltwater* (Stereopticon Pr, 1988,
    1982), *Poetry Now, And, Williwaw*

William Wells 🎤 ✈   P
4240 Campus Dr
Lima, OH 45804-3576, 419-995-8213
Internet: wellsw@ltc.tec.oh.us
    Pubs: *Conversing with the Light* (Anhinga Pr, 1988),
    *Prairie Schooner, Hudson Rev, Denver Qtly, Ohio Rev,
    Boulevard, Poetry NW, SPR, Poetry East, Stand,
    Cimmaron Rev, Yale Rev, Poetry Durham*

Milton White   W
325 E Vine St
Oxford, OH 45056, 513-529-5945

Dallas Wiebe 🎤 ✈   W
582 McAlpin Ave
Cincinnati, OH 45220-1534, 513-281-4767
    Pubs: *Our Asian Journey* (Canada; MLR Edtns, 1997),
    *Going to the Mountain, The Transparent Eye-Ball &
    Other Stories* (Burning Deck, 1988, 1982), *Paris Rev,
    NAR, First Intensity*

Austin Wright 🎤 ✈   W
3454 Lyleburn Pl
Cincinnati, OH 45220-1521, 513-751-2328
Internet: austin.wright@uc.edu
    Pubs: *Disciples, Telling Time, After Gregory, Tony &
    Susan* (Baskerville, 1997, 1995, 1994, 1993),
    Recalcitrance, Faulkner & the Professors (U Iowa Pr,
    1990)

Laura Yeager   W
3788 Kay Dr
Stow, OH 44224, 330-686-0760
    Pubs: *Kaleidoscope, Paris Rev, Missouri Rev*

David Young 🎤 ✈   P
English Dept, Oberlin College, Oberlin, OH 44074,
216-775-8576
    Pubs: *At the White Window, Seasoning, Night Thoughts
    & Henry Vaughn* (Ohio State U Pr, 2000, 1999, 1994),
    The Planet on the Desk: New & Selected Poems
    (Wesleyan, 1991)
Groups: Seniors, Nature/Environment

Thomas Young 🎤 ✈   P
2658 N 4 St
Columbus, OH 43202-2404, 614-267-1682
Internet: tygertom2@cs.com
    Pubs: *The Ohio Jrnl, Waves, Graffiti, You Gotta Suit
    Up for 'Em All, The Smudge*

Nancy Zafris   W
71 E Lincoln St
Columbus, OH 43215, 614-228-7251
    Pubs: *Into the Silence* (Green Street Pr, 1998), *Did My
    Mama Like to Dance?* (Avon Bks, 1994), *The People I
    Know* (U Georgia Pr, 1990), *Kenyon Rev, Witness,
    Missouri Rev*

Zena Zipporah   P
3544 Fairmount Blvd
Shaker Heights, OH 44118-4354, 216-932-1547
    Pubs: *In the Sacred Manner of the Buffalo, Lost Tribes,
    Victoriana–In Love with Words* (Zipporah, 1989, 1988,
    1987), *Akros Rev*

OKLAHOMA

Ivy Bloch   P
2109 E 25 Pl
Tulsa, OK 74114-2917, 918-742-8293
   Pubs: *Midwest Qtly, Plainsong, Nimrod, Chariton Rev, SPR, Mississippi Valley Rev*

William J. Bly   P
2701 S Juniper Ave, #101
Broken Arrow, OK 74012-7731
   Pubs: *Memories of Second Street, Land of the Living* (Pine Woods Pr, 1986, 1985), *Poetry Now*

Dorothea Condry   P&W
RR2, Box 71133
Calumet, OK 73014, 405-893-2615
   Pubs: *From Seed Bed to Harvest* (Seven Buffaloes Pr, 1986), *The Later Days* (Samisdat, 1980)

Mark Cox   P
Oklahoma State Univ, English Dept, 205 Morrill, Stillwater, OK 74078, 405-744-9474
   Pubs: *Thirty-Seven Years from the Stone* (U Pitt Pr, 1998), *Smoulder* (Godine, 1989), *Poetry, APR, NER, NAR, Poetry East, Poetry NW*

Mary Crescenzo   P&W
1411 E 20 St
Tulsa, OK 74120, 918-744-6828
   Pubs: *Women in Exile: Anth* (Milkweed Edtns, 1990), *West Wind Rev, Paragraph 7, La Bella Figura, Highlights for Children*

J. Madison Davis   W
1112 Lincoln Green
Norman, OK 73072-7521, 405-447-3756
   Pubs: *Red Knight, Bloody Marko, White Rook* (Walker & Co, 1992, 1991, 1990), *Conversations with Robertson Davies* (U Mississippi Pr, 1989)

George Economou 🎤 ✈   P
1401 Magnolia St
Norman, OK 73072-6827, 405-364-5797
   Pubs: *Century Dead Center & Other Poems* (Left Hand Bks, 1997), *Harmonies & Fits* (Point Riders, 1987), *Backwoods Broadsides, Cover, Grand St, Poetry NY, Sulfur, Texture, ACM, APR*
I.D.: Greek-American/Greek

Arn Henderson   P
1208 Barkley Ave
Norman, OK 73071, 405-364-6770
   Pubs: *Document for an Anonymous Indian, The Point Riders Great Plains Poetry Anth* (Point Riders Pr, 1974, 1982)

Geary Hobson   P&W
English Dept, Univ Oklahoma, Norman, OK 73019-0240, 405-325-6231
   Pubs: *Aniyunwiya* (Greenfield Rev Pr, 1995), *Deer Hunting & Other Poems* (Point Riders Pr, 1990), *The Remembered Earth* (U New Mexico Pr, 1981), *Quilt, Nimrod*

Sherry Lachance   P
4765 SE 23
Del City, OK 73115

Mike Lowery   P
State Farm Insurance, PO Box 55505, Tulsa, OK 74155-1505
   Pubs: *Masks of the Dreamer* (Wesleyan U Pr, 1979), *Nimrod, Cape Rock, Blue Unicorn, Quartet*

Janet McAdams   PW
760 Van Vlect Oval, Rm 113
Norman, OK 73019-0240, 405-325-5798
   Pubs: *The Island of Lost Luggage* (U Arizona Pr, 2000), *Crab Orchard Rev, Ascent Fall, Women's Rev of Books, Lullwater Rev*

Mary McAnally 🎤 ✈   P
76 N Yorktown
Tulsa, OK 74110-5214, 918-583-3651
   Pubs: *Stations* (Pemmican, 1995), *Fat Poems* (Cardinal Pr, 1990), *Coming of Age in Oklahoma* (Point Riders Pr, 1985), *The Absence of the Father & the Dance of the Zygotes* (Shadow Pr, 1981), *Poems from the Animal Heart* (Full Court Pr, 1979)
I.D.: Feminist

Susan Smith Nash   P&W
3760 Cedar Ridge Dr
Norman, OK 73072-4621, 405-366-7730
   Pubs: *Liquid Babylon* (Potes & Poets, 1994), *The Airport Is My Etude* (Paradigm Pr, 1993), *Pornography* (Generator Pr, 1992), *o.blek, Washington Rev, ACM, Aerial*

Perry Oldham   P
2940 Huntleigh Dr
Oklahoma City, OK 73120
   Pubs: *Higher Ground* (Mercury Pr, 1987), *Vinh Long* (Northwoods, 1977)

Rochelle Owens 🎤 ✈   P
1401 Magnolia
Norman, OK 73072-6827, 405-364-5797
   Pubs: *Luca: Discourse on Life & Death, New & Selected Poems 1961-1996* (Junction Pr, 2000, 1997), *Poems for the New Millennium Vol. 2: Anth* (U California Pr, 1998), *Sulfur, Abacus, Talisman, Temblor, ACM, Texture*

G. Palmer, Jr.   P
Rte 3
Carnegie, OK 73015, 405-654-2353
 Pubs: *American Indian Literature Anth* (U Oklahoma Pr,
 1979)

Alice Lindsay Price 🎤 ✈   P
3113 S Florence Ave
Tulsa, OK 74105-2407, 918-748-4411
Internet: blkpoodle2@aol.com
 Pubs: *Cranes* (La Alameda Pr, 2000), *Swans of the
 World* (Council Oak Bks, 1994), *Our Dismembered
 Shadow* (Ena Pr, 1980), *Nimrod, Rhino, Commonweal,
 Phoenix*
I.D.: Nature/Environment. Groups: Teenagers,
Nature/Environment

S. David Price   P
2542 NW 12
Oklahoma City, OK 73107-5418
 Pubs: *Summer Snow* (Daybreak, 1977), *Joyful Noise,
 Texas Rev, Writer, Encore, Driftwood East, Counsel*

Francine Ringold   P
3215 S Yorktown
Tulsa, OK 74105, 918-745-9234
 Pubs: *The Trouble with Voices: Selected Poetry,
 Making Your Own Mark* (Council Oak Bks, 1995, 1989),
 Nimrod, Phoenix, Borderlands, Puerto del Sol, SW Rev

Tim Tharp   W
800 N Mission Rd, #4
Okmulgee, OK 74447
 Pubs: *Falling Dark* (Milkweed Edtns, 1999)

Gordon Weaver   P&W
Cimarron Review, English Dept, Oklahoma State Univ,
Stillwater, OK 74078, 405-744-6140
 Pubs: *Men Who Would Be Good* (TriQtly Bks, 1991),
 Manoa, TriQtly

Ann E. Weisman   PP
Lawton Arts & Humanities Council, PO Box 1054, Lawton,
OK 73502, 405-581-3471
 Pubs: *Eye Imagine: Performances on Paper* (Point
 Riders Pr, 1991), *Moonrise, The Eloquent Object*
 (Philbrook Museum, 1989, 1987)

Carolyne Wright 🎤 ✈   P&W
English Dept, Univ Central Oklahoma, 100 W Univ Dr,
Edmond, OK 73034-5209, 405-624-3026
Internet: carolyne.eulene@juno.com
 Pubs: *Seasons of Mangos & Brainfire* (Lynx Hse Pr,
 2000), *9MM: Anth* (U Pitt Pr, 2000), *American
 Diaspora: Anth* (U Iowa Pr, 2000), *Agni, Amer Scholar,
 Crab Orchard Rev, Crazyhorse, Iowa Rev, Iron Horse
 Lit Rev, Kenyon Rev, New Yorker, Partisan Rev*
Lang: Spanish, Bengali; Bangla. I.D.: Latino/Latina, South
Asian. Groups: Women, Ethnic

OREGON

Howard Aaron   P
2428 NE 20
Portland, OR 97212, 503-282-4904
 Pubs: *Retina* (Confluence Pr, 1979), *What the Worms
 Ignore...* (Jawbone Pr, 1979), *Porch*

Diana Abu-Jaber   W
Dept. of English, Portland State Univ, Portland, OR 97207,
503-725-3554
 Pubs: *Arabian Jazz* (HB, 1993)

Cathy Ackerson 🎤 ✈   P
1850 Corina Dr SE
Salem, OR 97302-1624, 503-581-9075
Internet: ackerson@navicom.com
 Pubs: *Poets West: Anth* (Perivale Pr, 1976), *But Is It
 Poetry?: Anth* (Dragonfly Pr, 1972), *Dragonfly, Caprice,
 Outpost, Out of Sight, NW Rev*

Duane Ackerson 🎤 ✈   P&W
1850 Corina Dr SE
Salem, OR 97302-1624, 503-581-9075
Internet: ackerson@navicom.com
 Pubs: *The Bird at the End of the Universe* (TM Pr,
 1997), *The Eggplant* (Confluence Pr, 1977), *Yankee,
 NW Rev, Chelsea, Prairie Schooner, CSM*

Henry Melton Alley 🎤 ✈   W
Honors College, 1293 Univ Oregon, Eugene, OR 97403,
541-346-2513
Internet: halley@oregon.uoregon.edu
 Pubs: *Umbrella of Glass* (Breitenbush Bks, 1988), *The
 Lattice* (Ariadne Pr, 1986), *Virginia Qtly Rev, Seattle
 Rev, Outerbridge*
I.D.: G/L/B/T. Groups: G/L/B/T

Erland Anderson   P
565 Fairview
Ashland, OR 97520, 541-482-4029
 Pubs: *Searchings for Modesto* (Talent Hse Pr, 1993),
 Between Darkness & Darkness (Prescott St Pr, 1989),
 American Scholar, Calapooya Collage

Michael Anderson   P
158 Lincoln St
Ashland, OR 97520, 503-482-2441
 Pubs: *Wormwood Rev, Scree, Cape Rock, Hiram Rev,
 Kansas Qtly, Taurus*

Dori Appel   P&W
PO Box 1364
Ashland, OR 97520, 541-482-2735
 Pubs: *Girl Talk* (w/Myers; Samuel French, 1992), *At
 Our Core: Anth, Grow Old Along with Me: Anth*
 (Papier-Mache Pr, 1998, 1996), *Prairie Schooner,
 Yankee, Ascent, Calyx, Southern Humanities, Kalliope*

Lois Baker 🎤 ✈   P&W
6819 SW 32 Ave
Portland, OR 97219-1826, 503-244-1826
    Pubs: *Tracers* (Howlett Pr, 1992), *Partial Clearing*
    (Press-22, 1976), *Playing with a Full Deck: Anth* (26
    Bks, 1999), *Poetry, Poetry NW, Prism Intl, Calyx,
    Penthouse, Colorado State Qtly*

Tim Barnes   P
Portland Community College, PO Box 19000, Portland, OR
97280-0990, 503-977-4638
    Pubs: *Falling Through Leaves* (Marino Pr, 1995), *Star
    Hill Farm & the Grain of What Is Gone* (Skookum's
    Tongue Pr, 1994), *Fine Madness, Puerto del Sol*

Judith Barrington 🎤 ✈   P
622 SE 29 Ave
Portland, OR 97214-3026, 503-236-9862
Internet: soapston@teleport.com
    Pubs: *History & Geography, Trying to Be an Honest
    Woman* (8th Mtn Pr, 1989, 1985), *Poetry London, GSU
    Rev, Stand, Chattahoochee Rev, Americas Rev, Rialto,
    Kenyon, Sonora, American Voice, Ploughshares,
    Women's Rev of Bks, 13th Moon*
Groups: G/L/B/T, Women

Elizabeth Bartlett   P
5550 Bethel Heights Rd NW
Salem, OR 97304-9730
    Pubs: *Around the Clock* (St. Andrews, 1989), *Candles*
    (Autograph Edtns, 1988), *Harper's, Virginia Qtly, Denver
    Qtly, Ellery Queen's Qtly, NAR, Literary Rev, National
    Forum*

M. F. Beal 🎤 ✈   W
PO Box 161
Seal Rock, OR 97376-0161
    Pubs: *Angel Dance* (Crossing Pr, 1990), *End of Days*
    (H&R, 1982), *West Coast Fiction: Anth* (Bantam, 1979),
    Atlantic, Paris Rev, Calyx, Caprice

David Biespiel 🎤 ✈   P
The Attic, 4423 SE Hawthorne, Portland, OR 97215-3164,
503-963-8783
    Pubs: *Shattering Air* (BOA Edtns, 1996)

Kathleen M. Bogan   P
3523 SW Jerald Ct
Portland, OR 97201, 503-228-5663
    Pubs: *Prairie Hearts–Women's Writings on the Midwest:
    Anth* (Feminist Writers Guild, 1996), *Convolvulus,
    Confrontation, Writers' Forum, Alaska Qtly Rev,
    Encodings*

Karen Braucher   P
3326 SW 64 Pl
Portland, OR 97221, 503-291-1431
    Pubs: *Sending Messages Over Inconceivable Distances,
    Heaven's Net* (Bacchae Pr, 2000, 1997), *Spoon River
    Poetry Rev, Nimrod*

Julie Brown   W
1434 6 St
Astoria, OR 97103-5315
    Pubs: *Indiana Rev, Southern Rev, Madison Rev,
    Hayden's Ferry Rev, Cream City Rev, Michigan Rev*

Robert Brown   P
1434 6 St
Astoria, OR 97103-5315
    Pubs: *Sleepwalking with Mayakovsky* (Kent State U Pr,
    1994), *Poem, ELF, Poetry NW, New Virginia Rev,
    Kansas Qtly*

Douglas G. Campbell 🎤 ✈   P
9310 SW 18 Pl
Portland, OR 97219-6456, 503-246-3286
Internet: dcampbell@georgefox.edu
    Pubs: *When the Wind Stops* (Counterpoint Pub, 1992),
    In Our Own Voices: Anth (Oregon Writers Colony,
    1986), *The Dakota, This, TapJoe, Voices in the
    Wilderness, Urthkin, Gravida, A New Song*

Henry Carlile 🎤 ✈   P&W
7349 SE 30 Ave
Portland, OR 97202-8836, 503-774-0944
Internet: hcarlile@iccom.com
    Pubs: *Rain* (Carnegie Mellon, 1994), *Running Lights*
    (Dragon Gate, 1981), *Southern Rev, Poetry,
    Crazyhorse, Shenandoah, Ohio Rev, APR*

Deb Casey   P
Academic Learning Services, Univ Oregon, Eugene, OR
97403, 503-346-3226
Internet: wkcasey@oregon.uoregon.edu
    Pubs: *Daredevil Research* (Peter Lang Pub, 1997), *For
    a Living: Anth* (U Illinois Pr, 1995), *Zyzzyva, Kenyon
    Rev, River Styx, Ploughshares, Massachusetts Rev,
    Prairie Schooner, Graham Hse Rev, Calyx*

Kent Clair Chamberlain 🎤 ✈   P&W
625 Holly St
Ashland, OR 97520-2927, 541-482-2283
    Pubs: *Phaer Wind* (Pauper Pr, 1992), *Rarely Published*
    (Blue Willow Pr, 1977), *Object Lesson, Atrocity, Danger,
    GSC, Ozark Muse, Muse Letter, Carpe Laureate Diem,
    Sunflower Dream, New Observer, Poetic Realm, Blind
    Man's Rainbow, Bibleoppelus, Aim*

Sandra Cherches   W
2825 NE 39
Portland, OR 97212, 503-287-7404
    Pubs: *Taos Rev, New Delta Rev, American Fiction,
    Ms., Portland, Village Voice*

Walt Curtis　　　　　　　　　　　　P&W
Bridge City Books, 1717 SW Park Ave, Ste 616, Portland,
OR 97201, 503-220-4171
　　Pubs: *Mala Noche & Other Illegal Adventures* (Bridge
　　City Bks, 1997), *Rhymes for Alice Blue Light* (Lynx
　　Hse, 1984), *A New Geography of Poets: Anth* (U
　　Arkansas Pr, 1992), *Atlantic, Gay Sunshine, Clinton
　　Street Qtly*

Peter Ho Davies　　　　　　　　　　　W
Creative Writing Program, Univ Of Oregon, Eugene, OR
97403-1286, 503-346-3944
　　Pubs: *The Ugliest House in the World, Best American
　　Short Stories: Anths* (HM, 1997, 1996, 1995), *Paris
　　Rev, Story, Agni, Harvard Rev, Gettysburg Rev, Antioch
　　Rev*

Annie Dawid ♀ ✈　　　　　　　　　P&W
0615 SW Palatine Hill Rd, #58
Portland, OR 97219-7879, 503-768-7405
Internet: david@lclark.edu
　　Pubs: *Lily in the Desert* (Carnegie Mellon, 2001), *York
　　Ferry* (Cane Hill Pr, 1993), *American Fiction: Anth* (New
　　Rivers Pr, 1999), *Beyond Lament: Anth* (Northwestern
　　U Pr, 1998), *Arts & Letters, Phoebe, Art & Academe,
　　Toyon*

Sandy Diamond　　　　　　　　　　PP&P
PO Box 405
Grand Ronde, OR 97347-0405, 503-879-5672
　　Pubs: *Miss Coffin & Mrs. Blood* (Creative Arts Book
　　Co, 1994)

Steven Dimeo ♀　　　　　　　　　　W
800 NE 3 Ave
Hillsboro, OR 97124-2321, 503-640-1375
　　Pubs: *Great Midwestern Qtly, Indigenous Fiction,
　　Uncommon Reader, Wildfire, Seattle Times, Michigan
　　Qtly Rev, Amazing Stories, Descant, Crosscurrents*

John A. Domini　　　　　　　　　　W
1818 NE Halsey St
Portland, OR 97232-1440
　　Pubs: *Bedlam* (Fiction Intl, 1982), *Pushcart Prize: Anth*
　　(Pushcart, 1989), *Paris Rev, SW Rev, Ploughshares,
　　Threepenny Rev*

Thomas Doulis　　　　　　　　　　W
2236 NE Regents Dr
Portland, OR 97212, 503-287-3484
　　Pubs: *Landmarks of Our Past* (Holy Trinity, 1983),
　　Toward the Authentic Church: Anth (Light & Life, 1996)

Doug Draime　　　　　　　　　　　P
1096 Hillview Dr
Ashland, OR 97520
　　Pubs: *Lilliput Rev, Mind in Motion, Purple Patch,
　　Permafrost, L.A. Weekly, Struggle, Broken Streets, The
　　Temple, Pudding Mag, Angelflesh, Art Times, George &
　　Mertie's Place: Rooms with a View*

Albert Drake　　　　　　　　　　　P&W
9727 SE Reedway St
Portland, OR 97266-3738, 503-771-6779
　　Pubs: *Fifties Flashback* (Fisher Bks, 1999), *Flat Out,
　　Herding Goats* (Flat Out, 1994, 1989), *Epoch, Best
　　American Short Stories*

Barbara Drake ♀ ✈　　　　　　　　P&W
6104 NW Lilac Hill Rd
Yamhill, OR 97148-8328, 503-662-3373
　　Pubs: *Peace at Heart* (Oregon St U Pr, 1998), *Space
　　Before A* (26 Bks, 1996), *Bees in Wet Weather* (Canoe
　　Pr, 1992), *What We Say to Strangers* (Breitenbush,
　　1986), *Portland Lights: Anth* (Nine Lights, 1999), *Sumac
　　Reader: Anth* (MSU Pr, 1997)

David Elsey ♀ ✈　　　　　　　　　P
2139 W Burnside, #202
Portland, OR 97210-5543, 503-241-5404
　　Pubs: *Gray Light* (Smellfeast, 1995), *Off the Beaten
　　Track: Anth* (Quiet Lion Pr, 1992), *Poetry Now,
　　Hubbub, Small Pond Rev, Gryphon, Rhino*

Pat Enders　　　　　　　　　　　　P
Clackamas Press, 21730 SE Hwy 224, Clackamas, OR
97015
　　Pubs: *Pioneer Woman, Poetry Oregon, St. Andrews
　　Rev*

Elizabeth Engstrom　　　　　　　　W
1627 Charnelton St
Eugene, OR 97401
　　Pubs: *Lizard Wine* (Dell, 1995), *Nightmare Flower*
　　(TOR, 1992), *Fantasy & Sci Fi Mag, Cemetery Dance,
　　Bone*

Tess Enroth　　　　　　　　　　　P&W
8222 SW Capitol Hwy
Portland, OR 97219-3625, 503-977-2539
Internet: tessmce@aol.com
　　Pubs: *Her Soul Beneath the Bone: Anth* (U Illinois Pr,
　　1988), *Cottonwood, Lake Effect, Wide Open Mag*

Garrett Epps　　　　　　　　　　　W
Univ Oregon School of Law, Eugene, OR 97403
　　Pubs: *The Floating Island* (HM, 1985), *The Shad
　　Treatment* (Putnam, 1977)

Esther Erford　　　　　　　　　　　P
1313 Lincoln St, #1002
Eugene, OR 97401-3965
　　Pubs: *South Coast Poetry Jrnl, Connecticut River Rev,
　　Galley Sail Rev, Slant, Voices Intl*

Alice Evans   P&W
4635 Larkwood St
Eugene, OR 97405-3987
    Pubs: *Solo: Women Going It Alone in the Wilderness:
*Anth, Another Wilderness: New Outdoor Writing By
Women: Anth* (Seal Pr, 1996, 1994), *Clinton Street Qtly*

Sandra Foushee 🎤 ✈   P
PO Box 541
Manzanita, OR 97130-0541, 503-368-7228
    Pubs: *The Light That Stops Us* (Night Sky, 1990), *Back
to Essentials* (Bristlecone Pr, 1984), *Ploughshares,
Poetry & Prose, Westwind Rev, Prairie Schooner*

Vi Gale   P&W
Prescott Street Press, PO Box 40312, Portland, OR
97240-0312, 503-254-2922
    Pubs: *Odd Flowers & Short Eared Owls, The Prescott
St Reader: Anth* (Prescott St Pr, 1984, 1995),
Clearwater (Swallow, 1974), *Horisont* (Sweden)

Ken Gerner   P
PO Box 10881
Portland, OR 97210
    Pubs: *Throwing Shadows* (Copper Canyon Pr, 1985),
CutBank, Willow Springs

Martha Gies 🎤 ✈   W
2109 NE Rodney Ave
Portland, OR 97212-3739, 503-287-4394
    Pubs: *A Celestial Omnibus: Anth Beacon Pr, 1997),
Storming Heaven's Gate: Anth* (Plume/Penguin, 1997),
The World Begins Here: Anth (Oregon State U Pr,
1993), *The Time of Our Lives: Anth* (Crossing Pr,
1993), *Orion, Left Bank, Zyzzyva, Cream City Rev*

Jane Glazer 🎤 ✈   P
Adrienne Lee Press, PO Box 309, Monmouth, OR 97361,
503-838-1220
    Pubs: *Some Trick of Light* (Adrienne Lee Pr, 1993),
Fresh Water: Anth (Pudding Hse, 2000), *O Poetry, O
Poesia: Anth* (OCE, 1998), *Claiming the Spirit Within;
Anth* (Beacon Pr, 1996), *Twelve Oregon Poets 2: Anth*
(High St Pr, 1996), *Berkeley Poetry Rev*

Jim Grabill 🎤 ✈   P
9835 SW 53 Ave
Portland, OR 97219-5827, 503-977-0331
    Pubs: *Lame Duck Eternity* (26 Bks, 2000), *Listening to
the Leaves Form, Poem Rising Out of the Earth &
Standing Up in Someone* (Lynx Hse Pr, 1997, 1994),
Through the Green Fire (Holy Cow! Pr, 1995), *Poetry
East, Caliban, Kayak, Willow Springs, Poetry NW*

Jennifer Grotz   P
801 SW Broadway Dr
Portland, OR 97201, 503-224-8560
    Pubs: *TriQtly, Crab Orchard Rev, NER, Cimarron Rev,
Black Warrior Rev, Phoebe, Ploughshares, Sulphur
River Lit Rev, Hayden's Ferry Rev, Puerto del Sol,
Connecticut Rev, New Orleans Rev, Soundings East,
Sycamore Rev*

Cecelia Hagen   P&W
2972 Madison St
Eugene, OR 97405, 541-349-9002
    Pubs: *Fringe Living* (26 Books Pr, 1999) *From Where
We Speak: Anth of Oregon Poetry* (Oregon State U Pr,
1993), *Portlandia, Poet & Critic, Exquisite Corpse,
Prairie Schooner, Willow Springs, Seattle Rev, Puerto
del Sol*

John Haislip 🎤 ✈   P
925 Park Ave
Eugene, OR 97404-6502
    Pubs: *Seal Rock* (Barnwood Pr, 1987), *American Poets
in 1976: Anth* (Bobbs-Merrill, 1976)

James Byron Hall   P&W
1080 Patterson, #901
Eugene, OR 97401
    Pubs: *I Like It Better Now* (U Arkansas Pr, 1992),
Bereavements (Story Line Pr, 1991), *New Directions,
New Letters, Esquire*

Robert D. Hoeft   P
Blue Mountain Community College, PO Box 100,
Pendleton, OR 97801, 503-276-1260
    Pubs: *What Are You Doing?* (Trout Creek Pr, 1986),
Out of Work (Winewood Pub, 1983), *Green's Mag*

Michael Holstein   P
228 West St
Ashland, OR 97520, 503-488-1099
    Pubs: *Alura Qtly, Phoebus Mag, Poets On, BPJ,
Crosscurrents*

Garrett Kaoru Hongo   P
Univ Oregon, Program in Creative Writing, Eugene, OR
97405, 503-346-0545
    Pubs: *The River of Heaven* (Knopf, 1988), *The Open
Boat: Anth* (Anchor Bks, 1993), *Ploughshares, Zyzzyva,
Field, Antaeus, Bamboo Ridge, Agni*

Lawson Fusao Inada   P&W
Southern Oregon State College, English Dept, Ashland,
OR 97520, 541-552-6639
    Pubs: *Legends from Camp* (Coffee Hse Pr, 1993)

Stephen R. Jones   P
24407 Decker Rd
Corvallis, OR 97333, 503-929-5505
   Pubs: *Calapooya Collage, Eloquent Umbrella, NW Rev,
Oregon English Jrnl, Greenfield Rev, Fireweed*

Linda Valachovic Kay   P
PO Box 7781
Eugene, OR 97401
Internet: lkcoquille@aol.com
   Pubs: *Only Morning in Her Shoes: Anth* (Utah State U
Pr, 1990), *ByLine, Cold Mountain Rev, Jacaranda,
Prairie Schooner, Primavera, Slant, Voices Intl*

Susan Kenyon   P
2060 Willamette St
Eugene, OR 97405
   Pubs: *Western Humanities Rev, Accent, NW Rev,
Atlantic, California Rev*

Ken Kesey 🎤 ✈   W
85829 Ridgeway Rd
Pleasant Hill, OR 97455-9627, 541-746-1572
Internet: www.intrepidtrips.com
   Pubs: *Last Go Round, Sailor Song, Sometimes a Great
Nation, One Flew Over the Cuckoo's Nest* (Viking,
1994, 1992, 1964, 1962)

Lee Crawley Kirk 🎤 ✈   P
PO Box 5432
Eugene, OR 97405-0432, 541-683-7033
   Pubs: *From Here We Speak: Anth* (Oregon State U Pr,
1993), *Stafford's Road* (Adrienne Lee Pr, 1991),
*Portlander, Daughters of Nyx, Wormwood Rev,
Fireweed, Calapooya Collage*
Groups: Seniors, Prisoners

Mary Hope Whitehead Lee   P
12216 SE Oatfield Rd
Milwaukie, OR 97222, 503-238-8088
   Pubs: *Sombra, Sedicious Delicious, Yet Another Small
Mag, Writers' Haven Jrnl, Womanspirit, Plexus, Essence
Mag, Feminist Studies, Callaloo, Conditions*

Elio Emiliano Ligi   P
c/o Eric Blair, Uncommon Sense, PO Box 430, Banks, OR
97106-0430
Internet: dianaglampers@aol.com
   Pubs: *The Diversabomber* (Dehumanities, 1995), *How I
Shot Down KAL007* (Sodoms Insane Pub, 1994), *CSM*

Robert Hill Long   P&W
1910 Charnelton St
Eugene, OR 97405-2818, 541-686-6223
   Pubs: *The Effigies* (Plinth Bks, 1998), *The Work of the
Bow* (Cleveland State U Poetry Center, 1997), *Poetry,
Zyzzyva, Shenandoah, DoubleTake, Manoa, Prose
Poem*

Jack E. Lorts 🎤 ✈   P
PO Box 474
Fossil, OR 97830-0474, 541-763-3060
Internet: jclorts@transport.com
   Pubs: *Quantum Tao, Arizona Qtly, Kansas Qtly, English
Jrnl, Oregon English Jrnl, Abbey, Fireweed, Ninth Circle*

Manna Lowenfels   P
20950 SW Rock Creek Rd
Sheridan, OR 97378, 503-843-2465
   Pubs: *The New Woman Speaks & Other Poems*
(Buffalo Bks, 1979), *Sunbury, Connections*

Joan Maiers 🎤 ✈   P
PO Box 33
Marylhurst, OR 97036-0033, 503-636-8955
   Pubs: *Blooming in the Shade: Anth* (Media Weavers,
1997), *Out of Season: Anth* (Amagansett Pr, 1993), *If I
Had a Hammer: Anth* (Papier-Mache Pr, 1990), *Jrnl of
Pastoral Care, The Other Side, New Press Literary
Qtly, Hubbub, Paper Boat, Sistersong, Fireweed*

Katherine Marsh   P
PO Box 613
Salem, OR 97308-0613
   Pubs: *Voices from the White Noise* (Gaff Pr, 2000),
*Painting Daisies Yellow: Anth, Little Verse, Big
Thoughts: Anth* (Golden Apple Pr, 1995, 1995),
*Canadian Writers Jrnl, Hard Row to Hoe, Writers
Gazette, Writer's Exchange, Palo Alto Rev, Fighting
Chance Mag*

Robert McDowell   P
Story Line Press, Three Oaks Farm, Box 1108, Ashland,
OR 97520-0052, 541-512-8792
   Pubs: *The Diviners* (Peterloo Poets, 1995), *Quiet
Money* (H Holt, 1987), *At the House of the Tin Man*
(Chowder Pr, 1983), *Hudson Rev, Kenyon Rev,
Sewanee Rev, New Criterion, Harvard Rev, Poetry*

David Memmott   P&W
PO Box 3235
La Grande, OR 97850, 541-963-0723
   Pubs: *Within the Walls of Jericho* (26 Bks, 1998), *The
Larger Earth* (Permeable Pr, 1996), *Once Upon a
Midnight* (Unnameable Pr, 1995), *Nebula 27* (HB,
1993), *Oregon East, Co-Lingua, Airfish, Point No Point,
The Temple, Mag of Speculative Poetry*

Rob Hollis Miller   P
PO Box 865
Union, OR 97883, 503-562-5091
   Pubs: *The Boy Whose Shoesocks Ran Away*
(Primavera, 1982), *Shanghai Creek Fire* (St. Andrews,
1979)

Gary Miranda   P
1172 SE 55 St
Portland, OR 97215, 503-239-9174
   Pubs: *Grace Period* (Princeton, 1983)

Rodger Moody 🎤 ✈   P
PO Box 3541
Eugene, OR 97403-1697, 541-344-5060
Internet: sfrpress@aol.com
    Pubs: *Unbending Intent* (26 Bks Pr, 1997), *From Here
We Speak: Anth* (Oregon St U Pr, 1993), *Pleiades,
South Dakota Rev, Zyzzyva, Caliban*

F. A. Nettelbeck   P
PO Box 336
Sprague River, OR 97639, 503-533-2486
    Pubs: *Ecosystems Collapsing* (Inkblot Pubs, 1992),
Americruiser (Illuminati, 1983), *Gas, Bombay Gin,
Painted Bride Qtly, Rain City Rev*

Michael Niflis   P
6920 Whiskey Creek Rd
Tillamook, OR 97141-8316, 503-842-6755
    Pubs: *From Here We Speak: Anth* (Oregon St U Pr,
1993), *Poetry, Esquire, Partisan Rev, American Scholar,
Commonweal, CSM, Harper's, New Republic, Virginia
Qtly*

Verlena Orr   P
1907 NW Hoyt
Portland, OR 97209-1224, 503-224-1849
    Pubs: *Woman Who Hears Voices* (Future Tense Pr,
1998), *Graining the Mare: The Poetry of Ranch
Women: Anth* (Gibbs Smith, 1994), *From Here We
Speak: Anth* (Oregon State U Pr, 1993), *Poet & Critic,
Colorado Rev*

Robyn Parnell 🎤 ✈   W
343 NE 15 Ct
Hillsboro, OR 97124-3459, 503-681-9818
Internet: wagnell@teleport.com
    Pubs: *This Here & Now* (Scrivenery Pr, 2000),
Children's Storybook: Anth (Cherubic Pr, 1997), *Strictly
Fiction: Anth* (Potpourri, 1995), *Feminist Parenting: Anth*
(Crossing Pr, 1994), *Satire, Oasis, Lynx Eye, Mobius,
Bellowing Ark, Belletrist Rev, ProCreation*

A. B. Paulson   W
c/o English Dept, Portland State Univ, PO Box 751,
Portland, OR 97207, 503-725-3521
    Pubs: *Watchman Tell Us of the Night* (Viking Penguin,
1987), *Georgia Rev*

Jarold Ramsey 🎤 ✈   P
5884 NW Highway #26
Madras, OR 97741
    Pubs: *Hand-Shadows* (QRL, 1989), *Dermographia*
(Cornstalk Pr, 1982), *Atlantic, NW Rev, QRL, Poetry
NW, Nation, Chelsea, American Scholar*

Dan Raphael 🎤 ✈   P
6735 SE 78 St
Portland, OR 97206-7116, 503-777-0406
Internet: raphael@aracnet.com
    Pubs: *Clear to Where, Molecular Jam* (Jazz Police,
2000, 1996), *Isn't How We Got Here* (Unnum, 1999),
Trees Through the Road (Nine Muses, 1997), *The
Bones Begin to Sing* (26 Bks, 1993), *Here the Meat
Turns to the Audience* (Shattered Wig, 1991), *Strope,
Tight*

Carlos Reyes 🎤 ✈   P
3222 NE Schuyler
Portland, OR 97212-5131, 503-287-9806
Internet: isacar@aol.com
    Pubs: *A Suitcase Full of Crows* (Bluestem, 1995),
Nightmarks (Lynx Hse, 1990), *Men of Our Time: Anth*
(U Georgia, 1992), *West Coast Rev*
Lang: Spanish. Groups: Children, At-Risk Youth

Howard W. Robertson 🎤 ✈   P
854 Martin St
Eugene, OR 97405-4661, 541-344-6206
Internet: robertsons@uswest.net
    Pubs: *To the Fierce Guard in the Assyrian Saloon*
(Ahsahta Pr, 1987), *Ahsahta: Anth* (Ahsahta Pr, 1996)

Elaine Romaine 🎤   P
5017 SE 40 Ave
Portland, OR 97206-4221, 503-788-9034
    Pubs: *Breaking Up: Anth* (Crossing Pr, 1994), *Passion:
Anth* (Peconic Gallery, 1994), *The Dream Book: Anth*
(Schocken Bks, 1985), *Interim, Bellowing Ark, City
Primeval, New Letters, NAR, Oyez*

Helen Ronan   P
344 E 14 Ave
Eugene, OR 97401, 503-687-0419
    Pubs: *Petrified Thunder, Cloud Shadows* (Oregon State
Pr, 1989, 1989), *Brussels Sprout, Dragonfly, Modern
Haiku, Frogpond, Haiku Canada, New Cicada*

Lex Runciman 🎤 ✈   P
Linfield College, English Dept, McMinnville, OR 97128,
503-434-2583
Internet: lruncim@linfield.edu
    Pubs: *Continuo* (Salmon Pub, 2001), *The Admirations*
(Lynx Hse Pr, 1989), *Luck* (Owl Creek Pr, 1981), *Who
are the Rich & Where do They Live?: Anth* (Poetry
East Pr, 2000), *Verse, Fireweed, NER, Missouri Rev,
Willow Springs*

Vern Rutsala   P
2404 NE 24 Ave
Portland, OR 97212-4828, 503-281-5872
    Pubs: *Little-Known Sports* (U Massachusetts Pr, 1994),
Selected Poems (Story Line, 1991), *Ruined Cities*
(Carnegie Mellon, 1987)

Harley L. Sachs 🎤 ✈   P&W
2545 SW Terwilliger Blvd #222
Portland, OR 97201
Internet: www.hu.mtu.edu/~hlsachs
  Pubs: *Never Trust A Talking Horse* (Electric Umbrella,
2000), *Threads of the Covenant* (Isaac Nathan Pubs,
1995), *Irma Quarterdeck Reports* (Wescott Cove Pub,
1991), *Hadassah, Jewish Calendar, Passages North*
Lang: Swedish, Danish. Groups: Jewish, Seniors

Ralph Salisbury   P&W
2377 Charnelton
Eugene, OR 97405-2859, 541-343-5101
  Pubs: *The Last Rattlesnake Throw & Other Stories* (U
Oklahoma Pr, 1998), *One Indian & Two Chiefs* (Navaho
Comm College Pr, 1993), *Earth Song Sky Spirit*
(Doubleday, 1993), *Chariton Rev, Poetry Chicago, New
Yorker, Carolina Qtly, Massachusetts Rev*

Maxine Scates 🎤 ✈   P
1500 Skyline Park Loop
Eugene, OR 97405-4466, 541-687-2758
Internet: mscates@teleport.com
  Pubs: *Toluca Street* (U Pittsburgh Pr, 1989), *Poetry
East, APR, Agni, Crazyhorse, Ironwood*

Willa Schneberg   P
2524 SW Sheffield
Portland, OR 97201, 503-248-4136
  Pubs: *Each in Her Own Way* (Queen of Swords Pr,
1994), *Tikkun: Anth* (Tikkun, 1992), *Americas Rev,
Hawaii Pacific Rev, Exquisite Corpse, Bridges*

Sandra Scofield   W
PO Box 3329
Ashland, OR 97520, 541-488-0324
  Pubs: *Plain Seeing, A Chance to See Egypt* (HC,
1997, 1996), *Opal on Dry Ground* (Villard, 1994), *More
Than Allies, Walking Dunes, Beyond Deserving, Gringa*
(Permanent Press, 1993, 1992, 1990, 1989)

Peter Sears   P
2845 NW Royal Oakes Dr
Corvallis, OR 97330
  Pubs: *Saturday Rev, SPR, Field, Poetry NW, BPJ*

Dale Shank   W
PO Box 2870
Wilsonville, OR 97070-2870
  Pubs: *Powder, Joint Endeavor, Akros Rev, Before the
Sun, Croton Rev, U Portland Rev*

Brenda Shaw   P&W
3475 Harris St
Eugene, OR 97405
  Pubs: *The Dark Well* (Audenreed Pr, 1997), *Dog Music:
Anth* (St. Martin's Pr, 1996), *Each in Her Own Way:
Anth* (Queen of Swords Pr, 1994), *Scottish Stories
1985: Anth* (Collins, 1985), *Fireweed, Pacifica,
Mediphors, Northlight, Inscape, Word, Envoi, Spectrum*

Steven Sher 🎤 ✈   P&W
3930 NW Witham Hill Dr, #176
Corvallis, OR 97330-0900, 541-752-5949
Internet: ssher@eudoramail.com
  Pubs: *Thirty-Six* (Creative Arts Bk Co, 2001), *Flying
Through Glass* (Outloud Bks, 2000), *Traveler's Advisory*
(Trout Creek Pr, 1994), *Man with a Thousand Eyes &
Other Stories* (Gull Bks, 1989), *Trolley Lives* (Wampeter
Pr, 1985)
I.D.: Jewish. Groups: College/Univ, Jewish

Jim Shugrue 🎤 ✈   P
5344 SE 38 Ave
Portland, OR 97202-4208, 503-775-0370
Internet: jim.shugrue@reed.edu
  Pubs: *Icewater* (Trask Hse Bks, 1998), *Small Things
Screaming* (26 Bks, 1995), *Qtly West, Intl Qtly, Poetry
East, ACM*

Floyd Skloot 🎤 ✈   P&W
5680 Karla's Ln
Amity, OR 97101-2316, 503-835-2230
Internet: fskloot@viclink.com
  Pubs: *The Evening Light, The Open Door, The
Night-Side* (Story Line Pr, 2000, 1997, 1996), *Music
Appreciation* (U Pr Florida, 1994), *Atlantic, Harper's,
Poetry, American Scholar, New Criterion, Virginia Qtly
Rev*

Warren Slesinger   P
Oregon State Univ Press, 101 Waldo Hall, OSU, Corvallis,
OR 97331, 541-737-3873
  Pubs: *With Some Justification* (Windhover Pr, 1984),
*Antioch Rev, Iowa Rev, The Prose Poem, APR,
Georgia Rev, NAR, NW Rev*

Tom Smario   P
PO Box 221
Clackamas, OR 97015-0221
  Pubs: *Spring Fever, The Cat's Pajamas* (Gull Bks,
1984, 1982), *Portland Rev*

Angela Sorby   P
Dept of English, Linfield College, McMinnville, OR 97128,
503-435-1686
  Pubs: *Distance Learning* (New Issues Pr, 1998)

Primus St. John 🎤 ✈   P
Portland State Univ, PO Box 751, Portland, OR
97207-0751, 503-725-3578
  Pubs: *Communion, Skins on the Earth* (Copper Canyon
Pr, 1999, 1976), *Dreamer, Love Is Not a Consolation It
Is a Light* (Carnegie Mellon U Pr, 1990, 1982), *APR*
I.D.: African-American, Westerners. Groups: Children,
Prisoners

Kim R. Stafford   P
Northwest Writing Institute, Lewis & Clark College,
Campus Box 100, Portland, OR 97219, 503-768-7745
   Pubs: *Having Everything Right* (Sasquatch Bks, 1996),
   Lochsa Road: A Pilgrim in the West (Confluence Pr,
   1991), *Atlantic, Virginia Qtly Rev, The Sun*

Lisa Malinowski Steinman ♣ ✈   P
Reed College, English Dept, Portland, OR 97202-4208,
503-775-0370
Internet: lisa.steinman@reed.edu
   Pubs: *Ordinary Songs* (26 Bks, 1996), *A Book of Other
   Days, All That Comes to Light* (Arrowood Bks, 1993,
   1989), *Prairie Schooner, Chariton Rev, Michigan Qtly,
   Poetry East, Threepenny Rev*

Sandra Stone   P&W
2650 SW 106 Ave
Portland, OR 77225-4313, 503-292-3296
   Pubs: *Cocktails with Brueghel at the Museum Cafe*
   (Cleveland State U Poetry Ctr, 1997), *The Qtly, Ms.,
   Poetry NW, The New Republic*

Thomas Strand   P
PO Box 83706
Portland, OR 97283
   Pubs: *Oregon East* (Eastern Oregon State College,
   1985), *The Best of Poetic Space: Anth 1987-91* (Poetic
   Space, 1991), *Desperado, Incoming, Poetic Space*

Gloria Sykee   W
11057 SW Summerfield Dr, #10
Tigard, OR 97224, 503-684-1434
   Pubs: *Carolina Qtly, Prairie Schooner, Kansas Qtly*

Mark Thalman   P
3310 Hillside Way
Forest Grove, OR 97116, 503-357-4042
   Pubs: *Chariton Rev, Poetry, Fireweed, Pearl, From
   Here We Speak, Whetstone*

George Venn ♣ ✈   P
706 B Ave
La Grande, OR 97850-1133, 541-962-0380
Internet: venng@eou.edu
   Pubs: *West of Paradise* (Ice River Pr, 1999), *Marking
   the Magic Circle, From Here We Speak: Anth* (Oregon
   State U Pr, 1987, 1994), *Portland Lights: Anth* (Nine
   Lights, 1999), *Prescott St Reader: Anth* (Prescott St Pr,
   1995), *Hubbub, Idaho Yesterdays, The Kerf*

Doyle Wesley Walls ♣ ✈   P
English Dept, Pacific Univ, Forest Grove, OR 97116,
503-359-2992
Internet: wallsdw@pacificu.edu
   Pubs: *Sweet Nothings: Anth* (Indiana U Pr, 1994), *From
   Here We Speak: Anth* (Oregon State U Pr, 1993),
   NYQ, Poet & Critic, Cimarron Rev, Minnesota Rev, BPJ

Patricia J. Ware   P
4733 NE 17 Ave
Portland, OR 97211-5705, 503-232-9756
   Pubs: *CutBank, Slackwater Rev, Calyx, Portland Rev,
   Fedora, Poetry Seattle, Willamette Week*

Roger Weaver ♣ ✈   P
712 NW 13
Corvallis, OR 97330-5953, 541-753-9955
Internet: www.geocities.com/poetroger
   Pubs: *Standing on Earth, Throwing These Sequins at
   the Stars, Traveling on the Great Wheel* (Gardyloo Pr,
   1994, 1992, 1990), *Twenty-One Waking Dreams* (Trout
   Creek Pr, 1986), *The Orange & Other Poems*
   (Press-ZZ, 1978), *NAR, Massachusetts Rev, NW Rev*

Ingrid Wendt   W
2377 Charnelton
Eugene, OR 97405-2859, 541-343-5101
   Pubs: *Singing the Mozart Requiem* (Breitenbush Bks,
   1987), *Moving the House* (BOA Edtns, 1980), *No More
   Masks: Anth* (HC, 1993), *Poetry, Ms., Calyx,
   Massachusetts Rev*

Leslie What ♣ ✈   W
PO Box 5412
Eugene, OR 97405
Internet: what@radarangels.com
   Pubs: *Sweet & Sour Tongue* (Wildside Pr, 2000)
   Beyond Lament: Anth (Northwestern U Pr, 1998),
   Bending the Landscape: Anth (Overlook Pr, 1998),
   MacGuffin, Fiction Qtly, Lilith, Hysteria
Groups: Jewish, Writing Groups

Elizabeth Whitbeck   P&W
32200 SW French Prairie, A-106
Wilsonville, OR 97070, 503-694-5475
   Pubs: *Take This Woman* (Macmillan, 1947), *NE
   Corridor, Creativity Unlimited, Time of Singing, The
   Writing Self, Zantia, Pegasus Rev*

Hannah Wilson   P&W
2660 Emerald St
Eugene, OR 97403
   Pubs: *The Wedding Cake in the Middle of the Road:
   Anth* (Norton, 1992), *Prairie Schooner, Calyx, Earth's
   Daughters, Other Voices, Turnstile*

John Witte ♣ ✈   P
1170 Barber Dr
Eugene, OR 97405-4413, 541-346-3957
   Pubs: *Loving the Days* (Wesleyan, 1978), *Kenyon Rev,
   Ohio Rev, NER, New Yorker, Paris Rev, APR, Iowa
   Rev, Antaeus*

PENNSYLVANIA

Nathalie F. Anderson   P
3 Rutledge Ave
Morton, PA 19070, 610-690-1213
Pubs: *Following Fred Astaire* (Word Works Pr, 1999),
My Hand, My Only Map (House of Keys, 1978), *Paris
Rev, SPR, Madison Rev, Spazio Humano, Prairie
Schooner, Cimarron Rev*

Teresa Anderson ♀   P
PO Box 65
Starucca, PA 18462
Internet: michaels@interactive.net
Pubs: *Speaking in Sign* (West End Pr, 1978), *This
Same Sky: Anth* (S&S, 1996), *Pemmican, Manoa,
Paterson Lit Rev, New Poets: Women, Best Friends,
Anima, Sunsprout*
Lang: French, Spanish. I.D.: French-Canadian. Groups:
Children, Prisoners

Ron Androla   P
1624 W Grandview Blvd, Apt 1
Erie, PA 16509
Pubs: *Splattered in Erie* (Smiling Dog Pr, 1996), *It's a
Pretty World* (Non Compos Mentis Pr, 1996), *Poetry
Motel, Atom Mind, Chiron Rev, Wooden Head Rev*

Kenneth L. Arnold   P
6363 Germantown Ave
Philadelphia, PA 19144, 215-844-1892

Penelope Austin   P
29 Ross St
Williamsport, PA 17701, 717-326-7670
Pubs: *Waiting for a Hero: Poems, Devins Award Anth*
(U Missouri Pr, 1988, 1998), *Missouri Rev, Kenyon
Rev, The Jrnl, New Republic, Nightsun, Prairie
Schooner*

J. T. Barbarese ♀ ✈   P
7128 Cresheim Rd
Philadelphia, PA 19119-2429, 215-247-9575
Internet: barbares@crab.rutgers.edu
Pubs: *New Science, Under the Blue Moon* (U Georgia,
1989, 1985), *Sewanee Rev, Denver Qtly, Southern Rev,
Atlantic, NAR, Boulevard*

Gerald Barrax   P
805 Daisy Ln
West Chester, PA 19382-5702, 610-431-6660
Pubs: *From a Person Sitting in Darkness: New &
Selected Poems* (LSU Pr, 1998), *Leaning Against the
Sun* (U Arkansas Pr, 1992), *The Deaths of Animals &
Lesser Gods* (U Kentucky, 1984), *Callaloo, Hayden's
Ferry Rev, Georgia Rev, New Virginia Rev*

Sue Saniel Barry   P
6315 Forbes Ave, #202
Pittsburgh, PA 15217-1750, 412-521-1540
Pubs: *Bare as the Trees, Another Language*
(Papier-Mache Pr, 1992, 1989), *Kansas Qtly, Spoon
River Qtly, Negative Capability, Crosscurrents*

Constance Bartusis   W
129 S 17 St, #2
Pittsburgh, PA 15203
Pubs: *Shades of Difference* (St. Martin's Pr, 1968)

Marilyn Bates ♀ ✈   P&W
126 Swallow Hill Ct
Pittsburgh, PA 15220-1206
Internet: http://pitt.edu/~bbates
Pubs: *Mixed Blood* (Main St Rag, 1998), *And What
Rough Beast: Anth* (Ashland Poetry Pr, 1999), *Writing
on the Desk: Anth* (U Pitt Pr, 1998), *Paterson Lit Rev,
New Zoo Poetry Rev, Crab Creek Rev, Santa Clara
Rev, Pembroke Mag, Zuzu's Petals*

Jean Baur   P
29 Green Ridge Rd
Yardley, PA 19067, 215-493-4257
Pubs: *The Helen Rev, Confrontation, Green River Rev*

Robin Becker   P
215 Academy St
Boalsburg, PA 16827-1438, 814-466-3326
Pubs: *All-American Girl, Giacometti's Dog* (U Pitt Pr,
1995, 1990), *Backtalk* (Alice James Bks, 1982), *Prairie
Schooner, New Virginia Rev, APR, Kenyon Rev,
Ploughshares, Amicus Jrnl*

Stephen Berg   P
2005 Mt Vernon St
Philadelphia, PA 19130

Jonathan Mark Berkowitz   P&W
1030 E Lancaster Ave, #1008
Rosemont, PA 19010, 215-552-8167
Pubs: *New Renaissance, Heartlands Today, Black
Buzzard Rev, Northern Perspective, Riverrun, Green's
Mag, Art/Life, Rambunctious Rev, Appearances, Oyez
Rev*

Jane Bernstein ♀ ✈   W
English Dept, Carnegie Mellon Univ, Pittsburgh, PA
15213-3890, 412-268-6445
Internet: janebern+@andrew.cmu.edu
Pubs: *Loving Rachel* (Little, Brown, 1988), *Seven
Minutes in Heaven* (Fawcett, 1986), *Ms., The Sun,
Prairie Schooner*
I.D.: Jewish

Becky Birtha   P&W
32 Scottsdale Rd
Philadelphia, PA 19050
 Pubs: *The Forbidden Poems* (Seal, 1991), *Breaking Ice:
 Anth of Contemporary African-American Fiction* (Penguin
 1990), *We Are the Stories We Tell: Anth* (Pantheon,
 1990)

Lili Bita   P
326 Bryn Mawr Ave
Bala Cynwyd, PA 19004, 610-667-2224
 Pubs: *Striking the Sky* (European Arts Center, 1997),
 Excavations, Firewalkers (Lyra Pr, 1985, 1984), *Agenda,
 APR, Caprice, Intl Poetry Rev, Nea Hesperia, Mad
 Poets Rev*

Peter Blair   P
129 S Wade Ave
Washington, PA 15301, 804-977-7916
 Pubs: *Furnace Greens* (Defined Providence Pr, 1998),
 A Round, Fair Distance from the Furnace (White Eagle
 Coffee Store Pr, 1993), *And Rev, Poetry East,
 Crazyhorse, River City*

Karen Blomain   P
English Dept, Kutztown Univ, Kutztown, PA 19530,
215-683-4335
 Pubs: *Normal Ave., Borrowed Light* (Nightshade Pr,
 1998, 1993), *Coalseam: Poems* (U Scranton, 1993),
 *Pittsburgh Qtly, Passages North, Painted Bride Qtly,
 MacGuffin, Sun, Negative Capability, One Trick Pony*

Louise A. Blum   W
English Dept, Mansfield Univ, Mansfield, PA 16933,
717-662-4597
 Pubs: *Amnesty* (Alyson Pubs, 1995), *Love's Shadow:
 Anth* (Crossing Pr, 1992), *West, Cream City Rev,
 Poetic Space, Columbia, Sonora Rev*

William O. Boggs   P
English Dept, Slippery Rock Univ, Slippery Rock, PA
16057, 412-738-2348
 Pubs: *Eddy Johnson's American Dream* (Hiram Poetry
 Rev, 1990), *Swimming in Clear Water* (Dacotah
 Territory Pr, 1989), *Three Rivers Poetry Jrnl, Colorado
 Rev, Hiram*

Roger Bower   P
Cameron Star Rte
Waynesburg, PA 15370, 412-852-1448
 Pubs: *Editor's Choice II Anth, Space & Time, Abraxas,
 Pig Iron, Pudding, Colorado State Rev*

Greg Bowers   P
1010 Prospect Rd
Red Lion, PA 17356
 Pubs: *The Reunion* (Trunk Pr, 1977)

James Brasfield 🎤 ✈   P
Pennsylvania State Univ, 117 Burrowes, English Dept,
University Park, PA 16802-6200, 814-865-9795
Internet: jeb16@psu.edu
 Pubs: *Black Warrior Rev, Chicago Rev, Kestrel, Prairie
 Schooner, Qtly West*

Beth Phillips Brown   P
440 S Jackson St
Media, PA 19063, 610-566-2810
 Pubs: *A Celtic Daybook & Compendium of Lore,
 Invisible Threads* (White Pine Pr, 1987, 1983), *Painted
 Bride Qtly, U.S. 1 Worksheets, Full Moon, White Pine
 Jrnl*

Michael E. Burczynski   P&W
2116 Kater St
Philadelphia, PA 19146, 215-731-1114
 Pubs: *The Kerf, The Lucid Stone, The Poet's Attic,
 Coastal Forest Rev*

Richard Burgin   P&W
PO Box 30386
Philadelphia, PA 19103, 215-568-7062
 Pubs: *Private Fame, Man Without Memory* (U Illinois
 Pr, 1991, 1989), *Pushcart Prize XI: Anth* (Pushcart Pr,
 1987), *Witness, TriQtly, Mississippi Rev, Shenandoah*

Deborah Burnham   P
327 N 34
Philadelphia, PA 19104
 Pubs: *Anna & the Steel Mill* (Texas Tech, 1995),
 *Virginia Qtly Rev, West Branch, Literary Rev, Kansas
 Qtly*

Christopher Bursk 🎤 ✈   P
704 Hulmeville Ave
Langhorne Manor, PA 19047, 215-752-5101
 Pubs: *Cell Count* (Texas Tech, 1997), *The One True
 Religion* (Qtly Rev, 1997), *The Way Water Rubs Stone*
 (Word Works, 1989), *Places of Comfort, Places of
 Justice* (San Jose, 1987), *Making Wings* (State Street
 Pr, 1983), *APR*
Groups: Prisoners

Shulamith Wechter Caine   P
122 Grasmere Rd
Bala Cynwyd, PA 19004, 215-667-5990
 Pubs: *Love Fugue* (Silverfish Pr, 1998), *World & Local
 News* (Alms Hse Pr, 1988), *APR, American Scholar,
 Negative Capability, SPR, Kalliope*

Rosemary Cappello   P
1919 Chestnut St, #1721
Philadelphia, PA 19103, 215-568-1145
 Pubs: *Sig* (Peter Chaloner, 1988), *Pearl 22: Anth*
 (Pearl, 1995), *Voices in Italian Americana: Anth*
 (Bordighera, Inc, 1994), *Schuylkill Valley Jrnl*

Robert L. Carothers   P
English Dept, Edinboro State College, Edinboro, PA
16444, 814-732-2736

Jody Carr ♀ ✈   W
2210 Lehigh Pkwy N
Allentown, PA 18103, 610-820-5710
    Pubs: *Lost & Found* (Avon, 2001), *Song of Innocence,
    Monday's Child* (HC, 2000, 1999), *My Beautiful, Fat
    Friend* (Crosswinds, 1988), *No Regrets* (Dial Bks, 1982)
I.D.: Jewish. Groups: Seniors

Diana Cavallo ♀ ✈   W
1919 Chestnut St, #1015
Philadelphia, PA 19103-3415, 215-665-0698
    Pubs: *A Bridge of Leaves, The Voices We Carry: Anth*
    (Guernica Edtns, 1997, 1994), *From the Margin to the
    Center: Anth* (Purdue U Pr, 1990), *Confrontation*
I.D.: Italian-American, Women. Groups: Seniors

Joel Chace ♀ ✈   P
300 E Seminary St
Mercersburg, PA 17236, 717-328-3824
Internet: joel_chace@mercersburg.edu
    Pubs: *Greatest Hits* (Pudding Hse, 2000), *Uncertain
    Relations, The Melancholy of Yorick* (Birch Brook, 2000,
    1998), *Twentieth Century Deaths* (Singular Speech,
    1997), *Red Ghost* (Persephone, 1992), *Glossolalia, Big
    Bridge, Lost & Found Times, Coracle, Aught*

Diana Chang ♀ ✈   P&W
1400 Waverly Rd, Apt B126
Gladwyne, PA 19035-1263
    Pubs: *The Mind's Amazement* (Live Poets Society,
    1998), *Intersecting Circles: Anth* (Bamboo Ridge Pr,
    1999), *Yellow Light: Anth* (Temple U Pr, 1999), *Whelks
    Walk Rev, Montserrat Rev*
Groups: Visual Arts

Lisa Chewning   W
5427 Wilkins Ave
Pittsburgh, PA 15217, 412-683-9302
    Pubs: *Veri-Tales, Freed by Choice: Anth* (Fall Creek Pr,
    1994), *Walking the Twilight: Anth* (Northland Pub,
    1994), *Beloit Fiction Jrnl, Bluff City, Rosebud*

A. V. Christie   P
474 Conestoga Rd
Malvern, PA 19355, 610-725-1989
    Pubs: *Nine Skies* (U Illinois Pr, 1997), *Black & Blues*
    (Itinerant Pr, 1985), *The Bread Loaf Anth of New
    American Poets* (U Pr of New England, 2000), *Orpheus
    & Company: Anth* (U Pr of New England, 1999), *APR,
    Ploughshares, Excerpt, The Jrnl*

Michael Clark   W
Humanities Dept, Widener Univ, 1 University Pl, Chester,
PA 19013, 610-499-4354
    Pubs: *Our Roots Grow Deeper Than We Know: Anth*
    (U Pittsburgh Pr, 1985), *Arizona Qtly, Outerbridge*

John Clarke   P
RD 1, Stone Jug Rd
Biglerville, PA 17307, 717-677-7438
    Pubs: *Inland Tide* (Snowy Road Pr, 1981), *Texas Rev,
    Kansas Qtly, New Yorker, Atlantic, Colorado Qtly*

Lance Clewett ♀ ✈   P
8 Cave Hill Dr
Carlisle, PA 17013-1203, 717-249-6912
Internet: bluemoon51@juno.com
    Pubs: *One Fast Trout* (Paco Bks, 1997), *Diesel Flowers*
    (Warm Spring Pr, 1992)

Marion Deutsche Cohen   P
2203 Spruce St
Philadelphia, PA 19103, 215-732-7723
    Pubs: *Dirty Details* (Temple U Pr, 1996), *Epsilon
    Country* (Ctr for Thanatology Research, 1995), *The
    Sitting-Down Hug* (Liberal Pr, 1989), *Plain Brown
    Wrapper, Palo Alto Rev, Ikon, Abraxas*

James H. Comey   W
105 Treaty Rd
Drexel Hill, PA 19026
Internet: jcomey@bellatlantic.net
    Pubs: *The Eagle's Claw, The Dragon Singer, The
    Monster in the Woods* (Stages of Imagination, 1998,
    1997, 1996)
I.D.: Irish-American

Marjorie Lenore Compfort ♀   P
41 W Corydon St
Bradford, PA 16701-2233, 814-368-5742
    Pubs: *Comstock Rev, Poet's Page, Poetic Celebration,
    Cer*ber*us, Lucid Moon, Alpha Beat Soup, Tiotis,
    Parnassus, Arachne*

Julie Cooper-Fratrik   P
5553 Rte 412
Riegelsville, PA 18077
    Pubs: *Out of Season: Anth* (Amagansett Pr, 1993),
    Minnesota Rev, Slant, The Dickinson Rev

Anita R. Cornwell   W
3220 Powelton Ave
Philadelphia, PA 19104
    Pubs: *The Girls of Summer* (New Seed Pr, 1989),
    Black Lesbian in White America (Naiad Pr, 1983)

Gerald Costanzo ♀ ✈   P
366 Parker Dr
Pittsburgh, PA 15216-1324, 412-268-2861
    Pubs: *Great Disguise* (Aan, 2000), *Nobody Lives on
    Arthur Godfrey Boulevard* (BOA Edtns, 1993), *Devins
    Award: Anth* (U Missouri Pr, 1998), *Nation, APR,
    Ploughshares, NAR, Ohio Rev, Georgia Rev*

Barbara Crooker 🎤 ✈ P
7928 Woodsbluff Rd
Fogelsville, PA 18051, 610-395-5845
Internet: http://barbaracrooker.tripod.com
    Pubs: *In the Late Summer Garden* (H&H Pr, 1998),
    Obbligato (Linwood Pub, 1992), *Boomer Girls: Anth* (U
    Iowa Pr, 1999), *Thirteen Ways of Looking for a Poem:
    Anth* (AWL, 2000), *Worlds in Our Words: Contemporary
    American Women Writers: Anth* (Prentice Hall, 1997)
I.D.: Italian-American. Groups: Seniors, Children

David C. Cruse P
5220 W Master St
Philadelphia, PA 19139

Craig Czury P
914 Leiszs Bridge
Reading, PA 19605-2322, 610-921-0216
Internet: czury@aol.com
    Pubs: *Unreconciled Faces* (Foot Hills Pub, 1999),
    Shadow/Orphan Shadow, Obit Hotel (Pine Pr, 1996,
    1993), *Fine Line that Screams: Anth* (Endless
    Mountains Rev, 1993), *Five Finger Rev, Parnassus*

Susan Daily P
523 Magee Ave
Philadelphia, PA 19111, 215-725-5831
    Pubs: *Newsart, Hot Water Rev, Painted Bride Qtly,
    Palm of Your Hand, Ampersand Mag*

Jim Daniels P
Carnegie Mellon Univ, English Dept, Pittsburgh, PA 15213,
412-268-2842
    Pubs: *Niagara Falls* (Adastra Pr, 1994), *M-80* (U Pitt
    Pr, 1993), *Letters to America: Poetry on Race Anth*
    (Wayne State U Pr, 1994), *Iowa Rev, Ohio Rev*

Edmund Dantes 🎤 ✈ P
501 Franklin St
East Pittsburgh, PA 15112-1109, 412-241-0671
Internet: edantes@netscape.net

Almitra David 🎤 ✈ P
986 N Randolph St
Philadelphia, PA 19123, 215-922-4563
    Pubs: *Between the Sea & Home* (Eighth Mtn Pr, 1993),
    Impulse to Fly (Perugia Pr, 1998), *Annie Crow
    Road/Chesapeake* (Potter Pr, 1988), *Building the
    Cathedral* (Slash & Burn, 1986)

George Deaux W
English Dept, Temple Univ, Philadelphia, PA 19122,
215-787-7560
    Pubs: *Superworm* (S&S, 1968)

R. DeBacco P
Westmoreland Community College, College Sta,
Youngwood, PA 15697, 724-925-4033
    Pubs: *New Voices, Whiskey Island Mag, Atavist,
    MacGuffin, South Coast Poetry Jrnl, Tightrope,
    Loyalhanna Rev, Ecphorizer, Ko, Archer, Modern Haiku,
    Amelia*

Toi Derricotte P
6700 Edgerton Ave
Pittsburgh, PA 15208, 412-624-6527
    Pubs: *Captivity* (U Pitt Pr, 1995), *The Empress of the
    Death House* (Lotus Pr, 1988), *Callaloo, Paris Rev,
    Iowa Rev*

John Dewitt P
221 Buttonwood Way
Glenside, PA 19038
    Pubs: *Finger Food* (Synapse, 1982), *A New Geography
    of Poets: Anth* (U Arkansas Pr, 1992), *New American
    Rev, #, Spectrum, Painted Bride Qtly, Lace Rev,
    Hydrant*

Gregory Djanikian 🎤 P
English Dept, Univ Pennsylvania, 119 Bennett Hall,
Philadelphia, PA 19104, 215-898-7341
Internet: djanikia@english.upenn.edu
    Pubs: *Years Later, About Distance, Falling Deeply Into
    America* (Carnegie Mellon U Pr, 2000, 1995, 1989),
    *Poetry, American Scholar, Georgia Rev, Poetry NW,
    Shenandoah, Iowa Rev*

Patricia Dobler 🎤 ✈ P
English Dept, Carlow College, 3333 5th Ave, Pittsburgh,
PA 15213, 412-578-6032
Internet: pdobler@carlow.edu
    Pubs: *UXB* (Mill Hunk Bks, 1991), *Talking to Strangers*
    (U Wisconsin Pr, 1986), *Ploughshares, SPR,
    Mid-American Rev, 5 A.M.*

John Dolis 🎤 ✈ P
711 Summit Pointe
Scranton, PA 18508-1049, 570-961-9787
Internet: jjd3@psu.edu
    Pubs: *Time Flies: Butterflies, Bl()nk Space* (Runaway
    Spoon Pr, 1999, 1993), *Antennae, Logo, Daedalus,
    New Orleans Rev*

George Dowden P
c/o Corinne Thomas, 27 Ward St, Ridley Park, PA 19078,
215-532-6784
    Pubs: *A Message to Isis* (Moving I, 1977), *Renew
    Jerusalem* (Symra Pr, 1969), *Evergreen Rev*

Robert C. S. Downs 🎤 ✈ W
Pennsylvania State Univ, English Dept, University Park,
PA 16802, 814-234-0747
    Pubs: *The Fifth Season* (Counterpoint, 2000), *Living
    Together* (St. Martin's, 1983), *Cimarron Rev, Sundog*

Rachel Blau DuPlessis 🎤 ✈   P
211 Rutgers Ave
Swarthmore, PA 19081-1715, 610-328-4116
Internet: rdupless@astro.temple.edu
   Pubs: *Drafts 1-38, TOLL* (Wesleyan U Pr, 2001), *Drafts 15-XXX, The Fold; Drafts 3-14* (Potes & Poets, 1997, 1991), *The Pink Guitar* (Routledge, 1990), *Sulfur, Conjunctions, Hambone, Chain, Chelsea, Iowa Rev*

Howard Linn Edsall   W
105 Innis Way
Malvern, PA 19355-2135, 201-744-8434
   Pubs: *Successful Farming, Harper's, Saturday Evening Post, The American, London Graphic, Holland's*

W. D. Ehrhart 🎤 ✈   P
6845 Anderson St
Philadelphia, PA 19119-1423, 215-848-2068
Internet: wdehrhart@worldnet.att.net
   Pubs: *Beautiful Wreckage* (Adastra Pr, 1999), *APR, Virginia Qtly Rev, Poetry East*

Karen Elias   P
RD2, Box 279-C
Lock Haven, PA 17745, 717-748-1632
   Pubs: *Sinister Wisdom, 13th Moon, Second Wave, Feminist Studies, Women/Poems IV, Anima*

Edith Muesing Ellwood   P&W
RR1 PML 178
Bushkill, PA 18324, 717-588-3111
   Pubs: *Expressions Mag, Parent to Parent, Black Bough, Haiku Headlines, Brussels Sprout, Inkstone, Dragonfly*

Lynn Emanuel   P
Univ of Pittsburgh, Dept of English, Pittsburgh, PA 15260, 412-624-4036
Internet: emanuelt@pitt.edu
   Pubs: *Then, Suddenly* (U Pittsburgh Pr, 1999), *The Dig & Hotel Fiesta* (U Illinois Pr, 1995), *Best American Poetry: Anths* (Scribner, 1998, 1995), *Parnassus, Hudson Rev, Ploughshares, APR*

Aisha Eshe   P
Community College Philadelphia, 17 & Spring Garden, Philadelphia, PA 19130
   Pubs: *Grain* (Saskatchewan Writers Guild, 1994), *Life on the Line* (Negative Capability Pr, 1992), *Catalyst, Dream Network, Women's Recovery Network, Athena*

Joann Marie Everett   P
2224 Ogden Ave
Bensalem, PA 19020, 215-244-0525
   Pubs: *Angel Wisdom & a Woman's Song, Seasons in Thunder Valley, Whispered Beginnings* (Jasmine Pr, 1996, 1986, 1984), *Calliope*

Samuel Exler 🎤 ✈   P
307 E Roumfort Rd
Philadelphia, PA 19119-1031
   Pubs: *River Poems* (Slapering Hol Pr, 1992), *Ambition, Fertility, Loneliness* (Lintel, 1982), *Beyond Lament: Anth* (Northwestern U Pr, 1998), *Poetry East, Plainsong, NYQ, Literary Rev, And Rev*

Sascha Feinstein 🎤 ✈   P
Lycoming College, English Dept, Williamsport, PA 17701, 570-321-4279
   Pubs: *Misterioso* (Copper Canyon, 2000), *The Second Set: Anth* (Indiana U Pr, 1996), *The Jazz Poetry Anth* (Indiana U Pr, 1991), *APR, Ploughshares, NER, Missouri Rev, NAR, Denver Qtly, Hayden's Ferry Rev*

Al Ferber 🎤 ✈   P
1110 Sheffield Ct
Bensalem, PA 19020-4824, 215-638-2791
   Pubs: *Gus* (Cutting Edge Pub, 1994), *Badlands* (Johnston Green Pub, 1986), *Echos, Blue Buildings, Berkeley Poets Co-op, Painted Bride Qtly*

Charles Fergus   W
RD2, 340 Mountain Rd
Port Matilda, PA 16870, 814-692-5097
   Pubs: *Shadow Catcher* (Soho Pr, 1991)

Rina Ferrarelli   P
224 Adeline Ave
Pittsburgh, PA 15228, 412-341-8009
   Pubs: *A Whole Other Ball Game* (Noonday Pr, 1997), *Home Is A Foreign Country* (Eadmer Pr, 1996), *Dreamsearch* (malafemmina, 1992), *The Art of Life: Anth* (South-Western Educational Pub, 1998), *The Runner's Literary Companion: Anth* (Breakaway Pr, 1994)

Ken Fifer 🎤 ✈   P
5525 Spring Dr
Center Valley, PA 18034-9312
   Pubs: *Falling Man* (Ithaca Hse, 1979), *Partisan Rev, Ploughshares, New Letters, Poetry Now*

Gary Fincke   P&W
3 Melody Ln
Selinsgrove, PA 17870, 717-372-4164
   Pubs: *The Almanac for Desire* (BkMk Pr, 2000), *The Technology of Paradise* (Avisson Pr, 1998), *Emergency Calls* (U Missouri Pr, 1996), *Inventing Angels* (Zoland Bks, 1994), *Paris Rev, Harper's, Kenyon Rev, Poetry, Georgia Rev, Gettysburg Rev*

Sandra Gould Ford   W
7123 Race St
Pittsburgh, PA 15208, 412-731-7039
   Pubs: *ELF, Obsidian II, Confluence, James River Rev, Shooting Star Rev*

Cynthia Solt Frame 🎤 ✈   P
PO Box 101
Springtown, PA 18081, 610-346-6283
    Pubs: *Northern Pleasure, Abbey, Bogg, Visions*

Robert Freedman   P
30 E Market St, #3
Bethlehem, PA 18018, 610-868-5137
    Pubs: *Creeping Bent, Yarrow, Endless Mountains Rev,
    West Branch, Onthebus, Calapooya Collage, Four
    Quarters, NYQ, Poet Lore*

Catherine Gammon   W
Univ Pittsburgh, English Dept, Pittsburgh, PA 15260-0001
    Pubs: *Isabel Out of the Rain* (Mercury Hse, 1991),
    Cape Discovery: Anth (Sheep Meadow, 1994), *Manoa,
    Ploughshares, Kenyon, Central Park, Iowa Rev*

Tom Gatten 🎤 ✈   P&W
105 E Curtin St, #15
Bellefonte, PA 16823-1737, 814-353-0532
Internet: tomgatten123@hotmail.com
    Pubs: *Mapper of Mists* (Hre Lo Wambli Pr, 1974), *The
    Workshop: Anth* (Hyperion, 1999), *The Sumac Reader:
    Anth* (Michigan State U Pr, 1996), *Fiction Midwest,
    Shenandoah*

Greg Geleta 🎤 ✈   P
1017 S 48 St
Philadelphia, PA 19143-3508, 215-704-6969
    Pubs: *The Year I Learned to Drive, Jazz Elegies* (Axe
    Factory Pr, 1988, 1985), *Snail's Pace Rev, Artful
    Dodge, New Stone Circle, Onion River Rev, Axe
    Factory*
Groups: Children, Teenagers

Julia Geleta   P&W
427 Carpenter Ln
Philadelphia, PA 19119, 215-844-7678
    Pubs: *Meeting Tessie* (Singing Horse Pr, 1994),
    Artificial Memory (Leave Bks, 1994), *Parallelism*
    (Abacus/Potes & Poets Pr, 1989), *Topography* (Center,
    1983), *Aerial, Paper Air, 6IX, The World, Chain, Brief,
    Central Park*

Kathleen E. George 🎤 ✈   W
1213 Monterey St
Pittsburgh, PA 15212-4510
    Pubs: *The Man in the Buick* (BkMk Pr, 1999), *Rhythm
    in Drama* (U Pitt Pr, 1980), *Cimarron Rev, Alaska Qtly
    Rev, Great Stream Rev, NAR, American Fiction,
    Vignette*

Robert Gibb 🎤 ✈   P
5036 Revenue St
Homestead, PA 15120-1227, 412-243-5332
    Pubs: *Origins of Evening* (Norton, 1997), *Fugue for a
    Late Snow, The Winter House* (U Missouri Pr, 1993,
    1984), *Momentary Days* (Walt Whitman Ctr, 1988)

C. S. Giscombe   P
Pennsylvania State Univ, English Dept, Burrowes Bldg,
University Park, PA 16802, 814-865-6381
    Pubs: *Giscome Road, Here* (Dalkey Archive Pr, 1998,
    1994), *o.blek, River Styx, Obsidian II, Situation, NAW,
    ACM, Callaloo, Hambone*

Ann K. Glasner   W
Kennedy House 2209, 1901 J F Kennedy Blvd,
Philadelphia, PA 19103, 215-561-5874
    Pubs: *Summer Awakening* (Lancer Bks, 1971)

Patricia J. Goodrich 🎤 ✈   P
PO Box 473
Richlandtown, PA 18955-0473, 610-282-2822
Internet: pgoodric@bciu.k12.pa.us
    Pubs: *Sidelights* (Kali Moma Pr, 1995), *Intricate Lacing*
    (Nightshade Pr, 1992), *Zone 3, Yarrow, Mediphors,
    Folio, Footwork, New Jersey Jrnl*
Groups: Children, Disabled

Carol Granato   P
2506 S 18 St
Philadelphia, PA 19145, 215-334-5412
    Pubs: *The Universe & Beyond* (Garnet Pub, 1999),
    *Epiphany, Snake Nation, Seems, American Goat, The
    Formalist, Prophetic Voices, Midwest Qtly, Poem,
    Rockford Rev, Troubadour, Neo-Victorian, Riverrun, The
    Lyric*

Ray Greenblatt 🎤 ✈   P
Box 2000, Church Farm School
Paoli, PA 19301, 610-363-7500
    Pubs: *Puzzles in the Woods* (Meg Kennedy, 2000),
    *America, English Jrnl, Intl Poetry Rev, Midwest Qtly,
    Sulphur River Rev*

Sam Gridley 🎤 ✈   W
Box 13267
Philadelphia, PA 19101
    Pubs: *Free Parking* (Spirit That Moves Us Pr, 1990),
    *Huckleberry Press, Calapooya Collage, Epoch,
    Cottonwood, South Dakota Rev, Cimarron Rev,
    American Short Fiction*

Alexandra Grilikhes 🎤 ✈   P
4343 Manayunk Ave
Philadelphia, PA 19128-4930, 215-483-7051
    Pubs: *Shaman Body* (Branch Redd Bks, 1996), *The
    Reveries* (Insight to Riot Pr, 1994), *The Blue Scar*
    (Folder Edtns, 1988), *On Women Artists* (Cleis, 1981),
    Pleiades, Seattle Rev, TDR

Emily Grosholz   P
Pennsylvania State Univ, 240 Sparks Bldg, Philosophy,
University Park, PA 16802, 814-865-6397
    Pubs: *Eden* (Johns Hopkins U Pr, 1992), *Shores &
    Headlands* (Princeton U Pr, 1988), *Hudson Rev,
    Southern Rev, Poetry, Partisan Rev, New Virginia Rev*

Lee Gutkind W
5501 Walnut St, #202
Pittsburgh, PA 15232-1811, 412-688-0304
  Pubs: *Connecting: Anth* (Putnam, 1998)

John Haag P&W
379 Moose Run Rd
Bellefonte, PA 16823, 814-355-7578
  Pubs: *Stones Don't Float* (Ohio State U Pr, 1996),
Atlantis at $5 a Day (NAR, 1991), *The Brine Breather*
(Kayak Bks, 1971), *The Mirrored Man* (Reading U Pr,
1961), *Poetry, Talking River Rev, Fugue*

Sy Hakim P&W
3726 Manayunk Ave
Philadelphia, PA 19128-3705, 215-482-0853
Internet: syhakim@dellnet.com
  Pubs: *Michaelangelo's Call, Eleanor, Goodbye* (Poet
Gallery/Century Pr, 1998, 1988), *Dan River Anth* (Dan
River Pr, 2000), *California Qtly, American Writing*

William J. Harris P
103 Cherry Ridge
State College, PA 16803, 814-867-1381
  Pubs: *The Garden Thrives: Anth* (HC, 1996), *In Search
of Color Everywhere: Anth* (Stewart, Tabori & Chang,
1994)

Bim Harrison P&W
PO Box 97
Hegins, PA 17938-0097, 717-682-8764
  Pubs: *An Intricate Weave: Anth* (Iris Edtns, 1997), *Coal
Seam: Anth* (U Scranton Pr, 1994), *West Branch,
Spoon River, BPJ, Poetry Now*

Dev Hathaway W
314 N Morris St
Shippensburg, PA 17257, 717-530-5943
  Pubs: *The Widow's Boy* (Lynx Hse, 1992), *Black
Warrior Rev, Carolina Qtly, Missouri Rev, Greensboro
Rev*

G. W. Hawkes W
Lycoming College, English Dept, Williamsport, PA 17701,
570-321-4336
Internet: hawkes@lycoming.edu
  Pubs: *Gambler's Rose, Surveyor, Semaphore*
(MacMurray & Beck, 2000, 1998, 1998), *Playing Out of
the Deep Woods, Spies in the Blue Smoke: Stories* (U
Missouri Pr, 1995, 1992), *Atlantic, GQ, Ploughshares,
Missouri Rev*

Ann Hayes 🎤 ✈ P
English Dept, Carnegie Mellon Univ, Pittsburgh, PA
15213-3890, 412-268-2850
  Pubs: *Notes & Spectacles, Circle of the Earth, Progress
Dancing* (Robert Barth, 2000, 1990, 1986), *Letters at
Christmas & Other Poems* (Badger Pr, 1995)

Samuel Hazo 🎤 ✈ P&W
International Poetry Forum, 4415 Fifth Ave, Webster Hall,
Pittsburgh, PA 15213, 412-621-9893
  Pubs: *The Autobiographers of Everybody* (Intl Poetry
Forum, 2000), *As They Sail, The Holy Surprise of Right
Now, The Past Won't Stay Behind You* (U Arkansas Pr,
1999, 1996, 1993), *Spying for God* (Byblos Pr, 1999),
The Pages of Day & Night (Marlboro, 1994)

Sonya Hess P
Virginia Kidd Agency, 538 E Harford St, Box 278, Milford,
PA 18337, 717-296-6205
  Pubs: *Kingdom of Lost Waters* (Ahsata Pr, 1993),
Constellations of the Inner Eye (Puckerbrush Pr, 1991),
Grand St, Iowa Woman, Hiram Poetry Rev

Allen Hoey P
804 Bismark Way
King of Prussia, PA 19406-3214, 215-992-1088
  Pubs: *What Persists* (Liberty Street Bks, 1992), *A Fire
in the Cold House of Being* (Walt Whitman Ctr, 1987),
Georgia Rev, Hudson Rev, Poetry, Southern Rev

Daniel Hoffman 🎤 ✈ P
502 Cedar Ln
Swarthmore, PA 19081-1105, 610-544-4438
  Pubs: *Middens of the Tribe* (LSU, 1996), *Words to
Create a World* (U Michigan Pr, 1992), *Hudson Rev,
Sewanee Rev, Boulevard, Gettysburg Rev*

Cynthia Hogue 🎤 ✈ P
Bucknell Univ, Stadler Center For Poetry, Lewisburg, PA
17837, 570-577-1944
Internet: hogue@bucknell.edu
  Pubs: *The Never Wife* (Mammoth Pr, 1999), *The
Woman in Red* (Ahsahta Pr, 1990), *Where the Parallels
Cross* (White Knights Pr, 1984), *Southern Rev, APR,
NAR, Ploughshares, Spoon River Poetry Rev, Puerto
del Sol, Antioch Rev, The Jrnl, West Branch*

Margaret Holley P
1184A MacPherson Dr
West Chester, PA 19380, 610-344-4992
  Pubs: *Kore in Bloom, Morning Star* (Copper Beech Pr,
1998, 1992), *The Smoke Tree* (Bluestem Pr, 1991),
*Prairie Schooner, Boulevard, Poetry, Southern Rev,
Gettysburg Rev, Nation, Shenandoah*

Charlotte Holmes 🎤 ✈ W
Pennsylvania State Univ, English Dept, University Park,
PA 16802, 814-865-9126
  Pubs: *Gifts & Other Stories* (Confluence Pr, 1994), *The
Family Track: Anth* (U Illinois Pr, 1998), *New Stories
from the South: Anth* (Algonquin Bks, 1988), *Grand St,
Carolina Qtly, Epoch, Story, New Yorker, Antioch Rev,
New Letters, Columbia*

C. J. Houghtaling 🎤 ✈   P
RD2, Box 241
Middlebury Center, PA 16935, 570-376-2821
Internet: cjhoughtaling@usa.net
    Pubs: *Filtered Images: Anth* (Vintage 45 Pr, 1992),
Meanderings: Anth (Foothills, 1992), *Wild West, Literary
Jrnl, Wolf Head Qtly, Fox Cry, Open Bone, Byline Mag,
Endless Mountain Rev, Dogwood Tales, South Coast
Poetry Jrnl*

Carolyn Fairweather Hughes   P
548 Greenhurst Dr
Pittsburgh, PA 15243, 412-344-6850
    Pubs: *For She Is the Tree of Life: Anth* (Conari Pr,
1995), *We Speak for Peace: Anth* (KIT Pubs, 1993),
Pittsburgh Qtly, Slant, Wind, Poets On, Lactuca

Bruce Hunsberger   W
3616 Willingham Ave
Reading, PA 19605-1156, 610-929-2017
    Pubs: *Railroad Street* (Lyle Stuart, 1970), *Alfred
Hitchcock's Mystery, Nantucket Rev, Seattle Rev, John
O'Hara Jrnl, Redbook*

Mary Jean Irion 🎤 ✈   P
Chautauqua Writers' Center, 149 Kready Ave, Millersville,
PA 17551, 717-872-8337
    Pubs: *Holding On* (Heatherstone Pr, 1984), *Poetry,
Prairie Schooner, NER, Western Humanities Rev,
Southern Humanities Rev, Poet Lore*

Haywood Jackson   P
9A Carothers Dr
Turtle Creek, PA 15145, 412-824-6814
    Pubs: *Fellow Travelers* (Samisdat, 1981), *APR, Poetry
Now, NYQ, The Little Mag*

Susan S. Jacobson 🎤 ✈   P&W
3025 Mt Alister Rd
Pittsburgh, PA 15214-2603, 412-322-1072
    Pubs: *Other Testaments* (Incarnate Muse Pub, 1997),
Intergenerational Relationships: Anth (Papier-Mache Pr,
1998), *Life on the Line: Anth* (Negative Capability,
1992), *Pittsburgh Qtly, Heart Qtly, 5AM, Pittsburgh
Post-Gazette, Negative Capability*
Groups: Disabled, Native American

Annette Williams Jaffee   W
PO Box 26, River Rd
Lumberville, PA 18733
    Pubs: *The Dangerous Age* (Leapfrog Pr, 1999), *Recent
History* (Putnam, 1988), *Adult Education* (Ontario
Review Pr, 1981), *Ploughshares*

Martin James   W
Peekner Literary Agency, Inc, 3121 Portage Rd,
Bethlehem, PA 18017, 215-974-9158
    Pubs: *Zombie House, Night Glow* (Pinnacle Bks, 1990,
1989), *5 A.M., Mystery Scene, Cemetery Dance*

Nancy Esther James   P
267 Maple St
New Wilmington, PA 16142, 412-946-8761
    Pubs: *No Time to Hurry* (Dawn Valley Pr, 1979), *Pivot,
Stone Country, 13th Moon, Black Maria*

Lou Janac   P
PO Box 342
Mechanicsburg, PA 17055, 717-774-0253

Suzan Jivan   PP
818 N Taney St
Philadelphia, PA 19130-1817
    Pubs: *Long Pond Rev*

Julia Kasdorf 🎤 ✈   P
Penn State English Dept, Burrowes Building, University
Park, PA 16802-6200, 717-737-4996
Internet: jkasdorf@mcis.messiah.edu
    Pubs: *Eve's Striptease, Sleeping Preacher* (U Pitt Pr,
1998, 1992)

Susan Rea Katz 🎤 ✈   P
535 Valley Park Rd
Phoenixville, PA 19460, 610-933-3496
    Pubs: *Snowdrops for Cousin Ruth* (S&S, 1998), *Sutured
Words* (Aviva Pr, 1987), *Passages North Anth*
(Milkweed Edtns, 1990), *American Scholar, Louisville
Rev, Maryland Poetry Rev, Alaska Qtly Rev*
Groups: Children

Linda Keegan   P
141 Friar Ln
McMurray, PA 15317, 724-941-1279
    Pubs: *Heeding the Wind* (Still Waters Pr, 1995), *Greedy
for Sunlight* (M. Wurster, 1992), *Poet Lore, New
Virginia Rev, Zone 3, Cape Rock, Pittsburgh Qtly, The
Herb Companion*

Joseph J. Kelly   P
Pennsylvania Humanities Council, 325 Chestnut St, Ste
715, Philadelphia, PA 19106-2607, 215-925-1005
Internet: jkelly@libertynet.org
    Pubs: *Only Morning in Her Shoes: Anth* (Utah St U Pr,
1990), *Chariton Rev, Visions, Plains Poetry Jrnl,
Kansas Qtly, Poet Lore, Hiram Poetry Rev*

John A. Kessler   P
18 Birdie Ln
Reading, PA 19607, 610-796-0994
    Pubs: *Library of Congress Bicentennial: Anth* (Library of
Congress, 1999), *Reading Eagle, Bookends, Arts
Connection, Smile, Neovictorian, Riverrun*

Miriam Kessler 🎤 ✈   P
2008 Highland Cir
Camp Hill, PA 17011-5920, 717-761-4830
    Pubs: *Someone to Pour the Wine* (Ragged Edge Pr,
1996), *Blood to Remember: Anth* (Texas Tech U Pr,
1991), *Cries of the Spirit: Anth* (Beacon Pr, 1990)

Kerry Shawn Keys   P
14 Joseph Dr
Boiling Springs, PA 17007, 717-241-6033
    Pubs: *Ch'antscapes* (Pine Pr, 1998), *Krajina Supu
Vultures' Country* (Votobia, 1996), *Decoy's Desire*
(Pennywhistle Pr, 1993), *The Hearing* (Paco Bks, 1992),
*Nation, Ploughshares, Iowa Rev, Kayak, Wilderness,
100 Words, Blue Guitar, Michigan Qtly Rev*

Maurice Kilwien Guevara   P&W
Indiana Univ of Pennsylvania, Indiana, PA 15705-1094,
724-357-2261
    Pubs: *Poems of the River Spirits* (U Pittsburgh Pr
1996), *Postmortem* (U Georgia Pr 1994), *Learning By
Heart: Anth* (U Iowa Pr 1999), *The Best of Cream City
Rev: Anth* (U Wisconsin-Milwaukee, 1997), *Parnassus,
Ploughshares, JAMA, Poet Lore*

Yong Ik Kim   W
1030 Macon Ave
Pittsburgh, PA 15218, 412-243-9495
    Pubs: *Blue in the Seed & Other Stories* (Shi-Sa Yong
Wo Sa, 1989), *The Diving Gourd* (Knopf, 1963),
*Hudson Rev, New Yorker, Atlantic, TriQtly, Sewanee
Rev*

Dorothy E. King   PP
PenOwl Productions, PO Box 3872, Harrisburg, PA
17105-3872, 717-234-3886
    Pubs: *Love in Time* (PenOwl Pr, 1983), *Essence,
Chicago Sheet, Mobius*

Claude F. Koch   W
128 W Highland Ave
Philadelphia, PA 19118, 215-247-4270
    Pubs: *Light in Silence* (Dodd Mead, 1958), *O. Henry
Prize Stories: Anth* (Doubleday, 1985), *Sewanee Rev,
Antioch Rev, Southern Rev, Four Quarters, Spirit*

Sandra Kohler 🎤 ✈   P
225 S Market St
Selinsgrove, PA 17870-1813, 570-374-8497
Internet: hagendaz@ptd.net
    Pubs: *The Country of Women: Anth* (Calyx Bks, 1995),
*Gettysburg Rev, New Republic, Southern Rev, APR,
Countermeasures, West Branch, Calyx, Prairie
Schooner, Women's Rev of Bks*

William Krasner 🎤 ✈   W
538 Berwyn Ave
Berwyn, PA 19312, 610-647-1527
    Pubs: *The Gambler* (Harper Perennial, 1987), *Resort to
Murder* (Scribner Classic, 1985), *Harper's, Trans-Action,
Society*

Peter Krok   P
240 Golf Hills Rd
Haverton, PA 19083-1026, 610-789-4692
    Pubs: *Plains Poetry Jrnl, Midwest Qtly, Blue Unicorn,
Negative Capability, Schuylkill Valley Jrnl, America*

Will Lane   P
1420 Russel Tavern Rd
Gettysburg, PA 17325
    Pubs: *In the Barn of the God, Elegy for Virginia
Redding* (Mad River Pr, 1989, 1999), *Moonlight
Standinginas Cordelia, Hang Together: Anth* (Hanging
Loose Pr 1981, 1985), *Windless Orchard, Literary Rev,
Minnesota Rev*

Ursula K. Le Guin 🎤 ✈   P&W
Virginia Kidd Agency, Box 278, Milford, PA 18337
    Pubs: *The Telling* (Harcourt, 2000), *Sixty Odd*
(Shambhala, 1999), *Steering the Craft* (Eighth Mountain
Pr, 1998), *Unlocking the Air: Anth* (HC, 1996), *Kenyon,
Sunset, Amazing Stories, Playboy*

Audrey Lee 🎤   P&W
PO Box 16622
Philadelphia, PA 19139-6622
    Pubs: *The Workers, The Clarion People* (McGraw-Hill,
1969, 1968), *Black Amer Lit Forum: Anth* (Indiana St
U, 1989), *Our Roots Grow Deeper Than We Know:
Anth* (U Pitt, 1986), *What We Must See: Anth* (Ed
Oord Combs, 1971), *Essence, Sat Evening Post, Black
World*
I.D.: African-American

Harper Lee   W
c/o J. B. Lippincott Company, E Washington Sq,
Philadelphia, PA 19105, 215-238-4200

Bahman Levin   P&W
c/o Concourse Press, PO Box 8265, Philadelphia, PA
19101, 215-262-0497
    Pubs: *Dead Reckoning, Rooted in Volcanic Ashes, The
Night's Journey* (Concourse Pr, 1992, 1987, 1984),
Confrontation Anth (Long Island U, 1992)

Harriet Levin   P
Drexel University, Humanities Dept, McAlister Hall, 32nd &
Chestnut Sts, 5th Fl, Philadelphia, PA 19104,
215-895-2441
    Pubs: *The Christmas Show* (Beacon Pr, 1996), *West
Branch, Partisan Rev, New Letters, Nimrod, Iowa Rev,
American Voice*

Lynn Levin 🎤 ✈   P
1850 Dover Rd
Southampton, PA 18966-4550, 215-364-2423
    Pubs: *A Few Questions About Paradise* (Loonfeather
    Pr, 2000), *Touch Me There: A Yellow Silk Anth*
    (Warner Bks, 2000), *First Harvest: Anth* (Brodsky
    Library Pr, 1997), *Poetry NY, Kerem, NAR, New Laurel
    Rev, Loonfeather, Reconstructionist, JAMA, Potato Eyes*
Groups: Jewish, Writing Groups

Robert Lima 🎤 ✈   P
Pennsylvania State Univ, N 346 Burrowes Bldg, University
Park, PA 16802, 814-865-4252
Internet: www.personal.psu.edu/rxl2
    Pubs: *Sardinia/Sardegna* (Bordighera Intl, 2000),
    Mayaland (Editorial Betania, 1992), *The Olde Ground*
    (Society of Inter-Celtic Arts & Culture, 1985), *Fathoms*
    (Carnation Pr, 1981), *Uncommonplaces: Poems of the
    Fantastic: Anth* (Mayapple Pr, 2000)
Lang: Spanish

Jack Lindeman 🎤 ✈   P
133 S Franklin St
Fleetwood, PA 19522-1810, 215-944-9554
    Pubs: *From Both Sides Now* (Scribner, 1998),
    Twenty-One Poems (Atlantis Edtns, 1963), *Chiron Rev,
    Poetry Motel, Calapooya, Rhino, Bellowing Ark, New
    Authors Jrnl, Home Planet News, Eureka Lit Mag, Blue
    Unicorn, Poet's Page, San Fernando Poetry Jrnl*

Jeffrey Loo   P
1512 Pine St, #2R
Philadelphia, PA 19102, 215-546-6381
    Pubs: *Prayers to Protest: Anth, Unitarian Universalist
    Poets: Anth* (Pudding Hse, 1997, 1995), *African
    American Rev, Footwork, Synaesthetic, APR, Many
    Mountains Moving, SPR, Dis-Orient, Crab Orchard Rev,
    Rampike*

George Looney   P
Penn State Erie/The Behrend College, School of
Humanities and Social Sciences, Station Rd, Erie, PA
16563-1501, 814-898-6281
    Pubs: *Animals Housed in the Pleasure of Flesh*
    (Bluestem Pr, 1995), *Attendant Ghosts* (Cleveland State
    U Pr, 2000), *Kenyon Rev, Ascent, Willow Springs, High
    Plains Lit Rev, BPJ, Southern Rev*

Roger A. Lopata 🎤 ✈   W
1300 Medford Rd
Wynnewood, PA 19096-2419
    Pubs: *Other Voices, Painted Bride Qtly, Sou'wester,
    Hawaii Pacific Rev, Turnstile, Worcester Rev,
    Panhandler, Midland Rev, Pointed Circle, Hudson Valley
    Echoes*

Radomir Luza, Jr.   P
18 Golf Club Dr
Langhorne, PA 19047-2163, 215-741-5897
    Pubs: *Porch Light Blues* (B.T. Pubs, 1995), *This N'
    That, Handwriting from a Wounded Heart* (Dinstuhl,
    1994), *Poet, New Laurel Rev, Anterior Bitewing,
    Papyrus*

Jeanne Mahon 🎤 ✈   P
84 Yankee Ridge Rd
Mercer, PA 16137-2644, 412-346-6466
    Pubs: *The Wolf in the Wood* (Pangborn Bks, 1996),
    *English Jrnl, Cimarron Rev, Creeping Bent, Cutbank,
    Pig Iron, West Branch*
Groups: Women, Seniors

Jody Mahorsky   P&W
128 Mauch Chunk St
Nazareth, PA 18064, 610-759-8341
    Pubs: *See of Tranquility, The Creative Spirit, Spirit of
    the Muse, First Time, Golden Isis, Prophetic Voices,
    Cosmic Trend, Poetry Peddler, Me 2*

Jerre Mangione   W
3300 Darby Rd, #7315
Haverford, PA 19041-1075, 610-649-9609
    Pubs: *The Dream & the Deal: Federal Writers' Project*
    (U Pennsylvania Pr, 1983), *La Storia: Anth* (HC, 1992),
    VIA

Charles Edward Mann 🎤 ✈   P
PO Box 752
Langhorne, PA 19047, 215-943-3398
    Pubs: *After the Pledge of Allegiance* (Pudding Hse,
    2000), *American Poetry Rev, Threepenny Rev, Cream
    City Rev, Southern Humanities Rev, Greensboro Rev,
    NYQ*

Joanne M. Marinelli   P&W
158 N 23 St, Apt 514
Philadelphia, PA 19103
    Pubs: *Like Fire* (Crawlspace Pr, 1988), *Onionhead Lit
    Qtly, G.W. Rev, South Carolina Rev, Poetpourri,
    Pendragon, Parnassus Lit Jrnl.*

Gigi Marino   P
620 Devonshire Dr
State College, PA 16803, 814-234-7834
    Pubs: *Catholic Boys & Girls: Anth, Catholic Girls: Anth*
    (Penguin/NAL, 1994, 1992), *Willow Springs, Graham
    Hse Rev, South Florida Poetry Rev*

Paul Raymond Martin   P&W
18304 Porky St
Saegertown, PA 16433-9442, 814-763-1549
    Pubs: *Robo Frog: Killer Frog Anth* (Scavenger's
    Newsletter, 1993), *New Thought Jrnl, Gotta Write,
    Oceana, Eclipse*

Hilary Masters ⚲ ⊀ W
Carnegie Mellon Univ, Dept of English, Pittsburgh, PA
15213, 412-268-6443
Pubs: *In Montaigne's Tower* (U Missouri Pr, 2000),
Home Is the Exile (Permanent Pr, 1996), *Success: New
& Selected Stories* (St. Martin's, 1992, 1989), *Last
Stands: Notes from Memory* (David R. Godine, 1982),
Sewanee, NAR, Ohio Rev, Virginia Qtly Rev

Dawna M. Maydak P
Hickory On The Green, 7074 Clubview Dr, South Fayette,
PA 15017-1097
Pubs: *Ten: Poems* (R&R Pr, 1988), *Because the Death
of a Rose* (Earthwise Pub, 1983), *Eleven*

Jane McCafferty W
Allegheny College, Meadville, PA 16335
Pubs: *Director of the World* (U Pitt Pr, 1992), *Story,
Seattle Rev, West Branch, Alaska Qtly Rev*

Dorothy McCartney P&W
PO Box 29
Westtown, PA 19395
Pubs: *Lemmus Lemmus & Other Poems* (Branden Pr,
1973), *Poet Lore, Modern Haiku, Storytime*

Mark McCloskey P
663 Parkview Rd
Yeardon, PA 19050
Pubs: *Sometime the Cow Kick Your Head: Anth, Light
Year '87: Anth* (Bits Pr, 1988, 1987), *Poetry NW, Zone
3, Poetry/L.A., American Literary Rev*

Leslie Anne Mcilroy ⚲ ⊀ P
333 Pitt St, #2
Pittsburgh, PA 15221-3332, 412-241-2049
Internet: lesanne@ix.netcom.com
Pubs: *Gravel* (Slipstream, 1997), *American Poetry: Anth*
(Carnegie Mellon U Pr, 2000), *E: Emily Dickinson
Award Anth* (Universities West Pr, 1999), *MacGuffin,
Main St Rag, ACM, Ledge*

Louis McKee ⚲ ⊀ P
PO Box 11186
Philadelphia, PA 19136-6186, 215-331-7389
Internet: lmckee4148@aol.com
Pubs: *Right As Rain* (Nova Hse, 2000), *River
Architecture* (Cynic Pr, 1999), *The True Speed of
Things* (Nightshade Pr, 1990), *The New Geography of
Poets: Anth* (U Arkansas, 1992), *APR, Tar River Rev,
Lowell Rev*

Frank McQuilkin P
1708 S 16 St
Philadelphia, PA 19145
Pubs: *Southern Humanities Rev, San Jose Studies,
America, Painted Bride Qtly, Sparrow*

Robert Randolph Medcalf, Jr. P&W
185 N Main St, Apt 6, PO Box 746, Biglerville, PA 17307,
717-677-7437
Internet: bobmedcalfjr@blazenet.net
Pubs: *Eldritch Tales, Argonaut, Weirdbook, Beyond*

Diane Hamill Metzger P&W
c/o Caldwells, 240 W Ridley Ave, Norwood, PA 19074
Pubs: *Coralline Ornaments* (Weed Patch Pr, 1980),
*Pearl, South Coast Poetry Jrnl, Collages & Bricolages,
Anima, Philadelphia Poets, Hob-Nob, Long Islander*

Ann E. Michael ⚲ ⊀ P
2380 Brunner Rd
Emmaus, PA 18049
Internet: juanitafb@aol.com
Pubs: *The Swan King* (Limbo Bar & Grill, 1983),
Essential Love: Anth (Grayson Bks/Poetworks, 2000),
*Natural Bridge, Buckle &, Manhattan Rev, Painted Bride
Qtly, Pinchpenny, Cottonwood, Thema, Onset Rev,
Minimus, Amaranth*
Groups: Teenagers, Schools

David Milton W
3210 Garbett St
McKeesport, PA 15132

John Paul Minarik PW
1600 Walters Mill Rd
Somerset, PA 15510-0005, 724-847-9575
Internet: minarikl@asme.org
Pubs: *Past the Unknown, Remembered Gate*
(Greenfield Rev, 1981), *Pittsburgh & Tri-State Area
Poets: Anth* (Squirrel Hill Poetry Wkshp, 1992),
Confrontation

Carol Artman Montgomery P
3 Marshall Rd
Pittsburgh, PA 15214-2601, 412-231-7247
Pubs: *Starting Something* (Los Hombres Pr, 1992),
Outlines (Swamp Pr, 1990)

Dinty W. Moore ⚲ ⊀ W
916 26th Ave
Altoona, PA 16601, 814-949-5154
Pubs: *Toothpick Men* (Mammoth 1999), *The Accidental
Buddhist, The Emperor's Virtual Clothes* (Algonquin,
1997, 1995), *Catholic Girls: Anth* (Plume/Penguin,
1992), *Arts & Letters, Georgia Rev, Southern Rev, Iowa
Rev, Beloit Fiction Jrnl*

Edwin Moses W
1625 Almond St
Williamsport, PA 17701, 717-323-6496
Pubs: *Nine Sisters Dancing* (Fithian Pr, 1996),
Astonishment of Heart, One Smart Kid (MacMillan,
1984, 1982)

P. D. Murphy   P
English Dept, Univ Pennsylvania, Indiana, PA 15705
    Pubs: *CQ, Pinchpenny, Kindling, Gold Dust, Poetry
    Rev, Taurus, Asylum, Sonoma Mandala*

Manini Nayar   W
512 Brittany Dr
State College, PA 16803
    Pubs: *London Mag, Signals, Stand Mag, Malahat Rev,
    Parnassus*

Kirk Nesset ♦ ✈   P&W
Allegheny College, Dept of English, Meadville, PA 16335,
814-332-4331
    Pubs: *Antioch Rev, Chelsea, Cimarron Rev, Fiction,
    Folio, Green Mountains Rev, Hawaii Rev, Mudfish,
    NER, Nimrod, Paris Rev, Ploughshares, Poet Lore,
    Prarie Schooner, Seattle Rev, Spoon River Poetry Rev,
    Witness*

Felice Newman   P
Cleis Press, PO Box 8933, Pittsburgh, PA 15221,
412-937-1555
    Pubs: *The Second Coming* (Alyson, 1996), *Herotica 5:
    Anth* (Down There Pr, 1997)

Joseph Nicholson   P&W
RR3 Box 396E
Mill Hall, PA 17751-9519, 717-726-7635
    Pubs: *The Dam Builder* (Fault Pr, 1977), *Missouri Rev,
    West Branch, New Letters, Mississippi Rev, Poetry
    Now, Wormwood Rev*

Ed Ochester ♦ ✈   P
RD1, Box 174
Shelocta, PA 15774-9511, 724-354-4753
Internet: edochester@yourinter.net
    Pubs: *Land of Cockaigne* (Story Line Pr, 2001), *Snow
    White Horses* (Autumn Hse Pr, 2000), *Nation, Virginia
    Qtly Rev, Third Coast, Tin House, Ploughshares, Prairie
    Schooner, Poetry, Pearl*

Richard R. O'Keefe   P
PO Box 10506
State College, PA 16805
    Pubs: *Rumors of Autumn* (Hierophant Bks, 1984),
    Uccello's Horse (Three Rivers Pr, 1972)

Toby Olson ♦ ✈   P&W
275 S 19 St, Ste 7
Philadelphia, PA 19103-5710
    Pubs: *Human Nature* (New Directions, 2000), *Write
    Letter to Billy* (Coffee Hse, 2000), *Dorit in Lesbos* (Sun
    & Moon Pr, 1998), *At Sea* (S&S, 1993), *Unfinished
    Building* (Coffee Hse, 1993), *Seaview* (New Directions,
    1982), *Conjunctions, Gettysburg Rev*

Rebecca Ore   W
3511 Baring St, #3C
Philadelphia, PA 19104-2416
    Pubs: *Alien Bootlegger & Other Stories, The Illegal
    Rebirth of Billy the Kid, Being Alien* (Tor Bks, 1993,
    1991, 1989)

Peter Oresick   P
6342 Jackson St
Pittsburgh, PA 15206-2232, 412-741-6860 x411
Internet: poresick@aol.com
    Pubs: *For a Living: Anth* (U Illinois Pr, 1995),
    Pittsburgh Book of Contemporary American Poetry: Anth
    (U Pitt Pr, 1993)

Gil Ott ♦ ✈   P
Singing Horse Press, PO Box 40034, Philadelphia, PA
19106-0034, 215-844-7678
Internet: singinghorse@erols.com
    Pubs: *Traffic, Wheel* (Chax, 2000, 1992), *The Whole
    Note* (Zasterle, 1997), *Public Domain* (Potes & Poets,
    1989)

Karl Patten ♦ ✈   P
232 S 3 St
Lewisburg, PA 17837-1912, 717-522-0070
    Pubs: *Touch* (Bucknell U Pr, 1998), *The Impossible
    Reaches* (Dorcas Pr, 1992), *Yarrow, Amer Literary Rev,
    5 A.M., Graham Hse Rev, Pikeville Rev, Connecticut
    Rev, Mississippi Valley Rev, Cincinnati Poetry Rev,
    Greensboro Rev, Sucarnochee Rev*

Jean Pearson   P
PO Box 417
Bethlehem, PA 18016, 215-867-6447
    Pubs: *On Speaking Terms with Earth* (Great Elm Pr,
    1988), *Earth Prayers Anth, APR*

Pamela M. Perkins-Frederick   P
PO Box F-3
Feasterville, PA 19053-0003, 215-757-7229
    Pubs: *A Leaf Gnawed to Lace* (Petoskey Stone Pr,
    1992), *Medical Heritage, Other Poetry, BPJ, Images,
    The Sun*

James A. Perkins   P&W
Westminster College, Box 62, New Wilmington, PA 16172,
412-946-7347
    Pubs: *Snakes, Butterbeans, & the Discovery of
    Electricity* (Dawn Valley Pr, 1990), *Southern Rev,
    Footwork, U.S. 1 Worksheets, Mississippi Rev*

Walt Peterson   P
5837 Beacon St
Pittsburgh, PA 15217, 412-422-8129
    Pubs: *Image Song* (Seton Hill College, 1994),
    Rebuilding the Porch (Nightshade Pr, 1990), *Potato
    Eyes, Pittsburgh Qtly, Language Bridges, Samisdat*

Natalie L. M. Petesch W
6320 Crombie St
Pittsburgh, PA 15217-2511, 412-521-2802
  Pubs: *The Immigrant Train & Other Stories, Justina of
Andalusia & Other Stories* (Swallow Pr/Ohio U Pr,
1996, 1990), *Kansas Qtly, Chariton Rev, Confrontation*

Anthony Petrosky P
1109 DeVictor Pl
Pittsburgh, PA 15206, 412-361-5783
  Pubs: *Red & Yellow Boat* (LSU, 1994), *Georgia Rev,
Bastard Rev, Prairie Schooner, College English*

Sanford Pinsker 🎤 ✈ P
Franklin and Marshall College, English Dept, Lancaster,
PA 17603, 717-393-1483
  Pubs: *Sketches of Spain, Local News* (Plowman Pr,
1992, 1989), *Whales at Play* (Northwoods Pr, 1986),
Georgia Rev, Salmagundi, Centennial Rev

Kenneth Pobo P
123 Folsom Ave
Folsom, PA 19033
  Pubs: *A Barbaric Yawp on the Rocks Please* (Alpha
Beat Pr, 1996), *Ravens & Bad Bananas* (Osric Pubs,
1995), *Atlanta Rev, James White Rev*

Chaim Potok W
20 Berwick Rd
Philadelphia, PA 19131
  Pubs: *Davita's Harp, Book of Lights, Wanderings*
(Knopf, 1985, 1981, 1978)

David Poyer W
James Allen Agency, 538 E Harford St, Box 278, Milford,
PA 18337
  Pubs: *Tomahawk, The Passage* (St. Martin's Pr, 1998,
1995), *As the Wolf Loves Winter* (Forge, 1996), *Winter
in the Heart* (Tor, 1993)

Claudia M. Reder P
134 Edgehill Rd
Bala Cynwyd, PA 19004
  Pubs: *Chester H. Jones Anth* (Chester H. Jones Fdn,
1985), *Pennsylvania Rev, Nimrod, Quarry West, Kansas
Qtly, Poet Lore, NAR, Intl Qtly, Poetry NW, Literary
Rev*

Jad Reilly 🎤 ✈ P
2842 E Devereaux Ave
Philadelphia, PA 19149-3013, 215-289-3659
  Pubs: *Mozart Park* (Nightlight Pr, 1984), *Poets Theater:
Anth* (H&H Pr, 2000), *CPU Rev, Aloha, Impetus*

Barbara Reisner P
3026 Congress St
Allentown, PA 18104, 610-439-1610
  Pubs: *Poems* (Creeping Bent Pr, 1993), *MPR, Laurel
Rev, Blue Buildings, Shirim, Graham Hse Rev, Yarrow,
Wind, Bellingham Rev, River Styx*

John Repp 🎤 ✈ P
26598 Arneman Rd
Edinboro, PA 16412-5202
Internet: jrepp@edinboro.edu
  Pubs: *Things Work Out* (Palanquin Pr, 1998), *Thirst
Like This* (U Missouri Pr, 1990), *Puerto del Sol, Iowa
Rev, Greensboro Rev, Many Mountains Moving*

Michael D. Riley 🎤 ✈ P
1705 Lititz Pike
Lancaster, PA 17601-6509, 717-569-6377
Internet: mdr1@psu.edu
  Pubs: *Circling the Stones* (Creighton U Pr, 2000),
Scrimshaw: Citizens of Bone (Lightning Tree Pr, 1988),
*Poetry, Fiddlehead, Cumberland Poetry Rev, Poetry
Ireland Rev, Farmer's Market, Zone 3*
I.D.: Irish-American

Len Roberts P
2443 Wassergass Rd
Hellertown, PA 18055, 610-838-6716
  Pubs: *The Trouble-Making Finch, Counting the Black
Angels* (U Illinois Pr, 1998, 1994), *Dangerous Angels*
(Copper Beech Pr, 1993), *Partisan Rev, APR, Paris
Rev, Poetry, Hudson Rev, Georgia Rev*

Margaret A. Robinson P
Widener Univ, Chester, PA 19013
  Pubs: *A Woman of Her Tribe* (Fawcett, 1992), *Courting
Emma Howe* (Ballantine, 1989)

Rosaly DeMaios Roffman 🎤 ✈ P
English Dept, Indiana Univ Pennsylvania, Indiana, PA
15701, 412-349-2296
  Pubs: *Going to Bed Whole* (University Pr IV, 1993), *I
Am Becoming the Woman I've Wanted: Anth*
(Papier-Mache Pr, 1997), *Life on the Line: Anth*
(Negative Capability Pr, 1992), *A Gathering of Poets:
Anth* (Kent State U, 1992), *MacGuffin*

Judith Root P
Carnegie Mellon Univ Press, PO Box 21, Pittsburgh, PA
15213, 412-268-2861
  Pubs: *Weaving the Sheets* (Carnegie Mellon U Pr,
1988), *The Paris Rev Anth* (Norton, 1990), *Nation,
Commonweal, William & Mary Rev, Tar River Poetry,
Poetry, APR, New Republic*

Judith Rose 🎤 ✈ P&W
Allegheny College
Meadville, PA 16335
Internet: jrose@alleg.edu
    Pubs: *Prairie Schooner, Indiana Rev, Iowa Rev, Virginia Qtly Rev, Equinox, Carbuncle*
Groups: Women, Prisoners

Savina Roxas P
265 Sleepy Hollow
Pittsburgh, PA 15216, 412-561-3557
    Pubs: *Sacrificial Mix* (P. Gaglia Inc, 1992), *The Art of Life: Anth* (South Western Educational Pub, 1998), *Footwork: Paterson Lit Rev Anth* (Passaic Comm College, 1995), *For She Is the Tree of Life: Grandmothers Anth* (Conari Pr, 1994), *Whole Notes*

Gibbons Ruark 🎤 ✈ P
45 Morgan Hollow Way
Landenberg, PA 19350-1048, 610-255-3454
Internet: gruark@udel.edu
    Pubs: *Passing Through Customs, Rescue the Perishing* (LSU Pr, 1999, 1991), *Keeping Company* (Johns Hopkins, 1983), *New Republic, Shenandoah*

Sonia Sanchez P
Temple Univ, English Dept, Philadelphia, PA 19122, 215-787-1796
    Pubs: *Under a Soprano Sky* (Africa World, 1987), *Homegirls & Handgrenades* (Thunder's Mouth, 1984)

Walter Sanders W
266 Burley Ridge Rd
Mansfield, PA 16933
    Pubs: *Four-Minute Fictions: Anth* (WordBeat Pr, 1988), *NAR, West Branch, North Dakota Qtly*

Judy Schaefer 🎤 ✈ P
PO Box 90153
Harrisburg, PA 17109-0153, 717-651-0519
Internet: jschaefer@mindspring.com
    Pubs: *Harvesting the Dew* (Vista, 1997), *Between the Heartbeats* (U Iowa Pr, 1995), *Academic Medicine, Amer Jrnl of Nursing, Pediatric Nursing, The Lancet*

Peter Schneeman W
English Dept, Pennsylvania State Univ, 104 Burrowes Bldg, University Park, PA 16802, 814-865-6381
    Pubs: *Through the Finger Goggles: Stories* (U Missouri Pr, 1982), *Americas Rev, Salmagundi*

Michael Schneider 🎤 ✈ P
119 Gordon St
Pittsburgh, PA 15218-1605, 412-371-4523
    Pubs: *Sycamore Rev, Forklift Ohio, Yawp, Poet, Antietam Rev, Pittsburgh Qtly, Savannah Literary Jrnl, Notre Dame Rev, Atlanta Rev, Heart Qtly*

Adam Schonbrun P
English Dept, Pennsylvania State Univ, 103 Burrowes Bldg, University Park, PA 16802, 814-867-8735
    Pubs: *Not Always About Some People* (Ben-Adam, 1989), *We Held Each Other's Hand* (Haifa U, 1987)

Joel L. Schwartz W
1245 Highland Ave, Ste 202
Abington, PA 19001-3714
    Pubs: *Upchuck Summer's Revenge* (Delacorte, 1990), *The Great Spaghetti Showdown* (Dell, 1988)

Rhoda Josephson Schwartz P&W
1901 JFK Blvd, #2321
Philadelphia, PA 19103-1520, 215-563-3768
    Pubs: *Worlds of Literature: Anth* (Norton, 1994, 1989), *Chicago Rev, Nation, Kansas Qtly, APR*

Ruth Knafo Setton W
4759 Huckleberry Rd
Orefield, PA 18069
    Pubs: *Out of the Margins: Anth* (U Pr of New England, 1996), *Follow My Footprints: Anth* (Brandeis U Pr, 1992), *Mediterraneans, Intl Qtly, Lilith*

Kathleen M. Sewalk P
3589 Menoher Blvd
Johnston, PA 15905-5505
    Pubs: *Along the Way, Singing of Fruit, Generations of Excellence, On Holiday, Past the Conemaugh Yards* (Tunnel Pr Ltd, 1996, 1996, 1993, 1992, 1987)

Dr. M. P. A. Sheaffer 🎤 ✈ P
Millersville Univ, Humanities Division, Millersville, PA 17551
    Pubs: *Requiem Suite, Still a Miracle* (Millersville U Pr, 1992, 1987), *Moonrocks & Metaphysical Turnips* (MAF Pr, 1988), *Lacquer Birds & Leaves of Brass* (Four Seasons Pr, 1986), *Perspectives on Women: Anth* (Women's Ctr, Millersville U, 1995)

Ron Silliman P
262 Orchard Rd
Paoli, PA 19301-1116, 610-251-2214
    Pubs: *Xing* (Meow, 1996), *N/O* (Roof, 1994), *Toner* (Potes & Poets, 1993), *Jones* (Generator Pr, 1993), *Paris Rev, Poetry, Sulfur, Iowa Rev, Zyzzyva, Conjunctions, Object, Mirage, Grist On-Line, Object Permanence*

Randall Silvis W
PO Box 297
St Petersburg, PA 16054, 724-659-2922
    Pubs: *Dead Man Falling* (Carroll & Graf, 1996), *An Occasional Hell* (Permanent Pr, 1993), *Manoa, Destination Discovery, Pittsburgh Mag, CSM, Prism Intl*

Michael Simms 🎤 ✈   P
219 Bigham St
Pittsburgh, PA 15211-1431
Internet: simms@duq.edu
    Pubs: *The Fire-eater* (Del Rogers, 1987), *Migration*
(Breitenbush, 1985), *Café Rev, Mid-American Rev, West
Branch, SW Rev, Black Warrior Rev, 5 A.M., Pittsburgh
Qtly*

David R. Slavitt 🎤 ✈   P&W
523 S 41 St
Philadelphia, PA 19104-4501, 215-382-3994
    Pubs: *Falling from Silence, Ps3569.L3, A Gift* (LSU Pr,
2001, 1998, 1996), *A Crown for the King, Sixty-One
Psalms of David* (Oxford U Pr, 1998, 1996), *NER,
Pequod, Shenandoah, Partisan Rev*
I.D.: Jewish

Deloris Slesiensky   P&W
74 Dug Rd
Wyoming, PA 18644-9374
    Pubs: *Wild Onions, Plaza, Mobius, Psychopoetica,
Moments in Time, Pittston Thursday Dispatch*

David Small 🎤 ✈   W
532 Grandview Ave
Camp Hill, PA 17011-1812, 717-763-8328
    Pubs: *Alone, The River in Winter, Almost Famous*
(Norton, 1991, 1987, 1982)

Ronald F. Smits   P
Box 466
Ford City, PA 16226, 412-763-7024
    Pubs: *Mourning Dove* (Ball State U Pr, 1979), *Tar
River Poetry, Wilderness, Puerto del Sol, Free Lunch,
Connecticut River Rev, The Bridge*

Judith Sornberger   P
141 S Main St
Mansfield, PA 16933, 717-662-7735
    Pubs: *BiFocals Barbie: A Midlife Pantheon, Judith
Beheading Holofernes* (Talent Hse Pr, 1996, 1993),
Open Heart (Calyx Bks, 1993), *Prairie Schooner, Puerto
del Sol, West Branch, American Voice, Calyx, Hawaii
Pacific Rev*

Eileen Spinelli   P
Ray Lincoln, 7900 Old York Rd, 107B, Elkins Park, PA
19027
    Pubs: *Somebody Loves You, Mr. Hatch* (Bradbury,
1990), *A Room of One's Own, Muse, Footwork*

Will Stanton   W
925 Wilhelm Rd
Harrisburg, PA 17111, 717-564-1881
    Pubs: *The Old Familiar Booby Traps of Home*
(Doubleday, 1977), *New Yorker, Atlantic, Redbook*

Laurence Stapleton   P
229 N Roberts Rd
Bryn Mawr, PA 19010
    Pubs: *Some Poets & Their Resources: Anth* (U Pr
America, 1995), *Poetry Now*

Sharon Sheehe Stark   P&W
23 Blue Rocks Rd
Lenhartsville, PA 19534, 610-756-6048
    Pubs: *Wrestling Season, The Dealer's Yard & Other
Stories* (Morrow, 1987, 1985), *Atlantic*

Irving Stettner   P
RR2, Box 280
Harveys Lake, PA 18618
    Pubs: *Beggars in Paradise* (Writers Unlimited, 1991),
Self-Portrait (Sun Dog, 1991), *Anais, World Letter*

Alex Stiber   P
1133 Sunrise Dr
Pittsburgh, PA 15243-1945
    Pubs: *American Voice, Stone Country, Long Pond Rev,
Fiddlehead, Event, Louisville Rev*

Adrienne Su 🎤 ✈   P
English Dept, Dickinson College, PO Box 1773, Carlisle,
PA 17013-2896, 717-245-1347
Internet: ajsu@aol.com
    Pubs: *Middle Kingdom* (Alice James Bks, 1997), *New
American Poets: Anth* (U Pr of New England, 2000)
Best American Poetry: Anth (Scribner, 2000), *Crab
Orchard Rev, Indiana Rev, New Letters, Massachusetts
Rev, Prairie Schooner, Greensboro Rev*

John Taggart   P
295 E Creek Rd
Newburg, PA 17240, 717-423-5565
    Pubs: *Poems for the New Millennium: Anth* (U
California Pr, 1998), *Crosses* (Sun & Moon, 1998),
*Conjunctions, Five Fingers Rev, Hambone, Sulfur,
Talisman, To, Chicago Rev*

Charles A. Taormina   P&W
103 Camden Ave
Johnstown, PA 15904, 724-925-3254
    Pubs: *Moments* (1st Bks, 1998), *Rain Folio*
(Renaissance Workshop, 1998), *Blue Ridge Rev,
Gargoyle, William & Mary Rev, Samisdat, Fool's Jrnl*

Marcia M. Tarasovic   P
PO Box 10334
State College, PA 16805
    Pubs: *Piedmont Lit Rev, Touchstone, Wind, Mill Hunk
Herald, Interstate, Portland Rev*

Myron Taube   W
English Dept, Univ Pittsburgh, Pittsburgh, PA 15260,
412-624-6532
    Pubs: *Kansas Qtly, Texas Qtly, Wind, Cimarron Rev*

John Alfred Taylor   P
395 N Wade Ave
Washington, PA 15301, 412-228-0968
    Pubs: *Year's Best Horror Stories: Anth* (Daw, 1983),
    West Branch, New Letters, Twilight Zone Mag

Robert Love Taylor, Jr. ⚲ ✈   W
English Dept, Bucknell Univ, Lewisburg, PA 17837,
570-577-1440
Internet: www.facstaff.bucknell.edu/rtaylor
    Pubs: *Lady of Spain, The Lost Sister* (Algonquin Bks,
    1992, 1989), *Southern Rev, Hudson Rev, Shenandoah,
    Georgia Rev*

Philip Terman ⚲ ✈   P
4606 Scrubgrass Rd
Grove City, PA 16127-8716, 814-786-7270
Internet: terman@clarion.edu
    Pubs: *The House of Sages* (Mammoth Pr, 1998), *What
    Survives* (Sow's Ear Pr, 1993), *Poetry, Kenyon Rev,
    NER, NAR, Poetry NW, SPR*
I.D.: Jewish. Groups: Seniors, Prisoners

Elaine Terranova ⚲ ✈   P
1912 Panama St
Philadelphia, PA 19103
Internet: eterranova@ccp.cc.pa.us
    Pubs: *Damages* (Copper Canyon Pr, 1996), *The Cult of
    the Right Hand* (Doubleday, 1991), Sixty *Years of Amer
    Poetry: Anth* (Harry Abrams, 1997), *A Gift of Tongues:
    Anth* (Copper Canyon, 1996), *APR, Boulevard, Antioch
    Rev, New Yorker, River Styx, Virginia Qtly Rev*
Groups: Seniors, Women

Heather Thomas ⚲ ✈   P&W
Kutztown Univ, English Dept, Kutztown, PA 19530,
610-683-4337
Internet: hthomas@kutztown.edu
    Pubs: *Practicing Amnesia* (Singing Horse Pr, 2000),
    The Fray (Kutztown Pub, 2000), *Circus Freex* (Standing
    Stones Pr/Pine Pr, 1995), *Voiceunders* (Texture Pr,
    1993), *Five Fingers Rev, Chain, Key Satch(el),
    Itsyncast, Endless Mtns Rev, Big Allis, 6ix, Texture*

John A. Thompson, Sr. ⚲ ✈   P
137 Pointview Rd
Pittsburgh, PA 15227-3131, 412-885-3798
Internet: nitewriterarts@aol.com
    Pubs: *Medicinal Purposes, Droplet Jrnl, Poetic Soul,
    Broken Streets, Writer's Info, Green Feather, Wind Mag,
    Parnassus Lit Jrnl, Haiku Zasshi Zo, Prophetic Voices*

Sharon Thomson ⚲ ✈   PP&P
5401 Woodcrest Ave
Philadelphia, PA 19131-1331, 215-877-5628
Internet: sharonthomson@juno.com
    Pubs: *Home Again* (Pudding Hse, 2000), *Many Lights
    in Many Windows: Anth, Writer's Community: Anth*
    (Milkweed Edtns, 1997, 1997), *Grailville Poets: Anth*
    (Grailville, 1995), *Yrbk of Amer Poetry: Anth* (Monitor,
    1985), *Aspect, Poetry, Pequod, Christopher St*
Groups: Health-Related, Spiritual/Religious

J. C. Todd ⚲ ✈   P
339 S 4 St
Philadelphia, PA 19106-4219, 215-625-2449
    Pubs: *Nightshade, Entering Pisces* (Pine Pr, 1995,
    1984), *Meridian Bound: Anth* (Meridian Writers Coll,
    2000), *Paris Rev, Virginia Qtly Rev, Prairie Schooner,
    Puerto del Sol, BPJ*
Groups: Seniors, Schools

Ronald Tranquilla ⚲ ✈   P&W
Saint Vincent College, 300 Fraser Purchase Rd, Latrobe,
PA 15650-2690, 724-539-9761
Internet: tranquil@acad1.stvincent.edu
    Pubs: *Loyalhanna Rev, New Rev, West Branch, Great
    Stream Rev, Violent Milk, Marginal Rev, Hollins Critic,
    Rocky Mtn Rev, Small Pond Mag, Monmouth Rev,
    Haiku Highlights, New American & Canadian Poetry*

Tommy Trantino   W
Writers Unlimited, Inc, Box 280, Rte 2, Harveys Lake, PA
18618, 717-675-3447
    Pubs: *Lock the Lock* (Bantam, 1975), *Village Voice,
    People Mag, Stroker Mag*

Lee Upton ⚲ ✈   P
English Dept, Lafayette College, Easton, PA 18042,
610-330-5250
Internet: uptonlee@lafayette.edu
    Pubs: *Civilian Histories* (U Georgia, 2000), *Approximate
    Darling* (U Georgia, 1996), *No Mercy* (Atlantic Monthly,
    1989), *APR, Field, Yale Rev, Poetry*

Richard Vance   P&W
525C W 28 Div Hwy
Lititz, PA 17543
    Pubs: *Literary Rev, Poetry Wales, Poetry Australia,
    Oxford Mag, Karamu, Green Fuse Poetry*

William F. Vanwert   P&W
7200 Cresheim Rd, #C-1
Philadelphia, PA 19119, 215-248-4715
    Pubs: *Missing in Action* (York Pr, 1991), *The Discovery
    of Chocolate* (Word Beat Pr, 1987), *TriQtly, NAR,
    Western Humanities Rev, Chelsea, Boulevard, Georgia
    Rev*

Jack Veasey   P
37-A W 2nd St
Hummelstown, PA 17036, 717-566-9237
    Pubs: *Tennis with Baseball Bats* (Warm Spring Pr,
    1995), *A Loving Testimony: Anth* (Crossing Pr, 1995),
    Christopher St, Pittsburgh Qtly, Oxalis

Karen Volkman 🎤 ✈   P
U of Pittsburgh, 526 Cathedral of Learning, Pittsburgh, PA
15260, 412-422-2776
   Pubs: *Crash's Law* (Norton, 1996), *The Bread Loaf
Anthology of New American Poets* (U Prs of New
England, 2000), *New American Poets: Anth* (S Illinois U
Pr, 2000), *Best American Poetry 1996: Anth* (Scribner,
1996), *Paris Rev, New Republic, New American Writing*
Groups: College/Univ, Children

Jon Volkmer   P&W
English Dept, Ursinus College, Collegeville, PA 19426,
610-489-4111
   Pubs: *Painted Bride Qtly, Texas Rev, Folio, Dancing
Shadow Pr, South Dakota Rev, Crosscurrents, Carolina
Qtly, Hellas, Cimarron Rev, Prairie Schooner, Seattle
Rev*

Jeanne Murray Walker 🎤 ✈   P
742 S Latches Ln
Merion, PA 19066-1614
Internet: jwalker@udel.edu
   Pubs: *Gaining Time* (Copper Beech, 1998), *Stranger
Than Fiction* (QRL, 1993), *Coming Into History, Nailing
Up the Home Sweet Home* (Cleveland St U Pr, 1990,
1980), *APR, Poetry, Nation, Partisan Rev, Georgia Rev*
Groups: Spiritual/Religious, Women

T. H. S. Wallace 🎤 ✈   P
3032 Logan St
Camp Hill, PA 17011-2947, 717-780-2487
Internet: thswallace@safeconnect.com
   Pubs: *When the World's Foundation Shifts, Raw on the
Bars of Longing* (Rabbit Pr, 1998, 1994), *None Were
So Clear* (New Foundation Pub, 1996), *Voices from the
Peace Tree: Anth* (Rabbit Pr, 2000), *Midwest Qtly,
Cumberland Poetry Rev*

Mark Thomas Wangberg   P
593 Hansell Rd
Wynnewood, PA 19096, 215-649-6007
   Pubs: *The Third Coast: Anth* (Wayne State U Pr,
1976), *U.S. 1, Poets, Bellingham Rev, 5 A.M., South
Dakota Rev*

Robert G. Weaver   W
Box 194, RD 1
Petersburg, PA 16669, 814-667-3530
   Pubs: *Just Pulp, Manhunt*

Frances Webb   W
406 Crescent Rd
Wyncote, PA 19095
   Pubs: *Confrontation, Iowa Rev, New Renaissance,
Antioch Rev, Literary Rev, Feminist Studies*

Bruce Weigl   P
English Dept, Burrowes Bldg, Pennsylvania State Univ,
University Park, PA 16802, 814-865-7105
   Pubs: *Sweet Lorrain, What Saves Us* (TriQtly Bks,
1996, 1992), *Song of Napalm* (Atlantic Monthly Pr,
1988), *The Monkey Wars* (U Georgia Pr, 1985), *TriQtly*

Sanford Weiss   P
542 Headquarters Rd
Ottsville, PA 18942, 610-847-2238
Internet: sweiss@epix.net
   Pubs: *Poetry, Kayak, Poetry Now, Yankee, BPJ*

William Welsh 🎤 ✈   P&W
501 Franklin St
East Pittsburgh, PA 15112-1109, 412-824-0679
Internet: grapie@stargate.net
   Pubs: *Being Pretty Doesn't Help at All* (Ancient Mariner
Pr, 1989), *You Can't Get There from Here* (Neumenon
Pr, 1986), *Maple Leaf Rag: Anth* (Portals Pr, 1995),
*New Orleans Rev, Interstate, Maple Leaf Rag, Slow
Loris Reader, Pittsburgh Qtly, Gravida*

Richard Wertime 🎤 ✈   W
Beaver College, English Dept, Glenside, PA 19038-3295,
215-572-2963
Internet: wertime@beaver.edu
   Pubs: *The Ploughshares Reader: Anth* (Pushcart, 1985),
NE Corridor, Centerstage, Hudson Rev, Ploughshares

Kimmika L. H. Williams 🎤 ✈   PP
Temple Univ, Anthropology Dept, Philadelphia, PA 19122,
215-204-8414
Internet: kwilli01@thunder.ocis.temple.edu
   Pubs: *Signs of the Time: Culture Pop, Epic Memory:
Places & Spaces I've Been, Envisioning a Sea of Dry
Bones, Mine Eyes Have Seen Into the Millennium: Anth*
(Three Goat Pr, 1999, 1995, 1994, 2000), *Di-Verse City
2000: Anth* (AIPF, 2000), *Hip Mama, Sisters*
Groups: Adults, Seniors

Maureen Williams   P&W
RD3, Box 3292
Uniondale, PA 18470, 717-679-2745
   Pubs: *A Loving Voice: Anth* (Charles Pr, 1992), *Women
of the 14th Moon: Anth* (Crossing Pr, 1991), *Keltic
Fringe, Black Mountain Rev, Endless Mountain Rev,
Broomstick*

Craig Williamson   W
English Dept, Swarthmore College, Swarthmore, PA
19081, 215-328-8152
   Pubs: *Feast of Creatures* (U Penn Pr, 1982), *Senghor's
Poems* (England; Rex Collings Ltd, 1976)

Eleanor Wilner 🎤 ✈   P
324 S 12 St
Philadelphia, PA 19107-5947, 215-546-4237
Internet: pophys@aol.com
   Pubs: *Reversing the Spell* (Copper Canyon, 1998),
   Otherwise, Sarah's Choice, Shekhinah (U Chicago Pr,
   1993, 1989, 1984)

Jet Wimp   P
Math & Computers Dept, Drexel Univ, Philadelphia, PA
19104, 215-895-2658
   Pubs: *Against Infinity* (Primary Pr, 1978), *The Drowning
   Place* (Moore College of Art, 1974)

Sarah Winston   W
1801 Morris Rd, #C-110
Blue Bell, PA 19422, 215-699-6045
   Pubs: *Summer Conference* (Cornwall Bks, 1990), *Of
   Apples & Oranges* (Perma Pr, 1990), *Not Yet Spring*
   (Golden Quill Pr, 1976), *Literary Rev*

Michael Wurster 🎤 ✈   P
PO Box 4279
Pittsburgh, PA 15203-0279, 412-481-7636
   Pubs: *The Snake Charmer's Daughter* (Elemenope,
   2000), *The Cruelty of the Desert* (Cottage Wordsmiths,
   1989), *5AM, Old Red Kimono, Pittsburgh Qtly, Bone &
   Flesh, Cape Rock, Bogg, Pleiades, Poet Lore*

Yvonne   P
c/o Chameleon Productions, Inc, Greene Street Artists
Corp, 5225 Greene St, #16, Philadelphia, PA 19144
   Pubs: *Iwilla/Rise, Iwilla/Scourge* (Chameleon Prods,
   1999, 1987), *An Ear to the Ground: Anth* (U Georgia,
   1989)

Robert Zaller 🎤 ✈   P
326 Bryn Mawr Ave
Bala Cynwyd, PA 19004-2822, 610-667-2224
   Pubs: *For Empedocles* (European Arts Center, 1996),
   Invisible Music (Mavridis Pr, 1988), *Lives of the Poet*
   (Barlenmir Hse, 1974), *Meridian Bound: Anth* (Meridian
   Writers Collective, 2000), *Ekphrasis, Sea Change, Mad
   Poets Rev, Schuylkill Valley Rev, Agenda*

Anne Yusavage Zellars   W
RD2, Box 403
Valencia, PA 16059, 412-898-3019
   Pubs: *Oxford Mag, South Carolina Rev, Room of One's
   Own, West Branch, Women's Qtly Rev, Bloodroot*

PUERTO RICO

David Dayton 🎤 ✈   P
580 Cruz Maria/Bellas Lomas
Mayaguez, PR 00682-7571, 787-833-9242
Internet: ddayton@caribe.net
   Pubs: *The Lost Body of Childhood* (Copper Beech,
   1979)

Jose Emilio Gonzalez   P
Univ Puerto Rico, Box 2-3056, Rio Piedras, PR 00931,
809-751-8266

E. W. Northnagel   P&W
PO Box 6155
San Juan, PR 00914-6155
   Pubs: *Twenty-Five for Tony* (Cibola Studio, 1968),
   Phase & Cycle, Pegasus Rev, CQ, Poetry Motel

Carmen Puigdollers   P&W
Condominio Francia #5E, 1551 Rosario St, Santurce, PR
00911, 809-721-8379
   Pubs: *Homenaje Poetico A Josemilio Gonzalez: Anth* (U
   Puerto Rico, 1993), *Interamericana, A Proposito Revista
   Literaria*

Magaly Quinones 🎤   P
PO Box 22269, University Stn
San Juan, PR 00931-2269, 787-764-0000
Internet: mquinone@rrpac.upr.clu.edu
   Pubs: *Suenos de Papel* (Editorial Universidad de Puerto
   Rico, 1996), *Razon de Lucha, Razon de Amor,
   Nombrar* (Editorial Mairena, 1989, 1985)

Etnairis Rivera   P
Arrigoitia 515
San Juan, PR 00918-2648, 787-765-2888
   Pubs: *Entre Ciudades Y Casi Paraisos, Canto De La
   Pachamama* (Instituto De Cultura Puertorriquena, 1995,
   1976), *Ruptures, East Meets the West*

RHODE ISLAND

Tom Ahern 🎤 ✈   P
16 High St, #4
Westerly, RI 02891, 401-596-8480

William Allen   P
118 Gibbs Ave
Newport, RI 02840, 401-842-0832
   Pubs: *Sevastopol: On Photos of War* (Xenos, 1997),
   The Man on the Moon (NYU/Persea Pr, 1987), *Iowa
   Rev, Newport Rev, Spazio Humano, Denver Qtly,
   Prairie Schooner, American Voice*

Mark Anderson   P
English Dept, Rhode Island College, 600 Mt Pleasant Ave,
Providence, RI 02908, 401-456-8804
    Pubs: *Serious Joy* (Orchises Pr, 1990), *The Broken
    Boat* (Ithaca Hse, 1978), *Poetry, Hudson Rev*

Randy Blasing   P
44 Benefit St
Providence, RI 02904, 401-351-1253
    Pubs: *Graphic Scenes, The Double House of Life, To
    Continue* (Persea Bks, 1994, 1989, 1983)

Cathleen Calbert   P
English Dept, Rhode Island College, 600 Mt Pleasant Ave,
Providence, RI 02908, 401-456-8678
    Pubs: *Bad Judgment* (Sarabande Bks, 1999), *Lessons
    in Space* (U Pr Florida, 1997), *My Summer As a Bride*
    (Riverstone Pr, 1995), *Best American Poetry: Anth*
    (S&S, 1995), *Paris Rev, Nation, New Republic, Hudson
    Rev, Ploughshares*

David Cashman   P
23 Burlington St
Providence, RI 02906
    Pubs: *Modern Haiku, Brussels Sprout*

Tom Chandler 🎤 ✈   P
44 Summit Ave
Providence, RI 02906, 401-831-1401
Internet: tchandle@bryant.edu
    Pubs: *Wingbones* (Signal Bks, 1997), *One Tree Forest,
    The Sound the Moon Makes As It Watches* (The Poet's
    Pr, 1992, 1988), *Poetry, Ontario Rev, Boulevard,
    Literary Rev, NYQ*

Martha Christina 🎤 ✈   P
17 Union St
Bristol, RI 02809
    Pubs: *Staying Found* (Fleur de Lis, 1997), *Crab
    Orchard Rev, Defined Providence, Connecticut Rev,
    Louisville Rev, Poets On, Prairie Schooner, Tar River
    Poetry, Zone 3*

Geoffrey D. Clark 🎤 ✈   W
PO Box 43
Bristol, RI 02809-0043, 401-245-4369
    Pubs: *Rabbit Fever, All the Way Home* (Avisson Pr,
    2000, 1997), *Jackdog Summer* (Hi Jinx Pr, 1996),
    Schooling the Spirit (Asylum Arts, 1993), *Ruffian on the
    Stairs* (Story Pr, 1988), *Witness, NE Corridor,
    Ploughshares, Mississippi Rev, Pittsburgh Qtly*

Thomas Cobb   P
Rhode Island College, English Dept, Providence, RI
02908, 401-456-8115
    Pubs: *Crazy Heart* (H&R, 1987), *We Shall Curse the
    Dead* (Desert First Works, 1976)

Leonard Cochran   P
Providence College
Providence, RI 02918-0001, 401-865-2358
    Pubs: *Formalist, Tennessee Qtly, Atlantic, Harvard Mag,
    America, Spirit, Yankee, Christian Century*

Patricia Cumming 🎤 ✈   P
Box 251
Adamsville, RI 02801, 508-636-2403
    Pubs: *Mother to Daughter, Daughter to Mother: Anth*
    (Feminist Pr, 1984), *Letter from an Outlying Province,
    Afterwards* (Alice James Bks, 1976, 1974), *ACM,
    Riverrun, Home Planet News, Crone's Nest, Timber
    Creek Rev*

Tina Marie Egnoski 🎤 ✈   P&W
43 Nisbet St, #2
Providence, RI 02906, 401-273-0529
    Pubs: *Life on the Line: Anth* (Negative Capability Pr,
    1992), *Cimarron Rev, Dark Horse Lit Rev, Hawaii Paific
    Rev, Louisville Rev, Clackamas Lit Rev, Fish Stories,
    Rhode Islander Mag, Cream City Rev, Laurel Rev,
    Rockford Rev, Mississippi Valley Rev*

Caroline Finkelstein   P
170 Westminister St
Providence, RI 02903
    Pubs: *Germany* (Carnegie Mellon U Pr, 1995), *Windows
    Facing East* (Dragon Gate, 1986), *APR, Poetry,
    Antioch, TriQtly, Virginia Qtly Rev, Willow Springs*

Forrest Gander   P
351 Nayatt Rd
Barrington, RI 02806-4336
    Pubs: *Science & Steepleflower* (New Directions, 1998),
    Deeds of Utmost Kindness (Wesleyan, 1994),
    Lynchburg (U Pitt Pr, 1993), *Conjunctions, Grand St,
    Sulfur, First Intensity, Southern Rev, APR*

Lora Jean Gardiner   P
25 Glenwood Dr
North Kingstown, RI 02852
    Pubs: *In Native Woods* (Rhode Island State Poetry
    Society, 1985), *Chrysalis, Green's Mag, Lyric*

Christopher Gilbert 🎤 ✈   P
56 Ardoene St
Providence, RI 02907-3409, 401-461-5707
Internet: cgilbert@bristol.mass.edu
    Pubs: *Across the Mutual Landscape* (Graywolf, 1984),
    *Massachusetts Rev, African-American Lit Rev, Urbanus,
    Crab Apple Rev, Graham Hse Rev, Ploughshares,
    Indiana Rev, William & Mary Rev, Callaloo*
I.D.: African-American, Progressive

Ann Harleman P&W
55 Summit Ave
Providence, RI 02906, 401-272-7987
  Pubs: *Bitter Lake* (Southern Methodist U Pr, 1996),
  Happiness (U Iowa Pr, 1994), *Virginia Qtly Rev,*
  American Fiction, Southern Rev, Ploughshares,
  Shenandoah

Michael S. Harper P
Brown Univ, Box 1852, Providence, RI 02912,
401-863-2393
  Pubs: *Honorable Amendments* (U Illinois Pr, 1994),
  Every Shut Eye Ain't Asleep: Anth (Little, Brown, 1994),
  New Yorker, Obsidian

Edwin Honig P
Brown Univ, Box 1852, Providence, RI 02912,
401-863-2393
  Pubs: *The Imminence of Love* (Texas Ctr for Writers
  Pr, 1993), *Always Astonished* (City Lights, 1986),
  Interrupted Praise (Scarecrow Pr, 1984), *Mentor Book*
  of Major American Poets: Anth (Penguin, 1983), *Alea,*
  City Lights Rev, Agni

Peter Johnson P&W
Providence College, English Dept, Providence, RI 02918
  Pubs: *I'm a Man* (Raincrow Pr, 1998), *Pretty Happy!*
  (White Pine Pr, 1997), *Verse, Epoch, Qtly West, North*
  Dakota Qtly, Field, Web Del Sol, Denver Qtly

Caroline Knox P
Box 245
Adamsville, RI 02801-0245, 508-636-4138
Internet: cbjknox@aol.com
  Pubs: *Sleepers Wake* (Timken Pubs, 1994), *To*
  Newfoundland (U Georgia Pr, 1989), *Poetry, American*
  Scholar, New Republic, Harvard, Verse, Paris Rev

Kathryn Kulpa W
49 Shangri-la Ln
Middletown, RI 02842
  Pubs: *Indigenous Fiction, Florida Rev, Asimov's, Parting*
  Gifts, Madison Rev, Minimus, Seventeen, Larcom Rev,
  Quality Women's Fiction

Betsy Lincoln 🎤 ✈ P
247 Fishing Cove Rd
Wickford, RI 02852, 401-295-5547
Internet: blincoln@netsense.net
  Pubs: *News of the Living* (Premier Poets Chapbook
  Series, 1999), *Further Along* (Arbor Pr, 1990),
  Momentary Stays (Weaver Pubs, 1976), *Sojourner, NE*
  Jrnl, Newport Rev, Crone's Nest
Groups: Children, Seniors

Peter Mandel P
239 Transit St
Providence, RI 02906, 401-831-5227
  Pubs: *If One Lived on the Equator* (Nightshade Pr,
  1993), *Harper's, Yankee, Poetry NW, Laurel Rev,*
  Pulpsmith, Dusty Dog

Susan Onthank Mates W
52 Bluff Rd
Barrington, RI 02806
  Pubs: *The Good Doctor* (U Iowa Pr, 1994), *Pushcart*
  Prize XIX Anth (Pushcart Pr, 1994), *TriQtly, NW Rev,*
  Sou'wester, Arkansas Rev

F. X. Mathews W
497 Old North Rd
Kingston, RI 02881, 401-789-7338
  Pubs: *The Frog in the Bottom of the Well, The*
  Concrete Judasbird (HM, 1971, 1968)

Edward McCrorie 🎤 ✈ P
English Dept, Providence College, Providence, RI 02918
  Pubs: *Needle Man* (Chestnut Hills Pr, 1999), *After a*
  Cremation (Thorpe Springs Pr, 1974), *Ariel, Confluence,*
  Tennessee Qtly, NE Corridor, New Press Literary Qtly,
  BPJ, Little Mag, Spirit

Robert McRoberts P
8 Emery Rd
Warren, RI 02885, 401-245-5321

Tom Ockerse P
37 Woodbury St
Providence, RI 02906, 401-331-0783
  Pubs: *T.O.P.* (Tom Ockerse Edtns, 1970), *The A-Z*
  Book (Colorcraft-Brussel Pub, 1969)

Lawrence T. O'Neill P
PO Box 284
Kenyon, RI 02836
  Pubs: *Daguerreotypes, With Fire & Smoke* (Shadow Pr,
  1991, 1976)

Jane Lunin Perel P
English Dept, Providence College, Providence, RI 02918,
401-865-2490
  Pubs: *The Sea Is Not Full* (Le'Dory Pub Hse, 1990),
  Blowing Kisses to the Sharks (Copper Beech Pr, 1978),
  Alembic, 13th Moon, Poetry NW, Carolina Qtly, The
  Voice, West Coast Writer's Conspiracy, Choice,
  Massachusetts Rev

Paul Petrie P
200 Dendron Rd
Peace Dale, RI 02879, 401-783-8644
  Pubs: *The Runners* (Slow Loris Pr, 1988), *Strange*
  Gravity (Tidal Pr, 1984), *Atlantic, Poetry*

Nancy Potter   W
298 Hillsdale Rd
West Kingston, RI 02892, 401-539-2156
   Pubs: *Legacies* (U Illinois Pr, 1987), *Indiana Rev,*
Kansas Qtly, Cotton Boll, Paragraph, Alaska Qtly

Laurence J. Sasso, Jr.   P
145 Mann School Rd
Esmond, RI 02917, 401-231-1402
   Pubs: *The Olney Street Group Anth* (Olney Street Pr,
1989), *Italian-Americana, Texas Rev, Yankee, Santa Fe*
Literary Rev

John Shaw   W
28 Oaklawn St, #302
Cranston, RI 02920-9375, 401-944-5633
   Pubs: *Libido, New Renaissance, Turnstile, Brown Rev,*
NAR, Onion Head, New Oregon Rev, Phantasm,
Moosehead Rev, Spectrum, Back Bay View

Meredith Steinbach   W
English Dept, Brown Univ, Box 1852, Providence, RI
02912, 401-863-3526
Internet: meredith_steinbach@brown.edu
   Pubs: *The Birth of the World As We Know It; or*
Teiresias (Northwestern U Pr, 1996), *Zara* (TriQtly Bks,
1996), *Here Lies the Water* (Another Chicago Pr,
1990), *Prize Stories, 1990: The O. Henry Awards*
(Anchor, 1990), *Southwest Rev, Antioch Rev*

Nancy Sullivan   P
Hillsdale Rd
West Kingston, RI 02892, 401-539-2156
   Pubs: *Telling It* (Godine, 1976), *Treasury of English*
Short Stories: Anth (Doubleday, 1985), *Iowa Rev*

John Tagliabue 🎤 ✈   P
Wayland Manor Apt 412, 500 Angell St, Providence, RI
02906, 401-272-1766
   Pubs: *New & Selected Poems: 1942-1997* (National
Poetry Fdn, 1998), *The Great Day* (Alembic Pr, 1984),
The Doorless Door (Grossman, 1970), *American*
Scholar, Chelsea, NYQ, New Letters, Pacific Intl, Poetry
NW, Hudson Rev, Poetry, Kenyon Rev
Groups: College/Univ, Teenagers

Keith Waldrop   P
71 Elmgrove Ave
Providence, RI 02906, 401-863-3260
   Pubs: *The Locality Principle* (Avec, 1995), *Light While*
There Is Light (Sun & Moon, 1993), *The Opposite of*
Letting the Mind Wander (Lost Roads, 1990)

Rosmarie Waldrop 🎤 ✈   P
71 Elmgrove Ave
Providence, RI 02906-4132, 401-351-0015
   Pubs: *Reluctant Gravities, A Key Into the Language of*
America (New Directions, 1999, 1994), *Split Infinities*
(Singing Horse, 1998), *Another Language* (Talisman
Hse, 1997), *A Form/Of Taking/It All* (Station Hill, 1990),
Avec, Conjunctions, Grand St
Lang: German, French

Craig Watson 🎤 ✈   P
211 Conanicus Ave
Jamestown, RI 02835-1520, 401-423-2390
   Pubs: *Reason* (Zasterle, 1998), *Picture of the Picture of*
the Image in the Glass (O Pr, 1992), *Unsuspended*
Animation (Paradigm Pr, 1990), *After Calculus* (Burning
Deck, 1988)

Ed Weyhing 🎤 ✈   W
20 Murphy Cir
Middletown, RI 02842-6234, 401-846-1981
Internet: edweyhing@worldnet.att.net
   Pubs: *Generation to Generation: Anth* (Papier Mache
Pr, 1998), *How the Weather Was: Anth* (Ampersand Pr,
1990), *Short Story, Cimarron Rev, Witness, Glimmer*
Train, Crescent Rev, Nexus

Ruth Whitman   P
40 Tuckerman Ave
Middletown, RI 02842, 401-846-3737
   Pubs: *Hatshepsut, Speak to Me, Laughing Gas: New &*
Selected Poems (Wayne State U Pr, 1992, 1991), *New*
Republic, American Voice

Thomas Wilson   W
6 Bush St
Newport, RI 02840
   Pubs: *American Fiction, Ellery Queen, Paris Rev,*
Antaeus

C. D. Wright 🎤 ✈   P
351 Nayatt Rd
Barrington, RI 02806-4336, 401-245-8069
Internet: wrightcd@aol.com
   Pubs: *Deepstep Come Shining* (Copper Canyon, 1998),
Tremble (Ecco Pr, 1996), *Just Whistle* (Kelsey St Pr,
1993), *String Light* (U Georgia Pr, 1991), *Conjunctions,*
Sulfur, Arshile

SOUTH CAROLINA

Gilbert Allen 🎤 ✈   P&W
English Dept, Furman Univ, Greenville, SC 29613,
864-294-3152
   Pubs: *Commandments at Eleven, Second Chances*
(Orchises, 1994, 1991), *American Scholar, Cumberland*
Poetry Rev, Georgia Rev, Shenandoah, Southern Rev,
Tampa Rev

Paul Allen 🎤 ✈   P
English Dept, College of Charleston, Charleston, SC
29424, 843-953-5659
Internet: www.cofc.edu/~allenp/yourpage.html
   Pubs: *American Crawl* (U North Texas Pr, 1997), *Four
   Passes* (Glebe Street Pr, 1994), *Iowa Rev, Laurel Rev,
   Viet Nam Generation, Madison Rev, Ontario Rev*

Syed Amanuddin   P
790 McKay St
Sumter, SC 29150
   Pubs: *Poems* (Apt Bks, 1984), *World Poetry in English*
   (Humanities Pr, 1982)

Franklin Ashley   W
College of Applied Sciences, Univ South Carolina,
Columbia, SC 29208, 803-777-2560

Claire Bateman   P
Fine Arts Center, 1613 W Washington St, Greenville, SC
29601, 864-241-3327
   Pubs: *At the Funeral of the Ether* (Ninety-Six Pr 1998),
   Friction (Eighth Mountain Pr 1998), *The Bicycle Slow
   Race* (Wesleyan 1991), *The Wesleyan Tradition: Anth*
   (Wesleyan 1993, 1991), *The Kenyon Poets: Anth*
   (Kenyon Rev 1989), *Georgia Rev, NER, Paris Rev*

Alice Cabaniss   P
129 Grassmere Ln
Elgin, SC 29045, 803-713-0662
   Pubs: *The Dark Bus* (Saltcatcher Pr, 1975), *45/96: Anth*
   (Ninety-six Pr, 1996) *Portfolio, Circus Maximus, A Shout
   in the Street, Appalachian Heritage, The Devil's
   Millhopper, Points*

J. Clontz   P
PO Box 30302
Charleston, SC 29407-0302, 803-571-4683
   Pubs: *Haiku Headlines, Night Roses, Frogpond,
   Lamp-Post, Candelabrum*

Phebe Davidson 🎤 ✈   P
11 Inverness W
Aiken, SC 29803-5962, 803-642-3992
Internet: phebed@aiken.sc.edu
   Pubs: *Dreameater* (Delaware Valley, 1998),
   Conversations with the World (Trilogy Bks, 1998), *Two
   Seasons, Milk & Brittle Bone* (Muse-Pie Pr, 1993,
   1991), *Kenyon Rev, Literary Rev, Poetry East, Calliope,
   SPR*
Groups: Teenagers, Seniors

Kwame Dawes   P
4 Doral Ct
Columbia, SC 29229, 803-777-2096
   Pubs: *Resisting the Anomie* (Goose Lane Edtn, 1995),
   Prophets, Requiem, Jacko Jacobus, Shook Foil, (Peepal
   Tree Bks, 1995, 1996, 1996, 1997), *London Rev of
   Bks, West Coast Line, Poetry London Newsletter,
   Callaloo, Ariel, Black Renaissance/Renaissance Noire*

Kay Day   P
1036 Brentwood
Columbia, SC 29206
   Pubs: *Links: Anth* (PoetWorks Pr, 1999), *Herald Pr, Pif
   Magazine*

Fred Dings 🎤 ✈   P
Univ of South Carolina, Dept of English
Columbia, SC 29208, 803-777-7120
   Pubs: *Eulogy for a Private Man* (TriQtly Bks, 1999),
   After the Solstice (Orchises Pr, 1993), *TriQtly, Poetry,
   Paris Rev, New Republic, New Yorker, Western
   Humanities Rev*

John Matt Dorn   P
2363 Table Rock Rd
Pickens, SC 29761, 803-878-0350
   Pubs: *Prognosis: Fair* (Colonial Pr, 1992)

Scott Ely   W
Winthrop College, English Dept, Rock Hill, SC 29730,
803-323-2131
   Pubs: *Overgrown with Love* (U Arkansas Pr, 1993), *Pit
   Bull, Starlight* (Weidenfeld & Nicolson, 1988, 1987)

Marta Fenyves   P
937 Bowman Rd, #125
Mount Pleasant, SC 29464
   Pubs: *From a Distance* (Warthog Pr, 1981), *Celebrating
   Gaia: Anth* (Sweet Annie Pr, 2000), *Exile: Anth*
   (Milkweed, 1990), *Messages from the Heart, Home
   Planet News, Relativity, NYQ, Helen Rev*

Stephen Gardner 🎤 ✈   P
College of Humanities, Univ South Carolina, 471 University
Pkwy, Aiken, SC 29801, 803-641-3239
Internet: stephengardner@mindspring.com
   Pubs: *This Book Belongs to Eva* (Palanquin Pr, 1996),
   *Louisiana Literature, Texas Rev, Southern Rev,
   California Qtly, Kansas Qtly, Poetry NW, Connecticut
   Rev, Nebraska Rev, Widener Rev, New Delta Rev,
   SPR, Mississippi Rev*

Vertamae Grosvenor   P&W
c/o Penn Center, PO Box 126, Frogmore, SC 29920

Dan Huntley   P
1089 Cedar Spring Rd
York, SC 29745
   Pubs: *SPR, Kudzu, Graffiti, Hob-Nob*

Vera Kistler   W
123 Edwards Ave
Darlington, SC 29532, 843-393-3191
   Pubs: *Birds of a Feather, Deaf Violets* (Melantrich,
   1986, 1982), *Too Much Heaven* (C.S. Spisovatel, 1985),
   *Sandlapper, State, Zapad, Metamorphosis, Choice,
   Spektrum*

J. Calvin Koonts P
Professor Emeritus, Erskine College, Washington St, Due
West, SC 29639, 813-379-2360
 Pubs: *Lines: Opus 8* (Jacobs Pr, 1994), *Under the
 Umbrella* (Sandlapper Pr, 1971)

Margaret Lally 🎤 ✈ P
PO Box 30494
Charleston, SC 29417-0494, 843-953-7908
 Pubs: *Juliana's Room* (Bits Pr, 1988), *Ohio Rev,
 Literary Rev, Kenyon Rev, Hudson Rev*

John Lane P
Wofford College, Box 101, Spartanburg, SC 29303,
864-597-4518
 Pubs: *Against Information & Other Poems* (New Nature
 Pr, 1996), *In Short: Short Creative Nonfiction: Anth*
 (Norton, 1996), *Virginia Qtly Rev, Nimrod*

Bryan Eugene Lindsay P
109 Greenbriar Rd
Spartanburg, SC 29302, 803-573-7277
 Pubs: *New Orleans Rev, SPR, Epos, Human Voice
 Qtly, Foxfire, Prickly Pear*

Bret Lott W
English Dept, College of Charleston, Charleston, SC
29424, 803-953-5664
 Pubs: *The Hunt Club* (Villard, 1998), *Fathers, Sons, &
 Brothers* (HB, 1997), *Reed's Beach, Jewel* (Pocket Bks,
 1993, 1991), *Antioch Rev, Story, Prairie Schooner,
 Witness, New Letters, Iowa Rev, Gettysburg Rev,
 Southern Rev, Ascent, Notre Dame Rev*

Susan Ludvigson P
330 Marion St
Rock Hill, SC 29730, 803-328-9207
 Pubs: *To Find the Gold, The Beautiful Noon of No
 Shadow, The Swimmer* (LSU Pr, 1990, 1986, 1984)

Nelljean McConeghey P
c/o Rice, 203 Sherwood Dr, Conway, SC 29526
 Pubs: *BPJ, Calyx, Cold Mountain Rev, New Mexico
 Humanities Rev*

Susan Meyers 🎤 ✈ P
PO Box 1765
Pawley's Island, SC 29585-1765, 843-527-8669
 Pubs: *Lessons in Leaving* (Persephone Pr, 1998), *Word
 & Witness: Anth* (Carolina Academic Pr, 1999), *The
 South Carolina Collection: Anth* (South Carolina Writers
 Workshop, 1991), *Greensboro Rev, Crucible, Mount
 Olive Rev, Point, Wellspring, Pembroke Mag*

Horace Mungin P&W
152 McArn Rd
Ridgeville, SC 29472, 803-875-3886
 Pubs: *Sleepy Willie Talk About His Life* (R&M Pub,
 1991), *The Ninety-Six Sampler of South Carolina
 Poetry: Anth* (Ninety-Six Pr, 1994), *Essence*

Robert Parham P&W
Francis Marion College, Box 100547, Florence, SC 29501,
803-661-1500
 Pubs: *The Low Fires of Keen Memory* (Colonial Pr,
 1992), *The Ninety-Six Sampler of South Carolina
 Poetry: Anth* (Ninety-Six Pr, 1994), *SPR*

Eugene Platt 🎤 ✈ P&W
734 Gilmore Ct
Charleston, SC 29412-9043, 843-795-9442
 Pubs: *Summer Days with Daughter* (Hawkes Pub,
 1999), *Bubba, Missy & Me* (Tradd Street Pr, 1992),
 South Carolina State Line (Huguley Co, 1980), *Tar
 River Poetry, Crazyhorse, South Carolina Rev, Poet
 Lore, Poem, Christianity & the Arts*
I.D.: Southern Writer

Robert S. Poole W
2913 Kennedy St
Columbia, SC 29205, 803-799-3964
 Pubs: *Cardinal Anth* (Jaccar Pr, 1986), *Greensboro
 Rev, Fiction*

Ron Rash P&W
308 S Mechanic St
Pendleton, SC 29670, 864-646-3193
 Pubs: *Eureka Mill, The Night the New Jesus Fell to
 Earth* (Bench Pr, 1998, 1994)

Fran B. Reed W
PO Box 23481
Hilton Head Island, SC 29926, 212-592-3510
 Pubs: *Black Mexican Necklace* (Dominie, 1990), *A
 Dream with Storms* (New Readers Pr, 1990), *Female
 Patient*

Ennis Rees P
2921 Pruitt Dr
Columbia, SC 29204
 Pubs: *Selected Poems* (U South Carolina Pr, 1973),
 Southern Rev, New Republic

Rosa Shand W
189 Clifton Ave
Spartanburg, SC 29302-1435, 864-582-2302
 Pubs: *New Southern Harmonies: 4 Emerging Fiction
 Writers: Anth* (Holocene Pr, 1998), *Massachusetts Rev,
 Southern Rev, Indiana Rev, Chelsea, NW Rev, Chariton
 Rev, Virginia Qtly Rev, Shenandoah*

Bennie Lee Sinclair   P&W
PO Box 345
Cleveland, SC 29635, 864-836-8489
  Pubs: *The Endangered* (96 Pr, 1993), *The Lynching*
  (Walker & Sons, 1992), *New Rev, NAR, Ellery Queen,*
  Foxfire, South Carolina Rev, Asheville Poetry Rev

Mark Steadman   W
450 Pin du Lac Dr
Central, SC 29630, 864-639-6673
  Pubs: *Mcafee County* (U Georgia Pr, 1998), *Bang-Up*
  Season (Longstreet Pr, 1990), *Angel Child, An*
  American Christmas: Anth (Peachtree, 1987, 1986),
  South Carolina Rev, Southern Rev, Nova

Dennis Ward Stiles 🎤 ✈   P
656 Harbor Creek Dr
Charleston, SC 29412-3203, 843-762-2957
  Pubs: *Saigon Tea* (Palanquin Pr, 2000), *Asheville*
  Poetry Rev, Florida Rev, Hanging Loose, Laurel Rev,
  New Delta Rev, Poetry NW, Puerto del Sol, SPR

Lori Storie-Pahlitzsch   P&W
26 Partridge Ln
Greenville, SC 29601
  Pubs: *45/96: South Carolina Poetry Anth* (96 Pr, 1994),
  Looking for Home: Anth (Milkweed, 1990), *Poetry NW,*
  Pleiades, Blue Unicorn, Crescent Rev, Poet Lore,
  Laurel Rev

David Tillinghast 🎤 ✈   P&W
Clemson Univ, English Dept, Clemson, SC 29631-1366,
864-656-5412
  Pubs: *Women Hoping for Rain & Other Poems* (State
  St Pr, 1987), *Texas Rev, Southern Rev, Georgia Rev,*
  Virginia Qtly Rev, Ploughshares

Deno Trakas   P
Wofford College, 429 N Church St, Spartanburg, SC
29303
  Pubs: *Human & Puny, New Southern Harmonies, The*
  Shuffle of Wings (Holocene Pr, 1999, 1998, 1990),
  45/96: South Carolina Poetry Anth (96 Pr, 1994), *From*
  the Green Horseshoe: Anth (U South Carolina Pr,
  1987)

Laura Puccia Valtorta   W
2009 Lincoln St
Columbia, SC 29201, 803-765-0508
  Pubs: *Family Meal, A Living Culture in Durham*
  (Carolina Wren Pr, 1993, 1987)

Joy Walsh   P
31 S Hilton Head Cabanas
Hilton Head Island, SC 29928
  Pubs: *Undertow, My Trip West* (Textile Bridge, 1994,
  1992), *Mary Magdalene Visits the Flea Market of the*
  Mind (Alpha Beat Pr, 1993), *Alpha Beat Soup*

Tommy Scott Young   P
PO Box 11247
Columbia, SC 29211, 803-754-2075
  Pubs: *Tommy Scott Young Spins Magical Tales, Vols.*
  1 & 2 (Raspberry Recordings, 1986)

SOUTH DAKOTA

David Allan Evans   P&W
1326 2nd St
Brookings, SD 57006, 605-692-5214
  Pubs: *Double Happiness: Two Lives in China* (USD Pr,
  1995), *Hanging Out with the Crows* (BkMk Pr, 1991),
  Aethlon, Chariton Rev, English Jrnl, Poetry NW

Tom Hansen   P
1803 N Kline
Aberdeen, SD 57401, 605-225-0272
  Pubs: *Northern Centinel, Midwest Qtly, Kansas Qtly,*
  Great River Rev, Literary Rev, Iowa Rev, Anima, Prairie
  Schooner, Willow Springs, Changing Men

Donald Harington   W
Art Dept, Solberg Hall, South Dakota State Univ,
Brookings, SD 57007
  Pubs: *The Architecture of the Arkansas Ozarks* (Little,
  Brown, 1975), *Esquire*

Linda Hasselstrom   P&W
Box 169
Hermosa, SD 57744, 605-255-4064
  Pubs: *Dakota Bones: Collected Poems* (Spoon River
  Poetry Pr, 1993), *Land Circle: Writings Collected from*
  the Land (Fulcrum Inc, 1991), *Leaning Into the Wind:*
  Anth (HM, 1997), *Reader's Digest*

Allison Adelle Hedge Coke   P&W
PO Box 565
Rapid City, SD 57709-0565, 605-355-9147
  Pubs: *Dog Road Woman* (Coffee Hse Pr, 1997), *The*
  Year of the Rat (Grimes Pr, 1995), *Santa Barbara Rev,*
  Little Mag, Caliban, 13th Moon, Cross Culture Poetics,
  Gatherings

Adrian C. Louis   P
PO Box 1990
Pine Ridge, SD 57770-1990
  Pubs: *Wild Indians & Other Creatures* (U Nevada Pr,
  1996), *Skins* (Crown, 1995), *Ploughshares, New Letters,*
  Kenyon Rev, TriQtly, Exquisite Corpse, Chicago Rev

Janice H. Mikesell 🎤 ✈ P&W
PO Box 87945
Sioux Falls, SD 57105-7945
 Pubs: *No Redeeming Social Merit, Some People Don't Know That Barns Have Faces* (Hen's Teeth, 2000, 1998), *Fate Worse Than Death* (U South Dakota Pr, 1995)
I.D.: Irish-Catholic, Nurse. Groups: Women, Children

John R. Milton P&W
630 Thomas
Vermillion, SD 57069

Kathleen Norris P&W
PO Box 570
Lemmon, SD 57638
 Pubs: *The Cloister Walk* (Riverhead, 1996), *Little Girls in Church, The Middle of the World* (U Pitt Pr, 1995, 1981), *Dakota* (Ticknor & Fields, 1993)

Norval Rindfleisch W
21176 458 Ave
Volga, SD 57071-6213, 605-826-4102
 Pubs: *The Season of Letting Go* (Claritas Imprints, 1995), *In Loveless Clarity* (Ithaca Hse, 1970), *Epoch, Literary Rev, Yale Literary Mag, Northern New England Rev*

Geraldine A. J. Sanford P&W
306 W 36 St, #22
Sioux Falls, SD 57105, 605-332-6090
 Pubs: *Unverified Sightings* (Dakota East, 1996), *As Far As I Can See* (Windflower Pr, 1989), *Longneck, South Dakota Rev, Prairie Winds, South Dakota Mag*

Sylvia Wheeler P
English Dept, Univ South Dakota, Vermillion, SD 57069, 605-677-5229
 Pubs: *Counting Back: Voices of the Lakota & Pioneer Settlers, Dancing Alone* (BkMk Pr, 1992, 1992), *New Letters, Chariton Rev*

TENNESSEE

Deborah Adams P&W
Jin Publicists, 504 Cedar Forest Ct, Nashville, TN 37221, 615-356-3086
 Pubs: *All the Blood Relations, All the Deadly Beloved, All the Hungry Mothers* (Ballantine, 1997, 1996, 1994), *Murderous Intent, Funny Bones, Murder They Wrote 2, Deadly Women, Canine Capers, Malice Domestic 3*

Tina Barr 🎤 ✈ P
English Dept, Rhodes College, 2000 N Pkwy, Memphis, TN 38112-1690, 901-843-3979
 Pubs: *The Fugitive Eye* (Painted Bride Qtly, 1997), *At Dusk on Naskeag Point* (Flume Pr, 1984), *SW Rev, APR, Louisiana Lit, Harvard Rev, Pequod, Paris Rev, Chelsea, Crazyhorse, Boulevard*

Scott Bates P
Box 1263, 735 University Ave
Sewanee, TN 37375-1000, 615-598-5843
 Pubs: *Merry Green Peace, Lupo's Fables* (Jump-Off Mountain, 1990, 1983), *Delos*

John Bensko 🎤 ✈ P
PO Box 40042
Memphis, TN 38174-0042, 901-726-9187
 Pubs: *The Iron City* (U Illinois Pr, 2000), *The Waterman's Children* (U Mass Pr, 1994), *Green Soldiers* (Yale U Pr, 1981), *Poetry, Poetry NW, New Letters, NER, Iowa Rev, Georgia Rev*

Diann Blakely 🎤 ✈ P
3037 Woodlawn Dr
Nashville, TN 37215-1140, 615-297-6026
Internet: dblakely@aol.com
 Pubs: *Farewell My Lovelies* (Story Line Pr, 2000), *Hurricane Walk* (BOA Edtns, 1992)

Jane Bradley W
3120 Bellwood St
Nashville, TN 37403, 615-463-9476
 Pubs: *Living Doll* (Permanent Pr, 1994), *Power Lines & Other Stories* (U Arkansas, 1989), *Virginia Rev, The Literary Rev, NAR, Crazyhorse, Confrontation, Kansas Qtly*

Gaylord Brewer P
English Dept, Middle Tennessee St Univ, Murfreesboro, TN 37132, 615-898-2712
 Pubs: *Presently a Beast* (Coreopsis Bks, 1996), *Qtly West, NYQ, Lullwater Rev, Re:al, U of Windsor Rev, Puerto del Sol, Ellipsis, Chelsea, Conneticut Rev, Crab Orchard Rev, Poet Lore*

James Brooks 🎤 ✈ P&W
114 Malone Hollow Rd
Jonesborough, TN 37659, 615-753-7831
Internet: comeback@usit.net
 Pubs: *Comeback of the Bears* (Scruffy City, 2000), *South Carolina Rev, Davidson Miscellany, Cold Mountain Rev, Wisconsin Rev*

Melissa Cannon P
141 Neese Dr, #E18
Nashville, TN 37211-2750, 615-832-1813
 Pubs: *A Formal Feeling Comes, Sleeping with Dionysus* (Crossing Pr, 1994, 1994), *Bogg, Kenyon Rev, Lyric, Ploughshares, Shockbox, Tight*

Jill Carpenter ♀ ✈   P&W
PO Box 3271
Sewanee, TN 37375, 931-598-0795
Internet: jillc@infoave.net
   Pubs: *Fingerlings* (Catamount Pr, 1995), *Anth of Frogs
   & Toads: Anth* (Ione Pr, 1998), *Amelia, Birmingham
   Poetry Rev, Exquisite Corpse, New Mexico Humanities
   Rev, Utah Wilderness Assn Rev, Passager*

Blair Carr   W
PO Box 2138
Memphis, TN 38088-2138
   Pubs: *Flashbacks, A Case of Black or White* (Kudzu
   Pub, 1998, 1996)

Karyn Follis Cheatham   W
PO Box 150792
Nashville, TN 37215-0792
   Pubs: *The Best Way Out, Bring Home the Ghost* (HBJ,
   1982, 1980), *Panhandler, West Wind Rev*

Kevin Christianson   P
English Dept, Tennessee Tech Univ, Box 5053, Cookeville,
TN 38505, 931-372-3351
   Pubs: *Seven Deadly Witnesses* (Broom St Theatre Pr,
   1971), *Libido, Rockford Rev, The Formalist, Z Misc,
   Turnstile, Connecticut River Rev, Protea, Black Bear
   Rev, Lynx Eye, Minnesota Rev, New Letters*

Suzanne Underwood Clark ♀ ✈   P
721 Pennsylvania Ave
Bristol, TN 37620
   Pubs: *What a Light Thing, This Stone, Weather of the
   House* (Sow's Ear Pr, 1999, 1994), *Sketches of Home*
   (Canon Pr, 1998), *Quilt Anthology* (Quilt Digest Pr,
   1994), *Lullwater Rev, Shenandoah, SPR, Image,
   Appalachian Jrnl, Sow's Ear Poetry Rev*
Groups: Spiritual/Religious

Jay Clayton   W
English Dept, Vanderbilt Univ, Nashville, TN 37235,
615-322-2541
   Pubs: *Denver Qtly, SW Rev, Kansas Qtly, Southern
   Rev*

Robert Cowser   P
Univ Tennessee, Martin, TN 38238, 901-587-7280
   Pubs: *Backtrailing* (U Tennessee at Martin Pr, 1990),
   *Zone 3, Now, Old Red Kimono, American Literary Rev,
   Cape Rock, Lake Street Rev, Sow's Ear, English Jrnl,
   Sulphur*

Margaret Danner   P
Poet-In-Residence, Lemoyne Owen College, Memphis, TN
38126

Harry Norman Dean   P
920 Haywood Dr NW
Cleveland, TN 37312-3929, 423-476-6950
   Pubs: *A Sheltered Life* (Rowan Mountain Pr, 1991),
   Appalachia Inside Out: Anth (U Tennessee Pr, 1995),
   *Poetry Miscellany, Cumberland Poetry Rev, Appalachian
   Heritage, Samisdat, Number One, Mountain Ways*

Victor M. Depta   P
Blair Mountain Press, PO Box 147, Martin, TN 38237,
901-588-0079
Internet: sales@blairmtp.com
   Pubs: *Gate of Paradise, Silence of Blackberries* (Blair
   Mtn Pr, 2000, 1999) *A Doorkeeper in the House* (Ion
   Bks, 1993), *Idol & Sanctuary* (University Edtns, 1993),
   *Aura, Sonoma Mandala, Centennial Rev, Negative
   Capability*

Ora Wilbert Eads   P
812 W Hemlock St
LaFollette, TN 37766, 423-562-6330
   Pubs: *Tranquility, Heavenly Light* (Banner Bks, 1994,
   1993), *Crystal Rainbow, Omnific*

Neal Ellis   P
3561 Hanna Dr
Memphis, TN 38128, 901-386-2684
   Pubs: *Gayoso Street Rev, Voices Intl, Memphis
   Tennessee Anth*

Steve Eng   P&W
PO Box 111864
Nashville, TN 37222-1864
   Pubs: *All Aboard, SPWAO: Anth, Poets of Fantastic:
   Anth* (SPWAO, 1992, 1992), *Worlds of Fantasy &
   Horror, Beatlicks' Nashville Poetry Newsletter, Fantasy
   Commentator, Nashville Banner, Night Songs, Amanita
   Brandy, Nightmare Express*

David Flynn   P&W
303 Crestmeade Dr
Nashville, TN 37221, 615-354-1063
Internet: dflynn@vscc.cc.tn.us
   Pubs: *Stand, The Qtly, Intl Qtly, Panurge, Story Qtly,
   Confrontation, Paris Transcontinental*

Dorothy Foltz-Gray   P
5900 Wade Ln
Knoxville, TN 37912, 615-689-8160
   Pubs: *Homewords: Anth of Tennessee Writers* (U
   Tennessee Pr, 1986), *Mississippi Rev, Poet Lore,
   College English*

Shelby Foote   W
542 E Parkway S
Memphis, TN 38104-4362
   Pubs: *September, September* (Random Hse, 1977),
   *Jordan County, Shiloh, Love in a Dry Season, Follow
   Me Down, Tournament* (Dial Pr, 1954, 1952, 1951,
   1950, 1949)

Richard Fricks   P
134 Longwood Pl
Nashville, TN 37215, 615-385-9517
   Pubs: *A Feel for Words* (Tennessee Arts Commission, 1973)

Charlotte Gafford   P
7325 Walker Rd
Fairview, TN 37062-8142, 615-799-2546
   Pubs: *The Pond Woman* (Kudzu Pr, 1989), *SPR, Iowa Rev, NER*

Isabel Joshlin Glaser 🎤   PP&P&W
5383 Mason Rd
Memphis, TN 38120-1707, 901-685-5597
   Pubs: *Dreams of Glory: Anth* (Atheneum, 1995), *Cicada, Prairie Schooner, Greensboro Rev, Cricket, School Mag, Instructor, Mississippi Rev*
Groups: Children, Adults

Malcolm Glass   P
PO Box 137
Clarksville, TN 37041-0137, 615-648-7882
   Pubs: *The Dinky Line, Wiggins Poems* (Bucksnort, 1991, 1984), *In the Shadow of the Gourd* (New Rivers Pr, 1990), *Sewanee Rev*

George Grace 🎤 ✈ P&W
1030 Leatherwood Rd
White Bluff, TN 37187
Internet: gdgart@aol.com
   Pubs: *Buffalo Pr Anth, Pure Light, Textile Bridge Pr, Moody Street Irregulars: Jack Kerouac Newsletter*

Roy Neil Graves 🎤 ✈ P
Univ Tennessee, English Dept, Martin, TN 38238,
901-587-7301
Internet: ngraves@utm.edu
   Pubs: *Somewhere on the Interstate* (Ion Bks, 1987), *6 Tennessee Poets: Anth, Always at Home Here: Anth* (McGraw-Hill, 1998, 1998), *Homeworks: Anth* (U Tennessee Pr, 1996), *New Ground, Bean Switch, Manana, Distillery, Runner's World*

Larry D. Griffin 🎤 ✈ P&W
Dyersburg State Community College, 1510 Lake Rd,
Dyersburg, TN 38024, 901-286-3371
Internet: lgriffin@dscclan.dscc.cc.tn.us
   Pubs: *Larry D Griffin Gold* (Pudding Hse, 2000), *Airspace* (Slough, 1990), *A Gathering of Samphire* (Poetry Around, 1990), *Oyster Boy, 2 River Rev, Cimarron Rev, Riversedge, Poetry Ireland Rev, Blue Unicorn, Dock(s)*

Martha Whitmore Hickman 🎤 ✈ W
2034 Castleman Dr
Nashville, TN 37215, 615-292-9529
   Pubs: *Such Good People* (Warner Bks, 1996), *Fullness of Time: Short Stories of Women & Aging: Anth* (Abingdon Pr, 1997), *Weavings, Christian Century, Highlights, Pockets, Image*
Groups: Seniors

Cary Holladay 🎤 ✈ W
23 S Evergreen St
Memphis, TN 38104-3918, 901-278-7510
   Pubs: *The Palace of Wasted Footsteps* (U Missouri Pr, 1998), *The People Down South* (U Illinois Pr, 1989), *The O. Henry Awards: Anth* (Anchor Bks, 1999) *Kenyon Rev, Alaska Qtly Rev, Chelsea, Literary Rev, Oxford American, Chattahoochee Rev, Epoch, NW Rev*

Richard Jackson 🎤 ✈ P
3413 Alta Vista Dr
Chattanooga, TN 37411, 423-624-7279
Internet: svobodni@aol.com
   Pubs: *Half-lives* (Invisible Cities Pr, 2001), *Heartwall* (U Mass Pr, 2000), *Heart's Bridge* (Aureole Pr, 1999), *Alive All Day* (Cleveland State U Pr, 1992), *Worlds Apart, Dismantling Time* (U Alabama Pr, 1989, 1987), *Gettysburg Rev, Crazyhorse, NER, NAR*

Mark Jarman 🎤 ✈ P
English Dept, Vanderbilt Univ, Nashville, TN 37235,
615-322-2618
Internet: mark.jarman@vanderbilt.edu
   Pubs: *Unholy Sonnets, Questions for Ecclesiastes, Iris* (Story Line Pr, 2000, 1997, 1992), *APR, Hudson Rev, New Yorker, Southern Rev, New Criterion, Threepenny Rev, Atlantic, Kenyon Rev, Sewanee Rev*

Marilyn Kallet 🎤 ✈ P
Director, Creative Writing, Univ Tennessee, Knoxville, TN
37996, 865-974-6947
   Pubs: *Sleeping with One Eye Open: Women Writers & the Art of Survival: Anth* (U Georgia Pr, 1999), *How to Get Heat Without Fire* (New Messenger/New Millennium, 1996), *Worlds in Our Words: Anth* (Blair Pr/Prentice Hall, 1996), *New Letters, Prairie Schooner*
I.D.: Jewish. Groups: Women, Seniors

Richard Kelly   P
Univ Tennessee, McClung Tower, English Dept, Knoxville,
TN 37919, 615-974-5401
   Pubs: *Lewis Carroll, Daphne du Maurier* (G.K. Hall, 1990, 1987), *V.S. Naipaul* (Continuum, 1989)

Shara McCallum 🎤 ✈ P
Univ of Memphis, Dept of English, Memphis, TN 38152,
901-678-4771
Internet: sssmm@earthlink.net
   Pubs: *Water Between Us* (U Pitt Pr, 1999), *Beyond the Frontier: Anth* (Black Classics Pr, 2000), *New American Poets: Anth* (U Pr of New England, 2000), *Prairie Schooner, Iowa Rev, Verse, Antioch Rev, Caribbean Writer, Chelsea*
I.D.: Black, Afro-Caribbean

Ellis K. Meacham   W
414 S Crest Rd
Chattanooga, TN 37404, 615-624-1887
    Pubs: *For King & Company, On the Company's Service*
    (Little, Brown, 1976, 1968)

Corey J. Mesler 🎤   P&W
1954 Young Ave
Memphis, TN 38104-5643, 901-274-4718
Internet: burkes@netten.net
    Pubs: *Smashing Icons* (Avocet, 1998), *Full Court: Anth*
    (Breakaway Bks, 1996), *Yellow Silk, Green Egg, Poet
    Lore, Rhino, Crossroads, Visions Intl, Southern Voices,
    Slant, Epiphany, Agincourt, Irregular*

Gordon Osing   P
1056 Blythe St
Memphis, TN 38104
    Pubs: *A Town Down River* (St. Luke's Pr, 1984), *From
    the Boundary Waters* (Memphis State U, 1982)

William Page 🎤 ✈   P
5551 Derron Ave
Memphis, TN 38115-2323, 901-363-2216
Internet: wpagemem@aol.com
    Pubs: *Bodies Not Our Own* (Memphis St U Pr, 1986),
    *American Literary Rev, NAR, SPR, Literary Rev,
    College English, SW Rev*

Barbara Shirk Parish 🎤   P&W
4293 Beechcliff Ln
Memphis, TN 38128-3423, 901-388-4384
    Pubs: *Maverick Western Verse: Anth* (Gibbs Smith,
    1994), *The Kentucky Book: Anth* (Courier Journal,
    1979), *Small Pond, Green's Mag, Dry Crik Rev, Little
    Balkins Rev*

Wyatt Prunty   P
Sewanee Writers' Conference, Univ of the South, 310 St
Luke's Hall, Sewanee, TN 37383-1000, 615-598-1159
    Pubs: *Unarmed and Dangerous: New and Selected
    Poems, Since the Noon Mail Stopped, The Run of the
    House* (Johns Hopkins U Pr, 2000, 1997, 1993), *New
    Criterion, New Republic, New Yorker, Oxford American,
    Sewanee Review, Southern Rev, Yale Rev*

N. Scott Reynolds   P
301 28th Ave N Apt1206
Nashville, TN 37203
    Pubs: *First Songs from the Midden* (Nephtys Inc.),
    Something We Can't Name: Anth (Octus Orbus),
    *Kameleon, Tea Party Electronic Mag, Wired Art for
    Wired Hearts, Crumpled Papers, Beatlicks Nashville
    Poetry Newsletter, Flying Dog, Café Daze, Radio Beds*

J. C. Robison   W
Brentwood Academy, 219 Granny White Pike, Brentwood,
TN 37027
    Pubs: *Peter Taylor: A Study of the Short Fiction*
    (Twayne, 1988), *Texas Rev, Chariton Rev, Cimarron*

Abby Jane Rosenthal   P
650 S Greer
Memphis, TN 38111
    Pubs: *Ardor's Hut* (Alembic Pr, 1985), *Alaska Qtly Rev,
    Kalliope, CutBank, Bloomsbury Rev*

Frank Russell   P
501 Park Ctr
Nashville, TN 37205, 615-386-9731
    Pubs: *Dinner with Dr. Rocksteady* (Ion Bks, 1987),
    Poetry, Chariton Rev, Poetry NW

George Addison Scarbrough 🎤 ✈   P
100 Darwin Ln
Oak Ridge, TN 37830-4021, 865-482-2793
    Pubs: *Tellico Blue* (Iris Pr, 1999), *Southern Lit: Anth*
    (Prentice Hall, 2000), *Poetry, Southern Rev, Iron
    Mountain Rev, Emory Valley Rev, Now & Then,
    Appalachian Rev, New Orleans Rev, Atlantic, Harper's,
    Saturday Rev, New Republic*

Arthur Smith   P
Univ Tennessee, 301 McClung Tower/English Dept,
Knoxville, TN 37996, 865-974-5401
    Pubs: *Orders of Affection* (Carnegie Mellon U Pr,
    1996), *Elegy on Independence Day* (U Pitt Pr, 1985),
    Nation, Crazyhorse, NAR

Dorothy Stanfill   W
3131 N Highland Ave, #128M
Jackson, TN 38305-3408
    Pubs: *A Greater Love, Katharine & the Quarter Mile
    Drag* (Old Hickory Pr, 1985, 1978), *Amelia*

Rosemary Stephens   P&W
64 N Yates Rd
Memphis, TN 38120
    Pubs: *Eve's Navel* (South & West, 1976), *Seventeen,
    Mississippi Rev, SPR*

Arthur J. Stewart 🎤 ✈   P
2061 Crooked Oak Dr
Lenoir City, TN 37771-7898, 423-986-5935
Internet: astewart@utk.edu
    Pubs: *Songs from Unsung Worlds: Anth* (Birkhauser,
    1985), *Southern Voices in Every Direction: Anth* (Bell
    Buckle/Iris Pr, 1997), *Lullwater Rev, Quantum Tao, The
    Sow Ear Poetry Rev, ELF, Now & Then: The
    Appalachian Mag, New Millennium Writings*
I.D.: Scientist

James Summerville   W
2911 Woodlawn Dr
Nashville, TN 37215, 615-298-5830
    Pubs: *The Cormack-Cooper Shooting* (McFarland,
    1994), *Homewords: Anth* (U Tennessee, 1986), *North
    Dakota Qtly, Touchstone, Tennessee Historical Qtly,
    History News, Lake Superior Rev*

Frederick O. Waage 🎤   W
East Tennessee State Univ, Box 23081, Johnson City, TN
37614, 615-929-7466
Internet: waage@xtn.net
    Pubs: *Minestrone* (Pudding, 1983), *The End of the
World* (Gallimaufry, 1977), *SPR, California Qtly,
Antigonish Rev*

Jon Manchip White   P&W
5620 Pinellas Dr
Knoxville, TN 37919-4118, 423-558-8578
    Pubs: *Whistling Past the Churchyard, Journeying Boy*
(Atlantic Monthly Pr, 1992, 1991)

Lola White   P
5040 Villa Crest Dr
Nashville, TN 37220
    Pubs: *Thunder: Silence* (Red Girl Pr, 1992), *Potato
Eyes, New River Free Pr, Tendril, Aspect, Zeugma,
Cat's Eye, Pluma True, CSM, Dark Horse*

Allen Wier 🎤 ✈   W
English Dept, Univ Tennessee, 301 McClung Tower,
Knoxville, TN 37996-0430, 865-974-5401
Internet: awier@utk.edu
    Pubs: *Tehano* (Overlook Pr, 2001), *A Place for Outlaws*
(H&R, 1989), *Departing As Air* (S&S, 1983), *Southern
Rev, Texas Rev, Mid-American Rev*

Don Williams   W
PO Box 2463
Knoxville, TN 37901, 423-428-0389
    Pubs: *A Tennessee Landscape: Anth* (Cool Springs Pr,
1996), *Homeworks: Anth* (U Tennessee Pr 1996),
Voices from the Valley: Anth (Knoxville Writers Guild,
1994), *New Millennium Writings, Crescent Rev 10th
Anniversary Special*

Charles Wyatt   P&W
3810 Central Ave
Nashville, TN 37205, 615-385-2456
    Pubs: *Listening to Mozart* (U Iowa Pr, 1995), *NER,
TriQtly, Hanging Loose, BPJ, Florida Rev, The Qtly*

TEXAS

Virginia T. Abercrombie 🎤   P
2 Smithdale Ct
Houston, TX 77024
Internet: 229huck1574@msn.com
    Pubs: *Suddenly* (Martin Hse, 1998), *Songs for the
Century, Houston Party File, Leaf Raker* (Brown Rabbit
Pr, 1998, 1986, 1983), *Back to Your Roots: Anth*
(Houston Poetry Fest, 1991), *Visions Intl, Illyas Honey,
Raintown Rev, Pleiades*

Neal Abramson   P
1000 W Spring Valley Rd, #229
Richardson, TX 75080, 214-231-3732
    Pubs: *Sojourn, Lactuca, Amoeba, Unmuzzled Ox, City
West End, Confrontation*

Alan P. Akmakjian   P&W
2200 Waterview Pkwy, #2134
Richardson, TX 75080-2268
    Pubs: *And What Rough Beast: Poems at the End of
the Century* (Ashland U Pr, 1999), *California Picnic &
Other Poems* (Northwoods Pr, 1998), *Let the Sun Go*
(MAF Pr, 1993), *Ararat, Atom Mind, Black Bear Rev,
New Thought Jrnl, Onthebus, Wormwood Rev*

Silvia Berta Alaniz   P
821 Carver St
Alice, TX 78332
    Pubs: *Perceptions, Writing for Our Lives, Dream Intl
Qtly, Poetic Eloquence, Expressions, Tight, Moving Out,
Stone Drum, Up Against the Wall, Notebook, Aura,
Avocet, Pacific Coast Jrnl, Reflect, Mind in Motion*

Max Apple   W
Rice Univ, PO Box 1892, Houston, TX 77251,
713-527-8101
    Pubs: *Roommates, Zip* (Warner Bks, 1994, 1986), *The
Propheteers, Free Agents* (H&R, 1987, 1984),
Ploughshares

Terry Lee Armstrong   P
4219 Flint Hill St
San Antonio, TX 78230-1619
    Pubs: *When the Soul Speaks, Call it Love* (Armstrong
Pub, 1990, 1989), *Lone Stars Mag, Omnific Mag*

Carolyn Banks 🎤 ✈   W
223 Riverwood
Bastrop, TX 78602-7616, 512-303-1531
Internet: studio@onr.com
    Pubs: *Mr. Right* (Permanent Pr, 1999), *A Horse to Die
For, Death on the Diagonal, Murder Well Bred,
Groomed for Death, Death By Dressage* (Fawcett,
1996, 1996, 1995, 1994, 1993), *Tart Tales: Elegant
Erotic Stories* (Carroll & Graf, 1993)

Wendy Barker 🎤 ✈   P
Univ of Texas, 6900 North Loop 1604 West, San Antonio,
TX 78249-0643, 210-458-5362
Internet: wbarker@lonestar.utsa.edu
    Pubs: *Way of Whiteness* (Wings Pr, 2000), *Eve
Remembers* (Dark Arts Pr, 1996), *Let the Ice Speak*
(Ithaca Hse Bks, 1991), *Winter Chickens & Other
Poems* (Corona Pub, 1990), *Partisan Rev, Michigan
Qtly Rev, Poetry, NAR, American Scholar, Prairie
Schooner*
Groups: Seniors, Translation

Shulamith Bat-Yisrael   P
PO Box 852151
Richardson, TX 75085-2151
    Pubs: *Black Bear Rev, Nexus, Infinity Ltd., Harbinger,
    Bitterroot, Parnassus Literary Jrnl, Jrnl of New Jersey
    Poets, Response, Writers' Jrnl*

Charles Behlen 🎤 ✈   P
503 W Industrial Dr Apt B
Sulphur Springs, TX 75482-4646, 505-392-7005
Internet: cwbehlen@yahoo.com
    Pubs: *Texas Weather* (Trilobite Pr, 1999), *Roundup:
    Anth* (Prickly Pear Pr, 1999), *Borderlands*

Michael Berryhill   P
Fort Worth Star-Telegram, 400 W 7 St, Fort Worth, TX
76102

Michael C. Blumenthal   P
3311 Merrie Lynn Ave
Austin, TX 78722, 512-457-8856
Internet: mcblume@attglobalnet
    Pubs: *Dusty Angel* (BOA Edts, 1999), *The Wages of
    Goodness* (U Missouri Pr, 1992), *Against Romance*
    (Viking Penguin, 1987), *Marriage: Anth* (Poseidon,
    1991), *Poetry, Nation, Agni, American Scholar, Paris
    Rev, Ploughshares*

Bruce Bond   P
1505 Laurelwood
Denton, TX 76201, 940-565-0849
    Pubs: *Radiography* (BOA, 1997), *The Afternoon of
    Paradise* (QRL, 1991), *Independence Days* (Woodley
    Pr, 1990), *The Possible* (Silverfish Rev Pr, 1995)

Eugene G. E. Botelho   P
PO Box 925
Eagle Pass, TX 78853-0925
    Pubs: *For Better, for Worse* (All American Pr, 1981), *I
    Wonder As I Wander* (Northwoods, 1978)

David Breeden   P&W
Campus Box 4504, Schreiner College, 2100 Memorial
Blvd, Kerrville, TX 78028, 512-896-7945
    Pubs: *Another Number* (Silver Phoenix Pr, 1998),
    Guiltless Traveller, Building a Boat (March Street Pr,
    1996, 1995), *Double-Headed End Wrench* (Cloverdale
    Pr, 1992)

J. W. Brown   P
3500 Rankin St
Dallas, TX 75205, 214-739-6566
    Pubs: *Pawn Rev, DeKalb Literary Arts Jrnl, SW Rev,
    Texas Qtly*

William S. Burford   P
3001 W Gambrell
Fort Worth, TX 76133, 817-926-1480
    Pubs: *A Beginning* (Norton, 1968), *A World* (U Texas
    Pr, 1962), *The Poetry Anth: Sixty-Five Years of
    America's Distinguished Verse Mag* (HM, 1978), *Nation,
    Poetry Anth*

Robert Grant Burns   P
PO Box 763
Jacksonville, TX 75766
    Pubs: *Selected Poems* (Waltonhof, 1993)

Harry Burrus   P
1266 Fountain View
Houston, TX 77057-2204, 713-784-2802
Internet: HarryBurrus@juno.com
    Pubs: *Cartouche, The Jaguar Portfolio, Without
    Feathers* (Black Tie Press, 1995, 1991, 1990)

Bobby Byrd   P
2709 Louisville
El Paso, TX 79930, 915-566-9072
    Pubs: *On the Transmigration of Souls in El Paso*
    (Cinco Puntos Pr, 1993), *Get Some Fuses for the
    House* (North Atlantic Bks, 1987)

Jean Calkins 🎤   P
14281 Shoredale Ln
Farmers Branch, TX 75234-2045
Internet: nystxn@fastlane.net
    Pubs: *Passages, Win Place Show, Seasons of the
    Mind* (JC Pr, 2000, 1999, 1999), *Against All Odds,
    Portrait of Insomnia* (Inky Pr, 1995, 1995), *Black Creek
    Rev, Parnassus, Smile, Apropos, Potpourri, Haiku
    Headlines, Humoresque, Vantage Point, Pegasus*

Ewing Campbell   W
Texas A&M Univ, English Dept, College Station, TX
77843-4227, 409-845-8342
Internet: rec025b@venus.tamu.edu
    Pubs: *Madonna, Maleva* (York Pr, 1995), *The Tex-Mex
    Express* (Spectrum Pr, 1993), *London Mag, NER,
    Kenyon Rev, Chicago Rev, Cimarron Rev*

Vincent Canizarro, Jr.   P
8285 Collier Rd
Beaumont, TX 77706, 713-866-3612
    Pubs: *The Poet*

Warren Carrier 🎤   P
69 Colony Park Cir
Galveston, TX 77551-1737, 409-744-5511
    Pubs: *Risking the Wind* (Birch Brook, 2000), *Justice at
    Christmas, Death of a Poet* (Denlinger, 2000, 1999),
    *Harvard Mag, Formalist, Ohio Rev, Visions Intl,
    Pembroke Mag, Wallace Stevens Jrnl*

Jane Chance 🎤 ✈   P
English Dept, MS30, Rice Univ, 6100 Main St, Houston,
TX 77251-1892, 713-348-2625
Internet: jchance@rice.edu
   Pubs: *Christine de Pizan's Letter of Othea to Hector*
(Boydell & Brewer, 1997), *Literary Rev, Southern
Humanities Rev, Primavera, Ariel, New America*

Charlotte Cheatham   P
Galveston Arts Ctr On Strand, 202 Kempner, Galveston,
TX 77550, 713-765-6309
   Pubs: *Gjelsness, Joy Drake*

Paul Christensen 🎤 ✈   P
Texas A&M Univ, English Dept, College Sta, TX
77843-4227, 979-845-8330
Internet: p-christensen@tamu.edu
   Pubs: *Where Three Roads Meet* (Cedarshouse/Open
Theater, 1996), *In Love, In Sorrow* (Paragon Hse,
1990), *Weights & Measures* (University Edtns, 1985),
Texas Short Stories: Anth (Browder Springs Pr, 2000,
1997), *Antioch Rev, Connecticut Rev, SW Rev*

L. D. Clark   W
604 Main St
Smithville, TX 78957, 512-237-2756
   Pubs: *A Bright Tragic Thing* (Cinco Puntos Pr, 1992), *A
Charge of Angels* (Confluence Pr, 1987), *The Fifth
Wind* (Blue Moon Pr, 1981)

LaVerne Harrell Clark 🎤 ✈   W
604 Main St
Smithville, TX 78957, 512-237-2796
Internet: ldlhclark@aol.com
   Pubs: *21 Texas Women Writers: Anth* (Texas A&M U
Pr, 2001), *Keepers of the Earth* (Cinco Puntos Pr,
1997), *A New Dimension of an Old Affinity* (Writers on
the Plains Pr, 1996), *Pembroke, St. Andrews Rev,
Vanderbilt Street Rev, Southwestern Amer Lit*

Richard Cole   P
5125 McDade Dr
Austin, TX 78735, 512-891-9276
   Pubs: *Success Stories* (Limestone Bks, 1998), *The
Glass Children* (U Georgia Pr, 1986), *Chicago Rev,
New Yorker, Hudson Rev, Denver Qtly, The Sun*

Paul David Colgin   P
2308 Neeley Ave
Midland, TX 79705, 915-682-6609
   Pubs: *Yankee, Sulphur, Pearl, Nexus, Black Fly Rev,
Kinesis, Pittsburgh Qtly, Sou'wester, Oxford Mag,
Iconoclast, Tomorrow Mag, Xanadu*

Joe Coomer   W
1951 NW Parkway
Azle, TX 76020
   Pubs: *The Loop, Dream House* (Faber & Faber, 1992,
1992), *A Flatland Fable* (Texas Monthly Pr, 1986)

Carol Cullar   P&W
Rte 2, Box 4915
Eagle Pass, TX 78852-9605, 210-773-1836
   Pubs: *Inexplicable Burnings* (Pr of the Guadalupe,
1992), *Wind Eyes: A Woman's Reader & Writing
Source: Anth* (Plain View Pr, 1997), *Texas Short
Fiction: Anth, Texas In Poetry: Anth* (Ctr for Texas
Studies, 1996, 1994), *NYQ, RE:AL*

Chip Dameron   P
33 El Retiro Cir
Brownsville, TX 78520, 512-541-1983
   Pubs: *Night Spiders, Morning Milk, Definition of Hours*
(Hawk Pr, 1990), *In the Magnetic Arena* (Latitudes,
1987), *New Texas 95, Sulphur*

William Virgil Davis 🎤 ✈   P
2633 Lake Oaks Rd
Waco, TX 76710-1616, 254-772-3198
Internet: william_davis@baylor.edu
   Pubs: *One Way to Reconstruct the Scene* (Yale U Pr,
1980), *Poetry, New Criterion, Gettysburg Rev, Hudson
Rev, Atlantic*

Angela de Hoyos   P
M&A Editions, 10120 State Hwy 16 S, San Antonio, TX
78224
   Pubs: *Woman, Woman* (Arte Publico Pr, 1985),
Selected Poems/Selecciones (Dezkalzo Pr, 1979)

Nephtali Deleon   P&W
1411 Betty Dr
San Antonio, TX 78224

Jeffrey DeLotto   P
Texas Wesleyan Univ, 1201 Wesleyan, Fort Worth, TX
76105, 817-531-4909
   Pubs: *Anthology of New England Writers: Voices at the
Door* (Maverick Pr, 1995), *New Texas 91: Anth* (U
North Texas Pr, 1991), *Aura Literary/Arts Rev, College
English, Preying Mantis, Horny Toad*

Mark Doty   P&W
Creative Writing Program, Univ of Houston, English Dept,
Houston, TX 77204, 713-529-9586
   Pubs: *An Island Sheaf* (Dim Gray Bar Pr, 1998), *Sweet
Machine, Heaven's Coast, Atlantis* (HC, 1998, 1996,
1995), *My Alexandria* (U Illinois Pr, 1993), *New Yorker,
Paris Rev, Boulevard, DoubleTake*

Sharrard Douglass   P&W
PO Box 2107
Rockport, TX 78381, 512-729-9999
   Pubs: *The Music I Try to Become* (Maverick Pr, 1995),
Coastline, Preying Mantis, Culebra, Javelin, Paisano

Jerry Ellison ✈ P
Rte 3 Box 377
Gilmer, TX 75644-9537, 903-725-6283
Internet: peacewds@etex.net
Pubs: *Never Again Summer* (College Poetry Rev,
1969), *Death Chant: Anth* (Silver Spur, 1962), *Sulphur,
Borderlands, Avocet, Bellowing Ark*

Robert A. Fink P
Hardin-Simmons Univ, Box 15114, Abilene, TX 79698,
915-670-1214
Pubs: *The Tongues of Men & of Angels* (Texas Tech
U Pr, 1995), *The Ghostly Hitchhiker* (Corona Pub,
1989), *Azimuth Points* (Sam Houston State U, 1981),
*Poetry NW, Poetry, Michigan Qtly Rev, NER, TriQtly,
SW Rev*

Robert Flynn W
Trinity Univ, 715 Stadium Dr, San Antonio, TX 78212,
210-736-7575
Pubs: *Living with the Hyenas* (TCU Pr, 1995), *The Last
Klick* (Baskerville Pub, 1994), *A Personal War in Viet
Nam* (Texas A&M U, 1989), *Image*

Peter Fogo P
PO Box 7743
Pasadena, TX 77508-7743, 713-941-5227
Pubs: *A Language That Keeps Company with the Moon*
(Mackinations Pr, 1992), *Single Again* (Raspberry Pr,
1980), *Midwest Qtly, Black Bear Rev, Prairie Winds,
Ellipsis*

Ken Fontenot ♇ ✈ P
1221 Algarita, #162
Austin, TX 78704-4413, 512-442-7737
Pubs: *All My Animals & Stars* (Slough Pr, 1989), *After
the Days of Miami* (Longmeasure Pr, 1980), *APR,
Kenyon Rev, Southern Rev, NAR*

Larry L. Fontenot P
1911 Campwood Dr
Sugar Land, TX 77478-4117
Internet: poboy@hotmail.com
Pubs: *Choices & Consequences* (Maverick Pr, 1997),
*River Sedge, Minimus, El Locofoco, Bayousphere,
Treasure House, Arrowsmith, Maverick Pr, i.e. mag*

Margot Fraser W
Southern Methodist Univ Press, Box 415, Dallas, TX
75275, 214-768-1432
Pubs: *Careless Weeds, The Laying Out of Gussie Hoot*
(SMU Pr, 1993, 1990), *Negative Capability*

Laura Furman ♇ ✈ W
English Dept, Univ Texas, Austin, TX 78712-1164,
512-471-4991
Internet: ljfurman@mail.utexas.edu
Pubs: *What Would Buddha Do?, Watch Time Fly, The
Glass House, The Shadow Line, Tuxedo Park, Ordinary
Paradise* (Winedale Pub, 2001, 2001, 2001, 2000,
2000, 1998), *Threepenny Rev, Yale Rev, Preservation
Mag, New Yorker, Ploughshares, SW Rev*

G. N. Gabbard P&W
602 Cannon St
New Boston, TX 75570-2206, 903-628-2788
Pubs: *A Mask for Beowulf, Knights Errand, Daily Nous,
Dragon Raid* (Flea King Bks, 1992, 1992, 1991, 1985)

Roberto A. Galvan P
Southwest Texas State Univ, LBJ Dr, San Marcos, TX
78666, 512-245-2360
Pubs: *Poemas En Espanol Por Un Mexiamericano*
(Mexican American Cultural Center Pr, 1977)

Greg Garrett W
Baylor Univ, English Dept, Waco, TX 76798, 254-710-6879
Pubs: *Texas Short Fiction: Anth* (ALE Pub, 1995),
*Writers' Forum, High Plains Literary Rev, Grain, South
Dakota Rev, Laurel Rev, Negative Capability*

Daniel Garza P
5 Briarwood Cir
Richardson, TX 75080

Zulfikar Ghose P&W
Univ Texas, English Dept, Austin, TX 78712-1164
Pubs: *The Triple Mirror of the Self* (Bloomsbury, 1992),
Selected Poems (Oxford U Pr, 1991)

Miguel Gonzalez-Gerth P
Harry Ransom Humanities Center, Univ Texas, Austin, TX
78712, 512-471-8157
Pubs: *Palabras Inutilez* (Spain; Taller Fernandez
Ciudad, 1988)

Juan G. Guevara P
PO Box 446
Benavides, TX 78341, 512-256-3308

James Haining P
Salt Lick Press/LHB, PO Box 15471, Austin, TX
78761-5471, 512-450-0952
Pubs: *A Child's Garden* (Salt Lick Pr, 1987), *Beowulf to
Beatles & Beyond* (Macmillan, 1981)

Jim Hanson P
2114 Glenn Ln
Glenn Heights, TX 75115, 214-821-2740
Pubs: *Reasons for the Sky* (Toothpaste Pr, 1979),
Dental Floss, Mag City, Brilliant Corners

Devin Harrison   P
601 Petersburg St
Castroville, TX 78009-4538
    Pubs: *Lactuca, Riverrun, Passages North, Windless
    Orchard, Poem, Panhandler, South Dakota Rev*

Chris Haven   W
7302 Alabonson #1303
Houston, TX 77088, 281-591-0524
    Pubs: *Threepenny Rev, RE:AL, Massachusetts Rev,
    Hawaii Rev*

Don Hendrie, Jr.   W
714 Tuxedo Ave
San Antonio, TX 78209
    Pubs: *A Criminal Journey, Blount's Anvil* (Lynx Hse Pr,
    1990, 1980)

Edward Hirsch 🎤 ✈   P
Univ Houston, University Park, English Dept, Houston, TX
77204, 713-743-2956
    Pubs: *On Love, Earthly Measures, The Night Parade,
    Wild Gratitude* (Knopf, 1998, 1994, 1989, 1986), *New
    Yorker, Paris Rev, APR, DoubleTake*

Louise Horton   P&W
Brighton Gardens, 4401 Spicewood Springs Rd, #232,
Austin, TX 78759-8589
    Pubs: *Southern Humanities Rev*

Timothy Houghton   P
English Dept, Univ Houston, Creative Writing Program,
Houston, TX 77204-3012, 713-743-2390
    Pubs: *Below Two Skies* (Orchises Pr, 1993), *High
    Bridges* (Stride Pr, 1989), *Denver Qtly, Stand Mag,
    College English*

Diane Hueter   P
5210 15th
Lubbock, TX 79416, 806-795-2391
    Pubs: *Kansas: Just Before Sleep* (Cottonwood Rev,
    1978), *In the Middle: Midwestern Women Poets: Anth*
    (BKMK Pr, 1985), *Iris, Iowa Woman, Dekalb Lit Arts
    Jrnl, Kansas Qtly, Moons & Lion Tailes*

Albert Huffstickler   P
312 E 43 St, #103
Austin, TX 78751, 512-459-3472
    Pubs: *Quinlen, City of the Rain* (Press of Circumstance,
    1998, 1993), *Working on My Death Chant* (Back Yard
    Pr, 1992), *Poetry East, Poetry Motel, Heeltap, First
    Class, Rattle, Galley Sail*

Guida Jackson   W
Touchstone, PO Box 8308, Spring, TX 77387
    Pubs: *Virginia Diaspora* (Heritage Bks, 1992), *Women
    Who Ruled* (ABC-CLIO, 1990), *Heart to Hearth* (Prism,
    1989), *Passing Through* (S&S, 1989), *Suddenly: Anth*
    (Martin Hse, 1998), *Texas Short Stories: Anth* (Browder
    Springs Pub, 1997)

Dan Kaderli   P&W
English Division, Univ Texas, 6900 Loop 1604 W, San
Antonio, TX 78249-0691, 512-691-4165
    Pubs: *The Lyric, Tucumcari Rev, Reflect, Bogg,
    SPSM&H, Iota, Negative Capability, Star Poets 2,
    Plains Poetry Jrnl, Howling Mantra, Pegasus, Spitball*

T. J. Kallsen   P
600 Bostwick
Nacogdoches, TX 75961, 409-564-3347
    Pubs: *Making: Selected Poems* (Touchstone, 1981),
    Kansas Qtly, Green's Mag, Lightworks

Cynthia King 🎤   W
5306 Institute Ln
Houston, TX 77005-1820, 713-526-0232
    Pubs: *Sailing Home* (Putnam, 1982), *Beggars &
    Choosers* (Viking, 1980), *Good Housekeeping*

Judith Kroll   P
Univ Texas, Parlin 108, English Dept, Austin, TX 78712,
512-320-0546
    Pubs: *Our Elephant & that Child* (Qtly Rev Poetry
    Series, 1991), *In the Temperate Zone* (Scribner, 1974),
    Kenyon Rev, Southern Rev, American Voice

Patricia Clare Lamb   P
3614 Montrose Blvd, Ste 405
Houston, TX 77006-4651
Internet: harbottle@aol.com
    Pubs: *The Long Love, All Men By Nature* (Harbottle Pr,
    1998, 1993), *Plains Poetry Jrnl, Midwest Qtly Rev,
    Commonweal*

James Langdon   P&W
1202 Seagler Rd, #60
Houston, TX 77042, 713-266-1229
    Pubs: *Chicago Rev, Contempora, Descant, Maple Leaf
    Rag, New Orleans Rev, Rapport*

Barbara D. Langham 🎤 ✈   W
B.D. Langham Public Relations, 1 Riverway, Ste 2525,
Houston, TX 77056-1951, 713-961-4235
    Pubs: *NAR, Bellingham Rev, Descant, Fiction Texas,
    Crosscurrents, Pig Iron*

William Laufer 🎤   W
PO Box 8308
The Woodlands, TX 77387-3295
    Pubs: *P, Four Sea Interludes, Surrogates Fiction & Art*
(Third Coast Letterpress, 1998, 1996, 1995), *The
Indochina Suite* (Touchstone Pr, 1994), *Suddenly 2000:
Anth, Suddenly II: Anth* (Martin Hse, 2000, 1999)

Anne Leaton   W
3209 College Ave
Forth Worth, TX 76110, 817-923-7308
    Pubs: *Blackbird, Bye Bye* (Virago Pr, 1989), *Pearl*
(Knopf, 1989), *Esquire, Transatlantic Rev, Storia,
Cosmopolitan*

J. R. LeMaster   P
201 Harrington Ave
Waco, TX 76706-1519, 254-754-4358
    Pubs: *Purple Bamboo, First Person, Second* (Tagore
Inst of Creative Writing, 1988, 1983)

Jim Linebarger 🎤 ✈   P
210 Solar Way
Denton, TX 76207, 940-243-9020
Internet: jline@metronet.com
    Pubs: *Anecdotal Evidence* (Point Riders Pr, 1993), *The
Worcester Poems* (Trilobite Pr, 1991), *SW Rev,
Wormwood Rev, SE Rev, Southern Humanities Rev*

Paul Lisicky   W
1617 Branard St
Houston, TX 77006, 713-529-9586
    Pubs: *Lawnboy* (Turtle Point Pr, 1999), *Best American
Gay Fiction 2: Anth* (Little, Brown, 1997), *Men on Men
6: Anth* (Dutton, 1996), *Flash Fiction: Anth* (Norton,
1992), *Boulevard, Qtly West, Gulf Coast, Provincetown
Arts, Mississippi Rev*

Marianne McNeil Logan 🎤 ✈   P
7003 Amarillo Blvd, E, #16
Amarillo, TX 79107, 806-372-5032
    Pubs: *Designed by Heritage* (PR Pub, 1998), *Girls
Write Cowboy Poetry Too* (Nostalgic Nook Pr, 1990),
Pudgy Parodies (Tanglewood, 1988), *Country Mag,
Ellery Queen's Mystery Mag, Midwest Poetry*

Patricia Looker   P&W
PO Box 1551
Bellaire, TX 77401-1551, 713-432-7873
    Pubs: *Straight Ahead, Wellspring, Apalachee Qtly,
Forum, Quartet, Whetstone, Blonde on Blonde*

Marianne Loyd   P
3704 Tompkins
Baytown, TX 77521
    Pubs: *Stone Country, Uroboros, Tamarack, New Letters*

Grant Lyons 🎤   W
2923 Woodcrest
San Antonio, TX 78209-3047, 210-822-5409
    Pubs: *4.4.4.* (U Missouri Pr, 1977), *Negative Capability,
Seattle Rev, Confrontation, Cimarron Rev, NW Rev,
Redbook*

Cynthia Macdonald   P
1400 Hermann Dr, #8E
Houston, TX 77004, 713-520-6598
    Pubs: *Living Wills: New & Selected Poems, Alternate
Means of Transport* (Knopf, 1991, 1985)

Janet Marks   P
2718 Wroxton Rd, #3
Houston, TX 77005-1359, 713-660-8508
    Pubs: *Poets on Parnassus: Anth* (U California Pr,
1994), *Songs for Our Voices: Anth* (Judah L. Magnes
Museum, 1993), *Synapse, Houston Poetry Festival 1997
Anth*

Kenard Marlowe   P
3401 Cartagena Dr
Corpus Christi, TX 78418-3922, 512-937-5215
    Pubs: *Thinking Allowed* (Indiana Pub, 1994)

Lee Martin 🎤 ✈   W
English Dept, Univ of North Texas, Denton, TX
76203-6827, 940-565-2126
Internet: lmartin@unt.edu
    Pubs: *From Our House* (Dutton, 2000), *The Least You
Need to Know* (Sarabande Bks, 1996), *Harper's,
Georgia Rev, Story, DoubleTake, Glimmer Train*

Janet McCann 🎤 ✈   P
Texas A&M Univ, English Dept, College Station, TX
77843-4227, 409-845-8316
    Pubs: *Looking for Buddha in the Barbed Wire Garden*
(Avisson Pr, 1996), *Afterword* (Franciscan U Pr, 1990),
Borderlands, Christian Century
I.D.: Christian, Feminist

Cormac McCarthy   W
1510 N Brown
El Paso, TX 79902

Walt McDonald 🎤 ✈   P&W
English Dept, Texas Tech Univ, Lubbock, TX 79409,
806-742-2501
Internet: http://english.ttu.edu/faculty/McDonald
    Pubs: *All Occasions* (U Notre Dame Pr, 2000),
Blessings the Body Gave (Ohio State U Pr, 1998),
Counting Survivors (U Pitt Pr, 1995), *Night Landings*
(H&R, 1989), *American Scholar, Atlantic, Poetry,
Sewanee Rev, Southern Rev, APR*

Neill Megaw P
2805 Bowman Ave
Austin, TX 78703, 512-472-5522
    Pubs: *The Spectator, Negative Capability, Sequoia, Hellas, The Lyric, South Coast Poetry Jrnl, The Formalist*

James Michener W
2706 Mountain Laurel Ln
Austin, TX 78703-1143
    Pubs: *Space* (Random Hse, 1982), *Chesapeake*

Christopher Middleton P
Univ Texas, Dept Germanic Languages, Austin, TX 78712, 512-471-4123
    Pubs: *In the Mirror of the Eighth King* (Sun & Moon Pr, 1999), *Intimate Chronicles, The Balcony Tree* (Sheep Meadow Pr, 1996, 1992)

Bryce Milligan ♀ ✈ P&W
627 E Guenther
San Antonio, TX 78210-1134, 210-222-8449
Internet: milligan@wingspress.com
    Pubs: *Prince of Ireland* (Holiday Hse, 2001), *Comanche Captive, Battle of the Alamo* (Eakin Pr, 2000, 1999), *Lawmen* (Disney Pr, 1994), *Daysleepers & Other Poems* (Corona, 1984)

A. G. Mojtabai ♀ ✈ P&W
2102 S Hughes
Amarillo, TX 79109-2212, 806-376-9434
    Pubs: *Soon* (Zoland Bks, 1998), *Blessed Assurance* (Syracuse U Pr, 1997), *Called Out, Ordinary Time* (Doubleday, 1994, 1994)

Jane P. Moreland P&W
503 Shadywood
Houston, TX 77057, 713-975-6711
    Pubs: *Iowa Rev, Mademoiselle, Poetry, Poetry NW, Georgia Rev*

E'Lane Carlisle Murray P&W
433 Haroldson Pl
Corpus Christi, TX 78412, 512-991-5294
    Pubs: *The Lace of Tough Mesquite: A Texas Heritage* (Eakin Pr, 1993), *Southern Living, Texas Highways*

Jack Myers P
Southern Methodist Univ, English Dept, Dallas, TX 75275, 214-768-4369
    Pubs: *Blindsided, New American Poets of the '90s: Anth* (Godine, 1992, 1992), *Poetry, Esquire, APR*

Isabel Nathaniel ♀ ✈ P
18040 Midway Rd, Villa #215
Dallas, TX 75287, 972-380-6128
    Pubs: *The Dominion of Lights* (Copper Beech Pr, 1996), *Ravishing DisUnities: Anth* (Wesleyan U Pr, 2000), *Poetry, Nation, Field, Ploughshares, Prairie Schooner, The Jrnl*

Kim L. Neidigh P&W
231 Radiance Ave
San Antonio, TX 78218
    Pubs: *Poetry Forum Jrnl, Wicked Mystic, Realm of the Vampire, Ripples, Deathrealm, Bloodrake, Pursuit*

Sheryl L. Nelms ♀ ✈ P
PO Box 674
Azle, TX 76098-0674, 817-444-1149
Internet: slnelms@aol.com
    Pubs: *Aunt Emma Collected Teeth* (Sweet Annie Pr, 1999), *Friday Night Desperate* (IM Pr, 1997), *Land of the Blue Paloverde* (Shooting Star Pr, 1995), *Their Combs Turn Red in the Spring* (Northwoods Pr, 1984), *Kaleidoscope, Kansas Qtly*
I.D.: Women, Kansasan

Ben Norwood P&W
3046 Brown Lee Dr, #2016
Grand Prairie, TX 75052-7775, 817-695-4146
    Pubs: *Travois: An Anth of Texas Poetry* (Thorp Springs Pr, 1976), *Sulphur River, Negative Capability, Unity, Stone Drum*

Warren Norwood P&W
500 Green Tree
Weatherford, TX 76087-8909, 817-596-5201
    Pubs: *True Jaguar* (Bantam, 1988), *Space Opera: Anth* (Del Rey, 1996), *Twilight Zone, Lookout, Green Fuse*

Naomi Shihab Nye ♀ ✈ W
806 S Main Ave
San Antonio, TX 78204, 210-222-0504
Internet: nshihab@aol.com
    Pubs: *Come with Me* (Greenwillow, 2000), *Fuel, Red Suitcase* (BOA Edtns, 1998, 1994), *Words Under the Words* (Far Corner Bks, 1995), *Atlantic, Iowa Rev, Ploughshares, SW Rev, Wilderness, Five Points, Atlanta Rev, Georgia Rev, Indiana Rev*

David Offutt ♀ ✈ P
759 Redwood #3
Rockport, TX 78382-5961, 888-522-6464
    Pubs: *A Perishable Good* (Inflammable Pr, 1997), *Perceptions: Anth* (Write Technique, 1991), *Ship of Fools, Raintown Rev, Mother Earth Intl, Chachalaca, Poet House, Free Lunch, Poetry Motel, Maverick Pr, Tucumcari, Synaesthetic, Lost & Found Times, Aura*
I.D.: Catholic. Groups: Children, Literacy

Dave Oliphant 🎤 ✈   P&W
Univ Texas, Main 201, Austin, TX 78712, 512-331-1557
Internet: doliphant@mail.utexas.edu
    Pubs: *Memories of Texas Towns & Cities* (Host, 2000),
    *New Texas, New Letters, Colorado Qtly, College
    English, South Dakota Rev*

Joe Olvera   P&W
12400 Rojas Dr, #49
El Paso, TX 79927, 915-592-9870
    Pubs: *Drugs: Frankly Speaking* (SW Pub, 1980), *Voces
    de la Gente* (Mictla Pub, 1972)

Carolyn Osborn 🎤 ✈   W
3612 Windsor Rd
Austin, TX 78703-1538, 512-472-4533
    Pubs: *Warriors & Maidens* (Texas Christian U Pr,
    1991), *The O. Henry Awards: Anth* (Doubleday, 1991),
    Witness, SW Rev, Antioch Rev

Keddy Ann Outlaw 🎤 ✈   P&W
3003 Linkwood Dr
Houston, TX 77025-3813, 713-668-8273
    Pubs: *At Our Core: Anth, I Am Becoming the Woman
    I've Wanted: Anth* (Papier-Mache, 1998, 1994), *Texas
    Short Stories: Anth* (Browder Springs, 1999, 1997),
    Texas Short Fiction III: Anth (ALE Pub, 1996)

Leslie Palmer 🎤 ✈   P
Univ North Texas, English Dept, Denton, TX 76203,
817-387-5460
    Pubs: *Disgraceland* (Pine Tree Pr, 2000), *Swollen Foot,
    The Devil Sells Ice Cream* (Windy-Dawn, 1999, 1994),
    Ode to a Frozen Dog (Laughing Bear, 1992), *Poetry &
    Audience, Green's Mag, Blue Jacket, Cape Rock,
    Southern Humanities Rev, Linq*

Dave Parsons 🎤 ✈   P
414 Oak Hill
Conroe, TX 77304-1906, 409-539-2466
    Pubs: *Editing Sky* (Texas Rev Pr, 1999), *Texas Rev,
    Gulf Coast, Southwestern American Lit, Anth of
    Magazine Verse & Yearbook of Poetry, Louisiana Lit,
    Touchstone, Standpoints*

Tom Person   P
PO Box 613322
Dallas, TX 75261-3322, 817-283-6303
    Pubs: *Small Pr, NYQ, Nexus, Interstate, Iron,
    Coffeehouse Poets Qtly*

Estela Portillo   P&W
131 Clairemont
El Paso, TX 79912, 915-584-8841

Ron Querry   W
2415 E Musser
Laredo, TX 78043-2434, 11524-152-3542
    Pubs: *Bad Medicine, The Death of Bernadette Lefthand*
    (Bantam Bks, 1998, 1995), *I See By My Get-Up* (U
    Oklahoma Pr, 1994)

S. Ramnath   P&W
PO Box 371823
El Paso, TX 79937-1823, 915-592-3701
    Pubs: *Eye of the Beast* (Vergin Pr, 1986), *Rings in a
    Tree Trunk* (India; Writers Workshop, 1976), *Bedside
    Prayers: Anth* (Harper SF, 1997), *Willow Springs,
    Weber Studies, Press, Litspeak, Kerf, Arkansas Qtly,
    Quixote Qtly, Maverick Pr*

Pedro Revuelta   P
c/o Gutierrez Revuelta, Univ Houston, Spanish Dept,
Houston, TX 77204-3784, 713-749-3064
    Pubs: *Accidentes Y Otros Recursos* (Spain; Ediciones
    Libertarias, 1990), *Complejas Perspectivas* (Spain;
    Editorial Origenes, 1988), *Maize, el ultimo vuelo*

Clay Reynolds 🎤 ✈   W
909 Hilton Pl
Denton, TX 76201-8605, 940-566-2512
Internet: rclayr@aol.com
    Pubs: *Monuments* (Texas Tech U Pr, 2000), *Players*
    (Carroll & Graf, 1998), *Rage, Franklin's Crossing*
    (NAL/Signet, 1994, 1993), *Descant, Writers' Forum,
    Texas Rev, i.e. Mag, Cimarron Rev, Concho River Rev*

Brian Paul Robertson   P
516 Tamarack
McAllen, TX 78501

Del Marie Rogers   P
4804 Haverwood Ln, #922
Dallas, TX 75287, 972-735-0151
    Pubs: *Close to Ground* (Corona, 1990), *Anthology for
    Young Readers* (S&S, 1996), *Puerto del Sol, Texas
    Observer, Colorado Rev, Blue Mesa Rev, Nation,
    Epoch*

Amber Rollins 🎤 ✈   W
6618 Laura Ann Ct
Fort Worth, TX 76118-6278, 817-284-4322
Internet: amberrollins@hotmail.com
    Pubs: *EOTU, Paper Bag, Fiction Forum, The Torch,
    DC, After Hours, Being, Bahlasti Papers, Starsong,
    Outrage*

Paul Ruffin   P&W
Sam Houston State Univ, Sam Houston Ave, English
Dept, Huntsville, TX 77341, 409-294-1429
    Pubs: *Circling* (Browder Springs Pr, 1996), *The Man
    Who Would Be God* (SMU Pr, 1993), *Southern Rev,
    Michigan Qtly Rev, Georgia Rev, American Literary
    Rev, Alaska Qtly Rev, Poetry*

Annette Sanford W
Box 596
Ganado, TX 77962, 512-771-3654
Pubs: *Lasting Attachments, Common Bonds: Stories By & About Texas Women: Anth* (SMU Pr, 1989, 1990), *Story, American Short Fiction*

Rainer Schulte P
Center for Translation Studies, Univ Texas-Dallas, Box 830688, Richardson, TX 75083-0688, 214-690-2092
Pubs: *The Other Side of the Word* (Texas Writers, 1978), *Suicide at the Piano* (Sono Nis, 1970)

Daryl Scroggins 🎤 ✈ W
6200 Bryan Pkwy
Dallas, TX 75214-4302, 214-821-9317
Pubs: *elimae.com, web del sol.com, Pearl, Asylum Annual, The Qtly, NW Rev, Madison Rev, Carolina Qtly*

Jan Epton Seale 🎤 ✈ P
400 Sycamore
McAllen, TX 78501-2227, 956-686-4033
Internet: janseale@rgv.net
Pubs: *The Yin of It* (Pecan Grove Pr, 2000), *Airlift* (TCU Pr, 1992), *For She Is the Tree of Life: Anth* (Conari Pr, 1994), *Yale Rev, Texas Monthly, High Plains Lit Rev, Cape Rock, Nimrod, Passages North, Blue Mesa, COE Rev, Mesquite Rev*
Groups: Seniors, Women

Wendell P. Sexton P
4302 Rosebud Dr
Houston, TX 77053, 713-435-0867
Pubs: *Poets Corner* (Office Duplication Classes, 1975)

Samuel B. Southwell W
1217 W Main
Houston, TX 77006
Pubs: *Kenneth Burke & Martin Heidegger: With a Note Against Deconstructionism* (U Florida, 1988), *If All the Rebels Die* (Doubleday, 1966)

L. Sprague de Camp W
3453 Hearst Castle Way
Plano, TX 75025
Pubs: *Rivers of Time, The Enchanter Reborn* (w/C. Stasheff) (Baen Bks, 1993, 1992), *Analog, Asimov's Sci Fi, Command, Nature, Expanse*

Kristi Sprinkle P&W
2609 Nottingham Ln
Austin, TX 78704
Pubs: *Freelight, Paramour, Different Drummer, Austin Chronicle*

Cathy Stern 🎤 ✈ P
12427 Old Oaks Dr
Houston, TX 77024-4911, 713-465-8017
Pubs: *A Wider Giving: Anth* (Chicory Blue Pr, 1988), *Paris Rev, New Republic, Shenandoah*

Alex Stevens P
801 Rutland
Houston, TX 77007, 713-868-3716
Pubs: *New Yorker, Poetry, Georgia Rev, New Republic*

Gail Donohue Storey 🎤 ✈ P&W
3907 Swarthmore
Houston, TX 77005-3611, 713-669-9318
Pubs: *God's Country Club, The Lord's Motel* (Persea Bks, 1996, 1992), *Fiction, NAR, Chicago Rev, Gulf Coast, Ellipses, Mississippi Valley Rev*

James L. Stowe W
709 Baltimore
El Paso, TX 79902
Pubs: *Winter Stalk* (S&S, 1978)

Semon Strobos W
2281 Bretzke Ln
New Braunfels, TX 78132, 210-609-0527
Pubs: *NAR, Epoch, Chariton Rev, Antioch Rev, Descant, Alabama Literary Rev*

Belinda Subraman P
PO Box 370322
El Paso, TX 79937-0322, 915-566-1858
Internet: subraman1@msn.com
Pubs: *Notes of a Human Warehouse Engineer* (Nerve Cowboy, 1998), *Finding Reality in Myth* (Chiron Rev Pr, 1996), *Between the Cracks: Anth* (Daedalus, 1996), *Mondo Barbie: Anth* (St Martin's Pr, 1993), *Arkansas Rev, India Currents, Best Texas Writing*

Thea Temple P&W
3109 Caribou Ct
Mesquite, TX 75181, 972-222-3973
Pubs: *River Styx, Sycamore Rev, Yellow Silk, Chiron Rev, Beloit Fiction Jrnl, The New Press, Alabama Literary Rev, Japanophile*

Heriberto Teran P
2314 Baltimore St
Laredo, TX 78040, 512-722-7435

Larry D. Thomas 🎤 ✈ P
2006 Commonwealth
Houston, TX 77006-1804, 713-523-8147
Pubs: *Lighthouse Keeper* (Timberline, 2000), *Midwest Qtly, Louisiana Lit, Cottonwood, JAMA, Whole Notes, Plainsongs, Intl Poetry Rev, Southwestern Amer Lit, Green Hills Lit Lantern, Amer Indian Culture/Research Jrnl, Blue Violin, Modern Haiku*

Lorenzo Thomas 🎙 ✈   P
Box 14645
Houston, TX 77221, 713-221-8475
Internet: thomasl@zeus.dt.uh.edu
   Pubs: *The Bathers* (Reed & Cannon, 1981), *Chances
Are Few (Blue Wind Pr, 1979), *Postmodern American
Poetry: Anth* (Norton, 1994), *Ploughshares, Long News*

Ruby C. Tolliver   W
1806 Pin Oak Ln
Conroe, TX 77302, 409-756-4659
   Pubs: *Boomer's Kids, Blind Bess, Buddy & M*
(Hendrick-Long Pub, 1992, 1990), *Have Gun, Need
Bullets* (TCU Pr, 1991)

Frederick Turner   P&W
School of Arts & Humanities, Univ Texas-Dallas,
Richardson, TX 75083, 214-690-2777
   Pubs: *April Wind, Beauty* (U Pr Virginia, 1992, 1992),
Tempest, Flute & Oz (Persea Bks, 1991), *Harper's,
Poetry*

Leslie Ullman   P
Creative Writing Program, Univ Texas, English Dept, El
Paso, TX 79968, 505-874-3068
Internet: lullman@miners.utep.edu
   Pubs: *Slow Work Through Sand* (U Iowa Pr, 1998),
Dreams By No One's Daughter (U Pitt Pr, 1987),
Natural Histories (Yale U Pr, 1979), *Poetry, Kenyon
Rev, Bloomsbury Rev*

Leo Vroman   P
1600 Texas St
Fort Worth, TX 76102, 817-870-1172
   Pubs: *Psalmen en Andere Gedichten* (Amsterdam;
Querido, 1997), *Flight 800/Vlucht 800, Love, Greatly
Enlarged* (CCC, 1997, 1992)

Brian Walker   P
PO Box 5143
Lubbock, TX 79417
   Pubs: *Fiddlehead, Poetry Ireland Rev, Poetry Wales,
Transnational Perspectives, Bitterroot*

William Wenthe   P
Dept of English, Box 43091, Texas Tech Univ, Lubbock,
TX 79410, 806-742-2501
   Pubs: *Birds of Hoboken* (Orchises Pr, 1995), *Best
Texas Writing I: Anth* (Rancho Loco Pr, 1998), *Image,
Laurel Rev, Orion, Southern Rev, Meridian, Press, The
Georgia Rev, Texas Rev, Poetry East, Southern
Humanities Rev, Cimarron Rev, TriQtly*

Kenneth Wheatcroft-Pardue 🎙 ✈   P
1805 Robinwood Dr
Forth Worth, TX 76111-6110, 817-834-3341
Internet: kwheatcroftpardue@yahoo.com
   Pubs: *Sleepy Tree I: Anth* (Sleepy Tree Pr, 1980),
*California Qtly, Sulphur, Poetry Motel, Touchstone,
Maverick Press, Concho River Rev*

Thomas Whitbread   P
English Dept, Univ Texas, Austin, TX 78712,
512-471-4991
   Pubs: *Whomp & Moonshiver* (BOA Edtns, 1982), *Four
Infinitives* (H&R, 1964)

Brenda Black White   P
2508 Washington
Commerce, TX 75428, 903-886-3822
   Pubs: *Callahan County* (Plainview Pr, 1988), *New
Texas '95: Anth, Texas in Poetry: Anth* (Ctr for Texas
Studies, 1995, 1994), *RE:AL, Ms., Confrontation*

J. Whitebird   W
13815 Bay Gardens Dr
Sugar Land, TX 77478-1723, 281-494-1380
   Pubs: *Heat & Other Stories* (Arbiter Pr, 1990), *The
North Beach Papers* (Suck Egg Mule Pr, 1985),
Crosscurrents, Plainswoman, Poemail

Scott Wiggerman   P
1310 Crestwood Rd
Austin, TX 78722, 512-467-0678
   Pubs: *Borderlands: Texas Poetry Rev, Café Rev,
Limestone Circle, RFD: A County Journal, Paterson
Literary Rev, Will Work for Peace, @Austin, Entre
Nous, Modern Words*

Chris Willerton   P
English Dept, Abilene Christian Univ, Box 8242, ACU Sta,
Abilene, TX 79699, 915-674-2259
   Pubs: *Texas in Poetry: Anth* (U North Texas Pr, 1994),
New Texas '93: Anth (Ctr for Texas Studies, 1993),
Borderlands, Riversedge, Literary Rev, SPR

Lex Williford   W
English Dept; Hudspeth Hall Rm 113, U of Texas at El
Paso, 500 W University Ave, El Paso, TX 79968-0526,
915-747-5731
Internet: lex@utep.edu
   Pubs: *Macauley's Thumb* (U Iowa Pr, 1994), *Scribner's
Anth of Contemporary Short Fiction* (S&S, 1999),
*Glimmer Train, Sou'wester, Fiction, Qtly West, New
Texas, Laurel Rev, Virginia Qtly Rev, Story Qtly,
Southern Rev, Shenandoah*

Miles Wilson   P&W
906 Clyde St
San Marcos, TX 78666, 512-392-9643
   Pubs: *Line of Fall* (U Iowa Pr, 1989), *Gettysburg Rev,
Georgia Rev, Poetry, SW Rev, NAR, Iowa Rev*

Steve Wilson 🎙 ✈   P
English Dept, Southwest Texas State Univ, San Marcos,
TX 78666, 512-245-2163
Internet: sw13@swt.edu
   Pubs: *The Singapore Express, Allegory Dance* (Black
Tie Pr, 1994, 1991), *American Poetry: Anth* (Carnegie
Mellon U Pr, 2000), *What Have You Lost?: Anth*
(Greenwillow Bks, 1999), *Yankee Mag, Commonweal,
America, CSM, New Letters*
I.D.: Irish-American. Groups: Children, Travel

Marion Winik P
3808 Ridgelea Dr
Austin, TX 78731-6125
   Pubs: *Boy Crazy* (Sloughpress, 1986), *Nonstop* (Cedar Rock, 1981)

Bryan Woolley W
18040 Midway Rd, Villa 215
Dallas, TX 75287, 214-380-6128
   Pubs: *The Bride Wore Crimson, The Edge of the West* (Texas Western, 1993, 1990), *Time & Place* (TCU, 1985)

John Works W
1600 Forest Trail
Austin, TX 78703
   Pubs: *Thank You Queen Isabella* (Texas A&M U, 1986), *Humanities Rev, Cottonwood Rev*

Fabian Worsham P
English Dept, Univ Houston-Downtown, 1 Main St, Houston, TX 77002, 713-221-8115
   Pubs: *Vulture Woman* (Mac*Kinations Pr, 1994), *Aunt Erma's Country Kitchen & Bordello* (Signpost Pr, 1985), *New Texas, Southern Humanities Rev, Florida Rev*

UTAH

Margaret Pabst Battin W
Philosophy Dept, Univ of Utah, Salt Lake City, UT 84112, 801-581-6608
   Pubs: *The Least Worst Death* (Oxford U Pr, 1994)

Kenneth W. Brewer P
English Dept, Utah State Univ, Logan, UT 84322-3200, 435-797-3516
   Pubs: *The Place in Between* (Limberlost Pr, 1998), *To Remember What Is Lost* (Utah State U Pr, 1989), *Great & Peculiar Beauty, A Utah Reader: Anth* (Gibbs Smith, 1995), *Poetry NW, Kansas Qtly*

Alex Caldiero PP&P
1978 N 100 E
Orem, UT 84057, 801-224-8642
   Pubs: *Various Atmospheres* (Signature Bks, 1998), *Dictionary of the Text-Sounds Texts* (Morrow, 1980), *Avant-Guards: Anth* (A Capella Bks, 1994), *Clown War, Handbook, Screens & Tasted Parallels, Canyon Echo*

Lawrence Coates W
Southern Utah Univ, English Dept, Cedar City, UT 84720, 435-586-7835
   Pubs: *The Blossom Festival: Anth* (U Nevada Pr, 1999), *Connecticut Rev, Blue Mesa Rev, Contemporary Satire, Writers' Forum, Long Story, Toyon, Santa Clara Rev, Missouri Rev*

Brewster Ghiselin P
Univ Utah, English Dept 3500 LNCO, Salt Lake City, UT 84112, 801-581-6168
   Pubs: *Flame: Poems 1980-90, Windrose: Poems 1929-79* (U Utah 1990, 1980), *Poetry, Aperture, Letteratura, Hudson Rev, Story, Encounter*

Joan Gilgun W
1700 S 800 E
Lewiston, UT 84320
   Pubs: *The Uncle* (Cadmus Edtns, 1982), *Dialogue, New Voices, Innisfree, Western Humanities Rev*

Edward L. Hart P
1401 Cherry Ln
Provo, UT 84604, 801-375-0871
   Pubs: *To Utah* (Brigham Young U Pr, 1979), *BPJ, Western Humanities Rev*

Robert L. Jones P
Univ Utah, English Dept, 341 0SH, Salt Lake City, UT 84112
   Pubs: *Wild Onion* (Graywolf Pr, 1985), *The Space I Occupy* (Skywriting, 1977), *Kansas Qtly*

Lance Larsen 🎤 ✈ P
3077 JKHB, Brigham Young U
Provo, UT 84602, 801-378-8104
Internet: Lance_Larsen@byu.edu
   Pubs: *Erasable Walls* (New Issues Pr, 1998), *American Poetry: Anth* (Carnegie Mellon U Pr, 2000), *Threepenny Rev, Antioch Rev, Field, New Republic, Qtly West, Kenyon Rev, Paris Rev, Salmagundi, River Styx, Boulevard, Shenandoah, Western Humanities Rev*

David Lee 🎤 ✈ P
Dept of Language & Literature, Southern Utah State College, Cedar City, UT 84720, 801-586-7835
   Pubs: *A Legacy of Shadows, News from Down to the Café, Day's Work* (Copper Canyon Pr, 1999, 1999, 1990), *Paragonah Canyon, Autumn* (Brooding Heron Pr, 1988)

Harris Lenowitz P
Middle East Center, Univ Utah, Salt Lake City, UT 84112, 801-581-6181
   Pubs: *Transparencies: Jewish Pages* (Finch Lane, 1985), *The Sayings of Yakov Frank* (Tree, 1978)

Edward Lueders 🎤 ✈ P
958 S Windsor St
Salt Lake City, UT 84105-1308, 801-539-0430
   Pubs: *The Clam Lake Papers* (Wm. Caxton Ltd, 1996), *The Wake of the General Bliss* (U Utah Pr, 1989), *Poetry, Theology Today, Poetry Nippon, Terra Nova, Prairie Schooner, Weber Studies*
Groups: Translation

Lynne Butler Oaks   W
3945 S Wasatch Blvd, #260
Salt Lake City, UT 84124, 801-321-1808
  Pubs: *Missouri Rev, Fiction Intl, Story Qtly, The Qtly,*
  Utah Holiday

Jacqueline Osherow   P
Univ Utah, English Dept, 3500 LNCO, Salt Lake City, UT
84112
  Pubs: *With a Moon in Transit* (Grove Poetry, 1996),
  Conversations with Survivors, Looking for Angels in
  New York (U Georgia Pr, 1994, 1988), *Paris Rev, New*
  Republic, TriQtly, Partisan Rev, SW Rev, Boulevard

Donald Revell   P
English Dept, Univ Utah, Salt Lake City, UT 84112,
801-581-3392
  Pubs: *Beautiful Shirt, Erasures, New Dark Ages*
  (Wesleyan, 1994, 1992, 1990), *Antaeus, APR, Grand*
  St, Conjunctions, Partisan Rev, Kenyon Rev

Stephen Ruffus   P
c/o Utah Arts Council, 617 E South Temple, Salt Lake
City, UT 84102, 801-533-5895
  Pubs: *Qtly West, Westigan Rev, Western Humanities*
  Rev

Natasha Saje   P
Westminster College, 1840 1300 East, Salt Lake City, UT
84105, 801-488-1692
  Pubs: *Red Under the Skin* (U Pittsburgh Pr, 1994),
  Poetry, Shenandoah, American Voice, Denver Qtly,
  Ploughshares

Richard Schramm   P
Univ Utah, English Dept, Salt Lake City, UT 84112
  Pubs: *Rooted in Silence* (Bobbs-Merrill, 1972), *New*
  Yorker, Antaeus, APR

Emma Lou Thayne   P&W
1965 St Mary's Dr
Salt Lake City, UT 84108, 801-581-1260
  Pubs: *All God's Critters Got a Place in the Choir*
  (w/L.T. Ulrich; Aspen, 1995), *Things Happen: Poems of*
  Survival (Signature Bks, 1991), *Network*

Melanie Rae Thon ♦ ✈   W
Dept of English, Univ of Utah, 255 S Central Campus Dr,
Rm 3500, Salt Lake City, UT 84112-0494
  Pubs: *Sweet Hearts* (HM, 2001), *First, Body* (H Holt,
  1998), *Iona Moon* (Plume, 1994), *Girls in the Grass,*
  Meteors in August (Random Hse, 1991, 1990), *Granta,*
  Paris Rev, Ontario Rev, Antaeus, Hudson Rev,
  Ploughshares
Groups: At-Risk Youth, Teenagers

David Widup   P
1930 E Sunridge Cir
Sandy, UT 84093
  Pubs: *In Country: Anth* (w/Michael Andrews;
  Bombshelter Pr, 1994), *Over to You: Anth* (w/Stellasue
  Lee; Bombshelter Pr, 1991), *ACM, Icarus Rev, Spillway,*
  Onthebus, Rattle

VERMONT

Thomas Absher   P
Vermont College, Montpelier, VT 05679, 802-828-8820
  Pubs: *The Calling* (Alice James Bks, 1987), *Forms of*
  Praise (Ohio State U Pr, 1981), *Ploughshares, Poetry,*
  Nation

Laurie Alberts ♦ ✈   W
PO Box 258
Westminster, VT 05158
Internet: lalberts@sover.net
  Pubs: *Lost Daughters, The Price of Land in Shelby* (U
  Pr of New England, 1999, 1996), *Goodnight Silky*
  Sullivan (U Missouri Pr, 1995), *Tempting Fate* (HM,
  1987)

Joan Aleshire ♦ ✈   P
223 Mitchell Rd
Cuttingsville, VT 05738, 802-492-3550
  Pubs: *The Yellow Transparents* (Four Way Bks, 1997),
  This Far (QRL, 1987), *Cloud Train* (Texas Tech, 1982),
  Outsiders: Anth (Milkweed, 1999), *Staring Back: Anth*
  (Dutton, 1997), *Marlboro Rev, Barrow St, QRL, Nation,*
  Seneca Rev
Groups: Seniors, Prisoners

Frank Anthony ♦ ✈   P
151 Main St, PO Box 483
Windsor, VT 05089, 802-674-2315
  Pubs: *Down Gullah, The Conch Chronicle, The Brussels*
  Book, The Amsterdam Papers, The Magic Bench (New
  Vision Pubs, 2000, 1999, 1998, 1997, 1996)

Bob Arnold   P
1604 River Rd
Guilford, VT 05301, 802-254-4242
Internet: www.sover.net/~poetry
  Pubs: *Once in Vermont* (Gnomon Pr, 1999),
  Honeymoon (Granite Pr, 2000), *Home: Anth* (Abrams,
  1999), *Outsiders: Anth* (Milkweed Edtns, 1999),
  American Train Letters (Coyote/SUNY Buffalo, 1995),
  Where Rivers Meet (Mad River, 1990), *On Stone*
  (Origin Pr, 1988)

E. R. Barna 👤 ✈ P
80 Park St
Brandon, VT 05733, 802-247-3146
Internet: gotobarn@sover.net
  Pubs: *Atlanta Rev, Agni, Firehouse, Worcester Rev,
  Longhouse, Afterthought, Mothering, Softball, Gob*
Groups: Children, Seniors

Ben Belitt P
PO Box 88
North Bennington, VT 05257-0088, 802-442-5956
  Pubs: *Graffiti & Other Poems* (Erewhon, 1990),
  Nowhere But Light (U Chicago Pr, 1970), *Possessions*
  (Godine, 1986), *Salmagundi, Yale Rev, Southern Rev*

T. Alan Broughton 👤 ✈ P&W
124 Spruce St
Burlington, VT 05401-4522, 802-864-4250
Internet: tbrought@zoo.uvm.edu
  Pubs: *The Origin of Green, In the Country of Elegies,
  Preparing to Be Happy* (Carnegie Mellon U Pr, 2001,
  1995, 1988), *Jesse Tree* (Juniper Pr, 1988)

David Budbill P
4592 E Hill Rd
Wolcott, VT 05680-4149, 802-888-3729
  Pubs: *Moment to Moment* (Copper Canyon Pr, 1999),
  Judevine: The Complete Poems (Chelsea Green, 1991),
  Why I Came to Judevine (White Pine, 1987), *Green
  Mountains Rev, Harper's, New Virginia Rev, The Sun,
  Cedar Hill Rev, Graffiti Rag, Maine Times, Ohio Rev*

Rhoda Carroll P
RR5, Box 1030, 2047 Elm St
Montpelier, VT 05602, 802-229-0037
  Pubs: *Slant, Nebraska Rev, Green Mountains Rev, Poet
  Lore, Visions Intl, Lake Effect, Laurel Rev, Texas Rev,
  Northern Rev, Tar River Poetry, Louisville Rev*

George R. Clay W
Wild Farm
Arlington, VT 05250, 802-362-1656

Greg Delanty 👤 ✈ P
3 Berry St
Burlington, VT 05401, 802-862-1259
  Pubs: *The Fifth Province* (Traffic St Pr, 2000), *Leper's
  Walk* (Carcanet Pr, 2001), *The Hellbox* (Oxford U Pr,
  1998), *American Wake* (Dufour Edtns, 1995), *Southward*
  (Louisiana U Pr, 1992), *Cast in the Fire* (Dolmen Pr,
  1986)

Rickey Gard Diamond 👤 ✈ W
31 Hebert Rd
Montpelier, VT 05602, 802-223-7911
Internet: rdiamond@norwich.edu
  Pubs: *Second Sight* (Calyx Bks, 1997), *Other Voices,
  Writers' Bar-B-Q, Plainswoman, Kalliope, Sewanee Rev,
  Louisville Rev*
I.D.: Feminist, Environmentalist

Susan M. Dodd W
Bennington College, Bennington, VT 05201
  Pubs: *Hell-Bent Men & Their Cities, Mamaw, No
  Earthly Notion* (Viking, 1990, 1988, 1986), *New Yorker*

Ellen Dudley 👤 ✈ P
The Marlboro Rev, PO Box 243, Marlboro, VT 05344,
802-254-4938
  Pubs: *Slow Burn* (Provincetown Arts Pr 1997),
  Outsiders: Anth (Milkweed Edtns 1999), *TriQtly, Agni,
  Massachusetts Rev*

Margaret Edwards P&W
Univ of Vermont, English Dept, 400 Old Mill, Burlington,
VT 05405, 802-862-4468
  Pubs: *Best American Short Stories: Anth* (HM, 1986),
  Virginia Qtly Rev, Vermont History

Kenward Elmslie P&W
c/o Poets Corner, Calais, VT 05648, 802-456-8123
  Pubs: *Routine Disruptions* (Coffee Hse Pr, 1998), *Pay
  Dirt* (Bamberger Bks, 1992), *Sung Sex* (Kulchur Fdn,
  1989), *26 Bars* (Z Pr, 1987), *NAW, o.blek, Conjunctions*

John Engels P
221 Shelburne St
Burlington, VT 05401, 802-865-2543
  Pubs: *Walking to Cootehill* (U Pr of New England,
  1993), *Cardinals in the Ice Age* (Graywolf Pr, 1987),
  Weather-Fear (U Georgia Pr, 1982)

James Facos 👤 ✈ P&W
333 Elm St
Montpelier, VT 05602-2213
  Pubs: *The Silver Lady* (Thorndike Pr, 1995), *Morning's
  Come Singing* (American Poetry Pr, 1981), *Bk of Light
  Verse: Anth* (Norton, 1986), *New Press Lit Qtly,
  Negative Capability, Stories*

Terry Farish 👤 ✈ W
Steerforth Press, PO Box 70, South Royalton, VT 05068,
802-763-2808
Internet: www.terryfarish.com
  Pubs: *House in Earnest, If the Tiger* (Steerforth Pr,
  2000, 1995), *Talking in Animal, Shelter for a Seabird,
  Why I'm Already Blue* (Greenwillow, 1996, 1990, 1989),
  Flower Shadows (Morrow, 1992)

Alvin Feinman P
PO Box 655
North Bennington, VT 05257

Ellen Frye W
7 Third Ave
White River Jct, VT 05001
  Pubs: *Amazon Story Bones* (Spinsters Ink, 1994), *The
  Other Sappho* (Firebrand Bks, 1989), *Calyx, Short
  Fiction By Women*

Lyle Glazier   P&W
RD 3, Niles Rd
Bennington, VT 05201-4959, 802-442-9459
   Pubs: *Prefatory Lyrics* (Coffee Hse Pr, 1991), *Azubah
Nye* (White Pine Pr, 1988), *Origin, Longhouse,
Shadow/Play, Tel-Let, New Yorker, Story*

Florence Grossman   P
PO Box 352
Bondville, VT 05340-0352
   Pubs: *Listening to the Bells* (Heinemann Boynton/Cook,
1991), *Nation, Poetry, New Criterion*

Robert Hahn   P
155 College Hill
Johnson, VT 05656-9134, 802-635-1246
Internet: hahnr@badger.jsc.vsc.edu
   Pubs: *No Messages* (U Notre Dame Pr, 2001), *All
Clear* (U South Carolina Pr, 1996), *Ontario Rev, Paris
Rev, SW Rev, Yale Rev, Partisan Rev*

H. Douglas Hall   P
RD
Cuttingsville, VT 05738, 802-492-3517
   Pubs: *Road Apple Rev, Loon, The Sun, Poetry Now,
Northern New England Rev*

Pamela Harrison 🎤 ✈   P
PO Box 1106
Norwich, VT 05055-1106, 802-649-2946
   Pubs: *Noah's Daughter, The Panhandler* (U West
Florida Pr, 1988), *College Handbook of Creative
Writing: Anth* (HBJ, 1991), *BPJ, Yankee, Poetry,
Cimarron Rev, Laurel Rev, Green Mountains Rev,
Sow's Ear, Contemporary Rev*

Shelby Hearon 🎤 ✈   W
246 S Union
Burlington, VT 05401, 802-660-4349
   Pubs: *Ella in Bloom* (Knopf, 2000), *Footprints, Life
Estates, Hug Dancing* (Knopf, 1996, 1994, 1991),
Redbook, GQ, Cosmopolitan

Bruce Hesselbach   P&W
43 Bruce Brook Rd
Newfane, VT 05345, 802-254-0236
   Pubs: *The Lyric, Piedmont Lit Rev, Reflect, Waterways*

Geof Hewitt 🎤 ✈   P
PO Box 51
Calais, VT 05648-0051, 802-828-3111
   Pubs: *Only What's Imagined* (Kumquat Pr, 2000), *Just
Worlds* (Ithaca Hse, 1989)

Edward Hoagland   W
RR1, Box 2977
Bennington, VT 05201-9735, 802-442-2088
   Pubs: *Balancing Acts, Heart's Desire* (S&S, 1992, 1988)

David Huddle 🎤 ✈   P&W
34 N Willams St
Burlington, VT 05401-3304, 802-864-6111
Internet: dhuddle@zoo.uvm.edu
   Pubs: *Not: A Trio* (U Notre Dame Pr, 2000), *Story of a
Million Years* (HM, 1999), *Summer Lake* (LSU Pr,
1999), *Tenorman* (Chronicle Bks, 1995), *Intimates*
(Godine, 1992), *Story, APR, Kenyon Rev, Antioch,
Epoch, Field, Poetry*

John Irving   W
The Turnbull Agency, PO Box 757, Dorset, VT 05251
   Pubs: *A Widow for One Year* (Random Hse, 1998),
The Cider House Rules (Morrow, 1985)

Galway Kinnell   P&W
Sheffield, VT 05966
   Pubs: *When One Has Lived a Long Time Alone*
(Knopf, 1990), *The Past, Selected Poems* (HM, 1985,
1982)

Sydney Lea 🎤 ✈   P&W
PO Box 9
Newbury, VT 05051, 802-866-5458
Internet: leabaron@together.net
   Pubs: *Pursuit of a Wound: New Poems, To the Bone:
New & Selected Poems* (U Illinois Pr, 2000, 1996),
Hunting the Whole Way Home (U Pr of New England,
1995), *New Yorker, Atlantic, Georgia Rev*
Groups: Nature/Environment

Gary Lenhart 🎤 ✈   P
166 Beaver Meadow Rd
Norwich, VT 05055
   Pubs: *Father & Son Night, Light Heart* (Hanging Loose,
1999, 1991), *One at a Time* (United Artists, 1983),
*Greetings, The World, Hanging Loose, Poetry Flash,
Exquisite Corpse*

Daniel Lusk   P&W
PO Box 369
Jonesville, VT 05466, 802-434-5688
   Pubs: *Kissing the Ground: New & Selected Poems*
(Onion River 1999), *The Cow Wars* (Nightshade 1995),
*Painted Bride Qtly, Green Mountains Rev, APR, St.
Andrews Rev, New Letters, New American Rev*

Gary Margolis 🎤 ✈   P
Middlebury College, Carr Hall, Middlebury, VT 05753,
802-493-5141
   Pubs: *Falling Awake, The Day We Still Stand Here* (U
Georgia Pr, 1986, 1983), *Poetry, TriQtly*

Lynn Martin   P
43 Westgate Apartments
Brattleboro, VT 05301-8935, 802-257-7748
   Pubs: *Visible Signs of Defiance* (Out of the Kitchen Pr,
1995), *My Lover Is a Woman: Anth* (Ballantine, 1996),
*Green Mountains, Connecticut Rev, Centennial Rev,
Metis*

Jean R. Matthew W
Box 147
Marshfield, VT 05658
    Pubs: *Testimony: Stories* (U Missouri Pr, 1987),
*Missouri Rev, Black Warrior Rev, Crescent Rev,
Southern Humanities Rev*

Paul McRay P
PO Box 26
Strafford, VT 05072-0026, 802-765-4024
    Pubs: *As Though Traveling Backwards Were Natural* (U
Wisconsin Pr/Windfall Prophets Pr, 1990), *Sweet
Nothings: Anth* (Illinois U Pr, 1994), *Anth of Mag Verse
& Yearbook of American Poetry 1988, Poetry, Antioch
Rev, Crazyhorse, Mississippi Valley Rev*

Don Mitchell W
RD #2 Box 2680
Vergennes, VT 05491, 802-545-2278
    Pubs: *The Souls of Lambs* (HM, 1979), *Thumb Tripping*
(Little, Brown, 1970), *Boston Mag, Yankee, Country
Jrnl, Harper's, Atlantic, Esquire*

Patty Mucha P
RD 3
St Johnsbury, VT 05819
    Pubs: *See Vermont* (Poets Mimeo Co-op, 1979),
Telephone, New Wilderness Audiographics

Patrick O'Connor P
PO Box 296
Killington, VT 05751-0296, 802-422-9399
    Pubs: *No Poem for Fritz* (Colorado Qtly, 1978), *The
Prayers of Man: Anth* (Ivan Oblensky, 1960), *Dance
Mag, Voices Israel*

Robert Pack P
RD #2
Cornwall, VT 05753, 802-462-2441

Grace Paley P&W
PO Box 620
Thetford Hill, VT 05074-0620
    Pubs: *Just As I Thought, The Collected Stories* (FSG,
1998, 1994), *New & Collected Poems* (Tilbury Pr,
1992), *Long Walks & Intimate Talks* (Feminist Pr, 1991)

Verbena Pastor P&W
Graduate Program, Vermont College of Norwich Univ,
Montpelier, VT 05602, 802-828-8831
    Pubs: *Kiria Andreov* (Rain Crow Publishing, 1997),
*Penny Dreadful, Green's Mag, The European, 100
Words, Alfred Hitchcock's Mystery, Ellery Queen's
Mystery, Yellow Silk, Bostonia, Stories*

Linda Peavy P&W
169 Garron Rd
Middletown Springs, VT 05757-4222, 802-235-2844
    Pubs: *Women in Waiting in the Westward Movement*
(w/U. Smith; U Oklahoma Pr, 1994), *Hard Love: Anth*
(Queen of Swords Pr, 1997), *Word of Mouth Anth*
(Crossing Pr, 1990), *Kalliope, Poets On, Texas Rev,
Lesbian Short Fiction, Writers' Forum, Earth's Daughters*

John Pember ♣ ✈ P
PO Box 185
Dorset, VT 05251-0185, 802-362-8189
Internet: poemz2@sover.net
    Pubs: *Rope to the Barn* (White Eagle Coffee Store Pr,
1993), *Under a Gull's Wing: Anth* (Down the Shore
Pub, 1996), *Footwork, Fresh Ground, Sunrust, Jrnl of
New Jersey Poets, Calypso, Poetpourri, Without Halos,
Northern New England Rev*

Verandah Porche ♣ ✈ P
45 Old County Rd
Guilford, VT 09301, 802-254-2442
Internet: verandah@sover.net
    Pubs: *Glancing Off* (See-Through Pr, 1987), *The Body's
Symmetry* (H&R, 1975), *CSM, Chrysalis Reader, Ms.,
New Boston Rev*
Groups: Seniors, Literacy

Burt Porter ♣ ✈ P
1101 Heights Rd
Glover, VT 05839, 802-525-3037
    Pubs: *Rhymes of the Magical World* (Other Media Pr,
1995), *Crows & Angels* (Bread & Puppet Pr, 1993),
*Hellas, The Lyric, Poet, Classical Outlook, The
Formalist*

Martha Ramsey ♣ ✈ P
PO Box 1001
Putney, VT 05346, 802-387-2884
    Pubs: *Blood Stories* (Cleveland St U Poetry Ctr, 1996),
*Boulevard, Passages North, New Letters, American
Voice, Soundings East, Sojourner*

Julia Randall P
Rte 1, Box 64
North Bennington, VT 05257
    Pubs: *The Path to Fairview: New & Selected, Moving
in Memory* (LSU, 1992, 1987), *Ploughshares, Kenyon
Rev*

F. D. Reeve P&W
PO Box 14
Wilmington, VT 05363-0014
    Pubs: *The Blue Boat on the St. Anne* (Bayeux Arts,
1999), *The Red Machines* (Azul Edtns, 1999), *Concrete
Music* (Pyncheon Hse, 1992), *The White Monk*
(Vanderbilt, 1989), *Sewanee, Poetry, APR, Hudson,
New England, Free Lunch, Michigan Qtly*

Kate Riley   W
RD2, Box 455A
Johnson, VT 05656, 802-635-7021
    Pubs: *Other Voices, Green Mountains Rev, Kalliope*

Mary Ruefle   P
PO Box 864
North Bennington, VT 05257
    Pubs: *Cold Pluto* (Carnegie Mellon U Pr, 1996), *The
    Adamant* (U Iowa Pr, 1989), *Life Without Speaking* (U
    Alabama Pr, 1987)

Stephen Sandy ♪ ✈   P
PO Box 276
Shaftsbury, VT 05262, 802-442-8496
Internet: sandys@bennington.edu
    Pubs: *Scales, Black Box, The Thread* (LSU Pr, 2002,
    1999, 1998), *Thanksgiving Over the Water, Man in the
    Open Air* (Knopf, 1992, 1988), *Partisan Rev, Smartish
    Pace, Paris Rev, Ploughshares, New Yorker, Southern
    Rev, Atlantic, APR, Kenyon Rev, Mudfish*

Jim Schley ♪ ✈   P
Blue Moon Cooperative, 24 Blue Moon Rd, South
Strafford, VT 05070-7703
Internet: jschley@sover.net
    Pubs: *One Another* (Chapiteau, 1999), *Best American
    Spiritual Writing: Anth* (HC, 2000), *Articulations: Anth* (U
    Iowa Pr, 1994), *Orion, Northern Woodlands, Ironwood,
    Crazyhorse, Garrison Keillor's Writer's Almanac*
Groups: Children, Seniors

Roger W. Shattuck   P
231 Forge Hill Rd
Lincoln, VT 05443-9184
    Pubs: *Half Tame* (U Texas, 1964), *Harper's, New
    Republic, New Yorker, Poetry, Virginia Qtly Rev*

Neil Shepard   P
Writing & Literature Dept, Johnson State College, Johnson,
VT 05656
    Pubs: *I'm Here Because I Lost My Way, Scavenging
    the Country for a Heartbeat* (Mid-List Pr, 1998, 1993),
    *TriQtly, Chelsea, Western Humanities Rev, Poetry East,
    Denver Qtly, Southern Rev, Antioch Rev*

Allen Shepherd   W
487 S Willard St
Burlington, VT 05401, 802-863-5672
    Pubs: *Kansas Qtly, Colorado Qtly, New Yorker, New
    Arts Rev, Cimarron Rev*

Joe Sherman   W
Box 22
Montgomery, VT 05470
    Pubs: *Fast Lane on a Dirt Road* (Countryman Pr,
    1991), *A Thousand Voices* (Rutledge Hill, 1987), *The
    House at Shelburne Farms* (Paul Eriksen, 1986)

Jane Shore   P
RR1, Box 4
East Calais, VT 05650
    Pubs: *The Minute Hand, Eye Level* (U Mass Pr, 1987,
    1977), *New Republic, Ploughshares*

Frank Short   P
12 Burnell Terr
St Albans, VT 05478-1803, 802-524-3749
    Pubs: *Bits, Bitterroot, Blue Unicorn, Chowder Rev,
    High-Coo, Poet Lore, Poetry Now, Snakeroot*

Tom Smith ♪ ✈   P
PO Box 223
Castleton, VT 05735-0223, 802-468-2277
    Pubs: *Trash* (Red Moon, 2000), *Writing on Pentecost*
    (Birch Brook, 1999), *Cow's Leap* (Fithian, 1999), *Iowa
    Rev, Crazyhorse*

Wendy Stevens   P&W
PO Box 189
Waterbury Center, VT 05677
    Pubs: *True Life Adventure Stories: Anth* (Crossing Pr,
    1983), *Fight Back: Anth* (Cleis Pr, 1981), *Nimrod*

Floyd C. Stuart ♪ ✈   P
6 North St
Northfield, VT 05663
    Pubs: *The Spirit That Moves Us: Anth* (The Spirit That
    Moves Us Pr, 1982), *Travelling America with Today's
    Poets: Anth* (Macmillan, 1976), *BPJ*

Joyce A Thomas ♪   P
PO Box 24
Castleton, VT 05735-0024, 802-468-5104
    Pubs: *Orpheus & Company: Contemporary Poems on
    Greek Mythology: Anth* (U Pr of New England, 1999),
    *Of Frogs & Toads: Poems & Short Prose Featuring:
    Anth* (Ione Pr, 1998), *Each in Her Own Way: Anth*
    (Queen of Swords Pr, 1994), *Florida Rev, blueLINE*

Susan Thomas   P&W
1010 Ennis Hill Rd
Marshfield, VT 05658, 802-426-3749
    Pubs: *Kalliope, Midstream, Nimrod, Feminist Studies,
    Southern Humanities Rev, Spoon River Poetry Rev,
    Atlanta Rev*

Lynn Manning Valente ♪ ✈   P&W
PO Box 9
Marlboro, VT 05344-0009, 802-254-2876
Internet: lynnvalente@hotmail.com
    Pubs: *Dynamics of Choice: Anth* (Chrysalis Bks, 1999),
    *Anth of New England Writers, Longhouse, Northeast,
    Visions, Poetry Now, Jam To-Day, Pig Iron, Sistersong,
    Poetry Motel*

Ellen Bryant Voigt 🎤 ✈   P
Box 128
Marshfield, VT 05658-0128, 802-563-2707
    Pubs: *The Flexible Lyric* (U Georgia Pr, 1999), *Kyrie,
    Two Trees, The Lotus Flowers, The Forces of Plenty*
    (Norton, 1995, 1992, 1987, 1983), *Five Points, New
    Yorker, Atlantic*

Roger Weingarten   P
MFA in Writing, Vermont College, Montpelier, VT 05602,
802-828-8638
    Pubs: *Ghost Wrestling, Infant Bonds of Joy, Shadow
    Shadow* (Godine, 1997, 1990, 1986), *Poetry East,
    Missouri Rev, NAR, APR, Paris Rev, Poetry, New
    Yorker, Prague Revue*

Norman Williams   W
381 S Union St
Burlington, VT 05401
    Pubs: *The Unlovely Child* (Knopf, 1985), *New Yorker,
    Verse*

Nancy Means Wright 🎤 ✈   W
PO Box 182
Middlebury, VT 05753-9587, 802-462-2719
Internet: www.nancymeanswright.com
    Pubs: *Walking Up Into the Volcano* (Pudding Hse,
    2000), *Poison Apples, Harvest of Bones, Mad Season*
    (St. Martin's Pr, 2000, 1998, 1996), *Down the Strings*
    (Dutton, 1982), *Carolina Qtly, Wisconsin Rev, Redbook,
    Seventeen, Bellingham Rev, American Literary Rev*

VIRGINIA

B. Chelsea Adams   P&W
5510 Piney Woods Rd
Riner, VA 24149-1647, 540-382-1778
    Pubs: *Sampler: Anth* (Alms Hse Pr, 1993), *Lucid Stone,
    Potato Eyes, Thin Air, CQ, Poet Lore, Southwestern
    Rev, Union Street Rev, Albany Rev, Virginia English
    Bulletin*

Jennifer Atkinson   P
George Mason Univ, English Dept, MSN3E4, 4400
University Dr, Fairfax, VA 22030, 703-993-1177
    Pubs: *The Dogwood Tree* (U Alabama Pr, 1990), *The
    Drowned City* (Northeastern U Pr, 2000)

Judy Light Ayyildiz 🎤 ✈   P
4930 Hunting Hills Cir
Roanoke, VA 24014-4961, 703-774-8440
Internet: jayyildiz@aol.com
    Pubs: *Mud River* (Lintel Pr, 1988), *Smuggled Seeds*
    (Gusto Pr, 1981), *MacGuffin, New Renaissance, Pig
    Iron Pr, Blackwater Rev, Sow's Ear, Potato Eyes, NYQ*

Mary Balazs   P
English Dept, Virginia Military Institute, 411 Scott Shipp
Hall, Lexington, VA 24450, 703-464-7240
    Pubs: *Out of Darkness* (Phase & Cycle Pr, 1993),
    *Pierced By a Ray of Sun: Anth, Peeling the Onion:
    Anth* (HC, 1995, 1993), *Pivot, Shenandoah, Kalliope,
    Roanoke Rev, Christianity & Literature, Arts & Letters*

D. N. Baldwin   W
PO Box 82
Basye, VA 22810
Internet: dbaldwin@shentel.net
    Pubs: *American Short Fiction, Washington Rev, Hawaii
    Rev, Chiron Rev*

Dorothy Ussery Bass   P
Riverview Farm, Rte 1, Box 64
Rice, VA 23966, 804-392-4974
    Pubs: *NYQ, Gyre, Lyric, Hoosier Challenge, Archer,
    Mountainside Qtly, Appalachian Heritage*

Jefferson D. Bates 🎤   P
11939 Escalante Ct
Reston, VA 20191-1843, 703-758-0258
Internet: jefbates@netscape.net
    Pubs: *The Poets of Tallwood: Anth* (Learning In
    Retirement Institute, 1998), *Jazzbo Brown from Reston
    Town, Poems for Old Geezers & Young
    Whippersnappers* (Pogment Pr, 1993, 1990), *Qtly of
    Light Verse, Reston Rev*

Richard Bausch   W
George Mason Univ, English Dept, 4400 Univ Dr, Fairfax,
VA 22030, 703-349-0609
    Pubs: *Rare & Endangered Species, Rebel Powers*
    (Seymour Lawrence/HM, 1994, 1993), *The Fireman's
    Wife & Other Stories* (S&S, 1990), *New Yorker, Esquire*

Mel Belin 🎤 ✈   P
1600 N Oak St #1633
Arlington, VA 22209
    Pubs: *Flesh That Was Chrysalis* (Word Works, 1999),
    *Midstream, Connecticut River Rev, Phoebe, Cape Rock,
    Cumberland Poetry Rev, Poet Lore, Potomac Rev, Blue
    Unicorn, Wind Mag, Jewish Spectator, The Lyric, South
    Coast Poetry Jrnl*

Joe David Bellamy   P&W
1145 Lawson Cove Cir
Virginia Beach, VA 23455-6824, 757-490-7378
    Pubs: *Atomic Love: A Novella & Eight Stories* (U
    Arkansas Pr, 1993), *Suzi Sinzinnati* (Penguin, 1991),
    Story, Ploughshares, NAR, Paris Rev

Patsy Anne Bickerstaff   P
PO Box 156
Weyers Cave, VA 24486-0156
    Pubs: *City Rain* (Librado Pr, 1989), *Cumberland Poetry
    Rev, Piedmont Literary Rev, Ariel, Bellingham Rev,
    Caprice, Edge City Rev*

Dean Blehert 🎤 ✈   P
11919 Moss Point Ln
Reston, VA 20194, 703-471-7907
Internet: www.blehert.com
  Pubs: *Please, Lord, Make Me a Famous Poet or at
  Least Less Fat, I Swear He Was Laughing, No Cats
  Have Been Maimed or Mutilated* (Words & Pictures Pr,
  1999, 1996, 1996), *NYQ, Modern Haiku, Kansas Qtly
  Rev, Minimus, Light*

Adrian Blevins   P
3328 Forest Hill Ave NW
Roanoke, VA 24102, 540-362-1047
  Pubs: *The Man Who Went Out for Cigarettes* (Bright
  Hill Pr 1996, 1997), *Lucid Stone, Massachusetts Rev,
  Southern Rev, Sow's Ear Poetry Rev*

Edward Brash   P
1906 Windmill Ln
Alexandria, VA 22307, 703-765-1760
  Pubs: *Poetry, Atlantic, American Scholar, Partisan Rev,
  Mademoiselle*

David Bristol   P&W
1206 N Stuart St
Arlington, VA 22201, 703-841-1914
  Pubs: *Paradise & Cash* (Washington Writer's Pub Hse,
  1980), *Hayotzer, Kansas Qtly, Aerial, Washington Rev,
  New Laurel Rev*

Scott Cairns   P&W
Old Dominion Univ, English Dept, Norfolk, VA 23529,
757-683-4042
  Pubs: *Recovered Body* (Braziller, 1998), *Figures for the
  Ghost* (U Georgia Pr, 1994), *Paris Rev, New Republic,
  Atlantic, Image, Prairie Schooner, Colorado Rev*

Mary Patricia Carroll   P&W
528 Ocean Trace Arch, #H
Virginia Beach, VA 23451-5412
  Pubs: *The Creative Woman, Skylight, Black Bear Rev*

Travis Charbeneau   W
3421 Hanover Ave
Richmond, VA 23221-2735, 804-358-0417
  Pubs: *The Sun, Utne Reader, Esquire, Dallas Life Mag,
  Atlanta Constitution, World Monitor, In These Times*

Elaine Raco Chase 🎤 ✈   W
4333 Majestic Ln
Fairfax, VA 22033, 703-378-9580
  Pubs: *The Amateur Detective* (Writer's Digest Bks,
  1996), *Partners in Crime: Anth* (Signet Paperback,
  1995)

Emily Blair Chewning 🎤 ✈   P
6088 Leeds Manor Rd
Hume, VA 22639, 202-944-9644
Internet: twob1@aol.com
  Pubs: *Anatomy Illustrated* (S&S, 1980), *The Illustrated
  Flower* (Crown, 1979), *Family Life, Art & Antiques*

John I. Church   P
7216 Evans Mill Rd
McLean, VA 22101, 703-790-0428
  Pubs: *Hoosier College Poet* (The Friendly Pr, 1984),
  Windless Orchard, Patterns, Compass, Rhino

Rita Ciresi   W
Hollins College, PO Box 9642, Roanoke, VA 24020,
540-362-6318
  Pubs: *Mother Rocket* (U Georgia Pr, 1993), *Blue Italian:
  Anth* (Ecco Pr, 1996), *Prairie Schooner, South Carolina
  Rev, Oregon Rev, Alaska Qtly Rev, New Delta Rev,
  Italian Americana*

Mark Craver   P
Orchises Press, PO Box 20602, Alexandria, VA
22320-1602
  Pubs: *They Came for What You Love, Seven Crowns
  for the White Lady of the Other World & Blood Poems*
  (Orchises, 1998, 1992), *The Problem of Grace* (Lost
  Roads, 1986)

William Davey   P&W
Michelle Mordant, Literary Agent, PO Box 129, Keene, VA
22946, 804-977-0404
  Pubs: *Bitter Rainbow* (Edtns Carrefour, 2000), *Lost
  Adulteries, Trial of Pythagoras* (Alyscamps Pr, 1997,
  1996), *Angry Dust* (Beijing, 1993), *Dawn Breaks the
  Heart* (Howell, Soskin, 1941), *Arms, Angels, Epitaphs*
  (Rydal Pr, 1935), *Thalia, Massacre, Lyric*

Tom De Haven   W
14106 Huntgate Woods Rd
Midlothian, VA 23112-4355, 804-744-6288
  Pubs: *Walker of Worlds* (Bantam/Doubleday, 1990),
  Sunburn Lake, Freaks' Amour, Funny Papers (Penguin,
  1989, 1986, 1986)

R. H. W. Dillard 🎤 ✈   P&W
Hollins Univ, Box 9671, Roanoke, VA 24020-1671,
540-362-6316
Internet: rdillard@hollins.edu
  Pubs: *Omniphobia, Just Here, Just Now* (LSU Pr, 1995,
  1994)

Gregory Donovan   P&W
Virginia Commonwealth Univ, English Dept, PO Box
842005, Richmond, VA 23284-2005, 804-828-4507
  Pubs: *Calling His Children Home* (U Missouri Pr, 1993),
  *Mss., Hayden's Ferry Rev, Southern Rev, NER,
  CutBank, New Virginia Rev, South Coast Poetry Jrnl*

Rita Dove 🎤 ✈   P
PO Box 400121, Univ Virginia, English Dept, 219 Bryan
Hall, Charlottesville, VA 22904-4121, 804-924-6618
Internet: rfd4b@virginia.edu
    Pubs: *On the Bus with Rosa Parks, Mother Love,
    Grace Notes* (Norton, 2000, 1995, 1989), *The Darker
    Face of the Earth* (Oberon, 1999), *Selected Poems*
    (Pantheon, 1993), *Thomas & Beulah, Museum, Yellow
    House on the Corner* (Carnegie Mellon, 1986, 1983,
    1980)

John Elsberg 🎤 ✈   P
422 N Cleveland St
Arlington, VA 22201, 703-243-6019
    Pubs: *Sailor* (New Hope Intl, 1999), *Offsets* (Kings
    Estate Pr, 1998), *Broken Poems for Evita* (Runaway
    Spoon Pr, 1997), *Randomness of E* (Semiquasi Pr,
    1995), *Atom Mind, Plastic Tower, Onthebus, Lost &
    Found Times, Gargoyle, Spillway, Blue Unicorn*
Groups: Teenagers

Anthony Esler   W
History Dept, College of William & Mary, Williamsburg, VA
23187, 804-221-3741
    Pubs: *The Western World* (S&S, 1997), *The Human
    Venture* (2 Vols.) (Prentice Hall, 1992), *Bastion*
    (MacDonald, 1982), *Babylon* (Morrow, 1980)

Edward Falco   P&W
English Dept, Virginia Tech, Blacksburg, VA 24061-0112,
540-951-4112
    Pubs: *A Dream with Demons* (Eastgate Systems, 1997),
    Acid (U Notre Dame, 1996), *Atlantic, Ploughshares,
    TriQtly, Best American Short Stories 1995, Pushcart
    Prize: Anth* (Pushcart Pr, 1999), *Playboy*

Mark Farrington   W
13 E Windsor Ave
Alexandria, VA 22301
    Pubs: *Mountain Pr, Berkshire Writers Inc, Union St
    Rev, Phoebe, Bennington Booklet, The Louisville Rev*

Stanley Field   P&W
6315 Nicholson St
Falls Church, VA 22044
    Pubs: *The Freelancer* (Poetica Pr, 1984), *West Wind
    Rev, Women's Household, Minnesota Ink, Green's Mag,
    A Loving Voice, Animal Tales, Albatross, Cats*

Carolyn Forche   P
English Dept MS3E4, George Mason Univ, 4400 University
Dr, Fairfax, VA 22030, 301-320-2934
    Pubs: *The Angel of History, The Country Between Us*
    (HC, 1994, 1982)

Kathleen Ford   W
630 Ivy Farm Dr
Charlottesville, VA 22901-8848
    Pubs: *Jeffrey County* (St. Martin's Pr, 1986), *Ladies'
    Home Jrnl, Southern Rev, Redbook, Yankee*

Jay Bradford Fowler   P
3710 Lee Hwy, #220
Arlington, VA 22207-3721, 703-538-5892
    Pubs: *The Soul* (Shangri La Pubs, 1996), *Writing Down
    the Light* (Orchises Pr, 1988), *Poet Lore, Yankee,
    Shenandoah, Phoebe, APR, Cosmic Trend*

Edna Frederikson   W
130 Campbell St, #4
Harrisonburg, VA 22801
    Pubs: *Never Tomorrow* (Harrow Bks, 1988), *Three
    Parts Earth* (Threshold Bks, 1972), *Ms.*

Anne Hobson Freeman   P&W
PO Box 680
Callao, VA 22435-0680
    Pubs: *The Style of a Law Firm, Eight Gentlemen from
    Virginia* (Algonquin, 1989, 1989), *Virginia Qtly Rev, New
    Virginia Rev, Denver Qtly, Mademoiselle, Cosmopolitan*

Serena Fusek 🎤 ✈   P
PO Box 3095
Newport News, VA 23603-0095, 757-887-9253
    Pubs: *The Night Screams with Jaguar's Voice, Three in
    the Morning Songs* (Skiff's Creek Pr, 1998, 1992), *The
    Color of Poison* (Slipstream Pr, 1991), *Reflect, Poetry
    Motel, Poet Lore, Elegia, Impetus, Semi Dwarf Rev,
    Cedar Hill Rev, Rouge et Noir*

Louis Gallo ✈   P&W
Radford Univ, English Dept, Radford, VA 24142,
703-831-5264
    Pubs: *MacGuffin, Baltimore Rev, Green Hills Rev,
    Rhino, Evansville Rev, Mangrove, New Orleans Rev,
    Brownstone Rev, Maple Leaf Rag, Greensboro Rev,
    Habersham Rev, GAIA, Louisiana Lit, American Lit Rev,
    Glimmer Train, Rockford Rev*

David C. D. Gansz 🎤 ✈   P
229 Denny Ln
Lexington, VA 24450, 540-463-4324
Internet: dgansz@lib.rang.gen.va.us
    Pubs: *Millennial Scriptions* (OtherWind Pr, 2000), *Ashen
    Meal*

Patricia Garfinkel 🎤 ✈   P
900 N Stuart St, #1001
Arlington, VA 22203, 703-620-2945
    Pubs: *Making the Skeleton Dance* (George Braziller
    Pub, 2000), *From the Red Eye of Jupiter* (Washington
    Writer's Pub Hse, 1990), *Ram's Horn* (Window Pr,
    1980), *Seattle Rev, Hollins Critic, Pittsburgh Qtly,
    Visions Intl, Negative Capability, California Qtly*

George Garrett 🎤 ✈   P&W
1845 Wayside Pl
Charlottesville, VA 22903-1630, 804-979-5366
    Pubs: *Days of Our Lives Lie in Fragments* (LSU Pr,
    1998), *The King of Babylon Shall Not Come Against
    You, Whistling in the Dark* (HB, 1998, 1992)

Joseph Garrison   P
265 Thornrose Ave
Staunton, VA 24401, 540-885-7475
  Pubs: *Landscape & Distance: Poets from Virginia* (U Pr
  Virginia, 1975), *Hampden-Sydney Poetry Review: Anth*
  (Hampden-Sydney, 1990), *Carolina Qtly, South Carolina
  Rev, Poetry NW, SW Rev, SPR, Theology Today*

Beth George   P
13456 Muir Kirk Ln
Herndon, VA 22071, 703-435-3112
  Pubs: *Poet Lore, Wisconsin Rev, West Branch,
  Sou'wester, South Dakota Rev, Artemis, Kentucky
  Poetry Rev, Lip Service*

Bernadette K. Geyer   P
1020 N Stafford St #400
Arlington, VA 22201
  Pubs: *Red Owl Magazine, WordWrights!, The
  Mid-America Poetry Rev, Fodderwing, Independence
  Boulevard*

Wesley Gibson   W
342 S Laurel St, Apt B
Richmond, VA 23220
  Pubs: *Shelter* (Harmony Bks, 1992), *New Virginia Rev*

Robert L. Giron ♆ ⊁   P&W
5200 N 1 St
Arlington, VA 22203-1252, 703-351-0079
Internet: robtx@erols.com
  Pubs: *Texas: Anth* (Sam Houston St U Pr, 1979),
  Amphora Rev, Art Form Mag, The Great Lawn
  Lang: Spanish. I.D.: G/L/B/T. Groups: G/L/B/T

Courtenay Graham-Gazaway   P
PO Box 754
Earlysville, VA 22936-0754
  Pubs: *17 Syllables, Iona* (GramWel Studios & Stills Pr,
  1985, 1985), *Harvard Advocate*

Bernice Grohskopf   W
116 Turtle Creek Rd, #11
Charlottesville, VA 22901-6760, 804-296-8044
  Pubs: *End of Summer* (Avon, 1982), *Tell Me Your
  Dream* (Scholastic, 1981), *PEN Anth* (Ballantine, 1985),
  Harvard Library Bulletin, Virginia Qtly Rev

Cathryn Hankla ♆ ⊁   P&W
Hollins Univ, English Dept, Box 9677, Roanoke, VA
24020, 540-362-6278
Internet: chankla@hollins.edu
  Pubs: *Texas School Book Depository, Negative History,
  Afterimages, Yellow Shoe Poets: Anth* (LSU Pr, 2000,
  1997, 1991, 2000), *A Blue Moon in Poorwater* (U
  Virginia Pr, 1998), *Buck & Wing: Anth* (Shenandoah,
  2000), *Virginia Qtly Rev, Prairie Schooner*
  Groups: Women, G/L/B/T

Charles L. Hayes ♆ ⊁   W
PO Box 6995
Radford, VA 24142-6995, 703-831-5231
  Pubs: *Sou'wester, St Andrews Rev, Phoebe, Yellow Silk*

Ellen Herbert ♆ ⊁   W
2929 Rosemary Ln
Falls Church, VA 22042-1857, 703-532-4544
Internet: jhh1@msn.com
  Pubs: *Life on the Line: Anth* (Negative Capability Pr,
  1992), *Sonora Rev, Crescent Rev, First for Women,
  Iris, Thema, Pennsylvania English*

Susan Heroy   P
3133 Windsorview Dr
Richmond, VA 23225, 804-272-7111
  Pubs: *Prairie Schooner, SPR, Three Rivers Poetry Jrnl,
  New Virginia Rev, Artemis*

Neva Herrington ♆ ⊁   P&W
6712 W Wakefield Dr, #B-2
Alexandria, VA 22307-6746, 703-765-0388
  Pubs: *Blue Stone* (Still Point Pr, 1986), *Chariton Rev,
  Southern Rev, SW Rev, Wind, New Letters,
  Confrontation, Union Street Rev*

Edwin P. Hoyt   W
PO Box 520
North Virginia, VA 23128
  Pubs: *The Tempting of Confucius* (Zebra Bks, 1972),
  The Voice of Allah (John Day, 1969)

Lynn Dean Hunter ♆ ⊁   P&W
PO Box 4053
Virginia Beach, VA 23454, 804-496-8289
Internet: ldhunter@aol.com
  Pubs: *Excuses* (Watermark Literary Pr, 1996), *Powhatan
  Rev, Poet's Domain, Blackwater Rev, Crone's Nest,
  Ghent Mag, Virginian-Pilot, Crescent Rev, Thema*

Kaatje Hurlbut   W
PO Box 158
Franktown, VA 23354, 804-442-7942
  Pubs: *Best American Short Stories: Anth* (HM, 1979),
  Eve in Darkness: Anth (NAL, 1969), *SW Rev*

Lucky Jacobs   P
203 Santa Clara Dr
Richmond, VA 23229
  Pubs: *The Book of Love* (East Coast Edtns, 1993), *Our
  Eyes, Like Walls* (Konglomerati, 1981), *Poetry Now,
  Intro 7, Artemis, Hollins Critic, SPR*

Mark Jacobs　　　　　　　　　　　　　W
1130 Robert Carter Rd
Fairfax Station, VA 22039
　　Pubs: *The Liberation of Little Heaven, Stone Cowboy*
　　(Soho Pr, 1998, 1997), *A Cast of Spaniards* (Talisman
　　Hse, 1994), *Webster Rev, Pig Iron, Atlantic, Farmer's
　　Market, Sun, Kiosk, Nebraska Rev, Iowa Rev, Southern
　　Rev, South Dakota Qtly*

Kate Jennings　　　　　　　　　　　　P
12816 Cross Creek Ln
Herndon, VA 22071, 703-476-5814
　　Pubs: *Malice* (Devil's Millhopper Pr, 1988), *Birth Stories:
　　Anth* (Crossing, 1984), *Hudson Rev*

Edward P. Jones ⚲ ✈　　　　　　　　W
4300 Old Dominion Dr, #914
Arlington, VA 22207-3227, 703-522-6720
　　Pubs: *Lost in the City* (Morrow, 1992)

Paul Jones　　　　　　　　　　　　　P
5990 Buck Ridge Rd
Earlysville, VA 22936-9335
　　Pubs: *What the Welsh & the Chinese Have in Common*
　　(North Carolina Writers' Network, 1990), *Poetry,
　　Southern Rev, Georgia Rev, Southern Humanities Rev,
　　Hellas*

Ronnetta Bisman Kahn　　　　　　　　W
701 Locust Hill Dr
Harrisonburg, VA 22801, 703-434-0225
　　Pubs: *Anna's House, Apalachee Qtly, Sing Heavenly
　　Muse!, Second Wave, Moving Out, New Rev*

Samuel Kashner　　　　　　　　　　　P
College of William & Mary, Box 8795 English Dept,
Williamsburg, VA 23187-8795, 757-221-2439
　　Pubs: *Don Quixote in America, Hanging Loose 20 Year
　　Anth* (Hanging Loose Pr, 1997, 1988), *Harvard Mag,
　　riverrun, Verse, Salamander, Mudfish, William & Mary
　　Rev*

LuAnn Keener　　　　　　　　　　　　P
800 Maryland Ave
Salem, VA 24153, 540-389-4985
　　Pubs: *Color Documentary* (Calyx Bks, 1994), *Worlds in
　　Our Words: Anth* (Prentice Hall, 1997), *Poetry, Qtly
　　West, Chelsea, Shenandoah, Poetry NW, Sistersong*

William Keens　　　　　　　　　　　　P
The Keens Company, 200 N Little Falls St, #303, Falls
Church, VA 22046
　　Pubs: *Dear Anyone* (Penumbra Pr, 1977), *APR, Poetry,
　　Seneca Rev, Ohio Rev*

Helene Barker Kiser ⚲ ✈　　　　　　　P
1 W Princeton Cir
Lynchburg, VA 24503-1411, 804-846-1921
Internet: inkbiz@lynchburg.net
　　Pubs: *Topography* (Linear Arts Bks, 1998), *Salonika
　　Qtly, Hawai'i Rev, Chachalaca Poetry Rev, Indiana Rev,
　　Sycamore Rev, Borderlands Texas Poetry Rev, Poet
　　Lore*

Peter Klappert　　　　　　　　　　　P
MSN3E4 English Dept, George Mason Univ, Fairfax, VA
22030, 202-232-2874
　　Pubs: *The Idiot Princess of the Last Dynasty* (Carnegie
　　Mellon U Pr, 1998), *Lugging Vegetables to Nantucket*
　　(Yale, 1971), *Atlantic, Harper's, Antaeus, Ploughshares*

Carolyn Kreiter-Foronda ⚲ ✈　　　　P
5966 Annaberg Pl
Burke, VA 22015, 703-503-9743
Internet: foronda@erols.com
　　Pubs: *Death Comes Riding, Gathering Light* (SCOP
　　Pubs, 1999, 1993), *Contrary Visions* (Scripta
　　Humanistica, 1988), *Prairie Schooner, Antioch Rev,
　　Mid-American Rev, Poet Lore, Hispanic Culture Rev,
　　Antietam Rev*
Groups: Children, College/Univ

Elisabeth Kuhn ⚲ ✈　　　　　　　　　P
VA Commonwealth Univ, English Dept, Box 842005,
Richmond, VA 23284-2005, 804-828-4465
Internet: skronen@hotmail.com
　　Pubs: *Unbearable Uncertainty: Anth* (Pioneer Valley
　　Breast Cancer Network, 2000), *Formalist, Paterson Lit
　　Rev, LiNQ, 96 Inc, Ledge, Urban Spaghetti, Sow's Ear
　　Poetry Rev, Sweet Annie & Sweet Pea Rev, Stitches,
　　Chiron Rev, Potpourri, Herb Network*
Lang: German. Groups: Women, Cancer Survivors

Jeanne Larsen ⚲ ✈　　　　　　　　P&W
Hollins Univ, Box 9542, Roanoke, VA 24020-1542,
540-362-6276
Internet: jlarsen@hollins.edu
　　Pubs: *Manchu Palaces* (H Holt, 1997), *Silk Road* (H
　　Holt/BOMC, 1989), *NER, Georgia Rev, New Virginia
　　Rev, Yarrow, Greensboro Rev, 5 A.M.*

Monty S. Leitch ⚲ ✈　　　　　　　　W
113 Huffville Rd
Pilot, VA 24138-1679, 540-651-4502
　　Pubs: *Grandmother Histories: Anth* (Syracuse U, 1998),
　　*Writer's Yearbook '95, Hollins Mag, Artemis, Radford U
　　Mag, Virginia Country, Mountain Rev, Roanoker,
　　Window, Shenandoah, Union St Rev*

Janet Lembke ⚲ ✈　　　　　　　　　P
210 N Madison St
Staunton, VA 24401-3359, 540-886-4180
　　Pubs: *Euripides' Hecuba* (Oxford U Pr, 1991), *Looking
　　for Eagles* (Lyons & Burford, 1990), *Audubon, NAR,
　　Sierra*

Judy Longley P
1001 Wildmere Pl
Charlottesville, VA 22901, 804-973-0780
 Pubs: *My Journey Toward You* (Helicon Nine Edtns,
 1993), *Rowing Past Eden* (Nightshade Pr, 1993),
 Parallel Lives (Owl Creek Pr, 1990), *Poetry, Southern
 Rev*

James Lott W
Mary Baldwin College, Office of Dean of the College,
Staunton, VA 24401, 540-887-7030
 Pubs: *New Virginia Rev, Virginia Qtly Rev, Southern
 Rev, South Carolina Rev, Inlet*

Katie Letcher Lyle P&W
110 W McDowell St
Lexington, VA 24450, 540-463-5439
 Pubs: *The Foraging Gourmet* (Lyons & Burford, 1997),
 *The Men Who Wanted Seven Wives, Scalded to Death
 by the Steam* (Algonquin, 1986, 1983), *Virginia Qtly
 Rev, Shenandoah, Sierra Mag, Country Jrnl, Blue Ridge
 Country*

Edward C. Lynskey P
9503 Lees Mill Rd
Warrenton, VA 20186
 Pubs: *The Tree Surgeon's Gift* (Scripta, 1990), *Teeth of
 the Hydra* (Crop Dust Pr, 1986), *Atlantic, APR, Chicago
 Rev, Southwest, America, Commonweal*

Mike Maggio ⬤ ✈ P&W
1169 Cypress Tree Pl
Herndon, VA 22070
Internet: mikemaggio@aol.com
 Pubs: *Oranges from Palestine* (Mardi Gras Pr, 1996),
 Your Secret Is Safe with Me (Cassette; Black Bear
 Pub, 1988), *Blue Cathedral: Anth* (Red Hen Pr, 2000),
 Bedside Prayers: Anth (Harper, 1997), *For a Living:
 Anth* (U Illinois Pr, 1995), *Pleiades*
Lang: Arabic

Anita Mathias ⬤ ✈ P
104 Richard's Patent
Williamsburg, VA 23185-5118, 757-564-0355
Internet: mathias@widomaker.com
 Pubs: *The Best Spiritual Writing: Anth* (Harper SF,
 1999), *Tanzania on Tuesday: Anth* (New Rivers Pr,
 1997), *The Best of Writers at Work: Anth* (Northwest
 Pub, 1994), *Virginia Qtly Rev, Commonweal, New
 Letters, London Mag, America, Notre Dame Mag, The
 Jrnl*

Deirdra McAfee ⬤ ✈ W
1503 Willingham Rd
Richmond, VA 23233-4727, 804-750-1338
Internet: dhmca@aol.com
 Pubs: *Turnstile, Willow Springs, Ambergris,
 Confrontation*

David McAleavey ⬤ ✈ P
3305 N George Mason Dr
Arlington, VA 22207-1859, 703-532-8546
Internet: dmca@gwu.edu
 Pubs: *Holding Obsidian* (WWPH, 1985), *Antioch Rev,
 Poet Lore, Florida Rev, Ploughshares, Situation,
 Washington Rev*

Jane McIlvaine McClary W
Box 326
Middleburg, VA 22117, 703-687-6178
 Pubs: *Maggie Royal, A Portion for Foxes* (S&S, 1982,
 1972), *Middleburg Life, Virginia Country*

Heather Ross Miller P&W
402 Morningside Dr
Lexington, VA 24450, 540-464-6534
 Pubs: *In the Funny Papers, Friends & Assassins* (U
 Missouri Pr, 1995, 1993), *Witness, Sandhills Rev, Crab
 Orchard Rev, Potato Eyes, Southern Rev*

Elaine Moore W
702 Seneca Rd
Great Falls, VA 22066, 703-444-3499
 Pubs: *Phoebe, Virginia Country, Modern Short Stories*

Miles David Moore ⬤ ✈ P
5913 Mayflower Ct, #102
Alexandria, VA 22312, 703-256-9275
 Pubs: *Buddha Isn't Laughing* (Argonne Hotel Pr, 1999),
 *Winners: A Retrospective of the Washington Prize,
 Bears of Paris* (Word Works, 1999, 1995), *Pivot, Word
 Wrights, NYQ, Poet Lore, Sulphur, Bogg, Minimus,
 Writer's Jrnl*

Elizabeth Seydel Morgan P
504 Honaker Ave
Richmond, VA 23226, 804-285-2153
 Pubs: *The Governor of Desire, Parties* (LSU Pr, 1993,
 1988), *Southern Rev, Poetry, Prairie Schooner, Georgia
 Rev, Virginia Qtly, Iowa Rev*

Michael Mott ⬤ ✈ P&W
122 The Colony
Williamsburg, VA 23185-3157, 757-220-1042
 Pubs: *Woman & the Sea: Selected Poems, Counting
 the Grasses* (Anhinga, 1999, 1980), *Corday* (Black
 Buzzard Pr, 1995), *Georgia Rev, Sewanee Rev, Stand
 (U.K.), American Scholar, Verse, Tar River Poetry,
 Kenyon Rev*
Groups: College/Univ

Elisabeth Murawski ⬤ ✈ P
6804 Kenyon Dr
Alexandria, VA 22307-1535, 703-768-4504
Internet: emurawski@juno.com
 Pubs: *Troubled by an Angel* (Cleveland State U Pr,
 1997), *Moon & Mercury, Hungry As We Are: Anth*
 (Washington Writers Pub Hse, 1990, 1995), *Field, Qtly
 West, Crazy Horse, Virginia Qtly Rev, Literary Rev,
 American Voice, Grand Street, Ohio Rev, APR,
 Shenandoah*

Mary Hayne North P
6020 Piney Woods Rd
Riner, VA 24149
Pubs: *From Mt. San Angelo: Anth* (AAUP, 1987)

Tom O'Grady ♀ ✈ P
PO Box 126
Hampden-Sydney, VA 23943
Internet: thomaso@hsc.edu
Pubs: *Sun, Moon & Stars* (Tryon Pub, 1996), *In the Room of the Just Born* (Dolphin-Moon, 1989), *Poet Lore, Connecticut Rev, North Atlantic Rev, Maryland Poetry Rev, Chrysalis, New Letters*

Renee Ellen Olander ♀ ✈ P
Old Dominion Univ, Interdisciplinary Teacher Prep, College of Arts & Letters, Norfolk, VA 23529, 757-683-4044
Internet: rolander@odu.edu
Pubs: *Verse & Universe: Anth* (Milkweed Edtns, 1998), *13th Moon, Snake Nation Rev, Sistersong: Women Across Cultures, Artword Qtly, Amelia*
Groups: Women, Children

Bill Oliver ♀ ✈ W
Virginia Military Institute
Lexington, VA 24450, 540-464-7240
Pubs: *Women & Children First* (Mid-List Pr 1998), *Laurel Rev, Virginia Qtly Rev, Florida Rev, Descant, Indiana Rev, Kansas Qtly, Carolina Qtly, Cimarron Rev*

Marian Olson P
1501 Crystal Dr, #933
Arlington, VA 22202-4126
Pubs: *Letting Go, Songs of the Chicken Yard* (Honeybrook Pr, 1992, 1992), *Facing the Wind* (Raven Pr, 1990), *Modern Haiku, America, Plains Poetry Jrnl, Brussels Sprout, Kalliope, Trestle Creek Rev, Frog Pond*

Gregory Orr ♀ ✈ P
2006 Hessian Rd
Charlottesville, VA 22903-1219, 804-293-4831
Internet: gso@virginia.edu
Pubs: *The Caged Owl, Orpheus & Eurydice* (Copper Canyon Pr, 2003, 2000), *City of Salt* (U Pitt Pr, 1995)
Groups: Abuse Victims

Cheryl Pallant ♀ ✈ P&W
108 S Colonial Ave
Richmond, VA 23221-3518, 804-355-7524
Internet: cpallant@titan.vcu.edu
Pubs: *Uncommon Grammar: Anth* (Turtlemoon Bks, 2000), *Confrontation, NYQ, Coe Rev, Wormwood Rev, Crescent Rev, Oxford Mag, New Rain*

Eric Pankey ♀ ✈ P
4213 Lenox Dr
Fairfax, VA 22032, 703-993-1177
Pubs: *Cenotaph, Apocrypha, The Late Romances* (Knopf, 2000, 1998, 1997), *Heartwood* (Atheneum, 1988), *For the New Year,* (Atheneum, 1984)

Richard Peabody ♀ ✈ P&W
3819 N 13 St
Arlington, VA 22201, 703-465-9692
Internet: hedgehog2@erols.com
Pubs: *Sugar Mountain, Mood Vertigo* (Argonne Hotel, 2000, 1999), *Buoyancy* (Gut Punch, 1995), *Paraffin Days* (Cumberland, 1995), *Barcelona Rev, Bakunin, Spitball, Georgetown Rev, Atom Mind, Word Wrights, Potomac Rev, Hollins Critic, Articulate*

Jim Peterson ♀ ✈ P
555 Elmwood Ave
Lynchburg, VA 24503-4411, 804-845-2735
Internet: jepete1@aol.com
Pubs: *The Owning Stone* (Red Hen Pr, 2000), *An Afternoon with K, Carvings on a Prayer Tree* (Holocene Pr, 1996, 1994), *The Man Who Grew Silent* (Bench Pr, 1989), *Georgia Rev, Poetry, Prairie Schooner, Poetry NW*

Leslie Pietrzyk ♀ ✈ W
3201 Elmwood Dr
Alexandria, VA 22303
Internet: lpietr@aol.com
Pubs: *Pears on a Willow Tree* (Avon/Bard, 1998), *TriQtly, Epoch, Gettysburg Rev, Iowa Rev, NER, Shenandoah*
I.D.: Polish-American

Richard Plant ♀ ✈ W
English Dept, Mary Baldwin College, Staunton, VA 24401, 540-887-7284
Pubs: *Three Novellas: Anth* (Texas Rev Pr, 1997), *Sudden Fiction: Anth* (Norton, 1996), *The O. Henry Awards: Anth* (Doubleday, 1989), *Best Stories from New Writers: Anth* (Writer's Digest Bks, 1989), *South Dakota Rev, Cimarron Rev*

Simone Poirier-Bures W
7547 Cedar Grove Ln
Radford, VA 24141, 540-731-1814
Pubs: *That Shining Place, Candyman* (Oberon Pr, 1995, 1994), *Virginia Qtly Rev, Dalhousie Rev, Belles Lettres, Short Story, Emrys Jrnl, Florida Rev*

Barbara Ann Porte W
PO Box 16627
Arlington, VA 22215
Pubs: *Taxicab Tales* (Morrow, 1992), *Ruthann & Her Pig* (Orchard Bks, 1989), *Confrontation*

Ken Poyner 🎤 ✈ P
PO Box 14452
Norfolk, VA 23518, 757-473-0846
Internet: kpoyner@prodigy.net
Pubs: *Sciences, Social* (Palaquin Bks, 1995), *Cordwood* (22 Pr, 1985), *Iowa Rev, West Branch, Poet Lore, Western Humanities Rev, Yarrow, Black Fly Rev*

Philip Raisor P
PO Box 61623
Virginia Beach, VA 23466-1623, 804-489-3345
Pubs: *Kansas Qtly, Arete, Poetry NW, Literary Rev, Southern Rev, Tar River Poetry*

Paula Rankin P
89 Gum Grove Dr
Newport News, VA 23601-2705, 804-591-8350
Pubs: *Your Rightful Childhood, Divorce: A Romance, To the House Ghost* (Carnegie Mellon U Pr, 1996, 1990, 1985)

Kristen Staby Rembold 🎤 ✈ P&W
102 Bennington Rd
Charlottesville, VA 22901, 804-296-3086
Pubs: *Felicity* (Mid-List Pr, 1994), *Coming Into This World* (Hot Pepper Pr, 1992), *Artemis, Nimrod, South Dakota Rev, Iowa Woman, Appalachia, CQ*

Lisa Ress P
1414 5 St SW
Roanoke, VA 24016-4508
Pubs: *Flight Patterns* (U Pr Virginia, 1985), *Kalliope, Farmer's Market, Spoon River Qtly, Sycamore Rev, Denver Rev, Yarrow*

Kurt Rheinheimer W
1862 Arlington Rd SW
Roanoke, VA 24015-2859, 540-981-1307
Internet: krheinheimer@leisurepublishing.com
Pubs: *New Stories from the South: Anths* (Algonquin Bks, 1999, 1989, 1986), *Michigan Qtly Rev, Southern, Playgirl, Shenandoah, Carolina Qtly, Redbook, Story Qtly, Greensboro Rev*

Suzanne Rhodenbaugh P
3332 Kensington Ave
Richmond, VA 23221-2304, 804-354-9567
Pubs: *The Shine on Loss* (Painted Bride Qtly Pr, 1998), *Gardening Where the Land Remembers War* (Two Herons Pr, 1992), *A Gold Rain at Lonelyfarm* (Heatherstone Pr, 1990), *Hudson Rev, NER, American Scholar, Cimarron Rev, Salmagundi, Michigan Qtly Rev*

Evelyn Ritchie P
817 St Christopher's Rd
Richmond, VA 23226, 804-262-0664
Pubs: *New Virginia Rev, Richmond Qtly, Forms, Lyric, Midwest Poetry Rev*

Kim Roberts P
Ellipse Arts Center, 4350 Fairfax Dr, Arlington, VA 22203, 703-228-7710
Pubs: *The Wishbone Galaxy* (Washington Writers Pub Hse, 1994), *Ohio Rev, Sonora Rev, High Plains Literary Rev, Confrontation, New Letters, Crosscurrents*

Nickell Romjue W
410 Willow Oaks Blvd
Hampton, VA 23669-1470, 757-851-1644
Pubs: *Distillery, Writers' Forum, Karamu, Cream City Rev, Missouri Rev, Cimarron Rev, Sou'wester*

Renee Roper-Jackson P
380 E Washington St
Suffolk, VA 23434
Pubs: *Changes: Anth* (White Swan Pr, 1987), *Truly Fine, Abbey Mag, Columbia*

John B. Rosenman P
Norfolk State Univ, 2401 Corprew Ave, English Dept, Norfolk, VA 23504, 804-623-8891
Pubs: *The Best Laugh Last* (McPherson & Co, 1983), *Yankee, Croton Rev, Xanadu, Phoebe*

Irene Rouse 🎤 ✈ P
Box 310
Atlantic, VA 23303-0310, 757-824-4090
Internet: irbooks@dmv.com
Pubs: *Private Mythologies* (Argonne Hotel Pr, 1999), *Maryland Millennial Anth* (St Mary's College, 2000), *Poetry Baltimore: Anth* (Wordhouse, 1997), *Wordwrights!, Potato Eyes*

John D. Ruemmler W
815 W Main St
Charlottesville, VA 22901, 804-295-8393
Pubs: *Smoke on the Water* (Shoe Tree Pr, 1992), *Brothers in Arms* (Lynx Pr, 1988), *Albemarle, Stranger*

Viette Sandbank P
4800 Fillmore Ave, #419
Alexandria, VA 22311
Pubs: *Alive & Gazing at You* (Northwoods, 1984), *Coming Through the Wry* (Praying Mantis, 1982), *The Poet's Domain: Anth* (Road Pub, 1991), *The Lyric*

Ben Satterfield 🎤 ✈ P&W
403 Upham Pl NW
Vienna, VA 22180
Pubs: *Apocalypse Now: Anth* (Red Hen Press, 2000), *2000: Here's to Humanity: Anth* (People's Pr, 2000), *Light, Baltimore Rev, Rambunctious Rev, Art Times, American Dissident*

Roger Sauls P
513 N Boulevard #4
Richmond, VA 23220-3342, 804-358-2958
  Pubs: *Hard Weather* (Bench Pr, 1987), *Light* (Loom Pr,
  1975), *Ohio Rev, Ploughshares, Shenandoah*

Nancy Schoenberger P
College of William & Mary, PO Box 8795 English Dept,
Williamsburg, VA 23187-8795, 757-221-2439
  Pubs: *Long Like a River* (NYU Pr, 1998), *Girl on a
  White Porch* (U Missouri Pr, 1987), *Southern Rev,
  Poetry, NER, New Yorker, Ploughshares*

Nancy Scott P
PO Box 179
Sperryville, VA 22740-0179
  Pubs: *Rhino, Eleven, Windchimes, Phoebus,
  Womansong, Ten Years & Then Some, NYQ, Poetry
  Now, Modern Haiku, New Virginia Rev, Phoebe,
  Shades of Gray*

Tim Seibles 🎙 ✈ P
Old Dominion Univ, English Dept, Norfolk, VA 23529,
757-683-5120
Internet: tseibles@odu.edu
  Pubs: *Hammerlock, Hurdy-Gurdy* (Cleveland St U Pr,
  1999, 1992), *Ten Miles an Hour* (Mille Grazie Pr,
  1998), *Kerosene* (Ampersand Pr, 1995), *Body Moves*
  (Corona Pr, 1988), *Outsiders: Anth, Verse & Universe:
  Anth* (Milkweed Edtns, 1999, 1997), *New Letters*
I.D.: African-American. Groups: Prisoners

Richard Shaw P
1503 Scandia Cir
Reston, VA 20190
  Pubs: *Sleeping Beauty/Kabuki* (U Minnesota Pr, 1975)

Ellen Harvey Showell W
1200 N Cleveland St
Arlington, VA 22201, 703-525-8872
  Pubs: *Cecelia & the Blue Mountain Boy* (Lothrop, Lee
  & Shepard, 1983), *The Ghost of Tillie Jean Cassaway*
  (Four Winds Pr, 1978)

R. T. Smith 🎙 ✈ P
Washington & Lee Univ, Troubadour Theater, 2nd Fl,
Lexington, VA 24450, 540-463-8908
  Pubs: *Split the Lark* (Salmon, 1999), *Trespasser* (LSU
  Pr, 1996), *Hunter-Gatherer* (Livingston Pr, 1996),
  *Atlantic, Poetry, Georgia Rev, Gettysburg Rev, Southern
  Rev, Poetry Ireland Rev, Irish U Rev*
Groups: Prisoners, Irish-American

Ron Smith P
616 Maple Ave
Richmond, VA 23226
  Pubs: *Running Again in Hollywood Cemetery* (U Florida,
  1988), *Southern Rev, Virginia Qtly Rev, Kenyon Rev,
  Georgia Rev, Nation, NER*

Lisa Solod 🎙 ✈ W
310 Enfield Rd
Lexington, VA 24450-1756, 540-463-7637
Internet: lisa@rockbridge.net
  Pubs: *Summer's Love, Winter's Discontent: Anth*
  (Lonesome Traveller Pr, 1999), *The Inn Near Kyoto:
  Anth* (New Rivers Pr, 1998), *Lonzie's Fried Chicken,
  American Voice, Housewife-Writer's Forum, Tales of the
  Heart, Parting Gifts*

Margo Solod 🎙 ✈ P
PO Box 113
Lexington, VA 24450-0113, 540-464-6242
  Pubs: *Photo Cries Real Tears* (Talent Hse Pr, 1999),
  Still Life with Trucks (Tortilla Pr, 1996), *Outside the
  Kremlin* (Nightshade Pr, 1996), *What Have We Lost:
  Anth* (Green Willow, 1998), *Cedar Hill Rev, Defined
  Providence, New Frontiers of New Mexico*
I.D.: G/L/B/T, Jewish. Groups: Children, G/L/B/T

Katherine Soniat 🎙 ✈ P
Virginia Polytechnic Inst & SU, English Dept, Blacksburg,
VA 24061-0112, 703-231-6501
Internet: ksoniat@vt.edu
  Pubs: *Alluvial* (Bucknell U Pr, 2001), *A Shared Life* (U
  Iowa Pr, 1993), *Cracking Eggs* (U Pr Florida, 1990),
  *NAR, Poetry, Nation, New Republic, Southern Rev,
  Iowa Rev*
Groups: Schools

Lisa Russ Spaar P
English Dept, Univ Virginia, 219 Bryan Hall, Charlottesville,
VA 22903, 804-924-6675
  Pubs: *Blind Boy on Skates* (Trilobite Pr, 1987), *Cellar*
  (Alderman, 1983), *Poetry, Shenandoah, Poetry East,
  Crazyhorse, Virginia Qtly Rev, Tendril*

Bradley R. Strahan 🎙 ✈ P
1007 Ficklen Rd
Fredricksburg, VA 22405-2101
  Pubs: *Conjurer's Gallery* (CCC, 2000), *Crocodile Man*
  (The Smith, 1990), *First Things, Crosscurrents,
  Onthebus, Hollins Critic, Seattle Rev, Confrontation,
  Christian Century, Sources, America, Soundings East*

Dabney Stuart 🎙 ✈ P
30 Edmondson Ave
Lexington, VA 24450-1904, 540-463-5663
Internet: stuartd@wlu.edu
  Pubs: *Settlers, Long Gone, Light Years, Sweet Lucy
  Wine, Narcissus Dreaming* (LSU, 1999, 1996, 1994,
  1992, 1990), *The Way to Cobbs Creek, Second Sight*
  (U Missouri Pr, 1997, 1996)

Jitu Tambuzi P
Tambuzi Pub, 208 E Grace St, Richmond, VA
23219-1916, 804-649-3149
  Pubs: *A Voice Within* (King Pub, 1979), *New
  Renaissance, Universal Black Writer*

Eleanor Ross Taylor   P&W
1841 Wayside Pl
Charlottesville, VA 22903
    Pubs: *Days Going/Days Coming Back* (U Utah, 1992),
    New & Selected Poems (Stuart Wright, 1984),
    Parnassus, Seneca Rev, Ploughshares, Shenandoah,
    Virginia Qtly Rev

Henry Taylor 🎤 ✈   P
Box 23
Lincoln, VA 20160-0023, 540-338-3740
Internet: htaylor@american.edu
    Pubs: *Brief Candles: 101 Clerihews, Understanding*
    Fiction: Poems 1986-1996, The Flying Change (LSU Pr,
    2000, 1996, 1986), *Poetry, Sewanee Rev, New*
    Republic, Shenandoah

William Tester   W
8 Partridge Hill Rd
Richmond, VA 23233-6219
    Pubs: *Darling* (Knopf, 1992), *Grand St, Prairie*
    Schooner, Esquire, The Qtly, Fiction, TriQtly, NAR,
    Black Warrior, Witness

Hilary Tham   P&W
2600 N Upshur St
Arlington, VA 22207-4026, 703-527-4568
    Pubs: *Lane with No Name: Memoirs & Poems* (Lynne
    Rienner Pub, 1997), *Men & Other Strange Myths:*
    Poems (Three Continents Pr, 1994), *Mondo Barbie:*
    Anth (St. Martin's, 1993), *Antietam Rev, Metropolitan,*
    Encodings, Midstream

Carla Theodore 🎤   P
60 Ecology Ln
Woodville, VA 22749-1715, 540-987-8813
    Pubs: *Somebody's Brother, Rural Water, Peter & the*
    Guru (Samisdat, 1983, 1980, 1979), *Jewish Currents,*
    Kansas Qtly, Jump River Rev, Dark Horse, San
    Fernando Poetry Jrnl, Princeton Spectrum

Jack Trammell 🎤 ✈   P
241 Willow Brook Rd
Bumpass, VA 23024-3001, 804-556-4394
Internet: jtrammel@pen.k12.va.us
    Pubs: *Appalachian Dreams* (Escape, 1998), *Jessee*
    Poet, Fauquier Poetry Jrnl, Snowapple Jrnl
I.D.: Native American, White. Groups: Teenagers, Schools

Charles Vandersee 🎤 ✈   P
Dept of English, Univ Virginia, 219 Bryan Hall, PO Box
400121, Charlottesville, VA 22904-4121, 804-924-8877
Internet: cav7w@virginia.edu
    Pubs: *Ohio Rev, Georgia Rev, Sewanee Rev, Poetry*
    East, Poetry, Ironwood, Iris, Timbuktu
Groups: Spiritual/Religious

Angela Vogel   P
PO Box 36760
Richmond, VA 23235
    Pubs: *CQ, Evansville Rev, Cream City Rev, Cape*
    Rock, Black Dirt

Edward G. Williams   W
3837 Betsy Cre, PH
Virginia Beach, VA 23456-1610, 804-471-2781
    Pubs: *Not Like Niggers* (St. Martin's Pr, 1970), *A*
    Galaxy of Black Writing: Anth (Moore Pub Co, 1971),
    The Alumnus

Charles Wright 🎤 ✈   P
940 Locust Ave
Charlottesville, VA 22901-4030, 804-979-2373
    Pubs: *Negative Blue, Black Zodiac, Chickamauga, The*
    World of the 10,000 Things, (FSG, 2000, 1997, 1995,
    1990), *Halflife* (U Michigan Pr, 1988)

VIRGIN ISLANDS

Marty Campbell   W
5016 Estate Boetzberg
Christiansted, VI 00820-4516, 340-692-9935
    Pubs: *Companion to Senya* (MarCrafts, 1989), *Saint*
    Sea (Blondo, 1986), *Caribbean Writer, Hammers, Road*
    Map of My Soul, Collage, Magical Blend, Lilliput Rev

David Gershator 🎤 ✈   P
PO Box 303353
St Thomas, VI 00803-3353
Internet: gershator@islands.vi
    Pubs: *Palampam Day* (Cavendish, 1997), *Elijah's Child*
    (CCC, 1992), *Play Mas* (Downtown Poets, 1981),
    Frogpond, Home Planet News, Caribbean Writer
Lang: Spanish

Phillis Gershator 🎤 ✈   P&W
PO Box 303353
St Thomas, VI 00803-3353
Internet: gershator@islands.vi
    Pubs: *Only One Cowry, ZZZNG-ZZZNG-ZZZNG*
    (Orchard, 2000, 1998), *When It Starts to Snow* (H Holt,
    1998), *Sweet, Sweet Fig Banana* (Whitman, 1996),
    Caribbean Writer, Home Planet News, Cricket, Spider,
    Ladybug
Groups: Children

Joseph Lisowski   P
Univ Virgin Islands, 2 John Brewers Bay, Saint Thomas,
VI 00802-9990, 809-776-9200
    Pubs: *Looking for Lauren* (Amelia Pr, 1994), *Near the*
    Narcotic Sea (Cottage Wordsmiths, 1992), *Caribbean*
    Writer, Pittsburgh Qtly, Kansas Qtly

Oyoko Loving   P
Box 24742 Christiansted
St Croix, VI 00824, 809-778-7480
    Pubs: *Remember When* (Jet Publishing, 1974)

WASHINGTON

Catherine Austin Alexander ♀ ✈   W
9506 Ravenna Ave NE, #105
Seattle, WA 98115-2402, 206-616-7550
Internet: catalexander@yahoo.com
    Pubs: *Synapse, Mosaic, Children Churches & Daddies,
    Sidewalks, Mediphors, Spindrift, Amer Jones Building &
    Maintenance, North Atlantic Rev*

Jody Aliesan   P
5043 22 Ave NE
Seattle, WA 98105, 206-524-8365
    Pubs: *States of Grace* (Grey Spider Pr, 1992), *Grief
    Sweat* (Broken Moon Pr, 1991), *L.A. Times,
    Contemporary Qtly, Poetry NW, Yellow Silk, Calyx*

Judith Anne Azrael   P&W
PO Box 165
Lummi Island, WA 98262, 360-758-2042
    Pubs: *Twelve Black Horses* (Salmon Run Pr, 1998),
    Apple Tree Poems, Antelope Are Running (Confluence,
    1983, 1978), *Rosebud, Minnesota Rev, Nation, Yale
    Rev, CSM, Western Humanities Rev, SPR*

June Frankland Baker ♀ ✈   P
614 Lynnwood Ct
Richland, WA 99352-1860, 509-375-0842
    Pubs: *CSM, Flyway, Kansas Qtly, SPR, Oxford Mag,
    Gulf Stream Mag, Blueline, Kaleidoscope, Poetry NW,
    Commonweal, Webster Rev, Poet Lore*

Sharon Baker   W
1125 SW Normandy Terr
Seattle, WA 98166, 206-243-9004
    Pubs: *Burning Tears of Sassurum, Journey to Membliar*
    (Avon, 1988, 1987)

Christianne Balk ♀ ✈   P
PO Box 15633
Seattle, WA 98115-0633, 206-523-6543
    Pubs: *Desiring Flight* (Purdue U Pr, 1995), *Bindweed*
    (Macmillan, 1986), *New Yorker, Michigan Rev, Seattle
    Rev, Heartland, Pequod, Crazy Horse*

Carol Jane Bangs ♀ ✈   P&W
PO Box 92
Nordland, WA 98358, 360-379-0286
Internet: cbangs@olympus.net
    Pubs: *The Bones of the Earth* (New Directions, 1983),
    Verse & Universe: Anth (Milkweed Edtns, 1999), *Intro
    to Poetry: Anth* (Norton, 1995), *Colorado Rev, Indiana
    Rev, New Directions Annual, Ploughshares*

Heather Doran Barbieri   P&W
c/o Cine/Lit Representation, 7415 181 Pl SW, Edmonds,
WA 98026, 206-723-1058
    Pubs: *Pleasure Vessels: Anth* (Angela Royal, 1997),
    Writing for Our Lives: Anth (Running Deer Pr, 1996),
    The Pursuit of Happiness: Anth (Leftbank Bks, 1995),
    Amelia, Beacon Rev, Bellowing Ark, Crab Creek Rev

Mary Barnard   P&W
5565 E Evergreen Blvd, #3406
Vancouver, WA 98661-6672
    Pubs: *Nantucket Genesis, Time & the White Tigress*
    (Breitenbush Bks, 1988, 1986), *American Poetry, The
    20th Century, Vol 2: Anth* (LOA, 2000), *Paldeuma*

W. D. Barnes   P
7611-15th NE
Seattle, WA 98115, 206-523-8946
    Pubs: *Fragments, Vagabond, Phantasm, Harvest,
    Minnesota Poetry Jrnl*

Carol Barrett   P
310 SE 3 St
Battle Ground, WA 98604, 360-666-8801
    Pubs: *What's a Nice Girl Like You Doing in a
    Relationship Like This?: Anth* (Crossing Pr, 1992), *Anth
    of Mag Verse & Yearbook of Amer Poetry* (Monitor
    Bks, 1988), *Women's Rev of Bks, Christian Century,
    South Dakota Qtly, Crab Creek Rev, Blue Unicorn*

Bruce Beasley ♀ ✈   P
2225 Victor St
Bellingham, WA 98225, 360-738-4084
    Pubs: *Signs & Abominations* (Wesleyan U Pr, 2000),
    Summer Mystagogia (U Colorado Pr, 1996), *The
    Creation* (Ohio State U Pr, 1994), *Spirituals* (Wesleyan
    U Pr, 1988)

Sheila Bender   P
394 Colman Dr
Port Townsend, WA 98368, 360-385-7839
    Pubs: *Pockets Full of Garden Snails & Twigs* (Fithian
    Pr, 1999), *Love from the Coastal Route* (Duckabush Pr,
    1991), *Raven Chronicles, Women's Studies Qtly, Poetry
    NW, Seattle Rev, The World, Writers' Forum*

John Bennett ♦ ✈   W
605 E 5 Ave
Ellensburg, WA 98926, 509-962-8471
Internet: www.eburg.com/~vagabond
    Pubs: *The Moth Eaters* (Angelfish Pr, 1998), *Domestic
    Violence* (Foursep Pr, 1998), *Bodo* (Mata Pubs, 1997),
    Outlaw Bible of American Poetry: Anth (Thunder's
    Mouth Pr, 1999), *Rattle, Arkansas Rev, NW Rev,
    Pudding, Columbia, Pangolin Papers*

Beth Bentley   P
8762 25 Pl NE
Seattle, WA 98115, 206-525-3508
    Pubs: *Little Fires* (Cune Pr, 1998), *The Purely Visible*
    (Sea Pen Pr, 1980), *Country of Resemblances* (Ohio U
    Pr, 1976), *Best American Poetry: Anth* (Macmillan,
    1989), *Gettysburg Rev, Fine Madness, Poetry NW*

James Bertolino   P
PO Box 1157
Anacortes, WA 98221, 206-293-6274
    Pubs: *The Writer's Journal* (Dell Pub, 1997), *Snail
    River, First Credo* (QRL, 1994, 1986), *Amicus Jrnl,
    Wilderness, Onthebus, Raven Chronicles, Seattle Rev,
    Caliban, Ploughshares, Montserrat Rev, Gargoyle, The
    Temple*

Linda Bierds ♦ ✈   P
4326 NE Rhodes End
Bainbridge Island, WA 98110, 206-780-2015
Internet: lbierds@u.washington.edu
    Pubs: *The Profile Makers, Ghost Trio, Heart &
    Perimeter, The Stillness, The Dancing* (H Holt, 1997,
    1994, 1991, 1988), *Flights of the Harvest-Mare*
    (Ahsahta, 1985)

Laurie Blauner   P
7549 27 Ave NW
Seattle, WA 98117
    Pubs: *Self-Portrait in an Unwilling Landscape, Children
    of Gravity: Anth* (Owl Creek Pr, 1989, 1996), *APR,
    Poetry, New Republic, Nation, Georgia Rev, Poetry NW*
I.D.: Jewish

Alice Bloch ♦ ✈   W
4055 SW Henderson St
Seattle, WA 98136-2541
Internet: AliceBloch@home.com
    Pubs: *The Law of Return, Lifetime Guarantee* (Alyson
    Pub, 1983, 1981), *Hers2: Brilliant New Fiction By
    Lesbian Writers: Anth* (Faber & Faber, 1997)
I.D.: Jewish, G/L/B/T

Marian Blue ♦ ✈   P&W
PO Box 145
Clinton, WA 98236, 360-341-1630
Internet: www.blueudewritersservices.com
    Pubs: *Tiller & the Pen* (Eighth Moon Pr, 1994), *Cold
    Mountain Rev, Exhibition, Mankato Poetry Rev,
    Dominion Rev, Amaranth Rev, North Country Anvil*

Marcia Blumenthal   P&W
1134 Hendricks
Port Townsend, WA 98368-2309, 360-385-4560
    Pubs: *In the Heart of Town, Still Digging* (Barnwood Pr,
    1985), *Flying Island, Thema, Iowa Woman, Ms., Indiana
    Rev, Whiskey Island*

Malcolm J. Bosse   W
1407 E Madison, #30
Seattle, WA 98122
    Pubs: *The Vast Memory of Love, Mister Touch* (HM,
    1992, 1991), *Stranger at the Gate, Fire in Heaven*
    (S&S, 1988, 1986)

David Bosworth   W
Univ Washington, English Dept, GN-30, Seattle, WA
98115, 206-543-2682
    Pubs: *From My Father, Singing* (Pushcart Pr, 1986),
    The Death of Descartes (Pittsburgh Pr, 1981)

Maura Alia Bramkamp ♦ ✈   P
4756 U Vill Pl NE, #130
Seattle, WA 98105-5011
Internet: moxie_99@chickmail.com
    Pubs: *Resculpting* (Paper Boat Pr, 1995), *This Far
    Together: Anth* (Haight-Ashbury Literary, 1995),
    *Haight-Ashbury Jrnl, Exhibition, Synapse, Coffee Hse,
    Switched-on-Gutenberg, Convolvulus, Half Tones to
    Jubilee*

Randall Brock ♦   P
PO Box 1673
Spokane, WA 99210
    Pubs: *Weave* (Found Street Pr, 1994), *Deep Down
    Things: Anth* (Washington State U Pr, 1990), *Blind
    Man's Rainbow, Luna 1976, Olive Pit, Vagabond Rev,
    H.A.K.T.U.P., Lucid Moon, Vantage Point, Carpe
    Laureate Diem, Poetic Realm, Over the Transom,
    Poetalk*

James Broughton   P
PO Box 1330
Port Townsend, WA 98368-0018, 360-385-3748
    Pubs: *Packing Up for Paradise* (Black Sparrow Pr,
    1998), *Coming Unbuttoned, Making Light of It* (City
    Lights Bks, 1993, 1992), *Special Deliveries* (Broken
    Moon Pr, 1990)

John Brummet   P
8531 NW 24th
Seattle, WA 98117, 206-784-8393
    Pubs: *Negative Capability, Electrum, Common Ground,
    Concerning Poetry*

Thomas Brush   P
17217 SE 42 Pl
Issaquah, WA 98027, 206-746-9189
    Pubs: *Even Money* (Seapen Pr, 1988), *Opening Night*
    (Owl Creek Pr, 1981), *Poetry, Poetry NW, Indiana Rev,
    Tar River Rev, Fine Madness, Qtly West*

Sharon Bryan   P
125 Jackson St
Port Townsend, WA 98368, 036-055-5767
  Pubs: *Flying Blind* (Sarabande Bks, 1996), *Where We Stand: Anth* (Norton, 1994), *Paris Rev, Atlantic, Tar River Poetry, Nation, APR, Seattle Rev*

Gregory Burnham   W
PO Box 13129
Burton, WA 98013-0129, 206-463-4006
  Pubs: *Flash Fiction: Anth* (Norton, 1992), *Vital Lines: Anth* (St. Martin's Pr, 1991), *Harper's, Indiana Rev, Turnstile, Puerto del Sol, Black Ice*

E. G. Burrows ⏺ ✈   P
20319 92nd Ave W
Edmonds, WA 98020-2991, 425-775-5383
  Pubs: *The Birds Under the Earth* (Owl Creek Pr, 1996), *QRL 50th Anniversary: Anth* (QRL, 1993), *Wildsong: Anth* (U Georgia Pr, 1998), *Poet Lore, Emrys, Baybury Rev, North Dakota Rev, Abraxas, Wisconsin Rev, Comstock Rev, Santa Barbara Rev, Montserrat Rev*

Jack Cady ⏺ ✈   W
PO Box 872
Port Townsend, WA 98368-0872, 360-385-1670
Internet: erewhon@olympus.net
  Pubs: *The Night We Buried Road Dog* (Dreamhaven, 1998), *The Off Season, Street* (St Martin's, 1996, 1994), *Inagehi, The Sons of Noah* (Broken Moon Pr, 1994, 1992), *Omni, Glimmer Train, Fantasy & Sci-Fi, Portland Rev*

Janet Cannon   P
PO Box 715
Stanwood, WA 98292, 206-781-3378
  Pubs: *The Last Night in New York* (Homeward, 1984), *NYQ, Helicon Nine, Berkeley Poetry Rev, Slant, George Washington Rev, New Mexico Humanities Rev, Beatitude 33*

Gladys H. Cardiff   P
4216 Pasadena Pl NE, #1
Seattle, WA 98105, 206-632-3933
  Pubs: *Contemporary Native American Poets of the Twentieth Century* (H&R, 1988), *Seattle Rev*

Kris Christensen   P
2119 S Monroe St
Spokane, WA 99203, 509-363-1826
  Pubs: *Portland Rev Lit Jrnl, Heliotrope, Touchstone, Permafrost, Red Rock Rev, Hubbub, Passages North*

Chrystos ⏺ ✈   P
3900 Pleasant Beach Dr NE
Bainbridge Island, WA 98110-3215, 206-842-7207
  Pubs: *Fire Power* (Press Gang, 1995), *Reinventing the Enemy's Language: Anth* (Norton, 1996), *Fugitive Colors* (Cleveland State U Poetry Ctr, 1994)
I.D.: Native American, G/L/B/T. Groups: Native American, G/L/B/T

Thomas Churchill ⏺ ✈   W
PO Box 232
Langley, WA 98260-0232, 360-730-4634
Internet: pearlisl@whidbey.com
  Pubs: *Centralia Dead March* (Curbstone, 1980), *Island Independent, Rev of Contemporary Fiction*
I.D.: Playwright

Naomi Clark   P&W
140 Windship Dr, Kala Point
Port Townsend, WA 98368, 206-385-6732
  Pubs: *When I Kept Silence* (Cleveland State U Pr, 1988), *North Dakota Qtly, Indiana Rev, Prairie Schooner, Iowa Rev, Alaska Qtly Rev, Bellingham Rev, BPJ, South Dakota Rev*

Linda J. Clifton ⏺ ✈   P&W
Clifton Consulting, 4462 Whitman Ave N, Seattle, WA 98103-7347
  Pubs: *Shadowmarks* (Blue Begonia Pr, 1994), *Crab Creek Rev: Anth* (Crab Creek Rev, 1994), *Calyx, Gold Dust, Tinderbox*
I.D.: Jewish. Groups: Teenagers, Seniors

Jim Cody   P
1055 NW 96 St
Shoreline, WA 98177
  Pubs: *My Body Is a Flute* (A Place of Herons Pr, 1994), *A Book of Wonders* (Cedarshouse Pr, 1988), *Prayer to Fish* (Slough Pr, 1984), *Lynx, Exquisite Corpse*

Phyllis Collier   P
360 Stevens Ave SW
Renton, WA 98055
  Pubs: *Cape Rock, West Wind Rev, South Dakota Rev, Cumberland Poetry Rev, Mississippi Valley Rev, Puerto del Sol, Green Mountains Rev, Poet Lore, College English, Poetry NW, Nimrod*

Sharon Cumberland   P
Dept of English, Seattle Univ, Broadway & Madison, Seattle, WA 98122-4460, 206-296-5425
  Pubs: *The Arithmetic of Mourning* (Green Rock Pr, 1998), *Nelson Mandelamandela: Anth* (Three Continents Pr, 1989), *Ploughshares, Kalliope, BPJ, Iowa Rev, Mickle Street Rev, Contact II, Indiana Rev*

Madeline DeFrees 🎤 ✈   P
7548 11 Ave NW
Seattle, WA 98117-4143
   Pubs: *Double Dutch* (Red Wing Pr, 1999), *A Millennium*
   Reflection: Anth (Seattle Arts Commission, 1999),
   Southern California Anth, Possible Sibyls (Lynx Hse Pr,
   1991), *Imaginary Ancestors* (Broken Moon Pr, 1990),
   Paris Rev, Ploughshares

Judy Doenges   W
1402 N Steele
Tacoma, WA 98406-8013
   Pubs: *Our Mothers, Our Selves: Anth* (Bergin &
   Garvey, 1996), *Ohio Short Fiction: Anth* (Northmont,
   1995), *Permafrost, Green Mountains Rev, Phoebe,*
   Nimrod, Georgia Rev, Evergreen Chronicles, Equinox

Anita Endrezze 🎤 ✈   P
W 2411 Dell Dr
Spokane, WA 99208
   Pubs: *throwing fire at the Sun, water at the Moon* (U
   Arizona, 2000), *Lost Rivers* (Making Waves Pr, 1997),
   at the helm of twilight (Broken Moon Pr, 1992), *Harper*
   & Row's 20th Century of Native American Poetry: Anth
   (H&R, 1988)
I.D.: Native American. Groups: Native American, Women

Anita N. Feng   P
300 SW Forest Dr
Issaquah, WA 98027, 425-557-8764
   Pubs: *Internal Strategies* (U Akron Pr, 1996), *NW Rev,*
   Ploughshares, Primavera, Prairie Schooner, Black
   Warrior Rev, Nimrod

Lorraine Ferra 🎤 ✈   P
PO Box 93
Port Townsend, WA 98368-0093, 360-385-7568
Internet: lferra@waypt.com
   Pubs: *Eating Bread* (Kuhn Spit Pr, 1994), *Poet & Critic,*
   Qtly West, Florida Rev, Country Jrnl, Seattle Rev, Iris,
   Bellowing Ark
Groups: Children, G/L/B/T

Hollis Giammatteo 🎤 ✈   P&W
2911 1 Ave, #103
Seattle, WA 98121-1086
Internet: hoax@w-link.net
   Pubs: *Secrets* (Blue Heron Pub, 1996), *Left Bank, APR,*
   Prairie Schooner, Nimrod, Calyx, Feminist Studies,
   NAR, Ms., Salmagundi

Carole L. Glickfeld 🎤 ✈   W
731 Broadway E
Seattle, WA 98102-4674, 206-322-7953
Internet: clg@u.washington.edu
   Pubs: *Swimming Toward the Ocean* (Knopf, 2001),
   Useful Gifts (U Georgia Pr, 1989), *Her Face in the*
   Mirror: Anth (Beacon Pr, 1994), *Flannery O'Connor*
   Award Selected Stories: Anth (U Georgia Pr, 1992),
   Ohio Rev, Confrontation
Groups: Prisoners, Seniors

Samuel Green 🎤 ✈   P
101 Bookmonger Rd
Waldron Island, WA 98297, 360-202-6621
   Pubs: *Vertebrae* (Eastern Washington U Pr, 1994),
   Working in the Dark, Communion (Grey Spider Pr,
   1998, 1993), *Poetry, Poetry NW, Prairie Schooner,*
   SPR, Yellow Silk

Michael Gregory   P
1132 NW 56 St
Seattle, WA 98107
   Pubs: *The World Abandoned By Numbers* (Owl Creek
   Pr, 1992), *Denver Qtly, Western Humanities Rev, SPR,*
   Cape Rock, Phoebe, Telescope, Amelia, Nimrod,
   Crazyhorse, New Delta Rev, ACM, Passages North,
   Crab Creek Rev

Ben Groff 🎤 ✈   W
17832 66 Pl, W
Lynnwood, WA 98037-7115, 425-745-8855
Internet: bengroff@aol.com
   Pubs: *Pushcart Prize XVI: Anth* (Pushcart Pr, 1992),
   Alaska Qtly Rev, Crab Creek Rev, Permafrost, Iowa
   Rev, NW Rev

Carol Guess 🎤 ✈   P&W
Western Washington Univ, Dept of English, MS 9055,
Bellingham, WA 98225, 360-714-0216
Internet: guessc@cc.wwu.edu
   Pubs: *Switch* (Calyx Bks, 1998), *Seeing Dell* (Cleis Pr,
   1996), *Mankato Poetry Rev, Harvard Gay & Lesbian*
   Rev, Interim, Ilya's Honey, Poetry NW
I.D.: G/L/B/T. Groups: G/L/B/T, Women

Theodore Hall 🎤 ✈   P
PO Box 317
Rainier, WA 98576-0317
Internet: drtedhall@aol.com
   Pubs: *Intro I* (Bantam, 1968), *NYQ, Maps, Greenfield*
   Rev, NE Jrnl, Shenandoah, Stony Hills, Poet
I.D.: Activists

Mark W. Halperin 🎤 ✈   P
Central Washington Univ, English Dept, Ellensburg, WA
98926-7558, 509-963-3511
Internet: halperin@cwu.edu
   Pubs: *Time & Distance* (New Issues/Western Michigan
   U Pr, 2001), *A Measure of Islands* (Wesleyan, 1990), *A*
   Place Made Fast (Copper Canyon Pr, 1982), *Iowa Rev,*
   Seneca, Shenandoah, Seattle Rev, NW Rev
Lang: Russian

Sam Hamill 🎤 ✈   P
Copper Canyon Press, PO Box 271, Port Townsend, WA
98368, 206-385-4925
Internet: poetry@coppercanyon.org
   Pubs: *Gratitude* (BOA Edtns, 1998), *Destination Zero:*
   Poems 1970-1995 (White Pine Pr, 1995), *Tricycle, APR,*
   Poetry East, Ploughshares

Blaine Hammond 🎤 ✈   P
PO Box 543
Ocean Park, WA 98640-0543, 360-665-4248
Internet: padredoc@willapabay.org
    Pubs: *Sand Script: Anth* (North Coast Writers, 1998),
    *Byline, Minnesota Rev, Acorn, Pemmican, Prairie Jrnl,
    Crossroads, Psychopoetica, Kimera, Seattle Rev, South
    Dakota Rev, Poetalk, Antiskios, Fennel Stalk,
    Bouillabaisse, Free Lunch, Paisley Moon, Impetus*

Nixeon Civille Handy   P
262 Woodland Dr
Lacey, WA 98503, 206-438-5328
    Pubs: *River as Metaphor* (Gorham, 1992), *A Little
    Leaven* (Kings Pr, 1987), *NYQ, NER/BLQ, Oregon East,
    Chariton Rev, Skylark, Connecticut Rev, Bellowing Ark*

Edward Harkness 🎤 ✈   P
14903 Linden Ave N
Shoreline, WA 98133-6516, 206-367-6574
Internet: eharkness@ctc.edu
    Pubs: *Saying the Necessary* (Pleasure Boat Studio,
    2000), *Water Color Portrait of a Bamboo Rake*
    (Brooding Heron Pr, 1994), *Fiddle Wrapped in a
    Gunnysack* (Dooryard, 1984), *Seattle Rev, Portland Rev*

George W. Harper   W
1208 S 27 St, #C-2
Tacoma, WA 98409, 206-272-1034
    Pubs: *Gypsy Earth* (Doubleday, 1983)

Jana Harris 🎤 ✈   P&W
32814 120th St SE
Sultan, WA 98294-9605, 360-793-1848
Internet: jnh@u.washington.edu
    Pubs: *Pearl of Ruby City* (St Martin's Pr, 1998), *Dust
    of Everyday Life* (Sasquatch Pr, 1997), *Oh How Can I
    Keep on Singing?, Sourlands, Untitled Poetry* (Ontario
    Rev Pr, 1993, 1989, 1989), *Manhattan As a Second
    Language* (H&R, 1980)

Robin Hemley   W
English Dept, Western Washington Univ, Bellingham, WA
98225
    Pubs: *The Last Studebaker* (Graywolf, 1992), *All You
    Can Eat* (Atlantic Monthly Pr, 1988), *NAR, Prairie
    Schooner, Ploughshares, Story, Boulevard, Manoa*

Barbara Hiesiger   PP
202 NW 43 St
Seattle, WA 98107-4328

Alicia Hokanson   P
Box 10657
Bainbridge Island, WA 98110
    Pubs: *Mapping the Distance* (Breitenbush, 1989),
    Phosphorous (Brooding Heron, 1984), *Poetry USA,
    Exhibition, Literary Center Qtly*

Emily Newman Holt   P
1704 1st Ave N
Seattle, WA 98109, 206-283-3455
    Pubs: *Encore, Up Against the Wall Mother, Blue
    Unicorn*

A. J. Hovde   P
1400 Chuckanut Dr
Bellingham, WA 98226, 206-673-8073
    Pubs: *A.J. Hovde: Selected Poems* (Fairhaven College
    Pr, 1981), *New Laurel Rev, Kansas Qtly*

Christopher Howell 🎤 ✈   P
420 W 24th
Spokane, WA 99203-1922, 509-624-4894
Internet: cnhowell@ewu.edu
    Pubs: *Memory & Heaven* (Eastern Washington U Pr,
    1997), *Sweet Afton* (True Directions, 1991), *Pushcart
    Prize: Anth* (Pushcart Pr, 1999), *Harper's, Gettysburg
    Rev, NAR, NW Rev, Iowa Rev, Poetry NW, Hudson
    Rev, Ironwood*

Joan Howell   P
Colorado College, 1975 Wynoochee Valley Rd, Montesano,
WA 98563, 360-249-2005
    Pubs: *A Letter to Myself to Water* (Jonesalley Pr,
    1995), *Our Lady of the Harbor* (Seapen Pr, 1985), *Yale
    Rev, SPR, Poetry NW*

Robert Huff   P
English Dept, Western Washington Univ, Bellingham, WA
98225, 206-676-3236
    Pubs: *Shore Guide to Flocking Names* (Fanferon Pr,
    1985), *Western Humanities Rev, Interim, Poetry*

Paul Hunter 🎤 ✈   P
4131 Greenwood N
Seattle, WA 98103-7017, 206-633-5647
Internet: www.woodworkspress.com
    Pubs: *Clown Car, Lay of the Land* (Wood Works, 2000,
    1997), *It Loves Me It Loves Me Not* (Now Its Up To
    You Pr, 1992), *Mockingbird* (Jawbone Pr, 1981), *Alaska
    Fisherman's Jrnl, Fine Madness, NAR, Poetry, Poetry
    NW, Point No Point, Beloit*

Richard Ives 🎤 ✈   P
2693 SW Camano Dr
Camano Island, WA 98292-8205
    Pubs: *Evidence of Fire* (Owl Creek Pr, 1989), *Notes
    from the Water Journals* (Confluence Pr, 1980), *Iowa
    Rev, Poetry NW, NW Rev, Mississippi Rev, Virginia
    Qtly Rev*

Sibyl James   P&W
1712 22nd Ave, S
Seattle, WA 98144-4514, 206-323-7516
    Pubs: *The Adventures of Stout Mama* (Papier-Mache
    Pr, 1993), *In China with Harpo & Karl* (Calyx Bks,
    1990), *American Voice, Ironwood, Nebraska Rev*

Laura Jensen   P&W
302 N Yakima, #C-3
Tacoma, WA 98403-2213, 253-272-0541
    Pubs: *Shelter, Memory* (Dragon Gate, 1985, 1982), *Bad
    Boats* (Ecco, 1977), *APR, New Yorker, Crazyhorse,
    Poetry NW*

Ted Joans   P
513 Maynard Ave S, Studio #202
Seattle, WA 98104, 206-625-1399

Charles Johnson   W
English Dept, GN-30, Univ Washington, Seattle, WA
98195, 206-543-2690
    Pubs: *Middle Passage, Sorcerer's Apprentice*
    (Atheneum, 1990, 1986), *Dialogue, American Visions*

Douglas S. Johnson   P&W
PO Box 772
Auburn, WA 98071-0772, 206-351-9119
    Pubs: *Transformations* (Guyasuta Pub, 1994), *The
    Heartlands Today, Midwest Poetry Rev, Kansas English,
    Thomas Wolfe Rev, Ohioana Rev*

R. P. Jones   P
7102 Interlaaken Dr SW
Tacoma, WA 98499-1805, 206-531-7422
    Pubs: *The Rest Is Silence* (Broken Moon Pr, 1984),
    Waiting for Spring (Circinatum Pr, 1978)

Thom Jones   W
2438 31st Ave NW
Olympia, WA 98502, 360-866-8039
    Pubs: *Cold Snap, The Pugilist at Rest* (Little, Brown,
    1995, 1993), *New Yorker, Esquire, Harper's, Playboy,
    Buzz*

Jessie Kachmar   P
13739 15th Ave NE, #B-1
Seattle, WA 98125
    Pubs: *Snow Quiet* (Snow Pr, 1979), *Apertures to
    Anywhere* (Harper Square Pr, 1976), *Caprice, Redstart,
    Twigs, Chicago*

Sy M. Kahn   P
1212 Holcomb St
Port Townsend, WA 98368, 360-385-9499
    Pubs: *Between Tedium & Terror: A Soldier's Diary,
    1943-45* (U Illinois Pr, 1993), *Facing Mirrors* (Two
    Windows, 1980), *Another Time* (Sydon, Inc, 1968), *Jrnl
    of Modern Literature, Midwest Qtly, College English,
    South Carolina Rev*

Lonny Kaneko   P
Highline College, PO Box 98000, Des Moines, WA
98198-9800, 206-878-3710
    Pubs: *Coming Home from Camp* (Brooding Heron Pr,
    1986), *The Big Aiiieeee!: Anth* (NAL, 1991), *Seattle
    Rev, Written Arts, King County, An Ear to the Ground*

John E. Keegan 🎤 ✈   W
7722 22nd Ave NE
Seattle, WA 98115-4512
Internet: johnkeegan@dwt.com
    Pubs: *Piper* (Permanent Pr, 2001), *Clearwater Summer*
    (Carroll & Graf, 1994), *New Orleans Rev*

Richard L. Kenney   P
Univ Washington, English Dept, 354330, Seattle, WA
98195, 206-543-2690
    Pubs: *The Invention of the Zero* (Knopf, 1993), *Orrery*
    (Atheneum, 1985), *The Evolution of the Flightless Bird*
    (Yale U Pr, 1983)

Alex Kuo 🎤 ✈   P
PO Box 2237
Pullman, WA 99165, 509-335-4901
Internet: kuo@wsumix.wsu.edu
    Pubs: *This Fierce Geography* (Limberlost, 1999),
    Chinese Opera (Asia 2000, 1998), *Changing the River*
    (Reed & Cannon, 1986), *New Letters from Hiroshima*
    (Greenfield, 1974), *The Window Tree* (Windy Row,
    1971), *Chicago Rev, Caliban, Boundary 2, Malahat Rev*

Susan Landgraf   P
4828 51st Ave, S
Seattle, WA 98118, 206-721-0208
    Pubs: *Spoon River Qtly, South Florida Poetry Rev,
    Calyx, Ploughshares, Nimrod, Cincinnati Poetry Rev*

R. A. Larson   P
9600 Occidental
Yakima, WA 98903, 509-965-4547
    Pubs: *Of Wind, A Hawk, & Kiona* (Confluence Pr,
    1978), *Silverfish Rev, Brix, Kingfisher*

Alan Chong Lau 🎤 ✈   P
5005 Phinney Ave N, #302
Seattle, WA 98103-6047
    Pubs: *Blues & Greens* (U Hawaii Pr, 2000), *What
    Book!?: Anth* (Parallax Pr, 1998), *Highway 99: Anth*
    (Heyday Bks, 1996), *The Open Boat Poems from Asian
    America: Anth* (Anchor Bks, 1993), *American Dragons:
    Anth* (HC, 1993)
I.D.: Asian-American

Ellen Levine   P
838 NE 83 St
Seattle, WA 98115
    Pubs: *Poetry NW, Georgia Rev, SPR, Poetry Now,
    Calyx, Kansas Qtly*

Evelyn Livingston   W
71 Windship Dr
Port Townsend, WA 98368-9545, 360-385-2063
    Pubs: *Digging for Roots: Dalmo'ma 5 Anth* (Empty Bowl
    Pr, 1985), *Confrontation, Pennsylvania Rev, Indiana
    Rev, Georgia Rev, Crosscurrents, New Letters, Interim*

Jeanne Lohmann ♣ ✈ P
2501 Washington SE
Olympia, WA 98501-2962, 360-705-3735
Internet: jlohmann@olywa.net
  Pubs: *Flying Horses, Granite Under Water* (Fithian Pr,
  2000, 1996), *Between Silence & Answer* (Pendle Hill,
  1994), *Prayers to Protest* (Pudding Hse, 1998), *Wild
  Song: Anth* (U Georgia Pr, 1998), *Cries of the Spirit:
  Anth* (Beacon Pr, 1991), *Bitter Oleander*
  Groups: Seniors

Kenneth MacLean P
522 Decatur St SW
Olympia, WA 98502, 360-753-1175
  Pubs: *Blue Heron's Sky* (Latitudes Pr, 1990), *The Long
  Way Home* (Inchbird Pr, 1982), *Prism Intl, Poetry
  Seattle, Calapooya Collage, Concerning Poetry*

Jesus Maria Maldonado P
PO Box 471
Grandview, WA 98930, 509-882-6477
  Pubs: *In the Still of My Heart* (Canto Norteno Pubs,
  1993), *Americas Rev, Bilingual Rev, El Grito, Caracol,
  Metamorphoses, El Gato*

Stephen Manes ♣ ✈ W
1122 E Pike St, #588
Seattle, WA 98122-3916, 206-722-2525
Internet: steve@cranky.com
  Pubs: *An Almost Perfect Game, Comedy High*
  (Scholastic, 1995, 1992), *Make Four Million Dollars by
  Next Thursday* (Bantam, 1990), *Be a Perfect Person in
  Just Three Days!* (HM, 1982)

Laureen D. Mar P&W
3811 S Horton St
Seattle, WA 98144-7027, 206-722-3482
  Pubs: *Charlie Chan Is Dead: Anth* (Penguin, 1993),
  Breaking Silence: Anth (Greenfield Rev Pr, 1983),
  Contact II, Greenfield Rev, Seattle Rev

Carlos Martinez ♣ ✈ P
9116 1st Ave
Seattle, WA 98115-2705, 206-528-0543
Internet: carlmart1@yahoo.com
  Pubs: *Pitt Qtly, Black Bear Rev, Crab Creek Rev*

John Constantine Mastor ♣ P
401 NE Ravenna Blvd, #P122
Seattle, WA 98115-6428, 206-525-1081
  Pubs: *Studio Portrait, Glorious Morning, Bountiful Light*
  (The Plowman, 1999, 1996, 1995), *The Musing Place,
  Time of Singing, My Legacy, Broken Streets, Purpose,
  Rio Grande Pr, Bellowing Ark, Uprising, Aim Qtly,
  Poetic Realm*
  I.D.: Greek-American/Greek, Disabled. Groups: Mentally Ill,
  Disabled

William H. Matchett P
1017 Minor Ave, #702
Seattle, WA 98104-1303, 206-682-6730
  Pubs: *Fireweed* (The Tidal Pr, 1980), *Water Ouzel* (HM,
  1955), *New Yorker, Harper's, Harvard, New Republic,
  Ploughshares, SPR*

Rita Z. Mazur ♣ ✈ P
2332 Ferndale
Richland, WA 99352-1975, 509-375-4210
  Pubs: *The Great Blue Heron & Other Poems* (Adrienne
  Lee Pr, 1996), *Tanka Splendor* (AHA Bks, 1995), *Rain:
  Anth* (NW Region HSA, 1997), *Frogpond, American
  Tanka, Cherry Blossom, Black Bough, Modern Haiku,
  Passager*
  Groups: Children, Seniors

James J. McAuley P
1011 W 25 St
Spokane, WA 99203, 509-747-0896
  Pubs: *Coming & Going, New & Selected Work* (U
  Arkansas Pr, 1989), *Recital* (Dolmen/Colin Smythe,
  1982), *Irish Times, Shenandoah, Cimarron Rev, Poetry
  NW*

Joanne McCarthy P
1322 N Cascade
Tacoma, WA 98406-1113, 253-752-3462
  Pubs: *Shadowlight* (Broken Moon Pr, 1989), *At Our
  Core: Anth* (Papier-Mache Pr, 1998), *Calyx, Green
  Fuse, Kalliope, Writers' Forum*

Colleen J. McElroy ♣ ✈ P&W
c/o Elizabeth Wales, Wales Literary Agency, 108 Hayes,
Seattle, WA 98109, 206-284-7114
  Pubs: *Over the Lip of the World* (U Washington Pr,
  1999), *Travelling Music* (Story Line Pr, 1998), *A Long
  Way from St. Louie* (Coffee Hse Pr, 1997), *What
  Madness Brought Me Here* (Wesleyan U, 1990),
  Children of the Night: Anth (Little, Brown, 1995),
  Seneca Rev

John McFarland ♣ ✈ W
2320 10th Ave E, #5
Seattle, WA 98102-4076, 206-323-7053
Internet: jbmcfar@yahoo.com
  Pubs: *The Exploding Frog & Other Fables* (Little,
  Brown, 1981), *Contra/Diction: Anth* (Arsenal Pulp Pr,
  1998), *The Next Parish Over: Anth* (New Rivers Pr,
  1993), *Stringtown, Mediphors, Ararat, Caliban, Cricket*
  I.D.: G/L/B/T. Groups: Children, G/L/B/T

Heather McHugh P
English Dept, Box 354330, Univ Washington, Seattle, WA
98195-4330, 206-543-2483
  Pubs: *Hinge & Sign: Poems 1968-1993, Broken
  English: Poetry & Partiality, The Father of the
  Predicaments* (Wesleyan, 1994, 1993, 1999)

Robert McNamara ♟ ⊀ P
Univ Washington, English Dept, Box 354330, Seattle, WA
98195-4330, 206-543-7131
Internet: rmcnamar@u.washington.edu
  Pubs: *Second Messengers* (Wesleyan U Pr, 1990),
  *Ohio Rev, Agni, Missouri Rev, Field, Gettysburg Rev,
  Antioch Rev, NW Rev*

Linda Meyers P
15417 223rd Ave NE
Woodinville, WA 98072, 206-788-0336
  Pubs: *Poetry NW, Hawaii Rev, Calapooya Collage,
  Bottomfish, Impetus, Chambered Nautilus, Whole Notes,
  Chrysanthemum, Seattle Rev, Permafrost*

James Masao Mitsui P
6218 Latona Ave NE
Seattle, WA 98115
  Pubs: *From a Three-Cornered World* (U Washington Pr,
  1997), *After the Long Train* (Bieler Pr, 1986), *Crossing
  the Phantom River* (Graywolf, 1978), *A Year in Poetry:
  Anth* (Crown Pub, 1995)

Melinda Mueller ♟ ⊀ P
7704 16th Ave NW
Seattle, WA 98117-5419, 206-323-6600
  Pubs: *What the Ice Gets* (Van West Co, 2000),
  Apocrypha (Grey Spider Pr, 1998), *Asleep in Another
  Country* (Jawbone Pr, 1979), *Best American Poetry:
  Anth* (MacMillan, 1990)

Jo Nelson ♟ ⊀ P
11102 Crescent Valley Dr NW
Gig Harbor, WA 98335-9339, 206-851-7728
Internet: www.peninsula-art.com/poet/jo-nelson.html
  Pubs: *A Taste of Light,* (Ye Olde Font Shoppe, 2000),
  Seattle Five Plus One: Anth (Pig Iron Pr, 1995),
  *Chariton Rev, Confluence, Plainsong, Portland Rev,
  Main Street Rag, Willow Creek Jrnl, Pleiades, Wind
  Song*
Lang: Spanish, German

Carol Orlock ♟ ⊀ W
920 2nd Ave W
Seattle, WA 98119, 206-283-0680
  Pubs: *The Hedge, The Ribbon* (Broken Moon Pr,
  1993), *The Goddess Letters* (St. Martin's Pr, 1987),
  Century, Willow Springs, Calyx, Crab Creek Rev

Hans Ostrom ♟ ⊀ P&W
English Dept, Univ of Puget Sound, 1500 N Warner,
Tacoma, WA 98416, 206-756-3434
Internet: ostrom@ups.edu
  Pubs: *Subjects Apprehended: Poems* (Pudding Hse Pr,
  2000), *Metro* (Longman, 2000), *Water's Night*
  (Mariposite Pr, 1993), *Three to Get Ready* (Cliffhanger
  Pr, 1991), *Ploughshares, Poetry NW, Redbook,
  California Qtly, South Carolina Rev*

Lori Jo Oswald P&W
12401 SE 320th St, #HS
Auburn, WA 98092-3622
  Pubs: *Poetry North Rev, Day Tonight/Night Today,
  Alura, Negative Capability, Nettles & Nutmeg*

Eileen Owen P
2709 128th St SE
Everett, WA 98208, 206-337-1231
  Pubs: *Facing the Weather Side* (Basilisk Pr, 1985),
  Calyx, Cincinnati Rev, South Dakota Rev

Dixie Lee Partridge P
1817 Marshall Ct
Richland, WA 99351-2483, 509-943-4007
  Pubs: *Watermark* (Saturday Pr, 1991), *Deer in the
  Haystacks* (Ahsahta Pr, 1984), *Poetry, Commonweal,
  SPR, Ploughshares, Passages North, Georgia Rev,
  Northern Lights*

Lucia Perillo ♟ ⊀ P
James Rudy, 513 S Quince St, Olympia, WA 98501
  Pubs: *The Oldest Map with the Name America*
  (Random Hse, 1999), *The Body Mutinies* (Purdue U Pr,
  1996), *Dangerous Life* (Northeastern U Pr, 1989), *New
  Yorker, Ploughshares, Atlantic, Kenyon Rev, Poetry
  East*

Fred Pfeil W
6031 1st Ave NW
Seattle, WA 98107-2008
  Pubs: *Goodman 2020* (Indiana U Pr, 1985), *Georgia
  Rev, Fiction Intl, Sewanee Rev*

Anne Pitkin P
6809 Dayton Ave N
Seattle, WA 98103, 206-789-4623
  Pubs: *Yellow* (Arrowood Bks, 1989), *Poetry, Prairie
  Schooner, Ironwood, Malahat, Seattle Rev*

Randall Platt ♟ ⊀ W
1126 Pt Fosdick Dr NW
Gig Harbor, WA 98335-8810
Internet: www.plattbooks.com
  Pubs: *The Likes of Me* (Random Hse, 2000), *The 1898
  Baseball Fe-As-Ko, The Cornerstone, The Royalscope
  Fe-As-Ko, The Four Arrows Fe-As-Ko* (Catbird Pr, 2000,
  1998, 1997, 1991), *Honor Bright* (Doubleday, 1998),
  Out of the Forest Clearing (John Daniel, 1991)

Darryl Ponicsan W
PO Box 10036
Bainbridge Island, WA 98110
  Pubs: *The Ringmaster, Tom Mix Died for Your Sins*
  (Delacorte/Dell, 1978, 1975)

Charles Potts 🎤 ✈   P
PO Box 100
Walla Walla, WA 99362-0033, 509-529-0813
Internet: www.tsunami-inc.net
   Pubs: *Nature Lovers* (Pleasure Boat Studio, 2000), *Lost River Mountain* (Blue Begonia, 1999), *Little Lord Shiva* (Glass Eye Bks, 1999), *Fascist Haikus* (Acid Pr, 1999), *100 Years in Idaho, Pacific Northwestern Spiritual Poetry: Anth* (Tsunami, 1996, 1998)

Joseph Powell   P
221 Cross Creek Dr
Ellensburg, WA 98926, 509-925-5312
   Pubs: *Getting Here, QRL 50th Anniversary Anth* (QRL, 1997, 1993), *Counting the Change, Winter Insomnia* (Arrowhead, 1993, 1993), *Poetry, Seattle Rev, Tar River Poetry, Nebraska Rev*

Marjorie Power 🎤 ✈   P
508 O'Farrell Ave
Olympia, WA 98501-3470, 360-352-7025
Internet: birdbrane@home.com
   Pubs: *Cave Poems, Tishku After She Created Men* (Lone Willow Pr, 1998, 1996), *Living with It* (Wampeter Pr, 1983), *New Virginia Rev, SPR, Spoon River Poetry Rev, Puerto del Sol, Atlanta Rev, Poet Lore, Blue Unicorn, Malahat Rev*

Freda Quenneville   P
6348 S Island Dr E
Bonny Lake, WA 98390-8683, 206-236-2821
   Pubs: *Reflections on a Gift of Watermelon Pickle & Other Modern Verse* (Scott Foresman & Co, 1966), *Poetry NW, Nation, New Yorker, Prairie Schooner*

Belle Randall   P
1202 N. 42 St., Seattle, WA 98103, 206-633-2744
   Pubs: *Drop Dead Beautiful* (Wood Works Pr, 1998), *The Gift of Tongues: Anth* (Copper Canyon Pr, 1996), *Wallace Stegner Anth* (Stanford U Pr, 1989), *Contemporary Religious Poetry: Anth* (Paulist, 1988), *Threepenny Rev, Common Knowledge*

Bill Ransom 🎤 ✈   P&W
PO Box 284
Grayland, WA 98547-0284, 360-267-2018
Internet: www.sfwa.org/members/ransom
   Pubs: *Jaguar* (Wildside Press, 2000), *Learning the Ropes* (Utah State U Pr, 1995), *Burn* (Putnam-Berkley Pub, 1995), *In Praise of Pedagogy: Anth* (Calendar Pr, 2000), *Thirteen Ways of Looking for a Poem: Anth* (Longman, 1999), *Puerto del Sol, Tendril, NYQ*

Susan Rich 🎤 ✈   P
3417 60th Ave SW
Seattle, WA 98116-2819, 206-878-3710 x3253
Internet: srich@hcc.ctc.edu
   Pubs: *The Cartographer's Tongue* (White Pine Pr, 2000), *Alaska Qtly Rev, Bridges, DoubleTake, Glimmer Train, Harvard Mag, Hedgebrook Jrnl, Massachusetts Rev, Mercator's World, Poet Lore, SPR, Santa Barbara Rev, Sojourner*
I.D.: Jewish. Groups: Jewish, International

Sherry Rind 🎤 ✈   P
17301 NE 131 St
Redmond, WA 98052-2171, 425-869-9212
Internet: sherryrind@aol.com
   Pubs: *A Fall Out the Door* (Confluence Pr, 1994), *The Hawk in the Backyard* (Anhinga Pr, 1985), *Poetry NW, SPR*
I.D.: Jewish

Judith Roche 🎤 ✈   P
178 Lake Dell Ave
Seattle, WA 98122-6309, 206-329-4687
Internet: judith@onereel.org
   Pubs: *Myrrh, My Life as a Screamer* (Black Heron Pr, 1994), *Ghosts* (Empty Bowl Pr, 1984), *Willow Springs, Duckabush Jrnl, Yellow Silk*
Groups: Prisoners

Mary Elizabeth Ryan 🎤 ✈   W
WordCrafters Northwest, 4137 University Way NE, Ste 202, Seattle, WA 98105-6263, 206-632-2593
Internet: mary.e.ryan@gte.net
   Pubs: *Alias, The Trouble with Perfect, Me, My Sister, & I, My Sister Is Driving Me Crazy* (S&S, 1997, 1995, 1992, 1991), *I'd Rather Be Dancing* (Delacorte Pr, 1989), *Tails of Terror: Anth* (Lyrick, 1999)

Sal Salasin ✈   P
840 W Nickerson St, #11
Seattle, WA 98119-1448
   Pubs: *Optima Suavidad* (Greenbean Pr, 1999), *Casa de Caca* (Apathy Poets Pr, 1990), *Stepping Off the Plane* (Another Chicago Pr, 1988), *Exquisite Corpse, ACM, NAW, Sensitive Skin, Real Poetik*

Eric Schmidt   PP
1517 12th Ave, #Mezz
Seattle, WA 98122-3932
   Pubs: *The Freezing No to All Questions Prison of Bent Things: Verse Play*

Sandra Schroeder   P
4747 Univ View Pl NE
Seattle, WA 98105-4035
   Pubs: *Inventing the Cats* (BkMk Pr, 1973), *Seattle Rev, Fine Madness, Literary Arts Rev, Ergo!, Poetry NW, Bellowing Ark*

Julianne Seeman   P
English Dept, Bellevue Community College, Arts & Humanities Div, #A255M, Bellevue, WA 98004, 206-526-0698
   Pubs: *Enough Light to See* (Anhinga Pr, 1989)

Janet Seery   P
600 W Olympic Pl, Apt 512
Seattle, WA 98119-3661
   Pubs: *Washout Rev, Greenfield Rev, Kudzu, Wisconsin Rev, Nantucket Rev, Buckle, Bloodroot*

Sondra Shulman   W
934 E Allison St
Seattle, WA 98102, 206-329-6493
   Pubs: *Moon People* (Baskerville Pub, 1994), *Scrittori
   Ebrei Americani* (Tascabili Bom Pi Ant, 1989), *Ascent,
   Massachusetts Rev, Antioch Rev, Kansas Qtly,
   Bumbershoot*

Paul Red Shuttleworth 🎤 ✈   P
10482 Rd 16 NE
Moses Lake, WA 98837-9356, 509-766-9104
   Pubs: *Western Settings* (U Nevada Pr, 2000), *All These
   Bullets* (Logan Hse Pr, 1997), *Western Movie* (Signpost
   Pr, 1990), *Coyotes with Wings* (Gorse Pr, 1990), *Neon,
   Alaska Qtly Rev, New Mexico Humanities Rev, West
   Branch*

Sarah Singer 🎤   P
2360 43 Ave E, #415
Seattle, WA 98112-2703, 206-726-8103
   Pubs: *The Gathering, Of Love & Shoes* (William L.
   Bauhan, 1992, 1987), *Palomar Showcase: Anths*
   (Palomar Branch Pr, 1999, 1998, 1997), *Glimpses: Anth*
   (King Cty Public Art Prgm, 1997), *Shakespeare
   Newsletter, Voices Intl, Lyric, Judaism, Poets West,
   Penwoman*

Judith Skillman 🎤 ✈   P
14206 SE 45 Pl
Bellevue, WA 98006-2308, 206-644-4026
   Pubs: *Storm, Beethoven & the Birds* (Blue Begonia Pr,
   1998, 1996), *Worship of the Visible Spectrum*
   (Breitenbush Bks, 1988), *JAMA, Southern Rev, NW
   Rev, Iowa Rev, Prairie Schooner, Poetry, Laurel Rev*

James M. Snydal 🎤 ✈   P
11034 Old Creosote Hill Rd
Bainbridge Island, WA 98110-2154, 206-842-1273
Internet: jsnydal@webtv.net
   Pubs: *Blueberry Pie* (Wood Works, 1998), *Living in
   America* (New Thought Jrnl Pr, 1997), *To Range
   Widely Over Possibilities* (Full Moon Pub, 1996), *Near
   the Cathedral* (Dry Bones Pr, 1995), *NYQ, Poetry
   Wales, Onthebus, Chiron, Bloomsbury*

Maya Sonenberg 🎤 ✈   W
English Dept, Univ Washington, Box 354330, Seattle, WA
98195-4330, 206-543-7984
Internet: mayas@u.washington.edu
   Pubs: *Cartographies* (U Pitt Pr, 1989), *American Fiction
   X: Anth* (New Rivers Pr, 1999), *American Short Fiction,
   Cream City Rev, Grand Street, Chelsea, Santa Monica
   Rev*

Sandi Sonnenfeld 🎤 ✈   W
125 N 105 St
Seattle, WA 98133-8701
Internet: sanwar1@earthlink.net
   Pubs: *Sex & the City: Anth* (Serpent's Tail, 1989),
   *Onion River Rev, Voices West, This Mag, Salmon Mag,
   CPU Rev, Emrys Jrnl, Ion, Sojourner, Written Arts*
I.D.: Jewish

Michael Spence 🎤 ✈   P
5810 S 144 St
Tukwila, WA 98168-4550, 206-431-6874
   Pubs: *Adam Chooses* (Rose Alley Pr, 1998), *The Spine*
   (Purdue U Pr, 1987), *Poetry Comes Up Where It Can:
   Anth* (U Utah Pr, 2000), *Atlanta Rev, Nimrod, Southern
   Humanities Rev, Sewanee Rev, Poetry, American
   Scholar, Poetry NW*

Stephen Sundin 🎤 ✈   P
21 Alpine Way
Longview, WA 98632
Internet: stateofsss@aol.com
   Pubs: *Playing with a Full Deck: Anth* (26 Bks, 1999),
   *ACM, Artful Dodge, Denver Qtly, Key Satch(el), Luna,
   Mudfish, NYQ, Paragraph, Poet Lore, Prose Poem,
   Pivot, Quarter After Eight, Thin Air, Wolf Head Qtly*

Joan Swift 🎤 ✈   P
18520 Sound View Pl
Edmonds, WA 98020-2355, 425-776-2391
Internet: jayswift@msn.com
   Pubs: *The Tiger Iris* (BOA Edtns, 1999), *Intricate
   Moves* (Chicory Blue Pr, 1997), *The Dark Path of Our
   Names* (Dragon Gate, 1985), *Parts of Speech*
   (Confluence Pr, 1978), *Poetry, DoubleTake, Poetry NW,
   Ploughshares*

Gordon Taylor   W
3920 SW 109 St
Seattle, WA 98146-1652, 206-243-6768

Velande P. Taylor, Ph.D. 🎤 ✈   P&W
910 Marion St, #1008
Seattle, WA 98104-1273, 206-621-1376
   Pubs: *Zodiac Affair, Between the Lines, Copper
   Flowers, Tales from the Archetypal World* (WordCraft
   Bks, 2000, 1999, 1999, 1998), *Pacific Mag, Verses
   Mag, Extended Hands*
Groups: College/Univ, Seniors

Gary Thompson 🎤 ✈   P
875 Puget Dr SE
Port Orchard, WA 98366-8504
Internet: gary.thompson3@worldnet.att.net
   Pubs: *On John Muir's Trail* (Bear Star Pr, 1999), *As for
   Living* (Red Wing Pr, 1995), *Hold Fast* (Confluence Pr,
   1984), *Colorado Rev, Laurel Rev, Nebraska Rev,
   Writers' Forum, Hayden's Ferry Rev, Chariton Rev*

Gail Tremblay   P
The Evergreen State College, Olympia, WA 98505,
206-866-6000
   Pubs: *Indian Singing in 20th Century America* (Calyx,
   1990), *Harper's Anth of 20th Century Native American
   Poetry* (Harper SF, 1986), *Wooster Rev, Calyx, Denver
   Qtly, NW Rev*

Wayne Ude   W
PO Box 145
Clinton, WA 98236, 206-341-1630
  Pubs: *Maybe I Will Do Something* (HM, 1993), *Buffalo
  & Other Stories* (Lynx Hse Pr, 1991), *Three Coyote
  Tales* (Lone Oak Pr, 1989), *Ploughshares, NAR*

Michael Upchurch   W
9725 Sand Point Way NE
Seattle, WA 98115-2650
  Pubs: *Passive Intruder* (Norton, 1995), *The Flame
  Forest* (Available Pr/Ballantine, 1989), *Carolina Qtly,
  American Scholar, Glimmer Train*

Craig Van Riper 🎤 ✈   P
1630 E Lynn St
Seattle, WA 98112-2130, 206-329-5972
Internet: szbrook@aol.com
  Pubs: *Convenient Danger* (Pecan Grove Pr, 2000),
  Making the Path While You Walk (Sagittarius Pr, 1993),
  Seattle Poets & Photographers: Anth (U Washington Pr,
  1999), *Spoon River Qtly, Passages North, SPR,
  Onthebus, Five Fingers Rev, Coe Rev*

Nance Lee Van Winckel 🎤 ✈   P&W
12506 S Gardener
Cheney, WA 99004-9513, 509-448-6155
  Pubs: *Curtain Creek Farm* (Persea, 2000), *After a
  Spell, The Dirt* (Miami U Pr, 1998, 1994), *Limited
  Lifetime Warranty* (U Missouri Pr, 1994), *Field, New
  Letters, Georgia Rev, APR, Nation, NER, Denver Qtly,
  Shenandoah, NAR, Poetry NW*

David Wagoner   P&W
5416-154 Pl SW
Edmonds, WA 98026-4348, 206-745-6964
  Pubs: *Walt Whitman Bathing* (U Illinois Pr, 1996),
  Through the Forest (Atlantic Monthly Pr, 1987)

Edith M. Walden   P
PO Box 9493
Seattle, WA 98109
  Pubs: *Iowa Rev, Luna Tack, Calyx, Slackwater Rev,
  Rapunzel Rapunzel, Nethula Jrnl, Pig Iron*

Robert R. Ward   P
PO Box 45637
Seattle, WA 98145, 206-440-0791
  Pubs: *Notes on an Urban Ecology* (Primeval Pr, 1998),
  *Outposts Poetry Rev, Imago, MacGuffin, Permafrost,
  Santa Clara Rev, City Primeval, Kansas Qtly, Interim,
  Hawaii Rev, Cafe Solo, Farmer's Market, Connecticut
  River Rev, Snowy Egret, Marginalia*

Michael Frank Warlum   P
4412 50 Ave SW
Seattle, WA 98116, 206-935-8615
  Pubs: *The Keating Dynasty* (NAL/Signet, 1986), *A Bullet
  for Bradford* (Carousel, 1981)

Emily Warn   P
1723 27th Ave
Seattle, WA 98122, 206-322-8750
  Pubs: *The Novice Insomniac, The Leaf Path* (Copper
  Canyon Pr, 1996, 1982), *Kenyon Rev, Cream City Rev,
  SPR, CutBank, Mississippi Mud*

Irving Warner   W
PO Box 696
Carlsborg, WA 98324-0696
  Pubs: *From Timberline to Tidepool: Anth* (Copper
  Canyon, 1984), *Montana Rev, Cimarron Rev, Colorado
  Rev*

Jan Widgery   W
8605 NE 12 St
Medina, WA 98039-3904, 425-454-9358
Internet: jwidge@aol.com
  Pubs: *Trumpet at the Gates, The Adversary*
  (Doubleday, 1970, 1966), *Good Housekeeping*

Barbara Wilson   W
523 N 84 St
Seattle, WA 98103-4309, 206-781-9612
  Pubs: *Blue Windows* (Picador USA, 1997), *If You Had
  a Family* (Seal Pr, 1996)

Shawn H. Wong   P&W
Univ Washington, Asian American Studies, GN-80, Seattle,
WA 98195
  Pubs: *The Big Aiiieeee!: Anth* (NAL, 1991), *Before
  Columbus Fiction Anth, Before Columbus Poetry Anth*
  (Norton, 1992, 1992)

Sara Jorgenson Woodbury 🎤   P
PO Box 676
Spokane, WA 99210-4059, 509-458-0454
  Pubs: *Edge of Night* (Writer's Works, 1999), *Dreams,
  Shadows of the Moon* (Papermill, 1996, 1991), *All
  These Years* (B&N Cashon, 1995), *Still Window Profiles*
  (Implosion Pr, 1989)

WEST VIRGINIA

Jean Anaporte-Easton 🎤 ✈   P
110 Town Ct
Charleston, WV 25312-1130, 304-744-9776
  Pubs: *Free Songs* (Writers' Center Pr, 1992), *With a
  Fly's Eye, Whale's Wit, & Woman's Heart* (Cleis Pr,
  1989), *13th Moon, Mid-American Rev, Mildred, One
  Trick Pony, Kestrel, Callaloo*

Grace Cavalieri 🎤 ✈   P
PO Box 416
Hedgesville, WV 25427-0416, 304-754-8847
Internet: http://members.aol.com/grace7623/grace.htm
   Pubs: *Sit Down Says Love* (Argonne Hotel, 2000),
   Heart on a Leash (Red Dragon Pr, 1999), *Pinecrest
   Rest Haven* (Wordworks, 1998), *Migrations, Poems*
   (Vision Library Pubs, 1995, 1994), *Making Literature
   Matter: Anth* (Bedford Bks, 1999), *Paterson Lit Rev,
   APR*

Lillie D. Chaffin-Kash   P&W
4270 8th St Rd
Huntington, WV 25701-9424
   Pubs: *Catching the Wind, At Easter* (Edge of World Pr,
   1991, 1991), *We Be Warm Till Springtime* (Macmillan,
   1980)

Lloyd Davis   P
West Virginia Univ, Morgantown, WV 26506, 304-293-3107
   Pubs: *The Way All Rivers Run* (Une Pr, 1982), *Fishing
   the Lower Jackson* (Best Cellar, 1974)

Mark DeFoe 🎤 ✈   P&W
28 Central Ave
Buckhannon, WV 26201, 304-472-0667
   Pubs: *Air* (Grenn Tower Pr, 1998), *Palmate* (Pringle
   Tree Pr, 1988), *Bringing Home Breakfast* (Black Willow,
   1982), *Laurel Rev, Tar River Poetry, Poetry, Kenyon
   Rev, Paris Rev, Michigan Qtly Rev, Poet Lore, CSM,
   Tulane Rev, Poetry Intl*

Bill Garten   P
28 Twin Oaks Dr
Huntington, WV 25701, 304-523-2141
   Pubs: *And Now the Magpie* (Mtn State Pr, 1987), *What
   the Mountains Yield: Anth* (Jalamap Pub, 1986), *Potato
   Eyes, Poet Lore, Kumquat Meringue, Samisdat*

Marc Harshman 🎤 ✈   P
PO Box 1092
Moundsville, WV 26041-3092, 304-845-0689
Internet: www.hotyellow98.com/harshmac
   Pubs: *Rose of Sharon* (Mad River, 1999), *Turning Out
   the Stones* (State Street Pr, 1983), *Learning By Heart:
   Anth* (U Iowa Pr, 1999), *Wild Song: Anth* (U Georgia
   Pr, 1998), *Shenandoah, Wilderness, Sycamore Rev,
   Georgia Rev*

Robert G. Head   P
c/o Bookstore, 104 S Jefferson, Lewisburg, WV 24901
   Pubs: *Refuges of Value, Selected Poems* (Book &
   Mineral Investment Corp, 1993, 1988), *Jrnl of Sister
   Moon, Malcontent*

Norman Julian   W
Trillium Publishing, Rte 7, Box 222HH, Morgantown, WV
26505, 304-594-1765
   Pubs: *Snake Hill, Cheat* (Trillium Pub, 1993, 1984)

Russell Marano   P
314 Byrd Ln
Clarksburg, WV 26301
   Pubs: *Poems from a Mountain Ghetto* (Back Fork Bks,
   1979), *Poetry Now, Wind, Kansas Qtly*

Sandra Marshburn 🎤 ✈   P
201 Viking Rd
Charleston, WV 25302, 304-342-4450
   Pubs: *Undertow* (March Street Pr, 1992), *Controlled
   Flight* (Alms Hse Pr, 1990), *Flyway, Yankee, Cincinnati
   Poetry Rev, Devil's Millhopper, MacGuffin, Midwest Qtly,
   Tar River Poetry*

John McKernan 🎤 ✈   P
Marshall Univ, English Dept, Huntington, WV 25701,
304-696-6499
Internet: mckernan@marshall.edu
   Pubs: *Postcard from Dublin* (Dead Metaphor Pr, 1999),
   Walking Along the Missouri River (Lost Roads, 1977),
   *Paris Rev, Field, Harvard, Ohio Rev, Prairie Schooner,
   Virginia Qtly Rev*

Llewellyn T. McKernan 🎤   P
Rte 10, Box 4639B
Barboursville, WV 25504, 304-733-5054
   Pubs: *Short & Simple Annals* (West Virginia Humanities
   Council, 1983), *Bloodroot: Essays on Place by
   Appalachian Women Writers: Anth* (U Kentucky Pr,
   1998), *Kenyon Rev, SPR, Antietam Rev, Kalliope,
   Nimrod, Appalachian Jrnl*
Groups: Children, Seniors

Irene McKinney 🎤 ✈   P
Rte 1, Box 118C
Belington, WV 26250, 304-823-3041
Internet: McKinney_i@wvwc.edu
   Pubs: *Six O'Clock Mine Report* (U of Pittsburgh Pr,
   1989), *Kenyon Rev, Poetry, Salmagundi, NW Rev, MA
   Rev*

John S. Morris   P
English Dept, Davis & Elkins College, Elkins, WV 26241,
304-636-1900
   Pubs: *Bean Street* (Lost Roads, 1977), *America, Central
   Appalachian Rev, Shenandoah, Laurel Rev*

John O'Brien 🎤 ✈   P&W
PO Box 148
Franklin, WV 26807
   Pubs: *Country Jrnl, Massachusetts Rev, Gray's Sporting
   Journal, Hudson Rev, Iowa Rev, Madrona*

Barbara Smith   P&W
16 Willis Ln
Philippi, WV 26416, 304-457-3038
   Pubs: *Six Miles Out* (Mountain State Pr, 1981),
Appalachia Inside Out: Anth (U Tennessee Pr, 1995),
*Appalachian Heritage, Now & Then, Aethlon, Antietam
Rev, Anemone, Kansas Qtly, Hiram Poetry Rev,
Goldenseal, Agincourt Irregular*

Richard Thorman   W
325 Silver Rd
Berkeley Springs, WV 25411
   Pubs: *Hardly Working* (LSU Pr, 1990), *Bachman's Law*
(Norton, 1981), *Sewanee Rev, The Long Story*

Ed Zahniser 🎤 ✈   P&W
PO Box 955
Shepherdstown, WV 25443-0955, 304-876-2442
   Pubs: *A Calendar of Worship & Other Poems* (Plane
Bucket Pr, 1995), *Shepherdstown Historic Firsts* (Four
Seasons Bks, 1992), *Antietam Rev, December, Kestrel,
The Other Side*
I.D.: Nature/Environment. Groups: Spiritual/Religious,
Nature/Environment

WISCONSIN

Robert Alexander 🎤 ✈   P
3440 Lake Mendota Dr
Madison, WI 53705-1471, 608-238-5076
Internet: alex@mailbag.com
   Pubs: *White Pine Sucker River, The Talking of Hands:
Anth, The Party Train: Anth* (New Rivers Pr, 1993,
1998, 1996), *Luna, Flyway, The Prose Poem*

Shirley B. Anders   P
825 W 4 St
Appleton, WI 54914-5434
   Pubs: *The Bus Home* (U Missouri Pr, 1986), *Michigan
Qtly Rev, New Virginia Rev, Iris, Prairie Schooner, Fox
Cry*

Antler   P
c/o Inland Ocean, PO Box 11502, Milwaukee, WI 53211
   Pubs: *Selected Poems* (Soft Skull Pr, 2000), *Last
Words* (Ballantine Bks, 1986), *Factory* (City Lights,
1980), *NYQ, Kenyon Rev, Wilderness, Chiron Rev, The
Sun, Whole Earth Rev*

Norbert Blei   W
PO Box 33
Ellison Bay, WI 54210, 414-854-2413
   Pubs: *Chi Town, Neighborhood, The Ghost of
Sandburg's Phizzog, The Door* (Ellis Pr, 1990, 1987,
1986, 1985), *New Yorker, TriQtly, Chicago Mag*

Thomas Bontly   W
Creative Writing, English Dept, Univ Wisconsin-Milwaukee,
PO Box 413, Milwaukee, WI 53201-0413, 414-229-4530
   Pubs: *The Giant's Shadow* (Random Hse, 1989),
Celestial Chess (Ballantine, 1980), *Sewanee Rev,
Denver Qtly, Cream City Rev, Redbook, McCall's,
Esquire*

Harriet Brown   P
2515 Chamberlain Ave
Madison, WI 53705-3828, 608-233-6191
   Pubs: *The Good-Bye Window* (U Wisconsin Pr, 1998),
*Prairie Schooner, Wisconsin Poets Calendar, Ms.,
American Girl*

Gary C. Busha   P&W
3123 S Kennedy Dr
Sturtevant, WI 53177
   Pubs: *Willowdown* (Wolfsong Pub, 1995), *Root River
Poets Anth, Abraxas, Wisconsin Poet's Calendar, Page
5*

Alden R. Carter 🎤 ✈   W
1113 W Onstad Dr
Marshfield, WI 54449, 715-389-1108
Internet: www.tznet.com/busn/acarterwriter
   Pubs: *Crescent Moon* (Holiday Hse, 1999), *Bull
Catcher, Between a Rock & a Hard Place, Dogwolf*
(Scholastic, 1997, 1995, 1994), *RoboDad, Up Country,
Sheila's Dying* (Putnam, 1990, 1989, 1987)
Groups: Children

DeWitt Clinton 🎤 ✈   P
3567 N Murray
Shorewood, WI 53211-2525, 414-332-4582
   Pubs: *Divine Inspiration* (Oxford U Pr, 1998), *Wisconsin
Poetry: Anth* (Wisconsin Academy of Arts, Science &
Letters, 1991), *And What Rough Beast: Anth* (Ashland
Poetry Pr, 1999), *Southern California Jrnl, Southern
Anth, Image*
I.D.: Jewish. Groups: College/Univ, Jewish

Keith Cohen   W
149 Dayton Row
Madison, WI 53703, 608-238-2785
   Pubs: *Writing in a Film Age* (U Pr Colorado, 1991),
L'Esprit Createur

Mark Dintenfass   W
Lawrence Univ
Appleton, WI 54911
   Pubs: *A Loving Place, Old World, New World* (Morrow,
1986, 1982)

Karl Elder 🎤 ✈   P
Lakeland College, Box 359, Sheboygan, WI 53082-0359,
920-565-3871
Internet: kelder@excel.net
   Pubs: *A Man in Pieces* (Prickly Pear Pr, 1994), *Best
   American Poetry: Anth* (Scribner, 2000), *Chicago Rev,
   BPJ, High Plains Lit Rev*

Jean Feraca   P
1418 Winslow Ln
Madison, WI 53711, 608-273-0402
   Pubs: *Crossing the Great Divide* (Wisconsin Academy
   of Sciences, Arts & Letters, 1992), *The Dream Book:
   Anth* (Schocken Bks, 1985), *APR, Southern Rev, Nation*

Susan Firer   P
1514 E Kensington Blvd
Milwaukee, WI 53211, 414-332-7534
   Pubs: *The Lives of the Saints & Everything* (Cleveland
   State U Pr, 1993), *The Underground Communion Rail*
   (West End Pr, 1992), *Iowa Rev, Chicago Rev, Ms.*

Doug Flaherty   P
1011 Babcock St
Neenah, WI 54956-5114, 414-722-5826
   Pubs: *Last Hunt: Anth* (Wolfsong Pub, 1998), *Good
   Thief Come Home: Selected Poems* (Prickly Pear Pr,
   1990), *New Yorker, Nation, NAR, QRL, Poetry NW,
   Carolina Qtly*

Steven D. Fortney 🎤 ✈   P
501 W South St
Stoughton, WI 53589, 600-873-3917
   Pubs: *The Thomas Jesus: A Novella, Heg: A Novella*
   (Badger Bks, 2000, 1998), *This Sporting Life: Anth*
   (Milkweed Edtns, 1996), *East West A Poetry Annual:
   Anth* (Cape Cod Writers, 1992), *North Coast Rev,
   Visions Intl, Pulpsmith, Embers*

Frederick Gaines   P
621 N Badger Ave
Appleton, WI 54914, 414-731-0786

Brent Goodman 🎤 ✈   P
771 S Dickinson St
Madison, WI 53703, 608-256-5047
Internet: brentg@tos.net
   Pubs: *Wrong Horoscope* (Thorngate Rd, 1999), *Trees &
   the Slowest River* (Sarasota Poetry Theater Pr 1999),
   American Poetry at the End of the Millennium: Anth
   (Green Mountains Rev, 1997), *A First Light: Anth*
   (Calypso Pub, 1997), *Tampa Rev, Poetry, Zone 3*

George Gott   P
804 N 19 St
Superior, WI 54880-2902, 715-394-7512
   Pubs: *Here & There* (Linwood Pub, 1989), *Birds &
   Horses* (Poetry North Rev, 1984)

John Goulet 🎤 ✈   W
3489 N Frederick Ave
Milwaukee, WI 53211-2902, 414-332-5141
Internet: goulet@csd.uwm.edu
   Pubs: *Yvette in America* (Colorado U Pr, 2000), *Oh's
   Profit* (Morrow, 1975), *Brooklyn Rev, Alaska Qtly Rev,
   Denver Qtly, Crescent Rev, Folio, Sonoro Rev, Intro*

David M. Graham 🎤 ✈   P
215 Elm St
Ripon, WI 54971-1441, 920-748-5806
Internet: grahamd@mail.ripon.edu
   Pubs: *A Mind of Winter* (Flume Pr, 2000), *Doggedness*
   (Devil's Millhopper Pr, 1991), *Second Wind* (Texas Tech
   U Pr, 1990), *Magic Shows* (Cleveland St U Poetry Ctr,
   1986), *Poetry NW, Poetry*

S. C. Hahn   P
1053 Rutledge St
Madison, WI 53703, 608-251-9073
   Pubs: *The Party Train: Anth* (New Rivers Pr, 1996), *As
   Far As I Can See: Anth* (Windflower Pr, 1989), *Palo
   Alto Rev, Dominion Rev, Bridge, Exquisite Corpse,
   Chiron Rev, Wormwood Rev, Slant*

R. Chris Halla 🎤 ✈   P&W
1724 N Whitney Dr
Appleton, WI 54914, 920-731-2257
Internet: shagbark@vbe.com
   Pubs: *Water* (Wolfsong, 1994), *Northeast, Seems,
   Poetry Now*

Aedan Alexander Hanley   P
1917 N 18 St
Milwaukee, WI 53205, 414-933-0573
   Pubs: *Transactions Anth* (Wisconsin Academy, 1991),
   Boundaries of Twilight: Anth (New Rivers Pr, 1991),
   Iowa Rev, Callaloo, Cimarron Rev, Poet & Critic

C. J. Hribal 🎤 ✈   W
2831 W McKinley Blvd
Milwaukee, WI 53208-2928, 414-933-3555
Internet: cj.hribal@marquette.edu
   Pubs: *The Clouds in Memphis* (U Mass Pr, 2000),
   American Beauty (S&S, 1987), *Matty's Heart, The
   Boundaries of Twilight: Anth* (New Rivers Pr, 1984,
   1991)

Ellen Hunnicutt 🎤 ✈   W
PO Box 62
Big Bend, WI 53103-0062, 262-662-2740
Internet: wh@execpc.com
   Pubs: *Suite for Calliope* (Walker & Co, 1987), *In the
   Music Library* (U Pitt Pr, 1987), *The Whole Story: Anth*
   (Bench Pr, 2000), *Flash Fiction: Anth* (Norton, 1992),
   Story, Prairie Schooner, Cimarron Rev, Indiana Rev

John Judson   P
1310 Shorewood Dr
La Crosse, WI 54601
    Pubs: *The Inardo Poems, Muse(sic)* (Juniper Pr, 1996,
    1993), *The Baseball Poems, My Father's Brown
    Sweater: Anth* (Page Five, 1992, 1996), *The Long
    Story, Poem, Elysian Fields, NAR, Ohio Rev*

Reinhold Johannes Kaebitzsch   P
PO Box 3495
Madison, WI 53704-0495, 608-241-3949
    Pubs: *Red Snow, Quisconsin, Papagaio* (Red Mountain,
    1992, 1986, 1983), *Piankeshaw on Blue Horses* (White
    Anvil, 1983)

John Koethe   P
2666 N Hackett Ave
Milwaukee, WI 53211, 414-964-5107
    Pubs: *The Constructor, Falling Water* (HC, 1999, 1997),
    The Late Wisconsin Spring (Princeton U Pr, 1984),
    Domes (Columbia U Pr, 1974)

David Kubach   P
404 N Walbridge Ave, #6
Madison, WI 53714, 608-244-2538
    Pubs: *First Things* (Holmgangers Pr, 1980), *Wisconsin
    Poetry: Anth* (Wisconsin Academy of Sciences, Arts, &
    Letters, 1991), *Painted Bride Qtly, Slant*

Donald D. Kummings   P
Univ Wisconsin-Parkside, English Dept, Kenosha, WI
53141, 414-595-2525
    Pubs: *The Open Road Trip* (Geryon Pr, 1989), *The
    Dolphin's Arc: Anth* (SCOP Productions, 1989)

D. J. Lachance 🎤 ✈   W
1722 N 58 St
Milwaukee, WI 53208-1618, 414-453-4678
Internet: djlachance@usa.net
    Pubs: *Book Lovers, Art Forum, Poettalk, Collages &
    Bricolages, The Plaza, Pleiades, Philae*
Groups: Mentally Ill

Peg Carlson Lauber 🎤 ✈   P
1105 Bradley Ave
Eau Claire, WI 54701-6520, 715-835-0363
Internet: laubermc@uwec.edu
    Pubs: *Locked in the Wayne County Courthouse, A
    Change in Weather* (Rhiannon Pr, 1980, 1978),
    *Kalliope, Wind, Synaesthetic, Poetry Motel, Georgetown
    Rev, River Oak Rev, Windhover, Pike Creek Rev,
    Snail's Pace, Lucid Stone, Hodgepodge*

John Lehman 🎤 ✈   P&W
315 E Water St
Cambridge, WI 53523, 608-423-4141
    Pubs: *Shrine of the Tooth Fairy* (Cambridge Bk Rev Pr,
    1998), *Cambridge Book Rev, Rosebud*

Carl Lindner   P
Univ Wisconsin-Parkside, Box 2000, Kenosha, WI 53141,
414-595-2392
    Pubs: *Shooting Baskets in a Dark Gymnasium*
    (Linwood, 1984), *Vampire* (Spoon River Poetry Pr,
    1977), *Poetry, Slant, Literary Rev, Iowa Rev,
    Greensboro Rev*

Karen Loeb 🎤 ✈   P&W
Univ Wisconsin-Eau Claire, English Dept, Eau Claire, WI
54702, 715-836-3140
Internet: loebk@uwec.edu
    Pubs: *Jump Rope Queen & Other Stories* (New Rivers
    Pr, 1993), *100 Percent Pure Florida Fiction Anth* (U Pr
    Florida, 2000), *If I Had a Hammer: Anth* (Papier-Mache
    Pr, 1990), *Crania OnLine, Widener Rev, Lullwater Rev,
    South Dakota Rev, Footworks*

Arthur Madson   P
419 Pleasant
Whitewater, WI 53190, 414-473-4791
    Pubs: *Blue-Eyed Boy* (Lake Shore Pub, 1993), *Coming
    Up Sequined* (Fireweed Pr, 1990), *Midwest Poetry Rev,
    Samisdat, Anemone, South Carolina Rev, Wisconsin
    Academy Rev*

David Martin   P
7123 Cedar St
Wauwatosa, WI 53213
    Pubs: *Seattle Rev, Red Cedar Rev, Oyez Rev, Qtly
    West, Cream City Rev, Wisconsin Rev, College English,
    Slant, Poetry Motel*

Tom McKeown 🎤 ✈   P
1220 N Gammon Rd
Middleton, WI 53562-3806, 608-836-1612
    Pubs: *Three Hundred Tigers* (Zephyr Pub, 1994),
    Invitation of the Mirrors (Wisconsin Rev Pr, 1985), *New
    Yorker, Nation, Yale Rev, Atlantic, Harper's,
    Commonweal*
Groups: Children, College/Univ

Lee Merrill   P
217 E 3 St
Washburn, WI 54891, 715-373-2300
    Pubs: *Seven Lake Superior Poets: Anth* (Bear Cult Pr,
    1979), *Plainsong, Great Lakes Rev, Northeast*

Stephen M. Miller   P
Univ Wisconsin Press, 2537 Daniels St, Madison, WI
53718-6772, 608-224-3882
    Pubs: *Backwaters* (Peridot Pr, 1983), *The Last Camp in
    America* (Midwestern Writers Pub Hse, 1982),
    Midatlantic Rev, Stardancer, Rolling Stone

Oscar Mireles 🎙 ✈   P
1301 Wheeler Rd
Madison, WI 53704, 608-243-7969
   Pubs: *Black & Brown begin with the letter "B", I Didn't
   Know There Were Latinos in Wisconsin: 30 Hispanic
   Writers: Anth, Weehcohnson Latino Writers: Anth,
   Second Generation: Anth* (Focus Communications Inc,
   2000, 1999, 1998, 1985), *U.S. Latino Rev*
Lang: Spanish. I.D.: Latino/Latina. Groups: Prisoners

Mary Moran   P&W
PO Box 3012
Madison, WI 53704
   Pubs: *In Celebration of the Muse* (M Pr, 1987),
   Fireworks! (Women's Pr, 1987), *Sinister Wisdom*

Sandra Sylvia Nelson 🎙 ✈   P&W
4519 S Pine Ave
Milwaukee, WI 53207-5210, 414-294-0280
   Pubs: *Who are the Rich & Where do They Live?: Anth*
   (Poetry East Pr, 2000), *Hard Choices: Anth* (Iowa Rev
   Pr, 1996), *Yankee, Iowa Rev, Ms., Mid-American Rev,
   NAR, Virginia Qtly Rev, BPJ*

Mary F. O'Sullivan   W
N 1079 Lauterbach Rd
La Crosse, WI 54601
   Pubs: *Webs Inviolate, Common Lives/Lesbian Lives,
   Earth's Daughters, Touchstone*

Franco Pagnucci 🎙 ✈   P
Univ Wisconsin, 1 University Plaza, Platteville, WI 53818,
608-342-1921
Internet: pagnucci@am.uwplatt.edu
   Pubs: *Ancient Moves, I Never Had a Pet* (Bur Oak Pr,
   1998, 1992), *Out Harmsen's Way* (Fireweed Pr, 1991),
   Best American Poetry: Anth (Scribner, 1999), *American
   Voices: Anth* (Mayfield, 1996), *College English*

Angela Peckenpaugh   P
2513 E Webster
Milwaukee, WI 53211, 414-964-5644
   Pubs: *Always Improving My Appetite* (Sackbut Pr,
   1994), *A Heathen Herbal* (Artist's Bk Works, 1993),
   Eating Our Hearts Out: Anth (Crossing Pr, 1993),
   Gypsy Cab

Susan Peterson   P
Box 81
Ephraim, WI 54211
   Pubs: *Preparing the Fields* (Spoon River Poetry Pr,
   1985), *Cincinnati Poetry Rev, Calliope*

Sara Rath 🎙 ✈   P&W
1605 Legion Dr
Elm Grove, WI 53122-1706, 262-789-8618
Internet: sararath@aol.com
   Pubs: *Dancing with a Cowboy* (Wisconsin Academy of
   Sciences, Arts & Letters, 1991), *Remembering the
   Wilderness* (Northword Pr, 1983), *Boston Rev, Green
   Mountains, Arkham Collector, Contemporary Rev, Great
   River Rev, Wisconsin Academy Rev*

Jocelyn Riley   W
PO Box 5264
Madison, WI 53705, 608-271-7083
   Pubs: *Crazy Quilt, Only My Mouth Is Smiling* (Bantam,
   1986, 1986), *Wisconsin Woman, Wisconsin Trails,
   Wisconsin Academy Rev, Buffalo Spree, Spokane
   Woman, Crossing Press Anth*

Tobin F. Rockey   P
PO Box 795
Green Bay, WI 54305, 414-437-6608
   Pubs: *Bitterroot, Above the Bridge, Wisconsin Poets,
   Peninsula Rev, Around the Bay, Baybury Rev*

William Robert Rodriguez   P
1802 Redwood Ln
Madison, WI 53711-3332, 608-274-2096
   Pubs: *the shoe shine parlor poems* (Ghost Pony Pr,
   1984), *The Party Train: Anth* (New Rivers Pr, 1996),
   Abraxas, Critic, Epoch, North Coast Rev, Turnstile

Andrew J. Roffers   W
14022 W Tiffany Pl
New Berlin, WI 53151, 262-784-3729
   Pubs: *Short Story Forum, My Legacy, Penny-A-Liner,
   Expressions Jrnl*

Martin Jack Rosenblum 🎙 ✈   P
2521 E Stratford Court
Shorewood, WI 53211-2635, 414-332-7474
Internet: http://members.tripod.com/~holyranger/index.html
   Pubs: *No Freedom, Honey, Down on the Spirit Farm*
   (Wheel to Reel Pub, 2000, 1993), *The Holy Ranger:
   Harley-Davidson Poems* (Ranger Intl, 1989), *Conjunction*
   (Lion Pub, 1987)

Lisa M. Ruffolo   W
2125 Chamberlain Ave
Madison, WI 53705-3977
   Pubs: *Tanzania on Tuesday, Holidays* (New Rivers Pr,
   1997, 1987), *Voices That We Carry* (Guernica, 1993),
   From the Margin: Anth (Purdue U Pr, 1991),
   Mademoiselle, Cosmopolitan

R.M. Ryan 🎤 ✈ P&W
332 E Acacia Rd
Milwaukee, WI 53217-4234, 414-352-2902
  Pubs: *The Golden Rules* (Hi Jinx Pr, 1998), *Goldilocks in Later Life, Yellow Shoe Poets: Anth* (LSU, 1980, 1999), *Dreams & Secrets: Anth* (Woodland Pattern Bk Ctr, 1993), *Faultline, Light, New Republic, ACM, Exquisite Corpse, Wisconsin Acad Rev*
Lang: German

Carol Lee Saffioti P
Univ Wisconsin-Parkside, Kenosha, WI 53141, 414-595-2139
  Pubs: *Root River Anth, Anth of New England Writers, Rag Mag, Black Bear Rev*

Ted Schaefer 🎤 ✈ P&W
403 Center St
Lake Geneva, WI 53147-1905, 262-248-7729
Internet: trish@genevaonline.com
  Pubs: *The Summer People* (Singing Wind Pr, 1978), *After Drought* (Raindust Pr, 1976), *From A to Z: Anth* (Swallow, 1981), *Village Voice, Story Qtly, New Letters, Kansas Qtly, Wisconsin Rev, ACM, Chariton Rev, Webster Rev, NW Rev, Cottonwood Rev*

Willa Schmidt P&W
2020 University Ave, #317
Madison, WI 53705-3965
  Pubs: *Wisconsin Academy Rev, Ambergris, Iowa Woman, St. Anthony Messenger*

Robert Schuler 🎤 ✈ P
E 4549 479th Ave
Menomonie, WI 54751, 715-235-6525
  Pubs: *Red Cedar Suite* (Friends of the Red Cedar Trail, 1999), *Grace: A Book of Days* (Wolfsong Pr, 1995), *Music for Monet* (Spoon River, 1984), *Imagining Home, Inheriting the Earth: Anths* (U Minnesota Pr, 1995, 1993), *Dacotah Territory, Caliban, Northeast*

John Kingsley Shannon P&W
PO Box 245
Racine, WI 53401
  Pubs: *Loom, The Shrine of the White Owl, Randy, Hosea Jackson* (Caledonia Pr, 1992, 1991, 1983, 1980)

Lynn Shoemaker P
172 N Esterly Ave
Whitewater, WI 53190
  Pubs: *Hands* (Lynx Hse Pr, 1982), *Dreams & Secrets: Anth* (Woodland Pattern Book Center, 1993), *Poet Lore, Salthouse, Oxford Mag, Groundswell*

Alan Shucard P
Univ Wisconsin-Parkside, Box 2000, Kenosha, WI 53141-2000, 414-595-2392
  Pubs: *Modern American Poetry: 1865-1950, American Poetry: The Puritans Through Walt Whitman* (Twayne, 1989, 1988)

Mary Shumway P
PO Box 815
Plover, WI 54467-0815
  Pubs: *Legends & Other Voices: Selected & New Poems, Practicing Vivaldi* (Juniper Pr, 1992, 1981)

Shoshauna Shy 🎤 P
878 Woodrow St
Madison, WI 53711-1959, 608-238-7937
Internet: sschey@facstaff.wisc.edu
  Pubs: *Souped-Up on the Must-Drive Syndrome* (Pudding Hse, 2000), *Jane's Stories: Anth* (Wild Dove Studio & Pr, 2000), *Taproot Lit Rev, Rockford Rev, Whisky Island Mag, Midwest Poetry Rev, Fresh Ground*

Robert Siegel P&W
Univ Wisconsin, PO Box 413, English Dept, Milwaukee, WI 53201, 414-229-4511
  Pubs: *White Whale, Whalesong* (Harper SF, 1991, 1991), *In a Pig's Eye* (Florida, 1985), *Cream City Rev, Sewanee Rev, Atlantic*

Carol Sklenicka 🎤 ✈ W
332 E Acacia Rd
Milwaukee, WI 53217-2902
Internet: sklen@mixcom.com
  Pubs: *Dreams & Secrets: Anth* (Woodland Pattern, 1993), *Clackamas Lit Rev, Iowa Woman, Sou'wester, Confrontation, Cream City Rev, Military Lifestyle, Transactions*
Groups: Teenagers, Women

Thomas R. Smith 🎤 ✈ P
523 State St
River Falls, WI 54022-2237, 715-425-2137
  Pubs: *The Dark Indigo Current, Horse of Earth* (Holy Cow! Pr, 2000, 1994), *The Bitter Oleander, AGNI, Raccoon, Yellow Silk, Wilderness, Bloomsbury Rev, Sphinx*

Robert Spiess P
Modern Haiku, PO Box, Madison, WI 53701-1752, 608-233-2738
  Pubs: *Modern Haiku*

David Steingass P
1510 Drake St
Madison, WI 53711
  Pubs: *New Roads Old Towns: Anth* (U Wisconsin Platteville Pr, 1988), *Poetry, Mid-American Rev, Northeast*

Porter Stewart P
Milwaukee Inner City Council, 642 W North Ave, Milwaukee, WI 53212
  Pubs: *Passing By* (U Connecticut Lutheran Church, 1970), *Ethiop, The Flame*

Ingrid Swanberg 🎤 ✈ P
PO Box 260113
Madison, WI 53726-0113, 608-238-0175
Internet: http://www.geocities.com/Paris/4614
  Pubs: *Letter to Persephone & Other Poems* (Rhiannon
  Pr, 1984), *Northeast, Lips, Wisconsin Academy Rev,
  Orisis, Le Geupard*

Bruce Taylor P
Univ Wisconsin, English Dept, Eau Claire, WI 54702,
715-836-2639
  Pubs: *Why That Man Talks That* (Upriver Pr, 1994),
  This Day (Juniper Pr, 1993), *Poetry, Nation, Chicago
  Rev, NW Rev, Gulf Coast, NYQ*

Marilyn Taylor 🎤 ✈ P
2825 E Newport Ave
Milwaukee, WI 53211-2922, 414-332-3455
Internet: mlt@csd.uwm.edu
  Pubs: *Shadows Like These* (William Caxton, 1994), *Iris,
  Formalist, American Scholar, Hellas, Poetry, Poet Lore*

Daniel Tobin 🎤 ✈ P
Carthage College, 2001 Alford Park Dr, Kenosha, WI
53140-1994, 414-551-5943
Internet: tobind1@carthage.edu
  Pubs: *Where the World Is Made, New American Poets:
  Anth* (Middlebury/U Pr of New England, 1999, 2000),
  *Nation, Poetry, Ploughshares, Tampa Rev, Paris Rev,
  DoubleTake*

Alison Townsend P
5025 Lake Mendota Dr
Madison, WI 53705, 608-233-7619
  Pubs: *Loss of the Ground Note* (Clothespin Fever Pr,
  1992), *A Deer's Ear, Eagle's Song & Bear's Face*
  (Cleis Pr, 1990), *Claiming the Spirit Within: Anth*
  (Beacon Pr, 1996), *The Party Train: New Rivers, 1995),
  Prairie Schooner, Calyx, Georgia Rev*

Dennis Trudell P
309 N Brearly St
Madison, WI 53703-1601, 608-259-1958
  Pubs: *Fragments in Us: Recent & Earlier Poems* (U
  Wisconsin Pr, 1996), *Full Court: Basketball Literary
  Anth* (Breakaway Bks, 1996), *O. Henry Prize Stories:
  Anth* (Northwoods Pr, 1994), *Wisconsin Poetry: Anth*
  (Wisconsin Academy of Arts, 1991), *Chariton Rev*

Barbara Vroman 🎤 ✈ W
N4721 9th Dr
Hancock, WI 54943-7617, 715-249-5407
  Pubs: *Linger Not at Chebar: A Novel of Burma* (Angel
  Pr Wisconsin, 1992), *Sons of Thunder, Tomorrow Is a
  River* (Phunn Pub, 1981, 1977)

Ronald Wallace 🎤 ✈ P
Univ Wisconsin, English Dept, 600 N Park, Madison, WI
53706, 608-263-3705
Internet: rwallace@facstaff.wisc.edu
  Pubs: *Quick Bright Things* (Mid-List, 2000), *The Uses
  of Adversity, Time's Fancy, The Makings of Happiness*
  (U Pitt Pr, 1998, 1994, 1991), *Poetry, Nation, Poetry
  NW, Atlantic, Prairie Schooner, Laurel Rev*

Larry Watson P&W
English Dept, Univ Wisconsin, Stevens Point, WI 54481,
715-346-4757
  Pubs: *Justice, Montana 1948* (Milkweed Edtns, 1995,
  1993), *Leaving Dakota* (Song Pr, 1983), *NER, Black
  Warrior Rev, Cimarron Rev, Gettysburg Rev, Kansas
  Qtly*

Marvin Weaver P
Wisconsin Arts Board, 131 W Wilson St, #301, Madison,
WI 53702, 608-266-0190
  Pubs: *Hearts & Gizzards* (Curveship Pr, 1977),
  Contemporary North Carolina Poetry: Anth (Blair, 1977)

J. D. Whitney P
829 E Thomas St
Wausau, WI 54403-6448, 715-675-4848
  Pubs: *What Grandmother Says* (March Street Pr, 1994),
  sd (Spoon River Poetry Pr, 1988), *Word of Mouth*
  (Juniper, 1986)

Doris T. Wight P
122 8th Ave
Baraboo, WI 53913-2109, 608-356-6997
Internet: dwight@sauk.com
  Pubs: *Seeking Promethean Woman in the New Poetry*
  (Peter Lang, 1988), *Yale Jrnl of Law & Feminism,
  Language & Style, Wisconsin Rev, Dekalb Literary Arts
  Jrnl*

Jeffrey Winke 🎤 ✈ P
1705 N 68 St
Wauwatosa, WI 53213-2307, 414-453-3244
Internet: win9@earthlink.net
  Pubs: *Row of Pine* (Distant Thunder Pr, 1994), *Against
  Natural Impulse* (Boog Lit, 1992)

Karl Young P
7112 27th Ave
Kenosha, WI 53143-5218
Internet: www.thing.net/~grist/l&d/lighthom.htm
  Pubs: *Milestones Set 1* (Landlocked Pr, 1987), *To
  Dream Kalapuya* (Truck Pr, 1977), *Poems for the
  Millennium, Vol 2: Anth* (U California Pr, 1998)

Christina Zawadiwsky 🎤 ✈   P
1641 N Humboldt
Milwaukee, WI 53202-2111, 414-272-4592
Internet: xristia@hotmail.com
　　Pubs: *Desperation, Isolation, What Will Be, I Began to
　　Dream* (Where the Waters Meet, 1999, 1998, 1997,
　　1996), *The Hand on the Head of Lazarus* (Ion Bks,
　　1986)
I.D.: Ukrainian-American

Paul Zimmer   P
Box 1068, Rt 1
Soldiers Grove, WI 54655, 608-624-5742
　　Pubs: *Crossing to Sunlight: Selected Poems* (U Georgia
　　Pr, 1996), *Big Blue Train* (U Arkansas Pr, 1994),
　　*Georgia Rev, Southern Rev, Gettysburg Rev, Poetry
　　NW, NER, Prairie Schooner, Harper's*

WYOMING

Martha Clark Cummings   W
111 E Arapahoe #1
Thermopolis, WY 82443, 307-864-2235
　　Pubs: *Mono Lake* (Rowbarge Pr, 1995), *Love's Shadow*
　　(Crossing Pr, 1993), *Common Lives/Lesbian Lives,
　　Pearl, NAR, Kalliope, Hurricane Alice, Sojourner*

Richard F. Fleck   P&W
English Dept, Univ Wyoming, Laramie, WY 82071,
307-766-2650
　　Pubs: *Deep Woods* (Peregrine Smith, 1990), *Earthen
　　Wayfarer* (Writers Hse, 1988), *Trumpeter*

Dainis Hazners   P&W
PO Box 442
Story, WY 82842-0442
　　Pubs: *World Voice: Anth, Crab Creek Rev 10th
　　Anniversary: Anth* (Crab Creek Rev, 1996, 1994),
　　*Parting Gifts, Apocalypse, Prairie Winds, SPR,
　　Connecticut River Rev*

Charles Levendosky 🎤 ✈   P
714 E 22 St
Casper, WY 82601, 307-237-0884
　　Pubs: *Circle of Light* (High Plains Pr, 1995), *Hands &
　　Other Poems* (Point Riders Pr, 1986), *Dacotah Territory,
　　Poetry Now, Poetry On, Poetry Rev, APR, Northern
　　Lights*

Vicki Lindner   W
Univ Wyoming, Box 3353, Laramie, WY 82071,
307-766-2384
　　Pubs: *Outlaw Games* (Dial Pr, 1982), *Ploughshares,
　　Kenyon Rev, Northern Lights, South Dakota Rev, New
　　York Woman, Frontiers*

W. Dale Nelson 🎤 ✈   P&W
1719 Downey St
Laramie, WY 82072-1918, 307-742-0737
　　Pubs: *Interim, Imago, Small Pond, Western Humanities
　　Rev, New Yorker, Antietam Rev, NW Rev, Poetry NW,
　　Yankee, Blue Unicorn*

C. L. Rawlins   P&W
PO Box 51
Boulder, WY 82923, 307-537-5298
　　Pubs: *In Gravity National Park* (U Nevada Pr, 1998),
　　Broken Country, Sky's Witness (H Holt, 1996, 1993), *A
　　Ceremony on Bare Ground* (Utah State Pr, 1985),
　　Ploughshares, Poetry Ireland, Poetry Wales, NAR

Tom Rea 🎤 ✈   P
1756 S Chestnut St
Casper, WY 82601-4531, 307-235-9021
Internet: trea@trib.com
　　Pubs: *Smith & Other Poems* (Dooryard Pr, 1985), *Man
　　in a Rowboat* (Copper Canyon Pr, 1977), *What Have
　　You Lost?: Anth* (Greenwillow Bks, 1999)

Susan Richardson   P&W
5810 Osage #205
Cheyenne, WY 82009-3906
　　Pubs: *Rapunzel's Short Hair* (Embers, 1994), *Split
　　Verse: Anth* (Midmarch, 2000), *What's Become of Eden:
　　Anth* (Slapering Hol, 1994), *CQ, Faultline, Wisconsin
　　Rev*

David Romtvedt 🎤 ✈   P&W
457 N Main
Buffalo, WY 82834-1732, 307-684-2194
Internet: romtvedt@wyoming.com
　　Pubs: *Certainty* (White Pine Pr, 1996), *A Flower Whose
　　Name I Do Not Know* (Copper Canyon Pr, 1992)
Lang: Spanish

Tim Sandlin   W
Box 1974
Jackson, WY 83001, 307-733-1212
　　Pubs: *Social Blunders, Sorrow Floats, Skipped Parts* (H
　　Holt, 1995, 1992, 1991)

Stephen J. Thorpe   W
117 1/2 W Wentworth St
Newcastle, WY 82701
　　Pubs: *Walking Wounded* (Bantam, 1984), *Encounter,
　　California Qtly, Smackwarm*

OTHER COUNTRIES

ARABIAN GULF

Dione A. Tongal 🎤 ✈   P&W
c/o Dod M. Tongal, c/o NODCO, PO Box 50033, Boha,
Qatar, Arabian Gulf
Internet: cuddlycuttie13@hotmail.com
    Pubs: *That Morning Star Girl* (Upstream Productions
    1999)

AUSTRALIA

Jeri Kroll 🎤 ✈   P
29 Methuen St
Fitzroy, Adelaide 5082, South Australia
Internet: jeri.kroll@flinders.edu.au
    Pubs: *Beyond Blue, Better than Blue* (Longman, 1998,
    1997), *House Arrest, Monster Love* (Wakefield Pr, 1993,
    1990)

Laura Jan Shore   P&W
Lot 1 Johnsons Rd, Huonbrook 2482 NSW, Australia
    Pubs: *The Sacred Moon Tree* (Bradbury Pr, 1986),
    Croton Rev, Blue Unicorn, WomanSource

AUSTRIA

Herbert Kuhner 🎤 ✈   P&W
Gentzgasse 14/4/11
A-1180 Vienna, Austria, 01-479-2469
Internet: harry.k@vienna.at
    Pubs: *Love of Austria* (Vienna; Apple Pub, 1998), *Minki
    the Nazi Cat & the Human Side* (Verlag der Theodor
    Kramer Gesellschaft, 1998), *Will the Stars Fall* (Austrian
    Lit Forum, 1995)

BELGIUM

David Henson   P
Avenue Jacques Pastur 18, B-1180 Uccle, Belgium
    Pubs: *Wedging Oaks Into Acorns* (Uzza No Pr, 1979),
    Pikestaff Forum, Laurel Rev, Poetry Now

Phillip Sterling   P&W
Rue Garde Dieu, 33, 4031 Angleur, Belgium
    Pubs: *Passages North, Seneca Rev, South Florida
    Poetry Rev, Slant, MacGuffin, Hayden's Ferry Rev,
    Sucarnochee Rev*

BOLIVIA

Richard Hughes 🎤 ✈   W
Casilla 6572, Torres Sofer
Cochabamba, Bolivia
    Pubs: *Isla Grande* (Silver Mountain Pr, 1994)
Lang: Spanish

BOTSWANA

Keorapetse William Kgositsile   P
Univ Botswana, Private Bag 0022, Gabarone, Botswana

CANADA

Robert Allen   P
Box 169, Ayer's Cliff, Quebec J0B 1C0, Canada,
819-838-5921
    Pubs: *The Hawryliw Process: Vol II, Vol I* (Porcupine's
    Quill Pr, 1981, 1980)

Bert Almon   P
Univ of Alberta, English Dept, Edmonton, Alberta T6G
2E5, Canada, 403-492-7809
    Pubs: *Calling Texas* (Thistledown Pr, 1990), *Poetry
    East, Chicago Rev, Poetry Durham, Orbis*

George Amabile   P
Univ Manitoba, English Dept, Winnipeg, Manitoba R3R
2N2, Canada, 204-453-3107
    Pubs: *The Presence of Fire* (McClelland & Stewart,
    1982), *Ideas of Shelter* (Turnstone, 1981), *Saturday
    Night, Canadian Literature, Canadian Fiction Mag*

Margaret Atwood 🎤 ✈   P&W
c/o Oxford Univ Press, 70 Wynford Dr, Don Mills, Ontario
M3C 1J9, Canada
    Pubs: *Alias Grace* (Doubleday, 1996), *Morning in the
    Burned House* (HM, 1995), *The Handmaid's Tale* (HM,
    1986)
Lang: French

George I. Bernstein   P&W
220 Tecumseh Rd W
Windsor, Ontario N8X 1G1, Canada, 519-253-7531
    Pubs: *Jewish Frontier*

Michele Anne Birch-Connery   P&W
4006 8th Ave, North Island College, Port Alberni, BC V9Y
4S4, Canada

Peter Aroniawenrate Blue Cloud　　　P&W
Box 86, Kahnawake, Quebec J0L 1B0, Canada
　Pubs: *Clans of Many Nations, The Other Side of Nowhere, Elderberry Flute Song* (White Pine Pr, 1995, 1990, 1988)

Richard Emil Braun 🎤　　　P
PO Box 178
Errington, BC V0R 1V0, Canada
Internet: krbraun@bcsupernet.com
　Pubs: *The Body Electric* (Norton, 2000), *Last Man In* (Jargon Society, 1990), *Persius: Satires* (Corondo Pr, 1984), *Roman Poets of the Early Empire: Anth* (Penguin Bks, 1991)

Robert Bringhurst　　　P
PO Box 280, Bowen Island, BC V0N 1G0, Canada
　Pubs: *The Black Canoe* (U Washington, 1991), *Pieces of Map, Pieces of Music* (Copper Canyon, 1987)

Robert Clayton Casto　　　P
67 Forman Ave, Toronto, Ontario M4S 2R4, Canada
　Pubs: *The Arrivals* (The Studio Pr, 1980), *Midatlantic Rev, Waves, NYQ, New Orleans Rev*

Ann Copeland　　　W
c/o Carol Bonnett, MGA, 10 Saint Mary St, Ste 510, Toronto, Ontario M4Y 1-P9, Canada, 416-964-3302
　Pubs: *The Back Room* (HC, 1991), *The Golden Thread* (Viking Penguin, 1989)

James Deahl　　　P
237 Prospect St S, Hamilton, Ontario L8M 2Z6, Canada, 905-912-1779
　Pubs: *Even This Land Was Born of Light* (Moonstone Pr, 1993), *Heartland, Opening The Stone Heart* (Envoi Poets Pub, 1993, 1992)

John Ditsky　　　P
English Dept, Univ Windsor, Windsor, Ontario N9B 3P4, Canada, 313-963-6112
　Pubs: *Friend & Lover* (Ontario Rev, 1981), *New Letters, Ontario Rev, Fiddlehead, NAR*

Magie Dominic 🎤 ✈　　　P
c/o League of Canadian Poets, Toronto, ON M5T 1A5, 54 Wolsely St, Canada, 212-206-6418
　Pubs: *Countering the Myths: Anth, Outrage: Anth* (Women's Pr, 1996, 1993), *Greenwich Village; Anth* (St. Martin's Pr, 1995), *New York Times, Outrage, Pottersfield Portfolio, Prairie Jrnl, ARC*
Groups: Women, Children

Real Faucher　　　P
82 Main St N, Windsor, Quebec J1S 2C6, Canada, 819-845-4446
　Pubs: *Touching The Emptiness* (Ansuda Pr, 1983), *Fires & Crucifixions* (Samisdat Pr, 1980), *Wind*

John Bart Gerald　　　W
206 St Patrick's St, Ottawa, Ontario K1N 5K3, Canada, 613-241-1312
　Pubs: *Internal Exile, New Englanders, Geometry* (Gerald & Maas, 1992, 1992, 1989)

Roger Greenwald 🎤 ✈　　　P
Innis College, 2 Sussex Ave, Univ Toronto, Toronto, Ontario M5S 1J5, Canada, 416-978-2662
Internet: http://www.chass.utoronto.ca/~roger/rghome.html
　Pubs: *Men & Women: Together & Alone: Anth* (The Spirit That Moves Us Pr, 1988), *Atomic Ghost: Poets Respond to the Nuclear Age: Anth* (Coffee Hse Pr, 1995), *ARTES: An Intl Reader, Alcatraz, Dimension, Exile, Heat, Metamorphoses, Panjandrum, Pequod*
Groups: Scandinavian-American, Translation

Mark Holmgren　　　P
11119 72 Ave, Edmonton, Alberta T6G 0B3, Canada
　Pubs: *Poetry Now, Syncline, Paper Bag Poems, Nit Wit, Small Pond, Dark Horse*

Lewis Horne　　　W
1213 Elliott St
Saskatoon, SK S7N 0V5, Canada, 306-244-4145
　Pubs: *What do Ducks do in Winter* (Signature Bks, 1993), *The Seventh Day* (Thistledown, 1982), *Barrow Street, Other Voices, Fiddlehead, Colorado Rev, South Dakota Rev, Canadian Fiction Mag, Greensboro Rev, Southern Rev*

George Jonas　　　P
MGA, 10 St. Mary St, Ste 510, Toronto, Ontario M4Y 1P9, Canada, 416-964-3302
　Pubs: *Politically Incorrect* (Lester Pubs, 1991), *A Passion Observed* (Macmillan of Canada, 1989), *Saturday Night, The Idler*

Mary Stewart Kean　　　P&W
14981 Beachview Ave, White Rock, BC V4B 1P2, Canada
　Pubs: *Critical Minutes* (Rocky Ledge Cottage Edtns, 1985), *Bombay Gin, Windhorse, Camera*

W. P. Kinsella 🎤 ✈　　　W
9442 Nowell
Chilliwack, BC V2P 4X7, Canada, 604-793-9716
Internet: buzzard_299@yahoo.com
　Pubs: *Shoeless Joe* (Mariner Bks, 1999), *The Secret of the Northern Lights* (Thistledown Pr, 1998), *If Wishes Were Horses, The Winter Helen Dropped By, The Dixon Cornbelt League, Brother Frank's Gospel Hour, Box Socials* (HC, 1997, 1995, 1994, 1992, 1991)

William Kuhns　　　W
RR 1, Alcove, Quebec J0X 1A0, Canada, 819-459-2523

Carole Glasser Langille 🎙 ✈   P
Lunenburg County, PO Box 1531, Nova Scotia B0J 2C0,
Canada, 902-634-3187
Internet: carole.langille@ns.sympatico.ca
    Pubs: *In Cannon Cave* (Brick Bks, 1997), *All That
    Glitters in Water* (New Poetry Series, 1990), *Words Out
    There: Anth* (Roseway Pr, 2000), *Poetry Miscellany,
    Response, North Dakota Qtly*

Peter Levitt 🎙 ✈   P
121 Central Avenue, Salt Spring Island BC V8K 2P4,
Canada, 250-537-9795
Internet: levgram@saltspring.com
    Pubs: *One Hundred Butterflies; Bright Root, Dark Root*
    (Broken Moon Pr, 1992, 1991), *A Book of Light*
    (Amargi Pr, 1982), *Poetry/L.A.*

Judith McCombs   P
67 Sullivan St, Toronto, Ontario M5T 1C2, Canada
    Pubs: *Against Nature: Wilderness Poems* (Dustbooks,
    1981)

Eugene McNamara 🎙 ✈   P&W
English Dept, Univ Windsor, Windsor, Ontario N9B 2T3,
Canada
    Pubs: *Waterfalls* (Coteau Bks, 2000), *Forcing The Field:
    New & Selected Poems* (Mosaic Pr, 1998), *The Moving
    Light* (Wolsak & Wynn, 1986), *Best Canadian Stories
    90: Anth* (Oberon Pr, 1990), *Ontario Rev, Witness*

Albert F. Moritz 🎙 ✈   P
14 Alpha Ave
Toronto, Ontario M4X 1J3, Canada
Internet: tmoritz@chass.utoronto.ca
    Pubs: *Rest on the Flight Into Eqypt* (Brick Bks, 1999),
    Best American Poetry: Anth (Scribner, 1998), *Paris Rev,
    Partisan Rev, APR*

Joanna Ostrow   W
RR 2, North Gower, Ontario K0A 2T0, Canada

Pamela Porter 🎙 ✈   P
11347 Peregrine Pl
Sidney, BC V8L 5S3, Canada, 250-655-5204
Internet: westedge@netcom.ca
    Pubs: *Atlanta Rev, Clackamas Rev, Descant, 13th
    Moon, Iowa Woman, Borderlands, Theology Today,
    Seattle Rev, Phoebe, Equinox, The Other Side,
    Sojourner, Commonweal*
I.D.: Canadian

Rose Romano   P
Guernica Editions, PO Box 633, Station NDG, Montreal,
Quebec HYA 3R1, Canada
    Pubs: *Vendetta* (malafemmina pr, 1990), *Slipstream,
    Waterways, Common Lives, Footwork, Women's Studies
    Qtly, Italian Americana*

Leon Rooke   W
The Hotel, Eden Mills, Ontario N0B 1P0, Canada,
519-856-9014
    Pubs: *Who Do You Love?* (Canada; McClelland &
    Stewart, 1992), *A Good Baby* (Vintage, 1990), *How I
    Saved the Province* (Oolichan, 1989)

Aaron Schneider 🎙 ✈   P
RR4, Baddeck
Nova Scotia B0E 1B0, Canada, 902-929-2063
    Pubs: *Wild Honey* (Breton Bks, 1998), *Inner
    Visions-Outer Voices: Anth* (U College Cape Breton Pr,
    1988), *Antigonish Rev*

Robin Skelton   P
1255 Victoria Ave, Victoria, BC, V8S 4P3, Canada,
604-592-7032

Lynn Strongin 🎙 ✈   P
1370 Beach Dr
Victoria, BC V8S 2N6, Canada
Internet: yosunt@home.com
    Pubs: *Bones & Kim* (Spinsters Ink, 1980),
    Countrywoman/Surgeon (L'Epervier, 1979), *Visiting
    Emily: Anth* (U Iowa Pr, 2000), *Shenandoah, Southern
    Humanities Rev, Prism Intl*

W. D. Valgardson 🎙 ✈   W
Creative Writing Dept/Box 1700, Univ Victoria, Victoria, BC
V8W 2Y2, Canada, 250-721-7306
Internet: www.finearts.uvic.ca/~wvalgard
    Pubs: *Frances, The Divorced Kids' Club, Garbage
    Creek & Other Stories, Thor* (Groundwood, 2000, 1999,
    1998, 1995)

Ian Young   P
2483 Gerrard St E, Scarborough, Ontario, M1N 1W7,
Canada, 416-691-9838
    Pubs: *The AIDS Dissidents* (Scarecrow Pr, 1992), *Sex
    Magick* (Stubblejumper Pr, 1986), *The Son of the Male
    Muse* (Crossing Pr, 1983)

CAYMAN ISLANDS

David V. Hughey 🎙   P
International College, Newlands Campus, 595 Hirst Rd,
P0136SAU, Cayman Islands, 345-947-1100
Internet: dvhughley@mailcity.com
    Pubs: *Driftwood East, Orphic Lute, Piedmont Literary
    Rev*

DENMARK

Thomas E. Kennedy   P&W
Fragariavej 12, DK-2900 Hellerup, Denmark, 45-31-622269
    Pubs: *Crossing Borders* (Watermark, 1990), *American Fiction: Anth* (Birch Lane, 1990), *New Letters, Virginia Qtly Rev, New Delta Rev, Chariton Rev, Missouri Rev, Cimarron Rev*

EGYPT

David Graham Dubois   W
76 Nile St, Apt 24, Cairo, Giza, Egypt

ENGLAND

Dannie Abse ⚲ ⚲   P
85 Hodford Rd, London NW11 8NH, England,
44-71-458-196
    Pubs: *Be Seated, Thou* (Sheep Meadow Pr, 2000), *Remembrance of Crimes Past, White Coat, Purple Coat* (Persea Bks, 1992, 1990)

Joan Alexander   W
Coachman's Cottage/33 Grove Rd, Barnes, London SW13 OHH, England, 081-876-5338
    Pubs: *Voices & Echoes: Tales of Colonial Women: Anth* (Quartet, 1983)

Alba Ambert ⚲ ⚲   P&W
Orchard House, Queens Rd, Richmond Univ, Richmond, Surrey TW10 6JP, England, 44-208-332-0526
Internet: amberta@richmond.ac.uk
    Pubs: *The Eighth Continent & Other Stories, A Perfect Silence* (Arte Publico Pr, 1997, 1995), *The Mirror Is Always There, The Fifth Sun* (Cactus Pub, 1992, 1989), *Americas Rev, Mango Season, Southern California Anth*
I.D.: Puerto-Rican, Japanese-American. Groups: Children, Mental Health

Joan Montgomery Byles   P
The Coach House, Hinton NN135NF, England
    Pubs: *Wind, Blueline, Tickleace, The PEN*

Mary Carter   W
Amer Inst for Foreign Study, Dilke House, Malet St, London WC1E 7JA, England
    Pubs: *Tell Me My Name* (Morrow, 1975), *A Member of the Family* (Doubleday, 1974), *Mid-American Rev*

Judith Chernaik ⚲ ⚲   W
Poems on the Underground, 124 Mansfield Rd, London NW3, England, 020-7485-1930
    Pubs: *Love's Children* (Knopf, 1992), *Leah* (Macmillan, 1987), *The Daughter* (Harper, 1981), *TLS*

John T. Daniel   P
71 Alma Rd, Plymouth, Devon, England

Florence Elon   P
26 Whittlesex St, London SE1 8TA, England
    Pubs: *Self-Made* (Secker & Warburg, 1984), *Paris Rev, Poetry, Sewanee Rev, New Yorker*

Ruth Fainlight ⚲ ⚲   P
14 Ladbroke Terr, London W11 3PG, England,
020-7229-6758
    Pubs: *Selected Poems* (Sinclair-Stevenson, 1995), *Sugar-Paper Blue* (Bloodaxe Bks, 1997), *Sibyls* (Gehenna Pr, 1991), *The Knot* (England; Hutchinson, 1990), *New Yorker, Threepenny Rev*

Martha Gelhorn   W
72 Cadogan Sq, London SW1, England

Penelope Gilliatt   W
c/o A. P. Watt, 20 John St, London C1N 2DL, England
    Pubs: *New Yorker, Hic Haec Hoc, Fat Chance*

John Lahr   W
11A Chalcott Gdns, England's Lane, Hempstead, London NW3, England

Anne Lambton   W
15 Bellevue Rd, Wandsworth Common, London SW17 7EB, England, 081-767-4688
    Pubs: *Thoroughbred Style* (Salam Hse, 1987), *Lady* (Jove Pr, 1981), *The Daughter* (Berkley, 1978)

George Lamming   W
14A Highbury Pl, London N5, England, 212-534-2019
    Pubs: *Santeria, Bronx* (Atheneum, 1975)

Doris Lessing   W
Jonathan Clowes Ltd., 10 Iron Bridge House, Bridge Approach/London NW1 8BD, England
    Pubs: *The Real Thing: Stories & Sketches, African Laughter* (HC, 1992, 1992), *The Fifth Child, The Good Terrorist* (Knopf, 1988, 1987)

Liliane Lijn   P&W
99 Camden Mews
London NW1 9BU, England, 071-485-8524
    Pubs: *Crossing Map* (Thames & Hudson, 1983), *Six Throws of the Oracular Keys* (Edtns Nepe, 1983)

Tom Lowenstein P
c/o Deborah Rogers, 20 Powis Mews, Westbourn Pk Rd,
London, W11 1JN, England, 071-221-3717
Pubs: *Filibustering in Samsara* (London; Many Pr,
1987), *Eskimo Poems from Canada & Greenland: Anth*
(U Pittsburgh Pr, 1974)

Mairi MacInnes ♀ ⊁ P
31 Huntington Rd., York, Y031 8RL, England,
190-463-3362
Internet: mairimccormick@dial.pipex.com
Pubs: *The Pebble* (U Illinois Pr, 2000), *The Ghostwriter,*
Elsewhere & Back (Bloodaxe, 1999, 1993), *The*
Quondam Wives (Louisiana State U Pr, 1993), *The*
House on the Ridge Road (Rowan Tree, 1988),
Herring, Oatmeal (QRL, 1981), *New Yorker, Stand,*
Spectator

Joan Michelson P&W
8 Greig Close
London, N8 8PB, England, 44208-340-0008
Pubs: *Coming Late to Motherhood: Anth* (Thorsons
Pub, 1984), *Calyx, Alaska Qtly Rev, Bete Noire,*
Panurge

David Plante W
c/o Deborah Rogers, 20 Powis Mews, Westbourn Pk Rd,
London W11 1JN, England
Pubs: *The Accident* (Ticknor & Fields, 1991), *The*
Native, Difficult Women, The Woods, The Country
(Atheneum, 1987, 1983, 1982, 1981)

Frederic Michael Raphael W
The Wick, Langham, Colchester, Essex, England

Mary Jo Salter P
64 Muswell Rd, London N10 2BE, England
Pubs: *Henry Purcell in Japan* (Knopf, 1986), *New*
Yorker, Southwestern Rev, Atlantic

Clancy Sigal W
Elaine Greene Ltd., 31 Newington Green, London N16,
England
Pubs: *Zone of the Interior* (Crowell, 1975), *Going Away*
(HM, 1961)

Agnes Stein P&W
1 Carlingford Rd
London NW3 1RY, England, 071-435-4858
Pubs: *Color Composition, Windy Times* (Red Dust,
1985, 1984), *River City, Ambit, Rialto, Kansas Qtly*

Anne Stevenson ♀ ⊁ P
38 Western Hill
Durham DH1 4RJ, England, 191-386-2115
Pubs: *Granny Scarecrow,* (Bloodaxe Bks, 2000), *Four &*
a Half Dancing Men, The Other House (Oxford U Pr,
1993, 1990), *Hudson Rev, Michigan Qtly Rev, PN Rev,*
Partisan Rev, TLS, Stand, NER, Poetry Rev

Ted Walker P&W
David Higham Associates, Ltd, 115-8 Lower John St,
Golden Sq, London WIR 4HA, England
Pubs: *In Spain, Hands at a Live Fire* (Secker &
Warburg, 1987, 1987)

John J. Wieners P
Jonathan Cape, Ltd, 30 Bedford Sq, London NW3,
England
Pubs: *O! Khan Collar with Tong Tie, Selected Poems*
(Black Sparrow Pr, 1988, 1986), *San Francisco*
Sentinel, Ten Zone

FRANCE

Grace Andreacchi P&W
c/o E. Hadas, BP 11, 61320 Carrouges, France
Pubs: *Give My Heart Ease* (Permanent Pr, 1989),
Calapooya Collage

Samuel Astrachan W
La Juverde, 84220 Gordes, France, 90-72-00-66
Pubs: *Malaparte in Jassy* (Wayne State U, 1989),
Katz-Cohen (Macmillan, 1978), *Rejoice* (Dial, 1970)

Nina Bogin P
5 Rue Du Chantoiseau, Vescemont 90200 Giromagny,
France, 84-29-51-80
Pubs: *In the North* (Graywolf, 1989), *Ironwood, Agenda,*
Kenyon Rev, APR, Iowa Rev, Stand, CQ

Anthony Burgess W
44 Rue Grimaldi, Monte Carlo, Principality Of Monaco,
France

Roger Dickinson-Brown P
93, Rue De L'Eglise, Bethisy-St-Martin, 60320
Bethisy-St-Pierre, France, 03 44 39 72 04
Internet: euroformat@compuserve.com
Pubs: *Southern Rev, Canto, Agenda, Synthesis, Song,*
Intermuse
Lang: French

Michel R. Doret P
Editions Amon Ra, Ornex/Maconnex 01210,
Omex/Maconnex 01210, France, 50-41-44-87
Pubs: *Les Mamelles de Lutece* (Amon Ra, 1990),
Divagations, Hier et Domain, Degre Zero, Volutes (La
Nouvelle Proue, 1989, 1988, 1988, 1988)

James A. Emanuel 🎤 ✈   P
Boîte Postale 339
75266 Paris Cedex 06, France, 1-45-49-32-66
    Pubs: *Jazz from the Haiku King* (Broadside Pr, 1999),
    De la Rage au Coeur (France; Amiot-Lenganey, 1992),
    Whole Grain, Deadly James & Other Poems (Lotus,
    1991, 1987)
    Lang: French. I.D.: African-American

Susan Fox 🎤 ✈   P
La Bordelière, Segrie Fontaine 61100, France
    Pubs: *Poetry, Paris Rev, Boulevard, Minnesota Rev,*
    Chicago Rev, Women's Studies
    Lang: French

Jeffrey Greene 🎤 ✈   P
42 rue du Cherche-Midi
Paris 75006, France
Internet: jeffreygreene1@compuserve.com
    Pubs: *American Spirituals* (Northeastern U Pr, 1998),
    To the Left of the Worshiper (Alice James Bks, 1991),
    Glimpses of the Invisible World in New Haven
    (Coreopsis Bks, 1995), *Parnassus, New Yorker,*
    Ploughshares, Boulevard, Poetry

Yuri Mamleyev   W
142 rue Legendre, 75017 Paris, France, 42-63-51-61
    Pubs: *The Eternal House* (Fiction Literature, 1992), *The*
    Voice from Nothingness (Worker of Moscow, 1991),
    Drown My Head (Union Bks Ctr, 1990), *Lettre Intl*

Alice Notley 🎤 ✈   P
21 Rue de Messageries
Paris 75010, France, 014-523-0848
Internet: dougolly@aol.com
    Pubs: *Mysteries of Small Houses, The Descent of*
    Alette (Penguin, 1998, 1996), *The Scarlet Cabinet*
    (Scarlet Edtns, 1992), *Homer's Art* (Inst of Further
    Studies, 1990), *Margaret & Dusty* (Coffee Hse Pr,
    1985)

Judith Rosenberg 🎤 ✈   P
20 Quai de Béthune
Paris 75004, France, 004-329-0992
Internet: judyrosenberg@compuserve.com
    Pubs: *Paterson Lit Rev, Antigonish Rev, Atlanta Rev,*
    Louisville Rev, Women's Rev of Bks, Worcester Rev
    I.D.: Jewish. Groups: College/Univ, Seniors

Albert Russo 🎤   W
BP 640
75826 Paris cedex 17, France, 331-4766-4459
Internet: zapinet@worldnet.fr
    Pubs: *Eclipse over Lake Tanganyika, Mixed Blood*
    (Domhan Bks, 2000, 2000), *Zapinette à New York*
    (France; Edtns Hors Commerce, 2000), *L'amant de*
    mon pere (France; Le Nouvel Athanor, 2000), *Volcano*
    Rev, Short Story Intl, Amelia, Edinburgh Rev
    Lang: French

GERMANY

m. c. alpher   P
Seligenstaedter Str 17, 6113 Babenhausen 1, Germany,
11496-073-3510
    Pubs: *Bad Haircut, Parnassus Literary Jrnl, Riverrun,*
    On the Edge, Impetus, Anemone, Poetry Peddler,
    Electric Poets, Cathartic Infinity Limited

Jay Dougherty   P
Essener Str 73, 4320 Hattingen 16, Germany,
49-2324-42721
    Pubs: *The Process Poet Writes Back* (Parkville/Howling
    Dog, 1987), *Chiron Rev, Sonoma Mandala*

Gabriele Glang 🎤 ✈   P
Bonwiedenweg 21
73312 Geislingen-Türkheim, Germany, 114973-314-3695
Internet: gabiglang@compuserve.com
    Pubs: *Stark Naked on a Cold Irish Morning, In a*
    Certain Place: Anth (SCOP Pub, 1990, 2000), *Wenn*
    ich einen Vorschlag machen dürfte: Anth (Germany;
    Eislinger Edtns, 1996), *Eislinger Zeitung, Stuttgarrter*
    Zeitung, NWZ Geislingen, NWZ Göppingen, Quarry
    Lang: German

John Linthicum   P
Spichernstr 52, 4000 Dusseldorf 30, Germany,
0211-480709
    Pubs: *Fluchtige Landschaften* (Express Edtn, 1988),
    Love Poems 1976-1986 (Spheric Hse, 1987), *Stand,*
    Seneca Rev, TLR, Akzente

GREECE

Yannis A. Phillis   P
Aghiou Markou St, Technical Univ of Crete, Chania 73132,
Greece, 11308-216-4437
    Pubs: *Beyond the Symplegades* (Greece; Exantas,
    1991), *The Last Gasp of Planet Earth* (Greece;
    Boukoumanis, 1988), *Stone Country, Harbor Rev*

Ann Rivers   P
Hydra 180 40, Greece
    Pubs: *A World of Difference* (Persephone Pr, 1995),
    Samos Wine (Mammon Pr, 1987), *Pembroke Mag,*
    BRES, St. Andrews Rev, Prophetic Voices, Being

Jessie Schell   W
Anatolia College, Thessaloniki, Greece
    Pubs: *Sudina* (Avon, 1977), *O. Henry Awards: Prize*
    Stories Anth (Doubleday, 1978), *McCall's*

Vassilis Zambaras   P
21 K Fotopoulou, Melighala, Messenias, Greece,
0724-22313
  Pubs: *Out of the Blue, How the Net Is Gripped: Anth*
  (Stride Pubs, 1992, 1992), *Aural* (Singing Horse, 1985),
  The Rialto, Southeastern Rev, Longhouse

INDIA

Terry Kennedy 🎤 ✈   P&W
3/677 Coconut Grove, Prasanthi Nilayam AP 515134,
South India
  Pubs: *Open Letter to My Priest Perpetrator* (Tiger Moon
  Pubs, 1994), *Sexual Harassment: Anth* (Crossing Pr,
  1993), *Splitshift, Vol. No.*

INDONESIA

James Penha 🎤 ✈   P
Jakarta International School, PO Box 1078 JKS, Jakarta
12010, Indonesia
Internet: jpenha@yahoo.com
  Pubs: *Greatest Hits* (Pudding Hse, 2000), *Back of the
  Dragon* (Omega Cat Pr, 1992), *Columbia Rev, Poetry,
  Wired Art from Wired Hearts, Thema*

IRELAND

Chris Agee 🎤 ✈   P
102 N Parade
Belfast BT7 2GJ, Ireland, 44289-064-1644
  Pubs: *Sierra de Zacatecas* (w/R. Vargas; Edcns
  Papeles Privados/Bilingual, 1995), *In the New
  Hampshire Woods* (Dedalus, 1992), Bk *of
  Irish-American Poetry: Anth* (U Kentucky Pr, 2001),
  *APR, Orion, New Statesman, Irish Times, Poetry Ireland
  Rev*
Groups: Irish-American, Nature/Environment

Knute Skinner 🎤 ✈   P
Killaspuglonane
Lahinch, County Clare, Ireland, 1135365-707-2064
  Pubs: *Stretches* (Ireland; Salmon Pub, 2000), *An
  Afternoon Quiet* (Pudding Hse, 1998)

David S. Van Buren   P
24 Brompton Ct
Castleknock, Dublin 15, Ireland, 3531-821-0080
Internet: vanburen@indigo.ie
  Pubs: *Maryland Poetry Rev, Hiram Poetry Rev,
  Cutbank, Mid-Atlantic Rev, Spectrum, Wind*

ISRAEL

Karen Alkalay-Gut 🎤 ✈   P
Tel Aviv Univ, English Dept
Ramat Aviv 69978, Israel
Internet: gut22@post.tau.ac.il
  Pubs: *In My Skin, The Love of Clothes & Nakedness*
  (Israel; Sivan, 2000, 1999), *Harmonies/Disharmonies*
  (Israel; Etc. Edtns, 1994), *Ignorant Armies* (CCC, 1994)

Robert Friend   P
PO Box 4634, Jerusalem, Israel, 000-063-4998
  Pubs: *Dancing With a Tiger* (Beth-Shalom Pr, 1990), *5
  A.M., Jerusalem Post, Atlantic, West Hills Rev, Jewish
  Frontier, Midstream, Bay Windows, Ariel*

Hadassah Haskale   P
PO Box 9358
9190 Jerusalem, Israel, 119722-641-1951
  Pubs: *Inscape* (Laughing Moon Pubs, 1992; Cassette:
  Marcos Allen, 1992), *Between Me & Thee*
  (Illuminations, 1982), *Inkslinger's Rev, Cochlea, Seven
  Gates, Puerto del Sol, Beyond Baroque, Illuminations,
  Hoopoe*

Shirley Kaufman 🎤 ✈   P
7 Rashba St
92264 Jerusalem, Israel, 9722-561-8669
  Pubs: *Roots in the Air* (Copper Canyon Pr, 1996),
  Claims (Sheep Meadow Pr, 1984), *APR, Paris Rev,
  Field, Iowa Rev*

Sharon Kessler 🎤 ✈   P
49 Hashmonaim St
37000 Pardes Hanna, Israel, 9726-637-3351
Internet: sharkess@netvision.net.il
  Pubs: *Ghosts of the Holocaust* (Wayne State U Pr,
  1989), *Without a Single Answer: Anth* (J. Magnes
  Museum, 1990), *Exit 13, Hawaii Rev, Tel Aviv Rev,
  Jerusalem Post, Ariel, Response, Tikkun*

Ruth Finer Mintz   P
Neve Granot, Block 3, Ent 5, Rehov Avraham Granot,
Jerusalem 93706, Israel, 792-724
  Pubs: *Endor* (Massada, 1985), *Auguries Charm
  Amulets, Poems* (Jonathan David Pub, 1983)

Reva Sharon   P
13 Balfour St, Jerusalem 92102, Israel, 02-630608
  Pubs: *Pool of the Morning Wind* (Shemesh, 1989),
  Under Open Sky (Fordham U, 1986), *Ariel, Arc*

Lois Michal Unger 🎤 ✈   P
9 Bialik St
Tel Aviv 63324, Israel, 9723-525-5497
Internet: lois_michal_u@yahoo.com
   Pubs: *The Glass Lies Shattered All Around 9* (Sivan,
2000), *Tomorrow We Play Beersheva* (Lamed Bks,
1992), *White Rain in Jerusalem: Anth* (Yaran Golan
Pub Hse, 1997)
I.D.: Jewish

Linda Stern Zisquit 🎤 ✈   P
PO Box 8448
Jerusalem 91084, Israel, 9722-563-9567
Internet: mslz@pluto.mscc.huji.ac.il
   Pubs: *Unopened Letters* (Sheep Meadow Pr, 1996),
Ritual Bath (Broken Moon Pr, 1993), *Paris Rev,
Ploughshares, Boston Rev, Harvard Rev, Tikkun*

ITALY

Thomas Curley   W
Sarah Whitman Literary Agency, Via Della Croce 65,
Impruneta (FI), Italy, 113955-231-2466
   Pubs: *Libretto for "The Scarlet Letter"* (California State
U, 1994), *Camp Meeting* (Italy; Bastianelli, 1991),
Nowhere Man (H Holt, Rinehart & Winston, 1967), *Past
Eve & Adam's* (Atheneum, 1963)

Salvatore Galioto   P
Via Bruno Buozzi, 15, Montecatini Terme, 51016, Italy
   Pubs: *Is Anybody Listening* (Allicorn Pr, 1990), *Snow
Summits: Anth* (Cerulean Pr, 1988), *San Fernando
Poetry Jrnl, Imago*

Gerald Barttett Parks 🎤 ✈   P
CP 1879
Trieste 34125, Italy, 040-676-2346
Internet: parks@sslmit.univ.trieste.it
   Pubs: *Lumen* (Italy; Corbo e Fiore, 1992), *Epodi ed
Epigrammi* (Italy; Art Gallery Club, 1987), *World Order,
Mickle Street Rev*

Edmund Quincy   P
Via Grande Albergo, 6, San Remo, Imperia 18038, Italy,
9184-79881
   Pubs: *Lyrical Ways, Random Weirdness, Moana-Pacific
Qtly, Chock, Lyric, Country Poet*

Nat Scammacca   P&W
Co-op Ed Antigruppo Siciliano, Via Argenteria, Km 4,
Trapani, Sicily 91100, Italy, 000-126-7029
   Pubs: *Ericepeo III, II, I* (Co-op Ed Antigruppo
Siciliano/CCC, 1990, 1990, 1990), *Sikano l'Americano!,
Bye Bye America* (CCC, 1989, 1986)

JAPAN

William I. Elliott   P
4834 Mutsuura, Kanazawa-ku, Kanto Gakuin Univ,
Kamariya-cho, Yokohama 236, Japan, 45-786-7202
   Pubs: *62 Sonnets & Definitions* (Katydid Pr, 1992),
Doers of the Word, Floating the River in Melancholy
(Prescott Street Pr, 1991, 1989)

Morgan Gibson   P&W
c/o Keiko Gibson, 6-2-5-404 Isobe, Mihama-Ku, Chiba-shi,
Chiba-ken 260, Japan
   Pubs: *Among Buddhas in Japan, Tantric Poetry of
Kukai* (White Pine Pr, 1988), *World's Edge Anth,
Cold-drill, Blue Jacket, Farmer's Market*

Jesse Glass 🎤 ✈   P
Fukuoka Jo Gakuin College, 2409-1 Ogori, Ogori-shi,
Fukuoka 838-01, Japan
   Pubs: *The Book of Doll, Against the Agony of Matter,
Song for Arepo* (Revanche-Hoya, 1999, 1999, 1999),
The Life & Death of Peter Stubbe (Birch Brook Pr,
1995), *Asylum Annual, Confrontation, High Performance,
Literary Rev, Hambone, Shearsman*
Lang: Japanese. I.D.: Native American. Groups: Seniors,
Native American

Thomas Heffernan 🎤 ✈   P
1-52-1 Shimo-Ishiki-Cho, Kagoshima Kenritsu
Tanki-Daigaku, Kagoshima-Shi 890-0005, Japan, 81 99
258 7502
Internet: thomasheffernan@yahoo.com
   Pubs: *Gathering in Ireland* (New Hse Bks, 1996), *City
Renewing Itself* (Peloria Pr, 1983), *The Liam Poems*
(Dragon's Teeth, 1981), *At the Year's Turning: Anth*
(Dedalus Pr, 1998), *Wherever Home Begins: Anth*
(Orchard Bks, 1995), *Mainichi, Frog Pond*
Groups: Children, Seniors

Suzanne Kamata 🎤 ✈   W
113-6 Ninokoshi, Kitakawamukai, Aza,, Itano-gun,
Tokushima-ken 771-0220, Hiroshima, Matsushige-cho,
Japan, 8188-699-7574
Internet: kammy@mxs.mesh.ne.jp
   Pubs: *Beacon Best of 1999: Anth* (Beacon Pr, 1999),
Crab Orchard Rev, Kyoto Jrnl, Intl Qtly, Wingspan

Laurie Kuntz   P
PSC 76 Box 7627
Apo, AP 06319-7627, Japan
   Pubs: *Simple Gestures* (The Texas Rev Pr, 2000)

Drew McCord Stroud   P
Temple Univ, 1-16-7 Kamiochiai, Shinjuku-ku, Tokyo 161,
Japan
   Pubs: *The Hospitality of Circumstance, Poamorio, Lines
Drawn Towards* (Saru, 1988, 1984, 1980)

KENYA

Don Meredith W
Lamu Islands, PO Box 173, Kenya, AFRICA
Pubs: *Where the Tigers Were* (U South Carolina Pr, 2001), *Wing Walking & Other Stories* (Texas Rev Pr, 2001), *Home Movies, Morning Line* (Avon, 1982, 1980), *Folio, Kingfisher, Greensboro Rev, Texas Rev, Slipstream, Short Story Rev*

MEXICO

Jennifer Clement P&W
Tulipan 359 (esq. Azucena), Col El Toro, Del Magdalena Contreras, Mexico DF 10610, Mexico
Pubs: *Widow Basquiat* (Canongate Bks, 2000), *Newton's Sailor, The Next Stranger* (Ediciones El Tucan de Virginia, 1997, 1993), *A Ghost at Heart's Edge: Anth* (North Atlantic Pr, 1999), *Verse & the Universe: Anth* (Milkweed Edtns, 1998), *APR*

Kent Gardien P&W
Colonia Ranchos Cortes, Calle Nardo 137, 62120 Cuernavaca, Morelos, Mexico, 73-13-2269
Pubs: *The Way We Write Now: Anth* (Citadel Pr, 1995), *Antioch Rev, Qtly West, Glimmer Train, Writers' Forum, Paris Rev*

Michael Hogan 🎤 ✈ P&W
English Dept, Colegio Americano, Colomos 2100/APDO 6-280, Guadalajara, Jalisco, Mexico, 1563-642-0061
Internet: mhogan@vianet.com.mx
Pubs: *Imperfect Geographies* (Q-Trips, 1999), *Making Our Own Rules* (Greenfield Rev, 1989)

Robert O. Nystedt P
Apdo 377 Cuautitlan-Izcalli, Edo el Mexico 54701, Mexico
Pubs: *Stone Country, Taurus, Negative Capability, Nexus, Touchstone, Brushfire, Garcia Lorca Rev*

MOROCCO

Victor Hernandez Cruz 🎤 ✈ P
Secteur 8 #1027, Hay Salam Sale, Ouivvan, Morocco, 787-732-8458
Pubs: *Maraca: New & Selected Poems, Panoramas, Red Beans* (Coffee Hse Pr, 1998, 1991, 2001), *Paper Dance: Anth* (Persea Bks, 1995), *A Gathering of the Tribes, See, River Styx, Massachusetts Rev*
Lang: Spanish. I.D.: Puerto-Rican

NETHERLANDS

Lee Bridges P
Postbox 1346, 1000 BH Amsterdam, Netherlands, 020-6277482
Pubs: *The Blues Bird Sings* (K. T. Pub, 1989), *The Rhythm Man* (Conservatory of American Letters, 1987), *Archer, Poetalk, Paisley Moon, White Rose Literary Mag*

Rachel Pollack P&W
Balthasar Floriszstratt 30-III, 1071 VD Amsterdam, Netherlands, 000-076-3924
Pubs: *The New Tarot* (Aquarian, 1989), *Unquenchable Fire* (Century, 1988), *Interzone, Semiotext(e)*

PAKISTAN

Hashmi Alamgir P
House 40 Street 25, 6-10/2, Islamabad, Pakistan, +92 51-229-8951
Internet: alamgirhashmi@hotmail.com
Pubs: *A Choice of Hashmi's Verse* (Oxford U Pr England, 1997), *New Letters, Chelsea Rev, Washington Rev, Postmodern Culture*

SOUTH AFRICA

Sheila Roberts P&W
Justified Press, PO Box 5091 Rivonia, Johannesburg 2128, South Africa, 011-882-1408
Pubs: *Daughters & Other Dutiful Women: Poems, Coming In: Stories* (Justified Pr, 1995, 1993), *New Contrast, Printed Matter*

Mireya Robles P
Dept of Europe Studies, Univ Natal, King George Ave, Durban 4001, South Africa, 031-816-1086
Pubs: *Profecia Y Luz En La Poesia de Maya Islas* (M&A Edtns, 1987)

SOUTH KOREA

Tom Crawford P
Chonnam National University, 406 Kyosu #300, Yong-Bong Dong, Kwangju 500-757, South Korea, 062-520-6099
Pubs: *China Dancing, Lauds* (Cedar Hse Bks, 1996, 1993), *If It Weren't for These Trees* (Lynx Hse Pr, 1986), *I Want to Say Listen* (Ironwood Pr, 1980), *Malahat*

SPAIN

Neil Raymond Ricco   P
c/o Christine L. Wines, American Embassy, Madrid, PSC
61, Cons Box 0008, APO, AE 09642, Spain
   Pubs: *Between Wood & Water* (New Miami Poetry Pr,
   1992), *New World Rev*

TRINIDAD

Lennox Raphael   P
Home Theatre, Ten Pelham St, Belmont, Port-Of-Spain,
Trinidad

UNITED ARAB EMIRATES

Gerald Timothy Gordon   P
Dept. of English Language & Literature, The Univ of
Sharjah, P.O. Box 27272, Sharjah, U.A.E
   Pubs: *Out of Season: Anth* (Amagansett Pr, 1992),
   Mixed Voices: Anth (Milkweed Edtns, 1991), *Art Times,
   Spitball, Pacific Coast Jrnl, American Literary Rev*

483

Alphabetical Index
of All Writers

Porter, Joe Ashby 375
Porter, Melinda Camber 343
Porter, Pamela 475
Porterfield, Nolan 137
Portillo, Estela 435
Portnay, Linda 176
Portuges, Paul C. 57
Posamentier, Evelyn 57
Posner, Richard 267
Post, Jonathan V. 57
Poster, Carol 206
Potok, Chaim 412
Potter, Carol 176
Potter, Nancy 420
Potts, Charles 462
Pourakis, Cally 267
Powell, Dannye Romine 375
Powell, Enid Levinger 121
Powell, Joseph 462
Powell, Lynn 387
Powell, Padgett 103
Powell, Patricia 176
Powell, Shirley 267
Power, Marjorie 462
Powers, Charles F. 375
Poyer, David 412
Poyner, Ken 451
Prado, Holly 57
Prange, Marnie 209
Prasad, Prem Nagpal 267
Pratt, Minnie Bruce 225
Prefontaine, Joan Wolf 199
Prentice, Penelope 343
Preston, Elaine 267
Price, Alice Lindsay 392
Price, Nancy 131
Price, Phyllis E. 108
Price, Reynolds 375
Price, Richard 343
Price, Robert Earl 109
Price, Ron 344
Price, S. David 392
Price, V. B. 235
Price, William 344
Pringle, Robert 387

Pritchard, II, Norman Henry 225
Pritchard, Melissa 8
Prochaska, Robert 344
Proffitt, James S. 387
Proper, Stan 176
Prosen, Rose Mary 387
Providence, Wayne 344
Pruitt, William 268
Prunty, Wyatt 427
Puette, William J. 111
Puigdollers, Carmen 417
Pumphrey, Jean 58
Purdy, James 344
Purens, Ilmars 103
Purpura, Lia 154
Pynchon, Thomas 344
Quagliano, Tony 111
Quasha, George 268
Quatrone, Rich 225
Quenneville, Freda 462
Querry, Ron 435
Quick, Barbara 58
Quigley, Martin 206
Quincy, Edmund 480
Quinn, Fran 128
Quinn, John 131
Quinn, Sister Bernetta 199
Quinones, Magaly 417
Quintana, Leroy V. 58
Quintavalle, David 344
Quirk, Cathleen 206
Raab, Lawrence 176
Rabb, Margo 344
Rabbitt, Thomas 2
Rabby, Pat 176
Rabinowitz, Anna 344
Raborg, Jr., Frederick A. 58
Rachal, Patricia 190
Rachel, Naomi 80
Rachford, Fred 95
Rachlin, Nahid 344
Radavich, David 121
Rader, Dotson 344
Radford, Richard F. 176
Radin, Doris 225
Radke, Charles 58
Radner, Rebecca 58

Radowitz, Stuart P. 268
Radtke, Rosetta 109
Raeschild, Sheila 235
Raffa, Joseph 89
Raffel, Burton 142
Raffeld, David 176
Rafferty, Charles 89
Rafkin, Louise 176
Ragan, James 58
Rahmmings, Keith 344
Rain, Heidi 344
Raines, Helon Howell 202
Raintree, Diane 344
Raisor, Philip 451
Rakosi, Carl 58
Ramirez, Alice 344
Ramirez-De-Arellano, Diana 268
Ramjerdi, Jan Emily 225
Ramke, Bin 80
Ramnath, S. 435
Ramsey, Jarold 397
Ramsey, Martha 442
Rand, Peter 344
Randall, Belle 462
Randall, Dudley 190
Randall, Julia 442
Randall, Margaret 235
Randlev, Karen 58
Rangel-Ribeiro, Victor 345
Rankin, Paula 451
Rankine, Claudia 345
Ransom, Bill 462
Ranson, Nicholas 387
Ranzoni, Patricia Smith 146
Rapant, Larry 268
Raphael, Carolyn 345
Raphael, Dan 397
Raphael, Frederic Michael 477
Raphael, Lennox 482
Raphael, Phyllis 345
Rappleye, Greg 190
Ras, Barbara 109
Rash, Ron 422
Rasheed, Nefretete S. 268
Rass, Rebecca 345

Ratch, Jerry 58
Ratcliff, Carter 345
Ratcliffe, Stephen 58
Rath, Sara 469
Ratner, Rochelle 345
Rattee, Michael 8
Ratzlaff, Keith 131
Rawlins, C. L. 472
Rawlins, Susan 58
Ray, David 8
Ray, Judy 8
Rayher, Edward 176
Raymond, Monica E. 176
Raz, Hilda 211
Rea, Tom 472
Reader, Dennis J. 58
Rechy, John 345
Rector, Liam 176
Redel, Victoria 345
Reder, Claudia M. 412
Redmond, Eugene B. 121
Redmond, Glenis 375
Redshaw, Thomas Dillon 199
Reed, Carson 80
Reed, Fran B. 422
Reed, Ishmael 58
Reed, James 211
Reed, John R. 190
Reed, Kit 89
Rees, Ennis 422
Rees, Gomer 345
Reeve, F. D. 442
Reeves, Trish 135
Reevy, Tony 376
Regan, Jennifer 176
Regier, Gail 345
Reibstein, Regina 268
Reichick, Diane 58
Reid, Barbara 345
Reiff, A. E. 9
Reiff, Edward V. 268
Reiff, Robert L. 268
Reifler, Samuel 268
Reilly, Jad 412
Reinbold, James S. 176
Reineck, Gay Beste 59
Reis, Donna 268
Reisner, Barbara 412
Reiss, Barbara Eve 345

Index of
Performance Poets

Index of
Languages

Index of
Self-Identification

Key:
A.A.U.W. = The American Association of University Women
G/L/B/T = Gay/Lesbian/Bisexual/Transgender

Westerners

St. John, Primus   398

White

Selfridge, Bárbara   62
Trammell, Jack   453

Women

Anderson, Jean   3
Berman, Carol W.   286
Bernikow, Louise   286
Cavallo, Diana   402

DeLaurentis, Louise
  Budde   247
Donnelly, Susan   162
Finch, Annie   382
Friedman, Paula
  Naomi   30
Gilbert, Ilsa   307
Hejmadi, Padma   36
Hope, Akua Lezli   255
Jones, Patricia
  Spears   319
Joseph, Allison   118
Joseph, Joanne   319
Laux, Dorianne   260

Levin, Dana   233
Nelms, Sheryl L.   434
Peacock, Molly   341
Rodgers, Carolyn M.   121
Rosenthal, Barbara   347
Rudy, Dorothy   226
Sapphire   349
Slegman, Ann   135
Steinbergh, Judith
  W.   180
Taylor, Judith   68
Vanspanckeren,
  Kathryn   105
Winters, Mary   366

Zeiger, Gene   183

Working Class

Liebler, M. L.   188
Ranzoni, Patricia
  Smith   146

Zen Buddhist

Keenan, Terrance   258

Zen Judaist

Gach, Gary G.   30

Index of
Community Groups

Key:
A.A.U.W. = The American Association of University Women
G/L/B/T = Gay/Lesbian/Bisexual/Transgender

Index of Literary Agents